W9-CEI-403

Best Recipes from
AMERICAN COUNTRY INNS
and BED & BREAKFASTS

MORE THAN 1,500
MOUTHWATERING RECIPES
from 340 of AMERICA'S FAVORITE INNS

KITTY and LUCIAN MAYNARD

Rutledge Hill Press®
Nashville, Tennessee

A Division of Thomas Nelson Publishers, Inc.
www.ThomasNelson.com

Published by Rutledge Hill Press, a Division of Thomas Nelson, Inc., P.O. Box 141000, Nashville, Tennessee, 37214.

The authors and publisher of this book assume no liability for, and are released by readers from, any injury or damage resulting from the strict adherence to, or deviation from, the directions and/or recipes herein.

Art by Tonya Pitkin

Library of Congress Cataloging-in-Publication Data

Maynard, Kitty, 1955–
    Best recipe's from American country inns and bed & breakfasts / Kitty and Lucian Maynard.
        p. cm.
    ISBN 1-4016-0098-0 (hardcover)
    1. Breakfasts. 2. Hotels—United States. 3. Bed and breakfast accommodations—United States.
    I. Maynard, Lucian, 1952– II. Title.
    TX733.M44 2004
    641.5'2—dc22

                                                          2003020803

Printed in the United States of America
04 05 06 07 08—8 7 6 5 4 3 2 1

Contents

Preface

Almost twenty years have passed since our first bed and breakfast cook book, and the country inn and bed and breakfast industry continues to grow. Even though some of our old friends have since closed, new and exciting proprietors have taken the torch and run with it.

The biggest changes that we have seen in the industry over the past years is that inns and bed and breakfasts can be found all over the country instead of predominantly in New England or the West Coast. The inns are more sophisticated in some cases and in others they remain true to tradition.

Putting to words the splendor of these establishments is always both a pleasure and a challenge. Just saying that an inn is decorated with antiques is a given. But stating that the property is in the historic region of the town where legends walked the street makes all the difference. Innkeepers are experts on their homes, towns, and surrounding areas. They can tell you about all the points of interest and historical facts.

This book is written so you can experience more than the information about each inn and bed and breakfast. You also have the pleasure of regional recipes that are as culturally diverse as the people that run the inns. The recipes are used by innkeepers, caterers, and homemakers for special as well as everyday occasions. There are two indexes at the end of the book. One is an index of the cities that will guide you to the inns by location. The other index is of the recipes; it will guide you to your favorite foods.

You will find all different types of inns and bed and breakfasts in this book. If you want to be treated as visiting royalty, there is an inn to cater to your whims. If you thrive instead on the glory days, there are plenty of places that emphasize the traditional. Likewise, there are inns that cater to the technical, with high-speed Internet connections, and the weary, with complete day spas. But remember to have an open mind and a spirit of adventure when visiting bed and breakfasts. Even with costly renovations, you will still find the occasional wavy floor or chair in need of reupholstering; that's part of the charm.

When collecting the information for this book, we wanted to be fair yet maintain some scruples. We offered to our innkeeper friends the opportunity to be featured in our books at no cost to them. We understand the costs that go into running and maintaining these inns. We did, however, have a few guidelines when accepting a submission. The inns and bed and breakfasts had to . . .

- be authentic, with interesting histories and surroundings
- be in scenic or interesting locales that are reasonably accessible
- be comfortable, clean, and friendly
- serve *good* food (In this area some serve only breakfast and teas, but many are now combining full service restaurant services and private party dinners.)

It is impossible to write a book of this size without a lot of help and support.

The owners and managers of these establishments cannot be praised too highly. The pride they take in the numerous details is evident in the attention they give each guest. To greet guests cheerfully day and night, to forgo the travel and vacations to serve others is commendable. The bed and breakfast industry is booming and the credit goes to the hearty soles of the innkeepers. The proprietors of the many inns and bed and breakfasts have been more than generous with their time in answering our endless questions. The chefs have had to be patient with our confusion with some of the recipes. And we would be amiss if we did not thank the bed and breakfast associations of each state.

We also thank our children for understanding why Mom and Dad are functioning on four to six hours of sleep each day. Our children have put up with the letters, e-mails, and faxes that have interrupted everyone's life during the production of this book.

And many thanks go to our editor, Geoff Stone, who has survived our four relocations in the past year. We jokingly say, "If you want to find us, dial 411." We lead a very mobile professional life and Geoff has stood fast to keep us on track.

—KITTY *and* LOU MAYNARD

Introduction

As long as I can remember, I have loved old majestic homes. Part of my family's past time on Sundays was to drive by the stately homes in my hometown and admire their architectural beauty. I used to tell my family that some day I would own one of those homes. From then on I have had a love of architecture.

In 1974, I married my high school sweetheart and best friend. We had known each other since the fourth grade and sat together on the school bus everyday. Among our many shared interests, including a love of architecture and history, we both love to travel.

Our first bed and breakfast experience was right after college. We were on our way to North Carolina to visit family, and discover the South, when our car broke down. We were on the Blue Ridge Parkway late on a cold, rainy Sunday night. When we were all but resigned to spending the night in the car, a kind gentleman stopped to offer assistance. He assessed the car problem and invited us to come to his home for the night. His wonderful home had two guest rooms and a communal bath. The hospitality was warm and kind. The next day, the innkeeper not only found a mechanic for us, he took our car to the mechanic and brought it back before we had finished our breakfast. He charged us nothing for the stay and even made arrangements for us to send the mechanic payment at a later date. The bed and breakfast no longer exists and the home was torn down for a road expansion, but the memory of our first stay in a bed and breakfast had a lasting affect. We were hooked.

Since that first stay we have been traveling all over the United States visiting as many bed and breakfast and country inns that we can. We have kept a log of every establishment we visited and being an avid cook have collected recipes from the foods served. One day, while staying at the Governor's Inn in Vermont, Kitty shared the scrapbook with the innkeepers. They encouraged us to publish our collection. After talking about the idea with friends and family we were convinced it was what we should do. For the next three years we visited, called, wrote, collected, rewrote, experimented, and came up with our first book. *The American Country Inn and Bed & Breakfast Cookbook* was the result of a dream come true.

Over the years we stayed in touch with many of the inns and bed and breakfasts. We found that some establishments had closed and many new inns had taken their place. We also discovered that what was once a loose confederation of bed and breakfasts had grown into an industry. There were now bed and breakfast organizations that were taking up the campaign to help innkeepers reach the general public.

There are now Web sites with virtual tours and others that list practically all the bed and breakfasts in the United States, Canada, and Mexico. There are listings with each state's chamber of commerce. There are even historical locator signs on the interstates that tell you which exits to take to visit a bed and breakfast.

With the greater visibility of inns and bed and breakfasts comes greater competition. Today inns and bed and breakfasts compete by making themselves unique in a variety of ways from offering themes such as teddy bears to offering an adopt a cat program to offering expanded amenities such as teaching snorkeling and skiing. Some homes focus on their history, such as an inn in which Jessie James had a shootout or a haunted Inn. Some inns focus on their location, such as one with a bungalow with a private entrance and a viewing of whales migrating.

Of course, the main draw for us is the food. There are many homes that still do the traditional breakfasts. But more and more you will find that the meals are a point of interest as much as the antiques. Inns and bed and breakfasts, in most cases, serve at least a few of the regional dishes, but they also offer gourmet dishes that rival any five-star restaurants. Many of inns and bed and breakfasts are now owned either by chefs or employ trained chefs. Due to the generous nature of the innkeepers, they have been so kind as to share their prize-winning, crowd-pleasing recipes in this latest bed and breakfast cookbook. These recipes have been with some of the innkeepers' families for decades, even centuries.

We are pleased to present this book to you. Discover the wonderful world of inns and bed and breakfasts through the more than 1,500 recipes in this book. Or better yet, discover the inns and bed and breakfasts themselves by using the information given to make reservations for yourself. Enjoy the personal touch offered at an inn and bed and breakfast. Discover those majestic homes. Discover the wonderful world of country inns and bed and breakfasts for yourself.

Best Recipes from

AMERICAN COUNTRY INNS
and BED & BREAKFASTS

GORHAM'S BLUFF

101 Gorham Drive/Gorham's Bluff
Pisgah, AL 35765
(256) 451-8439
reservations@gorhamsbluff.com
www.gorhamsbluff.com

The Lodge on Gorham's Bluff is an up-scale country inn located in the northeast corner of Jackson County, Alabama. The lodge sits on the bluff overlooking the beautiful Tennessee River Valley. The six guest rooms each have fireplaces, whirlpool tubs and other amenities that provide comfort and privacy. The Lodge on Gorham's Bluff is patterned after vernacular architecture of the last century. It seeks to incorporate modern comforts with the best of an earlier time.

Breakfast Frittata

1 plus 1 tablespoon butter
2 medium baking potatoes,
    peeled and thinly sliced
Salt and pepper
6 large eggs, beaten
4 ounces shredded Cheddar cheese
2 ounces shredded Swiss cheese
1 cup sour cream
2 tablespoons chopped chives

1 large tomato
2 tablespoons grated Parmesan cheese

Melt 1 tablespoon butter in a skillet, add potatoes, and sauté until tender. Season with salt and pepper to taste. Transfer potatoes to 9-inch quiche plate or deep-dish pie plate that has been buttered or sprayed with cooking spray. In skillet, melt remaining butter and soft-scramble eggs, leaving them fairly liquid. Salt and pepper to taste. Sprinkle thin layer of Cheddar and Swiss cheese over potatoes. Spread sour cream over cheese. Sprinkle chives over sour cream. Add eggs and top with remaining cheese. Preheat oven to 400°. Peel and slice tomato. Place tomato slices in circle on top of frittata. Sprinkle grated Parmesan over the tomatoes. Bake about 35 minutes or until frittata is completely puffed and slightly browned. Slice and serve. Yields 6 to 8 servings.

Fallen Chocolate Soufflé

6 tablespoons unsalted butter
    plus extra for dishes
3 tablespoons all-purpose flour
    plus extra for dishes
3½ ounces bittersweet chocolate
2 eggs
½ cup sugar
Cocoa

Preheat oven to 350°. Butter and flour four custard dishes. Melt 6 tablespoons butter and chocolate. Beat eggs. While whisking, add sugar and whisk until foamy. Add 3 tablespoons flour and stir until just combined. Add chocolate and mix thoroughly. Pour into custard dishes and bake 8 to 10 minutes. Invert onto plates and dust with cocoa. Cut out a wedge to show the soft inside. The batter can be made 2 hours ahead of time. Yields 4 (4-ounce) soufflés.

Pan-Roasted Breast of Duck Salad

2 (6-ounce) boneless duck breasts
Kosher salt
White pepper
2 tablespoons garlic
2 tablespoons chopped shallots
⅛ cup extra virgin olive oil
½ pint fresh blueberries
½ pint fresh blackberries
¼ cup balsamic vinegar
1 teaspoon fresh thyme
1 teaspoon sugar (optional)
4 ounces mixed baby greens
6 tablespoons butter

Preheat oven to 350°. Season the fat side of duck breasts with kosher salt and white pepper to taste. In hot sauté pan, brown duck, fat-side down, until crispy. Place duck in casserole dish and bake until medium rare, about 8 minutes. In same sauté pan, sauté garlic and shallots until translucent. Add olive oil, blueberries, blackberries, vinegar, and thyme. Bring to a simmer and cook for 5 minutes. Add sugar if desired.

Remove from heat. When medium rare, remove duck from oven and slice each breast into 6 slices. Divide greens and duck among four plates. Fan out duck on top of greens. Whisk 6 tablespoons butter into sauce and ladle over duck slices. Yields 4 servings.

Mountain Laurel Inn

624 Road 948
P.O. Box 443
Mentone, AL 35984
(256) 634-4673 (phone/fax)
(800) 889-4244 (toll free)
info@mountain-laurel-inn.com
www.mountain-laurel-inn.com

Located in the woods on top of Lookout Mountain along the Little River, the Mountain Laurel Inn Bed & Breakfast is near the historic town of Mentone. The guest house is located in the woods about two hundred feet from the hosts. There are four rooms and an apartment, each with private entrance, bath, heat and air conditioning. Each set of rooms opens to a porch with rocking chairs. The area around Lookout Mountain and Mentone is perfect for exploring by foot, bike, or car. There is also fishing in the nearby lake, golfing and skiing as well.

Cinnamon Bread

½ cup vegetable oil
2 cups plus ½ cup plus 1 tablespoon sugar
2 eggs
2 cups buttermilk
2 teaspoons baking soda
4 cups all-purpose flour
2 tablespoons ground cinnamon
½ teaspoon salt

Preheat oven to 350°. Spray two loaf pans with nonstick spray. Mix together oil, 2 cups sugar, eggs, buttermilk, baking soda, and flour in large bowl. Pour a quarter of batter into each prepared pan. Combine ½ cup sugar, cinnamon, and salt in small bowl. Sprinkle a quarter of sugar mixture in each pan. Pour remaining batter equally between pans. Sprinkle with remaining sugar. Swirl a knife through batter. Bake 1 hour, or until a knife inserted in center comes out clean. Cool for 10 minutes and then remove bread from pans and place on wax paper. Slice when completely cool. Yields 2 loaves.

Sue's Hot Mixed Fruit

1 (16-ounce) can pineapple chunks
1 (16-ounce) can sliced pears
1 (16-ounce) can sliced peaches
1 (10-ounce) jar green Royal Cherries
¼ cup white raisins
3 oranges (sliced in half moons
    with zest left on)
¼ stick (2 tablespoons) butter
2 tablespoons all-purpose flour
¾ cup sugar

Preheat oven to 350°. Drain canned fruit well. Save juice. Place fruit in 2-quart casserole bowl with raisins and orange slices. Heat butter in saucepan. Add flour and sugar. Mix and add 1 cup of fruit juice. Put butter and sugar mixture on fruit. Mix well and bake 30 minutes. Stir halfway through cooking. Yields 8 servings.

Christmas French Toast

16 slices French bread
6 eggs
⅓ cup sugar
½ teaspoon ground cinnamon
2 cups eggnog (or buttermilk)
2 tablespoons melted butter
1 teaspoon ground nutmeg

Arrange 8 slices of bread in a single layer in two separate 9 x 13-inch pans. Beat the eggs and whisk in sugar, cinnamon, eggnog, butter, and nutmeg. Pour over bread. Turn slices to coat. Refrigerate bread overnight. Preheat oven to 400°. Bake bread for 10 minutes; turn slices of bread over and bake another 5 minutes. Broil briefly, if needed. Serve on a platter with eggs and sausage or bacon. Yields 8 servings.

Eggs Rancheros

1 (8-ounce) can tomato sauce
1 teaspoon chili powder
½ teaspoon cumin
8 eggs
¼ teaspoon pepper
¼ teaspoon paprika
1 cup (4 ounces) shredded Cheddar cheese
Sour cream
Jalapeño slices
Tortilla chips

Preheat oven to 350°. Combine tomato sauce, chili powder, and cumin in lightly greased, 9-inch pie plate. Break eggs evenly in dish and sprinkle with pepper and paprika. Cover with foil and bake 15 to 20 minutes until eggs are cooked. Top with cheese and bake an additional 5 minutes until cheese is melted. Top with sour cream and jalapeño slices. Serve with tortilla chips. Accompany with fresh fruit and biscuits. Great for breakfast or dinner. Yields 6 to 8 servings.

Breakfast in Bread

1 round sourdough loaf
4 to 6 ounces sliced ham
1 (2.5-ounce) can olives
1 (4-ounce) can mushrooms, or 8 ounces
    fresh, sliced, and cooked
3 ounces shredded Cheddar cheese
3 ounces shredded Monterey Jack cheese
6 eggs, wet scrambled
1 medium tomato, thinly sliced and
    slightly sautéed

Preheat oven to 350°. Cut top off loaf of bread. Remove crust with spoon. Set aside for the lid. Remove as much of soft interior of loaf as possible without breaking through crust. Layer interior of loaf with ham, adding a layer of olives and mushrooms, then a layer of Cheddar and Monterey Jack cheese. Add eggs. Use the back of a spoon to push eggs into all sections of loaf. Add more olives and layer of tomato. Add another layer of Cheddar and Monterey Jack cheese. Top with mushrooms. Put on the lid. Double wrap loaf tightly in heavy foil. Bake in the oven for about 45 minutes. After cooking, set aside for about 5 minutes to cool slightly. Cut the loaf into wedges. Yields 6 servings.

THE GOVERNOR'S HOUSE

500 Meadowlake Lane
Talladega, AL 35160
(205) 763-2186 (phone)
(256) 362-2391 (fax)
gaineslaw@aol.com
www.thegovernorshouse.us.com

The Governor's House bed and breakfast was built in Talladega in 1850 by Governor Parsons and was moved to the Polled Hereford farm on Logan Martin Lake. The home is furnished with antiques and has a wraparound porch.

The premises have a lighted plexi-paved tennis court, a bass- and brim-stocked pond with a picnic area, and pear trees and blueberry bushes to which guests may "help themselves." There is also a boat launch for boating and fishing on Logan Martin Lake. The Alabama Motorsports Superspeedway and Motorsports Hall of Fame are ten minutes from the Governor's House. A golf course is within thirty minutes of the house and the Robert Trent Jones Golf Trail is also near. The highest point in Alabama, Mt. Cheaha, is only forty-five minutes away.

Chocolate Cream Pie

1 (4-ounce) package German sweet chocolate
⅓ cup milk
2 tablespoons sugar
1 (3-ounce) package cream cheese, softened
1 (8-ounce) container Cool Whip
1 (8-inch) graham cracker crumb crust

Heat chocolate and milk, stirring until chocolate melts. Beat sugar into cream cheese, add chocolate mixture, and beat until smooth. Add Cool Whip and put all in a graham cracker crumb crust. Freeze 4 hours. Yields 6 to 8 servings.

Poppy Seed Bread

Bread:
3 cups all-purpose flour
2⅓ cups sugar
3 eggs
1½ cups milk
1½ cups vegetable oil
1½ teaspoons vanilla extract
1½ teaspoons almond extract
1½ teaspoons butter flavoring

Glaze:
½ teaspoon vanilla extract
½ teaspoon almond extract
½ teaspoon butter flavoring
¼ cup orange juice
¾ cup sugar

Preheat oven to 325°. To make bread, mix flour, sugar, eggs, milk, oil, vanilla and almond extracts, and butter flavoring with mixer and place in two greased loaf pans. Bake 1 hour. Let cool 10 minutes.

To make glaze, mix together vanilla and almond extracts, butter flavoring, orange juice, and sugar. Pour glaze over bread while still in pan. Leave bread in pans for about an hour. Yields 2 loaves.

Garlic Cheese Grits

1 cup uncooked grits
1 stick (½ cup) butter
1 (6-ounce) roll garlic cheese
2 eggs, beaten
½ cup milk
Salt

Cook grits (quick or regular) according to package directions. Preheat oven to 350°. Add butter and cheese and stir until melted. Add eggs, milk, and salt to taste. Pour mixture into buttered quart casserole dish and bake 30 minutes. Yields 4 servings.

Easy Bake Chocolate Cake

Cake:
2 cups self-rising flour
2 cups sugar
2 sticks (1 cup) butter
1 cup water
4 tablespoons cocoa
½ cup buttermilk
2 eggs
1 teaspoon baking soda
1 teaspoon vanilla extract

Frosting:
1 stick (½ cup) butter
4 tablespoons cocoa
6 tablespoons milk
1 (1-pound) box confectioners' sugar

To make the cake, preheat oven to 350° (325° if using a glass dish). Mix flour and sugar together in mixing bowl. Heat butter, water, and cocoa in double boiler until butter melts. Add to sugar/flour mixture. Add buttermilk and mix well. Add eggs, soda, and vanilla. Mix well, pour into 9 x 13-inch pan, and bake 40 minutes.

To make frosting, heat butter, cocoa, and milk until butter is melted. Add confectioners' sugar and mix well. Pour frosting over cake while still hot. Serve with whipped cream and a strawberry on top. Yields 24 (2-inch) squares.

Holly's Rolls

2 cups self-rising flour
1 cup sour cream
1½ sticks (¾ cup) butter, melted

Preheat oven to 400°. Mix flour, sour cream, and butter together and pour batter into small, greased muffin tins. Bake 10 to 15 minutes. Dip rolls in butter and serve. Yields 12 large rolls or 24 miniature rolls.

RED BLUFF COTTAGE BED & BREAKFAST

551 Clay Street
Montgomery, AL 36104
(334) 264-0056 (phone)
(334) 263-3054 (fax)
(888) 551-2529 (toll free)
RedblufBnB@aol.com
www.RedBluffCottage.com

Experience award-winning Southern hospitality "Alabama style." Red Bluff is a spacious and airy cottage located in downtown Montgomery's oldest historic neighborhood with four clean, comfortable, and cozy bedrooms with private baths. After a relaxing night's sleep, start your morning off with a bountiful and sumptuous breakfast. "Arrive as guests, depart as friends."

Activities in the surrounding area include Alabama Shakespeare Festival Theatre and Gardens; Alabama Cattlemen's Association "Mooseum"; Alabama Department of Archives and History; Alabama State Capitol; Betsy Ann Riverboat; Civil Rights Memorial; First White House of the Confederacy; F. Scott & Zelda Fitzgerald Museum; Fort Toulouse/Jackson Park; Hank Williams Memorial, Museum, and Statue; Jasmine Hill Gardens & Outdoor Museum; Montgomery Museum of Fine Arts; Montgomery Zoo; Old Alabama Town; Robert Trent Jones Golf Trail-Capital Hill; Rosa Parks Library & Museum; many annual festivals; several flea markets, antique galleries and malls.

Wild Rice Waffles

1 cup all-purpose, unbleached flour
1¾ cups cooked wild rice, well drained
⅓ cup dried cranberries
2 tablespoons sugar
2 tablespoons baking powder
½ teaspoon baking soda
¼ teaspoon salt
1¼ cups buttermilk
2 large eggs, separated
¼ cup melted unsalted butter
1 teaspoon almond extract
Fresh peaches, sliced
Whipped cream
Maple syrup

In large bowl, combine flour, rice, cranberries, sugar, baking powder, baking soda, and salt. In separate bowl, beat buttermilk, egg yolks, and melted butter. Add buttermilk mixture to dry ingredients, stirring well. Beat egg whites until stiff and fold into batter along with almond extract. Ladle batter onto heated waffle iron. Cook until brown and slightly crisp. (Baked waffles may be kept warm in a 200° oven while the rest of the waffles are being cooked.) Serve hot with peaches, whipped cream, and warm maple syrup. Yields 4 waffles.

Eggs Red Bluff

1 tablespoon olive oil
¼ cup finely chopped green onions
¼ cup sliced fresh mushrooms
¼ cup diced green bell pepper
6 eggs, beaten and seasoned
¼ cup canned, diced tomatoes, drained
1 tablespoon grated Parmesan cheese
1 cup grated Cheddar cheese
Fresh basil

Heat the olive oil in a medium, nonstick frying pan. Add the onions, mushrooms, and bell pepper. Sauté until vegetables are slightly softened, about 1 minute. Pour the eggs, seasoned to taste, over the vegetables and scramble, making certain the eggs remain moist. Gently stir in drained tomatoes until heated. Remove ingredients to serving dish and sprinkle with Parmesan cheese. Lightly top the serving dish with Cheddar cheese and garnish with fresh basil. Yields 4 servings.

Taste of Heaven Casserole

1 stick (½ cup) butter
½ cup all-purpose, unbleached flour
6 large eggs
1 cup milk
1 teaspoon baking powder
½ teaspoon salt
1 teaspoon sugar
⅛ teaspoon cream of tartar
1 pound Cabot's vintage white
    Cheddar cheese
3 ounces (6 tablespoons) cream cheese,
    softened
1 cup ricotta cheese
1 tablespoon chopped green onions

Preheat oven to 350°. Melt butter in saucepan. Add flour and cook until smooth. In large bowl beat eggs, milk, baking powder, salt, sugar, and cream of tartar. Stir in cheeses, green onions, and butter mixture until blended. Pour into two well-greased, 8 x 10-inch, ceramic baking dishes. Bake uncovered 30 minutes. Yields 12 servings.

Cranberry Orange Scones

Scones:
2 cups all-purpose, unbleached flour
7 teaspoons plus 1 tablespoon sugar
1 tablespoon grated orange peel
2 tablespoons baking powder
¼ teaspoon baking soda
½ teaspoon salt
⅓ cup cold butter
1 cup dried cranberries
¼ cup orange juice
¼ cup half-and-half
1 egg
1 tablespoon milk

Glaze:
½ cup confectioners' sugar
1 tablespoon orange juice

Orange Butter:
1 stick (½ cup) butter, softened
2 to 3 tablespoons orange marmalade

To make scones, in bowl combine flour, 7 teaspoons sugar, orange peel, baking powder, baking soda, and salt. Cut in butter until mixture resembles coarse crumbs. In small bowl, combine cranberries, orange juice, half-and-half, and egg. Add to flour mixture and stir until soft dough forms. On floured surface, gently knead dough 6 to 8 times. Preheat oven to 400°. Using rolling pin, roll dough to ¼- to ½-inch thickness. Cut into rounds using 2½-inch biscuit cutter. Place scones on ungreased cooking stone. Brush with milk and sprinkle with remaining 1 tablespoon sugar. Bake 12 to 15 minutes or until lightly browned.

To make glaze, combine sugar and orange juice and drizzle over scones.

To make orange butter, mix together butter and marmalade and serve with warm scones. Yields 8 scones.

Apple Nut Muffins

Filling:
2 tablespoons butter
⅓ cup packed brown sugar
1 tablespoon all-purpose, unbleached flour
½ teaspoon ground cinnamon
¼ teaspoon ground nutmeg
2 cups peeled, diced apples
½ cup finely chopped pecans

Muffins:
1½ sticks (¾ cup) butter, softened
1½ cups sugar
3 eggs
1½ teaspoons vanilla extract
3½ cups all-purpose, unbleached flour
1½ teaspoons baking powder
1½ teaspoons baking soda
¾ teaspoon salt
12 ounces (1½ cups) sour cream
Cinnamon sugar

To make filling, melt butter in saucepan. Stir in brown sugar, flour, cinnamon, and nutmeg until smooth. Add apples. Cook over medium-low heat 10 minutes or until tender, stirring frequently. Remove from heat. Add nuts and set aside to cool.

Preheat oven to 350°. To make muffins, cream butter and sugar in large mixing bowl. Add eggs, one at a time, beating well after each. Beat in vanilla. In separate bowl combine flour, baking powder, soda, and salt. Add to creamed mixture alternately with sour cream. Fill cups of a muffin tin half full with batter, making a well in the center. Add rounded teaspoon of apple mixture (do not spread) and top with remaining batter. Sprinkle with cinnamon sugar. Bake muffins 16 to 18 minutes. Cool 5 minutes before removing from pans to wire racks. Yields 2 dozen muffins.

The Martin House Bed & Breakfast Inn

212 East Commerce Street
Greenville, AL 36037
(334) 382-2011 (phone)
(877) 627-8465 (toll free)
themartinhouse@greenlynk.com

Filled with antiques and situated in the "Best Small Town in America," this 1895 Queen Anne house offers unsurpassed lodging and fine dining. Activities include world-class golf in Greenville, Alabama, at Cambrian Ridge-Robert Trent Jones Golf Trail; historic buildings, churches, and houses; hunting, birding, and nearby fishing.

Browned Butter Pecan Pie

½ cup butter
¾ cup light corn syrup
¼ cup honey
1 cup sugar
1 teaspoon vanilla extract
⅛ teaspoon salt
3 large eggs, beaten
1 cup toasted and chopped pecans
1 uncooked piecrust

Cook butter in small saucepan over medium-low heat until browned. Do not stir; watch very closely as butter goes from brown to burnt very quickly. Remove from heat. Preheat oven to 425°. Combine corn syrup, honey, sugar, vanilla, salt, and eggs. Stir well with wire whisk. Stir in butter and pecans. Pour into unbaked pie shell. Bake 10 minutes. Reduce heat to 325° and bake 40 to 45 additional minutes. Cool on wire rack. Yields 8 servings.

London Broil with Mustard Caper Sauce

1 plus 3 tablespoons butter
1 tablespoon olive oil
1½ pounds London broil steak
2 tablespoons vermouth
1 tablespoon Dijon mustard
¼ teaspoon Worcestershire sauce
1½ teaspoons capers
Fresh watercress sprigs

Melt 1 tablespoon butter and olive oil in skillet. Add steak and cook over medium heat 5 minutes each side or to desired degree of doneness. Remove steak to a serving platter, reserving drippings in skillet. Add remaining 3 tablespoons butter to skillet and melt. Combine vermouth, mustard, Worcestershire, and capers. Gradually add to skillet, stirring with a wire whisk until smooth. Slice steak diagonally across grain into thin slices. Pour sauce over steak. Garnish with watercress. Yields 4 to 6 servings.

Lemon Blueberry Cake

Cake:
2 sticks butter
2 cups sugar
4 eggs
3 cups all-purpose flour
½ teaspoon baking soda
½ teaspoon salt
1 cup buttermilk
Grated zest of 2 lemons
1 cup blueberries

Glaze:
½ cup confectioners' sugar
½ cup lemon juice
Grated zest of 3 lemons

Preheat oven to 325°. Cream butter and sugar. Add eggs one at a time. Blend flour, baking soda, and salt together. Add to batter alternately with buttermilk. Add zest. Fold in blueberries. Place into prepared tube pan. Bake 1 hour and 15 minutes or until cake tester comes out clean.

For glaze, mix together sugar, lemon juice, and lemon zest. Remove cake from oven and pour glaze slowly onto cake, poking holes into cake so glaze will be more easily absorbed. Yields 10 servings.

Alaska

Alaska Ocean View Bed & Breakfast Inn

1101 Edgecumbe Drive
Sitka, AK 99835
(907) 747-8310 (phone)
(907) 747-3440 (fax)
info@sitka-alaska-lodging.com
www.sitka-alaska-lodging.com

Overlooking magnificent Sitka Sound, Alaska Ocean View is home to whales, seals, sea lions, and otters. Guests enjoy the view in casual elegance and supreme comfort in the cheerful, cozy, serene ambience of one of Alaska's top-rated bed and breakfasts. The inn offers outstanding complimentary concierge service, library, and hot-tub spa in nonsmoking environment.

Authentic "Thin" German Pancakes

8 to 12 large eggs
2 cups nonfat or whole milk
2 cups all-purpose flour
Pinch of salt
1 stick (½ cup) butter

In bowl or blender mix all ingredients except butter. Cover and set in refrigerator 30 minutes to overnight (best). Batter keeps 2 to 3 days.

Heat crêpe pan or small frying pan over medium-high heat. When hot, smear entire bottom of pan with butter. It should be hot enough to smoke just a little when buttered. Pour small amount of batter, about ¼ cup depending on size of pan, to very thinly coat pan after swirling batter around. Place on burner and cook until golden, about 1 minute. Turn and cook briefly on other side. Serve immediately, open faced, directly onto warmed dinner plate. Fill delicious wafer-thin pancake with sweetened strawberry or peach slices and cottage cheese (optional), roll into a log, and top with whipping cream or warm maple syrup. Yields 12 to 15 servings.

Note: Since these crêpe-like, paper-thin pancakes cook very rapidly, it is best to cook them as you serve them, even when serving a crowd. Do not cook ahead; they are at their absolute best going from skillet to individual plate.

A Rabbit Creek Bed & Breakfast

P.O. Box 112842
4540 Rabbit Creek Road
Anchorage, AK 99511-2842
(907) 345-0733 (phone)
(907) 345-7600 (fax)
pamperyourself@arabbitcreekbandb.com
www.arabbitcreekbandb.com

A Rabbit Creek Bed & Breakfast is a peaceful inn with dramatic views. Located on the "prestigious hillside" and recognized in Arlington's Bed and Breakfast Journal as "Best of Alaska" and one of the top fifteen bed and breakfasts in the 2003 Book of Lists, this unique inn offers outstanding accommodations. Each of the bedrooms is isolated (no other bedrooms are located below, beside, or above). All include a king bed and large room, private bath, telephone, color TV, VCR, microwave, and refrigerator. Breakfast is a casual affair served in the breakfast room. You can watch the bore tides or, on a clear day, view Mt. Redoubt and Mt. Spur, two active volcanoes. The inn is open year-round. Activities in the area include glacier cruises, the Anchorage Museum, zoo, and the Native Cultural Center.

Bran Muffins

2 cups rolled oats
1 cup bran
1 cup wheat germ
2 cups boiling water
1 cup brown sugar
1 cup honey
1 cup vegetable oil
1 cup sesame seeds
1 cup blackstrap molasses
1 teaspoon salt
5 teaspoons baking soda
1 quart (4 cups) buttermilk
4 eggs
5½ cups whole wheat flour

Preheat oven to 350°. Mix oats, bran, wheat germ, and boiling water in mixing bowl. Add remaining ingredients and mix well. In sprayed muffin tins, pour batter two-thirds full and bake 12 to 14 minutes. Yields 7 dozen muffins.

Note: Batter will keep for 4 weeks in the refrigerator.

ALASKA CONNECTION BED & BREAKFAST

5224 Emmanuel Avenue
Anchorage, AK 99508
(907) 332-3332 (phone)
(907) 929-7821 (fax)
(888) 862-3332 (toll free)
www.ruralalaskaconnection.com

Alaska Connection Bed & Breakfast is a charming and affordable alternative to hotels when visiting Anchorage. It is also great for natives. Located in a quiet, safe neighborhood on the Chester Creek Greenbelt, the bed and breakfast provides gracious hospitality in this warm home decorated with antiques and special family treasures. Activities are endless in the Anchorage Area. You can shore fish for Salmon, discover the wetlands and woods abounding with birds and wildlife, rent a bike, take a walk, or go for a run. Relax over a delectable meal at one of Anchorage's many restaurants then top off your evening and relax at Alaska Connection over tea and one of the marvelous desserts.

Russian Alaska (Koulibiac)

This is a favorite Alaskan dish for guests, but especially for those who watch their cholesterol. It is a wonderful substitute protein meal instead of sausages, bacon, or ham.

1 pound fresh sockeye, silver, or king salmon fillets
1 small red onion, finely chopped
½ cup fresh mushrooms, sliced
2 tablespoons extra virgin olive oil
Salt and pepper
1 cup cooked brown rice
1 cup chopped cilantro or dill
1 hard-cooked egg, white only
¼ cup all-purpose flour
½ teaspoon pepper
2 tubes of refrigerator crescent rolls
1 egg white, beaten to a froth
Several whole cilantro springs
Several cherry tomatoes

Cut salmon into bite-size pieces. Sauté salmon, onion, and mushrooms in olive oil. Add salt and pepper to taste. Braise until salmon is just cooked. Mix salmon with rice, cilantro, and hard-cooked egg white. Mix flour and pepper and put on pastry cloth. Preheat oven to 350°. Open crescent rolls and spread out each section on pastry cloth as rectangles, not crescents. With rolling pin smooth eight rectangles slightly (each should be one solid rectangle). Place 1 cup of salmon mixture on top of four of the pastry rectangles. Place other four rectangles on top of mixture to form a top crust and seal edges thoroughly. Place pockets on oiled cookie sheet and baste with beaten egg white. Bake 20 minutes or until golden brown. Serve hot with sprig of cilantro and tomatoes for garnish, topped with dollop of sour cream. Yields 4 servings.

Smoked Salmon Gold Pans

An easy but yummy dish made especially for those looking for a taste of the North. Make the sauce first, cover, and hold aside in a warm spot until serving.

Sauce:
2 cups 2% milk
2 teaspoons Dijon mustard
½ teaspoon salt
¾ cup cornstarch
1 teaspoon ground basil leaves
1 teaspoon ground thyme
1 tablespoon butter
½ teaspoon pepper

Salmon:
1 pound smoked Alaskan salmon
½ sweet onion, finely cut
½ teaspoon pepper
½ teaspoon ground mustard
2 tablespoons mayonnaise
½ cup shredded, aged, sharp Cheddar cheese
4 English muffins, split into halves and toasted slightly
Parsley, cilantro, tomatoes for garnish

For the sauce, combine milk, mustard, salt, cornstarch, basil, thyme, butter, and pepper and mix well. Cook over low heat, stirring constantly until mixture boils. Continue stirring until mixture starts to thicken. Remove from heat.

Break salmon into crumbles and mix with onion, pepper, mustard, mayonnaise, and cheese. Place spoonful of mixture onto muffin halves, flattening out on top.

Broil until top of mixture appears golden brown, 7 to 10 minutes. To serve, place each muffin half onto plate and dribble sauce over it. Garnish with parsley or cilantro and slices of tomato. Serve with fresh fruit and a sweet bread. Yields 8 servings.

Hiker Energy Bars

Many of the guests take off on hiking, biking, or sight-seeing for the day. One energy bar taken along in their backpacks gives them a spurt of extra "oomph" to make it through the day. (Do not take into bear country!)

2½ cups Rice Krispies
2 cups oatmeal
1½ cups raisins
1 cup unsalted peanuts
½ cup chopped dried apricots
½ cup butter
½ cup peanut butter
1 (10-ounce) package large marshmallows

Preheat oven to 325°. Toast Rice Krispies and oatmeal 15 minutes. Add raisins, peanuts, and apricots and mix well. Melt butter and peanut butter in double boiler, mixing well. Add marshmallows and stir together until blended. Add to Rice Krispies mix. Pour into jelly-roll pan and press firmly in place. Cool before cutting into small rectangles. Store in refrigerator for freshness up to one month. Yields about 4 dozen rectangles.

Double French Toast

5 baked croissants
4 eggs, beaten
½ cup milk
½ teaspoon salt
¼ teaspoon fresh ground nutmeg
½ teaspoon ground cinnamon

Cut croissants as if to make into sandwiches. Beat eggs until light and fluffy. Add milk and spices and beat again. Place croissants one at a time in large bowl and pour egg mixture over them, making sure all are thoroughly wet. Rearrange croissants to assure all are in contact with egg mixture. Let soak in refrigerator 12 to 24 hours. Spray bottom of 9 x 12-inch glass pan with nonstick spray. Carefully lift each croissant onto the pan, placing the outer, baked-side down, being careful not to touch croissant sections (all the egg mixture should have been soaked up overnight, but the croissants are fragile). Bake at 350° for 30 minutes or until golden brown and puffy. Sprinkle with confectioners' sugar and serve with hot real maple syrup or fresh berries and slices of lime. Add crisp thick-sliced bacon and a fruit plate to the table, along with a citrus juice. Yields 5 servings.

Moose in a Raspberry Patch

8 low-fat graham crackers
½ cup boiling water
1 (¼-ounce) package unflavored gelatin
½ cup sugar
1 plus 1 cup fresh raspberries, chilled
1 (3.4-ounce) box chocolate fudge pudding mix
1¾ cups 1% milk
1 (8-ounce) package softened Neufchatel cheese
1 (8-ounce) bar bittersweet chocolate, broken into small pieces
1 (8-ounce) carton frozen whipped topping

Line pan (at least 12 x 12 inches) with wax paper. Place graham crackers side by side on bottom of pan, breaking apart along section lines. Cut three strings 1½ times length and three for width of pan. Lay strings along graham cracker section lines with ends hanging over pan, forming a grid. In bowl pour boiling water over gelatin and sugar and set aside until gelatin begins to set. Stir in 1 cup chilled raspberries, broken into small sections of berry (do not squash the berries).

While gelatin is cooling, cook pudding following directions on box, using 1¾ cups milk. Stir in cream cheese until it dissolves into pudding. Stir in broken chocolate pieces. Fold gelatin mixture into pudding until thoroughly mixed. Pour mixture onto graham crackers. Refrigerate 8 to 10 hours.

To serve hold each end of a string, one at a time, and pull up from the bottom of dessert, cutting through crackers and pudding mixture. Using a pliable spatula, place each dessert piece on a plate and top with whipped topping. Yields 16 servings.

ANNA'S BED & BREAKFAST

830 Jay Circle
Anchorage, AK 99504-1876
(907) 338-5331
annas@alaska.net
www.annasdreambreakfast.com

Anna's Bed & Breakfast is a multilevel home with a beautiful view of the Chugach Mountains. The inn offers three rooms, all with private baths. It is a non-smoking bed and breakfast. Off-street parking for guests is available. A full breakfast is served every morning, and waffles are made with real Alaskan sourdough.

Skillet Turkey Breakfast

12 slices turkey bacon, cut into ½-inch pieces
1 medium potato, peeled and cut into small cubes
2 green onions with tops, thinly sliced
¾ teaspoon chili powder
1 (4-ounce) carton egg substitute
4 eggs, beaten

Place turkey bacon and potato in nonstick skillet. Cook on medium about 12 minutes, stirring frequently until potato cubes are fork tender. Stir in onions and chili powder. Mix the egg substitute with the eggs and pour the mixture evenly over turkey/potato mixture. Cover. Turn heat to low and cook 5 minutes more, or until mixture is set. Spoon into serving bowl. Yields 4 servings.

Tropical Mini Muffins

1½ cups all-purpose flour
⅔ cup sugar
½ teaspoon salt
2 teaspoons baking powder
8 ounces lemon yogurt
½ cup vegetable oil
2 eggs, beaten
1 (11-ounce) can mandarin oranges, drained

Topping:
1 cup flaked coconut
½ cup sugar (or less)
½ teaspoon ground cinnamon

Combine flour, sugar, salt, and baking powder. Stir yogurt, oil, and eggs in a separate bowl. Add wet ingredients to dry ingredients. Stir just until blended. Fill lightly greased muffin pans one-fourth full. Place mandarin orange slices on top of batter.

Preheat oven to 350°. Combine in a small bowl the topping ingredients. Sprinkle over top of mandarin oranges. Bake 20 minutes. Yields 12 muffins.

Rhubarb Muffins

1½ cups brown sugar
¼ cup vegetable oil
1 egg
2 teaspoons vanilla extract
1 cup sour milk

1½ cups diced rhubarb
½ cup walnuts
2½ cups all-purpose flour
1 teaspoon baking soda
1 teaspoon baking powder
½ teaspoon salt
¼ cup applesauce

Topping:
2 teaspoons melted butter
⅔ cup sugar
1 teaspoon ground cinnamon

Beat together brown sugar, oil, egg, vanilla, and sour milk. Add rhubarb and walnuts. In a separate bowl mix flour, soda, baking powder, and salt. Add to liquid ingredients, stirring only until moistened. Spoon into greased muffin cups.

Preheat oven to 375°. Combine topping ingredients. Sprinkle over filled cups and lightly press into batter. Bake 20 to 25 minutes. Yields 20 large muffins.

Sourdough Pancakes

1 cup sourdough waffle mixture (see recipe below)
1 cup applesauce
½ teaspoon ground cinnamon

To waffle mixture add applesauce and cinnamon. Pour ¼ cup batter onto hot, lightly greased skillet and cook until bubbles appear. Turn and cook other side until lightly brown. Yields 8 to 10 pancakes.

Sourdough Waffles

2 cups sourdough starter
2 tablespoons sugar
1 egg
4 tablespoons vegetable oil
½ teaspoon salt
1 teaspoon baking soda

To sourdough starter, add sugar, egg, oil, and salt. Mix well. Dilute baking soda in about 3 to 4 tablespoons of warm water

and stir with your finger. Add to batter, but do not beat. Batter may double in volume. For each waffle, pour ¼ to ½ cup batter onto preheated waffle iron. Waffle is done when light on waffle iron goes out (1 to 2 minutes) or until golden brown. Serve with maple syrup and lemon yogurt. Yields 12 small or 6 large waffles.

Sourdough Starter

3½ cups all-purpose flour
1 package active dry yeast
2 cups warm water

Mix flour and yeast in 4-quart container. Gradually beat in water until smooth. Cover loosely with plastic wrap and let stand in warm place 2 to 4 days. Transfer to 2-quart plastic container with tight-fitting lid. Refrigerate until ready to use.

Note: To keep active, once a week beat in 1 tablespoon all-purpose flour and 1 tablespoon warm water. Cover and let stand 12 hours. To replenish, for each 1½ cups starter used, beat in 1⅓ cups flour and 1⅓ cups warm water until smooth. Cover and let stand 12 to 24 hours before refrigerating.

Turkey-Vegetable Frittata

1 (1-pound) package turkey sausage, thawed
1 medium onion, chopped
1 clove garlic, crushed or ½ teaspoon garlic powder
Pinch of cayenne
1 cup chopped broccoli florets
1 medium zucchini, cut into thin slices
½ teaspoon dried dill weed
3 tablespoons grated Parmesan cheese
2 (4-ounce) cartons egg substitute or 8 eggs, beaten
Paprika

Place sausage, onions, garlic, and cayenne in nonstick skillet. Cook on medium about 10 minutes, breaking sausage into small pieces and stirring frequently until lightly browned. Stir in vegetables and dill. Cover. Cook about 3 minutes, or until broccoli is bright green. Sprinkle with Parmesan cheese. Combine egg substitute and eggs in bowl and blend. Pour egg mixture evenly over the turkey and vegetable mixture. Sprinkle with paprika. Cover again. Continue to cook on low 15 minutes or until mixture is set. May be cut into slices or put into bowl and spooned out. Yields 8 servings.

BIG BEAR BED & BREAKFAST

3401 Richmond Avenue
Anchorage, AK 99508-1013
(907) 277-8189 (phone)
(907) 274-5214 (fax)
info@AlaskaBigBearBB.com
www.AlaskaBigBearBB.com

This inn offers old-fashioned Alaskan hospitality hosted by a lifelong Alaskan, a retired home economics teacher. It's a log home decorated with unique antiques and native art. The exceptional breakfasts feature Alaskan cuisine such as wild-berry specialties.

Apple Crisp Breakfast Pie with Reindeer Sausage

Crust:
2 cups all-purpose flour
1 teaspoon salt
¾ cup cold shortening
    (half butter-flavored)
5 tablespoons ice water

Filling:
5 cups sliced, tart pie apples
¼ cup brown sugar
½ cup granulated sugar
1½ tablespoons Minute Tapioca
½ teaspoon ground cinnamon
⅛ teaspoon ground nutmeg
2 tablespoons birch syrup (optional)
½ teaspoon vanilla extract
1 (8-ounce) polish sausage, chopped

Topping:
¼ cup (½ stick) firm butter or margarine
½ cup all-purpose flour
½ cup brown sugar
½ cup quick oats
½ teaspoon ground cinnamon
½ cup chopped walnuts

For crust, mix flour and salt and cut shortening into flour mixture with pastry blender until size of small peas. Sprinkle water over flour and toss with fork until it clings together. Roll out at least 3 inches wider than rim of 9-inch pie pan.

To make the filling, toss apples with sugars, tapioca, spices, and syrup to coat well. After juice forms, add vanilla and sausage and toss again to combine. Place in the crust. Fold up bottom crust to cover top of pie.

To make the topping, cut butter into flour, sugar, oats, and cinnamon and mix until crumbly. Add nuts. Sprinkle over apple filling.

Preheat oven to 425°. Trim off ragged edges of piecrust if necessary to even outer edge to about 2 inches past rim of pan. Fold edge of crust to center, partly covering edge of filling and topping, and forming waves evenly as needed to take up excess crust. Bake on bottom rack of oven 20 minutes. Reduce heat to 350° and continue 30 to 40 minutes longer until fruit is tender when tested with toothpick and filling has boiled at least 5 minutes. May place on top rack for last 15 minutes to increase browning if necessary. Yields 1 (9-inch) pie.

Note: A ceramic pie baking dish holds heat well and browns the bottom crust.

Crustless Individual Salmon Quiches

4 eggs
1 cup reduced-fat sour cream
1 cup reduced-fat cottage cheese
¼ cup all-purpose flour
⅓ cup Parmesan cheese
1 teaspoon onion powder
¼ teaspoon lemon pepper
⅛ teaspoon or dash of cayenne
1 tall can red (sockeye) salmon
    or 2 cups poached or baked
    and flaked
4 ounces canned mushroom stems
    and pieces, drained
1 cup tiny broccoli florets
4 ounces Cheddar cheese, grated
4 ounces Monterey Jack cheese, grated
½ teaspoon dill weed

In a blender combine eggs, sour cream, cottage cheese, flour, Parmesan cheese, onion powder, lemon pepper, and cayenne. Blend until smooth. Preheat oven to 350°. Drain canned salmon. Flake (not too small or mashed) salmon into large bowl. Drain mushrooms and combine with salmon. Blanch broccoli tips 30 seconds in boiling water or defrost frozen florets in microwave, and add to salmon and mushrooms. Toss cheeses to distribute evenly. Sprinkle dill weed over all. Gently fold in mixture from blender, being careful not to break up salmon flakes or broccoli. Fill ten individual ramekins or quiche dishes that have been sprayed with nonstick coating. Bake in pan of boiling water 30 to 45 minutes until eggs and cheese are set in center and top slightly browned. Can be covered with plastic wrap and refrigerated 8 to 10 hours prior to baking. Shorten baking time by warming ramekins in microwave on medium 2 to 3 minutes, and then finish in oven 20 to 30 minutes in pan of boiling water to prevent tough bottom crust. Yields 10 servings.

Variations: For shrimp or crab, use 8 ounces cocktail shrimp or snow, king, or imitation crab cut in chunks and flaked. Use only Monterey Jack cheese, increasing to 8 ounces, and add ½ teaspoon grated lemon peel and 1 tablespoon chopped chives, omitting dill. For ham quiche, use at least 1 cup chopped ham, 8 ounces Cheddar cheese, and omit Monterey Jack cheese, dill weed, and broccoli tips.

The crust should be rolled slightly thicker than usual so it will hold up well. Folding up the bottom crust is quicker than rolling a top crust, and it prevents the filling from boiling over.

Rhubarb Slush or Sorbet

2 quarts sliced fresh or frozen rhubarb
2 quarts water
3 cups sugar
1 (3-ounce) package strawberry gelatin
6 ounces pink or raspberry lemonade
    concentrate, thawed
Red food coloring (optional)

In large stainless steel or enamel saucepan, combine rhubarb and water. Bring to a boil. Reduce heat and simmer 5 minutes or until tender. Add the sugar, gelatin, and lemonade concentrate. Add red coloring if needed to give appetizing pink color. In blender, purée mixture 3 cups at a time, allowing room to incorporate air until becomes smooth and slightly thick. Freeze in convenient-size plastic containers.

Soften in refrigerator several hours, just enough to enable cutting into chunks to put in blender. Whip again on ice-crush speed to produce smooth ice crystals and incorporate air. Refreeze. Allow to soften a little at room temperature or 2 to 3 hours in refrigerator before serving as sorbet, more time for slush. Serve a small scoop (#30 ice scoop) of sorbet over a combination of fresh fruits and berries—whatever is available to provide contrast of color and texture—in a short-stemmed glass. Chunks of seedless watermelon, cantaloupe, honeydew, nectarine, kiwi, slices of strawberries and bananas, grapes halved, and whole raspberries and blueberries all make a great combination. Top scoop of rhubarb

sorbet with a little lemon-lime soda for sparkle and garnish with a sprig of mint, kiwi wedge, split strawberry, or a viola blossom. Yields about 3 quarts.

Blueberry Sausage Brunch Cake

Cake:
1 cup plus 1 tablespoon sugar
¾ cup butter-flavored shortening
3 eggs
3 cups plus 1 tablespoon all-purpose flour
1½ teaspoon baking powder
¾ teaspoon baking soda
1½ cups reduced-fat sour cream
1 pound mild breakfast sausage, fried in
    small pieces and well drained
1½ cups frozen or fresh wild blueberries

Crumb topping:
⅓ cup all-purpose flour
½ cup sugar
½ teaspoon ground cinnamon
¼ cup cold margarine
½ cup chopped walnuts

Blueberry sauce:
½ cup sugar
2 tablespoons cornstarch
¾ cup warm water
2 cups blueberries
½ teaspoon lemon juice
½ teaspoon ground cinnamon

For cake, cream 1 cup sugar, shortening, and eggs until light and fluffy. Combine 3 cups flour, baking powder, and baking soda. Add flour mixture and sour cream alternately to creamed mixture. Fold in drained sausage by hand. Divide in half. Spoon one-fourth into each of 2 greased and floured 9-inch cake pans. Combine remaining 1 tablespoon sugar and 1 tablespoon flour in small bowl. Pour in frozen blueberries and toss gently to coat them. Sprinkle half the blueberries and sugar mixture over batter in each pan. Top with small spoonfuls of remaining batter. Gently spread batter, leaving some blueberries

showing. Warming pans to room temperature prior to baking is best. Sprinkle crumb topping over batter before baking.

Preheat oven to 350°. To make crumb topping, mix together flour, sugar, and cinnamon. With pastry blender, cut mixture into margarine until crumbly. Mix in walnuts and sprinkle on batter. Bake 35 to 40 minutes. Test center with toothpick. Cut each cake into 6 wedges. Cake is soft and the first piece may be difficult to serve. Pie server works well. Serve hot with warm blueberry sauce.

To make the blueberry sauce, mix together sugar and cornstarch in small saucepan. Add water and blueberries. Stir constantly over medium heat until mixture boils, thickens, and clears, about 1 minute. Stir in lemon juice and cinnamon. Lemon juice may be omitted with wild blueberries. Also a delicious topping for Sourdough Waffles. Yields 12 servings.

ALASKA'S NORTH COUNTRY CASTLE BED & BREAKFAST

14600 Joanne Court
P.O. Box 111876
Anchorage, AK 99511
(907) 345-7296
nccbnb@customcpu.com
www.customcpu.com/commercial/nccbnb

Luxury awaits you in this unique Victorian home on forested acreage with sparkling mountain and ocean view. Enjoy bounteous gourmet breakfasts watching for munching moose.

Glacier Melter

6 tablespoons butter
12 slices wheat bread, trimmed
2 tablespoons mayonnaise
¾ cup plus 6 tablespoons grated
    Parmesan cheese
1 (7-ounce) can mild chiles, diced
1 teaspoon diced jalapeños
1 teaspoon garlic powder
6 artichoke hearts, drained and chopped
3 large eggs, beaten until creamy yellow
1¾ cups milk
6 tablespoons diced pimiento

Preheat oven to 350°. Melt butter in 9 x 13-inch casserole. Dip six bread slices in butter to cover lightly. Place remaining 6 slices in butter in casserole. Top bread with mixture of mayonnaise, ¾ cup cheese, mild and jalapeño chiles, garlic, and artichokes. Place remaining 6 bread slices, butter-side up, over cheese mix. Mix eggs and milk and pour over bread stacks. Top each bread slice with 1 tablespoon pimiento (We arrange it in a heart shape.) and 1 tablespoon Parmesan cheese. Cover and refrigerate 1 hour or overnight. Bake, uncovered, 45 minutes or until knife inserted in center comes out clean. Serve hot. Yields 6 servings.

Peaches 'N' Cream Bread Pudding

4 cups bread cubes
4 tablespoons melted butter
1 (8-ounce) package cream cheese,
    softened
½ plus ¼ teaspoon almond extract
½ cup plus 2 tablespoons sugar
1 tablespoon fresh lemon juice
½ teaspoon salt
Peaches
2 eggs
½ teaspoon ground nutmeg
1 cup milk

In an 8 x 8-inch casserole, toss bread cubes with butter. Leave 2½ cups in the bottom of pan, reserving 1½ cups for topping. In a separate bowl, mix softened cream cheese with ½ teaspoon almond extract, ½ cup sugar, lemon juice, salt, and peaches (reserve 8 nice slices of peaches for pinwheel decoration), chopped and mixed in. Beat eggs, 2 tablespoons sugar, ¼ teaspoon almond extract, nutmeg, and milk. Pour two-thirds of the egg mixture over 2½ cups of bread cubes; spoon peaches 'n' cream mixture over that; arrange reserved bread cubes on top, then 8 peach slices in pinwheel fashion, and dribble rest of egg mixture over all. Cover and refrigerate for 1 hour or overnight. Cook at 350° for 40 minutes covered, and at 400° for 10 minutes uncovered. Cut into four portions and serve warm. Final product may be mushy in middle, but no one will complain. Yields 4 servings.

CAMAI BED & BREAKFAST

3838 Westminster Way
Anchorage, AK 99508
(907) 333-2219 (phone)
(800) 659-8763 (toll free)
stay@camaibnb.com
www.camaibnb.com

Camai Bed & Breakfast is located in a quiet Anchorage residential neighborhood where moose are often seen. Camai's three suites, all with private baths, are ideal for families or travelers wanting spacious accommodations with many amenities. Things to do in Anchorage (all within five to twenty minutes from our door): Anchorage Museum of History and Art; Alaska Native Heritage Center; Alaska Botanical Gardens; Walking Tour of Anchorage; Anchorage Trolley Tour; Aviation Museum, at the airport; Alaska Zoo; hike Flattop or Powerline Trail; Alaska Native Hospital; Saturday Market; hike to University Lake along Chester Creek in our backyard; hike or bicycle the Coastal Trail; for kids, play at Castle Heights Park in the neighborhood. There are about a hundred other things to do south and north.

Make-Ahead Hash Brown Breakfast Pizza

4 cups dehydrated hash brown potatoes
4 cups water
⅓ cup melted butter (or vegetable oil)
1 cup shredded Parmesan cheese
1 pound bulk pork sausage, browned,
    crumbled, and drained
¾ cup chopped onions
2 cups sliced fresh mushrooms
1 cup quartered artichoke hearts
2 teaspoons crumbled dried sage leaves
½ teaspoon pepper
¼ teaspoon ground nutmeg
¼ teaspoon allspice
1 teaspoon cumin
2 cups shredded Cheddar cheese
8 eggs
1 cup milk
3 to 4 sprigs Italian flat parsley

Preheat oven to 425°. Place potatoes in mixing bowl. Cover with hot water to reconstitute potatoes. After about 10 minutes when potatoes have absorbed water, drain off excess water. Press potatoes into 15 x 10 x 2-inch pan. Drizzle butter or oil over potatoes. Spread Parmesan cheese over potatoes. Bake 25 minutes or until top is browned. Remove from oven and let cool on rack about 10 minutes.

While potatoes are cooking, brown and drain sausage. Sauté onions and mushrooms. Arrange sausage, onions, mushrooms, and artichokes on top of cooled potatoes. Sprinkle with sage, pepper, ground nutmeg, allspice, and cumin. Sprinkle with Cheddar cheese.

At this point pan can be stored in refrigerator 6 to 8 hours, or you can proceed with recipe. Beat eggs. Mix milk with eggs.

Pour over potatoes. Spread parsley leaves over top. Bake at 325° 45 minutes or until eggs are set. Serve with salsa. Yields 8 to 10 servings.

Layered Fresh Fruit with Citrus Sauce

Citrus sauce:
⅔ cup fresh orange juice
⅓ cup fresh lemon juice
⅓ cup packed brown sugar
1 stick cinnamon
1 teaspoon grated orange zest
1 teaspoon grated lemon zest

Fruit:
2 cups diced fresh pineapple
1 pint fresh strawberries,
    hulled and sliced
2 kiwifruits, peeled and sliced
2 large peaches, sliced
3 medium bananas, sliced
2 oranges, peeled and sectioned
1 cup red or green grapes

To make citrus sauce, combine in saucepan orange juice, lemon juice, brown sugar, cinnamon, orange zest, and lemon zest. Heat to boiling, reduce heat; simmer 5 minutes. Cool and then chill. Makes ⅓ cup. In a glass serving bowl, arrange layers of fruit. Remove cinnamon stick and pour citrus sauce over all. Cover bowl. Chill. Yields 8 servings.

Craig's Favorite Granola

½ cup honey
½ cup peanut butter
⅓ cup molasses
½ cup vegetable oil
4½ cups uncooked old-fashioned oats
1 cup wheat germ
½ cup instant nonfat dried milk
1½ cups dry roasted, unsalted peanuts
10 ounces dried mixed fruit, snipped

Combine honey, peanut butter, molasses, and vegetable oil in saucepan. Heat until it comes to a simmer. Preheat oven to 300°. Combine all remaining ingredients. Pour honey mixture over dry ingredients and mix well. Spoon mixture into 15½ x 10½ x 1-inch pan. Bake 30 to 40 minutes, stirring every 10 minutes. Remove from oven and allow to cool. Store in a cool, dry place in an airtight container. Yields 6 to 8 servings.

THE SILVERBOW

120 Second Street
Juneau, AK 99801
(907) 586-4146 (phone)
(907) 586-4242 (fax)
info@silverbowinn.com
www.silverbowinn.com

The Silverbow is a six-room, historic inn located in the heart of downtown Juneau, Alaska. The building contains Alaska's oldest bakery as well as a restaurant and arthouse cinema. Downtown Juneau includes the state capitol, a lively historic district, many important older buildings, and three museums. It is a walkable city with a well-educated population of thirty thousand. The surrounding area has world-class hiking, fishing, and other outdoor activities. Juneau's most visited attraction, the Mendenhall Glacier, is a ten-minute drive from downtown.

Famous Silverbow Challah

1 (¼-ounce) package yeast
2 cups warm water (110 to 115°)
1 plus 1 egg
5 ounces (½ cup + 2 tablespoons) milk
¼ cup sugar
1 tablespoon salt
½ cup canola oil (or vegetable oil)
7 cups bread flour
Poppy seeds

Dissolve yeast in ½ cup of water to activate. Mix all ingredients except 1 egg in large bowl. Knead by hand for 15 minutes, or mix in standing mixer with dough hooks for 10 minutes. Cover and let rise to double. Punch down and divide into 6 even pieces. Roll each piece into a long rope. Braid 3 strands together, pinching ends together and tucking under each end. Repeat with remaining 3 pieces. Cover again and let rise to double. Preheat oven to 375°. Before baking, beat remaining egg and brush on top of dough. Sprinkle with poppy seeds. Place on double baking pan in oven, or place pan on a baking stone. Bake for 35 to 40 minutes. Yields 2 loaves.

Silverbow Salmon Cake

1 pound Alaskan, hot, smoked sockeye
    salmon (meat only, discard bones
    and skin)
1 garlic bagel, torn into small pieces
    about the size of a dime
3 cloves garlic, minced
3 eggs
2 teaspoons parsley

Mix all ingredients together in bowl. To form into patties, pick up handful of salmon mix and press between your hands to squeeze out any excess egg. Flatten balls into round patties. Refrigerate patties for at least 15 minutes to set. Cook in butter in sauté pan until crisp. Flip with spatula and brown other side. Serve on single lettuce leaf with wedge of lemon and either mild tartar sauce or plain yogurt. Yields 5 large cakes or 12 to 16 small cakes.
Note: Often accompanied by pasta with cream sauce.

Thai Hot and Sour Soup

10 cups chicken or vegetable stock
2½ ounces Tom Yom Paste
    (available in Asian groceries)
¾ pound tomatoes, diced
½ pound mushrooms, sliced
¾ pound carrots, sliced
1 pound broccoli, cut in chunks
1 (12-ounce) can coconut milk
1 teaspoon salt
1 teaspoon pepper
1 tablespoon lime juice

Heat stock with Tom Yom Paste. Add vegetables and boil until soft. (about 30 minutes). Reduce to simmer and add coconut milk, salt, pepper, and lime juice. Yields 12 servings.

Almond Biscotti

1¾ cups (1½ sticks) butter
2 cups minus 2 tablespoons sugar
2 teaspoons vanilla extract
5 whole eggs
2 tablespoons almond extract
4½ cups all-purpose flour
1½ teaspoons baking powder
1½ teaspoons salt
1⅓ cups chopped almonds

Use a standing mixer with paddle attachment. Cream butter and sugar. Add vanilla, eggs, and almond extract. Mix for at least 5 minutes until airy and well whipped. Scrape bottom of bowl and mix another minute to fully mix. Mix flour, baking powder, and salt in separate bowl. Add dry ingredients to batter a little at a time, until just mixed. Do not overmix. Add chopped almonds; mix just a few seconds to blend through. Divide into two even portions and roll into tubes about 12 inches long. (Roll in flour if they are too sticky to work with). Refrigerate for at least 4 hours.

First bake: Bake loaves on cookie sheet at 350° about 40 minutes until golden brown across entire top of loaf. They will spread out quite a bit. Remove from oven and let cool completely to room temperature.

Second bake: With a sharp knife, cut each loaf into 12 even slices. Stand slices on bottom edge on cookie sheet. Bake about 35 minutes until center of each cookie is an even light brown. Yields 24 cookies.

7 GABLES INN & SUITES

4312 Birch Lane
Fairbanks, AK 99708
(907) 479-0751 (phone)
(907) 470-2229 (fax)
gables7@alaska.net
www.7gablesinn.com

The 7 Gables is a Tudor-style inn with choice rooms and/or separate apartments. The rooms have Jacuzzis, fireplaces, and complimentary canoes that make 7 Gables Inn a relaxing retreat. Nearby attractions include the Riverboat Discovery, University of Alaska Museum, and Alaskaland. Gold mines offer panning, and far north golf courses are close.

Salmon Broccoli Quiche

1 (9-inch) deep-dish piecrust
1 cup broccoli crowns
2 green onions, chopped
1 cup flaked cooked salmon
8 ounces Swiss cheese, grated
6 eggs
1 cup whipping cream
¼ teaspoon dried dill
⅛ teaspoon cayenne
¼ teaspoon cracked black pepper

Preheat oven to 350°. Cover bottom of piecrust with broccoli. Layer onions, salmon, and Swiss cheese over broccoli. Beat eggs in separate bowl and stir in whipping cream, dill, cayenne, and cracked pepper. Pour over layers. Bake for 1 hour, or until center tests done. Allow to cool 15 minutes. Cut into six slices. Yields 6 servings.

Sausage Tortilla Quiche

10 (6-inch) corn tortillas
12 ounces bulk sausage,
    cooked and crumbled
1 cup shredded Monterey Jack cheese
1 cup shredded Cheddar cheese
4 ounces chopped green chiles
12 eggs
1 cup milk
1 teaspoon ground chili powder

Grease two (9-inch) glass pie plates, and spread 5 tortillas in each plate to make a "crust," overlapping edges. Divide crumbled sausage evenly between pie plates. Spread ½ cup Monterey Jack over sausage in each dish, followed by Cheddar cheese. Divide green chiles over cheese. Preheat the oven to 350°. Place eggs in large bowl and beat well. Add milk and chili powder. Pour over layered ingredients. Bake 50 minutes, or until center tests done. Allow to stand 10 minutes before slicing each quiche into 6 wedges. Yields 12 servings.

7 Gables Inn & Suites

Cappuccino Chip Muffins

Muffins:
2 cups all-purpose flour
¾ cup sugar
1 tablespoon baking powder
2 teaspoons instant espresso coffee powder
½ teaspoon salt
½ teaspoon ground cinnamon
1 cup milk
½ cup (1 stick) butter, melted
1 egg, lightly beaten
¾ cup semisweet chocolate mini chips

Chocolate cream cheese espresso spread:
4 ounces cream cheese, softened
1 (1-ounce) square semisweet chocolate, melted
1 tablespoon sugar
½ teaspoon vanilla extract
½ teaspoon instant espresso coffee powder

Preheat oven to 350°. Grease tin for twelve large muffins. In large bowl, stir together flour, sugar, baking powder, coffee powder, salt, and cinnamon. In separate bowl, stir together milk, butter, egg, and vanilla until well blended. Add milk mixture to dry ingredients. Stir to combine. Mix in chips. Spoon batter into prepared muffin cups. Bake 20 minutes or until tops spring back when touched lightly. Remove from tin and cool on wire rack. Yields 12 large muffins.

To make the spread, place cheese, chocolate, sugar, vanilla, and espresso in small bowl and blend together thoroughly. Yields 12 servings.

Star Sausage Won Tons

2 cups (1 pound) cooked sausage, crumbled
1½ cups grated Cheddar cheese
1½ cups grated Monterey Jack cheese
½ cup dry ranch salad dressing mix
1 (4¼-ounce) can chopped ripe olives
½ cup chopped red pepper
1 (60-pack) package won ton wrappers

Preheat oven to 350°. Combine sausage, cheeses, salad dressing, olives, and red peppers in large bowl. Lightly grease regular-size muffin tins and press one wrapper in each cup. Brush with oil. Bake 5 minutes or until golden. Remove from tins and place on baking sheet. Fill each won ton three-fourths full with sausage mixture. Return to oven for 5 minutes until bubbly. Yields 4 to 5 dozen.

Lemon Squares

1 cup (2 sticks) butter
½ cup confectioners' sugar
2 cups plus ⅓ cup all-purpose flour
4 eggs
2 cups granulated sugar
⅓ cup frozen lemonade concentrate
1 teaspoon baking powder

Preheat oven to 350°. Cream butter and confectioners' sugar. Add 2 cups flour to butter mixture and blend. Spread evenly in a greased, 9 x 13-inch baking pan. Bake for 20 minutes. Beat eggs until light and foamy. Gradually add granulated sugar. Add lemonade concentrate, remaining ⅓ cup flour, and baking powder. Beat thoroughly. Pour mixture over baked crust. Bake additional 25 to 30 minutes. Cut into 2-inch squares. Sprinkle with additional confectioners' sugar after removing from oven. Yields approximately 26 squares.

ALASKAN FRONTIER GARDENS BED & BREAKFAST

P.O. Box 241881
Anchorage, AK 99524-1881
(907) 562-2923 (phone)
(907) 345-6556 (fax)
afg@alaska.net
www.alaskafrontiergardens.com

The Frontier Gardens is an elegant Alaskan hillside estate on a peaceful, scenic three acres by Chugach State Park. Spacious luxury suites have a king-size bed, large Jacuzzi, sauna, fireplace, and double shower—getaway for honeymooners and special occasions. Count on gourmet breakfasts, museum-like environment with Alaskan hospitality, and exceptional comfort. Open year-round, special services and events at the inn include spa services such as massages, including Swedish, therapeutic deep tissue, aromatherapy, reflexology, and facial massage at extra cost; murder mystery events; golf; hiking; mountain biking; and cross country and downhill skiing. Other attractions include Chugach State Park, City Lights, mountains (Mt. McKinley), zoo, and Cook Inlet.

Crème Brûlée French Toast

1 stick (½ cup) unsalted butter
1 cup packed brown sugar
2 tablespoons corn syrup
1 (8- to 9-inch-round) loaf country-style bread
5 large eggs

1½ cups half-and-half
1 teaspoon vanilla extract
1 teaspoon Grand Marnier
¼ teaspoon salt

In small heavy saucepan melt butter with sugar and corn syrup over moderate heat, stirring until smooth, and pour into 13 x 9 x 2-inch baking dish. Cut six 1-inch-thick slices from the center portion of bread, reserving ends for another use, and trim crusts. Arrange bread slices in one layer in baking dish, squeezing them slightly to fit. In bowl whisk together eggs, half-and-half, vanilla, Grand Marnier, and salt until combined well and pour evenly over bread. Chill mixture, covered, at least 8 hours and up to 24. Preheat oven to 350° and bring bread to room temperature. Bake 30 to 40 minutes, or until set. Yields 4 to 6 servings.

Sausage and Potato Breakfast Casserole

1 pound bulk breakfast sausage
2 tablespoons all-purpose flour
1½ cups milk (do not use low-fat or nonfat)
1 (1-pound) package frozen, shredded hash brown potatoes
4 green onions, finely chopped
1¼ cups grated sharp Cheddar cheese

Preheat oven to 350°. Butter 8 x 8 x 2-inch glass baking dish. Cook sausage in large, heavy skillet over medium-high heat until brown, breaking into small pieces with back of spoon, about 5 minutes. Mix in flour and milk. Cook until mixture thickens and comes to a boil, stirring occasionally, about 5 minutes. Arrange potatoes in prepared dish. Top with one-third of green onions, 1 cup cheese, another one-third of

green onions, sausage mixture, and remaining ¼ cup cheese. Bake casserole until potatoes are tender, about 45 minutes. Sprinkle with remaining green onions and serve. Yields 6 servings.

Wildberry French Toast

1 loaf French bread, cut in 1-inch-thick slices
6 eggs, beaten
¾ cup milk
1 tablespoon vanilla extract
¼ teaspoon baking powder
1 (16-ounce) bag mixed frozen berries
1 cup sugar
1 tablespoon cornstarch
1 tablespoon pumpkin pie spice
1 tablespoon cinnamon sugar

Place bread slices in large, shallow baking dish. Combine eggs, milk, vanilla, and baking powder and pour over bread. Cover and chill 8 to 10 hours. Remove from refrigerator 30 minutes before baking. Preheat oven to 400°. In a bowl combine berries, sugar, cornstarch, and pie spice. Pour into greased 9 x 13 x 2-inch baking dish. Arrange prepared bread on top. Sprinkle with cinnamon sugar. Bake uncovered for 35 to 40 minutes. Yields 6 servings.

Sausage and Tomato Quiche

1 (8-inch) frozen piecrust, baked
1 cup shredded mozzarella
3 sweet Italian sausages, cooked and crumbled
2 egg yolks plus 1 whole egg
½ teaspoon salt
⅛ teaspoon dried red pepper flakes
2 cups whipping cream
1 large tomato, halved crosswise, seeded, and thinly sliced
1 teaspoon dried oregano

Preheat oven to 425°. Place piecrust on cookie sheet and put cheese and sausage in crust. Beat together yolks and egg, salt, and red pepper flakes. Mix in cream. Pour into piecrust. Place tomato slices in circular pattern on top. Sprinkle with oregano. Bake 15 minutes. Reduce oven temperature to 300°. Bake until tester inserted in center comes out clean, about 40 minutes. Let stand 10 minutes. Serve warm. Yields 6 to 8 servings.

Never-Fail Piecrust

1 pound lard
5 cups all-purpose flour
1 teaspoon salt
1 teaspoon baking powder
2 tablespoons sugar
1 egg
2 tablespoons vinegar

Mix lard, flour, salt, baking powder, and sugar until lard is mixed in thoroughly. In separate bowl beat egg and vinegar. Add water to fill to 1 cup. Add egg mixture to the dough. Roll out and arrange in pie plate. Yields 4 piecrusts.

Casa Tierra Adobe Bed & Breakfast

11155 West Calle Pima
Tucson, AZ 85743
(520) 578-3058 (phone)
(866) 254-0006 (toll free)
info@casatierratucson.com
www.casatierratucson.com

Casa Tierra Adobe Bed & Breakfast has three rooms plus two bedroom suites beautifully decorated featuring Mexican furniture, private Talavera tile baths, queen-size beds with luxurious linens, and viga and latilla ceilings. The inn is a true hacienda-style, exposed adobe structure with an open central courtyard with fountain, which is beautifully landscaped and invites you to sit, relax, and enjoy the sights and sounds. There is an additional courtyard with fountain and desert garden on the eastern side of the inn, perfect for watching sunrises and birds.

Casa Tierra Scrambled Egg Enchiladas

1 dozen eggs or equivalent egg substitute
2 tablespoons butter
1 (8-ounce) package shredded Mexican-style cheese
1 dozen (8- to 10-inch) flour tortillas
½ teaspoon adobo spice*
2 cups light cream sauce (or 1 package country gravy mix prepared per instructions on package)
1 (10-ounce) package frozen chopped spinach, cooked per directions and drained well
1 teaspoon ground nutmeg
½ cup diced sweet red pepper
Cilantro leaves

Scramble eggs with butter until set. Spread some cheese on entire surface of tortilla. Put 2 heaping tablespoons of scrambled egg mixture on tortilla, sprinkle lightly with adobo, and roll up tightly. Place seam-side down in a buttered pan. Continue until all egg mixture is used.

Preheat oven to 350°. Make cream sauce and fold in spinach and ground nutmeg. Spoon over enchiladas and top with remaining cheese. Bake covered for about 30 minutes or until bubbly. Uncover and put under a low broiler for a few minutes to brown the cheese slightly. Garnish with chopped sweet red pepper and cilantro. Yields 12 servings.

*If adobo is not available, use equal parts of salt, pepper, oregano, and garlic.

Casa Tierra Green Chile Polenta

1 cup quick-cooking grits
2 tablespoons butter
2 large eggs
2 cups shredded sharp Cheddar cheese
1 cup diced green chiles
1 clove garlic, minced or pressed
½ teaspoon adobo spice
¾ teaspoon pepper
1 teaspoon hot sauce
¼ cup chopped red bell pepper
¼ cup chopped green bell pepper
⅓ cup fresh cilantro leaves

In 2- to 3-quart pan blend the grits with 4 cups water. Bring to a boil over high heat, stirring often. Add butter. Cover pan and reduce heat to low. Stir often until grits are tender, about 5 to 6 minutes. In large bowl, beat eggs to blend. While stirring add cheese, chiles, garlic, adobo, pepper, and hot sauce. Add grits and pour mixture into buttered, shallow, 9 x 13-inch baking dish or 2½- to 3-quart casserole. Preheat oven to 350° and bake until lightly browned for 40 to 45 minutes. Let stand about 5 minutes. Garnish with red and green bell peppers and cilantro. Cut into pieces and serve with a wide spatula. Yields 8 servings.

Casa Tierra Stuffed French Toast

1 (8-ounce) package light cream cheese
1 loaf day-old French bread sliced into
    16 thick slices
1 (6-ounce) jar prickly pear marmalade
1 cup fat-free French vanilla
    coffee creamer
32 ounces egg-white product
    (or 1 dozen eggs)
1 teaspoon vanilla extract
Prickly pear syrup for garnish
Confectioners' sugar

Spread cream cheese evenly on 8 pieces of bread. Place 1 teaspoon marmalade on other 8 and make a sandwich. Place sandwiches into a deep, heavily buttered baking pan. In blender, mix coffee creamer, eggs, and vanilla. Pour mixture over the bread. Turn bread several times to coat evenly. For best results, soak the bread 8 to 10 hours before baking.

Preheat oven to 350°. After turning sandwiches one final time, butter tops and cover with foil. Bake on center rack of oven for 1 hour. Uncover for the last few minutes to brown the tops. Drizzle syrup on a serving plate. Place French toast in center and sprinkle with confectioners' sugar. Serve with additional syrup if desired. Yields 8 servings.

Light-as-a-Feather Biscotti

¾ cup sugar
5 ounces (10 tablespoons) butter
½ teaspoon vanilla extract
1 cup egg white product (or 4 eggs)
2½ cups all-purpose baking mix
1¼ cups bread flour
1 cup diced, dried apricots
1 cup pistachio nut meats

Mix all ingredients by hand or in electric mixer. Shape dough into a smooth ball.

Using a sharp knife, cut into 2 or 3 pieces. Sprinkle your working surface with sugar and roll pieces into 12-inch logs, adding enough sugar to coat surface of logs. Preheat oven to 350°. Space logs on nonstick cookie sheet with enough space between to allow spreading. Bake 15 to 25 minutes until golden brown. Let cool. Cut biscotti at an angle. Yields 3 dozen.

THE ROYAL ELIZABETH BED & BREAKFAST INN

204 South Scott Avenue
Tucson, AZ 85701
(520) 670-9022 (phone)
(520) 629-9710 (fax)
(877) 670-9022 (toll free)
info@royalelizabeth.com
www.royalelizabeth.com

The Royal Elizabeth Bed & Breakfast Inn has a touch of the southwest and also offers accommodations with a southern background as well. The pristine white and green exterior opens to a warm and inviting inside. Conveniently located within minutes of government offices and major Tucson attractions, the Royal Elizabeth is perfect for business as well as leisure guests.

Nearby destinations include El Presidio Historic District, Tucson Museum of Art, Sonoran Desert Museum, Convention Center, and the University of Arizona. The inn is housed in a totally renovated, 1878 adobe mansion, complete with pool, spa, garden areas, and so much more.

The Best Banana Pudding

Vanilla wafers for crust
½ cup all-purpose flour
⅔ cup sugar
¼ teaspoon salt
2 eggs, separated
2 cups milk
1 teaspoon vanilla extract
3 ripe bananas
¼ teaspoon cream of tartar for meringue
2 tablespoons sugar for meringue

Butter 9- to 10-inch pie plate. Line plate with vanilla wafers. Mix all dry ingredients, add egg yolks, and slowly add milk. Heat mixture on medium, stirring frequently. After it thickens, add vanilla. While mixture cools, cut bananas in slices and put over vanilla wafers. Pour pudding mixture over bananas. Beat egg whites until peaks are stiff and add cream of tartar and sugar. Top pudding mixture with beaten egg whites. Preheat oven to 400° and bake until meringue is delicate brown, about 8 to 10 minutes. Yields 4 servings.

Quick Moravian Sugar Cake

4 cups biscuit baking mix
¼ cup sugar
¼ cup skim milk powder
    (Do not mix with water.)
½ cup instant potatoes, uncooked
2 eggs
3 tablespoons vegetable oil
1 (12-ounce) can beer
2 cups light brown sugar, for topping
1¼ teaspoons ground cinnamon,
    for topping
1½ sticks butter, melted for topping

Mix together dry ingredients, except those for topping. Beat eggs. Add oil and beer to eggs. Combine egg mixture with dry ingredients. Spread in lightly oiled, 17 x 11 x 1-inch pan. Let stand 10 to 15 minutes. Preheat oven to 350°. Mix brown sugar and cinnamon. Spread over cake, making small depressions with a floured finger. Drizzle butter on top. Bake 20 to 25 minutes. Yields 12 to16 servings.

Cranberry Scones

⅓ cup chilled margarine or butter
1¼ cups all-purpose flour
4 tablespoons sugar
2½ teaspoons baking powder
¼ teaspoon salt
1 plus 1 egg, beaten
½ cup dried cranberries (may substitute currants or raisins)
4 to 6 tablespoons half-and-half

Preheat oven to 400°. Cut butter into flour, sugar, baking powder, and salt until mixture resembles fine crumbs. Stir in 1 egg, cranberries, and just enough half-and-half so dough leaves side of bowl. Turn dough onto lightly floured surface and knead 10 times. Form into biscuit-size pieces or cut into diamond shapes. Place on ungreased cookie sheet. Brush dough with remaining egg. Bake 10 to 12 minutes or until golden brown. Yields 4 to 6 servings.

Spinach and Artichoke Dip

1 (9-ounce) package creamed spinach at room temperature
½ plus ¼ cup freshly grated Parmesan cheese
1 (14-ounce) can artichoke hearts, drained and chopped
¼ teaspoon white pepper
1 teaspoon fresh lemon juice
1 cup shredded mozzarella cheese

Preheat oven to 400°. Combine all ingredients, using just ½ cup Parmesan cheese, and blend thoroughly. Place in ovenproof dish and top with remaining ¼ cup Parmesan

cheese. Bake until hot and bubbly, about 25 minutes. Serve with crackers, chips, pita points, or whatever you choose. Yields about 1 quart.

Southern Pimiento Cheese

1½ pounds cheese (½ pound each of medium sharp Cheddar, mild Cheddar, and Swiss or mozzarella), grated
2 (7-ounce) jars chopped pimientos, not drained
Mayonnaise
Salt, cayenne, and fresh lemon juice

Mix cheeses with pimientos and liquid. Add enough mayonnaise to make a spreadable mixture. Add salt, cayenne, and lemon juice to taste. Wonderful for afternoon snacks on bread or crackers. Store in refrigerator; the cheese will keep for 2 to 3 weeks.

DESERT DOVE BED & BREAKFAST

11707 E. Old Spanish Trail
Tucson, AZ 85730
(520) 722-6879 (phone)
(877) 722-6879 (toll free)
info@desertdovebb.com
www.desertdovebb.com

The Desert Dove is an old west adobe situated on four acres—a lush desert setting within walking distance from the Saguaro National Park. Guests enjoy gourmet breakfasts and romantic country ambience. Area attractions include Saguaro National Park,

Sonoran Desert Museum, Colossal Cave, Mt. Lemmon, San Xavier Mission, Old Tucson Movie Studio, Sabino Canyon, and Kitts Peak Observatory. Day trips include Tombstone and the OK Corral, Bisbee and the Copper Queen Mine, and Nogales, Mexico.

Southwestern Frittata

The frittata should be prepared the day before and allowed to "cure" in the refrigerator overnight.

1 pound bulk sausage, cooked (ground turkey or chicken can be used in place of pork; for vegetarians, leave out meat)
1 pod garlic, pressed
1 (or more) cans chopped, mild green chiles
8 corn tortillas, sliced into small strips
1½ cups shredded pepper Jack cheese
9 large eggs
1 cup milk
1 teaspoon salt
¼ teaspoon black pepper
½ teaspoon onion salt
½ teaspoon cumin
Chili powder
1 large ripe tomato, thinly sliced for top
Reduced-fat sour cream

Brown sausage and drain any excess fat. Add pressed garlic to meat and cook for a few more minutes. Grease 9 x 13-inch baking dish and evenly line the bottom of dish with half of the chopped chiles, half of the tortilla strips, half of the sausage, and half of the cheese. Repeat layering with other half of chiles, tortilla chips, sausage, and cheese. In a medium bowl, whisk eggs, milk, salt, pepper, onion salt, and cumin until well mixed. Pour mixture over top of dish. Sprinkle with chili powder to taste. Place tomato slices over top. Cover with plastic wrap. Place in refrigerator overnight to cure.

The next day, preheat oven to 375°. Remove plastic wrap from dish and bake frittata 45 to 50 minutes, or until top is

Desert Dove Bed & Breakfast

golden and sides are a rich brown color. Cut into equal pieces and serve with a dollop of sour cream and salsa. Serve with warmed flour tortillas or your favorite toast. Yields 6 to 8 servings.

Orange French Toast

⅓ cup butter
½ cup pecan pieces
4 eggs
⅔ cup orange juice
⅓ cup milk
¼ cup sugar
¼ teaspoon ground nutmeg
½ teaspoon vanilla extract
8 (1-inch) slices French bread
    or double thin slices
Confectioners' sugar
Orange slices for garnish

Melt butter in 9 x 13-inch glass casserole or baking dish, making sure sides are well buttered. Place pecan pieces evenly in butter. Whisk together eggs, orange juice, milk, sugar, ground nutmeg, and vanilla. In shallow dish dip bread, one piece at a time, in egg mixture. Nestle bread over the melted butter and pecans and pour any leftover milk mixture over bread. Cover with plastic wrap and refrigerate 8 to 10 hours. When ready to bake, heat oven to 375°. Remove plastic wrap and bake 30 to 35 minutes or until puffed up and lightly brown. Dust with confectioners' sugar and top with a thin slice of orange, rind removed. Serve with maple syrup. Yields 4 servings.

No-Bake
Fudge Cookies

1 cup granulated sugar
1 cup brown sugar
½ cup (1 stick) butter
½ cup milk
1 cup chocolate chips
2 cups oatmeal
½ cup coconut
½ cup chopped walnuts

Into a saucepan put sugars, butter, and milk. Cook 2 minutes and remove from heat. Stir in the chips to melt, then add oatmeal, coconut, and nuts. Mix until thick and drop in small mounds on wax paper. Cool. These freeze well. Yields 2 dozen cookies.

Baked Oatmeal
Delight

½ cup (1 stick) melted butter
2 eggs
½ cup brown sugar
3 cups oatmeal
2 teaspoons baking powder
1 teaspoon salt
1 cup milk
1 teaspoon ground cinnamon
1 teaspoon vanilla extract
½ cup raisins or dried cranberries
½ cup coconut
(You can substitute apples and walnuts)

Preheat oven to 350°. Put butter, eggs, sugar, oatmeal, baking powder, and salt in bowl. Make a well in the center and add milk, cinnamon, vanilla, raisins, and coconut. Blend well. Pour into greased 9 x 13-inch pan. Bake 20 to 30 minutes. Do *not* overbake. Serve hot with fresh fruit and milk on the side. I serve it with a scoop of vanilla yogurt. Yields 8 servings. Recipe can be cut in half for 4 servings.

Bountiful Brunch

1 (24-ounce) package frozen shredded
    hash browns
7 eggs plus 1 egg
Salt and pepper
½ cup milk
4 ounces (1 cup) ham, chopped,
    or bacon (½ cup), cooked and
    crumbled
½ cup chopped green bell pepper
½ cup chopped red and yellow peppers
½ cup sliced mushrooms
¼ cup sliced green onions
1 cup shredded Cheddar cheese

Preheat oven to 400°. Oil 9 x 13-inch pan or 12-inch round, cast-iron skillet. Warm the baking dish. Thaw potatoes and combine with 1 egg, lightly beaten, and salt and pepper to taste in a 2-quart bowl. Mix well. Spread potato mixture in prepared pan and pat down evenly. Bake 15 minutes. Remove potatoes from oven. Reset oven to 375°. Whisk remaining 7 eggs and milk in 1-quart bowl. Season with salt and pepper if desired. Microwave on high 3 minutes and stir. Eggs should not be completely set. Do not overcook. Spread partially cooked egg mixture evenly over potato crust. Add chopped ham and vegetables. Cover with shredded cheese. Bake 15 to 20 minutes. Cut and serve. Garnish with a sprig of fresh parsley or cilantro. Serve with your favorite toast and salsa. Yields 6 servings.

Betty's B & B Cookies

1 cup (2 sticks) butter
1 cup granulated sugar
1 cup brown sugar
2 eggs
1 teaspoon vanilla extract
2 cups all-purpose flour
2½ cups blended oatmeal
    (measure oatmeal and
    blend "in blender" to
    fine powder)
½ teaspoon salt
1 tablespoon wheat germ
1 teaspoon baking powder
1 teaspoon baking soda
12 ounces chocolate chips
1 cup or ½ bag of English toffee bits
1½ cups nuts of choice
    (the inn uses pecans)

In a bowl, cream butter with both sugars. Add eggs and vanilla. In another large bowl, mix together flour, oatmeal, salt, wheat germ, baking powder, and soda. Blend the two mixtures. Add chips, toffee bits, and nuts. Preheat oven to 375°. Spread cookies two inches apart on cookie sheet (or baking stone). Bake 7 to 10 minutes. Yields 56 cookies.

THE HONEY HOUSE

5150 North 36th Street
Phoenix, AZ 85018
(602) 956-5646(phone)
(602) 224-9765 (fax)
HoneyHouse@aol.com
www.travelguides.com/home/honeyhouse

This historic property is located on an acre of lush, verdant land on the Arizona Canal. It was homesteaded in 1895, and the original owner was the first agricultural agent for Arizona to teach beekeeping to the farmers. At one time there were 1,500 beehives on this property. There are three rooms available with The Honey House, which has a Civil War library, wood floors with oriental carpets, and a charming kitchen that overlooks a wooded area. The inn has bikes for the guests and is within walking distance of the Biltmore Hotel, a shopping center, and wonderful restaurants of all kinds.

Pankannugen

6 pieces bacon
2 cups milk
5 large eggs
2 tablespoons sugar
1 cup all-purpose flour

Preheat oven to 350°. In baking dish sprayed with nonstick coating, cut up bacon and microwave until semi-crisp. While it is cooking, in bowl whisk milk, eggs, sugar, and flour. Add to bacon dish. Bake 25 minutes. Cut into squares. Serve with warm syrup and butter. Yields 4 servings.

THE PLEASANT STREET INN

142 South Pleasant Street
Prescott, AZ 86303
(928) 445-4774 (phone)
(928) 777-8696 (fax)
(877) 226-7128 (toll free)
info@pleasantbandb.com
www.pleasantstreetinn-bb.com

The inn is a lovely Victorian house in a residential neighborhood of historic downtown Prescott. Guests are treated to bright, spacious rooms with rich, traditional furnishings and private bathrooms. Prescott was twice the territorial capital of Arizona and is rich in pioneer lore. There are museums, art galleries, and the historic Court House Square. Explore the Prescott National Forest and area lakes with hiking, climbing, bike trails, kayaking, and fishing. Relax in Prescott with shopping, dining, walking, antiquing, day spas, golf, and tennis. There's something for everybody in Prescott.

Pleasant Street Fruit Parfait

4 tablespoons plain granola
    (no raisins or nuts or flavoring)
4 wide-mouth stemmed glasses
8 ounces vanilla yogurt
8 ounces fresh strawberries, sliced
    (save two whole berries for top)
1 banana, sliced
8 ounces fresh blueberries,
    washed and drained

Place 1 tablespoon granola in the bottom of each stemmed glass. Layer 1 to 2 tablespoons yogurt on top of granola. Layer sliced fruit on top of yogurt in this order: strawberries, then banana, then blueberries. Place small dollop of yogurt on top of blueberries. Halve remaining two strawberries and place a half on top of each parfait. Serve immediately. Yields 4 servings.

Note: For a lovely presentation, place the stemware on a paper doily on a saucer.

Candy Apple French Toast

½ cup (1 stick) butter
1 cup brown sugar
2 tablespoons corn syrup
2 tart apples, peeled and sliced
¼ cup golden raisins
¼ cup chopped walnuts (optional)
1 loaf French bread, cut in 1-inch slices
5 eggs
1½ cups milk
1 teaspoon vanilla extract

Sugar-cinnamon topping:
3 tablespoons sugar
1½ teaspoons ground cinnamon

Cook butter, sugar, and corn syrup in saucepan over medium heat until it thickens to a syrup consistency. Pour into 9 x 13-inch baking dish that has been prepared with cooking spray. Spread apple slices, raisins, and walnuts over syrup. Place bread on top. Whisk together eggs, milk, and vanilla. Pour over bread. Cover and refrigerate 8 to 10 hours. Before baking, preheat oven to 350°.

Sprinkle top with mixture of sugar and cinnamon. Bake, uncovered, 40 minutes. Cut in squares and serve with Apple Cider Syrup (see recipe below). Yields 8 to 9 servings.

Apple Cider Syrup

½ cup sugar
1½ teaspoons biscuit mix
½ teaspoon ground cinnamon
1 cup apple cider
1 tablespoon lemon juice
2 tablespoons butter

Mix all ingredients except butter in saucepan. Cook, stirring constantly, until mixture thickens and boils. Boil 1 minute. Remove from heat and stir in butter. Serve hot. Leftover syrup will keep in refrigerator for a few weeks. Yields about 1¼ cups.

Pleasant Street Inn

Pleasant Street Breakfast Scones

2 cups all-purpose flour
2 teaspoons baking powder
½ teaspoon baking soda
¼ teaspoon salt
3 plus 1 tablespoons sugar
⅓ cup butter or margarine
½ cup sour cream
1 large egg, lightly beaten
⅔ cup chopped dried apricots
   (or golden raisins)
2 teaspoons milk

Combine flour, baking powder, soda, salt, and 3 tablespoons sugar. Stir well. Cut in butter with pastry blender until mixture is crumbly. Add sour cream and egg, stirring just until dry ingredients are moistened. Stir in dried fruit. Preheat oven to 400°. Turn dough out onto lightly floured surface and knead lightly 4 to 5 times. Pat dough into two 6-inch circles on greased baking sheet. Brush top with milk and sprinkle with remaining 1 tablespoon sugar. Cut circles into 6 wedges each,

using a sharp knife. Separate wedges slightly. Bake for 14 to 16 minutes or until lightly browned. Serve scones warm with strawberry butter or lemon curd. Yields 12 scones.

Breakfast Enchiladas

2 cups shredded cheese
   (sharp cheese, Jack cheese,
   pepper Jack, or combination)
8 to 10 (8-inch) flour tortillas
½ cup chopped green onions
1 (4-ounce) can diced green chiles
1 tablespoon all-purpose flour
2 cups milk
6 eggs, beaten

Place about 2 tablespoons cheese evenly on a tortilla. Top with 1 teaspoon green onions and 1 teaspoon diced chiles. Roll up and place seam side down in a greased 13 x 9 x 2-inch baking dish. Repeat until all tortillas are filled. Combine flour, milk, and eggs in bowl until smooth. Pour mixture over tortillas. Cover and refrigerate 30 minutes before baking. Preheat oven to 350°. Cover and bake 25 minutes. Uncover and bake additional 10 minutes. Sprinkle with remaining cheese and bake 3 minutes longer. Let stand 10 minutes before serving. Yields 4 to 6 servings.

THE INN AT 410

410 North Leroux Street
Flagstaff, AZ 86001
(928) 774-0088 (phone)
(928) 774-6354 (fax)
(800) 774-2008 (toll free)
info@inn410.com
www.inn410.com

Relax at the "Place with the Personal Touch." There are nine distinctive guest rooms with private bath, some with fireplace, and Jacuzzi. Explore the Grand Canyon, ancient Indian ruins, Sedona, and Oak Creek Canyon. Venture into historic, downtown Flagstaff. Visit the Museum of Northern Arizona, Riordan Mansion, and Lowell Observatory. Hike, mountain bike, and ski nearby.

Ginger Scones

Scones:
½ cup whipping cream
1¼ cups all-purpose flour
½ cup whole wheat flour
⅓ cup confectioners' sugar
1¼ teaspoons baking powder
½ teaspoon salt
½ cup finely chopped crystallized ginger
Finely grated zest of 1 medium orange
½ cup cold butter, cut into small pieces
1½ teaspoons pure vanilla extract

Topping:
1 teaspoon whipping cream
¼ teaspoon vanilla extract
1 tablespoon finely chopped
    crystallized ginger
1 teaspoon sugar

For scones, coat a large baking sheet with nonstick spray. Preheat oven to 400°. Let ½ cup whipping cream sit at room temperature while you continue. In bowl of food processor, pulse together flours, confectioners' sugar, baking powder, salt, ginger, and orange zest until well combined. Add butter pieces and pulse food processor on and off until mixture resembles coarse sand. Combine room-temperature whipping cream and vanilla and add to flour mixture, stirring only until dry ingredients are moistened. Dough will be very sticky. Turn dough onto floured work surface and gently press together. With floured hands, pat into a circle about ¾-inch thick.

For topping, in small bowl, combine whipping cream and vanilla for topping. In another small bowl, mix together ginger and sugar. Brush cream mixture over top of dough. Sprinkle with ginger-sugar

mixture. Use a sharp knife to cut dough circle into 8 wedges. Place wedges, 2 inches apart, on prepared baking sheet. Bake about 15 minutes, or until golden brown. Yields 8 scones.

Bananas Bombay

½ cup low-fat sour cream or plain yogurt
1 tablespoon honey
1 tablespoon chutney
½ teaspoon curry powder
6 bananas
2 tablespoons toasted and chopped
    unsalted cashews
6 dates, each cut into 3 to 4 pieces

Mix sour cream, honey, chutney, and curry powder until well blended. Cover and refrigerate at least 1 hour to allow flavors to blend. Just before serving, peel and slice bananas into large mixing bowl. Toss gently with sour cream sauce until bananas are well coated. Distribute bananas among six fruit dishes or small bowls. Garnish with cashews and dates. Yields 6 servings.

THE Inn at 410
BED & BREAKFAST

Mexican Cactus Cooler

3 cups guava juice or mango nectar
2 cups ice cubes
2 tablespoons cactus syrup
1 lime, freshly squeezed

Put guava juice, ice cubes, and cactus syrup into blender. Add lime juice. "Froth to a frenzy" until ice cubes are puréed. Yields 6 servings.

Three Sisters Frittata with Tomatillo Sauce

Tomatillo Sauce:
1 small yellow onion, peeled and
    quartered
4 medium tomatillos, husked, washed,
    quartered
1 clove garlic, peeled
2 tablespoons canola oil
⅛ teaspoon ground black pepper
1 jalapeño pepper, washed, stemmed,
    seeded
2 tablespoons coarsely chopped cilantro
1 cup chicken stock

Frittata:
1 small zucchini, cubed (about ½ cup)
½ cup frozen corn kernels, thawed
½ cup frozen green beans, thawed
3 green onions, coarsely chopped
6 eggs
½ cup ricotta cheese
¼ cup milk
½ teaspoon dried Mexican oregano
½ teaspoon ground cumin
½ teaspoon salt
¼ teaspoon white pepper
½ cup shredded Cheddar
    or Colby Jack cheese
1 red bell pepper, minced for garnish
6 sprigs cilantro for garnish
1 small zucchini, sliced for garnish

For sauce, preheat oven to 400°. Toss onion, tomatillos, and garlic with oil. Spread on baking tray. Roast until well cooked, about 20 minutes. Cool slightly. Purée roasted vegetables, black pepper, jalapeño, and cilantro in food processor. Pulse until most of the chunks are gone. While processor is running, slowly add chicken broth in a steady stream through feed tube. Pour into airtight container and refrigerate 8 to 10 hours. When ready to use, put sauce in saucepan and heat over medium-low.

For frittata, spread zucchini on paper towels, sprinkle with salt, and let stand for 30 minutes. After 30 minutes, rinse salt from zucchini and set on paper towels to drain. Combine zucchini, corn, green beans, and onions in bowl. Preheat oven to 325°. Coat 9-inch pie pan with nonstick spray. In large mixing bowl, beat together eggs and ricotta just until mixed. Stir in milk, oregano, cumin, salt, and white pepper. Fold in vegetable mixture with shredded cheese. Pour into prepared pan and bake, uncovered, for 45 minutes. Remove frittata from oven and let sit for 5 minutes. Cut into 6 wedge-shaped servings. Top each serving with spoonful of Tomatillo Sauce and sprig of cilantro. Garnish plate with 2 slices of zucchini and a sprinkling of minced red pepper. Yields 6 servings.

Whole Wheat Carrot Pancakes with Orange Sauce

Orange Sauce:
3 whole eggs
3 egg yolks
1 cup sugar
6 tablespoons strained lemon juice
1 cup strained orange juice
2 teaspoons lemon oil
2 teaspoons orange oil
10 tablespoons butter, cut into
    small pieces

Pancakes:
2¼ cups whole wheat flour
3 teaspoons baking powder
1 teaspoon salt
1 teaspoon ground cinnamon
2¼ cups buttermilk
2 eggs
¼ cup honey
2 tablespoons canola oil
2 cups grated carrots
½ cup chopped pecans for garnish
½ cup raisins for garnish

For sauce, in medium saucepan, whisk together eggs, egg yolks, and sugar to combine. Stir in lemon juice, orange juice, lemon oil, and orange oil. Stirring constantly, cook over low heat. Stir in pieces of butter, a few at a time, until they melt and mix in. Continue stirring and turn heat to medium. Cook over medium heat until mixture thickens. Remember, thickening is a gradual process; it does not need to boil. This will take about 20 minutes. Pour into airtight container and refrigerate 8 to 10 hours. When ready, transfer sauce to saucepan and heat gently over low heat. You do not need to boil it, just reheat past lukewarm. Do not leave sauce unattended over heat, since it may cause eggs to curdle if it gets too hot.

Preheat griddle to 350°. In medium bowl, mix flour, baking powder, salt, and cinnamon together. In small bowl, whisk together buttermilk, eggs, honey, and canola oil. Add to flour mixture and stir just until mixed. Let sit until ready to cook. Just before cooking, fold in grated carrots. Using a ⅓-cup measure, drop batter onto hot griddle. When surface of pancakes is filled with bubbles, flip and continue cooking until done. Serve 2 on a plate. Use ¼-cup measure to spoon Orange Sauce over pancakes. Garnish with a sprinkling of chopped pecans and raisins. Yields 7 servings, 14 pancakes.

WHITE MOUNTAIN LODGE

P.O. Box 143
140 Main Street
Greer, AZ 85927
(928) 735-7568 (phone)
(928) 735-7498 (fax)
(888) 493-7568 (toll free)
bast@cybertrails.com
www.wmlodge.com

Built in 1892, the lodge reflects its country heritage. Guests enjoy magnificent views, luxury accommodations, and exceptional breakfasts in the heart of Arizona's White Mountains.

Shrimp Puffs

½ cup butter or margarine
1 cup water
1 cup flour
¼ teaspoon salt
4 eggs
¾ cup sharp Cheddar cheese
¼ cup chopped green onions, including
    part of green tops
1 (6-ounce) can small shrimp
¼ teaspoon garlic granules

Preheat oven to 400°. In medium saucepan, heat butter and water until it comes to a boil. Remove pan from heat and add flour and salt. Mix until flour is completely incorporated. Beat in eggs, one at a time, until thoroughly blended. Add cheese, onions, shrimp, and garlic; mix well. Drop dough by tablespoons about 1 inch apart onto two, ungreased cookie sheets. Bake for 30 minutes. Serve warm. Yields 45 to 48 puffs.

White Mountain Royal Eggs

3 tablespoons butter or margarine
¼ cup red bell pepper
¼ cup green bell pepper
2 tablespoons all-purpose flour
1 cup milk
½ teaspoon salt
1 teaspoon garlic granules
¼ teaspoon black pepper
½ cup shredded Cheddar cheese
4 hard-cooked eggs, peeled and sliced

In a 4-quart saucepan, melt butter or margarine. Put bell peppers into pan and sauté for 2 or 3 minutes until peppers start to soften. Add flour and mix to thicken. Gradually blend in milk with whisk to

...mps. Add salt, garlic, and pepper ...her over low heat until mixture thickens, about 8 minutes. Add cheese and stir until melted. Gently mix in sliced eggs. Serve hot over English muffins or buttermilk biscuits. Yields 4 servings.

Tortellini-Chicken Salad

When a group requests a light lunch, this is a great summer meal.

1 (20-ounce) package frozen, cheese-filled tortellini
½ cup virgin olive oil
¼ cup lemon juice
¼ cup red wine vinegar
2 tablespoons sugar
1 tablespoon dried parsley flakes
1 teaspoon dried oregano
½ teaspoon garlic
½ teaspoon salt
½ teaspoon pepper
1 large bunch spinach leaves, cleaned, dried, and crisp
4 cooked, boneless chicken breasts, cut in strips and chilled
1 cup shredded Italian cheese blend (4- or 6-cheese mix) or feta cheese
½ large red onion cut in thin rings
6 hard-cooked eggs, peeled and quartered

Prepare tortellini according to package directions, drain, and set aside in large bowl. Combine oil, lemon juice, wine vinegar, sugar, parsley, oregano, garlic, salt,

and pepper. Mix well and pour over tortellini until coated. Cover bowl and chill at least 2 hours or up to 1 day ahead.

To assemble, mix spinach, chicken, and cheese with tortellini and mound on individual serving plates. Arrange onion rings and eggs on top or around edge of plate. Yields 6 servings.

Strawberry Muffins

½ cup (1 stick) butter at room temperature
½ cup butter-flavored shortening
1 cup sugar
2 eggs
1 cup strawberry yogurt
1 teaspoon vanilla extract
2 cups all-purpose flour
1 teaspoon baking soda
½ teaspoon salt
1 cup fresh strawberries, cut in small pieces

Preheat oven to 350°. Grease and flour 24 muffin cups or use paper cupcake liners. In large mixing bowl, cream together butter, shortening, and sugar until well blended. Add eggs, yogurt, and vanilla and

beat well about 2 minutes. Stir in flour, baking soda, and salt and mix until flour is completely blended. Fold in strawberries. Pour into muffin cups until about half full. Bake for 20 minutes or until center springs back when touched. Yields 24 muffins.

Mary's Swiss Omelet Casserole

8 slices of bread, cut in ½-inch cubes
½ cup diced onion
1 cup grated mild Cheddar cheese
1½ cups grated Swiss cheese
¼ cup diced green bell pepper
¼ cup diced red bell pepper
¼ cup sliced mushrooms
1 cup milk
1 cup sour cream
6 eggs
½ teaspoon ground mustard
½ teaspoon granulated garlic
½ teaspoon black pepper

Grease 9 x 13-inch baking pan, and lace cubed bread evenly in bottom. Layer onions, cheeses, peppers, and mushrooms evenly over bread. Beat milk, sour cream, eggs, mustard, garlic, and pepper in medium bowl until well blended, about 2 minutes. Pour egg mixture evenly over layers and cover with plastic wrap. Place in refrigerator overnight. In the morning, preheat oven to 350° and bake casserole until eggs are set, about 30 to 40 minutes. Let casserole sit for 15 minutes before cutting. Serve with sliced ham and fruit garnish. Yields 12 servings.

Arkansas

MORNINGSTAR RETREAT

370 Star Lane
Eureka Springs, AR 72632
(479) 253-5995 (phone)
(800) 298-5995 (toll free)
office@morningstarretreat.com
www.MorningstarRetreat.com

The Morningstar mission statement: "Morningstar Retreat exists as a country retreat for the purpose of offering an environment in which people can slow down from the hectic pace of our modern lives. We believe that the natural setting, the absence of TVs and ringing phones exert a powerful healing influence in our lives. Simplicity, nature, peace and quiet, and the additional aids of therapeutic Jacuzzi baths and massage allow us to offer a healthy stress-free alternative to the usual pace of the many see-it-all, do-it-all vacations. It is our sincere hope that those who stay here will find an escape from the ordinary patterns of their lives. We offer an interlude of peace and potential, from which they may heal their relationships, reevaluate their priorities, and find delight and meaning in the simple things that nature has to offer."

Eureka Springs is a unique Ozark Mountain village. There are art galleries, craft stores, and fine restaurants here. Also you are surrounded by nature. You can enjoy hiking, mountain biking, and enjoy the lakes, rivers, and views everywhere you look.

Aunt Rose's Cookies

½ cup (1 stick) butter
½ plus ½ cup sugar
1 egg
1 tablespoon orange zest
3 tablespoons milk
1½ teaspoons baking powder
1¾ cups all-purpose flour
½ cup golden raisins
½ cup chopped English walnuts
1 egg white, slightly beaten

Cream butter with ½ cup sugar and add egg, orange zest, and milk. Add baking powder to flour and stir into the wet mixture. Stir in raisins and chopped walnuts. Chill dough 1 hour. Preheat oven to 400°. Roll dough into walnut-size balls. Dip tops into egg white and then remaining ½ cup sugar. Place sugar-side up on a dry cookie sheet. Bake for 12 to 15 minutes. Cool completely on wire rack and store in an airtight container. Yields about 30 cookies.

Sweet Potato Muffins

½ cup (1 stick) butter
1¼ cups sugar
2 eggs
1¼ cups cooked and mashed sweet potato
1½ cups unbleached all-purpose flour
2 teaspoons baking powder
¼ teaspoon salt
1 teaspoon ground cinnamon
¼ teaspoon ground nutmeg
1 cup milk
¼ cup chopped pecans
½ cup chopped raisins or dates

Preheat oven to 375°. Coat muffin tins with nonstick spray. Cream butter and sugar. Add eggs and mix well. Blend in sweet potatoes. Blend flour, baking powder, salt, cinnamon, and ground nutmeg. Add alternately to flour mixture with milk. Do not overmix. Fold in nuts and raisins. Fill muffin tins two-thirds full. Bake 25 minutes or until done. Cool in tins for 5 minutes before moving to wire rack to cool. Yields 18 regular-size muffins.

Morningstar Fudgy Brownies

Brownies:
4 ounces unsweetened chocolate
1½ sticks butter
2 cups sugar
3 eggs
1 teaspoon vanilla extract
1 cup all-purpose flour

Frosting:
3 tablespoons butter
3 tablespoons light corn syrup
1 cup chocolate chips
20 pecan halves

Melt chocolate and butter in heavy saucepan over low heat. Put sugar in large bowl and stir in melted chocolate and butter. Mix in eggs and vanilla. Add flour, mixing well. Preheat oven to 350°. Grease 9 x 13-inch pan with shortening. Spread brownie mixture evenly in pan. Bake for 25 minutes.

For the frosting, melt butter in a small saucepan over medium heat and add corn syrup and chocolate chips, stirring until completely melted. Spread frosting over brownies and evenly space pecans on top. Cool completely before cutting. Yields 20 servings.

Harvest Moon Cookies

2 cups all-purpose flour
1 teaspoon salt
1 teaspoon baking soda
1 cup (2 sticks) butter
¾ cup granulated sugar
⅔ cup packed brown sugar
2 eggs
1 teaspoon vanilla extract
2 cups uncooked oat flakes
½ cup chopped black walnuts
½ cup dried cranberries

Blend the flour, salt, and baking soda. Beat butter, sugars, eggs, and vanilla until light and fluffy. Stir into flour mixture along with oats until well blended. Add walnuts and cranberries. Preheat oven to 375°. Drop dough by rounded teaspoonfuls onto cookie sheet, two inches apart. Bake 10 minutes until golden brown. Let stand 1 minute before cooling on a wire rack. Yields 6 dozen cookies.

THE HEARTSTONE INN & COTTAGES

35 Kings Highway
Eureka Springs, AR 72632
(479) 253-8916 (phone)
(800) 494-4921 (toll free)
info@heartstoneinn.com
www.heartstoneinn.com

This award-winning, handsomely restored, Victorian house with wraparound porches is located in the historic district and is known for its one-of-a-kind breakfasts. Nestled in the Ozarks, the inn offers ample outdoor activities, including fishing, canoeing, horseback riding, and hiking. The historic downtown is bustling with art galleries, quaint shops, and antiques. The inn offers golf and massage packages to rejuvenate the guests. Music shows and concerts, including the world famous passion play, abound.

Praline Brunch Toast

½ cup butter
¾ cup plus 1 tablespoon packed brown sugar
½ cup maple syrup
¾ cup coarsely chopped pecans
6 cups cubed sourdough bread
8 eggs
1½ cups half-and-half
2 teaspoons vanilla extract

Lightly grease 9 x 13-inch baking dish. Combine butter, ¾ cup brown sugar, and maple syrup in medium saucepan. Cook over medium heat until butter is melted and sugar is dissolved. Pour mixture in the bottom of greased pan and sprinkle pecans evenly over the top. Arrange cubed bread on top of pecans. Beat eggs, half-and-half, vanilla, and remaining 1 tablespoon brown sugar together until frothy. Ladle over bread so that all pieces are soaked. Cover and refrigerate 8 to 12 hours. When ready to bake, bring to room temperature and preheat oven to 350°. Bake for approximately 45 minutes or until set. Invert onto cookie sheet, leaving baking dish on for several minutes to allow topping to set up. Remove baking dish, cut, and serve. Yields 8 servings.

Surprise Bran Muffins

This batter is best prepared the night before baking, then covered tightly and refrigerated.

4 cups all-purpose flour
4 cups all-bran cereal
2 cups sugar
4 teaspoons baking soda
2 teaspoons salt
3 eggs
4 cups milk
1½ cups vegetable oil
2 (8-ounce) tubs honey-nut cream cheese or flavor of your choice

In large bowl, mix flour, cereal, sugar, soda, and salt. Beat together eggs, milk, and oil. Add to dry ingredients and mix just until blended. When kept overnight cereal will dissolve and make a thick batter. Stir again before use. Prepare muffin tins with nonstick spray. Preheat oven to 400°. Spoon about 2 tablespoons batter into each of the muffin cups. Drop 1 rounded teaspoon cream cheese into center and then add batter on top to three-fourths full, covering cream cheese. Bake 15 to 20 minutes or until browned. Batter will keep in refrigerator for up to 2 weeks if you wish to make fewer muffins at a time. Yields 4 dozen muffins.

Pear Bread

3 cups all-purpose flour
1 tablespoon ground cinnamon
1 teaspoon baking soda
1 teaspoon salt
¼ teaspoon baking powder
1 cup chopped pecans
3 eggs, beaten
2 cups sugar
2 cups peeled and grated ripe pears
¾ cup vegetable oil
2 teaspoons vanilla extract

Preheat oven to 325°. Grease and flour two
9 x 5-inch loaf pans. Combine flour, cinnamon, baking soda, salt, baking powder,
and pecans in bowl. Make a well in dry
ingredients. Combine remaining ingredients in separate bowl, blending well. Add
wet ingredients to dry ingredients, stirring
until just moistened. Pour into prepared
pans. Bake for 1 hour 15 minutes or until
done. Cool in pans 10 minutes before
turning out onto rack to cool completely.
Yields 2 loaves.

Artichoke-Potato Quiche

12 eggs
½ cup Parmesan cheese
1 (10¾-ounce) can mushroom soup
1 teaspoon dried basil
1 teaspoon seasoned salt
¼ teaspoon pepper
2 cups Monterey Jack cheese
2 cups Cheddar cheese
1 (16-ounce) can artichoke hearts,
    chopped
½ cup medium chunky salsa
    plus extra for garnish
¼ cup chopped onion
4 cups frozen hash brown potatoes

Preheat oven to 350°. Lightly grease 9 x
13-inch baking dish. Beat together eggs,
Parmesan cheese, soup, basil, salt, and
pepper until well mixed. Stir in cheeses,
artichoke hearts, salsa, and onion. Add
potatoes, breaking up and distributing
them evenly. Pour into prepared pan and
bake for 1 hour until set and slightly
browned. Let stand a few minutes before
cutting and garnish with more salsa. Yields
8 servings.

POND MOUNTAIN LODGE & RESORT

1218 Highway 23 S
Eureka Springs, AR 72632
(479) 253-5877 (phone)
(800) 583-8043 (toll free)
info@pondmountainlodge.com
www.pondmountainlodge.com

Mountaintop breezes, pastoral and
panoramic views, a leisurely pace, country
breakfast, and warm hospitality await you
at Pond Mountain. Relax in your cabin or
private Jacuzzi suite or enjoy horseback
riding, fishing, swimming, Ping-Pong, or
billiards. Or simply listen to the wind
rustling through the 150 acres of woods,
the crackling of your private fireplace,
cicadas singing the life beat, birds calling
their partners, and the gentle sounds of
silence for your soul. Located at the highest point in Carroll County, Pond Mountain enjoys a thirty-mile view of the Ozark
Mountains, ridges, and valleys. Our two
spring-fed, landscaped ponds at the mountain's top are stocked for your catch-and-
release fishing pleasure.

"After the Fall" Pancakes

1 cup all-purpose flour
½ cup whole wheat (or graham) flour
3 tablespoons brown sugar
1½ cups ricotta cheese
¼ cup slivered almonds
2 cups finely diced Rome, McIntosh,
    or Jonathan apples
1 teaspoon ground nutmeg
1 teaspoon ground cinnamon
Dash of salt
7 or 8 eggs, well beaten

Mix together flours and brown sugar. Add
cheese and almond extract. Fold in apples,
nutmeg, cinnamon, and salt. Add eggs and
mix well. Pour batter in ¼- to ½-cup portions onto medium hot iron skillet in small
amount of butter or light oil. Cook until
golden brown. Serve with yogurt or sour
cream (and a little syrup for the tradition-
alist). For the adventuresome, serve with
tart Cranberry Chutney (see recipe below).
Yields 8 servings.

Cranberry Chutney

1 cup whole cranberries
½ cup brown sugar or ¼ cup honey
1 tablespoon water
¼ teaspoon vanilla extract
¼ teaspoon orange zest
2 tablespoons Cointreau
½ cup walnuts (optional)

Simmer cranberries, brown sugar, and
water over medium heat about 10 minutes

(cranberry skins should pop open slightly). Add remaining ingredients. Let flavors meld at room temperature for 15 minutes. Refrigerate. Good with pancakes, seafood. Yields about 1½ cups.

Sweet Potato/Pecan Buttermilk Pancakes

2 cups all-purpose flour
½ teaspoon salt
1½ teaspoons baking soda
1 teaspoon sugar
2 tablespoons melted butter
2 cups buttermilk
¼ cup chopped pecans
1 cup cooked and mashed
    sweet potatoes
1 teaspoon ground nutmeg
1 teaspoon ground cinnamon
2 (or 3) egg yolks (reserve whites)

Mix together all ingredients except egg whites. Beat egg whites and fold into batter just until well blended; do not overmix. Let batter be lumpy. Pour batter by ¼ or ⅓ cup and fry on medium-hot iron skillet in small amount of butter or light oil until golden brown. Yields 8 servings.

Slumbering Volcanoes

4 large tomatoes
4 canned artichoke hearts
4 eggs

Topping:
4 tablespoons Parmesan cheese
4 tablespoons breadcrumbs seasoned
    with 1 teaspoon dill, ½ teaspoon
    garlic, ½ teaspoon onion powder

Preheat oven to 350°. Carefully scoop out insides of tomatoes and drain juice from shells. Place tomatoes, hole-side up, in baking dish and put in oven for 8 to 10 min-utes. Remove shells from oven and put 1 artichoke heart into center of each. Break 1 egg over each artichoke heart and then sprinkle with 1 tablespoon Parmesan and 1 tablespoon seasoned breadcrumbs. Place "volcanoes" back into oven and bake approximately 20 minutes. (Time depends on how you prefer eggs cooked; if you want hard yolks, bake for ½ hour.) Serve hot with side condiments of sour cream, chopped chives, green chili salsa, or others of your imagination. Yields 4 servings.

Simply Chic Seafood Bisque

¼ pound fresh shrimp, shelled,
    deveined, cooked, and chilled
¼ pound crabmeat
    (or imitation crabmeat)
½ pound whitefish, lightly sautéed in
    ½ cup chicken or vegetable broth
4 cups homemade tomato soup
    (or low-salt canned tomato soup)
1½ tablespoons curry, mild or hot
    according to your preference
2 cups evaporated skim milk
    or 1½ cups sour cream
3 tablespoons fresh lemon juice
1 teaspoon ground nutmeg

Place all ingredients in large, non-aluminum soup pot over medium heat. Heat just until slightly steaming; don't boil. Serve either hot or chilled, depending on taste. Garnish with thin slice of lemon and sprinkle of parsley. Yields 8 servings.

Cuban Black Bean Chili

2 pounds ground chuck or ground
    round, browned and drained
1 large onion, diced
1 large green pepper, diced
3 cloves garlic, crushed
3 carrots, finely grated
Black beans (1 pound dry beans that
    have been precooked in chicken
    or beef broth or 4 cans beans)
1 (28- to 32-ounce) can crushed tomatoes
2 (20-ounce) cans peeled, diced tomatoes
Juice of 3 fresh limes
    or 6 tablespoons frozen lime juice
Dash of Tabasco or Louisiana Hot Sauce
1 tablespoon cumin
1 tablespoon garlic powder
    (optional but suggested)

In large iron pot or Dutch oven, sauté ground chuck, onion, green pepper, garlic, and carrots for 5 to 8 minutes to blend. Add beans and remaining ingredients. Simmer for at least 35 minutes, adding a little of cook's sipping beer to achieve desired thickness of chili. Serve with slice of lime, sprig of mint, and dollop of sour cream or plain yogurt floated on top. Serving with thick and crusty hot French bread is an extra treat. Yields 8 servings.

1884 BRIDGEFORD HOUSE

263 Spring Street
Eureka Springs, AR 72632
(479) 253-7853 (phone)
(479) 253-5497 (fax)
(888) 567-2422 (toll free)
innkeeper@bridgefordhouse.com
www.bridgefordhouse.com

Southern hospitality combined with Victorian charm awaits you at our beautiful Queen Anne/Eastlake home (circa 1884). The Bridgeford House is nestled in the very heart of Eureka Springs in a quiet neighborhood. The Ozark Mountain vistas are your backdrop. The inn is within a few blocks of the historic downtown with numerous gift boutiques, antique shops,

1884 Bridgeford House

Baked Swiss Corn

3 cups freshly cut corn or 2 (9-ounce)
    packages frozen corn
1 (5½-ounce) can evaporated milk
1 egg, beaten
2 tablespoons chopped onion
½ teaspoon salt
Dash of pepper
¾ plus ¼ cup shredded Swiss cheese
½ cup soft breadcrumbs
1 tablespoon melted butter

Preheat oven to 350°. Cook corn in salted
water until tender. Combine corn, milk,
egg, onion, salt, pepper, and ¾ cup of the
cheese. Mix and pour in greased baking
dish. Toss breadcrumbs with melted butter
and remaining ¼ cup cheese. Sprinkle over
corn mixture and bake 25 to 30 minutes.
Yields 4 to 6 servings.

massage spas, fine restaurants, and art
emporiums. Located on the trolley car and
horse-drawn carriage routes, you are
within easy access to all interesting sights.
Almost every month, there is an art or
music festival in Eureka Springs. In addition, there is the Turpentine Creek Wildlife Refuge for lions, tigers, and bears—oh,
my!

Baked Bananas

4 bananas
½ cup orange juice
¼ cup brown sugar
½ cup granola-type cereal

Preheat oven to 375°. Cut bananas into
½-inch-thick round pieces and arrange in
ovenproof dish. Pour orange juice over
bananas and toss to coat. (Bananas will
darken if not covered well.) Sprinkle
evenly with brown sugar. Bake 10 minutes.
Do not overcook or bananas will be mushy.
Just before serving, sprinkle with granola.
Yields 8 servings.

Spring Street Grape-Cran Breakfast Daiquiri

1 (12-ounce) can frozen white or
    purple grape juice concentrate,
    not prepared
1 (12-ounce) can frozen cranberry juice
    concentrate, not prepared
12 ounces (1½ cups) chilled water
½ cup sugar
26 ice cubes
Mint sprigs or orange slices for garnish

Combine all ingredients except ice cubes
in blender. Blend 1 to 2 minutes. Decant
half mixture into pitcher or other container. Add 12 to 13 ice cubes to blender.
Blend until ice cubes have been incorporated smoothly. Decant this mixture
into serving pitcher. Repeat process with
remaining mixture. Serve beverage in
6-ounce, tall juice glasses. Garnish with
mint sprigs or orange slices on rim of
glass. Yields 10 (6-ounce) servings.

Cinnamon Chip Scones

2 cups all-purpose flour
2 teaspoons baking powder
½ teaspoon baking soda
½ teaspoon salt
2 tablespoons sugar, plus additional
    for dusting scones
1 stick butter
1 cup packaged cinnamon chips
1 egg, separated
1 teaspoon vanilla extract
¾ cup buttermilk

Preheat oven to 375°. In large bowl, combine flour, baking powder, baking soda,
salt, and sugar. Cut in butter until mixture
resembles coarse meal. Stir in cinnamon
chips. In another bowl, combine egg yolk,
vanilla, and buttermilk. Stir into dry
ingredients just until combined. Turn
dough onto a floured surface, handling it
as gently as possible. Do not use rolling
pin; pat into 10-inch circle that is ½-inch
thick. Cut into wedges or cut with 2-inch
cookie cutter. Place scones on ungreased

baking sheet. Lightly beat egg white and brush tops of scones. Dust with sugar. Bake 18 to 22 minutes until golden brown. Remove from pan and cool on wire rack. After 5 minutes, cover loosely with dish-towel until completely cool. Yields 12 scones.

1890 WILLIAMS HOUSE BED & BREAKFAST

420 Quapaw
Hot Springs National Park, AR 71901
(501) 624-4275
bnb@1890williamshouse.com
www.1890williamshouse.com

The 1890 Williams House Bed & Break-fast was the first bed and breakfast in the state of Arkansas, established in 1980. This is a grand mansion built in 1890. Master-fully constructed and located in the Historic District, the 1890 House offers a high level of comfort and privacy. The bed and break-fast is located five blocks from historic downtown. Sites and activities in the surrounding area include: the historic downtown shopping area; world famous Bathhouse Row; fine restaurants; art gal-leries; Oaklawn thoroughbred horse rac-ing; National Park with breathtaking mountains; hiking; beautiful lakes; boat-ing; fishing; carriage rides; horseback rid-ing; sightseeing tour of Historic City and National Park; and Magic Springs-Crystal Falls amusement and water park.

Cheese & Egg Brunch Pie

5 eggs, beaten
¼ cup all-purpose flour
8 ounces cream-style cottage cheese
1 (4-ounce) can chopped green chiles
2 tablespoons melted butter
½ teaspoon baking powder
2 cups shredded Monterey Jack cheese

1890 Williams House Bed & Breakfast

Preheat oven to 400°. Combine eggs, flour, cottage cheese, and green chiles in mixing bowl; beat well at medium speed with elec-tric mixer. Stir in remaining ingredients and pour into well-greased, 9-inch pie plate. Bake 10 minutes, reduce heat to 350°, and bake 20 to 22 minutes until set. Cut into wedges. Yields 6 to 7 servings.

Note: This recipe can be made the night before and baked in the morning. You can serve warm salsa on the side. Served with a biscuit and sausage links, this is a favorite at the Williams House.

Overnight French Toast

1 (1-pound) loaf French bread
4 eggs
2 cups milk
1 teaspoon ground cinnamon
4 tablespoons (¼ cup) vanilla extract
½ cup sugar
3 tablespoons butter or margarine, divided into 8 slices

Crumb topping:
¼ cup brown sugar
¼ cup (½ stick) butter or margarine, softened
¼ cup oatmeal
½ teaspoon ground cinnamon
¼ cup chopped pecans

Prepare large 10 x 15-inch baking dish lightly with coating spray. Cut bread into 8 slices, each 1½-inch thick. Any leftover bread can be saved for breadcrumbs for other recipes. Place slices in pan. Combine eggs, milk, cinnamon, vanilla, and sugar. Pour egg mixture over bread slices. Flip over each slice after eggs are partially absorbed. When all mixture is absorbed, top each slice with thin slice of butter. Wrap pan tightly with plastic wrap and freeze 8 to 10 hours.

For crumb topping, combine all ingredi-ents. To bake, preheat oven to 500°. Bake 15 minutes. Remove pan from oven and flip pieces over. Add crumb topping and return to oven to bake additional 10 minutes. Yields 4 servings.

Six Weeks Muffins

1 (15-ounce) box Raisin Bran cereal
3 cups sugar
5 cups all-purpose flour
5 teaspoons baking soda
2 teaspoons salt
1 teaspoon ground cinnamon
½ teaspoon allspice
1 cup vegetable oil
4 eggs, beaten
Melted butter
Cinnamon sugar

Mix dry ingredients in large bowl, add wet ingredients, and mix well. Store in covered container in refrigerator to use as needed. Batter will keep for six weeks. Preheat oven to 375°. To bake, fill greased muffin cups two-thirds full and bake 15 to 20 minutes.

Dip tops in melted butter and sprinkle with cinnamon sugar. Yields five dozen muffins depending on cup size.

Fresh Berry Cobbler

1 cup raspberries
3 cups blackberries
1 cup sugar
3 tablespoons cornstarch
¼ cup fruit juice
  (white grape juice or apple juice)

Topping:
2 cups all-purpose flour
3 teaspoons baking powder
½ teaspoon salt
4 tablespoons sugar
⅔ cup milk
3 tablespoons melted butter

Preheat oven to 400°. Combine berries and sugar. Put in 9 x 14-inch glass dish

and bake 10 minutes. While oven, mix cornstarch and juice When you remove berries from oven, stir in cornstarch mixture and mix well.

For topping, mix flour, baking powder, salt, and sugar together. Stir in milk and butter and beat well. Spoon dough onto prepared berry mixture. Bake 20 minutes or until top is golden brown. Cool on rack, slightly, before serving. Yields 8 servings.

California

The Inn at Schoolhouse Creek

7051 N. Highway One
Little River, CA 95456
(800) 731-5525 (toll free)
innkeeper@schoolhousecreek.com
www.schoolhousecreek.com

Stay on the quiet side of Mendocino and capture a slower pace at one of the oldest inns on the Mendocino Coast. Our historic bed and breakfast is set within eight acres of spectacular gardens. The inn is wedding, family reunion, and pet-friendly, and the Thyme Cottage is wheelchair accessible. Family antiques and collectibles appoint this comfortable coastal retreat. The inn is minutes to fine dining, sea kayaking, canoeing, hiking, biking, golf, botanical gardens, state parks, theater, and galleries.

Schoolhouse Creek Merlot Lamb Balls

<u>Lamb balls:</u>
3½ pounds ground lamb
1½ cups breadcrumbs
2 tablespoons seasonings (combination of dried basil, dried sweet marjoram, minced fresh parsley, dried minced garlic, and red pepper flakes)
2 to 3 tablespoons minced fresh rosemary
1 bunch green onions, minced
6 to 8 cloves garlic, minced
½ cup Merlot
½ cup soy sauce
⅓ cup brown sugar
1 cup currants

<u>Dipping sauce:</u>
½ cup Merlot
½ cup soy sauce
¼ cup honey
2 tablespoons hot pepper oil or sesame oil
2 teaspoons grated fresh ginger

Preheat oven to 450°. Combine lamb, breadcrumbs, seasonings, rosemary, onions, garlic, Merlot, soy, brown sugar, and currants and mix well. Form into small balls using approximately 1 to 1½ teaspoons of mixture. Bake on parchment-lined cookie sheet for 8 to 10 minutes. Serve with heated dipping sauce. Yields 75 pieces.

Combine ingredients for sauce well and simmer for 3 to 4 minutes until heated through.

Apple, Rosemary, and Cheddar Muffins

1½ cups all-purpose flour
¼ cup rolled oats
1 tablespoon sugar
2 teaspoons baking powder
½ teaspoon baking soda
½ teaspoon salt
⅛ teaspoon white pepper
⅛ teaspoon ground cardamom
¼ teaspoon allspice
½ teaspoon minced fresh rosemary
¾ cup nonfat milk
2 large eggs
¼ cup melted margarine
1 large Granny Smith or Pippin apple, peeled, cored, and cut in ⅛-inch pieces
¾ cup finely grated Cheddar cheese

Preheat oven to 400°. Mix all dry ingredients together. In medium bowl, whisk rosemary, milk, eggs, and margarine together well. Stir in apple and cheese. Add dry ingredients and stir just until blended. Using an ice cream scoop, fill oiled muffin tins two-thirds full. Bake 15 to 20 minutes or until toothpick comes out clean. Yields 12 muffins.

BRIDGE CREEK INN

5300 Righetti Road
San Luis Obispo, CA 93401
(805) 544-3003 (phone)
(805) 544-2002 (fax)
info@bridgecreekinn.com
www.BridgeCreekInn.com

Nestled in the vineyards just minutes from San Luis Obispo, our inn offers a view of the Santa Lucia Mountains from our redwood deck and a nightly show of brilliant stars from our hot tub. The craftsman-style home features two luxurious rooms on ten acres of land.

Bruschetta with White Beans, Tomatoes, and Olives

1 cup dried white beans
3 tomatoes, diced
¼ cup chopped kalamata olives
1 tablespoon minced garlic
¼ cup chopped fresh basil
4 plus 2 tablespoons olive oil
Salt and pepper
1 (18-inch) baguette,
    cut in ½-inch rounds
5 to 6 ounces goat cheese
Basil for garnish

Place beans in a large saucepan. Add water to cover. Boil and remove from heat. Let stand 1 hour. Drain and return to pan. Add cold water to cover. Boil and then turn down to a simmer for 1 hour 10 minutes. Drain and cool. Transfer 1½ cups beans to large bowl and mix with tomatoes, olives, garlic, basil, and 4 tablespoons olive oil. Season to taste with salt and pepper. Preheat broiler. Place bread on baking sheet and brush or spray with remaining 2 tablespoons olive oil. Broil until browned, about 1 minute. Spread with goat cheese and then top with about 2 teaspoons of bean mixture on each bread slice. Garnish with basil leaves to serve. Yields 36 appetizer servings.

Brie with Raspberries in Pastry

½ cup plum/raspberry jam
    (or raspberry or strawberry)
¼ cup fresh raspberries or sliced
    strawberries
½ teaspoon finely chopped fresh
    rosemary
Pepper
1 sheet frozen puff pastry, thawed
1 (6 to 7-inch) wheel of Brie
1 egg, beaten for glaze
Crackers or baguette slices

Stir jam, berries, and rosemary in small bowl. Season with pepper. Roll out pastry on floured board to about 12 inches. Cut top rind off Brie and discard. Preheat oven to 325°. Place Brie, rindless side up, in center of pastry. Spoon jam/berry mix on top. Fold pastry over cheese and press to seal. Brush pastry with egg glaze. Place on baking sheet and bake 30 minutes. Let cool for 15 minutes before serving. Garnish with fresh rosemary sprigs and either raspberries or strawberries and surround with crackers or baguettes to serve. Yields 30 to 45 appetizer servings.

Crabmeat Canapés

I freeze these with about 12 triangles to a Zip-loc bag and then just take out what I need for that evening's appetizer.

2 tablespoons butter
8 ounces crabmeat (or imitation crabmeat)
1 (6-ounce) jar Old English Cheddar
    Cheese spread
1 tablespoon mayonnaise
½ teaspoon seasoned salt
¼ teaspoon garlic salt
6 white English muffins, split

Soften butter, shred crabmeat, and combine with cheese, mayonnaise, and salts. Spread mixture on 12 muffin halves and freeze 10 minutes. Take out of freezer and cut each muffin half into 6 triangles. Broil 5 minutes until cheese is bubbly and slightly browned. Yields 72 pieces.

Couscous Baked Eggs

2 cups couscous, cooked according
    to package directions
9 mushrooms, sliced and cooked in a little
    butter (microwave for 1 minute)
1 cup whipping cream, whipped
6 eggs
Salt
Grated Swiss cheese
Ground nutmeg

Preheat oven to 425°. Divide cooked couscous into six ramekins or glass dishes. Divide mushrooms equally and mix into couscous. Divide whipping cream and top the couscous mix, making a well in the center for egg. Break egg into each depression and sprinkle slightly with salt. Put a little grated cheese and ground nutmeg on top of each. Bake about 12 to 14 minutes. If you wish yolk hard, 14 to 15 minutes. Serve warm. Yields 6 servings.

Serving suggestions: Garnish with sprigs of fresh rosemary and complete the meal with hashed brown potatoes and muffins of various types.

HOWARD CREEK RANCH

40501 North Highway One
P.O. Box 121
Westport, CA 95488
(707) 964-6725 (phone)
(707) 964-1603 (fax)
www.howardcreekranch.com

Howard Creek Ranch is alive with the rural splendor of sweeping ocean and mountain view, 60 acres of peace and beauty on the beach near the Lost Coast, a sixty-mile-long wilderness. The ranch was settled in 1867 as a land grant of thousands of acres and included a sheep and cattle ranch and a blacksmith shop. Horses, cows, sheep, and llamas graze the pastures.

In the middle of wide green lawns sits a large 1871 farmhouse filled with antiques. A seventy-five-foot swinging bridge spans Howard Creek as it flows past barns and cabins to the beach 200 yards away.

Overwhelmingly Delicious Baked Pears

Healthy pears (any variety, experiment)
Fresh apple cider or frozen apple juice
Ground cinnamon and sticks

Preheat oven to 350°. Slice pears in half lengthways. Remove any dark spots and core. Place upside down in pan and cover with cider or defrosted frozen apple juice. Cover with aluminum foil. Bake for 1 hour, longer if pears are hard as a rock or much less if pears are soft. Remove from oven and place upright on a plate. Add dash of cinnamon and place cinnamon sticks around plate here and there. Yields 2 servings per pear.

Variations: You can substitute juices. If you use blueberry juice or grape juice, the pears will look "funny," so add blueberries scattered over and around the plate and dark grapes for grape juice. You can also liven up the plate with fuchsias to pick up the various colors.

Baked Oranges

3 large oranges, halved and separated
    from skin into bite-size pieces
6 teaspoons cherry or blackberry brandy
Dab of butter
Brown sugar
6 maraschino cherries or 1 cup blackberries
6 teaspoons maraschino cherry syrup

Cut oranges in half. Arrange oranges pulp-side up on baking dish. Cut up pulp into pieces so that sections can be easily lifted to eat. The evening before serving, add brandy, butter, and brown sugar to taste. Refrigerate 8 to 10 hours. When ready to use, preheat oven to 350° and bake 20 minutes, or until tops begin to brown and pulp is very juicy. Remove earlier if oranges begin to burn. Add cherries and cherry syrup. Bake another 5 minutes. Arrange on serving platter with nasturtium leaves, flowers, and cinnamon sticks or blackberries. Serve warm with pretty silver spoons. Yields 6 servings.

Variation: Grapefruit makes an excellent dish also, and can be substituted for the oranges.

Baked Bananas

3 cups maple syrup
2 cups orange juice
1 tablespoon butter
6 large firm bananas, each cut into
    bite-size pieces
Dash of ground cinnamon

Preheat oven to 350°. In large pot warm syrup, orange juice, and butter. When it just begins to bubble, pour in with bananas in ovenproof dish. Mix in cinnamon and bake 5 to 10 minutes or just until the bananas begin to soften. Do not overcook. You want bananas to be firm, not mushy. Serve very hot. Yields 6 servings.

Variations: Add nuts (slivered or cut up), raisins, dried cranberries, or dates with the pits removed and cut up into small pieces.

Howard Creek Ranch

Salsa Puff

12 eggs
2 to 3 tablespoons sour cream
   (if you are cooking for thirty people
   you can use up to 1½ cups sour
   cream; never use nonfat)
Salt and pepper
2 cups fresh tomato salsa, medium
   strength, never hot
1 cup grated mozzarella or Monterey
   Jack cheese
Sour cream
Cilantro for garnish

Preheat oven to 350°. Beat eggs, sour cream, and salt and pepper until airy and fluffy. Layer bottom of small baking dish with the salsa. Pour egg mixture over this and sprinkle with cheese. Bake 45 to 50 minutes or until center is firm. To serve, cut away browned edges and cut into various-size pieces. Serve with sour cream on side and cilantro as garnish, or if you don't like cilantro, try mint leaves, nasturtium leaves, or some other green edible herbs. Yields 6 servings.

PACKARD HOUSE BED & BREAKFAST

45170 Little Lake Street
Mendocino, CA 95460-1065
(707) 937-2677 (phone)
(888) 453-2677 (toll free)
info@packardhouse.com
www.packardhouse.com

Packard House is a beautiful 1878 Victorian located in Mendocino Village, surrounded by gardens and ocean views. It is exquisitely decorated with fireplaces, jet tubs, luxury linens, and Italian tile. Activities in the area include bicycling, hiking, canoeing, kayaking, boating, fishing, whale and bird watching, shopping, wine tasting, garden touring, golfing, and tennis, to name but a few.

Peach Tarts for Six

9 ounces fresh, ready-made
   puff pastry
2 tablespoons butter plus extra
   for brushing
8 teaspoons light brown sugar
1 tablespoon finely chopped
   preserved ginger
3 peaches, peeled, cored, and halved
Crème fraîche

On lightly floured or sugared surface, roll out dough. Cut into six 3 x 4-inch pastry pieces. Place on large cookie sheet. Cream together butter and brown sugar in small bowl and stir in ginger. Prick pastry rounds all over with fork and mound a little of ginger mixture onto middle of each. In small saucepan, boil water and put each peach in for just a few seconds. Remove from water and remove skin from peach. Slice peaches in half. Keeping halves intact at the tip, carefully fan out slices slightly. Place fanned out peach halves on top of each dough round. Make small flutes around edge of dough rounds and generously brush peach half with melted butter. Preheat oven to 400° and bake 15 to 20 minutes until pastry is risen and golden in color. Serve warm with a little crème fraîche or yogurt. Yields 6 servings.

Spinach Frittata for Fourteen

¼ package previously frozen spinach
1 large zucchini
½ pound Monterey Jack cheese
1 cup Parmesan cheese
16 to 18 eggs

Preheat oven to 375°. In large bowl, combine spinach, zucchini, cheeses, and eggs. Mix well. Fill individual ramekins that have been coated with nonstick spray three-fourths full. Cook for 25 minutes. Yields 14 servings.

Potato-Mushroom Frittata

1 small onion, chopped
1 pound mushrooms (preferably
   crimini), sliced
1 tablespoon olive oil and butter,
   blended
1 (1-pound) package frozen grated
   potatoes
12 eggs
1 cup Parmesan cheese
1½ cups shredded Monterey Jack cheese

In large skillet over medium heat, sauté onion and mushrooms in oil-butter until onion is caramelized. Add potatoes and mix well. Add more butter or oil if needed. Cook until potatoes are tender. Cool. In large bowl beat the eggs, add cheeses, and fold in potato mixture. Preheat oven to 375°. Fill sprayed, nonstick ramekins three-fourths full and bake 30 minutes, or until set. Yields 6 servings.

Packard House Chocolate Chip Cookies

1 pound (4 sticks) soft butter
2 cups packed dark brown sugar
1½ cups granulated sugar
6 cups all-purpose flour
1½ teaspoons salt
1½ teaspoons baking soda
2 cups chocolate chips
1 cup pecans
½ cup coconut
½ cup dates

Mix by hand—no beaters. Cream butter and brown sugar. Add granulated sugar and beat for 3 to 4 minutes. Blend in a separate bowl flour, salt, and soda. Add dry ingredients to butter mixture. Beat well. Stir in chocolate chips, pecans, coconut, and dates. Preheat oven to 400°. Use small ice cream scoop or large spoon to place batter onto greased sheets. Cook 8 to 10 minutes (cookies don't look done). Let cool 5 minutes on sheet and remove and enjoy. Yields 4 to 5 dozen cookies.

BLAIR HOUSE CAROUSEL INN

2985 Clay Street
Placerville, CA 95667
(530) 626-9006 (phone)
(530) 295-9034 (fax)
info@blairhousecarouselinn.com
www.blairhousecarouselinn.com

Lumberman James B. Blair built this turreted Queen Anne with original woodwork, clinker-brick fireplace, and garden stonework in 1901 for his bride, Erla. Within the historic district of downtown Placerville the inn is near river rafting, gold mines, shopping, wineries, art galleries, antique shops, restaurants, hiking trails, and 45 minutes from Sacramento, the state capital, one hour's driving distance to Lake Tahoe for boating, fishing, gambling casinos, and more.

Eggs Carousel

3 English muffins, halved and cubed
1 cup shredded Swiss cheese
1 cup cooked Black Forest ham, cut in ¼-inch cubes
9 eggs
1 cup milk

Pepper
Hollandaise sauce
Paprika

Hollandaise sauce:
1 stick butter
3 egg yolks
1 tablespoon fresh lemon juice
3 dashes cayenne

Spray six ramekins with nonstick spray. Cover bottom of each ramekin one layer deep with muffin cubes. Next, sprinkle layer of Swiss cheese, then layer of ham cubes, and then another layer of Swiss cheese. Beat together eggs, milk, and pepper to taste. Then pour equal amounts into ramekins. Cover with plastic wrap and refrigerate 8 to 10 hours. When ready to bake, preheat oven to 350°. Uncover ramekins and bake 30 minutes. Top with hollandaise sauce and sprinkle with paprika. Serve with hash browns and fresh fruit. Yields 6 servings.

For sauce, melt butter in saucepan until almost boiling. In blender mix egg yolks, lemon juice, and cayenne. With blender running, pour butter slowly into blender and mix all ingredients. Sauce may be kept warm over warm water. Yields 6 servings.

Egg Puff

¼ cup sour cream
¼ cup milk
3 eggs
2 drops Tabasco
Pinch of dry mustard
½ cup shredded sharp Cheddar cheese

Preheat oven to 325°. Spray 2 (8-ounce) ramekins with nonstick spray. Beat together sour cream, milk, eggs, Tabasco, and dry mustard. Stir in cheese. Pour into prepared ramekins. Bake 35 minutes. Serve immediately. Yields 2 servings.

Blair House Carousel Inn

Sandy's Praline French Toast

2 tablespoons dark corn syrup
1 cup packed brown sugar
½ cup (1 stick) butter
¾ cup roasted chopped pecans
1 large loaf sweet French bread,
    cut into 1-inch-thick slices
8 eggs
¾ cup milk
¾ cup half-and-half
1 teaspoon vanilla extract
Dash of ground cinnamon
Dash of ground nutmeg
Strawberries and confectioners' sugar
    for topping

In saucepan, stir together corn syrup, brown sugar, and butter and cook until mixture thickens and coats the back of spoon. Spray 9 x 13-inch glass baking pan with butter-flavored nonstick spray. Pour sugar mixture in pan and immediately top with pecans, pressing nuts lightly into mixture. Arrange bread slices in two rows, six slices per row. Beat together eggs, milk, half-and-half, vanilla, cinnamon, and nutmeg. Pour over bread, cover with plastic wrap, and refrigerate 8 to 10 hours. When ready to bake, preheat oven to 350°. Remove wrap and bake 50 minutes or until golden brown. Let sit 5 minutes before cutting. Serve praline side up, top with strawberries, and sprinkle with confectioners' sugar. Serve with maple-flavored sausage and Strawberry Parfaits (see recipe below). Yields 6 servings.

Strawberry Parfait

¾ cup sliced strawberries
½ cup vanilla yogurt
¼ cup of oats granola, crushed
Mint sprigs for garnish

In a long-stemmed glass layer ingredients, starting with strawberries, yogurt, and granola. Top with a strawberry half and a sprig of mint. Makes an elegant presentation with very little work. You may also use other berries or seasonal fruits. Yields 1 serving.

Hangtown Onion Bites

½ cup freshly grated Parmesan cheese
½ cup finely chopped green onions,
    white part only
1 teaspoon dry mustard
½ cup mayonnaise
36 deli-style rye Triscuits

Mix cheese, onions, dry mustard, and mayonnaise together and refrigerate 8 to 24 hours. Preheat oven to 350°. Spread 1 rounded teaspoon of the cheese mixture on each Triscuit. Place on ungreased cookie sheet. Bake for 10 minutes or until golden brown. Yields 36 servings.

THE SHELFORD HOUSE BED & BREAKFAST INN

29955 River Road
Cloverdale, CA 95425
(707) 894-5956 (phone)
(707) 894-8621 (fax)
(800) 833-6479 (toll free)
info@shelford.com
www.shelford.com

This 1885 Victorian inn is in the heart of the Alexander Valley Wine Country and beautifully decorated with turn-of-the-century antiques. Come feast on our award-winning cookies, and let us pamper you with gourmet breakfasts of special breads, quiches, and stuffed French toast.

Blueberry Stuffed French Toast

1 loaf sourdough bread cut in
    1-inch squares
2 to 3 cups blueberries
1 (8-ounce) package cream cheese
9 eggs
1½ cups milk
⅓ cup maple syrup

Blueberry sauce:
1 cup sugar
1 cup water
1 to 2 cups blueberries
1 tablespoon cornstarch

Line bottom of 13 x 9 x 2-inch glass pan with sourdough. Top with fresh or frozen blueberries and small squares of cream cheese. Add another layer of cubed sourdough. Beat eggs, milk, and syrup until well blended and pour over layers. Cover dish with foil and refrigerate until ready to bake. When ready, preheat oven to 350° and bake covered about 30 minutes. Remove foil and bake additional 10 minutes until lightly browned and top of bread in center feels slightly dry. Cut into serving-size pieces. May be served with blueberry sauce. Yields 10 generous servings.

For sauce, mix sugar and water in a small saucepan. Bring to a slow boil for 10 minutes. Add berries and reduce heat when mixture returns to boiling. Simmer for about 30 minutes. While French toast bakes, just before serving, thicken with a lump-free mixture of cornstarch and a small amount of water. Stir constantly until thickened to desired consistency. Yields 3½ cups.

Spicy Baked Eggs with Green Chiles

½ stick butter
¼ cup all-purpose flour
½ teaspoon baking powder
¼ teaspoon salt
5 eggs
2 tablespoons diced green chiles
1 cup cottage cheese
2 cups grated Monterey Jack cheese

In saucepan melt butter and add flour, baking powder, and salt. Beat eggs well and add butter/flour mixture to eggs. Stir in chiles. Add cheeses and mix well. Preheat oven to 350°. Spray 8 x 8-inch glass baking dish or quiche pan with non-stick spray. Bake 40 minutes to 1 hour until center is firm. Serve with Dill Cheese Sauce (see recipe below). Yields 4 servings.

Dill Cheese Sauce

1 tablespoon butter
½ cup milk
½ cup heavy cream
Salt
¼ cup white Cheddar cheese
Freshly chopped dill weed

Heat butter, milk, and cream. Bring to a boil until rolling softly and turn heat to low. Add salt to taste, cheese, and dill. Yields about 1 cup.

Almond Poppy Seed Cake

½ cup shortening
1 cup (2 sticks) butter
3 cups sugar
5 eggs
3 cups all-purpose flour
½ teaspoon baking powder

1 cup milk
1 teaspoon vanilla extract
1½ to 2 teaspoons almond extract
2-plus teaspoons poppy seeds

Glaze:
1 cup confectioners' sugar
1 to 2 tablespoons half-and-half
Slivered almonds

Cream shortening, butter, and sugar until light and fluffy. Add eggs one at a time. Add flour and baking powder alternately with milk. Add extracts and poppy seeds. Bake in greased and floured tube pan at 325°. Do not preheat oven. Bake 1½ hours or longer. Make glaze with confectioners' sugar and half-and-half, and spread over cake. Top with slivered almonds. Yields 12 to 16 servings.

Santa Nella House Bed & Breakfast

12130 Highway 116
Guerneville, CA 95446
(707) 869-9488 (phone)
(800) 440-9031 (toll free)
info@santanellahouse.com
www.santanellahouse.com

An 1870s Victorian house with a grand wraparound veranda set among the redwoods in the Sonoma Wine Country, Santa Nella boasts four elegantly appointed guest rooms. Whether for a weekend getaway or a honeymoon, you will find many things to do in the area: Tour and taste award-winning wines at over fifty wineries nearby; go canoeing, kayaking, or swimming on the beautiful Russian River; bicycle through vineyards on quiet country roads; shop the fine boutiques of Healdsburg; go horseback riding and hiking through the ancient redwoods; stroll miles of pristine beaches along the Sonoma Coast; hunt for antiques in nearby Sebastopol; or just relax and enjoy the unhurried pace of life in a Victorian country inn.

Artichoke Soufflés

2 medium, cooked artichokes, chilled, or 1 (14-ounce) can quartered artichokes in water
5 large eggs, separated
¼ cup (½ stick) butter
¼ cup all-purpose flour
1½ cups milk
½ teaspoon salt
1 teaspoon Worcestershire sauce
⅛ teaspoon cayenne
⅛ teaspoon white pepper
½ pound Swiss cheese, grated
2 scallions, chopped finely

If using fresh artichokes, prepare them as follows: Pull off leaves and cut off lower portion of each leaf, leaving any fibrous part behind. Scoop out chokes and discard. Cut hearts in ¼-inch dice. If using canned artichokes, drain well and chop coarsely. Beat egg whites until stiff peaks form. In large saucepan over low heat, melt butter, add flour, and stir with wire whisk until blended. Meanwhile, bring milk to a boil and add all at once to butter-flour mixture, stirring vigorously with whisk until no lumps remain and mixture is thickened. Season to taste with salt, Worcestershire sauce, cayenne, and white pepper. Turn off heat. Add cheese and stir until melted. Beat in egg yolks. Add artichokes and scallions to egg mixture. Fold egg whites into the mixture. Turn into six individual, heatproof soufflé dishes, ungreased. Fill roasting pan half full of hot tap water. Preheat oven to 325°. Place soufflés in pan and bake on top shelf of oven until set, about 30 minutes. Serve immediately with Roasted Lemon Potatoes (see next recipe) and croissants. Yields 6 to 8 servings.

Roasted Lemon Potatoes

    2 pounds small white or red potatoes,
        scrubbed
    2 teaspoons garlic salt
    2 teaspoons lemon pepper
    ⅓ cup olive oil
    6 teaspoons sour cream

Preheat oven to 450°. Cut potatoes in quarters, or 1- to 1½-inch dice. Place in 9 x 12-inch baking pan. Sprinkle with garlic salt, lemon pepper, and drizzle oil on top. Turn potatoes with spatula to coat. Bake 1 hour, turning every 15 minutes to prevent sticking. Top each serving with 1 teaspoon sour cream. Yields 6 servings (allow 2 to 3 potatoes per person).

"Kitchen Sink" Soufflés

These soufflés are easy to prepare and you can use whatever you have on hand as filling: mushrooms, tomatoes, chopped sausage, asparagus tips.

    1 tablespoon olive oil
    8 ounces mushrooms, sliced
    Salt and pepper
    2 green onions, thinly sliced
    4 ounces ham or 3 slices bacon,
        chopped and cooked
    1 (8-ounce) package grated Cheddar
        or Swiss cheese
    4 eggs
    1¼ cups milk
    ½ cup flour

Preheat oven to 375°. Heat oil in skillet over medium heat. Sauté mushrooms with salt and pepper to taste until they have released their liquid and are nicely browned. Spray 6 shallow individual heat-proof dishes with nonstick spray. Distribute green onions, mushrooms, ham, and shredded cheese equally among dishes. In a food processor, blend eggs, milk, and flour. Pour over other ingredients in dishes. Bake 20 to 25 minutes until puffed and slightly browned around edges. Remove immediately before serving. Yields 6 servings.

Lemon Muffins

    1 lemon
    1 cup plus 1 tablespoon sugar
    2 cups all-purpose flour
    2 teaspoons baking powder
    1 teaspoon salt
    2 eggs
    1 cup buttermilk
    ½ cup melted butter

Preheat oven to 375°. Zest lemons and chop zest. Slice lemons in half crosswise and squeeze out juice, removing any seeds. Mix lemon juice with 1 tablespoon sugar. In bowl combine remaining 1 cup sugar, flour, baking powder, salt, and lemon zest. In separate bowl, mix eggs, and buttermilk. Stir in butter. Add to dry ingredients and stir just until mixed. Batter will be lumpy. Spray 12-cup muffin tin with cooking spray. Fill muffin cups until all batter is used up. Bake 25 minutes, or until lightly browned on top. Let cool in muffin tin 10 minutes. Brush tops of muffins with lemon juice mixture. Remove muffins from tin and serve with butter. Yields 12 muffins.

THE GOOSE & TURRETS BED & BREAKFAST

835 George Street
Montara, CA 94037
(650) 728-5451
rhmgt@montara.com
http://goose.montara.com

The Goose is a historic, earth-friendly inn catering to readers, nature lovers, pilots, and enthusiastic eaters. It specializes in pampering fast-lane folks with slow-lane comforts. Activities at the inn include bird watching, reading in the hammock, playing bocce ball, and listening to the rose garden fountain from the Appalachian courting swing. In the area there is biking, hiking, kayaking, golfing, surfing, shopping at boutiques, and art galleries. Viewing elephant seals at Año Nuevo, visiting lighthouses, and trying out new restaurants are just a few activities for guests to explore.

Foul Madamas

This is a traditional Egyptian dish that is cooked by Fedayeen over fires at the dumps and delivered to the doors of Cairenes in time for breakfast.

    3 cups dried fava beans
    1 teaspoon baking soda
    1 tablespoon salt
    12 tablespoons chopped onion
    12 teaspoons ground cardamom
    12 teaspoons ground cumin
    3 teaspoons salt
    3 teaspoons coarsely ground black pepper
    12 tablespoons lemon juice
    12 tablespoons extra virgin olive oil
    12 hard-cooked eggs, whole

The day before serving, soak fava beans in water with baking soda 8 hours or overnight. Cook in pressure cooker according to directions (probably with water to cover and 1 tablespoon salt about 20 to 30 minutes). For each serving, place 1 cup beans in a soup plate. Make dent in center and put in it: 1 tablespoon onion, 1 teaspoon ground cardamom, 1 teaspoon ground cumin, ¼ teaspoon salt, ¼ teaspoon black pepper, 1 tablespoon lemon juice, 1 tablespoon olive oil, and 1 egg. Mash everything together. Serve with soup spoon and hot Arabic (or pita) bread. Yields 12 servings.

Bellila

This barley recipe is simple, and the dish is called Bellila *in Arabic.*

   ½ cup dry pearl barley
   Milk to cover barley
   ¼ cup sugar or more

The night before, place dry barley in saucepan and cover with water. Bring to a boil and remove from heat. Let soak overnight. The next morning, add milk to barley. Add sugar. Stir well and cook over low heat. Let it boil gently, very gently. More milk may have to be added if barley has absorbed all liquid (always keep enough liquid to cover barley). Taste and add more sugar if necessary. Barley is done when it is tender and creamy. Remove from heat. Serve hot and with dash of your favorite spice—ground nutmeg, clove, cinnamon. Yields 2 servings.

Blackberry Buckle

   Pastry:
   2 cups all-purpose flour
   ½ teaspoon salt
   4 teaspoons baking powder
   ½ cup shortening
   ½ cup sugar
   1 egg, beaten
   ½ cup milk

   Fruit:
   2 teaspoons lemon juice
   2 cups blackberries or blueberries
   ⅓ cup sugar
   ⅓ cup all-purpose flour
   ½ teaspoon ground cinnamon
   ¼ cup (½ stick) butter

Mix together flour, salt, and baking powder. Cut in shortening. Beat sugar, egg, and milk until light and fluffy. Mix with dry ingredients until dough is formed. Reserve some for topping. Roll out and line eight ramekins (ungreased), approximately 3 inches in diameter.

Preheat oven to 350°. Sprinkle lemon juice over fruit. Mix sugar, flour, and cinnamon and cut in butter. Toss fruit in sugar/flour mixture. Divide among pastry-lined ramekins. Sprinkle reserved pastry over top. Bake in oven 1 hour. Serve warm. Whipped cream on top is a luscious addition. Yields 8 servings.

Olive Tartlets

   Tartlets:
   1¼ cups all-purpose flour
   ½ teaspoon salt
   ½ cup cold vegetable shortening
   ¼ cup cold water

   Filling:
   2 cups chopped green olives (not stuffed)
   4 tablespoons sour cream
   3 tablespoons mayonnaise
   Grated cheese (Cheddar, mozzarella, or Parmesan)

Preheat oven to 375°. Mix all ingredients lightly. Roll out to ¼-inch thickness. Cut to fit six 3½- to 4-inch-diameter pie plates. Shape and trim. Place baking weights over dough to prevent puffing. Bake 10 minutes. Remove weights and continue baking 5 to 7 minutes. Let cool.

Mix filling ingredients together well. Place in pre-baked tartlet shells and top with cheese. Raise oven temperature to 400° and bake 8 to 10 minutes until cheese is melted. Yields 6 servings.

ABELLA GARDEN INN BED & BREAKFAST

210 Oak Street
Arroyo Grande, CA 93420
(805) 489-5926 (phone)
(800) 563-7762 (toll free)
info@abellagardeninn.com
www.abellagardeninn.com

The Abella Garden Inn is a luxury, romantic inn near San Luis Obispo, decorated with Laura Ashley prints and antiques. In-room spa and fireplace, gourmet breakfast, a lovely garden with waterfall, a gazebo, and a creek add to the comfort of the inn. Activities in the area include Hearst Castle, wineries, Pismo Beach, and horseback riding on the beach.

Mexican Quiche

   10 eggs, beaten
   ½ cup all-purpose flour
   1 tablespoon baking powder
   ½ teaspoon salt
   7 ounces diced green chiles
   2 cups cottage cheese
   1 pound Jack cheese, grated
   ½ cup melted butter

Preheat oven to 400°. Mix ingredients in order given, adding butter last. Bake in lightly greased 13 x 9 x 2-inch glass dish 15 minutes. Lower heat to 350° and continue baking 20 minutes more or until knife comes out clean. Yields 12 servings.

Orange Date Nut Bread

Bread:
2 eggs
2 tablespoons butter
¾ cup sugar
1 small unpeeled orange, cut into pieces and seeded
1 cup pitted, chopped dates
1¾ cups all-purpose flour
1 teaspoon baking soda
1 teaspoon salt
1 cup chopped pecans

Sauce:
½ cup orange juice
½ cup sugar

Preheat oven to 325°. For bread, place eggs, butter, sugar, orange pieces, and dates in blender or food processor. Cover and process with on/off motions until finely chopped. Remove to large mixing bowl. In separate bowl, sift together flour, baking soda, and salt. Add to orange mixture and mix until well blended. Stir in pecans. Pour batter into greased 9 x 5 x 3-inch baking pan. Bake 1 hour or until bread tests done. If bread begins to darken, cover with foil during last few minutes of baking.

For the sauce, heat orange juice and sugar until sugar melts. When bread comes out of oven, prick with wooden pick and pour hot sauce over top. Let bread stand 15 minutes before removing from pan. Cool on wire rack. Yields 1 loaf.

Oatmeal Coffee Cake

1½ cups boiling water
1 stick butter
1 cup oatmeal
2 eggs
1 cup granulated sugar
1 cup packed brown sugar
1 teaspoon vanilla extract
1 teaspoon baking soda
½ teaspoon salt
1½ cups all-purpose flour

Topping:
1 tablespoon butter
1 tablespoon all-purpose flour
½ cup packed brown sugar
½ teaspoon ground cinnamon

Mix boiling water, butter, and oatmeal and let sit 20 minutes. Preheat oven to 350°. Mix remaining ingredients and add to oatmeal mixture. Pour in greased and floured pan and bake 25 minutes.

Prepare topping by crumbling butter, flour, sugar, and cinnamon together with your fingers. Remove cake from oven about 5 minutes before it is done and crumble mixture on top. Return to oven to brown. Insert knife in center to test for doneness. Yields 12 servings.

Cheese Soufflé

6 eggs
2 cups cottage cheese
¼ cup sugar
1 tablespoon baking powder
1 to 2 teaspoons vanilla extract
1 stick butter, melted

Preheat oven to 350°. Mix together eggs, cottage cheese, sugar, baking powder, and vanilla until well blended. Add butter and bake 45 minutes. Top with jams, fresh fruit syrups, fresh berries, or try the Fresh Strawberry Sauce (see next recipe). Yields 6 to 8 servings.

Fresh Strawberry Sauce

2 pints strawberries, hulled
4 to 6 tablespoons sugar
2 tablespoons strawberry or orange-flavored liqueur (optional)

Blend all ingredients until sugar is dissolved. Yields 2 pints.

Puffed Apple Pancakes

4 large eggs
1 cup whole milk
3 tablespoons granulated sugar
1 teaspoon vanilla extract
½ teaspoon salt
1 teaspoon ground cinnamon
⅔ cup all-purpose flour
¼ cup butter
2 Golden Delicious apples, peeled and sliced thin
3 tablespoons packed light brown sugar

Preheat oven to 425°. Whisk eggs, milk, sugar, vanilla, salt, and cinnamon in large bowl until well blended. Add flour and whisk until batter is smooth. Place butter in 13 x 9-inch baking dish in oven until melted, about 5 minutes. Remove dish from oven, and place apple slices in overlapping rows atop melted butter. Return to oven and bake until apples begin to soften slightly and butter is bubbling and beginning to brown around edges of dish, about 10 minutes. Pour batter over apples and sprinkle with brown sugar. Bake 20 minutes more until puffed and brown. Yields 6 to 8 servings.

SOUTHPORT LANDING

444 Phelan Road
P.O. Box 172
Loleta, CA 95551
(707) 733-5915
southprt@northcoast.com
www.northcoast.com/southprt

Southport Landing is a seven-bedroom, colonial revival mansion built in the 1890s on the shores of Humboldt Bay at the end of a country lane. In a traditional, country-manor atmosphere with period antiques, guests enjoy individual, decorated rooms with dynamic views of the hillside or Humboldt Bay. Guests enjoy uninterrupted silence and the bounty of wildlife. Hiking, kayaking, bicycling, bird watching, and beach combing can be enjoyed at your doorstep.

Oatmeal Soufflé

  1 cup milk
  2 tablespoons butter
  1 cup oats (quick or regular)
  ⅓ cup cream cheese (regular or low-fat)
  ¼ teaspoon salt
  ¼ cup brown sugar
  ½ teaspoon ground cinnamon
  ½ teaspoon ground nutmeg
  3 eggs, separated
  ½ cup raisins or diced dried mixed fruit
      (optional)
  ½ cup chopped walnuts

Preheat oven to 325°. Oil or butter a 1½-quart soufflé dish. Heat milk and butter in small saucepan until barely boiling. Stir in oats. Cook, stirring often, until oatmeal is done (do not overcook; it becomes too mushy). Remove from heat and stir in cream cheese, salt, sugar, cinnamon, and ground nutmeg. Beat egg yolks slightly and slowly add them to oatmeal mixture, stirring constantly. Mix in raisins and walnuts. (Both raisins and walnuts can be omitted for an equally delicious soufflé.) Beat egg whites until stiff (peaks form, but still moist). Mix about one-quarter of beaten egg whites into oatmeal mixture. Use rubber spatula to gently fold in rest of egg whites. Don't overmix. Spoon mixture into prepared soufflé dish. Bake 35 to 40 minutes (20 to 25 minutes for a 1-quart dish; 15 minutes for individual ramekins) until risen and set but center still trembles a bit. Serve immediately. Wrap pretty tea towel around dish and set it on table for guests to spoon into pre-warmed bowls. Serve with warm milk and extra brown sugar. This is also good with Baked Fruit Compote (see recipe below) served on side or spooned on top. Yields 4 to 6 servings.

Baked Fruit Compote

You can use whatever fruit is in season or on hand, fresh and/or canned. Both slightly overripe, as well as somewhat under ripe, fruit works just fine.

  3 to 4 cups sliced uncooked fruit*

  To the sliced fruit add:
  ¼ cup juice from fruit (or water)
  Zest of 1 orange
  Freshly squeezed juice from orange
      (or ¼ cup orange juice)
  1 or 2 tablespoons honey (optional)
  Butter

Preheat oven to 325°. Combine fruit, juice, orange zest and juice, and honey in baking dish. Dot with several pats of butter. Bake about 35 minutes. Serve warm (it is also good with a little half-and-half poured on top). For a fancy presentation on table or buffet, transfer to stemmed compote dish for serving. Yields 4 servings.

  *A good summer combination is pears, peaches, plums, and dried cherries. Or try prunes, apricots (both can be dry-soaked overnight) and in the morning add raisins and bananas, sliced thick.

MAISON FLEURIE

6529 Yount Street
Yountville, CA 94599
(707) 944-2056 (phone)
(707) 944-9342 (fax)
(800) 788-0369 (toll free)
info@foursisters.com
www.foursisters.com/inns/maisonfleurie.html

Napa Valley's Maison Fleurie features French country decor, lush gardens, full breakfast, afternoon wine and hors d'oeuvre, pool, and spa. Many rooms offer romantic fireplaces. California's famous Napa Valley is one of the world's leading wine producing regions; visitors take full advantage of Maison Fleurie's proximity to hundreds of excellent wineries for tasting and tours. The inn provides bicycles for guests' use to explore the surrounding countryside and take a picnic along for a vineyard repast. The village of Yountville (where Maison Fleurie is situated) offers tempting antiques and other shops, plus a variety of excellent restaurants. Visitors also enjoy hot-air ballooning, the Napa Valley Wine Train, the Culinary Institute of America at Greystone, and the American Center for Wine, Food, and the Arts, in Napa.

Pumpkin Muffins

1¼ cups all-purpose flour
½ cup wheat flour
¼ teaspoon baking powder
1 teaspoon baking soda
1 cup sugar
½ teaspoon ground nutmeg
3 teaspoons ground cinnamon
½ cup finely chopped walnuts
½ cup raisins
2 eggs
½ cup vegetable oil
1 cup canned pumpkin
⅓ cup water
2 tablespoons maple syrup

Preheat oven to 375°. Mix together flours, baking powder, baking soda, sugar, ground nutmeg, cinnamon, and walnuts. In separate bowl, beat together raisins, eggs, oil, pumpkin, water, and maple syrup. Add wet ingredients to dry ingredients and mix just until combined. Spoon into greased muffin tins, three-quarters full. Bake 25 to 30 minutes. Yields 1 dozen muffins.

Sour Cream Coffee Cake

1 cup (2 sticks) sweet butter
2 plus ½ cups sugar
2 eggs, beaten
2 cups sour cream
1 tablespoon vanilla extract
1 cup wheat flour
1 cup all-purpose flour
1 tablespoon baking powder
¼ teaspoon salt
2 cups finely chopped pecans
1½ teaspoons ground cinnamon

Preheat oven to 350°. Cream butter and 2 cups sugar. Add eggs and mix well. Add sour cream and vanilla. In separate bowl, sift together flours, baking powder, and salt. Add to creamed mixture just until blended, being careful not to overbeat. Mix together remaining ½ cup sugar with pecans and cinnamon. Pour half the batter into well-greased and floured Bundt pan. Sprinkle with half the pecans and sugar mixture. Add remaining batter and top with remaining pecan mixture. Bake 1 hour. Serve warm or at room temperature. Yields 1 Bundt cake.

Peanut Butter Squares

1 cup (2 sticks) sweet butter
2 cups peanut butter
1 pound confectioners' sugar
12 ounces semisweet chocolate

Melt butter and peanut butter over low flame. Stir in confectioners' sugar. Pat into 9 x 13-inch pan. Melt chocolate in double boiler and pour over top. Chill until firm and then remove from refrigerator. Cut into 2-inch squares. Yields 25 squares.

Special K Cookies

1 cup sweet butter
1 cup sugar
1 teaspoon vanilla extract
1½ cups all-purpose flour
1½ teaspoons baking powder
2 cups Special K cereal

Preheat oven to 350°. In large bowl, cream butter and sugar until fluffy and add vanilla. In separate bowl, combine flour and baking powder and add to butter mixture. Fold in cereal. Bake 10 to 15 minutes. This recipe is also delicious with raisin bran cereals. Yields 2 dozen cookies.

Persimmon Pudding Cakes

3 Hachiya persimmons, ripened
3 eggs
1 cup packed brown sugar
1 cup all-purpose flour
¾ cup cream
½ cup (1 stick) sweet butter, melted
½ cup currants
2 teaspoons ground cinnamon
1 teaspoon baking soda
1 teaspoon baking powder
1 teaspoon ginger
½ teaspoon ground nutmeg
½ teaspoon salt
Confectioners' sugar for topping

Preheat oven to 325°. Use only very ripe persimmons and cut them in half, scoop out insides and purée in food processor. Whisk in all remaining ingredients and pour into muffin tins. Fill three-quarters full. Cakes will fall a little during baking. Allow to cool completely and sprinkle confectioners' sugar on top. Bake 45 minutes. Yields 1 dozen cakes.

JAMESTOWN HOTEL

18153 Main Street
Jamestown, CA 95327
(209) 984-3902 (phone)
(209) 984-4149 (fax)
(800) 205-4901 (toll free)
info@jamestownhotel.com
www.jamestownhotel.com

The Jamestown Hotel is the centerpiece of the quaint Gold Rush town. Offering fresh and innovative contemporary dining with friendly service, there are eleven antique-filled guest rooms with private bathrooms, claw-foot tubs, whirlpool tubs, air conditioning, TVs, and breakfast is included.

Crab Cakes with Chipotle Aïoli & Watermelon Salsa

Crab Cakes:
½ cup diced red bell pepper
1 teaspoon canola oil
⅓ cup mayonnaise
1 egg yolk
2 teaspoons lemon juice
1 pound Dungeness crab claw meat
1½ plus 1 cups panko breadcrumbs
Zest of 1 lemon

Chipotle Aïoli:
2 cups mayonnaise
2 chipotle peppers (canned in
    adobo are best)

Watermelon Salsa:
1½ cups diced watermelon
½ cup diced jicama
⅓ cup diced yellow bell pepper
⅓ cup diced red onion
½ bunch cilantro, stems removed
    and roughly chopped
1 ounce tequila
Pinch of salt

Mix crab cake ingredients, using 1½ cups breadcrumbs in large mixing bowl and combine thoroughly. Make 4 cakes and press in remaining 1 cup panko crumbs. (These may be made ahead and frozen for up to 1 month.)

Combine aïoli ingredients in food processor on high speed for 1 minute. Put aïoli through a strainer to remove seeds. Put resulting aïoli in squeeze bottle for decorating plates. (This may be made 1 week in advance.)

Combine all salsa ingredients in bowl and toss lightly.

Crab cakes should be thawed if frozen and cooked with small amount of oil over medium heat about 1½ minutes per side. Use squeeze bottle of aïoli to draw on plate. Place cooked crab cakes on plate and top with salsa. Yields 4 servings.

Oatmeal-Stout Bread

8 cups hi-gluten flour
1 cup oatmeal
3 tablespoons dry yeast
1 teaspoon salt
3 cups Guinness or other stout beer
½ cup buttermilk
3 tablespoons packed brown sugar

Preheat oven to 375°. Combine flour, oatmeal, yeast, and salt in mixer with dough hook. Heat beer, buttermilk, and sugar to 130° and add to mixer. Mix on low speed until thoroughly combined. Place dough in oiled bowl and cover with clean, damp towel. After dough has risen 20 to 45 minutes, punch down and make loaves. When loaves have risen until doubled in size, bake 16 to 20 minutes. Yields 4 to 6 loaves, depending on size.

THE INN AT FAWNSKIN

P.O. Box 378
880 Canyon Road
Fawnskin, CA 92333
(909) 878-2249 (fax)
(888) FAWNSKIN (toll free)
fawnskininn@earthlink.net
www.fawnskininn.com

The Inn at Fawnskin is a beautiful log-home bed and breakfast nestled in its own pine forest on the quiet peaceful north shore of Big Bear Lake. Decorated in period antiques, the inn offers a tranquil setting just minutes away from ski areas, shops, restaurants, boating, fishing, golf, hiking trails, and picnic areas.

Tapenade (Olive Spread)

1 cup pitted kalamata olives
2 to 3 tablespoons olive oil
2 tablespoons rinsed capers
2 teaspoons fresh lemon juice
½ teaspoon anchovy paste
    (or 2 anchovy fillets, rinsed)
1 to 2 cloves garlic, pressed
¼ teaspoon each dried oregano
    and thyme
1 (12-inch) baguette

In food processor, combine all ingredients except baguette. Slice baguette in ¼-inch slices. Spread slices with olive oil with pastry brush and sprinkle dried thyme over slices. Preheat oven to 350° and bake 15 minutes. Spread toasts with tapenade. Enjoy! Yields 48 appetizer servings.

Melt-in-Your-Mouth Pancakes

4 eggs, separated
1 cup sour cream
1 cup small-curd cottage cheese
¾ cup all-purpose flour
¾ teaspoon baking soda
½ teaspoon salt
1 tablespoon sugar

Beat egg whites until stiff and set aside. Beat egg yolks until creamy. Add sour cream and cottage cheese to the egg yolks and blend. Mix flour, baking soda, salt, and sugar and add to cottage cheese mixture. Gently fold in egg whites. Drop batter onto hot greased griddle. Brown and turn to cook the other side. (Centers should be slightly moist.) Yields 18 (3- to 4-inch) pancakes.

Fresh Strawberry Waffles

3 eggs, separated
½ cup plain yogurt
½ cup small-curd cottage cheese
1¼ cups all-purpose flour
1 cup buttermilk
2 tablespoons sugar
1 tablespoon vanilla extract
1¼ teaspoons baking powder
½ cup chopped fresh strawberries,
    plus 4 to 5 sliced for garnish

Preheat waffle iron and lightly spray with vegetable oil. Beat egg whites until stiff and set aside. In large mixing bowl, blend all remaining ingredients. Fold egg whites into this mixture. Pour approximately 1 cup batter onto hot waffle iron, and cook until golden brown. Serve garnished with fresh strawberry slices and warm pure maple syrup. Yields 3 to 5 waffles.

Note: A Belgian waffle iron works great.

RIDENHOUR RANCH HOUSE INN

12850 River Road
Guerneville, CA 95446
(707) 887-1033 (phone)
(707) 869-2967 (fax)
(888) 877-4466 (toll free)
innkeeper@ridenhourranchhouseinn.com
www.ridenhourranchhouseinn.com

Towering redwoods and informal gardens surround this 1906 farmhouse along the Russian River in Sonoma Wine Country. The inn offers gourmet country breakfast, outdoor hot tub, and homemade cookies.

Activities in the area include wine tastings (more than seventy Sonoma County wineries are located within a short drive); swimming, fishing, canoeing, and kayaking on the Russian River; beachcombing and whale watching at the Sonoma Coast and Bodega Bay; numerous state parks and Armstrong Woods (redwood forest) offering extensive hiking and biking trails; horseback riding in the redwoods and on the beach; golfing; hot-air ballooning; shopping and antiquing; day spa; Charles M. Shulz Museum; Luther Burbank Home and Garden; annual blues and jazz festivals at Johnson's Beach in Guerneville.

Ranch House Cobbler

¾ cup (1½ sticks) butter
1½ cups all-purpose flour
1½ cups sugar
1 tablespoon baking powder
¼ teaspoon salt
1¼ cups milk
6 cups fresh or frozen blackberries, or
    3 cups berries and 3 cups peaches

Preheat oven to 375°. Melt butter in 9 x 13-inch baking pan in warm oven. In bowl, blend together flour, sugar, baking powder, and salt. Stir in milk and blend until smooth. Pour mixture into pan of melted butter. Sprinkle fruit on top of mixture and bake about 55 minutes or until top is browned and crisp. Serve with splash of fresh cream. Yields 10 to 12 servings.

"Love Child" Quiche

Our ham and vegetarian quiches got together in the oven and had a "love child"— a medley quiche containing ingredients from the other two.

1 (9-inch) unbaked pastry shell, or your
    own piecrust recipe
1 cup mixed, grated cheeses
    (Swiss, Monterey Jack, Cheddar)
¼ cup diced, sautéed leek

½ cup each diced ham, chopped
    mushrooms, diced asparagus
4 eggs
1 cup half-and-half
Sprinkle of ground pepper
Dash of ground nutmeg

Preheat oven to 375°. Place pie shell on cookie sheet. Spread cheese evenly in bottom of shell and top with sautéed leek, ham, mushrooms, and asparagus. (Note: To prevent crust from becoming soggy, we recommend placing chopped mushrooms and diced asparagus in microwaveable bowl, cover with plastic wrap, and microwave on high about 2 to 3 minutes. Let cool and then strain or squeeze out water before adding veggies to pie shell.) Place eggs, half-and-half, pepper, and nutmeg in bowl and whip together. Pour mixture into pastry shell and bake 45 minutes or until puffed, golden, and firm in center. Let it rest a few minutes before slicing. Yields 6 generous wedges.

Ridenhour Ranch House Inn

Stuffed French Toast served with Mini-Soufflés

4 ounces cream cheese
¼ cup orange marmalade
⅓ cup chopped pecans
8 slices buttermilk bread
¾ cup apricot preserves
Orange juice
4 eggs, beaten
¾ cup heavy cream
1 teaspoon vanilla extract
Dash of ground nutmeg
Sliced bananas
Orange slices and mint sprigs for garnish

Mix together cream cheese, orange marmalade, and chopped pecans. Spread equally on 4 slices of bread. Top with remaining slices to make 4 sandwiches. To make topping sauce, heat apricot preserves in small saucepan. Thin with orange juice to desired consistency. Mix together eggs, cream, vanilla, and nutmeg and dip sandwiches into mixture. Cook in butter in frying pan over medium heat until browned on both sides. Arrange on plate by slicing toast diagonally and fan banana slices on top. Spoon warm sauce over toast. Garnish with orange slices and mint sprigs. Add "Mini-Soufflé" (see recipe below) to plate and serve immediately. Yields 4 servings.

Mini-Soufflés

½ cup grated cheese
½ cup diced ham
4 thinly sliced mushrooms
Dash of ground nutmeg
4 eggs
1 cup heavy cream

Preheat oven to 350°. Butter four ramekins and place them on cookie sheet. Sprinkle grated cheese to cover bottoms of ramekins. Add ham and mushrooms and dash of ground nutmeg to each ramekin. Whip eggs well and slowly add cream. Pour mixture equally into ramekins and bake about 30 minutes or until soufflés are puffed and golden. The soufflés will hold in warm oven about 20 minutes before they begin to deflate. Yields 4 servings.

The National Hotel Bed & Breakfast

18183 Main Street
P.O. Box 502
Jamestown, CA 95327
(209) 984-3446 (phone)
(209) 984-5620 (fax)
(800) 894-3446 (toll free)
info@national-hotel.com
www.national-hotel.com

The National Hotel Bed & Breakfast (1859) is in the heart of the Gold Rush area near Yosemite, where rooms have been restored to the casual elegance of a simpler, romantic era. The hotel boasts of a gourmet restaurant with full bar, and outdoor recreation abounds, from water-skiing to snow skiing, from fishing to hiking, from golfing to antique shopping. Yosemite National Park, Columbia State Park and Railtown 1897 State Park are all within a pleasant day-trip distance.

Gazpacho

2 cucumbers, peeled, seeded,
    and diced
1½ jalapeño peppers, seeded and diced
1 bell pepper, diced
1 medium yellow onion, diced
64 ounces canned, diced tomatoes
    with juice
24 ounces tomato juice
1½ teaspoons chopped cilantro
1½ tablespoons salt
½ teaspoon black pepper
¼ cup balsamic vinegar
2 tablespoons lemon juice
1½ teaspoons Tabasco
1 tablespoon Worcestershire sauce
Cilantro leaves for garnish

Purée half the cucumbers, jalapeños, bell pepper, and yellow onion, and pour into large mixing bowl. Add remaining diced ingredients, tomatoes, tomato juice, and cilantro. Stir and season with salt, pepper, vinegar, lemon juice, Tabasco, and Worcestershire. Stir and chill. Garnish with cilantro leaves. Yields approximately ½ gallon.

Raspberry Vinaigrette

1 large or extra large egg
¼ cup red wine vinegar
2 cups salad oil
¾ cup sugar
¾ cup puréed and strained raspberries

Combine egg and vinegar in blender. Slowly add salad oil. Add sugar and raspberries. Mix well. Yields approximately 1 pint or 16 one-ounce servings.

Chicken Patrice

All-purpose flour
1 (6-ounce) boneless chicken breast,
    cut in half, pounded, and floured
2 tablespoons olive oil
1 teaspoon chopped shallots
Small handful of fresh spinach
3 small apricot halves (canned)
1 tablespoon apricot brandy
3 tablespoons chicken stock
1 teaspoon packed brown sugar
¼ cup heavy cream
1 ounce bay shrimp
½ teaspoon butter
Salt and pepper

Flour chicken breast and place in hot oil; cook until brown. Pour off grease. Remove from heat (pan will catch fire when brandy is added). Add shallots, spinach, apricots, and apricot brandy. Place pan back on heat (very carefully, flame will be high), sauté until brandy has burned away (4 to 6 seconds). Add chicken stock, brown sugar, and heavy cream. Reduce until enough sauce is left to cover chicken. Stir in bay shrimp, a little butter, and salt and pepper to taste. Warm thoroughly. To serve, place half a chicken breast on a plate. Spoon over a portion of sauce and two of the apricot halves. Place other breast piece over apricots and top with remaining apricot half and rest of sauce. Yields 1 serving.

Loin of Pork Madagascar

1½ boneless pork loins
2 tablespoons olive oil
Flour to coat pork
1 tablespoon chopped shallots
2 tablespoons Madagascar
    Green Peppercorns
¼ cup brandy
½ cup heavy cream
⅓ cup brown sauce*
1 tablespoon French mustard
Pinch of coriander
¼ cup melted butter
Optional garnish: small sprig of
    watercress and julienne-style
    red peppers

Slice pork into ¼-inch medallions. Flatten each piece slightly with back of heavy skillet. Heat oil in medium saucepan. Flour each slice of pork and sauté. Evenly brown and then turn. Brown second side and add shallots and green peppercorns. Cook until shallots are soft. Remove pan from flame and carefully pour in brandy. Return pan to burner and flame brandy. Add cream and begin to reduce. Blend in brown sauce and add mustard, coriander, and butter. Remove meat and place on serving platter. Reduce sauce to desired consistency. Pour sauce over meat and garnish with watercress and peppers. Yields 6 servings.

*Note: To make the brown sauce, sauté 1 chopped scallion in a tablespoon of butter. Gradually add ⅓ cup red wine and ⅓ cup beef broth. Let it come to a boil and add tarragon, thyme, salt, and pepper to taste. Cook down for a few minutes. Add beurre manié to thicken. Let simmer for a few minutes and strain.

STRAWBERRY CREEK INN

P.O. Box 1818
Idyllwild, CA 92549
(909) 659-3202 (phone)
(800) 262-8969 (toll free)
www.strawberrycreekinn.com

Strawberry Creek Inn is a large mountain home surrounded by pines and oaks with nine guest rooms, all with private baths, most with fireplaces, some with TVs. The inn offers gourmet breakfasts. There are more than 100 miles of nearby hiking trails and dozens of restaurants; antique, art, and craft shops; and galleries.

German French Toast

3 egg yolks
2 cups milk
1 tablespoon sugar
Salt
Zest of 1 lemon, grated
6 to 8 thickly cut slices day-old
    French bread
3 egg whites, slightly beaten
2 cups breadcrumbs
6 tablespoons cinnamon/sugar mixture
3 to 4 Granny Smith apples,
    sliced and sautéed

Preheat oven to 375°. Combine egg yolks, milk, sugar, salt, and lemon zest. Dip bread slices into mixture and then into egg whites, lightly coating with breadcrumbs. Arrange on greased baking pans and bake 15 minutes. Turn slices over and bake another 15 minutes. Arrange toasts on plates, sprinkle with cinnamon/sugar mixture, top with sautéed apples, and serve with bacon or sausage, preferably smoked bratwurst. Provide maple syrup if desired. Yields 3 to 4 servings.

Strawberry Creek Inn

Baked Sour Cream Omelet

½ loaf of sliced bread
3 tablespoons soft margarine
4 ounces Gruyère cheese, shredded
4 ounces Monterey Jack cheese, shredded
12 slices bacon, cooked and crumbled
2 scallions, finely chopped
8 eggs
1⅓ cups milk
⅓ cup white wine
1 teaspoon Dijon-style mustard
⅛ teaspoon cayenne
¾ cup sour cream
½ cup grated Parmesan cheese

Coat bottom and sides of 9 x 13-inch baking dish with nonstick spray. Place bread slices in dish and spread with margarine. Sprinkle Gruyère and Monterey Jack cheeses, bacon, and scallions over bread slices. In medium bowl beat together eggs, milk, wine, mustard, and cayenne until foamy. Pour mixture evenly over cheese and bread. Cover tightly with foil and refrigerate overnight or 8 to 10 hours. Remove mixture from refrigerator when ready to cook and let stand covered at room temperature 30 minutes. Preheat oven to 350°. Bake, covered, 45 minutes or until egg mixture is set. Remove foil, spread mixture with sour cream, sprinkle with Parmesan cheese and return to oven uncovered for another 10 minutes or until lightly browned. Serve immediately. Yields 12 servings.

BACKYARD GARDEN OASIS

P.O. Box 1760
24019 Hilderbrand Dr.
Middletown, CA 95461
(707) 987-0505
bygoasis@jnb.com
www.backyardgardenoasis.com

Backyard Garden Oasis provides serenity, privacy, and romance in three cottages tucked away in the mountains north of the Napa Valley, away from the crowds. Activities include wineries, spas, glider rides, casino, concerts at Konocti, paddle wheel on Clear Lake, golf, hiking, biking, and bird-watching.

Vegetable Frittata

12 eggs
1 pint cottage cheese
8 ounces shredded mozzarella
1 small onion, finely diced
2 carrots, thinly sliced
2 cloves garlic, minced
½ red or yellow bell pepper
1 cup finely sliced asparagus
1 cup sliced mushrooms
1 tablespoon butter
1 tablespoon dried basil
1 tablespoon dried dill
Fresh Garden Salsa

Beat eggs, cottage cheese, and mozzarella together. Stir well. Sauté onions, carrots, and garlic until slightly softened. Add bell pepper and asparagus. Sauté mixture until soft. Add to egg mixture. In separate pan sauté mushrooms in butter until lightly softened. Add mushrooms and herbs to egg mixture. Preheat oven to 325° and bake in 9 x 13-inch pan about 45 minutes, or until toothpick inserted in center comes out clean. The frittata is best served with Fresh Garden Salsa (see recipe below). Yields 8 servings.

Fresh Garden Salsa

3 medium tomatoes, diced
1 onion, diced
1 bunch cilantro, finely chopped
2 cloves garlic, minced
Juice of 1 lime
1 jalapeño pepper
½ cup diced tomatoes
Salt

Mix tomatoes, onion, and cilantro together and blend until smooth. Add remaining ingredients. Allow to sit in refrigerator overnight. Yields approximately 3 cups.

THE WINDROSE INN

1407 Jackson Gate Road
Jackson, CA 95642
(209) 223-3650 (phone)
(209) 223-3793 (fax)
(888) 568-5250 (toll free)
info@windroseinn.com
www.windroseinn.com

The inn is an elegant 1897 Victorian house amid an acre of lush gardens. Creek, patio, and gazebo make a romantic country setting near historic Jackson and Sutter Creek.

Gourmet breakfast and wine hour are included. Activities in the area include antique and art attractions, cavern and gold mine tours, biking, fine dining, fishing, hiking, historic Gold Rush towns, shopping, theater, and award-winning wineries.

A Bed and Breakfast

THE WINDROSE INN

Baked Bananas

¼ cup melted unsalted butter
2 lemons
8 firm, but ripe, bananas
¾ cup packed brown sugar
2 tablespoons ground cinnamon
½ teaspoon ground ginger
½ cup shredded coconut
½ cup heavy cream

Preheat oven to 325°. Pour butter into baking dish large enough to hold 8 bananas. Slice 1 lemon thinly into 8 pieces for garnish. Squeeze juice from remainder of this lemon and second lemon and pour into baking dish. Swirl butter and lemon juice together. Peel each banana gently to keep it whole. Place bananas in baking dish and turn until coated with butter mixture. In small bowl, combine brown sugar, cinnamon, and ginger, using a ricer or whisk to thoroughly blend. Sprinkle top of each banana with about 1 teaspoon of mixture. Bake bananas 8 to 10 minutes. Remove from oven and turn them over. Sprinkle each banana with another teaspoon of brown sugar mixture and top with shredded coconut. Return to oven 8 to 10 more minutes. Remove bananas from baking pan, slice them in half, and place two halves in each bowl. Pour 1 tablespoon of cream into each bowl, around banana not on top of it. Add lemon garnish and serve immediately. Yields 8 servings.

Decadent French Toast

8 day-old croissants
1½ cups heavy cream
¼ cup Triple Sec liqueur
3 tablespoons sugar
2 tablespoons ground cinnamon
½ teaspoon vanilla extract
6 large eggs
Zest of 1 orange, finely chopped
Butter
Confectioners' sugar
Ground cinnamon
Orange slices, strawberries
    or raspberries for garnish

Slice croissants in half. Combine cream, liqueur, sugar, cinnamon, vanilla, eggs, and orange zest in large, shallow bowl and whisk until fully blended. Preheat oven to 200° for warming serving plates. Melt butter on griddle or in large frying pan on medium heat. Drench each slice of croissant in the batter and place on griddle. Keep cooked croissants warm in oven on plates. Dust croissants with confectioners' sugar and cinnamon before serving. Garnish with sliced oranges, strawberries or raspberries and serve with maple syrup or other fruit syrups. Yields 8 servings.

Souflatta

1 teaspoon butter
10 large eggs
¼ cup plus 2 tablespoons all-purpose
    flour
1 teaspoon baking powder
½ teaspoon salt
2 cups shredded sharp Cheddar cheese
    (reserve 2 tablespoons for garnish)

1 cup shredded fresh
    Parmigiano-Reggiano cheese
    (reserve 2 tablespoons for garnish)
8 ounces fresh ricotta cheese
1 cup finely chopped scallions
    (reserve 2 tablespoons for garnish)
½ cup finely chopped red bell pepper
    (reserve 8 slices for garnish)
Chopped parsley
4 tablespoons sour cream

Preheat oven to 350°. Butter (or dust with cooking spray) a 9-inch glass or ceramic pie pan. Beat eggs in mixer at medium-high speed 8 to 10 minutes until light and fluffy, double in volume. Sift flour, baking powder, and salt in small bowl and add to eggs. Mix 2 minutes. Add cheeses, scallions, and peppers and mix for 2 more minutes. Pour into pie pan and bake 55 minutes. Remove from oven and let stand 5 minutes before serving. Slice like pie and arrange each wedge on a plate. Garnish with sprinkles of Cheddar and Parmesan cheese and scallions. Place sliced piece of red bell pepper on top of each wedge, sprinkle with parsley, and add dollop of sour cream at edge of each wedge. Serve immediately. Yields 8 servings.

Tomatoes with Balsamic Vinaigrette

6 to 8 ripe hothouse tomatoes,
    thinly sliced
16 to 20 thin slices fresh mozzarella cheese
¼ cup fresh basil leaves
2 tablespoons freshly grated
    Parmigiano-Reggiano

Vinaigrette dressing:
⅓ cup balsamic vinegar
2 tablespoons extra virgin olive oil
1 teaspoon salt
2 teaspoons pepper
½ teaspoon garlic powder
2 teaspoons Dijon mustard

Arrange tomato and cheese slices on platter with cheese on bottom. Roll basil leaves

together before slicing very thinly, reserving extra "flowers" and "leaves" for garnish. Sprinkle sliced basil over tomato and cheese slices. May be refrigerated covered with plastic up to 2 hours. When ready to serve, drizzle dressing over each tomato/cheese section. Finish off with dusting of Parmigiano-Reggiano over each tomato/cheese section and arrange basil leaves and flowers as garnish. Serve immediately. Yields 8 servings.

For vinaigrette dressing, mix all ingredients well and set aside until serving time. Yields about 5 ounces.

THE GABLES WINE COUNTRY INN

4257 Petaluma Hill Road
Santa Rosa, CA 95404
(707) 585-7777 (phone)
(707) 584-5634 (fax)
(800) GABLES-N (toll free)
innkeeper@thegablesinn.com
www.thegablesinn.com

The Gables is an elegant Victorian inn sitting grandly in the center of the Sonoma Wine Country. It provides gracious accommodations and incomparable hospitality to the wine-country traveler.

...ly's Cherry Trifle

1 Buttermilk Pound Cake (see recipe below)
2 (1-pound) cans Bing cherries
    in heavy syrup
1 (12-ounce) jar premium quality
    cherry preserves
1 pint heavy whipping cream
⅓ cup confectioners' sugar
1 teaspoon vanilla extract
½ cup cherry brandy, cherry wine,
    or cream sherry
1 recipe blancmange (see next recipe)

To assemble, cut pound cake into 1-inch cubes, cutting off any dark edges or crust. Drain 1 can of cherries, but save juice from other can and stir cherries and juice into preserves. Whip the cream and add confectioners' sugar and vanilla. Place one-third of cake pieces in serving dish and sprinkle with one-third of the brandy. Spoon about one-third of cherry mixture over cake pieces, then spread approximately one-third of blancmange over cherries. Spoon scant 1 cup whipping cream over blancmange and spread evenly. Repeat twice more with cake, brandy, cherries, blancmange, and whipping cream, ending with whipping cream. Refrigerate for a few hours for flavors to blend. In spring and summer, this is terrific with fresh strawberries, blueberries, raspberries, blackberries, or peaches, or a combination of fruits. Yields 12 servings.

Buttermilk Pound Cake

1 cup (2 sticks) butter
2 cups sugar
4 eggs
1 teaspoon vanilla extract
1 teaspoon almond extract
2¾ cups all-purpose flour
½ teaspoon baking powder
½ teaspoon baking soda
½ teaspoon salt
1 cup buttermilk or sour milk

Blancmange:
6 tablespoons cornstarch
4 tablespoons sugar
¼ teaspoon salt
4 cups milk
2 eggs, beaten
2 teaspoons vanilla extract

Preheat oven to 350°. Grease (or use non-stick spray) large loaf pan plus 1 small loaf pan, or tube cake pan. Cream butter, add sugar, eggs, and extracts, and beat well. Mix dry ingredients together and add butter mixture alternately with buttermilk, beginning and ending with flour mixture. Bake approximately 1 hour or until golden. (Take care not to overbake; small loaf pan will be done at least 15 minutes before large loaf and you don't want "dark" edges to spoil the look of your trifle. Top each piece of cake with blancmange. Yields 1 small and 1 large loaf.

For blancmange, mix cornstarch, sugar, and salt, and stir in milk in saucepan. Cook over medium-low, stirring constantly, until mixture is thickened and smooth. Remove from heat. Take 1 cup of blancmange and whisk into eggs. Strain egg mixture through a sieve (takes out little pieces of "cooked" eggs) and stir back into blancmange. Put back on heat and stir a minute or two until cooked through. It's easy to scorch at this point, so keep heat low and stir constantly. Remove from heat, stir in vanilla and put mixture into bowl. Press plastic wrap down on top to keep "skin" from forming and refrigerate until ready to assemble trifle. To quick-chill mixture, put bowl into larger bowl of ice. Yields 12 generous servings.

Variation: Use a purchased pound cake instead of making your own.

Strawberry Streusel Bar

1 cup (2 sticks) butter, softened
1 cup sugar
1 egg
2 cups all-purpose flour
1 (10-ounce) jar strawberry jam
    (raspberry or apricot is also good)

Streusel:
1 cup all-purpose flour
¼ cup cold butter
¼ cup sugar

Icing:
1 cup confectioners' sugar
1 tablespoon milk
¼ teaspoon vanilla extract

In medium mixing bowl beat butter and sugar with electric mixer or by hand until fluffy. Beat in egg. Add flour gradually until fully incorporated. Press this mixture into bottom of greased 9 x 13-inch or 10 x 10-inch baking pan. Spread jam to within ½ inch of the edges. Preheat oven to 350°.

Make streusel by combining flour, butter, and sugar with a pastry blender or two forks until crumbly. Sprinkle evenly over jam and bake 40 to 45 minutes until top is lightly golden brown. Cool on wire rack.

When cool, combine icing ingredients until very smooth and drizzle over bars. Let sit 1 to 2 hours before cutting into bars. Yields 24 bars.

Individual Sourdough Vegetable Strata

6 (½-inch-thick) slices sourdough bread
6 eggs
1 cup milk
1 teaspoon Dijon mustard
6 slices Canadian bacon
½ to 1 cup chopped or sliced onions,
    sautéed in 1 teaspoon butter
12 tomato slices
12 to 18 asparagus spears (if fresh, cook
    for about 2 minutes and drain;
    if frozen, thaw but do not cook)
Peppercorns
Nutmeg, preferably whole
1½ cups grated mozzarella cheese, or
    mozzarella and Cheddar combined
Parmesan cheese

Grease 9 x 13-inch pan with nonstick spray, or use six oval ramekins large enough to hold bread slice. Trim crusts off bread and place slices on bottom of pan or in ramekins. In blender, whip eggs, milk, and Dijon mustard and pour half of this mixture evenly over bread slices. Put 1 slice Canadian bacon on each bread slice and top with onion, then 2 tomato slices, then asparagus spears. Grind pepper and grate small amount of nutmeg over each slice. Pour remaining egg/milk mixture over vegetables. Top with mozzarella and sprinkle with Parmesan. Let stand about 1 hour for bread to absorb milk/egg mixture, or can be made the night before and refrigerated. Bake at 375° about 35 minutes. (Add 5 minutes baking time if refrigerated.) Serve with dollop of sour cream and sprinkling of diced tomatoes and scallions, or other colorful garnish on side. Yields 6 servings.

THE PHILO POTTERY INN

P.O. Box 166
8550 Highway 128
Philo, CA 95466
(707) 895-3069
info@philopotteryinn.com
http://philopotteryinn.com

It is time to visit The Philo Pottery Inn, in the lovely and secluded Anderson Valley, and Mendocino County, California. The inn is only 2½ hours from San Francisco and the Bay area. Surrounded by rolling hills, majestic redwoods, and the Navarro River, the inn offers the perfect getaway from a busy life. There are five spacious and comfortable rooms, a living room with plenty of books and games for you to enjoy, and the lovely garden, which invites contemplation, meditation, and relaxation.

The historic town of Mendocino and the Northern California coast are only 30 minutes away. Enjoy a hike at Hendy Woods State Park, a picnic at the Navarro River, or mountain biking on the scenic coastal loop.

Poppy Seed Waffles with Lemon Cream

Lemon cream:
1 large egg plus 2 large egg yolks
⅓ cup sugar
1 cup heavy cream
½ cup fresh lemon juice
1 tablespoon lemon zest

Poppy seed waffles:
1 cup all-purpose flour
1 cup cake flour
½ cup sugar
¾ teaspoon baking powder
½ teaspoon baking soda
2 tablespoons poppy seeds
1 cup sour cream
½ cup milk
3 large eggs, separated,
    at room temperature
4 tablespoons (½ stick) butter,
    melted
⅛ teaspoon pure almond extract

For the Lemon Cream, in medium-size bowl, whisk together egg, egg yolks, and sugar. Slowly add cream, whisking until well blended. Transfer mixture to medium-size saucepan and cook over medium heat, whisking constantly, 8 to 10 minutes, or until mixture begins to thicken. Remove pan from heat and stir in lemon juice and zest. Transfer mixture to shallow bowl and let cool to room temperature. Refrigerate for 2 hours, or until thoroughly chilled.

For the waffles, in medium-size bowl sift together both flours, sugar, baking powder, and baking soda. Stir in poppy seeds. In another medium-size bowl, whisk together sour cream, milk, egg yolks, butter, and almond extract. Pour mixture into dry ingredients, stirring in with a few quick strokes to form a lumpy batter. In another medium-size bowl,

using electric mixer set at high, beat egg whites until stiff peaks form. Using rubber spatula, gently and thoroughly fold egg whites into batter. Lightly grease or spray grids of waffle iron. Follow manufacturers instructions, or spoon about ⅓ cup batter (amount varies with size of iron) onto hot iron. Spread it almost to corners of grids. Close lid and bake 2 to 3 minutes, or until waffles are golden brown, edges look dry, and they do not stick to grids. Transfer waffles to oven, placing them directly on rack so they will stay crisp. Repeat with remaining batter. Transfer waffles to serving plates and top each serving with Lemon Cream. Yields 8 to 10 waffles.

Corn Cakes

1 dozen ears fresh corn, shucked and
    stripped off cobs
5 plus 3 tablespoons milk
1¼ cups yellow cornmeal
1¼ cups unbleached all-purpose flour
1 teaspoon salt
1½ tablespoons baking powder
3 egg yolks
5 eggs whole
¾ cup melted butter
1½ cups chopped green onions
Sour cream

Mango-Tomato Salsa:
1 large mango, peeled and cubed
4 tomatoes, cubed
Fresh mint, finely chopped
Olive oil
Salt and Pepper

Put 3 cups corn kernels in blender with 5 tablespoons milk; blend until puréed. In separate bowl, sift together cornmeal, flour, salt, and baking powder. In another bowl put together 3 tablespoons remaining milk, egg yolks, whole eggs, and melted butter. Whisk until well combined. Add mix to dry ingredients and stir until well mixed (do not overstir). Add 3 cups corn kernels and chopped green onions and mix well. Bake on griddle or in nonstick pan until golden brown on both sides. Top with sour cream and Mango-Tomato Salsa. Yields approximately 20 corn cakes.

For salsa, mix together ingredients. Drizzle in a bit of olive oil and add salt and pepper to taste.

Ginger-Cider Lemonade

2 cups water
½ cup sugar
1 (1-inch) piece fresh ginger, peeled and thinly sliced
5 lemons, halved
2 cups apple cider

Bring water, sugar, and fresh ginger to a boil in a saucepan. Cook for 1 minute. Remove from heat. Add lemons to pan and let mixture stand 30 minutes. Squeeze juice from lemons. Strain mixture through a sieve into a bowl. Discard solids. Stir in cider and chill before serving. Yields 1 large pitcher.

Miniature Sausage Muffins

¼ pound ground pork sausage
3 tablespoons chopped onions
¼ cup biscuit mix
¼ teaspoon dry mustard
⅛ teaspoon ground red pepper
¼ cup milk
¼ cup (1 ounce) finely shredded Cheddar cheese

Combine sausage and onions in a medium skillet and cook over medium heat, stirring until sausage crumbles. Drain well. Combine biscuit mix, dry mustard, and red pepper. Add milk, stirring just until moistened. Stir in sausage mixture and cheese; mixture will be thick. Spoon into greased, miniature (1¾-inch) muffin pans, filling two-thirds full. Bake at 400° 12 to 14 minutes or until muffins are golden.

Remove from pans immediately. Serve warm. Yields 1 dozen muffins.

MELITTA STATION INN

5850 Melitta Road
Santa Rosa, CA 95409
(707) 538-7712 (phone)
(800) 504-3099 (toll free)
info@melittastationinn.com
www.melittastationinn.com

An 1880 country store and then a historic railroad depot, Melitta Station Inn has been lovingly restored to a six-room bed and breakfast inn and family home. You are invited to relax and enjoy your visit to Santa Rosa, the Sonoma Wine Country, and the beauty of the Valley of the Moon.

Apple Omelet

1 plus 2 tablespoons butter or margarine
1 large apple, peeled, cored, and sliced
2 teaspoons raisins
2 teaspoons slivered almonds
3 teaspoons brown sugar
1 teaspoon vanilla extract
1 tablespoon lemon or lime juice
4 eggs, beaten
Confectioners' sugar
1 tablespoon sour cream for garnish

In small skillet, melt 1 tablespoon butter. Sauté apples, raisins, and almonds and add brown sugar, vanilla, and lemon juice. In another skillet melt remaining 2 tablespoons butter, and add eggs. Cook as you would an omelet and place apple mixture in middle. Cook until bottom is crusty and then turn omelet into skillet in which

you prepared apple mixture. Slide to warm platter and sprinkle with confectioners' sugar and garnish with sour cream. Yields 2 open-face servings.

Pineapple Oatmeal Muffins

2 eggs
½ cup vegetable oil
¼ cup orange juice
1 cup unsweetened crushed pineapple with juice
½ cup brown sugar
1 cup old-fashion rolled oats
1½ cups all-purpose flour
1 tablespoon baking powder
½ teaspoon baking soda
½ teaspoon salt

Preheat oven to 400°. Combine eggs, oil, and juices in large bowl. Combine remaining ingredients and gently fold together with egg mixture until just mixed. Spoon into greased pan. Bake 20 to 25 minutes. Yields 10 muffins.

Variation: Sprinkle with cinnamon sugar before baking and add a walnut half to each muffin.

Dark Chocolate Mint Bread

3 eggs
½ cup vegetable oil
½ cup chocolate syrup
¼ cup cocoa powder
½ cup warm water
½ teaspoon salt
1 cup sugar
2 cups all-purpose flour
3 tablespoons baking powder
1 cup dark chocolate mint chips

Whisk together eggs, oil, chocolate syrup, cocoa, water, salt, and sugar in large mixing bowl. Combine flour, baking powder, egg mixture, and chips and stir to mix. Pour batter into greased 2-quart baking dish, and bake at 350° until bread is firm in center when touched, about 45 minutes. Center of bread may fall slightly during last 10 minutes of baking. Yields 8 servings.

Strata

12 slices bread, crusts removed
   and cut into cubes (sour French
   works well)
2 full cups Cheddar cheese or more
   to cover well (can use half
   Monterey Jack)
1½ cups diced ham (turkey ham works)
1 pound fresh or canned asparagus,
   cut into 1- to 2-inch pieces (if using
   fresh, boil 4 minutes only)
7 eggs
2 tablespoons minced onion
1 teaspoon salt
2 teaspoons dry mustard
3 cups milk

Grease well with butter 9 x 13-inch glass pan and place bread in two layers on bottom. Layer as follows: first a little cheese on bread, then chopped ham, asparagus, cheese, egg mixed with onion, salt, mustard, and milk. Cover with plastic wrap and let sit 8 to 10 hours or overnight in refrigerator. When ready to prepare, bake in 350° oven about 50 minutes. Yields 10 to 12 servings.

SIERRA HOUSE BED & BREAKFAST

4981 Indian Peak Road
Mariposa, CA 95338
(209) 966-3515 (phone/fax)
libby@sierrahousebnb.com
www.sierrahousebnb.com

Sierra House Bed & Breakfast is nestled in the Sierra Nevada Mountains convenient to Yosemite National Park. Luxury rooms are individually appointed for your comfort. Pan for gold in Mariposa, hike in Yosemite, or enjoy water sports on Bass Lake.

Egg Sausage Casserole

8 cups cubed, crustless
   sourdough bread
2 cups grated Cheddar cheese
1 pound bulk hot sausage,
   browned and crumbled
½ cup sautéed mushrooms
   (or 8-ounce can, drained)
4 eggs
1½ cups milk
½ teaspoon dry mustard
1 (10¾-ounce) can cream of
   mushroom soup
½ (soup) can milk

Place bread in bottom of 9 x 13-inch pan. Add cheese, sausage, and mushrooms. Mix eggs, milk, and mustard together and add to casserole. Cover and refrigerate 8 to 10 hours. Bring to room temperature. Mix soup with milk. Pour over casserole. Bake, uncovered, for 1 hour at 325°. Let sit before cutting. Yields 6 to 8 servings.

French Breakfast Puffs

⅛ teaspoon salt
1½ cups all-purpose flour
½ cup sugar
1½ teaspoons baking powder
¼ teaspoon ground nutmeg
1 egg, beaten
½ cup milk
⅓ cup melted butter, plus additional
   for top
Sugar/cinnamon mix

Preheat oven to 350°. Combine dry ingredients and add egg, milk, and butter. Stir until moistened. May be lumpy. Pour in lightly greased muffin cups. Bake 20 to 25 minutes. Top with melted butter and sprinkle with sugar and cinnamon. Yields 12 muffins.

Mountain High Herb-Baked Eggs

¼ pound flaked ham
8 large eggs
2 teaspoons Dijon mustard
½ cup sour cream
1 teaspoon chopped fresh chives
2 teaspoons chopped fresh parsley
¾ cup shredded sharp Cheddar cheese

Preheat oven to 375°. Grease four 1-cup ramekins. Divide ham among the ramekins. Whisk together eggs, mustard, and sour cream. Stir in herbs and top with cheese. Bake for 25 to 30 minutes until golden and set. Yields 4 servings.

HOLLY TREE INN BED & BREAKFAST

Box 642
Point Reyes, CA 94956
(415) 663-1554 (phone)
(415) 663-8566 (fax)
(800) 286-4665 (toll free)
info@hollytreeinn.com
www.hollytreeinn.com

Located in a nineteen-acre private valley, the Holly Tree Inn has offered guests a casually elegant retreat for over 23 years. Guests choose from one of four rooms or three storybook cottages, each in a unique setting. Organic gardens, a creek-side gazebo, an outdoor hot tub and inspired, served breakfasts leave guests feeling renewed. Located one mile from the Point Reyes National Seashore Park headquarters, guests can choose from a variety of outdoor activities—abundant hiking, world-renowned birding, annual whale migrations, breathtaking spring wildflowers, kayaking on the waters of Tomales Bay, biking and swimming. Local artists and craftspeople make shopping the locally-owned stores a great option. Napa and San Francisco are day trips. Oysters are a local delicacy, and the local cheese producers are getting international recognition.

Broiled Grapefruit with Brown Sugar

1 grapefruit
½ teaspoon brown sugar
Sprig of mint

Halve a grapefruit and section with a knife. Sprinkle ½ teaspoon brown sugar on top.

Place under a broiler until sugar starts to brown. Serve with sprig of mint and edible flowers. Yields 2 servings.

Vanilla French Toast

8 eggs
2 teaspoons vanilla extract
¾ cup milk
1½-inch-thick sourdough baguette slices
Unsweetened coconut
Sliced bananas
Fresh strawberries
Maple syrup

Mix eggs, vanilla, and milk in large bowl. Soak bread in mixture until moist throughout. Transfer slices to a warm, buttered griddle. Cook on medium heat until golden brown. Sprinkle plates with coconut and bananas. Place toast on plates and top with strawberries. Serve with warm syrup. Yields 4 to 6 servings.

Chile Egg Puff

8 eggs
1 cup milk
2 cups cottage cheese
1 (7-ounce) can diced green chiles
¾ pound grated Jack cheese
3 tablespoons melted butter
¾ cup biscuit mix
Sour cream and salsa for serving (optional)
Garnish with avocado and tomato (optional)

Mix all ingredients except biscuit mix together in large bowl. This can be done the night before. Preheat oven to 375°. Before baking, add ¾ cup biscuit mix and stir. Pour mixture into greased baking dish 9 x 13-inch or 8-inch round casserole or individual dishes. Bake 50 minutes (less for individual dishes) or until center is set and top is lightly browned. Serve with sour cream and salsa or garnish with avocado and tomato. Yields 6 to 8 servings.

Holly Tree Inn Bed & Breakfast

Holly Tree Inn Berry Scone

5 plus 1 cups all-purpose flour
1 cup sugar
1½ teaspoons baking soda
1 tablespoon baking powder
¾ teaspoon salt
2 sticks (½ pound) butter
3 cups frozen blueberries
2 cups milk

Combine 5 cups flour, sugar, baking soda, baking powder, and salt. Cut in butter until well combined. Roll berries in remaining 1 cup flour until coated. Transfer berries to dry mixture leaving remaining flour. Add milk. Mix all together with floured hands. Do not overhandle. Preheat oven to 425°. Form tennis-ball-size balls and place on baking sheets lined with parchment paper. Bake until golden brown. Remove and cool on rack. Yields 12 scones.

Vanilla Poached Pears

4 pears, halved, peeled, and cored
Apple juice
½-inch fresh vanilla bean
Ground cinnamon
Sprig of mint

Place pears in a large saucepan and cover with apple juice. Add vanilla bean. Simmer until pears are tender. Serve cool. Top with sprinkle of cinnamon and sprig of mint. Yields 8 servings.

FOOTHILL HOUSE

3037 Foothill Blvd.
Calistoga, CA 94515
(707) 942-6933 (phone)
(707) 942-5692 (fax)
(800) 942-6933 (toll free)
Gus@calicom.net
www.foothillhouse.com

Foothill House is nestled among the western foothills just north of Calistoga. The inn offers beautiful views across the valley of wooded hills and Mount St. Helena. In the foothills, nature abounds with such wildlife as quail, hummingbirds, and hawks. Guests will find a wide variety of things to do because Foothill House is close to every attraction of the Napa Valley. Regardless of the day's activity, one simple pleasure is to enjoy the picturesque scenery of this world-famous wine region.

Decadent French Toast Soufflé

4 large or 5 medium, baked croissants
6 ounces cream cheese, softened
½ cup softened butter
¼ plus ½ cup maple syrup
10 eggs
3 cups half-and-half
Ground cinnamon

Sauce:
½ cup butter
½ cup maple syrup
Chopped pecans
Confectioners' sugar

In food processor, coarsely chop croissants and distribute them evenly in greased, 1-cup soufflé dishes, or 9 x 12-inch glass dish. In food processor, combine cream cheese, butter, and ¼ cup maple syrup. Dollop heaping tablespoon in the middle of croissant crumbs. In large bowl, beat eggs, the remaining ½ cup maple syrup, and half-and-half; pour over the croissant mixture. Sprinkle with cinnamon. Cover and refrigerate 8 to 10 hours. Remove from refrigerator. Preheat oven to 350°. Uncover and bake 45 to 50 minutes or until golden.

For the sauce, heat butter and maple syrup in small saucepan. Pour over warm soufflé. Sprinkle with chopped pecans and confectioners' sugar. Garnish with edible flowers or berries. Yields 8 servings.

Foothill House

Foothill House Sweet Dream Cookies

1 cup (2 sticks) butter
1½ cups firmly packed light
    brown sugar
1 egg at room temperature
1 teaspoon vanilla extract
2½ cups all-purpose flour
1 teaspoon baking soda
1 teaspoon ground cinnamon
1 teaspoon ground ginger
½ teaspoon salt
1 (12-ounce package) semisweet
    chocolate chips
1 cup chopped walnuts
1 cup confectioners' sugar

Cream butter. Beat in brown sugar, egg, and vanilla. Combine flour, baking soda, cinnamon, ginger, and salt. Blend into butter mixture. Fold in chips and walnuts. Refrigerate until firm. (Can be prepared 1 day ahead.) Preheat oven to 375°. Lightly grease baking sheets. Break off small pieces of dough. Roll between your palms into 1-inch rounds. Dredge rounds in confectioners' sugar. Arrange rounds on greased baking sheets, spacing at least 2 inches apart. Bake 10 minutes. Let cool 5 minutes on sheets. Transfer to racks and cool. Store in airtight container. Yields 2 dozen cookies.

Hungarian Casserole

1½ pounds bulk pork sausage,
    crumbled and cooked
3 large potatoes, peeled and boiled
2 to 3 large tomatoes, cored, peeled,
    and sliced
4 hard-cooked eggs, peeled and sliced
1 (single-pack-size) ranch dip mix
    combined with 2 cups sour cream
¾ pound Monterey Jack cheese, sliced
Hungarian paprika

Preheat oven to 350°. In 1-cup soufflé dishes or individual ramekin dishes, layer enough crumbled sausage to cover bottom of dish. Slice potatoes the same thickness as the meat and place them on the sausage layer. Cover with tomato slices. Cover tomatoes with egg slices. Spread ranch dressing to cover all and top with slice of Jack cheese. Sprinkle generously with paprika and bake 30 minutes. Yields 8 servings.

Fruit Soup

3 pints sliced strawberries
3 pints blackberries
2 pints blueberries
3 pints raspberries
1 pound pitted cherries
2 (10-ounce) packages frozen
    sweetened raspberries, thawed
Juice of 6 oranges
Juice of 3 lemons
4 cups sugar

Combine all ingredients in a bowl and refrigerate 8 to 10 hours. Taste for sweetness before serving. Garnish with a fanned strawberry, mint leaf, and a dollop of whipped cream with a blueberry. Yields 8 servings.

Foothill House Gold Rush Brunch Breakfast

1 (8-patty) package frozen
    hash browns, thawed
1 (10¾-ounce) can potato soup,
    undiluted
2 cups sour cream
1 bunch green onions, including tops
10 slices Canadian bacon, chopped
4 hard-cooked eggs, sliced
12 ounces shredded sharp
    Cheddar cheese

Preheat oven to 350°. Combine hash browns with soup, sour cream, and green onions. Lightly grease 9 x 13-inch baking dish or 1-cup soufflé ramekins. Assemble with hash-brown mixture first, then bacon, and then eggs. Top with cheese and bake for 45 minutes. Yields 8 servings.

❧   ❧   ❧

THE INN OF IMAGINATION

470 Randolph Street
Napa, CA 94559
(707) 224-7772
kim@innofimagination.com
www.innofimagination.com

The inn is dedicated to individuals who created new and fanciful worlds through their works. Come explore the imaginations of Lewis Carroll, Dr. Seuss, and Jimmy Buffet. In the area enjoy wine tasting, hot-air ballooning, mud baths, the wine train, and many gourmet restaurants.

The Duchess' Fruit Dipping Sauce

2½ cups Cabernet Sauvignon
1¼ cups balsamic vinegar
1 cup fresh peach juice
4 tablespoon brown sugar
Your choice of fresh fruit,
    cut for dipping

Combine all ingredients in saucepan and cook over medium heat until sauce thickens and reduces to approximately ¾ cup. Do not burn. Serve at room temperature and dip away. Great on strawberries, melons, stone fruits, bananas, mangoes. Yields ¾ cup sauce.

A Nutty Queen of Tarts

Sweet tart dough:
1 cup all-purpose flour
Pinch of salt
1 tablespoon sugar
½ teaspoon grated orange peel
4 ounces unsalted butter, room
    temperature
1 tablespoon water
½ teaspoon vanilla extract

Filling:
⅓ cup almonds
⅓ cup sugar
Pinch of salt
2 eggs
1 teaspoon vanilla extract
Few drops almond extract
½ cup unsalted butter at room
    temperature
2 tablespoons all-purpose flour
½ teaspoon baking powder
3 to 4 tablespoons raspberry
    or apricot jam
½ cup pine nuts
Confectioners' sugar

Prepare Sweet Tart Dough by combining in food processor flour, salt, sugar, and orange peel. Then add butter. Cut in small pieces and process until a coarse meal has formed, 10 to 15 seconds. Combine water and vanilla and pour into flour mixture while machine is running for just 5 seconds. Do not let dough form a ball. Empty ingredients onto work surface, gather them together with your hands, and press dough into ball. Flatten into disk, wrap in plastic, and set aside for ½ hour in refrigerator. (Dough can be kept frozen for 4 to 6 weeks.) Do not roll out. Use your hands to line 9-inch tart pan, sides first and then bottom. After getting general shape, go back and reshape sides and any areas that need evening out. Partially bake. Yields 1 (9-inch) tart.

Bring small pan of water to boil, add almonds, turn off heat, and let sit for 1 minute. Drain, slip off skins, and rub in clean towel to dry. Put almonds in food processor with metal blade about 45 seconds. Add sugar, salt, eggs, vanilla, and almond extract. Add butter, flour, and baking powder. Process long enough to make smooth batter, about 10 seconds. Preheat oven to 375°. Spread thick layer of jam over tart shell and cover with filling. Set pine nuts over the top and bake until surface is firm and browned, about 30 minutes. Remove from oven and let cool. Dust with confectioners' sugar. Serve by itself or with soft mounds of crème fraîche. Yields 6 servings.

Jack's Citrus Flaps with Pumpkin Sauce

Pumpkin sauce:
4 cups coarsely cubed, unpeeled
    pumpkin (or 1½ cups canned
    pumpkin)
¾ cup sugar
¾ teaspoon ground cinnamon
⅛ teaspoon ground nutmeg
¼ teaspoon ground cloves
½ teaspoon salt
⅓ cup raisins
¼ cup milk

Pancakes:
2 eggs
1 cup milk
2 tablespoons lemon juice
1 cup all-purpose flour
½ teaspoon salt
1 teaspoon baking powder
½ teaspoon baking soda
1 tablespoon shortening

To make pumpkin sauce, cook pumpkin, covered, in boiling salted water until tender, 15 to 20 minutes. Drain. Remove rind. Mash pulp and press through sieve. Measure 1½ cups pumpkin (or use canned pumpkin). Mix pumpkin, sugar, spices, and salt. Stir in raisins and milk. Heat through and keep warm. Sauce will be thick. Spoon on pancakes.

To make pancakes, beat eggs until creamy. Add milk and lemon juice and blend. In separate bowl, mix flour, salt, baking powder, and baking soda. Fold into egg mixture. Heat griddle to hot and coat with shortening. Pour approximately 1½ tablespoons batter thinly on griddle. Flip when bubbles stop forming in batter. These should be more crêpe-like than thick pancakes. Yields 10 to 12 pancakes.

TIFFANY HOUSE BED & BREAKFAST

1510 Barbara Road
Redding, CA 96003
(530) 244-3225
tiffanylise@aol.com
www.sylvia.com/tiffany.htm

The Tiffany House is Victorian-furnished with antiques throughout and a private cottage behind the main house. There is a lovely view of Mount Lassen from the rooms and gardens. Activities in the area include championship golf, hiking, water sports, camping, fishing, biking, and skiing; Turtle Bay Exploration Park and Museum; Sacramento River Trail; Mount Shasta, Lake Shasta, Shasta Dam, Shasta Caverns; Shasta State Historical Park; Whiskeytown Lake; McArthur-Burney Falls State Park; Lassen Volcanic National Park; Win River Casino.

Rebecca's Surprise

2 to 3 tablespoons olive oil
1½ teaspoons black peppercorns
1 tablespoon chopped fresh rosemary
3 cloves garlic, chopped
Lemon zest from ½ lemon
7 ounces goat cheese
1 sourdough baguette, sliced
Kalamata olives
Cherry tomatoes

Heat olive oil in large nonstick skillet over medium temperature. Add peppercorns and cook a few minutes to soften. Add rosemary and garlic, stirring until soft and fragrant, about 5 minutes. Add lemon zest and continue cooking another minute. Break up cheese on center of platter. Pour peppercorn mixture over cheese. Surround cheese with baguette slices. Top cheese with kalamata olives and cherry tomatoes. Yields 12 to 14 appetizers.

Spicy Smoked Salmon Corn Cakes

¼ cup plus 2 tablespoons yellow cornmeal
3 tablespoons all-purpose flour
¼ teaspoon baking soda
¼ teaspoon salt
1 large egg, beaten lightly
3 tablespoons softened cream cheese
¼ cup plus 2 tablespoons buttermilk
1 ear fresh sweet corn, cut from cob
    with knife
3 tablespoons finely chopped fresh chives
¼ cup seeded and finely chopped
    pepperoncini
3 ounces finely chopped smoked salmon
Sour cream
1 red onion, chopped
Lemon slices

In small bowl whisk together cornmeal, flour, baking soda, and salt. In medium bowl whisk together egg, cream cheese, and buttermilk. Coarsely chop corn and stir into buttermilk mixture with chives, pep-peroncini, salmon, and cornmeal mixture until just combined. Drop by ¼-cup measure onto hot griddle, spreading slightly to form 3½- to 4-inch cakes. Cook 2 to 3 minutes on each side, or until golden brown. For each serving, place about 2 tablespoons sour cream on plate and sprinkle with 1 tablespoon chopped red onion. Arrange lemon slices beside the cream. Serve 3 corn cakes each. Yields 2 servings.

Kathy's Beans

1 pound ground beef
1 pound bacon, chopped
1 onion, chopped
½ cup ketchup
½ cup barbecue sauce
1 teaspoon salt
4 tablespoons prepared mustard
4 tablespoons molasses
1 teaspoon chili powder
¾ teaspoon pepper
2 (16-ounce) cans red kidney beans
2 (16-ounce) cans pork and beans
2 (16-ounce) cans butter beans

Brown beef, bacon, and onion. Drain excess fat. Combine all other ingredients except beans; stir well. Add beans with juice from cans and combine thoroughly. Bake 1 hour at 350°. Yields 20 to 24 servings.

Buffet Cheese-Scalloped Carrots

1 small onion, minced
¼ cup (½ stick) butter
¼ cup all-purpose flour
1 teaspoon salt
¼ teaspoon dry mustard
2 cups milk
½ teaspoon pepper
½ teaspoon celery salt
12 medium carrots, pared, sliced,
    and parboiled
½ pound sharp Cheddar cheese, sliced
3 cups buttered fresh breadcrumbs

Preheat oven to 350°. Cook onion in butter for 2 to 3 minutes. Stir in flour, salt, mustard, and milk. Cook, stirring, until smooth. Add pepper and celery salt. In a 2-quart casserole dish arrange layer of carrots, then layer of cheese. Repeat until all are used, ending with carrots. Pour sauce over carrots and top with breadcrumbs. Bake uncovered 25 minutes or until golden brown. Yields 10 to 12 servings.

APPLE FARM INN

2015 Monterey Street
San Luis Obispo, CA 93401
(805) 544-2040 (phone)
(805) 546-9495 (fax)
(800) 255-2040 (toll free)
info@applefarm.com
reservations@applefarm.com
www.applefarm.com

Experience the "good old American" virtues of friendliness, cleanliness, honest value, homemade food, and cozy rooms in the surroundings of country Victorian charm. Each beautifully appointed room in our four-diamond-rated inn features a fireplace, cozy seating areas, and most have canopy beds. Enjoy homestyle meals in our restaurant and bakery, shopping in our elaborate three-level gift shop, and tour our picturesque antique millhouse.

Cashew Crusted Salmon with Fresh Herb Pesto

2 plus ½ ounces (⅓ cup plus
    1 tablespoon) roasted cashews
1 cup panko breadcrumbs

½ ounce freshly grated Parmesan cheese
3 to 4 sprigs fresh thyme
3 to 4 leaves fresh sage
2 cups loosely packed fresh basil leaves
1 clove garlic
1 tablespoon fresh lemon juice
⅓ cup extra virgin olive oil
Salt and pepper
4 (8-ounce) salmon fillets
¼ pound (1 stick) butter, clarified

For crust, place 2 ounces cashews in a food processor. Process for 30 seconds or until cashews are chopped medium fine. Mix with breadcrumbs. For pesto, place ½ ounce cashews and Parmesan cheese in food processor. Process 30 to 40 seconds until mix is finely chopped. Add thyme, sage, basil, and garlic. Process 15 to 20 seconds and add olive oil and process 45 seconds more. Salt and pepper to taste. For the salmon, brush each salmon fillet with clarified butter. Dip fillets in cashew crust and place skin side up in hot pan. Cook about 4 minutes, and then turn salmon and finish cooking 4 to 5 minutes. To present salmon, place on plate and put dollop of pesto on center of fillet. Serve with rice pilaf and vegetable medley. Garnish with lemon wheels and fresh herbs. Yields 4 servings.

Pork Chops and Apple Sauce with Fried Onions

2 teaspoons salt
2 teaspoons pepper
1 teaspoon garlic powder
1 teaspoon French thyme
1 (3½- to 4½-pound) center-cut
    pork loin, rack bone on
Vegetable oil
1 yellow onion, thinly sliced
1 cup all-purpose flour
Salt and pepper

Preheat oven to 350°. Combine salt, pepper, garlic powder, and thyme. Sprinkle seasoning mix all over pork. Place on oven rack with pan underneath and bake 55 to 60 minutes or until meat thermometer registers 165°. While pork is cooking heat about 3 inches of oil in deep saucepan. Mix sliced onion with flour and salt and pepper. Shake off excess flour and when oil is hot enough, drop onions into oil and cook until golden brown, stirring often. When pork is done, remove from oven and let sit 10 minutes. Cut pork into individual chops by slicing between bones. Place two chops on each plate and drape fried onions over bones. Top with your favorite chunky applesauce and serve with mashed potatoes and green beans. Garnish with a cherry tomato and chopped parsley. Yields 4 servings.

OLD MONTEREY INN

500 Martin Street
Monterey, CA 93940
(831) 375-8284 (phone)
(831) 375-6730 (fax)
(800) 350-2344 (toll free)
omi@oldmontereyinn.com
www.oldmontereyinn.com

A historic, boutique, hotel-style bed and breakfast inn, Monterey Inn is the perfect accommodation for travelers headed to Monterey Peninsula, Carmel, Pebble Beach, and Big Sur. It is an award-winning establishment, a perfect choice for those seeking a romantic honeymoon destination or a California vacation. Nearby are some of the best golf courses in the world.

Chiles Con Queso

Custard:
1½ cups milk
¾ cup all-purpose flour
Dash of salt
3 eggs

1 (4-ounce) can whole green chiles,
    drained and cut into chunks
    (seeds can be left in)
¾ pound provolone cheese, sliced
    or shredded
¾ pound Cheddar cheese, sliced
    or shredded
4 ounces queso fresco cheese, crumbled
    (found in Hispanic section)

Blend custard ingredients together in blender. Preheat oven to 375°. To assemble, spray casserole dish with nonstick spray. Layer chiles, provolone, chiles, Cheddar, chiles, provolone, chiles, queso fresco. Slowly pour in custard, lifting cheese with fork as you fill dish. Bake about 40 minutes or until casserole is puffed and top is golden brown. Serve immediately or freeze for later use. To cook frozen casserole, leave in refrigerator overnight and then bake as above, or place frozen in oven and cook 60 minutes until center is hot and casserole is browned. Cut into squares. We serve this with a light corn bread or muffin for breakfast. A mango, papaya, pineapple, and avocado salad adds some zesty flavors and looks very festive. Yields 6 to 10 servings.

Apricot Chutney

1 tablespoon salad oil
1 large onion, chopped
1 tablespoon grated ginger
1 tablespoon mustard seed
1 teaspoon curry powder
⅛ teaspoon cayenne
2 cups coarsely chopped dried apricots
⅔ cup golden raisins
½ cup apple cider vinegar
⅓ cup sugar
⅓ cup chopped cilantro

In 3-quart, nonstick frying pan, combine oil, onion, and ginger. Cook until lightly brown. Add mustard seed, curry powder, and cayenne to pan and stir 4 minutes before adding remaining ingredients except cilantro. Let cook for 7 minutes, taste, sample, and add salt if desired while stirring in cilantro. Remove from heat and let cool. Package and place in refrigerator. Chutney will keep for several months if kept in a securely covered container. Serve with cream cheese on bread slices or crackers. This is an excellent condiment served with Indian curries.

Spanikopita

9 eggs
16 ounces ricotta cheese
16 ounces cream cheese
2 teaspoons ground nutmeg
2 teaspoons salt
2 teaspoons pepper
2 yellow onions, julienned, sautéed, and caramelized
3 pounds frozen spinach, drained and chopped
2 sticks butter
1 (1-pound) package phyllo dough

Combine and mix eggs, cheeses, and spices in large bowl. Add onions and spinach. Line couple of sheet pans with waxed paper. Place two sheets of waxed paper side by side on the counter. Melt butter. Unwrap phyllo dough. Lay flat. Slice dough in half vertically so that you now have twice as many slices of dough. Place slightly damp cloth over exposed dough to prevent it from drying out. Peel one sheet of phyllo dough off stack and place it on wax paper. Cover remaining dough. Generously brush sheet of dough with melted butter. Place another sheet of phyllo on top of buttered sheet. Generously brush second sheet with melted butter. Place generous tablespoon of spinach mixture on one end of each strip of dough. Pick up one end of dough and fold it over spinach mixture to form triangle. Continue turning package over, keeping triangle shape until you reach end.

Either trim remaining end or fold edge under. Place on lined sheet pan or directly into large plastic bag to freeze for future use. Continue with remaining dough and spinach mixture. Take frozen triangles from freezer, brush triangles with butter. Bake at 375° 25 minutes until golden brown. Serve with béarnaise sauce if desired. Garnish with tomatoes, spinach leaves, diced bell pepper, or anything that brightens the plate. Yields 80 servings.

OAK CREEK MANOR BED & BREAKFAST

4735 Olive Hill Road
Fallbrook, CA 92028
(760) 451-2468 (phone)
(760) 451-2791 (fax)
(877) 451-2468 (toll free)
johannes.c.zachbauer@gte.net
www.oakcreekmanor.com

The Oak Creek Manor is secluded on eight acres with beautiful gardens and a romantic gazebo overlooking the fish-stocked pond and dock. It is the perfect place to relax, spend your honeymoon, have small executive meetings, or the perfect place for a hideaway.

Spinach Feta Strudel

2 pounds fresh baby spinach, including stems
¼ cup (½ stick) butter
12 green onions, white part only, minced to make ½ cup
6 ounces (1½ cups) chilled feta cheese, coarsely chopped
½ cup fresh breadcrumbs
¼ cup minced parsley leaves
4 egg whites
4 tablespoons fresh dill weed or 2 tablespoons dried
Salt and freshly ground pepper
¾ pound phyllo pastry sheets
1 cup (2 sticks) melted unsalted butter

Wash spinach and cut off root. Cook spinach quickly in uncovered pot only in water clinging to leaves, turning twice to promote even cooking. As soon as spinach wilts transfer to colander and run under cold water until spinach is cool to the touch. Transfer to processor and purée. Melt butter in small skillet. Add onions and sauté 5 minutes. Using food processor, combine spinach purée, onion, feta cheese, 2 tablespoons of breadcrumbs, parsley, egg whites, dill weed, and salt and pepper to taste. Blend well. Taste for seasoning; mixture should be highly seasoned. Preheat oven to 375°. Butter baking sheet. Place 1 phyllo sheet lengthwise in front of you on wax paper on damp towel. Cover remaining sheets with wax paper and wrap in another damp towel. Brush phyllo with some of the melted butter and sprinkle with 1 teaspoon of remaining breadcrumbs. Repeat buttering and crumbing process using three additional phyllo sheets. Spread one-third spinach mixture on phyllo sheets ¼ inch from long edge closest to you. Roll tightly and firmly, using waxed paper to assist. Transfer to prepared baking sheet. Brush top lightly with some of remaining melted butter. Repeat twice for a total of three strudel rolls. Bake until golden brown, about 30 to 35 minutes. Cut in 1-inch slices, using serrated knife. Yields 36 portions.

ALEGRIA

44781 Main Street
P.O. Box 803
Mendocino, CA 95460
(707) 937-5150 (phone)
(800) 780-7905 (toll free)
inn@oceanfrontmagic.com
www.oceanfrontmagic.com

Alegria—the state of being joyful and happy—is an inn that welcomes you by putting your cares to rest and applying thoughtful attention to the myriad details of your stay so that you can focus on more important things, like the hummingbird out the window, the fragrance of ocean on the breeze, sunlight across the garden path which leads to the ocean beach. Alegria is an ocean-front bed and breakfast inn located in the village of Mendocino, California. It features ocean-view rooms and cottages, fireplaces, decks, a hot tub, and a path to the beach. Interesting shops, beautiful galleries, fine restaurants, and the ocean are just a stroll away.

More-Than-Chocolate-Chip Cookies

1 cup unsalted butter
¾ cup granulated sugar
1 cup brown sugar
2 eggs
1½ teaspoons vanilla extract
2¼ cups all-purpose flour
1 teaspoon baking soda
1 teaspoon ground cinnamon
½ teaspoon salt
1 cup oatmeal
2 cups semisweet chocolate chips
½ cup dried cranberries
½ dried apricot, chopped
¼ cup cacao nibs (by Scharffen Berger)

Preheat oven to 350°. Cream together butter, sugar, and brown sugar. Add eggs and vanilla. Add flour, baking soda, cinnamon, and salt. After blended thoroughly, fold in oatmeal, chips, cranberries, apricot, and cacao nibs. Drop dough by teaspoonfuls onto nonstick or greased cookie sheet. Bake 8 to 10 minutes. Cool on racks. Yields approximately 60 cookies.

Blueberry Cream Cheese Coffee Cake

1 cup fresh or frozen blueberries
¼ cup apple juice
1 teaspoon cornstarch
2 teaspoons water
⅓ cup butter
2¼ cups all-purpose flour
¾ plus ¼ cup sugar
½ teaspoon baking powder
½ teaspoon baking soda
¼ teaspoon salt
¾ cup plain low-fat yogurt
1 teaspoon almond extract
2 plus 1 eggs
6 ounces cream cheese
½ cup sliced almonds

In small saucepan, bring to boil blueberries and apple juice and then simmer on very low 3 minutes. Combine cornstarch and water and add to blueberries. Continue to simmer until reduced to 1 cup blueberry mixture. (Won't take long.) Cut butter into small pieces and pulse with flour and ¾ cup sugar in food processor until mixture resembles coarse crumbs. Reserve 1 cup. Pour remaining into large bowl. Stir in baking powder, baking soda, and salt. Add yogurt, almor.. 2 eggs. Batter will be sticky. Spread along bottom of greased and floured 9- or 10-inch spring form pan. Batter should be up sides of pan about ¼-inch. Use small offset stainless steel spatula. Preheat oven to 350°. In food processor, mix cream cheese, remaining ¼ cup sugar, and remaining egg together. Whirl until smooth. Spread over well of batter. Carefully spread blueberry mixture over cream cheese mixture. Toss together reserved crumb mixture and sliced almonds. Sprinkle over blueberry mixture and batter edge. Bake 45 minutes or until filling is set and cake is golden brown. Cool 15 minutes before removing sides. Yields 10 to 12 servings.

Peach and Walnut Corn Scones

3½ cups all-purpose flour
¾ cup cornmeal
¾ cup sugar
2 tablespoons baking powder
½ teaspoon salt
2 teaspoons ground nutmeg
¼ teaspoon ground cinnamon
½ cup (1 stick) butter
1¼ cups peeled and diced peaches
1 cup toasted walnuts
⅔ cup half-and-half plus extra
    for brushing
4 eggs
2 teaspoons vanilla extract
Vanilla sugar for topping

Place in food processor flour, cornmeal, sugar, baking powder, salt, nutmeg, and cinnamon. Pulse to mix. Add butter to processor and pulse to cut in. Empty mixture into large bowl. Add peaches and walnuts. Toss to blend. Beat together in medium-size bowl half-and-half, eggs, and vanilla. Add to large bowl and mix lightly. Preheat oven to 425°. Use ice cream scoop to drop onto cookie sheet sprayed with nonstick spray. Brush with half-and-half. Sprinkle with vanilla sugar. Bake 17 minutes. Yields 12 to 15 servings.

Spinach-Porcini Mushroom Quiche

1 (10-ounce) package frozen
    chopped spinach
1 tablespoon sun-dried tomatoes
    packed in olive oil, garlic,
    and herbs
2 eggs
½ cup mayonnaise
½ cup milk
1 tablespoon cornstarch
½ cup Swiss cheese
½ cup Cheddar cheese
½ cup Monterey Jack cheese
½ bunch green onions, chopped
3 tablespoons chopped dried
    porcini mushrooms
1 (8-inch) piecrust

Thaw spinach and squeeze dry. Place sun-dried tomatoes in sieve, rinse with hot water, and let drain. Chop. Preheat oven to 350°. Whip together eggs, mayonnaise, milk, and cornstarch. Add cheeses, onions, and mushrooms, mixing well. Pour into piecrust. Bake 35 minutes or until firm in center and crust is done. Yields 6 servings.

Vanilla Bean-Pecan Waffles

2 cups all-purpose flour
½ cup rice flour
1 tablespoon baking powder
¾ teaspoon salt
¼ cup sugar
½ vanilla bean(sliced in half lengthwise
    and scraped out)
5 egg yolks
2 cups milk
1 tablespoon vanilla extract
4 tablespoons melted butter
5 egg whites
1½ cups chopped toasted pecans

Stir together flours, baking powder, salt, and sugar. In separate bowl stir in vanilla bean and egg yolks. Beat in milk and vanilla. Add to dry mixture. Stir melted butter into batter. Beat egg whites until stiff but not dry. Fold into batter. Fold pecans into batter. Follow waffle iron instructions for cooking waffles. Serve with sliced organic strawberries in season and a rosette of whipped cream sprinkled with finely chopped pecans. Yields 6 large waffles.

THE BABBLING BROOK INN

1025 Laurel Street
Santa Cruz, CA 95060
(831) 427-2437 (phone)
(800) 866-1131 (toll free)
babblingbrook@innsbythesea.com
www.bbonline.com/ca/babblingbrook/

Tucked into a wooded one-acre hillside, the Babbling Brook, with its cascading waterfall, meandering brook, gardens, decks, and working waterwheel, is a relaxing sanctuary in downtown Santa Cruz.

World-Famous Cookies

2½ cups chocolate chips
1 cup white chocolate chips
1 cup raisins
2½ cups chopped walnuts
2½ cups rolled oats
2 cups orange-almond granola
2 cups softened butter
2 cups packed brown sugar
2 cups white sugar
4 eggs
2 teaspoons vanilla extract
½ cup water
4 cups all-purpose flour
2 teaspoons baking powder
2 teaspoons baking soda
1 teaspoon salt

In small bowl, mix together chips, raisins, walnuts, oats, and granola. In large mixing bowl blend with electric mixer until creamy butter, brown sugar, and white sugar. Beat in eggs, vanilla, and water. In separate bowl, whisk together flour, baking powder, baking soda, and salt. Add dry ingredients to wet mixture using a rubber spatula. Add chocolate mixture. Preheat oven to 375°. Place nine ice cream scoops of cookie dough on cookie sheet. Bake 7 to 8 minutes, turn, and bake 4 to 5 minutes. Remove from oven and cover with foil. After 5 minutes, loosen cookies with spatula, cool, and serve. Repeat with the rest of the dough. Yields 20 cookies.

THE INN AT DEPOT HILL

250 Monterey Avenue
Capitola, CA 95010
(831) 462-3376 (phone)
(800) 572-2632 (toll free)
DepotHill@innsbythesea.com
www.innatdepothill.com

The Inn at Depot Hill is an elegant restored train depot, and each of its twelve rooms is designed to be a romantic destination. Nestled above Capitola Beach, the four-diamond, four-star inn has also received the Four Kiss Award from the Best Places to Kiss in Northern California Guide.

Savory Artichoke Dip

2 (8-ounce) jars marinated artichoke
    hearts, drained and chopped
4 green onions, including tops, chopped

1 cup shredded Parmesan cheese
½ cup mayonnaise
1 cup shredded mozzarella or Jack cheese
3 cloves garlic, minced
1 tablespoon pesto

Preheat oven to 350°. Combine all ingredients. Bake 20 to 25 minutes. Serve with sliced baguettes. Yields about 4 cups.

ADAGIO INN

1417 Kearney Street
St. Helena, CA 94574
(707) 963-2238 (phone)
(707) 963-5598 (fax)
(888) 8-ADAGIO (toll free)
innkeeper@adagioinn.com
www.adagioinn.com

Welcome to Adagio Inn, an 1890s Edwardian home nestled in the quiet neighborhoods of picturesque Saint Helena in the heart of the Napa Valley Wine Country. The inn offers three luxurious suites that are decorated with impeccable European elegance. Period antiques, spa tubs, spacious sitting areas, and the ultimate in fine linens are just some of the surprises that await guests.

Mango Mousse

3 ripe mangoes, seeded, peeled,
    and cut up (3 cups)
⅓ cup sugar
1 teaspoon unflavored gelatin
¼ cup cold water
1 cup whipping cream
¼ teaspoon coconut extract
1 kiwifruit, peeled and sliced
Coconut flakes

Chill medium mixing bowl and beaters of an electric mixer. In food processor blend 2 mangoes until smooth. Measure 1 cup purée and set aside. Combine sugar and gelatin in medium saucepan. Stir in water. Cook and stir over low heat just till gelatin is dissolved. Remove from heat. Stir in 1 cup purée. Cool a few minutes to room temperature. Beat whipping cream and coconut extract in chilled bowl with electric mixer on low speed until peaks form. By hand, fold mango mixture into whipped cream. Chill till mixture mounds when spooned. Divide half of the mango mixture among six parfait dishes. Divide kiwi slices and remaining cut-up mango among the dishes. Top with remaining mango mixture and coconut flakes. Cover and chill 4 hours or until set. Yields 6 servings.

Spinach and Artichoke Cheese Custard

This can be prepared a day ahead through step 3 and chilled; bake 10 to 15 minutes longer.

10 large eggs
2 cups small-curd, low-fat
    cottage cheese
1 plus 1 cups shredded Jack cheese
    (½ pound)
½ cup grated Parmesan cheese
    (2½ ounces)
½ teaspoon salt
¼ teaspoon ground nutmeg
1 (13¼-ounce) can quartered artichoke
    hearts, drained
1 (10-ounce) package frozen, chopped
    spinach, thawed

Preheat oven to 350°. In large bowl, whisk eggs, cottage cheese, 1 cup Jack cheese, Parmesan cheese, salt, and nutmeg until well blended. Coarsely chop artichoke hearts. With your hands, squeeze as much liquid as possible from spinach. Stir in artichoke hearts. Stir artichokes and spinach into egg mixture. Spread mixture level in buttered, shallow, rectangular 2½- to 3-quart casserole. Sprinkle remaining 1 cup Jack cheese evenly over top. Bake until custard is firm to touch in the center, 30 to 40 minutes. Let stand about 10 minutes and cut into portions. Yields 8 to 10 servings.

Herbed Cheesecake Appetizers

1 cup premium round-cracker crumbs
3 tablespoons melted butter
    or margarine
2 (8-ounce) packages cream cheese,
    softened
1 (16-ounce) container sour cream,
    divided
2 (3-ounce) packages goat cheese
3 large eggs
¼ cup chopped fresh chives
2 tablespoons minced fresh thyme
Fresh spinach leaves
Fresh thyme sprigs

Stir together crumbs and melted butter. Press mixture evenly into bottom of 4 (4-inch) springform pans. Preheat oven to 325°. Beat cream cheese, 1 cup sour cream, and goat cheese at medium speed with electric mixer until smooth. Add eggs, one at a time, beating until blended. Stir in chives and thyme and pour into prepared pans. Bake 30 minutes or until almost set. Cool on wire rack. Cover and chill 8 hours or freeze up to 1 month. Spread tops evenly with remaining sour cream. Remove from pans. Place on bed of spinach leaves and garnish with thyme sprigs. Allow to soften for 30 minutes before serving. Serve with assorted crackers. Yields about 6 cups.

Mushroom Crust Quiche

3 plus 2 tablespoons butter
½ pound mushrooms, coarsely chopped
½ cup finely crushed saltine crackers
¾ cup chopped green onion
2 cups shredded Swiss cheese
1 cup cottage cheese
3 eggs
¼ teaspoon cayenne
¼ teaspoon paprika

In frying pan over medium heat, melt 3 tablespoons butter. Add mushrooms and cook until limp. Stir in crackers and turn mixture into well-greased 9-inch pie pan. Press mixture evenly over pan bottom and up sides. In same frying pan over medium heat, melt remaining 2 tablespoons butter; add onions and cook until limp. Spread onions over mushroom crust; sprinkle evenly with Swiss cheese. Preheat oven to 350°. In blender, whip cottage cheese, eggs, and cayenne until smooth. Pour into crust and sprinkle with paprika. Bake 25 to 30 minutes or until knife inserted just off-center comes out clean. Let stand 10 minutes before cutting. Yields 4 to 6 servings.

Russian Cream with Fresh Berries

¾ cup sugar
1½ teaspoons plain gelatin
½ cup water
1 cup whipping cream
1½ cups sour cream
1 teaspoon vanilla extract
Blackberries, raspberries, blueberries, or any combination of berries
Whipped cream for topping

In small pan blend sugar, gelatin, and water. Let stand 5 minutes. Bring to boil. Remove from heat and add cream. Mix sour cream and vanilla together and gradually beat into sugar/cream mixture. Using parfait glasses alternate cream and berries. Cover with plastic wrap. Chill at least 4 hours. Top with additional berries and whipped cream before serving. Yields 6 servings.

LAVENDER HILL BED & BREAKFAST

683 S. Barretta Street
Sonora, CA 95370
(209) 532-9024 (phone)
(800) 446-1333 x290 (toll free)
lavender@sonnet.com
www.LavenderHill.com

Enjoy a restful time, a beautiful stay at the Lavender Hill Bed & Breakfast Inn. There are four rooms to choose from, including the Lavender Room, the Cabbage Rose Room, the Wild Flower Room, and the Primavera Room. The area activities include live theater and historic carriage rides, and the inn is happy to arrange for dinner-theater packages, scheduled rides, or massages.

Lavender Hill Bed & Breakfast

Smoothie

2 cups cranberry juice
1 (8-ounce) carton raspberry yogurt
1 whole banana (frozen is good)
2 to 3 cups frozen fruit (raspberries, strawberries, blueberries, mixed)
Cinnamon

Blend in blender the juice, yogurt, and banana. Add frozen fruit until consistency of milk shake. Add cinnamon to taste. Serve in pretty, longstemmed glasses or 12-ounce tumblers. A great first course for a country breakfast. Yields 4 servings.

Swiss Breakfast Parfait

1 cup quick or old-fashioned, uncooked oats
2 (8-ounce) cartons vanilla yogurt
1 (8-ounce) can crushed pineapple in juice, not drained
2 tablespoons sliced almond
2 cups sliced fresh or frozen strawberries, thawed

In medium bowl, combine oats, yogurt, pineapple, and almonds; mix well. Cover and refrigerate 8 to 10 hours or up to 1 week. To serve, layer oat mixture and strawberries in parfait glasses. Garnish with additional sliced almonds, if desired. Serve chilled. This is a low-calorie, low-fat dish that is light and filling and does not require large servings. Yields 5 servings.

Note: Yogurt can be low-fat or nonfat. Other fruit like blueberries or fresh peaches may be substituted for strawberries.

CINNAMON BEAR INN

113 Center Street
P.O. Box 3338
Mammoth Lakes, CA 93546
(760) 934-2873 (phone/fax)
(800) 845-2873 (toll free)
cinnabear1@aol.com
www.cinnamonbearinn.com

Who needs the Ritz?" That's the message written by one of the guests on a thank-you card. Enjoy the friendly atmosphere, comfort, style, and coziness of this lodge, located next to a large wooded area. Rooms feature full baths and free HBO. There's even an outdoor Jacuzzi. A full breakfast and wine and cheese are also included. A friendly inn located in Mammoth Lakes.

Raspberry Cream Cheese-Stuffed French Toast

2 (8-ounce) packages cream cheese
1 (10-ounce) package frozen
    raspberries
1 dozen eggs
1 quart milk
¼ cup vanilla flavoring
1 tablespoon ground cinnamon
2 loaves sliced bread
Butter
Confectioners' sugar
Syrup

Heat skillet over medium heat. Microwave cream cheese and raspberries about 2 minutes at low wattage, until you can blend them together. Use 1 egg for every two servings. To make the batter, blend eggs and milk and flavor with vanilla and cinnamon. Spread about 1 tablespoon cream cheese mix on a piece of bread and put another piece of bread on top. Then dunk the sandwich in batter and toss in skillet. Brown both sides, top with butter, and sprinkle with confectioners' sugar. Serve with hot syrup and garnish the plate to complete your masterpiece. Quick, easy, and delicious. Yields 24 servings.

THE INN AT THE PINNACLES

P.O. Box 1204
Soledad, CA 93960
(831) 678-2400
info@innatthepinnacles.com
www.innatthepinnacles.com

The Inn at the Pinnacles is a newly built, Mediterranean-style bed and breakfast located within our family-owned vineyard in the foothills of Monterey County, California. Hiking and rock climbing are popular attractions in our area as is the Pinnacles National Monument. Located next to world-famous Chalone Winery, it is also within reasonable driving distance to other local wineries.

Orange Pecan Belgian Waffles

1 large egg
6 tablespoons canola oil
1¼ cups milk
¼ cup chopped pecans
1 tablespoon grated orange peel
1¼ cups all-purpose flour
2 teaspoons baking powder
Dash of salt

In large bowl, beat egg with wire whip. Add canola oil and milk. Mix well. Mix in pecans and orange peel. In another bowl, mix dry ingredients. Stir into liquid mixture. Heat Belgian waffle maker. When hot, brush with melted butter and add about 1½ cups batter. Bake. Remove from griddle and place on warm plate. Top with confectioners' sugar and pecan halves. Place sliced oranges, zest removed and sectioned, on the side. Serve with maple syrup. Yields 2 to 3 servings.

Lemon Soufflé Pancakes

Blueberry sauce:
1 cup real maple syrup
1 cup frozen blueberries
2 tablespoons butter

Pancakes:
2 cups all-purpose flour
2 tablespoons sugar
1 teaspoon baking soda
½ teaspoon salt
2 large eggs, separated
1½ cups buttermilk
2 teaspoons grated lemon peel
3 tablespoons lemon juice
2 tablespoons melted butter

To make sauce, in small saucepan over medium heat, combine maple syrup, blueberries, and butter. Heat until butter melts. Keep warm.

To make pancakes, in large bowl, mix together flour, sugar, baking soda, and salt. In small bowl, beat egg yolks with wire whip and add buttermilk, lemon peel, lemon juice, and melted butter. Add flour mixture to buttermilk mixture and blend. In another bowl, whip egg whites to stiff moist peaks. Gently fold egg whites into batter and carefully blend. Heat pancake griddle. Lightly coat griddle with butter. Add about ½ cup batter per pancake to griddle. Cook until golden on each side, turning once. Remove from griddle. Place on warm plate and top with blueberry sauce and confectioners' sugar. Serve extra sauce on the side. Yields 3 to 4 servings.

Cheese and Herb Quiche

Piecrust:
1½ cups all-purpose flour
½ teaspoon salt
½ cup Saffola margarine
4 to 5 tablespoons very cold water

Filling:
½ cup shredded Swiss cheese
½ cup shredded Cheddar cheese
½ cup shredded mozzarella cheese
5 eggs
½ cup ricotta cheese
1 cup half-and-half
1 teaspoon dried dill
1 teaspoon parsley
1 teaspoon instant minced onion
½ teaspoon dried thyme
½ teaspoon dried chives
¼ teaspoon salt

Preheat oven to 425°. To make piecrust, combine flour and salt in food processor. Cut in margarine. With processor running, slowly add 1 tablespoon cold water at a time until dough starts to form a ball. Remove from processor and roll out on lightly floured surface. Assemble in 9-inch pie pan. Prick bottom of crust with fork. Line with foil and pie weights and bake about 12 minutes. Remove from oven and let cool.

To make filling, combine shredded cheeses and place in bottom of piecrust. Beat eggs with wire whip and add ricotta and half-and-half. Mix well. Combine remaining ingredients and add to egg mixture. Pour over cheeses. Bake at 350° for 1 hour 15 minutes. Can also be made with egg substitute. Baking time may very slightly. Yields 6 servings.

JOSHUA GRINDLE INN

44800 Little Lake Road
P.O. Box 647
Mendocino, CA 95460
(707) 937-4143 (phone)
(800) GRINDLE (toll free)
stay@joshgrin.com
www.joshgrin.com

Romantic ocean-view rooms, fireplaces, a full breakfast, and excellent service make the Joshua Grindle the most revisited inn on the north coast of California.

Mandarin Almond French Toast

12 slices sourdough bread
1 tablespoon grated orange peel
2 teaspoons ground nutmeg
1 cup sliced almonds
4 ounces cream cheese (cubed)
1 (11-ounce) can mandarin oranges, diced
10 eggs
⅓ cup maple syrup
1½ cups milk
½ cup orange juice

Remove crusts and cube bread. Place half the cubes in greased 9 x 13-inch pan. Sprinkle with orange peel and nutmeg. Layer with almonds, cream cheese, and oranges. Place remaining bread cubes on top. Combine eggs, syrup, milk, and orange juice. Pour over bread, and cover with plastic wrap. Press down firmly so that bread soaks up egg mixture. Refrigerate overnight or 8 to 10 hours. When ready to serve, preheat oven to 350° and bake 40 to 50 minutes or until golden brown. Cut into ten squares and serve with maple syrup, a dab of sour cream and half an orange slice on top. Yields 10 servings.

Spinach, Mushrooms, Pesto Quiche

Also known as Pizza Quiche.

½ cup polenta
1½ cups water
¼ plus ¼ cup grated Parmesan cheese
½ teaspoon salt
1 heaping tablespoon fresh
    or frozen pesto
1 cup shredded mozzarella
1 cup thinly sliced mushrooms
3 cloves garlic, minced
¼ cup chopped sun-dried tomatoes
3 eggs, beaten
1¼ cups milk
½ cup cottage cheese
5 ounces frozen spinach, thawed with
    liquid squeezed out
1 Roma tomato, thinly sliced

Lightly oil bottom of pie plate. In small saucepan, mix polenta and water and bring to a boil. Reduce heat and stir until thickened. Add ¼ cup Parmesan and salt and mix well. Pour into pie plate, covering bottom. Let cool until solidified, 5 to 10 minutes. Spread pesto over polenta and sprinkle with mozzarella. Sauté mushrooms, garlic, and sun-dried tomatoes. Preheat oven to 350°. Beat together eggs, milk, and cottage cheese. Add sautéed mushroom mixture and spinach. Mix well. Pour into pie plate. Top with remaining ¼ cup Parmesan and decorate with tomato slices. Bake 45 minutes until center is set. Yields 10 to 12 servings.

Arlene's Spicy Baked Pears with Yogurt

½ cup dark brown sugar
Ground cinnamon
Mace
Pinch of ground cloves
5 large ripe pears
¾ cup orange juice
    (or enough to make ½-inch
    liquid in baking dish)
¼ cup (½ stick) butter
Vanilla yogurt

Preheat oven to 350°. Line bottom of 10 x 15-inch baking dish with brown sugar. Sprinkle sugar layer generously with cinnamon, mace, and cloves. Slice pears in half; remove cores and stems. Lay pears cut-side down on sugar mixture. Pour orange juice over pears and dot with butter. Bake 15 to 20 minutes, or until pears are tender.

To serve, place pear cut-side down on serving dish and pour some juice mixture over the pear. Place a dollop of yogurt beside pears and top with nutmeg. Yields 10 servings.

Note: This recipe can be prepared in advance by combining all ingredients except orange juice. Pour over just before baking.

Cinnamon Bran Muffins

1 box bran buds
2 cups boiling water
3 cups sugar
4 eggs, beaten
1 cup vegetable oil
5 cups all-purpose flour
1½ teaspoons ground cinnamon
1½ tablespoons baking soda
2 teaspoons salt
1 tablespoon grated orange peel
2 cups raisins
4 cups buttermilk
Cinnamon sugar

In very large bowl, mix together bran buds and water and let stand 10 minutes. Mix together sugar, eggs, and oil and add bran buds. Mix together flour, cinnamon, baking soda, salt, orange peel, and raisins. Add to bran mixture alternately with buttermilk until well mixed. Preheat oven to 375°. Spoon batter into muffin tins for number desired, sprinkle with cinnamon sugar mixture. Bake 15 to 20 minutes, or until tester comes out clean. Serve with apple or honey butter. Yields 40 muffins.

Chocolate Zucchini Cake

¾ cup (1½ sticks) butter
2 cups sugar
3 eggs
2 teaspoons vanilla extract
1 tablespoon grated orange peel
2 cups grated raw zucchini
2¾ cups all-purpose flour
⅓ cup cocoa
2½ teaspoons baking powder
1½ teaspoons baking soda
1 teaspoon salt
1 teaspoon ground cinnamon
½ cup low-fat milk
1 cup chopped walnuts

Lemon orange glaze:
1 tablespoon vanilla extract
1 cup confectioners' sugar
Grated orange peel
Lemon juice

Preheat oven to 350°. Grease and flour a 10-inch Bundt pan. Cream butter and slowly add sugar, beating until smooth. Beat in eggs and mix thoroughly. Stir in vanilla, orange peel, and zucchini and blend well. Mix together flour, cocoa, baking powder, baking soda, salt, and cinnamon. Add to zucchini mixture alternately with milk and beat until thoroughly mixed. Fold in nuts. Pour batter in prepared pan and bake 60 minutes, or until toothpick inserted in center comes out clean.

To make glaze, stir vanilla into sugar until a thick paste is forme... and enough juice to make g... When cake is completely co... of pan onto serving plate and drizzle glaze over the top. Garnish with fresh flowers. Yields 8 to 10 servings.

THE TURRET HOUSE

556 Chestnut Avenue
Long Beach, CA 90802
(562) 983-9812 (phone)
(562) 437-4082 (fax)
(888) 4-TURRET (toll free)
innkeepers@turrethouse.com
www.turrethouse.com

Indulge in Victorian hospitality and antique finery in this elegant 1906 home in Long Beach, California. Five romantic guestrooms, private baths, and gourmet candlelit breakfasts await you. Pleasant stroll to ocean beaches, aquarium, convention center, theaters, fine dining, antique stores, and specialty shops. Convenient to all Southern California attractions.

Saffron Serenade

2 (5-ounce) bags saffron rice
2 cups marinated artichoke hearts,
    drained and chopped
3 cups shredded sharp Cheddar cheese
½ cup reserved artichoke marinade
10 large eggs
1 cup milk
1 teaspoon dry mustard
¼ teaspoon black pepper
Paprika

Preheat oven to 350°. Prepare saffron rice according to package directions. Mix together rice, artichoke hearts, cheese, and marinade. Whisk together eggs, milk, mustard, and pepper. Combine artichoke mixture and egg mixture. Pour into greased 9 x 13-inch baking dish. Sprinkle paprika over top. Bake 50 to 60 minutes or until done. Serve with pineapple salsa or other fruit-flavored salsa. Yields 12 servings.

Spinach Parasol Pie

Olive oil pastry crust:
2⅔ cups all-purpose flour
1 teaspoon salt
⅔ cup olive oil (if sun-dried tomatoes for filling are packed in olive oil, you can use some oil from those)
2 tablespoons cold water

Filling:
1 (10-ounce) package frozen chopped spinach, cooked, and drained well
3 eggs
1 (16-ounce) container ricotta cheese or blend of ricotta and cottage cheese
½ cup grated sharp Cheddar cheese
½ cup grated Jack cheese
½ cup feta cheese
¼ cup shredded Parmesan cheese
¼ to ½ cup milk
½ cup chopped sun-dried tomatoes
2 tablespoons oregano leaves
2 tablespoons bacon bits

To make crust, mix flour, salt, and oil in bowl until all flour is moistened. Sprinkle with water, 1 tablespoon at a time. Toss with fork until all water is absorbed and dough holds together easily. Divide dough in half. Press each half in bottoms and up sides of two 9-inch pie pans. You might like to use a tablespoon to press down the dough once you've distributed the crust mixture.

Preheat oven to 350°. To make filling, combine spinach, eggs, cheeses, milk, tomatoes, oregano, and bacon bits. Pour into piecrusts and bake about an hour or until done. Yields 2 (9-inch) quiches.

Tomato, Bacon, and Leek Pie

4 to 6 slices bacon, cut in ½-inch pieces
3 tablespoons butter
5 leeks, white and pale green only, thinly sliced
6 eggs
1 cup whipping cream
¼ cup milk
½ teaspoon ground nutmeg
1 teaspoon salt
White pepper
1 large tomato, seeded and diced

Cook bacon in medium-size skillet over medium-high heat, stirring often, until brown but not crisp, about 6 minutes. Set aside on paper towels to drain. Discard grease but do not wipe out pan. Melt butter in same pan over medium heat. Add leeks. Cook until softened but not browned, stirring often, about 8 to 10 minutes. Preheat oven to 300°. Put eggs, cream, milk, nutmeg, and salt and pepper to taste in bowl. Whisk until well mixed. Stir in bacon and leeks. Adjust seasoning to taste. Set 9-inch pie pan on baking sheet and ladle bacon mixture into pie pan. Fill to within ⅛ inch from top. Dot top with diced tomato. Bake in lower area of oven until set, browned, and puffy, 50 to 60 minutes. To serve, cut into wedges. This can be made with a piecrust. Yields 5 to 6 servings.

Wintertime Brie

¾ cup chopped pitted dates
1 small apple peeled, cored, diced
1 small firm pear, diced
½ cup currants or dried cranberries
½ cup chopped pecans
⅓ cup sweet wine (Marsala or other dessert wine)
1- to 2-pound wheel Brie, well chilled

Combine dates, apple, pear, currants, pecans, and wine. Set aside for at least two hours or overnight is even better, adding more wine as it is absorbed. Cut Brie in half horizontally to make two layers. Place one layer rind-side down in medium-deep dish. Spread with half the fruit mixture. Place remaining Brie on top with rind-side facing up. Spoon remaining fruit mixture on center top of Brie. Seal with plastic wrap and refrigerate up to two days. Preheat oven to 350°. Transfer Brie to baking dish and bake uncovered until cheese melts at edges, 25 to 30 minutes. (May be made with combination of summer fruits—peaches, apricots, and nectarines—instead of winter fruits.) Serve warm out of the oven with assortment of crackers and toasted breads. Yields 20 to 25 servings.

Watermelon with Hot Strawberry Vinaigrette

Watermelon balls (½ average-size, seedless watermelon)
⅓ cup balsamic vinegar
2 tablespoons sugar
1 cup sliced strawberries or whole fresh raspberries

Using a melon baller, prepare individual dishes of melon balls. In a 1- to 1½-quart pan over high heat, bring vinegar and sugar to boil. Lower heat and stir in strawberries until heated through. Spoon berry mixture over melon balls while hot. Serve immediately. Yields 4 to 6 servings.

CHICHESTER-McKEE HOUSE

800 Spring Street
Placerville, CA 95667-4424
(530) 626-1882 (phone)
(800) 831-4008 (toll free)
info@innlover.com
www.innlover.com

You can begin an adventure winding through Placerville's historic district to find this elegant and romantic grand, Victorian Painted Lady home, circa 1892.

Ham and Asparagus Crêpes

Crêpes:
1 cup milk
3 eggs
⅔ cups all-purpose flour

Filling:
12 thin slices Black Forest ham
4 slices Muenster cheese, cut in thirds
3 (16-ounce) cans asparagus

Cheese sauce:
3 tablespoons melted butter
3 tablespoons all-purpose flour
1 cup milk
1 cup grated sharp Cheddar cheese
Dash of white pepper
Paprika

To make crêpes, mix milk, eggs, and flour in blender. Heat 8-inch pan to medium-high. Pour batter in pan and roll around to cover pan thinly. Cook until bubbles appear and edges start to turn brown. Flip over and cook other side a few seconds. Repeat 12 times.

Preheat oven to 325°. Lay crêpes flat. Place thin slice of ham, ⅓ slice of cheese, and 2 or 3 asparagus spears on each crêpe. Roll up crêpe and place in 9 x 13-inch pan. Cover with foil. Bake for 30 minutes. Brown the last few minutes. Serve two on plate with cheese sauce.

To make cheese sauce, microwave butter, flour, and milk and whip with wire whisk until smooth. Add cheese and white pepper. Spoon 2 or 3 tablespoons sauce over crêpes and decorate with sprinkle of paprika. A nice touch is to decorate the plate with an orange slice, twisted, a sprig of parsley, and a pansy. Yields 6 servings.

Doreen's Quiche

4 eggs, beaten
1 (15-ounce) can evaporated milk
⅓ (10-ounce) package frozen, chopped spinach, thawed and drained
1 cup grated sharp Cheddar cheese
½ medium zucchini, chopped
4 link sausages, thinly sliced
9 medium mushrooms, sliced and sautéed

Mix ingredients together. Pour into baked crust and cook in microwave on high for approximately 16 minutes (900 watt oven). Adjust time according to microwave wattage. Test for doneness by inserting a knife into pie. If it comes out clean, it's done. Yields 6 servings.

Easy, Quick, and Delicious Eggs

2 large cans chiles
1 cup grated Cheddar cheese
1 dozen eggs
¾ cup heavy cream
Salt and pepper

Layer chiles and cheese in greased 9 x 9-inch pan. Beat eggs and add cream and salt and pepper and pour over cheese. Bake at 350° for 30 minutes. Don't allow to brown.

Let sit 10 minutes before cutting into small pieces. Serve as finger food. Yields 6 servings.

Heath Brunch Coffee Cake

2 cups all-purpose flour
¼ pound (1 stick) butter
1 cup brown sugar
½ cup granulated sugar
1 cup buttermilk
1 teaspoon soda
1 egg
1 teaspoon vanilla extract
½ cup finely crushed English toffee
¼ cup finely crushed pecans or almonds

Preheat oven to 350°. Blend flour, butter, and sugars. Take out ½ cup of mixture and set aside. Add remaining ingredients. Blend well. Pour into greased and floured 9 x 9-inch cake pan. Mix together toffee and nuts with the set-aside ½ cup cake mixture. Sprinkle over the top of batter and bake 45 minutes. Yields 16 servings.

Erma's Bundt Cake

1 (18-ounce) package yellow cake mix
1 (3.4-ounce) package instant vanilla pudding mix
¾ cup butter-flavored oil
¾ cup cream sherry
4 eggs
1 tablespoon butter flavoring
¼ cup sugar
½ cup chopped walnuts
2 teaspoons ground cinnamon

Beat cake and pudding mixes with oil, sherry, eggs, and flavoring together 7 minutes. Grease and flour Bundt pan. Mix remaining ingredients together and sprinkle half of mixture in bottom of pan. Pour batter on top. Sprinkle rest of sugar mixture on top and pour remaining batter over all. Bake in a 350° oven for 50 minutes. Yields 10 servings.

THE 1801 INN

1801 First Street
Napa, CA 94559
(707) 224-3739 (phone)
(707) 224-3932 (fax)
(800) 518-0146 (toll free)
innkeeper@the1801inn.com
www.the1801inn.com

Among Napa California's finest bed and breakfast inns, the 1801 combines luxury and historic refinement. Also known as the distinguished Hunter-Prouty House, it is a stunning Victorian located in the heart of downtown Napa, the gateway to the world-famous Napa Valley Wine Country.

Ramona's French Toast

1½ loaves buttermilk bread
    (cut into 1-inch squares)
1½ (8-ounce) packages cream cheese,
    softened
¼ cup maple syrup
18 eggs
3 cups milk
⅛ teaspoon ground nutmeg
⅛ teaspoon ground cinnamon

Blueberry sauce:
2 tablespoons cornstarch
¼ plus ¾ cup cold water
1 tablespoon butter
¾ cup sugar
1 cup fresh or frozen blueberries

Preheat oven to 350°. Grease 4-quart baking dish with cooking spray and place half the bread on bottom of dish. Mix cream cheese and syrup in blender until creamy. Spread over bread in dish. Top with remaining bread. Mix eggs, milk, nutmeg, and cinnamon. Pour over bread mixture. Sprinkle top with a little extra cinnamon.

Cover with foil and bake 30 minutes. Uncover and bake another 30 minutes. The dish will be done when it is set in the middle and has puffed up in the center. Serve with blueberry sauce.

To make the sauce, mix cornstarch with ¼ cup of water and add back to ¾-cup full. Pour into small saucepan and add butter. Heat on medium heat until butter has melted. Add sugar and stir until bubbling. Add blueberries and turn heat to simmer. Sauce is done when blueberries have popped and sauce has thickened. Yields 16 servings.

Apple Cinnamon Tart Soufflé

8 ounces cream cheese
16 to 18 ounces (2 to 2¼ cups) applesauce
Ground cinnamon
6 eggs
Sour cream for serving

Preheat oven to 350°. In electric mixer, combine cream cheese and applesauce, spooning applesauce a little at a time until desired consistency. Sprinkle cinnamon to taste into mixer. Remove from mixer and hand-beat eggs into mixture. Grease 9-inch pie pan and pour in mixture. Bake 40 to 50 minutes. Serve with sweetened sour cream. Yields 6 servings.

Basil Brie Torte

1 (14-ounce) round Brie cheese
½ cup softened butter
1 to 2 large cloves garlic
⅓ cup chopped walnuts
⅓ cup pitted and chopped black olives
2 tablespoons chopped fresh basil
    (oregano, parsley, or other herbs
    can be substituted)

Freeze Brie for 30 minutes or until firm. In small bowl, combine butter and garlic. Add walnuts, olives, and basil and mix

well. Cut Brie rounds in half horizontally to get a top and bottom. Spread mixture evenly on cut side of one of the halves. Top with other half, cut-side down. Lightly press together, wrap in foil or plastic wrap, and refrigerate. When ready to serve, bring cheese to room temperature. We serve this with Carr's crackers, but you can use any water wafers, saltines, or other plain crackers. Yields about 24 appetizer servings.

HERITAGE PARK INN

2470 Heritage Park Row
San Diego, CA 92110
(619) 299-6832 (phone)
(619) 299-9465 (fax)
(800) 995-2470 (toll free)
innkeeper@heritageparkinn.com
www.heritageparkinn.com

Come for a glimpse of the past, stay and be pampered at Heritage Park Inn. Snuggle in a featherbed . . . unwind in the bubbles of a claw-foot tub . . . awaken to a homemade gourmet breakfast served on the veranda. It's all here in sunny San Diego, just minutes from the zoo, Sea World, and our beautiful beaches.

Danish Pecan Cake

¾ cup (1½ sticks) soft butter
    or margarine
1½ cups sugar
3 eggs
1½ teaspoons vanilla extract
3 cups all-purpose flour
1½ teaspoons baking powder
1½ teaspoons baking soda
¼ teaspoon salt
1½ cups sour cream

Filling:
½ cup packed brown sugar
½ cup chopped pecans
1½ teaspoons ground cinnamon

Preheat oven to 350°. Grease two 9 x 5 x 3-inch loaf pans. Cream butter and sugar thoroughly; beat in eggs and vanilla. In another bowl, stir flour, baking powder, baking soda, and salt together. Mix into creamed mixture alternately with sour cream.

Combine filling ingredients. Spread one-fourth batter (about 1½ cups) into each pan. Sprinkle each with one-fourth filling (about 5 tablespoons) and repeat the steps. Bake 50 to 60 minutes. Cool slightly in pans before removing. Yields 2 loaves.

Hot Fruited Tea

5 cups boiling water
5 teaspoons loose tea or 5 tea bags
10 whole cloves
¼ teaspoon ground cinnamon
¼ cup sugar
¼ cup lemon juice
⅓ cup orange juice
3 unpeeled orange slices, cut in half

Pour boiling water over tea, cloves, and cinnamon. Cover and let steep 5 minutes. Strain tea and stir in sugar and fruit juices. Heat to just below boiling. Serve hot with orange slice in each cup. Yields 6 servings.

Zucchini Bread

2½ cups all-purpose flour
3 eggs, lightly beaten
1 cup mayonnaise
1 cup sugar
2 cups grated, drained zucchini
2 teaspoons vanilla extract
1 teaspoon baking powder
1 teaspoon baking soda
1 tablespoon ground cinnamon
1 teaspoon salt
⅔ cup raisins
1 cup chopped toasted pecans or walnuts

Preheat oven to 350°. Blend all ingredients in mixing bowl until thoroughly combined. Divide batter between two greased 9 x 5-inch loaf pans. Bake 1 hour. Let cool 10 minutes and remove from pans. Yields 2 (9 x 5-inch) loaves.

Spicy Chicken Roll-ups

2 (6-inch) pita bread rounds
¼ pound boneless cooked chicken
2 teaspoons mango chutney
2½ tablespoons mayonnaise
½ teaspoon curry powder
1 teaspoon lime juice
Salt

With a serrated bread knife, split pita rounds in half horizontally. Stack the halves between layers of dampened paper towels and cover with plastic wrap. Let bread sit at room temperature for about an hour until softened. Chop chicken into small pieces. Chop up large pieces of fruit in chutney. In medium bowl, combine chutney with mayonnaise, curry powder, lime juice, and salt. Mix together well. Stir in chopped chicken. Working with 1 pita half at a time, spread chicken filling on rough side of each half. Roll up tightly, jelly-roll style, and wrap tightly with plastic wrap. Chill rolls for several hours. To serve, cut rolls crosswise into ¼-inch-thick slices. Yields 24 slices.

Shortbread

½ cup sugar
½ cup cornstarch
2 cups all-purpose flour
1 cup (2 sticks) butter, melted

Preheat oven to 300°. Sift sugar, cornstarch, and flour together. Mix in butter. Knead slightly; press into two, 8-inch round cake pans. Prick all over with fork. Bake until set but not browned (30 to 40 minutes). Remove from oven and score into wedges. Allow to cool. Yields 16 wedges.

BLUE SPRUCE INN

2815 South Main Street
Soquel, CA 95073
(831) 464-1137 (phone)
(831) 475-0608 (fax)
(800) 559-1137 (toll free)
info@bluespruce.com
www.BlueSpruce.com

The Blue Spruce Inn offers amenities such as robes, afternoon wine service, spa tubs, fireplaces, data ports, a hearty breakfast and quiet gardens for our guests' relaxation.

Good Morning Cheese Cake

1½ cups grated Jack cheese
    or Cheddar mixture
5 eggs
1½ cups 2% cottage cheese
¾ cup milk
¾ cup all-purpose flour
¼ cup melted butter

...oven to 350°. Butter 8 x 8-inch pan. Sprinkle bottom of pan with cheese. In blender or mixer or food processor beat eggs and add cottage cheese, then milk. Blend until smooth. Add flour and butter slowly. Pour over cheeses. Bake uncovered for 45 to 60 minutes, depending on serving size. Cool slightly before cutting. Best if served at room temperature. Serve with fruit and whipped cream, croissants and jam. Yields 6 servings.

Gingerbread Waffles

2 cups all-purpose flour
½ teaspoon salt
1 teaspoon baking powder
1 teaspoon ginger
1 teaspoon ground cinnamon
¼ teaspoon cloves
1 cup molasses
1 cup milk
1 egg, beaten
½ cup vegetable oil

Combine flour, salt, baking powder, ginger, cinnamon, and cloves. Mix together molasses, milk, egg, and oil and stir into dry ingredients, adding additional milk if necessary. Bake in hot greased waffle iron until golden brown. Serve with sweetened whipped cream, lemon curd, and maple syrup. This recipe can be easily doubled for larger crowds. Yields 4 to 6 waffles, depending on size of waffle iron.

Peach Vanilla French Toast

¾ cup (1½ sticks) butter
1½ cups packed brown sugar
2 plus 3 teaspoons vanilla extract
3 (15-ounce) cans peaches, drained
8 cups torn French bread
1 cup chopped pecans
16 eggs, beaten
2½ cups milk
½ cup half-and-half

Preheat oven to 350°. Melt butter with brown sugar and vanilla, boil 2 minutes, and cool slightly. Pour mixture into well-greased pan (sides, too). Line with peaches and sprinkle with bread and nuts. Beat eggs, milk, and half-and-half and pour over bread and nuts. Cover and refrigerate 8 to 10 hours. Bake 40 to 50 minutes. Serve with syrup. Yields 12 servings.

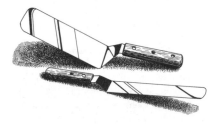

Best-Ever Chocolate Chip Cookies

1½ cups sifted all-purpose flour
1 teaspoon baking soda
1 teaspoon ground cinnamon
1 cup (2 sticks) butter, softened
½ cup firmly packed light brown sugar
1 cup granulated sugar
1 large egg
1 teaspoon vanilla extract
1½ cups old-fashioned rolled oats
1 cup semisweet chocolate chips
½ cup nuts

Mix together flour, baking soda, and cinnamon. Beat together butter and sugars at medium speed until light and fluffy. Beat in egg and vanilla. At low speed, beat in flour mixture until blended. Fold in oats, chips, and nuts. Cover with plastic wrap; chill for 1 hour. Preheat oven to 350°. Grease two baking sheets. Shape dough into 1-inch balls. Place cookies, two inches apart, on prepared baking sheets. Flatten each cookie slightly. Bake cookies until lightly browned around edges, 10 to 12 minutes. Transfer baking sheets to wire racks to cool slightly. Transfer cookies to racks to cool completely. Yields 4 dozen cookies.

Blue Spruce Sour Dough Pancake Batter

4 eggs
½ cup vegetable oil or canola oil
1 tablespoon dry yeast, dissolved in
   ¼ cup warm water
1 quart buttermilk
½ teaspoon salt
1 tablespoon baking powder
1 teaspoon baking soda
4 tablespoons sugar
4 cups all-purpose flour

Add eggs and oil to yeast mixture and buttermilk. Add all dry ingredients and mix well. Seal bowl with plastic wrap and put in refrigerator overnight. This batter will keep up to 2 weeks. It will get dark on top while in refrigerator during this time, but just mix it all in. Sprinkle with confectioners' sugar and dollop of whipped butter. Yields 6 to 8 servings.

AGATE COVE INN

P.O. Box 1150
11201 Lansing Street
Mendocino, CA 95460
(707) 937-0551 (phone)
(707) 937-0550 (fax)
(800) 527-3111 (toll free)
info@agatecove.com
reservations@agatecove.com
www.agatecove.com

Perched on a bluff, Agate Cove Inn features cottages with ocean views, fireplaces, and decks surrounded by gardens. Breakfast is in the ocean-view dining room.

Chocolate-Walnut Biscotti

2 cups all-purpose flour
1 cup sugar
½ teaspoon baking powder
½ teaspoon baking soda
½ teaspoon salt
½ teaspoon ground cinnamon
¼ teaspoon ground cloves
¼ cup cooled strong coffee
1 tablespoon milk
1 large egg
1 teaspoon vanilla extract
1¼ cups semisweet chocolate chips
¾ cup chopped walnuts
¾ cup dried cranberries
   or chopped dried cherries

Preheat oven to 350°. In large mixing bowl, combine all dry ingredients and blend well. In small bowl, whisk together all liquids and add to dry ingredients with mixer. You may want to add a few more drops of coffee to get gooey mixture. Turn dough out onto well-floured board and add chips, walnuts, and cranberries. Form into ½ x 3½-inch flat logs (biscotti will double in size during cooking). Grease and lightly flour a large cookie sheet. Bake 20 to 25 minutes. Yields 32 biscotti.

Note: For a harder biscotti, after baking, cut logs into ½-inch pieces, lay them cut-side down on cookie sheet and bake another 6 to 8 minutes at 300° on one side only.

Chocolate Cheesecake Muffins

1 cup all-purpose flour
½ cup sugar
3 tablespoons unsweetened cocoa
2 teaspoons baking powder
½ teaspoon salt
½ cup chocolate chips (optional)
1 egg, beaten
¾ cup milk
⅓ cup canola oil
8 ounces cream cheese
2 tablespoons sugar

Preheat oven to 375°. Mix dry ingredients (and chips if using) in bowl. Mix egg, milk, and oil in separate bowl. In small bowl, blend cream cheese and sugar until fluffy. Make well in center of dry ingredients. Add wet ingredients all at once to dry mixture, stirring until moistened. Batter should be lumpy. Assemble muffins in lightly greased muffin pan. Fill muffin cups with 3 tablespoons batter, spoon in 1 teaspoon cream cheese mixture, and top with 2 tablespoons batter. Bake 20 minutes. Dust with confectioners' sugar. Yields 12 muffins.

Mexican Strata

6 (8-inch) corn tortillas
2 cups grated pepper Jack cheese
1 cup grated Cheddar cheese
4 ounces green chiles, drained
   and chopped
1 bell pepper, red or yellow, diced
¼ cup green onions (optional)
2 eggs, beaten
1½ cups milk
1 tablespoon cumin powder
Salt

Preheat oven to 350°. Grease 9-inch glass pie dish. Put layer of tortillas on bottom of dish, completely covering bottom (okay to overlap). Sprinkle generously with Jack and Cheddar cheeses; add chiles and bell pepper. Repeat another layer (2 layers total), ending with diced bell pepper, chiles and onions (optional). Top with cheese. Combine eggs, milk, cumin, and salt, and pour slowly over the layers. Bake uncovered 30 minutes, or until the strata is slightly puffed and bubbly. Let the strata cool for 15 minutes before slicing. Yields 1 strata, serves 6.

Granola

8 cups rolled oats
1⅓ cups coconut
⅔ cup sesame seeds
½ cup sunflower seeds
1 cup chopped cashews, almonds,
   or walnuts
⅔ cup honey
2 teaspoons vanilla extract
½ teaspoon salt

Preheat oven to 300°. In large bowl, mix oats, coconut, sesame seeds, sunflower seeds, and nuts. In smaller saucepan, combine honey, vanilla, and salt. Heat together until smooth and pour over dry mix and toss. Spread mix on greased cookie sheet. Bake 35 to 45 minutes or until golden brown. Yields 10 servings.

Note: Stir the granola every 10 to 15 minutes to ensure even browning.

Fruit Parfaits

1 cup granola
1½ cups vanilla yogurt
1½ cups fresh fruit

Layer ingredients in order given in parfait glass, 2 tablespoons per layer. Continue layers until serving dish is filled. Top with pieces of fresh fruit. Refrigerate until ready to serve. Yields 6 servings.

Agate Cove Blueberry Bread Pudding

4 eggs
2 cups milk
½ plus ¼ cup sugar
1½ teaspoons vanilla extract
1 teaspoon ground cinnamon
¼ to ⅓ teaspoon ground nutmeg
1 loaf cinnamon raisin bread
1 (12-ounce) package cream cheese,
    softened
½ plus ¼ cup frozen blueberries
¼ cup blueberries

Preheat oven to 325°. Whisk together the eggs, milk, ½ cup sugar, vanilla, cinnamon, and nutmeg in large bowl until sugar dissolves. Cut bread into ½-inch cubes and add to egg mixture. Mix well. Distribute half bread mixture in bottom of buttered pans. Combine cream cheese with remaining ¼ cup sugar and spread on top of bread mixture. Place ¼ cup blueberries on top and cover with remaining bread mixture. Finish with remaining ½ cup blueberries sprinkled on top. Bake until pudding is browned on top and set, about 45 minutes. Cool to room temperature, about 40 minutes. Yields 10 servings.

Pesto Benedict

4 cups basil leaves
1 cup olive oil
⅓ cup pine nuts
4 cloves garlic
1 teaspoon salt
1 cup grated Parmesan cheese
⅓ cup grated Romano cheese
½ cup (1 stick) butter, softened
1 slice English muffin, lightly toasted
1 slice Canadian bacon, browned
1 egg, poached

In blender, purée basil, olive oil, pine nuts, garlic, and salt. Using a spoon, stir in both cheeses. Finally, stir in butter with a spoon. It's very important to stir in cheeses and butter to ensure the desired texture. Place the muffin on a plate, top with bacon and egg, and pour pesto on top. Yields 1 serving.

Variation: For the vegetarian version, replace Canadian bacon with a tomato slice and steamed spinach.

Colorado

RIVER RUN INN BED & BREAKFAST

8495 County Road 160
Salida, CO 81201
(719) 539-3818 (phone)
(800) 385-6925 (toll free)
riverrun@amigo.net
www.riverruninn.com

River Run Inn Bed & Breakfast is in an 1890s historic large home that was originally the county poor farm. The inn sits on five acres on the Arkansas River overlooking a valley surrounded by fourteen-thousand-foot majestic mountains just outside Salida, Colorado. The innkeeper takes pride in serving hearty breakfasts that sustain guests for days of hiking, rafting, kayaking, fishing, biking, hunting, skiing, snowshoeing, and horseback riding, all available in the area. In town, quaint art galleries, antique shops, boutiques, and quality restaurants beckon for relaxation.

❧ ❧ ❧

Fourteeners Granola

4 cups old-fashioned oats
¼ cup brown sugar
2 teaspoons ground cinnamon
½ cup chopped walnuts
½ cup sunflower seeds
¼ cup orange juice
2 tablespoons honey
1 tablespoon vanilla extract
½ cup raisins
½ cup craisins (dried cranberries)
⅓ cup chopped dried apricots

Preheat oven to 350°. In large bowl mix together oats, sugar, cinnamon, walnuts, and sunflower seeds. In microwaveable bowl, mix orange juice, honey, and vanilla. Microwave 1 minute or just until honey is melted and mixture is blended. Pour orange juice mixture over oat mixture and stir well to coat. Spread mixture into large baking pan. Bake 30 minutes, stirring every 10 minutes until mixture is golden. Remove from oven and add raisins, craisins, and apricots. Cool well before storing. Yields 5 cups.

Note: When making oatmeal, add 1 to 2 tablespoons granola just before it is totally cooked.

River Run Inn Bed & Breakfast

Rolled Oven Omelet

6 eggs
¾ cup all-purpose flour
3 tablespoons melted butter
1½ cups milk
Salt and pepper

Fillings (choose one):
Ham and chives with Swiss cheese
Bacon, tomato, and red onion with
     Cheddar cheese
Sausage and green chilies with
     Monterey Jack cheese
Salsa and sautéed mushrooms
     with Brie

Preheat oven to 350°. Line with foil a large cookie sheet with sides. Grease well. In medium bowl, whisk together eggs, flour, butter, and milk thoroughly. Season with salt and pepper to taste. Pour egg mixture into foil-lined pan. Sprinkle with filling ingredients except the cheese. Bake for 18 minutes, or until omelet puffs and eggs are set. Remove from oven and sprinkle with cheese. Using spatula and foil as an aid, roll the omelet and transfer to large platter. Sprinkle top with additional cheese, and any herbs. Yields 4 to 6 servings.

Note: Bacon and sausage should be cooked and crumbled prior to adding to omelet.

Baked Streusel Plums

1¼ pounds plums (assorted
     or whatever is in season)
2 tablespoons all-purpose flour
2 tablespoons sugar

Streusel:
⅓ cup all-purpose flour
¼ cup brown sugar
½ teaspoon ground cinnamon
3 tablespoons butter

Pit and slice plums. Toss with flour and sugar and place in small greased casserole. Preheat oven to 350°.

To make streusel, in separate bowl mix together flour, brown sugar, and cinnamon. Cut in butter until mixture is pebbly. Top plums with streusel and bake 30 minutes. Cook until top is browned and plums are bubbly. Yields 4 to 6 servings.

Note: You can make a big batch of streusel and keep it in the refrigerator for about 10 days. This makes preparation even easier in the morning. Any leftovers are great on vanilla ice cream. Try this same procedure with other fresh fruits like peaches or pears.

BROSS HOTEL BED & BREAKFAST

312 Onarga Street
P.O. Box 85
Paonia, CO 81428-0085
(970) 527-6776
brosshotel@paonia.com
www.paonia-inn.com

The Bross Hotel is a vintage, western-style hotel with two rocking-chair front porches. Period antiques and handmade quilts grace each room. Local activities include music (chamber to bluegrass); art galleries; antiquing; scenic byways (West Elk Loop and Grand Mesa); fruit picking; bicycling and motorcycling; hiking; hunting and fishing; skiing, snowshoeing, and Nordic skiing; painting and photography;

Black Canyon of the Gunnison National Park; Ute Indian Museum; Colorado National Monument.

Baked Chile Relleños

1 (16-ounce) can green chiles
8 ounces Cheddar cheese, grated
8 ounces Monterey Jack cheese, grated
1 dozen eggs
1 pint sour cream
Salt

Clean chiles and arrange single layer in bottom of greased 9 x 13-inch cake pan. Preheat oven to 325°. Layer cheeses over the chiles. In bowl, whisk eggs and sour cream and salt to taste. Pour over cheeses. Bake 25 to 30 minutes, or until egg mixture is set. Yields 6 servings.

THE INN ON MAPLETON HILL

1001 Spruce Street
Boulder, CO 80302
(303) 449-6528 (phone)
(303) 415-0470 (fax)
(800) 276-6528 (toll free)
Maphillinn@aol.com
www.innonmapletonhill.com

The inn was built in 1899 and dramatically remodeled several years ago, winning a historic preservation award. You can choose from seven individually-decorated rooms; they and the common areas are furnished with antiques. The Inn's location represents the best of both worlds. One block from the festive Pearl Street Mall, a promenade of shopping and dining, it also borders a quiet residential street. Boulder abounds with mountainous trails, falls, resorts, and the Rocky Mountain National Park just forty-five miles northwest.

Inn on Mapleton Hill Signature Cookies

2½ cups all-purpose flour
1 generous teaspoon baking soda
1 teaspoon salt
2 sticks butter, softened
¾ cup packed brown sugar
¼ cup granulated sugar
2 extra large eggs
1 tablespoon pure vanilla extract
Zest of 2 large oranges, finely grated
2 cups semisweet chocolate chips
2 cups uncooked oats (do not use instant or quick cooking)

Preheat oven and baking stone* to 350°. Blend together flour, soda, and salt. In large bowl, cream together butter and sugars. Add eggs and vanilla and beat until creamy. Slowly mix in dry ingredients. Mix in orange zest. Mix in chocolate chips and oats (it will be hard to mix since the dough is very stiff). Drop small amounts of dough on a preheated baking stone and bake 13 minutes per batch. Yields 2 to 3 dozen cookies.

Note: Use a baking stone for this recipe rather than a cooking sheet. It prevents the cookie bottoms from burning and allows the cookies to bake more evenly throughout. This recipe is for high altitude. If they are too chewy, reduce the flour by ¼ cup.

Lavender Sugar Cookies

If you have ever wondered what to do with fresh lavender, other than putting it in sachets, here's a wonderful cookie. As you bite into these cookies the aroma is marvelous— especially when they're warm out of the oven.

1 cup (2 sticks) unsalted butter
½ cup sugar
2 large eggs, beaten
3 cups all-purpose flour
3 to 4 tablespoons fresh lavender florets or 2 tablespoons slightly chopped dried culinary lavender
Superfine sugar for sprinkling

Cream together butter and sugar until light and fluffy. Mix eggs into butter/sugar mixture. Stir in flour and lavender until mixture becomes soft ball. Cover ball of dough and place in refrigerator 15 minutes to set. Preheat oven and baking stone to 400°. Break off small pieces of dough and roll out on lightly floured surface until dough is ⅛ inch thick or less, preferably less. Use cookie cutter to shape. Place the cookies on preheated baking stone and bake approximately 10 minutes. Cookies should be just browning around the edges. Once done, sprinkle with superfine sugar and let cookies sit on baking stone about 5 minutes to set. Then transfer cookies to

rack to cool. Can be stor[...] container in a freezer for [...] Yields 4 to 6 dozen cookies.

Note: This recipe is for [...] If they are too chewy, reduce the flour by ¼ cup.

Judi's Chocolate Cinnamon Swirl Cake

1½ cups plus ½ cup sugar
5 teaspoons unsweetened cocoa powder (a good brand)
2 tablespoons ground cinnamon
2 sticks butter, softened
8 ounces cream cheese, softened
1½ teaspoons pure vanilla extract
4 eggs, beaten
2¼ cups all-purpose flour
1½ teaspoons baking powder
1 cup high-quality, semisweet chocolate chips

The Inn on Mapleton Hill

In small bowl, mix ½ cup sugar, cocoa, and cinnamon. Spray 9 x 13-inch glass baking dish with nonstick spray. In large bowl, blend butter and cream cheese. When well blended, cream in remaining 1½ cups sugar and vanilla. Add eggs and blend well. Mix in flour and baking powder. When well blended, mix in chocolate chips. Preheat oven to 325°. Pour half the batter into pan. Sprinkle with cinnamon/sugar mixture. Pour remaining batter into pan and spread evenly over first layer. Sprinkle entire top of batter with remaining cinnamon/sugar. Bake 45 minutes or until wooden toothpick comes out clean. Yields 12 to 14 servings.

Spinach, Mushroom, Cheese Strudel

This makes a wonderful, savory breakfast dish and is quite easy to make. The trick is putting it together quickly so the phyllo dough doesn't dry out.

2 cups finely chopped spinach
    (Use only fresh and chop just before
    putting together. Frozen spinach
    doesn't work well at all.)
1 cup finely chopped mushrooms
⅓ cup grated cheese (extra sharp
    Cheddar, Parmesan, Gruyère,
    Swiss, Gouda)
4 tablespoons melted butter
6 single sheets phyllo dough,
    folded in half

Mix together spinach, mushrooms, and cheese. Brush baking sheet with melted butter. Lay the first sheet of phyllo on baking sheet. Brush with butter. Place another sheet of dough on top of the first and brush with butter. Repeat until you have all six folded sheets in layers. Toward the right side of the layers, place the mixture of spinach, mushrooms, and cheese in a line. Be sure to leave about 1 inch on top and bottom of layers so that you will be able to fold the ends under. Preheat oven to 350°. Roll the layers of veggie/cheese mixture into a log. Fold the ends under

and brush with butter. Pierce top of log several times with a thin knife to let steam escape. Bake approximately 30 minutes. Let cool slightly after baking and cut log into 4 to 6 pieces. Yields 1 log (4 servings).

THE MARY LAWRENCE INN

601 North Taylor
Gunnison, CO 81230
(970) 641-3343 (phone)
(888) 331-6863 (toll free)
marylinn@gunnison.com

The Mary Lawrence Inn is a two-story, Italianate home built in 1885. It now features seven guest rooms, each with a private bath. The Mary Lawrence Inn is perfectly located to be a "home base" for outdoor recreational activities, including alpine skiing, snowboarding, and cross-country skiing; gold medal fishing on the Taylor, East, and Gunnison rivers; mountain biking, hiking, fall-color tours and sightseeing. The Black Canyon of the Gunnison National Park and Blue Mesa Reservoir are nearby.

Egg Casserole

6 eggs, beaten
2 cups grated Cheddar cheese
2 cups grated mozzarella cheese
2 cups cottage cheese
1 cup biscuit mix
½ cup (1 stick) margarine
Dash of black pepper
Chives

Preheat oven to 350°. Blend together all ingredients except chives. Bake in pie plate sprayed with nonstick spray for 45 min-

utes. Serve in wedges garnished with chopped chives. Serve with salsa or catsup. Yields 6 servings.

Variations: Add chiles and browned chorizo for "South of the Border Baked Eggs." Add sautéed vegetables such as onions, bell peppers, and mushrooms for a vegetarian presentation.

"Homemade" Biscuits

8¾ cups all-purpose flour
⅓ cup baking powder
¼ cup sugar
1 tablespoon salt
2 cups vegetable shortening
½ cup cold milk

Combine flour, baking powder, sugar, and salt. Cut in shortening to make baking mix. Preheat oven to 450°. Combine 2 cups mix and milk and turn dough onto lightly floured surface. Knead ten times. Pat to ½-inch thickness and cut into rounds. Brush tops with melted butter if desired. Bake 10 to 15 minutes. Yields 10 to 12 biscuits.

Note: When measuring baking mix do not pack. The remaining baking mix does not need to be refrigerated. Store in airtight container.

Variations: For cheese biscuits, add ⅓ cup grated cheese, any flavor; for onion biscuits, add ¼ cup chopped, sautéed onions; for ham or bacon biscuits, add ⅓ cup crisp bacon bits or ¼ cup finely chopped, cooked ham.

BEARS INN BED & BREAKFAST

27425 Spruce Lane
Evergreen, CO 80439
(303) 670-1205 (phone)
(303) 670-8542 (fax)
(800) 863-1205 (toll free)
www.bearsinn.com

Nestled in the pine trees at eight thousand feet, this eleven-guest room inn invites you to enjoy a true mountain lodging experience. Things to do in the area include hiking, biking, horseback riding, white-water rafting, and even golf.

Apple Cider Syrup

1 cup sugar
8 teaspoons cornstarch
1 teaspoon ground cinnamon
2 cups apple cider or apple juice
2 tablespoons lemon juice
4 tablespoons butter

In saucepan, stir together sugar, cornstarch, and cinnamon. Stir in cider and lemon juice. Cook and stir mixture over medium heat until thickened and bubbly. Cook and stir for 2 minutes more. Remove from heat and stir in butter until melted. Serve with French toast. Yields 2½ cups syrup.

Sticky Buns

¾ cup chopped pecans
24 frozen bread rolls
1 box vanilla pudding (not instant)
¾ cup (1½ sticks) butter
¾ cup firmly packed brown sugar

Cover the bottom of greased 10 x 14-inch baking pan with pecans. Place frozen rolls over nuts. Sprinkle dry pudding mix over rolls. Bring butter and brown sugar to rolling boil and pour over rolls. Cover with plastic wrap and let stand 8 to 10 hours. Bake at 350° 25 to 30 minutes. Let stand 2 minutes and invert onto cookie sheet. Yields 24 buns.

Bacon Rings

A unique twist on traditional eggs Benedict.

12 slices bacon
12 eggs
½ teaspoon garlic powder
½ teaspoon dill
1 cup shredded Cheddar cheese
6 large croissants
Hollandaise sauce for serving

Preheat oven to 400°. Coat 12-count muffin pan with nonstick spray. In large skillet fry bacon until almost crisp. Drain bacon slices and quickly (while bacon is pliable) place in circle around inside edge of muffin cups. Break 1 egg into each cup. Sprinkle with garlic powder and dill. Top with cheese. Bake 12 to 20 minutes, depending on desired degree of doneness. Cut croissants in half and place bacon wrapped egg on top drizzled with Hollandaise sauce. Yields 6 servings.

HUNT PLACER INN

P.O. Box 4898
275 Ski Hill Road
Breckenridge, CO 80424
(970) 453-7573 (phone)
(800) 472-1430 (toll free)
reservations@huntplacerinn.com
www.huntplacerinn.com

Tucked in the mountainside on Breckenridge Ski Resort's "Peak 8," the Hunt Placer Inn Bed & Breakfast is the ideal lodging option for the discerning traveler. World-class skiing, snowboarding, hiking, biking, fly-fishing, and golf are just a few of the full range of summer and winter activities available.

Potato and Goat Cheese Frittata

3 medium new potatoes
2 teaspoons olive oil
1 small red onion, peeled and diced
1 small clove garlic, chopped
8 to 10 basil leaves, slivered
6 eggs, lightly beaten
Salt and pepper
¼ cup heavy whipping cream
4 ounces goat cheese, broken in pieces

Boil potatoes in salted water until tender. Drain, cool, and cut into 1-inch cubes. Preheat oven to 400°. In skillet heat oil over medium and sauté onion until tender, 5 to 6 minutes. Add potatoes, garlic, and basil. Sauté, stirring occasionally, 1 minute more. Add eggs, salt and pepper to taste, cream, and goat cheese. Stir until mixed. Transfer mixture to greased oven pan and bake 30 minutes. Yields 6 servings.

Crispy Almond Brittle

1½ cups sugar
½ cup honey
7 tablespoons softened butter
½ pound slivered almonds
Vegetable oil
4 squares semisweet baking
    chocolate, softened

Melt sugar and honey in saucepan together, stirring occasionally. Add butter while constantly stirring. Mix well until ingredients are combined. Carefully fold slivered almonds into sugar mixture. Cook a few minutes, still stirring. Quickly and carefully spread nut mixture evenly on baking sheet lined with lightly oiled baking parchment. Allow brittle to cool slightly. Before brittle has hardened completely, cut it into pieces with sharp knife. Melt chocolate in double boiler. Dip each piece almost halfway into chocolate. Cool on wire rack. Yields 70 pieces.

Hawaiian Pancake

4 eggs
¼ stick butter, melted
1 cup milk
1 cup all-purpose flour
¼ teaspoon salt
¼ teaspoon ground cinnamon
½ teaspoon vanilla extract
Lemon juice
Confectioners' sugar
Coconut syrup, warmed

In blender mix eggs until light yellow. In large bowl mix well eggs, butter, milk, flour, salt, cinnamon, and vanilla. Let batter rest and mix again. Preheat oven to 400°. Pour batter into oven dish and bake 20 minutes. Cut in pie-shaped slices. Butter and sprinkle with lemon juice, confectioners' sugar, and warm coconut syrup. Yields 6 servings.

HOLDEN HOUSE 1902 BED & BREAKFAST INN

1102 W. Pikes Peak Avenue
Colorado Springs, CO 80904
(719) 471-3980 (phone)
(719) 471-4740 (fax)
(888) 565-3980 (toll free)
mail@holdenhouse.com
www.holdenhouse.com

Holden House is a Pikes Peak treasure, a romantic Victorian inn boasting queen beds, sitting areas, fireplaces, and "tubs for two." Nearby are shopping areas, restaurants, and activities. The AAA/Mobil Awards inn offers a full gourmet breakfast. Located in the heart of the Pikes Peak region, Holden House is one mile west of downtown near Old Colorado City Historic District; four miles east of historic Manitou Springs; ten miles from the south entrance of the Air Force Academy; and thirteen miles from Colorado Springs Airport. The inn is two hours from Denver International Airport; five miles (5 to 10 minutes) from the Broadmoor, Cheyenne Mountain Zoo, Garden of the Gods, the Olympic Training Center, Cheyenne Cañon and Seven Falls hiking trails; and one hour from Royal Gorge Bridge, Cripple Creek, Florrissant Fossil Beds and petrified redwood forest.

Ruffled Crêpes Isabel

Crêpes:
1¼ cups all-purpose flour
2 tablespoons sugar
Pinch of salt
3 eggs
1½ cups milk
2 tablespoons melted butter
1 teaspoon lemon extract (optional)

Egg mixture:
7 eggs
1½ cups milk
½ teaspoon salt
¼ teaspoon pepper
1 tablespoon all-purpose flour
Sharp Cheddar cheese
6 slices turkey bacon, cooked
    and crumbled
Sour cream for garnish
Fresh dill, parsley, or tarragon
    for garnish

Blend or mix all crêpe ingredients well. Let rest for approximately 5 minutes. Make 5-inch crêpes, using either a well-greased skillet or crêpe maker. Extra crêpes may be stored in refrigerator for later use.

Mix eggs with milk, salt, pepper, and flour. Generously grease 24 muffin tins with nonstick spray. Press crêpes into tins, lightly ruffling edges but being careful not to tear them. Place small square of cheese in bottom of each tin and pour egg mixture carefully into tins, filling just to below top of rim. Top with crumbled bacon (vegetarian bacon bits may be substituted). Preheat oven to 375° and bake 15 to 20 minutes or until mixture is firm and crêpes are just lightly brown. Let cool

Holden House 1902 Bed & Breakfast Inn

slightly and carefully loosen cups from tins with a fork or knife, taking care not to break edges. Remove from tins with a spoon, place two on each plate, and top with a small dab of sour cream and chopped fresh dill, parsley, or tarragon (we try to use herbs fresh from the garden). Yields 24 crêpes (2 per serving).

Italiano Eggs Florentine

3 ready-to-bake piecrusts
12 (12-ounce) quiche dishes
7 eggs
3 cups milk
6 tablespoons all-purpose flour
1½ (16-ounce) packages frozen
 spinach, thawed
1 cup shredded Swiss, Jack, or
 mozzarella cheese
6 slices turkey bacon, sliced in half
Italian seasoning
Nutmeg
1 (12-ounce) jar marinara sauce
Shredded Parmesan cheese for garnish
Fresh parsley for garnish

Preheat oven to 325°. Divide each piecrust into fourths and place each quarter into a greased quiche dish (will form a triangular shaped crust). Beat eggs, milk, and flour together. Evenly divide spinach and place on top crusts. Pour egg mixture over spinach, top with shredded cheese, lay half slice of bacon over cheese, and sprinkle with a dash of Italian seasoning and nutmeg. Bake 30 to 40 minutes or until quiche is firm and slightly brown on top. Remove from oven and place on plate with lace doily if desired. Garnish each quiche with 3 tablespoons marinara sauce, a sprinkle of Parmesan cheese, and sprig of fresh parsley. Yields 12 servings.

Southwestern Eggs Fiesta

12 individual soufflé dishes
 (5- to 8-ounce size)
24 eggs
6 (4-inch) flour tortillas, cut in half
12 ounces Cheddar cheese
Bacon bits or crumbled cooked
 turkey bacon
Cilantro (fresh if available)
Sour cream for topping
Mild picante sauce for topping
Parsley for garnish

Preheat oven to 375°. Well grease soufflé dishes with nonstick spray and break 2 eggs into each dish. Slice tortillas in half and place a half in each dish with cut edge down and outside eggs to form a U-shape around outer edge of dish. Top with cheese and bacon and sprinkle with a dash of cilantro. Bake for 30 minutes or until eggs are done, cheese is melted, and tortilla is slightly brown. Top with a dab of sour cream and teaspoon of picante sauce. Sprinkle cilantro on top and serve on a plate. Garnish with parsley if desired. Yields 12 servings.

Sallie's Puff Pastry Eggs Goldenrod

12 hard-cooked eggs, chopped
24 puff pastry shells
4 tablespoons butter
4 tablespoons all-purpose flour
2 cups milk
Bacon, cooked and crumbled
Paprika for garnish
Salt and pepper
Fresh tarragon for garnish

Cook eggs the night before if desired. Prepare pastry shells as directed on package. While pastry shells are baking, prepare white sauce: Melt butter over low heat, add flour, and stir until well blended, about 4 minutes; slowly add milk and stir constantly until slightly set. Keep warm on the stove. Wash the fresh tarragon (dried can be used if necessary) and dry. When pastry shells are puffed and slightly brown, remove from oven. Place on plates and remove scored top from shells. Cover chopped eggs with plastic wrap and heat until warm in the microwave, about 1 to 2 minutes. Spoon eggs over and into pastry shells. Liberally drizzle with white sauce. Sprinkle bacon, dash of paprika, salt, pepper, and tarragon over the shell. Push shell top upright onto lower shell to make clamshell effect. Garnish plate with colorful fruit and serve. Yields 12 servings.

BEAR PAW INN

871 Bear Paw Drive
P.O. Box 334
Winter Park, CO 80482
(970) 887-1351 (phone/fax)
bearpaw@rkymtnhi.com
www.bearpaw-winterpark.com

Rick and Sue Callahan, innkeepers of the Bear Paw Inn, Winter Park, Colorado, know just what their guests like—from delicious morning gourmet surprises to featherbeds, Jacuzzis, and a spectacular view of the Rocky Mountain National Park.

Bear Paw Blintz Soufflé

8 to 9 frozen cherry or blueberry blintzes
    (homemade or in the freezer section)
½ cup melted butter
6 eggs, beaten
2 cups sour cream
5 tablespoons orange juice
1 tablespoon vanilla extract
2 teaspoons sugar

Lay frozen blintzes in a 2-quart baking dish or deep quiche pan. Pour melted butter over all. In separate bowl, combine eggs, sour cream, orange juice, vanilla, and sugar. Whisk briskly for a few moments. Pour over blintz mixture. Cover with plastic wrap and store in refrigerator 8 to 10 hours. When ready to cook preheat oven to 350°. Remove wrap and bake about 1 hour 15 minutes. Yields 6 servings.

Eggs in a Hatch

6 frozen puff pastry shells
    (in freezer section)
¾ pound bacon
1 clove garlic, chopped
1½ pounds mushrooms, finely chopped
6 eggs
Hollandaise sauce (see next recipe)
Fresh parsley, minced

Bake puff pastry shells according to directions. When done, take top off and take out insides and discard. Keep warm. Cut bacon in small pieces and cook until crisp. Drain on paper towels. Pour off most of the bacon grease, but keep a few tablespoons. Sauté garlic in grease (not too hot) for 1 minute. Add mushrooms and cook 8 to 10 minutes on low; drain mushrooms and keep warm. When ready to serve, poach eggs. Put pastry shells on plates. Divide bacon equally among plates, putting inside the pastry shells and a little outside the shell. Divide mushrooms same way. Put a poached egg on top of bacon and mushrooms in each shell and top with hollandaise. Garnish with minced parsley. Yields 6 servings.

Bear Paw Eggs Blackstone

2 large tomatoes, each sliced into
    4 thick slices, salted and
    peppered, and drained
All-purpose flour
Bacon drippings
4 English muffins, split and buttered
7 to 8 pieces of bacon, cooked crisp
    and drained
4 eggs, poached

Hollandaise sauce:
3 large egg yolks
1 tablespoon lemon juice
¼ plus ¼ cup firm butter

Ten minutes before eating, dip tomato slices in flour and sauté on medium heat in the bacon drippings, not more than 4 minutes a side or they will get mushy. Place muffins on plates and top with sautéed tomato. Crumble 2 pieces of bacon on each tomato, top with poached egg (drained, so it won't be soggy).

For Hollandaise sauce, in saucepan vigorously stir egg yolks and lemon juice. Add ¼ cup butter and heat over very low heat, stirring constantly until butter is melted. Add remaining ¼ cup butter. Continue vigorously until sauce thickens. Pour on top of eggs and serve. Yields 4 servings.

High Noon Huevos Rancheros

1 (15-ounce) can black beans
1 (15-ounce) can refried beans
1 (4½-ounce) can green chiles
¾ to 1 pound pork sausage, cooked and
    crumbled
1 (12-ounce) jar salsa
4 (8-inch) flour tortillas
8 eggs
1½ cups Monterey Jack cheese
1½ cups Cheddar cheese
Sour cream
Green onions, finely chopped
Cilantro for garnish
Avocado and salsa for serving

Put black beans, refried beans, green chiles, sausage, and salsa in separate bowls and microwave for 1 or 2 minutes. Warm tortillas in foil in oven for 15 minutes or set them on top of the stove in a steamer. When ready to serve, fry eggs 2 at a time. While eggs are frying, cover tortillas with refried beans to ¼-inch of the edge. Then divide evenly on top of tortillas sausage, black beans, green chiles, and eggs. Dab some salsa around each tortilla. Divide both cheeses among the tortillas. Place tortillas under broiler for cheese to melt. Top with sour cream and a few green onions. Sprinkle with cilantro and serve with sliced avocado and salsa on the side. Yields 4 servings.

THE LEADVILLE COUNTRY INN

127 East Eighth Street
Leadville, CO 80461
(719) 486-2354 (phone)
(719) 486-0300 (fax)
lcinn@bemail.com
www.leadvillebednbreakfast.com

Journey back in time at this beautiful Victorian inn. A breakfast to remember greets our guests in the morning, while the garden hot tub is the perfect end to the day. Acclaimed for its mining history, Leadville is a year-round paradise for outdoor enthusiasts, history buffs, or antique hunters. Whether it is skiing, snowshoeing, hiking, or mountain biking that strikes your fancy, there are many trails to explore. With different levels of difficulty, from the highest majestic peaks in Colorado to crisp alpine lakes and backcountry trails to the historic mining district, there is something for everyone.

Breakfast Fritters

Vegetable oil for frying
1 cup all-purpose flour
1½ teaspoons baking powder
½ teaspoon salt
⅓ cup milk
1 egg
¼ cup sugar
1 cup fruit pieces of choice
    (Granny Smith apple, pineapple
    tidbits, banana slices, dried
    cranberries)
Confectioners' sugar

Heat oil until hot and bubbly in fryer or deep pan. Mix together for batter the flour, baking powder, salt, milk, egg, and sugar. Add fruit and mix. Drop tablespoonfuls into hot oil and cook until golden brown, about 4 to 5 minutes. Keep warm until ready to serve and then sprinkle with confectioners' sugar. Yields 4 to 6 servings.

Shoofly Cake

4 cups all-purpose flour
1 pound brown sugar
Pinch of salt
¼ cup vegetable oil
1 cup molasses
1 tablespoon baking soda
2¼ cups boiling water

Preheat oven to 350°. Mix flour, sugar, salt, and oil together with a fork. Set aside 1½ cups for crumb topping. In separate bowl combine molasses and soda. Carefully add boiling water to molasses/soda; it will fizz. Add this to large crumb mixture and stir until mixed; it will be lumpy. Pour into greased, 9 x 13-inch baking pan. Top with remaining 1½ cups crumb mixture. Bake 50 minutes until toothpick comes out clean. Best served warm for breakfast or afternoon tea. Yields 15 servings.

Chocolate Butter Cream Pie

1 stick butter
¾ cup sugar
2 squares unsweetened chocolate
1 teaspoon vanilla extract
2 eggs
1 (8-inch) crumb pie shell
Whipped cream
1 mint sprig

Cream butter and sugar well until sugar dissolves. Melt unsweetened chocolate in a double boiler, and cool before adding to butter mixture. Add vanilla and eggs, one at a time, while blending on a medium speed for 5 minutes after each addition. Pour into pie shell. Chill. For serving, top with whipped cream and fresh mint. This pie can be made ahead and freezes well. Yields 8 servings.

Luscious Lemon Cake

1½ cups all-purpose flour
1 cup sugar
1 teaspoon baking powder
½ teaspoon salt
2 eggs
½ cup vegetable oil
Grated zest of 1 lemon

Lemon glaze:
Juice of 1 lemon
⅓ cup sugar

Preheat oven to 350°. Mix together all ingredients and pour into greased, 7 x 11-inch baking pan. Bake for 30 minutes, or until golden brown.

For glaze, mix together lemon sugar and pour on top of hot cake. Sprinkle with confectioners' sugar and top with thin slice of lemon to garnish, if desired. Yields 10 servings.

Whistle Stop Bed & Breakfast

P.O. Box 418
Winter Park, CO 80482
(970) 726-8767
whistle@rkymtnhi.com
www.winterparkbandb.com

At the Whistle Stop Bed and Breakfast, you will find that you have entered a bright and contemporary home designed for casual living where guests can enjoy the sun room and spacious living area with breathtaking views of the Continental Divide.

Susan's Surprise Quiche

1½ cups sliced onions
2 tablespoons butter
2 tablespoons olive oil
½ plus 1 cup grated Gruyère cheese
⅛ cup diced sun-dried tomatoes
Salt and pepper
4 to 5 large eggs
1½ to 2 cups half-and-half
Prebaked 9-inch pastry shell
Freshly grated nutmeg

Sauté onions in butter and oil over very low heat until caramelized, approximately 30 minutes. Preheat oven to 350°. Spread ½ cup cheese over crust, then spread onions evenly over cheese, and then spread tomatoes over onions. Season well with salt and pepper. Put eggs in a 4-cup measure and beat lightly. Add enough half-and-half to the eggs to measure 2½ cups liquid. Mix thoroughly. Pour egg mixture into piecrust. Add remaining 1 cup cheese and sprinkle top liberally with nutmeg. Use aluminum foil to keep rim of piecrust from burning. Bake in preheated oven for 35 to 40 minutes, or until completely set around edges and only slightly wiggly in center; should be browned and puffed. Let cool 10 minutes. Yields 6 servings.

Oatmeal Brûlée

"Even oatmeal haters like this."

¼ cup water
¼ cup sugar
2 cups frozen mixed berries
¼ plus ¼ cup well-chilled whipping cream
2 large eggs
⅓ cup packed brown sugar, divided
¼ teaspoon salt
3 cups water
1½ cups rolled oats
Mint sprigs

Boil water and sugar together to make simple syrup. Let syrup cool and pour over berries. Whisk ¼ cup of whipping cream with eggs and 2 tablespoons of brown sugar. Whip remaining ¼ cup whipping cream to stiff peaks and fold into cream, egg, and brown sugar mixture. Preheat oven to 400°.

Bring salted water to a boil; add oats, stir, and cook 5 minutes until thickened. Divide among four ovenproof bowls and smooth the surface of the oatmeal with back of spatula. Pour custard over the oatmeal. Arrange bowls on cookie tray and bake 6 minutes; rotate trays and bake 6 more minutes, or until custard is lightly browned. Remove bowls from oven and raise oven temperature to low broil. Sprinkle tops of custards evenly with remaining brown sugar. Return bowls to broiler and watch them (don't take your eyes off) until the sugar melts; be careful the sugar doesn't burn. Spoon berries on top of each oatmeal brûlée. Serve while warm and berries are cold. Garnish with sprigs of mint. Yields 4 servings.

Whistle Stop Nutty Granola

5 cups rolled oats
4 cups quick oats
2 cups soy flour
2 cups honey
2 cups vegetable oil
2 tablespoons vanilla extract
1½ cups wheat germ
1 cup flaked coconut
1 cup sunflower seeds
1 cup sesame seeds
1 cup pumpkin seeds
1 cup walnuts
1 cup hazelnuts
1 cup cashews
1 cup slivered almonds
1 cup raisins
1 cup craisins

In your largest mixing bowl, mix rolled oats, quick oats, flour, honey, oil, vanilla, wheat germ, and coconut. Add sunflower seeds, sesame seeds, pumpkin seeds, walnuts, hazelnuts, and cashews. Mix thoroughly. Preheat oven to 375°. Spray two dark metal 9 x 13-inch baking pans with nonstick spray. Spread mixture into pans. Bake, stirring every 5 minutes until mixture is lightly golden brown. Divide the almonds between the two pans and continue to bake until almonds are lightly browned. The whole mixture should be golden brown at this point. Remove from oven and stir every 5 minutes until mixture is cooled completely. Add raisins and craisins and stir to incorporate. Yields 6 quarts.

Note: The whole process takes about an hour, but it makes a lot of granola. Freeze the portion you aren't going to eat within a week.

TWO SISTERS INN

Ten Otoe Place
Manitou Springs, CO 80829
719-685-9684 (phone)
(800) 2-SIS-INN (toll free)
info@twosisinn.com
www.twosisinn.com

Two Sisters is a gracious, award-winning, traditional bed and breakfast and cozy honeymoon cottage, sitting at the base of Pikes Peak in the Colorado Rockies. Caring, fun owners offer creative, beautifully presented gourmet breakfasts. It's a magical experience. In and around the Pikes Peak area you can enjoy hiking, biking, driving, and cog training on Pikes Peak, in the Garden of the Gods, and at Mueller State Park. Explore Miramont Castle, Cave of the Winds, the Cliff Dwellings Museum, the Iron Springs Château Melodrama, and the Mineral Springs. Also around the area are the U.S. Air Force Academy, the U.S. Olympic Training Center, the Broadmoor Hotel,

Cheyenne Mountain Zoo, the Flying W Ranch, the Royal Gorge, and Cripple Creek.

Canadian Corncakes

1 cup cornmeal
1 cup all-purpose flour
¼ cup sugar
1 teaspoon baking soda
1 teaspoon salt
3 eggs
2 cups buttermilk
½ cup plain yogurt
¼ cup melted unsalted butter
½ pound sharp Cheddar cheese, grated
1 pound bacon, crisply cooked
    and crumbled
Sour cream and chives for garnish

Whisk together dry ingredients in a large bowl. In separate bowl, whisk together eggs, buttermilk, yogurt, and melted butter. Blend buttermilk mixture into flour mixture just until combined. Do *not* overmix. Heat a nonstick griddle over medium heat and lightly grease with oil (do not use nonstick spray). Using large soup spoon,

Two Sisters Inn

drop batter onto griddle in rounds about 2 inches apart, and sprinkle each round with 1 tablespoon each of cheese and bacon. Cook pancakes until golden on each side, about 1 to 2 minutes each. Transfer cooked pancakes to a baking sheet and keep warm in oven until ready to serve. Place five pancakes per plate and top with dollop of sour cream and a sprinkle of minced chives. Yields 50 small pancakes.

Signature Nutty Apples

1 cup apple cider
1 teaspoon vanilla extract
3 apples, peeled (save the peels for
    garnish), cored, and cut into halves

Raspberry sauce:*
1 (10-ounce) package frozen sweetened
    red raspberries
2 tablespoons fresh lemon juice
½ cup finely chopped pistachio nuts
2 tablespoons vanilla yogurt

Bring cider and vanilla to a boil in a nonstick pan large enough to hold apples in one layer. Place apples in boiling liquid, reduce heat to low, and simmer, basting frequently, until apples are tender but still holding their shape, about 6 to 8 minutes. Remove and cool on a plate.

For raspberry sauce, thaw raspberries and purée in blender. Put through a fine sieve to remove all seeds, and then add lemon juice. Pool 1 tablespoon of raspberry sauce on bottom of each of six plates. Allowing half an apple per person, slice each apple into ¼-inch-thick slices, and roll outside edge of each slice in pistachios. Arrange apple slices in a fan shape over the sauce. Place 3 drops of vanilla yogurt in sauce under apple fan and drag a knife through the drops creating hearts. Yields 6 servings.

*Note: You can refrigerate or freeze the raspberry sauce for future use. Yields 1½ cups.

Parsnip Lemon Muffins

1 stick butter, softened
1 cup granulated sugar
3 eggs
1 cup puréed cooked parsnips
    (1½ cups uncooked cubed parsnips)
1 teaspoon vanilla extract
¼ cup buttermilk
2 cups all-purpose flour
1½ teaspoons baking powder
½ teaspoon baking soda
½ teaspoon salt
4 teaspoons finely grated lemon and
    orange zest, mixed
½ cup confectioners' sugar
¼ cup lemon juice

Preheat oven to 375°. Grease and flour a 12-cup muffin tin. Cream butter and granulated sugar until fluffy. Cream in eggs, one at a time. Stir in parsnips, vanilla, and buttermilk. Whisk together the flour, baking powder, baking soda, and salt in large mixing bowl, and stir in lemon and orange zest. Stir into butter/sugar mixture just until combined. Spoon into muffin cups making each cup almost full. Bake until toothpick inserted into center of a muffin comes out clean, about 18 to 20 minutes. Place on rack. Using a wooden skewer, pierce deeply the surface of muffins. Combine confectioners' sugar and lemon juice and heat in microwave until boiling. Stir until sugar is completely dissolved. Brush evenly over very hot muffins. Let cool in pan 10 minutes. Turn out and let cool on rack, glazed side up. Yields 12 muffins.

THE WYMAN HOTEL & INN

1371 Greene Street
Silverton, CO 81433
(970) 387-5372 (phone)
(970) 387-5745 (fax)
thewyman@frontier.net
www.silverton.org/wymanhotel

Come home to The Wyman Hotel & Inn, Silverton's finest inn. You will experience a stunning contrast between the ruggedness of the San Juan Mountains and the luxury of the Wyman. All rooms have featherbeds, goose down pillows and comforters on either queen- or king-size beds, and private bathrooms. Many rooms have floor to ceiling arched windows with spectacular views of the mountains and all are furnished with one-of-a-kind antiques. Five romantic rooms have two-person whirlpools. Serving gourmet breakfasts and candlelight dinners and being listed on the National Register, the Wyman is a historic jewel of Colorado.

Silverton Eggs Supreme

6 (8- or 10-inch) flour tortillas (not
    refrigerated), handmade if available
6 ounces sharp Cheddar cheese,
    shredded
1 small onion, chopped
3 medium roasted green chiles, diced
1 medium tomato, chopped
2 sprigs fresh basil, finely chopped
9 large eggs
1 teaspoon dry mustard
½ teaspoon garlic powder
½ teaspoon freshly ground black pepper
½ teaspoon salt

Using jumbo muffin pans lightly sprayed with a nonstick spray, fold tortillas to fit each muffin hole (somewhat like an inverted cone with a flat tip). Preheat oven to 350°. Distribute half the cheese equally into each tortilla cone. Distribute onion, chiles, tomato, and basil evenly into each cone. Beat eggs; add dry mustard, garlic powder, pepper, and salt. Pour egg mixture equally into each cone. Distribute remaining cheese on top of egg mixture. Bake 40 to 50 minutes until edges of tortillas are golden brown and cheese is light brown. Yields 6 servings.

Note: This entrée has a habit of rolling around on the plate, so use an orange wedge on one side and a nice arrangement of tarragon roasted potatoes on the other side. To enhance the presentation, place a small dollop of sour cream close to the entrée, sprinkle a small amount of paprika on top of the sour cream.

Brandied Chicken Breasts

4 boneless, skinless chicken breasts,
    dried on paper towels
1 teaspoon freshly ground black pepper
2 tablespoons butter
2 tablespoons extra virgin olive oil
1 medium onion, coarsely chopped
1 clove garlic, coarsely chopped
1 pound button mushrooms, sliced
¼ cup brandy
½ cup heavy cream
Salt and freshly ground black pepper

Preheat oven to 250°. Place chicken on plate and press black pepper into them. In heavy skillet, heat butter and olive oil and slowly cook chicken until light brown. Remove chicken and place in warm oven, retaining pepper crust and juices in skillet. In same skillet, brown onion and garlic, adding more olive oil if necessary. Try not to brown garlic too much. Add mushrooms and sauté until most of the liquid has evaporated. Remove pan from the stove and add brandy. Ignite and sauté for 1 minute. Add cream and stir. Salt and pepper to taste. Remove chicken from oven, place in skillet, and reheat for 2 minutes, letting the chicken absorb the brandy sauce. Serve on a bed of wild rice surrounded by sliced grape tomatoes and steamed broccoli. Yields 4 servings.

Note: You can substitute sour cream for the heavy cream and cook as indicated above.

Wyman Wedding Pop-Ups

7 frozen puff pastry squares, thawed
4 ounces shredded mozzarella cheese
2 tablespoons capers, drained and dried
⅓ cup julienned sun-dried tomatoes*
9 large eggs
¼ teaspoon fresh ground black pepper
⅛ teaspoon garlic powder
½ small onion, grated
Pinch of salt
Egg wash (1 egg yolk, 2 teaspoons water,
    and a dash of salt—less than
    ⅛ teaspoon—beaten together)

Roll out pastry to about 8-inches square. Using jumbo muffin pans lightly sprayed with nonstick spray, place pastry square into each muffin cup, molding the pastry sheet to the contour of the cup. Combine cheese, capers, and tomatoes and divide equally among cups. Beat eggs and add pepper, garlic, onion, and salt. Pour egg mixture over cheese mixture. Preheat oven to 375°. Using medium-size biscuit cutter, cut six circles from seventh pastry square, and place over top of egg/cheese mixture. Moisten pastry dough edges and corners with water and twist corners of each muffin cup together, forming a spiral. Brush each spiral with egg wash and twist another one-eighth turn to seal in mixture. Bake 55 to 65 minutes until golden brown. Place one pop-up in the center of each plate surrounded by rosemary-roasted russet and sweet potatoes. Garnish with chopped chives and a dash of paprika. Yields 6 servings.

*Note: To reconstitute sun-dried tomatoes, in a heavy saucepan over high heat, add tomatoes, 1 cup water, and ½ teaspoon balsamic vinegar and boil for 2 minutes. Remove from heat and let stand 3 minutes and drain completely.

Crème Brûlée

2 to 3 quarts boiling water
2½ cups heavy fresh cream*
½ cup sugar plus ¼ cup for topping
3 vanilla beans, split
6 egg yolks
1½ teaspoons vanilla extract

Preheat oven to 300° and have boiling water ready. In a heavy saucepan, place cream, sugar, and vanilla beans. Warm on medium heat, lightly whisking until steam rises. Let cool 5 minutes. In separate bowl beat egg yolks and vanilla until blended. Strain cream mixture into yolk bowl a small portion at a time, lightly whisking until entire mixture is totally blended and smooth. Line baking pan with cloth and place four to six ramekins in pan. Evenly pour cream mixture into ramekins. Pour boiling water into pan and bake loosely covered with aluminum foil until set, about 35 minutes. Remove ramekins, cool to room temperature, and refrigerate covered with plastic wrap.

To prepare for serving, remove from refrigerator and, if condensation is visible on top, gently blot moisture up with a paper towel. Sprinkle about 2 teaspoons sugar on top of each ramekin and shake from side to side to spread sugar evenly across top. Caramelize the sugar with a propane torch or under the broiler. Yields 4 to 6 servings.

*Note: Use fresh cream with a minimum 50 percent butter-fat content.

Gazebo Country Inn Bed & Breakfast

507 E. Third Street
Salida, CO 81201
(719) 539-7806 (phone)
(800) 565-7806 (toll free)
info@gazebocountryinn.com
www.gazebocountryinn.com

Quiet front porch, bubbling hot tub, yummy breakfasts, freshly baked cookies, and fabulous mountain views are all here at the Gazebo Country Inn in historic Salida. Activities available in the area include art galleries, winery, antique shops, rafting, skiing, mountain biking, fishing, hot springs—all within 5 to 30 minutes from our breakfast table.

Chocolate Toffee Slices

1 cup shortening
½ cup granulated sugar
½ cup packed brown sugar
2 eggs
1½ teaspoons vanilla extract
2 squares unsweetened (can use semisweet) chocolate, melted and cooled
3 cups all-purpose flour
½ teaspoon baking soda
1 teaspoon salt
1 cup toffee pieces

Combine shortening, sugars, eggs, vanilla, and chocolate until mixed. Add flour, soda, salt, and toffee gradually. Divide dough into two to four portions. Roll into logs about 2 inches thick. Wrap in plastic and chill or freeze. When ready to bake, preheat oven to 400°. Cut dough into ¼-inch slices. Place on ungreased cookie sheet and bake 8 to 10 minutes. Dust with confectioners' sugar and enjoy. Yields 2 to 3 dozen cookies.

Eggs Gazebo

4 to 6 medium potatoes, peeled and diced
1 tablespoon butter
1 tablespoon olive oil
2 tablespoons chopped onion
6 eggs
Milk or cream
White pepper
Salt
1 teaspoon oregano

Spray six individual au gratin dishes with nonstick spray. Sauté potatoes in butter and olive oil until browned, about 20 minutes. Add onion in last 5 minutes to slightly cook and brown. Divide potato and onion mixture among dishes. Preheat oven to 350°. Mix eggs and enough milk to bring to 3 cups total liquid. Season with white pepper and salt to taste and oregano. Pour ½ cup into each dish. Bake until golden and bubbling. Serve immediately with fresh baked muffins and fruit. Yields 6 servings.

Note: Can prepare potatoes ahead and cover with water in container in refrigerator.

Variation 1: Arrange slices of zucchini or chopped fresh spinach and tomato on top and sprinkle with oregano.

Variation 2: Rinse 2 to 3 cups fresh baby spinach and pile on top of nearly cooked potatoes. Allow the water on the spinach to finish steaming the potatoes and cook the spinach a bit. After... pour the egg/milk mixture on the p... crumble about 1 tables... each dish.

❧ ❧

The Quilt House Bed & Breakfast

310 Riverside Drive
P.O. Box 339
Estes Park, CO 80517
(970) 586-0427
hgraetzen@aol.com

The Quilt House Bed & Breakfast in Estes Park, Colorado, is a home-stay bed and breakfast. There are three rooms upstairs and a guest house beside the main house, all with private baths. The inn offers lovely views, full breakfasts, and homemade quilts on the beds. Estes Park is the gateway city to the Rocky Mountain National park. Activities are hiking, fishing, golfing, shopping, wildlife viewing, and enjoying fresh mountain air.

Yorkshire Sausage

1 pound pork sausage
4 large eggs
1 cup all-purpose flour
1 cup milk

In skillet brown sausage on medium heat, stirring to break up meat. When all red color is gone, drain off fat and discard. You can do this part early and then cover and refrigerate. An hour before serving time, oil a 7 x 11-inch pan with lecithin mix (see note). Preheat oven to 350°. Distribute cooked sausage evenly on bottom of pan. In small mixing bowl, beat eggs until foamy. Add flour and milk and continue mixing. Pour over sausage, starting around the edges of pan. Push down with spatula any sausage that wants to protrude too high. Bake 45 to 55 minutes. Cool slightly and cut into eight pieces. Fresh apple slices make a pretty, edible garnish. Yields 8 servings.

Note: To oil your pans for casseroles or baking use the following process: In a wide-mouthed jar, mix 2 parts liquid lecithin (available at health food stores) and 1 part vegetable oil. Store covered in the refrigerator. Use a nylon cooking brush, and lightly brush on the bottom and sides of pan you are using. Your baked products will slide out nicely.

Morning Fruit Cup

1 diced apple
1 peeled and diced orange
1 cup strawberries plus extra for garnish
6 scoops orange sherbet

Divide fruit among six dishes. Put apple on bottom, then orange, and then the strawberries last. Top with scoop of orange sherbet. Do this about 30 to 45 minutes before serving time. You want the sherbet to melt and mix in with the fruit. Garnish with slice of strawberry on top. Yields 6 servings.

Steamboat Bed & Breakfast

442 Pine Street
P.O. Box 775888
Steamboat Springs, CO 80477
(970) 870-8787 (fax)
(877) 335-4321 (toll free)
info@steamboatb-b.com
www.steamboatb-b.com

Come experience steamboat hospitality at the beautiful Victorian-style Steamboat Bed & Breakfast. The historic building dates back to 1891 as Steamboat's First Congregational Church. It is centrally located two blocks from downtown, two miles from the ski resort, and convenient to all-year-long activities. As you awaken to the aroma of custom-blended coffees, you begin your morning with freshly baked breads, select fruits, and a delicious, full breakfast. Nestled in the lush green Yampa Valley, Steamboat Springs is surrounded by mountains and alpine beauty. Gaze upon Steamboat sunsets and spectacular stars from the hot tub.

Uncle Carlos' Apple Cake

2 eggs
½ cup vegetable oil
2 cups sugar
2 cups all-purpose flour
2 teaspoons baking soda
2 teaspoons ground cinnamon
¼ teaspoon salt
¼ cup chopped walnuts
2 teaspoons vanilla extract
4 cups peeled and chopped tart apples

Frosting:
2 (3-ounce) packages cream cheese
1½ cups confectioners' sugar
2 teaspoons vanilla extract
1 tablespoon butter
⅛ teaspoon salt

Preheat oven to 325°. In large bowl beat together eggs and oil. Mix together the sugar, flour, baking soda, cinnamon, salt, walnuts, and vanilla. Stir in the apples and egg mixture. Bake 45 minutes in 9 x 13-inch glass pan.

To make the frosting, beat together the cream cheese, sugar, vanilla, butter, and salt until creamy and smooth. Frost cake when it cools. Yields 12 servings.

Paula's Baked Pear Frittata

2 firm pears
2 tablespoons butter
6 large eggs
⅓ cup milk
¼ cup all-purpose flour
¼ cup granulated sugar
1 tablespoon vanilla extract
¼ teaspoon salt
¼ cup whipped cream cheese
1 to 2 tablespoons brown sugar

Peel and dice pears. Over medium-high heat melt butter, add pears, and turn occasionally until lightly brown and tender. This should take 7 to 8 minutes. Whisk eggs, milk, flour, sugar, vanilla, and salt in a bowl. Remove pan from heat and cool a few minutes. Pour egg mixture over pears. Preheat oven to 425°. Put pear mixture in an 8 x 8-inch glass pan and bake until golden brown, 8 to 10 minutes. Cut into wedges and serve with dollops of cream cheese and brown sugar. Yields 6 servings.

Aunt Frieda's Coffee Cake

1 (18-ounce) package yellow cake mix, do not prepare
1 (3.4-ounce) package vanilla instant pudding, do not prepare
¼ cup vegetable oil
¾ cup water
4 eggs
2 teaspoons vanilla extract

1 cup sour cream
½ cup sugar
2 teaspoons ground cinnamon
½ cup chopped walnuts

Grease an angel food cake pan. Preheat oven to 350°. Mix together the cake mix, pudding, oil, water, eggs, vanilla, and sour cream in bowl until thoroughly wet. In separate bowl mix together sugar and cinnamon. Place walnuts on bottom of cake pan. Pour some batter on top of the walnuts. Put some sugar mixture next, and then alternate with batter, finishing off with sugar mixture. Pull a knife through the mixture to create a swirl effect. Bake 60 minutes. Serve upside down. Yields 12 servings.

ELIZABETH STREET GUEST HOUSE

202 East Elizabeth Street
Fort Collins, CO 80524
(970) 493-2337 (phone)
(970) 416-0826 (fax)
bbinnkeeper@earthlink.net
www.bbonline.com/co/elizabeth

Built in 1905 and established as a bed and breakfast in 1984, Elizabeth Street Guest House is located one block east of Colorado State University. Restored to its original luster, the oak woodwork and leaded windows add a historic accent. The unique eighteen-room, three-story miniature house in the entry hall is a treasured family heirloom.

Fort Collins is sixty-five miles north of Denver along the front range of the Rocky Mountains. Home of Colorado State University, Fort Collins benefits from the intellectual influence of a major university.

Nearby national forests and parks offer outdoor activities ranging from camping, fishing, and hiking to river-rafting.

Popover Muffins

1 cup all-purpose flour
⅛ teaspoon salt
2 large eggs
1 cup milk

Coat a 12-cup, heavy muffin tin with canola oil spray and place in freezer 15 minutes (or overnight) before baking. A half hour before serving, place flour and the salt in a mixing bowl over to one side of the bowl. On the other side of the mixing bowl, break eggs and add milk. With a fork (not a whisk) beat eggs and milk together and incorporate the flour and salt as you beat. Beat until mixed together but batter is still lumpy. Take muffin tin out of freezer and spoon or pour batter evenly into tin. Place tin in cold oven and turn oven to 450°. Set timer for 20 minutes and do not peek. After 20 minutes, check muffins to see if brown enough. Serve immediately with butter and jam. Yields 12 muffins.

Note: Salt is very important; it is needed to make the popover rise but too much will make it tough.

German Blueberry Pancake

6 eggs
1½ cups all-purpose flour
1½ cups milk
½ teaspoon salt
6 tablespoons butter
¾ cup blueberries

Preheat oven to 450°. Place medium iron skillet in oven 5 to 10 minutes. In mixing bowl, whisk eggs, flour, milk, and salt together until well blended and smooth. Place butter in hot skillet to melt and put

Elizabeth Street Guest House

vate cottages. It is an uncommonly memorable 1885 oasis. Spring Cottage is a nationally registered historic district with a view of Pikes Peak from the cottage porches. It is also close to nine naturally flowing springs and scenic wonders. Area attractions include Pikes Peak Cog Train; Indian Cliff Dwelling; Cove of the Winds; Castle; Garden of the Gods; Seven Falls; Olympic Training Center; Santa's North Poll Workshop; Pikes Peaks Highway; and spectacular trails.

Scrambled Eggs in a Cream Puff Bowl

Cream puff bowls:
½ cup water
¼ cup (½ stick) butter
½ cup all-purpose flour
⅛ teaspoon salt
2 eggs

Filling:
8 eggs
6 tablespoons cream
½ cup small-curd cottage cheese
1 tablespoon finely snipped chives
¼ teaspoon dry mustard
½ teaspoon salt
3 tablespoons butter
Parsley for garnish

Preheat oven to 400°. Grease either 9-inch glass pie pan or four glass baking dishes or bowls. Heat water and butter to rolling boil. Sir in flour and salt. Stir vigorously until mixture leaves the side of pan and forms a ball, about 1 minute. Remove from heat and cool slightly. Add 2 eggs all at once, beating until smooth and glossy. Spread batter evenly in pie pan or baking dishes. Have batter touch sides but do not spread up the sides. Indent center with spoon spreading towards sides and making the center thinner like a bowl. Bake 30 to 40 minutes (less time for individual dishes), or until puffed and golden.

For the filling, beat eggs thoroughly and stir in cream, cottage cheese, chives,

back in oven for 30 seconds or until butter is melted. Remove the hot skillet and pour in batter. Sprinkle blueberries on top. Place skillet in oven and turn temperature to 400°. Bake 20 minutes and then check for doneness. Pancake should have risen above skillet all around and be brown on the edges; it may need a few minutes longer. Remove from oven (it will fall immediately), slice into eight sections, and arrange on a serving platter along with cooked sausage links. Serve immediately with warmed maple syrup. Yields 8 servings.

Preheat oven to 400°. Combine in bowl flour, baking powder, salt, and sugar. Cut in butter until well combined and crumbly. Pat mixture over bottom and sides of a 10-inch pie pan. Arrange peach halves in pastry. Sprinkle blueberries on top. Mix the sugar and cinnamon and sprinkle on top of fruit. Bake 15 minutes. Combine the egg and sour cream until well blended. Pour over fruit and bake 30 minutes longer. Yields 8 servings.

Peach Blueberry Kuchen

1⅓ cups all-purpose flour
¼ teaspoon baking powder
½ teaspoon salt
2 tablespoons sugar
⅓ cup butter
8 to 12 peach halves, canned or frozen
½ cup blueberries
½ cup sugar
1 teaspoon ground cinnamon
1 egg
1 cup sour cream

SPRING COTTAGE

113 Pawnee Avenue
Manitou Springs, CO 80829
(719) 685-9395 (phone)
(888) 588-9395 (toll free)
lancaster@springcottage.com
www.springcottage.com

A time and a place to count as your own, Spring Cottage offers extraordinarily pri-

mustard, and salt. Heat butter in skillet until just hot enough to sizzle a drop of water. Pour egg mixture into skillet. As mixture sets, gently lift cooked portions so the thin, uncooked portion can flow to bottom. Avoid constant stirring. Cook until thickened but moist. Mound in cream puff bowl or bowls. Top with small sprig of fresh parsley. Serve immediately. Yields 4 servings.

Puffed Apple Pancakes

6 eggs
1½ cups milk
1 cup all-purpose flour
3 tablespoons sugar
1 teaspoon vanilla extract*
½ teaspoon salt
¼ teaspoon ground cinnamon
6 tablespoons butter
2 Granny Smith apples, peeled and
   sliced very thinly
1 plus ¾ cup firmly packed brown sugar
½ cup orange juice
1 tablespoon very finely grated orange peel

Heat oven to 425° or lower if your oven "bakes hot." Whisk together the eggs, milk, flour, sugar, vanilla, salt, and cinnamon. Melt 1 tablespoon butter (or margarine) in each of five or six (6 x 1½ inch) individual dishes as oven preheats. When butter is melted and sizzles (do not brown), remove dishes from oven and brush sides of dishes with the melted butter, leaving extra in the bottom. Place apple slices in the bottom of each dish and return to oven. When apples and dishes are hot, remove from the oven and immediately pour a scant 1 cup batter into each dish. Sprinkle 2 tablespoons brown sugar on the top of each. Return immediately to the oven while dish is still hot. Bake 20 minutes until puffed and golden. Combine the remaining 1 cup brown sugar, orange juice, and orange peel and simmer 5 minutes. Pour over the pancakes and serve immediately. Yields 5 to 6 servings.

*Note: Vanilla butternut flavoring is a great alternative.

Spicy Oven-Baked Irish Potato Chips

1 teaspoon ground coriander
½ teaspoon fennel seeds
½ teaspoon dried oregano
½ teaspoon dried hot red pepper flakes
1 teaspoon salt
3 tablespoons vegetable oil
2 pounds Irish potatoes, pared,
   cut in half, then cut into
   ½-inch wedges

Preheat oven to 400°. Mix together spices, salt, and oil on flat cookie sheet (with a lip). Toss potato wedges in mixture to thoroughly coat. Roast 20 to 30 minutes or more until tender and browned, turning as needed. Serve immediately. Yields 4 to 6 servings.

Spring Cottage Apple Pie

Crust:
3 cups all-purpose flour
1 teaspoon salt
1 cup butter-flavored shortening
1 egg
1 teaspoon vinegar
Milk to make 1 cup with the egg
   and vinegar

Filling:
6 to 7 medium apples, equal
   number of Golden Delicious
   and Granny Smith
2 tablespoons all-purpose flour
1 cup granulated sugar
½ cup brown sugar
Dash of salt
1 teaspoon ground cinnamon
¼ teaspoon ground nutmeg
2 tablespoons butter

Cut together the flour, salt, and shortening with a pastry blender. Add the egg, vinegar, and milk. Mix well to form a ball. If dough sits while you peel apples it will be easier to work with. Use adequate flour to roll out the dough for a two-crust pie. Line individual pie shells or a large pie plate with pastry.

For filling, peel apples, cut into quarters, core, and slice each quarter crosswise. Mix flour, sugars, salt, cinnamon, and nutmeg and toss with apples. Put apples into pie shell(s). Dot with butter. Cover with a top crust. Preheat oven to 375°. Flute edges of crust, cutting off excess not needed to facilitate a tuck under the edge. Pierce top to release steam. Place on tray to catch spillover in oven. Bake 1 hour or until bubbly edges look thickened and top is golden brown. Yields 6 to 8 servings.

OLD TOWN GUESTHOUSE

115 South 26th Street
Colorado Springs, CO 80904
(719) 632-9194 (phone)
(719) 632-9026 (fax)
(888) 375-4210 (toll free)
luxury@oldtown-guesthouse.com
www.oldtown-guesthouse.com

Old Town GuestHouse is a newly built bed and breakfast that offers upscale amenities to discerning business and leisure guests. "Experience historic Old Town in urban luxury." The GuestHouse has been awarded AAA Four Diamonds, Select Registry, and Distinctive Inns of Colorado. The private conference center now offers worldwide videoconferencing. Activities in the area include sightseeing (Garden of the Gods, Air Force Academy, Olympic Training Center, Focus on the Family, Pikes Peak, Cripple Creek gold mines), hiking, birding, white water rafting, horseback riding, and golf, to mention a few.

Old Town Chocolate Chip Pumpkin Bread

3 cups all-purpose flour
2 teaspoons ground cinnamon
1 teaspoon salt
1 teaspoon baking soda
4 eggs
2 cups sugar
2 cups canned pumpkin
1¼ cups vegetable oil
1½ cups chocolate chips

Preheat oven to 350°. In large bowl, combine flour, cinnamon, salt, and soda. In another bowl, beat eggs, sugar, pumpkin, and oil. Add dry ingredients, stirring just until moistened. Fold in chocolate chips. Pour into two greased 8 x 4 x 2-inch loaf pans. Bake for 60 to 70 minutes or until a toothpick inserted near center comes out clean. Cool 10 minutes before removing from pans to cooling racks. Yields 2 large loaves.

CREEKSIDE INN BED & BREAKFAST

P.O. Box 4835
51 West Main Street
Frisco, CO 80443
(970) 668-5607 (phone)
(970) 668-8635 (fax)
(800) 668-7320 (toll free)
creeksideinn@earthlink.net
www.creeksideinn-frisco.com

In the heart of the Colorado Rockies, Creekside Inn is a comfortable and friendly adult retreat—seven rooms with private bathrooms, outdoor hot tub, and great breakfasts. Activities include boating, concerts, dogsledding, film festivals, fly-fishing, golf, hiking, horseback riding, hot-air ballooning, jeep tours, kayaking, gold mine tours, mountain biking, Nordic skiing, outlet shopping, river rafting, sailing, skiing, sleigh rides, snowmobiling, snowshoe tours, tennis, trail biking, and wildflower walks.

Spicy Baked Pears with Yogurt

½ cup dark brown sugar
½ teaspoon ground cinnamon
¼ teaspoon mace
Pinch of ground cloves
5 large ripe pears or 10 canned halves
¾ cup orange juice (enough to make
    ½ inch of liquid in baking dish)
¼ cup (½ stick) butter
Vanilla yogurt
Strawberries and raspberries

Preheat oven to 350°. Line bottom of 10 x 15-inch baking dish with brown sugar. Sprinkle sugar layer with cinnamon, mace, and cloves. Slice fresh pears in half; remove cores and stems. Lay pears cut side down on sugar mixture. Pour orange juice over pears and dot with butter. Bake 30 minutes, or until pears are tender. To serve, place 2 pear halves on serving dish and pour juice mixture over the pears. Place dollop of yogurt and berries on top. Yields 5 servings.

Cranberry Cake

Topping:
⅔ cup packed brown sugar
½ cup all-purpose flour
1 teaspoon ground cinnamon
4 tablespoons softened butter
    or margarine
⅔ cups toasted and chopped walnuts
½ cup cranberries

Cake:
2½ cups all-purpose flour
2 teaspoons baking powder
½ teaspoon baking soda
½ teaspoon salt
1½ cups sugar
6 tablespoons softened butter
    or margarine
2 large eggs
1 teaspoon almond extract
1⅓ cups sour cream
2 cups cranberries

Preheat oven to 350°. Grease 13 x 9-inch metal baking pan; dust with flour.

Prepare topping in medium bowl; with fork, mix sugar, flour, and cinnamon until blended. With fingertips, work in butter until evenly distributed. Stir in walnuts and cranberries.

Prepare cake in another medium bowl; combine flour, baking powder, baking soda, and salt. In large bowl, with mixer at low speed, beat sugar with butter until blended, scraping bowl often with rubber spatula. Increase speed to high; beat 2 minutes, occasionally scraping bowl. Reduce speed to low; add eggs, one at a time, beating well after each addition. Beat in almond extract. With mixer at low speed, alternatively add flour mixture and sour cream, beginning and ending with flour mixture, until batter is smooth, occasionally scraping bowl. With rubber spatula, fold in cranberries. Spoon batter into pan; spread evenly. Sprinkle with topping. Bake cake 55 to 60 minutes or until toothpick inserted in center comes out clean. Cool cake in pan on wire rack 1 hour. Yields 1 cake.

Connecticut

ANOTHER SECOND PENNY INN

870 Pequot Trail
Stonington, CT 06378-2234
(860) 535-1710
innkeepers@secondpenny.com
www.secondpenny.com

It is said, "If you have two pennies, with the first buy bread and with the second buy hyacinths for your soul." Another Second Penny Inn, a 1710 colonial house, offers three large guest rooms, private jetted baths, fireplaces, gardens, and a quiet country setting near the heart of Mystic. Area attractions include Mystic Seaport, Mystic Aquarium, historic Stonington Borough, the Mashantucket Pequot Museum, Foxwoods and Mohegan Sun Casinos, beaches, hiking, shopping, antiquing, boating, and a wealth of historical sites.

Jim's Sautéed Apples

2 apples
3 tablespoons butter
1 cup loosely packed brown sugar
1 cup hard apple cider
Ground cinnamon

Peel and core apples and slice thinly (¼ inch). In sauté pan or large nonstick fry pan put in butter, sugar, and cider, stirring until sugar is dissolved. Bring sauce to a full boil and add apple slices. Reduce heat to simmer and cook apples, stirring very occasionally (so as not to break up slices) until apples are tender and sauce is reduced by three-fourths. Sprinkle with cinnamon before serving. May be served either hot or cold as desired with dollop of vanilla yogurt or splash of cream. Yields 4 servings.

Hard Apple Cider Cake

This recipe dates to the 1830s and is quite similar to pound cake.

6 cups all-purpose flour
1 teaspoon baking soda
½ teaspoon salt
1 teaspoon grated nutmeg
1 cup softened butter
3 cups sugar
4 eggs
1 cup cider (dry, not sweet)

In bowl, mix together flour, soda, salt, and nutmeg. In electric mixer, cream butter well and add sugar gradually, creaming until fluffy. Add eggs one at a time and beat thoroughly. On low speed, add the flour mixture alternately with the cider, beating until smooth after each addition.

Preheat oven to 350°. Grease two loaf pans (or 4 smaller ones) and distribute batter evenly. Bake about 1 hour (gas ovens take 10 minutes longer). Keep moist with chunk of apple placed in your cake container. Freezes well. Yields 2 large loaves or 4 small.

LIGHTHOUSE INN

Six Guthrie Place
New London, CT 06320
(860) 443-8411
www.lighthouseinn-ct.com

Lighthouse Inn is exceptional in that it attracts locals as well as out-of-town guests. Recent renovations have restored the inn to the grandeur of its past. The inn comprises of two buildings: the original Guthrie Mansion and the Carriage House. The mansion has twenty-seven spectacular guest rooms, many have ocean views and all are filled with period antiques. The

Carriage House has twenty-four comfortable rooms decorated in country French décor. Guests have access to the inn's private beach, outdoor pool, salon, and day spa.

Award-winning food and service is the trademark of Timothy's Restaurant. Chef Timothy Grills offers inspiring American continental cuisine. Enjoy your repast in the restaurant among the original hand-carved chandeliers and Victorian ambience in the casual comfort of the 1902 tavern or on our beautiful outdoor patio overlooking Long Island Sound.

Delmonico Potatoes

5 pounds red potatoes
1 pint (16 ounces) light cream
Salt and pepper
1½ cups dry breadcrumbs
1 cup grated Romano cheese
¼ cup melted butter

The day before potatoes are to be eaten, wash and boil with skins on. Cook just until fork will go in easily. Do *not* overcook. Peel and place in refrigerator overnight to firm slightly. Next day, chop finely and place in pot with light cream, enough to cover. Season with salt and pepper to taste. Cook over a low heat, stirring occasionally. Cook until cream thickens, remove from heat, and leave in same pot for 1 to 2 hours. The liquid will thicken a bit more. When ready to serve, place in shallow casserole dish, sprinkle with dry breadcrumbs, grated Romano cheese, and a little melted butter. Preheat oven to 350°. Place pota-

toes in oven and bake until thoroughly heated and a golden brown on top. Yields 10 to 12 servings.

HOMESPUN FARM BED & BREAKFAST

306 Preston Road
Griswold, CT 06351
(860) 376-5178 (phone)
(888) 889-6673 (toll free)
www.homespunfarm.com

Homespun Farm is listed on the National Register of Historic Places. From the hand-crafted beds to the hand-hewn beams, Homespun Farm Bed & Breakfast warms you with the spirit of hardworking men and women. It is a part of the National Wildlife Federation Backyard Habitat. The grounds are completely alive with Koi Pond—a habitat for snails, frogs, and freshwater clams, hardy water lilies, tropical lilies, and grasses. There are all types of flowers, such as iris, Russian sage, corriopsis, sunflowers, mints, and heathers. Homespun is a delight for all who enjoy nature and harmony. Activities nearby include Mystic, Foxwoods Casino, Mohegan Sun Casino, golf, New London Submarine Base, Coast Guard Station, antiquing, horseback riding, and state parks.

Warm Winter Fruit Soup

½ gallon apple juice
4 teaspoons small pearl tapioca
1 pound dried fruit slices
    (prunes, pears, apricots, peaches)

1 (16-ounce) can cherries
    (not pie filling)
4 teaspoons sugar
Stick cinnamon
Whole nutmeg

Heat juice and tapioca in pot. Add fruit slices, cherries, sugar, cinnamon, and nutmeg. Serve when tapioca is absorbed and mixture is hot. Remove cinnamon stick and nutmeg. Yields 10 to 12 cups.

Note: Works great in a slow cooker and makes the whole house smell great. A loaf of French bread goes nicely with this.

Homespun Farm Upside-Down French Toast

1 cup pecans
1 stick butter
1 cup packed brown sugar
2 tablespoons corn syrup
6 to 8 (¾-inch thick) slices sweet bread
5 eggs
1½ cups half-and-half
1 teaspoon vanilla extract
¼ teaspoon salt

Spray 9 x 13-inch pan with nonstick spray or grease well with butter. Spread pecans in bottom. Melt butter, brown sugar, and corn syrup and pour over pecans evenly. Fit slices of bread tightly on top, covering pecans. Beat eggs, half-and-half, vanilla, and salt together and pour over bread. Cover and chill at least 8 hours. Preheat oven to 350° and bake 35 to 40 minutes. Let sit for a minute or two until butter stops bubbling and then flip pan over onto cookie sheet. Slide back into pan with nuts now on top. This helps to stop the brown sugar from caramelizing and sticking to pan when cooled. Serve with bacon or sausage. Yields 6 servings.

TAYLOR'S CORNER

880 Route 171
Woodstock, CT 06281
(860) 974-0490 (phone)
(860) 974-0498 (fax)
(888) 503-9057 (toll free)
peggy@TaylorsBB.com
www.TaylorsBB.com

Experience the country at Taylor's Corner, a lovingly restored eighteenth century farmhouse, decorated and furnished with antiques and reproductions. Bed & Breakfast at Taylor's Corner provides smoke-free lodging in three air-conditioned guest rooms with fireplaces, phones, private baths, and queen-size beds. Nine fireplaces invite winter guests to warm hearts and souls by the crackling fires. Taylor's Corner is listed on the National Register of Historic Places. Nearby are excellent restaurants and four wonderful state parks for hiking, swimming, and picnicking. Also nearby are museums, antiquing, the Connecticut Audubon Center, trails for cross-country skiing, picturesque countryside as only New England can provide, and much more. The University of Connecticut, Old Sturbridge Village, and Brimfield antique shows are within twenty minutes of the inn.

Vegetarian Oven Omelet

6 slices white bread
2 medium zucchini squash,
    sliced and steamed
1 cup grated Swiss
    or sharp Cheddar cheese
6 eggs
2 cups milk
Salt and pepper

Coat 9 x 13-inch pan with nonstick spray. Layer bread to cover bottom of pan. Place zucchini and then cheese on bread. Beat eggs with milk using wire whisk. Pour over all. Salt and pepper to taste. Cover with plastic wrap and place in refrigerator 8 to 10 hours or overnight. When ready to bake, heat oven to 350° and bake 35 minutes. Yields 6 to 8 servings.

Variation: When the garden isn't producing, replace squash with canned mushrooms and onion flakes.

Mike's Irresistible Cookies

2 cups (4 sticks) butter
2 cups light brown sugar
2 cups granulated sugar
4 eggs
2 teaspoons vanilla extract
4 cups all-purpose flour
2 teaspoons baking powder
2 teaspoons salt
2 teaspoons baking soda
12 ounces chocolate chips
2 cups raisins
1 cup chopped nuts
2 cups old-fashioned rolled oats

Preheat oven to 375°. Blend butter with sugars until creamy. Add eggs and vanilla. Beat until well mixed. Sift flour, baking powder, salt, and baking soda together in bowl. Add to egg mixture and beat well. Stir in remaining ingredients. When well mixed, shape into balls and bake on ungreased cookie sheet 8 to 10 minutes or until barely golden. Best when slightly undercooked and served warm from oven. Yields 4 to 6 dozen cookies.

Peg's Baked Beans

2 pounds dry navy beans
1 teaspoon baking soda
1 (12-ounce) can V-8 juice
1 cup dark brown sugar
1 large onion, sliced in wedges
1 teaspoon prepared mustard
¼ cup dark molasses or maple syrup
1 teaspoon salt
⅛ teaspoon pepper
⅛ teaspoon garlic powder
Salt pork, scored

Soak beans in water overnight. Add baking soda and bring to a boil. Simmer until skins split when you blow on them, about 10 minutes. While beans are simmering, mix remaining ingredients, except salt pork, in bean pot. Preheat oven to 350°. Drain beans and add to mixture in bean pot. Stir. Add hot water just to cover. Place salt pork on top, pushing into beans. Cover and bake about 5 hours until beans are tender. Check pot 3 or 4 times during baking and add water if you don't see the juice bubbling on the edges. Yields 10 to 12 servings.

Pannukakku (Finnish Pancake)

4 to 5 tablespoons butter
1 quart milk
4 eggs
½ cup sugar
1½ cups all-purpose flour
1 teaspoon salt (optional)

Preheat oven to 350°. Melt butter in 9 x 13-inch pan in oven. Mix remaining ingredients in a large bowl with whisk. Pour over melted butter. Bake 55 to 65 minutes. Yields 6 to 8 servings.

MANOR HOUSE

69 Maple Avenue
Norfolk, CT 06058
(860) 542-5690
innkepper@manorhouse-norfolk.com
www.manorhouse-norfolk.com

Indulge yourselves at the Manor House, designated as "Connecticut's Most Romantic Hideaway." The inn exudes Victorian elegance with its Tiffany windows and antique furnishings. There is much for guests to do and see. Besides relaxing amidst our spacious grounds and gardens, the inn is within walking distance of the Yale School of Music and Art. There is also hiking, biking, and swimming. Just a short drive from the Manor House are Tanglewood, Music Mountain, summer theater, antique and craft shops, vineyards, historic homes, museums, splendid perennial gardens, alpine and cross-country skiing, riding stables, carriage and sleigh rides, and Lime Rock Park.

Baked French Doughnuts

1½ cups pastry flour
2¼ teaspoons baking powder
½ teaspoon salt
½ teaspoon ground nutmeg
5 tablespoons vegetable shortening
½ plus ½ cup sugar
1 egg, beaten
½ cup milk
1 teaspoon ground cinnamon
6 tablespoons melted butter

Preheat oven to 375°. Grease 12-cup muffin tin. In large mixing bowl sift together flour, baking powder, salt, and nutmeg. In separate bowl, cream together shortening and ½ cup sugar. Add egg to shortening mixture and beat well. Add sifted ingredients alternately with milk. Refrigerate overnight. Fill muffin cups half full of doughnut batter. Bake 20 to 25 minutes or until toothpick inserted comes out clean. Remove from pan immediately. Mix remaining ½ cup sugar with cinnamon. Brush melted butter on top and roll in cinnamon/sugar mixture. Yields 1 dozen.

Variation: Fill muffin tins one-fourth full with batter, top with a thin layer of jam, and cover with batter, filling the tins half full.

Poached Eggs with Lemon-Butter-Chive Sauce

4 eggs
1 tablespoon vinegar
⅓ cup butter
2 tablespoons finely chopped fresh chives
1 tablespoon lemon juice
¼ teaspoon freshly ground black pepper
2 English muffins, halved and toasted

Poach the eggs for 3 to 4 minutes in simmering water to which vinegar has been added. (Or use a poacher if available.) For the sauce melt the butter in a small saucepan, add the chives, lemon juice, salt, and pepper, and beat thoroughly. When the eggs are just set, remove them from the pan. Drain on paper towel if they were cooked directly in the water. To serve, place a poached egg on muffin half and spoon sauce over the top. Yields 2 to 4 servings.

A to Z Bread

3 cups all-purpose flour
1 teaspoon baking soda
1 teaspoon salt
1 tablespoon ground cinnamon
½ teaspoon baking powder
3 eggs
1 cup vegetable oil
2 cups sugar
2 cups A to Z mix*
3 teaspoons vanilla extract
1 cup chopped walnuts or almonds

Preheat oven to 325°. Sift the flour, baking soda, salt, cinnamon, and baking powder. Beat eggs in a large bowl. Add oil and sugar and cream well. Add A-to-Z mix and vanilla to the egg mixture. Add the dry ingredients and mix well. Stir in the nuts. Spoon into two, well-greased loaf pans. Bake for 1 hour. Yields 2 loaves.

Variation: Fill muffin tins halfway and bake for approximately 25 minutes.

*A to Z Mix: Use one or more ingredients to equal 2 cups. Anything from grated apples or carrots to grated sweet potatoes or zucchini.

Orange Waffles

1 cup all-purpose flour
1 tablespoon sugar
1½ teaspoons baking powder
2 eggs
½ cup milk
Grated zest of 1 orange
2 tablespoons butter

Combine dry ingredients and add eggs, milk, and zest. Add butter to batter. Cook waffles in heated iron. Slice on the diagonal and serve with orange slices, raspberries, or any fresh, colorful fruit. Yields 2 servings.

INN AT LOWER FARM BED & BREAKFAST

119 Mystic Road
North Stonington, CT 06359
(860) 535-9075 (phone)
(866) 535-9075 (toll free)
info@lowerfarm.com
www.lowerfarm.com

Located in the heart of southeastern Connecticut, the Inn at Lower Farm is a bed and breakfast that blends the charm of yesterday with the comforts of today. The Inn, a 260 year old center chimney colonial farmhouse, features four comfortable guest rooms, each with a private bath. Wake up each morning to a full country breakfast served by candlelight in front of the original hearth. Take a walk through the four acre grounds or admire the lovely gardens. Area attractions include Downtown Mystic, with the renowned Mystic Seaport and the world class Mystic Aquarium. The Inn is also convenient to the quaint seaside village of Stonington Borough.

Summer Fruit Salad

2 cups seedless grapes cut in half
    (mix red and white)
2 cups blueberries
2 cups sliced strawberries
2 cups sliced fresh peaches
½ cup dark brown sugar
1 cup low-fat sour cream

Mix all the fruit in large bowl. In small bowl mix together brown sugar and sour cream. Pour mixture over fruit until all the fruit is coated. Serve in wine glasses. Yields 6 servings.

Cheesy Broccoli Casserole

1 (10-ounce) package frozen
    broccoli, thawed and
    drained
1 cup low-fat sour cream
1 cup low-fat cottage cheese
½ cup biscuit mix
¼ cup (½ stick) melted butter
2 eggs
1 tomato, thinly sliced
¼ cup grated Parmesan cheese

Preheat oven to 350°. Coat an 8-inch-square glass dish with cooking spray. Spread broccoli in bottom of pan. Mix together sour cream, cottage cheese, biscuit mix, melted butter, and eggs. Beat for 1 minute with a hand-held electric mixer. Pour over the broccoli. Arrange tomato slices on top and sprinkle with Parmesan cheese. Bake 30 minutes or until golden brown. Cool 5 minutes. Cut into pieces and serve. Yields 4 to 6 servings.

Lemon Blueberry Biscuits

2 cups all-purpose flour
⅓ cup sugar
2 teaspoons baking powder
½ teaspoon baking soda
¼ teaspoon salt
1 egg, lightly beaten
1 (8-ounce) carton lemon yogurt
¼ cup melted butter
1 teaspoon grated lemon peel
1 cup fresh or frozen blueberries

Preheat oven to 400°. In large bowl, combine flour, sugar, baking powder, baking soda, and salt. In small bowl combine the egg, yogurt, butter, and lemon peel. Stir yogurt mixture into dry ingredients just until moistened. Fold in blueberries. Coat a baking sheet with cooking spray. Drop the dough by tablespoonfuls onto the baking sheet. Bake 15 to 18 minutes or until lightly brown. Serve with preserves and butter. Yields about 18 biscuits.

Delaware

DELAWARE INN

55 Delaware Avenue
Rehoboth Beach, DE 19971
(302) 227-6031 (phone)
(800) 246-5244 (toll free)
Innkeeper@DelawareInn.com
www.delawareinn.com

For more than seventy years the Delaware Inn, an AAA-approved establishment, has welcomed and delighted guests, making it one of the oldest continuously operating bed and breakfasts in Rehoboth Beach. The inn is just steps to the town's sandy white beaches and many fine restaurants, clubs, shops, and boutiques. The inn is decorated to make your stay relaxing and enjoyable. The common rooms are in country colonial with a collection of straw baskets, dried flowers, and country herbs adorning a cedar-beamed ceiling.

Zucchini Bread

3 eggs
1 cup vegetable oil
2 cups sugar
2½ cups all-purpose flour
2 teaspoons baking soda
½ teaspoon baking powder
3 teaspoons ground cinnamon
1 teaspoon salt
2 cups grated zucchini
2 teaspoons vanilla extract
1 cup walnuts or pecans
1 cup raisins

Preheat oven to 350°. Combine eggs, oil, and sugar. Mix with electric mixer until well blended. Sift together flour, baking soda, baking powder, cinnamon, and salt. Add to creamed mixture, alternating with zucchini. Add vanilla, nuts, and raisins. Pour into greased and floured loaf pans. Bake 60 minutes. Yields 2 large or 3 small loaves.

Tomato Basil Quiche

1 refrigerated unbaked piecrust
½ plus 2 cups shredded mozzarella cheese
5 Roma tomatoes
1 cup loosely-packed fresh basil leaves
4 cloves garlic
2 cups mayonnaise
⅓ cup grated Parmesan cheese
⅛ teaspoon white pepper

Preheat oven to 450°. Unfold piecrust and place in a 9-inch quiche dish. Line crust with a double thickness of foil. Bake 8 minutes. Remove foil and bake 4 to 5 more minutes until set and dry. Remove from oven and reduce oven temperature to 375°. Sprinkle crust with ½ cup mozzarella cheese. Cool slightly on rack. Cut tomatoes into wedges and drain on paper towels. Arrange tomato wedges atop cheese in pie shell. In food processor combine basil and garlic. Cover and process until coarsely chopped and sprinkle over tomatoes. In medium mixing bowl combine remaining 2 cups mozzarella cheese, mayonnaise, Parmesan cheese, and pepper. Spoon mixture over basil mixture, spreading to evenly cover top. Bake 35 to 40 minutes. Yields 6 to 8 servings.

Crustless Spinach Quiche

3 ounces light cream cheese, softened
1 cup skim milk
Egg substitute equal to 4 eggs
¼ teaspoon pepper
3 cups shredded, reduced-fat
    Cheddar cheese
1 (10-ounce) package chopped spinach,
    thawed and squeezed dry
1 (10-ounce) package frozen chopped
    broccoli, thawed and drained
1 small onion, chopped
1 (4-ounce) can mushroom pieces

Preheat oven to 350°. In small mixing bowl, beat cream cheese, milk, egg substitute, and pepper. Beat until smooth. Stir in remaining ingredients. Transfer to 10-inch quiche pan coated with nonstick spray. Bake 55 to 60 minutes. Yields 6 to 8 servings.

BARRY'S GULL COTTAGE BED & BREAKFAST

116 Chesapeake Street
Dewey Beach, DE 19971
(302) 227-7000 (phone)
(302) 645-1575 (off-season)
innkeeper@gullcottage.com
www.gullcottage.com

Barry's Gull Cottage Bed & Breakfast is located one-and-a-half blocks from the Atlantic Ocean in Dewey Beach, Delaware. It is a contemporary Victorian beach house that won the "National Architects Award" when it was built in 1962 and selected the "Best Place to Stay" by the *Washingtonian* magazine and QVC poll. Romance is in the air and the innkeepers delight in pampering guests. Activities are all forms of water sports on the ocean and in the bay, along with fishing and whale/dolphin watching.

Chocolate LUV Cake

1 (18-ounce) box Devil's Food
    cake mix (do not prepare
    according to directions)
1 (3.4-ounce) box instant chocolate
    pudding mix (do not prepare
    according to directions)
3 eggs
½ cup canola oil
1¼ cups strong coffee or half bourbon
    and half coffee
2 cups chocolate chips

Preheat oven to 350°. Mix all ingredients except chips. Pour into greased Bundt pan and sprinkle with chocolate chips. Bake for 35 to 45 minutes. Yields 8 to 10 servings.

Delaware Corn Pudding

3 (15-ounce) cans cream-style corn
2 (15-ounce) cans whole kernel corn,
    drained
3 eggs, beaten
¼ cup sugar
2 tablespoons all-purpose flour
    to thicken
1 cup half-and-half or 2% milk

Preheat oven to 350°. Mix all ingredients and pour into sprayed 2-quart crock or casserole. Bake for 1 hour or until set. Serve hot. Yields 10 servings.

Baked Almond Pear Brie

1 round Brie
1 jar pear preserves
1 cup sliced, toasted almonds

Preheat oven to 350°. Scrape top rind of Brie, exposing the cheese. Spoon preserves over top of Brie. Add almonds and bake until soft and almonds golden. Do not overcook. Serve with water wafers or French bread. Yields up to 20 servings.

Delaware Sweet Cakes

1 (16-ounce) can creamed corn
1 (16-ounce) can whole kernel corn,
    drained
1 egg, beaten
1 tablespoon sugar
2 tablespoons canola oil
½ cup biscuit mix
1 cup half-and-half or 2% milk
Cinnamon sugar
Confectioners' sugar
Maple syrup

Mix corn, egg, sugar, oil, biscuit mix, and half-and-half. Batter will be loose like for crêpes. Butter hot grill and scoop batter to make a small cake two inches in diameter. Sprinkle with cinnamon sugar and grill to golden; turn and grill other side until golden. Sprinkle with confectioners' sugar for presentation. Serve with maple syrup. Yields 8 servings.

SEA WITCH MANOR INN & SPA

71 Lake Avenue
Rehoboth Beach, DE 19971
(302) 226-WITCH (phone)
(866) SEA-WITCH (toll free)
innkeeper@seawitchmanor.com
www.seawitchmanor.com

Fall back into the time of elegance and romance by the sea, quietude, charm, hospitality, comfort, and attention to detail. An adult-only bed and breakfast, we strive to be everything the discriminating traveler has come to expect. We have been selected by *Delaware Today* magazine as the 2002 Best of Delaware, *Delaware Bride's* 1st Choice, and we have been awarded AAA Three Diamond Awards. Our goal is to provide a quiet romantic year-round getaway for our guests. The Sea Witch sits on a beautiful, quiet tree-lined street that meets the sea. Victorian elegance and romance, the warmth of delicious food, and accommodations that marry character and comfort.

...itch Beer and Onion Pancakes

Pancakes:
4 tablespoons unsalted butter,
   plus more for cooking
   pancakes
½ Vidalia onion, chopped
1 cup beer, at room temperature
3 eggs
1 teaspoon vanilla extract
2 cups biscuit mix (recommended:
   Bisquick)
1 teaspoon ground cinnamon
1 teaspoon ground nutmeg

Syrup:
1 cup light brown sugar
¼ cup beer
¼ cup chopped walnuts
2 tablespoons unsalted butter
1 tablespoon maple syrup
¼ teaspoon ground cinnamon

For pancakes, heat butter in medium skillet over medium-high heat. Add onions and cook until softened, about 4 minutes. In mixing bowl whisk beer, eggs, and vanilla. Stir in onions and butter. Add biscuit mix, cinnamon, and nutmeg and stir just to combine. Let stand 3 to 5 minutes.

For syrup, combine all ingredients in small saucepan and bring to simmer, stirring. Remove from heat and keep warm. Heat large skillet over medium heat and add enough butter to coat well. Working in batches, pour ¼ cup of batter into skillet for each pancake. Cook until browned on bottom and bubbles begin to form on top. Turn pancakes and cook until browned on bottom. Add more butter between batches as needed. Serve immediately with syrup. Yields 4 servings.

Sea Witch Strata

5 tablespoons olive oil
1 large red onion sliced
6 scallions, white and green parts
   thinly sliced separately
1 each red, yellow, and orange bell
   peppers, roasted, peeled, and diced
½ pound fresh shiitake mushrooms,
   stemmed and caps sliced
½ pound fresh button mushrooms,
   stemmed and caps sliced
½ pound Portobello mushrooms,
   stemmed and caps sliced
8 large eggs or Eggbeaters
2 cups half-and-half
2 tablespoons chopped fresh thyme
1½ teaspoons salt
¾ teaspoon ground black pepper
1½ loaves challah bread sliced lengthwise
9 ounces soft fresh cream cheese
1 cup shredded sharp white and yellow
   Cheddar & Parmesan cheese
1 jar pepper & onion relish
   (Harry & David's)

Hollandaise sauce:
3 large egg yolks
1 tablespoon lemon juice
¼ plus ¼ cup firm butter

Preheat oven to 350°. Pour olive oil in large nonstick skillet over medium-high heat.

Add all onions and sauté for about 2 minutes. Add peppers and sauté until tender, about 8 minutes. Add mushrooms and sauté until tender, about 4 minutes. Season to taste and cool.

In bowl whisk together eggs, half-and-half, thyme, salt, and pepper. Coat 13 x 9 x 2-inch glass baking dish with nonstick spray. Cut ½-inch-thick slices from center portion of challah bread, reserving ends. Spread cream cheese on all bread slices.

Arrange half the bread slices in one layer in baking dish, squeezing them slightly to fit. Top with half the mushrooms mixture. Sprinkle half the Cheddar & Parmesan cheese on top. Pour half the egg mixture evenly over top. Repeat layering with remaining bread. Spread pepper and onion relish over top. Cover and refrigerate. Bring the Strata to room temperature before baking. Preheat oven to 350° and bake uncovered until puffed and edges are pale golden, about 60 minutes.

For hollandaise sauce, in saucepan vigorously stir egg yolks and lemon juice. Add ¼ cup butter and heat over very low heat, stirring constantly until butter is melted. Add remaining ¼ cup butter. Continue stirring vigorously until sauce thickens. Serve over strata. Yields 10 to 12 servings.

Easy Chocolate Chip Banana Bread

1 cup mashed ripe bananas
   (2 large bananas)
¾ cup sugar
¼ cup half-and-half
½ teaspoon vanilla extract
3 eggs
3 tablespoons olive oil
2 cups Bisquick
½ cup chocolate chips

Preheat oven to 350°. Grease 9 x 5 x 3-inch loaf pan. Combine bananas, sugar, half-and-half, vanilla, eggs, and olive oil. Stir in Bisquick and chocolate chips. Pour mixture into loaf pan and bake 50 to 60 minutes until toothpick comes out clean. Yields 1 loaf.

Florida

COQUINA GABLES OCEANFRONT BED & BREAKFAST

1 F Street
St. Augustine Beach, FL 32080-6915
(904) 461-8727
gables@aug.com
www.coquinagables.com

Situated on over an acre of oceanfront lawns and gardens, this home has been lovingly preserved since the early 1900s. Featuring cypress cathedral ceilings and detailed hardwood floors, the main house

offers three ocean-view king rooms. The private garden house offers three queen rooms, all with private baths. A gourmet breakfast and afternoon beverage are served in the main house great room. During the day enjoy the large pool, eight-person hot tub, a stroll on the beach, beach furniture and bikes, or a five-minute drive to historic St. Augustine.

Peaches and Cream French Toast

1 loaf French bread
5 eggs
1 cup half-and-half
2 tablespoons peach preserves
½ teaspoon nutmeg
2 (18- to 20-ounce) bags frozen peaches
½ cup sugar
1 teaspoon ground cinnamon
2 teaspoons cornstarch
Melted butter
Maple syrup
Whipped cream
    or confectioners' sugar for topping

Cut bread in 1-inch slices and lay in a 15 x 10-inch pan. Squeeze bread together to get about 14 to 16 slices. Beat together eggs, half-and-half, preserves, and nutmeg. Pour over bread, turning slices to coat both sides. Cover with plastic and refrigerate 8 to 10 hours or overnight. When ready to serve, preheat oven to 450°. Butter 15 x 10-inch pan. Mix peaches, sugar, cinnamon, and cornstarch and spread in pan. Top with bread slices and brush with butter. Bake 20 to 25 minutes, until golden brown. Place two pieces French toast on plate. Spoon peach sauce from pan over toast. Add maple syrup and dollop of whipped cream or confectioners' sugar. Garnish with whole strawberries and serve with ham, sausage, or bacon. Yields 7 to 8 servings.

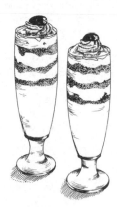

Granola and Yogurt Parfait

½ cup granola
½ cup strawberry yogurt
Sliced strawberries, bananas, and walnut
    halves for garnish

In parfait glass layer granola, then yogurt, twice. Garnish top with sliced strawberries, bananas, and walnut halves. Serve with a muffin and egg dish. Yields 1 serving.

Note: Crunchy granola with raisins and blended, creamy yogurt work best.

THE CURRY MANSION INN

511 Caroline Street
Key West, FL 33040
(305) 294-5349 (phone)
(305) 294-4093 (fax)
(800) 253-3466 (toll free)
www.currymansion.com

Nestled on the grounds of the former Curry estate in Key West, Florida, the Curry Mansion Inn offers guests a relaxed, yet luxurious setting, recalling the graciousness of an earlier era. Adjoining the mansion are elegant rooms surrounding a tropical courtyard and sun-drenched heated pool. The inn is located at the southern tip of the Florida Keys. A picturesque village of architectural gems and riotous tropical foliage, Key West also boasts some of the most sophisticated shops, restaurants, and entertainment anywhere in Florida. Fabulous Duval Street is less than half a block from the Curry Mansion Inn, and guests love exploring the Ernest Hemingway House Museum, the Audubon House, and the Mel Fisher Maritime Museum. Offshore lies the only living coral reef in North America with an abundance of opportunities for fishing, diving, and snorkeling.

Key Lime Pie

Key Lime Pie was first created in this house by Aunt Sally, a cook who worked for the Curry family in 1894.

4 eggs, separated
½ cup Key lime juice
1 (14-ounce) can sweetened condensed milk
1 graham cracker crust
¼ teaspoon cream of tartar
⅓ cup sugar

Preheat oven to 350°. Beat egg yolks until light and thick. Blend in lime juice, then condensed milk, stirring until mixture thickens. Pour mixture into piecrust. Beat egg whites with cream of tartar until stiff. Gradually beat in sugar, beating until glossy peaks form. Spread egg whites over surface of pie to edge of crust. Bake until golden brown, about 20 minutes. Chill before serving. Yields 8 servings.

GREYFIELD INN OF CUMBERLAND ISLAND, GEORGIA

Box 900
Fernandina Beach, FL 32035-0900
(904) 261-6408 (phone)
(904) 321-0666 (fax)
seashore@greyfieldinn.com
www.greyfieldinn.com

Greyfield Inn, a graceful mansion tucked away on Cumberland Island and accessible only by private ferry, offers guests the gracious elegance of a bygone era. The inn provides the perfect setting for lounging on a porch swing; bicycle riding along eighteen miles of unspoiled beaches; fishing in the surf; and learning about the island's fragile ecosystem on a wilderness tour with our staff naturalist.

Grilled Tuna Steaks with Tequila-Citrus Marinade

1 ounce tequila
Juice of 2 oranges
Juice of 4 limes
1 tablespoon chili powder
1 (8-ounce) can crushed pineapple

The Curry Mansion Inn

1 jalapeño pepper, seeded and diced
4 (8-ounce) tuna steaks, cut 1- to
   1½-inches thick
Salt and pepper
Black Bean and Mango Salsa
   (see recipe below)

Combine tequila, orange and lime juices, chili powder, pineapple, and jalapeño and mix well. Add tuna to marinade and refrigerate for 1 hour. Remove tuna from marinade, brush lightly with oil, and season with salt and pepper to taste. Over high heat, place steaks on grill and cook 2 to 3 minutes on each side. This will produce a steak that is crispy on the outside and cooked to rare on the inside. Serve with Black Bean and Mango Salsa. Yields 4 servings.

Black Bean & Mango Salsa

1 cup cooked black beans
1 small red onion, diced
1 red pepper, seeded and diced
¼ cup olive oil
2 ripe mangoes, peeled and diced
2 tablespoons minced garlic
Juice of 2 limes
¼ cup freshly chopped cilantro

Combine all ingredients in medium bowl. Toss gently and refrigerate. A few dashes of your favorite hot sauce can be added to increase the spicy flavor. Yields about 4 cups.

Honey-Mustard Sweet Potato Salad

2 pounds sweet potatoes
12 ounces fresh greens, collard, mustard,
   or spinach, rinsed and trimmed
4 ounces honey
2 ounces Dijon mustard
2 cloves garlic, minced

1 tablespoon allspice
1 teaspoon Kosher salt
½ teaspoon freshly cracked
   black pepper

Peel and cut sweet potatoes into ¾-inch cubes. Add potatoes to 6 quarts cold water. Bring to a boil. Continue cooking until soft. Drain and chill. Steam the greens until wilted. Chill and top with potatoes. Mix honey, mustard, garlic, allspice, salt, and pepper. Adjust flavor to personal taste. Toss with potatoes and greens. Yields 8 servings.

THE DRIFTWOOD INN

HC3 Box 982105
Mexico Beach, FL 32456
(850) 648-5126
peggy@driftwoodinn.com
www.driftwoodinn.com

The Driftwood Inn is located in the quiet little town of Mexico Beach, Florida. It is a beach Victorian-style establishment with a red tin roof and gingerbread details surrounding. There are fourteen in-house rooms, six apartment-style rooms, and four Victorian houses. The main office is lined with glass shelves filled with antique gift items. The inn itself sits directly on the beach with every room opening to the Gulf.

   The entire inn is encircled with lush gardens, beautiful statues, and benches and chairs for relaxing. The boardwalks (off the back of the motel) have covered areas featuring wooden swings and paths directly to the emerald-green waters and sugar-white sands.

   This is a one-of-a-kind inn, and its location in a town with no stoplights or com-

mercialization just puts icin
cake—a beautiful setting with
sand beaches.

Chicken Salad

6 boneless, skinless chicken breasts,
   cooked and chopped into small
   chunks
½ cup halved red grapes
½ cup halved white grapes
1 (20-ounce) can pineapple chunks,
   drained
½ cup raisins
1 (8-ounce) bottle poppy seed dressing

Mix all ingredients well and chill. Serve on a lettuce leaf and top with a fanned strawberry and a few slices of melon. Yields 12 servings.

Strawberry Dressing

¼ cup balsamic vinegar
¼ cup poppy seed dressing
12 large strawberries
3 kiwifruit, chopped
½ avocado
½ cup chopped pecans

Mix all ingredients together and chill for about 2 hours. Serve over a bed of romaine lettuce. Yields 6 servings.

The Azalea House Bed & Breakfast

220 Madison Street
Palatka, FL 32177
(386) 325-4547
azaleahouse@gbso.net
www.theazaleahouse.com

The 125–year-old Victorian Azalea House has six guest rooms. The inn is filled with needlework and boasts an onsite counted cross-stitch shop and pastry-chef owner. The Azalea House accommodations include six rooms on two floors. Within ninety minutes or less you can visit Daytona Beach, the Kennedy Space Center, and more.

The Azalea House Bed & Breakfast

Stuffed French Toast with Blueberry Topping

1 (1½-pound) loaf challah bread
8 ounces cream cheese
12 large eggs
3 cups half-and-half
½ cup maple syrup
10 tablespoons melted unsalted butter
Blueberry Topping

Cut bread into ½-inch cubes and scatter half the cubes in greased 11 x 14-inch baking dish. Cut cream cheese into chunks and scatter on top of bread. Cover with remaining bread cubes. Whip together eggs, half-and-half, maple syrup, and butter. Pour over bread, pushing down so bread gets soaked. Cover and refrigerate 8 to 10 hours or overnight. When ready to serve, preheat oven to 350°. Bake 35 to 40 minutes. Serve with Blueberry Topping (see next recipe). Yields 12 servings.

Blueberry Topping

1 quart blueberries
½ cup plus 4 tablespoons water
4 tablespoons sugar
2 tablespoons cornstarch

Place blueberries, ½ cup water, and sugar in saucepan. Cook over medium heat until mixture is boiling. Mix together 4 tablespoons water and cornstarch and add to blueberries while boiling. The mixture will thicken. Keep warm until ready to serve over French toast. Yields about 4 cups.

Azalea House Granola Chocolate Cherry Cookies

1½ cups coarsely chopped pecans
1½ cups dried tart cherries
1¾ cups granola with no added sugar
1¼ cups old-fashioned oatmeal
2½ cups semisweet chocolate chips
1 cup coconut
1⅜ cups all-purpose flour
1 teaspoon baking soda
1 teaspoon baking powder
½ teaspoon salt
1 cup (2 sticks) unsalted butter
¾ cup granulated sugar
1 cup firmly packed light brown sugar
2 large eggs
1 teaspoon vanilla extract

In large bowl, toss together the pecans, cherries, granola, oats, chocolate chips, and coconut. In small bowl, sift together flour, baking soda, baking powder, and salt. Soften butter, add sugars, and beat until smooth and creamy. Beat in eggs and vanilla until incorporated. On low speed of electric mixer, add flour mixture and beat in just until incorporated. Add granola mixture to batter and combine well. Preheat oven to 375°. On cookie sheets lined with parchment paper, place 1¾-inch-diameter balls of dough 2 inches apart.

Bake 12 to 15 minutes until golden around the edges but still soft in the middle. Yields 2 dozen cookies.

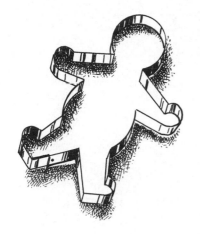

Individual Blueberry Cream Cheese Strudels

8 ounces cream cheese, softened
1 large egg
¼ cup sugar
2 tablespoons honey
1 teaspoon lemon juice
Pinch of nutmeg
14 sheets of phyllo dough, thawed
Melted butter
Breadcrumbs
Fresh blueberries

Mix together cream cheese, egg, sugar, honey, lemon juice, and nutmeg. Unroll phyllo. Take 1 sheet (keep phyllo covered with towel or and brush with melted butter and spr with breadcrumbs. Fold in half lengthwise. Place 2 tablespoons of cream cheese mixture on bottom of short side, leaving 1-inch edge on bottom and sides, and sprinkle with 12 blueberries. Turn up edge, fold in sides, and roll up. Place seamside down on parchment-lined cookie sheet. Repeat with remaining phyllo sheets and filling. Brush with melted butter. Preheat oven to 375° and bake for 15 minutes or until crisp and light brown. Yields 6 to 7 servings.

❧ ❧ ❧

THE VILLAGE INN BED & BREAKFAST

992 Ridge Avenue
Stone Mountain, GA 30083
(770) 469-3459 (phone)
(800) 214-8385 (toll free)
villageb@bellsouth.net

The Village Inn was built in the 1820s as a roadside inn. The Village is the oldest structure in historic Stone Mountain Village. The inn survived Sherman's fiery torch because of its use as a Confederate hospital during the Civil War. If these walls could talk, what stories they would have to tell. Completely renovated in 1995, the inn now offers guests six comfortable guest rooms with modern amenities. Each of the rooms is warmly decorated with period antiques. Indulge yourself in a reverie of yesteryear made complete by our present-day amenities. Soothe your senses before a blazing fire, while delighting in a delectable cup of steaming tea. Reflect on the flawless details that encompass you. Surrender your stresses and abandon your cares. Immerse yourself in swirling bath salt, surrounded by bubbles and candlelight. Guests enjoy complimentary snacks, beverages, and a full breakfast each morning.

Strawberries Romanoff French Toast

9 slices thick French bread
3 eggs
½ cup milk
1 tablespoon vanilla extract
2 cups crushed cornflakes cereal
4 tablespoons melted butter
Romanoff Sauce
⅔ cup sliced strawberries
6 sprigs fresh mint

Romanoff Sauce:
½ cup sour cream
1 cup heavy whipping cream
¼ cup confectioners' sugar
¼ to ½ cup spiced rum

Preheat oven to 450°. Cut each slice of bread diagonally to form 18 triangular pieces. Combine eggs, milk, and vanilla. Place cornflakes in pie pan. Dip each piece of bread into egg mixture and then into cornflakes, coating both sides. Place bread on cookie sheet that has been coated with nonstick spray. Drizzle butter over French toast. Bake 15 minutes or until crispy.

While French toast is baking, prepare Romanoff sauce. Whip sour cream, whipping cream, confectioners' sugar, and rum together. To serve arrange French toast on plate. Place strawberries on top of toast. Drizzle Romanoff Sauce over strawberries and toast. Top with sprig of mint. Yields 6 servings.

Raspberry Cheesecake Stuffed French Toast

4 eggs
¼ plus ½ cup sugar
½ cup milk
2 tablespoons vanilla extract
2 tablespoons ground cinnamon
4 ounces softened cream cheese
½ cup raspberry preserves
1 loaf French bread, sliced 1 inch thick
Confectioners' sugar
Grated nutmeg

Combine eggs, ¼ cup sugar, milk, vanilla, and cinnamon with a wire whisk. Combine softened cream cheese, remaining ½ cup sugar, and raspberry preserves with hand mixer. Slice each piece of bread almost in half horizontally. Using butter spreader, spread the raspberry filling in the middle of each slice. Dip each piece of bread into egg batter and place on hot griddle. Cook each side until golden brown. Arrange pieces on plate and sprinkle with confectioners' sugar and nutmeg. Yields 4 servings.

Harvest Bread

1 (15-ounce) can pumpkin purée
4 eggs
1 cup vegetable oil
⅔ cup water

3 cups sugar
3½ cups all-purpose flour
2 teaspoons baking soda
1½ teaspoons salt
¼ teaspoon cardamom
1 teaspoon ground cinnamon
1 teaspoon nutmeg
½ teaspoon ground cloves
¼ teaspoon ground ginger
¼ cup chopped pecans

Coat two 8 x 5-inch loaf pans with non-stick spray. Preheat oven to 350°. Mix together pumpkin, eggs, oil, water, and sugar. In separate bowl, whisk together flour, baking soda, salt, cardamom, cinnamon, nutmeg, cloves, and ginger. Stir dry ingredients into pumpkin mixture until just blended. Fold in pecans. Pour into pans. Bake about 50 minutes. Loaves are done when toothpick inserted in center comes out clean. Yields 2 loaves.

Cheesy Green Chile Grits

3 cups water
2 teaspoons salt
1 teaspoon pepper
2 tablespoons butter
¾ cup grits
½ cup milk
1 cup Cheddar cheese
1 (4½-ounce) can diced green chiles

Place water, salt, pepper, and butter in a saucepan over medium heat until the butter is melted. Add grits and stir very well. Reduce heat to low. Stir occasionally, breaking up any lumps until thickened. Add milk and continue to cook until desired consistency. Add cheese and mix until melted. Stir in chiles and pour into small ramekins. May serve with pat of butter and sprinkle of pepper on top. Yields 6 to 8 servings.

THE SKELTON HOUSE BED & BREAKFAST

97 Benson Street
Hartwell, GA 30643
(706) 376-7969 (phone)
(706) 856-3139 (fax)
skeltonhouse@hartcom.net
www.theskeltonhouse.com

The Skelton House is an 1896 Victorian house remodeled in 1996 and listed on the National Historic Register. It offers seven guest rooms with private baths and queen beds and a gourmet breakfast greets guests every morning. Activities in the area include: historic downtown Hartwell; Lake Hartwell, offering sailing, boating, skiing, and swimming; Hart State Park; Cateechee, an Audubon signature golf course; Hartwell Marina; Hart County Historical Society and Museum; Bluegrass Music Express; Ty Cobb memorial and museum, and the Hart County Community Theatre.

Skelton House Belgian Waffles

½ cup warm water
1 tablespoon dry yeast
2 cups lukewarm milk
½ cup vegetable oil
1 teaspoon salt
1 tablespoon sugar
2 cups all-purpose flour
2 eggs, beaten
1 teaspoon vanilla extract
¼ teaspoon baking soda
1½ cups sliced fresh peaches for topping (optional)
Whipped cream or maple syrup (optional)

Stir water and yeast together. Add milk, oil, salt, and sugar. Beat in flour. Let stand on countertop 8 to 10 hours or overnight. When ready to cook, stir in eggs, vanilla, and soda. Beat well. Bake on waffle iron until golden brown. Top with fresh peaches and whipped cream or hot buttered maple syrup. Yields 4 servings.

SHELLMONT INN

821 Piedmont Avenue
Atlanta, GA 30308
(404) 872-9290 (phone)
(404) 872-5379 (fax)
www.shellmont.com

Shellmont is a treasure chest of stained, leaded, and beveled glass. Impeccably restored. wicker-laden verandas overlook manicured lawns and gardens, including a Victorian fishpond. The inn is located near the Botanical Gardens, Margaret Mitchell house, High Museum of Art, and Piedmont Park to mention a few.

Blueberry Bread

1¾ cups sugar
3 cups all-purpose flour
1½ teaspoons baking soda
1 teaspoon salt
1 tablespoon ground cinnamon
4 eggs, beaten
1¼ cups vegetable oil
2 (10-ounce) bags frozen blueberries, drained

Preheat oven to 350°. Mix all dry ingredients. Add eggs and oil, mixing well after each addition. Add blueberries. Coat two loaf pans with nonstick spray. Pour mixture into pan. Bake 1 hour. Yields 2 loaves.

Victorian Raspberry Treats

1 cup all-purpose flour
1 teaspoon baking powder
½ teaspoon salt
1 stick butter, softened
1 plus 1 egg, beaten
1 tablespoon milk
1 (12-ounce) jar seedless raspberry jam
1 stick butter, melted
1 cup sugar
1 cup coconut

Preheat oven to 325°. Coat 11 x 7-inch pan with nonstick spray. Blend flour, baking powder, and salt. Add softened butter, 1 beaten egg, and milk. Beat until smooth. Spread mixture into pan. Spread jam on dough. Mix melted butter, sugar, coconut, and remaining beaten egg. Spread on top of jam. Bake 35 minutes or until golden. Cool and cut into squares. Yields 14 to 16 servings.

Chicken and Dressing Casserole

1 (8-ounce) package cornbread dressing
1 stick butter, melted
1 cup chicken broth
½ cup chopped onion
½ cup chopped celery
½ cup mayonnaise
2½ cups chopped chicken
1 egg
1 cup milk
1 (10¾-ounce) can cream of
   chicken soup

Mix dressing, butter, broth, onion, celery, mayonnaise, and chicken. Mix egg and milk together. Put dressing in greased 9 x 12-inch pan. Pour egg mixture over dressing. Refrigerate 8 to 10 hours or overnight. When ready to cook, preheat oven to 325°. Pour soup on top and bake 45 minutes. Yields 4 to 6 servings.

Bakeless Fruitcake

½ pound graham cracker crumbs
½ pound dates, finely chopped
1 cup whipping cream
½ pound marshmallows, finely chopped
1 cup chopped pecans
10 maraschino cherries
8 ounces candied mixed fruit

Mix all ingredients. Line loaf pan with wax paper. Pour mixture into 8 x 4-inch pan and press firmly. Cover and refrigerate overnight or longer. Serve sliced with additional whipped cream and sprigs of holly. Yields 10 to 12 servings.

THE BELLAIRE HOUSE

1234 Bellaire Drive, NE
Atlanta, GA 30319
(404) 262-1173 (phone)
(404) 262-1174 (fax)
bellairedrive@aol.com

Located in the upscale Buckhead area, the Bellaire House replaces the hurried hotel with a cozy, comfortable bedroom, antiques, and a morning treat served on china and silver. Located near Atlanta's famous Phipps Plaza, Lenox Square Shopping Center, and the best restaurants in town, the Bellaire is convenient to the MARTA rail line.

Bellaire House Sock-It-To-Me Coffee Cake

1 (18-ounce) box yellow cake mix
1 cup sour cream
4 eggs
½ cup granulated sugar
⅔ cup vegetable oil
1 plus 1 tablespoon vanilla extract
1 cup pecan pieces
¼ cup brown sugar
2 tablespoons ground cinnamon
½ cup milk
¼ cup confectioners' sugar

Preheat oven to 350°. Grease and flour Bundt pan. In large bowl, combine cake mix, sour cream, eggs, granulated sugar, oil, 1 tablespoon vanilla, and pecans. In separate bowl, mix brown sugar and cinnamon. In small bowl mix the milk, confectioners' sugar, and remaining tablespoon vanilla. Pour half cake batter into Bundt

The Bellaire House

pan and sprinkle cinnamon sugar mixture over batter, avoiding edges of Bundt pan. Add remaining batter. Bake for 40 to 45 minutes. After cooling, turn cake onto cake plate and top with confectioners' sugar glaze. Yields 8 servings.

BONNIE CASTLE BED & BREAKFAST

2 Post Street
P.O. Box 359
Grantville, GA 30220
(770) 583-3090 (phone/fax)
bocastle@mindspring.com
www.bonnie-castle.com

Bonnie Castle Bed & Breakfast is a refurbished, 1896 brick and granite Victorian mansion in downtown Grantville. Restored in 1992, the Castle is still a step back in time so guests can enjoy simpler days when the veranda was the place to pass the time and relax. A favorite place for honeymooners to start their lives—in a castle. Full southern breakfast is served on china and crystal each morning. The Castle is convenient to Atlanta, Warm Springs, Callaway Gardens, and Pine Mountain.

Castle Breakfast Potatoes

2 to 3 tablespoons extra virgin olive oil
1 to 2 teaspoons minced garlic
2 cups diced, cooked potatoes
    with skins on
1 tablespoon freshly chopped rosemary
Kosher salt
Black pepper

In skillet, heat oil and add garlic and potatoes. Stir frequently until potatoes start to brown and add rosemary, salt and pepper to taste. When potatoes are browned, place on platter or "country" bowl and serve hot with a sprig of fresh rosemary. Yields 2 to 4 servings.

Castle Cheese Eggs

Our guests always wonder how the eggs got the tang.

10 to 12 large eggs
¼ cup water
1 tablespoon butter
½ (8-ounce) package cream
    cheese, diced
Chives (optional)

Whip eggs and water in bowl. Heat skillet and melt butter. Add eggs and let the bottom set slightly. Stir and gently fold in cream cheese. Finish cooking eggs. The texture is a little different, so do not overcook. Place on serving dish with chives or your favorite herb, and salt and pepper to taste. Serve hot. Yields 6 servings.

Bonnie Castle Angel Flake Biscuits

3 cups all-purpose flour
1 tablespoon baking powder
1 teaspoon salt
1 teaspoon baking soda
¼ cup sugar
1½ teaspoons bread-making yeast
1 cup butter-flavored shortening
2 cups low-fat buttermilk

Stir flour, baking powder, salt, baking soda, sugar, and yeast together. Cut in shortening until size of small peas. Make a well in center and add buttermilk. This forms a very light batter; cover and refrigerate 8 to 10 hours or overnight. When ready to bake, preheat oven to 400°. On well-floured board, place as much batter as you will need for that meal and knead, incorporating flour as needed to make firm, non-sticky ball. Pat out with hand to about ¼ inch and cut out biscuits. Place on clay baking dish or lightly greased cookie sheet. Bake 12 to 15 minutes until brown. Yields 24 biscuits and will keep in refrigerator for seven days so you can have fresh biscuits every morning.

THE STOVALL HOUSE

1526 Highway 255N
Sautee, GA 30571
(706) 878-3355
info@stovallhouse.com
www.stovallhouse.com

This 1837 country farmhouse is located in the historic Sautee Valley. It was restored in 1983 as a country inn and retreat for its guests to escape from the rigors of their normal lifestyles. Whether staying as a guest or just enjoying a creative dinner with a fresh difference, it's a country experience.

The Stovall House is located in one of the top one hundred, small arts communities in the U.S. The Sautee-Nacoochee Arts Center is one mile from the inn and has a gallery featuring local art in all media, a museum with Indian artifacts, gold mining and logging exhibits, and a theater featuring music and drama performances throughout the year. We offer dinner and theater packages for events at the Center.

❧   ❧   ❧

Tomato Soup

1½ cups olive oil
2 cups chopped onions
3 cups chopped celery
½ cup all-purpose flour
2 quarts water
1 (46-ounce) can V-8 juice
4 (26½-ounce) cans (13 cups) whole
    peeled tomatoes
2 tablespoons parsley
2 tablespoons sugar
1 teaspoon thyme
½ teaspoon pepper
2 bay leaves
1 tablespoon basil
Parmesan cheese

In skillet heat oil over medium and sauté onions and celery. Stir in flour until well mixed. Add water and vegetable juice and mix. Grind tomatoes and add to liquid. Add parsley, sugar, thyme, pepper, bay leaves, and basil. Simmer to let flavors blend. Remove bay leaves before serving. Serve in cups or bowls and garnish with Parmesan cheese. Yields about 8 quarts, 32 (1-cup) servings.

Stuffed Chicken Breasts

1 pound (16 ounces) cream cheese
1 tablespoon basil
1 tablespoon chives
1 tablespoon chopped garlic
8 (6- to 8-ounce) boneless, skinless
    chicken breasts
All-purpose flour
Egg wash
Herbed breadcrumbs
Canola cooking oil

Soften cream cheese and add basil, chives, and garlic, mixing well. Trim chicken breasts and cut a pocket in each. Stuff with heaping tablespoon of herb mixture. Dredge each breast in flour. Dip in the egg wash and roll in the breadcrumbs. In large skillet add 3 tablespoons oil and sauté breasts until browned (no more than four at one time). Preheat oven to 350°. Place sautéed breasts on greased baking pan and bake for about 20 minutes. Yields 8 servings.

Apple-Praline Pie

1½ cups sugar
¼ cup all-purpose flour
½ teaspoon nutmeg
½ teaspoon ground cinnamon
2 eggs, beaten
½ cup (1 stick) melted margarine
1 teaspoon vanilla extract
3 cups peeled and chopped apples
1 deep-dish unbaked pie shell
½ cup chopped pecans

Preheat oven to 375°. Mix sugar, flour, nutmeg, and cinnamon. Add eggs, margarine, and vanilla. Stir in apples and pour filling into pie shell. Sprinkle pecans on top and bake 40 minutes. Yields 1 pie, 6 to 8 servings.

THE INN AT FOLKSTON

509 West Main Street
Folkston, GA 31537
(912) 496-6256 (phone/fax)
(888) 509-6246 (toll free)
info@innatfolkston.com
www.innatfolkston.com

The Inn at Folkston is a luxurious, yet comfortable, 1920s bungalow with four spacious and uniquely decorated guest rooms. Situated on two acres in Folkston, Georgia—gateway to the Okefenokee Swamp—the inn is a perfect destination for romantic getaways, nature tours and boating, business travelers, and train watching.

Individual Georgia Peach Pancakes

2 eggs
½ cup all-purpose flour
½ cup milk
Pinch of salt
3 teaspoons butter
2 Georgia peaches (only the best
    for this recipe)
Confectioners' sugar
Maple syrup
Whipped cream
Ground cinnamon
Mint sprigs

Preheat oven to 450°. Beat together eggs, flour, milk, and salt with a whisk until very smooth. Melt about a teaspoon of butter in each of three (6-inch) iron skillets to coat bottom. As soon as butter begins to sizzle, pour one-third of the batter (about ½ cup) into each skillet and put skillets in oven. Bake until pancakes are brown and crisp, about 15 to 20 minutes. Pancakes will puff up as they cook. Remove from oven.

Remove pancakes from skillets and set them on individual plates (they will not stick to the skillet if you poured the batter into hot, buttered skillets). Peel and slice peaches and divide among pancakes. (For color, add blueberries or raspberries.) Sprinkle confectioners' sugar over rims of pancakes. Pour maple syrup on the side for your sweet tooth. Top each pancake with spoonful of whipped cream, cinnamon, and sprig of mint. Yields 3 servings.

Note: Add any combination of fresh fruits on hand. The more color in the combination of fruits, the better. But most importantly, the quality of fruit makes or breaks this dish.

Georgia Pecan Chocolate Chip Cookies

1⅓ cups soft butter
1 cup granulated sugar
1 cup packed brown sugar
2 eggs
1 teaspoon vanilla extract
3¾ cups all-purpose flour
1 teaspoon baking soda
1 cup chopped Georgia pecans
2 cups chocolate chips

Preheat oven to 350°. Mix together butter, sugars, eggs, and vanilla until thoroughly mixed. Add flour and baking soda, mixing well. Add pecans and chocolate chips until well combined. Drop by spoonfuls onto cookie sheet. Bake 9 to 12 minutes. Remove to racks to cool. As with all chocolate cookies, do not overbake. Yields about 3 dozen cookies.

Mandarin Orange Yogurt Fruit Cup

1 (8-ounce) carton mandarin orange
    yogurt
1 (8¼-ounce) can mandarin oranges
Fresh blueberries
2 mint sprigs

Divide yogurt between two glass fruit cups. Top each with about five mandarin orange sections and a few fresh blueberries. Top with a sprig of mint (or an edible flower from your garden). Yields 2 servings.

THE LODGE ON LITTLE ST. SIMONS ISLAND

P.O. Box 21078
Little St. Simons Island, GA 31522
(912) 638-7472 (phone)
(912) 634-1811 (fax)
(888) 733-5774 (toll free)
LSSI@mindspring.com
www.LittleStSimonsIsland.com

At The Lodge on Little St. Simons Island, the pristine barrier island setting and the food are inseparably linked. To dine on Little St. Simons Island is not just to experience the tastes of this low-country southern island, but to immerse oneself in the culture, history, and beautiful surroundings the island has to offer. One of the richest estuaries in the United States surrounds Little St. Simons Island in miles of salt marshes, rivers, and tidal creeks, all feeding into the Atlantic Ocean. These bountiful natural resources spawned what is commonly known as low-country cuisine, rich in local ingredients and drawing heavily from the surrounding waters for a variety of seafood and shellfish.

Mealtime gatherings on Little St. Simons highlight traditions that date back to the early 1900s. Today, with no more than thirty overnight guests on the island at any one time, meals remain social occasions. A cast-iron bell still alerts guests to gather.

Low-Country Boil

A Low-Country favorite, this is a great feast to serve on picnics, barge cruises or in your own dining room. Be sure to have plenty of napkins on hand!

Cayenne
Cloves
Garlic
Bay leaves
Old Bay seasoning
Black pepper
Tabasco sauce
3 tablespoons lemon juice or vinegar
3 small new potatoes
1 carrot cut into fourths
½ pound kielbasa
2 small onions
1 ear of corn
1 to 2 crabs (optional)
½ pound raw shrimp in shell

Boil water (about 1 quart) in very large steam kettle on stove or on outdoor cooker. Season water to taste. Add lemon juice or vinegar. Add potatoes, carrots, sausage and onions. Bring back to a boil and boil until almost tender. Add corn and crabs, if using, and boil 5 minutes longer. Add shrimp and simmer 3 to 4 minutes more, or until shrimp are just cooked. Enjoy with corn bread, slaw and watermelon. Yields 2 to 3 servings.

Old South Blackberry Cobbler

¼ pound (1 stick) unsalted butter
¾ cup whole milk
1 cup all-purpose flour
1 plus ½ cup sugar
2 teaspoons baking powder
8 cups blackberries

Preheat oven to 350°. Melt butter in 9 x 12-inch baking pan. Beat together milk, flour, 1 cup sugar, and baking powder. Pour batter over butter. Sprinkle berries over batter. Sprinkle remaining ½ cup sugar over berries. Bake about 1 hour. Yields about 4 servings.

Tomato-Date Chutney

Chutney, relishes, and chow-chow are traditional on Low-County dining tables—a testament to the influence of the slave and spice trade on Southern cuisine.

2 teaspoons olive oil
1 tablespoon mustard seeds
1 cup finely diced onion
2 cups peeled, diced tomatoes
2 cups chopped, pitted dates
Hot sauce

Heat oil over medium and sauté mustard seeds until they darken and "pop." Add diced onion and cook until translucent. Add tomatoes, dates, and hot sauce to taste. Simmer slowly 1 hour. Cool and refrigerate. Serve at room temperature with fish, pork, or rice and vegetables. Yields about 4 cups (8 servings).

Gazpacho

One of our favorite ways to cool down on a warm summer day is with Chef Charles' homemade gazpacho, which serves as a zesty starter for one of our delicious beach picnics.

6 large ripe tomatoes
2 sweet red peppers
2 medium-size Vidalia onions
2 large shallots
2 large cucumbers
½ cup balsamic vinegar
½ cup olive oil
1 (14½-ounce) can tomato juice
½ cup chopped fresh dill
Pinch of cayenne
Salt and ground pepper
1 bunch scallions, chopped
½ cup sour cream

Wash and prepare vegetables. Core and coarsely chop tomatoes; save juice. Core, seed, and coarsely chop red peppers. Peel and coarsely chop onions and shallots. Peel, seed, and coarsely chop cucumbers. In bowl, whisk together vinegar, olive oil, reserved tomato juice and canned tomato juice. In food processor slightly purée* the vegetables in small batches, adding tomato juice mixture as necessary to keep blades from sticking. Stir in dill and cayenne, salt, and pepper to taste. Cover and chill 4 hours. To serve, stir, taste and correct seasoning if necessary. Ladle into chilled soup bowls or mugs. Garnish with crisp fresh scallion and teaspoon of sour cream. Yields 6 to 8 servings.

*Note: Gazpacho should retain some of its crunch.

HISTORIC BANNING MILLS

205 Horseshoe Dam Road
Whitesburg, GA 30185
(770) 834-9149 (phone)
(770) 214-3729 (fax)
(866) 447-8688 (toll free)
info@historicbanningmills.com
www.historicbanningmills.com

Historic Banning Mills is located on eighty unique, secluded acres on one-hundred-foot-wide Snake Creek with two hundred years of history. Explore the ruins. Enjoy wonderful cuisine prepared by an award-winning chef. The Mills specializes in romantic getaways, business, and church retreats. It is forty-five minutes from Atlanta with its myriad of activities, including Six Flags over Georgia and Stone Mountain. Visit local attractions such as the West William McIntosh State Park and Reserve; the Susan Haywood Memorial; numerous golf courses; historic Carrolton and Newnan with lots of antique shopping just eight miles away. Stop in at world famous Sprayberry's Barbecue, in operation since World War II, where GIs on their way to Fort Benning would stop to eat.

Whole Roasted Rib-Eye of Beef

3 to 4 pound rib-eye roast
    (½ pound per person)
Balsamic or red wine vinegar
½ cup kosher salt
    (if using table salt, use ⅓ cup)
3 tablespoons ground black pepper
¼ cup dried rosemary
¼ cup dried thyme leaves
    (2 tablespoons if using
    powdered thyme)
¼ cup granulated garlic

Let roast come to room temperature for about 1 hour before roasting. Preheat oven to 450°. Trim off a good bit of visible fat, but leave some to give flavor and moisture to roast. Rub roast on all sides with balsamic or red wine vinegar. Combine remaining ingredients. Coat roast on all sides with the dry mix. Store unused portion in airtight container for up to two weeks. Place on rack in roasting pan or on baking sheet. Spray lightly with nonstick spray and place in oven. After 20 minutes turn oven temperature down to 350° and continue roasting until internal temperature reaches 130° in thickest part of roast, about 1 hour 15 minutes. Remove from oven, cover loosely with foil, and let rest 15 minutes before slicing and serving. The roast should continue to cook to about 150° or so; this will give you medium-done meat, depending upon the thickness of the roast where you are slicing. Yields 6 to 8 servings.

Note: Cooking time will vary depending on quality of meat, thickness, and amount of fat in the roast.

Chicken Salad

2 pounds boneless, skinless chicken
    breasts or chicken tenders
¾ cup mayonnaise
2½ teaspoons white vinegar
1 tablespoon chopped onion
¼ cup chopped celery
1¼ teaspoons salt
1¼ teaspoons granulated garlic
¼ teaspoon ground black pepper
1 hard-cooked egg, chopped

Place chicken in pot of cold water. Bring to a boil, reduce heat, and let simmer until cooked through, approximately 12 minutes. Chicken should be white all the way through. Drain and place chicken in ice water to stop the cooking process (known as "shocking"). When completely cool, drain well and cut into desired-size pieces, removing any fat or tendons. Combine mayonnaise and vinegar. Combine chicken, onion, celery, salt, garlic, and pepper in mixing bowl. Gently fold in egg and mayonnaise. Cover and refrigerate. Yields 4 servings.

Chicken Noodle Soup

3 whole chickens
1½ gallons water
1½ cups margarine
1½ cups all-purpose flour
1 tablespoon granulated garlic
1 tablespoon black pepper
2 teaspoons onion powder
½ cup chicken base
16 ounces fettuccine, cut in
    1-inch pieces
1 bunch green onions, chopped in
    ⅛-inch pieces

Cook chickens in water until tender. Remove and pull meat from bones, removing fat. Chop into ¼-inch pieces and add back to broth. In a separate pan melt margarine and add flour while stirring. Add garlic, pepper, and onion powder. Cook 5 minutes until blond in color. Add chicken base to roux, stirring, and then add roux to broth. Bring to a boil to thicken. Stir in fettuccine and green onions. Yields about 8 quarts, 16 (2-cup) servings.

Banana Pudding

2 eggs, beaten
2½ cups milk
½ cup sugar
2 tablespoons cornstarch
¼ teaspoon salt
1 teaspoon vanilla extract
1 tablespoon margarine
32 vanilla wafers
4 bananas, sliced

In double boiler over simmering water, combine eggs, milk, sugar, cornstarch, and salt. Stir constantly and cook until thick, 10 to 15 minutes. Remove from heat and stir in vanilla and margarine. Place 16 wafers in glass serving dish. Top with half the bananas. Top with half the pudding. Repeat layers. Serve immediately or refrigerate until serving. Yields 4 servings.

Hawaii

MARA'S DIVE BED & BREAKFAST

P.O. Box 4
Captain Cook, HI 96704
(808) 328-8373 (phone)
(877) 627-2348 (toll free)
mara@marasdive.com
www.marasdive.com

Mara's Dive is a comfortable and affordable bed and breakfast in the green, coffee hills of Mauna Loa overlooking South Kona's magnificent Pacific Ocean. "PADI Scuba" certifications; introductory dives; snorkeling; kayak and dive tours; and more are all just down the road from our great place to stay and watch the sunset. Accommodations include diver's continental breakfast, sunset lanai and barbecue, indoor and outdoor showers, and cable TV. A short drive down our winding road takes you to an awesome variety of shore diving sites, including the well-known site of the Captain Cook Monument in Kealakekua Bay Marina. Many other recreational areas are within reach, including beautiful gray sand beaches, the Kona Historical Museum and the Greewell Ethnobotanical Gardens.

Kona Coffee Banana Bread

Butter for greasing pan
Sesame seeds
1 cup softened butter
1⅓ cups brown Hawaiian sugar
3 eggs, room temperature
2 teaspoons vanilla extract
¼ teaspoon almond extract
2 cups unbleached all-purpose flour
2 cups whole wheat flour
1 teaspoon salt
½ teaspoon baking soda
3 teaspoons baking powder
¼ teaspoon nutmeg
2 teaspoons ground cinnamon
1½ cups ripe mashed bananas soaked
   in ⅔ cup 100% Kona coffee
¾ cup chopped Macadamia nuts
¾ cup raisins

Preheat oven to 350°. Butter two loaf pans generously and sprinkle with sesame seeds (they will stick). Beat in large bowl butter and sugar. Add eggs one at a time and then the extracts. Beat until light in color. In separate bowl blend together flours, salt, baking soda, baking powder, nutmeg, and cinnamon. Add flour mixture and bananas alternately to wet ingredients, starting and ending with dry. Mix each addition gently to combine; do not overbeat. Add nuts and raisins. Divide batter into two loaf pans and bake 1 hour. Toothpick will come out clean when done. Cool in pan for 10 minutes; then remove and cool on rack to finish. Yields 2 loaves.

WAIPIO WAYSIDE INN

P.O. Box 840
Honokaa, HI 96727
(808) 775-0275 (phone)
(800) 833-8849 (toll free)
wayside@bigisland.net
www.waipiowayside.com

Located on the temperate northeastern coast of the Island of Hawaii, Waipio Wayside Inn's location is ideal for the Hawaii visitor. The Inn is located just minutes from Historic Waipio Valley and its mile-long black sand beach. It's also centrally located to Kona, Hilo, and Volcano National Park. This historic 1932 sugar plantation is set in a tropical garden of fruit and nut trees, and brilliant-flowering, sweet-smelling shrubs. Extensive decks offer panoramic views of the Hamakua Coast of the Island of Hawaii.

Waipio Wayside Signature Chocolate Cake

4 tablespoons butter
1 tablespoon Hawaiian White honey

2 tablespoons Ohana Plantation
  pepper jelly
2 tablespoons cream or "fruit brandy"
¼ cup all-purpose flour
½ cup Macadamia nuts
¼ teaspoon baking soda
Pinch of salt
1 plus ½ cup chocolate chips
1 small egg

Preheat oven to 310°. Line bottom of 6-inch springform pan with parchment paper. Bring butter, honey, jelly, and cream to a boil for 1 minute. Cool for 10 minutes. In a separate bowl, use food processor to pulse chop flour, nuts, soda, and salt 3 to 5 times and set syrup mixture aside. Mix 1 cup of chocolate chips into warm syrup mixture and process it 10 seconds. Add small egg and process 5 seconds. Pulse the syrup mixture, nut mixture, and remaining ½ cup of chocolate chips 3 to 4 times. Spread into prepared pan and cook 50 minutes or until center of the cake is done. Check with cake tester, it should come out clean. (Do not overcook.) Yields 1 cake.

HALE LANI BED & BREAKFAST

283 Aina Lani Place
Kapaa, Kauai, HI 96746
(808) 823-6434
innkeeper@halelani.com
www.halelani.com

Hale Lani is a luxurious bed and breakfast in the heart of Kauai, Hawaii. Four suites, each uniquely decorated in island themes, and with private entrances, full baths, kitchens, and hot tubs await the visitor seeking tranquility in paradise. Your day begins with a delicious breakfast delivered every morning and ends with a relaxing soak under the stars in your own hot tub.

Note: The honey can be ordered from www.volcanoislandhoney.com and the jelly from www.ohanaplantation.com.

Zesty Hawaiian Scallops

3 tablespoons olive oil
16 ounces mushrooms, cleaned
  and quartered
2 large onions, peeled and quartered
2 bell peppers, washed and quartered
2 slicing tomatoes, washed and quartered
24 sea scallops
3 avocados
2 cups sour cream
2 cups salsa

Heat oil in skillet over medium heat. Sauté vegetables. Charbroil scallops on outdoor grill or stove top, 3 minutes per side. (Be careful not to overcook.) Arrange scallops and vegetables on serving plate in a single layer. Slice avocados in strips and arrange on top of scallops and vegetables. Drizzle sour cream over top of plate. Serve with salsa of your choice on the side. Yields 6 servings.

Fabulous Frittata

1 plus 1 tablespoon vegetable oil
½ cup chopped onion
½ cup mushrooms, green pepper,
  or other vegetable
6 large eggs
½ cup ham
½ plus ½ cup grated Swiss
  or Cheddar cheese

Preheat oven to 350°. Heat 1 tablespoon oil in skillet over medium heat and sauté onions and vegetables until soft. Mix eggs, ham, and ½ cup cheese. Add remaining tablespoon oil to pan and add egg mixture. Cook over medium heat until egg mixture is slightly firm on sides but soft in middle. Remove skillet from heat, add remaining cheese and place in oven. Be careful not to disturb egg mixture. Cook approximately 10 minutes until eggs fluff and cheese turns light brown. Remove from oven and let cool about 5 minutes before serving. Garnish and serve. Yields 3 to 4 servings.

Potato Bacon Casserole

4 cups frozen shredded hash browns
½ cup finely diced onion
12 cooked bacon slices
1 cup shredded Cheddar
  or Swiss cheese
12 ounces evaporated milk
2 large eggs
Salt and pepper

Preheat oven to 350°. Layer half of potatoes, onion, bacon, and cheese in lightly greased baking dish. Repeat layers. Combine evaporated milk, eggs, and salt and pepper to taste. Pour egg mixture over layers. Cover and bake 50 to 60 minutes. Uncover and bake 5 to 10 minutes to brown mixture. Let cool 15 minutes before serving. Garnish and serve with a side of fresh fruit. Yields 4 servings.

HAWAIIAN OASIS BED & BREAKFAST

74-4958 Kiwi Street
Kailu-Kona, HI 96740
(808) 327-1701
info@hawaiianoasis.com
www.hawaiianoasis.com

Hawaiian Oasis Bed & Breakfast is a hidden gem located on the Big Island of Hawaii in Kailua-Kona. It is located on two acres of lush tropical landscaping including over fifty varieties of palms, fragrant tropical flowers, waterfalls, koi ponds, and fruit orchards where guests can help themselves to strawberry papaya, limes, passionfruit, cherimoya and pineapple. Hawaiian Oasis has almost everything the active or laid-back traveler could desire: a forty-foot lap pool, hot tub, tennis court, workout room, and an assortment of beach gear including snorkels, masks, fins, boogie boards, and beach chairs.

Oasis Tropical Loaves

It's our most requested recipe of all times.

> 2½ cups all-purpose flour
> 2½ teaspoons ground cinnamon
> 1 tablespoon baking powder
> 1½ cups sugar
> ½ teaspoon salt
> ¼ cup shredded coconut
> ½ cup chopped dried apricots or
>   golden raisins
> ¼ cup chopped dried mango
> ¼ cup chopped dried papaya
> ⅛ cup chopped dried ginger
>   (or any dried fruit)
> ⅜ cup chopped macadamia nuts
>   (or nuts of your choice)
> 3½ eggs (room temperature)
> 1¼ teaspoons vanilla extract
> 1¼ cups canola oil
>   (or applesauce for low-fat)
> 1 cup cubed mango
> ¼ cup crushed pineapple

Preheat oven to 350°. Grease and flour 5 small (6 x 3 x 2-inch) loaf pans. Sift together the flour, cinnamon, baking powder, sugar, and salt in large bowl. (Sifting will aerate and lighten flour to help prevent an overly compact texture.) Add the dried fruit and nuts. Mix thoroughly and set aside. Mix together the eggs, vanilla, oil, mango, and pineapple. Add the dry ingredients to the wet ingredients and stir only until the batter is thoroughly blended. (Mixing less helps the batter rise appropriately.) Pour into the prepared pans and bake on the middle rack of oven 30 to 45 minutes, or until a toothpick inserted in the center of the loaves comes out clean. (Once mixed get into the oven right away. The ingredients will start reacting right away with each other and need to get into the heat. Try to avoid opening the oven as much as possible.) Remove from the oven and let cool in pan 5 minutes, then turn on wire rack and let cool completely. Yields 5 small loaves.

Note: The loaves freeze wonderfully for up to a month.

The Maples Bed & Breakfast

P.O. Box 1
Star, ID 83669
(208) 286-7419 (phone)
(877) 286-7419 (toll free)
maplesbb@mindspring.com
www.mindspring.com/maplesbb

The Maples Bed & Breakfast, an 1888 farmhouse located in Star, Idaho, offers the best of a small town location and proximity to the state capitol. Area attractions include the state capitol, State Historical Museum, State Art Museum, World Center for Birds of Prey, Idaho Shakespeare Theater, and Boise Zoo. Boise State University, Northwest Nazarene University, and Albertson's College are all close by. Desert, canyon, and mountain day trips are all options from this location. White-water rafting, tubing, fishing, skiing, snowmobiling, golfing, and other sports abound.

Basque Breakfast

4 Basque chorizo sausages, casing
    removed and diced
4 Idaho baking potatoes, diced
1 large onion, chopped
8 large eggs
Salsa

Place diced chorizo in frying pan and fry on medium until begins to draw grease. Add potatoes and onion; stir and cover. Check and stir periodically. When potatoes are almost done, make eight depressions in surface of mixture with gravy ladle. Break an egg into each depression. Cover and continue cooking until eggs are done. Serve with salsa. Yields 4 to 6 servings.

Note: This recipe is also wonderful done in a Dutch oven while camping.

Maples Muffins

4 English muffins, split and toasted
8 large eggs
2 tablespoons water
1 tablespoon finely chopped
    fresh parsley
½ cup chopped fresh mushrooms
½ cup crabmeat
2 tablespoons butter
½ cup shredded Cheddar cheese
½ cup shredded Monterey Jack cheese

Coat broiler pan with nonstick spray. Place muffins split side up on pan and toast under broiler. Mix eggs, water, parsley, mushrooms, and crabmeat in bowl. Melt butter in coated frying pan. Pour egg mixture into frying pan and scramble. Divide egg mixture evenly among the toasted muffin halves. Mix the two cheeses together and put on top of egg mixture. Place under the broiler just until the cheese melts. Serve immediately. Yields 4 servings.

Gingerbread Waffles with Lemon Sauce

Waffles:
¼ cup (½ stick) butter
½ cup firmly packed light brown sugar
½ cup light corn syrup
2 large eggs, separated
1 cup milk
2 cups all-purpose flour
1½ teaspoons baking powder
1 teaspoon ground ginger
¼ teaspoon ground cloves
¼ teaspoon salt
1 teaspoon ground cinnamon

Lemon Custard Sauce:
3 large eggs
1 cup sugar
¼ cup fresh lemon juice
1 teaspoon grated lemon zest
Dash of salt
2 tablespoons melted butter

Preheat waffle iron. Cream together the butter and brown sugar. Beat in the corn syrup, egg yolks, and milk. Sift dry ingredients together and add to the liquid mixture. Making sure beaters are completely clean, beat egg whites until soft peaks form. Fold egg whites into batter. Pour batter into waffle iron and bake until waffles are golden brown.

For Lemon Custard Sauce, using electric mixer, beat eggs and sugar until thick and pale yellow. Beat in remaining ingredients. Pour mixture into the top of a double boiler and cook, stirring over simmering water about 15 minutes, or until mixture is slightly thickened and coats a spoon. Serve with waffles. Yields 4 (6 x 10 ½-inch waffles).

Ham and Egg Casserole

1 pound Black Forest ham, cut into
   ¼-inch cubes
1 large onion, chopped fine
2 cups frozen hash brown potatoes,
   thawed
1 cup shredded Cheddar cheese
8 extra large eggs
½ cup milk
1 cup ranch dressing

Preheat oven to 350°. In coated frying pan, fry ham and onion until onion is soft. Set aside to cool. Transfer to large bowl. Add potatoes and cheese. Mix eggs, milk, and ranch dressing and add to mixture. Spoon into a greased, ovenproof casserole (or individual casseroles). Bake about 30 minutes until eggs are set and golden. Serve with salsa. Yields 4 to 6 servings.

The Roosevelt Bed & Breakfast Inn

THE ROOSEVELT BED & BREAKFAST INN

P.O. Box 2379
Coeur d'Alene, ID 83816
(208) 765-5200 (phone)
(208) 664-4142 (fax)
(800) 290-3358 (toll free)
info@therooseveltinn.com
www.therooseveltinn.com

The Roosevelt was once an elementary school that the innkeeper actually attended. The inn has fifteen rooms and suites, one of which encompasses the bell tower of the school. The Roosevelt is open year-round. The submitted recipe is the signature dessert treat that is brought to the guests in their rooms upon check-in.

Custard Bread Pudding

4 cups milk
2 tablespoons butter
2 cups finely crumbled breadcrumbs
1 cup sugar
4 eggs
½ teaspoon salt
1 tablespoon vanilla extract
Grated nutmeg

Scald milk and butter in saucepan. Add breadcrumbs and let sit at least 10 minutes. In medium-size bowl, mix sugar, eggs, salt, and vanilla and add to cooled milk mixture. Pour into 8 x 12-inch baking dish and place that dish into larger baking dish half-filled with water. This creates a water bath that will allow your custard to cook slowly and evenly. Preheat oven to 350°. Sprinkle nutmeg on top before baking. Bake 40 to 45 minutes, or until a knife comes out clean when inserted into the center of the custard. Top bread pudding with caramel sauce. Yields 6 servings.

WOLF LODGE CREEK BED & BREAKFAST

515 S. Wolf Lodge Creek Road
Coeur d'Alene, ID 83814
(208) 667-5902 (phone)
(208) 667-1133 (fax)
(800) 919-9653 (toll free)
wlebb@wolflodge.com
www.wolflodge.com

With twenty-seven acres backing national forest, this five-room property provides romance, solitude, and glorious mountain scenery. All rooms offer private baths and fireplaces. Guests are treated to a plentiful breakfast buffet guaranteed to satisfy the most hearty appetites. Activities close by include hiking, horseback riding, skiing, biking, restaurants, and Coeur d'Alene Lake.

Lemon Snappers

1 (18-ounce) package lemon cake mix
   (do not prepare according
   to directions)
2 cups frozen whipped topping, thawed
1 egg, beaten
½ cup sifted confectioners' sugar

Preheat oven to 350°. Grease cookie sheet. Mix cake mix, topping, and egg. Mix well. Drop by teaspoonfuls into sugar to coat. Place on cookie sheet 1½ inches apart. Bake 10 to 15 minutes, until golden brown. Yields 3 to 4 dozen cookies.

Wolf Lodge Creek Breakfast Mexigrands

½ pound pork sausage
1 (1¼-ounce) package taco seasoning mix
¼ cup scallions, chopped, including
   green part
6 eggs, beaten
¼ cup picante sauce
1 teaspoon salt
1 plus ½ cup shredded Monterey
   Jack cheese
1 (8-count) package refrigerated
   jumbo biscuits

Preheat oven to 375°. Sauté pork sausage, taco seasoning, and scallions in skillet, stirring to break up chunks. Drain the skillet, add the eggs, and scramble. When almost cooked through, add sausage, picante sauce, and salt. Stir to blend flavors. Add 1 cup cheese. Roll out 6 biscuits, each to about 5½-inch circle. Mold into greased Texas muffin cups (3½ x 1¾-inch). Put ½ cup sausage mixture into each biscuit. Top with remaining ½ cup cheese. Roll out remaining 2 biscuits. Using 3-inch cookie cutter, cut 3 rounds from each. Place on top of the filled biscuits. Bake for 12 minutes. Serve with a side of salsa. Yields 6 servings.

BRIERWREATH MANOR BED & BREAKFAST

216 North Bench Street
Galena, IL 61036
(815) 777-0608
brierw@galenalink.com
www.brierwreath.com

Brierwreath Manor (circa 1884) is a Queen Anne-style house with a wrap-around porch, located only one short block from Galena's historic Main Street shopping district. The Galena area has something for everyone: history, pre-Civil War buildings, museum, Grant's home, golfing, the Mississippi River, gambling, ski resort, two state parks, and hundreds of shops.

Brierwreath's Upside-Down Pancake

1 stick butter
1 cup brown sugar
1 cup pecans
2 apples
3 cups biscuit mix
1½ cups milk
3 eggs
1 teaspoon ground cinnamon

Preheat oven to 350°. Spray 9 x 13 x 2-inch pan with nonstick pan coating. Melt butter in microwave on 50 percent power and pour into pan. Sprinkle brown sugar and pecans over melted butter. Slice apples and arrange over brown sugar and pecans. Make batter from biscuit mix, milk, eggs, and cinnamon. Pour over apple slices. Bake 30 minutes. Remove from oven and flip over onto a cookie sheet or plate. Cut and serve, plain or with maple syrup. Yields 6 to 8 servings.

Brierwreath's Fruit and Nut Pancake

3 cups biscuit mix
½ cup sugar
1 teaspoon ground cinnamon
1½ cups milk
3 eggs

¾ cup walnuts
¾ cup blueberries or cranberries
1 large apple, chopped

Apple Syrup:
1 cup sugar
2 tablespoons biscuit mix
2 cups apple juice
4 tablespoons butter

Preheat oven to 350°. Mix biscuit mix, sugar, cinnamon, milk, and eggs together in bowl. Add walnuts, berries, and apple and pour into greased 13 x 9-inch pan. Bake 30 minutes.

For syrup, mix ingredients in small saucepan and bring to a boil. Serve over pancake. Yields 6 to 8 servings.

HILLENDALE BED & BREAKFAST

600 Lincolnway West
Morrison, IL 61270
(815) 772-3454 (phone)
(815) 772-7023 (fax)
hillend@clinton.net
www.hillend.com

The Hillendale is a large Tudor mansion built in 1891 with ten guest rooms and loaded with artifacts from the owner's travels. Unwind at a beautiful setting and let your cares dissolve. Activities available in the area includes traveling the Lincoln Highway National Scenic Byway, the Great River Road National Scenic Byway, the Blackhawk Chocolate Trail, theater, antiquing, fishing, biking, cross-country skiing, Morrison Rockwood State Park, and gambling in Clinton, Iowa.

Blueberry Muffins

3 cups all-purpose flour
3 cups sugar
1 tablespoon baking powder
1 stick (½ cup) butter
2 eggs
1 cup milk
1 teaspoon vanilla extract
2 cups blueberries
2 tablespoons melted butter

Preheat oven to 350°. Grease 24 muffin cups. Put flour, sugar, baking powder, and butter in large bowl. Mix well. With your fingers squeeze mixture until it is in crumbs. Set aside 1 cup flour mixture in small bowl. To mixture in large bowl, add eggs, milk, and vanilla. Beat until smooth. Gently stir in berries. Fill muffin cups two-thirds full with batter. Dribble melted butter over mixture in small bowl and toss with fork. Sprinkle crumbs over batter. Bake 20 minutes until light golden brown. Muffins may be frozen for later use. Yields 24 muffins.

Cranberry Walnut Coffee Cake

3 cups fresh or frozen cranberries
1 cup chopped walnuts
¾ plus 1 cup sugar
¾ cup (1½ sticks) butter, softened
3 eggs, lightly beaten
1 teaspoon vanilla extract
1½ cups all-purpose flour
1 teaspoon baking powder
½ teaspoon salt

In greased, 9-inch round pan combine cranberries, walnuts, and ¾ cup sugar. In mixing bowl, cream butter and remaining 1 cup sugar until light and fluffy. Add eggs and vanilla. Mix well. Combine flour, baking powder, and salt in separate bowl. Add to creamed mixture and mix well. Preheat oven to 350°. Drop batter by rounded tablespoonfuls over cranberry mixture. Carefully spread to cover. Bake 50 to 60 minutes or until toothpick inserted near the center comes out clean. Yields 8 to 10 servings.

Cranberry Chocolate Chip Muffins

3 cups all-purpose flour
1 cup sugar
4 teaspoons baking powder
2 eggs
½ cup vegetable oil
1 cup milk
2 cups frozen or fresh cranberries
¾ cup chocolate chips

Preheat oven to 350°. Mix together flour, sugar, and baking powder. Mix together eggs, oil, and milk. Add the dry ingredients. Mix until moistened. Add cranberries and chocolate chips. Mix well. Fill greased muffin tins two-thirds full. Bake 20 to 30 minutes. Yields 18 muffins.

PINEHILL INN

400 Mix Street
Oregon, IL 61061
(815) 732-2067 (phone)
(815) 732-1348 (fax)
(800) 851-0131 (toll free)
info@pinehillbb.com
www.pinehillbb.com

Nestled among century-old pine trees, the Pinehill Inn beckons you with light, color, space—the Rock River's most comforting oasis. Activities include hiking and cross-country skiing at four state parks; John Deere Historic Site; Black Hawk Statue; "Pride of Oregon" paddlewheel boat rides; antiquing; canoe rentals and fishing in the Rock River; Ronald Reagan's boyhood home; Autumn on Parade festival; Let Freedom Ring festival; Byronfest; and "Feather Boas and Fedoras" murder mystery weekends.

Artichoke and Caper Bread Spread

1 (14-ounce) can artichokes, drained
6 tablespoons extra virgin olive oil
1½ tablespoons lemon juice
3 tablespoons capers, drained
2 cloves garlic, peeled
1 teaspoon dill
⅛ teaspoon cayenne
2 teaspoons parsley
2 teaspoons roasted red pepper (optional) for color
Pinch of salt, if needed
Crusty French bread, sliced

Place all ingredients except the French bread in bowl of food processor fitted with knife blade. Pulse on and off to a slightly coarse texture. Serve at room temperature with warm French bread. May be refrigerated up to a week. Yields 4 to 6 servings.

Pinehill Inn Peach Melba Crêpes

<u>Crêpes:</u>
⅔ cup milk
⅔ cup cold water
3 large eggs
¼ teaspoon salt
3 tablespoons melted butter
1 cup all-purpose flour

<u>Filling:</u>
1 cup frozen peach slices
1 plus 2 tablespoons sugar
16 ounces small-curd cottage cheese
1 egg yolk
⅛ teaspoon salt
1 teaspoon finely diced lemon peel
Melted butter

<u>Sauce:</u>
1 (12-ounce) jar red raspberry
    preserves
6 ounces red currant jelly

For crêpes, mix all ingredients in blender until smooth. Chill 30 minutes. Heat a skillet over medium heat until hot. Brush lightly with butter. Pour about 3 tablespoons batter into hot pan and swirl pan to cover bottom of pan evenly. Cook until browned on the bottom (this is when bubbles on the topside pop). Turn. Cook briefly on other side. Cool on rack.

For filling, coat frozen peaches with 1 tablespoon sugar and thaw in microwave for 2½ minutes on medium. Dice. Preheat oven to 375°. Mix with cottage cheese, egg yolk, salt, and lemon peel. Stuff crêpes with approximately 2 tablespoons filling. Roll. Place seam-side down on parchment-paper-lined cookie sheet. Brush with melted butter and cover with foil. Bake 20 minutes or more, or until filling is firm.

To serve, make the sauce by mixing preserves and jelly in small saucepan and bring to boil. Strain. Place 2 crêpes on plate and top with about 2 tablespoons raspberry sauce. Serve immediately. Yields 12 to 14 (10-inch) crêpes.

Note: Store between sheets of wax paper. You can easily make the crêpes in advance and store in the refrigerator.

Spinach Bread Pudding

1 small onion, diced
1 tablespoon butter
1 tablespoon olive oil
½ cup dry white wine
1 (10-ounce) package frozen spinach,
    thawed and squeezed very dry
6 large eggs
1¼ cups half-and-half
¾ teaspoon salt
½ teaspoon thyme
¼ teaspoon pepper
1½ cups grated Swiss cheese
8 pieces good white bread, cubed

<u>Onion and tomato sauce:</u>
1 small onion, diced
1 tablespoon olive oil
1 tablespoon butter
1 tablespoon brown sugar
1 (14½-ounce) can diced tomatoes,
    drained
Pinch of salt
Dash of pepper
1 tablespoon dried parsley

Make one day ahead of serving. Sauté onion in butter and olive oil until translucent. Add white wine and reduce by half. Mix in spinach and toss. While onion and wine are cooking, beat eggs, half-and-half, salt, thyme, and pepper. Add spinach mix and stir. Add cheese and stir. Add bread cubes and stir. Pour into 8 x 8-inch pan sprayed with cooking oil. Cover with foil and refrigerate overnight. On serving day, preheat oven to 350°. Bake bread pudding 45 minutes covered. Bake 10 to 15 minutes more uncovered, or until lightly browned. Let pudding rest 10 to 15 minutes. Cut into pieces.

For onion and tomato sauce, sauté onion in oil and butter. Add brown sugar and cook until onion caramelizes. Add tomatoes, salt, pepper, and parsley. Heat through. Taste and adjust seasoning, if needed. Serve with the pudding. Yields 4 to 6 servings.

1877 HOUSE COUNTRY INN BED & BREAKFAST

2408 Utica-Sellersburg Road
Jeffersonville, IN 47130
(812) 285-1877 (phone)
(888) 284-1877 (toll free)
house1877@peoplepc.com
www.bbonline.com/in/1877house

The 1877 House is a historic farmhouse built in 1877 on 2½ scenic acres. Fireplaces and private baths grace every room, and there is a fantastic view of the Louisville, Kentucky, skyline as well as a beautiful view of the countryside. Guest cottage has a whirlpool tub.

Breakfast Pudding

3 cups whole or 2% milk
½ cup cream of wheat
⅓ cup sugar
2 eggs
2 teaspoons almond extract
Fruit preserves for garnish
Mint sprigs for garnish

In medium saucepan over medium-low heat stir milk and cream of wheat together with whisk until thickened. While stirring, add sugar. Add eggs, 1 at a time, stirring constantly. Cook about 1 minute and remove from heat. Stir in almond extract. Pour immediately into six dessert bowls and let cool. Serve cold with a dollop of fruit preserves and a mint leaf. Yields 6 servings.

Holiday French Toast

6 beaten eggs
1 cup eggnog
1 tablespoon rum
12 slices bread

Peach-butter syrup:
1 (10-ounce) package frozen sliced peaches or (1-pound) can peaches
1 cup fresh cranberries (optional)
¼ cup (½ stick) butter or margarine
⅓ cup honey or maple syrup
1 teaspoon lemon juice
2 teaspoons cornstarch
2 tablespoons water
¼ teaspoon almond extract

Heat griddle coated with cooking spray. Mix eggs, eggnog, and rum together in shallow bowl. Dip bread and brown on both sides. Serve with Peach Butter Syrup.

For syrup, put frozen peaches or canned peaches with juice (and cranberries, if using) into small saucepan. Add butter, honey, and lemon juice. Cook over low

1877 House Country Inn Bed & Breakfast

heat, stirring occasionally, until mixture begins to boil. Mix cornstarch with water until smooth and gradually stir into hot peaches. Continue to cook, stirring constantly, until smooth and thickened. Remove from heat and stir in almond extract. Serve hot over pancakes, waffles, or French toast. Yields 6 servings, 2 slices each.

Hash Brown Casserole

1 (2-pound) package frozen shredded hash browns
1 teaspoon salt
1 cup sour cream
1 (10¾-ounce) can cream of chicken soup
1½ cups shredded Cheddar cheese
Topping: Parmesan cheese and/or breadcrumbs

Preheat oven to 350°. Mix all ingredients except topping together in large bowl. Put into large casserole dish coated with non-stick spray. Sprinkle topping heavily onto mixture. Bake 1 hour and 15 minutes. Yields 8 servings.

Ham and Cheese Crescents

1 (8-count) package crescent rolls
½ pound thin-sliced deli ham
½ pound Cheddar cheese

Preheat oven to 375°. Separate rolls and place 1 or two slices of ham on each. Top with cheese. Roll up and place onto cookie sheet. Bake 20 to 25 minutes, or until lightly browned. Serve with Hash Brown Casserole (see recipe above) and fresh fruit. Yields 8 rolls.

Orange Dream Beverage

1 (6-ounce) can frozen orange juice concentrate
1 cup milk
1 cup water
⅓ cup sugar
1 teaspoon vanilla extract
10 to 12 ice cubes

Put all ingredients except the ice cubes into a blender and mix. Add ice cubes 1 at a time and blend on "frappé" until frothy. Serve in a stemmed glass with a sprig of mint. Yields 4 servings.

Ivy House Bed & Breakfast

304 North Merrill
Fortville, IN 46040
(317) 485-4800
relax@ivyhousebb.com
www.ivyhousebb.com

This 1920s Dutch Colonial was destined to become a bed and breakfast. With three beautiful rooms all with private baths, the Ivy House will beckon you to stay. Just blocks from the bed and breakfast is Dolly Mama's Toy and Doll Museum, the most comprehensive collection of toys and dolls in the Midwest. There is also Connor Prairie, a living history museum in Fishers, Indiana, just fifteen minutes from the Ivy House. Everyone enjoys spending the day meandering through the village, an all-day event.

Ivy House Buttery Skillet Apples

4 medium cooking apples
⅓ cup butter
½ cup sugar
2 tablespoons cornstarch
1½ cups apple juice
Freshly ground nutmeg

Peel, core, and slice apples. Make a sauce by melting the butter in medium skillet over medium heat; stir in sugar. Add cornstarch. Mix well and add water. Add apples to sauce, cover, and cook over medium heat. Occasionally spoon the sauce over the apples as they cook. Serve warm. Sprinkle with nutmeg. Yields 4 servings.

Ivy House Peach Delight

½ plus ½ cup brown sugar
½ cup chopped pecans
½ cup oatmeal
½ cup granola
½ cup melted butter
2 (26-ounce) cans peach halves or 7 fresh peaches in season
1 cup vanilla yogurt

Combine ½ cup brown sugar, pecans, oatmeal, granola, and butter. Mix well. Arrange layer of peaches in shallow pan. Using remaining ½ cup brown sugar, place ½ teaspoon sugar in center of each peach half. Broil until sugar is melted. Remove from broiler and place a heaping spoonful of topping in center of each peach. Place under broiler for 1 minute. Be careful not to burn. Remove from broiler and top each peach with a tablespoon of yogurt. Serve warm. Yields 8 to 10 servings.

Date Nut Orange Bread

2 eggs
½ cup sugar
½ cup honey
⅔ cup orange juice
6 tablespoons melted butter
    (no substitutes)
1 teaspoon vanilla extract
2 cups all-purpose flour
2 teaspoons baking powder
½ teaspoon baking soda
1 cup chopped dates
¾ cup pecans

Orange Marmalade Butter:
½ cup softened butter
¼ cup orange marmalade
2 tablespoons finely chopped pecans

Preheat oven to 350°. Beat together eggs, sugar, honey, orange juice, butter, and vanilla. Blend well. Add flour, baking powder, baking soda, dates, and pecans all at once and stir until mixture is just moistened. Do not overmix. Pour mixture into three, small, greased loaf pans (6 x 3 x 2-inch) and bake 25 minutes. Lower oven temperature to 325° and bake 10 minutes. Test with toothpick for doneness. Cool in pans 10 minutes and remove and cool on rack. Serve with Orange Marmalade Butter.

For marmalade butter, beat butter and marmalade until fluffy. Add pecans until blended. Yields 3 small loaves.

Bee Hive Bed & Breakfast

P.O. Box 1191
Middlebury, IN 46540
(574) 825-5023 (phone)

Bee" yourself at the Swarm's Hive, built with hand-sawed, rough timber. Snuggle under handmade quilts. Wake to the smell of a country breakfast being prepared. Back-road tours and separate cottage are available.

Refrigerator Bran Muffins

1 (10-ounce) package raisin bran cereal
5 cups all-purpose flour
5 teaspoons baking soda
2 teaspoons salt
3 cups sugar
1 quart buttermilk
1 cup vegetable oil
4 eggs, beaten

Combine in large bowl raisin bran, flour, soda, salt, and sugar. Add buttermilk, vegetable oil, and eggs. Mix until all ingredients are moistened. Store in covered container in refrigerator; will keep for 6 weeks. To bake, preheat oven to 325°. Fill muffin tins three-fourths full and bake 15 to 20 minutes. Yields 3 or more dozen muffins.

Breakfast Omelet

1 dozen eggs, beaten
½ teaspoon dill
½ teaspoon thyme
1 tablespoon Worcestershire sauce
1 cup heavy cream
¼ cup bacon-horseradish dip
4 tablespoons vegetable oil
1 (32-ounce) package frozen
    hash brown potatoes
½ cup chopped red pepper
½ cup chopped green pepper
1 (8-ounce) jar mushrooms
½ cup sliced green onions
2 cups shredded cheese

Preheat oven to 350°. Beat eggs, dill, thyme, and Worcestershire sauce until foamy. Add cream and dip. Heat oil in skillet over medium heat. Add potatoes, peppers, mushrooms, and onions. Cook until tender. Place in greased 9 x 13-inch baking dish. Pour egg mixture over potato mixture and stir to mix evenly. Bake 25 to 35 minutes until set in center. Pour cheese over top and return to oven until melted. Serve with salsa. Yields 12 servings.

Sorghum Cookies

5 cups sugar
3 cups shortening
4 eggs
8 teaspoons baking soda dissolved in
    1 cup buttermilk
1 cup sorghum
2 teaspoons baking powder
4 teaspoons ground cinnamon
1 teaspoon salt
12 cups all-purpose flour

Preheat oven to 400°. Cream sugar and shortening until fluffy. Add eggs and beat until combined with shortening mixture. Add buttermilk mixture and beat until combined. Add sorghum to mixture. Combine baking powder, cinnamon, and salt with flour. Add to creamed mixture. Chill dough and roll into small balls. Dip in granulated sugar, pressing slightly. Bake 8 to 10 minutes on a slightly greased cookie sheet. Yields 4 dozen cookies.

Baked Oatmeal

1 cup brown sugar
½ cup (1 stick) melted butter
2 eggs, beaten
3 cups quick-cooking oatmeal
2 teaspoons baking powder
1 teaspoon salt
1 cup milk

Preheat oven to 350°. Beat together brown sugar, butter, and eggs. Add oatmeal, baking powder, salt, and milk. Grease 6 x 9-inch baking pan. Put batter in pan and bake 30 minutes. Yields 4 servings.

Amish Peanut Butter

1¼ pounds peanut butter
4 cups marshmallow crème
¾ cup brown sugar
¾ cup warm water
1 cup light corn syrup
¼ pound (1 stick) butter, melted
½ teaspoon vanilla extract

Mix all ingredients together in large mixing bowl. Store in covered container in refrigerator. Yields approximately 8 cups.

Prairie Manor Bed & Breakfast

Prairie Manor Bed & Breakfast

66398 US 33 South
Goshen, IN 46526
(574) 642–4761 (phone)
(800) 791-3952 (toll free)
jeston@npcc.net
www.prairiemanor.com

Prairie Manor is an elegant, historic, English country manor home on twelve acres in the center of northern Indiana Amish country with private baths and full breakfast. The Manor is located in an area where you can enjoy Amish-made furniture, quilts, antiquing, shopping, golf, fishing, biking, boating, Shipshewana flea market and antique auction, Notre Dame, Elkhart County Fair, and Mennonite Relief Sale.

Fresh Vegetable Frittata

1 large sweet red or green pepper, chopped
1 cup sliced fresh mushrooms
¾ plus ¾ cup (6 ounces) shredded Cheddar cheese
¼ pound asparagus, cooked and cut in 1-inch pieces
7 large eggs, lightly beaten
½ cup mayonnaise
½ teaspoon salt
2 tablespoons chopped fresh basil or 2 teaspoons dried
1 tomato, sliced

Preheat oven to 375°. Layer pepper, mushrooms, and ¾ cup cheese in a lightly greased, 9½-inch, deep-dish pie plate. Top with asparagus and remaining ¾ cup cheese. Combine eggs, mayonnaise, salt, and basil and pour evenly over cheese. Top with tomato slices. Bake 30 minutes or until a knife inserted in center comes out clean. Let stand 5 minutes. Serve hot or at room temperature. Yields 6 servings.

Whoopie Pies

2 cups all-purpose flour
1 cup sugar
¾ cup milk
½ cup unsweetened cocoa
6 tablespoons melted butter
1 teaspoon baking soda
1 teaspoon vanilla extract
¼ teaspoon salt
1 large egg

Marshmallow Crème Filling:
6 tablespoons softened butter
1 cup confectioners' sugar
1 (7-ounce) jar marshmallow crème
1 teaspoon vanilla extract

Preheat oven to 350°. Grease two large cookie sheets. In large bowl, with spoon mix all ingredients except the filling until smooth. Drop 12 heaping tablespoons batter 2 inches apart on each cookie sheet. Bake cookies 12 to 14 minutes until puffy and toothpick inserted in center comes out clean, rotating cookie sheets between upper and lower racks halfway through baking time. Remove cookies to wire racks to cool completely.

To make the filling, in large bowl with mixer at medium speed, beat butter until smooth. With mixer at low speed, gradually beat in confectioners' sugar. Then beat in marshmallow crème and vanilla until smooth. Spread 1 rounded tablespoon of filling on flat side of 12 cookies. Top with remaining cookies. Yields 12 servings.

Raspberry Chocolate Chip Muffins

2 cups all-purpose flour
2 teaspoons baking powder
1 cup semisweet chocolate chip mini-morsels
½ pound (1 stick) butter, softened
¾ cup sugar
1 teaspoon vanilla extract
1 tablespoon finely grated orange zest (optional)
½ cup milk
2 cups fresh or unsweetened frozen raspberries

Preheat oven to 375° and coat 12-cup muffin tin with nonstick spray. Sift flour with baking powder. Mix in mini-morsels. With electric mixer, beat butter with sugar until pale and fluffy. Add vanilla and orange zest. Mix into dry ingredients in two additions, alternating with milk. Fold in raspberries. Dough will be very stiff like cookie dough. Spoon into muffin tin and bake 25 to 30 minutes or until toothpick comes out clean. Cool 10 minutes before removing from tin. Yields 12 muffins.

Variation: Substitute raspberry chocolate chips for the mini-morsels.

Peaches and Cream Cheesecake

¾ cup all-purpose flour
1 teaspoon baking powder
1 (3.4-ounce) package dry vanilla pudding mix (not instant)
3 tablespoons softened margarine
1 egg
½ cup milk
1 (15- to 20-ounce) can sliced peaches, or equal amount fresh

1 (8-ounce) package cream cheese, softened
½ cup plus 1 tablespoon sugar
3 tablespoons reserved juice (if using fresh peaches, use orange juice)
½ teaspoon ground cinnamon

Preheat oven to 350°. Combine flour, baking powder, pudding, margarine, egg, and milk. Beat 2 minutes at medium speed. Pour into greased 9- to 10-inch pie pan or round cake pan. Place fruit over batter. Combine cream cheese, ½ cup sugar, and reserved juice; beat 2 minutes at medium speed. Spoon over fruit to within one inch of edge. Combine remaining tablespoon sugar with cinnamon and sprinkle over top. Bake 30 to 35 minutes or until cheese is set. Store in refrigerator. Yields 6 to 8 servings.

BLUEBIRD HOUSE

107 East Market Street
North Liberty, IN 46554
(574) 656-8080

You are cordially invited to enjoy the Bluebird House, an 1894 faithfully restored and charmingly decorated Victorian guest house. Enjoy complete privacy in a quiet residential neighborhood located in a quaint and friendly northern Indiana main-street town. The home's thoughtful, whimsical, and artistic decorating results in an enchanting and intriguing experience with various treasures and surprises for you to discover and enjoy. Bluebird House is located within four miles of Potato Creek State Park and eighteen miles from the University of Notre Dame and St. Mary's College. It is also located near South Bend, Plymouth, Michigan City, Shipshewana, Amish country, and Southern Michigan.

Oven French Toast with Nut Topping

1 loaf French bread cut into 1-inch slices
8 large eggs
2 cups half-and-half plus 2 cups milk
2 teaspoons vanilla extract
½ teaspoon ground nutmeg
½ teaspoon ground cinnamon
¾ cup softened butter
1⅓ cups brown sugar
3 tablespoons dark or light corn syrup
1 cup coarsely chopped nuts
Maple syrup (optional)

Butter 13 x 9-inch baking pan. Fill pan with bread slices within 1½ inches of top. In blender mix eggs, half-and-half, milk, vanilla, nutmeg, and cinnamon. Pour over bread slices. Refrigerate covered 8 to 10 hours or overnight. Mix topping by combining butter, brown sugar, corn syrup, and nuts. Can store in refrigerator but needs to be room temperature when time to bake. When ready to bake, preheat oven to 350°. Spread topping on bread mixture and bake about 1 hour, until puffed and golden. Serve with maple syrup if desired. Yields 8 to 10 servings.

CHESTNUT CHARM BED & BREAKFAST

1409 Chestnut St.
Atlantic, IA 50022
(712) 243-5652
chestnut@metc.net
www.chestnutcharm.org

Chestnut Charm is an enchanting 1898 Victorian country inn with romantic carriage house suites. There is a serene atmosphere with affordable and luxurious accommodations at this award-winning Roman escape. There are plenty of wonderful activities in the area for you to enjoy. Come and golf at championship golf courses, go antique shopping, visit the specialty shops, or take quiet walks in the many parks. Sightseeing includes many historical attractions, including a Danish Windmill Museum or the short drive to see the famous bridges of Madison County.

Florentine Benedict

4 medium potatoes, washed and pierced several times with a fork
Vegetable oil for frying
1 tablespoon butter or margarine
1½ to 2 tablespoons all-purpose flour
⅛ teaspoon white pepper
¼ teaspoon dry mustard
1 tablespoon chopped chives
1½ cups skim milk
½ cup shredded Cheddar cheese
1 pound fresh young spinach leaves, washed and torn into small pieces
8 slices bacon, cooked, drained on paper towels, broken into small pieces
¼ pound mushrooms, cleaned, bottoms trimmed, sliced
4 thin red onion slices
8 eggs, poached

Bake unpeeled potatoes about 15 minutes in microwave. Dice in medium cubes and then fry in vegetable oil until browned. Remove from pan and drain on paper towel. Keep warm. Make sauce by melting butter or margarine in sauté pan over very low heat. Stir in flour, pepper, mustard, chives, and mix until smooth; add milk gradually, stirring constantly. Add cheese and continue to stir until mixture is thick. If mixture is too thick, add more milk. If mixture is not thick enough, carefully add more flour paste (flour mixed with milk) and stir well. Keep warm.

To assemble, divide potatoes into four equal portions and place on dinner plates. Place spinach on top of potatoes. Sprinkle with bacon, mushrooms, and onion slices. Put two poached eggs per plate. Add sauce and serve immediately. Serve toast as a side attraction to this very healthy dish. Yields 4 servings.

Chicken-Almond Puff Appetizers

½ cup (1 stick) butter
1 cup chicken stock and 1 teaspoon chicken bouillon
1 cup all-purpose flour
¼ teaspoon salt
4 eggs
¾ cup finely diced, cooked chicken
3 tablespoons toasted and sliced almonds
Pinch of paprika

Combine butter, chicken stock, and bouillon in medium saucepan. Heat over low heat until butter is melted. Add flour and salt all at once and stir vigorously over low heat until mixture forms a ball and leaves the sides of pan. Remove from heat and cool to room temperature. Add eggs one at a time, beating thoroughly after each addition. Continue beating until a thick dough is formed. Stir in chicken, almonds, and paprika and mix well. Preheat oven to 450°. Drop dough by small teaspoonfuls onto a greased baking sheet. Bake 10 minutes and reduce heat to 350° for about 5 to 10 minutes longer or until golden brown. Serve warm. These are award-winning appetizers that will earn you rave reviews at any party. Yields 4 to 5 dozen.

Tomatoes and Egg Brunch

1 teaspoon melted butter
1 teaspoon olive oil
4 large tomatoes
2 cloves garlic, crushed
1 teaspoon salt
½ teaspoon black pepper
1 ounce cooked ham, finely chopped
4 eggs
4 tablespoons heavy cream
1 teaspoon dried basil
¼ cup grated Parmesan cheese

Grease baking sheet with butter and olive oil. Slice off tops of tomatoes. Set tomato lids aside to be cored, diced, and used as garnish later. Scoop out and discard seeds from tomatoes. Set tomato shells upside-down on paper towels to drain. Then turn the shells upright on baking sheet and sprinkle insides with garlic, salt, and pepper.

Preheat oven to 350°. Place one-fourth of the ham in each tomato. Gently break an egg into tomato shell, being careful not to break the yolk. Add 1 tablespoon cream to each tomato shell. Sprinkle each with basil and Parmesan cheese. Bake about 15 to 20 minutes or until eggs just set. Remove baking sheet from oven. Transfer tomatoes to individual plates and serve immediately. This is a great brunch dish served with crusty French bread and an assortment of fresh fruit. Yields 4 servings.

Easy Ham and Cheese Soufflé

This makes a light and tasty supper dish. It is delicious served with garden fresh salad and crusty French bread.

12 slices white bread, cubed
½ plus ½ cup milk
3 tablespoons butter
3 eggs, separated
1½ tablespoons all-purpose flour
2 cups shredded Cheddar cheese
½ teaspoon salt
½ teaspoon paprika
⅛ teaspoon cayenne
3 ounces finely chopped cooked ham
½ cup half-and-half

Coat shallow baking dish with vegetable spray. Put in half the bread cubes and sprinkle in ½ cup milk. In separate bowl, soak remaining bread cubes with remaining ½ cup milk. In large bowl, cream butter with wooden spoon and mix in egg yolks, one at a time, stirring well after each addition. Stir in flour, then cheese, salt, paprika, cayenne, and soaked bread cubes. Blend well. Stir in ham and half-and-half. Preheat oven to 350°. In clean, grease-free, medium bowl, place room temperature egg whites. Beat egg whites with a wire whisk until stiff. Lightly fold them into cheese mixture. Pour into baking dish with the soaked bread cubes. Bake about 35 to 40 minutes. Serve immediately. Yields 4 servings.

Orange Tea Bread

2 large oranges (lemons can be used instead)
½ cup plus 1 cup sugar
2 eggs
¾ cup milk
½ cup melted butter
3 cups all-purpose flour
1 teaspoon baking soda
1 teaspoon baking powder
½ teaspoon salt
½ teaspoon ground ginger
½ cup chopped walnuts
½ cup confectioners' sugar
⅛ teaspoon vanilla extract

Pare oranges with a sharp knife and cut peel into slivers. Place in small saucepan and cover with cold water. Bring orange slivers to a boil. Reduce heat and simmer for 5 minutes. Drain off water and add ½ cup sugar. Continue to simmer for 5 minutes or until mixture becomes thick and syrupy, stirring constantly. Remove from heat and cool completely in pot. In large bowl, beat eggs with a wire whisk until light. Add remaining 1 cup sugar and whisk until well blended. Beat in milk before stirring in the candied orange peel and butter or margarine. Sift flour, baking soda, baking powder, salt, and ground ginger in medium bowl. Put flour mixture into batter and mix until batter is just blended. Stir in nuts. You do not want to overmix this batter or you will have a tough bread. Preheat oven to 325°. Pour bread batter into greased 9 x 5 x 3-inch loaf pan. Bake about 1 hour and 20 minutes, or until wooden toothpick inserted in the center comes clean. Cool in pan on wire rack for 10 minutes. Remove to serving plate. Mix confectioners' sugar, vanilla, and enough milk to make glaze. Drizzle on the cooled loaf. Yields 1 loaf.

THE SCHRAMM HOUSE BED & BREAKFAST

616 Columbia Street
Burlington, IA 52601
(319) 754-0373 (phone/fax)
(800) 683-7117 (toll free)
visit@schramm.com
www.visit.schramm.com

A stay in the Schramm House is a delight in its own right. This fine Victorian home, built in the 1860s by department store founder John Siegmund Schramm, features architectural details that make it stand out from others in the area. Inside, its high ceilings, parquet floors, original woodwork, and antique furnishings evoke the elegant comfort of a bygone era. Areas available for guest use include two parlors for relaxation and conversation, a library with fireplace, and a large dining room where your full breakfast is served. In good weather, you'll enjoy our outside porches with wicker furniture and swing. You're in the heart of the nationally recognized Heritage Hill Historic District with mighty oaks and maples arching cathedral-like over streets lined with stately homes and churches. Close by are vistas of the Mississippi River. Just a block away is Snake Alley, proclaimed "the crookedest street in the world."

Pumpkin Muffins

2 eggs
1 cup milk
1 cup mashed or canned pumpkin
½ cup melted butter
3 cups all-purpose flour
1 cup sugar
4 teaspoons baking powder
1 teaspoon salt
1 teaspoon ground cinnamon
1 teaspoon ground nutmeg
1 cup raisins (optional)

Preheat oven to 400°. Grease bottom of two (12-cup) muffin tins or use paper liners. Mix eggs, milk, pumpkin, and butter. Blend dry ingredients and add to liquid just until flour is moistened. Fold in raisins, if using. Fill muffin cups two-thirds full. Bake 18 to 20 minutes. Yields 24 muffins.

Freezer Biscuits

4 cups all-purpose flour
8 teaspoons baking powder
4 tablespoons sugar
1 teaspoon cream of tartar
1 cup shortening
1½ cups milk
1 teaspoon salt
1 egg

Mix dry ingredients and cut in shortening with pastry blender, or use two forks until shortening is pea-size. Add milk, salt, and

egg and stir until combined. Cut into desired shapes. Freeze on an ungreased cookie sheet. When frozen, place in airtight bag to store in the freezer. When ready to bake, preheat oven to 375°. Place frozen biscuits on greased cookie sheet or baking stone. Take out as many as needed for breakfast and bake 15 to 20 minutes. Yields 3 dozen (2-inch) biscuits.

Blueberry Crumb Cake

Cake:
2 cups all-purpose flour
1 cup sugar
1 tablespoon baking powder
¼ teaspoon salt
½ cup shortening
1 cup milk
2 eggs, beaten
1½ cups fresh or frozen blueberries

Topping:
1 cup sugar
½ cup all-purpose flour
¼ cup (½ stick) melted butter

Coat 9 x 12-inch pan with nonstick spray. For cake, blend flour, sugar, baking powder, and salt and cut in shortening. Combine milk and eggs and add to dry ingredients. Mix lightly and fold in berries. Spread in pan. Preheat oven to 350°.

For the topping, combine sugar, flour, and butter. Mix until crumbly and spread on top of batter. Bake 25 minutes, or until cake tests for doneness with cake tester. Cut in squares to serve. Yields 10 servings.

FULTON'S LANDING GUEST HOUSE ON THE MISSISSIPPI

1206 East River Drive
Davenport, IA 52803
(563) 322-4069
www.fultonslanding.com

Fulton's Landing Guest House is a magnificent old mansion with beautiful Mississippi River views, four large bedrooms furnished with antiques, and a convenient location for all area attractions—the ultimate in rest and relaxation. The Quad Cities' greatest attraction is the Mississippi River. Home of the John Deere International headquarters and many jazz and music festivals along the river, the area offers excursion dinner boats, gambling boats, golf, museums, sporting events, and concerts at the civic center.

Fulton's Landing Guest House on the Mississippi

Victorian French Toast

1½ cups packed brown sugar
½ cup (1 stick) butter or margarine
4 tablespoons light corn syrup
1 (16-ounce) loaf good French or Italian
    bread, cut in 1-inch slices
8 to 10 eggs
2½ cups milk
¼ cup sugar
1 teaspoon ground cinnamon

In small saucepan, cook and stir brown sugar, butter, and corn syrup just until butter is melted. Pour mixture into ungreased 9 x 13-inch casserole dish. Arrange slices of bread in a single layer on top of brown sugar mixture. Mix the eggs and milk and pour over bread. Mix sugar and cinnamon and sprinkle over all. Cover and refrigerate 8 to 10 hours or overnight. When ready to serve, preheat oven to 350°. Remove cover and bake 55 minutes. Combine sugar and cinnamon and sprinkle on top. Yields 12 servings.

Dutch Babies

1 tablespoon unsalted butter
1 egg
¼ cup low-fat milk
¼ cup unbleached all-purpose flour
¼ teaspoon almond extract

Preheat oven to 400°. Place butter in a 4-inch baking dish or ramekin and heat until butter is melted. Beat egg until light and gradually beat in milk and flour until smooth. Stir in almond extract. Pour batter into melted butter and bake until pancake is puffed and golden, about 10 minutes. Serve at once. Yields 1 serving.
   Note: The traditional topping is simply lemon juice and confectioners' sugar. At Christmas, sliced strawberries and sliced kiwis, sprinkled with confectioners' sugar, make a festive topping. Any berries or fruit are good on top.

Rhubarb Coffee Cake

½ cup softened margarine
1½ cups brown sugar
1 cup milk
2 cups all-purpose flour
1 teaspoon baking powder
⅓ cup old-fashioned oats
1 teaspoon vanilla extract
1 egg
2 cups rhubarb, cut into ½-inch chunks
½ cup sugar
1 teaspoon cinnamon

Preheat oven to 375°. Mix margarine, sugar, milk, flour, baking powder, oats, vanilla, egg, and rhubarb together, adding rhubarb last. Pour into greased and floured 9 x 13-inch baking dish. Mix sugar and cinnamon and sprinkle over top. Bake 35 minutes. Yields 8 servings.

Pecan Waffles

2 cups all-purpose flour
1 tablespoon baking powder
1 teaspoon baking soda
½ teaspoon salt
4 eggs
2 cups buttermilk
½ cup melted butter
3 tablespoons chopped pecans

Combine flour, baking powder, baking soda, and salt. In mixing bowl, beat eggs until light. Add buttermilk and mix well. Fold in dry ingredients and beat until batter is smooth. Stir in butter. Pour ¾ cup batter onto a lightly greased, preheated waffle iron and sprinkle with pecans. Yields 7 waffles.

THE RICHARDS HOUSE

1492 Locust Street
Dubuque, IA 52001-4714
(563) 557-1492
info@therichardshouse.com
www.TheRichardsHouse.com

Surround yourself with elegance and craftsmanship at their best in this High Victorian home. Constructed in 1883 by manufacturer and financier B. B. Richards, this four-story, Stick-style house with Eastlake effects is one of the finest and most original Victorian homes in Dubuque. Occupied by the same family from its completion until 1989, the Richards House features a dazzling display of nearly ninety stained-glass windows, eight ornate fireplaces, seven types of woodwork, patterns of embossed wall coverings, original chandeliers, hand-painted tiles, elaborate built-ins, and more. Enjoy a full breakfast by the fireplace in the dining room, surrounded by pocket doors with breathtaking stained-glass inserts, an inviting bay window, and ornate fretwork. Adventurous souls can ride the steepest inclined railway in the world, enjoy a peaceful river cruise on one of the paddle wheelers, or take a horse and carriage tour of the historic districts.

Scalloped Pineapple

1 stick butter or margarine
3 eggs
¾ cup sugar
1 (20-ounce) can pineapple
    chunks, drained
8 slices bread, toasted and cubed

Preheat oven to 350°. Melt butter. Mix eggs and sugar together. Add pineapple and bread and mix well. Pour batter in

...le dish and bake about 30 minutes ...til top is golden brown. Yields 8 to 10 se...ings.

Pumpkin Roll

Roll:
3 eggs
1 cup sugar
⅔ cups pumpkin
1 teaspoon lemon juice
¾ cup all-purpose flour
1 teaspoon baking powder
½ teaspoon salt
½ teaspoon ground nutmeg
1½ teaspoons ground cinnamon
Nuts (optional)

Filling:
1 cup confectioners' sugar
8 ounces cream cheese, room
    temperature
4 tablespoons margarine
½ teaspoon vanilla extract

Preheat oven to 375°. Mix together all roll ingredients, except nuts, if using. Line 10½ x 15-inch cookie sheet with wax paper. Trim excess wax paper to minimize smoking. Pour batter onto cookie sheet and spread evenly. Bake 12 to 15 minutes. (May sprinkle with nuts before baking.) Heavily sprinkle linen towel with confectioners' sugar. After baking, turn cake onto towel and roll up in towel. Cool 30 to 40 minutes while rolled.

Prepare filling while roll cools. Mix filling ingredients thoroughly. After roll has cooled, unroll and spread filling evenly. Reroll cake and slice before serving. Yields 10 to 12 servings.

Pear Coffee Cake

Cake:
¾ cup sugar
¼ cup (½ stick) margarine
1 teaspoon vanilla extract
3 egg whites
1¾ cups all-purpose flour
1 teaspoon baking powder
½ teaspoon baking soda
½ teaspoon ground cumin
¼ teaspoon salt
1 cup low-fat sour cream
2 cups chopped pears

Streusel:
⅓ cup granulated sugar
⅓ cup packed brown sugar
2 tablespoons all-purpose flour
½ teaspoon ground cinnamon
2 tablespoons margarine

Glaze:
½ cup confectioners' sugar
2 to 3 teaspoons skim milk
¼ teaspoon vanilla extract

For cake, beat sugar, margarine, vanilla, and egg whites in a large bowl until well mixed. Mix flour, baking powder, baking soda, cumin, and salt. Alternately mix flour mixture and sour cream into sugar mixture with mixer on low speed. Fold in pears. Spread batter into 13 x 9-inch pan coated with nonstick spray. Preheat oven to 350°.

For streusel, mix sugars, flour, and cinnamon. Cut in margarine until crumbly. Sprinkle batter with streusel. Bake 45 to 55 minutes. Cool.

For glaze, mix ingredients until smooth. Drizzle cake with glaze. Yields 8 to 12 servings.

The Richards House

THE RIVER'S EDGE BED & BREAKFAST

611 Grand Avenue
Keokuk, IA 52632
(319) 524-1700 (phone)
(888) 581-3343 (toll free)
NToering@aol.com
www.riversedge.itgo.com

Situated on a bluff overlooking the mighty Mississippi River, The River's Edge

Bed & Breakfast enthralls guests with its spectacular view. This 1915 Tudor-style mansion has four spacious guest rooms (two are suites), each with private bath. Boats glide by in the summer and bald eagles abound in the winter.

Activities and attractions include Civil War Reenact-ment in April; Bald Eagle Appreciation Days in January; Lock & Dam and barges on the Mississippi; walking tours of Grand Avenue's "Miracle Mile" of historic homes; rock-hunting for geodes; the first national cemetery west of the Mississippi; historic riverboat museum tour; and the historic Mormon settlement at Nauvoo, Illinois, just twenty minutes away.

Baked Apple Pancakes

    4 eggs
    1½ cups milk
    ½ teaspoon salt
    2 tablespoons sugar
    2 tablespoons vegetable oil
    2 cups sifted all-purpose flour
    ½ cup sugar mixed with
        1 tablespoon cinnamon
    3 Granny Smith apples, peeled and sliced
    ¼ cup brown sugar
    4 tablespoons butter
    Syrup (optional)

Beat eggs until thick and add milk, salt, sugar, and oil. Sift in flour, mixing well. Let batter stand for 30 minutes. Preheat oven to 375°. Butter two 9-inch round cake pans and sprinkle with some of cinnamon sugar mixture. Arrange apples in pans and sprinkle with remaining cinnamon sugar and brown sugar. Dot with butter. Pour batter over apples, dividing evenly between pans. Bake 30 to 35 minutes or until top is golden and set. Cut into wedges and serve hot with warm syrup if desired. Yields 8 to 10 servings.

Chocolate Zucchini Muffins

    1 cup packed brown sugar
    1 cup granulated sugar
    1½ cups whole wheat flour
    1½ cups all-purpose flour
    1 teaspoon baking soda
    1 teaspoon baking powder
    1 teaspoon salt
    1 teaspoon ground cinnamon
    3 ounces grated Hershey bar
    1 cup mini chocolate chips
    3 eggs, beaten
    1 cup vegetable oil
    1 tablespoon vanilla extract
    2½ cups grated zucchini

Mix dry ingredients in large bowl. In medium bowl, mix together eggs, oil, vanilla, and zucchini. Add to dry ingredients. Preheat oven to 400°. Grease muffin cups and fill about three-quarters full with batter. Bake 18 to 20 minutes. Yields 24 muffins.

THE BLUE BELLE INN

513 West 4th Street
P.O. Box 205
St. Ansgar, IA 50472
(641) 713-3113
innkeeper@bluebelleinn.com
www.BlueBelleInn.com

The Blue Belle Inn is a vintage Victorian house set in a quaint country village. Recapture the romance of the 1890s with intimate candlelight dining, fireplaces, private whirlpools for two, and creatively decorated, storybook-themed rooms. The Blue Belle Inn is located just one hour from Rochester, Minnesota, and forty-five minutes from Clear Lake, Iowa. Hunt for treasures in our antique Victorian, country primitive, craft, or quilting shops or hunt, hike, canoe, or golf along the Cider River.

Peachy Bread Pudding with Amaretto Sauce

    8 cups cubed bread
    8 eggs
    3 cups milk
    ¾ cup sugar
    1 teaspoon almond extract
    1 (26-ounce) can sliced peaches in
        heavy syrup, drained
    1 teaspoon ground cinnamon
    3 tablespoons packed brown sugar
    3 tablespoons almonds

    Amaretto Sauce:
    1 cup sugar
    1 tablespoon all-purpose flour
    ½ cup (1 stick) butter
    ½ cup half-and-half
    4 teaspoons Amaretto

Preheat oven to 350°. Spray 9 x 13-inch pan and spread in bread cubes. Whisk eggs, milk, sugar, and almond extract. Stir in peaches. Pour mix over bread. Press in with spoon. Mix cinnamon and brown sugar and sprinkle on top. Add almonds. Bake 50 to 55 minutes until knife comes out clean. Serve warm with Amaretto Sauce. Garnish with fresh raspberries in season and fresh mint. Yields 10 to 12 servings.

To make sauce, stir together sugar and flour in a small pan. Add butter and half-and-half. Bring to boil. Remove from heat. Stir in Amaretto. Yields 2 cups.

Mucky Mouth Pie

There once was a naughty boy who sneaked from the icebox a piece of a wild berry and apple pie his mother had made for a tea party. When his mother discovered the piece was missing, she lined the children up and asked whoever was responsible to confess. The little boy did not speak up, but the wise mother could tell by the stains on the lips of the boy's "Mucky Mouth" that it was he who was guilty.

1⅓ cups sugar
⅓ cup all-purpose flour
2 cups thinly sliced apples
1 cup fresh or frozen raspberries
1 cup fresh or frozen blueberries or
    blackberries
1 cup fresh or frozen rhubarb,
    cut in 1-inch pieces
Fresh mint, cut in tiny pieces
2 (9-inch) unbaked piecrusts
Confectioners' sugar
Milk

Preheat oven to 350°. Stir sugar and flour together in a large bowl. (Use a little more flour if using frozen fruit.) Add apples, berries, rhubarb, and mint. Toss together and turn into piecrust. Cover with second crust. Trim and seal edges. Cut vents in top. Bake about 45 minutes until crust is golden brown and filling is bubbling. Make a glaze of confectioners' sugar and milk. Drizzle over pie and let dry. Garnish with fresh mint and fresh raspberries. Yields 1 (9-inch) pie.

Strawberry Dumplings

⅓ cup plus 2 tablespoons plus
    1 tablespoon sugar
⅔ cup water
½ teaspoon vanilla extract
1 cup sifted all-purpose flour
1½ teaspoons baking powder
½ teaspoon salt
4 tablespoons butter or margarine
½ cup milk
1 pint strawberries, hulled (May use
    half peach slices if desired.)
Fresh mint

Combine ⅓ cup sugar and water in pan. Bring mixture to boiling. Reduce heat and simmer, uncovered, 5 minutes. Stir in vanilla. Preheat oven to 400°. To make dough sift together flour, 2 tablespoons sugar, baking powder, and salt. Cut in butter until crumbly. Add milk and stir just until well combined. Place berries in 1½-quart casserole and pour hot sugar water over them. Immediately drop dumpling dough in 8 to 10 spoonfuls over berries. Sprinkle dumplings with remaining 1 tablespoon sugar. Bake 25 to 30 minutes until dumplings are done. Serve warm from the casserole into individual dessert dishes. Garnish with fresh mint. Yields 4 to 5 servings.

Sirloin Fillet with Chardonnay Cream Sauce

2 pounds sirloin steak
All-purpose flour for dredging
Salt and pepper for dredging
2 tablespoons butter
1 tablespoon olive oil
2 large onions, thinly sliced
1 clove garlic
1 cup white wine
1 cup beef broth
1 teaspoon Worcestershire sauce
1 teaspoon soy sauce
⅛ teaspoon pepper

Chardonnay cream sauce:
6 small shallots, finely chopped
¼ cup (½ stick) butter
1 cup Chardonnay
½ cup heavy cream
¾ cup half-and-half
¼ pound Gorgonzola cheese, crumbled
⅛ teaspoon garlic
⅛ teaspoon beef concentrate
⅛ teaspoon white pepper
Dash of salt

Cut steak into four (8-ounce) fillets. Dredge in flour seasoned with salt and pepper. Brown fillets on both sides in butter and oil in a heavy pan. Remove from pan, add onions, and sauté until golden. Stir in garlic, wine, broth, Worcestershire sauce, soy sauce, and pepper, being careful to stir up all the browned bits from the bottom of the pan. Return fillets to pan, cover, and simmer slowly for 1½ hours until meat is very tender. To serve, ladle Chardonnay cream sauce on individual

The Blue Belle Inn

plates and top with steak and boiled new potatoes.

To make sauce, sauté shallots in butter until soft. Add wine. Reduce 15 minutes at a good boil. Add heavy cream and half-and-half and reduce for 5 minutes. Add cheese. Stir and reduce until creamy and smooth. Add garlic, beef concentrate, pepper, and salt. Garnish with sprig of fresh basil and a colorful nasturtium blossom. Yields 4 servings.

McGregor Manor Bed & Breakfast

320 4th street
McGregor, IA 52157
(563) 873-2600 (phone)
(563) 873-2218 (fax)
innkeeper@mcgregorinn.com
www.mcgregorinn.com

McGregor Manor Bed & Breakfast is a restored Victorian home that transports one back to an era of elegance and charm. Share the warmth and hospitality of our home by relaxing on the wraparound porch and enjoying the panoramic beauty of scenic McGregor. There are four rooms, all with private baths and queen-size beds.

There are many activities available in the surrounding area. There is magnificent hiking and scenery at Pikes Peak State Park, Effigy Mounds National Monument, and Yellow River State Forest. Spook Cave, Villa Louis Victorian Mansion, and the Prairie du Chien Medical Museum are wonderful stops, and the many antique shops and unique boutiques will entice you to stay in our beautiful area. There are also a number of good restaurants plus a riverboat casino.

Lemon Scones

3 cups all-purpose flour
⅓ cup sugar
2½ teaspoons baking powder
Zest of 1 lemon
¾ cup (1½ sticks) butter (no substitute)
1 cup buttermilk
½ cup dried cranberries, cherries, raisins, or currants

Combine flour, sugar, baking powder, and lemon zest. Cut in butter with a pastry blender. Add buttermilk and fruit and mix well. Turn dough out on well-floured surface and gently knead. Press dough into round, 9-inch, floured cake pan to form it. Take out and cut into twelve wedges. Preheat oven to 425°. Place wedges on baking sheet lined with parchment paper. Bake 15 minutes or until golden brown. Yields 12 scones.

Note: When cool, glaze with blend of confectioners' sugar and milk and serve with Devonshire cream or jam.

Glazed Bacon

1 pound bacon
½ cup light brown sugar
1 tablespoon Creole or Dijon mustard
1 tablespoon red or white wine

Preheat oven to 350°. Put bacon on large baking sheet, bake 10 minutes, and drain off fat. Bacon should be almost crisp—be sure not to underbake. In small bowl mix together brown sugar, mustard, and wine. Pour half this glaze over bacon and return to oven. Bake 10 minutes more, turning bacon over and covering with remaining glaze. Continue to bake until golden brown. Remove and place on wax paper to cool. (Do *not* drain on paper towels as bacon will stick and be almost impossible to remove.) Serve warm or cooled. Yields 8 servings.

Muesli

1 cup uncooked oatmeal
½ cup plain yogurt
Juice of 1 lemon
⅔ cup milk
½ cup sugar
1 peach, sliced and cubed
½ cup seedless grapes
1 cup fresh strawberries
1 apple, coarsely grated
1 pear, chopped
1 orange, peeled and cut into small pieces
1 cup slivered almonds
½ cup whipped cream

Combine oatmeal, yogurt, lemon juice, milk, and sugar. Add fruits and almonds. Just before serving fold in whipped cream. Yields 10 to 12 servings.

Sausage-Hash Brown Bake

2 pounds pork sausage, spicy or regular
1 (32-ounce) package frozen hash browns
3 (10¾-ounce) cans cream of celery soup
2½ cups sour cream
Paprika

Brown sausage and drain grease. Cook hash browns according to package directions, being sure to brown them well. Preheat oven to 350°. Mix soup and sour cream in large bowl, add sausage and hash browns, and mix well. Pour into greased, 9 x 13-inch glass pan and top with paprika. Bake 1 hour. Yields 15 servings.

Note: This can be made the day before, covered, and refrigerated overnight. It can also be frozen. Set out 1 hour or longer before baking; bake uncovered.

La Corsette Maison Inn

Separately cook sausage until crumbly. Pour off fat. Preheat oven to 350°. Stir in soup, celery, onion, salt, and pepper. Add rice. Put mixture in buttered casserole and cover. Bake 30 minutes. Yields 4 servings.

LA CORSETTE MAISON INN

629 First Avenue East
Newton, IA 50208
(641) 792-6833

Historic La Corsette Maison Inn is nationally renowned, not only for its exquisite furnishings and hospitality, but also award-winning gourmet cuisine. Places of interest in Newton and surrounding areas include Jasper County Historical Museum, the Maytag Company, Maytag Park, and Maytag pool, tennis courts, golf courses, horseback riding, and cross-country skiing.

Swedish Rice Pudding

3 cups cooked rice
¾ cup brown sugar
¼ teaspoon salt
½ teaspoon ground cinnamon
1 teaspoon vanilla extract
2 cups heavy whipping cream
¼ cup plumped raisins

Put all ingredients in saucepan. Cover. Heat slowly until some of the cream is absorbed by mixture. Serve in pretty dish and dust with cinnamon. (To plump raisins, pour hot water over them and let sit 10 minutes. Drain well.) Yields 8 servings.

Sausage and Wild Rice Casserole

½ cup wild rice
½ cup white rice
1 medium onion, finely chopped
1 cup finely chopped celery
2 tablespoons vegetable oil
1 pound bulk sausage
1 (10¾-ounce) can cream of
   mushroom soup
1 teaspoon salt
¼ teaspoon pepper

Cook wild rice 45 minutes and white rice 10 minutes. Drain. In small pan sauté onion and celery in oil for 10 minutes.

THE HANCOCK HOUSE BED & BREAKFAST

1105 Grove Terrace
Dubuque, IA 52001-4644
(563) 557-8989 (phone)
(563) 583-0813 (fax)
www.thehancockhouse.com

Victorian elegance comes alive for you at the Hancock House, nestled in the bluffs of historic Dubuque. The Hancock House, listed on the National Register of Historic Places, shows Queen Anne architecture at its finest. Built in 1891 by the Midwest's largest wholesale grocer and distributor, Charles T. Hancock, the Hancock House offers unique rooms, each with its own charm and character. All of the rooms are authentically decorated in period antique furnishings to maintain the integrity of the original Hancock House.

Experience history at the Woodward Riverboat Museum and the Ham House Museum—home of Mathias Ham, early founder of the city. The areas attractions do not end with warm weather. You will find a masterpiece of nature as she paints the brilliant hues of fall. In winter, the Mississippi Mountains afford the finest downhill skiing in the Midwest. For nature lovers, the skies above the Mississippi Valley provide a majestic view of soaring eagles. Other activities include biking, golfing, hiking, tennis, swimming, picnics, canoeing, fishing, boating, skiing, museums, arboretum, and shopping.

Caramel French Toast

1 cup brown sugar
½ cup (1 stick) butter
2 tablespoons light corn syrup
12 pieces day-old Texas Toast (thick bread)
8 eggs
2 cups milk
1 teaspoon vanilla

Cook sugar, butter, and corn syrup over medium heat for 10 minutes, stirring constantly. Pour into a 9 x 13-inch baking pan. Place bread over mixture 2 pieces deep.

Combine eggs, milk, and vanilla, pour over bread, cover, and place in refrigerator 8 to 10 hours or overnight. When ready to bake, preheat oven to 350° and bake for 45 minutes until golden brown. Serve upside down. Yields 6 to 8 servings.

Honey Puffed Pancake

6 eggs
1 cup milk
3 tablespoons honey
3 ounces cream cheese, softened
1 cup all-purpose flour
½ teaspoon salt
½ teaspoon baking powder
1 plus 2 tablespoons butter

Honey-butter sauce:
½ cup honey
½ cup confectioners' sugar
½ cup softened butter
Cinnamon

Preheat oven to 400°. In blender mix eggs, milk, honey, cream cheese, flour, salt, and baking powder. Blend ingredients at high speed for 1 minute or until smooth. Grease 10-inch, ovenproof pie dish with 1 tablespoon butter. Add remaining 2 tablespoons and heat in oven until butter sizzles. Pour batter in dish and bake for 25 minutes or until puffed and golden brown. (Pancake will flatten to about 1 inch after being removed from the oven.)

While pancake is baking, make honey-butter sauce. Beat honey, confectioners' sugar, butter, and cinnamon to taste together until well mixed. Dust pancake with confectioners' sugar and serve with sauce (or syrup if desired). Yields 4 to 5 servings.

Breakfast Bread Pudding with Warm Berry Sauce

Bread pudding:
2 eggs
¾ cup sugar
3 cups low-fat milk
1 cup heavy (whipping) cream or light cream (half-and-half)
½ cup (1 stick) melted unsalted butter
1 tablespoon vanilla extract
¾ cup dried currants or raisins
1 teaspoon freshly grated nutmeg
8 ounces stale Texas Toast or French bread, preferably whole wheat, sliced ½-inch thick

Warm berry sauce:
2 cups fresh or frozen raspberries
2 cups fresh or frozen strawberries
⅓ cup sugar
⅓ cup freshly squeezed orange juice
⅓ cup freshly squeezed lemon juice
Confectioners' sugar for dusting
Whole fresh raspberries and strawberries for garnish

To make pudding, combine eggs, sugar, milk, cream, butter, vanilla, currants, and nutmeg in a bowl. Whisk to blend well. Pour mixture over bread slices in large bowl

The Hancock House Bed & Breakfast

and let stand, turning bread as necessary, until bread is soft and saturated, about 20 minutes. Preheat oven to 350°. Arrange bread slices in lightly greased 4-quart baking dish and pour any unabsorbed custard mixture over the bread. Bake, uncovered, until the custard is set and top is lightly browned, about 45 minutes.

To make the sauce, combine berries, sugar, and orange and lemon juices in saucepan over medium heat. Cook, stirring continuously, until fruit begins to break up, about 5 minutes. Purée in food processor or blender, return to saucepan, and heat until warm. To serve, dust top of pudding with confectioners' sugar. Pass sauce and fresh berries at the table. Yields 8 servings.

CARRIAGE HOUSE BED & BREAKFAST

1133 Broad Street
Grinnell, IA 50112
(641) 236-7520 (phone)
(641) 236-5085 (fax)
irishbnb@iowatelecom.net
www.BedandBreakfast.com/bbc/p216752.asp

Guests are welcomed to a Victorian home with the aura of an English manor house. Your hosts are from the British Isles and offer you fine china, crystal, and linens. The house is on the edge of the Grinnell College campus and within walking distance of several fine restaurants. Situated halfway between Des Moines and Iowa City on Interstate 80, the inn is easy driving distance to tourist attractions such as Amana colonies and Pella.

Escalloped Pineapple Casserole

2 sticks real butter
2 cups sugar
4 eggs
¼ cup whole milk
4 cups bread cubes
1 (20-ounce) can crushed pineapple (do not drain)

Preheat oven to 325°. Cream together butter and sugar. Beat eggs and milk together and add to creamed mixture. Fold in bread cubes, then pineapple, then juice. Pour into buttered 9 x 13-inch pan. Bake for approximately 45 minutes until puffy and slightly browned around the edges. Yields 15 servings.

Irish Wheaten Bread

2 cups all-purpose flour
¾ cup wheat flour
2 teaspoons baking soda
1 teaspoon salt
3 tablespoons sugar
1⅔ cups buttermilk

Preheat oven to 380°. Mix dry ingredients in medium bowl. Add buttermilk all at once. Mix to a soft dough (if necessary, use 1 to 2 tablespoons more buttermilk). Turn out onto floured surface and form into a flat ball by turning over several times in flour. Put in 9-inch, metal cake pan dusted with flour. Mark a deep X across the top with floured knife. Bake immediately for 25 to 30 minutes until the top is crusty. Cool 10 minutes and then turn out onto cooling rack. Serve by cutting along the lines of the X so that you have four quarters and then slice each quarter into thin slices. Serve with butter and homemade jam. Yields 12 servings.

Potatoes Supreme

1 (28-ounce) bag frozen hash browns
¼ cup frozen chopped onion
1 teaspoon pepper
1 (10¾-ounce) can cream of chicken soup
1 (soup) can whole milk
½ pint sour cream
2 cups grated sharp Cheddar cheese

Topping:
2 cups coarsely crushed cornflakes
¼ cup melted butter

Preheat oven to 350°. Mix ingredients together and put in greased, 9 x 13-inch baking pan. Bake 1 hour.

For topping, mix together cornflakes and butter and sprinkle on casserole during last half-hour of baking. Yields 6 to 8 servings.

Asparagus Wraps

1 sheet puff pastry, thawed
Grated Swiss cheese
18 stalks frozen or cooked asparagus
1 egg
2 tablespoons cold water

Preheat oven to 400°. Unfold puff pastry and cut along fold lines. Cut each strip in three squares. Turn the square a quarter turn so it is diamond shaped. Place a teaspoon of cheese on square and 2 stalks asparagus on top of cheese. Fold over pastry corners so that stalks are wrapped with tips and bottoms sticking out of pastry. Press the pastry together slightly to seal. Beat the egg and cold water together and brush on pastry. Bake until puffy and brown. Serve immediately. These make a fancy extra on a breakfast plate with egg casserole and bacon. Cook asparagus to crisp tender since it will cook more in the oven. Yields 8 servings.

Kansas

PEACEFUL ACRES BED & BREAKFAST

Route 5, Box 153
Great Bend, KS 67530
(316) 793-7527

Peaceful Acres is a comfortable, sprawling, old farmhouse with two bedrooms on the ground level and a possible third upstairs. Bed and breakfast guests share the bathroom. A working windmill, small livestock, chickens and guineas, dogs and cats are all part of the ten acres. Your complimentary breakfast will consist of homemade breads, fresh eggs, juice, hot coffee or tea, milk, and cereal if desired. It is a quiet stay at Peaceful Acres, reminding one of days spent at the grandparents' home. Children are welcome and will enjoy the animals and the sturdy swing set and teeter-totter. The bed and breakfast is located about five miles from Great Bend, which has a zoo, tennis courts and a museum.

❧   ❧   ❧

Caramel Pecan Rolls

1 (¼-ounce) package yeast
1 cup warm water
¼ plus ½ cup sugar
1 teaspoon salt
2 tablespoons margarine
1 egg
2 plus 1¼ to 1½ cups all-purpose flour
2 teaspoons ground cinnamon

Topping:
⅔ cup pecan halves
2 tablespoons melted butter
1 tablespoon corn syrup
½ cup brown sugar

In mixing bowl dissolve yeast in warm water. Stir in the ¼ cup sugar, salt, margarine, egg, and 2 cups flour. Beat until smooth. With spoon or hand, work in enough of remaining flour until dough is easy to handle. Place in greased bowl, greased side up, and cover tightly. May be refrigerated up to 4 days. To make into cinnamon rolls, roll dough into rectangle, put remaining ½ cup sugar and cinnamon on dough, roll up, and cut.

For topping, place pecans in bottom of greased 10 x 15 x 2-inch baking pan. Put the butter, syrup, and brown sugar over pecans and place cut rolls on top. Let rise a little and then refrigerate. When ready to bake, preheat oven to 350° and bake about 30 minutes, or until golden brown. Turn out onto waxed paper on a tray, nut side up. Yields 18 large cinnamon rolls.

THE BRICKYARD BARN INN

4020 N. W. 25th Ave.
Topeka, KS 66618
(785) 235-0057 (phone)
(785) 234-0924 (fax)
umoo2me@cjnetworks.com
www.brickyardbarninn.com

The Brickyard Barn Inn is a magnificent 1927 dairy barn with a unique red brick exterior and attached silo. It has been converted into an elegant bed and breakfast situated on four scenic acres on the north edge of Topeka, Kansas. Relax with a hot cup of tea and a good book next to a warm, crackling fire in the Inn's living room. Wake up to fresh coffee and the day's newspaper in the country kitchen.

Christmas Pecan & Cranberry Snack Mix

Use this recipe for a very fast holiday snack. Be adventuresome to create your own favorites by adding pretzel sticks, walnuts, wheat chex. Have fun!

2 tablespoons Worcestershire sauce
2 tablespoons melted butter
½ teaspoon ground red pepper
½ teaspoon ground cumin
½ teaspoon garlic powder
½ teaspoon seasoned salt
¼ teaspoon dried oregano
3 cups pecan halves
1½ cups dried cranberries
    (or substitute dried cherries)

Preheat oven to 350°. Stir together Worcestershire sauce, butter, and spices. Add pecan halves and toss to coat. Spread mixture on cookie sheet. Bake 15 minutes; stir every 5 minutes. Stir in cranberries. Bake 5 minutes more or till pecans are toasted. Spread on paper towels or a paper grocery sack to cool. Store in an airtight container. Yields 4 cups.

Scott's Quick Shrimp Scampi

This recipe is virtually foolproof. You will love the quick simplicity, flexibility, and great flavor.

8 ounces dry pasta
½ cup extra virgin olive oil
1 large onion, diced
6 cloves garlic, minced or crushed
1 cup white wine
1 pound precooked shrimp, preferably
    the jumbo size, thawed
6 tablespoons butter
Salt and freshly ground pepper
1 tablespoon parsley (optional)
2 teaspoons paprika (optional)
1 lemon, cut into wedges (optional)

Cook pasta in boiling salted water until al dente. Heat olive oil in skillet over medium-high heat and sauté onions and garlic until onions are translucent. (Don't let them brown.) Add wine, turn to medium heat and reduce for 5 minutes. (The alcohol will evaporate.) Add shrimp; heat until warmed through. Stir in butter until melted. Turn heat to low. Add salt

and pepper to taste and parsley, paprika, and lemon, if using. Cover and simmer until pasta is ready. Serve over pasta. Yields 4 servings.

Note: This recipe is very flexible. Vegetarians can omit the meat and throw in vegetables. Be adventurous by adding tomatoes or pea pods. Garnish with parsley, cilantro, or lemon slices. If you are not a wine drinker, substitute low sodium chicken or vegetable broth.

Tango Salad

This is a great recipe to use to keep the kitchen cool and still serve your family a nutritious, balanced meal. Let the kids mix the salad, Mom does the dressing, and Dad gets to play with the grill.

6 cups salad greens
½ cup julienned cucumber
½ cup halved grape tomatoes
⅓ cup chopped red onions (or if you
    prefer use a red bell pepper)
¼ cup chopped olives
½ cup croutons
½ cup Honey-Lime Vinaigrette
    (see recipe below)
6 ounces smoked or grilled salmon
    (can substitute other meats)
4 tablespoons crumbled feta cheese

Toss salad greens, cucumber, tomatoes, red onions, olives, and croutons with honey-lime vinaigrette. Evenly distribute salmon on the top of salad and sprinkle with crumbled feta cheese. Yields about 6 servings.

Honey-Lime Vinaigrette

¼ cup freshly squeezed lime juice
¼ cup champagne vinegar
1 egg
1 cup vegetable oil
¼ cup honey
Salt and pepper

Place the lime juice, vinegar, and egg in a blender. Run on low and slowly drizzle in the oil and honey until the mixture is slightly thick. Add salt and pepper. Place the dressing mixture in a medium-size bowl. Place the bowl over a saucepan of simmering water (double boiler style) and whisk until the dressing reaches a temperature of 165°. (This last step is to thicken the dressing as well as pasteurize the raw egg.) Refrigerate for 12 hours before serving; thin if necessary with more lime juice or vinegar. Yields 1¾ cups.

Note: You can make a substitute for this dressing by mixing a bottled Italian dressing and adding the honey and lime juice; whisk together.

Chocolate Crème Brûlée

I enjoy garnishing this recipe with raspberries, strawberries, or coffee beans.

2 cups heavy cream
1 tablespoon instant espresso powder
    (or 1 teaspoon instant coffee)
5 ounces bittersweet chocolate
6 egg yolks
5 tablespoons granulated white sugar
1 teaspoon pure vanilla extract
¼ cup granulated white sugar
    (for the caramelized tops)
Whipped cream
Chocolate-covered coffee beans
    for garnish

Preheat oven to 300°. Combine cream and espresso powder in a heavy, medium saucepan. Bring to a simmer, whisking to dissolve espresso powder. Remove from heat. Break up chocolate and add to hot cream mixture, whisking until smooth. Set aside. Whisk yolks, sugar, and vanilla in a large bowl until well blended. Gradually whisk in chocolate mixture. Strain into a clean bowl, skimming off any foam or bubbles. Divide mixture among 6 ramekins or custard cups. Pour boiling water into square baking pan to a depth of about ½ inch.

Place the filled ramekins in the water bath, put all in the oven, and bake until set around the edges, but still loose in the center, about 40 to 50 minutes. Remove from oven and leave in the water bath until cooled. Remove cups from water bath.

These custards can be served warm or chilled. To chill, refrigerate for at least 2 hours, or up to 2 days. When ready to serve, sprinkle about 2 teaspoons of sugar over each custard. For best results, use a small, hand-held torch to melt sugar. If you don't have a torch, place under the broiler until sugar melts (watch carefully!).

To serve warm, dry off bottoms of ramekins as soon as you remove them from the hot water bath, and present them plain. If desired, top warm crème brûlée with a generous dollop of freshly-whipped cream, or serve with vanilla ice cream. Garnish with chocolate-covered coffee beans. Yields 6 to 8 servings.

LYONS' VICTORIAN MANSION BED & BREAKFAST & SPA

742 South National
Fort Scott, KS 66701
(620) 223-3644 (phone)
(620) 223-0062 (fax)
(800) 78-GUEST (toll free)
miss_pat@lyonsmansion.com
www.lyonsmansion.com

Welcome to Lyons' Victorian Mansion in Fort Scott, Kansas! This landmark 1876 Victorian mansion embraces business and leisure travelers with king-size beds in spacious suites. In-room phone, desk, mini-refrigerator, television, and VCR provide convenience for the road-weary. Front porch, butterfly gardens, fish pond, and barbeque grill invite guests for picnics on the lawn to the music of the waterfall dished up with a hearty measure of southern hospitality. To add to guests' comfort discover Paradise, a full-service spa offering massage therapy, and full spa services, including manicure, pedicure, facials, and wraps. A party barn with big screen TV and an enclosed Starlit Hot Tub complete the luxurious getaway. Guests are invited to enjoy the parlors that are trimmed in classical black walnut millwork. Wood trim has its original finish, a testimony of more than a century of loving care by the owners.

Lyons' Wild Rice Casserole

Grand served with Cornish game hens for dinner or as an accompaniment to an omelet or frittata for breakfast.

3 (6-ounce) boxes Uncle Ben's Original Long Grain and Wild Rice
24 ounces real sour cream
2 sticks real butter
2 (8-ounce) cans sliced water chestnuts, drained
3 cups shredded colby or Monterey Jack cheese
1 cup sliced almonds

Make rice according to package directions, including seasoning package. Mix in sour cream, butter, water chestnuts, and cheese. Preheat oven to 350°. Pour rice mixture into greased 9 x 13-inch pan. Bake 25 minutes. Top with raw sliced almonds and continue to cook 10 to 15 more minutes to allow almonds to toast as the casserole bakes. Yields 15 hearty servings.

PRAIRIE QUEEN BED & BREAKFAST

221 Arch Street
Leavenworth, KS 66048
(913) 758-1959 (phone/fax)
prairiequeen@attglobal.net
www.prairiequeen.com

The Prairie Queen is the premier bed and breakfast in Leavenworth, Kansas, and takes its name from a Missouri River riverboat that docked at Leavenworth. Take a step back in time as you drive up the brick driveway and receive your welcome under the porte cochere. Relax in one of the three elegant bedrooms, as you enjoy the warm personal hospitality of your hosts and indulge in a delicious home-cooked breakfast. Unwind in a soothing hot tub or by a cozy fireplace. Take a stroll along the beautiful Missouri River, tour historic Fort Leavenworth, or even enjoy a workout at the Riverfront Community Center.

The three individually decorated guest rooms include private baths. All rooms offer king-size beds and furniture built for comfort. The outdoor hot tub is the perfect place for soaking tired muscles after a day of shopping or touring.

Bob's Baked Apple

1 apple (Granny Smith or Rome)
1 tablespoon butter or margarine
½ plus ½ tablespoon cinnamon sugar
Raisins and walnuts
Whipped cream for garnish

Peel and core apple leaving bottom intact. A melon baller works well. Place butter in hole. Place apple in microwave-safe dish. Fill hole with ½ tablespoon cinnamon sugar.

Add raisins and nuts to taste. Sprinkle remaining cinnamon sugar on and around the apple. Cover apple with plastic wrap. Microwave on high 3 minutes. (Adjust time for multiple apples and turn frequently.) Be careful of hot steam when you uncover the apples. Garnish with whipped cream (smother with ice cream for your midnight snack). Yields 1 serving.

Potato Egg Skillet

2 tablespoons olive oil
1 medium potato, cubed
¼ cup chopped green pepper
¼ cup chopped red pepper
½ cup chopped mushrooms
¼ cup chopped onion
⅓ cup chopped cooked ham,
    bacon, or sausage
2 eggs, beaten with a splash of milk
¼ cup shredded Cheddar cheese

Prairie Queen Bed & Breakfast

Heat oil in skillet over medium-high heat. Pan fry potato until golden brown. In separate skillet sauté green pepper, red pepper, mushrooms, and onion until tender crisp. Preheat oven to 390°. Combine potato, vegetables, and meat at last minute in an oven-safe baking dish. Pour eggs over top of potato mixture. Bake until center is firm, about 15 minutes. Top with cheese. Yields 1 serving.

Stuffed Puffed French Toast

2 ounces cream cheese
Sliced fruit (apples, peaches,
    or strawberries)
2 slices French bread
Fruit topping to match
    stuffing choice (or just
    use maple syrup)

Batter:
2 cups all-purpose flour
4 teaspoons baking powder
½ cup sugar
½ teaspoon salt
1 teaspoon ground cinnamon
½ teaspoon ground nutmeg
1 egg
1 teaspoon vanilla extract
1½ cups milk
⅛ cup vegetable oil

Spread cream cheese and fruit layer on one slice. (If using apples, microwave the slices for 20 seconds before layering.) Put other slice on top. (This can be done ahead of time as having bread dry out a little is even better.)

For batter, mix together flour, baking powder, sugar, salt, cinnamon, and nutmeg. Add egg, vanilla, and milk. Blend until smooth. Heat the oil in skillet over medium-high heat. Dip each sandwich in batter and fry in hot oil, turning once until golden brown. Drain on paper towel and serve. I serve with Twisted Bacon (see recipe below). Yields 1 serving.

Note: The batter makes enough for 8. I keep the dry mixture on hand and just take enough to make the amount of batter I think I'll need. A little extra egg doesn't hurt the mixture. I just add the milk a little at a time to get the right batter thickness.

Twisted Bacon

½ cup brown sugar
Cracked black pepper
8 slices thick bacon

Preheat oven to 325°. Mix brown sugar and pepper in plastic bag. Add bacon and coat. Twist each end of bacon. Lay on rack over baking pan and bake about 40 minutes. Do not burn.

Kentucky

TRINITY HILLS FARM CHRISTIAN RETREAT

10455 Old Lovelaceville Road
Paducah, KY 42001
(800) 488-3998 (toll free)
www.trinityhills.com

Trinity Hills has many romantic amenities, which include fireplaces and stained glass, candlelight dining, and decks with gazebo and swings. The inn also offers corporate meeting rooms, lodging, and recreation.

Mr. Mike's Specialty Biscuits

4¼ cups biscuit mix
1¼ cups cold milk
½ cup bacon pieces
½ cup colby or Monterey Jack cheese

Preheat oven to 450°. Combine ingredients and mix, using electric mixer with dough hook or by hand. If dough is dry, add water until moist, but not sticky. Coat ice cream scoop with nonstick spray and drop biscuits on baking sheet. Bake 10 to 12 minutes. Yields 24 biscuits.

Almond Drizzle

1 to 2 tablespoons milk
½ cup confectioners' sugar
1 drop almond flavoring

Mix milk and confectioners' sugar, adding milk if necessary until desired consistency is achieved. Stir in flavoring. Drizzle over hot crescent rolls or croissants. Yields 8 servings.

Lady Anne's Egg Strata

Leftover bread pieces
  (rolls, buns, loaf bread)
1 (8-ounce) can sliced water chestnuts
½ cup real bacon pieces
1 cup colby or Monterey Jack cheese
1 slice green pepper, chopped
7 eggs
1½ cups milk
½ cup half-and-half
Salt and pepper

Spray two pie plates or one 9 x 11-inch pan. Line bottoms with bread pieces. Layer water chestnuts, bacon, cheese, and green pepper. Beat eggs together, add milk, half-and-half, and season with salt and pepper to taste. Pour mixture over base and let sit for 10 minutes. Preheat oven to 350° and bake 45 minutes, or until knife inserted comes out clean. Yields 8 servings.

Crescent Roll-Ups

1 (8-count) package crescent rolls
4 slices cooked sausage, finely chopped
  (can use food processor)
3 ounces softened cream cheese
1 tablespoon brown mustard

Preheat oven to 375°. Separate crescent rolls. Mix sausage, cream cheese, and mustard. Put 1 tablespoon mixture in middle of short end of roll triangle and roll up. Bake 9 to 11 minutes until golden brown. Yields 8 servings.
Note: Delicious with scrambled egg casserole (stir in bacon with eggs and scramble until fluffy) and baked spiced pears.

Cincinnati's Weller Haus Bed & Breakfast, Inc.

319 Poplar Street
Newport, KY 41073
(856) 431-6829 (phone)
(859) 431-4332 (fax)
(800) 431-4287 (toll free)
innkeepers@wellerhaus.com
www.wellerhaus.com

Savor the charm of the 1880s with a stay in this preservation-awarded bed and breakfast listed on the National Register of Historic Places. The house features original millwork and eighteenth-century period pieces. Weller Haus is two Victorian Gothic homes in Taylor Daught's historic district directly across the Ohio River from downtown Cincinnati. Enjoy a small town atmosphere with all of the conveniences of downtown Cincinnati. Antique-appointed guest and sitting rooms with private baths have all the amenities you could want.

Orange French Toast

8 eggs
½ cup orange juice
¼ teaspoon salt
Zest of half an orange
½ teaspoon ground cinnamon
Texas Toast

Orange-honey butter:
½ cup (1 stick) melted butter
¼ cup honey
Zest of half an orange

Whisk all ingredients, except toast and honey butter in wide bowl. Spray griddle with cooking spray and heat to 400° or until water sizzles on it. Dip toast into batter and brown both sides. Cut each slice in half diagonally.

For honey butter, combine all ingredients. Serve over French toast. Yields 4 servings.

The Rocking Horse Manor Bed & Breakfast

1022 South Third Street
Louisville, KY 40203
(502) 583-0408 (phone)
(502) 583-6077 (fax)
(888) HORSE-BB (toll free)
rockinghorse1888@cs.com
www.rockinghorse-bb.com

The Manor is a beautifully restored Victorian mansion in historic Old Louisville that has all the modern conveniences today's traveler requires. Two-course breakfast is served when you choose. Activities in the surrounding area include antiquing, wineries, riverboats, Churchill Downs, Louisville Slugger Museum, fairgrounds and exposition center, fine dining, and airport.

Brad's Hickory Bacon

½ cup brown sugar
¼ cup all-purpose flour
¼ teaspoon pepper
16 thick slices bacon
    (the thicker the better)

Preheat oven to 325°. Mix sugar, flour, and pepper in a sealable bag. Shake well. (Adjust brown sugar to taste.) Add bacon, one piece at a time, and toss to coat. Lay bacon on cookie sheet sprayed with nonstick spray and bake about 30 minutes. Use a pan with edges to prevent dripping. Yields 8 servings.

Rocking Horse Manor Quiche

3 eggs
1½ cups milk
⅓ cup melted margarine
½ cup biscuit mix
½ teaspoon lemon pepper
1 teaspoon dehydrated minced onion
1 cup cheese
2 cups "throw-ins" (new potatoes, broccoli, bacon, mushrooms)

Preheat oven to 350°. Mix eggs, milk, margarine, biscuit mix, lemon pepper, and onion in blender for about 1 minute. Pour over cheese and "throw-ins" in large bowl. Stir gently. Pour into pie pan coated with nonstick spray. Bake 40 minutes. Let stand 10 minutes before serving. This recipe is easily made the night before, refrigerated, and heated up before serving time. Yields 4 to 6 servings.

Pecan Twists

2 (8-ounce) cans refrigerated
    crescent rolls
4 plus 2 tablespoons melted butter
½ cup chopped pecans
¼ cup sugar
1 teaspoon ground cinnamon
⅛ teaspoon nutmeg
½ cup confectioners' sugar
2 tablespoons maple syrup or milk

Preheat oven to 375°. Unroll crescent rolls and separate each can into four rectangles, pressing perforations to seal. Brush evenly with 4 tablespoons butter. Stir together pecans, sugar, cinnamon, and nutmeg. Sprinkle 1 tablespoon mixture on each rectangle, pressing in gently. Roll up, starting at long side, and twist. Cut six shallow, ½-inch-long, diagonal slits in each roll. Shape rolls into rings, pressing ends together; place on lightly greased baking sheet. Brush rings with remaining 2 tablespoons butter. Bake 12 minutes or until golden brown. Stir together confectioners' sugar and maple syrup or milk until glaze is smooth. Drizzle over warm twists. Yields 8 servings.

Apple Brunch Biscuit

½ plus ½ cup sugar
1 cup ricotta cheese
1 egg
½ teaspoon ground cinnamon
1 (17.3-ounce) can large refrigerated biscuits
1 small apple, peeled and cut into wedges
½ cup sliced almonds

Preheat oven to 375°. Coat eight jumbo muffin cups or eight (6-ounce) custard cups with nonstick spray. In small bowl, combine ½ cup sugar, cheese, and egg and beat at high speed for 1 minute. In small bowl, combine remaining ½ cup sugar and cinnamon; mix well. Separate biscuits and turn each in cinnamon sugar. Press biscuits in bottom and up sides of muffin cups. Place 1 apple wedge in each biscuit, add almonds to cinnamon sugar, and sprinkle each biscuit with 1 tablespoon cinnamon mixture. Bake 20 to 25 minutes or until biscuits are deep golden brown and apples are crisp tender. Remove biscuits from cups. Cool 15 minutes. Serve warm. Store in the refrigerator. Yields 8 servings.

The Rocking Horse Manor Bed & Breakfast

ALEKSANDER HOUSE BED & BREAKFAST

1213 S. First St.
Louisville, KY 40203
(502) 637-4985 (phone)
(502) 635-1398 (fax)
alekhouse@aol.com
www.bbonline.com/ky/aleksander

Aleksander House Bed & Breakfast, a gracious 1882 Victorian home, is centrally located in historic Old Louisville near shops, restaurants, museums, and many other attractions. The three-story brick building is completely restored and listed on the National Register of Historic Landmarks. Inside are fourteen-foot ceilings, original hardwood floors, light fixtures, stained glass, and fireplaces. The walls of the spacious dining room are lined with French toile paper and prints of the nineteenth-century French impressionists. Area attractions and activities include viewing the wonderful old Victorian homes of Old Louisville; the delightful JB

Speed Art Museum; Churchill Downs; a paddleboat ride on the Ohio River; a dinner train ride through scenic Kentucky; a relaxing trip to the Huber Wineries; visit to a Shaker Village or to one of the many other small quaint villages just one hour away.

Grand Marnier French Toast

French toast:
French bread, large slices, thickly cut
3 cups heavy cream
1 cup orange juice
4 eggs
4 tablespoons Grand Marnier
4 tablespoons sugar
2 tablespoons orange zest
Melted butter
Confectioners' sugar

Orange butter:
6 ounces butter
Juice of 1 orange
½ cup confectioners' sugar
Zest of 1 orange
1 tablespoon Grand Marnier
Mint leaves for garnish

Put 12 to 16 pieces bread in large rectangular baking dish. Mix cream, orange juice, eggs, Grand Marnier, sugar, and orange zest and pour over bread. Put in refrigerator for several hours. Turn over and soak 8 to 10 hours or overnight. When ready to bake, preheat oven to 350°. Brush cookie tins generously with melted butter. Lay pieces of bread onto buttered pans. Brush tops with melted butter. Bake about 45 minutes to 1 hour. Turn halfway through the cooking process. Remove from pans to plates and sprinkle with confectioners' sugar.

For orange butter, soften butter. Add remaining ingredients. Mix and form into ball or mold. Garnish with mint leaves and serve with French toast. Yields 8 servings.

Cranberry Orange Frappé

2 cups cranberry juice
1 cup orange juice
¼ cup whipping cream
Sugar
1 tablespoon lemon juice
2 bananas
¾ cup crushed ice
Mint leaves

Combine all ingredients, except the mint leaves, in a blender. Process on high for 1 minute. Garnish with mint leaves and serve in stemmed goblets. Yields 4 servings.

Tomato-Onion Quiche

2 cups shredded Cheddar and
    mozzarella cheese
1 (9-inch) partially baked pie shell
3 tomatoes, thinly sliced
1 onion, thinly sliced
1 teaspoon dried basil
¼ teaspoon garlic salt

Cracked pepper
2 eggs
¾ cup milk
3 tablespoons grated Parmesan

Preheat oven to 350°. Sprinkle cheese on bottom of pie shell. Layer tomatoes and onions over cheese. Sprinkle basil, garlic salt, and pepper to taste on top. Beat eggs and milk together and pour over tomatoes and onions. Sprinkle Parmesan on top. Bake 45 to 50 minutes. Yields 8 servings.

Eggs Florentine

1 (16-ounce) package chopped spinach
8 eggs
½ cup (1 stick) melted butter
8 ounces shredded Swiss cheese
8 ounces crumbled feta cheese
⅛ teaspoon ground nutmeg

Cook spinach as directed on package. Drain well and squeeze in paper towels until water is removed. Preheat oven to 350°. Beat eggs and add butter, cheeses, and nutmeg. Mix well. Add spinach and blend thoroughly. Pour into greased, 9 x 12-inch baking pan. Bake 30 minutes. Cut into squares and serve. Yields 8 servings.

Pears in White Zinfandel

8 pears
3 cups white Zinfandel
2 tablespoons lemon juice
1 cup sugar
2 teaspoons ground cinnamon
Zest of 1 lemon
1 teaspoon vanilla extract
Crème fraîche
Mint leaves

Peel and core pears. In a deep saucepan, combine wine, lemon juice, sugar, cinnamon, lemon zest, and vanilla. Bring to a boil. Add pears, stems up, and scoop spoonfuls of liquid over them. Simmer until pears are tender, 10 to 20 minutes. Remove pears and place in individual serving dishes. Strain liquid and boil until reduced by half. Pour wine sauce over pears. Let cool. Serve with crème fraîche on the side. Garnish with mint leaves. Yields 8 servings.

GRATZ PARK INN

120 West Second Street
Lexington, KY 40507
(859) 231-1777 (phone)
(859) 233-7593 (fax)
(800) 752-4166 (toll free)
gratzparkinn@gratzparkinn.com
www.gratzparkinn.com

Venture back in time to an oasis of elegance in spacious, appointed, forty-four guest rooms. Escape, yet feel the comforts of your setting in one of the luxurious suites, and relax in the elegant sitting rooms. Each of the guest rooms is individually decorated in nineteenth-century style and illuminates unique color schemes. Included are antique reproductions, mahogany four-poster beds, and regional artwork. Gratz Park Inn, located in the heart of Lexington's historic district and "The Horse Capital of the World," is listed on the National Register of Historic Sites. The inn lies mere blocks from Lexington's downtown business and legal district, Rupp Arena, Victorian Square, historical sites and museums, private and public educational institutions and churches. Jonathan at Gratz Park creates a menu of refined regional cuisine as well as offering multiple fine wines and spirits.

Black-Eyed-Pea-Crusted Scallops

2 cups crispy black-eyed peas
2 tablespoons cornmeal
1 teaspoon black pepper
1 teaspoon garlic powder
1 teaspoon onion powder
Salt
16 very large scallops, more if they are medium size
2 tablespoons olive oil

Place crispy peas in food processor and purée until they develop a moist texture and stick to sides of bowl. Scrape down sides of bowl; add cornmeal, pepper, garlic powder, and onion powder and process for a few seconds more. Continue scraping sides of bowl and processing until a smooth meal is achieved. Add salt to taste and pour mixture onto a large plate. Pat mixture on scallops until well coated. The scallops should be cooked about four at a time or they will cook too slowly and become soggy. Heat oil almost to a smoking point over medium-high heat. Add scallops and sauté quickly to lightly brown on both sides. Finish in 325° oven if not cooked through. Cook remaining scallops in same manner. Yields 4 servings.

Note: The black-eyed-pea crust can be used with any white fish. Jonathan's serves the scallops with caramelized onions, arugula wilted in browned butter, and jasmine rice cooked with stock and browned butter.

Crispy Black-Eyed Peas

4 cups dried black-eyed peas
12 cups water
6 cups vegetable oil
Salt

Soak peas in water for 24 hours. Drain off water and spread on paper towels to dry.

Heat oil in a deep skillet and fry peas until they are light brown and crispy to the bite. Drain peas in a colander with a drip pan to catch oil, and salt generously. Yields 8 to 10 cups.

Note: These are great for snacks or salad toppings.

INN AT WOODHAVEN

401 South Hubbards Lane
Louisville, KY 40207
(502) 895-1011 (phone)
(888) 895-1011 (toll free)
info@innatwoodhaven.com
www.innatwoodhaven.com

Enjoy comfortable, elegant lodging in an 1853 Gothic Revival home listed on the National Register of Historic Places. Take your choice of beautifully appointed rooms in the main house as well as the carriage house.

Victorian Lace Cookies

⅔ cup butter
2 cups quick oats
1 cup sugar
⅔ cup all-purpose flour
¼ cup milk
1 teaspoon vanilla extract
¼ teaspoon salt
12 ounces chocolate morsels, melted

Preheat oven to 350°. Melt butter in a medium saucepan over medium heat. Remove from heat. Stir in all ingredients but chocolate. Drop by teaspoonfuls three inches apart on foil-lined cookie sheets.

Bake about 7 minutes or until lightly browned. Cool and spread melted chocolate on top of half the cookies and cover with remaining half. Yields about 16 cookies.

Savory Herb Cheesecake

Crust:
2 tablespoons softened butter
¼ cup finely crushed dry breadcrumbs
½ cup Parmesan cheese

Inn at Woodhaven

Cheesecake:
16 ounces cream cheese at
    room temperature
1 cup crumbled goat cheese
3 large eggs, room temperature
1 cup sour cream
6 green onions, chopped
1 tablespoon chopped roasted garlic
1 teaspoon each basil, parsley, and tarragon
Fresh herbs to garnish

For crust, grease 9-inch springform pan with butter. Mix remaining ingredients and coat bottom of pan. Set aside any remaining mixture.

For cheesecake, preheat oven to 375°. In food processor beat cream cheese until creamy. Add goat cheese, eggs, and sour cream. Beat until smooth. Add onions, garlic, and herbs and blend well. Spoon mixture into prepared pan and bake for 40 minutes or until golden brown. Cool to room temperature and chill for at least 2 hours. Remove from pan and pat remaining crumb mixture around the sides. Garnish with sprigs of fresh herbs. Serve with toasted crackers. Yields 8 servings.

Shrimp Puffs

10 ounces cooked shrimp
8 ounces cream cheese, softened
¼ teaspoon curry powder
2 teaspoons melted butter
1 (1-pound) package frozen puff pastry

Preheat oven to 350°. Blend the shrimp, cream cheese, curry powder, and butter in food processor. Cut pastry into 3 x 3-inch squares, place teaspoonful of mixture in center and fold into triangles, sealing edges well. Place on lightly buttered baking sheet and bake for 20 minutes until brown. Yields 4 to 5 dozen.

CHRETIEN POINT PLANTATION

665 Chretien Point Road
Sunset, LA 70584
(337) 662-7050 (phone)
(337) 662-6751 (fax)
reservations@chretienpoint.com
www.chretienpoint.com

Chretien Point, rich in Civil War history, is a lovely 1831 plantation home that operates as a bed and breakfast point of interest for tourists and as a special events venue. The twelve-room mansion includes twenty acres of comfort and serenity, a pond, swimming pool, and gift shop. Rate includes cocktails, hors d'oeuvre, home-cooked plantation breakfast, and tour. Activities in the surrounding area of interest to our guests include antique shopping, swamp tours, museums, state parks, historic site tours, hunting and fishing, gaming, amusement and water parks, aquarium, zoo, local food and music, and many festivals year-round.

♣   ♣   ♣

Anna Maria Pancakes

½ stick butter
5 eggs, beaten
1¼ cups all-purpose flour
1¼ cups milk
1 tablespoon vanilla extract
Fresh berries (optional)
Lime juice (juice of approximately
    2 limes)
Confectioners' sugar

Preheat oven to 415°. In large ovenproof skillet, melt butter. In medium bowl, combine eggs, flour, milk, and vanilla. Mix well. Pour batter into skillet. Do not stir. At this point you may add fresh berries if you choose. Bake 20 minutes. Pancake will be big and puffy. Immediately pour or squeeze lime juice all over pancake and sprinkle liberally with confectioners' sugar. This will make a deliciously tart syrup. You may add fresh fruit on top or leave plain. Slice and serve. Yields 8 to 10 servings.

Persimmon Pudding Bread

½ cup vegetable oil
1 cup sugar
2 eggs, beaten
3 large, ripe persimmons
2 cups all-purpose flour
½ teaspoon baking powder
1 teaspoon baking soda
½ teaspoon salt
1 teaspoon ground cinnamon
3 tablespoons milk
⅓ teaspoon vanilla extract
Confectioners' sugar

Preheat oven to 350°. Combine oil and sugar. Add eggs and persimmons and mix well. Mix flour, baking powder, baking soda, salt, cinnamon, milk, and vanilla. Combine with sugar mixture. Pour into greased and floured loaf pan. Cook 1 hour. Bread will come out very moist, almost pudding-like. Cut into slices and serve with confectioners' sugar. This makes a good morning bread to serve with coffee. Yields 1 loaf.

Cranberry Pecan Scones

6 cups biscuit mix
1½ cups sugar
3 cups pecans, broken into pieces
4 cups craisins (dried cranberries)
2 teaspoons salt
2 eggs, beaten
2 cups milk
1 stick butter, melted
1 tablespoon vanilla extract

Preheat oven to 425°. Butter two cookie sheets. In large bowl, blend biscuit mix and sugar together. Add pecans and craisins. Add salt and stir well. In separate bowl or large measuring cup, mix eggs, milk, butter, and vanilla. Pour liquid mixture into dry mixture and mix well. Dough should be sticky (a bit softer than dough you would roll out). Drop by teaspoonfuls (about size of a large egg) on buttered cookie sheet. Space one inch apart. Bake 14 to 18 minutes or until golden brown. Yields about 2½ dozen scones.

Mint Juleps

8 cups water
3½ cups sugar
2 teaspoons mint extract
Bourbon
Fresh mint sprigs

Measure water into a large pot. Stir sugar into water. Bring water to a boil, stirring occasionally. Remove from heat and let cool completely. Add mint extract to sugar water. This is the syrup that you will use to mix with bourbon. Syrup can be stored in refrigerator until ready to mix. When ready to serve, mix 2 to 3 parts syrup to 1 part bourbon. Serve with fresh mint sprigs. Yields about 3 quarts.

Hearty Brunch Casserole

4 to 6 slices sourdough bread
2 cups shredded Cheddar cheese
1 pound breakfast sausage
8 eggs
1 teaspoon dry mustard
2¼ cups plus ⅓ cup milk
2 tablespoons dried onion flakes
1 (10¾-ounce) can cream of
    mushroom soup

Grease 9 x 13-inch baking pan. Cover with bread slices, using just enough to cover entire bottom. Sprinkle cheese over bread. Brown sausage, drain, and let cool slightly. Sausage should be well crumbled. Sprinkle sausage crumbles over cheese. In large bowl, mix eggs, mustard, 2¼ cups milk, and onion flakes. Pour over bread, cheese, and sausage. Cover and refrigerate over-night. When ready to bake preheat oven to 350°. Mix soup with remaining ⅓ cup milk and pour over casserole. Bake 1 hour. Let stand 5 to 10 minutes before serving. Cut into squares. Serve with crusty bread and fruit salad. Yields 8 to 10 servings.

THE BARROW HOUSE INN

9779 Royal, Box 2550
St. Francisville, LA 70775
(225) 635-4791 (phone)
(225) 635-1863 (fax)
website@topteninn.com
www.topteninn.com

The Barrow House Inn offers antiques and ambience in the heart of a fairy-tale historic district. Two houses (circa 1800) offer luxurious rooms and suites. Included is our unique cassette-tape walking tour. The area is rich in plantation tours. These include Rosedown Plantation; Oakley Plantation; Greenwood Plantation; Afton Villa; Cottage Plantation; Butler Greenwood Plantation; and The Myrtles Plantation.

Praline Parfait

Sauce:
1½ sticks butter or margarine
1 cup granulated sugar
2 cups packed light brown sugar
½ cup heavy cream
1 cup milk
1¼ plus 1¼ cups chopped pecans
1 teaspoon vanilla extract

Parfaits:
Vanilla ice cream
Whipped cream
Chopped pecans

For sauce, melt butter or margarine in large pot. Add sugars and cream; cook for 1 minute while stirring. Add milk and 1¼ cups pecans. Cook 4 minutes, stirring occasionally. Reduce heat to medium and cook another 5 minutes. Add remaining 1¼ cups pecans and vanilla. Continue to cook for another 15 to 20 minutes.

For parfaits, place 1 scoop vanilla ice cream in a footed glass. Pour 2 tablespoons sauce on top. Decorate with a spoonful of whipped cream and chopped pecans. Yields 25 servings.

Note: Sauce can also be used on bananas. Heat and serve as Bananas Foster for breakfast. The inn calls this "Bananas Praline."

Veal Scaloppine with Wild Mushrooms and Tasso

1 teaspoon Creole seasoning
4 (3-ounce) slices veal, pounded to
    ⅛-inch thickness (boneless chicken
    or turkey breasts can be substituted)
2 tablespoons olive oil
½ cup all-purpose flour
½ pound sliced, mixed wild mushrooms
¼ pound tasso (turkey or ham), chopped
½ cup Marsala wine
½ cup veal or chicken stock
4 slices low-fat mozzarella cheese

Sprinkle seasoning on meat and melt oil in large skillet. Dredge veal in flour and sauté in oil heated to medium for 1 to 2 minutes per side; remove meat from skillet. Add mushrooms and tasso to skillet and cook for 2 minutes. Add wine and stock. Boil mixture about 5 minutes, or until it is reduced by half. Preheat oven to 350°. Place veal in baking pan and put mushroom-tasso mixture on top. Cover each slice with mozzarella and bake for 10 minutes or until cheese melts. Yields 4 servings.

Ricotta Breakfast Quiche

Topping:

1½ cups all-purpose flour
½ cup sugar
½ cup (1 stick) butter or margarine
1 teaspoon ground cinnamon

Filling:

¾ cup (1½ sticks) butter or margarine
¾ cup sugar
6 eggs, extra large to jumbo
1 teaspoon orange extract
1 teaspoon vanilla extract
2 pounds ricotta cheese
2 (9-inch) uncooked piecrusts
1 egg white, beaten

For topping, mix flour, sugar, butter, and cinnamon in food processor. Preheat oven to 350°.

For filling, cream butter and sugar. Add eggs, one at a time, and mix in with electric mixer. Mix in orange extract and vanilla. Add ricotta and mix well again. Brush piecrusts with egg white, and pour in filling. Sprinkle on topping. Bake 1 hour. Let pies cool at least 10 minutes before serving. Yields 2 pies, 8 servings each.

Linzertorte Cheese Cups

1 cup (2 sticks) butter
1 cup all-purpose flour
1½ cups ground almonds
½ cup sugar
2 egg yolks
12 ounces cream cheese, softened
¾ cup sugar
2 eggs, separated
2 teaspoons vanilla extract
2 plus 2 tablespoons raspberry liqueur
4 ounces raspberry chocolate chips
1 (8-ounce) jar seedless raspberry preserves
1 tablespoon cornstarch
4 ounces white chocolate chips

Mix butter and flour and add almonds. Mix in sugar and egg yolks to blend. Refrigerate dough for 4 hours or overnight. Press 1 rounded teaspoon dough into each of 4 dozen greased, mini-cupcake molds.

Preheat oven to 375°. Blend cream cheese with sugar, egg yolks, vanilla, and 2 tablespoons liqueur. With electric mixer at medium speed, beat until smooth. Place 3 raspberry chocolate chips into each cup and fill with 1 teaspoon cheese mixture. Bake 20 minutes. Remove from oven and cool. Melt raspberry preserves in saucepan and add remaining 2 tablespoons liqueur. Bring to a boil and add cornstarch mixed with 1 tablespoon water. Spoon ½ teaspoon preserves on top of each cup. Place 3 white chocolate chips on top of preserves. Refrigerate. Yields 4 dozen cups, or 2 dozen regular tarts or 2 standard pies.

Delta Queen Steamboat Company, Inc.

1380 Port of New Orleans Place
New Orleans, LA 70130-1890
(504) 586-0631 (phone)
(800) 543-1949 (toll free)
www.deltaqueen.com

Delta Queen Steamboat Company, the oldest U.S. flag cruise line, offers three-night to eleven-night cruises aboard America's only authentic, steam-powered, overnight paddlewheelers: the legendary Delta Queen, the magnificent Mississippi Queen, and the grand American Queen. Each steamboatin' vacation includes four sumptuous meals a day, award-winning Broadway-style entertainment, the services of our all-American crew, and varied shore excursions. A variety of special theme cruises are also offered, such as Spring Pilgrimage vacations, Civil War vacations, big band vacations, and old-fashioned holiday vacations.

Fried Green Tomatoes

3 green tomatoes (unripe red tomatoes), sliced in ⅜- to ¼-inch-thick slices
Seasoned flour
Egg wash (2 parts egg and 2 parts water) or buttermilk, beaten slightly
1 cup fish-fry coating
Vegetable oil for frying
½ to 1 pound peeled crawfish tails
Cajun Beurre Blanc*

Dredge tomato slices in seasoned flour. Dip in egg wash or buttermilk. Dredge again in 1 cup fish-fry coating. Fry in vegetable oil; drain on paper towel. Place 3 slices tomato on serving plate; top with peeled crawfish tails and 1 ounce Cajun Beurre Blanc. Yields 6 servings.

*Note: *Beurre blanc,* which means "white butter," is composed of a wine, vinegar, and shallot reduction to which chunks of butter are added to make a thick and smooth sauce.

Louisiana Pork Roast with Sweet Potatoes

1 pork loin, center cut, with 9 to 10 bones
1 pint cane syrup
1 pint Creole mustard
½ cup diced onion
¼ cup each diced celery and carrots

Sweet potatoes:

2 large raw sweet potatoes
Vegetable oil

Trim excess fat from pork. Combine syrup and mustard; rub pork loin liberally with mixture. Marinate overnight. Preheat oven to 375°. Place pork loin in roasting pan with onion, celery, and carrots. Cook pork loin uncovered for 15 minutes; reduce heat to 300° and cook until brown, about 45 minutes to 1 hour (internal temperature of 155°). Five minutes prior to removing from oven, add 1 cup water or stock to bottom of pan to increase pan drippings. Remove pork loin from roasting pan; let stand for 15 minutes; cut into chops.

While pork chops are cooking, julienne sweet potatoes. Fry in small batches in vegetable oil until crisp. To serve, place pork chop on plate, pour 2 tablespoons pan drippings over chop; top with nest of sweet potatoes. Yields 9 to 10 servings.

Spinach Salad with Duck and Andouille Sausage Dressing

2 duck breasts (12 ounces total)
Salt and pepper
½ pound andouille sausage,
    cut in ¼-inch dice

Dressing:
¼ cup diced red onion
3 cloves garlic, crushed
1 cup red wine
1 teaspoon basil
1 teaspoon thyme
1 teaspoon oregano leaves
½ cup red wine vinegar
1¼ cups vegetable oil
2 pounds fresh spinach leaves
½ pound shiitake mushrooms,
    thinly sliced
½ pound feta cheese, cut in ¼-inch dice

Preheat oven to 350°. Season outside of duck breast with salt and pepper to taste. In oven pan, brown very well for 20 to 30 minutes. Pour off grease. Add 1½ cups water and cover. Simmer in oven for 1 to 1½ hours or until duck is tender. Remove. Reserve stock. Remove skin and dice breast meat in ½-inch cubes.

For dressing, in sauté pan over medium-high heat, sauté sausage in 2 tablespoons duck fat until brown. Add onion and garlic and cook until onions are clear. Add red

wine, reserved duck stock, and herbs, and reduce liquid by one-fourth. Add diced duck breast and mix well. Remove from heat. Add red wine vinegar and whip in oil. Keep in warm area or over warm heat. Clean and wash spinach. Drain well. Divide onto six to eight salad plates and top with equal amounts of mushrooms and cheese. Serve with 2 to 2½ ounces warm dressing. Yields 6 to 8 servings.

Mississippi Mud Pie

Coffee ice cream:
2 cups whole milk
3 cups heavy cream
1¼ cups sugar
4 whole eggs
½ teaspoon vanilla
¼ cup coffee reduction
    (4 cups reduced to ¼ cup)

Chocolate pecan brownie:
4 ounces unsweetened chocolate
1 cup (2 sticks) softened
    unsalted butter
2 cups sugar
4 whole eggs
½ teaspoon salt
1 teaspoon vanilla extract
1 cup all-purpose flour
1 cup pecan pieces
2 cups heavy whipping cream
1 cup confectioners' sugar
2 teaspoons chocolate liqueur
Hershey's syrup
Pecan pieces for garnish

For coffee ice cream, scald milk and cream. Add sugar and dissolve. In separate bowl, beat eggs, vanilla, and coffee reduction. Slowly add milk mixture to eggs, whipping continuously. Return to heat and cook for about 15 minutes over low heat, or until mixture coats a spoon. Stir constantly. Let cool 8 to 10 hours and freeze in ice cream freezer.

For brownie, preheat oven to 375°. Melt chocolate and let cool. Whip butter and add sugar, eggs, salt, and vanilla. Mix well. Add melted chocolate and flour and mix

well. Fold in pecans and blend evenly through batter. Pour into 9 x 13-inch glass baking pan that has been buttered and floured. Bake about 30 minutes, turn out on flat surface, and cool.

To serve, whip together cream, sugar, and liqueur, and chill in mixing bowl until stiff. Top brownie with ice cream and freeze until set. Top with whipping cream and freeze. Cut into 6 to 8 equal portions and top with warm Hershey's syrup. Garnish with pecan pieces. Yields 6 servings.

2439 FAIRFIELD, A BED & BREAKFAST

2439 Fairfield Avenue
Shreveport, LA 71104
(318) 424-2424 (phone)
(877) 251-2439 (toll free)
2439fair@bellsouth.net

The elegant Twenty-Four Thirty-Nine Fairfield Bed & Breakfast, circa 1905, is situated in the historical district on a beautiful avenue of splendid avenue of splendid mansions and fine homes built around the turn of the century. Landscaped English rose and herb gardens, a Victorian swing, gazebo, and water fountain are nestled among the oak trees. Downtown Shreveport and the Bossier City Municipal Complex, the Shreveport Regional Airport, Barksdale Air Force Base, all medical facilities, museums, art galleries, Louisiana Downs, and river boat casinos are only minutes away. The Line Avenue shopping corridor of many unique shops are just two blocks with many quaint restaurants also to savor and to enjoy.

Tomato Quiche

6 to 8 tomatoes, sliced
    (Roma tomatoes work well)
1 (9-inch) pie shell, prebaked until
    slightly golden
½ teaspoon sweet basil
¼ cup chopped green onions
Salt and pepper
1 cup shredded Cheddar cheese
1 cup mayonnaise

Preheat oven to 350°. Place layer of tomatoes in pie shell. Sprinkle with sweet basil, green onions, and salt and pepper to taste. Add another layer of tomatoes. Add more sweet basil, salt, pepper, and green onions. Keep adding layers until pie shell is full. Spread cheese over top. Spread mayonnaise over cheese layer. Bake 45 minutes or until golden brown. Let stand for 20 minutes before slicing. Yields 8 servings.

Note: Use piecrust protectors about half way through cooking time to keep crust from burning. If you don't have piecrust protectors, use aluminum foil.

Sautéed Mushrooms

¼ cup (½ stick) butter or margarine
16 ounces mushrooms, cleaned
    and sliced
1 teaspoon black pepper
1 to 2 tablespoons ham, sausage,
    or bacon drippings

Put butter, mushrooms, black pepper, and drippings in large skillet. Cook, covered, on medium heat for about 10 minutes. Remove lid and continue to cook on medium heat until liquid has evaporated. Yields 4 to 6 servings.

Banana Bread

1 (18-ounce) package butter-recipe
    cake mix
4 bananas, mashed
3 eggs, slightly beaten
½ cup (1 stick) melted butter
½ cup chopped nuts
1 teaspoon vanilla extract

Preheat oven to 350°. Mix all ingredients together well and divide into two loaf pans coated with nonstick spray. Bake 45 minutes to 1 hour. Yields 2 loaves.

Note: Each loaf serves 6 to 10 guests, depending on how generous the slices are

Hash Brown Casserole

1 (2-pound) package frozen
    hash brown potatoes, thawed
1 (16-ounce) carton sour cream
1 (10¾-ounce) can cream of celery soup
1 cup shredded sharp Cheddar cheese
½ cup chopped green onions
½ cup (1 stick) melted butter
    or margarine
1 teaspoon salt
1 teaspoon pepper
½ cup cracker crumbs

Preheat oven to 350°. Combine hash browns, sour cream, soup, cheese, green onions, butter, salt and pepper. Spoon into a lightly greased 13 x 9 x 2-inch baking dish. Bake 40 to 45 minutes or until bubbly. Remove from oven and top with cracker crumbs. Bake for 5 minutes or until crumbs turn lightly golden. Yields 10 to 12 servings.

Hint: Once you mix this recipe together, you can divide the mixture into two separate pans. Don't freeze longer than a month.

OAK ALLEY PLANTATION RESTAURANT & INN

3645 Highway 18
Vacherie, LA 70090
(225) 265-2151 (phone)
(225) 265-7035 (fax)
(800) 442-5539 (toll free)
ContactUs@OakAlleyPlantation.com
www.OakAlleyPlantation.com

Oak Alley Plantation beckons the visitor to discover fascinating moments from three centuries reflected in the colorful cultures and traditions unique to life along the banks of the lower Mississippi River. The story of Oak Alley begins with the trees. Sometime in the early 1700s, an unknown French settler built a small house on the site of the present mansion. It was he who planted the twenty-eight live oak trees in two well-spaced rows, reaching from his house to the Mississippi.

Enjoy the cottages (circa 1900) that are located in the residential quarters of the plantation grounds, not far from the antebellum mansion. They are tastefully furnished and cheerfully decorated with the fresh charm of country living. The absence of a television and telephone further enhances this peaceful setting. As for activities, the plantation offers tours and many points of interest on the twenty-five acres of the Oak Alley Foundation, seventy-five acres surrounding the foundation's property; 600 acres leased for sugarcane, and 450 acres of virgin woodlands.

Chicken and Sausage Gumbo

½ cup vegetable oil
½ cup all-purpose flour
1 cup diced onion
½ cup diced celery
½ cup diced bell pepper
1 tablespoon Italian seasoning
1 tablespoon parsley flakes
½ pound andouille, sliced
1½ pounds boneless chicken breasts, cut up
½ pound smoked sausage, sliced
4 cups water
2 tablespoons Creole seasoning
1 tablespoon sugar
¼ cup piquant sauce*
1 bay leaf
2 cups chicken broth

Heat oil in heavy, 8-quart pot. Add flour, stirring constantly until roux is the color of a copper penny. Lower flame and add onion, celery, bell pepper, Italian seasoning, parsley flakes, andouille, chicken, and sausage. Add water slowly, stirring constantly, until well mixed. Stir in Creole seasoning, sugar, piquant sauce, bay leaf, and chicken broth. Cover pot and cook on low for 30 minutes, stirring every 15 minutes or so to prevent sticking. Skim off grease and remove bay leaf before serving. Serve over steamed white rice. Yields 10 servings.

*Note: A piquante sauce is 1 part cider vinegar and 8 parts brown sauce. Sauté some onions in liberal amount of butter and simmer with vinegar and sauce for 30 minutes. Add some chopped pickles

and simmer 10 minutes. Remove from heat and add parlsey.

Shrimp Creole

2 pounds raw shrimp
½ gallon water
½ cup vegetable oil
½ cup all-purpose flour
1½ cups diced onion
½ cup diced celery
¾ cup diced bell pepper
16 ounces mushroom slices
1 (6-ounce) can tomato paste
1 (14½-ounce) can diced tomatoes
1½ tablespoons sugar
½ tablespoon Creole Seasoning*
1 teaspoon basil
1 tablespoon parsley flakes
½ tablespoon minced garlic
Juice of 1 lemon
½ teaspoon Tabasco Sauce*
½ cup shrimp stock

Boil shrimp in water until shrimp turns pink. Peel and set aside, reserving liquid for stock. Heat oil in heavy saucepan. Add flour, stirring constantly until roux is the color of a copper penny. Lower flame and add onion, celery, bell pepper, and mushrooms; sauté until tender. Add remaining ingredients and cook on medium heat for 20 minutes. Add shrimp and cook an additional 10 minutes. Serve over steamed rice. Yields 8 servings.

*Note: Tony Chachere's Creole Seasoning and Tabasco Sauce may be purchased through the online gift shop for Oak Alley.

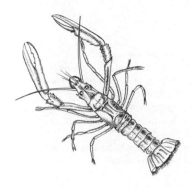

Crawfish Étouffée

½ cup (1 stick) margarine
2 onions, chopped
1 bell pepper, chopped
2 ribs celery, chopped
1 tablespoon chopped garlic
1 (10-ounce) can Ro-Tel Tomatoes
1 (10¾-ounce) can cream of
   mushroom soup
Salt and pepper
1 pound crawfish, peeled and boiled
½ cup chopped green onion
2 tablespoons chopped parsley

Melt margarine in Dutch oven. Add onions, bell pepper, celery, and garlic and sauté until tender. Add tomatoes and soup, and salt and pepper to taste. Cook over low heat for 1 hour, stirring constantly to prevent sticking. Add crawfish, green onion, and parsley. Cook for another 20 minutes. Serve over steamed white rice. Yields 6 servings.

The Captain Jefferds Inn

P.O. Box 691, 5 Pearl Street
Kennebunkport, ME 04046
(207) 967-2311 (phone)
(207) 967-0721 (fax)
(800) 839-6844 (toll free)
captjeff@captainjefferdsinn.com
www.captainjefferdsinn.com

Captain Jefferds Inn is a magnificent, federal-style mansion within easy walking distance of art galleries, unique gift shops, restaurants, and the harbor. Each guest room is individually decorated and amenities include tiled baths, super-soft linens, terry robes, fireplaces, and whirlpool tubs. Outstanding candlelit breakfasts served by the fire with friendly personal service make this a very special place.

Apricot-Stuffed French Toast with Orange Syrup

1 (1-pound) loaf crusty French bread
6 ounces cream cheese, softened
⅓ cup part-skim-milk ricotta cheese
⅓ cup apricot preserves
½ cup chopped dried apricots
5 eggs
1¼ cups milk
½ teaspoon vanilla extract
¼ teaspoon ground cinnamon
Dash of ground nutmeg
2 tablespoons butter or margarine

Orange syrup:
½ cup (1 stick) butter
½ cup sugar
3 ounces (⅓ cup) frozen
    orange juice concentrate

Cut bread into diagonal slices about 1 inch thick. Cut a pocket in each slice, cutting from top crust side almost to bottom crust side. In small mixing bowl beat together cream cheese, ricotta, preserves, and apricots. Spoon about 1 tablespoon mixture into each pocket. Mix together eggs, milk, vanilla, cinnamon, and nutmeg. Dip stuffed bread slices into egg mixture. Melt butter in medium skillet and cook bread over medium heat until golden brown, turning once. Allow about 1½ to 2 minutes for each side.

For orange syrup, combine all ingredients in saucepan. Heat over low heat, stirring occasionally, until butter is melted. (Do *not* boil.) Remove from heat and cool 10 minutes. Using rotary beater, beat until slightly thickened. Serve warm over Apricot-Stuffed French Toast. Yields 7 servings, two pieces toast per serving.

Variation: Substitute blueberry preserves for the apricot preserves. Add 1 cup frozen or fresh wild blueberries and mix gently. Stuff bread slices and proceed with recipe as directed. Serve with maple syrup.

Artichoke Frittata

1 tablespoon butter
2 tablespoons olive oil
1 large onion, chopped
⅔ cup chopped red pepper
3 tablespoons chopped fresh basil
    or 2 teaspoons dried basil
2 teaspoons dried Italian seasonings
Salt and freshly ground pepper
1 cup grated Cheddar cheese
2 (14-ounce) cans artichoke hearts,
    well drained and cut into sixths
3 cups southern-style hash brown
    potatoes, thawed and drained
3 tablespoons all-purpose flour
8 eggs
1 cup ranch dressing
½ cup milk
Paprika (optional)
Chopped parsley (optional)
2 cups commercially prepared tomato
    salsa, heated
Sour cream
Diced fresh tomato
Fresh chives, cut into 2-inch pieces

Heat butter and oil in large frying pan over medium heat. Sauté onion, pepper, and basil until slightly limp but not browned. Add Italian seasoning, salt, and pepper. Add sautéed mixture, cheese, and artichokes to potatoes and toss to mix well. (You may cover and refrigerate this mixture overnight before proceeding with recipe.) Preheat oven to 325°. Add flour to potato mixture and mix well. In separate medium-size bowl, beat eggs very well. Add dressing and milk to eggs. Blend well and add to potato mixture. Thoroughly mix and pour into 9 x 13-inch, greased baking dish. If desired, sprinkle casserole with paprika and finely chopped, fresh parsley. Bake about 40 minutes or until knife inserted in center comes out clean. Allow frittata to sit for 10 to 15 minutes before cutting into 12 servings.

To serve, ladle warmed salsa onto serving plate. Place frittata on top of salsa. Garnish with dollop of sour cream, diced tomatoes, and chives. Yields 12 servings.

Pineapple Bread Pudding with Bourbon Sauce

2 cups hot water
1½ cups sugar
1 (12-ounce) can evaporated milk
4 large eggs
1 cup flaked coconut
½ cup crushed drained pineapple
½ cup raisins or chopped nuts
⅓ cup melted butter or margarine
1 teaspoon vanilla extract
½ teaspoon ground nutmeg
9 slices firm white (or crusty French)
    bread, cut into ½-inch cubes

Bourbon sauce:
1 cup light corn syrup
¼ cup (½ stick) butter or margarine
¼ cup bourbon
½ teaspoon vanilla extract

Combine water and sugar. Stir to dissolve. Add milk and eggs. Stir with whisk until blended. Stir in coconut, pineapple, raisins or nuts, butter, vanilla, and nutmeg. Add bread cubes. Let stand 30 minutes, stirring occasionally. Preheat oven to 350°. Pour mixture into greased, 13 x 9-inch baking dish or 2-quart casserole. Bake for 45 minutes or until knife inserted in middle comes out clean.

For bourbon sauce, bring syrup to boil in medium saucepan over medium-high heat. Remove from heat and cool slightly.

Stir in butter, bourbon, and vanilla with whisk. Serve warm or at room temperature with warm bourbon sauce. Yields 12 to 15 servings.

Sour Cream Coffee Cake

Topping:
2 teaspoons ground cinnamon
1 cup packed light brown sugar
1 cup finely chopped nuts

Cake:
1 cup (2 sticks) softened butter
1 cup sugar
3 eggs
1 teaspoon vanilla extract
2½ cups all-purpose flour
3 teaspoons baking powder
1 teaspoon baking soda
1 cup sour cream

Preheat oven to 350°. Grease and flour 10-inch tube pan. Mix topping ingredients together. Cream butter and sugar together. Add eggs and vanilla and beat well. Sift flour, baking powder, and soda into separate bowl. Add to creamed mixture alternately with sour cream. Pour one-third of batter into pan. Sprinkle with one-third of topping mixture. Repeat layers, ending with topping. Bake 40 to 45 minutes. Allow to cool in pan before loosening sides and transferring to serving plate. Yields 16 servings.

Scones

2½ cups all-purpose flour
½ cup sugar plus ⅓ cup for topping
2 teaspoons baking powder
1 teaspoon baking soda
½ cup dried cranberries, raisins,
    currants, or chopped dates
1 stick unsalted butter, slightly softened
½ cup sour cream
1 egg
4 tablespoons heavy cream

Mix flour, ½ cup sugar, baking powder, and soda with pastry blender in large bowl. Add dried fruit. Cut butter into dry ingredients using pastry blender to make uniform, crumbly mixture. In separate bowl, blend sour cream, egg, and heavy cream together and add to flour mixture. Mix gently to form soft dough. (Handle like piecrust dough.) Place on lightly floured surface and knead several times until dough is no longer sticky. Divide dough in half and shape into two balls. Flatten each ball to ½-inch thick circle. Cut each round into eight pie-shaped wedges (sixteen pieces total). Transfer scones to cookie sheet and sprinkle lightly with remaining ⅓ cup sugar. Preheat oven to 375° and bake about 20 minutes or until scones are firm and lightly browned. Yields 16 scones.

THE WELBY INN

92 Ocean Avenue
P.O. Box 774
Kennebunkport, ME 04046
(207) 967-4655 (phone)
(800) 773-4085 (toll free)
innkeeper@welbyinn.com
www.welbyinn.com

The Welby Inn Bed & Breakfast, located in the seaport town of Kennebunkport, Maine, has seven comfortable bed and breakfast accommodations, each with private bath and one with a fireplace. A full breakfast and afternoon tea is served every day.

The Eye-Opener

We are known for the juice mixtures that we make each morning. They are very simple, but our guests enjoy guessing the juice of the day. This is one that is a particular favorite at the inn.

1 cup strawberries, hulled
1 to 2 bananas
¾ gallon orange juice

Mix ingredients in blender until very smooth. Pour into jug and let stand 30 minutes in refrigerator. Skim off foam. Yields 12 to 14 servings.

Dolores' Special Peach French Toast

<u>Toast (must be made the night before):</u>
16 slices white bread
6 ounces cream cheese, softened
2 cups sliced peaches
14 eggs, well beaten
⅓ cup maple syrup
1 cup half-and-half or light cream
1 cup milk

<u>Sauce:</u>
2 cups water
¾ cup sugar
4 tablespoons cornstarch
½ teaspoon ground nutmeg
2 cups diced peaches
1 tablespoon butter

Grease 9 x 13-inch baking pan thoroughly. Cut crusts from bread. Generously spread cream cheese over six slices of bread and lay them cheese-side up in pan. Arrange peach slices on top. Cut remaining bread into small cubes and arrange on top. Mix eggs, syrup, half-and-half, and milk. Pour over bread covering all cubes and press down lightly to make sure bread will be saturated. Cover and refrigerate 8 to 10 hours or overnight. When ready to bake, preheat oven to 350°. Cover toast with foil and bake 30 minutes. Remove cover and bake another 30 minutes. Let stand in warm oven 10 minutes before serving.

For sauce, stir together water, sugar, cornstarch, and nutmeg in saucepan over medium heat until mixture comes to boil and is clear. Add peaches and cook over low heat about 10 minutes. Add butter and stir. Yields 8 to 10 servings.

Welby Inn Rolled Oat Cookies

1½ cups all-purpose flour
2 cups rolled oats
¾ cup packed brown sugar
¾ cup granulated sugar
1 teaspoon baking powder
½ teaspoon baking soda
½ cup melted butter
½ cup melted shortening
2 eggs, beaten with 1 teaspoon salt

Preheat oven to 350°. Mix ingredients together with hands. Drop small balls (teaspoon size) on greased baking sheet and flatten with fork. Bake about 10 minutes. Yields 30 cookies.

Note: These store beautifully in tins in freezer. You can also add dried fruits such as cranberries or raisins, nuts, or white chocolate chunks to mixture if you wish.

Welby Inn Ginger Snaps

These are old-fashioned cookies that are very attractive to look at and taste as if they came from Grandmother's kitchen.

½ cup vegetable shortening
1 cup sugar
1 egg
⅓ cup molasses
2 cups all-purpose flour
2 teaspoons baking soda
2 teaspoons ginger
1 teaspoon ground cinnamon

Preheat oven to 350°. Using electric mixer at low speed, cream shortening and sugar together in large bowl. Beat in egg and molasses. Stir in remaining ingredients, mixing just until they are combined. Roll dough into small balls and place on cookie sheet. Dust tops with a little sugar. Bake on greased cookie sheet 12 to 15 minutes. Yields about 18 cookies.

Welby Inn French Scrambled Eggs

These are rich and very creamy. We usually serve them with a muffin and slice of cantaloupe for garnish.

12 eggs
¼ cup half-and-half
1 teaspoon salt
¾ teaspoon white pepper
½ cup soft cream cheese
2 tablespoons very finely chopped
    fresh parsley
2 tablespoons very finely chopped fresh dill
2 tablespoons very finely chopped scallions
2 tablespoons butter

Beat eggs, half-and-half, salt, and pepper together thoroughly. In separate bowl mash cream cheese with herbs. Melt butter in large saucepan and pour in egg and cheese mixtures. Over low heat, stir constantly just until cheese begins to incorporate. Turn off heat and let mixture sit about 20 minutes. Just before serving, turn on heat and scramble. (The resting period makes a difference and gets the flavors well blended together. Don't skip it.) Yields 4 servings.

Cape Neddick House

Cape Neddick House

1300 Route 1
P.O. Box 70
Cape Neddick, ME 03902
(207) 363-2500 (phone)
(207) 363-4499 (fax)
capeneddickhouse@aol.com
www.capeneddickhouse.com

The Cape Neddick House (aka Nubble Light) is an 1885 Victorian house on ten acres of woods and gardens. There are five rooms with air conditioning and some with fireplaces. Breakfast feasts invite guests to enjoy almond pear tortes, blueberry scones, and orange thyme pancakes. This is a year-round area with beaches, boutiques, the Kittery Outlets, and Perkins Cove, a working fishing village with a magnificent walk—Marginal Way—adjacent to the ocean.

Mystery Bed and Breakfast Pillows

1 (8-count) can crescent rolls
Ground cinnamon
1 large banana, thinly sliced
Butterscotch morsels

Preheat oven to 350°. Separate rolls and sprinkle lightly with cinnamon. Cover each roll with thinly sliced banana. Place 4 butterscotch morsels on top of banana. Roll from small side to large and pinch ends closed. Place on greased cookie sheet. Bake 12 to 16 minutes or until golden. Yields 8 rolls.

Note: This works fine using peaches or pears with chocolate chips, too.

The Captain Fairfield Inn

Corner of Pleasant & Green Streets
P.O. Box 2690
Kennebunkport, ME 04046
(207) 967-4454 (phone)
(800) 322-1928 (toll free)
jrw@captainfairfield.com
www.captainfairfield.com

The Captain Fairfield Inn is a romantic bed and breakfast inn with nine spacious rooms featuring antiques, four-poster beds, and fireplaces. The living room has a comforting and timeless warmth in which to visit or just relax. Other public rooms are the Music Room with a grand piano and the historic Gathering Room. A gourmet breakfast is served in two lovely dining areas overlooking the garden. Of course, in warmer weather the garden patio is set for breakfast alfresco.

The Captain Fairfield is a classic 1813 Federal ship captain's home in the heart of Kennebunkport's historic district. The inn is within walking distance of the ocean, restaurants, shops, and galleries. Attractions in the area include the Brick Store Museum, Seashore Trolley Museum, Walder's Point, Kennebunkport Historical Society, Cape Arundel Golf Club, Rachel Carson National Refuge, to name only a few.

Apple Oatmeal Pancakes

2 tablespoons butter
    plus melted butter
    for cooking pancakes
3 tablespoons packed brown sugar
2 tablespoons maple syrup
1 teaspoon ground cinnamon
1 baking apple, chopped
1 cup old-fashioned rolled oats
2 cups boiling water
2 eggs, beaten
1¼ cups whole milk
1 cup unbleached all-purpose flour
1½ teaspoons baking soda
1 teaspoon salt

Put 2 tablespoons butter in medium skillet over medium-high heat. Immediately add brown sugar, maple syrup, and cinnamon. Stir to mix and cook until bubbly and then add apple. Reduce the heat to medium and cook just until apple is tender and set aside to cool. While apple is cooking, stir oats into boiling water and set aside off heat to cool about 10 minutes.

To prepare pancake batter, whisk eggs and milk in large mixing bowl. In another bowl mix flour, baking soda, and salt. Gradually add dry ingredients to liquid ingredients, stirring just until blended. (Do *not* overmix.) Fold oatmeal, then apples, into batter. Batter should be a little runny. Heat griddle or heavy skillet over medium heat and with pastry brush coat heated surface with melted butter. Ladle batter onto hot pan. When pancakes bubble and are browned on bottom, flip them. Serve immediately or keep warm in a 250° oven for a short time before you serve. Dust warm plate with cinnamon sugar and place pancakes on dusted plate. Yields 4 servings.

French Crêpes with Fruit Compote Topping

Crêpes:
6 eggs
3 tablespoons sugar
2 tablespoons cottage cheese
3 tablespoons melted butter
1 cup half-and-half
1¾ cups all-purpose flour

Fruit compote:
2 cups fresh or frozen fruit
(blueberries, strawberries, or peaches)
⅓ cup sugar
¼ cup lemon juice
3 tablespoons cornstarch, mixed with water

Combine eggs, sugar, cottage cheese, butter, and half-and-half in blender at medium-speed. Add flour in small amounts and process until smooth. Let batter sit for 1 hour. Heat heavy small frying pan or crêpe pan to medium-high heat. Lightly brush melted butter on pan. Gently whisk batter before cooking. Fill 2-ounce ladle and pour into pan. Immediately roll pan to cover the bottom. Cook to golden brown and dry on top. Flip and brown on other side. Keep warm stacked on top of each other in 200° oven. Cover to keep from drying. Serve with fruit compote. Simply roll a small amount of filling into crêpe.

For fruit compote, slightly cook fruit with sugar and lemon juice. Add cornstarch mixture to hot berries to thicken. Serve warm with crêpes or as topping for French toast or ice cream. Yields 8 servings, 16 crêpes.

Note: If you use strawberries or peaches, you will need more than 2 cups. Strawberries and peaches will cook down more than blueberries because of higher water content. Use about 3 to 4 cups. Add pinch of ginger powder and 2 tablespoons orange marmalade to fresh peach compote. The marmalade will thicken compote, so you will not need to use cornstarch. (Blueberries are our choice at the Captain Fairfield Inn. The small Maine blueberries are the sweetest.)

The Captain Fairfield Inn

THE OXFORD HOUSE INN

105 Main Street
Fryeburg, ME 04037
(207) 935-3442 (phone)
(800) 261-7206 (toll free)
innkeeper@oxfordhouseinn.com
www.oxfordhouseinn.com

Oxford House is a country inn in a village setting with a gourmet restaurant and spectacular mountain views. Open year-round, the inn is near a national forest and offers four-season sports, activities, antiquing, and shopping. Experience the comforts and pleasures of a charming country inn with friendly service and hospitality.

Venison Medallions with Port & Dried Cherries

2½ to 3 pounds venison, cut into
1-ounce medallions
(3 to 4 ounces per person)
All-purpose flour
1 cup port
½ cup currant jelly
¼ cup guava jelly
1 lemon, juice and zest of rind
¼ teaspoon ground allspice
¼ teaspoon cloves
¼ teaspoon ground cinnamon
1 teaspoon Worcestershire sauce
2 cups rich stock or consommé
1 cup halved dried cherries

Flour venison and pan-fry in hot oil until medium to rare. Remove to warm plate. Pour off oil in pan. Add remaining ingredients and simmer to make a thin sauce. Add venison to sauce and heat quickly before serving. Yields 8 servings.

The Oxford House Inn

Pork-and-Apple-Stuffed Pheasant

2 pounds fresh ground pork
2 tablespoons chopped parsley
2 Granny Smith apples, peeled,
    cored, and chopped
Salt and pepper
6 boneless pheasant breasts
1 cup crème fraîche
1 tablespoon minced fresh sage

Preheat oven to 400°. Combine pork, parsley, apple, salt, and pepper. Between two pieces of plastic wrap, pound each breast to ¼ inch thickness. Place portion of stuffing on flesh side of breasts and roll up. Place on buttered baking sheet and bake 20 to 30 minutes. Com-bine crème fraîche and sage and spoon on just before serving. Yields 6 servings.

Maine Lobster Croustades

Butter for greasing and spreading
24 slices white bread,
    cut into 3-inch rounds
½ pound cooked lobster meat,
    cut into small pieces

1 tablespoon finely chopped
    red bell pepper
1 teaspoon lemon juice
4 drops Tabasco sauce
1½ tablespoons mayonnaise
Salt and pepper

Preheat oven to 350°. Brush 12-cup muffin tin with melted butter. Fit bread rounds into tin to form cups. Brush bread with softened butter. Combine lobster, pepper, lemon juice, Tabasco, mayonnaise, and salt and pepper to taste. Spread into bread cups and bake for 10 minutes. Serve immediately. Yields 12 servings.

Galen C. Moses House

1009 Washington Street
Bath, ME 04530
(207) 442-8771 (phone)
(888) 442-8771 (toll free)
stay@galenmoses.com
www.galenmoses.com

Being a guest at the Galen C. Moses House is like dwelling in a living museum, surrounded by reminders of the vast wealth that flowed through the city of Bath 150 years ago. Indeed, the history of Bath, the ambiance of Washington Street, and the special design of the Galen C. Moses House becomes a total immersion in history for those who visit. Historic Bath invites the traveler to spend a few relaxing days strolling through the pleasant parks overlooking the Kennebec River or rummaging through the many antique stores on Front Street. Beach lovers will find two sandy state park beaches within a short drive. The nationally acclaimed Maritime Museum, the Chocolate Church, or the Art Gallery of Bowdoin College furnish exciting diversions on a rainy afternoon, while short drives to Wiscasset, Boothbay Harbor, or Freeport (home of L. L. Bean) can satisfy every shopper's appetite. And speaking of appetites, the restaurants in the area serve marvelous seafood on tables overlooking the great bays and charming coves.

Snow Grapes

2 pounds black seedless grapes
½ cup sour cream
2 tablespoons ground cinnamon
¼ cup brown sugar
Orange slices and mint for garnish

Wash and stem grapes and place in bowl. Mix with sour cream, cinnamon, and sugar. Place in small cups and garnish with orange slices and mint. Yields 6 to 8 servings.

Baked Eggs in Maple Toast Cups

2 tablespoons maple syrup
2 tablespoons butter
8 slices white bread, crusts removed
8 eggs
Salt and pepper

Preheat oven to 400°. Combine syrup and butter in saucepan and heat until butter is melted. Press out bread with rolling pin. Brush each slice with syrup mixture and press down into greased muffin cups. Break 1 egg into each cup and sprinkle with salt and pepper to taste. Bake 15 minutes. Yields 4 servings.

Egg Casserole

1 cup half-and-half
2 teaspoons Dijon mustard
1 tablespoon freshly chopped parsley
1½ cups grated Cheddar cheese
Salt and pepper
1 dozen eggs

Blend half-and-half, mustard, and parsley and place in refrigerator for an hour or so. Preheat oven to 325°. Spread grated cheese in bottom of oiled casserole dish. Spread mustard mixture over cheese. Whisk salt, pepper, and eggs and pour into casserole. Bake for 45 to 60 minutes. For creative additions, add artichoke hearts and basil. Yields 6 servings.

Zucchini Casserole

9 cups shredded zucchini
    (3 to 4 pounds)
1 large onion, chopped
1 garlic clove, chopped
10 eggs
2 cups grated Parmesan
¾ cup vegetable oil
Pepper
2 cups biscuit mix

Preheat oven to 350°. Mix all ingredients together, adding biscuit mix last. Grease casserole pan and dust with flour. Pour in zucchini and bake 1 hour. Yields 6 to 8 servings.

Variation: Add Cheddar cheese and spices of choice.

Kenniston Hill Inn

P.O. Box 125
Boothbay, ME 04537
(207) 633-2159 (phone)
(800) 992-2915 (toll free)
innkeeper@maine.com
www.kennistonhillinn.com

This two-hundred-year-old center chimney, Georgian colonial inn sits on four acres. Ten rooms have private baths; five have working fireplaces. The golf course is next door.

Best-Ever Banana Muffins

3 large bananas
¾ cup granulated sugar
1 egg, slightly beaten
½ cup melted butter
1 teaspoon baking soda
1 teaspoon baking powder
½ teaspoon salt
1½ cups all-purpose flour

Preheat oven to 375°. Coat 12-cup muffin tin with nonstick spray. Mash bananas. Add sugar and egg. Add melted butter. Add dry ingredients and pour into muffin cups. Bake 20 minutes. Yields 12 servings.

Ham and Cheese in Puff Pastry

4 (5 x 5-inch) puff pastry squares
2 tablespoons finely chopped onion
1 tablespoon butter
1 egg, beaten
1 cup shredded Swiss cheese (or a mix)
⅔ cup coarsely chopped, cooked ham
1 tablespoon snipped fresh parsley
1 teaspoon dried dill weed or
    1 tablespoon snipped fresh dill weed
Dash of garlic powder
Dash of freshly ground pepper
1 egg yolk mixed with 2 tablespoons
    water for egg wash

Preheat oven to 400° to 425°. If using frozen puff pastry, let pastry come to room temperature. In small saucepan, cook onion in butter till tender but not browned. For filling, in medium mixing bowl combine egg, cheese, ham, parsley, dill, garlic powder, and pepper. Stir in onion mixture. Place 2 to 3 tablespoons filling just off center on each square. Moisten pastry edges with water and fold in half diagonally. Seal edges by pressing with fingers or tines of fork. Place pastry on ungreased baking sheet. Coat with egg wash. Place in oven and immediately drop temperature to 375°. Cook 20 to 25 minutes until nicely browned. Served with broiled tomatoes and scrambled eggs and chives. Yields 4 servings.

Note: For vegetarian dish substitute 1 box spinach, squeezed dry, for ham.

Three-Cheese Pie with Tomato and Sweet Basil

1 cup shredded Cheddar cheese
1 cup shredded Monterey Jack cheese
1 cup Swiss cheese
1 tablespoon all-purpose flour
6 eggs, beaten
½ cup half-and-half
1 medium tomato, diced
2 tablespoons dried, sweet basil
    or ½ cup freshly chopped
3 to 6 strips cooked bacon, well drained
    and crumbled

Preheat oven to 350°. Coat 8-inch quiche dish with nonstick spray. Combine the cheeses. In small bowl, toss 1 cup cheeses with flour. Place in bottom of dish. Spread remaining cheese on top. Lightly whisk eggs together in bowl. Add half-and-half and whisk until frothy. Pour over cheese and sprinkle with tomato and basil. Top with crumbled bacon. Bake 35 to 40 minutes or until center is domed and nicely browned. Let stand out of oven 20 to 30 minutes to allow eggs to set up. Yields 6 to 8 servings.

THE FIVE GABLES INN

Murray Hill Road
P.O. Box 335
East Boothbay, ME 04544
(207) 633-4551 (phone)
(800) 451-5048 (toll free)
info@fivegablesinn.com
www.fivegablesinn.com

For more than a century the Five Gables Inn has perched on a garden-framed hillside just down the lane from the East Boothbay General Store. It still has a broad verandah with a hammock and plenty of comfortable chairs overlooking a quiet cove where lobster boats tug at their moorings. And guests still linger in welcoming wing chairs in front of a big fireplace in the common room. If guests from the past were to return today, however, they would certainly be struck by all of the inn's modern luxuries. All of the rooms afford spectacular views of Linekin Bay, its islands, and the sea beyond. Five of the rooms also have working fireplaces. Guests of the inn

choose from a variety of activities, including whale-watching excursions, trips to Monhegan Island, windjammer sailing and scenic boat cruises.

Cream Cheese Quiche

1 (9-inch) piecrust
1 onion, chopped
2 tablespoons vegetable oil
¼ cup milk
8 ounces cream cheese, cubed
4 eggs
1 cup finely diced ham
2 ounces diced pimiento
½ teaspoon fresh dill or thyme
⅛ teaspoon pepper
1 tomato for garnish

Bake pie shell at 350° for 12 minutes. Sauté onion in oil until well caramelized. Add milk and cream cheese. Stir over low heat until cheese melts. Remove from heat and pour into bowl. Assemble eggs, ham, pimiento, dill or thyme, and pepper. Remove pulp from tomato and dice. Combine all ingredients except tomato. Adjust seasoning and pour into piecrust. Garnish top with diced tomato. Bake 30 to 35 minutes. Yields 4 to 6 servings.

Spoon Bread with Chorizo

1 onion, chopped
1 plus 1 tablespoon butter
5 ounces chorizo, cut in ½-inch dice
2 cups fresh corn kernels
1½ teaspoons salt
5 eggs
1½ cups cream
1 cup cornmeal
¼ cup cilantro, chopped

Fry onion in 1 tablespoon butter over medium heat, stirring occasionally until

soft, about 4 minutes. Add chorizo and sauté until meat is slightly browned, about 4 minutes more. Drain off grease and let sausage mixture cool. Combine corn kernels, salt, and remaining 1 tablespoon butter. Whip eggs and cream together. Bring 4 cups water to boil in small saucepan. Slowly pour in cornmeal, stirring constantly. Reduce heat to low and cook until thickened, immediately to 2 minutes. Combine cornmeal with sausage mixture. Add corn and butter mixture. Add egg and cream mixture. Mix well. Preheat oven to 350°. Divide between two greased pie plates. Bake 50 minutes. Garnish with cilantro. Yields 8 servings per pie.

Plum Tart

Crust:
1¼ cups all-purpose flour
2 tablespoons sugar
¼ teaspoon salt
½ cup (1 stick) cold butter
3 tablespoons ice water

Topping:
2 pounds plums
4 plus 1 plus 1 tablespoon sugar
½ teaspoon ground ginger
¼ teaspoon ground cinnamon
1 tablespoon all-purpose flour
2 tablespoons butter
1 egg, beaten
¼ cup apricot preserves

For crust mix flour, sugar, and salt in food processor. Cut butter into small pieces and add to flour mix. Add ice water until mixture forms moist dough. Flatten dough ball into disk shape, wrap in plastic, and cool in refrigerator.

For topping, pit and slice plums. Toss with 4 tablespoons sugar, ginger, and cinnamon. Roll out dough on parchment paper to 12-inch round. Keeping dough on parchment paper, place on baking sheet. Mix 1 tablespoon sugar with 1 tablespoon flour and sprinkle over dough. Arrange plums on dough leaving a 1-inch border. Melt butter in microwave. Sprinkle over plums. Fold edges of dough to make border. Beat egg and brush border with egg glaze. Sprinkle border with remaining tablespoon sugar. Melt apricot preserves and brush over plums. Preheat oven to 350° and bake 30 to 45 minutes. Yields 6 to 8 servings.

Spiced Rice Cereal with Mangos and Bananas

1 cup Arborio rice
2 cups milk
⅓ cup sugar
¼ teaspoon salt
¼ cup crystallized ginger, diced
¼ teaspoon ground cardamom
½ teaspoon ground cinnamon
¼ teaspoon ground allspice
1 pint cream
2 mangos
1 lemon
2 bananas

Boil rice (2 cups water per 1 cup rice) for 15 minutes. It should be just undercooked. Drain any excess water. Add milk, sugar, and salt to rice. Bring to boil and reduce heat. Cook 5 minutes stirring frequently. Add ginger and spices. Cook another 5 minutes until rice is fully cooked. Whip cream until it peaks. Peel mangos, dice, and soak in a little lemon juice to preserve color. Peel and slice bananas. Spoon rice into serving bowl, layer banana slices on top, cover with layer of whipped cream, and sprinkle with diced mangos. Serve hot. Yields 8 servings.

Sweet Potato Biscuits

2 tablespoons melted butter
Orange rind strip, 2 x 1-inch
2 cups all-purpose flour
1 tablespoon baking powder
½ teaspoon baking soda
¾ teaspoon salt
3 tablespoons brown sugar
¼ teaspoon ground ginger
1 tablespoon grated orange zest
6 tablespoons cold butter, cubed
1 cup cooked and mashed sweet potato
⅔ cup buttermilk

In small bowl combine melted butter and orange rind. Leave for 1 hour. Preheat oven to 350°. Combine all dry ingredients and orange zest. Mix well. Using a pastry cutter, cut butter into dry mixture. Make well in center of dry mixture. Using a fork, stir in sweet potato. Add buttermilk. Stir just until dough comes together. (Do *not* overmix.) Dust dough with flour. Turn dough onto lightly floured surface. Knead gently 6 to 8 times. Roll out dough to ½-inch thickness, and cut biscuits using 1½-inch biscuit cutter. Transfer cut biscuits to greased baking sheet. Brush tops with orange butter. Bake 15 to 20 minutes. Yields 20 biscuits.

MAPLES INN

16 Roberts Ave
Bar Harbor, ME 04609
(207) 288-3443
info@maplesinn.com
www.maplesinn.com

Maples Inn is a 1903 Victorian-era bed and breakfast that features "classic tranquility," gourmet breakfasts, and a welcoming atmosphere offering six distinctly decorated rooms with queen-size beds and private baths. The inn is located two blocks from the ocean on a residential, tree-lined street in the village of Bar Harbor. Guests enjoy the convenience of walking to quaint shops, intimate restaurants, and all of the activities that the town has to offer: whale-watching trips, nature tours, sea kayaking tours, and sunset sails. Surrounding the town of Bar Harbor is the breathtaking beauty of Acadia National Park.

Stuffed Sour Cream Coffee Cake

1 cup chopped pecans
2 cups plus 1 tablespoon sugar
1 teaspoon ground cinnamon
½ cup coarsely chopped raisins, apricots, or pitted dates
2 cups all-purpose flour
¼ teaspoon salt
1 teaspoon baking powder
1 cup (2 sticks) butter at room temperature
2 eggs
1 cup sour cream
½ teaspoon vanilla extract

Preheat oven to 350°. Butter and flour a 9-inch tube or Bundt pan. In small bowl, stir together pecans, 1 tablespoon sugar, cinnamon, and dried fruits. In medium bowl, combine flour, salt, and baking powder. Using an electric mixer on medium speed beat together butter and remaining 2 cups sugar. Beat until mixture is light and fluffy. Beat in eggs, one at a time, beating well after each addition. Reduce beater speed to low and mix in sour cream and vanilla. Beat in flour mixture at low speed, one-third at a time just until mixed. Spoon one-third of batter into pan. Place nut/fruit mixture in middle of ring of batter, being careful not to touch center or sides of pan. Spoon remaining batter over mixture, smoothing out top. Bake until golden brown, about 1 hour. Let cool completely in pan on wire rack and then invert onto platter. Yields 20 servings.

Pineapple, Kiwi, and Orange in Mint Syrup

Since mint can be quite prolific in the garden, this is a perfect recipe to use the abundance of this wonderful herb. The mint syrup is light, refreshing, and a wonderful accent for the fruit.

cup sugar
½ cup water
1 cup loosely packed mint leaves
3 navel oranges
1 whole fresh pineapple, peeled, cored,
    and sliced
4 kiwifruit, peeled, sliced, quartered
Shredded coconut for topping
Mint sprigs for topping

Bring sugar, water, and mint to boil in small saucepan over high heat, stirring until sugar is dissolved. Remove from heat and let steep, covered, 10 minutes. Pour syrup through sieve into large serving bowl, pressing and discarding mint. Allow syrup to cool to room temperature. Cut and peel white pith from oranges with sharp knife. Hold oranges over bowl of syrup to catch any juices as sections are cut free from membranes, and let them fall into syrup. Squeeze orange membranes to extract as much juice as possible. Cut pineapple into ¾-inch, bite-size pieces. Add oranges, pineapple, and kiwi to syrup bowl. Stir to coat with syrup. Cover and set in refrigerator to chill 8 to 10 hours. To serve, divide fruit evenly among serving bowls, using slotted spoon. Top with shredded coconut and sprig of mint. Yields 6 servings.

Chocolate
Snickerdoodles

1½ cups plus 2 tablespoons sugar
½ cup (1 stick) butter
1 teaspoon vanilla extract
1 egg
2¼ cups all-purpose flour
½ cup unsweetened cocoa powder
1 teaspoon cream of tartar
½ teaspoon baking soda
¼ teaspoon salt
2 tablespoons ground cinnamon

Preheat oven to 400°. In large bowl, combine 1½ cups sugar and butter; beat until light and fluffy. Add vanilla and egg. Blend well. Add flour, cocoa, cream of tartar, baking soda, and salt. Mix well. In a small bowl,

combine remaining 2 tablespoons sugar with cinnamon. Shape dough into 1-inch balls and roll in cinnamon sugar. Bake 14 to 16 minutes. Immediately remove from cookie sheets. Yields 4 dozen cookies.

Variation: Combine minced nuts with cinnamon sugar.

Caramelized-Pear
French Toast

This dish is prepared the night before and baked the next morning. The pears add a delicious blend of flavors and provide a wonderful presentation.

3 Bosc pears
1 cup water
1 teaspoon cloves
¼ cup granulated sugar
1 cup firmly packed brown sugar
½ cup (1 stick) butter
1¾ tablespoons dark corn syrup
6 slices Texas Toast, crusts removed
7 eggs, beaten
1½ cups milk
1 teaspoon vanilla extract
¼ teaspoon salt
Whipped cream

Peel pears and cut in half. Remove seeds and core. In saucepan over medium-high heat, combine water, cloves, and granulated sugar, stirring as mixture comes to a boil. Reduce heat to simmer and place pears in liquid. Cover and simmer pears until soft. (Cooking time will vary depending on ripeness of pears. Test by inserting knife into pear to check firmness.) When done, remove pears from liquid and set on paper towel to cool. Coat 13 x 9 x 2-inch, glass baking dish with nonstick spray. Combine brown sugar, butter, and corn syrup in heavy saucepan. Stir mixture constantly over medium-low heat until butter melts and sugar dissolves. Increase heat to medium-high and bring to boil. Pour into dish, spreading mixture to coat bottom evenly. Allow to cool. Take pear halves and make several slices from top to bottom. Do

not slice through top of pear so that slices remain joined, allowing the pear to fan when laid flat. Place 1 pear half, round-side down, into one corner of cooled caramel. Fan pears slightly so they will lay flat. Place remaining pears fanned and evenly spaced, one on each corner and in middle of pan. Arrange bread in single layer on top of pears. One slice of bread should be centered on top of each pear. Whisk eggs, milk, vanilla, and salt in bowl to blend. Pour over bread. Cover and refrigerate 8 to 10 hours or overnight.

When ready to bake, preheat oven to 350°. Bake uncovered until bread is puffed and light golden brown, about 45 minutes. Let stand 5 minutes. Cut into six portions using bread as a guide. Using spatula, invert each portion onto plate so that caramel side faces up. Top with dollop of whipped cream. Yields 6 servings.

Panna Cottas with
Raspberry Sauce

Panna Cottas:
2 teaspoons unflavored gelatin
½ cup milk
2 cups heavy cream
¼ cup sugar
¾ teaspoon vanilla extract

Raspberry sauce:
¾ cup water
1 cup sugar
¼ cup lemon juice
6 ounces frozen raspberries
1½ tablespoons cornstarch
2 tablespoons hot water
Fresh raspberries and mint

To make Panna Cottas, spray six 2- or 4-ounce tart molds with vegetable oil, very light coating to help with release of Panna Cottas from molds. Wipe any excess oil from molds with paper towel. In medium bowl, sprinkle gelatin over milk and let stand. Combine cream and sugar in heavy saucepan. Cook over medium-high heat, stirring constantly to dissolve sugar. Continue stirring until small bubbles begin to form around edges of pan. Slowly add heated cream to gelatin mixture, stirring until smooth. Stir in vanilla. Pour mixture into molds, dividing equally and filling each to just below the rim. Place molds in plastic food storage container, cover, and refrigerate 8 to 10 hours or overnight.

To make raspberry sauce, in small saucepan stir water, sugar, and lemon juice together and bring to a boil. Reduce heat and simmer for 2 minutes. Add raspberries and return to boil. Remove from heat, cover, and let stand 10 minutes. Strain liquid without pressing raspberries, discard berries, and return liquid to saucepan. Add cornstarch to hot water and stir until dissolved and smooth. Stir cornstarch liquid into raspberry sauce. Stir sauce constantly over medium heat until mixture slowly thickens. Chill sauce.

To serve fill small bowl with hot water and dip bottom of molds briefly in water to loosen Panna Cottas. Do *not* submerge. Invert each mold onto serving place. The molds may need additional quick dip in hot water or gentle shake to separate. When Panna Cottas are on plates, pour raspberry sauce around them and garnish with fresh raspberries and sprig of mint. Yields 6 servings.

THE PRYOR HOUSE BED & BREAKFAST

360 Front St.
Bath, ME 04530
(207) 443-1146
pryorhse@suscommaine.com
www.gwi.net/~pryorhse

The Pryor House Bed & Breakfast is a comfortably elegant Federal-style home located in the heart of Bath, a city in midcoast Maine rich in shipbuilding. Located just several blocks from downtown and within easy walking distance of shops and restaurants, activities include Maine Maritime Museum; Popham Beach; Reid State Park; Pemaquid Point Lighthouse; antique shopping; lobster eating; L. L. Bean and surrounding outlets; Bowdoin College; Joshua Lawrence Chamberlain Museum (for Civil War buffs) and much more.

Valentine's Fruit Tart

Crust:
1 cup all-purpose flour
5 tablespoons butter, softened
⅛ teaspoon salt
2 tablespoons sugar
2 tablespoons water

Cream cheese filling:
2 (8-ounce) packages cream cheese, softened
¼ cup sugar
4 teaspoons milk
½ teaspoon vanilla extract
Fresh fruit or pie filling

For crust, preheat oven to 400°. In medium bowl knead flour, butter, salt, sugar, and water until dough forms ball, adding more water if needed. Pat pastry into bottom and up sides of 9-inch pie pan or tart pan shaped like a heart with removable bottom. Bake 20 minutes. Take out pan after it has cooled.

The Pryor House Bed & Breakfast

For filling, combine all except fruit in mixing bowl. Beat until smooth. Spread in cool crust. Top with fresh fruit or pie filling. This makes a very elegant centerpiece on your table. Yields 6 to 8 servings.

LAKESHORE INN

184 Lakeview Drive
Rockland, ME 04841
(207) 594-4209 (phone)
(207) 596-6407 (fax)
(866) 540-8800 (toll free)
info@lakeshorebb.com
www.lakeshorebb.com

Lakeshore Inn is a 1767 New England farmhouse overlooking Lake Chickawaukie. It offers a full gourmet breakfast, enclosed outdoor hot tub/Jacuzzi, and Ladies Spa Weekends featured on Boston's *Chronicle* TV show. Activities include schooner trips, lighthouses, museums, antiquing, art galleries, hiking, biking, fishing, canoeing, and kayaking.

Egg Soufflé with Three Cheeses

7 eggs
1 cup milk
28 ounces shredded Cheddar cheese
4 ounces cream cheese, cubed
1 pound small curd cottage cheese
⅔ cup melted butter (or margarine)
½ cup flour
1 teaspoon baking powder

Preheat oven to 350°. Coat a 3-quart baking dish with nonstick spray. Beat together eggs and milk. Add cheeses and melted butter and mix well. Mix in flour and baking powder, then pour into baking dish. Bake 45 to 50 minutes or until knife inserted in center comes out clean. Cut into rectangles to serve. Yields 12 servings.

Note: May be prepared in advance and refrigerated, covered. If put in oven directly from refrigerator, uncover and bake up to 60 minutes.

Cranberry-Apple Coffee Cake

l (18.5-ounce) box yellow cake mix
l can cranberry-apple pie filling
4 eggs, beaten
⅔ cup all-purpose flour
½ cup sugar
5 tablespoons butter
1½ teaspoons ground cinnamon
⅔ cup confectioners' sugar
2 tablespoons milk

Grease a 9 x 13-inch baking dish. Preheat oven to 350°. Combine cake mix, pie filling, and eggs. Mix well and pour into prepared pan. Combine flour, sugar, butter, and cinnamon and blend with a pastry blender until moist and crumbly. Sprinkle on top of batter. Bake 45 minutes. Cool in pan. Mix confectioners' sugar and milk to make glaze. When cake is cooled, drizzle glaze over top. Yields 10 servings.

Feta Cheese Pie

3 tablespoons butter
3 tablespoons all-purpose flour
1½ cups milk
½ pound feta cheese
3 eggs
¼ cup chopped parsley
1 (10-inch) piecrust
1 large tomato, sliced

Preheat oven to 350°. Melt butter in small saucepan over low heat. Remove from heat. Stir in flour until smooth. Gradually stir in milk. Turn heat to high and bring to a boil, stirring constantly. Reduce heat and simmer for 1 minute. Remove from heat. Crumble cheese in medium bowl, mix on low speed until smooth, and add white sauce. Add eggs and beat just until combined. Stir in parsley. Pour into pie shell. Bake 50 minutes or until filling feels firm. Top with thin slices of tomato the last 10 minutes of cooking. Yields 4 to 6 servings.

BRUNSWICK BED & BREAKFAST

165 Park Row
Brunswick, ME 04011
(207) 729-4914 (phone)
(207) 725-1759 (fax)
(800) 299-4914 (toll free)
info@brunswickbnb.com
www.brunswickbnb.com

Brunswick Bed & Breakfast features gracious lodging in a historic Greek revival home overlooking the town green. Relax on the wraparound porch or in front of a crackling fire. Some local attractions include antiquing, L. L. Bean, museums, and Bowdoin College.

Morning Granola

5 cups rolled oats
1 cup walnuts or pecans
½ cup packed brown sugar
1½ teaspoons ground cinnamon
½ teaspoon ground nutmeg
⅓ cup maple syrup
1 cup melted butter
½ cup golden raisins

Preheat oven to 350°. In large bowl, stir together oats, nuts, brown sugar, and spices. Mix maple syrup with melted butter and heat gently. Pour this over oat mixture and mix well. Spread mix into buttered 10 x 15-inch baking pan. Bake until golden brown, about 30 minutes. May take longer depending on pan. Set timer for every 10 minutes to stir granola for even browning. Let cool in pan. When completely cooled, stir in raisins. Yields 8 cups.

Note: Can be stored in airtight container up to 1 month. Also freezes well.

Hearty Breakfast Bake

4 cups frozen shredded hash browns
1 pound bacon, diced
6 eggs, lightly beaten
2 cups shredded Cheddar cheese
1½ cups cottage cheese
1¼ cups shredded Swiss cheese
½ teaspoon salt
¼ teaspoon pepper
½ teaspoon dill weed
¼ teaspoon paprika

Thaw hash browns. In large skillet over medium heat cook bacon until crisp and drain. (Cook bacon day before to make preparation very quick.) Preheat oven to 350°. In bowl, combine hash browns with bacon and remaining ingredients. Transfer to greased 9 x 13-inch baking dish. Bake uncovered 35 to 40 minutes or until set and bubbly. Best to check after 30 minutes. Let stand 5 to 10 minutes before cutting into meal-size servings for breakfast buffet. Yields 10 to 12 servings.

Banana Pecan Pancakes

1 ripe banana
⅔ cup all-purpose flour
1 tablespoon baking powder
2 tablespoons sugar
½ teaspoon salt
⅓ cup yellow cornmeal
⅓ cup lightly toasted chopped pecans
¾ cup milk
1 large egg
3 tablespoons vegetable oil

Chop banana. Mix dry ingredients and add pecans. Mix milk, egg, oil, and banana. Add to dry mix. Heat griddle. Drop batter by scant ¼ cup on hot griddle. Cook until bubbles appear on surface and undersides are golden brown. Flip pancakes with spatula and repeat. Serve with warm maple syrup on the side. Yields 10 pancakes.

Lemon Soufflé Pancakes with Blueberry Syrup

2 cups all-purpose flour
2 tablespoons sugar
1 teaspoon baking soda
½ teaspoon salt
2 large eggs, separated
1½ cups buttermilk
2 teaspoons grated lemon peel
3 tablespoons lemon juice
2 tablespoons melted butter
1 cup blueberries
1 cup maple syrup

In large bowl, mix flour, sugar, baking soda, and salt. In small bowl, whisk together egg yolks, buttermilk, lemon peel, lemon juice, and butter. In deep bowl with mixer on high speed, whip egg whites until they hold stiff, moist peaks. Pour buttermilk mixture into flour mix; stir to blend. Add beaten egg whites and fold gently to blend. On buttered griddle over medium heat, pour ¼-cup portions of batter onto griddle. Cook until bubbles appear on top. Flip pancakes and continue cooking until golden brown on both sides. In 1-quart saucepan over medium heat, combine blueberries and syrup. Heat, stirring occasionally, until heated through, about 3 minutes. Serve 3 to 4 pancakes overlapping each other; drizzle syrup on top, and garnish with mint leaf. Yields 3 to 4 servings.

Very Berry Streusel French Toast

6 eggs
4 tablespoons granulated sugar
1 teaspoon vanilla extract
2¼ cups milk
1 loaf Italian bread, sliced
2 cups blueberries, raspberries,
    or strawberries
¼ cup (½ stick) margarine
⅓ cup all-purpose flour
½ cup brown sugar
Confectioner's sugar for sprinkling

Beat together eggs, sugar, vanilla, and milk. Put bread slices in greased 9 x 13-inch pan. Make sure bread slices cover as much of pan as possible; may need to cut smaller pieces to fit in some open spaces between slices. Pour egg mixture over bread. Cover and refrigerate 8 to 10 hours or overnight.

When ready to bake, preheat oven to 375°. Sprinkle fruit on top of bread. Combine margarine, flour, and brown sugar until crumbly (food processor works great). Sprinkle over fruit. Bake 35 to 40 minutes until golden and puffed. Let sit a few minutes; then cut into servings and sprinkle with sifted confectioner's sugar. Serve with warmed maple syrup on the side. This can be served as main dish or cut into small portions for brunch buffet. Yields 8 servings.

BRASS LANTERN INN

81 West Main Street
Searsport, ME 04974
(207) 548-0150 (phone)
(800) 691-0150 (toll free)
stay@BrassLanternMaine.com
www.BrassLanternMaine.com

Guests staying at our Victorian sea captain's home are treated to unsurpassed personal attention and hospitality. Gourmet breakfasts served by candlelight are the perfect beginning to a day exploring the coast of Maine. Searsport is rich in maritime history, with 10 percent of the nation's sea captains coming from this small town. The harbor is a short walk from the inn, and at low tide, beachcombing is a relaxing way to get away from it all. Acadia National Park and Bar Harbor are an easy day-trip away, as are many other of Maine's picturesque towns and harbors. There are museums, galleries, antique shops, and flea markets nearby. Hiking, biking, and sea kayaking are some of the other activities enjoyed by our guests.

Fruit 'n' Spice Scones

2 cups all-purpose flour
¼ cup sugar
3 teaspoons baking powder
⅛ teaspoon salt
½ teaspoon ground cinnamon
½ teaspoon ground nutmeg
⅓ cup chilled butter
½ cup raisins or dates
½ cup heavy cream
1 large egg
1½ teaspoons vanilla extract

Preheat oven to 350°. Combine flour, sugar, baking powder, salt, cinnamon, and nutmeg in electric mixer. Mix and gradually add butter until mixture resembles coarse crumbs. Add raisins or dates and mix. Combine cream, egg, and vanilla in small bowl and add to flour mixture all at once. Mix just until all is incorporated. Knead four or five times on floured board. Roll out to about ¾-inch thickness and cut with biscuit cutter. Bake about 20 minutes or until just slightly browned. Serve while warm on a plate with doily. Yields 4 servings.

Almond Poppy Seed Bread

3 cups all-purpose flour
1½ teaspoons salt
2 tablespoons poppy seeds
1½ teaspoons baking powder
3 eggs
2¼ cups sugar
1½ cups milk
1⅛ cups vegetable oil
1½ teaspoons almond extract
1½ teaspoons vanilla extract
1½ teaspoons butter flavoring

Glaze:
¾ cup sifted confectioners' sugar
¼ cup orange juice
½ teaspoon almond extract
½ teaspoon vanilla extract
½ teaspoon butter flavoring

Preheat oven to 350°. In large bowl, mix flour, salt, poppy seeds, and baking powder. With electric mixer, beat together eggs, sugar, milk, oil, and almond, vanilla, and butter flavorings. Mix in flour. Beat on medium or medium-high speed for 2 minutes. Pour batter into two buttered 9 x 5-inch bread pans. Bake about 1 hour or until toothpick inserted in center comes out clean. Remove pans from oven and cool for no longer than 5 minutes while preparing glaze.

For glaze, in small bowl, mix confectioners' sugar, orange juice, and almond, vanilla, and butter flavorings until smooth. Pour over bread while hot and still in pans. Cool bread another 15 minutes before turn-ing out onto wire rack to cool completely. Slice and serve. Yields 2 loaves.

Blueberry Surprise French Toast

1 cup firmly packed brown sugar
½ cup (1 stick) butter
2 tablespoons light corn syrup
1 cup chopped pecans
8 to 10 cups cubed Italian bread, about 10 slices, ¾ inch thick, divided
2 ounces cream cheese (can substitute light cream cheese)
3 cups fresh or frozen blueberries (can substitute thinly sliced apples or other fruit)
1 cup sugar
1 teaspoon ground cinnamon
½ teaspoon freshly grated nutmeg
6 large eggs
2 cups milk
1 teaspoon vanilla extract
¼ teaspoon salt

Combine brown sugar, butter, and corn syrup in a small saucepan and cook over medium heat until thickened, stirring constantly. Pour into 13 x 9-inch baking dish, and sprinkle pecans over syrup. Place 4 heaping cups bread evenly over caramel pan. Slice cream cheese into four thin slices. Cut each one in half lengthwise and then cut into small cubes. Arrange cubes evenly over bread. Sprinkle blueberries over top of bread and cheese cubes. Mix sugar, cinnamon, and nutmeg together and pour over blueberries. Finish with remaining bread cubes, forming a layer over blueberries and sugar. Beat eggs, add milk, vanilla, and salt, and pour evenly over entire dish, making sure bread is moistened. Cover baking dish and chill in refrigerator 8 hours or overnight. Take dish out about 30 minutes before baking. Preheat oven to 350°. Bake uncovered 1 hour or until lightly browned. Let stand 15 to 20 minutes to firm. Turn upside down onto serving platter and cut into pieces. Yields 8 to 10 servings.

Pumpkin Blueberry Bread

4 cups all-purpose flour
3 cups sugar
2 teaspoons baking soda
2 teaspoons baking powder
1½ teaspoons salt
1 teaspoon ground cloves
1 teaspoon ground cinnamon
1 tablespoon ground nutmeg
½ cup orange marmalade
1 cup vegetable oil
4 eggs
1 can pumpkin
1 cup water
1 cup fresh or frozen blueberries
1 cup chopped walnuts or pecans

Preheat oven to 350°. Mix together dry ingredients. Beat together marmalade, oil, eggs, pumpkin, and water. Add to dry ingredients, mixing well. Stir in blueberries and walnuts. Put into three, 9 x 5-inch, greased and floured bread pans. Bake 1 hour or until cake tester inserted in center comes out clean. Yields 3 loaves.

Variation: In the fall fresh cranberries can be used instead of blueberries. Lemon marmalade can be used instead of orange.

Flapjacks

1 stick butter
2 tablespoons dark brown sugar
2 tablespoons golden syrup
5 ounces quick-cooking oats
3 tablespoons all-purpose flour

Preheat oven to 350°. Melt butter, sugar, and syrup over low heat, stirring until dissolved. Remove from heat. Mix in oats and flour. Press into well-greased 8 x 8-inch pan. Bake 15 to 20 minutes until golden brown. (Do not overcook.) Mark into bars. Leave to cool before removing from pan. (If you wish, you can add chopped pecans and raisins or mini chocolate chips.) Yields 4 servings.

BRAMPTON BED & BREAKFAST INN

25227 Chestertown Road
Chestertown, MD 21620
(410) 778-1860 (phone)
(866) 305-1860 (toll free)
innkeeper@bramptoninn.com
www.bramptoninn.com

Brampton Bed & Breakfast Inn is a magnificent National Register 1860 plantation house on thirty-five acres near Chestertown's historic district. Spacious guest and common rooms feature antiques and oriental rugs. Most guest rooms have wood-burning fireplaces and whirlpool baths. Attention to detail, personal service, and friendly innkeepers assure a relaxing and memorable visit.

Brampton Tea Cookies

4 cups all-purpose flour
½ teaspoon salt
2 cups (4 sticks) unsalted butter at
    room temperature
1 cup confectioners' sugar
2 teaspoons pure vanilla
¾ cup homemade jam (fig, strawberry
    jam, or orange marmalade)
Confectioners' sugar

Preheat oven to 325°. Blend flour and salt. Cream butter and sugar with electric mixer until well blended, scraping down sides of bowl as needed. Add vanilla and mix again. Add flour mixture and mix until thoroughly combined. Roll dough into 1-inch balls. Place balls on lightly buttered cookie sheet. Press down on ball with thumb to make indentation. Fill each indentation with ¼ teaspoon jam. Bake about 15 minutes or until barely golden brown. Cool cookies completely on flat surface before dusting with confectioners' sugar. Yields 4 dozen.

Blueberry Bread Pudding

6 eggs
1½ cups half-and-half
½ cup real maple syrup
1 tablespoon grated lemon zest
1 loaf French bread, cut into
    1-inch cubes
½ pint blueberries
2 tablespoons ground cinnamon
2 tablespoons sugar

Butter 8-inch square glass dish. In blender combine eggs, half-and-half, syrup, and zest and mix well. Put bread cubes in large bowl. Pour egg mixture over cubes. Soak until absorbed. Preheat oven to 325°. Gently fold in blueberries and distribute mixture evenly in pan. Combine cinnamon and sugar and sprinkle on top. Bake 40 to 50 minutes until golden and toothpick comes out clean. Yields 6 servings.

Rum and Raisin Pound Cake

1½ cups raisins
¼ cup good rum
1½ cups (3 sticks) butter at
    room temperature
1½ cups sugar
4 large eggs
2 teaspoons vanilla extract
½ teaspoon baking powder
¼ teaspoon salt
3 cups all-purpose flour
¾ cup sour cream

Soak raisins in rum while preparing batter. Preheat oven to 325°. Beat butter until light. Add sugar and beat until fluffy. Add eggs, one at a time, beating well to mix. Add vanilla, baking powder, and salt and beat well. Add flour and mix well. Add sour cream and mix well. Fold in raisins. Pour batter into well-greased Bundt or tube pan and bake about 1 hour. Test for doneness. Yields 10 to 12 servings.

❧   ❧   ❧

Chocolate Chip Pumpkin Muffins

1¾ cups unbleached all-purpose flour
1 cup sugar
1 teaspoon baking soda
1 teaspoon baking powder
½ teaspoon salt
1 tablespoon pumpkin pie spice
2 large eggs
1 cup plain pumpkin
½ cup melted unsalted butter
½ cup chocolate chips

Preheat oven to 375°. Grease muffin tin with spray. In large bowl, combine flour, sugar, baking soda, baking powder, salt, and pumpkin pie spice; mix well. In another bowl whisk together eggs, pumpkin, and melted butter. Pour over dry ingredients and mix gently just until moistened. Sprinkle with chocolate chips. Fold in without overmixing. Scoop into prepared tin and bake 20 to 25 minutes until golden brown. To cool, turn out onto rack. Yields 8 giant or 12 medium muffins.

Dutch Babies

Batter:
1 cup half-and-half
1 cup unbleached all-purpose flour
4 large eggs

Toppings:
Fried apples
Fresh peaches
Fresh blueberries
Fruit of choice

Mix batter ingredients very well without overbeating. Keep refrigerated until ready to bake. Preheat oven to 450°. Put 1 tablespoon batter into each of four ramekin dishes. Heat dishes 30 seconds in hot oven. Pour ⅓ cup prepared batter in each dish. Bake 7 to 9 minutes until nicely puffed and golden brown. Serve with topping of choice. Yields 4 servings.

STRAWBERRY INN

P.O. Box 237
17 W. Main Street
New Market, MD 21774
(301) 865-3318
www.newmarketmd.com/straw.htm

Built in 1837, the Strawberry Inn is located in the center of the nationally-registered town of New Market. The inn has four great guest rooms, each with private bath and each furnished in antiques. Breakfast is served in our dining room, or on pleasant days, on the grapevine, café-style back porch. Afternoons and evenings may be spent relaxing in the Victorian gazebo. Additionally, Mealey's Restaurant, voted number one in Frederick County, is located across the street. The inn is fifty miles east of Washington, DC and thirty-five miles from Baltimore. The area is surrounded by Civil War history and battlefields.

Molasses Refrigerator Muffins

1⅓ cups shortening
1 cup sugar
4 eggs
1 cup molasses
1 cup buttermilk
4 cups all-purpose flour
2 teaspoons baking soda
1 teaspoon salt
1 teaspoon ground cinnamon
1 teaspoon ground ginger
¼ teaspoon ground cloves
¼ teaspoon ground allspice
¼ teaspoon ground nutmeg
1 cup raisins

Cream shortening and sugar together until fluffy. Add eggs, one at a time, beating well. Blend in molasses and buttermilk. Add dry ingredients, stirring just to moisten. Add raisins. Store in covered container in refrigerator up to three weeks, always ready to scoop out as many muffins as you need "instantly." When ready, preheat oven to 350° and bake in greased muffin tin(s) for 20 minutes. Yields 3 dozen muffins.

Strawberry Inn

Corn Spoon Pudding

1 (8½-ounce) box corn muffin mix
1 (7½-ounce) can whole kernel corn
1 (7½-ounce) can creamed corn
1 cup sour cream
2 large eggs, beaten
½ cup melted unsalted butter
½ cup grated Swiss cheese

Preheat oven to 350°. Combine all ingredients except cheese in large mixing bowl. Pour into slightly greased 9 x 13-inch baking dish. Bake 35 minutes. Sprinkle cheese on top and Bake 10 minutes. Pudding is done when toothpick inserted in center comes out clean. Serve warm. Yields 12 servings.

THE INN AT MITCHELL HOUSE

8796 Maryland Parkway
Chestertown, MD 21620
(410) 778-6500

Surrounded by woods and overlooking Stoneybrook Pond, this eighteenth-century manor offers guests a touch of tranquility and a chance to step back in time. Shop and tour historic Chestertown, visit Eastern Neck Island National Wildlife Refuge, sail, fish, hunt, kayak, canoe, swim (private beach ½ mile away), bird watch, horseback ride, hike, bike, or play a round of sporting clays or golf.

Chesapeake Poppers

2 goose or 4 duck breasts*
1 (5-ounce) package taco
    seasoning mix
⅛ cup lime juice
⅛ cup water
¼ cup light olive oil
10 pickled jalapeños,
    cut in half lengthwise
10 slices bacon, cut in half
Picante sauce (optional)

Thinly slice breasts and cut into strips 4 inches long. Mix taco seasoning, lime juice, water, and olive oil to make marinade. Add meat and refrigerate 1 to 4 hours. Wrap piece of meat around half a jalapeño. Wrap piece of bacon around meat. Secure with toothpick. Grill over medium coals about 10 minutes until bacon is crisp, turning frequently. Serve poppers with picante sauce for dipping and plenty of frosty ale as an extinguisher. Yields 20 poppers.

*Note: Venison is also excellent. Should game not be available, lean beef or chicken strips can be substituted.

Chestertown Crab Quiche

1 piecrust, unbaked
½ cup milk
½ cup mayonnaise
2 eggs
3 tablespoons all-purpose flour
1½ tablespoons Old Bay seasoning
1 large shallot, chopped
1 tablespoon chopped parsley
1 teaspoon dry mustard
2 tablespoons sherry
Dash of cayenne
1½ cups shredded Swiss cheese
1 pound crabmeat
    (canned may be substituted)

Preheat oven to 350°. Put crust in 9-inch, deep-dish pie pan sprayed with nonstick pan coating. Mix together milk, mayonnaise, eggs, and flour. Stir in remaining ingredients, being careful not to break up crabmeat. Pour in pie shell. Bake 1 hour. Serve warm. Yields 6 servings.

Mitchell House Home Fries

2 white potatoes
2 large red potatoes
2 medium sweet potatoes
⅓ cup bacon drippings
3 green onions, including
    green part, chopped
1 to 2 tablespoons lemon pepper

Clean and chop potatoes. Heat bacon drippings in large fry pan over medium-high heat. Add potatoes and fry until golden brown. Add onions and fry several minutes. Add lemon pepper and stir. Serve hot. Yields 6 servings.

Aunt Gay's Crustless Quiche

1 medium onion, sliced
4 ounces fresh mushrooms, sliced
½ red pepper, sliced
½ green pepper, sliced
4 tablespoons butter
8 eggs
½ cup milk
1 teaspoon pepper
1 teaspoon seasoned salt
1 teaspoon chives
1 cup shredded sharp Cheddar cheese

Preheat oven to 375°. Spray 8-inch round cake pan with nonstick spray. Sauté onion, mushrooms, and peppers in butter until soft. Mix eggs, milk, pepper, salt, and chives. Add vegetables and cheese. Pour into prepared pan. Bake 45 minutes or until set. Holds very well in warm oven. Yields 6 servings.

THE INN AT NORWOOD

7514 Norwood Avenue
Sykesville, MD 21784
(410) 549-7868
Kelly@innatnorwood.com
www.innatnorwood.com

Built in 1906, this Colonial Revival home retains much of its original charm. Five beautifully decorated rooms have canopy beds, two-person Jacuzzi tubs, and fireplaces. Included is a full, three-course breakfast. The town of Sykesville is on the National Register of Historic Places. There is a restored railroad station that is the home of one of Maryland's best restaurants, Baldwin's Station. Sykesville has much to offer: great restaurants, a museum, many festivals throughout the year, hiking and biking trails, fishing, antique shops, and much more.

Old-Fashioned Potato Pancakes

3 medium potatoes, grated
½ onion, grated
1 egg
3 tablespoons all-purpose flour
Salt and pepper
½ teaspoon baking powder
2 tablespoons vegetable oil

Mix potatoes and onions. Add egg, flour, salt and pepper to taste, and baking powder. Heat oil in frying pan until really hot. Drop full tablespoon of mixture into hot oil to test (should cook and bubble quickly). Spoon ¼ cup batter into frying pan and cook until top is bubbly and bottom is browned; flip and brown on other side. Yields 4 servings.

Fruit Pudding Granola

1 (3.9-ounce) box instant
   French vanilla pudding
1 (8-ounce) container whipped topping
Mini vanilla wafers
1 banana, sliced
1 (20-ounce) can pineapple chunks
Granola
Cherries

Prepare pudding according to directions on box and refrigerate until chilled. Fold in whipped topping. Layer wafers in dessert cups. Layer pudding, banana, pudding, pineapple, pudding, granola. Serve with cherry on top. Yields 4 servings.

Best-Ever French Toast

1 cup packed brown sugar
⅓ cup butter
2 tablespoons light corn syrup
1½ teaspoons ground cinnamon
1 loaf (1-inch-thick) sourdough bread
5 eggs
1¼ cups milk
Strawberries
Confectioners' sugar

In saucepan, cook and stir brown sugar, butter, corn syrup, and cinnamon until melted. Pour in ungreased 8 x 8 x 2-inch pan. Cut bread to fill the baking dish and put in single layer on top of sugar. In mixing bowl, beat eggs and milk. Pour over bread, cover, and refrigerate 8 to 10 hours or overnight. When ready to bake, preheat oven to 350°. Remove cover and bake 35 to 45 minutes or until bread rises. Top with strawberries and confectioners' sugar. Yields 6 servings.

Chocolate Chip Pound Cake

1 (18-ounce) box chocolate cake mix
1 (3.9-ounce) box chocolate
   instant pudding
2 eggs
1¾ cups milk
1 (12-ounce) bag mini chocolate chips
Confectioners' sugar

Preheat oven to 350°. Beat all ingredients, except confectioners' sugar, by hand. (Do *not* use mixer.) Put into Bundt cake pan sprayed with nonstick pan coating. Bake for 1 hour. Top with confectioners' sugar. Yields 12 to 15 servings.

WATERLOO COUNTRY INN

28822 Mt. Vernon Road
Princess Anne, MD 21853
(410) 651-0883 (phone)
(410) 651-5592 (fax)
innkeeper@waterloocountryinn.com
www.waterloocounryinn.com

The Waterloo Country Inn is a restored, 1750s waterfront estate offering six luxury suites/rooms with private baths. Canoeing, swimming, and bicycling are available. The inn offers the best of two worlds nestled in a rural setting, but just a short distance away from the sandy beaches of Ocean City, Chincoteague, and Assateague Islands, known worldwide for their wild ponies. Fishing in Crisfield or a boat ride to Tangier and Smith islands will add adventure to your trip.

Waterloo Country Inn

Zurich Geschnetzeltes (a traditional Swiss Dish)

21 ounces veal, thinly sliced by hand
2 tablespoons butter
Salt and pepper
1 onion
¾ cup white wine
¾ cup cream
Lemon juice
1 tablespoon chopped parsley

Sauté in saucepan over high heat the thinly sliced veal on both sides in very hot butter. Remove from pan, sprinkle with salt and pepper, and keep warm. Slightly reduce heat. Finely chop onion and add to fat from meat. Sauté briefly and pour in wine. Simmer until liquid is reduced by half. Add cream and bring to boil. Add meat juices and season with salt, pepper, and a few drops of lemon juice. Reheat meat in sauce, but do *not* let it boil. Serve topped with parsley. Delicious with pasta. Yields 4 servings.

Apple Strudel Waterloo

2 pounds apples, peeled, cored, and chopped
½ cup sugar
1 teaspoon ground cinnamon
⅔ cup raisins
2 tablespoons rum
½ cup pine nuts or hazelnuts
1 ready-to-bake puff pastry sheet
⅓ cup cream
1 to 2 egg yolks
Peppermint sprigs

Blend apples with sugar, cinnamon, raisins, rum, and nuts. Spread cloth on table and dust with flour. Roll out puff pastry on cloth, and stretch sheet with your hands until it is paper thin. Trim edges of puff pastry if thick or uneven. Distribute apples evenly over sheet. Hold cloth on one side with both hands and lift it up little by little so puff pastry sheet rolls itself up around filling. Preheat oven to 375°. Arrange strudel on baking sheet and press sheet together along sides. Mix cream and egg yolks and pour over strudel. Bake 30 minutes. It should be brown and crisp when done. When serving, cut strudel into slices and serve with vanilla sauce or vanilla ice cream. Garnish with peppermint. Yields 4 servings.

Shrimp Waterloo

8 to 10 large shrimp
Lemon juice
Salt and pepper
2 teaspoons oil
¼ cup plus 2 tablespoons plus
    1 tablespoon butter
¼ cup dry vermouth
1 to 2 garlic cloves, crushed
Parsley
Dill or thyme, if desired
½ cup white wine

Sprinkle shrimp with lemon juice and salt and pepper to taste. Heat saucepan on medium-high and add oil and 1 to 2 tablespoons butter. Add shrimp and sauté on both sides until pink. Add ¼ cup dry vermouth, and ignite it. Flambé shrimp. Take out shrimp immediately after flame has died and keep warm. Add 1 tablespoon butter to pan. Sauté 1 to 2 garlic cloves, parsley, and dill or thyme if desired. Pour in white wine and dash of lemon juice and reduce sauce by half. Stir remaining ¼ cup butter into sauce and add salt and pepper to taste. Add shrimp and heat, but do *not* boil sauce. Place sauce on plates and arrange shrimp. Serve with rice and asparagus. Garnish with 1 to 2 tomato slices. Yields 2 servings.

Swiss Cheese Fondue

1 clove garlic, crushed
1½ cups dry white wine
14 ounces Emmenthaler cheese, grated
14 ounces Gruyère cheese, grated
2 teaspoons potato flour
3 teaspoons Kirsch
Freshly ground pepper and nutmeg
2 pounds white bread, cut into
    bite-size cubes

Rub inside of heat-proof casserole with crushed garlic clove. Add white wine and warm on low heat on top of stove. Add grated cheeses and bring to just under boiling point over medium heat. Stir with spatula until cheese is melted. Add Kirsch to flour, stirring until smooth. Stir into fondue mixture. Season with pepper and nutmeg to taste. Remove from stove and set on alcohol burner at table. Stir while dipping small pieces of bread speared on fondue forks into cheese. Serve with a side of spring leaf salads. Enjoy an evening of conversation and good food. Yields 6 servings.

INN AT WALNUT BOTTOM

120 Greene Street
Cumberland, MD 21502
(301) 777-0003 (phone)
(301) 777-8288 (fax)
(800) 286-9718 (toll free)
iwb@iwbinfo.com
www.iwbinfo.com

If visiting the terminus of the C&O Canal in Cumberland, be sure to try the Inn at Walnut Bottom for its historic charm, proximity to the canal, and friendly staff, who go out of their way to make you feel at home. You will feel like you are in a comfortable historic home as you enjoy one of our twelve lovely guest rooms. The Inn at Walnut Bottom combines charming accommodations, delicious food, and friendly service with affordable pricing to create an outstanding value. Wake up to a delightful breakfast served with joyful courtesy in the inn's bright dining room, after which you may want to stroll the historic district, ride the scenic train, or venture out to tour Frank Lloyd Wright's Fallingwater. The inn is located only 2½ hours from Washington, DC, Baltimore, and Pittsburgh.

Chocolate Gems

1 stick butter
12 ounces Nestle semisweet
  chocolate chips
1 (14-ounce) can sweetened
  condensed milk
1 cup all-purpose flour
1½ teaspoons vanilla extract
1 cup chopped nuts

Preheat oven to 350°. Melt butter, chocolate chips, and condensed milk together in double boiler over high heat. Stir in flour, vanilla, and chopped nuts. Drop by teaspoonfuls onto greased pan. Bake 7 minutes. These cookies taste almost like a confection and are very easy to make. Yields 3 dozen gems.

Bran Muffins with Cream Cheese Filling

Filling:
8 ounces cream cheese, softened
⅓ cup sugar
2 tablespoons all-purpose flour
1 teaspoon vanilla extract

Batter:
2½ cups all-purpose flour
2 cups sugar
2½ teaspoons baking soda
1 teaspoon salt
1 tablespoon ground cinnamon
½ teaspoon freshly grated nutmeg
3½ cups raisin bran cereal
2 large eggs, beaten lightly
2 cups well-shaken buttermilk
½ cup vegetable oil
½ cup raisins

Preheat oven to 400°. Grease muffin tins or line tins with paper liners. In small bowl stir together filling ingredients until combined well. Filling keeps, covered and chilled, 1 week.
  For batter, sift together flour, sugar, baking soda, salt, cinnamon, and nutmeg in large bowl and stir in cereal. Add eggs, buttermilk, oil, and raisins, stirring just until combined well. Batter keeps, covered and chilled, 1 week. Spoon 1 heaping tablespoon batter into each muffin cup and top with 2 teaspoons filling. Spoon 1 heaping tablespoon batter over filling, spreading to cover filling completely. Bake muffins in middle of oven 20 to 25 minutes, or until tester comes out clean. Yields about 24 muffins.

Golden Raisin Buns

Batter:
1 cup water
½ cup (1 stick) butter or margarine
1 teaspoon sugar
¼ teaspoon salt
1 cup all-purpose flour
4 eggs
½ cup golden raisins plumped
  (cover with hot water
  and let stand 5 minutes)

Lemon frosting:
1 tablespoon butter
1½ tablespoons heavy cream
1 cup confectioners' sugar
½ teaspoon each lemon juice
  and vanilla

Preheat oven to 375°. Combine water, butter, sugar, and salt in saucepan and bring to boil. Add flour all at once and over low heat beat with wooden spoon about 1 minute, or until mixture leaves sides of pan and forms smooth dough. Remove from heat. Continue beating about 2 minutes to cool slightly. Add eggs, one at a time, beating after each until mixture has a satiny sheen. Stir in raisins. Drop heaping tablespoons about 2 inches apart on greased baking sheet. Bake 30 to 35 minutes or until doubled, golden, and firm.

For lemon frosting, melt butter and stir in heavy cream. Remove from heat. Stir in confectioners' sugar until smooth. Stir in lemon juice and vanilla. Add more cream if necessary to make spreading consistency. While buns are still warm, gently spread frosting over tops and sides. Yields 20 to 24 buns.

Fruit and Spice Granola

4 cups old-fashioned rolled oats
1 cup unsweetened desiccated coconut
    (available at natural food shops)
1 cup slivered almonds
1 cup coarsely chopped pecans
¼ cup raw sunflower seeds
1½ teaspoons ground cinnamon
½ teaspoon freshly ground nutmeg
½ cup (1 stick) unsalted butter
½ cup honey
2 cups mixed fruits such as cranberries,
    cherries, currants, golden raisins,
    apricots, prunes, and/or dates

Preheat oven to 300°. In large bowl stir together oats, coconut, almonds, pecans, sunflower seeds, and spices. In small saucepan melt butter with honey over low heat, stirring occasionally. Pour mixture over oat mixture and toss to combine well. Spread granola evenly in two shallow baking pans and bake in upper and lower thirds of oven, stirring frequently and switching positions of pans halfway through baking, until golden brown, about 20 to 30 minutes. In large bowl, combine granola with dried fruits and cool, stirring occasionally. Yields about 10 cups.

Note: Granola keeps in an airtight container, chilled, 1 month.

Massachusetts

NANTUCKET HOUSE OF CHATHAM

2647 Main Street
South Chatham, MA
(508) 432-5641 (phone)
(866) 220-2547 (toll free)
jgordon1@cape.com
www.chathaminn.com

Lovingly restored to retain its historic charm, the Nantucket House of Chatham is a year-round comfortable and affordable inn. Breakfasts are a great start to your day. Nestled in peaceful Chatham, the busy Chatham shops and attractions are only minutes away. The town of Chatham is surrounded by water on three sides providing cool summers, exquisite autumns, and mild winters. Activities include fishing, of course, but also band concerts in the park, antique shopping, and much more. This is a year-round town and a year-round inn.

Wonderful Popovers!

3 large eggs
1 cup milk
1 cup all-purpose flour
2 tablespoons melted butter
Pinch of salt

Place eggs, milk, flour, butter, and salt in medium-size bowl or blender. If using bowl, use electric mixer at low speed to moisten ingredients. Beat 1 minute at high speed. Let sit up to 1 hour.

Preheat oven to 475° and adjust oven rack to top-third position. Place cast iron popover pan in oven to heat for a few minutes. (Very important to use this kind of pan.) Remove hot pan from oven and generously coat with vegetable spray. Immediately pour batter into prepared cups, filling each about two-thirds full. Bake 10 minutes. Reduce heat to 400° and bake 15 minutes more or until puffed, brown, and crisp. Don't open oven until popovers are fully baked or they won't rise. Serve at once with butter, jam, or honey. Yields about 8 popovers.

Upside-Down French Toast

1 cup packed brown sugar
1 stick butter
2 tablespoons white corn syrup
Challah or white bread
8 large eggs
2 teaspoons vanilla extract
2¼ cups milk
Fresh fruit for garnish

Combine brown sugar, butter, and corn syrup in a saucepan. Stir over medium heat until butter melts and sugar dissolves. For 1 or 2 minutes bring to a boil; then put into 13 x 9-inch pan and tilt to coat bottom of pan. Cut crusts off bread and arrange in layers over caramel. Make a second layer of bread. Whisk eggs, vanilla, and milk and pour over all. Cover with foil and refrigerate 8 to 10 hours or overnight.

When ready to cook, preheat oven to 350° and bake uncovered 40 to 60 minutes. Slice and invert to serve. Cover with foil and keep warm between servings. Garnish with fresh fruit. Yields 6 servings.

Nan's Great Chocolate Cake

3 cups all-purpose flour
2 cups sugar
7 tablespoons cocoa powder
1 teaspoon salt
2 teaspoons baking soda
1 cup vegetable oil
2 cups cold water
2 tablespoons vinegar
1 teaspoon vanilla extract

Preheat oven to 350°. Mix flour, sugar, cocoa powder, salt, and baking soda in bowl and blend well. Add vegetable oil, cold water, vinegar, and vanilla. Coat 13 x 9-inch pan with vegetable spray and dust with flour. Bake about 30 minutes. Frost with your favorite frosting and decorate with chocolate chips, sprinkles, and so forth—use your imagination. Yields 12 servings.

Fourth of July Berry Mini-Breads

½ cup (1 stick) butter, softened
1 cup sugar
2 eggs
3 cups all-purpose flour
1 teaspoon baking soda
1 teaspoon baking powder
1 teaspoon salt
1 cup buttermilk
1 cup whole-berry cranberry sauce
1 cup fresh or frozen blueberries

Preheat oven to 350°. In mixing bowl cream butter and sugar. Add eggs, one at a time, beating well after each addition. Combine dry ingredients and add to creamed mixture alternately with buttermilk. Stir in cranberry sauce and blueberries. Pour into four greased 5¾ x 3 x 2-inch loaf pans. Bake 25 to 30 minutes or until toothpick inserted comes out clean. Cool 10 minutes before removing from pans to wire rack. Yields 4 loaves.

THE CAPTAIN FREEMAN INN

15 Breakwater Road
Brewster, Cape Cod, MA 02631
(508) 896-7481 (phone)
(800) 843-4664 (toll free)
stay@captainfreemaninn.com
www.captainfreemaninn.com

The Captain Freeman Inn is a historic sea captain's mansion a short stroll from Cape Cod Bay. Surrounded by a graceful wrap-around porch, gardens, and pool, the inn serves guests breakfast on the porch or in front of the fireplace depending on the season. Winter cooking-school weekends feature international cuisine and include wine tasting and dinner. Activities in the area include beach walking, swimming, kayaking, sailing, whale watching, theater, golf, antiquing, auctions, and, of course, our cooking classes.

Cinnamon and Corn Pancakes

1¾ cups all-purpose flour
½ cup yellow cornmeal
2 teaspoons baking powder
1 teaspoon baking soda
2 teaspoons ground cinnamon
1½ cups milk
1 (15-ounce) can whole kernel corn
½ cup liquid reserved from corn
2 tablespoons vegetable oil
2 egg whites

Mix all ingredients in large bowl until well blended. Scoop onto hot griddle and cook until bubbles appear and sides begin to dry. Then turn pancakes over and cook until golden, 2 to 3 minutes per side. Serve with hot apple compote and crème fraîche or real maple syrup. Yields 4 servings.

Grilled Shrimp with Basil and Prosciutto

1 large shallot, minced
¼ cup dry vermouth
3 tablespoons olive oil
1 tablespoon balsamic vinegar
1 tablespoon lemon juice
1 tablespoon freshly chopped basil
Fresh ground pepper
16 large raw peeled shrimp
16 very thin slices of prosciutto
16 large or 32 small fresh basil leaves

Mix shallot, vermouth, oil, vinegar, lemon juice, basil, and pepper together and marinate shrimp refrigerated for 1 hour. Drain shrimp thoroughly. Place slice of prosciutto on work surface and cover with basil. Lay shrimp on top of basil at one end of prosciutto and roll up shrimp. Grill or broil shrimp four inches from heat for 2 minutes, or just until shrimp are pink. Do *not* overcook. For presentation several shrimp may be threaded onto bamboo skewers before grilling or grilled individually. Yields 4 appetizer or 2 main course servings.

Sweet Potato and Corn Chowder

1 large onion, sliced
4 large sweet potatoes, peeled and diced
3 tablespoons olive oil
2 cloves garlic, minced
8 cups vegetable or chicken stock
4 ears corn, stripped and kernels removed
1 tablespoon salt
½ teaspoon hot sauce
1 tablespoon cracked peppercorns
4 tablespoons brown sugar
4 tablespoons minced fresh dill weed
½ cup plain yogurt
1 tablespoon cornstarch

In large Dutch oven or soup pot sauté onion and sweet potatoes in olive oil for 5 minutes. Add garlic and stock. Bring to a boil and reduce heat to simmer just until potatoes are done. Purée potatoes, onion, and garlic and return to stock. Add corn, salt, hot sauce, peppercorns, sugar, and dill. Turn off heat. Mix yogurt and cornstarch together and add to stock, mixing well. Return to simmer for 2 to 3 minutes. Serve warm with Cheddar Cheese Biscuits (see recipe below). Yields 8 servings.

Note: For a one-dish meal, add 1 pound fresh scallops or shrimp during final simmer. Do *not* overcook.

Cheese Biscuits

2 cups all-purpose flour
1 tablespoon baking powder
1 teaspoon salt
2 tablespoons cold unsalted butter
¾ cup grated sharp white Cheddar
cheese, kept cold until used
1 cup cold buttermilk

Preheat oven to 425°. Combine flour, baking powder, and salt together in large open bowl. Cut butter into dry ingredients until mixture looks like coarse cornmeal. Toss grated cheese with dry ingredients. Stir in buttermilk to form soft dough. Turn dough out onto floured board and knead quickly 6 to 8 times. Pat dough into ¾-inch thickness and cut with 2-inch round cutter to form biscuits. Be careful not to handle dough too much or it will be tough. Bake biscuits on ungreased cookie sheet 10 to 12 minutes or until lightly browned and puffy. Serve warm. Yields 8 to 10 biscuits.

Old-Fashioned Almond Shortcakes

2 cups all-purpose flour
4 teaspoons baking powder
½ teaspoon salt
2 tablespoons sugar
⅓ cup finely ground almonds
⅛ teaspoon ground nutmeg
¼ cup unsalted cold butter,
cut into small pieces
¾ cup very cold milk
½ teaspoon almond extract

Mix dry ingredients together in mixing bowl. With fingers or pastry cutter, work butter into flour mixture until it resembles coarse cornmeal. Add milk and almond extract, mixing with a fork just until dough holds together. Preheat oven to 325°. Turn dough out onto floured board and pat to 1-inch thickness. Cut with cookie cutter into 3-inch circles. Place on ungreased cookie sheet and bake 8 to 10 minutes or just until golden. Serve warm or at room temperature with fresh sliced strawberries and sweetened cream. Yields 8 servings for dessert or breakfast.

THE WILDFLOWER INN BED & BREAKFAST

167 Palmer Avenue
Falmouth, MA 02540
(508) 548-9524 (phone)
(800) 294-5459 (toll free)
wldflr167@aol.com
www.wildflower-inn.com

A tastefully restored Cape Cod Inn in Falmouth, Massachusetts's, quaint historic district, the Wildflower Inn Bed & Breakfast is well known for its edible flower breakfasts. The Wildflower Inn, where guests can enjoy an atmosphere of relaxation and comfort, is a home away from home. Enjoy long summer evenings on the wraparound porch. Whatever the season or reason, relax with the Wildflower Inn.

Orange Blossom Bread Pudding

1 plus 1 cup orange juice
1 tablespoon Grand Marnier
⅓ cup dried cranberries, soaked
1 teaspoon orange blossom water,
if available
1 pound bread, broken into
2-inch cubes
8 large eggs
2 egg yolks
¼ cup brown sugar
3 cups milk
1 cup heavy cream
1 teaspoon vanilla extract
1 tablespoon orange extract
1 tablespoon grated orange zest
1 teaspoon freshly grated nutmeg

The Wildflower Inn Bed & Breakfast

<u>Grand Marnier sauce:</u>
1 stick butter
1 cup confectioners' sugar
2 egg yolks
⅓ cup orange juice
1 teaspoon Grand Marnier

Two days before preparing recipe, plump up cranberries by soaking in 1 cup orange juice and Grand Marnier. Let sit 8 to 10 hours or overnight.

To make orange water infuse orange blossoms by pouring boiling water over them and let sit in covered container 8 to 10 hours in refrigerator.

Eight to 10 hours before serving, grease 9 x 13-inch pan with nonstick spray. Tear bread into 2-inch pieces. Line pan with half the bread pieces, covering bottom of pan. Strain all liquid off cranberries. Beat eggs, yolks, and sugar until very frothy. Add milk, cream, vanilla, orange extract, orange zest, and remaining 1 cup orange juice, and orange blossom water, if available. Beat until frothy. The longer you beat, the better. Make sure there are bubbles on top of egg mixture. Pour half the milk mixture over bread, sprinkle on cranberries evenly, and add remaining egg mixture. Make sure all bread is covered with milk mixture. Sprinkle nutmeg over top. Cover and refrigerate 8 to 10 hours or overnight.

When ready to cook, preheat oven to 350°. Place 9 x 13-inch pan inside 11 x 13-inch pan with warm water three-fourths up smaller pan. Bake 50 to 60 minutes until set. Remove from oven and let stand 10 minutes.

For Grand Marnier sauce, melt butter over medium heat, add sugar, and whip until all sugar is absorbed. Remove from heat and add egg yolks. Whisk thoroughly. Whisk in orange juice and Grand Marnier. Put the sauce back on low heat to cook off alcohol, whisking occasionally. Cut pudding into twelve squares, pour Grand Marnier sauce over the pudding, and serve hot. Garnish with orange mint or an orange slice. Yields 12 squares.

Note: Orange blossom water can be purchased in Middle Eastern markets or gourmet specialty shops.

HARBOUR HOUSE INN BED & BREAKFAST

725 North State Road
Cheshire, MA 01225
(413) 743-8959
harbourhouseinn@aol.com
www.harbourhouseinn.com

The Harbour House Inn Bed & Breakfast is a beautiful and historic eighteenth-century Georgian Colonial nestled in the heart of the picturesque Berkshire Hills in western Massachusetts. From its beginning in the late 1700s, the house has evolved from a small homestead to a stately center hall colonial in the 1800s, and then, in the early 1900s, it was transformed by the Walter Penniman family into an elegant gentleman's farmhouse. In the beginning the Harbour House was said to be a stagecoach stop and tavern. It is also thought that it served as a "safe harbour" on the Underground Railroad, hence comes the name. The Harbour House is a relaxing retreat far removed from the hustle and hurry of everyday life.

Harbour House Granola

4 cups oats
1½ cups sliced almonds
½ cup brown sugar
1 teaspoon ground cinnamon
½ teaspoon salt
¼ cup vegetable oil
¼ cup honey
1 teaspoon vanilla extract
1½ cups craisins

In large bowl mix together oats, almonds, sugar, cinnamon, and salt. In small saucepan heat oil and honey, stirring to mix well. Add vanilla. Pour over oat mixture, stirring well with a wooden spoon. Preheat oven to 350°. Spread mixture in 15 x 10 x 1-inch cookie sheet coated with cooking spray. Reduce oven to 300°. Bake 10 minutes. Take out and stir thoroughly. Repeat four times, baking for a total of 40 minutes. Take out and let oven cool to 250°. Turn oven off and return pan to oven. Leave 8 to 10 hours or overnight. This assures crunchiness. Transfer to bowl and add craisins. Store in an airtight container. Yields about 8 cups.

Variation: Use walnuts and raisins or any combination of nuts and dried fruit.

Eggs in Crêpe Cups

½ cup "complete" pancake mix
1 egg
½ cup water
6 ounces mushrooms, sliced
2 tablespoons butter
2 tablespoons sour cream
Salt and pepper
6 jumbo eggs
Fresh snipped chives

Combine pancake mix, egg, and water. Stir to form batter. Cook in crêpe pan, removing crêpes to wax paper when done. Spray deep muffin or popover pan with nonstick spray and preheat oven to 350°. Place crêpe in each cup so that crêpes are evenly ruffled. Sauté mushrooms in butter until slightly dried and golden. Place in a bowl and add sour cream. Salt and pepper to taste. Place 1 tablespoon mushroom mixture in bottom of each crêpe. Break 1 egg into each cup and top with chives. Bake 15 to 20 minutes depending on your oven and size of eggs. Yields 5 to 6 crêpes.

KENBURN ORCHARDS BED & BREAKFAST

1394 Mohawk Trail
Shelburne, MA 01370
(413) 625-6443 (phone/fax)
info@kenburnorchards.com
www.kenburnorchards.com

Kenburn Orchards Bed & Breakfast offers three gracious guest rooms in a lovingly restored farmhouse that has been in our family for generations. We serve an elegant "candlelight and crystal" breakfast in our dining room, except on summer days when guests may choose to eat on the porch. The inn is in western Massachusetts, where the hills rise out of the Connecticut River valley to form the Berkshires. There are excellent schools and colleges, museums, ski areas, white-water rafting, hiking nearby, and the picturesque village of Shelburne Falls with its glacial potholes and famous bridge of flowers is fifteen minutes away.

Grapes Vineyard

½ cup sour cream
2 tablespoons dark brown sugar
¼ teaspoon vanilla extract
1 pound seedless green grapes
4 strawberries
Mint sprigs

Combine sour cream, brown sugar, and vanilla in small bowl. Cover and refrigerate at least 1 hour to overnight.

Wash grapes; remove stems and pat dry. Stir prepared sauce to ensure brown sugar is thoroughly dissolved and gently mix with grapes. Serve in parfait glasses or dessert dishes garnished with fresh strawberries in season and sprigs of fresh mint. Yields 4 servings.

Cranberry Coffee Cake

¼ cup brown sugar
½ cup walnuts
½ cup raisins (optional: delicious,
    but sticky in pan)
Fresh or frozen cranberries
    to cover pan bottom
1 cup all-purpose flour
1 cup sugar
2 eggs
1 teaspoon almond extract
¾ cup melted butter
Confectioners' sugar or whipped cream
    for topping

Preheat oven to 350°. Cover bottom of lightly greased 9- or 10-inch pie plate with brown sugar, walnuts, raisins, and cranberries. Mix flour, sugar, eggs, almond extract, and butter together in medium bowl. Pour mixture into pie plate, filling in around cranberries and walnuts. Bake 35 minutes, or until knife inserted in center comes out clean. Remove from oven. Either serve in pan or run spatula around sides of pan and turn out upside down on serving plate. Sprinkle with confectioners' sugar or top with fresh whipped cream— ½ cup heavy cream with 1 tablespoon sugar. Yields 8 servings.

Pumpkin Flan

¾ plus ½ cup sugar
½ teaspoon salt
1 teaspoon ground cinnamon
1 cup canned pumpkin (or 1 cup cooked
    and mashed fresh pumpkin)
5 large eggs, lightly beaten
1½ cups undiluted evaporated milk
⅓ cup water
1½ teaspoons vanilla extract

Topping:
½ cup heavy cream
1 tablespoon sugar
¼ teaspoon ground ginger

Melt ½ cup sugar in small pan over medium-low heat until it forms a golden

Kenburn Orchards Bed & Breakfast

syrup, stirring constantly to prevent burning. Pour immediately into 8 x 8 x 2-inch pan, turning and rolling pan from side to side to coat with caramel. Set aside to use later. Do *not* stick your finger in caramel.

Preheat oven to 350°. Combine remaining sugar, salt, and cinnamon. Add pumpkin and eggs. Mix well. Stir in evaporated milk, water, and vanilla. Mix well and turn into caramel-coated pan. Bake in a water bath about 1 hour or until knife inserted in center comes out clean. Remove from oven, cool, and refrigerate several hours until well chilled. To serve, run spatula around the sides of the pan, turn out on serving plate, and cut into squares.

For topping, whip heavy cream with sugar and ground ginger until thick and fluffy. Pour over flan and garnish with fresh strawberry or other fruit if available. Yields 8 servings.

BIRCHWOOD INN

7 Hubbard Street
Lenox, MA 01240
(800) 524-1646 (toll free)
innkeeper@birchwood-inn.com
www.birchwood-inn.com

Did Washington and Lafayette stay at Birchwood Inn? It is quite possible since they were friends of an early owner. If they were guests today, they would receive a warm welcome at the oldest home in Lenox, circa 1767. They would savor the country breakfast and afternoon tea prepared by the inn's prize-winning chef and baker.

Nancy's Monday Morning Blueberry Buckle

This incredible coffee cake is a wonderful addition to both breakfast and afternoon tea.

Buckle:
¾ cup sugar
¼ cup softened butter
1 egg
1⅓ plus ⅓ cups all-purpose flour
2 teaspoons baking powder
½ teaspoon salt
⅓ cup milk
⅓ cup fresh blueberries

Topping:
½ cup sugar
½ cup all-purpose flour
½ teaspoon ground cinnamon
½ stick chilled butter

Preheat oven to 375°. Butter and flour 9-inch-square baking pan. In large bowl cream together sugar and butter. Add egg and beat until light. In medium bowl combine 1⅓ cups flour, baking powder, and salt. Add flour mixture to egg mixture alternately with milk, beginning and ending with flour. Mix until just combined. Lightly fold remaining ⅓ cup flour in with blueberries and fold floured blueberries into batter. Spread batter in baking pan.

For topping, blend sugar, flour, and cinnamon in food processor. Cut chilled butter into chunks and add to sugar mixture, processing until mixture is crumbly. Sprinkle topping over batter. Bake 45 to 50 minutes. The buckle can be served warm or at room temperature. Yields 8 to 10 servings.

Raspberry Flan Tart

This recipe is derived from a similar clafouti created by the Troisgros brothers for their restaurant in Roanne, France.

Pastry:
1¾ cups unbleached cake flour
¼ teaspoon salt
½ cup sugar
1 stick chilled unsalted butter, cut into pieces
4 egg yolks
2 tablespoons ice water

Filling:
4 egg yolks
1 cup crème fraîche
6 tablespoons sugar
2 cups fresh raspberries

In food processor mix together flour, salt, and sugar. Add the chilled butter and blend in short spurts until mixture resembles coarse meal. In small bowl beat egg yolks together with ice water. Add egg mixture to flour mixture in food processor. Blend in short spurts, being careful not to overblend. Transfer dough to a floured board and shape dough into a ball, kneading with heel of your hand to distribute the butter evenly. Reshape into a ball, dust lightly with flour, and wrap loosely in wax paper. Refrigerate for 15 minutes. Preheat oven to 400°. Cut chilled dough in half, wrapping one piece in wax paper and refrigerating or freezing it for future use. Roll out other half on lightly floured surface, creating a 10-inch circle. Transfer circle of dough to 9-inch, fluted flan pan with removable bottom, being careful not to stretch dough. With floured hands, pat dough into flan pan, pushing dough into corners and up to top of flan rim. Prick dough with fork in several places and line with buttered foil, buttered side down. Fill with thick layer of rice, dried beans, or baking weights. Bake in the lower third of the oven 10 to 15 minutes, or until golden. Remove rice and foil. Carefully remove shell from pan and cool on a wire rack. Reduce oven temperature to 350°.

To make filling, combine egg yolks, crème fraîche, and sugar in small mixing bowl. Whisk until blended. Arrange raspberries in concentric circles in pastry shell, filling entire shell. Spoon custard mixture over the berries. Bake 20 minutes. Reduce heat to 325° and bake additional 5 to 10 minutes, or until pastry is golden. Serve warm or at room temperature. Yields 6 to 8 servings.

Rise and Shine Soufflé

This is our signature breakfast entrée. We prepare it the night before, wake up, bake it in the oven, and graciously accept the rave reviews.

   6 cups firm, day-old French bread, cubed
   2 cups (½ pound) shredded aged
       Cheddar cheese
   10 eggs, lightly beaten
   4 cups (1 quart) milk
   ½ cup minced fresh parsley
   1 teaspoon dry mustard
   1 teaspoon Maggi seasoning or salt
   ¼ teaspoon onion powder
   2 tablespoons fines herbs or freshly
       chopped chives
   Freshly ground pepper
   ½ cup chopped tomatoes
   6 to 8 slices bacon, cooked and
       crumbled (optional)

Generously grease eight 8-ounce ramekins. Arrange bread cubes in ramekins and sprinkle with cheese. Beat together eggs, milk, parsley, mustard, Maggi, onion powder, fines herbs, and pepper and pour evenly over cheese and bread. Sprinkle with tomatoes and bacon, if using. Cover with plastic wrap and chill up to 24 hours.

   When ready to bake, preheat oven to 350°. Bake soufflé uncovered until it rises and is lightly browned on top, about 45 to 50 minutes. Serve immediately. Yields 8 servings.

❧ ❧ ❧

Peach Upside-Down French Toast

   ½ cup melted butter
   1 cup packed brown sugar
   2 tablespoons water
   2 cups fresh peach slices
   8 large challah (egg bread),
       preferably loaf style, cut into
       squares with crusts cut off
   5 eggs
   1½ cups milk
   3 teaspoons vanilla extract
   Ground cinnamon or nutmeg
   1 cup peach slices

Mix butter, brown sugar, and water to make syrup. Pour syrup into greased 9 x 13-inch baking dish. Arrange peach slices in overlapping rows on top of syrup. Place bread slices in a layer over peaches. Mix eggs, milk, vanilla, and cinnamon and pour over bread. Cover and refrigerate French toast 8 to 10 hours or overnight.

   When ready to prepare, preheat oven to 350°. Bake 45 to 55 minutes. Cut toast into eight servings and place on individual

Bunker Hill Bed & Breakfast

plates. Garnish with fresh peach slices. Spoon pan liquid over each serving. Yields 8 servings.

   Note: This recipe is also wonderful with apples, pineapples, or plums.

BUNKER HILL BED & BREAKFAST

80 Elm Street
Charlestown, MA 02129
(617) 886-9367 (phone/fax)
crawolff@cs.com
www.bunkerhillbedandbreakfast.com

The Bunker Hill Bed & Breakfast is a Victorian-style bed and breakfast built in 1885 within the heart of historic Boston. It is only ten minutes from the airport and Boston's many historic landmarks: home of the USS Constitution, the Bunker Hill Monument, and the Charlestown Navy Yard. Our motto is: My house is your house.

The Bunker Hill Dessert

   1 (8-ounce) package pistachio
       (vanilla or chocolate) pudding mix
   32 ounces plain or vanilla yogurt
   Fruit (any kind), sliced
   Whipped cream for topping
   Sprig of mint for topping
   Cherry for topping

Mix pistachio pudding mix into yogurt container. Refrigerate overnight. Layer fruit slices alternately with yogurt in fancy goblet. Top with whipped cream, sprig of mint, and cherry. Yields 4 to 6 servings.

CAPTAIN'S CHOICE BED & BREAKFAST

212 Greenwood Ave.
P.O. Box 78
Hyannis Port, MA 02647-0078
(508) 775-0101 (phone)
(508) 778-4235 (fax)
(866) 775-0101 (toll free)
BandB@captchoice.com
www.captchoice.com

Unique services are the hallmark at Captain's Choice Bed & Breakfast. The famous, yet quiet, Hyannis Port location is within a half mile of beaches, boating, shops, restaurants, golf, and nightlife. It is ideally suited to offer a complimentary area tour, drop-off/pick-up service to ferries serving the islands of Martha's Vineyard and Nantucket and fresh floral designs for each of the guest rooms from the bountiful gardens that surround the property. Made-to-order breakfasts featuring unique recipes and fine organic ingredients highlight the mornings.

Captain's Choice Frittata

We bake in individual ramekins, but this recipe can be used to make one casserole to generously serve six.

3 eggs
1 (16-ounce) carton egg substitute
½ cup diced onion
½ cup chopped ham
½ cup shredded cheese
½ cup diced cooked potato
½ teaspoon black or white pepper

Preheat oven to 325° to 350°. In large bowl, beat eggs and add egg substitute. Micro-wave diced onion for 20 seconds, and add to egg mixture together with ham, cheese, potato, and pepper. Spray 9-inch quiche pan or six individual ramekins and bake 35 minutes or until frittata puffs and browns on top. Yields 6 servings.

Captain's Choice Pumpkin Muffins

In the interest of good health, the Captain's Choice uses organically grown grains and other organically produced products including flax oil, which gives the muffins a light texture and requires a lower baking temperature. This recipe is wheat-free and excellent for those with dietary concerns.

2 cups spelt flour* (or half spelt/half all-purpose flour)
½ cup oat bran
¼ cup unsweetened shredded coconut
1 teaspoon baking soda
1 teaspoon baking powder
¾ cup Rice Dream (or milk)
½ cup flaxseed oil
1 cup canned or cooked pumpkin
¼ teaspoon ground nutmeg
½ teaspoon ground cinnamon
⅓ cup raisins

Preheat oven to 325°. In large bowl combine flour, bran, coconut, baking soda, and baking powder and stir to mix well. In a blender combine Rice Dream, oil, pumpkin, nutmeg, and cinnamon and purée until smooth and creamy. Add raisins and pulse to chop. Add pumpkin mixture to dry ingredients and stir until well moistened. Spray, or oil, muffin pans and bake 35 minutes or until done. Test for doneness with cake tester. Yields 12 muffins.

*Note: Spelt flour is made from spelt grain, which is from the grass family. It is good for those with an aversion to wheat flour. Spelt flour does not rise as much as other flours, but that's what makes it easier to digest. Spelt flour and Rice Dream may both be found in specialty sections of your local grocery store.

CROWNE POINTE HISTORIC INN

82 Bradford Street
Provincetown, MA 02657
(508) 487-6767 (phone)
(508) 487-5554 (fax)
(877) CROWNE-1 (toll free)
welcome@crownepointe.com
www.crownepointe.com

Crowne Pointe is a distinguished AAA Four-Diamond property, complete with heated pool and spas. Most rooms feature fireplaces, whirlpool tubs, and period antiques. A complimentary, unsurpassed, hot breakfast is served daily. The inn is set high on a bluff in the heart of Provincetown overlooking Provincetown Harbor. The inn boasts luxurious rooms and suites as well as wedding, meeting, and conference facilities. Activities in the area include whale watching, kayaking, boating, tennis, beaches, squash/racquetball, golf, charter fishing, bike rental, dune tours, and sight-seeing airplanes.

Yummy Orange Marmalade French Toast with Grand Marnier

3 teaspoons grated orange zest
2 cups freshly squeezed orange juice
¼ cup sugar
2 teaspoons pure vanilla
6 eggs
½ cup half-and-half
1 package maple-favored English muffins

Orange butter sauce:
3 teaspoons clarified melted butter
5 teaspoons sweet orange marmalade
2 teaspoons Grand Marnier liqueur

Whisk together zest, orange juice, sugar, vanilla, eggs, and half-and-half. Arrange muffins, split in half, in large container and pour mixture over muffins and soak chilled 8 to 10 hours or overnight.

When ready to serve, preheat oven to 375°. Arrange muffins on greased cookie sheet and bake about 15 minutes.

For orange sauce, mix together butter, marmalade, and Grand Marnier. Serve muffins on individual plates and drizzle with sauce. Yields 6 servings.

Mom's Cinnamon Croissant French Toast

4 large eggs
4 cups half-and-half
2 tablespoons sugar
1 teaspoon vanilla extract
1 tablespoon ground cinnamon
6 day-old croissants, sliced
3 cups blueberries
1 cup toasted almonds
Confectioners' sugar as needed
3 cups whipped cream

Whisk together eggs, half-and-half, sugar, vanilla, and cinnamon. Soak croissants in egg batter 10 minutes. Grill croissants on griddle until golden brown and cooked through. To serve, top with fresh blueberries, toasted almonds, confectioners' sugar, and freshly whipped cream. Serve on individual plates and add strawberries to plate for color accents if desired. Yields 6 servings.

WINTERWOOD AT PETERSHAM

19 North Main Street
Petersham, MA 01366-9500
(978) 724-8885 (phone)
(978) 724-8884 (fax)
winterwoodinn@juno.com
www.winterwoodinn.com

Winterwood is an elegantly restored, historic 1842 Greek Revival mansion with six beautifully appointed guest rooms with fireplaces. Winterwood is available for weddings and cocktail receptions. The town of Petersham is nestled in the heart of New England in central Massachusetts, about seventy miles west of Boston and thirty miles from Worcester and Amherst. The town of Petersham is often referred to as a museum of Greek Revival architecture and reminiscent of a picture perfect "Norman Rockwell" town. There are plenty of activities nearby, including hiking, mountain biking, downhill skiing, antique shopping, horseback riding, golfing, and bird-watching.

Anise Biscotti

½ cup shortening
½ cup softened butter
1 cup sugar
2 eggs
3 cups all-purpose flour
2 teaspoons baking powder
½ teaspoon salt
1 teaspoon vanilla extract
4 teaspoons anise extract

Preheat oven to 350°. Grease large cookie sheet. In large mixer bowl combine all ingredients. Mix well to form a stiff dough. Divide dough in half. On prepared cookie sheet, shape dough into two long bars about ½ inch thick. Bake about 25 minutes. Retain oven temperature at 350°. Let bars cool on cookie sheet about 15 minutes. Slice bars across to make the cookies. Lay them down on cut side. Bake an additional 15 minutes or until cut side is golden brown. Let cool on pan. These cookies will keep well in plastic container or cookie tin. Yields about 3 dozen biscotti.

Winterwood Chocolate Banana Torte

Crust:
¾ package Oreos
¼ cup melted butter

Filling:
1½ cups heavy cream
2 cups semisweet chocolate chips
5 pounds ripe, but still firm, bananas

Topping:
3 cups heavy cream
1 (3.8-ounce) package vanilla instant pudding
Unsweetened cocoa

Lightly grease 9-inch or 10-inch springform pan. To prepare crust, grate Oreos in blender or food processor to fine crumbs. Mix butter into crumbs and spread into bottom of prepared pan, pressing until firm. Put into refrigerator until ready to use.

For filling, heat heavy cream to full boil, watching constantly. Add semisweet chocolate chips. Remove from heat and let sit about 5 minutes. Mix until well blended and pour into crust. Chill in refrigerator 2 hours or overnight. Peel and slice bananas, making some slices into triangles. Starting at edge of prepared pan, place banana slices on their sides and make a circle using triangle pieces to fill in spaces. Repeat to form an inner circle. Keep repeating until you have completely filled pan, making a complete layer of bananas.

For topping, beat cream until almost firm. Beat in instant pudding. Spread onto banana layer to cover completely. Sprinkle top with cocoa in a fine strainer. Yields 10 to 12 servings.

Chocolate Cherry Truffle Torte

Torte:
2 (10-ounce) jars maraschino cherries, drained, reserving ½ cup juice
2 cups (4 sticks) butter, cut into pieces
12 ounces semisweet chocolate, broken into pieces
1 cup sugar
½ teaspoon almond extract
8 large eggs at room temperature

Ganache:
⅔ cup heavy cream
2 tablespoons softened butter
8 ounces (1¼ cups) semisweet chocolate chips

Preheat oven to 325°. Butter bottom and sides of 10 x 3-inch pan. Do *not* use springform pan. Reserve sixteen of best-looking cherries and place on plate lined with paper towel to drain. Coarsely chop remaining cherries. In heavy, large saucepan, over low heat, combine butter, chocolate, and sugar. Using wooden spoon, stir constantly until mixture is smooth. Remove pan from heat. Stir in reserved cherry juice and almond extract. Whisk in eggs one at a time. At first, mixture may look separated, but it will become smooth as remaining eggs are added. Stir in chopped cherries. Scrape mixture into prepared pan. Set pan in large roasting pan in oven and pour hot water in roasting pan to come halfway up sides of cake pan. Bake torte 60 to 70 minutes or until cake tester inserted in center comes out clean. Cool torte about an hour on cooling rack and remove to serving plate. It will come out easier if still warm. If it sticks in spots, just take a knife and smooth it over. The frosting will hide any indentations. Let cool completely and wrap with plastic wrap. Chill thoroughly, even overnight.

For ganache, bring cream to a boil in small, heavy saucepan over low heat, watching carefully. Remove pan from heat and immediately add butter and chocolate. Let mixture sit about 5 minutes. Whisk mixture until all chocolate is melted and smooth. Cover ganache with plastic wrap and refrigerate until it thickens to pudding-like consistency. This should take 30 to 45 minutes. Stir occasionally.

To decorate torte, spread ganache over top and sides. Pipe sixteen rosettes through pastry bag around edge of torte and place cherry on each rosette. If you don't have a pastry bag, cut a small hole out of corner of a small plastic bag, and squeeze a dollop of ganache on torte. Yields 8 to 10 servings.

WHALEWALK INN

220 Bridge Road
Eastham, MA 02642
(598) 255-0617 (phone)
(508) 240-0017 (fax)
(800) 440-1281 (toll free)
reservations@whalewalkinn.com
information@whalewalkinn.com
www.whalewalkinn.com

Get away from the hustle and bustle of your every day life. Come and relax at one of Cape Cod's most romantic and secluded country Inns—quietly tucked away on a country road, but close enough to all the attractions that make the Cape so special. Walk the "Outer Cape" beaches, listening to the soothing sound of the waves lapping on Cape Cod Bay or crashing at the National Seashore. Partake in some of the finest dining that the Cape has to offer, beginning here each day with a gourmet breakfast served to you at your own private table. Explore the Cape by bicycle, swimming, and shopping, then end your day with an in-room massage.

Grand Marnier Oatmeal Pie

¾ cup skim milk
3 eggs, beaten
½ cup orange juice
¼ cup sugar or 2 tablespoons honey
½ cup quick oats
2 tablespoons margarine or butter, melted and cooled
1 tablespoon orange zest, soaked in 1 tablespoon Grand Marnier
1 (9-inch) pie shell

Preheat oven to 325° to 350°. Mix together all ingredients and pour into pie shell. Bake 30 to 35 minutes. Can also be cooked without shell in pie pan or quiche dish that has been coated with nonstick spray. Yields 6 servings.

Whalewalk Inn Italian Stuffed Mushrooms

2 tablespoons olive oil
2 tablespoons butter
½ small onion, diced (about ¼ cup)
2 cloves garlic, minced
3 to 6 pepperoncini peppers, seeded and minced
3 ounces prosciutto (about 3 slices), diced
1 medium tomato, seeded and diced
½ cup Italian seasoned breadcrumbs
½ cup plus 1 tablespoon grated Parmesan
36 large white mushrooms, stems removed

Preheat oven to 350°. Heat medium-size skillet over medium heat. Add oil, butter, and onion. Stir occasionally until onion is translucent, about 5 minutes. Add garlic, pepperoncini, and prosciutto. Stir constantly for 2 minutes and add tomato. Stir occasionally for 2 to 3 minutes and add breadcrumbs. Remove from heat and stir until breadcrumbs are thoroughly mixed and moistened. Add ½ cup Parmesan and stir until incorporated. Firmly pack generous tablespoon of mixture into each mushroom. Sprinkle tops with remaining 1 tablespoon Parmesan and bake 20 minutes. Yields 36 stuffed mushrooms.

Granola Breakfast Pizza

This pancake is baked in a pizza pan with a little lip and topped with bananas, brown sugar, fresh seasonal fruits, and sour cream. It is a great dish to add a splash of color, especially for the Fourth of July.

Topping:
1 cup brown sugar
2 tablespoons butter
¼ cup water

Pancake:
2 eggs
1¼ cups milk
2 tablespoons olive oil
1 teaspoon maple syrup
2 cups pancake mix
¾ cup granola (without raisins)
¾ cup chopped macadamia nuts
    (pecans, walnuts, or almonds
    may be substituted)
Banana, strawberry, and peach slices
Blueberries or blackberries
Sour cream for topping

Preheat oven to 425°. Combine brown sugar, butter, and water in saucepan. Bring to low boil, stirring occasionally.

For pancake, in large bowl beat eggs, milk, oil, and maple syrup. Add pancake mix and beat mixture by hand until smooth. Coat 12- to 14-inch pizza pan with nonstick spray. Pour batter into pan and sprinkle granola and nuts evenly over batter. Bake in lower third of oven for 10 to 12 minutes. Cut pizza into six wedges and top with sliced bananas on left-hand corner of slice. Spoon brown sugar mixture over bananas and pizza. Add strawberry slices to right corner, 3 slices of peach to point of slice, and decorate with a few blueberries or blackberries for added color. Add dollop of sour cream on bananas, strawberries, and peaches. Yields 6 servings.

Whalewalk Inn Granola

5 cups oats
1 cup sesame seeds
1 cup sunflower seeds
1 cup wheat germ
1 cup instant milk powder
1 cup honey
¾ cup vegetable oil
1 cup each nuts, raisins, dates, and craisins

Preheat oven to 375°. Mix together dry ingredients, combine honey and oil, and add to dry ingredients. Bake on cookie sheet about 30 minutes. Remove from oven and add fruits and nuts. When cool store in airtight containers. Yields 3½ quarts.

CAPTAIN EZRA NYE HOUSE

152 Main Street
Sandwich, MA 02563
(508) 888-6142 (phone)
(508) 833-2897 (fax)
(800) 388-2278 (toll free)
captainnye@adelphia.net
www.captainezranyehouse.com

The Captain Ezra Nye House is an award-winning 1829 sea captain's home in the heart of Sandwich Village, renowned for fine hospitality and good food in a historic setting. Sandwich, Cape Cod's oldest town, established in 1637, is the site of fine museums, including Sandwich Glass Museum. Other fine attractions are: Thornton Burgess Museum, Green Briar Nature Center, and the Hoxie House, Cape Cod's oldest house. Beaches, whale watching, and antiquing also beckon the traveler.

Captain Ezra Nye House

Baked Blueberry Pancakes

1 cup baking mix
½ cup unprocessed bran
2 heaping tablespoons sugar
½ cup blueberries (fresh or frozen)
1 egg
½ cup milk
4 tablespoons (½ stick) butter
4 tablespoons apricot preserves
1 tablespoon water

Preheat oven to 475°. Mix baking mix, bran, and sugar together in bowl. Add blueberries and mix to cover blueberries. Add egg and milk and mix gently but thoroughly. Prepare pie plate by spraying with Pam and then melting ½ stick butter in microwave for 30 seconds. Pour pancake mixture into buttered pie plate and bake 12 to 15 minutes. Cut into quarters, dust with confectioners' sugar, and scatter with blueberries on plate. Place a strawberry and mint sprig on top. Serve with Vermont syrup. Yields 4 servings.

Eggs Portugal

8 slices bread cubed
1 cup grated cheddar cheese
½ pound sausage, crumbled
4 eggs, beaten
2½ cups milk
¾ teaspoons prepared mustard
1 (10¾-ounce) can cream of
    mushroom soup
¼ cup dry vermouth
1 can chopped mushrooms

Layer bread, cheese, and sausage in 9 x 13-inch casserole. In bowl beat eggs with milk and mustard. Pour egg mixture over sausage in casserole. Refrigerate 8 to 10 hours or overnight. When ready to make, preheat oven to 300°. In mixing bowl blend soup, vermouth, and mushrooms. Pour over casserole and bake 1½ hours. Yields 4 servings.

Finnish Baked Pancakes

½ cup (1 stick) butter
6 eggs
4 cups milk
4 tablespoons sugar
1 teaspoon salt
1 cup all-purpose flour
Maple syrup and confectioners' sugar
    for topping

Preheat oven to 475°. Melt and slightly brown butter in 12 x 16-inch baking dish. Whisk together remaining ingredients. Pour into baking dish and bake 20 to 25 minutes. Cut into eight pieces and serve on warmed plates with maple syrup and sprinkle with confectioners' sugar. Serve with blueberries on the side, or dab of cranberry sauce, if desired. Yields 8 servings.

THE NAUSET HOUSE INN

143 Beach Road
P.O. Box 774
East Orleans, MA 02643-0774
(508) 255-2195 (phone)
(508) 240-6276 (fax)
(800) 771-5508 (toll free)
info@nausethouseinn.com
www.nausethouseinn.com

At the Nauset House Inn you will find the gentle amenities of life are still observed. This 1800s farmhouse with glass conservatory is a half mile from the ocean and a little more than fifteen miles from the beach. Activities include: hiking, biking, fishing, whale and seal watching, swimming (ocean, bay, and fresh water), museums, galleries, great restaurants, and much more.

Spinach & Artichoke Dip for Slow Cooker

2 cups chopped fresh baby spinach
1 (14-ounce) can artichoke hearts, diced
½ cup store-bought Alfredo sauce with
    roasted garlic
½ cup mayonnaise
¾ teaspoon garlic salt
¼ teaspoon pepper
1 cup shredded Swiss cheese

Mix all ingredients in large bowl and put in slow cooker coated with nonstick spray. Mixture can be combined ahead and refrigerated. Heat in slow cooker on low 2 hours before serving. This recipe can be doubled. Yields about 3½ cups.

Oatmeal Butterscotch Muffins

1 (18-ounce) box oatmeal or 7 cups
1 quart low-fat buttermilk
2¼ cups light brown sugar
1½ cups (3 sticks) margarine
6 eggs, slightly beaten
9 cups all-purpose flour
4 tablespoons baking powder
1½ tablespoons baking soda
1 teaspoon salt
1½ cups butterscotch chips

Put oatmeal in large bowl, pour buttermilk over oats, and mix. Add brown sugar on top of oatmeal. Mix again and let stand 1 hour. Preheat oven to 375°. In separate bowl, melt margarine and cool. In another bowl beat eggs. Add margarine to oats and mix well. Add eggs and mix again. Mix flour, baking powder, baking soda, and salt together and mix with oats and eggs. Fold in chips. Pour into three greased muffin pans. Bake for 18 minutes or until done. This batter can be mixed a day ahead and refrigerated. Yields 3 dozen muffins.

Zucchini Bread

3 cups or more grated zucchini
3¼ cups all-purpose flour
½ teaspoon baking soda
1½ teaspoons baking powder
1 teaspoon salt
1 teaspoon ground cinnamon
4 eggs
2 cups sugar
1 cup corn oil
1 tablespoon vanilla extract
1 cup raisins
1 cup chopped walnuts

Grate zucchini. In large bowl, combine flour, soda, baking powder, salt, and cinnamon. In separate medium bowl, beat together eggs, sugar, corn oil, and vanilla. Mix zucchini alternately with wet ingredients into dry ingredients. Add raisins and walnuts. Preheat oven to 350°. (You can substitute cranberries and pecans for the raisins and walnuts.) Bake about 1 hour in two greased 9 x 5 x 2¾-inch loaf pans. Test with wire that should come out clean. Yields 2 loaves.

GATEWAYS INN & RESTAURANT

51 Walker Street
Lenox, MA 01240
(413) 637-2532 (phone)
(413) 637-1432 (fax)
gateways@berkshire.net
www.gatewaysinn.com

A former Gilded-Age Mansion, Gateways offers luxurious guest rooms with antiques, romantic canopy beds, and fireplaces. Candlelit dining rooms showcase fine cui-sine and world-class wines. The Berkshires of western Massachusetts are known for their spectacular natural beauty, rolling green hillsides, and splendid fall foliage. Known as "America's Premier Cultural Resort" the area abounds with the arts, the highlight being the Tanglewood Music Festival, the summer home of the Boston Symphony. World-class dance, theater, and performing arts can be found in the region, as well as many noted museums.

Almond-Date Granola

⅓ cup plus 2 tablespoons canola oil
3 cups old-fashioned oats
1 cup wheat flakes
1 cup wheat germ
½ cup quinoa flakes (found in most
    health-food stores)
1 cup unsweetened flaked coconut
2 cups blanched and sliced almonds
2 cups finely chopped pitted dates
2 to 3 lemons, squeezed to yield
    ½ cup juice
½ cup honey
Pinch of salt
1 teaspoon ground cinnamon
1 tablespoon vanilla extract
1 tablespoon pure almond extract

Preheat oven to 350°. Lightly grease large cookie sheet with 2 tablespoons canola oil. In large bowl blend oats, wheat flakes, wheat germ, quinoa flakes, coconut, almonds, and dates. Place juice, honey, salt, cinnamon, extracts, and remaining ⅓ cup oil in medium-size saucepan. Heat over low flame just to boiling point. Remove from heat and pour over dry ingredients. Mix well. Spread mixture evenly on cookie sheet. Bake in center of oven for 30 minutes, stirring frequently, so that mixture is evenly browned and toasted. Cool, pour into sealed containers, and store. Granola will stay fresh about two weeks if stored in refrigerator. Yields about 8 cups.

Gateways Inn Apple Pie

Crust:
2 cups all-purpose flour
1 teaspoon salt
6 tablespoons cold unsalted butter,
    cut into cubes
6 tablespoons vegetable shortening
⅓ cup ice water

Filling:
½ cup sugar
½ cup dried cranberries (craisins)
Juice and grated zest of 1 lemon
½ teaspoon cinnamon
2 tablespoons all-purpose flour
2 pounds (about 6 to 8) Cortland, Paula
    Red, Spy or other tart apples, such as
    Granny Smith, depending on size

Gateways Inn & Restaurant

Topping:
1 cup firmly packed light brown sugar
¼ cup (½ stick) unsalted butter
2 tablespoons all-purpose flour

Using a food processor, blend flour and salt. Add butter and shortening and blend until crumbly. Slowly add ice water, blending until smooth. Divide dough into two balls, flatten them, and wrap each tightly in plastic film. Refrigerate for at least 4 hours.

For filling, place sugar, cranberries, lemon juice and zest, cinnamon, and flour into large bowl and mix together. Core, peel, and slice apples into wedges, approximately eight pieces per half apple or ¼-inch slices. Add to bowl with other ingredients, mixing well to coat apples.

For topping, mix brown sugar, butter, and flour together with fingertips until crumbly. On a well-floured board with rolling pin, roll out 1 chilled crust to a 12-inch circle (keep other refrigerated) for bottom crust. This will fit 9-inch pie tin. Re-flouring while rolling out will be necessary since dough will stick often. Carefully fold rolled-out crust circle in half, then in quarters. Carefully lay into pie tin and unfold. Spoon filling onto piecrust, spreading evenly. Spread topping evenly over filling. Divide remaining top crust in half. Again, roll out on well-floured board with rolling pin. Roll each half to 11-inch circle. They will be very thin. Using a fluted pastry wheel, cut into strips 1 inch wide. Weave strips into lattice on top of pie. (Or lattice can be woven separately on parchment paper and transferred whole onto pie.) Trim ends evenly with bottom crust edges. Fold up bottom crust edges over lattice edges and crimp together. Roll out scrap dough and cut decorative shapes, such as leaves, etc. Using pastry brush, brush undersides of shapes with milk and attach to top of pie decoratively. Brush pie top all over with milk, about 2 tablespoons. Sprinkle sugar, about 1 tablespoon, over top.

Preheat oven to 350° and bake for 1 hour 15 minutes. If top and edges begin to brown too much, cover loosely with aluminum foil. Remove from oven and allow to cool on rack for at least ½ hour. Yields 8 servings.

Caramelized Onion and Goat Cheese Tart

1 tablespoon yeast
3 cups warm water (80°)
4 plus 2 tablespoons olive oil
4 to 4½ cups all-purpose flour
8 ounces goat cheese
½ cup heavy cream
1 tablespoon lemon juice
1 teaspoon plus dash of salt
Dash of white pepper
3 large yellow or Spanish onions, thinly sliced
1 clove garlic, crushed
1 teaspoon black pepper
1 teaspoon sugar
2 teaspoons finely chopped Italian parsley

Sprinkle yeast over warm water in bowl. Stir and let rest for 5 minutes. Stir in 4 tablespoons of oil. Gradually add and mix in flour. Scrape down bowl. Cover with plastic wrap. Let rest in warm place for about 1½ hours.

Punch down dough. Separate into balls approximately 3 ounces each. (the dough should yield about 15 balls). Preheat oven to 350°. Lightly flour board and roll out each ball to ⅛-inch-thick circle. Using a fork, pierce dough randomly. Brush lightly with olive oil. Bake 5 to 7 minutes. Remove from oven and cool.

Mix goat cheese, cream, lemon juice, dash of salt, and white pepper and set aside. In large sauté pan, heat remaining 2 tablespoons of olive oil. Add onions and cook over low flame until translucent. Add garlic, 1 teaspoon salt, black pepper, and sugar. Continue cooking until onions are dark brown and caramelized. Add parsley and cool topping. Spread goat cheese topping thinly and evenly on tart. Spread caramelized onions on top of goat cheese. Warm in 350° oven 5 to 7 minutes. Cut in pie shape wedges and serve. Yields 8 pieces.

Gingerbread Mascarpone Petit Fours

Gingerbread:
1 pound brown sugar
6 eggs
3 tablespoons molasses
2½ cups all-purpose flour
2 tablespoons baking powder
1 teaspoon baking soda
4 tablespoons ground cinnamon
2 teaspoons ground cloves
1 teaspoon salt
1½ cups melted butter
⅓ cup half-and-half
¾ cup buttermilk

Filling:
2 pounds mascarpone cheese
8 ounces white chocolate, shaved
2 tablespoons confectioners' sugar
8 to 10 ounces white chocolate, melted

Preheat oven to 350°. Whip sugar and eggs until foamy. Add molasses. Sift together dry ingredients and add to egg mixture. Combine butter, half-and-half, and buttermilk and add to mixture. Spread batter on greased and floured sheet or cookie pan with ½-inch sides. Bake about 15 minutes, or until springy and toothpick inserted comes out clean.

For filling, using standing mixer with paddle attachment, mix cheese and white chocolate until light and fluffy, about 5 minutes. Mix in confectioners' sugar. With long, thin serrated knife, slice gingerbread in half, creating 2 layers. Carefully separate them, laying top layer aside. Spread mascarpone filling evenly on bottom layer of gingerbread. Put second layer on top of filling. Cut gingerbread into desired shape, squares or diamonds, approximately 1-inch in size. Place cut pieces onto cake rack placed inside a baking sheet and coat with white chocolate. Allow white chocolate to dry and repeat to thoroughly and evenly coat. Yields 2 to 3 dozen petit fours.

Mint Chocolate Chip Biscotti

8 tablespoons softened butter
¾ cup sugar
2 eggs
1 teaspoon vanilla extract
2 teaspoons pure peppermint extract, or
    4 tablespoons peppermint liqueur
3 cups all-purpose flour
½ teaspoon salt
2 teaspoons baking powder
1 cup semisweet chocolate chips

Using wooden spoon, cream together butter and sugar until fluffy. Beat in eggs and add extracts. Sift together flour, salt, and baking powder. Add to butter/sugar mixture, blending thoroughly. Dough will be stiff. Use back of spoon to aid in mixing, or you can use electric mixer on low speed. Stir in chocolate chips. Divide dough into thirds. Drop each third by spoonfuls onto sheet of plastic film. Shape dough into log about 2 x 10 x 1-inch high. Wrap plastic neatly and tightly around log, closing long sides first, then ends. Place in freezer for 10 to 15 minutes. Preheat oven to 350°. Line large baking sheet with parchment paper or aluminum foil. Unwrap logs and place onto lined sheet. Bake 25 minutes until logs are lightly browned. Remove from oven. Reduce heat to 300°. Slide paper or foil with logs off baking sheet and onto cutting board. Let cool for 5 to 10 minutes. Using thin, sharp knife cut logs at an angle into slices about ¾ to 1 inch wide. Slide paper and slices back onto baking sheet. Lay each cookie slice on its side. Return to oven. Bake 10 minutes. Remove from oven. Turn each cookie slice to opposite side and bake again for 10 minutes. Yields 3 dozen cookies.

Michigan

BRIGADOON BED & BREAKFAST

207 Langlade Street
P.O. Box 810
Mackinaw City, MI 49701
(231) 436-8882
info@mackinawbrigadoon.com
www.mackinawbrigadoon.com

Brigadoon is a premier bed and breakfast located in a quiet residential area of beautiful Mackinaw City, Michigan. Built in 1998, the suites offer old-world enchantment amongst modern luxury. Join us to celebrate a special event in your life or just visit on a quiet weekend, and you will remember your stay. Merriment, hospitality, and warmth are the values awaiting guests at Brigadoon.

Easy Elegant Eggs Florentine

9 eggs
2 cups cottage cheese
2 cups grated Swiss cheese (or use 1 cup
     Swiss and 1 cup Cheddar)
8 ounces feta cheese
4 tablespoons melted butter
2 (10-ounce) packages frozen chopped
     spinach, thawed and drained
1 teaspoon ground nutmeg

Preheat oven to 350°. Grease 9 x 13-inch pan. In large bowl, beat eggs slightly and add cottage, Swiss, and feta cheeses, and butter. Mix well. Stir in spinach and nutmeg. Pour into prepared pan. Bake for 1 hour or until knife inserted in center comes out clean. Delightful served with sliced ham, fresh fruit slices, and small dish of yogurt. Yields 8 servings.

Wild Rice & Mushroom Crustless Quiche

1 cup cooked wild or
     long-grain wild rice
½ cup diced red pepper
½ cup diced green onions
¼ cup dried onion
1 (4-ounce) can sliced mushrooms
1 cup shredded cheese (Cheddar, Swiss,
     or Monterey Jack)
8 eggs
½ cup half-and-half
½ teaspoon salt
½ teaspoon dried tarragon or other herb

Preheat oven to 350°. Coat 9-inch, deep-dish pie plate with cooking spray. Place rice, peppers, and onions in bottom of pan. Next layer mushrooms and then cheese over rice mixture. Beat eggs in medium bowl, and add half-and-half, salt, and tarragon. Pour over cheese/rice mixture. Bake for 1 hour or until center is set. This quiche goes well with crisp bacon curls or sausage links, a parfait of yogurt and fresh fruit, a raspberry and blackberry muffin, and a steaming mug of hazelnut coffee. Yields 6 servings.

Autumn's Caramel Apple French Toast

4 large Granny Smith apples
½ cup apple juice or water
1 teaspoon ground cinnamon
Granulated sugar (optional)
¾ cup packed brown sugar
3 tablespoons light corn syrup
3 tablespoons butter or margarine
¾ cup chopped walnuts or pecans
12 slices firm white bread
3 eggs, beaten
1¼ cups skim milk
1 teaspoon vanilla extract
⅛ teaspoon ground nutmeg

Vanilla sauce:
½ cup sugar
1 tablespoon cornstarch
1 cup water
2 tablespoons butter or margarine
1 tablespoon vanilla extract

Peel, core, and slice apples. Place in a medium-size skillet over medium heat. Pour apple juice over apples. Simmer 4 to 5 minutes until apples are softened. Drain apples in colander. Place in bowl and add cinnamon and a little sugar if apples are tart. Remove from skillet. In same skillet, combine brown sugar, corn syrup, and butter. Cook and stir over medium heat until sugar melts and mixture just begins to come to slow boil. Pour into 13 x 9-inch baking dish. Sprinkle with nuts. Place half the bread slices on top of syrup and nuts. Divide apples among bread slices and top with remaining bread slices. Whisk together eggs, milk, vanilla, and nutmeg. Pour over "apple sandwiches." Cover and refrigerate 8 to 10 hours or overnight. When ready to serve, preheat oven to 325° and bake uncovered for 40 minutes. Remove from oven, cover with a serving platter, and invert.

For vanilla sauce, mix sugar, cornstarch, and water in small saucepan. Cook, stirring often, over medium heat until thick and bubbly. Remove from heat and add butter and vanilla. Stir until butter melts. Cut each sandwich in half diagonally and drizzle with vanilla sauce. Serve this wonderful dish on a chilly fall morning with crisp bacon curls, fresh fruit slices, a small dish of vanilla yogurt sprinkled with Halloween candy corn, and a mug of hot amaretto-flavored hot chocolate. Yields 6 servings.

Big Bay Lighthouse Bed & Breakfast

BIG BAY LIGHTHOUSE BED & BREAKFAST

3 Lighthouse Road
Big Bay, MI 49808
(906) 345-9957
keepers@bigbaylighthouse.com
www.bigbaylighthouse.com

High on a cliff overlooking Lake Superior, the Lighthouse beckons adults looking for a retreat from the stress of modern life. Sitting on fifty acres a half mile off of Lake Superior's shore, the inn offers a wide range of outdoor activities. Guests can relax their bodies and renew their spirits in the unsurpassed setting of the Serenity Massage Hut overlooking the lake.

Oatmeal Raisin Pancakes with Cinnamon Sour Cream

1 cup old-fashioned oats
1 cup all-purpose flour
2 teaspoons baking powder
½ teaspoon baking soda
1 teaspoon ground cinnamon
¼ cup packed light brown sugar
1⅔ cups buttermilk
2 large eggs
4 tablespoons melted unsalted butter
½ teaspoon vanilla extract
1 cup plump raisins

Cinnamon sour cream:
1 cup sour cream
1 tablespoon plus 1 teaspoon brown sugar
1 teaspoon ground cinnamon
½ cup chopped walnuts for garnish

In medium bowl, whisk oats, flour, baking powder, soda, cinnamon, and light brown sugar. In another bowl whisk together buttermilk, eggs, butter, and vanilla and blend thoroughly. Pour liquid ingredients over dry ingredients and mix with whisk just until combined. Don't worry if batter is lumpy. With rubber spatula, gently fold in raisins. Batter will thicken as it stands. If it becomes too thick, add more buttermilk.

For cinnamon sour cream, combine in small bowl sour cream, brown sugar, and cinnamon and thoroughly mix using rubber spatula. Store covered in refrigerator until ready to serve. Will keep for 5 days refrigerated.

Heat griddle to 350° and lightly spray with oil. Spoon ¼ cup batter onto griddle for each pancake, allowing space for spreading. When underside of pancake is golden and top speckled with bubbles that pop, flip pancake. Cook until other side is golden brown. Serve immediately, top with a spoonful of cinnamon sour cream and sprinkle with walnuts. Yields 14 pancakes.

BONNIE'S PARSONAGE 1908 BED & BREAKFAST

6 East 24th Street
Holland, MI 49423
(616) 396-1316

Since opening in 1984, the Parsonage 1908 guests' compliments have put the bed and breakfast on the top of the list with Michigan's best lodging facilities. The Parsonage was built as a parsonage by one of Holland's early Dutch churches, in order to call its first minister. The inside still glows with the original dark oak woodwork, pocket doors, and leaded glass windows that were so lovingly and masterfully crafted for such an important mission. Situated in a lovely residential neighborhood, guests can relax and enjoy the two sitting rooms, summer porch, and outdoor garden-patio with a glass of lemonade. Or in winter we serve hot spiced cider in front of the fire in the country kitchen. In the morning guests awake to the tantalizing aroma of our famous baked pancakes, which a judge guest "ruled" are a culinary masterpiece. Guests enjoy Tulip Time in May, Lake Michigan beaches, boating, swimming, golf, tennis, biking/hiking trails, art and antique shops, summer theater, exceptional dining, fall colors, and cross-country skiing in the winter.

Parsonage Famous Baked Pancakes

3 eggs, beaten
½ cup all-purpose flour
½ cup milk
¼ stick butter

Preheat oven to 400°. Mix together eggs and flour with beaters. Add milk and mix until smooth. Melt butter in baking pan. Pour in batter. Bake 20 minutes. Serve with sausages, fresh fruit, juice, and coffee. Yields 2 to 3 servings.

THE INN AT LUDINGTON

701 East Ludington Ave.
Ludington, MI 49431
(231) 845-7055 (phone)
(800) 845-9170 (toll free)
www.inn-ludington.com

The Inn at Ludington is a historic Queen Anne painted lady. An atmosphere of casual elegance makes guests feel right at home. The six guest rooms and common areas are decorated with a happy mix of period antiques and comfortable reproductions. Treasured collections are displayed throughout, so there is always something to discover. A private garden is a wonderful place for relaxing on a summer day, and the inn's four fireplaces are welcoming and cozy after snow-time activities. The bountiful breakfast is the pride and joy of the award-winning cook, and a not-to-be-missed start to the day.

The Inn at Ludington

Maple Cream Cake

Cake:
1 cup (2 sticks) soft butter
2 cups granulated sugar
1 cup sour cream (may use low-fat)
2 large eggs
1 teaspoon vanilla or maple flavoring
2 cups all-purpose flour
1 teaspoon baking powder

Filling:
3 tablespoons maple sugar
½ cup finely chopped pecans or walnuts

Frosting:
2 tablespoons soft butter
1 cup confectioners' sugar
¼ cup pure maple syrup

In large mixing bowl, beat butter and sugar until creamy. Add sour cream and eggs and beat until fluffy. Add vanilla or maple flavoring. Add flour and baking powder that have been mixed together and beat 1 minute.

For filling, combine maple sugar and nuts in small bowl. Grease and flour tube pan. Preheat oven to 350°. Spread half of batter in pan and sprinkle with half of sugar-nut mixture. Spread remaining batter over and sprinkle with remaining sugar-nut mixture. Bake about 45 minutes until toothpick inserted in center of cake comes out clean. Cool cake in pan 10 minutes, and then remove sides (if using pan with removable sides) or loosen sides and around tube with knife. Allow to cool an additional 10 minutes and invert on serving plate.

Mix frosting ingredients well with spoon until smooth. Add more syrup if frosting is stiff. It should be soft enough to spread smoothly and drip down sides of cake. Frost while still slightly warm. Allow to set before slicing cake. Yields 16 slices.

Baked Spicy Pears with Vanilla Cream

½ cup brown sugar
1 teaspoon ground cinnamon
½ teaspoon ground nutmeg
¼ teaspoon cloves
6 pears, halved and cored
½ cup apple juice
1½ cups Post Cranberry Almond
     Crunch cereal
2 tablespoons all-purpose flour
¼ cup soft butter
1½ cups low-fat sour cream
½ cup heavy cream
2 teaspoons vanilla extract

Preheat oven to 350°. Grease 9 x 13-inch baking pan. Mix brown sugar, cinnamon, nutmeg, and cloves and spread over bottom of baking pan. Place pears, cut-side down, over sugar mixture. Pour apple juice over pears. In separate bowl, mix cereal and flour. Mix in butter with fork until crumbly. Spread over pears. Bake about 20 minutes until topping is lightly browned and pears are tender when pierced with a fork. While pears are baking, mix sour cream, heavy cream, and vanilla in small bowl. Allow to blend at room temperature. Serve pears warm, topped with cream mix. May be served directly from baking pan on the buffet with cream alongside or in individual dishes with cream on top. Yields 12 servings.

Nutmeg Pecan Muffins

1½ cups all-purpose flour
⅔ cup sugar
¾ teaspoon baking soda
1 teaspoon ground nutmeg
1 large egg
⅔ cup buttermilk
⅓ cup butter, melted
1 teaspoon vanilla extract
⅓ cup chopped toasted pecans

Preheat oven to 350°. Spray 12-cup muffin pan with cooking spray. In large bowl, mix flour, sugar, baking soda, and nutmeg. In small bowl whisk egg, buttermilk, melted butter, and vanilla with whisk. Stir liquid ingredients into dry ingredients until just mixed. Stir in pecans. Fill muffin cups two-thirds full. Bake about 20 minutes until lightly browned. Cool in pan. Best when served warm, although these muffins freeze well and can be wrapped in foil and reheated in oven or toaster oven. Yields 12 muffins.

Sausage Strata Deluxe

1 pound bulk sausage
2 cups croutons or toasted bread cubes
6 eggs
1 (10¾-ounce) can cream of mushroom soup
1½ soup cans milk
¼ teaspoon dry mustard
¼ teaspoon crushed dried rosemary
     or 1 teaspoon fresh
1 (10-ounce) package frozen spinach,
     thawed and squeezed dry
2 cups shredded Colby Jack cheese
¼ cup sliced mushrooms

Cook sausage in skillet over medium heat until browned, stirring frequently to break up into small pieces. Spread croutons on bottom of 9 x 13-inch greased pan. Drain sausage well and spread over croutons. In large bowl, whisk eggs, mushroom soup, milk, mustard, and rosemary. Stir in spinach, cheese, and mushrooms. Pour over sausage. Cover with plastic wrap and re-frigerate 8 to 10 hours or overnight. When ready to serve, preheat oven to 350°, uncover, and bake about 1 hour, or until set and lightly browned on top. Yields 6 servings.

Ham Hash Topped with Eggs in Mustard Cream Sauce

3 plus 1 tablespoons butter
3 tablespoons oil
3 large potatoes, peeled, cooked,
     and cubed
½ pound ham, chopped
1 tablespoon finely minced onion
1 tablespoon all-purpose flour
1 tablespoon Dijon mustard
1 cup milk
4 hard-cooked eggs, peeled and sliced

In large skillet, heat 3 tablespoons butter with oil until butter is melted. Add potatoes, ham, and onion. Cook over medium heat, stirring and turning mixture until crispy brown. To make mustard cream sauce, melt remaining tablespoon butter in small saucepan. Stir in flour and mustard. Add milk and continue cooking until sauce is thick. Add sliced eggs to sauce, but do *not* stir. When hash is finished cooking, place in serving bowl. Pour sauce over middle of hash. Serve at once. Nice with toast or biscuits. Yields 4 servings.

THE STATE STREET INN

646 State Street
Harbor Beach, MI 48441
(989) 479-3388 (phone)
(866) 424-7961 (toll free)

The State Street Inn is a century-old, country Victorian in a quaint lakeside town in Michigan's thumb. Gracious, old-fashioned hospitality, warm and inviting guest rooms, great amenities, and hearty, homemade breakfasts make this bed and breakfast a favorite getaway spot.

German Apple Pancake (aka Dutch Baby)

8 eggs
1 cup all-purpose flour
1 teaspoon baking powder
¾ plus ¼ cup plus 2 tablespoons sugar
Pinch or two of salt
2 cups light cream or milk
¼ cup melted unsalted butter
2 teaspoons vanilla extract
½ plus ½ teaspoon ground nutmeg
½ cup (1 stick) unsalted butter
1 teaspoon ground cinnamon
2 large tart apples, peeled, cored, and sliced

In large bowl blend eggs, flour, baking powder, 2 tablespoons sugar, and salt. Gradually mix in cream, stirring constantly. Add melted butter, vanilla, and ½ teaspoon nutmeg. Let batter stand for at least 30 minutes or overnight. Preheat oven to 425°. Melt ½ cup butter in large ovenproof skillet, brushing butter up sides of pan. In small bowl, combine ¼ cup sugar, cinnamon, and remaining ½ teaspoon nutmeg. Sprinkle mixture over butter in pan. Line pan with apple slices and sprinkle remaining ¾ cup sugar over apples. Bake 20 to 30 minutes until apples are tender. Yields 8 servings.

Eggs in a Basket

12 very thin, but not shaved, slices
    Black Forest ham
8 eggs
1½ cups half-and-half or light cream
½ teaspoon lemon pepper
½ teaspoon garlic powder
½ teaspoon onion powder
6 ounces shredded sharp
    Cheddar cheese

Preheat oven to 325°. Spray nonstick muffin pan very lightly with vegetable oil spray. Place ham slice in each muffin cup, carefully arranging it to form a basket. Beat eggs, cream, and seasonings in bowl with electric mixer. Pour egg mixture into large measuring cup with spout. Fill ham baskets about three-fourths full with egg mixture. Sprinkle heaping tablespoon shredded cheese on top of each basket. Bake 30 minutes or until toothpick comes out clean. Yields 12 servings.

Cowboy Cookies

1 cup softened butter or margarine
1 cup packed brown sugar
1 cup sugar
2 eggs
1 cup peanut butter
1½ cups all-purpose flour
1 teaspoon baking soda
1 teaspoon baking powder
1 cup rolled oats
1 cup dark raisins
1 cup coconut
1 cup chopped walnuts

Preheat oven to 325°. Cream butter and sugars together with electric mixer. Add eggs and peanut butter and continue beating. Mix flour, baking soda, and powder together. Add flour by hand to butter mixture. Then add oats, raisins, coconut, and walnuts. Mix well. Bake 12 to 15 minutes or until lightly golden brown. Cool a few minutes before you take cookies off cookie sheet. Store in airtight container. Yields 3 dozen cookies.

Carrot Raisin Muffins

2 cups all-purpose flour
1 tablespoon baking powder
¾ cup packed dark brown sugar
¾ cup shredded carrots
¾ cup dark raisins
½ cup chopped walnuts
2 eggs
½ cup canola oil
⅔ cup low-fat buttermilk
2 teaspoons vanilla extract

Preheat oven to 350°. Combine flour, baking powder, and brown sugar thoroughly in bowl. Add carrots, raisins, and walnuts to dry mixture and blend well. In another bowl, beat eggs, oil, buttermilk, and vanilla thoroughly for a minute or so. Pour wet ingredients into dry ingredients and mix just until blended. Fill paper-lined muffin pans about three-fourths full and bake about 20 minutes or until muffins test done with a toothpick. Delicious served warm with butter. Yields about 20 to 24 muffins.

Banana Chocolate Chip Muffins

2 cups all-purpose flour
1 tablespoon baking powder
½ cup granulated sugar
½ cup light brown sugar
2 very ripe bananas, mashed
2 eggs
1 teaspoon vanilla extract
½ cup canola oil

½ cup half-and-half, light cream,
    or milk
½ to ¾ cup semisweet chocolate chips

Preheat oven to 350°. Combine flour, baking powder, and sugars in bowl thoroughly. In another bowl, combine mashed bananas, eggs, vanilla, oil, and half-and-half with electric mixer until thoroughly blended and creamy, about 1 minute. Pour wet ingredients into flour mixture and stir until just combined. Add chocolate chips to batter and blend again gently until chips are evenly mixed into batter. Fill paper-lined muffin pans about three-fourths full and bake 20 minutes or until golden brown on top. These are best when served warm because chocolate chips are still gooey. Yields 18 to 24 muffins.

SLEEPING BEAR BED & BREAKFAST

11977 Gilbert Road
Empire, MI 49630
(231) 326-5375
www.sleepingbearbb.com

Sleeping Bear Bed & Breakfast is situated on four rolling acres in Michigan's Leelanau Peninsula. This circa 1889 home has five beautiful bedrooms, gourmet breakfasts, and close proximity to the Sleeping Bear Dunes National Lakeshore. Activities available in the area include Dune climbs; swimming in Lake Michigan; boating; bird-watching; hiking; cycling; fishing; Interlochen; fall colors; wineries; cross-country skiing; snowshoeing; and snowmobiling.

Southwestern Breakfast Burritos

Chicken hash:
¼ teaspoon cayenne
1 teaspoon cumin
1 teaspoon garlic salt
1 tablespoon minced onion
2 cloves garlic, chopped
1 jalapeño, chopped
2 whole chicken breasts

Black bean & corn salsa:
½ yellow onion, chopped
½ red bell pepper, chopped
2 tablespoons olive oil
1 (16-ounce) can black beans,
    drained
4 ears of corn, cut from cob
    (or 1 cup canned)
½ teaspoon cumin
3 tablespoons chopped fresh cilantro
Salt and pepper
1 tablespoon lemon juice

Scrambled Mexican eggs:
4 tablespoons butter
8 eggs
4 tablespoons green chiles
½ cup Monterey Jack/Cheddar
    cheese combo
8 scallions, chopped
Salt and pepper
Flour tortillas
Green chile sauce
Sour cream
Cilantro

For chicken hash, combine spices, onion, garlic, and pepper and rub mixture on chicken breasts. Grill. Cool. Pulse in food processor until consistency of hash. (Prepare extra for dinner and make hash in morning.) Microwave until warm just before assembly.

For salsa, sauté onions and peppers in olive oil until onions are transparent. Add black beans, corn, spices, and lemon juice. Set aside to cool.

For scrambled eggs, melt butter in nonstick pan over medium heat. Whisk eggs for scrambling in large bowl. When butter is melted and hot, scramble eggs, adding other ingredients as eggs begin to cook. Salt and pepper to taste. When scrambled, set aside for assembly.

To assemble, heat oven to 300°. Warm flour tortilla for 10 minutes in oven while preparing eggs. For each serving, spread 1 tortilla with green chile sauce. Add one-eighth of chicken hash and one-eighth of scrambled eggs and roll tortilla. Place in center of plate. Top with sour cream, Black Bean & Corn Salsa, and cilantro. Garnish with fresh melon. Yields 8 servings.

Sleeping Bear French Toast

6 eggs
2 cups half-and-half
½ cup sugar
1 teaspoon ground cinnamon
Pinch of freshly grated nutmeg
2 tablespoons orange liqueur
    (optional)
Grated zest of 1 orange
¼ cup tonic water
Unsalted butter
18 slices Texas toast
Confectioners' sugar
Seasonal fruit

Beat together in large bowl eggs, half-and-half, sugar, cinnamon, nutmeg, orange liqueur, and zest. Add tonic water and pour mixture into shallow pan or pie plate. Heat griddle; when hot, melt thin layer of butter. Dip slices of Texas toast in batter. Place on griddle to brown. Preheat oven to 350°. After brief cooking on both sides, place on baking sheet and bake 15 minutes or until puffed. Cut slices diagonally and place four halves on each plate. Dust with confectioners' sugar and top with seasonal berries or fruit. Typically we serve with blueberries, raspberries, peaches, or apples sautéed with apple butter. Accompany each serving with local cherry-pecan sausage or apple-smoked bacon. Yields 9 servings.

DEWEY LAKE MANOR BED & BREAKFAST

11811 Laird Road
Brooklyn, MI 49230
(517) 467-7122 (phone)
(517) 467-2346 (fax)
info@deweylakemanor.com
www.deweylakemanor.com

A "country retreat" awaits guests at this century-old, lakeside home in the Irish Hills of southern Michigan. Private baths, fireplaces, and tranquility await guests. Activities include picnics; paddleboats; bonfires on site; golf; antiquing; botanical gardens; and a nearby theater.

Joe's Waffles

1 large egg
1 tablespoon vegetable oil
⅛ teaspoon baking powder
1 cup buttermilk
¼ cup pecan pancakes mix
½ cup buckwheat pancake mix

In medium bowl, beat egg well with wire whisk. Whisking constantly, add oil, baking powder, buttermilk, and pancake mixes and mix until well blended. Pour batter (approximately ½ cup per waffle) onto hot waffle iron. (A Belgium waffle iron works well.) Close cover and bake 4 minutes until steaming nearly stops. Gently lift waffle from iron with fork and serve immediately. Serve with real butter and pure Michigan maple syrup. This is a real favorite with our guests. Yields 4 waffles.

❧ ❧ ❧

CHICAGO PIKE INN

215 East Chicago Street
Coldwater, MI 49036
(517) 279-8744 (phone)
(800) 471-0501 (toll free)
www.chicagopikeinn.com

A stay at Chicago Pike Inn is lodging in Victorian elegance. The turn-of-the-century, reformed colonial mansion is adorned with period antiques. The inn features oak parquet floors, sweeping cherry staircase, stained-glass windows, and eight beautifully restored guest houses. We take pride in our "knack" of making your stay a memorable one. Full breakfasts served feature old family recipes.

Cheese Straws

1 cup shredded Cheddar cheese
½ cup (1 stick) butter, softened to room temperature
1 cup all-purpose flour
¼ teaspoon salt

Preheat oven to 400°. Mix all ingredients. Knead and roll out like pie dough on floured surface. Cut into strips about 4 inches long. Using spatula place on cookie sheet. Bake 8 to 10 minutes or until golden. Serve warm or cool. Store in tin container. Yields 1½ dozen straws.

Peaches and Cream Stuffed French Toast

12 eggs
1 cup milk or half-and-half
1 teaspoon vanilla extract
2 loaves French bread cut into 1½-inch slices with pocket sliced into each
1 (16-ounce) tub soft cream cheese
1 cup brown sugar
3 ripe fresh peaches, peeled and thinly sliced
1 pint whipping cream
¼ cup confectioners' sugar
½ cup peach preserves
Ground nutmeg and cinnamon

In bowl combine eggs, milk, and vanilla. Gently open bread pockets. Spread one side of each pocket with 1 tablespoon cream cheese. Spoon 1 tablespoon brown sugar into each pocket and top with 3 to 4 fresh peach slices. Close pockets and dip

Chicago Pike Inn

into egg mixture. Fry on hot buttered griddle. In another bowl, whip cream until fluffy and add confectioners' sugar and preserves. Stir until mixed well. Put dollop of cream on toast and sprinkle with nutmeg and cinnamon. Yields about 20 servings, 2 slices per person.

Summer Fruit Soup

6 cups hot water
⅔ cup tapioca
5 cups chopped dried fruit
    (peaches, pineapple, white raisins,
    apple rings, apricots, papaya,
    coconut, or tropical fruit mix)
2 cinnamon sticks
6 cups pineapple juice
Dried banana chips, broken or crushed

In large saucepan over medium-high heat, combine water, tapioca, dried fruit, and cinnamon sticks. Bring to a boil. Reduce heat and simmer until transparent. Soup will be thick. Remove from heat and add pineapple juice. Serve warm in sherbet bowls with banana chips sprinkled on top. Keeps up to 1 week in refrigerator. Yields 18 to 24 servings.

Frozen Berry Delight

2 (12-ounce) bags frozen raspberries,
    thawed
2 (16-ounce) bags frozen strawberries,
    thawed
2 (12-ounce) jars raspberry preserves
1 (12-ounce) jar strawberry preserves
1 teaspoon lemon juice
Heavy cream

In food processor purée thawed fruit. Strain to remove seeds. In saucepan cook preserves until liquid. Strain to remove seeds. Mix fruit and preserves together. Strain again to remove any remaining seeds and add lemon juice. Pour into 9 x 13-inch metal pan. Cover and freeze overnight. Remove just before serving. Use

ice cream scoop to dish out. Pour heavy cream over top to form glaze. Yields 25 to 30 servings.

Topliff's Tara

251 Noble Road
Williamston, MI 48895
(517) 655-8860
info@topliffstara.com
www.topliffstara.com

Topliff's Tara is located in the 1905 farmhouse portion of this grand country estate. Topliff's Tara is in rural Ingham County, within easy driving distance of charming downtown Williamston, numerous antique shops, golf courses, shopping, and fine dining. In addition, you can reach the campus of Michigan State University in just ten minutes. As well as enjoying a beautiful and charming setting you can also see llamas. Included in the gift shop on the premises are hand-spun llama yarn and llama wool products, as well as dried and pressed floral arrangements and maple syrup from the family farm.

Cherry-Cheese Stuffed French Toast

1 cup dried tart cherries
½ cup rum
6 to12 slices French bread
    (based on diameter of loaf),
    bias cut 1½ inches thick
1 egg
4 tablespoons mascarpone cheese
1 tablespoon confectioners' sugar

Egg mixture:
2 eggs, beaten
1 cup milk
1 teaspoon vanilla extract
1 teaspoon ground cinnamon
1 teaspoon grated nutmeg
1 to 2 tablespoons butter

Buttered cherry sauce:
½ cup reserved dried tart cherries
¼ cup (½ stick) butter
2 cups cherry juice blend
    (or cranberry juice)
2 tablespoons sugar
2 tablespoons cornstarch
2 tablespoons water

Combine dried cherries and rum in a small saucepan. Simmer, covered, 5 minutes, or until cherries are soft and rum is

Topliff's Tara

absorbed. Half the cherries will be used to stuff bread and the other half for cherry sauce. Cut pockets through side of each slice of bread. Combine egg, mascarpone cheese, confectioners' sugar, and ½ cup cherries in small bowl. Mix well. Spoon cherry-cheese mixture into pockets of bread slices. Cover and chill, if desired.

Preheat griddle and oven to 350°. Prepare egg mixture by combining eggs, milk, vanilla, cinnamon, and nutmeg in a large bowl. Mix well. Melt butter on hot griddle. Dip stuffed bread slices into egg mixture and transfer to griddle. Cook until golden brown on both sides. Transfer to sheet pans sprayed with nonstick spray. Bake 20 minutes, or until bread slices are puffed and filling is hot. While baking toast combine remaining cherries, butter, cherry juice blend (or cranberry juice), and sugar in small saucepan. Simmer, stirring occasionally, until butter is completely melted. Combine cornstarch and water. Add slowly to hot liquid, whisking constantly. Increase heat and bring to a boil, stirring often, until thickened. Reduce heat; simmer about 5 minutes. Serve sauce over each serving of Cherry-Cheese French Toast. Yields 6 servings.

Rhubarb Bread

¾ cup granulated sugar
½ cup brown sugar
⅔ cup vegetable oil
1 egg
3 cups all-purpose flour
1 teaspoon baking soda
½ teaspoon salt
1 cup sour cream
1 teaspoon vanilla extract
2 cups diced rhubarb
½ cup chopped pecans

Topping:
½ cup brown sugar
½ teaspoon ground cinnamon
1 to 2 tablespoons butter or margarine

Preheat oven to 350°. Mix together thoroughly sugars, oil, and egg. Sift together flour, soda, and salt. Combine sour cream and vanilla. Alternately add dry ingredients and sour cream mixture to sugar mixture. Blend in rhubarb and pecans. Pour into greased and floured Bundt pan, or one regular and one small bread pan.

Prepare topping by combining sugar, cinnamon, and butter into fine crumbs. Sprinkle over rhubarb mixture. Bake 55 to 60 minutes. Cool 10 minutes before removing from pans. Yields 16 servings.

Harvest Eggs

Fresh salsa:
¼ medium sweet onion, diced
½ jalapeño pepper, diced
3 medium tomatoes, seeds removed and diced
2 tablespoons chopped fresh cilantro
½ teaspoon cumin
1 tablespoon lemon juice
1 teaspoon salt

Eggs:
½ green pepper, thinly sliced
½ red pepper, thinly sliced
½ sweet onion, thinly sliced
Chopped mushrooms (optional)
6 eggs, lightly beaten
1 cup grated Cheddar cheese

For salsa, sauté onion and jalapeño pepper in olive oil. Add tomatoes, cilantro, cumin, lemon juice, and salt.

For eggs, sauté peppers, onion, and mushrooms. Spray quiche dish with nonstick spray. Lightly scramble eggs without overcooking. Spread eggs in quiche dish. Remove liquid from salsa and cover eggs with salsa. Cover salsa with sautéed vegetables. Sprinkle cheese over vegetables. Broil until cheese is melted. Serve with toast and homemade jam. Yields 6 servings.

Apple-Nut Coffee Cake

½ cup shortening
1 cup sugar
2 eggs
1 teaspoon vanilla extract
2 cups all-purpose flour
¼ teaspoon salt
1 teaspoon baking soda
1 cup sour cream
2 cups peeled and diced apples

Topping:
½ cup chopped pecans
½ cup brown sugar
1 teaspoon ground cinnamon
2 tablespoons melted butter

Cream together shortening and sugar. Add eggs and vanilla. Beat well. Stir in flour, salt, and baking soda. Add sour cream. Fold in apples. Spread in well greased 13 x 9 x 2-inch pan.

Preheat oven to 350°. For topping, combine topping ingredients. Sprinkle over batter. Bake 35 to 40 minutes or until toothpick comes out clean. Yields 12 to 14 servings.

GRAND HOTEL

286 Grand Avenue
Mackinac Island, MI 49757
(906) 847-3331 (phone)
(906) 847-3259 (fax)
(800) 33-GRAND (toll free)
khayward@grandhotel.com
www.grandhotel.com

Glimmering like a diamond on an island of brilliant green, Grand Hotel beckons you to a bygone era of old world hospitality and charm. It will take you back to a time of horse-drawn carriages, afternoon tea, and croquet on an endless lawn, an era of dining to chamber music and dancing the evening away. Here, no automobiles are permitted, and nothing intrudes on the serenity and natural beauty of the island. The crown jewel of pristine secluded Mackinac Island, Grand Hotel has been America's summer place since 1887.

Sweet Potato and White Corn Soup

2 tablespoons butter
1 large white onion, diced
1 cup white kernel corn
⅓ cup white wine
3 large sweet potatoes, baked, peeled, and mashed
4 cups chicken stock
½ cup herbs de Provence
Salt and pepper
1 tablespoon pickled ginger
1 cup half-and-half
¼ cup celery root, boiled and diced
¼ cup white kernel corn, cooked
¼ cup white potatoes, boiled and diced
¼ cup chives, diced

Heat stockpot and add butter, onions, and 1 cup white kernel corn. Sauté for about 10 minutes on medium heat and add white wine, sweet potato pulp, chicken stock, herbs, salt, pepper, and ginger. Continue to simmer for another 10 minutes. Add half-and-half and simmer another 5 minutes. Remove from heat, pour into blender, and blend until smooth. Strain soup through colander, and add celery root, ¼ cup cooked corn, and potatoes. Pour into serving bowls, and garnish with diced fresh chives. Yields 6 servings.

Scallops and Shrimp on Herb Linguine

2 pounds bay scallops
2 pounds broken shrimp pieces
2 ounces lemon juice
¼ cup olive oil
1 tablespoon chopped fresh basil
1 tablespoon chopped fresh ginger
¼ cup red onion julienne
1 tablespoon minced fresh garlic
4 large vine-ripened tomatoes, peeled and cut into fine dice with juice
1 tablespoon diced fresh cilantro
1 tablespoon diced fresh thyme
¼ cup balsamic vinegar
¼ cup margarine
8 ounces mascarpone cheese
1½ cups heavy cream
Salt and pepper
32 ounces herb linguine, cooked and drained

Marinate scallops, shrimp pieces, lemon juice, basil, and ginger in bowl. Cover and let marinate for 15 minutes. Heat sauté pan, add olive oil, and sauté onions and garlic over medium heat until onions are tender. Add tomatoes, cilantro, thyme, and balsamic vinegar. Reduce heat and simmer for 15 minutes. Drain scallops and shrimp. Cook in margarine in separate skillet over medium heat until seafood is opaque, about 3 minutes. Then add mascarpone cheese, heavy cream, and tomato mixture. Season with salt and pepper to taste. Pour over herb linguine and toss to coat. Garnish dish as desired. Yields 8 servings.

Buffalo Tenderloin with Wild Mushroom Salad

Wild mushroom salad:
1 tablespoon butter
1 shallot, diced
1 clove garlic, minced
⅓ cup sliced shiitake mushrooms
⅓ cup cremini mushrooms
⅓ cup morels
1 teaspoon curry
2 tablespoons chopped herbs (tarragon, parsley)
Salt and pepper
⅓ cup hazelnut oil
⅓ cup olive oil
⅓ cup rice vinegar

Blackberry sauce:
1 tablespoon olive oil
2 shallots, diced
2 tablespoons pickled ginger
1 tablespoon tomato paste
3 tablespoons blackberry jam
2 tablespoons soy sauce
1 cup meat stock
2 tablespoons thyme
⅓ cup fresh blackberries

Wild rice:
1 tablespoon butter
1 shallot, diced
1 cup cooked wild rice
2 tablespoons pecans
1 tablespoon chopped basil
Salt and pepper
3 (2-ounce) medallions of buffalo tenderloin

For mushroom salad, in skillet over medium heat melt butter and sauté shal-

Grand Hotel

lots and garlic. Add wild mushrooms, curry, herbs, salt, and pepper. Add oils and rice vinegar to skillet, remove from heat, and pour mixture into bowl to infuse.

For blackberry sauce heat olive oil in saucepan and add shallots and ginger. Sauté for 1 minute. Add tomato paste, blackberry jam, soy sauce, meat stock, and thyme and reduce by half. Strain and adjust seasonings. Add fresh blackberries and set sauce aside.

For wild rice, in sauté pan over low heat, melt butter. Add shallots, wild rice, pecans, basil, and seasonings and heat. Finally season buffalo medallions with salt and pepper and sear in skillet over medium-high heat until medium rare. Serve with sauce, wild rice, and mushroom salad. Yields 1 serving.

Wild Mushrooms on Puff Pastry

2 puff pastry sheets
2 tablespoons margarine
2 shallots
1 cup shiitake mushrooms
1 cup portobello mushrooms
1 cup chanterelle mushrooms
3 tablespoons mixed herbs
½ cup sherry
½ cup half-and-half
1 cup mascarpone cheese
Salt and pepper
12 ounces fresh spinach, cleaned
    and stemmed
1 cup vegetable stock
¼ cup diced chives
4 edible flowers

Using cookie cutter or knife, cut puff pastry sheets into shapes like hearts or circles and bake until golden brown. Remove from oven and keep warm. Heat a sauté pan over medium heat, add margarine and shallots, and sauté several minutes. Add all mushroom varieties and herbs. Let simmer until all fluids have evaporated. Add sherry to deglaze pan and mix in half-and-half, mascarpone cheese, and salt and pepper to taste. Simmer until sauce coats bottom of spoon. Heat another saucepan and cook spinach with salt and pepper to taste in vegetable stock until soft. Slice puff pastry in half horizontally and place spinach and wild mushroom mixture on bottom half of pastry. Replace top piece of pastry. Garnish with chives and flowers and serve. Yields 4 servings.

Minnesota

THE COTTON MANSION

2309 East First Street
Duluth, MN 55812
(218) 724-6405 (phone)
(800) 228-1997 (toll free)

From the breathtaking entry with its hand-carved wooden angels and stunning stained-glass dome to the amazing, imported marble fireplaces, you will thoroughly enjoy use of our common areas. Built in 1908 for Joseph Bell Cotton, attorney for John D. Rockefeller, the mansion is a unique Italian Renaissance structure that, at sixteen thousand square feet, features a formal library, sunroom, and dining room. Relax in the living room with its exquisite alabaster fireplace, beautifully carved woodwork, and grand piano, or step into the sunroom and enjoy the morning sunshine.

Blueberry Puff Pancakes

4 tablespoons butter
¾ cup all-purpose flour
¾ cup milk
1 teaspoon salt
3 eggs
1 cup blueberries
¼ cup sugar
Confectioners' sugar

Preheat oven to 400°. Melt butter and divide between two 8-inch round pans. Rotate pans until butter has coated sides and bottom. Beat flour, milk, salt, and eggs. Divide blueberries between pans. Divide batter evenly between pans. Sprinkle with sugar. Bake for 25 minutes or until golden brown. Transfer to plate immediately and dust with confectioners' sugar. Serve with warm maple syrup. Yields 2 servings.

Note: Place blueberries as though you were making a pizza, so you have a 1½-inch crust area around the pan.

Rosemary Pork Chops

4 double-rib, extra thick pork chops, 1 to 1½ inches thick
Garlic salt
Freshly ground pepper
Fresh or dried rosemary
1 cup garlic mashed potatoes
1 packet peppercorn sauce, mixed per packet instructions

Preheat broiler. Place chops on cookie sheet and sprinkle with garlic salt, pepper and rosemary. Place chops under broiler for 4 to 5 minutes per side. Do *not* over-cook. Serve chops on top of mashed potatoes and top with peppercorn sauce. This recipe is best when served with sweet onions and red and yellow peppers rubbed with olive oil and roasted. Yields 4 servings.

Kimberly's Salad

Dressing:
¼ cup olive oil
2 tablespoons sugar
2 tablespoons balsamic vinegar

Salad:
1 cup pecans
½ cup sugar
1 head Romaine lettuce, torn into small pieces
¼ cup thinly sliced red onions
½ cup dried cranberries
1 (8-ounce) package crumbled blue cheese or feta cheese

Combine dressing ingredients and mix well. Sprinkle pecans with sugar and cook over low heat until pecans are caramelized and place on wax paper. Divide lettuce among six salad plates and top with red onions, dried cranberries, crumbled cheese, and caramelized pecans. Spoon dressing over salad and serve. Yields 6 servings.

LINDGREN'S BED & BREAKFAST

5552 County Road 35
P.O. Box 56
Lutsen, MN 55612-0056
(218) 663-7450
info@lindgrensbb.com
www.lindgrensbb.com

Located just off scenic Highway 61 in Lutsen, Minnesota, on the Lake Superior Circle Tour, all of the rooms at Lindgren's Bed & Breakfast have views of Lake Superior. The great room overlooking the big lake has a magnificent stone fireplace.

Lindgren's has been a bed and breakfast since 1988. The accommodations will enhance your vacation and make you wish you could stay longer. Whatever the season, you will enjoy the comforts of this lakeshore home. Nearby activities include: snow skiing, fishing, canoeing, championship golf, moose or bird-watching, hunt-ing, berry picking, mountain biking, sailing, snowmobiling, tennis, swimming, horseback riding, antiquing, and much more.

Wild Raspberry Muffins

Muffins:
1¼ cups sugar
½ cup (1 stick) margarine
2 eggs
1 cup sour cream
1 teaspoon vanilla extract
2 cups all-purpose flour
1 teaspoon baking powder
⅛ teaspoon baking soda
¼ teaspoon salt
1 cup fresh or frozen wild raspberries

Topping:
2 tablespoons sugar
¼ teaspoon ground cinnamon
¼ teaspoon ground nutmeg

Preheat oven to 375°. For muffins, cream sugar and margarine. Add eggs, sour cream, and vanilla. Add sifted dry ingredients and mix just until moist. Fold in berries. Place batter in two muffin pans coated with nonstick spray. Mix topping ingredients and sprinkle ¼ teaspoon on each muffin. Bake 25 to 30 minutes. Yields 24 muffins.

Banana and Wild Blueberry Bread

⅔ cup sugar
1½ cups all-purpose flour
2 teaspoons baking powder
¼ teaspoon salt
¾ cup quick-cooking oatmeal
⅓ cup corn oil or canola oil
2 eggs, slightly beaten
2 large bananas, mashed
¾ cup wild blueberries, fresh or frozen

Preheat oven to 350°. In large bowl sift together sugar, flour, baking powder, and salt. Stir in oatmeal. Mix in oil, eggs, and mashed bananas, stirring only until all ingredients are moist. Fold in blueberries. Pour batter into greased, lightly floured, 9 x 5-inch loaf pan. Bake 60 to 65 minutes, or until toothpick inserted in middle comes out clean. Remove from oven. Cool in pan 15 minutes and remove from pan and place on wire rack. Yields 12 servings.

Lindgren's Bed & Breakfast

Nippy Cheese-Baked Eggs in Toast Cups

12 thin slices fresh bread
9 tablespoons melted butter
12 eggs

Nippy cheese sauce:
3 tablespoons butter
3 tablespoons all-purpose flour
1 plus 1 cup whole milk
½ teaspoon salt
⅛ teaspoon pepper
2 teaspoons Worcestershire sauce
Dash of hot pepper sauce
Dash of cayenne
2 cups shredded Cheddar cheese

Preheat oven to 350°. Trim crusts from bread and brush both sides of each slice with melted butter. Press gently into 3-inch muffin tins. Bake 10 to 15 minutes until lightly browned. Break an egg into each toast cup. Bake 15 to 20 minutes until eggs are set.

For cheese sauce, melt butter in upper part of double boiler over low heat. Add flour and blend. Heat 1 cup milk. Add remaining 1 cup cold milk to flour mixture and blend. Stir in hot milk, salt and pepper, sauces, and cayenne. Cool until thick and smooth, stirring constantly. Water should not touch top of pan. Cover and cook 4 to 8 minutes. Turn off heat. Add cheese and let stand until cheese melts. Stir enough to blend and serve with the toast cups. Yields 6 to 8 servings.

Caramel Torte

6 egg yolks
1½ cups sugar
1 teaspoon baking powder
2 teaspoons vanilla extract
6 egg whites, beaten stiff
2 cups finely crushed graham
    cracker crumbs
1¼ cups chopped nuts, pecans preferred
1 pint heavy cream, whipped

Caramel sauce:
1¼ cups lightly packed brown sugar
1 tablespoon all-purpose flour
¼ cup (½ stick) butter
¼ cup orange juice
¼ cup water
1 egg, beaten
1 teaspoon vanilla extract

Line two, 9-inch round cake pans with wax paper. Preheat oven to 325°. Beat egg yolks well, adding sugar, baking powder, and vanilla. Fold egg whites into yolk mixture. Fold in crumbs and nuts. Blend. Pour batter into pans and bake 35 minutes. Cool on wire racks.

For caramel sauce, combine sugar, flour, butter, orange juice, water, and egg in top of double boiler. Cook, uncovered, over low heat, stirring until boiling and thickened. Add vanilla. Cut each layer in half to make four layers. Stack each layer with whipped cream and spread top with whipped cream. Drizzle entire cake with caramel sauce. Yields 10 servings.

GOLDEN LANTERN INN

721 East Ave.
Red Wing, MN 55066
(651) 388-3315 (phone)
(888) 288-3315 (toll free)
info@goldenlantern.com
www.goldenlantern.com

Built by Red Wing Shoe Company's owner, this bed and breakfast offers a wonderful setting for your next getaway. Whirlpools, fireplaces, balconies, and breakfast-in-bed are a few amenities to enjoy. Red Wing is a beautiful town to visit anytime of the year. There is unique shopping, breathtaking bluffs for hiking, downhill and cross-country skiing, golfing, and fascinating history.

Vegetable Oven Omelet

¼ cup melted butter
27 eggs or 5½ cups liquid eggs
1½ cups sour cream
1½ cups milk
2 teaspoons salt
½ teaspoon basil
3 cups shredded Cheddar cheese
6 to 8 ounces sliced mushrooms, drained
½ cup chopped green onion

Preheat oven to 325°. Spread melted butter in 15 x 10-inch baking dish. In very large bowl beat eggs and add sour cream, milk, salt, and basil. Stir in cheese, mushrooms, and onions. Pour mixture into prepared baking dish. Bake 55 minutes until edges are slightly brown and knife comes out clean when inserted in middle. Garnish with tomato slices or wedges. Can vary recipe with chopped peppers or other chopped vegetables. Yields 10 to 12 large pieces.

Curried Fruit

2 (15-ounce) cans peach slices
1 (15-ounce) can pear halves
1 (20-ounce) can pineapple chunks
½ cup (1 stick) butter
1 cup packed brown sugar
1 teaspoon curry
3 tablespoons cornstarch

Preheat oven to 350°. Drain fruit, and cut peaches and pears into bite-size pieces. Put fruit in 9 x 13-inch baking dish. In small bowl add butter and melt in microwave. Add brown sugar, curry, and cornstarch to butter and mix. Spoon mixture over fruit and mix. Bake 1 hour. Yields 10 to 12 individual serving cups/bowls.

Morning Coffee Cake

1 cup sugar
1 cup vegetable oil
4 eggs
2 cups all-purpose flour
1 teaspoon baking powder
1 (16-ounce) can peach, apple, or
    cherry pie filling
Cinnamon sugar
Confectioners' sugar and milk for frosting

Preheat oven to 350°. Coat 9 x 13-inch baking dish with cooking spray. Cream sugar and oil. Beat eggs well and add to sugar mix. Mix flour and baking powder and add to egg/sugar mix. Spread half of mixture over bottom of prepared pan. Pour pie filling in pan and spread evenly. Put remaining batter over pie filling.

Sprinkle top with cinnamon sugar. Bake 35 to 40 minutes. When cool, drizzle with frosting of confectioners' sugar and milk mixed to thin consistency. Cut into triangles or squares. Yields 6 to 8 servings.

Blueberry Oven Pancake

3¾ cups all-purpose flour
3 teaspoons baking powder
1½ teaspoons baking soda
3 plus 1 teaspoons ground cinnamon
3 tablespoons sugar
4 cups buttermilk
1½ teaspoons vanilla extract
3 tablespoons vegetable oil
3 eggs
1 cup fresh or frozen blueberries
1 cup packed brown sugar
Blueberry Syrup

Preheat oven to 350°. Spray 15 x 10-inch baking dish with cooking spray. In large bowl combine flour, baking powder, baking soda, 3 teaspoons cinnamon, and sugar. Add buttermilk, vanilla, oil, and eggs. Stir until well blended with no lumps. Add more buttermilk if mixture is too thick. It should run off a spoon in a consistent stream. Stir in blueberries. Pour mixture into baking dish and top with brown sugar and remaining 1 teaspoon cinnamon. Bake 35 to 40 minutes or until wooden pick inserted comes out clean. Serve hot with Blueberry Syrup (see recipe below) or butter and syrup. Yields 10 to 12 large servings.

Blueberry Syrup

1½ cups sugar
3 tablespoons cornstarch
1½ cups water
1½ cups blueberries, fresh or frozen
3 tablespoons butter

Combine sugar, cornstarch, water, and blueberries in saucepan. Cook over medium-high heat, stirring for 15 minutes or until berries burst. Remove from heat and add butter, stirring until melted. Serve warm over Blueberry Oven Pancakes. Yields 10 servings (about 4 cups).

LOWELL INN

102 North Second Street
Stillwater, MN 55082
(612) 439-1100 (phone)
(612) 439-4686 (fax)

The Lowell Inn offers fine dining for business or pleasure and twenty-two newly restored rooms in beautiful downtown Stillwater, Minnesota. There are three unique fine dining rooms: The George Washington Room boasts an American Fare menu; The Garden Room features the first natural spring-fed trout pool; and The Matterhorn Room includes Swiss Fondue and elaborate Swiss carvings.

Red Cabbage

1 medium head red cabbage
1 medium sweet onion
2 large apples
1 full tablespoon bacon fat
1 teaspoon salt
½ cup sugar
1½ cups water
1 cup vinegar
1 bay leaf
2 whole allspice berries
2 cloves, heads removed
6 peppercorns
Cornstarch

Wash and remove outer leaves of cabbage. Remove core and slice cabbage. Peel and slice onion. Peel and quarter apples. Toss all together. Add remaining ingredients except cornstarch. Simmer in saucepan for

1½ hours covered. Thicken slightly with small amount of cornstarch mixed with a little juice from saucepan. The cornstarch gives cabbage a nice glow. Yields 6 servings.

Lowell Inn Crescent Rolls

2 ounces yeast
¼ cup plus 1 teaspoon sugar
1 plus 1 cup warm water
1 tablespoon salt
¼ cup melted butter
7 to 8 cups all-purpose flour, divided
3 eggs

Sprinkle yeast with 1 teaspoon sugar and soften in 1 cup warm water and set aside to proof. Dissolve the remaining ¼ cup sugar with salt in the remaining 1 cup warm water. Add butter and 2 to 3 cups flour. Mix in eggs and yeast mixture and add remaining flour until stiff but soft. Let rise until double in size. Punch down. Let rise again. Turn out on floured board and let rest 10 minutes.

Preheat oven to 400°. Fold dough to less than ¼-inch thickness. Cut in full quarters with dough or pizza cutter. From each quarter cut elongated triangles of dough, rolling each triangle from one cut quarter before starting the next quarter. Gently twist the dough triangles into knots and place on greased pans. Bake 10 to 15 minutes, or until golden brown. Yields 50 rolls.

Lemon Angel Pie

12 egg whites
2 cups sugar

Filling:
12 egg yolks
1½ cups sugar
6 teaspoons lemon zest
¾ cup lemon juice
1 pint cream

Preheat oven to 275°. Beat egg whites until stiff. Add sugar slowly and blend. Place in pie tin. Bake for 1 hour. Remove and cool.

For filling, beat egg yolks. Add sugar, lemon zest, and lemon juice. Whip cream until firm. Spread small amount over meringue in pie shell. Spread in cool lemon filling. Refrigerate for 6 hours to set. Top with remaining whipped cream. Yields 8 servings.

Cream of Wild Rice Soup

2 cups cooked wild rice
1 large onion, finely diced
1 carrot, finely diced
1 rib celery, finely diced
½ cup chopped ham
½ cup (1 stick) butter
4 tablespoons all-purpose flour
8 cups chicken broth
Herb seasoning
Salt and white pepper
1 cup light cream or half-and-half

Prepare wild rice according to package directions. Sauté onion, carrot, celery, and ham in butter in large saucepan about 3minutes, or until vegetables have softened slightly. Sift in flour, a bit at a time, stirring and cooking until flour is well blended, but do *not* let brown. Slowly add chicken broth, stirring until flour-vegetable mixture is blended well. Add wild rice, herb seasoning, salt, and white pepper to taste. Heat thoroughly. Add cream and reheat gently, but do *not* boil. Yields 12 servings.

Brittle Maple Frango

¾ cup maple syrup
¼ cup molasses-flavored syrup
4 egg yolks
3 cups whipping cream

Pour egg yolks into saucepan and warm over low heat. Pour syrups into saucepan and warm slightly before adding to warm egg yolks. Bring mixture to a gentle boil and cook until thick; set aside to cool. Whip the cream and fold into cooled maple mixture. Pour into 8- or 9-inch square pan. Freeze for 48 hours. Slice and serve. Store leftovers in freezer. Yields 8 to 10 servings.

Olcott House Bed & Breakfast

OLCOTT HOUSE BED & BREAKFAST

2316 East 1st Street
Duluth, MN 55812
(218) 728-1339 (phone)
(800) 715-1339 (toll free)
info@olcotthouse.com
www.olcotthouse.com

Constructed in 1904 by master craftsmen, the ten-thousand-square-foot, brick, Georgian colonial home and carriage house showcases soaring pillars, rich mahogany wood, beamed ceilings, hardwood floors, bay windows, eleven antique fireplaces, and a grand staircase. The home is situated on five city lots surrounded by a brick-and-wrought-iron wall. There are six comfortable suites, all with fireplaces and private baths, completely renovated and refurbished within the last five years. AAA approved, the Olcott House is located in Duluth's historic East End Mansion District, just four blocks from Lake Superior and minutes from Duluth's attractions and the beautiful North Shore. Don't miss the Lakewalk, the Harbor, and Aerial Lift Bridge; the Rose Gardens, Canal Park, Glensheen Mansion, the Depot Museum, Enger Tower, Gooseberry Falls, and Split Rock Lighthouse; and miles of incredible hiking, biking, and skiing trails.

Caramel/Maple Syrup

2 cups brown sugar
½ cup (1 stick) butter
1 cup milk
1 teaspoon vanilla extract
½ cup maple syrup

Stir all ingredients together in saucepan. Cook on medium heat for about 15 minutes. Do *not* boil. Put into pretty syrup pitcher and let guests pour on top of stuffed, toasted croissants. Yields approximately 4 cups.

Amaretto Stuffed French Croissants

12-ounces cream cheese
1 healthy shot Amaretto
6 large or 12 small croissants,
    sliced three-quarters open
12 medium fresh strawberries,
    sliced
6 eggs
⅓ cup milk or cream
1 teaspoon vanilla extract
1 teaspoon ground cinnamon

Heat griddle to 350°. Combine cream cheese and amaretto using a microwave-safe dish. Soften about 1 or 2 minutes until spreading consistency. Spread cream cheese mixture on inside of each croissant and add sliced strawberries on top as if making a sandwich. Close croissants. Mix together eggs, milk, vanilla, and cinnamon. Lightly dip both sides of croissants in egg mixture and put on greased or buttered griddle, turning so all four sides are toasted. The entire process will take about 5 to 6 minutes. Serve immediately by arranging croissants on plate with remaining strawberry slices placed on top. Sprinkle with confectioners' sugar. Yields 6 servings.

Snuggle Inn Bed & Breakfast

8 Seventh Ave. W.
P.O. Box 915
Grand Marais, MN 55604
(218) 387-2847 (phone)
(800) 823-3174 (toll free)
info@snuggleinnbb.com
www.snuggleinnbb.com

Built in 1913, the Snuggle Inn Bed & Breakfast is naturally inviting. Each room is charmingly decorated with original prints by local artists. The inn is located on Minnesota's North Shore of Lake Superior, just one block from the harbor and close to the Boundary Waters Canoe Area Wilderness. The area is made for those who love to hike, canoe, cross-country ski, snowshoe, or stroll through the art galleries and antique shops, or just plain relax.

Cashew Peach Cereal

2 bananas, thinly sliced
2 peaches, coarsely chopped
½ cup cashew halves
4 tablespoons shredded coconut
2 tablespoons sesame seeds
¾ cup golden raisins
¼ cup currants
4 teaspoons maple syrup
¼ teaspoon ground cinnamon
Pinch of ground allspice
Milk or yogurt

In medium bowl, combine bananas and peaches. In food processor, combine cashews, coconut, and sesame seeds. Process with on/off turns until coarsely ground (Do *not* over-process). Sprinkle mixture over fruit. Stir in raisins, currants, maple

syrup, cinnamon and allspice. Serve topped with milk or yogurt. Yields 2 to 3 servings.

Pumpkin-Apple Muffins with Streusel Topping

Streusel:
½ cup all-purpose flour
½ cup sugar
½ teaspoon ground cinnamon
3 tablespoons butter, melted

Muffins:
1¼ cups all purpose flour
1 cup sugar
1 teaspoon pumpkin pie spice
¼ teaspoon salt
½ teaspoon baking soda
1 egg, beaten
½ cup canned pumpkin
¼ cup vegetable oil
4 ounces cream cheese, softened
1 cup peeled and finely chopped
    Braeburn apples

Preheat oven to 375°. In small bowl, combine flour, sugar, and cinnamon for streusel topping. Add melted butter, mixing thoroughly with fork.

For muffins, in medium bowl, combine flour, sugar, pumpkin pie spice, salt, and baking soda. In large bowl, mix egg with pumpkin and oil. Add flour mixture to egg mixture and stir batter well. Place cream cheese in small microwave-safe bowl and

covered, 30 to 45 seconds or
_____ oft. Add cream cheese to batter
and blend well. Fold in apples. Fill well-
greased muffin pan cups three-quarters
full and sprinkle with streusel topping.
Bake 20 to 25 minutes. Let cool on wire
rack. Yields 12 muffins.

Rhubarb-Strawberry Coffee Cake

½ cup (1 stick) butter, softened
1½ cups sugar
1 egg
2½ cups all-purpose flour
1 teaspoon baking soda
½ teaspoon salt
1 cup buttermilk
2½ cups sliced fresh rhubarb
1 cup chopped fresh strawberries
1 teaspoon vanilla extract
1 cup packed brown sugar
½ cup chopped walnuts

Glaze:
1 cup sugar
½ cup butter
3 tablespoons milk
1 teaspoon vanilla extract

Preheat oven to 350°. In large mixing
bowl, cream butter and sugar. Beat in egg.
In medium mixing bowl, combine flour,
baking soda, and salt. Add flour mixture
and buttermilk alternately to butter/sugar/
0egg mixture. Mix well. Stir in rhubarb,
strawberries, and vanilla. Pour into greased
13 x 9 x 2-inch baking pan. Sprinkle with
brown sugar and nuts. Bake 45 minutes, or
until a toothpick inserted comes out clean.

For glaze, combine sugar, butter, and
milk in small saucepan. Bring to a boil.
Remove from heat and stir in vanilla. Pour
warm glaze over hot cake. Serve immediately. Yields 8 to 12 servings.

RIVERTOWN INN

306 West Olive Street
Stillwater, MN 55082
(651) 430-2955 (phone)
(651) 430-2206 (fax)
rivertown@rivertowninn.com
www.rivertowninn.com

The Rivertown Inn is a grand three story
mansion that was built by lumber baron
John O'Brien in 1882, when lumber was
big and the logging industry flourished. It
sits high upon historic Chestnut Hill, overlooking picturesque Stillwater and the St.
Croix River Valley. The inn has been completely and lovingly restored and lavishly
furnished with gasolier light fixtures, hardwood parquet floors, plush hand woven
oriental rugs, leaded glass doors, arched
stained glass windows, eleven fireplaces
set in period mantels, a mahogany grand
piano, and gothic European furnishings
throughout. Each of the nine luxury guest
rooms is uniquely decorated and designed
in the spirit of nineteenth-century poets
and offers every plush amenity imaginable
for romance and comfort. It is a step back
to the Victorian splendor of the nineteenth century.

Scented Geranium Poached Pear with Sweetened Ricotta Filling

Pears:
1½ cups water
1½ cups sugar
½ lemon, juiced
1 sprig fresh scented geranium
3 Anjou pears

Sweetened ricotta:
1 cup ricotta cheese
1 tablespoon brown sugar
1 teaspoon honey
1 drop vanilla extract
1 pinch sea salt
6 mint leaves for garnish

In saucepan combine water, sugar, lemon
juice, and geranium. Peel pears and slice in
half. Remove core and stems. Place pear
halves in sugar water and bring to a boil.
Reduce heat and simmer until tender,
about 20 to 30 minutes. Pour hot pears
and cooking liquid into container and
allow to steep and cool. (Can be refrigerated up to one week.)

For sweetened ricotta, in stainless steel
bowl, combine all ingredients and mix
well. (Can be made ahead of time.) Using
slotted spoon, place each pear half in
bowl. Place scoop of ricotta filling in center, garnish with mint leaf, and serve
immediately. Yields 6 servings.

Almond Crêpe with Apricot Sauce

Crêpe filling:
1 (8-ounce) package cream cheese,
    cubed and softened
2 tablespoons cream
2 drops almond extract
2 drops vanilla extract
1 tablespoon toasted slivered almonds
1 pinch sea salt

Apricot sauce:
½ cup water
½ cup sugar
1 lemon, juiced
6 fresh apricots, halved and pits removed
Sea salt
6 crêpes
18 slices apricot
¼ cup toasted slivered almonds
2 tablespoons confectioners' sugar

Combine filling ingredients in mixer and
using paddle attachment mix until com-

bined. (This can be done ahead of time.)

Combine apricot sauce ingredients in pot over medium-high heat and bring to a boil. Lower heat, simmer for 5 minutes, and remove from heat. Using slotted spoon scoop out apricots and transfer to blender. Purée and strain through fine-mesh sieve. Season with salt to taste. (This can be made ahead of time.)

Preheat oven to 350°. Lay crêpes on counter and divide almond filling generously and evenly along middle of each crêpe. Roll into cylinder, and transfer to parchment-lined sheet pan. (This can be made ahead of time.) Warm crêpes in oven about 5 minutes. Ladle 2 to 3 ounces apricot sauce in middle of serving plate and swirl around to make a circle. Place warm crêpe in center of sauce and place apricot slices on top of crêpe. Sprinkle toasted almonds on top of apricots, and sprinkle confectioners' sugar over plate. Serve immediately. Yields 6 servings.

Huevos "Sombrero" Rancheros

3 (12-inch) tortillas (your favorite flavor)
1 cup fresh salsa
6 large eggs
1 teaspoon lime juice
6 tablespoons cream
2 tablespoons unsalted butter
6 shallots, minced
1 tablespoon chopped cilantro
Sea salt
1 piece parchment paper
1 (8-ounce) can refried beans
1 cup salsa fresca
Scrambled eggs
2 cups grated Cheddar cheese
6 sprigs fresh cilantro

Stack tortillas. Using a 3½-inch ring cutter, cut 6 rounds for a total of 18 tortilla rounds. (This can be done ahead of time). In saucepan over medium heat bring salsa to a simmer. Blend in blender, return to pan, and keep warm. Crack eggs in stainless steel bowl. Add lime juice and cream and beat eggs. Place nonstick pan over medium-high heat and melt butter. Add shallots and stir until translucent. Add egg mixture and cilantro and cook until scrambled, stirring often. Remove from heat and season with salt to taste.

Preheat oven to 350°. To assemble, on parchment-lined sheet pan, lay out six tortilla rounds. Spread beans and salsa on top and place another tortilla layer on top. Spoon on some scrambled eggs and then salsa on top of eggs. Place another tortilla layer on top. Spoon on more eggs, cover with cheese, and bake 5 minutes. Ladle some salsa onto center of serving plate, put hot sombrero on top, garnish with sprig of cilantro, and serve immediately. Yields 6 servings.

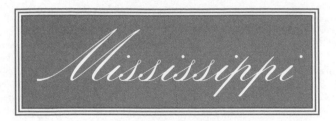

MILLSAPS BUIE HOUSE

628 N. State Street
Jackson, MS 39202
(601) 352-0221 (phone)
(800) 784-0221 (toll free)
info@millsapsbuiehouse.com
www.millsapsbuiehouse.com

A splendid Southern welcome awaits you at this stately Queen Anne mansion, a landmark that has remained in the same Mississippi family for four generations. There are eleven unique guest rooms, each with private bath, cable television, and telephone with computer data port. There are nearby upscale restaurants, antique and specialty shops, the Art Museum, Planetarium, Natural History Museum, Agriculture and Forestry Museum, Northpark and Dogwood Festival shopping malls, Mynelle Gardens, good public golf courses, and zoo.

Pralines

½ pint (1 cup) whipping cream
1 (1-pound) box light brown sugar
2 tablespoons butter
1 cup pecan halves

Combine all ingredients, mixing well with wooden spoon. Cook in microwave on high for 5 minutes. (Make sure container is deep enough, since candy bubbles up. We use an 8-cup glass measuring cup). Stir well with wooden spoon. Cook 11 more minutes on high, testing for soft ball stage in small amount of ice water (candy may possibly need 1 additional minute of cooking). Add pecan halves and continue stirring candy until it starts to thicken. Drop onto aluminum foil by the tablespoon. If candy gets too thick while you are dropping it, add 1 to 2 tablespoons cream to thin it as you go. Yields 2 to 2½ dozen pralines.

Note: Wrap pralines individually and freeze in plastic wrapping bag.

Texas Torte

2 heaping tablespoons sifted
     all-purpose flour
5 eggs
¾ cup milk
1 (4-ounce) can chopped green chiles
1 cup grated Cheddar cheese
1 cup grated Monterey Jack or pepper
     Jack cheese
1½ cups chopped cooked sausage
     or combination of cooked
     sausage and ham

Preheat oven to 350°. Coat 3-quart round casserole dish with nonstick spray. Put flour in large mixing bowl. Beat together well eggs and milk. Whisk into flour, getting rid of as many lumps as possible. Add remaining ingredients. Bake, uncovered, 45 minutes to 1 hour, or until done in center. Yields 6 servings.

Note: This casserole can be prepared a day ahead, then baked next morning. Cut in six wedges and serve on buffet table in chafing dish to keep casserole warm. It also reheats well in microwave at 50 percent power.

Pecan Horns

½ pound cold butter, cut in pieces
     (2 sticks cut into tablespoons)
2 cups all-purpose flour
8 ounces cream cheese, cut in pieces
½ cup granulated sugar
1 tablespoon ground cinnamon
2 tablespoons melted butter
¼ cup chopped pecans
¼ cup currants
½ cup confectioners' sugar
¼ teaspoon vanilla extract
1 tablespoon milk

Process butter and flour in food processor (pulse) until size of small peas. Process continuously just until dough begins to form a ball. Add cream cheese. Divide into three balls, flatten, wrap, and freeze, or use immediately. Dough does not need to rest.

To assemble, roll dough out ¼-inch thickness. Combine the sugar and cinnamon. Brush dough with melted butter, and sprinkle with cinnamon sugar. Sprinkle with chopped pecans and currants. Cut into pie-shaped wedges (six or eight, de-pending on how large you want them) and roll up, starting at wide end, rolling toward point. Place seam-side down on baking sheet and freeze or bake immediately. These can be stored in plastic freezer bags.

Count out number of horns needed and place frozen on ungreased cookie sheet. Preheat oven to 350°. Bake horns about 35 minutes or until light brown. Cool on rack. Mix together confectioners' sugar, vanilla, and milk and drizzle glaze on baked pastries when cool. (Drizzling icing from a fork works well.) Serve warm or at room temperature on a crystal cake stand or shiny silver tray. Yields 12 crescents.

Cheese Grits

3 cups water
½ stick butter, cut in pieces
    (Do *not* use margarine.)
1 cup quick (5-minute) grits
8 ounces cubed processed cheese,
    more or less as desired
Pinch of salt
Dash of garlic powder (optional)

Bring water to slow boil and add butter. When butter has melted, slowly add grits, stirring continually as they are added to avoid lumps. Cook, stirring occasionally, on low heat until grits are done, about 5 minutes. Add processed cheese, pinch of salt, and dash of garlic powder, if using. Continue stirring, cooking on very low heat, until all cheese is melted and grits are thick. Yields 6 to 8 servings.

CEDAR GROVE MANSION INN

2200 Oak Street
Vicksburg, MS 39180
(601) 636-1000 (phone)
(601) 634-6126 (fax)
(800) 862-1300 (toll free)
info@cedargroveinn.com
www.cedargroveinn.com

Make Cedar Grove your next romantic escape. Capture *Gone with the Wind* elegance and romance in exquisite guest rooms/suites in the Mansion or one of the restored, historic, patio cottages, the Carriage House or Poolside Garden Cottage, all nestled in five acres of gardens. Each room is lavishly decorated and furnished with period antiques combined with the conveniences of private baths, cable TV, telephones, and air conditioning. Relax with a Mint Julep or cocktail in the Piano Bar, the perfect prelude to a romantic gourmet candlelight dinner in Cedar Grove's restaurant.

Raspberry Sorbet

2 cups water
1 cup sugar
1 pint fresh raspberries
⅓ cup lemon juice
Pinch of salt
1½ tablespoons Kirsch

Combine water, sugar, and raspberries in saucepan. Stir over high heat to dissolve sugar. Bring to a boil for 5 minutes without stirring. Remove from heat and let cool to room temperature. Purée raspberries in blender and strain. Stir lemon juice, salt, and Kirsch into ⅔ cup of raspberry juice. Pour into shallow, 9-inch square, metal pan. Freeze. Yields 4 servings.

Citrus Salsa

1 medium lemon, zest removed
    and minced
1 medium lime
1 medium navel orange
1 medium ruby red grapefruit
1 tangerine
¾ cup light corn syrup
½ cup cane vinegar or white
    distilled vinegar
2 jalapeño peppers, seeds and
    membrane removed, diced
Kosher salt and freshly ground pepper
1 red, 1 yellow, and 1 green bell pepper
½ large red onion, cut in very small dice
½ bunch green onions, thinly sliced
    on bias
2 tablespoons chopped fresh cilantro

Section all citrus fruit by slicing off rinds with sharp paring knife and removing any pieces of bitter white pith. Slice on either side of each dividing membrane to free citrus segments. Squeeze into small bowl juice from membranes that may remain after sectioning. Strain. Add to this any juice that has accumulated underneath citrus segments. Should have about ½ cup. Combine citrus juice, corn syrup, and vinegar in medium saucepan. Cook over medium heat, reducing liquid by three-fourths, or until it coats back of spoon. Remove from heat. This reduced mixture will be base of salsa. Add minced lemon zest and jalapeño, season lightly with salt and pepper to taste, and set aside to cool. Roast bell peppers with olive oil, salt, and pepper at 450° for 25 minutes. Cut into medium dice. Combine reduced citrus liquid, citrus segments, roasted peppers, red onions, and green onions in bowl. Stir in cilantro and season salsa to taste with salt and pepper. This salsa is particularly good over crispy grilled halibut. Place in center of plate and spoon salsa over top. Add fresh cilantro leaves for garnish. Yields about 3 to 4 cups salsa, enough for 6 halibut.

Halibut with Tomato-Tarragon Cream Sauce

½ yellow onion
3 plum tomatoes
2 plus 1 tablespoons olive oil
Kosher salt
Freshly ground pepper
3 sun-dried tomatoes
½ cup boiling water
¼ cup heavy cream
1 tablespoon sherry vinegar
1 tablespoon roughly chopped
   fresh tarragon
4 (7- to 8-ounce) halibut fillets about
   1 inch thick

Cut onion crosswise into ½-inch-thick slices. Core tomatoes and cut crosswise into ½-inch-thick slices. Brush onion and tomato slices with 1 tablespoon olive oil. Season with salt and pepper to taste. Grill onion slices directly over medium heat until soft, turning once, 12 to 14 minutes total. Grill tomato slices directly over medium heat, turning once, until grill marks are clearly visible, 8 to 10 minutes total. Place sun-dried tomatoes in bowl and add boiling water. Allow to soften about 15 minutes. Remove sun-dried tomatoes, reserving liquid. Place sun-dried tomatoes in food processor. Add cream, vinegar, and tarragon. Add enough reserved sun-dried tomato liquid to make sauce smooth. Season with salt and pepper to taste. Transfer to small saucepan and keep warm over low heat. Brush halibut fillets with remaining 2 tablespoons olive oil. Season with salt and pepper to taste. Grill halibut directly over medium heat, turning once, until flesh just begins to flake when tested with a fork, about 8 minutes total. Serve warm with sauce. Yields 4 servings.

Missouri

Captain Wohlt Inn Bed & Breakfast

123 E. Third Street
Hermann, MO 65041
(573) 486-3357
matwilkns@aol.com
www.captainwohltinn.com

In the heart of Historic Hermann—restored 1840s and 1886 buildings listed on National Register of Historic Sites—the Captain Wohlt Inn has five rooms, all with private baths; three of the suites have private baths and private entrances and one has a two-person Jacuzzi. The Captain's Home is wheelchair accessible.

Fresh Blueberry French Toast

12 slices homemade-type white bread,
    cut into 1-inch cubes (no crusts)
1 (8-ounce) package cold cream cheese,
    cut into 1-inch cubes
1 cup fresh blueberries
12 large eggs

⅓ cup syrup or honey
2 cups milk

Sauce:
1 cup sugar
2 tablespoons cornstarch
1 cup water
1 cup fresh blueberries
2 tablespoons butter

To make toast mixture, arrange half of bread cubes in buttered 9 x 13-inch glass baking dish. Scatter cream cheese over bread. Sprinkle blueberries over cream cheese. Arrange remaining bread cubes over blueberries. In large bowl, whisk together eggs, syrup, and milk. Pour egg mixture evenly over bread. Cover. Chill 8 to 10 hours or overnight. When ready to bake, preheat oven to 350°. Cover with foil coated with nonstick spray to keep toast from sticking. Place in middle of oven. Bake 30 minutes. Remove foil. Bake 30 minutes longer, or until puffed and golden.

For sauce, in small saucepan mix together sugar, cornstarch, and water. Cook over moderate high heat, stirring occasionally, for 5 minutes or until thickened. Stir in blueberries. Simmer, occasionally stirring for 10 minutes or until berries burst. Add butter, stirring until it melts. Yields 8 to 12 servings.

Rock Eddy Bluff Farm

10245 Maries Road #511
Dixon, MO 65459
(573) 759-6081 (phone)
(800) 335-5921 (toll free)
welcome@rockeddy.com
www.rockeddy.com

Scenic views, solitude, and relaxing country pleasures are specialties at Rock Eddy Bluff Farm. Tucked into the wooded Ozark hills, the inn features secluded cottages, cabins, and a bed and breakfast, all boasting magnificent views into the Gasconade River Valley. Relax in bucolic surroundings, fish, canoe, nature watch, or explore the hills and hollows. Other enjoyments include, river floating, caving, swimming, antiquing, golfing nearby, and visiting an Amish settlement. Find peaceful days and starry nights at the end of a long country lane.

Salmon Chowder

1 small onion, chopped fine
½ cup diced celery
¼ cup diced green pepper
Vegetable oil
2 to 3 small potatoes, chopped
1 cup water

can red or pink
not drained

2 tablespoons butter
Garlic, minced
Paprika

Sauté onion, celery, and green pepper in oil in soup pot over medium heat until onion is transparent. Add potatoes and water and cook until potatoes are tender. Shred salmon with fork as it is added to pot along with milk and cream. Let simmer 1 hour and add butter and garlic to taste. (Do *not* boil.) Sprinkle with paprika for added color. Yields 4 to 6 servings.

Chicken Lasagna

1 pound skinless, boneless chicken
 breasts, cooked and cubed
2 cups finely chopped onion
3 cups sliced mushrooms
2 (9-ounce) packages hollandaise
 sauce mix
8 cooked lasagna noodles
½ teaspoon salt
⅛ teaspoon pepper
2 (10½-ounce) cans cut asparagus
2 plus ½ cups shredded
 Cheddar cheese
¼ teaspoon basil
¼ teaspoon oregano
1 cup Parmesan cheese

Brown chicken in skillet over medium-high heat. In small skillet sauté onions and mushrooms in butter over medium heat until onions are translucent. Prepare hollandaise sauce mix and lasagna noodles according to package directions. Preheat oven to 350° and coat 13 x 9-inch baking dish with nonstick spray. Spread ½ cup hollandaise sauce in dish. Layer four lasagna noodles, chicken, salt and pepper, mushrooms, and onions. Add remaining sauce, asparagus, 2 cups Cheddar cheese, and remaining noodles. Top with remaining ½ cup Cheddar cheese, basil, and oregano. Bake uncovered 35 to 40 min-

utes, topping with Parmesan cheese after 15 minutes. Yields 8 servings.

Savory Vegetable Soup

1 large onion, chopped
¼ cup (½ stick) butter or margarine
3 medium sweet potatoes, peeled
 and chopped
3 medium zucchini, chopped
1 bunch broccoli, chopped
2 quarts chicken broth
2 medium potatoes, peeled and shredded
2 teaspoons celery seed
2 teaspoons ground cumin
1 teaspoon pepper
2 cups light cream

In large kettle, sauté onions in butter until transparent. Add sweet potatoes, zucchini, and broccoli. Sauté 5 minutes and then stir in broth and simmer for several minutes. Add potatoes, celery seed, cumin, and pepper and cook another 10 minutes until vegetables are tender. Stir in cream and heat through. Yields 12 to 16 servings.

Maine Pancakes

2 large eggs, lightly beaten
½ cup all-purpose flour
½ cup milk
Pinch of salt
Pinch of freshly grated nutmeg
1 tablespoon unsalted butter
Confectioners' sugar

Heat oven to 425°. Whisk eggs, flour, milk, salt, and nutmeg until well combined. Batter may be slightly lumpy. Melt butter in 12-inch, cast-iron skillet over medium heat. Pour batter into pan and transfer to oven. Bake until pancake is golden brown and puffy, 10 to 12 minutes. Transfer to serving plate and dust with confectioners' sugar. Top as desired with jams, jellies, preserves, or syrup. Yields 2 servings.

THE DICKEY HOUSE BED & BREAKFAST, LTD

331 South Clay Street
Marshfield, MO 65706
(417) 468-3000 (phone)
(417) 859-2775 (fax)
info@dickeyhouse.com
www.dickeyhouse.com

The Dickey House is a 1910 Greek Revival mansion on two acres of gardens. Choose from three rooms and four romantic suites at this AAA Four-Diamond inn. The house is located in the Ozark Mountains in Southwest Missouri. Our location offers a wide selection of activities from fishing to the opera. Branson, the entertainment capital of the Midwest, is only forty-five minutes away. Swimming, boating, caving, fishing, and canoeing are here for you. Branson shows and water parks are only a few of the activities available in the area.

Dickey House Fast 'n' Easy Baked Pears

3 tablespoons softened butter
3 tablespoons granulated sugar
 (you may substitute brown sugar)
8 medium-size Bartlett pears with stem,
 firm and not too ripe
Maple syrup
Freshly ground allspice
2 tablespoons brown sugar
¼ cup raisins or dried cranberries
¼ cup heavy cream
Fresh mint and whole strawberries
 for garnish

Rub 9 x 13-inch baking dish with butter. Leave any extra butter in dish. Sprinkle sugar over bottom of pan. Note: butter and sugar will cook together and form syrup, which is used when serving. Peel pears, leaving stems on top intact. Cut small slice off bottom of pears so they sit flat and straight. Place pears in prepared baking dish. Pour about 2 tablespoons maple syrup over each pear. Sprinkle with allspice and brown sugar. Sprinkle raisins around pan. Place uncovered dish in microwave. Microwave on high about 8 to 12 minutes. Use paring knife to test for doneness. Flesh should be firm but easily pierced. Cook for an additional 2 minutes at a time until done. Transfer each pear to serving dish. Spoon some syrup and raisins from baking dish over each pear. Pour 2 tablespoons heavy cream on top of each pear. Garnish with fresh mint sprig and strawberry fan. Yields 8 servings.

Dickey House Breakfast Braid

4 ounces cream cheese
½ cup milk
1 egg, separated
7 eggs
¼ teaspoon salt
Dash of ground black pepper
¼ cup chopped red bell pepper
2 tablespoons sliced green onions with tops
1 teaspoon butter or margarine
2 (8-ounce) packages crescent rolls
¼ pound thinly sliced deli ham (or sliced turkey or cooked breakfast sausage)
Freshly sliced button or Portobello mushrooms
½ cup shredded Cheddar cheese

Preheat oven to 375°. Place cream cheese and milk in 2-quart, microwaveable bowl. Microwave on high 1 minute. Whisk together until smooth. Reserve egg white of separated egg in small cup and add yolk and 7 whole eggs, salt, and black pepper to cream cheese and milk mixture. Whisk to combine. Add bell pepper and green onions. Melt butter in 10-inch nonstick frying pan over medium-low heat. Add egg mixture and cook, stirring occasionally, until eggs are set but still moist. Remove pan from heat.

Unroll 1 package crescent dough but do *not* separate. Arrange longest side of dough across width of 12 x 15-inch cookie sheet. Repeat with remaining package of dough. Roll or pinch dough to seal perforations. On longest sides of pan, cut dough into strips 1½ inches apart, 3 inches deep, leaving 6 inches of dough in center for filling. Arrange ham evenly over middle of dough. Spoon eggs over ham. Top with mushrooms and half of Cheddar cheese. Lay strips of dough across filling to meet in center, twisting each strip one turn. Press ends together. Continue alternating strips to form a braid. Brush dough lightly with beaten egg white. Bake 30 to 35 minutes or until deep golden brown. Cool 5 minutes. Cut into slices and serve. Yields 8 to 10 generous servings.

Dickey House Baked Hash Browns

6 to 8 cups fresh or frozen shredded potatoes
2 cups whole milk
4 eggs
1 cup chopped fresh (or frozen) red pepper
1 teaspoon salt
Dash of black pepper
½ teaspoon granulated garlic
2 cups shredded Cheddar cheese
6 bacon strips, cooked until crisp and crumbled (optional)
¼ cup (½ stick) butter, cut into small pieces (optional)

Place potatoes in large mixing bowl. Add remaining ingredients one at a time, mixing after each. When all is mixed and thoroughly moist, place in buttered 9 x 13-inch baking dish (you may also use a cooking spray), pressing down with spoon to combine mixture. Preheat oven to 375°. Dot top with butter if you choose. Bake about 45 minutes until top is browned and puffed. Yields 10 to 12 generous servings.

Dickey House Stuffed Pancakes

3 cups prepared pancake mix
2 ripe bananas
2 tablespoons vegetable oil
1 tablespoon vanilla extract
1 teaspoon almond or rum extract
½ teaspoon orange zest or dried orange peel
3 cups milk
2 eggs

Cream cheese filling:
8 ounces cream cheese, softened
2 teaspoons vanilla (or other flavoring such as lemon)
4 tablespoons confectioners' sugar
Half-and-half or heavy cream

Fruit sauce:
1 quart strawberries
1 quart blueberries
¼ to ½ cup sugar
½ to 1 cup cranberry juice
Confectioners' sugar
Whipped cream

Measure pancake mix into large bowl. Put all remaining ingredients into blender and blend on high until thoroughly mixed and smooth. Pour blended mixture into pancake mix and mix thoroughly.

For cream cheese filling, place cream cheese in medium mixing bowl and blend with mixer until smooth. Add flavoring and confectioners' sugar. Blend with mixer, adding half-and-half or heavy cream a little at a time until mixture is smooth and spreads easily.

For fruit sauce, wash and prepare all fruit. Place all fruit and sugar in blender or food processor and process until smooth and even, adding cranberry juice as needed for consistency. Transfer mixture to medium saucepan and bring to a boil, stirring constantly. Reduce heat and simmer about 15 minutes, stirring occasionally to prevent burning. Let cool.

Cook pancakes on griddle or fry pan. Remove and spread thin layer of cream cheese filling over entire pancake. Roll up pancake and place on plate. I usually serve two pancakes per person. Sprinkle pancakes with confectioners' sugar. Top with dollop of whipped cream and 2 or 3 tablespoons of fruit sauce. Yields 14 to 18 servings.

Note: The filling and fruit sauce may be made up to one week in advance and kept in an airtight container in refrigerator. Fruit sauce may be divided and frozen for up to 6 months. Thaw 8 to 10 hours, reheat, and stir thoroughly before using.

Down to Earth Lifestyle Bed & Breakfast

12500 NW Crooked Road
Parkville, MO 64152
(816) 891-1018

Down to Earth is a country retreat at a city's doorstep. With eighty-six acres of privacy and peacefulness and an indoor heated swimming pool, guests can relax year-round. Fishing ponds are on the premises for the avid sportsman. Nature, wildlife, and all kinds of animals share the property. The bed and breakfast has a guest entrance. Special order breakfasts are no problem. Located between Kansas City International Airport and Kansas City, which is four miles from Parkville, sightseeing and activities in the area include a national golf course, a NASCAR race track, antiquing, skiing, sports, and arts.

Egg-Stuffed Zucchini

1½ pounds zucchini, about 4 medium
½ cup water
1 cup chopped tomato
2 tablespoons margarine
4 eggs, beaten
½ cup chopped walnuts, toasted
¼ teaspoon salt
¼ teaspoon basil leaves
Dash of pepper
1 cup shredded American
    or sharp Cheddar cheese

Cut zucchini lengthwise in half. Scoop out pulp, leaving ¼-inch shell, and chop pulp. Place shells, cut-side down, in large skillet. Pour in water. Simmer until crisp tender, about 5 minutes. Drain and turn shells cut-sides up. Season with salt. Cook zucchini pulp and tomato in margarine in skillet over medium-heat until tender, about 3 minutes. Stir in eggs, walnuts, salt, basil, and pepper. Cook, lifting thickened portions, to let eggs flow to bottom until set, but still moist, 3 to 5 minutes. Spoon mixture into zucchini shells. Sprinkle with cheese, cover, and cook over low heat just until cheese is melted, about 2 minutes. Yields 8 servings.

Baked Fruit

1 (11-ounce) can mandarin oranges,
    drained
1 (13¼-ounce) can pineapple tidbits,
    drained
1 (28-ounce) can pear halves,
    not drained
1 (33-ounce) can cherry pie filling
1 (33-ounce) can apple pie filling
1 (28-ounce) can sliced peaches, drained
1 (12-ounce) package pitted prunes
Salt
¼ cup (½ stick) butter or margarine
¼ cup orange liqueur or ⅓ cup brandy
    (optional)

Preheat oven to 350°. Combine all fruit. Place in buttered 13 x 9-inch baking pan.

Sprinkle with salt and dot with butter and brandy. Bake 1 hour. Serve with egg dishes and breads for brunch. Yields 12 to 14 servings.

Corned Beef Wheels

Filling:
½ cup chopped onion
1 (4-ounce) can mushroom stems
    and pieces, drained
½ cup sour cream
⅓ cup tomato soup (reserve remainder
    of 10½-ounce can)
1 (12-ounce) can corned beef,
    finely chopped
1 tablespoon Worcestershire sauce
½ teaspoon hot pepper sauce

Biscuit dough:
2 cups sifted all-purpose flour
3 teaspoons baking powder
1 teaspoon dry mustard
½ teaspoon salt
½ cup (1 stick) butter
1 egg
2 teaspoons caraway seeds
½ cup milk

For filling, sauté onions and mushrooms and stir in sour cream, tomato soup, corned beef, Worcestershire, and pepper sauce. Chill.

For dough, mix dry ingredients and cut in butter until particles are fine. Add remaining ingredients. Stir until dough clings together. Roll out on floured wax paper to 14 x 12-inch rectangle. Spread with corned beef filling. Roll up like a jelly roll. Cut into twelve slices. Preheat oven to 425°. Place wheels in greased 12 x 8-inch baking dish. Bake 25 to 30 minutes. Yields 12 servings.

Sausage Sandwich

12 slices buttered bread
1 pound bulk sausage, browned
¼ cup chopped onion
1½ cups grated cheese
6 eggs
½ cup milk

Preheat oven to 325°. Butter flat, 9 x 13-inch, glass casserole or baking dish. Put in 6 slices bread, buttered side down. Put sausage over bread. Sprinkle onion on sausage. Add half of cheese. Cover with remaining 6 slices bread, buttered side up. Combine eggs with milk and cover bread with mixture. Sprinkle remaining cheese on top. Bake 30 minutes or until done. Yields 6 servings.

VICTORIAN VERANDA BED & BREAKFAST

207 E. School St.
Bonne Terre, MO 63628
(573) 358-1134 (phone)
(800) 343-1134 (toll free)
info@victorianveranda.com
www.victorianveranda.com

The Victorian Veranda is an elegant 1880 Victorian mansion with large wraparound veranda and spacious gazebo. Four romantic guest rooms boast private baths and thermal massage tubs for two. Enjoy one of two parlors or large dining room where warm homemade goodies wait for you. The Victorian is located in a small town in the middle of the Parklands. We have eight state parks anywhere from three to thirty miles away. Guests enjoy hiking or canoeing. There are also antique shops and flea markets close by. The world's largest man-made cavern—the Bonne Terre Mine—is just one block away and tours are available.

French Breakfast Muffins

1½ cups plus 2 tablespoons
    all-purpose flour
2 teaspoons baking powder
¼ teaspoon ground nutmeg
¾ cup sugar
¼ teaspoon salt
½ cup milk
⅓ cup melted butter
1 egg, beaten

Topping:
½ cup sugar
1 teaspoon ground cinnamon
½ teaspoon vanilla extract
⅓ cup melted butter

Preheat oven to 400°. Combine flour, baking powder, nutmeg, sugar, and salt in large mixing bowl. Add milk, butter, and egg and mix well. Grease and flour small muffin tins. Fill half full and bake for 20 minutes or until lightly browned. Remove from pan immediately.

For topping, combine sugar, cinnamon, and vanilla. Dip muffins in melted butter and roll in sugar mixture. Serve warm. Yields 24 small muffins.

Chocolate Zucchini Bread

3 eggs
1 cup vegetable oil
2 cups sugar
1 tablespoon vanilla extract
2 cups peeled and shredded zucchini,
    about 1 medium
½ cup cocoa
1 teaspoon salt
1 teaspoon baking soda
1 teaspoon ground cinnamon
¼ teaspoon baking powder
2½ cups all-purpose flour

Preheat oven to 350°. Beat eggs, oil, sugar, and vanilla. Stir in zucchini. Combine dry ingredients, add to zucchini mixture, and mix well. Pour into two greased 8 x 4 x 2-inch loaf pans. Bake for 1 hour or until bread tests done. Yields 2 loaves.

Note: Add ½ cup chocolate chips to the batter to sweeten the deal.

Victorian Veranda Bed & Breakfast

Gooey Butter Cookies

1 (18.25-ounce) box yellow cake mix
½ cup (1 stick) butter or margarine
8 ounces cream cheese
1 egg
1 teaspoon vanilla extract
Confectioners' sugar

Preheat oven to 350°. Blend cake mix, butter, cream cheese, egg, and vanilla in mixer. Form into small balls and roll in confectioners' sugar. Place on cookie sheet and bake 10 minutes. Yields 3 to 4 dozen cookies.

The Southern Hotel

The Southern Hotel

146 South Third Street
Ste. Genevieve, MO 63670
(573) 883-3493 (phone)
(800) 275-1412 (toll free)
mike@southernhotelbb.com
www.southernhotelbb.com

At the Southern Hotel the graciousness of the past is carefully blended with modern comforts to make your stay a very special experience. This graceful Federal building operated as a hotel in 1805 and was known for the finest accommodations between Natchez and St. Louis. It was famous for fine food, busy gambling rooms, and the first pool hall west of the Mississippi. It closed in 1980 and stood empty until 1986, when we became the owners. Now after a total renovation, this magnificent building is the bed and breakfast inn of our dreams. There are eight romantic guest rooms with private baths. Each guest room contains unique collections of country Victorian antiques and delightful "whimsies." The large front parlor has been restored and the spacious dining room and one of the game rooms have also been restored so that guests experience all the charms of the past.

Oranges Grand Marnier

12 medium-size navel oranges
⅓ to ½ cup Grand Marnier or other
orange-flavored liqueur
1½ quarts orange sherbet, softened

Trim bottoms of oranges slightly, so they will sit flat. Cut ½-inch slice from stem end of each orange. Scoop out pulp, removing membrane and seeds. Chop pulp and drain well. Combine drained pulp, Grand Marnier, and sherbet. Stir until well blended. Spoon mixture into orange shells, mounding as much as possible. Place in muffin tins and freeze 8 hours or overnight. Remove 20 to 30 minutes before serving. Garnish with sprig of mint. These will keep in freezer up to one month. After initial freezing, remove from muffin tins and pack in cardboard box in one layer. Cover tightly with plastic wrap and then foil. Yields 12 servings.

Green Herb Kookoo

1 cup chopped leeks or scallions,
including some green stems
2 lettuce leaves, chopped
½ cup chopped dill weed
1 cup chopped parsley
¼ cup chopped coriander
or 1 cup chopped fresh spinach
1 plus 1 tablespoon butter
8 eggs
½ teaspoon baking soda
½ teaspoon turmeric or saffron
⅛ teaspoon ground cinnamon
½ teaspoon salt
¼ teaspoon pepper
3 tablespoons chopped walnuts
for garnish
3 tablespoons currants for garnish
Plain yogurt for garnish

Preheat oven to 350°. Sauté leeks, lettuce, dill weed, parsley, and coriander for 5 minutes in 1 tablespoon butter, stirring frequently. Beat eggs well and add baking soda, turmeric, cinnamon, salt, and pepper. Melt remaining 1 tablespoon butter in 8 x 11-inch, 2-quart glass baking dish. Combine egg mixture with sautéed herbs and pour into prepared pan. Bake 45 to 60 minutes until Kookoo is crisp on bottom and light brown on top. Garnish with walnuts, currants, and dollop of yogurt. Yields 6 servings.

Ginger Persimmon Muffins

1¼ cups all-purpose flour
¾ teaspoon baking soda
¾ teaspoon ginger
¾ teaspoon ground cinnamon
¼ teaspoon ground nutmeg
¼ teaspoon ground cloves
½ cup (1 stick) butter
½ cup sugar
⅓ cup molasses
1 egg
¼ cup hot, brewed coffee
2 tablespoons sour cream
1½ teaspoons grated orange zest
½ cup fresh persimmon purée

Sift together flour, baking soda, ginger, cinnamon, nutmeg, and cloves. With an electric mixer, cream together butter and sugar until light and fluffy. Add molasses and egg and continue beating until smooth. Add dry ingredients and mix just until combined. Fold in coffee, sour cream, and orange zest. Fold in purée. Preheat oven to 375°. Divide batter equally in nonstick-sprayed muffin tins. Bake 25 to 30 minutes. Cool 5 minutes. Remove from pans to wire rack to cool. Yields 12 muffins.

Cold Cherry Soup

4 cups pitted sour cherries or an equal amount canned, drained
1 cup sugar
1 cinnamon stick
3 cups plus 2 tablespoons cold water
1 tablespoon arrowroot
¼ cup chilled heavy cream
¾ cup chilled red wine

In heavy saucepan, simmer cherries, sugar, and cinnamon stick in 3 cups water 35 to 40 minutes if fresh, or 10 minutes if canned. Mix arrowroot and remaining 2 tablespoons water to form paste. Off heat, beat paste into soup. Return to heat and stir until thickened. Pour into shallow pan and chill overnight. Before serving, stir in cream and wine. Yields 8 servings.

Boursin Cheese

2 (8-ounce) packages cream cheese, room temperature
1 package cheese-garlic salad dressing
½ cup (1 stick) sweet butter, room temperature
4 tablespoons grated Parmesan cheese

Combine all ingredients in food processor fitted with steel blade. Process until completely smooth. Form into balls or pack into molds. Chill and age at least 24 hours before serving. Freezes beautifully. Yields about 2½ cups.

THE BRANSON HOTEL BED & BREAKFAST INN

214 West Main Street
Branson, MO 65616
(417) 335-6104 (phone)
(417) 339-3224 (fax)
(800) 933-0651 (toll free)
info@bransonhotelbb.com
www.bransonhotelbb.com

Located in historic downtown Branson, this elegant little hotel, built in 1903, offers seven distinct guest rooms, each with private baths. Renovated in 1992, each room is uniquely decorated with antiques and antique reproductions. In the morning, guests gather around the harvest table in the glass-enclosed breakfast room to enjoy a full gourmet breakfast. Branson has a wide range of activities, including live theater, Silver Dollar City Theme Park, water park, shopping at three outlet malls, antique and craft shopping, go-carts, miniature golf, scenic railway, and much more.

Bacon Mushroom Quiche

1 (9-inch) unbaked piecrust
½ cup grated Cheddar cheese
⅓ cup grated mozzarella cheese
½ cup sliced mushrooms
6 to 8 bacon slices, fried and crumbled
8 eggs
1 (10¾-ounce) can cream of onion soup
½ cup milk

Preheat oven to 350°. Spray 2-quart casserole dish with vegetable oil. Gently press piecrust into dish. Layer grated cheeses (reserving a small amount for topping), sliced mushrooms, and crumbled bacon on piecrust. In separate bowl beat eggs, onion soup, and milk until well blended. Pour egg mixture on top of cheese/bacon layer. Top with cheese. Bake 50 to 60 minutes or until lightly browned. A sharp knife will come out clean when done. Slice quiche and serve with bacon and fresh fruit. Yields 6 servings.

The Inn at Harbour Ridge Bed & Breakfast

6334 Red Barn Road
P.O. Box 496
Osage Beach, MO 65065
(573) 302-0411 (phone)
(877) 744-6020 (toll free)
info@harbourridgeinn.com
www.harbourridgeinn.com

The Inn at Harbour Ridge is a country nautical design located on Lake of the Ozarks. The inn offers four themed guest rooms in the bed and breakfast and one guest cottage in the Big Red Barn; all have private baths, TV/VCRs, and private decks or patios. Enjoy fireplaces, twosome tubbies and the "innside" hot tub in its own private, decorated room. Guests can enjoy quiet surroundings and a peaceful cove yet are close to an array of exciting activities. Fourteen golf courses, 110 outlet mall stores, thirteen hundred miles of shoreline, and award-winning customer service at The Inn at Harbour Ridge are waiting for you.

Macintosh Muffins

1¼ cups applesauce
2 cups sugar
2 cups all-purpose flour
1 cup whole wheat flour
3 eggs
2 teaspoons vanilla extract
1 teaspoon baking soda
1 teaspoon ground cinnamon
1 teaspoon salt
2 cups chopped apples
    (Macintosh or Granny Smith)
1 cup chopped walnuts
1 cup coconut
Fresh chopped mint (optional)
Brown sugar and cinnamon mix or
    granulated sugar and cinnamon mix

Preheat oven to 350°. In large bowl mix all muffin ingredients together until blended. Fill sprayed muffin tins about two-thirds full. Sprinkle with cinnamon sugar mixture. Bake for about 25 minutes or until golden brown. These muffins don't "crown" very much and are very dense. Can be made into mini-muffins. Bake 18 to 20 minutes. Yields 12 large or 24 mini-muffins.

Reagan's Queen Anne

313 North Fifth Street
Hannibal, MO 63401
(573) 221-0774 (phone)
(888) 221-1251 (toll free)
info@reagansqueenanne.com
www.reagansqueenanne.com

Enjoy a bit of the privileged lifestyle of a nineteenth century lumber baron at the Inn at Reagan's Queen Anne Bed & Breakfast in Hannibal, Missouri. Step inside this graceful Painted Lady and find magnificently carved woodwork, original gas and electric fixtures, fireplace mantles, and stained glass windows. Or relax outside on the wraparound verandah and let your mind drift back to a simpler time. Experience the sights and sounds of this famous Mississippi River town, as Mark Twain did one hundred years before. Imagine what life was like for young Sammy Clemens, who surely frequented this Victorian neighborhood, and the street which was designated as Millionaires Row.

Norm's Beefy Quiche

½ pound ground chuck
½ cup chopped scallions,
    tips included
1 teaspoon salt-free seasoning
½ teaspoon oregano
½ teaspoon garlic powder
3 large eggs
1 cup heavy whipping cream
½ cup mayonnaise
1 cup finely shredded Cheddar cheese
1 cup finely shredded Swiss cheese
1 unbaked 9-inch pastry shell

In skillet over medium-high heat cook ground chuck until browned and add scallions. Cook until scallions are tender and drain. Stir in seasoning, oregano, and garlic powder. Make sure to thaw pastry shell if frozen. Preheat oven to 350°. In mixing bowl beat eggs, whipping cream, and mayonnaise. Fold in cheeses. Pour into pastry shell. Bake uncovered 35 to 40 minutes or until a knife inserted near center comes out clean. Let stand six minutes before cutting. Yields 5 servings.

The Queen's French Toast Marmalade

8 large eggs
⅔ cup milk
1⅓ cups orange juice
1 plus ½ cup sugar
2 teaspoons vanilla extract
¼ teaspoon ground nutmeg
3 tablespoons butter
16 (1-inch-thick) slices French bread
1 cup (2 sticks) unsalted butter
⅔ cup frozen orange juice concentrate
Confectioners' sugar for topping
Nutmeg for topping

Beat eggs, milk, orange juice, ½ cup sugar, vanilla, and nutmeg until combined. Melt 3 tablespoons butter in two 9 x 13 x 1-inch pans. Dip each bread slice into egg mixture, being careful not to soak up too much liquid, and arrange bread in one layer in pans. Cover and refrigerate for 2 to 24 hours.

In saucepan make orange syrup by combining unsalted butter, remaining 1 cup sugar, and concentrate. Heat, stirring frequently. Do *not* boil. Cool 10 minutes and beat to thicken. Heat syrup briefly in microwave to warm before serving, watching so it does not boil. (Optional: Stir in ½ cup chopped pecans.)

When ready to serve, preheat oven to 350°. Bake toast for 20 minutes. Bottom should be golden brown. Flip toast onto plate with browned side up and sprinkle with confectioners' sugar and pinch of nutmeg. Garnish plate with orange peel and fresh blueberries and serve with orange syrup. Yields 8 servings.

Butter Pecan Muffins

2 cups plus 3 tablespoons
    all-purpose flour
½ teaspoon salt
½ cup brown sugar
2 teaspoons baking powder
⅔ cup whole milk or half-and-half
½ cup melted unsalted butter
½ cup butter pecan syrup
¼ cup sour cream
1 large egg
½ teaspoon vanilla extract
3 tablespoons granulated sugar
3 tablespoons chopped pecans
½ teaspoon ground cinnamon
2 tablespoons cold butter

Mix 2 cups flour, salt, brown sugar, and baking powder in medium bowl. In another bowl combine milk, melted butter (cooled), syrup, sour cream, egg, and vanilla. Stir into dry ingredients just until moistened. Do *not* overmix. For topping combine remaining 3 tablespoons flour, granulated sugar, cinnamon, and nuts and cut in butter until crumbly. Preheat oven to 375°. Grease 6-cup muffin tin with pan spray. Spoon mixture into tin, distributing evenly and filling cups approximately two-thirds full. Sprinkle topping on each cup. Bake 16 to 20 minutes until well risen and golden brown. Allow to cool 5 minutes before removing from tin. Yields 6 large muffins.

VIRGINIA ROSE BED & BREAKFAST

317 East Glenwood Street
Springfield, MO 65807
(417) 883-0693 (phone)
(800) 345-1412 (toll free)
vrosebb@sisna.com
bbonline.com/mo/virginiarose

The Virginia Rose is nestled on a tree-covered acre on a quiet street only minutes from Bass Pro Shop, Missouri one attraction, and thirty-five Branson's shows and lakes. The one-hundred-year-old farmhouse features four cozy rooms with quilts on queen-size beds and private baths. Guests are served a full breakfast, family style, on Virginia Rose china.

Brunch Fruit Cup

1 (3-ounce) package lemon gelatin
2 cups boiling water
1 (16-ounce) can pineapple chunks
1 (8-ounce) can mandarin oranges
1 (6-ounce) can frozen orange
    juice, thawed
Grapes
Bananas

Dissolve lemon gelatin in water. Add pineapple with juice, mandarin oranges with juice, thawed orange juice, and grapes. Stir well, cover, and keep in refrigerator 8 to 10 hours or overnight. Just before serving, add sliced banana (may add other fruits in season). Yields 6 servings.

Virginia Rose Bed & Breakfast

Light Breakfast Burritos

½ pound ground sausage
1 (16-ounce) package hash browns
1 cup egg substitute (equals 4 eggs)
4 large flour tortillas
1 cup Cheddar cheese
1 large tomato, cut up
Salsa

Cook sausage in large skillet over medium-high heat, breaking up into small pieces. Add hash browns and continue cooking until brown. Drain fat, if necessary. Scramble egg substitute. Warm tortillas in microwave 15 seconds. Lay each tortilla on plate and divide sausage mixture, eggs, cheese, and chopped tomato among them. Top each tortilla with 1 tablespoon salsa and fold, securing with toothpick. Decorate plate with sliced kiwi and serve with small bowl of extra salsa. Yields 4 servings.

Red Bud Cove Bed & Breakfast Suites

162 Lakewood Drive
Branson, MO 65672
(417) 334-7144 (phone)
(417) 337-8823 (fax)
(800) 677-5525 (toll free)
redbudcove@aol.com
www.redbudcove.com

Red Bud Cove Bed & Breakfast offers the peaceful serenity of scenic Table Rock Lake just minutes from Branson. At Red Bud Cove you will experience luxury from the minute you enter the main house with the great room. And it continues as you step into your spacious, private suite. Enjoy the morning with a breathtaking view of the lake. After breakfast choose from the many Branson area attractions or spend the day at Red Bud Cove enjoying the abundant wildlife and magnificent flower gardens or just relaxing on a glider at the lake's edge watching the boats go by.

Cheesecake Crêpes with Fruit Sauce

Batter:
1 cup all-purpose flour
2 eggs
½ cup milk
½ cup water
¼ teaspoon salt
2 tablespoons melted butter
    or margarine

Filling:
1 beaten egg
1 cup dry cottage cheese
    (drain regular cottage cheese)
1 (8-ounce) package cream cheese,
    softened
2 tablespoons sugar
1 teaspoon vanilla extract

Fruit sauce:
1 (15¼-ounce) can pineapple tidbits
Orange juice
¼ cup sugar
1½ cups sliced strawberries or whole
    raspberries or cherry pie filling

Place batter ingredients in blender. Blend 30 seconds, stop, and stir down sides. Blend 30 to 60 seconds until smooth. Make crêpes with electric crêpe maker or small crêpe pan. You can also purchase ready-made crêpes.

Preheat oven to 350°. Beat all filling ingredients. Spoon 1 rounded tablespoon in center of crêpe. Fold envelope style. Place filled crêpes in 9 x 13-inch, slightly greased, baking dish. Cover with foil and bake 20 minutes. Can make/fill day before and refrigerate. Bake 10 minutes instead of 20 minutes.

For topping, drain pineapple tidbits, reserving juice. Add orange juice to pineapple juice to make 1¼ cups liquid. In medium saucepan over low heat combine sugar and juices and cook 2 minutes. Gently stir in sliced strawberries and pineapple tidbits and cook 2 minutes more. Serve over the crêpes. Yields 7 to 8 servings.

Orange Yogurt Muffins

Zest of 3 large oranges
¼ plus ¼ cup sugar
2 tablespoons water
5 tablespoons unsalted butter
2 cups all-purpose flour
1¼ teaspoons baking powder
1 teaspoon baking soda
½ teaspoon plus pinch of salt
2 eggs
¾ cup plain yogurt
¾ cup milk
1 cup sifted confectioners' sugar
2 tablespoons orange juice

Grease two 6-cup muffin tins. Finely grate zest, using only bright orange portion of peel, to make ¼ cup plus 2 teaspoons. Combine ¼ cup zest, ¼ cup sugar, and water in small saucepan. Stir over medium heat for 2 minutes until sugar is dissolved. Add butter and stir until melted, about 1 minute more. Preheat oven to 375°. In medium bowl stir together flour, baking powder, baking soda, ½ teaspoon salt, and remaining ¼ cup sugar. In larger bowl, whisk together eggs, yogurt, milk, and reserved orange mixture until smooth. Add dry ingredients and stir until blended. Spoon into prepared tins three-fourths full. Bake for 15 to 20 minutes. Cool in tins for 3 minutes and remove. If glazing, put glaze on muffins while slightly warm. Combine confectioners' sugar, orange juice, 2 teaspoons of remaining orange zest, and pinch of salt until ingredients are smooth. If too stiff, add few more drops of juice. Yields 12 muffins.

Stuffed Ham Rolls with Cheese Sauce

Ham rolls:
2 (10-ounce) packages frozen, chopped
    spinach
2 cups cornbread stuffing
2 cups sour cream
24 thin slices deli ham

Cheese sauce:
½ cup (1 stick) butter
½ cup flour
4 cups milk
1 to 2 cups grated Cheddar cheese
Parmesan cheese
Paprika

Cook spinach until thawed and drain. Combine spinach, stuffing, and sour cream. Spread spoonful on each ham slice. Roll up and place seam-side down in individual au gratin dishes or large casserole dish. Preheat oven to 350°.

For cheese sauce, melt butter in saucepan over low heat, add flour, and blend well. Add milk, stirring until thick. Add cheese and remove from heat. Stir until cheese is melted. Pour over ham rolls, being sure to cover all exposed ham to avoid crisping during baking. Sprinkle with Parmesan cheese and paprika and bake for 20 minutes covered with foil. Uncover 10 minutes before done. Yields 12 to 24 servings.

Hash-Brown Potato Bake

32 ounces hash browns, thawed
½ plus ¼ cup melted butter
1 (10¾-ounce) can cream of chicken soup
1 cup sour cream
1 cup shredded Cheddar cheese
2 cups crushed cornflakes

Preheat oven to 350°. Combine hash browns, ½ cup melted butter, soup, sour cream, and cheese. Press into two 9 x 13-inch casserole dishes. Combine cornflakes and remaining ¼ cup melted butter and sprinkle on top of casserole. Bake 50 minutes. Ingredients can be mixed ahead and refrigerated, but do *not* add topping until ready to bake. Yields 12 servings.

THE PORCH SWING INN

702 East Street
Parkville, MO 64152
(816) 587-6282
theporchswinginn@kc.rr.com
www.theporchswinginn.com

The Porch Swing Inn is located just blocks from the restaurants and shops of historic downtown Parkville, Missouri. Our four guest rooms are equipped with private bathroom, queen-size bed, TV, telephone, and computer hookup. A full breakfast is served in the morning. The inn is located within walking distance of shops, restaurants, day spa, walking trails, mini golf, and much more. Within a short drive are downtown Kansas City, the Plaza, area golf courses, casinos and the NASCAR track.

Lemon Scones

2 cups all-purpose flour
¼ cup sugar
2 teaspoons baking powder
½ teaspoon baking soda
¼ teaspoon salt
3 tablespoons cold margarine
1 medium lemon, zest and juice
1 (8-ounce) carton vanilla yogurt

Preheat over to 400°. Combine flour, sugar, baking powder, soda, and salt in large bowl. Cut in margarine with pastry blender until mixture resembles coarse meal. Mix in lemon zest. Add yogurt and lemon juice, stirring just until dough is moist and sticks together. Form small blobs with greased hands (spray oil works well) and place on greased cookie sheet. Bake 13 minutes or until golden brown. Serve warm. Yields 1 dozen scones.

Montana

GIBSON MANSION BED & BREAKFAST

Missoula, MT
(406) 251-1345 (phone)
(866) 251-1345 (toll free)
info@gibsonmansion.com
www.gibsonmansion.com

Located in Missoula, Montana, the Gibson Mansion is your bed and breakfast destination. Built in 1903, the Gibson Mansion combines Victorian elegance of the past with the modern conveniences of today to make your stay comfortable and enjoyable. Exquisite original antique leaded stained-glass windows and hardwood floors welcome you upon entry. The grand oak staircase invites guests to their private quarters. There are four guest rooms furnished with the finest quality iron beds and down comforters. Each room has hardwood floors with mosaic bathroom tile floors. Gibson Mansion is conveniently located just minutes away from the University of Montana, historic museums, live theater, center-city shopping, and the historical downtown area. Activities such as nature trails, golfing, and skiing are just a few of the many activities out our front door.

❧   ❧   ❧

Dutch Babies

2 teaspoons butter
2 eggs
½ cup all-purpose flour
½ cup milk
¼ teaspoon salt
6 tablespoons Montana Huckleberry
    pie filling
Whipped cream
Confectioners' sugar

Place two ramekins with 1 teaspoon butter in each into oven as it preheats. Blend eggs, flour, milk, and salt. When ramekins are hot and oven is to 425°, swirl ramekins to coat bottoms with butter. Divide batter evenly between ramekins. Bake approximately 20 minutes, or until batter has puffed and is golden brown. Remove from oven and set ramekins on serving plate. Fill each with 3 tablespoons warm pie filling and top with whipped cream (three little puffs). Dust with confectioners' sugar. Serve Dutch Babies with ham. Yields 2 servings.

GOOD MEDICINE LODGE

5337 Wisconsin Ave.
Whitefish, MT 59937
(406) 862-5489 (fax)
(800) 860-5488 (toll free)
info@goodmedicinelodge.com
www.goodmedicinelodge.com

Built in 1979 and expanded in 1993 and 2000, this sixty-five-hundred-square-foot cedar lodge is decorated in a Montana motif with fabrics influenced by Native American textiles. Individually appointed accommodations, some with balconies and all with air conditioning, are especially designed with our guests' comfort in mind. The rooms feature Montana Wood Designs custom-made lodgepole beds and are characterized by mountain or garden views.

Good Medicine Lodge

Good Medicine Granola

4½ cups old-fashioned oats
2 cups shredded coconut
1 cup brown sugar
¾ cup chopped pecans

¾ cup sliced almonds
¼ cup plus 2 tablespoons
    vegetable oil
¼ cup plus 2 tablespoons honey
½ cup dark raisins
½ cup dried cranberries
½ cup dried blueberries and cherries

Preheat oven to 350°. Mix first oats, coconut, sugar, pecans, and almonds. Heat oil and honey in small, heavy saucepan over medium heat until warm. Pour over oat mixture and stir to coat. Transfer to cookie sheet, spreading evenly. Bake until coconut and nuts are golden, stirring occasionally, about 20 minutes. Cool. Add raisins and dried fruit. Stir to combine. Store in airtight container at room temperature. Can be prepared 2 weeks ahead. Yields 4 servings.

Good Medicine Lodge Montana-Size Cookies

1 cup (2 sticks) butter
¾ cup dark brown sugar
¾ cup granulated sugar
2 eggs
1 teaspoon vanilla extract
1 teaspoon baking powder
1 teaspoon baking soda
½ teaspoon salt
2 cups all-purpose flour
2½ cups oats
1 cup chopped walnuts
1 cup chocolate chips

Preheat oven to 350°. Cream butter and sugars. Beat in eggs and vanilla until very light and fluffy. Combine baking powder, baking soda, salt, and flour. Mix dry ingredients with butter mixture until blended. Mix in oats, walnuts, and chocolate chips. Use ¼ cup batter per cookie. Bake on greased cookie sheet for 16 minutes. (For oatmeal raisin cookies, substitute raisins for chocolate chips and add 1 teaspoon cinnamon.) Yields 18 cookies.

Asparagus Eggs

½ cup grated Swiss cheese
4 tablespoons butter
1 cup cream
½ teaspoon salt
Dash of pepper
1½ teaspoons dry mustard
10 eggs, slightly beaten
10 asparagus spears, cut in
    1-inch pieces

Preheat oven to 325°. Coat 9 x 12 inch baking dish with nonstick spray. Sprinkle cheese in bottom of dish. Dot with butter. Mix cream with salt, pepper, and mustard. Pour half of mixture over cheese. Add eggs and then remaining cream mixture. Arrange asparagus pieces on top. Bake 40 minutes. Yields 6 servings.

COUGAR RANCH BED & BREAKFAST

P.O. Box 9431
Missoula, MT 59807
(406) 726-3745 (phone)
(406) 726-3747 (fax)
cougarranch@blackfoot.net
www.bbonline.com/mt/cougar/

Peace and quiet are yours while surrounded by mountains near and far in all directions, along with brook trout, an Indian reservation, and national forest lands outside your door. At the Cougar Ranch you will stay in a five-thousand-square-foot custom home with floor-to-ceiling windows, located in the middle of 160 acres of trees and pastures. You are only half a mile off the highway and ten miles from the Missoula airport.

Charlotte's Homemade Mincemeat

2 pounds lean stew meat (venison)
1½ cups suet or shortening
4 cups peeled, cored, and chopped apples
2½ cups raisins
1½ cups chopped currants
2½ cups sugar
3 cups pitted pie cherries
1½ pints strong cold coffee
1 pint cider
2 teaspoons ground cinnamon
1 teaspoon ground nutmeg
6 teaspoons salt
½ teaspoon cloves
1 tablespoon mace
1 tablespoon allspice

Cook meat in low oven (250°) or slow cooker (6 to 7 hours on low) until tender. In large pan, add all ingredients except meat and simmer 30 minutes. Add meat and stir well. Yields 4 quarts, about 8 servings.

GASTHAUS WENDLINGEN BED & BREAKFAST

700 Monegan Road
Whitefish, MT 59937
(406) 862-4886 (phone/fax)
(800) 811-8002 (toll free)
gasthaus@aboutmontana.net

A place for all seasons and sports, the Gasthaus Wendlinger reflects western German hospitality. Located on eight private acres on Haskill Creek, there is plenty of room to relax. All bedrooms have ski trail, water, and mountain views. A magnificent breakfast, many from family recipes, greets you every morning. In the afternoon appetizers are served, and in the evening you can relax in front of the beautiful river-rock fireplace or on the front porch or creek-side patio.

German Crumb Cake

1 cup sugar
Pinch of salt
2 cups flour
2 teaspoons baking powder
¼ pound (1 stick) butter or margarine
1 teaspoon vanilla extract
2 eggs
½ to ¾ cup milk

Crumb topping:
1 cup sugar
2 to 2½ cups all-purpose flour
½ pound (2 sticks) butter (or a little less)

Preheat oven to 350°. Mix together sugar, salt, flour, baking powder, butter, vanilla, and eggs. Add milk until batter is desired consistency. (It should not be too thin.) Spread dough into prepared 13 x 9-inch baking dish.

For crumb topping, mix together the sugar and flour. Cut the butter into the flour mixture. Knead until firm but moist consistency. Sprinkle large crumbs over the entire top of dough in baking dish. Bake 30 to 35 minutes, or until light brown. Yields 4 to 6 servings.

BEAR CREEK LODGE

1184 Bear Creek Trail
Victor, MT 59875
(406) 642-3750
info@bear-creek-lodge.com
www.bear-creek-lodge.com

Bear Creek Lodge is located adjacent to the Selway-Bitterroot Wilderness in Montana's Bitterroot Valley. It is a small, intimate log lodge offering a civilized approach to a wilderness experience. Its guests all share a love of the spectacular outdoors that makes western Montana such a special place to visit. The Lewis and Clark Trail is only six miles east and the Big Hole Battlefield is an hour south. The love of nature, luxury accommodations, and fine dining are the reasons our guests return year after year.

Pan-Seared Filet Mignon with Cabernet Sauce

Cabernet sauce:
½ cup chopped shallots
¼ cup chopped garlic
1 plus 1 teaspoon butter
1 to 2 cups cabernet sauvignon
1 to 2 cups beef broth
1 teaspoon all-purpose flour

Mushrooms:
½ teaspoon olive oil
½ cup chopped fresh rosemary
2 pounds assorted wild mushrooms, halved
½ cup red wine
½ cup white wine

4 (8-ounce) filet mignon steaks
Fresh ground pepper

For the sauce, sweat shallots and garlic in 1 teaspoon butter over low heat about 10 minutes. Add red wine and reduce by half. Add beef broth and simmer 20 minutes. (The longer it simmers, the more flavorful it will become.) Make a roux by melting remaining teaspoon butter over medium heat. Add flour and cook until deep golden brown. Thicken sauce with roux. Strain sauce through a fine mesh bowl-shaped sieve and discard garlic and shallots. Keep sauce warm until ready to serve.

For mushrooms, heat olive oil over medium-high heat and cook chopped rosemary 5 to 10 minutes, stirring occasionally. (Rosemary will be bitter if not cooked long enough.) Add mushrooms and toss well. Add red wine and reduce until liquid is gone. Add white wine and reduce again until liquid is gone.

For the filets, slice each filet into 4-ounce medallions, being sure to slice against the grain. Using a pepper mill on coarse setting, pepper each side of the medallions. Sear steaks in hot olive oil 2 to 3 minutes on each side for medium-rare. Place filets on a bed of wild mushrooms and top with cabernet sauce. Garnish with rosemary sprigs. Yields 4 servings.

SILVER FOREST INN

15325 Bridger Canyon Road
Bozeman, MT 59715
(406) 586-1882 (phone)
(406) 582-0492 (fax)
(877) 394-9357 (toll free)
info@silverforestinn.com
www.silverforestinn.com

The Silver Forest Inn is located fifteen miles from Bozeman, Montana, in the Bridger Canyon. We have six guest rooms and five bathrooms. There is a great room and sunroom and outside deck with a hot tub for all guests to enjoy. A gourmet breakfast is served each morning. The inn is very close to skiing, hiking trails, golf, fly-fishing, horseback riding, and the Gallatin National Forest.

Mexican Quiche

5 eggs
2 tablespoons vegetable oil
¼ cup all-purpose flour
½ teaspoon baking powder
8 ounces cottage cheese
2 cups shredded Monterey Jack cheese
½ cup chopped chiles
Sour cream and salsa

Preheat oven to 350°. Combine eggs, oil, flour, and baking powder and mix well. Stir in cheeses and chiles and mix well. Coat individual ramekins with nonstick spray and fill with batter. Bake 20 minutes or until set and golden brown. Serve with sour cream and salsa on side. Yields 4 servings.

Baked Eggs With Three Cheeses

7 eggs
1 cup milk
2 teaspoons sugar
28 ounces shredded Monterey
    Jack cheese
4 ounces cream cheese, cubed
28 ounces small curd cottage cheese
⅔ cup melted butter
½ cup all-purpose flour
1 teaspoon baking powder

Preheat oven to 350°. Beat together eggs, milk, and sugar. Add cheeses and melted butter and mix well. Mix in flour and baking powder, then pour into 3-quart baking dish coated with nonstick spray. Bake 45 to 50 minutes or until knife comes out clean. Yields 10 to 12 servings.

Note: May be prepared in advance and refrigerated covered overnight. If baked directly from refrigerator, cook uncovered for 60 minutes.

Key Lime Pie

Crust:
1¼ cups graham cracker crumbs
4 tablespoons melted butter
1 to 2 tablespoons brown sugar

Filling:
4 limes
1 (14-ounce) can sweetened
    condensed milk
1 cup whipping cream

For crust, preheat oven to 375°. Mix cracker crumbs, butter, and sugar. Pour into 9-inch pie plate. Bake 10 minutes and let cool.

For filling, grate 1 tablespoon lime peel and squeeze ½ cup lime juice. In large bowl mix lime juice, peel, and sweetened condensed milk until blended. Beat cream until stiff peaks form. Gently fold into lime mixture one third at a time. Pour filling into cool crust. Freeze at least 2 to 3 hours or until firm. Serve garnished with whipped cream and a lime slice on top. Yields 6 servings.

Atwood House Bed & Breakfast

740 S. 17th Street
Lincoln, NE 68508
(402) 438-4567 (phone)
(402) 477-8314 (fax)
larry@atwoodhouse.com
www.atwoodhouse.com

Experience the elegance of a suite in this more than seventy-five-hundred-square-foot, 1894 Neoclassical Georgian Revival mansion. Fireplaces, whirlpools, private sitting areas, fresh-cut flowers, and Victorian furnishing are just a few of the extraordinary amenities of the Atwood. Activities in the surrounding area include downtown Lincoln; the Lied Center; Pershing auditorium; historic Haymarket district; the University of Nebraska; some of Lincoln's most elegant dining; and the Nebraska State Capitol.

Poached Pear

1 large Bosc pear
4 tablespoons butter
Brown sugar
Raspberry syrup
3 fresh raspberries

Peel pear with potato peeler. Make sure bottom is flat so pear will sit upright. Score single line down length of pear so that it can be stacked after cooking. Slice pear into five or six ½-inch sections perpendicular to height of pear. Core each "ring." Melt butter in large flat-bottom pan over medium-low to medium heat. Place pear rings in butter, being sure order of stacking is maintained to restack pear rings easily. Cook about 20 minutes, turning periodically. (Do *not* get pan too hot or butter will burn.) Sprinkle approximately ⅓ cup brown sugar over rings. Allow sugar to "melt" with butter and cook on medium-low heat for approximately 5 to 8 minutes. Starting with bottom ring, restack, aligning score mark on each ring. Place on plate with bed of raspberry syrup and three fresh raspberries spaced around pear. Spoon small amount of brown sugar "sauce" over pear and serve immediately. Yields 1 serving.

Note: If brown sugar sauce becomes hard, heat was too high.

Atwood House Egg Mountain

2 eggs
2 slices bread

Preheat oven to 350°. Separate eggs, being careful not to break yolks. Beat whites until stiff peaks form. Cut a 3-inch circle from each slice of bread, removing any crust and discarding. On each piece of bread shape egg white into majestic mound about 3 inches high. Place on cookie sheet. Hollow out place for yolk and carefully place yolk into hole. Cook about 14 minutes or until egg whites turn a golden brown. Can be served plain or with cream cheese or hollandaise sauce. Yields 1 serving.

Atwood Dutch Eggs

Cheese sauce:
2 tablespoons butter
¼ cup all-purpose flour
1½ cups milk
5 to 6 ounces processed cheese, cubed
Salt and pepper

Pancake:
1 plus 1 egg
¼ cup milk
¼ cup all-purpose flour
⅛ teaspoon salt
1 tablespoon butter
Salt and pepper
2 slices bacon, cooked and cut in
    small pieces

For sauce, in top pan of double boiler melt butter. When to a boil, add flour and immediately begin stirring with whip. Add milk, continuing to stir and bring to boil again. When sauce thickens and boils, add cheese. Stir until cheese melts. Turn heat to low to keep sauce from burning. Season to taste with salt and pepper.

Preheat oven to 475°. For pancake, in blender mix 1 egg (other egg to be cooked separately), milk, flour, and salt. Coat six-inch soufflé dish with nonstick spray, place butter in dish, and place in oven 3 to 4 minutes, until butter is completely melted. Pour in batter. Cook 2 minutes. After 2 minutes, put remaining egg in small custard dish that has been sprayed and sprinkle with salt and pepper. Cook 10 additional minutes along with pancake. As pancake cooks it will rise, forming pocket in center. Remove from soufflé dish top-side up. Put bacon into "pocket," keeping small amount for garnish. Insert egg in pocket and top with cheese sauce. Garnish with remaining bacon. Serve immediately. Yields 1 serving.

Sugared Rhubarb Muffins

2 cups all-purpose flour
1 plus ¼ cup sugar
2 teaspoons baking powder
½ teaspoon salt
1 egg
1 cup milk
⅓ cup canola oil
1 cup chopped fresh or frozen rhubarb

Preheat oven to 375°. Coat muffin pan with nonstick spray. In large mixing bowl, combine flour, 1 cup sugar, baking powder, and salt. In separate bowl, beat egg, milk, and oil. Add to dry mixture and stir just until moistened. Fold in rhubarb. Spoon/pour batter into greased muffin pan two-thirds to three-fourths full. Sprinkle with remaining ¼ cup sugar. Bake 28 minutes, or until slightly golden and toothpick inserted in middle comes out clean. Let muffins stand on cooling rack for about 3 minutes before removing from pans. Yields 10 to 12 muffins.

UPPER ROOM BED & BREAKFAST

409 North Wilson Street
Ainsworth, NE 60210
(402) 387-0107
upperroom@bloomnet.com
www.bbhost.com/UpperRoom

Return to the charm and romance of the Victorian Era in this historic 1910 landmark. Located in the Nebraska outback where the sand hills meet the scenic Niobrara River, rated top ten in the nation for tubing and canoeing, Candlelight breakfasts await you. Activities in the area include trail rides, hunting, fishing, canoeing, tubing, hiking, biking, scenic drives, antiquing, stargazing, history, golf, three state parks, wildlife refuge, birding, geographically unique sand dunes, museums, and much more.

Homemade Granola

4 cups smoked almonds
3 cups sunflower seeds
2 cups sesame seeds
4 tablespoons ground cinnamon
16 cups old-fashioned oats
1 cup canola oil
1 cup honey
4 cups raisins
4 cups M&Ms

Preheat oven to 375°. Add almonds, sunflower and sesame seeds, and cinnamon to dry oats and mix well. Add oil and honey a little at a time and mix well. Mix again and again. Spread thin on cookie sheets. Bake 10 minutes. Remove from oven and turn mixture over several times. Bake 10 more minutes, turning several times again and

let cool. Add raisins and M&Ms. Mix by turning until evenly distributed throughout baked ingredients. Makes a great snack or can be served with yogurt at breakfast buffet. Yields enough to serve 30 people.

Stuffed French Toast

8 slices heavy bread (cottage), crusts cut off and cubed
2 (8-ounce) packages cream cheese, cubed
12 eggs
2 cups milk
1⅓ cups maple syrup
8 slices cooked bacon, cut into ½- or 1-inch squares

In ungreased 9 x 13-inch pan, layer half the bread and add cream cheese. Top with remaining bread. Mix eggs, milk, and syrup. Pour over bread. Cover with plastic wrap. Refrigerate 8 hours or overnight.

When ready to serve, preheat oven to 375°. Bake 45 minutes. Sprinkle bacon over French toast, garnish with fruit, and serve with warm syrup. Yields 10 servings.

French Silk Pie

½ cup (1 stick) butter, room temperature
¾ cup sugar
2 squares unsweetened chocolate
2 egg beaters (¼ cup equals 1 egg)
2 (8-ounce) tubs Cool Whip
1 (9-inch) graham cracker piecrust
Chocolate shavings

Cream butter and sugar together. Melt chocolate in microwave and slightly cool. Mix chocolate with butter mixture. Add ¼ cup egg beaters and beat for 5 minutes. Add remaining ¼ cup egg beaters and beat 5 minutes more. Fold in 2 to 3 cups Cool Whip and fill piecrust. Top with thick layer of remaining Cool Whip. Sprinkle chocolate shavings on top of pie and cut chocolate curlicues for center with potato peeler. Yields 1 pie.

Wassail

4 individual bags black tea
5½ quarts plus 2 cups water
4 (46-ounce) cans orange juice
2 (46-ounce) cans grapefruit/orange juice
4 (46-ounce) cans pineapple juice

Steep tea in 2 cups boiling water. Pour into large soup pan with juices and remaining water. Cook, but do *not* boil and add tea. Serve hot. Yields about 60 servings.

Upper Room B & B Favorite Casserole

The amounts you use will depend on size of dish. This allows you to make as little or as much as you need to serve 1 person or 10 people with no leftovers.

Frozen hash browns
Sausage, cooked and crumbled
American cheese, cubed
Eggs
Half-and-half

Preheat oven to 350°. Spray any size casserole dish with cooking oil. Layer hash browns up about ¾ inch in casserole dish. Then layer an equal amount of sausage. Place cubed cheese about 1 or 2 inches apart to make cheese layer. Mix enough eggs and half-and-half together to cover hash browns, sausage, and cheese and pour on top. Bake 30 to 40 minutes until heated through and egg mixture is set.

THE KIRSCHKE HOUSE BED & BREAKFAST

1124 W. Third Street
Grand Island, NE 68801
(308) 381-6851
www.kirschkehouse.com

A turn-of-the-century showplace, the Kirschke House was built in 1902 by the prominent contractor, Otto Kirschke, as his family home. The vine-covered, two-story brick home features architectural highlights including a windowed cupola, turret, and stained-glass windows over the open oak staircase. The guest rooms, accented with Victorian lace, period furnishings, and antique accessories, reflect the ambience of the exterior vines and roses.

Wheat Germ Zucchini Bread

3 eggs, beaten light and fluffy
1 cup vegetable oil
1 cup granulated sugar
1 cup brown sugar
3 teaspoons maple flavoring
2 cups coarsely shredded zucchini
2½ cups all-purpose flour
½ cup toasted wheat germ
2 teaspoons baking soda
1½ teaspoons salt
½ teaspoon baking powder
1 cup chopped walnuts
⅓ cup sesame seeds

Preheat oven to 325°. Add ingredients, except sesame seeds, to mixing bowl in order listed. Mix well. Pour into two 9 x 5-inch or three 7 x 4-inch loaf pans. Sprinkle sesame seeds on top of batter. Bake for 1 hour. Yields 2 or 3 loaves.

Nevada

Deer Run Ranch Bed & Breakfast

5440 Eastlake Blvd
Carson City, NV 89704
(775) 882-3643
www.bbonline.com/nv/deerrun/

Deer Run Ranch Bed & Breakfast is located on a working alfalfa ranch overlooking Washoe Lake and the Sierra Nevada Mountains, midway between Reno and Carson City. This elegant timber framed contemporary home is earth bermed to the north and east, with expansive views to the south and west. The private guest wing has two comfortable guest rooms with private baths, a large sitting room with TV, VCR, guest refrigerator, library, fireplace, and private entry. The bountiful ranch breakfast might include frittatas with garden vegetables and homemade muffins or coffee cakes. Activities in the area include swimming, sailing, biking, hiking, skiing, golfing, and antiquing. Fine dining, nightlife, and casinos are all nearby.

❧   ❧   ❧

Breakfast Quesadillas

This is, quite simply, the "grilled cheese" of Mexico, recreated as a tasty southwest style breakfast.

1 package 10-inch flour tortillas
(flavored or plain)
1 (8-ounce) package grated
Mexican cheeses
6 large eggs, lightly beaten
1 (7-ounce) tin diced Ortega chiles
1 plus ½ cup finely chopped onion
1 to 2 cloves garlic, finely minced
1 cup diced deli-style ham
Salt and pepper
Cumin
1 or 2 fresh tomatoes, chopped
2 cups finely cut lettuce
(romaine or iceberg)

Lay out all 6 tortillas. Sprinkle 1 tablespoon cheese on half of each tortilla. Divide eggs, chiles, ½ cup onion, garlic, and ham in thirds. Pour one-third of eggs in a hot 10-inch skillet coated with nonstick spray. When ready flip eggs and add one-third chiles, onion, garlic, and ham. Season to taste. When eggs completely cooked remove omelets and repeat with remaining ingredients to make 3 omelets. Cut each omelet in half and lay on top of cheese on tortillas. Sprinkle more cheese over omelets and fold tortillas in half. Heat a little vegetable oil in large skillet. Fry folded tortillas until lightly brown on both sides, turning once. Check to make sure cheese is melted. (It takes about 1 or 2 minutes per side to cook.) Garnish with remaining 1 cup onion, tomato, and lettuce. Serve with salsa, hot sauce, guacamole, and sour cream. Yields 6 servings.

Note: You may leave out the ham for vegetarian guests.

Chili Cheese Puff

Make this the night before and refrigerate overnight.

1 large green bell—or pasilla
—pepper, seeded, and
sliced thin
1 large red bell pepper, seeded
and sliced thin
1 large yellow onion, sliced thin
1 tablespoon canola oil
4 eggs
1½ cups milk
2 teaspoons chili powder
1 teaspoon salt
5 (1-inch thick) slices sourdough bread,
crusts removed and cubed
1 cup grated Cheddar (mild
or medium) cheese

Lightly sauté peppers and onion in oil. Coat 2-quart baking dish with cooking spray. In medium bowl beat eggs with milk and add chili powder and salt. Spread cubed bread on bottom of baking dish; cover with cooked peppers and onion. Top with cheese and pour egg mixture over top. Refrigerate at least 1 hour. (Overnight is best.) When ready, preheat oven to 350° and bake about 45 minutes, or until puffed and golden. Yields 4 to 6 servings.

Lake View Cottage Bed & Breakfast

P.O. Box 1
99 Route 113
Silver Lake, NH 03875
(603) 367-9182 (phone)
(800) 982-0418 (toll free)
info@lakeviewcottage.com
www.lakeviewcottage.com

Lake View Cottage Bed & Breakfast offers the best of the lakes and mountain regions. Commanding a majestic view of Silver Lake, this bed and breakfast has been in the Knowles family since it was built as an inn in 1876. The inn is known for its hospitality, service, views, and sumptuous

Lake View Cottage Bed & Breakfast

full breakfasts. Activities available include boating, swimming, fishing, cross-country and downhill skiing, ice-skating, snow-mobiling, hiking, Mount Washington auto road, and rock climbing.

Lake View Cottage Granola

6 cups old-fashioned oats
1 cup wheat germ
2 cups shredded coconut
½ cup sesame seeds
1 cup sliced almonds
1 cup chopped pecans
⅔ cup firmly packed brown sugar
⅔ cup water
⅔ cup canola oil
¼ cup honey
¾ teaspoon salt
1 teaspoon ground cinnamon
1 teaspoon vanilla extract

Preheat oven to 300°. In large bowl, combine oats, wheat germ, coconut, sesame seeds, almonds, and pecans. Blend well. In large saucepan, mix sugar, water, canola oil, honey, salt, cinnamon, and vanilla. Heat until sugar dissolves, but do *not* boil. Pour liquid mixture over dry ingredients and stir until well coated. Spread in two large ungreased cookie sheets with sides. Bake 1 hour and 30 minutes, stirring every 15 minutes after the first 30 minutes. Cool on pans and store in airtight container. Dried fruit or raisins may be added for variety. Can be served alone or with milk or yogurt. Yields 11 cups.

Blueberry Scones

2 cups all-purpose flour
3 tablespoons sugar, plus extra for sprinkling tops
1 tablespoon baking powder
¾ teaspoon salt
6 tablespoons cold unsalted butter (¾ cup), cut in pieces
1½ cups fresh or frozen blueberries, not thawed
1 teaspoon grated lemon zest
⅓ cup heavy cream, plus extra for brushing tops
2 large eggs, lightly beaten

Adjust rack to center of oven and preheat to 400°. Place parchment paper on baking sheet (or grease and flour). In food processor, place flour, sugar, baking powder, and salt. Process 10 seconds on high. Add butter pieces and process until largest butter pieces are size of small peas. Place mixture in large bowl and stir in berries and zest. Whisk together cream and eggs. Make a well in center of dry ingredients and pour in cream and egg mixture. Stir lightly with fork until dough comes together. Turn out onto lightly floured surface and knead several times to mix well. (Too much mixing can make scones tough.) Pat dough into 6-inch square. Using floured knife, cut into four 3-inch squares. Cut squares in half on diagonal to form two triangles from each square. Transfer to baking sheet, spacing triangles 2 inches apart. Brush tops with cream and sprinkle lightly with sugar. Bake until golden brown, 20 to 22 minutes. Cool on wire racks. Serve warm with butter, fruit preserves, or clotted cream. Serve with lemon curd for afternoon tea. Yields 8 servings.

Croissant French Toast

½ cup sliced almonds
6 stale croissants
2 eggs
1 cup half-and-half
¼ teaspoon vanilla extract

Heat electric griddle to 350° (or cast iron griddle until drops of water spatter on the surface). Place sliced almonds on dinner plate. Cut croissants in half, front to back so that you have two crescent shapes from each. Beat well eggs, half-and-half, and vanilla. Dip croissant halves in mixture, coating both sides. Press cut-side of each half into almonds and bake on griddle 3 to 4 minutes, turning once or until golden on each side. Serve with warmed real maple syrup. Yields 3 servings.

Blueberry Buttermilk Pancakes

2 cups all-purpose flour
2 teaspoons baking powder
1 teaspoon baking soda
3 tablespoons sugar
2 large eggs, lightly beaten
3 cups buttermilk
4 tablespoons melted butter, plus some for griddle
1 cup fresh or frozen blueberries
 (Do not thaw.)

Heat electric griddle to 350°. In large bowl, whisk together flour, baking powder, baking soda, and sugar. In medium bowl, whisk together eggs, buttermilk, and butter. Gently fold egg mixture into dry ingredients; some lumps will remain. (Too much mixing makes pancakes tough.) Fold in blueberries. Butter griddle and pour batter by ¼-cup measure. Cook until edges look dry and there are bubbles over entire surface. Turn and cook 2 to 3 more minutes. Serve with warmed real maple syrup. Yields about 18 (¾-inch-thick) pancakes.

Maple Pecan Scones

3 cups all-purpose flour
1½ tablespoons baking powder
¾ teaspoon salt
¾ cup (1½ sticks) cold unsalted butter
1 cup chopped pecans
⅔ cup maple syrup, plus additional for brushing scones
⅓ cup heavy cream

Place parchment paper on (or grease and flour) baking sheet. Preheat oven to 350°. Put flour, baking powder, and salt in food processor and process on high 10 seconds. Add butter, cut in pieces. Process until ingredients resemble coarse meal and put into large mixing bowl. Add pecans. In medium bowl, whisk syrup and cream together. Make a well in dry ingredients and gently mix in syrup and cream with fork, just until mixture holds together. Put on floured board and knead several times. (Too much makes scones tough.) Pat into 8-inch square. Cut into four squares and then cut each square into two triangles. Place on baking sheet and brush with maple syrup. Bake 20 to 25 minutes or until tips are lightly browned. May be served warm or at room temperature with butter. Yields 8 servings.

EASTMAN INN

P.O. Box 882
Route 16
North Conway, NH 03860
(603) 356-6707 (phone)
(603) 356-7708 (fax)
innkeeper@eastmaninn.com
www.eastmaninn.com

The Eastman Inn bed and breakfast is a Georgian Colonial built in 1777 which has operated as an Inn since the early 1900s. Breakfast at the Eastman Inn is not traditional country inn fare but a gastronomic adventure with a menu changing daily. Experience views of the Moat Mountains from the parlor or wraparound porch of the Eastman Inn.

Chicken Pecan Quiche

2 cups finely chopped cooked chicken*
1 cup grated Monterey Jack cheese
¼ cup finely chopped scallions**
1 tablespoon chopped fresh parsley
1 tablespoon all-purpose flour
1 unbaked 9-inch pie shell
3 eggs, beaten
1¼ cups half-and-half
½ teaspoon Dijon mustard
½ cup chopped pecans

Preheat oven to 350°. In large bowl, combine chicken, cheese, scallions, parsley, and flour. Sprinkle into pie shell. In medium bowl, combine eggs, half-and-half, and mustard. Pour over chicken mixture and top with pecans. Bake for 60 minutes. Yields 4 servings.

Substitutions: *1 can chicken breast, drained and flaked; **1 tablespoon dehydrated onion.

Eastman Inn

Biscuits with Chocolate Gravy

2 cups all-purpose flour
1 tablespoon sugar
1 tablespoon baking powder
½ teaspoon baking soda
¾ teaspoon salt
½ cup shortening
1½ cups buttermilk

Chocolate gravy:
1 cup sugar
1½ tablespoons cocoa
3 tablespoons flour
¼ teaspoon salt
3½ cups milk, preferably whole milk
¼ cup (½ stick) butter

Lightly grease cookie sheet or baking pan. Preheat oven to 425°. In large bowl, mix dry ingredients. Cut shortening into dry ingredients with pastry blender until mixture resembles coarse meal. Form a well in center of mixture and add buttermilk all at once. Mix lightly and turn onto floured board. Knead lightly and roll to about ½-inch thickness. Using biscuit cutter or glass, cut dough into biscuits and place on prepared pan. Bake for about 15 minutes, or until lightly browned.

For chocolate gravy, mix dry ingredients together, add milk, and mix until smooth. Melt butter in large skillet over medium heat. Slowly add mixture and cook until desired consistency, stirring frequently to prevent sticking. Serve over biscuits. Yields 15 to 20 biscuits.

Eggplant and Mushroom Frittata

2 tablespoons olive oil
2 cloves garlic, minced
⅓ cup chopped green onions, including tops
5 medium zucchini, thinly sliced
1 medium eggplant, not peeled, thinly sliced
¾ pound mushrooms, thinly sliced
3 eggs, beaten
1 teaspoon Italian seasoning
1 teaspoon salt
Freshly ground pepper
3 cups grated Monterey Jack cheese
1 cup freshly grated Parmesan cheese

Coat 9 x 13-inch baking dish with nonstick spray. Preheat oven to 350°. Heat olive oil in large skillet over medium heat and sauté garlic and onions until translucent. Add zucchini, eggplant, and mushrooms. Sauté, turning with spoon for about 6 to 7 minutes. Remove from heat and drain. Beat eggs, Italian seasoning, salt, and pepper to taste until frothy. Add egg mixture to vegetable mixture, stir well, and pour into prepared baking dish. Spread Monterey Jack cheese evenly over mixture and sprinkle with Parmesan cheese. Bake for 35 to 40 minutes. Yields 4 to 6 servings.

Monte Cristo Sandwiches with Warm Chutney

Chutney:
½ cup diced dried apricots
3 small ripe peaches, pitted and diced
1 cup apple juice concentrate
1 inch fresh peeled ginger root
Zest of 1 lemon
Few pinches of ground nutmeg
¼ teaspoon ground cinnamon

Sandwiches:
3 eggs, beaten
½ cup milk or half-and-half
1 tablespoon sugar
¼ teaspoon ground nutmeg
8 slices white toasting bread
1 (6 to 8-ounce) block Vermont sharp Cheddar cheese, thinly sliced
1 Gala or Golden Delicious apple, quartered, cored, and thinly sliced
¾ pound deli-sliced smoked turkey breast
Melted butter

Put chutney ingredients in medium saucepan over medium heat and bring to a boil. Reduce heat and let chutney simmer for about 10 minutes. Remove ginger root. Remove from heat.

Thoroughly mix eggs, milk, sugar, and nutmeg in shallow pan. Preheat nonstick griddle or large skillet over moderate heat. Coat griddle with butter, dip four pieces of bread on both sides into egg mixture, and place on griddle or pan. Cook 2 minutes and turn two slices over. Top these with thin layer of cheese, apple, turkey, and finally another slice of cheese. Top sandwich filling with remaining two slices of bread in pan, keeping uncooked side up. Turn entire sandwich over to cook opposite side. Gently press down on sandwich as it grills for 1 to 2 minutes. Repeat process with remaining ingredients. Cut sandwiches on diagonal and serve with small ramekins of warm fruit chutney for topping. Yields 4 servings.

Eastman Inn
Fresh Corn Loaf

When summer vegetables are plentiful, slices of corn loaf provide a beautiful combination of colors.

    2 cups fresh corn, cut off cob
    1 cup chopped fresh tomato
    1 cup chopped onion
    1 cup chopped green pepper
    2 teaspoons salt
    2 tablespoons canned,
        chopped green chiles
    1 cup yellow cornmeal
    1 cup grated Cheddar cheese
    2 eggs
    ½ cup evaporated milk
    ½ cup water

Preheat oven to 375°. Mix together all ingredients except eggs, milk, and water. Combine well and let mixture sit for 30 minutes. Beat eggs and add evaporated milk and water, mixing well. Add egg mixture to vegetable/cornmeal mix. Pour into greased loaf pan and Bake 1 hour. Serve hot or cold. Yields 4 to 6 servings.

SUGAR HILL INN

Route 117
P.O. Box 954
Franconia, NH 03580
(603) 823-5621 (phone)
(800) 548-4748 (toll free)
info@sugarhillinn.com
www.sugarhillinn.com

Your travels to Sugar Hill will take you over mountain highways and glorious views of towering peaks and clear lakes. The Sugar Hill Inn is a historic farmhouse built in 1789 and over the years impeccably restored to its present beauty. This charming country inn offers a relaxing vacation experience with attentive service and exceptional meals. Recent additions to the inn include two luxury suites, each with a fireplace, whirlpool bath, and private deck. There are eight rooms in the main house, six guest rooms in the country cottages, and two master suites. All rooms have private baths and breathtaking views of the White Mountain Presidential Range. Year-round activities can be enjoyed at Sugar Hill Inn. Activities include skiing, sleigh rides, golfing, hiking, concerts and much more.

Chocolate Pâte

    18 ounces bittersweet chocolate,
        broken into pieces
    1 cup heavy cream
    4 tablespoons cold butter,
        cut into tablespoon slices
    4 egg yolks
    1 cup confectioners' sugar
    ½ cup dark rum
    Berry purée and hazelnuts for serving

In bowl set over simmering water, combine chocolate, cream, and butter. Cook, stirring occasionally, until melted and smooth, about 10 minutes. Remove from heat and whisk in egg yolks one at a time.

Gradually whisk in sugar and then rum. Line bottom and sides of 3-cup loaf pan with plastic wrap. Pour in chocolate, cover, and freeze. Unwrap and cut into ½-inch-thick slices. Serve with berry purée and sprinkle with toasted and chopped hazelnuts. Yields 10 (3-slice) portions.

Maple Walnut
Muffins

    1¼ cups all-purpose flour
    ½ teaspoon salt
    1 teaspoon baking powder
    ½ teaspoon baking soda
    ⅓ cup firmly packed brown sugar
    1 cup old-fashioned oats
    1 cup chopped walnuts
    1 cup sour cream
    5 tablespoons softened butter
    2 eggs
    ⅓ cup real maple syrup

Preheat oven to 350°. Mix dry ingredients together. Mix wet ingredients together in separate bowl. Add wet ingredients to dry ingredients. Spoon batter into well-greased muffin tin, filling cups two-thirds full. Bake 20 to 30 minutes, turning pan 15 minutes into cooking time, until toothpick comes out clean. Let stand 10 minutes after removing from oven and remove muffins from tin. Yields 12 medium muffins.

Mushroom Dill Soup

Served nightly at the Sugar Hill Inn.

    3 cups sliced onions
    8 tablespoons butter
    Salt and freshly ground pepper
    4 cups sliced fresh mushrooms
    1 teaspoon dried dill weed
    3 cups vegetable broth
    1 tablespoon tamari sauce
        (natural soy sauce)
    2 teaspoons sweet Hungarian paprika
    ¼ cup sour cream

In medium-size saucepan, sauté onions in butter over medium heat. Stir occasionally, until soft but not brown. Sprinkle lightly with salt and pepper. Add mushrooms and sweat until softened, about 15 minutes. Add dill weed, broth, tamari, and paprika. Cover pan and simmer 15 minutes. Taste and adjust seasoning if needed. Just before serving, whisk in sour cream. (Do *not* boil.) Stir until blended. Yields 6 to 8 servings.

THE CROWES' NEST BED & BREAKFAST

P.O. Box 427
Thorn Mountain Road
Jackson, NH 03846
(603) 383-8913 (phone)
(603) 383-8241 (fax)
(800) 511-8383 (toll free)
tcnest@crowesnest.net
www.crowesnest.net

The Crowes' Nest is located within walking distance of everything in picturesque Jackson, New Hampshire. The bed and breakfast offers the best of the three *Rs*—romance, relaxation, and recreation. Seven guest rooms, each with private bath, air conditioning, queen or king bed, and some with sitting rooms, balconies, fireplaces, or Jacuzzis. Breakfasts change daily.

Cranberry Chutney

1 cup water
¾ cup dark brown sugar
½ cup granulated sugar
1 cup sliced onions
¾ cup cider vinegar
2 tart apples, peeled, seeded, and diced
1 teaspoon grated fresh ginger
½ teaspoon mace
½ teaspoon curry powder
½ teaspoon salt
Grated zest of 2 oranges
4 cups cranberries
½ cup currants
½ cup strained juice of fresh oranges
    or ½ cup packaged orange juice

Combine water, sugars, and onions in heavy pot over medium-high heat. Simmer 30 minutes. Stir in vinegar, apples, ginger, mace, curry, salt, and orange zest. Boil slowly 30 minutes longer and stir in cranberries, currants, and orange juice. Boil slowly about 15 minutes, or until cranberries burst. Season if desired. Allow to cool. Use as garnish for any egg dish. Yields about 4 cups.

Lemon Thyme Bread

2 cups all-purpose flour
1½ teaspoons baking powder
⅛ teaspoon freshly ground nutmeg
¾ cup skim milk
2 tablespoons chopped fresh lemon balm
2 tablespoons chopped fresh thyme
½ cup softened butter
1 cup sugar
2 large eggs
1 tablespoon fresh lemon zest
½ cup confectioners' sugar
2 tablespoons fresh lemon juice

Mix flour, baking powder, and nutmeg. Combine milk, lemon balm, and thyme in saucepan, bring to a boil, and remove from heat. Let stand, covered, until cool. Preheat oven to 325°. Beat butter until creamy. Add sugar gradually, beating constantly until light and fluffy. Add eggs, one at a time, beating well after each. Add flour mixture alternately with milk mixture, beginning and ending with flour. Stir in lemon zest. Pour into greased and floured 5 x 9-inch loaf pan. Bake 50 minutes or until tests done. Cool in pan 10 minutes. Combine the confectioners' sugar and lemon juice and glaze the cake when partially cooled. Yields 10 to 12 servings.

Christine's Hot Fruit Compote

1 cup pitted, cut-up prunes
1 cup cut-up dried apricots
½ cup dried cranberries
1 (20-ounce) can pineapple chunks, not drained
1 (16-ounce) can drained mandarin oranges
1 (21-ounce) can cherry pie filling
1 cup vermouth or Campari

Mock Devonshire cream:
½ cup whipped heavy cream
½ cup sour cream
¼ cup brown sugar
3 tablespoons milk

Preheat oven to 350°. Combine all ingredients in 2-quart casserole. Bake 45 minutes.

For Mock Devonshire cream, whip heavy cream to soft peaks. Combine sour cream, brown sugar, and milk. Fold into whipped cream. Will last, refrigerated, for 3 weeks. Spoon fruit into individual serving dishes and top with Mock Devonshire Cream. Yields 8 to 10 servings.

Florentine Frittata

6 eggs
1 tablespoon snipped fresh chervil or parsley
¼ teaspoon salt
1 tablespoon butter
1 tablespoon olive oil
3 scallions, thinly sliced (white part only)
½ cup fresh spinach leaves, washed and torn into medium-size pieces

Beat eggs, chervil, and salt. In medium cast-iron skillet over low heat melt butter with oil. Add scallions and cook for 5 to 7 minutes or until tender. Turn off heat. Top with spinach. Pour in egg mixture. Preheat oven to 350° and bake 18 to 20 minutes or until browned on top. Serve immediately. Yields 4 servings.

Pears in Mascarpone Custard

3 medium pears, peeled, cored, and sliced
2 tablespoons Scotch whisky (optional)
½ cup plus 1 tablespoon sugar
4 tablespoons butter or margarine
1 egg
⅔ cup mascarpone cheese
2 tablespoons flour
Fresh mint sprigs

Preheat oven to 350°. Arrange pears in buttered 6- or 8-ounce ramekins. Sprinkle with Scotch and 1 tablespoon sugar. Cream butter and remaining sugar. Beat in egg, then mascarpone. Stir in flour last and mix well. Spoon over fruit. Bake until just set, about 50 minutes. Check time; ovens may vary. Garnish with sprig of mint. Yields 6 servings.

Inn at Crystal Lake

Route 153
Eaton Center, NH 03832
(603) 447-2120 (phone)
(603) 447-3599 (fax)
(800) 343-7336 (toll free)
stay@innatcrystallake.com
www.innatcrystallake.com

Inn at Crystal Lake is tucked away in a quiet New England village with complete country store, little white church, and sparkling Crystal Lake.

Mammy's Blueberry Muffins

½ cup (1 stick) butter
1¼ cups sugar
2 eggs
2 cups all-purpose flour
2 teaspoons baking powder
½ teaspoon salt
½ cup cream
2½ cups blueberries

Grease large muffin tin, including the tops. Preheat oven to 350°. Using paddle on electric mixer, cream butter and sugar until light and fluffy. Add eggs and beat well after each addition. In separate bowl, blend the flour, baking powder, and salt. Add alternately with cream to butter mixture, starting with flour and ending with flour. Do *not* overmix. Add blueberries and spoon into muffin tin (an ice cream scoop works well). Bake 30 minutes. Yields 6 large muffins.

Eaton Everythings

1 cup brown sugar
½ cup granulated sugar
1 cup (2 sticks) unsalted butter, softened
2 cups all-purpose flour
½ teaspoon salt
½ teaspoon ground cinnamon
1 teaspoon baking powder
1 teaspoon baking soda
3 cups old-fashioned oats
2 eggs
3 tablespoons heavy cream
1 tablespoon vanilla extract
1 cup raisins or dried cranberries
1 cup semisweet chocolate chips
1 cup chopped pecans or walnuts

Cream both sugars and butter until light and fluffy. Combine flour, salt, cinnamon, baking powder, baking soda, and oats. Mix eggs, cream, and vanilla together and add gradually to butter and sugar mixture. Add dry mixture and mix until it just comes together. Fold in raisins or cranberries, chocolate chips, and nuts. Preheat oven to 350°. Scoop cookie dough by tablespoonfuls onto parchment-paper-lined baking sheet. Bake until golden, approximately 10 to 15 minutes. Yields 50 to 55 cookies.

Bobby's Blueberry Bread

½ cup softened butter
1½ cups sugar plus additional for pan
1 cup sour cream
3 eggs
3 cups all-purpose flour
4 teaspoons baking powder
1 teaspoon salt
2 cups fresh blueberries

Preheat oven to 350°. Mix butter with sugar and sour cream and add eggs. Add flour, baking powder, and salt. Mix until batter just comes together and then fold in berries. Pour into greased and floured tube/Bundt pan. Sprinkle on layer of sugar. Bake 1 hour, checking after 45 minutes. (Instead of blueberries, try substituting fresh cranberries and walnuts.) Makes 1 Bundt or tube cake. Yields 12 to 14 servings.

Crystal Lake Spicy Cilantro Shrimp

Juice of 1 lemon
Juice of 2 limes
3 to 4 cloves garlic
2 to 3 small jalapeño peppers
1 bunch fresh cilantro
2 pounds fresh shrimp, shelled and deveined

Put lemon and lime juices into 9 x 12-inch glass pan or glass bowl. Finely chop garlic and jalapeños and add to juices. Remove cilantro leaves from stem and rinse. Finely chop cilantro until you have about ½ cup

juices. Grill shrimp 1 to 2 minutes each side until no longer translucent. Add shrimp to pan and completely coat with marinade. Chill 1 hour, making sure to stir periodically. Tastes best fresh since cilantro will start to wilt after several hours. You can sauté shrimp or even use frozen cooked shrimp, but fresh ones on grill are best. Also, use food processor to chop garlic, jalapeños, and cilantro for ease. This is a perfect summer appetizer when served with chilled white wine or margaritas. Yields 6 servings.

Tim's Double Chocolate Chip Cookies

2½ cups oatmeal
1 cup (2 sticks) butter
1 cup granulated sugar
1 cup brown sugar
1 teaspoon vanilla extract
2 eggs
2 cups all-purpose flour
½ teaspoon salt
1 teaspoon baking powder
1 teaspoon baking soda
1 (4-ounce) chocolate bar, melted
12 ounces semisweet chocolate chips
1½ cups chopped walnuts

Blend oatmeal in blender or food processor to a fine powder. Preheat oven to 350°. Cream butter, both sugars, and vanilla. Beat in eggs. Mix together with flour, oatmeal, salt, baking powder, and baking soda. Add melted chocolate bar and completely incorporate. Add chocolate chips and nuts. Roll into balls and place two inches apart on cookie sheet. Bake 10 minutes. Yields 50 to 55 cookies.

MT. WASHINGTON BED & BREAKFAST

421 State Route 2
Shelburne, NH 03581
(603) 466-2669 (phone)
(877) 466-2399 (toll free)
mtwashbb@yahoo.com
www.mtwashingtonbb.com

Come be pampered at this late 1800s Federal-style farmhouse with wonderful sunset views of Mt. Washington, Mt. Madison, and Mt. Adams. Seven guest rooms all have private baths and two deluxe suites have whirlpool tubs. Come for a romantic or relaxing getaway or to hike the White Mountains of New Hampshire. You can also hike, bike, golf, swim, fish, canoe, kayak, moose watch, snowshoe, ski—cross-country or downhill—rent a snowmobile, build a snowman, sightsee, shop, antique, or visit one of the many other area attractions. The Mt. Washington Bed & Breakfast is within fifteen minutes of Mt. Washington Auto Road, Great Glen Outdoors Center, and Wildcat Mountain. The Appalachian Trail is only about three-quarters of a mile from our door; Sunday River Ski Resort is thirty minutes away. Area attractions also include Six Gun City, Santa's Village, Heritage New Hampshire, and Storyland.

Frangelico French Toast

8 eggs
½ cup half-and-half

¼ cup Frangelico hazelnut liqueur
2 loaves Italian bread
Nutella
Confectioners' sugar

Whisk eggs, half-and-half, and Frangelico until well blended. Slice bread into 16 slices ½- to 1-inch-thick. Dip both sides of bread in mixture. Brown on both sides on lightly greased hot griddle. Smear top side with coating of Nutella as thick, or thin, as you prefer. Sprinkle very lightly with confectioners' sugar. Decorate with sliced strawberry for an elegant look. Serve with warm maple syrup for sweeter version. Yields 8 servings, 2 pieces per serving.

Auntie May's Oatmeal Spice Cookies with Chocolate Chips

1 stick margarine
½ cup applesauce
1 cup firmly packed brown sugar
½ cup granulated sugar
2 eggs (egg substitutes work well)
1 teaspoon vanilla extract
1½ cups all-purpose flour
1 teaspoon baking soda
1 teaspoon ground cinnamon
½ teaspoon ground allspice
3 cups old-fashioned oatmeal
1 cup or more chocolate chips

Preheat oven to 350°. Beat together margarine, applesauce, and sugars until creamy. Add eggs or egg substitute and vanilla; beat well. Combine flour, baking soda, cinnamon, and allspice. Add flour mixture to margarine mixture; mix well. Stir in oatmeal and chocolate chips. Drop by rounded tablespoonfuls onto ungreased cookie sheet. Bake 10 to 12 minutes until light golden brown; edges should be golden brown. Cool 1 minute and move to wire cooling rack. Get out the milk. Yields 5 dozen cookies.

THE HILLTOP INN

1348 Main Street
Sugar Hill, NH 03585
(603) 823-5695 (phone)
(603) 823-5518 (fax)
(800) 770-5695 (toll free)
info@hilltopinn.com
www.hilltopinn.com

The Hilltop Inn is a charming Victorian country inn built circa 1895. Antique furnishings throughout make each of the six guest rooms unique and the common rooms cozy and inviting. All guest rooms include full private bath. The inn is nonsmoking. There are lovely sunset views from the deck and strolls along quiet country lanes. Relax in comfortable porch rockers or in the Victorian sitting room. There is an assortment of books, magazines, and games, or join in for a friendly conversation by the fireside. The Hilltop Inn is close to all the area attractions—alpine and Nordic skiing, Cannon, Loon, Bretton Woods & Attitash. There is also swimming, canoeing, fishing, biking, hiking, waterfall trails, horseback riding, windsurfing, glider and plane rides, summer stock theater, and antiquing, just to mention a few.

White Gazpacho Soup

9 medium cucumbers, peeled and
    cut into 2-inch chunks
9 cups chicken broth
9 cups sour cream
6 tablespoons white vinegar
2 tablespoons salt or to taste
3 cloves garlic, crushed
1½ cups sliced scallions
1½ cups freshly chopped dill
6 tomatoes, finely chopped

Whirl cucumbers in food processor or blender with a little chicken broth until thickly puréed. Combine with remaining broth and all other ingredients, reserving one-fourth of chopped tomatoes. Refrigerate overnight and serve garnished with remaining tomatoes. Yields 18 to 20 servings.

Fresh Berry Soufflé

1 large loaf white bread,
    crusts removed, and each
    slice cut into 4 squares
1 quart fresh berries
    (Frozen berries may be used,
    but defrost and strain liquid.)
6 tablespoons sugar
1 tablespoon ground cinnamon
10 eggs
3 cups half-and-half
1 teaspoon vanilla extract
¼ cup maple syrup

In two greased pie pans or two 4-cup soufflé dishes, place layer of bread squares and layer of berries. Mix sugar and cinnamon and sprinkle with half this mixture. Beat eggs, half-and-half, vanilla, and maple syrup together. Pour half egg mixture over bread and berries. Repeat with remaining bread, berries, and egg mixture. Sprinkle top with remaining sugar/cinnamon mix. Cover and refrigerate 8 to 10 hours or overnight. When ready to serve, preheat oven to 375° and bake 45 to 60 minutes until puffed and light brown. Serve with warm maple syrup. Yields 6 to 8 servings.

The Hilltop Inn

THE INN ON GOLDEN POND

Route 3, P.O. Box 680
Holderness, NH 03245
(603) 968-7269 (phone)
(603) 968-9226 (fax)
innongp@lr.net
www.innongoldenpond.com

The Inn on Golden Pond is an impressive country home built in 1879 and located near Squam Lake, setting for the classic film *On Golden Pond*. The inn is known

...gly friendly, yet profes-
...re. The inn sits on twenty-
... spotted with meandering
...d split-rail fences, and a
variety of ... rs, shrubs, and shade trees.
All rooms are tastefully decorated with
private baths, air conditioning, and individual heat. Each morning guests are
treated to a full breakfast featuring homemade breads and muffins and Bonnie's
signature rhubarb jam. Although the inn
has no lake frontage itself, a mile away are
swimming, boating, a historic covered
bridge, and tours of Squam Lake. The area
offers miles of hiking trails, and guests
enjoy simply sitting and relaxing on the
sixty-foot-long, screened-in porch.

Puffed Apple Pancake

6 eggs
1½ cups milk
1 cup all-purpose flour
3 tablespoons granulated sugar
1 teaspoon vanilla extract

½ teaspoon salt
½ teaspoon ground cinnamon
¼ pound (1 stick) butter
3 large apples, peeled and sliced
¼ cup brown sugar

Preheat oven to 425°. Mix eggs, milk, flour,
granulated sugar, vanilla, salt, and cinnamon together in medium mixing bowl.
Melt butter in 13 x 9 x 2-inch glass baking
dish. Add apples. Pour batter over apples
and sprinkle with brown sugar. Bake 25 to
30 minutes. Serve hot with maple syrup.
This is a favorite with the fall foliage
crowd. Yields 6 to 8 servings.

Pear Bread

½ cup (1 stick) margarine
1 cup sugar
2 eggs
2 cups all-purpose flour
½ teaspoon salt
½ teaspoon baking soda
1 teaspoon baking powder

⅛ teaspoon ground nutmeg
¼ cup plain yogurt
1 cup coarsely chopped pears
    with peeling on
1 teaspoon vanilla extract

Preheat oven to 350°. In mixing bowl
cream together margarine and sugar. Beat
in eggs one at a time. Combine flour, salt,
baking soda, baking powder, and nutmeg.
Add to egg mixture, alternating with
yogurt. Stir in pears and vanilla. Pour into
a greased 9 x 5 x 3-inch loaf pan. Bake for
1 hour. Turn onto rack to cool. Yields 10 to
12 servings.

Rhubarb Coffee Cake

Topping:
4 tablespoons butter
½ cup light brown sugar
⅔ cup all-purpose flour
¾ cup coconut
¼ cup chopped walnuts

Cake:
⅔ cup all-purpose flour
1¼ cups sugar
1 teaspoon baking soda
1 teaspoon salt
¼ teaspoon ground cloves
1 teaspoon ground cinnamon
¼ teaspoon ground allspice or nutmeg
2 large eggs
¼ cup vegetable oil
⅓ cup milk
2 cups diced fresh rhubarb

Prepare topping by creaming butter and
sugar in medium bowl. Add flour, coconut, and nuts. Mix well.
  Preheat oven to 350°. For cake, sift dry
ingredients together in a bowl. Mix eggs
and oil together in another bowl and add to
dry ingredients. Blend in milk and fold in
rhubarb. Pour into greased 9 x 13 x 2-inch
pan. Spread topping over unbaked cake and
bake 50 minutes. Yields 10 to 12 servings.

The Inn on Golden Pond

THE POST AND BEAM BED & BREAKFAST

18 Centre St.
Sullivan, NH 03445
(603) 847-3330 (phone)
(603) 847-3306 (fax)
(888) 3-ROMANCE (toll free)
postandbeambb@earthlink.net
www.postandbeambb.com

Guests at this 1797 New England colonial farmstead enjoy a comfortable, relaxed atmosphere. Seven charming guest rooms, decorated with quilts and braided rugs, provide guests with a great night's sleep. The outdoor hot tub provides a welcome massage following a hike up Mt. Monadnock, the most climbed mountain in North America. In the surrounding countryside local crafters, quiet back roads, unspoiled woodland, old bookstores, covered bridges, and small villages offer a sense of the way life used to be.

Very Berry Muffins

2 cups all-purpose flour
4 teaspoons baking powder
¾ cup sugar
½ teaspoon salt
1 cup fresh or frozen berries
    (⅓ cup blueberries; ⅓ cup
    raspberries; ⅓ cup strawberries)
2 eggs
½ cup melted butter
1 cup milk

Combine flour, baking powder, sugar, and salt in large mixing bowl. Cut raspberries in half if large and strawberries into small pieces the size of raspberries. Add fruit to flour mix and stir to coat evenly. In small bowl beat eggs and add butter and milk. Lightly combine egg mixture with flour mixture, stirring just enough to blend. Allow batter to sit a minute or two while greasing 12 muffin cups. Preheat oven to 400°. Fill muffin cups three-fourths full. Bake 12 to 15 minutes until lightly browned on top. Yields 12 muffins.

Fruit Smoothie

3 cups mixed fruit pieces
1 cup lemon yogurt
4 ice cubes
Mint leaves and berries for garnish

Place four attractive ten-ounce glasses in freezer 10 to 15 minutes. Put fruit in food processor and blend to liquefy. Add yogurt and blend another 15 to 30 seconds. Add ice cubes and blend until ice is crushed. Pour into chilled glasses. Garnish with mint leaves and a berry or two. Yields 4 (1-cup) servings.

Darcy's Granola

4 cups long-cooking oats
2 cups long-cooking rye or wheat flakes
½ cup oat bran
½ cup wheat germ
1 cup sesame seeds
1 cup sunflower seeds
1 cup pumpkin seeds
½ cup soy nuts
½ cup vegetable oil
¼ cup honey or maple syrup
¼ cup brown or natural sugar
½ teaspoon ground cinnamon
1 teaspoon maple flavoring
½ cup raisins
½ cup dried cranberries
½ cup dried cherries

Preheat oven to 275°. Combine grains, seeds, and nuts in large bowl. Place oil, honey, sugar, and cinnamon in small saucepan and heat slowly until sugar is melted. Remove from heat and add maple flavoring. Pour over grain mixture and stir to lightly coat. Scoop into two large, ungreased baking pans. Bake 1½ to 2 hours, stirring every 20 minutes until toasty. Remove from oven and add fruits. Cool completely and store in tightly covered container until ready for use. Yields 24 low-fat, half-cup servings.

THE LAVENDER FLOWER INN

1657 East Main Street
Route 302
Center Conway, NH 03813
(603) 447-3794 (phone)
(800) 729-0106 (toll free)
lavenderflower@adelphia.net
www.lavenderflowerinn.com

The Lavender Flower Inn is a rambling farmhouse built in the early 1800s. This colonial home has been restored and consists of eight guest rooms, seven of which are located in the main part of the inn. It is beautifully designed with wide pine flooring, wainscoted ceilings, and a wrap-around porch. The guest rooms are delightful, each one with a different flair and decorated with handmade quilts and treasures from the past. There is also a master suite, which is a totally private getaway with its own entrance and deck overlooking the gardens and grounds. A full breakfast is artfully served each morning as well as delectable snacks each afternoon. Recreational opportunities in the area include hiking, canoeing, horseback riding, skiing, snowmobile trail, sleigh rides, and tax-free shopping.

Cinnamon-Apple French Toast

1 tablespoon butter
6 medium firm apples, peeled, cored,
    and sliced
¼ cup cinnamon sugar
    or enough to cover apples
1 tablespoon apple cider
3 eggs
¼ cup whole milk
½ teaspoon vanilla extract
½ teaspoon cinnamon sugar
8 slices thickly-cut bread

Melt butter in medium skillet. Mix apples and cinnamon. Sauté in butter over medium heat for approximately 5 minutes until slightly softened. Add apple cider, stir, and turn off heat. Whisk together in medium-size bowl eggs, milk, vanilla, and cinnamon sugar. Dip bread into egg mixture and cook on griddle until browned on both sides. Arrange two slices toast on each plate and cover with apple mixture. Garnish plate with red and green apples and serve while warm. Yields 4 servings.

CANDLELITE INN

5 Greenhouse Lane
Bradford, NH 03221
(603) 938-5571 (phone)
(603) 938-2564 (fax)
(888) 812-5571 (toll free)
candlelite@conknet.com
www.candleliteinn.com

This award-winning, circa 1897, country Victorian inn is located in the Lake Sunapee region and has all the grace and charm for that perfect getaway. Enjoy your three-course breakfast—down to dessert— each morning in the sunroom overlooking the pond. Sit on the gazebo porch sipping lemonade on a hot, lazy summer day. Or walk the back roads of Bradford as the leaves change. In the wintertime enjoy downhill or cross-country skiing or snowshoe the hills as you explore the beautiful scenery here in town. Come and experience the relaxed atmosphere and the quiet elegance of this all-season inn.

Pear Pie with Streusel Topping

Streusel topping:
⅔ cup all-purpose flour
⅓ cup firmly packed light brown sugar
⅓ cup butter

Filling:
¼ cup sugar
¼ teaspoon ginger
4 teaspoons flour
1 (9-inch) unbaked piecrust
5 ripe pears
4 teaspoons lemon juice
¼ cup light corn syrup

For topping, combine flour and brown sugar in small bowl. Cut in butter with pastry blender until mixture is like coarse cornmeal. Preheat oven to 450°.

For filling, combine sugar, ginger, and flour and sprinkle one-third of mixture over bottom of pie shell. Peel and core pears. Slice thinly into bowl. Arrange half the pears in crust and top with a third of sugar mixture. Arrange remaining pears; top with remaining sugar mixture. Drizzle lemon juice and corn syrup over top. Cover with streusel topping. Bake 15 minutes. Reduce oven temperature to 350° and bake 30 minutes. Yields 6 servings.

Chocolate Raspberry Muffins

1½ cups all-purpose flour
¼ cup granulated sugar
¼ cup packed brown sugar
1 teaspoon baking powder
2 teaspoons salt
½ cup melted butter
½ cup milk
1 egg
2 cups milk chocolate chips
    (11½-ounce package)
⅓ cup seedless raspberry jam

Heat oven to 350°. Line 12-muffin tin with paper baking cups. In large bowl, stir together flour, sugar, baking powder, and salt. In small bowl, combine butter, milk, and egg. Add to flour mixture, stirring just until combined. Stir in chips. Spoon half the batter into muffin cups, filling half full. Spoon 1 teaspoon raspberry jam into each muffin and cover with remaining batter. Bake 20 to 25 minutes or until golden brown. Serve warm with additional jam, if desired. Yields 12 muffins.

Lemonade-Stand Pie

1 (6-ounce) can frozen lemonade
    or pink lemonade concentrate,
    partially thawed
1 pint vanilla ice cream (2 cups), softened
1 (8-ounce) container nondairy whipped
    topping, thawed
1 prepared graham cracker crumb crust

Beat concentrate in large mixer bowl with electric mixer on low speed about 30 seconds. Gradually spoon in ice cream; beat until well blended. Gently stir in whipped topping until smooth. If necessary, freeze until mixture will mound. Spoon into crust. Freeze 4 hours or overnight until firm. Let stand at room temperature 30 minutes or until pie can be cut easily. Garnish with strawberries, if desired. Store leftover pie in freezer. Yields 6 servings.

Zucchini & Egg Bake

1 medium zucchini, chopped
1 tablespoon butter
5 eggs
6 to 8 fresh basil leaves, cut into strips
½ teaspoon oregano
½ cup cottage cheese
3 plus 2 tablespoons Parmesan cheese
1 (8-ounce) package cherry tomatoes
Salt and pepper
Parsley

Sauté zucchini in butter in small pan over medium heat until soft. In large bowl combine eggs, basil, oregano, cottage cheese, and 3 tablespoons Parmesan cheese. Add zucchini. Divide egg mixture among four mini quiche dishes. Cut tomatoes in half and place on top of egg mixture. Preheat oven to 350°. Sprinkle remaining 2 tablespoons Parmesan cheese and salt and pepper to taste on top. Bake 20 minutes or until browned and puffed. Serve with parsley garnish. Should be served immediately. Yields 4 servings.

Cheese, Broccoli, Egg Bake

Herb bread
1 cup broccoli florets
2 cups Swiss cheese
¼ cup Parmesan cheese
1/4 cup Monterey Jack
      or Muenster cheese
5 large eggs
1 cup milk
1 tablespoon chives
White pepper

Butter four mini casserole dishes. Preheat oven to 375°. Place slice of bread on bottom. Microwave broccoli about 2 minutes, just to soften slightly. Divide among dishes. Sprinkle dishes with cheeses, leave a little for sprinkling top. In medium bowl combine eggs, milk, chives, and white pepper. Divide among dishes. Sprinkle with remaining cheeses. Bake about 25 minutes until brown and puffed. Yields 4 servings.

THREE CHIMNEYS INN

17 Newmarket Road
Durham, NH 03824
(603) 868-7800 (phone)
(603) 868-2964 (fax)
(888) 399-9777 (toll free)
chimney3@aol.com
www.threechimneysinn.com

The Three Chimneys Inn is a 1649 homestead with twenty-three guest rooms, fireplaces, four posters, and colonial fine dining. This inn was *Yankee* magazine's "Editor's Pick." The inn offers unique, authentic, colonial lodging convenient to antique and outlet shopping, the Strawbery Banke Museum, several historic mansions on tour, beaches, and the rugged coastline of Maine.

Three Chimneys Chowder

½ pound quality bacon, diced and
      rendered until golden
1 stalk celery, diced
4 large Spanish onions, diced
1 pound unsalted butter
3 cups all-purpose flour
1 pound red potatoes, rinsed and diced
3 (6-ounce) cans chopped clams,
      drained, liquid reserved
Thyme sprigs

Few bay leaves
3 quarts heavy cream
1½ gallons milk
Black pepper
Worcestershire sauce
Celery salt
Parsley
Tabasco

Using a heavy gauge five-gallon bucket and wooden spoon, mix bacon, celery, onions, butter, and flour. Rinse and dice potatoes. Boil potatoes in reserved clam broth. Add water if needed to cover potatoes. Add thyme sprigs and bay leaves to potatoes and cook just until tender. Remove bay leaves and thyme sprigs and add potatoes to bacon, vegetables, butter, and flour. Add the 3 quarts of heavy cream and milk, heat. Season with lots of black pepper, salt, Worcestershire sauce, celery salt, parsley, and Tabasco to taste. Add the chopped, drained clams. Heat and serve. Yields about 5 gallons.

ROSEWOOD COUNTRY INN

67 Pleasant View Road
Bradford, NH 03221
(603) 938-5253 (phone)
(800) 938-5273 (toll free)
info@rosewoodcountryinn.com
www.rosewoodcountryinn.com

Tucked away on a meandering country lane, the Rosewood Country Inn is set against a backdrop of rolling fields and hills. Here lies an extraordinary treasure for the discerning traveler. With elegant guest rooms and inspired cuisine, the inn is noted for its warmth and charm. The Mt. Sunapee area abounds with seasonal activities. During the winter months, there is downhill skiing at Mt. Sunapee and X-C, nd snowmobiling right from door. Summer brings con-...een, hiking, League of New Hampshire Craft Fair (America's oldest craft fair), summer stock theater, historic sites, golf, and tax-free shopping. Autumn brings New England's best leaf-peeping and foliage, and spring wouldn't be complete without maple sugar shack tours.

Butternut Apple Bisque

2 (16-ounce) cans butternut
    squash purée
1½ teaspoons ground cinnamon
½ teaspoon ground cloves
½ cup apple cider
¼ cup maple syrup
2 cups heavy cream
Paprika

Combine squash purée, cinnamon, cloves, apple cider, and maple syrup in large saucepan and simmer over medium heat 5 to 10 minutes. Add cream and heat through. Serve with dusting of paprika. Great first course for Thanksgiving dinner. Yields 8 servings.

Hot Artichoke Dip

1 (5½-ounce) can artichokes, drained
1 cup grated Parmesan cheese
½ cup mayonnaise
½ cup sour cream
1 teaspoon lemon juice
¼ teaspoon garlic powder

Place artichokes in food processor and pulse a few times. Transfer to small bowl and add cheese, mayonnaise, sour cream, lemon juice, and garlic powder. Place mixture in small casserole dish and microwave on high 1 minute. Stir and microwave additional 1 to 2 minutes until cheese has melted and mixture is hot. Serve with garlic pita crackers. Yields about 3 cups.

Cherry Granola

2½ cups old-fashioned oats
1 cup large-shred coconut
1 cup coarsely chopped pecans
    or almonds
½ cup pumpkin seeds
1 teaspoon ground cinnamon
1 cup packed dark brown sugar
¼ cup water
3 tablespoons vegetable oil
¾ cup dried cherries

Position rack in top third of oven. Grease a heavy, large baking sheet. Combine oats, coconut, pecans, pumpkin seeds, and cinnamon in large bowl. Bring sugar, water, and oil to boil in heavy saucepan. Add sugar mixture to oat mixture and stir with a fork until well combined. Preheat oven to 275°. Spread mixture evenly on prepared baking sheet and bake 15 minutes. Stir and bake 10 minutes longer. Stir in dried cherries. Bake until golden brown, stirring frequently, about 10 minutes longer. Stir mixture and cool completely. Store in airtight container. Yields 7½ cups.

Piña Colada Muffins

2 cups all-purpose flour
1 cup sugar
2½ teaspoons baking powder
½ teaspoon salt
1 stick margarine, melted and cooled
2 eggs, lightly beaten
8 ounces low-fat sour cream
½ teaspoon coconut extract
3 ounces grated sweet coconut
¼ cup chopped maraschino cherries
1 (6-ounce) can crushed pineapple,
    drained well

Preheat oven to 375°. Combine flour, sugar, baking powder, and salt. Combine margarine, eggs, sour cream, coconut extract, coconut, cherries, and pineapple. Add to dry ingredients. Pour into greased muffin tins and bake 25 to 30 minutes. Yields 12 muffins.

Rosewood Egg Soufflé

8 slices tomato bread
    or any dense herb bread, cubed
1 teaspoon minced scallions
1 cup broccoli florets
8 ounces Swiss cheese, grated
4 ounces Cheddar cheese, grated
6 large eggs
1½ cups milk
1 teaspoon salt
Dash of pepper
½ teaspoon onion powder
Parsley
Paprika
Grated Parmesan cheese

Preheat oven to 425°. Spray six individual, 8-ounce casserole dishes with nonstick spray. Divide cubed bread, scallions, broccoli, and cheeses among the dishes. Place eggs, milk, salt, pepper, and onion powder in blender and blend on low. Pour over casseroles. Sprinkle with parsley, paprika, and Parmesan cheese. Bake about 20 minutes or until puffed and golden brown. Yields 6 servings.

THE BERNERHOF INN

P.O. Box 240
Route 302
Glen, NH 03838
(603) 383-9132 (phone)
(603) 383-0809 (fax)
(800) 548-8007 (toll free)
inn@bernerhofinn.com
www.bernerhofinn.com

The perfect getaway, the Bernerhof is a charming Victorian-style inn at the gateway to the White Mountains, a favorite destination for travelers and diners since 1880. The inn is surrounded by a dozen Nordic and Alpine ski areas, with great hiking, biking, foliage, canoeing, kayaking, snowshoeing, horseback riding, and so much more. Go on a waterfall tour, snuggle by a fire and watch the snow fall, or relax in a Jacuzzi after a hard day of play. We have the perfect escape for you. Recipes are from the Rare Bear Bistro Dining Room at the Bernerhof Inn.

Wild Mushroom and Goat Cheese Terrine

2 tablespoons olive oil
3 cups sliced wild mushrooms
Salt and pepper
1 tablespoon chopped herbs
      (thyme, rosemary, tarragon)
1 small shallot, finely diced
6 ounces goat cheese
1 tablespoon chives

In large skillet on high heat, heat oil until smoking. Add mushrooms and let cook until golden. Add salt, pepper, herbs, and shallot and stir 30 seconds, being careful not to burn shallots. Remove from pan and cool completely. In mixer with paddle attachment, beat goat cheese just until smooth. Add mushrooms and chives and mix just until blended, scraping down sides once. Put mushroom mixture on parchment paper and wrap to form a log. Roll parchment around, leaving 1 inch paper on both ends. Wrap parchment in plastic wrap and twist each end to form a tight log. Chill overnight. Unwrap terrine and slice. Yields 4 servings.

Wild Mushroom and Ramp Risotto

1 small onion, diced
2 cloves garlic, minced
2 cups Arborio rice
½ cup white wine
6 cups chicken stock
½ cup cream
½ cup Parmesan cheese
Olive oil or butter
2 cups sliced wild mushrooms
1 cup chopped wild ramps
1 shallot, minced
1 tablespoon chopped herbs
Salt and pepper

In large sauce pan, sauté onions and garlic until translucent. Add rice and stir until you hear popping. Add wine and reduce until dry. Add 1 cup stock and stir constantly. When rice has absorbed the stock, add another cup. Continue until rice is al dente. Add cream and Parmesan. In large sauté pan heat oil or butter over medium heat. Add mushrooms and ramp, and sauté until soft. Toss with shallots, herbs, and salt and pepper to taste. Stir into rice. Season to taste. Yields 8 servings.

Sautéed Salmon with Brown Butter Citrus Sauce

Oil
4 (8-ounce) salmon fillets,
      seasoned with salt and pepper
4 tablespoons butter
4 segments each of orange, grapefruit,
      lime, and lemon
1 tablespoon shallots
1 tablespoon chives
Salt and pepper

Cover bottom of large sauté pan with oil over high heat. Just before smoking point, add salmon. Cook on each side about 3 minutes. In separate pan over medium heat, add butter and cook until it browns. Immediately add citrus and remove from heat. Add shallots and chives. Season with salt and pepper to taste. Serve sauce over salmon. Yields 4 servings.

Homemade Chicken Fennel Hash

3 skinless chicken breasts, diced
5 strips bacon, diced
½ cup each small-dice onion, turnip,
      Yukon gold potato, and red pepper
1 cup small-dice fennel
1 shallot, minced
3 cloves garlic, minced
1 cup heavy cream
1 tablespoon chopped fresh thyme
½ teaspoon chopped rosemary
Salt and pepper

In food processor, add chicken and pulse until it resembles ground chicken. In large

The Bernerhof Inn

sauté pan over medium heat render bacon and remove, leaving fat in pan. Add onion, turnips, and potatoes and sauté until tender. Add red peppers and fennel and cook until tender. Remove from pan and add chicken. Cook thoroughly and add shallot, garlic, cream, thyme, and rosemary. Cook 2 minutes or until cream is absorbed and season with salt and pepper to taste. Yields 4 servings.

FOXGLOVE, A COUNTRY INN

Route 117 at Lover's Lane
Sugar Hill, NH 03585
(603) 823-8840 (phone)
(603) 823-5755 (fax)
(888) 343-2220 (toll free)
foxgloveinn@compuserve.com
www.foxgloveinn.com

Foxglove is elegance atop Sugar Hill— a newly renovated, designer decorated, turn-of-the-century country home. Cozy, romantic bedrooms and suites along with private baths, crackling fireplaces, park-like woodland setting, hideaway porches, terraces and quiet glades are provided. There are trickling fountains, soft music, swaying hammocks, and fabulous sunsets. Foxglove offers guests a tranquil and impeccable setting from which they may explore and enjoy the charm of this historic little mountain village with its magnificent views and vistas and the natural beauty that lies at its feet.

Goat Cheese Spread with Lemon

2 cloves garlic, minced
4 teaspoons lemon zest
Freshly ground black pepper
4 teaspoons chopped fresh thyme
½ cup soft goat cheese
½ cup soft cream cheese
¼ cup olive oil

Mix garlic, lemon zest, pepper, and thyme in small bowl. Divide and blend half with cheeses thoroughly. Put in serving bowl. Add olive oil to remaining half of garlic mixture and spoon on top of cheese mixture. Serve with crackers. Yields 1½ cups.

Banana Nut Bread

¼ pound (1 stick) butter, softened
1 cup sugar
2 eggs, beaten
3 ripe bananas, mashed
2 cups all-purpose flour
1 teaspoon baking soda
1 teaspoon salt
1 teaspoon vanilla extract
¼ cup orange juice
½ teaspoon grated orange zest
½ cup toasted chopped pecans

Preheat oven to 350°. Cream butter and sugar, add eggs and mashed bananas, and beat until foamy. Add flour, baking soda, salt, vanilla, orange juice, and orange zest. Stir in pecans. Put in large loaf pan and bake 1 hour or until toothpick comes out clean. Cool 10 minutes and remove from pan. Yields 1 large loaf.

Kathy's Famous Stuffed Mushrooms

2 pounds stuffing mushrooms
6 plus 4 tablespoons melted butter
1 cup shredded mozzarella cheese
⅓ cup Parmesan cheese
¼ cup breadcrumbs (optional)
Pimiento-stuffed green olives, halved (optional)

Preheat broiler. Wipe mushroom caps with damp paper towel and discard stems. Brush with 4 tablespoons butter and place under broiler, top-side up. Let tops broil just to soften slightly. In separate bowl add cheeses, remaining 6 tablespoons butter, and breadcrumbs. Stuff mushroom caps with mixture and top with olive half. When ready to serve, place mushrooms under broiler until brown and bubbly. Serve immediately. Yields 24 mushrooms.

Foxglove, A Country Inn

Kathy's Roasted Pork Loin

5-pound boneless pork roast

Marinade:
½ cup soy sauce
½ cup sherry
1 teaspoon minced garlic
1 teaspoon ground ginger
1 teaspoon thyme

Sauce:
1 jar current jelly
2 tablespoons sherry
1 tablespoon soy sauce

Place pork roast in large plastic bag. Mix marinade ingredients together and pour over pork. Marinate overnight or at least 8 hours, turning occasionally.

When ready to cook, preheat oven to 350°. Place roast in 9 x 11-inch baking pan and bake until meat thermometer registers pork is done, from 155 to 160°, (20 to 25 minutes per pound). Internal temperature will rise another 5 to 10° after removing from oven. Discard marinade.

For sauce, heat jelly, sherry, and soy sauce in small pan over low heat until jelly melts. Serve with pork. Yields 12 to 15 servings.

Mom Riley's Best and Easiest Carrot Cake

3 jars strained baby carrots
2 cups sugar
1½ cups vegetable oil
4 large eggs
3 cups all-purpose flour
2 teaspoons baking soda
1 teaspoon salt
1 (20-ounce) can crushed pineapple, drained
1 cup raisins
1 cup chopped walnuts

Cream cheese icing:
8 ounces cream cheese, softened
1 stick butter, softened
½ box confectioners' sugar
1 teaspoon vanilla extract
Chopped walnuts (optional)

Preheat oven to 350°. Mix ingredients in order given. Pour into greased tube pan. Bake for 1 hour or until toothpick comes out clean. Cool before icing.

For icing, beat all ingredients until creamy, frost cake, and cover with chopped walnuts, if desired. Spread over cake. Yields 16 to 18 servings.

25 minutes per pound). Internal temperature will rise another 5 to 10° after removing from oven. Discard marinade.

For sauce, heat jelly, sherry, and soy sauce in small pan over low heat until jelly melts. Serve with pork. Yields 12 to 15 servings.

New Jersey

The Chalfonte Bed & Breakfast

301 Howard Street
Cape May, NJ 08204
(609) 884-8409 (phone)
(609) 884-4588 (fax)
(888) 411-1998 (toll free)
chalfontnj@aol.com
www.chalfonte.com

The Chalfonte is Cape May's oldest continually operating hotel, serving guests since 1876. The Magnolia Room restaurant in the Chalfonte is acclaimed for its southern style fare made famous by generations of chefs beginning with the late Miss Helen Dickerson, and now presided over by her daughters, Dot Burton and Lucille Thompson. Cape May is a resort for all seasons, and is America's only National Landmark City, with more than six hundred registered landmarks. It's a Victorian wonderland, situated on an island with superb beaches, dining, entertainment, and lots of open natural space for birders, naturalists, and bicyclists.

Dot's Buttermilk Biscuits

2 cups all-purpose flour
2 teaspoons baking powder
½ teaspoon salt
Pinch of sugar
¼ teaspoon baking soda
4 tablespoons shortening
¾ cup buttermilk

Mix flour, baking powder, salt, sugar, and baking soda. Cut shortening into dry ingredients. Gradually add buttermilk until dough is manageable. Do not make it too sticky. Preheat oven to 400°. Roll on floured board until dough is ¼ inch thick. Cut out biscuits about size of silver dollars. Bake in greased or sprayed pan until golden brown, about 20 minutes. Yields 2 dozen biscuits.

Lucille's Onion Soup

4 cups thinly sliced, large, mild onions
5 tablespoons margarine or butter
¼ teaspoon pepper
5 beef bouillon cubes
1 cup boiling water
5⅓ cups chicken stock
1 teaspoon salt
5 (2-inch) toast rounds
Parmesan cheese (optional)

Sauté onions in butter until golden brown. Sprinkle with pepper. Dissolve bouillon cubes in boiling water. Add stock, onions, and salt. Simmer, covered, about 1 hour. If there's time, let soup sit overnight—it enhances flavor. Lightly spread toasts with garlic butter and broil until browned. Place rounds in bowls and cover with soup. If desired, sprinkle with Parmesan cheese. Yields 5 servings.

Helen's Macaroni & Cheese

Cream sauce:
2 tablespoons butter
2 tablespoons all-purpose flour
¼ teaspoon salt
Pinch of pepper
1 cup milk

½ pound macaroni
2 cups grated sharp Cheddar cheese
½ cup breadcrumbs
Paprika

Melt butter in small saucepan over medium heat. Mix flour, salt, and pepper and blend with butter. Add milk gradually, stirring constantly. Bring to a boil point and cook 2 to 3 minutes, stirring constantly. Butter casserole dish. Cook macaroni according to package directions. Preheat oven to 350°. Place layer of macaroni in bottom of dish. Sprinkle with half the cheese. Pour half the cream sauce over macaroni. Repeat and sprinkle breadcrumbs and paprika on last layer. Bake until brown on top, 20 to 30 minutes. Yields 6 to 8 servings.

250

CHIMNEY HILL FARM ESTATE

207 Goat Hill Road
Lambertville, NJ 08530
(609) 397-1516 (phone)
(800) 211-4667 (toll free)
info@chimneyhillinn.com
www.chimneyhillinn.com

Chimney Hill Farm Estate, 1820 Field-stone Manor House, and the Ol' Barn Inn sit on eight and a half acres of wooded landscaped grounds on a country road one minute from the antique mecca of Lambertville, New Jersey, and the artistic funky nightlife of New Hope, Pennsylvania. The inn offers private baths, fireplaces, Jacuzzis, and alpacas.

Blueberry Sour Cream Coffee Cake

1⅔ cups sour cream
1½ sticks butter, softened
3 eggs
1 tablespoon almond extract
3 cups plus 2 tablespoons all-purpose flour
1½ cups sugar
1½ tablespoons baking powder
1½ teaspoons baking soda
1 teaspoon salt
1 cup blueberries, fresh or frozen
Confectioners' sugar

Preheat oven to 350°. Coat 10-inch tube pan with nonstick spray. In large bowl mix together sour cream, butter, eggs, and almond extract. In medium bowl mix together 3 cups flour, sugar, baking powder, baking soda, and salt. Add dry ingredients to wet ingredients and mix well. This makes a very stiff dough. Toss blueberries with remaining 2 tablespoons flour. Gently fold berries into dough. Do *not* overmix; that will cause cake to be green. Place dough into prepared pan, smoothing top. Bake 1 hour. Cool cake in pan. Once cool, run a knife around edge of pan to release cake. Place on cake plate and sprinkle with confectioners' sugar. Yields 12 servings.

Chimney Hill Farm Estate's Own Alpaca Cookies

(No actual alpacas are used in the recipe.)

1 cup softened butter
1 cup sugar
1 egg
2 tablespoons orange juice
1 tablespoon vanilla extract
2½ cups all-purpose flour
1 teaspoon baking powder
1 teaspoon ground cinnamon

Glaze:
2½ cups confectioners' sugar
2 tablespoons orange juice
1 tablespoon softened butter
1 tablespoon light corn syrup
½ teaspoon vanilla extract

In large mixing bowl combine butter, sugar, and egg, beating at medium speed for 1 to 2 minutes until creamy. Add orange juice and vanilla. Continue beating, scraping bowl often for additional 1 to 2 minutes. Reduce speed to low. In separate bowl combine flour, baking powder, and cinnamon. Add to egg mixture and beat, scraping bowl often, until well mixed. Divide dough into thirds. Shape each third into a ball and place onto sheet of saran wrap. Flatten ball to ½ inch. Wrap in plastic and refrigerate for 2 to 3 hours until firm.

Preheat oven to 400°. Roll out dough on lightly floured surface ⅛- to ¼-inch thickness. (Use a third of dough at a time, keeping remaining dough in fridge until time to roll out.) Cut out with Place 1 inch apart on ungre sheet. Bake 6 to10 minutes or until are lightly browned. Cool completely.

For glaze, combine ingredients in small mixing bowl. Beat at medium speed until smooth. Spread over cooled cookies and let harden. Yields 4 to 6 dozen servings.

Betty's Heavenly Bananas

½ cup sour cream
2 tablespoons sugar
1 teaspoon orange peel
1 tablespoon orange juice
2 large bananas, sliced
4 tablespoons granola

In small bowl combine sour cream, sugar, orange peel, and orange juice, and mix well. Add bananas and toss gently. Put one-fourth mixture in each of four ice cream sundae dishes. Top each serving with 1 tablespoon granola. Yields 4 (½-cup) servings.

Baked Apple French Toast

½ cup (1 stick) butter
½ cup brown sugar
1 tablespoon white corn syrup
3 large apples
½ cup currants
12 slices bread (wheat, bran, or white)
6 eggs, beaten
4 cups milk
2 tablespoons vanilla extract
Ground cinnamon

Preheat oven to 350°. Coat 13 x 9-inch pan with nonstick spray. In small saucepan over low heat melt butter and add sugar and syrup. Slice apples thinly, leaving peel on, but discard seeds and core. Simmer apples in butter mixture 1 to 2 minutes.

Pour apple mixture into prepared pan and sprinkle currants over top. On cutting board, stack bread slices and cut each in half. Laying slices over apple mixture, making sure all bread and bread crust is wet. Mix eggs, milk, and vanilla and pour over bread. Sprinkle with cinnamon. Bake 40 to 50 minutes until golden brown and puffy. Yields 8 to 12 servings.

Low-Fat Vegetable Quiche

2 cups diced vegetables (zucchini, broccoli, tomato, onion)
1 cup shredded low-fat Cheddar cheese
5 eggs (or egg substitute to equal 5 eggs or 8 egg whites and 1 whole egg)
2¼ cups skim milk
1¼ cup low-fat biscuit mix
1 teaspoon fresh or dried herbs (such as basil, dill, tarragon)

Preheat oven to 400°. Coat 10-inch pie or quiche pan with nonstick spray. Place veggies in pan. Place cheese on top of veggies. In medium bowl beat together eggs, milk, biscuit mix, and herbs. Pour over vegetables and cheese. Bake 40 minutes, or until lightly browned and knife inserted in center comes out clean. Let stand 5 minutes before cutting into wedges. Fresh herbs, cherry tomato cup filled with parsley, and a sprinkle of dried herbs around the plate make a nice presentation. Yields 6 servings.

THE MAINSTAY INN

635 Columbia Avenue
Cape May, NJ 08204
(609) 884-8690
reservations@mainstayinn.com
www.mainstayinn.com

Once a private club for wealthy gamblers, the Mainstay Inn is now an elegant, but friendly, bed and breakfast. Spacious rooms, wide verandas, and lovely gardens await the guests. Mainstay is located in the historic district of a national landmark community, but is just a brief walk from beautiful beaches, excellent birding trails, and award-winning restaurants. Golf and tennis are available nearby, as is a day spa and numerous shops.

Poached Pears with Brandied Cranberries

Pears:
2 cups cranberry juice
2 tablespoons brown sugar
½ teaspoon ground cinnamon
½ teaspoon ground nutmeg
4 firm medium pears, peeled, cored, and halved

Brandied cranberries:
1½ (12-ounce) packages fresh cranberries (18 ounces total)
1½ cups sugar
¼ cup brandy

To prepare pears bring cranberry juice, sugar, cinnamon, and nutmeg to a boil in saucepan over medium-high heat. Add pear halves and simmer 30 minutes. Refrigerate for 1 hour or until thoroughly chilled.

To make brandied cranberries, preheat oven to 350°. Lightly grease 15 x 10-inch jellyroll pan. Arrange cranberries in single layer in prepared pan. Top with sugar. Cover tightly with foil and Bake 45 minutes. Spoon into bowl and add brandy, tossing to combine. Refrigerate 1 hour or until thoroughly chilled. Serve cranberries over pears. Yields 8 servings.

Apple-Sausage Ring

2 pounds bulk sausage
2 eggs, lightly beaten
¼ cup minced onion (½ small onion)
½ cup milk
1½ cups seasoned herb stuffing
1 cup peeled, chopped apple (1 medium)

Preheat oven to 350°. Grease baking sheet. Mix all ingredients until thoroughly combined. Form mixture into ring on prepared baking sheet and bake 1 hour or until browned. Drain and cut into serving slices. Serve hot. Yields 8 servings.

Lemon-Frosted Pecan Bars

1½ plus ¼ cups all-purpose flour
⅓ cup confectioners' sugar
¾ cup (1½ sticks) butter
2 cups brown sugar
4 eggs, beaten
1 cup chopped pecans
½ teaspoon baking powder

Frosting:
¾ cup softened butter
3 cups confectioners' sugar
1½ teaspoons grated lemon zest
2 tablespoons fresh lemon juice

Preheat oven to 350°. Grease 13 x 9-inch baking pan. Combine 1½ cups flour with confectioner's sugar. Cut in butter with pastry blender or two knives until mixture is crumbly. Press onto bottom of prepared pan and Bake 15 minutes. In large bowl combine brown sugar, remaining ¼ cup flour, eggs, pecans, and baking powder. Mix well. Spread evenly over baked crust and bake 20 to 25 minutes or until lightly browned. Cool. To prepare frosting, with electric mixer beat butter, confectioners' sugar, lemon zest, and lemon juice until well blended and spreading consistency. Spread frosting over cooled base and cut into bars. Yields 36 servings.

Fruit Pizza

Filling:
1 (14-ounce) can sweetened
    condensed milk
½ cup sour cream
¼ cup lemon juice
1 teaspoon vanilla extract

Dough:
½ cup softened butter
¼ cup brown sugar
1 cup all-purpose flour
¼ cup quick-cooking rolled oats
¼ cup finely chopped walnuts

Glaze:
½ cup apricot preserves
2 tablespoons brandy
4 cups thinly sliced fresh fruit (such as
    kiwis, strawberries, bananas)

For filling mix milk, sour cream, lemon juice, and vanilla. Refrigerate for at least 30 minutes. Preheat oven to 375°. Lightly oil 12-inch pizza pan.

To make dough, beat butter and sugar until fluffy. Mix in flour, rolled oats, and walnuts. Place dough on prepared pizza pan and press into a circle, forming rim around edge. Prick with fork and bake 10 to 12 minutes. Cool.

For glaze, melt apricot preserves in small saucepan over low heat. Add brandy and mix. Strain. Spoon chilled filling over cooled crust. Arrange fruit slices in circular pattern over filling. Brush glaze over fruit. Cover and refrigerate 1 hour. Cut into wedges and serve. Yields 8 servings.

Feta Cheese Corn Muffins

1 cup cornmeal
⅔ cup all-purpose flour
1 teaspoon baking powder
½ teaspoon baking soda
½ teaspoon salt
1 tablespoon finely chopped fresh basil
1 cup crumbled feta cheese (4 ounces)
1 cup milk
1 egg
½ cup (1 stick) butter, melted

Preheat oven to 425°. Grease 12 muffin cups. In large bowl, whisk together cornmeal, flour, baking powder, baking soda, and salt. Add basil and cheese and toss well. In small bowl, whisk together milk, egg, and butter. Add to cornmeal mixture, stirring just until batter is combined (Do not overmix). Scoop batter into prepared muffin cups and bake 18 to 20 minutes or until golden and springy to touch. Turn out on a wire rack to cool. Serve warm or at room temperature. Yields 12 muffins.

THE QUEEN VICTORIA® BED & BREAKFAST

Cape May, NJ 08204
(609) 884-8702
www.queenvictoria.com

The Queen Victoria Bed & Breakfast offers twenty-one inviting rooms and suites all with private baths in two historic homes located in the center of Victorian Cape May, New Jersey, one block from the Atlantic Ocean. The bed and breakfast is open all year with special winter packages.

Cape May is known for historic tours, exceptional birding, unique shopping, antiquing, gourmet dining, and numerous festivals, including the Cape May Music Festival, Jazz Festival, Food and Wine Festival, and the popular Victorian Week.

Poppy Seed Bread

4 eggs
2 cups sugar
1 (13-ounce) can evaporated milk
    (not sweetened condensed milk)
3 ounces milk or half-and-half
2 cups vegetable oil
4 cups all-purpose flour
4 teaspoons baking powder
½ cup poppy seeds
1 teaspoon salt

Preheat oven to 325°. Beat together eggs, sugar, milks, and oil. Add flour, baking powder, poppy seeds, and salt. Batter will be quite liquid. Pour into four greased loaf pans and bake 45 to 60 minutes or until tester inserted in center comes out clean. Yields 4 loaves.

Applesauce Bread Pudding

16 slices cinnamon or raisin bread
½ cup softened butter
2 cups applesauce
1 cup brown sugar
4 teaspoons ground cinnamon
½ teaspoon ground nutmeg
1 cup raisins (optional)
4 cups milk
4 eggs
2 teaspoons vanilla extract
Whipped cream (optional)

Spread bread with butter. Fit half on bottom of 3-quart glass baking dish that has been sprayed with nonstick pan coating. Cut bread to fit as necessary. Spread applesauce on top. Mix sugar, cinnamon, and nutmeg and sprinkle on top of applesauce, followed by raisins, if using, and remaining buttered bread. In separate bowl, blend milk, eggs, and vanilla. Pour over ingredients in baking dish. May be prepared in advance to this point and refrigerated, covered. When ready to serve, preheat oven to 350° and bake 45 to 60 minutes until lightly puffed and browned. Serve with whipped or light cream if desired. Yields 12 servings.

Walnut Blue Cheese Spread

8 ounces cream cheese, softened
3 ounces blue or Stilton cheese
1 tablespoon dry sherry
½ cup chopped walnuts
2 tablespoons minced parsley
⅛ teaspoon garlic powder

In food processor, cream cheeses together with sherry. Add remaining ingredients and process just until blended. Walnuts should be good-size pieces, not flakes. If softer mixture is desired, thin with sour cream. Serve with crackers or stuff cucumbers, celery, shrimp, or apple slices. Store in refrigerator up to two weeks, covered. Yields 2 cups.

No-Bake Chocolate-Topped Nut Chews

6 cups (about 90) finely crushed
  vanilla wafers
1 cup ground toasted almonds
1 cup melted and cooled butter
½ cup sweetened condensed milk
¼ teaspoon salt
2 cups chocolate chips

Combine crumbs, nuts, butter, condensed milk, and salt. Mix well. Press into greased, rimmed, 10 x 15-inch cookie pan. Melt chocolate chips and stir until smooth. Spread melted chips over crumb layer. Chill until firm. Cut into 2 x 1-inch bars. Yields 72 bars.

Rancho Arriba Bed & Breakfast

P.O. Box 338
Truchas, NM 87578
(505) 689-2374
rancho@ranchoarriba.com
www.ranchoarriba.com

Rancho Arriba is a small farm in the mountains of northern New Mexico. Located on a Spanish Land Grant (1752) adjacent to the Pecos Wilderness, the adobe hacienda affords an informal rural getaway with spectacular views in every direction. A full breakfast is cooked on the wood-burning stove with eggs from our chickens.

Chicken Enchiladas

6 (10-inch) flour tortillas
2 tablespoons olive oil
1 large onion, chopped
2 to 3 garlic cloves, chopped
3 (8-ounce) boneless chicken breasts,
    boiled or grilled

Dampen tortillas by wrapping in wet paper towel. Heat oil in skillet over medium-high heat. Sauté onion a couple minutes. Add garlic in skillet and continue to sauté until onion is translucent. Preheat oven to 350º. Shred the cooked chicken. Divide onion, garlic, and chicken among tortillas. Roll up and place in lightly oiled pan. Cover with Cheddar cheese. Bake about 10 minutes. Once cheese melts cover with enchilada sauce and bake a couple minutes more. Yields 3 servings (2 enchiladas a piece).

Fairfield's Bread

1½ to 1¼ cups all-purpose flour
    (some wheat germ can
    be substituted)
1 cup bran
1 teaspoon baking powder
½ teaspoon salt
⅓ cup sugar
½ teaspoon ground cinnamon
½ teaspoon ground clove
½ teaspoon ground nutmeg
⅓ cup oil or butter
2 to 3 tablespoons molasses
1 cup milk or water
¼ cup fruit or nuts of your choice

Preheat oven to 375º. Combine dry ingredients in mixing bowl. In another bowl combine butter, molasses, milk, and fruit or nuts. Add wet mixture to dry mixture and knead with hands. Put dough in loaf pan and bake 20 to 30 minutes. Yields 1 loaf.

Gandy Dancer Bed & Breakfast Inn

299 Maple Avenue
Chama, NM 87520
(505) 756-2191
(800) 424-6702
frontdesk@gandydancerbb.com
www.gandydancerbb.com

The Gandy Dancer Bed & Breakfast Inn is an historic 1912 Victorian with seven luxurious rooms, each with private bath, television and VCR. Bountiful breakfasts are served daily, featuring our fresh baked treats and savory dishes. Situated in the beautiful village of Chama, New Mexico, nestled in the Rockies, you'll step back in time to a Western town surrounded by nature unspoiled. We have hundreds of species of indigenous birds to watch. Fish in the lakes, rivers & streams or explore the hiking paths, abundant wildlife reserves and national forests on horseback, snowmobile, 4 x 4, on foot, cross-country skis or snowshoes. Experience the historic Cumbres and Toltec scenic railway that takes you through the Rockies. Don't miss the incredible fall colors!

Ira's German Buttercake

Dough:
½ cup milk
3 tablespoons sugar
2 teaspoons salt
3 tablespoons butter
2 packages active dry yeast
1½ cups warm water (105–115°)
6 cups all-purpose flour
2 (8-ounce) cans almond pie filling

Topping:
¾ cup sugar
1 teaspoon ground cinnamon
¼ pound (1 stick) butter
4 ounces sliced almonds

Preheat oven to 400°. For dough, scald milk and stir in sugar, salt, and butter. Let mixture cool to about 115°. In warmed bowl, dissolve yeast in warm water. Add milk mixture and add 4½ cups of flour. Knead dough and add remaining flour as needed until dough is no longer sticky. Lightly oil inside of large bowl so dough won't stick and let dough rise 1 hour in bowl covered with a towel. Divide dough in half and let each half rise 10 more minutes. Roll out half of dough on greased cookie sheet to about ¼ inch thick. Spread almond filling on top of dough. Roll out second half of dough, again to ¼ inch thickness and lay over the first layer; crimp edges.

For Topping, mix sugar and cinnamon together. Slice stick of butter into ⅛ inch thick slices and lay them on top of cake. Press each piece lightly into dough. Sprinkle cinnamon sugar over cake and lay almond slices on top. Bake 20 to 30 minutes or until golden brown and toothpick poked in center comes out clean. Yields 1 buttercake.

Savory Sausage Casserole

2 pounds spicy pork sausage (uncased)
12 eggs, lightly beaten
12 ounce sour cream
1 large yellow pepper, diced
1 large orange pepper, diced
1 onion, diced
3 medium zucchini, diced
3 cups sliced mushrooms
3 cups cubed sharp Cheddar cheese

Preheat oven to 400°. Brown sausage; drain grease. In large bowl, lightly beat eggs, stir in sour cream, leaving small lumps. Add diced vegetables, cheese, and sausage and mix well. Finally, add sliced mushrooms and lightly stir. Coat 10 x 15-casserole dish with nonstick spray and pour in mixture. Bake 60 minutes or until golden brown and center is firm. Yields 12 servings.

Note: This recipe is high altitude specific. You may need to adjust temperature and cooking time slightly for lower altitudes.

Gandy Dancer Roast Potatoes

8 large baking potatoes
2 large lemons
4 tablespoons rosemary leaves
2 tablespoons coarse sea salt
Olive oil

Preheat oven to 425°. Clean potatoes, leaving skin on. Cut potatoes into wedges, lengthwise (about ½ inch thick on skin-side). Lightly grease large baking sheet with olive oil. Place potato wedges on baking sheet and rotate them so olive oil coats both sides lightly. Cut lemons in half and squeeze the juice over potatoes. Sprinkle rosemary leaves and sea salt over potatoes. Bake 35 to 40 minutes or until golden. Yields 12 servings.

New York

SOUTH WINDS BED & BREAKFAST

91 Potunk Lane
Westhampton Beach, NY 11978
(631) 288-5505 (phone)
(631) 288-5506 (fax)
(866) 332-3344 (toll free)
info@southwindsbnb.com
www.southwindsbnb.com

South Winds Bed & Breakfast is a century-old restored country colonial home in the heart of Westhampton Beach. Decorated with family antiques and original watercolor paintings, each of four bedrooms features private bath, A/C, hair dryer, cable TV, and ceiling fan. There is a large front porch, a fireplace in the parlor, and a swimming pool for your use. A full breakfast

and afternoon snacks are available daily. Open year-round, South Winds offers things to do in the area: North and South Fork wineries, outlet center, aquarium, fishing, ocean beach, shopping, antiques, nature trails, golf, and tennis.

Country Scones

¼ cup dried currants
¼ cup dried cranberries
2 cups all-purpose flour
3 tablespoons plus 1 teaspoon sugar
2 teaspoons baking powder
⅔ teaspoon salt
½ teaspoon baking soda
½ teaspoon orange zest
5 tablespoons butter
1 (8-ounce) container sour cream
1 egg, separated
¼ teaspoon ground cinnamon

In small bowl pour hot water over currants and cranberries just to cover and let stand 5 minutes. Drain well and set aside. In large bowl, combine flour, 3 tablespoons sugar, baking powder, salt, soda, and orange zest. Cut in butter with knives until mixture resembles coarse meal. Stir in currants and cranberries. In small bowl, blend sour cream and egg yolk. Add all at once to flour mixture. Stir just until dough sticks together. Knead on lightly floured surface about 2 minutes. Preheat oven to 425°. Divide dough into five or six portions and pat each into a circle about ½-inch thick. With knife, score each circle into quarters but do not separate. Place on ungreased

baking sheet. Beat egg white and brush dough. Mix remaining teaspoon sugar and cinnamon and sprinkle over top. Bake 15 to 20 minutes. Serve warm with butter and jam. Yields 6 servings.

Zucchini Nut Bread

3 cups all-purpose flour
1½ teaspoons ground cinnamon
1 teaspoon baking soda
½ teaspoon baking powder
½ teaspoon salt
3 eggs
2 cups sugar
1 cup canola oil
1 tablespoon vanilla extract
2 cups shredded zucchini
½ cup chopped nuts (walnuts or pecans)

Preheat oven to 350°. In large bowl combine flour, cinnamon, baking soda, powder, and salt. In another bowl beat eggs, sugar, oil, and vanilla. Add to dry ingredients. Stir just until combined. Fold in zucchini and nuts. Grease and flour two 8 x 4 x 2-inch loaf pans. Pour mixture evenly into pans. Bake 55 to 60 minutes until brown and toothpick inserted in center comes out clean. Cool 10 minutes and remove to wire rack. Cut in slices and serve. Wrap in foil to store. Refrigerate to keep for up to a week. Freezes very well. Great recipe to make ahead. Freshen refrigerated bread in toaster oven and serve with butter. Yields 2 loaves.

MAXWELL CREEK INN

7563 Lake Road
Sodus, NY 14551
(315) 483-2222
mcinnbnb@worldnet.att.net
www.maxwellcreekinn-bnb.com

Maxwell Creek Inn is a historic, 1846 cobblestone house on six acres of peace and tranquil beauty surrounded by woodland wildlife and apple orchards on the shores of Lake Ontario and the Seaway Trail. The property includes a historic gristmill and is rumored to have been on the Underground Railroad. Tennis court, canoe rental, walking trails, and one-quarter mile of prime shoreline fishing are just a few activities that await you at Maxwell Creek. There are five guest bedrooms with two efficiency suites. Each room provides private bath, air conditioning, private guest TV sitting room, and king/queen/or full beds. A full gourmet breakfast by candlelight greets you each morning. And don't forget the Murder Mystery Dinner Theater.

Broccoli Puffs

Crêpes:
1 cup all-purpose flour
½ teaspoon salt
1 cup whole milk
3 large eggs
2 tablespoons melted butter
　　or margarine

Batter:
6 large eggs, separated
1 cup whole milk
3 tablespoons light or fat-free mayonnaise
¼ teaspoon salt
2 cups shredded extra sharp
　　Cheddar cheese
1 (12-ounce) package frozen broccoli
　　florets, cooked according to
　　package directions
Salt and white pepper

For crêpes, lightly spray small sauté pan with canola oil. Heat pan over medium heat. Mix all ingredients and pour ¼ cup at a time in pan. Swirl batter to cover bottom of pan. Cook 30 to 35 seconds or until lightly brown on each side. Take out of pan and let cool on wax paper. Crêpes are easier to work with cold. Stack with wax paper in between and store in plastic bag.

For batter, beat egg yolks, milk, mayonnaise, and salt together. Beat whites in separate bowl until stiff and fold into yolk mixture. Preheat oven to 350°. Lightly butter cups and edges of 6-cup muffin pan. Tuck crêpe into each cup. Put shredded cheese in bottom of crêpe cup, then some broccoli. Top with cheese and season with salt and white pepper to taste. Pour egg batter into each crêpe cup, being careful not to allow seepage. Bake 30 minutes until golden and eggs are set. Carefully remove from muffin pan. Serve with bacon and toast. Yields 6 servings.

Ham and Egg Cups

¾ pound portobello
　　or mushrooms of your choice
¼ cup chopped onion
Salt and pepper
2 tablespoons butter
6 thin slices Virginia baked ham
6 large eggs

In food processor finely chop the mushrooms. In heavy pan cook onion, mushrooms, salt and pepper to taste, and butter on high heat until the liquid from the mushrooms is evaporated. Remove from heat. Preheat oven to 400° and lightly grease 6-cup muffin tin. Tuck 1 slice of ham into each muffin cup. Ham slices will hang over side. Spoon in 1 teaspoon mushroom pâté and drop 1 egg into each ham cup. Bake 15 minutes. Carefully remove ham cup from muffin tin and place on serving dish. Whites will be cooked but yokes will still be somewhat runny. Serve 2 ham cups with fresh fruit slices, toast, and homemade jam. Yields 3 servings.

Note: Can do individual servings or a whole bunch at a time.

Maxwell Creek Inn

Western Omelet Breakfast Braid

1 (8-ounce) package refrigerated crescent
    rolls
¼ pound ham, diced
4 ounces low-fat or fat-free cream cheese
½ cup milk
8 large eggs plus 1 egg white
1 teaspoon margarine or butter
¼ cup chopped red bell pepper
¾ cup sliced mushrooms
2 tablespoons sliced green onions
    with tops
Salt and pepper
½ cup shredded Cheddar cheese

On flat baking stone roll out 4 crescent
rolls, two deep and two wide, so that perforations are sealed. On longest side cut
dough into six strips on each side. Preheat
oven to 375°. Arrange ham in middle of
dough. In medium-size bowl microwave
cream cheese and milk on high for 1½ minutes. Beat in eggs. Sauté in margarine red
bell pepper, mushrooms, and green onions.
Add egg mixture to pan, season with salt
and pepper to taste, and cook until set but
still relatively wet and able to be spooned
out and arranged over ham. Sprinkle
Cheddar cheese over top of eggs. Lift strips
of dough across filling to meet in center,
twisting each strip one turn, and pinch
together. Do this all the way down pinching ends together. Beat egg white and brush
lightly over dough. Bake 25 to 28 minutes
or until golden. Cover with aluminum foil
after 15 to 20 minutes so that dough does
not burn. Cut into slices and serve with
toast and fresh fruit and homemade jam.
Yields 6 servings.

FRIENDS LAKE INN

Friends Lake Road
Chestertown, NY 12817
(518) 494-4751 (phone)
(518) 494-4616 (fax)
www.friendslake.com
friends@friendslake.com

Friends Lake is an Adirondack inn with
seventeen luxury guest rooms, some with
Jacuzzis, fireplaces, and lake views; an
imaginative new-American cuisine; a
superior wine collection; and thirty-two
kilometers of groomed, wooded snow-
shoe/ski trails. Activities available on
premises include swimming at our beach
or heated pool, canoeing or kayaking on
Friends Lake, and hiking on our wooded
trails. Close by is Gore Mountain, antiquing, outlet shopping, the racetrack in
Saratoga Springs, the sights and scenery of
Lake George, and the Olympic venues of
Lake Placid.

Braised Rabbit Cannelloni

1 whole rabbit, cleaned and dressed
Salt and pepper
2 tablespoons 10% olive oil blend
6 whole garlic cloves
2 peeled carrots, roughly cut
4 celery stalks, roughly cut
1 yellow onion, roughly cut
6 sprigs fresh thyme
2 sprigs fresh rosemary
1 bay leaf
2 cups white wine
1½ quarts veal stock
¾ cup caramelized yellow onion
20 pieces 3 x 3-inch pasta sheets
1 cup grated Parmesan cheese

Use sharp boning knife to cut rabbit into
manageable-size cooking pieces. Season
rabbit pieces with salt and pepper to taste.
Heat heavy medium-size pan and add oil
and rabbit pieces. Sear rabbit over moderately high heat. Remove pieces from pan.
Preheat oven to 350°. While pan is still hot,
add garlic, carrots, celery, onions, thyme,
rosemary, and bay leaf. Stir to coat ingredients with remaining oil in pan. Add wine
and reduce by half. Add rabbit back to pan,
cover with veal stock, and bake 2 hours, or
just until the rabbit is fork tender. When
meat is tender, remove pan from oven.
Carefully remove rabbit pieces from braising liquid and set aside to cool. Strain liquid, reserving liquid and discarding solids.
Divide liquid in half and place in two separate saucepans. Put one on medium-high
heat and reduce by half. Reserve other half
of liquid to make sauce. While first liquid
is reducing, carefully pick rabbit meat from
bones in small pieces to ensure all bones
are removed. Place meat in mixing bowl
and set bones aside to use later in sauce.
Add caramelized onions to mixing bowl
with rabbit meat. When braising liquid is
reduced by half, add to bowl with rabbit
and onion mixture. Mix together and place
in refrigerator to cool.

Heat oven to 350° again. Blanch pasta
sheets in boiling, salted water for about
1 minute each. Pat them lightly with clean
towel to remove excess water. Spread grated
Parmesan cheese on flat, clean work surface. Place pasta sheets flat on work surface
on top of cheese. This will keep pasta from
sticking to counter and makes a delicious
crust for cannelloni. Take rabbit mixture
from refrigerator and spoon 1 to 1½ tablespoons onto each pasta sheet. Carefully roll
each rabbit-filled pasta sheet into cannelloni. Roll tightly and place on lightly oiled
baking sheet. Sprinkle lightly with any remaining cheese from work surface and
bake 12 to 15 minutes or until cannelloni
are heated through and slightly browned
on top. Yields 4 servings.

Note: This is good served with oven-
dried tomatoes and artichoke tapenade
(see next recipe).

Artichoke Tapenade

6 whole fresh large artichokes
1 gallon hot water
2 tablespoons kosher salt
½ cup all-purpose-flour
1 tablespoon chopped fresh garlic
1 tablespoon balsamic vinegar
½ teaspoon chopped fresh thyme
2 teaspoons chopped fresh basil
¼ cup 100% olive oil
Salt and pepper

Cut stems off artichokes at base of choke. Don't cut meat of artichoke. Cut one inch off top of artichokes. Peel and snap off about a dozen leaves at base of each artichoke. Place artichokes in large pot with hot, salted water. Add flour and stir. After it comes to a boil, reduce to a simmer and cook until artichoke hearts are tender, when knife pierces easily and the blade slides back out with little resistance. Remove artichokes from water and place in ice water to rapidly cool. When completely cooled clean artichokes and peel all leaves away, then scoop out "choke". Discard leaves and choke. Place cleaned artichoke hearts into food processor and pulsate briefly. Add chopped garlic, balsamic vinegar, thyme, and basil and pulsate to make a paste. With machine running, slowly drizzle in olive oil. When all olive oil has been incorporated, adjust seasoning with salt and pepper to taste. Keep hot until ready to serve or cool rapidly. Store it covered and heat it up in a sauté pan when ready to use. Yields 4 servings.

Sautéed Rainbow Trout

Trout:
4 cleaned trout, cut into fillets
Salt and pepper
4 tablespoons all-purpose flour
2 tablespoons olive oil
¼ cup white wine

Lemon-thyme sauce:
¼ cup (½ stick) whole butter
1 clove fresh garlic, finely chopped
6 to 8 sprigs fresh thyme, finely chopped
2 tablespoons white wine
1 fresh whole lemon
⅓ cup chicken stock or broth

Orzo:
1 cup orzo pasta
4 cups water
1 teaspoon salt
1 tablespoon butter
1 clove fresh garlic, finely chopped
1 small red onion, diced

Rinse trout fillets with cold water and pat dry with paper towel. Season each fillet with salt and pepper to taste and dredge lightly in flour. Heat oil in large sauté pan or skillet over medium-high heat and add trout skin side down. Cook about 2 minutes, turn trout over, add wine, and cook for 1 more minute. Remove trout from pan.

For lemon-thyme sauce, brown butter in pan in which you cooked trout. Add garlic and thyme. Stir with wooden spoon and add wine. Reduce wine by half and add juice of lemon and chicken stock. Bring to a boil, stir, and remove from heat. Emulsify sauce by using hand-held blender or by whisking rapidly. Adjust seasoning if necessary with salt and pepper.

Toast orzo in 350° oven on flat baking sheet until lightly browned. Bring water and salt to rapid boil and add pasta. Cook until al dente and strain pasta in colander. While straining orzo, use pan to melt butter and add garlic and onion. Cook 1 minute and add orzo back to pan. Stir to incorporate and you're ready to serve. Start by putting small mound of orzo in center of each plate. Next arrange fillets of 1 whole trout on top of each mound of orzo. Use spoon to drizzle butter emulsion sauce over fish and around plate. Garnish with colorful and tasty quick sauté of crisp bacon, tomatoes, and spinach. Yields 4 servings.

✿   ✿   ✿

ANCESTORS INN

215 Sycamore Street
Liverpool, NY 13088
(315) 461-1226 (phone)
(888) 866-8591 (toll free)
innkeeper@ancestorsinn.com
www.ancestorsinn.com

Ancestors Inn is a bed and breakfast located just outside of Syracuse, New York, in the quiet village of Liverpool. The historic Bassett House is a beautiful, large, brick Italianate, which was built in the late 1850s and later lovingly restored. Take a walk in Onondaga Lake Park or visit the Gleason Mansion or Salt Museum, and then enjoy afternoon tea or lemonade relaxing on a wicker chair on the wide front porch. All of the rooms have queen-size beds and private bath and TV/VCRs. There are movies, magazines, and books to borrow and complimentary soft drinks and juices. Activities guests like most when visiting, other than sitting on the porch, are walking, running, and biking in Onondaga Lake Park. This beautiful park is just two blocks away and has paved paths that run along the lake. Other activities include Syracuse Symphony concerts, Syracuse University activities, meeting with friends and family, our annual summer Antiquefest, and our Christmas Lights on the Lake.

Ham and Potato Casserole

¾ cup diced potatoes with
    peppers and onions
½ cup diced ham
Tarragon
Salt and pepper
3 eggs
½ to ¾ cup milk or half-and-half
½ cup shredded Cheddar cheese

Preheat oven to 325°. Coat two individual (12-ounce) casseroles or au gratin dishes with cooking spray. Divide potatoes and ham between casseroles. Sprinkle with tarragon, salt, and pepper to taste. Break eggs into measuring cup and add enough milk to equal 1 cup (a little extra is OK) and mix well. Divide between dishes, pouring over potatoes and ham. Bake about 30 minutes until set. Sprinkle cheese on top and return to oven just until cheese melts. Yields 2 servings.

GREENWOODS BED & BREAKFAST INN

8136 Quayle Road
Honeoye, NY 14471
(585) 229-2111 (phone)
(800) 914-3559 (toll free)
innkeeper@greenwoodsinn.com
www.greenwoodsinn.com

Greenwoods is a five-guest-room, log inn rich in the tradition of the "Great Camp" style lodge. Relive the era where the rustic romance of log beams, fieldstone, fine china, and linens are all brought together to create a symphony to sooth the soul and refresh the senses. Located in New York's Finger Lakes Region, the inn has year-round activities to interest all. Enjoy winery tours and tasting, boating, fishing, swimming, hiking, biking, Alpine and Nordic skiing. Golf courses, antique stores, museums, historical homes, and gardens abound.

Lemon-Poppy Seed Pancakes

1½ cups all-purpose flour
4 tablespoons sugar
1 tablespoon baking powder
½ teaspoon salt
1 tablespoon poppy seeds
1½ cups buttermilk
1 tablespoon fresh lemon juice
1 large egg
1 tablespoon vegetable oil
1 teaspoon vanilla extract

In large mixing bowl combine flour, sugar, baking powder, salt, and poppy seeds. In a separate bowl combine buttermilk, lemon juice, egg, oil, and vanilla. Whisk until smooth. Pour liquid ingredients into dry ingredients and stir until smooth. Using ladle or large spoon, pour batter onto lightly greased, hot griddle. Turn each pancake when there are bubbles across top and edges are slightly browned. Pancakes are done when they spring back if touched. Serve with warm raspberry syrup and garnish with fresh raspberries. Yields 8 pancakes.

Peaches 'n' Cream Strata

10 slices challah bread, cubed
8 ounces mascarpone cheese
4 cups plus 1 cup chopped fresh peaches
12 eggs
2 cups milk
¼ cup maple syrup
½ teaspoon ground cinnamon
½ teaspoon ground ginger
1 cup sugar
2 tablespoons Peach Schnapps
Cornstarch
Confectioners' sugar
Whipped cream
Toasted sliced almonds

Place half the bread cubes in bottom of greased 9 x 13-inch baking dish or eight individual ramekins. Dot top with cheese, then 1 cup peaches. Top with remaining bread cubes. Combine eggs, milk, maple syrup, cinnamon, and ginger. Beat with hand blender until very smooth. Pour over layered bread, cheese, and peaches. Cover and refrigerate 8 to 10 hours or overnight. When ready to bake, remove from refrigerator 30 minutes before baking. Preheat oven to 350°. Cover baking dish with aluminum foil and bake 40 minutes, covered. Remove foil and bake another 15 minutes. While strata is baking, combine remaining 4 cups peaches, sugar, and Peach Schnapps in medium saucepan over high heat. Bring to a boil, stirring frequently, and reduce to simmer. Cook until you uncover strata. Thicken with a little cornstarch and water to desired consistency. Cut into eight equal portions. To serve, dust edges of each plate with confectioners' sugar and place serving of strata on plate. Top with about ½ cup of peach sauce, dollop of whipped cream, and sprinkle of almonds. Yields 8 servings.

THE EDGE OF THYME

6 Main Street, P.O. Box 48
Candor, NY 13743
(607) 659-5155
innthyme@twcny.rr.com
edgeofthyme.com

The Edge of Thyme, located in a quiet rural village, is a large Georgian home with leaded-glass-windowed porch, marble fireplaces, period sitting rooms, gardens and pergola. Activities in the nearby area include silversmith; pumpkin farm attraction in the fall; Cornell University with the largest herb garden in the country; plantations; Ithaca College; theater; farmers market; Binghamton University; Corning; Mark Twain country; Watkins Glen; many wineries, events, tastings, and sales; waterfalls and state parks; Finger Lakes hiking trails and cross-country skiing; antiques, historic homes, and beautiful countryside year-round.

Gifford Family Fruit Tart

1¼ cups all-purpose flour
¼ cup sugar
¼ pound (1 stick) butter
1 egg yolk
1 teaspoon vanilla extract
Sliced apples
1 cup chopped dried apricots
½ cup water
½ cup sugar
1 teaspoon lemon juice

Preheat oven to 350°. Cream together flour, sugar, and butter. Add egg yolk and vanilla. Press into tart pan. Place sliced apples decoratively on top. Bake 30 minutes. Combine apricots, water, sugar, and lemon juice in saucepan over high heat and boil down to syrup. When cool, put glaze on top of tart. Yields 6 to 8 servings.

Tears of Joy Onion, Mushroom, & Ham Tart

1½ cups all-purpose flour
1 tablespoon sugar
1 stick plus 2 tablespoons butter
1 egg yolk
2 large Vidalia (sweet) onions, thinly sliced
1 tablespoon caraway seeds
2 cups portobello baby mushrooms
¼ pound sliced ham, cut in squares
¼ cup all-purpose flour
4 eggs
½ cup half-and-half
4 tablespoons apricot preserves

Combine in food processor flour, sugar, 1 stick butter and egg yolk. Pat into quiche pan. Sauté onions, reserving 4 slices, in remaining butter for 20 minutes. Do not brown. Add caraway seeds, mushrooms, and ham and cook for 10 minutes more. Add flour. Beat eggs and add half-and-half. Add onion mixture. Pour into quiche pan. Preheat oven to 350° and bake 30 min-

utes. Add remaining 4 slices raw onion on top of tart and bake 15 minutes more. Then spoon apricot preserves over top and bake another 15 minutes. Let sit 10 to 15 minutes before cutting. Yields 6 to 8 servings.

Reverend DeCamp's Fondue *Au Fore*

6 tablespoons butter
8 slices Monk's bread, crust removed
8 ounces Swiss cheese
2 eggs
1½ cups milk
1 teaspoon salt
¼ teaspoon white pepper
¼ cup sesame seeds

Preheat oven to 350°. Butter bread on one side. Cut into strips 1-inch wide. Cut cheese same size. Layer bread and cheese in baking dish. Whisk eggs, milk, salt, and pepper. Pour over bread and cover with sesame seeds. Bake 40 minutes. Serve at once. Yields 8 servings.

The Edge of Thyme

WHISPERING PINES BED & BREAKFAST

60 Cedar Hill Road
High Falls, NY 12440
(845) 687-2419
info@whisperingpinesbb.com
www.whisperingpinesbb.com

Whispering Pines is a quiet, nature-inspired retreat. Surrounded by fifty acres of private woods, this light-filled, relaxing bed and breakfast features firm queen beds,

Whispering Pines Bed & Breakfast

cool before using. Cream butte in sugar. Mix in chocolate. Beat egg rately and mix in. Add slightly warm sour cream and water. Mix flour, salt, baking powder, and baking soda separately and add to butter mixture. Preheat oven to 350° and bake in greased and flour-dusted, 9-inch-round pan 30 to 35 minutes or until center springs back.

For frosting, cream butter and add chocolate. Add sour cream, vanilla, and sugar. Use a little hot water if mixture gets too thick. Frost cake when cool. Makes one layer. Yields 8 to 10 servings.

private bathrooms, Jacuzzis, living room fire-place, huge deck, and outdoor hot Spa open all winter. The inn is close to Minnewaska, Mohonk Mountain House, golfing, hiking, swimming, sports, shopping, and restaurants.

Georgia Toasted Pecans

1 cup fresh pecan halves
¼ cup (½ stick) melted butter
Salt

Mix pecans and melted butter in small mixing bowl until pecans are coated. Spread pecans flat and separate on cookie sheet. Pour any leftover (or extra, if desired) melted butter on top. Sprinkle with salt. Toast under broiler or in toaster oven 1 to 2 minutes. Watch them constantly. As soon as pecans get a little brown, take them out and flip them over, using spatula or tongs. Salt second side. Toast again briefly until brown. Cool and serve in glass candy dish. Yields 1 cup.

Sour Cream Chocolate Cake

All ingredients should be about room temperature or the chocolate will fragment.

<u>Cake:</u>
2 ounces unsweetened chocolate
2 tablespoons (¼ stick) butter
1 cup sugar
1 egg
⅜ cup warmed sour cream
½ cup water
1 cup all-purpose flour
½ teaspoon salt
¼ teaspoon baking powder
¾ teaspoon baking soda

<u>Frosting:</u>
3 tablespoons butter
2 ounces unsweetened chocolate, melted and cooled
¼ cup room-temperature sour cream
1 teaspoon vanilla extract
1½ cups confectioners' sugar

Melt chocolate slowly in heavy saucepan or double boiler, stirring until melted. Let

GENESEE COUNTRY INN CIRCA 1833

948 George Street Box 340
Mumford-Rochester, NY 14511-0340
(716) 538-2500 (phone)
(716) 538-4565 (fax)
room2escapeinn@aol.com
www.innbook.com/genesee.html

Step back in time to a quieter, gentler time as you enjoy our unique water setting on Spring Creek. Enjoy our new sunroom and hydra spa or visit the nearby Genesee Country Village Museum, the third largest historic museum in the United States. The inn, a former plaster-paper mill during the 1800s with 2½-foot-thick walls, is located near Rochester, New York, just three hours from Toronto at the edge of the Finger Lakes. From our guests' diaries: "A fine inn indeed. You are on a par with the better country inns of England." The inn offers hospitality and beauty. There are ten rooms total—three garden rooms, six Old Mill rooms, and one king two-room suite.

White Cookie Cake

Cake:
1 (18-ounce) package white cake mix
1¼ cups water
⅓ cup vegetable oil
3 egg whites
1½ cups crushed Oreo cookies

Frosting:
1 cup shortening
1 tablespoon vanilla extract
2¼ plus 2¼ cups sifted confectioners'
    sugar
3 plus 2 tablespoons milk

Preheat oven to 350°. Mix cake with water, oil, and egg whites and fold in cookies. Fill two cake pans and bake 28 to 30 minutes. Let cool.

For frosting, beat shortening and vanilla together until creamed. Add 2¼ cups confectioners' sugar. Add 3 tablespoons milk. Cream together. Then add remaining 2¼ cups sugar and remaining 2 tablespoons milk. Beat until frosting is desired consistency. Frost cake and enjoy. Top with fresh strawberries or more crushed cookies if desired. Yields 10 to 12 servings.

Innkeepers' Best Bean Recipe

4 slices bacon
1 onion, chopped
1 (28-ounce) can baked beans
    in tomato sauce
1 (16-ounce) can kidney beans, drained
1 (16-ounce) can lima beans, drained
1 cup sharp Cheddar cheese, cubed
½ cup brown sugar
½ cup ketchup
1 tablespoon Worcestershire sauce
Parmesan cheese for topping

Fry bacon and crumble. Preheat oven to 350°. In bacon drippings, sauté onion. Mix with remaining ingredients except cheese. Put in casserole and sprinkle top with Parmesan cheese. Bake uncovered 1 hour. Yields 6 to 8 servings.

New York State Wine-Parmesan Crackers

1 cup mayonnaise
½ teaspoon Worcestershire sauce
¼ teaspoon onion salt
1 tablespoon New York State
    sherry wine
24 Ritz crackers
⅓ cup grated Parmesan cheese

Fold mayonnaise, Worcestershire sauce, onion salt, and sherry wine together. Spread on crackers. Sprinkle with Parmesan cheese. Brown under hot broiler. Serve hot. Yields 24 appetizers.

FOX 'N' HOUND

142 Lake Avenue
Saratoga Springs, NY 12866
(518) 584-5959 (phone)
(518) 584-2594 (fax)
(866) 369-1913 (toll free)
innkeeper@foxnhoundbandb.com
www.foxnhoundbandb.com

Come visit the Fox 'n' Hound Saratoga Springs Bed & Breakfast located in downtown Saratoga, New York. The Fox 'n' Hound is unlike any other. A restored colonial mansion that offers comfortable elegance with a cosmopolitan flair, European hospitality with the warmth of home, attention to detail found in the finest resorts, and the convenience of in town location. To enhance your stay, we will delight you with a multi-course breakfast that changes daily and is prepared to order by your hostess, Marlena.

Eggs in Shrimp Nests

4 hard-cooked eggs
2 tablespoons olive oil
4 tablespoons unsalted butter
4 scallions, white and green part,
    cleaned and diced
1 cup chicken broth
½ cup dry white wine
    (Sauvignon Blanc)
24 medium shrimp, peeled
    and deveined
¼ cup lemon juice
¼ cup chopped parsley
¼ teaspoon salt
⅛ teaspoon white pepper
Toasted English muffins or bagels

In small pan over high heat cover eggs with water and bring to a boil. Continue cooking 4 minutes. Remove from stove. Drain off water. Cool with cold water. Peel and cut with egg cutter in ¼-inch slices. In sauté pan add olive oil and butter. Heat on medium flame till butter melts. Add scallions and sauté until limp. Add chicken broth. Increase heat and reduce liquid by one-third. Add wine. Reduce liquid by half. Add shrimp and cook until they start to turn pink. Add lemon juice and chopped parsley. Add salt and pepper. Remove from heat.

To serve place six shrimp in center of plate to form a nest. Fan egg slices in center of nest. Drizzle with 2 tablespoons sauce in which shrimp was cooked. Place English muffin or bagel on side of plate. Yields 4 servings.

Note: The inn serves this with small scoop of spiced goat cheese beside nest. (To make spiced goat cheese mix 2 ounces goat cheese with 2 tablespoons sour cream, pinch of salt, pinch of black pepper, and ⅛ teaspoon paprika.)

QUINTESSENTIALS BED & BREAKFAST SPA

8985 Main Road
P.O. Box 574
East Marion, NY 11939
(631) 477-9400 (phone)
(877) 259-0939 (toll free)
innkeeper@quintessentialsinc.com
www.quintessentialsinc.com

Quintessentials, built by Captain Leek, a wealthy sea captain, is a gloriously restored, spacious, fifteen-room house complete with charming widow's walk and is furnished with an eclectic collection of fine antiques and yard sale finds. At Quintessentials, we cater to rejuvenation of your mind, body, and spirit. Surrounded by almost an acre of mature, landscaped grounds, there is a full-service, day spa staffed by licensed, experienced professionals, whirlpool baths, private decks, and a Japanese meditation garden. Our ideal location in East Marion, between the historical villages of Greenport and Orient, fulfills your desire for fresh country air, unspoiled beaches, sleepy fishing villages, farmlands, vineyards, and challenging sports and activities.

Calaloo and Salted Codfish

2 bunches (16 ounces) calaloo
    or fresh spinach
1 pound dried codfish
1 large onion
1 large tomato
2 cloves garlic
3 tablespoons canola oil
3 to 5 thin slices Jamaican Scotch
    Bonnet pepper

Clean, bundle together, and thinly slice calaloo. Boil codfish, pouring off water three times to get rid of saltiness. Peel and slice onion thinly, dice tomato, and finely chop garlic. In saucepan over medium heat add oil and sauté onion, garlic, and Scotch Bonnet pepper. Add diced tomatoes. Flake fish with fork and add to saucepan. Add calaloo and steam until tender. Stir and steam another 8 minutes. Serve with fried green plantains as breakfast or light lunch. Yields 4 servings.

ADAMS BASIN INN

425 Washington Street
Adams Basin, New York
(888) 352-3999
Halya@Adamsbasininn.com
www.adamsbasininn.com

Adams Basin Inn is nestled along the towpath of the Historic Erie Canal. The post-and-beam constructed building still holds the original tavern that served its travelers and workers. The inn is a delight to lovers of antiques, exceptional food, and relaxation. Guest rooms include private baths, terry robes, and slippers. Located fifteen minutes west of Rochester, it is a haven for cyclists and boaters.

Baked Eggs with Mushroom Sauce

8 slices bacon
8 eggs
8 tablespoons heavy cream
Salt and pepper
¼ cup chopped chives
French baguette slices, toasted

Sauce:
2 to 3 slices bacon, thinly chopped
2 tablespoons unsalted butter
2 cups sliced mushrooms
3 tablespoons chopped chives
2 to 3 tablespoons sour cream
1 cup heavy cream
2 tablespoons chopped fresh tarragon
Salt and pepper
Sprigs of tarragon

Preheat oven to 350°. Cut bacon slices into sections to line bottom and sides of 8-cup muffin tin (not a shallow one). Bake 8 to 10 minutes until lightly browned. Remove pan and cool. Break eggs carefully into muffin cups, rearranging bacon so it falls slightly. Pour 1 tablespoon heavy cream over each egg, lightly sprinkle with salt and pepper, and top with chives. Bake 15 to 20 minutes or until eggs test done. Check with fork if necessary.

For sauce, in medium pan sauté bacon slices over medium-high heat until crispy, remove bacon, and pour out drippings. Add butter, mushrooms, and chives and sauté about 10 minutes. Add sour cream and bacon, stirring until well blended and heated through. Add heavy cream and tarragon. Simmer on low heat 2 to 3 minutes. Add salt and pepper to taste.

To assemble arrange two slices baguette on plate. Scoop out two eggs a plate on bread, ladle sauce over eggs, and garnish with sprigs of tarragon. The inn serves with roasted asparagus and slices of crispy bacon. Yields 4 servings.

1871 HOUSE

130 East 62nd Street
New York, NY 10021
(212) 756-8823 (phone)
(212) 588-0995 (fax)
info@1871house.com
www.1871house.com

Nestled among the residences of the fashionable East Side of Manhattan on a quiet tree-lined street, this charming brownstone is just a stroll away from Central Park, Madison Avenue shopping, museums, and business areas. The 1871 House offers three two-bedroom suites and three studio apartments as well as a hidden cottage that once served as a carriage house.

Ratatouille

1 large onion, chopped
2 zucchini, not peeled, sliced
3 potatoes, thinly sliced
3 green peppers, cut in large dice
2 tomatoes, sliced
1 jalapeño pepper, chopped
5 mini eggplants, sliced
Olive oil
Salt

Combine all ingredients and cook over medium-low heat until vegetables are cooked through. Yields 5 servings.

Sara's Pasta

Vegetable oil
½ tablespoon plus 1 teaspoon
    minced garlic
2 medium bell peppers (red/yellow)
1 (3-ounce) package sun-dried
    tomatoes
1 (10-ounce) package
    triple-washed spinach
½ tablespoon lemon juice
Cooked shrimp
1 (1-pound) box penne pasta, cooked

Heat oil and ½ tablespoon garlic in medium saucepan over medium heat. Add peppers and cook for 2 minutes. Add tomatoes. Sauté approximately 5 minutes or until almost tender. Add spinach, lemon juice, and remaining teaspoon garlic. Sauté until spinach is completely wilted. Add shrimp and heat for 3 minutes. Toss with cooked pasta. Yields 8 servings.

THE GOLDEN PINEAPPLE

201 Liberty Avenue
Port Jefferson, NY 11777
(631) 331-0706 (phone)
(631) 474-5311 (fax)
info@goldenpineapplebandb.com
www.goldenpineapplebandb.com

The Golden Pineapple is an elegant and charming bed and breakfast nestled in the hills of the quaint harbor-side village of Port Jefferson. Gourmet breakfasts are served each morning. Boating, fishing, golfing, museums, wineries, and live theater thrive in this beautiful Long Island community. Interesting art galleries, shops, and great dining make this an ideal spot for a weekend getaway or more.

Golden Pineapple Personalized Breakfast Casserole

1 small red onion, chopped
½ large sweet red pepper, chopped
½ cup sliced white mushrooms
¼ cup chopped fresh parsley
2 or 3 large croissants
1 cup shredded Mexican blend cheese, or
    cheese of choice
Pinch of salt
Pinch of pepper
Pinch of dry mustard
1 dozen eggs
2 cups whole milk

Sauté onion, pepper, mushrooms, and parsley in butter in frying pan over medium heat. Spray ceramic or glass 9 x 13 x 2-inch baking dish with nonstick coating. Line bottom of baking dish with croissants that have been pulled apart gently. Top croissants with sautéed vegetables. Top vegetables with shredded cheese, spreading evenly across baking dish. Sprinkle with salt, pepper, and dry mustard. In separate bowl, beat eggs with milk about 2 minutes. Pour egg mixture over casserole and refrigerate 8 to 10 hours or overnight. When ready to bake, preheat oven to 350° and bake 1 hour. Serve with slices of fruit, parsley sprigs, and whole wheat toast. Yields 6 to 8 servings.

Creole Bread Pudding

1 large loaf very crispy French bread
1 quart whole milk
1½ cups sugar
3 eggs
1 teaspoon ground cinnamon
2 tablespoons pure vanilla extract
1 cup raisins
3 tablespoons butter
1½ cups heavy cream

Confectioners' sugar
6 large strawberries, halved
8 fresh mint sprigs

In large bowl, break bread into small pieces. Cover with milk and let soak for 1 to 2 hours. Add sugar to soaked bread and mix well. In separate bowl, beat eggs until foamy. Add to bread and sugar. Add cinnamon, vanilla, and raisins and stir together. Melt butter in microwave and coat 13 x 9-inch baking dish, taking care to coat bottom and sides. Pour pudding mixture into dish. Cover with plastic wrap and refrigerate 8 to 10 hours or overnight. When ready to bake, preheat oven to 375° and bake 1 hour. Remove from oven and let cool for 30 minutes to 1 hour. Pudding should still be warm, but not hot, when serving. While pudding is cooling, whip cream until peaks form. Cut pudding into wedges and dust with confectioners' sugar. Top with sliced strawberries and mint. Whipped cream may be spooned on top or served on the side. Yields 6 generous portions or 8 smaller portions.

North Carolina

PINECREST

249 Cumberland Avenue
Asheville, NC 28801
(828) 281-4275 (phone)
(828) 281-2215 (fax)
innkeeper@pinecrestbb.com
www.pinecrestbb.com

Located in the Montford Historic District of Asheville, North Carolina, this turn-of-the-century home has been elegantly restored. Pinecrest has four beautifully appointed bedrooms with private baths. The beds are dressed in fine linens. Gourmet breakfasts await guests each morning.

Blueberry Pexto Pumpkin Muffins

Muffins:

1⅔ cups flour
1 teaspoon baking soda
1 teaspoon ground cinnamon
½ teaspoon baking powder
¼ teaspoon salt
½ teaspoon allspice
1 cup canned pumpkin
¼ cup evaporated milk
⅓ cup butter
1 cup brown sugar
1 egg, beaten
1 cup fresh or frozen blueberries

Topping:

2 tablespoons flour
2 tablespoons sugar
¼ teaspoon ground cinnamon
1 tablespoon butter

Preheat oven to 350°. Combine flour, baking soda, cinnamon, baking powder, salt, and allspice. Blend together pumpkin and milk. Cream together butter, sugar, and egg. Combine pumpkin and creamed mixtures together. Gently combine with dry mixture. Add blueberries. Spoon into prepared muffin cups.

For topping, combine flour, sugar, cinnamon, and butter. Sprinkle over muffins. Bake 40 minutes. Yields 12 muffins.

Eden's Delight Muffins (Apple)

¼ cup sugar
2 eggs
¼ cup vegetable oil
½ teaspoon vanilla extract
2 cups all-purpose flour
½ teaspoon baking powder
½ teaspoon baking soda
¼ teaspoon salt
½ teaspoon ground cinnamon
2½ cups finely chopped Granny Smith apples (2 to 3)
1 cup chopped nuts

Preheat oven to 400°. In a large bowl beat together sugar and eggs until blended. Beat in oil and vanilla. In another large bowl combine flour, baking powder, baking soda, salt, and cinnamon. Stir in apples and nuts and add to egg mixture. Beat 5 minutes with mixer at medium speed. (This batter needs extra beating to release apple juices needed for moistness.) Fill prepared muffin cups full and bake 20 minutes or until golden brown. Yields 12 muffins.

Walnut-Pear Sour Cream Cake

1 plus ½ cup broken walnuts
⅓ cup packed brown sugar
1 teaspoon ground cinnamon
1 plus ½ stick butter, softened
1¾ cups plus ⅓ cup all-purpose flour
2 medium pears, peeled, cored and sliced (about 2 cups)
2 teaspoons lemon juice
¾ teaspoon baking powder
½ teaspoon baking soda
¼ teaspoon salt
1 cup granulated sugar
1 teaspoon vanilla extract
2 eggs
1 (8-ounce) container sour cream

Preheat oven to 350°. Combine 1 cup walnuts, brown sugar, and cinnamon. For topping, cut ½ stick butter into ⅓ cup flour to make coarse crumbs. Stir in three-fourths cup of nut mixture. Toss pears with lemon juice. In medium bowl, combine remaining 1¾ cups flour, baking powder, baking soda, and salt. In large bowl beat remain-

268

ing 1 stick butter for 30 seconds. Beat in granulated sugar and vanilla. Add eggs, one at a time, beating after each addition until combined. Spread two-thirds of batter into prepared 9-inch springform pan or 9 x 9 x 2-inch baking pan. Sprinkle with remaining nut mixture. Layer pears over top. Gently spread remaining batter over pears. Sprinkle with reserved topping. Bake 10 minutes. For chunky top, sprinkle with remaining ½ cup nuts. Bake 45 to 50 minutes more or until toothpick comes out clean. Cool in pan on rack about 10 minutes. Remove sides of springform pan. Cool at least 1 hour. Drizzle with sour-cream for icing. Yields 16 servings.

1904 Secret Garden Bed & Breakfast

56 North Main Street
Asheville, NC
(828) 658-9317 (phone)
(828) 645-6420 (fax)
(800) 797-8211 (toll free)
innkeeper@secretgardenNC.com
www.secretgardenNC.com

This 1904 former mayors' home is a popular village inn just steps to excellent dining and quaint shops on Main Street. Gourmet breakfasts, refreshments, and elegant bedroom suites with private baths await you. The inn is ten minutes from downtown Asheville.

The Garden's French Toast

6 eggs, beaten
½ cup orange juice
2 tablespoons orange zest
⅛ teaspoon orange extract
1 teaspoon vanilla extract
2 cups milk
2 ounces Grand Marnier or Triple Sec
Dash of salt
8 (1-inch-thick) slices French bread
Orange slices for garnish

Spiced Honey Syrup:
2 cups maple syrup
¼ cup honey
¼ teaspoon ground cinnamon
Dash of nutmeg

Mix eggs, orange juice, zest and extract, vanilla, milk, Grand Marnier, and salt together in large bowl. Place bread slices in mixture to coat. Coat griddle with cooking spray and cook bread until golden brown on both sides.

For syrup, stir all ingredients in microwaveable bowl until mixed thoroughly and heat in microwave 1 minute on high. Place orange sections on top of French toast as garnish and serve with Spiced Honey Syrup. Yields 4 servings, 2 slices per serving.

Marinated Steak Bites

½ cup soy sauce
½ tablespoon dried dill
½ cup honey
¼ cup wine vinegar
5 tablespoons ginger
4 cloves garlic, crushed
1 medium onion, sliced
2 whole medium flank steaks

Mix ingredients, including steaks, in large freezer bag. Refrigerate 3 days, turning over

once daily. On day three, drain marinade and cook steaks on hot grill 7 to 10 minutes on one side. Remove and cool 10 minutes. Slice very thinly, roll up each slice, and secure with toothpick. Arrange on large platter of fancy lettuce and serve with cherry tomatoes. Yields 4 to 6 servings.

Blake House Inn

150 Royal Pines Drive
Asheville, NC 28704
(828) 681-5227 (phone)
(828) 681-0420 (fax)
(888) 353-5227 (toll free)
blakeinn@aol.com
www.blakehouse.com

Blake House Inn, originally Newington, was built c.1847. Conveniently located in the Historic Royal Pines Area, Blake House Inn was one of the beautiful summer homes built by wealthy lowlanders to take advantage of the cool summer breezes in the mountains of North Carolina. Surrounded by 150 year old pine and sycamore trees, this fine example of Italianate architecture with Gothic Revival influence will bring you back in time to the more relaxed atmosphere of the 1800s. It is minutes away from the Biltmore Estate and the entrance to the Blue Ridge Parkway.

Baked Macaroon Pears

1 large red pear, peeled, quartered,
    cored, and sliced
¼ cup dry vermouth
¼ cup apricot or mixed-berry preserves
1 macaroon, chopped
1 teaspoon butter

Preheat oven to 350°. Divide pear slices between two ramekins. Mix vermouth and preserves and pour over fruit. Top each with ½ macaroon and pat of butter. Bake about 15 to 20 minutes; topping should just start to brown. Serve within 30 minutes. Yields 2 servings.

Note: These freeze very well for weeks. Take out 8 to 10 hours before baking and defrost in refrigerator. Fold a napkin into a lotus flower, place on dinner plate, add flowers to folds, and place ramekin in center.

Baked Grapefruit Topped with Meringue

5 ruby red grapefruits
10 tablespoons brown sugar
5 egg whites
¼ teaspoon cream of tartar
½ cup granulated sugar

Preheat oven to 375°. Halve grapefruits and loosen sections with knife. Cut thin slice off bottom of each grapefruit half to keep from sliding on plate. Sprinkle each half with 1 tablespoon brown sugar. Beat egg whites, cream of tartar, and sugar until stiff peaks form. Top grapefruit halves with meringue. Bake 5 to 6 minutes, just until peaks are light brown. Yields 10 servings.

Brie Baked Eggs

1 tablespoon chopped fresh parsley
1½ tablespoons minced ham or 1 link cooked & sliced breakfast sausage
1½ tablespoons cubed Brie
2 eggs
1 tablespoon heavy cream
Salt and pepper

Preheat oven to 400°. Toss parsley, meat, and Brie together and place in 3-inch ramekin. Break eggs over top and drizzle cream over eggs. Sprinkle with salt and pepper to taste. Place ramekin in water bath and bake 15 to 20 minutes depending on how set you want eggs. Serve immediately with toast points or an herb popover. Presentation: Use dinner plate with folded napkin, maybe lotus fold, with bouquet of herbs in upper left fold and place ramekin in center. Yields 1 serving.

INN ON MAIN STREET

88 South Main Street
Weaverville, NC 28787
(828) 645-4935
relax@innonmain.com
www.innonmain.com

Inn on Main Street is a romantic, small-town bed and breakfast about ten minutes from downtown Asheville in the quiet, artsy town of Weaverville, North Carolina. It has seven rooms with private baths, all furnished in comfortable antiques, most with fireplaces, and some with whirlpool tubs. Weaverville is home to the twice-yearly Art Safari studio tour and a yearly literary fair.

Bruschetta Fresca

2 garlic cloves, minced
3 cups diced fresh tomatoes
⅓ to ½ cup olive oil
¼ teaspoon salt
4 to 5 leaves fresh basil
1 baguette, thinly sliced
¼ cup grated Parmesan cheese or ½ cup grated mozzarella (optional)

Mix garlic with tomatoes, olive oil, and salt. Chop basil and add to mixture. Spoon mixture onto sliced bread, which may be lightly toasted (broiled) on each side. Optional serving suggestion is to sprinkle on Parmesan or mozzarella and broil until cheese melts. Yields 6 to 8 servings.

Mango Salsa

2 mangoes, diced
1 jalapeño, finely diced
2 tablespoons finely chopped red pepper
Juice of 1 lime
¼ sweet onion, diced
1 teaspoon salt
3 tablespoons chopped cilantro
½ teaspoon ground cumin
Tortilla chips

Peel mangoes, cut fruit away from pit, and dice. Add jalapeño, red pepper, lime juice, onion, salt, cilantro, and cumin. Chill. Serve with chips or as a topping on grilled fish or with your favorite Mexican dish. Yields about 1¼ cups.

Dan's Famous Frittata (Regular and Vegetarian)

1 medium red potato
1 tablespoon chopped onion
1 tablespoon chopped green pepper
1 plus 1 teaspoon olive oil
½ teaspoon freshly chopped rosemary
Pinch of salt
Freshly ground pepper
3 eggs, beaten
2 very thin slices tomato
2 tablespoons grated Parmesan cheese

Microwave potato 3 to 4 minutes and dice. Sauté onions, then green pepper in 6-inch, cast iron pan with 1 teaspoon oil. Then fry potato in remaining 1 teaspoon oil, adding rosemary, salt, and pepper. Cover with eggs, then with tomato slices and Parmesan. Cook on stovetop until eggs firm and then put pan under broiler until fully set and Parmesan starts to brown. Check for doneness. Serve on well-insulated trivet. Yields 2 servings.

Herren House Bed & Breakfast

94 East Street
Waynesville, NC 28786
(800) 284-1932
herren@brinet.com
www.herrenhouse.com

Herren House is a unique nineteenth-century boardinghouse located on a quiet residential street just one block from downtown shopping. It has been exquisitely restored and features beautiful English gardens and exceptional food. Fine English china, lovely old silver plate, and crisp white linens are part of the ambience of every meal. The gourmet dinner on Saturday is not just a meal—it's an event.

Blackberry-Glazed Tenderloin of Pork

2 (1-pound) pork tenderloins
⅓ cup olive oil
2 tablespoons chopped fresh rosemary
1½ teaspoons dried sage
1 teaspoon salt
½ teaspoon freshly ground black pepper

Glaze:
¾ cup seedless blackberry jam
¼ cup sweet vermouth

Place tenderloins in heavy-duty plastic storage bag. In small bowl, whisk together oil, rosemary, sage, salt, and pepper. Pour oil mixture into bag and coat all surfaces of tenderloins. Close bag and refrigerate at least 4 hours.

When ready to cook, preheat oven to 450°. Remove tenderloins from bag and place on rack in open roasting pan. Roast 15 minutes. Lower temperature to 300° and continue to roast. Baste every 10 to 15 minutes with glaze until meat thermometer reaches 150°. Remove from oven, tent with foil, and let rest at least 15 minutes.

For glaze, combine jam and vermouth in small saucepan. Warm over low heat, stirring frequently until smooth. Serve with warm glaze on side. Yields 4 to 6 servings.

Provolone & Prosciutto-Stuffed Chicken Breast

4 boneless, skinless chicken breast halves
4 slices prosciutto
4 slices provolone cheese
⅓ cup fresh breadcrumbs
½ teaspoon dried oregano
½ teaspoon dried basil
2 tablespoons freshly grated Romano cheese
2 tablespoons minced fresh parsley
½ teaspoon salt
½ teaspoon freshly ground black pepper
2 egg whites
1½ teaspoons olive oil

Place chicken breast skin-side down on cutting board. Make horizontal slit along thinner, long edge of breast, cutting nearly through to opposite side. Open breast so it forms two flaps hinged at center. Place 1 slice prosciutto and 1 slice cheese on one flap, leaving a ½-inch border at the edge. Press remaining flap down firmly over cheese and set aside. Repeat with remaining breasts. In shallow dish, mix breadcrumbs, oregano, basil, Romano cheese, parsley, salt and pepper. In another bowl, lightly beat egg whites with fork. Holding stuffed breast together firmly, dip in egg whites, and then roll in breadcrumbs. Repeat with remaining breasts.

Preheat oven to 400°. In large oven-proof skillet, heat oil over high heat until almost smoking. Carefully add chicken and cook until browned on one side, about 2 minutes. Turn breasts over and place skillet in oven. Bake until chicken is no longer pink in center, about 20 minutes. Serve with Wild Mushroom Sauce (see recipe below). Yields 4 servings.

Wild Mushroom Sauce

1 ounce dried wild mushrooms (porcini, morel, shitake, etc.)
3 tablespoons plus 1 tablespoon butter
8 ounces fresh mushrooms
¼ cup minced shallots
2 cloves garlic, minced
1 tablespoon all-purpose flour
½ cup beef or chicken stock
¼ cup sherry
¼ cup heavy cream
2 tablespoons chopped fresh parsley
Salt and pepper

Place dried mushrooms in small saucepan and cover with water. Bring to boil over high heat. Remove from heat, cover, and allow to cool about 30 minutes. Meanwhile, melt 3 tablespoons butter in medium skillet over medium heat. Add fresh mushrooms, shallots, and garlic and sauté until mushrooms are almost cooked. Remove from skillet. In same skillet, melt remaining 1 tablespoon butter. Stir in flour and cook over medium-low heat until mixture becomes golden. Stir in stock and bring to simmer. Remove from heat and add sherry. Place skillet back on heat and simmer about 5 minutes. Add heavy cream and continue to simmer over low heat 5 minutes. Drain reconstituted wild mushrooms, reserving liquid. Chop any large pieces and add to skillet. Stir in fresh mushroom mixture and parsley. Add salt and pepper to taste. For thinner sauce, stir in some reserved mushroom liquid. Yields 4 to 6 servings.

Ginger Peach Muffins

2 cups all-purpose flour
2 teaspoons baking powder
1 teaspoon ground ginger
½ teaspoon salt
½ teaspoon ground cinnamon
¼ teaspoon ground cloves
½ cup sugar
½ cup unsweetened applesauce
¼ cup apple juice
¼ cup molasses
1 egg
2 tablespoons canola oil
1½ cups chopped fresh peaches

Coat twelve regular-size muffin cups with cooking spray. Preheat oven to 400°. In large bowl, combine flour, baking powder, ginger, salt, cinnamon, and cloves. In small bowl, whisk together sugar, applesauce, apple juice, molasses, egg, oil, and peaches. Stir applesauce mixture into dry ingredients just until combined. Spoon into prepared muffin cups. Bake 20 minutes or until done. Remove from pan and cool on wire rack for 10 minutes before serving. Yields 12 muffins.

BIG MILL BED & BREAKFAST

1607 Big Mill Road
Williamston, NC 27892
(252) 792-8787
info@bigmill.com
www.bigmill.com

The Big Mill Bed & Breakfast sits shaded amid eighty-year-old pecan trees overlooking a three-acre lake in the tranquil Carolina countryside, just minutes from major highways. Big Mill is a good place to stop on the way to North Carolina's outer banks. The Carolina countryside is lush farmland with numerous rivers and creeks that meander slowly toward the sea, and this has made canoeing and eco-tourism popular. The Senator Bob Martin Agriculture Center hosts diverse horse shows during the year. The area is rich in history and historic places, including historic Bath, New Bern, Edenton, and Hamilton. East Carolina University and Medical School are also in the area.

Almond Biscotti

2½ cups all-purpose flour
1¼ cups sugar
1 teaspoon baking powder
3 medium eggs
2 egg yolks
1 teaspoon vanilla flavoring
1 teaspoon almond flavoring
1¼ plus ¼ cups slivered almonds
Zest of 1 lemon or lime

Preheat oven to 275°. Mix flour, sugar, and baking powder in large mixing bowl. In another large bowl mix eggs and egg yolks together. Add vanilla and almond flavoring, 1¼ cups almonds, and zest to eggs. Gradually add dry mixture to wet mixture, stirring until just barely blended. Grease heavy cookie sheet. Using greased hands, form dough into three 4 x 9-inch rolls two inches thick. Place on greased cookie sheet, making sure rolls are several inches apart. Press reserved almonds on top of shaped dough. Bake 20 to 25 minutes. Remove from oven and cool slightly. (You must not cool biscotti too much because they will get too hard to cut.) When cooled slightly, cut each roll at an angle into 1½-inch pieces. Turn each piece on its side and place on cookie sheet. Bake again 10 to 15 minutes. Remove from oven and turn each piece onto other side. Bake 10 more minutes. If you prefer softer biscotti, omit last 10 minutes of baking. Biscotti will keep for several weeks if stored in airtight container. Serve with morning or evening coffee. Also great with afternoon tea. Yields 36 to 40 biscotti.

Yellow Squash Bread

3 eggs
2 cups sugar
1 cup vegetable oil
1 tablespoon vanilla extract
2 cups all-purpose flour
1 teaspoon ground cinnamon
¼ teaspoon baking soda
2 teaspoons baking powder
2 cups coarsely grated yellow
   summer squash
1 cup chopped pecans
Ginger-Pineapple Spread

Preheat oven to 350°. Grease and dust with flour four mini loaf pans. Beat eggs in large bowl. Add sugar, oil, and vanilla to eggs. Sift together the flour, cinnamon, baking soda, and baking powder and add to egg mixture. Fold in squash and nuts and stir until just mixed. Pour into mini loaf pans, filling half full. Bake 25 to 30 minutes. This is a moist bread and cooking times may vary depending on moisture of squash. Cool before slicing. Serve with Ginger-Pineapple Spread (see recipe below). Yields 4 small loaves.

Ginger-Pineapple Spread

1 (8-ounce) container pineapple cream
   cheese at room temperature
1 tablespoon kumquat
   or orange marmalade
Peel of 1 orange, grated
1 teaspoon grated or finely chopped
   crystallized ginger

Combine all ingredients in mixing bowl. Using hand mixer, whip ingredients for several minutes. Chill. Serve with specialty sweet breads such as Yellow Squash Bread or Cranberry Bread. Yields 1 cup.

Sweet Potato Biscuits

1 cup canned, unsweetened, mashed
　　sweet potatoes or yams
1 cup packed light brown sugar
¼ cup water
2¼ cups packed biscuit mix

Grease or spray cookie sheet. Mix together sweet potatoes, brown sugar, water, and biscuit mix. Mixture will be very sticky. Preheat oven to 350°. Dust countertop or cutting board with flour. Place mixture on floured surface and roll to ½ inch thick. Cut with a 1½-inch biscuit cutter and place on greased cookie sheet, allowing some space between biscuits. Bake 12 to 15 minutes. Cool on cooling rack before storing. Biscuits will be moist even when done. To make larger biscuits, increase baking time to 16 to 18 minutes. Split biscuits and stuff with salty, shaved Virginia or country ham. Yields 70 small biscuits.

　　Note: One pound ham will stuff 70 biscuits. These may be served warm or at room temperature.

Cranberry Liqueur

1 cup water
2 cups sugar
2 cups cranberries, washed,
　　and chopped
1 tablespoon grated lemon rind
1 tablespoon frozen orange juice
　　concentrate
2 cups vodka

Combine water and sugar in heavy saucepan and bring to a boil. Lower heat and simmer sugar syrup 5 minutes, making sure sugar is completely dissolved. Stir in cranberries, lemon rind, and orange juice concentrate. Remove syrup mixture from heat and cool enough so to safely pour mixture into blender. Use chop setting but make sure berries are just barely chopped. Allow mixture to cool. Add vodka and stir. Pour into glass jar and store in cool, dark place for three weeks, stirring every so often. Strain mixture several times using mesh strainer or cheesecloth until mixture comes out clean. Pour into glass jars and store liqueur and pulp in refrigerator. Reserve pulp for other things. Serve at room temperature as an after-dinner liqueur or pour over desserts such as hot apple pie. Pulp is excellent served over ice cream, as a surprise in a chocolate truffle, or baked in an acorn squash. Yields 2½ to 3 cups liqueur.

The Moss House Bed & Breakfast

129 Van Norden Street
Washington, NC 27889
(252) 975-3967 (phone)
(252) 975-1148 (fax)
(888) 975-3393 (toll free)
info@themosshouse.com
www.themosshouse.com

The Moss House continues a family tradition of easy Southern style in coastal Carolina. Located one block from the Pamlico River and in the heart of the historic district, this beautiful 1902 Victorian home was built by the innkeeper's great-grandparents, Frank Adams Moss and Mary Bonner Moss. Activities in the area include sailing, kayaking, historic tours, and a variety of antique and gift shops as well as local art galleries. A newly renovated waterfront with thirty-eight public docking slips is only a block from the bed and breakfast.

Momma's Sweet Potato Muffins

1 cup mashed cooked sweet potatoes
1 cup raisins
1 cup chopped walnuts
1½ cups sugar
1½ cups canola oil
4 eggs
3 cups self-rising flour
1½ teaspoons ground cinnamon
¼ teaspoon ground cloves

Preheat oven to 350° and bake sweet potatoes for 1 hour. Rinse raisins and walnuts in colander by pouring boiling water over them. Combine sweet potatoes, sugar, and oil and beat with wire whisk. Add eggs one at a time, beating well after each addition.

The Moss House Bed & Breakfast

Combine flour, cinnamon, and cloves with walnuts and raisins. Stir into potato mixture just until moistened. Grease muffin pans with thin coating of shortening or margarine. Fill each muffin cup three-quarters full. Bake 18 to 20 minutes. Muffins will be done when top springs back when gently pressed. Do *not* over-bake. Batter may be refrigerated and used as needed. Cooked muffins freeze well. Thaw in refrigerator 8 to 10 hours or overnight and reheat on cookie sheet in 350° oven 10 to 15 minutes. Yields 15 to 18 muffins.

Country Ham & Broccoli Quiche

    1 fill-and-bake pie shell
    1 cup chopped country ham
    ⅓ cup finely minced onion
    1 cup precooked fresh broccoli, chopped
    1 cup shredded Swiss cheese
    ¼ cup shredded sharp Cheddar cheese
    3 eggs, beaten
    1 cup half-and-half
    1 teaspoon sugar
    ¼ teaspoon cayenne

Preheat oven to 375°. Following directions on box for fill-and-bake method, unfold and press pie shell into 9-inch glass pie plate. Sprinkle country ham evenly on bottom, then minced onion, broccoli, and finally cheeses. Beat eggs, half-and-half, sugar, and cayenne and pour slowly and evenly into pie shell. Bake 30 minutes or until set. Let stand a good 10 minutes before serving. Yields 8 servings.

Note: It presents well with thinly sliced fresh tomatoes and a sprinkle of alfalfa or broccoli sprouts. If you cannot find good tomatoes out of season, you can usually find good cherry tomatoes. Cut a couple in half and leave a few whole. Scatter on one side of quiche slice and use sprouts on top of slice.

VICTORIAN COUNTRY BED & BREAKFAST

711 Sunset Avenue
Asheboro, NC 27203
(336) 626-4706 (phone)
(336) 963-2673 (mobile)
vcbb@asheboro.com
www.victoriancountrybb.com

January 2003 was the two-year anniversary for this beautiful Victorian charmer. Even though the Queen-Anne-style home took on a new look several years ago, the grace of bygone years can never be replaced by a "cosmetic" makeover. Each floor is tastefully and romantically decorated. Special touches and unique features, such as stained glass and breathtaking light fixtures, are just a few of our luring details. In Asheboro there are a variety of activities. Antique shopping is always a favorite. Of course, Seagrove, the Pottery Capital of the world, is only ten minutes away. The renowned North Carolina Zoo is only ten minutes away.

Mama Joyce's *True* Southern Gal's Biscuits

    8 cups self-rising flour
    ½ to ¾ cup shortening
    1 tall glass (16 ounces) buttermilk
    1 cup water added if more liquid needed

Sift flour and place in center of large bowl. Work in shortening by hand. Adding about ¼ to ½ cup buttermilk at a time, start making dough. Keep wet with buttermilk until you form consistency to make bis-

cuits. Fold over until smooth. Mama Joyce uses her hands to roll out dough and uses her fingers to form the biscuits, each about 2 to 3 inches around. Preheat oven to 375°. Place biscuits in greased pan about 1 inch apart. Bake until bottoms of biscuits are brown, 12 to 14 minutes. Then put pan on top rack to brown tops. Yields generous amount of biscuits for 8 guests. Nobody cooks like Mama!

C. W. WORTH HOUSE

412 South Third Street
Wilmington, NC 28401
(910) 762-8562 (phone)
(910) 763-2173 (fax)
(800) 340-8559 (toll free)
info@worthhouse.com
www.worthhouse.com

The C. W. Worth House, located in the historic district, is a Victorian charmer with fanciful shingles and turrets reminding one of a castle. Walk tree-lined streets to the riverfront, where upscale shops and fine dining await visitors. Spend the day shopping antique shops and art galleries; go on a walking tour, historic home tour, or a carriage ride along cobblestone streets. Beautiful beaches and world-class golf courses are only a short drive away.

Rosemary and Goat Cheese Strata

    Butter
    1 loaf rustic bread such as ciabatta, sliced
    8 to 10 sprigs rosemary
    6 to 8 ounces goat cheese, feta, or
        combination of cheeses to your liking
    12 large eggs

3½ cups half-and-half
¼ teaspoon cayenne
¼ to ½ teaspoon dried thyme
Crème fraîche
Paprika
Sprigs of rosemary

Butter eight ½-cup ramekins. Preheat oven to 350°. In large bowl, tear sliced bread into 1-inch pieces. Chop rosemary leaves finely and sprinkle over bread. Over this, crumble goat cheese. Mix gently with large slotted spoon. In medium bowl whisk together eggs, half-and-half, and spices. Pour egg mixture over bread mixture and combine well by gently mixing with large slotted spoon. Divide mixture evenly among ramekins, filling three-quarters full. Put on baking sheet and bake in middle of oven until puffed and golden, 25 to 35 minutes. Remove from oven and let rest 5 minutes. Remove from ramekins with flexible spatula and place on plates. Drizzle crème fraîche over individual casseroles, sprinkle on a little paprika, and top with sprig of rosemary. Serve with bacon strips and broiled tomato. Yields 6 to 8 servings.

Artichoke Mushroom Flan

1 (10-inch) piecrust, frozen prepared or homemade
1 (16-ounce) can whole artichokes
1 (4-ounce) can sliced mushrooms
1 cup shredded Swiss cheese
3 eggs plus 2 egg whites
1 cup whipping cream
¼ to ½ teaspoon dried thyme
¼ teaspoon cayenne
1 teaspoon dry mustard

Prepare piecrust according to directions for 10-inch glass pie plate. Preheat oven to 350°. Drain artichokes well, squeeze out liquid, and roughly chop. Spread on bottom of piecrust. Drain mushrooms, roughly chop, and spread on top of artichokes. Spread shredded cheese over artichokes and mushrooms. In medium bowl, mix eggs and egg whites together. Add cream and spices. Mix well. Gently pour egg mixture over all. Bake in center of oven 40 to 50 minutes until risen and

nicely browned. A knife inserted in middle will come out clean. Remove from oven and let sit 5 minutes. When set, slice and serve with bacon or sausage and broiled tomato. Garnish with fresh thyme. Yields 6 to 8 servings.

NORTH LODGE ON OAKLAND

84 Oakland Road
Asheville, NC 28801
(828) 252-6433 (phone)
(877) 222-1200 (toll free)
NLodgeonOakland@aol.com

North Lodge is an always affordable luxury. One mile from the Biltmore Estate and one mile from downtown Asheville, you can enjoy the elegance of this 1904 stone house with fireplaces. Amenities such as private baths, cable TV, gardens, and bountiful breakfasts await each guest.

Crêpes with Sherry Cheese Sauce

Crêpes:
1 cup milk
4 eggs
1 cup all-purpose flour
½ teaspoon salt
2 tablespoons melted butter

Sherry Cheese Sauce:
3 tablespoons butter
3 tablespoons all-purpose flour
1¼ cups warm milk
1 cup grated sharp Cheddar cheese
Pinch of dry mustard
¼ cup sherry
12 eggs, scrambled

C. W. Worth House

Blend well all ingredients in a blender 30 seconds. Let mixture stand 30 minutes. Preheat small, nonstick pan for 2 minutes, making sure it is very hot. Pour ¼ cup batter in pan and tilt and turn pan until batter covers entire bottom of pan. Cook each crêpe 30 seconds until nicely browned. Using spatula, lift crêpe and flip to other side. Cook that side 20 seconds. Slide cooked crêpes onto wax paper and stack them on a plate.

For sauce, melt butter in saucepan over low heat and add flour. Cook 2 minutes. Add warm (not boiling) milk to mixture slowly and stir for 1 minute. Add cheese, dry mustard, and sherry. Spoon scrambled eggs onto each crêpe. Roll like a cigar. Drip sauce over crêpe. Yields 6 servings, 2 crêpes per guest.

Crustless Spinach Quiche

1 (10-ounce) package frozen chopped spinach, thawed
6 large eggs
8 ounces shredded sharp Cheddar cheese
16 ounces small curd cottage cheese
6 tablespoons unbleached all-purpose flour
1 teaspoon salt

Preheat oven with central rack to 350°. Hand-squeeze most water from thawed spinach and place in large mixing bowl. Mix in eggs. Add cheeses, flour, and salt. Mix thoroughly. Place contents in round baking dish. Bake 45 minutes or until top browning is apparent. Yields 8 servings.

dens. New Bern is also the home of Pepsi-Cola, born in the Carolinas in 1898 by local pharmacist Caleb Bradham.

Heavenly Bananas

½ cup sour cream
2 tablespoons sugar
1 teaspoon orange peel
1 tablespoon orange juice (fresh if available)
2 to 3 large bananas
1 tablespoon granola or Grape Nuts
Fresh mint

In small bowl, combine sour cream, sugar, orange peel, and orange juice and blend well. Add bananas and gently toss to evenly coat. Spoon into serving dish and sprinkle with granola or Grape Nuts. Garnish with fresh mint from the garden. Yields 4 (½-cup) servings.

BLOOMING GARDEN INN

543 Holloway Street
Durham, NC 27701
(919) 687-0801 (phone)
(888) 687-0803 (toll free)
bloominggardeninn@msn.com
www.bloominggardeninn.com

The Blooming Garden Inn is an 1890 gated Victorian home with a wraparound, columned porch in the central historic district. There are antiques, gardens, and gracious hosts to cater to your needs. Gourmet breakfasts greet guests each morning. Suites have two-person Jacuzzis. Options are available for extended stays.

THE AERIE INN BED & BREAKFAST

509 Pollock Street
New Bern, NC 28562
(252) 636-5553 (phone)
(252) 514-2157 (fax)
(800) 849-5553 (toll free)
aerieinn@aol.com
www.aerieinn.com

The Aerie Inn Bed & Breakfast is an 1880s Victorian inn with herbal gardens one block from the Tryon Palace and located in historic New Bern. Enjoy a mouthwatering breakfast with a choice of three hot entrées. New Bern was the colonial capital of the Carolinas. The Tryon Palace, the English Governors' house, has been fully restored, along with eleven acres of gar-

ARROWHEAD INN

106 Mason Road
Durham, NC 27712
(919) 477-8430 (phone)
(919) 471-9538 (fax)
(800) 528-2207 (toll free)
info@arrowheadinn.com
www.arrowheadinn.com

Relax in the comfort of our eighteenth-century plantation inn, which rests on six acres of gardens and venerable trees. Each of our nine elegant rooms/suites and log cabin provides a serene respite with the amenities of a fine hotel—fireplaces, whirlpool tubs, TV/VCR, luxury robes, phones and data ports, and gourmet breakfasts. Fine dining is provided at the inn and it is ideal for seminar and business retreats and small weddings. Activities in the area include Duke University; UNC, Chapel Hill; North Carolina Museums of Life and Science; North Carolina Museum of Art; Eno River State Park; Brightleaf Square; and the Streets of Southpoint for shopping.

Ginger Scones

3 cups all-purpose flour
⅓ cup sugar
4 teaspoons baking powder
¼ teaspoon grated lemon zest
⅔ cup cubed, chilled unsalted butter
¾ cup plus 2 tablespoons whipping
    cream or buttermilk
⅔ cup diced crystallized ginger

Lightly butter baking sheet. Preheat oven to 400°. Blend flour, sugar, baking powder, and lemon zest in processor. Add butter and cut in flour mixture using on/off turns until mixture resembles coarse meal. Transfer mixture to large bowl. Make well in center and add ¾ cup cream or buttermilk. Using fork, stir until just moist. Mix in ginger. Transfer dough to floured surface and gently knead until smooth, about eight turns. Divide dough in half and pat each portion into ¾ inch thick round. Cut each round into six wedges and transfer to prepared baking sheet, spacing 1 inch apart. Brush tops with remaining 2 tablespoons of cream or buttermilk. Bake until lightly browned, about 18 minutes. Yields 12 servings.

Note: Can be made 1 day ahead. Cool completely. Store in airtight container at room temperature. Warm in 350° oven before serving.

Fresh Apple Cake

5 medium cooking apples
    (about 1½ pounds) peeled, cored,
    and sliced into ½-inch pieces
5 tablespoons plus 2 cups sugar
5 teaspoons ground cinnamon
4 large eggs
1 cup vegetable oil
¼ cup orange juice
1 tablespoon grated orange zest
1 teaspoon vanilla extract
3 cups all-purpose flour
3½ teaspoons baking powder
½ teaspoon salt
Confectioners' sugar

Grease and flour twelve-cup angel food pan. Preheat oven to 350°. Mix apple slices, 5 tablespoons sugar, and ground cinnamon in medium bowl. Combine 2 cups sugar, eggs, vegetable oil, orange juice, orange zest, and vanilla in large bowl and whisk to blend. Stir flour, baking powder, and salt into egg mixture. Spoon 1½ cups batter into prepared pan. Top with half of apple mixture. Cover with 1½ cups batter. Top with remaining apples, then remaining batter. Bake cake until top is brown and tester inserted near center comes out with moist crumbs attached, about 1 hour 30 minutes. Cool cake in pan on rack 15 minutes. Run knife around sides of pan to loosen. Turn cake out onto rack. Cool at least 45 minutes. Dust with confectioners' sugar. Serve slightly warm at room temperature. Yields 8 to 10 servings.

Smoky Black Bean Dip

4 slices bacon
1 medium onion, chopped
1 red bell pepper, seeded and chopped
½ teaspoon ground cumin
½ teaspoon dried oregano
2 (15-ounce) cans black beans, drained
1 tablespoon chopped and seeded
    canned chipotle chiles*
Salt and pepper
½ cup sour cream
2 teaspoons chopped fresh cilantro
Tortilla or tostado chips

Cook bacon in heavy large skillet over medium heat until crisp, about 6 minutes. Coarsely chop bacon. Pour off all but 1 tablespoon drippings from skillet. Add onion and bell pepper and sauté until onion is soft, about 6 minutes. Add cumin and oregano and sauté 1 minute. Add beans and chipotles. Simmer over medium-low heat until slightly thickened, stirring occasionally, about 4 minutes. Transfer bean mixture to processor. Blend until smooth.

Arrowhead Inn

Season with salt and pepper. Transfer to bowl. Cover and refrigerate 2 hours. (Can be made 2 days ahead. Chill dip and bacon separately.) Stir half of bacon into dip. Top with sour cream. Sprinkle with cilantro and remaining bacon. Serve dip chilled or at room temperature with tortilla chips or tostado chips. Yields 3 to 4 cups.

*Note: Chipotle chiles canned in a spicy tomato sauce, sometimes called *adobo*, can be found in most supermarkets in Mexican or Latin American specialty sections.

803 Elizabeth Bed & Breakfast

803 Elizabeth Lane
Matthews, NC 28105
(704) 847-8900 (phone)
(704) 847-5094 (fax)
(800) 327-4843 (toll free)
mwkrauss@carolina.rr.com
www.803elizabeth.com

Eight Hundred Three Elizabeth is a small, friendly bed and breakfast nestled on five acres of woods and informal rose, flower, and herb gardens. Something is in bloom every day of the year. Activities include, for sports fans, NASCAR, Panthers football, Charlotte Knights baseball, the Sting basketball and the Checkers ice hockey; for the museum seeker, Discovery Place Science Museum, the Levine Museum of the New South, the Mint Museum and the Museum of Arts and Crafts. Theater and orchestra and Broadway plays as well as historical sites are nearby.

Bran Flake Drop Cookies

½ cup (1 stick) butter at room temperature
½ cup granulated sugar
½ cup packed brown sugar
1 egg
1 teaspoon vanilla extract
1⅓ cups unbleached all-purpose flour
1 teaspoon baking soda
Pinch of salt
1 cup bran flakes cereal
½ cup coarsely chopped nuts

Preheat oven to 350°. Beat butter and sugars until fluffy. Mix in egg and vanilla until creamy. Mix together flour, baking soda, and salt and add to creamed mixture. Stir in cereal and nuts. Bake 10 minutes or until lightly browned. Yields about 3 dozen cookies.

Cousin Theo's Muffins

This is a very different coarse muffin, but a tasty nutritious change from sweet muffins.

3½ cups old-fashioned oats (not instant)
¾ cup milk
1 cup orange marmalade
2 medium eggs
1 tablespoon canola oil
1 tablespoon baking powder
1 cup chopped dates
1 cup coarsely chopped nuts

Mix oats, milk, and jelly and allow to stand for at least 30 minutes. Preheat oven to 375°. Add remaining ingredients to oats mixture, one at a time, and stir until completely blended. Spray regular-size muffin tins with cooking oil. Fill tins even with top. Bake 20 minutes or until lightly brown. Remove from oven and allow to cool about 15 minutes before removing from pan. Yields 12 muffins.

Variation: Substitute any kind of jelly or jam for orange marmalade and any dried fruit for chopped dates. Serve with fresh fruit and mint garnish.

Pecan Crunch Cookies

1 cup (2 sticks) butter, room temperature
¾ cup brown sugar
½ cup granulated sugar
1 egg
1 teaspoon vanilla extract
2¼ cups unbleached all-purpose flour
½ teaspoon baking soda
½ teaspoon cream of tartar
1½ cups chopped pecans

Preheat oven to 350°. Beat butter and sugars until fluffy. Add egg and vanilla and beat well. Mix flour, baking soda, and cream of tartar and add gradually to creamed mixture. Stir in chopped nuts. Drop by teaspoonful onto parchment paper cut to fit cookie sheet. Bake about 10 minutes or until lightly browned. Yields about 6 dozen cookies.

The Inn at Bingham School

P.O. Box 267
Chapel Hill, NC 27514
(919) 563-5583 (phone)
(919) 563-9826 (fax)
(800) 566-5583 (toll free)
fdeprez@aol.com
www.chapel-hill-inn.com

Operating from 1845 to 1865, the Bingham School served as a preparatory school for young men seeking entrance to

The Inn at Bingham School

the University of North Carolina at nearby Chapel Hill. Although the school itself is no longer standing, the headmaster's home, listed in the National Historic Registry, has received an award for its meticulous restoration. Your hosts, the Deprez family, invite you to step back in time. Furnished in period antiques, the Inn at Bingham School is nestled among pecan trees in the rolling farmland of central North Carolina. A combination of Greek and Federal styles, the inn offers five spacious guest rooms with modern private baths. Relax on one of our porches after roaming the surrounding acres of woodland. Join in a game of croquet or find peace gently swinging in a hammock. Or spend your time indoors, curling up with a good book, playing games in the parlor, or watching a classic old movie.

Madeleines

2 eggs
Zest of 1 lemon, grated
½ cup sugar
¾ cup all-purpose flour
1 teaspoon baking powder

Whisk together eggs, lemon zest, and sugar until lightened in color. Blend flour and baking powder with egg mixture and stir to combine. Cover batter and rest at room temperature for 2 hours or over-

night in refrigerator. Butter madeleine molds well and dust with flour. When ready to bake, preheat oven to 375°. Spoon 1 tablespoon batter into each mold and bake until top is lightly brown. Remove from molds and cool on rack. Yields 16 (3-inch) Madeleines.

Lemon Poppy Seed Scones

3 cups all-purpose flour
1 cup plus 1 tablespoon sugar
3 tablespoons poppy seeds
1 tablespoon baking powder
2 teaspoons grated lemon peel
1 teaspoon salt
10 tablespoons chilled unsalted butter, cut in small pieces
1 large egg
2 tablespoons fresh lemon juice
⅓ cup whole milk plus milk for brushing dough

Position rack in top third of oven. Preheat oven to 375°. Mix flour, 1 cup sugar, poppy seeds, baking powder, lemon peel, and salt in food processor. Add butter and cut in, using on/off turns, until mix resembles coarse meal. Whisk egg and lemon juice in small bowl. Add to flour mixture. Using on/off turns, process until clumps form together. Using floured hands, set out on

floured board. Gather dough into ball. Add milk. Process just until dough comes together. Divide in half. Flatten each half into 8-inch round. Cut into six wedges. Transfer scones to baking sheet coated with cooking spray. Brush with milk and sprinkle with remaining 1 tablespoon sugar. Bake until scones are brown, about 25 minutes. Transfer to rack and cool. Yields 12 scones.

German Apple Pancake

1 cup milk
3 large eggs
¾ cup all-purpose flour
2 plus 1 tablespoons sugar
2 tablespoons butter
2 Granny Smith apples, peeled, cored, and sliced into ¾-inch wedges
1 teaspoon ground cinnamon
Confectioners' sugar

Preheat oven to 375°. In bowl whisk milk, eggs, flour, and 2 tablespoons sugar. In cast-iron skillet melt butter. Add apples, cinnamon, and remaining 1 tablespoon sugar. Cook until apples are soft. Pour batter over apples. Bake until puffy and brown, about 30 minutes. Remove from oven and dust with confectioners' sugar. Yields 2 to 4 servings.

MADELYNS IN THE GROVE

1836 West Memorial Highway
P.O. Box 249
Union Grove, NC 28689-0249
(704) 539-4151 (phone)
(800) 948-4473 (toll free)
innkeepers@madelyns.com
www.madelyns.com

Encircled by chestnut oaks, the inn sits on nine peaceful acres in the foothills of

North Carolina. Madelyn serves delicious afternoon snacks and evening desserts and, in the morning, "A No Need for Lunch" breakfast. The five beautifully appointed bedchambers and private baths have all the modern conveniences and luxury amenities that guests need. There are bluegrass jam sessions every week, music festivals and plays, the burgeoning wine country, antique malls, gem mining, horseback riding, and furniture shopping for the guests to enjoy.

Broccoli Breakfast Pie

8 to 10 slices bread
1 (10-ounce) package frozen chopped broccoli, thawed and drained
1 cup shredded cooked ham (optional)
2 cups shredded Swiss cheese
½ cup Parmesan cheese
3 tablespoons butter
3 tablespoons all-purpose flour
1 cup milk
1 teaspoon dried chopped basil
1 teaspoon dried chopped parsley
5 eggs, slightly beaten
1½ cups milk

Spray a 10-inch, deep pie dish with vegetable coating. Arrange half the bread in bottom and up sides of dish. Layer broccoli on bread. Top with ham and cheese. In small saucepan, melt butter and add flour. Cook 2 to 3 minutes to take raw taste from flour Add milk. Bring to a boil, stirring constantly. When thickened, remove white sauce from heat and pour over broccoli and ham. Sprinkle basil and parsley over sauce. Cover this with remaining bread slices. You may have to cut bread to fit top of dish. Mix eggs and milk together. Carefully pour mixture over bread and broccoli. Cover with plastic wrap and refrigerate 8 to 10 hours or overnight. When ready to bake, preheat oven to 350°. Bake casserole until golden brown, 35 to 40 minutes. Remove from oven and allow to rest for about 15 minutes before serving in pie-shaped wedges. Garnish with chopped cherry tomatoes. Yields 6 to 8 servings.

Lemon Chess Pie

1 cup sugar
¾ cup (1½ sticks) melted butter
3 large eggs
Grated zest and juice of 1 large lemon
1 (9-inch) piecrust
2 tablespoons graham cracker crumbs
Mint sprigs
Whipped cream

Preheat oven to 350°. In bowl, combine sugar, butter, eggs, and lemon zest and juice. Blend well with electric mixer. Pour into piecrust. Sprinkle with graham cracker crumbs and bake 50 to 55 minutes. Garnish with sprig of mint and dollop of whipped cream. Yields 6 to 8 servings.

Morning Poppy Pizza Pie

2 plus 3 tablespoons melted butter
2 tablespoons Dijon mustard
1 tablespoon poppy seeds
3 (7-inch) prepared gourmet pizza crusts
¼ cup diced onion
10 to 12 mushrooms, sliced
1 cup ham cut in small cubes
15 large eggs
½ cup cottage cheese
1 tablespoon Worcestershire sauce
4 to 5 drops of Tabasco
2¼ cups shredded Cheddar and Jack cheeses

Preheat oven to 400°. Combine 2 tablespoons butter, Dijon mustard, and poppy seeds. Spread mixture over pizza crusts. Place in oven while preparing egg mixture. In large frying pan over medium heat, add remaining 3 tablespoons butter and diced onion. Sauté and add mushrooms and cook 3 more minutes. Add ham and cook another 2 minutes. Combine eggs, cottage cheese, Worcestershire, and Tabasco in bowl. Mix well and pour over ham mixture in pan. Scramble eggs until just set

and light and fluffy. Remove pizza crusts from oven and divide egg mixture equally over crusts. Sprinkle each pizza with cheese mixture. Return to oven and bake 8 to 10 minutes or until cheese is completely melted. Remove from oven and serve. Cut each pizza into four wedges. Yields 6 servings, 2 wedges per person.

Chocolate, Chocolate Chip Waffles with Peanut Butter Syrup

3 tablespoons coconut
1 tablespoon cocoa
1 tablespoon sugar
2 tablespoons vegetable oil
1 cup oatmeal
½ cup hot water
1 egg
1 cup skim milk
2 cups pancake mix
¼ cup mini chocolate chips
⅓ cup real maple syrup
⅓ cup smooth peanut butter
Confectioners' sugar

Preheat waffle iron. Place coconut in small frying pan and toast until golden brown. Watch carefully because this will burn easily. When golden, remove from heat and set aside. In large bowl, combine cocoa, sugar, and oil. Stir well. Add oatmeal and water, mixing all ingredients together very well. Allow to sit for 5 minutes. After oatmeal has absorbed water, add egg, milk, and pancake mix. Stir well. Fold in chips. Use batter required by waffle iron directions. Cook until steam stops. While waffle cooks, combine syrup and peanut butter. Place waffle on plate and dust with confectioners' sugar. Top with peanut butter mixture and garnish with toasted coconut. Yields 4 large waffles or 6 to 8 small waffles.

❧   ❧   ❧

HIGHLAND LAKE INN

P.O. Box 1026
Flat Rock, NC 28731
(828) 693-6812 (phone)
(800) 635-5101 (toll free)
frontdesk@HLInn.com
www.HLInn.com

Highland Lake Inn is a country retreat. Nestled in the Blue Ridge Mountains, this enchanted location offers an inn, lodge, cabins, cottages, and an award-winning restaurant to accommodate one and all. Families, weddings, reunions, banquets, and business retreats are welcome. Surrounding activities include Flat Rock Playhouse and the Carl Sandburg home. There are many on-site activities such as hiking, biking, swimming, horseshoes, volleyball, and much more.

Pecan-Crusted Mountain Trout

This mountain favorite is our most popular dish. Long-grain rice or Grilled Potato and Charred Pepper Salad makes a great side dish for this entrée.

3 cups chopped pecans
1 cup Japanese breadcrumbs (panko)
1 tablespoon chopped mint
Kosher salt
Fresh ground black pepper
2 ounces melted butter
6 (8-ounce) trout fillets
Flour as needed, seasoned with
    salt and pepper
Egg wash (3 eggs plus ½ cup water)
Canola oil

Combine pecans, breadcrumbs, and mint. Season with salt and pepper to taste. Add butter and mix by hand until combined. Season trout fillets with salt and pepper to taste. Dredge trout, flesh-side only, in seasoned flour. Dip in egg wash. Press flesh side of trout into crumb mixture. Sauté over medium to medium-high heat in pan coated with canola oil. When pan is hot, place trout, skin-side up so that pecan crust can brown 1 to 2 minutes. When crust is brown, turn trout to brown, and finish cooking about 2 minutes more. Yields 6 servings.

Grilled Potato and Charred Pepper Salad

Need a new alternative for mashed potatoes? Try this great side dish. It's a crowd pleaser and goes well with beef, chicken, and seafood.

1 pound medium potatoes
½ medium red onion, peeled
2 tablespoons plus ½ cup olive oil
1 each red and green roasted bell
    peppers, peeled and seeded
Kosher salt
Fresh ground black pepper
2 tablespoons whole grain mustard
⅓ bunch parsley, chopped
2 tablespoons chopped chives
¼ cup balsamic vinegar
2 tablespoons honey

Preheat oven to 350°. Wash and quarter potatoes. Slice onions and peppers ¾-inch thick. Toss potatoes and onions in 2 tablespoons olive oil until lightly coated. Season with salt and pepper to taste. In medium baking pan, roast potatoes and onions 25 minutes. Fold roasted peppers into potato and onion mixture. Make vinaigrette by combining mustard, parsley, chives, balsamic vinegar, and honey. Slowly whisk in remaining ½ cup olive oil until well blended. Toss potato mixture in vinaigrette. This can be served hot or at room temperature. Yields 6 servings.

Key Lime Flummery

A deliciously light dessert perfect for summer.

½ ounce unflavored gelatin
½ cup key lime juice
1 plus 1 cup heavy cream
1 cup sugar
2 teaspoons vanilla extract
1 quart plain yogurt
Zest of 2 limes, chopped (optional)

In medium bowl, soak gelatin in lime juice. In small saucepan over high heat, scald 1 cup cream with sugar and vanilla. Pour over "bloomed" gelatin and whisk until gelatin is fully dissolved. Whisk in yogurt and lime zest. Whip remaining cup cream to medium-stiff peaks and fold into yogurt mixture. Pour into plastic-lined mold. Refrigerate until set. Yields 10 to 12 servings.

CORNER OAK MANOR BED & BREAKFAST

53 Saint Dunstans Road
Asheville, NC 28803
(828) 253-3525 (phone)
(888) 633-3525 (toll free)
info@corneroakmanor.com
www.corneroakmanor.com

Corner Oak Manor Bed & Breakfast is a 1920 Tudor home located just a half mile from Biltmore House. Chef-prepared, gourmet breakfasts using seasonal ingredients, vegetarian, and healthful menus are available. The bed and breakfast is also close to downtown Asheville with many galleries and antique stores. Nearby are the Blue Ridge Parkway and Appalachian Mountains with hiking, biking, and river rafting.

Smoked Trout Frittata

3 medium red potatoes
6 large eggs
⅛ teaspoon salt
¼ teaspoon pepper
¼ cup milk
1 tablespoon prepared horseradish
1 tablespoon chopped fresh dill
    or 1 teaspoon dried
1 large onion, chopped
2 teaspoons extra virgin olive oil
¾ cup flaked smoked trout

Place potatoes in small pot with cold water to cover. Bring to a boil over high heat and then simmer just until tender. Cool. Slice potatoes in half lengthwise and then into ¼-inch-thick slices. Whisk together eggs, salt and pepper, milk, horseradish, and dill. Sauté onion in olive oil until tender. Add potatoes and season with salt and pepper to taste. Pour eggs over potato-onion mixture and top with trout. Preheat oven to 350° and bake 20 minutes or until eggs are set. If desired you can broil for 1 or 2 minutes to slightly brown top. Cut in wedges and serve hot or at room temperature. Yields 4 to 6 servings.

Cinnamon Crumb Cake

1¼ cups all-purpose flour
⅔ cup packed brown sugar
¾ teaspoon ground cinnamon
⅛ teaspoon salt
¼ cup (½ stick) butter, cut in tiny pieces
½ teaspoon baking powder
½ teaspoon baking soda
½ cup low-fat buttermilk
1 teaspoon vanilla extract
1 large egg

Preheat oven to 350°. Coat 8-inch cake pan with spray. Combine flour, brown sugar, cinnamon, and salt in bowl. Cut in butter until mixture resembles coarse remaining flour mixture, add baking powder and soda. Combine buttermilk, vanilla, crumbs. Reserve ½ cup for topping. To and egg. Add to flour mixture and beat until well blended. Spoon batter into cake pan. Sprinkle reserved ½ cup flour mixture over batter. Bake 30 minutes or until cake springs back when touched lightly in center. Cool on wire rack. Yields 8 wedges.

Cranberry-White Chocolate Oatmeal Cookies

½ cup (1 stick) butter, softened
1½ cups sugar
2 large eggs
1 teaspoon vanilla extract
1¾ cups all-purpose flour
1 cup old-fashioned oats
1½ teaspoons baking soda
½ teaspoon salt
1 cup dried cranberries
⅔ cup chopped white chocolate

Cream butter and sugar until well blended. Beat in eggs and vanilla. Combine flour, oats, baking soda, and salt. Add dry ingredients to butter mixture just until blended. Fold in cranberries and chocolate pieces. Chill dough; it will be sticky. Preheat oven to 350°. When chilled, shape dough into 1-inch balls. Place on greased cookie sheets. Bake 9 to 11 minutes. Yields 48 cookies.

Corner Oak Manor Bed & Breakfast

BED & BREAKFAST AT LAUREL RIDGE

3188 Siler City-Snow Camp Road
Siler City, NC 27344
(919) 742-6049 (phone)
(800) 742-6049 (toll free)
info@laurel-ridge.com
www.laurel-ridge.com

Laurel Ridge, a distinct post-and-beam home with a separate cottage, is located on twenty-six forested acres and sits adjacent the Rocky River in central North Carolina. Laurel Ridge is convenient to the Seagrove potters, furniture shopping, the North Carolina Zoo, many antique vendors and antique fairs, world-class golf courses, or just relaxing on the gazebo overlooking the river.

Eggs Florentine

Potatoes:
4 Yukon gold potatoes
2 tablespoons butter
Salt and pepper
Paprika
Fresh thyme

Spinach topping:
1 cup fresh mushrooms,
    mixed varieties
2 tablespoons butter
1 tablespoon olive oil
2 cups fresh spinach,
    cut in bite-size pieces
Salt and freshly ground pepper
½ teaspoon balsamic vinegar
4 poached eggs

Slice potatoes about ¼ inch thick. Parboil potatoes in slightly salted water just until fork tender. Cool immediately. In sauté pan or griddle over medium heat add butter and potatoes and season to taste with salt, pepper, paprika, and thyme. Finish cooking potatoes until golden brown on both sides.

For topping, slice mushrooms and sauté in fry pan over medium heat with butter and olive oil. Add spinach and season with salt and pepper to taste. Add balsamic vinegar and remove from heat. Place 4 or 5 potato rounds on plate. Put spinach mixture on top of potatoes. Place poached egg on top of spinach. Spoon Hollandaise Sauce (see next recipe) over top of poached eggs and finish with dash of paprika. Yields 4 servings.

Hollandaise Sauce

4 egg yolks
1 cup melted unsalted butter
2 teaspoons fresh lemon juice
Hot sauce
Salt

Place egg yolks and about 1 tablespoon tepid water in medium stainless steel mixing bowl. Place bowl over poaching pan at low to medium heat. Whisk yolks until thickened and pale yellow. Do *not* overcook yolks or they will not accept melted butter. Remove pan from heat immediately and while constantly whisking, very slowly add warm butter to thicken sauce. Add fresh lemon juice and drops of hot sauce and salt to taste. Keep sauce warm, but not hot, or it will separate. Yields about 2 cups sauce.

Lemon-Zucchini-Rosemary Muffins

⅔ cup sugar
½ cup vegetable oil
2 eggs
Grated zest of 1 lemon
Juice of 1 lemon
1½ cups unpeeled, grated zucchini
1 teaspoon finely chopped
    fresh rosemary
2 cups all-purpose flour
2 teaspoons baking powder
½ teaspoon baking soda
½ teaspoon salt
¼ teaspoon ground nutmeg

Preheat oven to 400°. In large bowl mix sugar, oil, eggs, lemon zest, lemon juice, zucchini, and fresh rosemary. In smaller bowl, blend flour, baking powder, baking soda, salt, and nutmeg. Spray nonstick coating in 12-cup muffin tin and fill each cup about three-fourths full. Bake for 15 to 18 minutes depending on oven. Do *not* overbake. Remove from pan and cool on rack. Yields 12 muffins.

Apple Apricot Crunch

Crunch:
6 large tart apples, peeled,
    cored, and sliced
¾ cup apricot preserves
Zest and juice of 1 lemon
½ teaspoon ground cinnamon
½ teaspoon ground nutmeg
2 tablespoons light brown sugar
Whipped cream for garnish
Mint sprigs for garnish

Topping:
1 cup all-purpose flour
⅔ cup brown sugar
½ teaspoon ground cinnamon
¼ teaspoon salt
1 stick cold butter,
    cut into small pieces
½ cup pecans
1 cup old-fashioned oats

Preheat oven to 375°. Combine apples, preserves, lemon zest and juice, cinnamon, nutmeg, and brown sugar in large mixing bowl. Put mixture in buttered ramekins. Place ramekins on sheet pan to prevent mixture from spilling on oven while baking. Bake about 20 minutes.

For topping, in food processor, add flour, brown sugar, cinnamon, and salt. Pulse until mixed. Add butter and pecans and pulse until crumbly. Do *not* overmix. Pour into large bowl and add oats and mix thoroughly. Spoon 2 tablespoons topping on apples and finish baking for another 20 minutes until bubbly. Cool 10 minutes before serving. Garnish each ramekin with 1 tablespoon whipped heavy cream. Sprinkle ground cinnamon on top of cream and add sprig of fresh mint. Yields 4 servings.

HARBORLIGHT GUEST HOUSE

332 Live Oak Drive
Cape Carteret, NC 28584-9268
(252) 393-6868 (phone)
(252) 393-6868 (fax)
(800) 624-8439 (toll free)

The Harborlight, a secluded waterfront inn located on the central coast, offers romantic suites with Jacuzzis, fireplaces, and stunning water views. Breakfast is served in-suite or deck-side. Favorite guest activities include excursions to barrier islands (only accessible by boat) that offer incredible shelling and pristine private beaches; a catamaran sail to the Cape Lookout lighthouse; horseback riding on the beach; exploring the waterfront shops of Beaufort and Swansboro; and ending the day with a romantic sunset sail.

Rum-Runner French Toast

¾ cup melted coffee ice cream
3 eggs, beaten
1 tablespoon dark rum
¼ teaspoon ground cinnamon
10 slices cinnamon raisin bread
Butter for grilling
8 scoops coffee ice cream

Combine melted ice cream, eggs, rum, and cinnamon in bowl. Whisk until blended. Dip raisin bread into egg mixture, coating on both sides. Melt butter on electric griddle at 300° and grill bread about 5 minutes per side until golden brown. Slice bread diagonally, layer five half-slices on each plate, and top with 2 scoops coffee ice cream. Maple syrup can be served with this dish if desired. Yields 4 servings.

Honeybee Ambrosia

½ cup orange juice
¼ cup honey
2 tablespoons lemon juice
2 (12-ounce) cans mandarin oranges
2 bananas
Grated coconut and cherries with stems

Mix orange juice, honey, and lemon juice until blended. Layer mandarin oranges and bananas in sherbet bowls and top with juice mixture. Sprinkle coconut on top and top with cherry. Serve in bowl presented on crystal plate topped with paper doily. Yields 4 servings.

Quick Potato Casserole

1 (2-pound) package frozen hash browns
2 cups (1 pint) sour cream
1 onion, chopped
1 teaspoon salt
½ cup melted butter
2 cups shredded sharp Cheddar cheese
1 (10¾-ounce) can cream of chicken soup

Preheat oven to 375°. Mix all ingredients and bake in greased, 9 x 13-inch pan 45 minutes or until brown. Yields 10 to 12 servings.

Note: Served at the inn in individual ramekins and topped with cheese. Delicious as an accompaniment for breakfast or as a dinner dish.

THE CAROLINA INN

211 Pittsboro Street
Chapel Hill, NC 27516
(919) 918-2722 (phone)
(919) 918-2760 (fax)
Marcie@carolinainn.com
www.carolinainn.com

The Carolina Inn is listed on the National Register of Historic Places. From the day that it opened in 1924, the inn has played an important role in the life of the University of North Carolina and the Chapel Hill community. The inn was built by John Sprunt Hill, a UNC graduate, who, in 1935, gave the inn to the University to serve as "a cheerful inn for visitors, a town hall for the state, and a home for returning sons and daughters of alma mater." The inn continues to be owned by UNC.

Braised Veal Short Ribs

2 pounds short ribs
½ gallon chicken or veal stock
½ bunch thyme
½ teaspoon black peppercorns
1 shallot, diced
1 clove garlic, split
¾ cup roasted red pepper purée
½ pound all-purpose flour
3 eggs
Pinch of nutmeg
Salt and pepper
4 ounces black trumpet mushrooms (can be substituted)
4 ounces fresh corn
4 ounces collard greens

Preheat oven to 300°. In hot sauté pan over high heat, sear ribs until golden brown on all sides. Cover ribs with stock and add thyme, peppercorns, shallot, and garlic. Cover and place in oven. Cook until fork tender, about 2 hours. Remove from braising liquid and strain liquid through sieve into saucepan. Reduce braising liquid until flavorful. While braising liquid is reducing, prepare spaetzle. In bowl combine red pepper purée, flour, eggs, nutmeg, and salt and pepper and mix thoroughly. Bring seasoned water to simmer and slowly add small pinches of spaetzle batter to water. Cook until spaetzle float, remove from water, and drain. Sauté in large pan over medium heat mushrooms, corn, spaetzle, and collards together and season with salt and pepper. Warm short ribs in reduced braising liquid. Place sautéed vegetables in middle of plate and short ribs on top. Drizzle reduced braising sauce around plate and serve. Yields 4 servings.

Gala Apple and Chive Slaw

8 ounces lump crabmeat
1 each red and yellow peppers
4 scallions
1 clove garlic
2 ounces brandy
¼ cup (½ stick) butter
1 tablespoon Dijon mustard
2 whole eggs
Salt and pepper
1 cup breadcrumbs
2 Gala apples
¼ sweet onion
10 chives
⅓ cup olive oil
2 tablespoons cider vinegar

Pick through crabmeat and remove all shells. Finely dice red and yellow peppers. Thinly slice scallions. In hot sauté pan over medium-high heat, add red and yellow peppers and sauté for 2 minutes. Add garlic and brandy and reduce volume by half. Add butter and mustard and cook until butter is melted. Remove from heat and

cool thoroughly. When cool combine with crabmeat, eggs, scallions, and salt and pepper to taste in bowl. Separate mixture into four portions and coat with breadcrumbs. Refrigerate until needed. Thinly slice apples and onion. Dice chives. Combine olive oil, vinegar, apples, onions, and chives. Season with salt and pepper. Sear crab cakes in medium-hot sauté pan with small amount of oil until golden brown on both sides. Divide slaw and place in middle of two plates, and divide hot crab cakes on top of slaw to serve. Yields 2 servings.

Butternut Squash Bisque

2 medium butternut squash
1 large yellow onion
2 plus 2 tablespoons olive oil
4 cloves garlic
¼ cup sugar
1 quart herb stock or chicken stock
1 pint half-and-half
Salt and pepper
1 teaspoon wine vinegar
1 teaspoon butter
1 ounce pumpkin seeds
Cayenne (optional)
1 Gala apple

Peel and coarsely chop squash and yellow onion. Place on stove and warm to medium-high temperature in thick-bottom soup pot. Add 2 tablespoons olive oil, squash, garlic, and onion. Stir to avoid browning and add sugar. Cover pot, reduce heat to medium-low, and let mixture steep in its juices for 20 minutes. Add stock and bring to simmer. Continue to simmer for another 20 minutes. Remove from heat and blend thoroughly. Strain through fine sieve and return to soup pot. Add half-and-half and bring to simmer over low heat, stirring occasionally. Season soup with salt and pepper and vinegar. In warm sauté pan add butter, seeds, and cayenne, if using. Sauté over medium heat until seeds are toasted to golden brown. Remove to paper towel. Slice apple very

thinly and in medium hot sauté remaining 2 tablespoons oil s until golden brown and crisp. To serve, ladle hot soup in bowl, lay crisp apple slice in middle of bowl, and sprinkle roasted pumpkin seeds on top of apple. Yields 4 servings.

Herb-Crusted Loin of Lamb

1 bunch parsley
4 sprigs fresh rosemary
1 cup breadcrumbs
½ cup olive oil
1 (16-ounce) loin of lamb
3 tablespoons Dijon mustard
1 medium beet
¼ cup brown sugar
1 cinnamon stick
2 cloves
2 medium whole shallots
    and 1 chopped
2 sweet potatoes
¼ cup (½ stick) sweet butter
Salt and pepper
⅛ teaspoon ground cinnamon
4 cloves garlic
1 cup red wine
1 quart lamb stock

In food processor, place leaves from parsley along with 1 sprig rosemary and breadcrumbs and blend for 5 minutes until combined. In hot sauté pan with small amount of olive oil sear loin of lamb on all sides and remove from pan to cool. Brush mustard over cooled loin and coat with seasoned breadcrumbs. In saucepan place whole, washed, unpeeled beet, cover with water, sugar, cinnamon stick, and cloves and bring to a boil. Reduce pan to simmer, cover, and continue to cook until beet is soft. Once beets are done, remove from liquid to cool. Preheat oven to 250°. Continue to reduce cooking liquid until it is reduced by two-thirds. Remove and reserve for later.

Roast whole shallots in pan covered with olive oil for 30 minutes or until soft.

Remove from oil. Peel and coarsely chop sweet potatoes. Boil in water until soft and whip together with butter, salt, pepper, and cinnamon. Keep warm to serve.

Sauté remaining shallot and garlic until shallots are glossy. Add red wine and reduce until wine has evaporated. Add lamb stock and rosemary sprig. Continue to reduce to two-thirds, strain, and season with salt and pepper. Set oven to 350° and roast lamb until internal temperature is 125° (about 10 minutes). Remove from oven when done and let rest for 5 minutes. Warm beet mixture with reserved syrup and place on plate along with remainder of items. Garnish with rosemary sprig and serve. Yields 2 servings.

THE COLBY HOUSE & COTTAGE

230 Pearson Drive
Asheville, NC 28801
(828) 253-5644 (phone)
(828) 259-9479 (fax)
(800) 982-2118 (toll free)
colbyhouse@cs.com
www.colbyhouse.com

Contemporary comfort complements historic colonial elegance at the Colby House and Cottage. Guests enjoy beautiful gardens, sitting porch, inviting fireplaces, and bountiful breakfasts. The bed and breakfast is in the Appalachians, near the Blue Ridge Parkway, Biltmore Estate, and a city of great diversity and arts.

Irish Frittata

3 medium potatoes, peeled and sliced
1 medium onion, chopped
2 tablespoons olive oil
12 eggs
1 teaspoon dried rosemary or
    2 teaspoons fresh minced rosemary
3 scallions, finely chopped
Salt and pepper
2 tablespoons milk
2 tablespoons cubed cream cheese
¾ cup shredded Cheddar cheese

Place potatoes in saucepan and cover with water. Bring to a boil over high heat and cook about 10 minutes until tender but firm. Drain well. Sauté onion in olive oil in large skillet. Add potatoes and heat through. Preheat broiler on low setting. Beat eggs with rosemary, scallions, salt and pepper, milk and cream cheese. Pour into pan with potatoes. Cook and stir lightly on top of stove until partially cooked. Sprinkle with cheese and broil until set. Cut into wedges. Garnish with rosemary sprigs. Yields 6 servings.

Lemon-Ricotta Pancakes

Pancakes:
3 eggs, separated
¼ cup all-purpose flour
¼ cup vegetable oil
¾ cup ricotta cheese
2 tablespoons sugar
¼ teaspoon salt
1 tablespoon grated lemon zest

Mixed berry sauce:
1½ cups frozen mixed berries
    (strawberries, blueberries, raspberries)
2 teaspoons sugar
1 teaspoon cornstarch
2 teaspoons cold water

Beat egg whites to soft peak. Beat together yolks, flour, oil, ricotta, sugar, salt, and lemon zest. Gently fold in egg whites. Pour ¼ cup batter per pancake onto hot griddle, and cook for about 2 minutes. Flip each for 1 minute.

For sauce, thaw berries in saucepan with sugar. Cook over medium heat 5 minutes. Combine cornstarch with water and add to mixture. Stir until thickened. Serve with pancakes. Yields 10 to 12 pancakes.

Cranberry-Orange Pecan Muffins

2 cups bread flour
½ teaspoon salt
1 tablespoon baking powder
1 cup sugar
1 egg, beaten
½ cup orange juice
½ cup milk
⅓ cup vegetable oil
2 tablespoons grated orange peel
½ cup chopped pecans
1 cup dried cranberries

Preheat oven to 400°. Blend together flour, salt, baking powder, and sugar. Stir in, just until moistened, egg, juice, milk, and oil. Fold in orange peel, pecans, and cranberries. Fill greased muffin tins and bake about 15 minutes. Yields 12 muffins.

Black Olive Hummus

2 cups cooked or canned chickpeas
2 cloves garlic, minced
2 tablespoons chopped parsley
4 to 6 kalamata olives, pitted and chopped
¼ cup liquid from chickpeas
¼ cup lemon juice
3 tablespoons tahini (sesame paste)
2 tablespoons olive oil

Purée all ingredients in food processor. Sprinkle with parsley and serve with pita wedges or water crackers. Best made ahead to allow flavors to blend. Yields 3 cups.

THE INN ON MILL CREEK

P.O. Box 185
Ridgecrest, North Carolina 29770
(828) 668-1115 (phone)
(828) 668-8506 (fax)
(877) 735-2964 (toll free)
Jim@inn-on-mill-creek.com
www.inn-on-mill-creek.com

Nestled between Horse Ridge and Bernard Mountain, the Inn on Mill Creek sits on seven beautiful acres in the midst of the Pisgah National Forest. Guests are invited to help themselves to the harvest from the onsite orchard, the bounty of which also graces the breakfast table. Well-rested guests can often be found canoeing or fishing by the lake edge, picking fruit in the 170-tree orchard, or hiking or mountain biking through the National Forest at the edge of the property. Creek play, whitewater rafting, waterfall hikes, and beautiful drives and picnic spots on the Blue Ridge Parkway, plus the world-famous Biltmore Estate, are all available nearby.

Apple Nut Bread

2 cups sugar
1¼ cups vegetable oil
3 eggs
3 cups all-purpose flour
1 teaspoon baking soda
1 teaspoon salt
4 tablespoons vanilla extract
3 cups chopped apples
1 cup quick oatmeal
1 teaspoon ground cinnamon
½ cup chopped nuts

Preheat oven to 325°. Mix sugar, oil, and eggs. Add flour, baking soda, and salt and mix well. Add vanilla, apples, oatmeal, cinnamon, and nuts. Bake in Bundt pan 1 hour 15 minutes. This is wonderful with coffee. Yields 10 to 12 servings.

Cinnamon-Peach Bread

3 cups all-purpose flour
1½ cups granulated sugar
½ cup packed brown sugar
1½ teaspoons ground cinnamon
¼ teaspoon mace
1 teaspoon baking soda
1 teaspoon salt
2 peaches, peeled and chopped
4 eggs
1 cup vegetable oil

Preheat oven to 350°. Grease two 4½ x 8½-inch loaf pans and line with wax paper. In large bowl, combine flour, sugars, cinnamon, mace, baking soda, and salt. In mixing bowl, beat peaches, eggs, and oil until well blended. Add flour mixture to peach mixture and stir until well blended. Spoon batter into prepared pans. Bake 50 to 60 minutes or until toothpick inserted in center of bread comes out clean. Cool in pans 10 minutes. Remove from pans and cool completely or slice and serve warm. Yields 2 loaves.

Maple Syrup Custard

1 cup milk or half-and-half
4 eggs
Salt
½ cup maple syrup

Preheat oven to 375°. Butter (or use non-stick spray) four custard cups. For water bath, put paper towel in bottom of shallow baking dish and fill it three-fourths full with boiling water. Beat all ingredients together in bowl and fill custard cups. Place them in water bath and bake 20 minutes or until custard is barely set. Remove from oven. Run knife around edges and turn custards out onto serving plate; serving in cups is easier and a very nice alternative. Yields 4 cups.

The Inn on Mill Creek

THE WICKLOW INN

Highway 64/74A
P.O. Box 246
Chimney Rock, NC 28720-0246
(828) 625-4038 (phone)
(877) 625-4038 (toll free)
wicklowinn@earthlink.com
www.thewicklowinn.com

The Wicklow Inn is a riverside bed and breakfast with an Irish accent. It offers individually decorated rooms with private entrances on Rocky Broad River two blocks from Chimney Rock Park. And there is a delightful breakfast.

Nearby you will find fishing, tubing, and canoeing on Rocky Broad River; hiking in Chimney Rock Park; swimming, boating, and fishing at Lake Lure; browsing through quaint shops filled with antiques, pottery, and crafts in the village of Chimney Rock; horseback riding; two championship golf courses; the Blue Ridge Parkway; Asheville and Biltmore Estates; Hendersonville and the Flat Rock Playhouse; the Carl Sandburg Home; the Brevard Music Center; Pisgah National Forest and Sliding Rock; and DuPont State Forest.

Mary McGee's Scones

¼ pound (1 stick) butter, softened
2 cups self-rising flour
½ cup sugar
2 teaspoons baking powder
1 cup golden raisins
1 cup milk
1 plus 1 egg, beaten
Sugar

Preheat oven to 350°. In mixing bowl, add softened butter to flour, sugar, and baking powder. Using pastry attachment blend with mixer on slow, scraping sides until crumbly. Add raisins, milk, and 1 beaten egg and continue blending until mixture forms a dough. Spread dough on floured surface. Knead very lightly and roll out to ½-inch thick. Cut scones out with pastry cutter and place on warmed, buttered baking sheet. Brush remaining beaten egg on top and sprinkle with sugar. Bake 20 minutes or until lightly brown. Yields 8 to 10 scones.

Note: The proper way to eat scones is to split them in half and spread the bottom with Devonshire Cream (see next recipe), then raspberry or strawberry preserves. Place the top back on the bottom and enjoy.

Devonshire Cream

5 ounces cream cheese, softened
1 cup heavy cream
½ cup confectioners' sugar

Whip all ingredients until blended. Yields about 2 cups.

Poached Cinnamon Pears

4 pears
Lemon juice
Cinnamon sugar
Whipped cream for topping
Cinnamon for topping
Kiwi or strawberry for garnish

Peel pears carefully with vegetable peeler. Slice pears in half lengthwise, trying to retain some stem if possible on each slice (just for aesthetics). Place pears flat-side down in baking dish. Sprinkle with lemon juice. Sprinkle liberally with cinnamon and sugar mix. Microwave until fork tender, not mushy. Remove from dish and place each pear half on individual serving dish. Top with whipped cream. Sprinkle cinnamon over cream. Garnish with kiwi slice, strawberry, or whatever is in season. Yields 4 servings.

The Wicklow Inn

MEADOWS INN BED & BREAKFAST

212 Pollock Street
New Bern, NC 28560
(252) 634-1776 (phone)
(877) 551-1776 (toll free)
meadowsinnbnb@earthlink.net
www.meadowsinn-nc.com

History and hospitality await you at this colonial bed and breakfast. Visit New Bern, North Carolina, and enjoy the charm of Meadows Inn. Walk to historic sites, restaurants, and waterfront. Private baths, full breakfasts, and TV/VCRs make the inn family friendly. Create history by planning a reunion or event and discover the coast while staying at the Meadows Inn.

Scrambled Egg Enchiladas

1 tablespoon butter or margarine
12 large eggs, lightly beaten
16 ounces processed cheese-spread loaf
    with peppers, cut and divided
1½ cups chopped, cooked ham
12 (8-inch) flour tortillas
2 tablespoons milk
Salsa and sour cream for topping

Melt butter in large skillet and cook eggs over medium heat without stirring until eggs begin to set on bottom. Draw spatula across bottom of pan to form large curds. Continue cooking until eggs are thickened but still moist. Remove from heat. Add half of cheese to eggs, stirring until cheese melts; chill remaining cheese. Stir chopped ham into egg mixture. Spoon mixture evenly down center of each tortilla, and roll up jellyroll fashion. Place seam-side down in lightly greased 13 x 9-inch baking dish. Cover and chill 8 hours. Let stand at room temperature 30 minutes. Preheat oven to 350° and bake 35 to 40 minutes or until thoroughly heated. Combine remaining cheese and milk in small saucepan and cook until cheese melts. Spoon over enchiladas and serve with salsa and sour cream. Yields 12 servings.

Meadows Inn Oatmeal Custard

½ cup milk
½ cup heavy cream
    (or 1 cup milk or
    1 cup half-and-half)
4 eggs
Salt
5 teaspoons sugar
1 teaspoon vanilla extract
½ cup quick oatmeal
½ teaspoon ground nutmeg
3 tablespoons chopped raisins
    or 4 teaspoons chopped nuts
    (optional)
Cinnamon

Preheat oven to 375°. Butter four custard cups and set in shallow baking dish half filled with hot water. In large bowl combine milk, cream, eggs, and salt. Add sugar, vanilla, oatmeal, and nutmeg. Add raisins if desired. Fill prepared cups to ½ inch from top. Sprinkle with pinch of cinnamon. Bake 20 to 25 minutes until set. Remove from oven and let stand 5 minutes. Yields 4 servings.

Note: This may be prepared the night before and baked in the morning.

Stuffed French Toast Strata

1 (1-pound) loaf French bread
1 (8-ounce) package cream cheese, cubed
8 eggs
2½ cups milk, cream, or half-and-half
6 tablespoons melted butter
    or margarine
¼ cup maple syrup
1 teaspoon ground cinnamon

Cut bread into cubes, about 12 cups. Grease 13 x 9-inch baking pan and put in half of bread cubes. Top with cream cheese and remaining bread cubes. With blender or mixing bowl with rotary beater, mix together eggs, milk, butter, maple syrup, and cinnamon until well combined. Pour egg mixture evenly over bread and cheese cubes. Using spatula, slightly press layers down to moisten. Cover with plastic wrap and refrigerate 2 to 24 hours. When ready to bake, preheat oven to 325°. Remove plastic wrap and bake 40 to 45 minutes or until center appears to be set and eggs are golden. Let stand 10 minutes. Yields 6 to 8 servings.

Note: May add blueberries after cream cheese and serve with blueberry syrup.

CEDAR CREST VICTORIAN INN

674 Biltmore Avenue
Asheville, NC 28803
(828) 252-1389 (phone)
(800) 252-0310 (toll free)
stay@cedarcrestvictorianinn.com
www.cedarcrestinn.com

Step back in time while enjoying the comforts of the present at Cedar Crest Victorian Inn. This magnificent Queen Anne mansion offers exquisite Victorian decor with lavish interior woodwork and glass. The inn is conveniently located to all area attractions, including Biltmore Estate, arts and crafts, antiquing, galleries, as well as outdoor activities such as hiking, biking, and river rafting.

Peaches and Cream French Toast

½ cup (1 stick) butter
1 cup brown sugar
2 tablespoons corn syrup
1 (29-ounce) can peach halves in
    light syrup, drained
1 loaf French bread, cubed
8 ounces cream cheese, frozen and
    shaved
12 large eggs
1 cup half-and-half
1 teaspoon vanilla extract

Heat butter, sugar, and syrup in saucepan over medium-high heat until bubbly. Pour into greased 9 x 13-inch baking dish. Cover caramel sauce with peaches. Spread cubed bread over peaches. Scatter cream cheese through bread. Combine eggs, half-and-half and vanilla well. Pour over bread and cream cheese. Cover and refrigerate for at least 1 hour or overnight. When ready to bake, preheat oven to 350° and bake uncovered 50 to 60 minutes. Yields 12 servings.

Fresh Blueberry Cream Pie

10 graham crackers (1½ cups crushed)
½ cup pecans
¼ plus ¾ cup sugar
½ cup melted butter
¼ teaspoon salt
12 ounces cream cheese, softened
1½ teaspoons vanilla extract
1½ cups heavy cream
2 pints plus 1 pint blueberries
3 tablespoons blueberry jelly

Preheat oven to 350°. In food processor crumble graham cracker and grind to fine crumbs. Add pecans, ¼ cup sugar, butter, and salt and pulse until nuts are finely chopped. Press crumb mixture evenly onto bottom and side of glass 10 x 2-inch, deep-dish pie plate and bake in middle of oven 8 minutes. Cool shell in plate on rack. Combine cream cheese, remaining ¾ cup sugar, and vanilla in bowl and mix well. Whip cream and fold into cream cheese mixture. Add 2 pints berries to cream filling. Spoon into crust. Arrange remaining pint blueberries on top. Heat jelly in pan and with pastry brush glaze top of pie with jelly. Chill 3 to 4 hours. Yields 1 pie.

Cranberry Apple Cobbler

8 cups peeled, cored, and sliced apples
3 cups fresh cranberries
1⅓ cups brown sugar
1½ cups broken pecans
1 teaspoon ground cinnamon
1 cup all-purpose flour
½ cup sugar
¼ cup (½ stick) cold butter
1 large egg, lightly beaten

Preheat oven to 400°. Combine apples and cranberries, brown sugar, pecans, and cinnamon. Toss to coat. Divide into twenty 4-ounce ramekins or put in 9 x 13-inch casserole dish. (Can be covered, refrigerated, and baked later.) Combine flour, sugar, butter, and egg. Cut butter and egg into flour until mixture resembles coarse crumbs. Separate with fingers and sprinkle over apple mixture. Place ramekins on one or two half-sheet pans, or if using casserole dish just place in oven, and bake 25 to 30 minutes. Keep warm in oven (200°) until ready to serve. Yields 20 servings.

ALBEMARLE INN BED & BREAKFAST

86 Edgemont Road
Asheville, NC 28801
(828) 255-0027 (phone)
(828) 236-3397 (fax)
(800) 621-7435 (toll free)
info@albemarleinn.com
www.albemarieinn.com

Albemarle Inn is an elegant, 1907 Greek Revival mansion in the residential Grove Park section of Asheville. The inn features an exquisite carved oak staircase, exceptionally spacious guest rooms with period furnishings, fine linens, televisions, telephones, and private baths. Rooms with whirlpool and fireplace are available. Full gourmet breakfasts and evening refreshments are included. Area activities include the Blue Ridge Parkway; Biltmore Estate; downtown just a mile away; Grove Park Inn and Resort in walking distance; outdoor activities including hot-air balloon rides, hiking trails, mountain biking, waterfall tours, horseback riding, and whitewater rafting; art galleries; and antique shops.

Apple Cheddar Quiche

3 Granny Smith apples, peeled and diced
3 tablespoons butter
1 partially-baked, 10-inch pie shell
1½ cups grated sharp Cheddar cheese
4 eggs plus 2 egg yolks
1 cup whole milk ricotta cheese
1½ cups half-and-half
1 teaspoon sugar
¼ teaspoon ground cinnamon
Dash of salt

Preheat oven to 375°. In medium pan over medium-high heat sauté apples in butter for 5 minutes and place in pie shell. Top with cheese. Beat together eggs, egg yolks, ricotta, and half-and-half. Pour over apples and cheese. Combine sugar, cinnamon, and salt and sprinkle on top. Bake 30 to 45 minutes until quiche is firm. Yields 6 servings.

Lime Tea Cakes

Have all ingredients at room temperature.

Cakes:
1½ cups all-purpose flour
1¼ teaspoons baking powder
¼ teaspoon baking soda
¼ teaspoon salt
2 tablespoons tea leaves, steeped in
    ¾ cup hot milk for 10 to 15 minutes
8 tablespoons (1 stick) unsalted butter
1 cup sugar
2 eggs, beaten
½ teaspoon vanilla extract
Grated zest of 2 limes
Confectioners' sugar

Lime glaze:
3 tablespoons cream cheese at
    room temperature
2½ cups confectioners' sugar
3 to 4 limes, juiced

Position rack in lower third of oven and preheat to 325°. Butter and flour wells of swirl cake pan and tap out excess flour. Sift flour, baking powder, baking soda, and salt onto sheet of wax paper. Pour tea mixture through fine-mesh sieve into small bowl. Press liquid from tea leaves and discard leaves. In bowl of electric mixer, beat butter on medium speed until creamy, about 30 seconds. Add sugar and continue beating until light and fluffy, 3 to 5 minutes. Stop mixer and scrape bowl occasionally. Add eggs, a little at a time, beating well after each addition. Add vanilla and lime zest. On very low speed, add flour mixture in three additions, alternating with milk and ending with flour. Blend each addi-

tion just until incorporated, scraping sides of bowl occasionally. Fill wells in pan a little more than halfway. Bake until cake springs back when touched and pull out of pan. Repeat with remaining batter. Dust cakes with confectioners' sugar. Put small bowl of glaze in center of plate. Slice tea cakes and overlap them around bowl.

For glaze, in mixer with paddle attachment, beat cream cheese until soft. Slowly add confectioners' sugar and mix until all is incorporated. Add lime juice a little at a time, pausing between additions, until a pouring consistency is reached. Garnish plate with lime twists and drizzle small amount of glaze in arches over tea cakes. Yields 12 servings.

Apple Inn

1005 White Pine Drive
Hendersonville, NC 28739
(828) 693-0107 (phone)
(828) 693-0173 (fax)
(800) 615-6611 (toll free)
appleinnkeepers@aol.com
www.appleinn.com

Come stay at Apple Inn, where life is a little sweeter. Relax on our wide porch outfitted with wicker rockers that are perfect for enjoying one of our "famous" homemade cookies and a nice cool drink. Read a book or enjoy the wide variety of birds on our three-plus-acre estate. And after a busy day hiking in the Pisgah Forest or antiquing downtown, you can enjoy a game of billiards before retiring to your room enhanced with period antiques. Your private bath is thoughtfully appointed with modern plumbing, fluffy bath towels, and luscious apple soap.

Eggs Foo Yung

¾ pound mushrooms
2 tablespoons chicken stock
¼ cup chopped onions
1 cup diced celery
¾ cup drained bean sprouts
4 eggs
¼ teaspoon salt
¼ teaspoon pepper

Cook mushrooms in chicken stock in sauté pan over medium heat for 1 minute. Add onions and celery, stir, and sauté 5 minutes. Cool. Add bean sprouts. Beat eggs. Add salt and pepper and cooked vegetables. Heat small iron skillet until very hot and add large spoonful of mixture. When pancakes are brown on bottom, turn and brown other side. Serve immediately with soy sauce. Yields 2 servings.

Ginger-Mint Cooler

1 cup water
1 tablespoon liquid sugar substitute
¼ cup chopped mint leaves
½ cup lemon juice
2 cups orange juice
1 quart ginger ale

Combine water, sugar substitute, and mint and bring to a boil. Strain and cool. At serving time, add lemon and orange juices and ginger ale. Pour over finely crushed ice in tall glasses. Yields 8 servings.

Eggs Louisiana

1 small green pepper, diced
2 teaspoons chopped onion
2 eggs, well beaten

Preheat oven to 350°. Steam pepper and onion in small amount of water in small pan for approximately 15 minutes, drain, and turn vegetables into single-serve ramekin. Season eggs to taste and pour over steamed vegetables. Bake in oven 15 minutes at 350°. Yields 1 serving.

German Apple Pancake

3 eggs
½ cup milk
⅓ cup all-purpose flour
¼ teaspoon salt
Juice of ½ lemon
2 apples, peeled, cored, and thinly sliced
2 plus 2 tablespoons butter
¼ cup sugar
½ teaspoon ground cinnamon

In blender mix eggs, milk, flour, and salt. Blend until smooth. Let stand 1 hour. Sprinkle lemon juice over apple slices. Preheat oven to 375°. In large, heavy skillet over medium heat melt 2 tablespoons butter. When bubbly, pour in batter. Cover with apple slices and bake 10 to 15 minutes. Mix sugar and cinnamon together. When done, dot with remaining 2 tablespoons butter and sprinkle cinnamon sugar over apples. Return to oven for 2 minutes. Cut into squares and serve immediately. Yields 4 servings.

THE GROVE PARK INN

290 Macon Ave.
Asheville, NC 28804
(828) 252-2711 (phone)
(800) 438-5800 (toll free)
www.groveparkinn.com

The Grove Park Inn was built in 1913 and overlooks Asheville's skyline and the Blue Ridge Mountains. Architecturally unique, the historic Main Inn is constructed of native granite boulders quarried from nearby mountainsides. On the National Register of Historic Places and a member of Historic Hotels of America, the inn houses the world's largest publicly displayed collection of arts and crafts antiques under its red-tile roof.

Grilled Chicken Paillard

Chicken & marinade:
4 boneless chicken breast halves, pound to about ½ inch
1 shallot, minced
2 tablespoons vegetable oil
Juice of 1 lime

Peach salsa:
2 ripe peaches, pitted and chopped (may substitute 3 ripe nectarines)
1 small red bell pepper, cored, seeded, and diced
½ small red onion, diced
¼ cup chopped fresh parsley
1 medium clove garlic, minced
¼ cup pineapple juice
6 tablespoons lime juice
1 jalapeño, stemmed, seeded, and minced
Salt

Jalapeño butter:
1 cup (2 sticks) unsalted butter, softened
1 handful cilantro leaves, chopped
2 small jalapeños, seeded and chopped
1 tablespoon lime juice
2 teaspoons salt
Freshly ground black pepper

Combine chicken & marinade ingredients and chill 1 to 2 hours.

For peach salsa, combine all ingredients except salt and toss in medium bowl. Cover and refrigerate to blend flavors at least 1 hour or up to 4 days. Add salt to taste when ready to serve.

Place jalapeño butter ingredients in food processor or blender and pulse until well blended. Roll in foil or plastic wrap and freeze. Remove from freezer and slice into ½-inch slices as needed. Can be made up to 2 months in advance.

Broil or grill chicken for about 2 minutes per side or until desired doneness. Place pat of jalapeño butter on top of chicken and serve with peach salsa on side. Yields 4 servings.

Sautéed Trout with Sweet Potato/Smoked Trout Hash

2 plus 2 tablespoons butter
½ cup chopped celery
½ cup chopped red onion
1 green bell pepper, chopped
1 sweet potato, cut in ¼-inch slices and blanched
2 ounces smoked trout, flaked
Salt and pepper
½ teaspoon minced fresh thyme
½ teaspoon minced fresh sage
½ cup plus 1 teaspoon all-purpose flour
8 trout fillets
Lemon and fresh herbs for garnish

Melt 2 tablespoons butter in sauté pan and cook celery, onion, and bell pepper for 2 minutes until soft. Add blanched potato and cook 2 minutes or until hot throughout. Add smoked trout, salt, pepper, herbs, and 1 teaspoon flour. Toss lightly, cover, and keep warm. Melt remaining 2 tablespoons butter in nonstick sauté pan over medium heat. Dredge trout fillets in remaining ½ cup flour and place in sauté pan skin-side up. Sauté 3 minutes and turn over gently. Season fillets with salt and freshly ground pepper to taste. Divide hash in center of four dinner plates and place 2 trout fillets on each. Garnish with lemon, fresh herbs, and green vegetable (broccoli spear). Yields 4 servings.

Collard Greens with Shrimp and Red Rice

4 strips bacon, diced
1½ pounds shrimp, peeled and deveined
2 onions, chopped
1 bell pepper, chopped
1 teaspoon garlic, minced
1 (6-ounce) can tomato paste
1 (6-ounce) can tomato juice
3 teaspoons salt
2 teaspoons sugar
½ teaspoon pepper
3 cups cooked white rice
12 collard green leaves, blanched in
    boiling, salted water

Preheat oven to 350°. Sauté bacon in skillet until crisp. Add shrimp, onions, and pepper and sauté 2 minutes. Add garlic and cook 1 minute. Add tomato paste, tomato juice, salt, sugar, and pepper and blend. Stir in rice, tossing to mix, and cool. Wrap collard leaves around rice mixture as you would an egg roll or burrito. Place in ovenproof casserole with a little water in bottom and bake covered 15 minutes. Yields 4 servings.

CUMBERLAND FALLS BED & BREAKFAST

254 Cumberland Avenue
Asheville, NC 28801
(828) 253-4085 (phone)
(828) 253-5566 (fax)
(888) 743-2557 (toll free)
fallsinn@aol.com
www.cumberlandfalls.com

The exquisite detail of the decor, special "extras" that you will enjoy as our guest,

including fresh flowers, home baked goodies, snuggly robes in your room, a turn-down served with chocolates on the pillow and the personal attention of our concierge service will leave you feeling like royalty. Three miles from Biltmore Estates.

Simply Perfect Breakfast Pecan Pie

⅔ cup granulated sugar
⅓ cup (5 tablespoons) melted butter
1 cup white corn syrup
1 tablespoon real vanilla extract
½ teaspoon salt
3 eggs, beaten
1 cup toasted pecan halves
1 (9-inch) pie shell

Preheat oven to 375°. Beat together sugar, butter, and corn syrup. Add vanilla, salt, eggs, and pecans. Pour into unbaked pie shell. Bake 40 to 50 minutes. Serve warm if desired. Yields 6 to 8 servings.

Cumberland Falls Key Lime Cream Cheese Pie

1 (14-ounce) can sweetened
    condensed milk
8 ounces cream cheese, softened
1 cup Key lime juice
1 teaspoon vanilla extract
Dash of angostura bitters
1 (9-inch) piecrust, baked
Whipped cream
Lime slices

Put condensed milk, cream cheese, lime juice, vanilla, and bitters in food processor and process for 10 minutes. Spoon filling into piecrust and refrigerate 8 to 10 hours or overnight. (You can also use regular piecrust recipe and make a deep-dish pie. If you are using dough, cook piecrust first

and let cool before spooning filling into pie. Refrigerate as with prepared crust. You can also make a deep-dish graham cracker crust and deep-dish pie if you prefer.) Garnish with whipped cream either in aerosol container or make your own using 1 pint whipping cream and ¼ cup sugar. Garnish with twisted lime slices. Yields 8 servings.

Nana's Cranberry Pumpkin Bread

2 cups sugar
½ cup (1 stick) unsalted butter, softened
2 eggs, slightly beaten
1 cup pumpkin (not pumpkin pie filling)
1 tablespoon vanilla extract
2¼ cups all-purpose flour
1 teaspoon baking soda
½ teaspoon salt
1 tablespoon pumpkin pie spice
Pinch of coriander
1 cup chopped fresh cranberries

Preheat oven to 350°. Cream sugar and butter until light and fluffy. Add eggs, pumpkin, and vanilla. Combine flour, baking soda, salt, pie spice, and coriander together and add to butter mixture. Fold in cranberries. Grease two 8½ x 4½ x 2½-inch loaf pans. Bake 50 minutes and check with toothpick. It should be clean. Do *not* overbake. Yields 2 loaves.

ACORN COTTAGE BED & BREAKFAST

25 Saint Dunstans Circle
Asheville, NC 28803
(828) 253-0609 (phone)
(800) 699-0609 (toll free)
acorncott@aol.com
www.acorncottagebnb.com

This cozy 1920s bungalow is tucked away on a hillside in the heart of Asheville. The relaxed, informal atmosphere provides the perfect weekend or vacation getaway. Nearby activities include the Biltmore Estate, Thomas Wolfe Memorial, Asheville Urban Walking Trail, North Carolina Arboretum, Botanical Gardens, WNC Nature Center, WNC Farmer's Market, Carl Sandburg home, Chimney Rock Park, Blue Ridge Parkway, horseback riding, rafting, canoeing, antiquing, art galleries, and Smith-McDowell House.

Banana Almond Oatcakes

1 tablespoon melted butter or margarine
1 overripe banana, mashed
1 tablespoon brown sugar
Pinch of salt
1 egg
1 cup all-purpose flour
1½ cups quick oats
½ teaspoon baking powder
¼ cup toasted sliced almonds
2 cups milk

Beat together all ingredients until smooth, and let sit 10 minutes or more (can be prepared night before and stored in refrigerator). Batter will be thicker than normal pancake batter. If too thick, stir in small amount of water. Heat griddle to 450°. Pour about ¼ cup batter per pancake and let cook until bubbles appear on top and edges are set, about 7 minutes. Flip and cook about 3 minutes more. Serve warm with maple syrup and fruit of choice. Yields 16 pancakes.

Double Chocolate Brownies

⅔ cup sugar
2 eggs
½ cup all-purpose flour
1 teaspoon vanilla extract
1 cup chocolate chips
4 tablespoons cocoa
1 stick butter, melted
Confectioners' sugar

Preheat oven to 350°. Grease 9 x 9-inch baking dish. In medium bowl combine sugar, eggs, flour, vanilla, and chocolate chips. Stir cocoa into melted butter and stir until mixed well. Pour over dry mix and mix just until moist. Pour into baking dish. Bake 25 minutes. Brownies will be gooey when removed from oven. Let cool 20 to 30 minutes. Sprinkle with confectioners' sugar. Yields 16 squares.

Roulade (or Rolled Omelet)

2 cups plus ½ cup milk
8 eggs
¾ cup plus 1 tablespoon all-purpose flour
½ plus ½ cup grated mild Cheddar cheese
1½ cups filling of choice: fresh bulk
    sausage, peppers, finely chopped
    ham, chopped bacon, tomatoes, etc.
1 tablespoon butter
Seasonings (salt, pepper, chives, basil)

Preheat oven to 400°. Line large cookie sheet with foil. Grease well. Beat together 2 cups milk, eggs, ¾ cup flour, and seasonings to taste and pour onto cookie sheet. Bake about 15 minutes or until edges are slightly brown and eggs are puffed. Remove from oven and sprinkle cheese and filling ingredient(s) over egg mixture. Using knife, loosen egg mixture at narrow end of cookie sheet and roll up like a jellyroll. Slice. Using medium microwave-safe dish, melt butter and stir in remaining 1 tablespoon flour. Gradually add remaining ½ cup milk, stirring until smooth. Add remaining ½ cup cheese and heat in microwave on high 45 seconds. Stir and heat 45 seconds more and season to taste. Serve roulade slices with cheese sauce. Yields 6 to 8 servings.

Variation: Rolled Omelet: Follow same instructions, except from long side of cookie sheet, loosen egg mixture with knife and fold over twice. Sprinkle top with cheese. Cover and return to oven for 2 minutes until cheese is melted. Garnish with salsa and herbs, if desired.

TURN OF THE CENTURY VICTORIAN BED & BREAKFAST

529 South Fulton Street
Salisbury, NC 28144
(704) 642-1660 (phone)
(800) 250-5349 (toll free)
info@turnofthecenturybb.com
www.turnofthecenturybb.com

Turn of the Century Victorian Bed & Breakfast provides elegant accommodations in this Preservation North Carolina award-winning 1905 home. Located in the heart of the Salisbury National Register West Square Historic District, Turn of the Century is the perfect location to explore the local museums, galleries, shops, attend a concert or play, research genealogy at the local library, shop for antiques, and to visit restaurants. It's just a short drive to see the North Carolina State Transportation Museum, shop for furniture in High Point or Hickory, or visit Concord Mills, Lowes Motor Speedway, or Charlotte.

Tarragon Breakfast Crêpes with Mushroom Sauce

Crêpes:
1¼ cups all-purpose flour
3 eggs, beaten
1½ cups milk
2 tablespoons melted butter
Pinch of salt

Mushroom sauce:
2 tablespoons water
2 tablespoons lemon juice
2 teaspoons parsley
2 teaspoons chives
⅛ teaspoon cayenne
½ teaspoon salt
3 tablespoons minced onions
4 tablespoons melted butter
½ pound minced mushrooms
2 tablespoons all-purpose flour
1 cup half-and-half
Eggs
Salt
Pepper
Tarragon

Mix crêpes ingredients in blender. Let batter sit for 1 hour. Make crêpes in hot crêpe pan or iron skillet. Pour just enough batter (about ¼ cup) to cover pan, tilting and rotating pan quickly in all directions to coat entire surface evenly. In about 1 to 2 minutes edges of crepe will be lightly browned and pull away slightly from pan. Top will be set and almost dry. Turn to cook other side lightly. (Crêpes may be stored in refrigerator after cooled with piece of wax paper between each one.)

For mushroom sauce, mix water, lemon juice, parsley, chives, cayenne, and salt in bowl. Place onions in microwave-safe dish and add water to cover. Microwave for 1 minute to reconstitute. Place butter in saucepan. Add onions, and sauté over medium heat. Add mushrooms and cook 10 to 15 minutes until moisture is gone. Do not overcook or mushrooms will become very dark. Remove from heat, add flour, and blend well. Add half-and-half and return to heat. Bring to a boil, reduce heat, and simmer 2 minutes. Remove mixture from heat. Add lemon juice mixture, mix well, and cover. Mix 2 eggs per person with salt, pepper, and tarragon to taste. Scramble but do not overcook. Place single crêpe on plate, place eggs in center of crêpe from top to bottom, and fold each side of crepe over eggs. Spoon mushroom sauce over crêpes and garnish plate with sliced mushrooms and tarragon. Yields 4 to 6 servings.

Turn of the Century Victorian Bed & Breakfast

Pineapple Boats

Pineapple
Strawberries, sliced
Kiwifruit, peeled and sliced

Cut fresh pineapple, including top, into quarters. Cut each quarter in half for eight servings. Carefully cut out pineapple and cut flesh into bite-size pieces. Mix cut pineapple with strawberries and kiwifuit. Place mixed fruit into pineapple boats to serve. Yields 8 servings.

Lemon Bread

6 tablespoons shortening
1 plus ½ cup sugar
2 eggs
1⅓ cups flour
1 teaspoon baking powder
½ teaspoon salt
½ cup milk
Grated zest and juice of 1 lemon

Preheat oven to 325°. Cream shortening and 1 cup sugar. Mix in eggs. Mix flour, baking powder, salt, milk, and lemon zest and add to egg mixture. Coat bread pan with nonstick spray or shortening. Bake for 1 hour. Mix remaining ½ cup sugar and lemon juice. Pour mixture over hot bread. Yields 1 loaf.

THE 1900 INN ON MONTFORD

296 Montford Avenue
Asheville, NC 28801
(800) 254-9569 (toll free)
info@innonmontford.com
www.innonmontford.com

The 1900 Inn on Montford was designed by Biltmore's supervising architect. Nestled in the heart of the historic district, the inn recaptures a warmth and graciousness reminiscent of Biltmore's gilded age. Activities in the area include the Biltmore Estate, Chimney Rock, Blue Ridge Parkway, waterfalls, hiking, Asheville's architecture, shopping, and music venues.

Brunch Enchiladas

1 cup ground cooked ham
¼ cup sliced green onions
¼ cup finely chopped red pepper
¼ cup finely chopped green pepper
1 tablespoon cooking oil
4 (10-inch) flour tortillas
1¼ cups shredded sharp Cheddar cheese
2 large eggs
2 cups half-and-half
½ tablespoon all-purpose flour
⅛ teaspoon garlic powder
1 to 2 drops hot pepper sauce
Salsa
Sour cream

In skillet over medium heat sauté ham, onions, red and green pepper in oil until vegetables are tender. Place about ⅓ cup down center of each tortilla and top with 3 heaping tablespoons cheese. Roll up and place seam down in a greased 11 x 7 x 2-inch baking dish, or use individual oven-proof dishes. In bowl beat eggs. Add half-and-half, flour, garlic powder, and hot pepper sauce. Mix well and pour over tortillas. Cover and chill 8 hours or overnight.

When ready to bake, remove from refrigerator 30 minutes before. Preheat oven to 350°. Bake, uncovered, 35 to 40 minutes or until knife inserted near center comes out clean. Top with salsa and sour cream. Yields 4 servings.

Apricot Cream Cheese Danish

2 (8-count) packages refrigerated crescent rolls
⅓ plus ⅓ cup slivered almonds, divided
6 eggs, separated
8 ounces cream cheese
½ plus ¼ cup sugar
Cinnamon sugar
2 teaspoons almond extract or to taste
8 ounces apricot jam
1 tablespoon peach schnapps

Preheat oven to 375°. Spray two 7½-inch tart pans with removable bases with non-stick spray, being generous to fluted edges. Line tart pans with half a package of crescent-roll pastry. Cover bottom of crust with ⅓ cup slivered almonds. Separate eggs, setting aside egg whites for meringue. Beat together cream cheese, ½ cup sugar, almond extract, and yolk of 1 egg until smooth. Divide between tart pans. Mix apricot jam and peach schnapps and spread over cream cheese filling. Roll remaining pastry and cut two 7-inch circles. Sprinkle with cinnamon sugar and cover tarts. Bake 15 minutes or until golden brown. While tarts are baking, beat egg whites in aluminum bowl. Start at slow speed gradually adding remaining ¼ cup sugar. Increase speed of mixer until egg whites reach desired volume. (Egg whites beat best at room temperature.) Remove tarts from oven, cover with meringue, sprinkle with remaining ⅓ cup almonds, and cinnamon sugar and return to oven until brown. Remove from oven, let sit 5 to 10 minutes and turn tarts onto silver tray. Let stand 30 minutes before serving. Yields 8 servings.

Blackberry Starry Nights

1 (15-ounce) package refrigerated piecrusts
½ cup water
⅔ cup sugar
2 tablespoons cornstarch
2 plus 2 tablespoons butter
3 cups fresh blackberries
1 (3-ounce) package cream cheese, softened
1 teaspoon vanilla extract
1 cup confectioners' sugar

Preheat oven to 350°. Unfold piecrusts and press out fold lines with rolling pin on lightly floured surface. Cut piecrusts with a 2½ to 3-inch star shape cutter and fit into lightly greased miniature muffin pans. Bake 7 minutes or until golden. Remove from pans and cool on wire racks. Bring water, sugar, cornstarch, 2 tablespoons butter, and blackberries to a boil in heavy saucepan over medium heat. Boil, stirring constantly, for 1 minute. Remove from heat. Stir together cream cheese, remaining 2 tablespoons butter, vanilla, and confectioners' sugar. Spoon blackberry mixture into tart shells and pipe or dollop with cream cheese mixture. Sprinkle with additional confectioners' sugar, if desired. Yields 36 tarts.

The 1900 Inn on Montford

IVIVI LAKE & MOUNTAIN LODGE

161 Waterside Drive
Lake Lure, NC 28746
(828) 625-0601 (phone)
(828) 625-8841(fax)
ivivi@blueridge.net
www.ivivilodge.com

Enjoy the European contemporary atmosphere and spectacular views at Ivivi Lake and Mountain Lodge. The inn has seven exquisitely furnished rooms and suites, many with terraces and balconies. Nearby activities include water sports on Lake Lure, Chimney Rock Park, two 18-hole championship golf courses, horseback riding, Asheville, the Biltmore Estate, and the Blue Ridge Parkway.

Hummus

4 cups chickpeas, drained
½ cup tahini
⅓ cup extra virgin olive oil
⅓ cup warm water
Juice of 2 lemons, divided
5 to 6 cloves garlic
1 teaspoon salt
2 teaspoons ground cumin
1 teaspoon cayenne
1 teaspoon curry
Freshly ground black pepper

Combine chickpeas, tahini, olive oil, warm water, and half of lemon juice in food processor bowl. Process till smooth and creamy. Add garlic, salt, cumin, cayenne, curry, and pepper to taste. Add remaining lemon juice to taste. Scrape into storage container, cover, and refrigerate until ready to use. Serve with vegetables and baked pita crisps. Yields about 1 quart.

Caramelized Bacon

1 pound thickly sliced lean bacon
1 cup dark brown sugar

Put bacon and sugar together in airtight container. Keep at room temperature until mixture becomes syrupy. (Bacon can be baked then or stored in refrigerator for a day or two.) To cook preheat oven to 350°. Place bacon flat on broiler pan and bake until bacon cooks, 15 to 20 minutes. Broil 2 to 3 minutes just to make bacon crisp. Transfer to paper towels to drain. Cut into bite-size pieces and serve with toothpicks. Yields 16 to 20 appetizer servings.

Ivivi Sunrise

Orange juice
Cranberry juice
Mint sprigs

Fill juice glass to three-fourths full with freshly squeezed orange juice and top remaining fourth with cranberry juice. Do *not* stir—it will resemble a marbleized swirl—like a pretty sunrise. Serve with sprig of fresh mint. Yields 1 serving.

THE LODGE ON LAKE LURE

P.O. Box 519
Lake Lure, NC 28746
(828) 625-2789 (phone)
(828) 625-2421 (fax)
(800) 733-2785 (toll free)
info@lodgeonlakelure.com
www.lodgeonlakelure.com

Boat, swim, fish, unwind, and be spoiled at this magnificently-renovated, elegant, sixteen-room getaway with fabulous views, stone fireplaces, and a beautiful lakeside dock. Nearby activities include water sports on Lake Lure; Chimney Rock Park; two 18-hole championship golf courses, one 9-hole municipal course; horseback riding; Asheville and the Biltmore Estate, the Blue Ridge Park-way; historic Hendersonville; and the Flat Rock Playhouse.

Cheese Petit Fours

1 cup (2 sticks) margarine or butter
6 (6-ounce) jars Old English cheese spread
1½ teaspoons Worcestershire sauce
1 teaspoon hot sauce
1 teaspoon onion powder
1 teaspoon garlic salt
Cayenne
3 loaves sandwich bread, crusts removed
Dill weed for garnish

Cream margarine, cheese, Worcestershire sauce, hot sauce, onion powder, garlic salt, and cayenne to taste with beater until consistency of icing. Spread mixture on bread slice, top with another, spread mixture on second slice, and top with third. Quarter and spread mixture over sides and top. Repeat. (Each petit four is three slices

Sprinkle each petit four with dill or garnish. Freeze on cookie sheets and put into plastic bags in freezer. Do not defrost until ready to bake. Preheat oven to 400°. Bake 15 to 20 minutes. Yields 2 dozen petit fours.

Chilled Tortilla Bites

3 (8-ounce) packages cream cheese, softened
1 (8-ounce) carton sour cream
1 (8-ounce) package shredded mild Cheddar cheese
2 tablespoons lime juice
3 tablespoons hot salsa
6 chopped scallions
1 (4-ounce) can green chiles
8 to 10 (6-inch) flour tortillas

Mix all ingredients together except tortillas. Spread mixture on tortillas. Roll up, wrap each roll in wax paper, and refrigerate 24 hours. Cut tortillas in 1-inch sections and serve with salsa. Yields 4 to 5 dozen bites.

Caramelized Apple Crêpes

1 large Granny Smith apple, peeled, and sliced lengthwise
¼ cup plus 1½ tablespoons sugar
¼ teaspoon ground cinnamon
1 tablespoon melted unsalted butter
2 large eggs
½ cup whole milk
¼ cup amber rum
¼ cup vegetable oil
¾ cup all-purpose flour
¼ teaspoon salt

Mix apple slices, 1½ tablespoons sugar, cinnamon, and butter together and cook 5 minutes in large skillet over medium heat. Mix together eggs, milk, rum, oil, flour, remaining ¼ cup sugar, and salt. Stir in apple mixture. Brush crêpe pan with butter, just enough to keep batter from sticking. Heat pan over medium-high heat until hot, but not smoking. Remove pan from heat and ladle in ¼ cup batter, tilting and rotating pan quickly in all directions to coat entire surface evenly. Return pan to heat. Cook until edges are lightly brown and top dry. Sprinkle sugar on crêpe before turning. Sprinkle first time; flip twice. Yields 6 to 8 crêpes.

THE INN ON CHURCH STREET

201 3rd Avenue West
Hendersonville, NC 28739
(828) 693-3258 (phone)
(828) 693-3741 (fax)
(800) 330-3836 (toll free)
innonchurch@inspiredinns.com
www.innspiredinns.com

Since opening its doors in 1921, this gracious inn has specialized in Southern hospitality. The inn was built during the Roaring Twenties that gave way to the Great Depression when it was sold on the courthouse steps for $25 dollars. In 2000, this National Register Historic property escaped demolition and was completely renovated. Now boasting nineteen gracious guest rooms, two luxurious suites with fireplaces, and Jacuzzi tubs, the inn is again a bustling bed and breakfast.

Brown Sugar and Oatmeal Crème Brûlée

3½ cups half-and-half
2 cups quick oats
½ cup brown sugar
3 tablespoons maple syrup
Pinch of allspice
Pinch of nutmeg
Pinch of kosher salt
¼ cup Amish butter
1 pint organic local strawberries
Splash of Triple Sec (optional)
¼ plus ¼ cup sugar
4 mint sprigs for garnish

In medium saucepan over medium-high heat, bring half-and-half up to just below boiling point. Stir in oats and mix well.

The Inn on Church Street

Add brown sugar, syrup, allspice, nutmeg, and salt and cook about 2 minutes. Take pan off heat and stir in butter. Pour oatmeal into four serving bowls and let sit at room temperature. Wash strawberries, cut green tops off, and quarter. Place berries, Triple Sec, and ¼ cup sugar in bowl to macerate 10 minutes. Sprinkle tops of oatmeal with remaining ¼ cup sugar. With butane torch caramelized sugar until lightly browned. (Optionally, place bowls under broiler.) Set bowls in refrigerator for 1 minute. Garnish tops of brûlées with small pile of strawberries and a mint sprig. Yields 4 servings.

Farmhouse Soup

3 tablespoons olive oil
3 pieces smoked bacon,
    cut into small pieces
1 sweet onion, diced
4 cloves garlic, crushed
3 carrots, peeled and diced
1 large turnip, peeled and diced
1 large rutabaga, peeled and diced
1 red bell pepper, diced
1 (14-ounce) can diced tomatoes
1 tablespoon tomato paste
¼ cup chopped fresh parsley,
    divided in half
¼ cup torn basil leaves, divided in half
1 teaspoon dried oregano
1 teaspoon chile flakes
1 tablespoon kosher salt
1 teaspoon freshly cracked pepper
8 cups chicken stock
½ cup small ziti pasta
1 (14-ounce) can red kidney beans,
    rinsed
½ cup freshly grated Parmesan cheese

Heat oil in medium-size saucepan over medium heat. Add bacon, then onion and garlic and cook for 5 to 7 minutes. Add carrots, turnip, rutabaga, red pepper, canned tomatoes, tomato paste, half of each fresh herb, dry herbs, and chile flakes and stir in salt and pepper. Pour in stock, bring to a boil, and stir well. Cover and lower heat to simmer and cook 25 min-

utes, stirring occasionally. Add pasta and bring back to a boil, stir 2 or 3 times, and then cook until pasta is al dente. Add beans, cook 5 more minutes, and add other half of fresh herbs. Adjust seasonings. Place soup in bowls and add cheese to garnish. Serve with crusty Italian Ciabatta loaf. Yields 6 to 8 hearty portions.

Roasted Organic Butternut Squash Pansotti

1 butternut squash
4 tablespoons plus 1 tablespoon
    balsamic vinegar
1 plus 1 tablespoon kosher salt
1 teaspoon freshly cracked pepper
3 whole cloves
4 fresh thyme sprigs
2 tablespoons Amish butter
1 cup ricotta cheese
1 tablespoon fresh thyme leaves
2 tablespoons brown sugar
½ teaspoon white pepper
½ teaspoon freshly ground nutmeg
1 package small wonton skins
2 eggs, whipped for egg wash
½ cup (1 stick) butter
12 sage leaves

Preheat oven to 350°. Cut squash in half and scoop out seeds. Place squash halves, cut-side up, on sheet pan and drizzle with 1 tablespoon balsamic vinegar. Cover with 1 tablespoon salt, cracked pepper, cloves, thyme sprigs, and Amish butter. Bake 35 to 45 minutes. When soft remove from oven and let rest 15 minutes. Scoop pulp into medium-size bowl. Add ricotta, thyme leaves, brown sugar, remaining 1 tablespoon salt, pepper, and nutmeg to bowl with squash and mix well. Lay wonton wrappers out on large work surface and place small amount of squash mixture in center of each skin. Brush only two edges with egg wash and fold into triangle. Seal around edges with fork. Make as many won tons as mixture permits. In sauté pan

over medium heat add stick of butter and let brown. Add sage and remaining 4 tablespoons balsamic vinegar. Cook Pansotti (pumpkin wraps) in boiling salted water until they float. Add to balsamic brown-butter sauce and divide among plates to serve. Yields 4 to 6 servings.

Savory Cranberry, Fontina, and Roasted Turkey Bread Pudding

6 farm-fresh eggs
1 tablespoon kosher salt
1 teaspoon freshly ground pepper
2 cups heavy cream
¼ cup grated Parmesan cheese
1 cup milk
Pinch of fresh ground nutmeg
½ cup sun-dried cranberries
2 cups roasted turkey in small shreds
2 tablespoons fresh thyme leaves
1 tablespoon chopped fresh sage
1½ cups fontina cheese, cut into
    small to medium cubes
1 sweet onion, cut medium-dice
1 day-old crusty Italian loaf,
    cut into cubes
½ cup (1 stick) butter

Preheat oven to 350°. Mix together in bowl with whisk eggs, salt and pepper, cream, Parmesan, milk, and nutmeg. In separate bowl, mix remaining ingredients. Use 2 tablespoons butter to grease inside of casserole dish or individual ramekins. Place bread mixture into casserole or ramekins and pour cream/egg mixture over bread. Place remaining 6 tablespoons butter in little nubs around top and let sit at room temperature 15 minutes. Place in oven and bake 35 minutes or until top gets golden brown. Serve warm. Yields 8 to 10 servings.

Fire-Grilled Filetto Di Manzo

4 (6- to 8-ounce) beef tenderloin steaks
2 tablespoons olive oil
1 teaspoon plus 1 plus 2 tablespoons
    kosher salt
1 teaspoon freshly ground pepper
2 cups peeled garlic cloves
2 fresh rosemary sprigs
3 fresh thyme sprigs
5 fresh sage leaves
Balsamic vinegar
½ cup sugar
1 teaspoon freshly cracked pepper
6 large Idaho potatoes, peeled,
    and cut to medium dice
¼ cup heavy cream
½ cup Amish butter
½ teaspoon white pepper
½ cup mascarpone cheese
2 tablespoons olive oil
2 bunches fresh spinach, washed
    three times

Rub steaks with olive oil, 1 teaspoon salt, and ground pepper. Heat grill. In small saucepan place garlic, rosemary, thyme, sage, and balsamic vinegar to cover by one inch. Add sugar, 1 tablespoon salt, and cracked pepper and cook over medium heat. Let garlic mixture simmer 25 to 30 minutes or until soft. Let sit off heat to cool to room temperature. Pull out herb stems and discard. Place potatoes in enough cold water to cover by three inches, add remaining 2 tablespoons salt, and let cook over medium-high heat 20 to 25 minutes or until potatoes are soft and ready to mash. Drain water from potatoes and return to pan. Add cream, butter, and white pepper and mash well. Fold in mascarpone cheese. Adjust seasoning and keep warm. In sauté pan heat olive oil until very hot and drop spinach in. Season with salt and pepper and splash a little water in pan to wilt leaves. Remove from pan. Place steaks on grill and grill to desired temperature. Let rest on plate for 5 minutes. Place scoop of mashed potatoes in center of plate, place spinach on mashed potatoes, and top with steak. Garnish with candied garlic mix and pour balsamic reduction over steak to serve. Yields 4 servings.

THE CHALET INN

285 Lone Oak Drive
Whittier, NC 28789
(828) 586-0251
paradisefound@chaletinn.com
www.chaletinn.com

The Chalet Inn is known for its fabulous views, bountiful breakfasts, twenty-two acres, pond, trails, hammocks for two, picnic area, and lawn games. The inn offers rooms and fireplace suites, whirlpool for two, private balconies, and baths. Activities near the Chalet Inn include the Great Smoky Mountains Railroad; quaint village of Dillsboro; Great Smoky Mountains National Park; Blue Ridge Parkway; Cherokee Indian Reservation and Casino; whitewater rafting and tubing; gem mining; trout fishing; horseback riding; golf; Tsali mountain bike area; antiquing; Biltmore Estate; Fontana Dam and Reservoir; Joyce Kilmer Memorial Forest; and Whiteside Mountain and Whiteside Falls.

Dutch Eggs

Whipping cream
Grated aged Gouda cheese
1 or 2 eggs per person
Salt and pepper
Dill weed
Dried parsley flakes

Preheat oven to 325°. Coat glass baking ramekin dishes (one ramekin dish for each person) liberally with nonstick spray. Pour 1 tablespoon whipping cream (not whipped) into each ramekin dish. Sprinkle cheese over cream. Gently break 1 egg into each dish. Add salt, pepper, and dill weed to taste. Pour dollop of cream over each egg. Sprinkle parsley flakes on top. Bake until eggs are just set (12 to 20 minutes). Yield will depend on number to be served.

Apfelkuchen (German Apple Cake)

2½ cups self-rising flour
¾ plus ⅜ cups sugar
5 ounces (1 stick plus 2 tablespoons)
    butter
2 egg yolks
Pinch of salt
1 pound cooking apples
    (or drained, canned apples)
Juice of 1 lemon
Pinch of ground cinnamon
2 tablespoons raisins
2 tablespoons ground hazelnuts
2 tablespoons ground almonds
2 tablespoons apricot jam
2 ounces (¼ cup) vanilla icing
    (homemade or canned)
2 tablespoons cherry liqueur
    (Kirsch)

Sift flour into bowl. Stir in ¾ cup sugar and knead in butter. Add egg yolks and salt and mix to smooth dough. Chill 20 minutes. Preheat oven to 400°. Roll out half of dough to cover bottom of 9½ x 3-inch-high springform pan. Bake 15 minutes. Peel, core, and slice apples and mix with remaining ⅜ cup sugar. Add lemon juice, cinnamon, raisins, and nuts. Moisten with just enough water to blend. Spoon evenly onto baked pastry shell in springform pan. Roll out remaining half of dough and cover filling (you can also make decorative strips to cover the filling). Bake in oven 30 minutes. Cool in pan 8 to 10 hours or overnight. An hour before serving, remove from pan and allow cake to reach room temperature. Shortly before serving, warm jam and spread over cake. Combine icing and cherry liqueur and dribble over jam. Yields 6 to 8 servings.

Home Waffle Mix

1 (¼-ounce) package dry yeast
2 cups lukewarm milk
4 eggs
1 teaspoon vanilla extract
2½ cups all-purpose flour
½ teaspoon salt
1 tablespoon sugar
½ cup (1 stick) melted butter

Put yeast in lukewarm milk in large bowl and dissolve. Add eggs and vanilla. Add flour, salt, and sugar. Beat well by hand. Add melted butter. Set in warm place 45 minutes or store in refrigerator 8 to 10 hours or overnight. If refrigerated, bring dough to room temperature before baking. Bake in waffle iron according to directions. Yields 8 to 10 servings.

THE FRYEMONT INN

P.O. Box 459
Bryson City, NC 28713
(828) 488-2159 (phone)
(828) 488-5769 (fax)
(800) 845-4879 (toll free)
fryemont@dnet.net
www.fryemontinn.com

Listed on the National Register of Historic Places and built in 1923, the Fryemont Inn is built mostly of chestnut and covered with poplar bark. The inn features gleaming hardwood floors and enormous stone fireplaces big enough to burn nine-foot logs. The Fryemont is situated on a mountainside overlooking the Great Smoky Mountains National Park.

Vegetable Strudel with Fresh Tomato Sauce

Strudel:
1 sheet puff pastry
2 (3-ounce) packages cream cheese
2 tablespoons Parmesan cheese
1 teaspoon chopped garlic
1 (10-ounce) package frozen chopped
   spinach, thawed
½ cup walnut pieces
1 medium tomato, sliced paper thin

Cheese sauce:
1 tablespoon butter
1 tablespoon all-purpose flour
1 cup half-and-half
3 tablespoons Parmesan cheese
½ cup shredded Monterey Jack cheese
¼ teaspoon dry mustard
Salt and pepper

Fresh tomato sauce:
1 tablespoon olive oil
¼ cup finely chopped onion
½ cup julienned green pepper
½ cup julienned red pepper
½ teaspoon chopped garlic
1 large tomato, peeled and diced
2 tablespoons chopped fresh basil
2 tablespoons fresh parsley

Thaw puff pastry according to package instructions. Preheat oven to 350°. Combine cream cheese, Parmesan cheese, and garlic in small bowl. Mix well. Spread to within 1 inch of edges of pastry. Press all water out of spinach. Distribute over cheese layer. Sprinkle with walnuts and top with thinly sliced tomatoes. Roll up

lengthwise and place on parchment-lined baking sheet. Bake for 30 minutes or until puffed and browned.

For cheese sauce, in small saucepan melt butter, add flour, and stir constantly for 30 seconds. Add half-and-half and continue stirring until mixture thickens. Turn off heat and add cheese, dry mustard, and salt and pepper to taste. Stir until cheese is melted.

For tomato sauce, heat olive oil in small sauté pan over medium heat. Add onion and peppers and sauté 1 minute. Add garlic and sauté 1 minute more. Add tomato and basil and cook for an additional 3 minutes. Remove from heat and add chopped parsley.

To serve, puddle a little of cheese sauce on each of six warm plates. Using sharp serrated knife, slice strudel into six pieces. Place slice in center of each cheese-sauce puddle. Top with fresh tomato sauce. Yields 6 servings.

Variation: For hot and spicy use pepper Jack cheese in cheese sauce and 2 tablespoons chopped jalapeño peppers in tomato sauce.

Trout in Cashew Crust

4 trout fillets
Salt and pepper
½ cup cashews
½ cup all-purpose flour
½ teaspoon paprika
2 tablespoons milk
1 large egg
4 tablespoons butter
¼ cup orange juice
¼ cup white wine
½ teaspoon grated fresh ginger
1½ teaspoons soy sauce
1½ teaspoons Dijon mustard
1 teaspoon cornstarch
¼ cup orange marmalade
Chopped fresh parsley

Rinse trout fillets and pat dry. Sprinkle with salt and pepper. Combine cashews, flour, and paprika in food processor. Pulse on and off several times until cashews are coarsely ground. Spread out in shallow dish. Combine milk and egg in small bowl and whisk until frothy. Pour into another shallow dish. Dip fillets, skin-side up, in egg mixture and lay fillets in flour mixture, skin-side up. Press gently into flour mixture. Over medium heat in medium-size skillet, sauté trout in butter (cashew-side up) 2 minutes. Turn over and cook 3 or 4 minutes more or until done. (Cashews can easily burn, so keep heat moderate.) Just before removing trout from pan, carefully remove bottom skin; it should peel off easily. Pierce bottom of trout with knife point. Flesh should no longer be translucent. Flip over onto warmed plate, cashew-side up. Combine orange juice, wine, ginger, soy sauce, and mustard in small saucepan and cook over medium-high heat, stirring constantly, until mixture comes to a boil. Dissolve cornstarch in a little water and add to saucepan. Cook 30 seconds more or until thickened. Remove from heat. Add marmalade and stir until melted completely. To serve, spoon sauce over fish, sprinkle with parsley, and serve. Yields 4 servings.

Braised Lamb Shanks

4 lamb shanks, about 1 pound each
Flour seasoned with salt and pepper
2 tablespoons olive oil
1 (14-ounce) can diced tomatoes in juice
1 small onion, diced
1 cup thinly sliced celery
2 carrots, peeled and julienned
1 cup white Vermouth
    or other dry white wine
1 teaspoon dried oregano
1 teaspoon chopped garlic
1 bay leaf

Dredge lamb shanks in seasoned flour. Heat olive oil in large heavy skillet over medium-high heat. Add shanks and cook, turning slightly every 2 or 3 minutes until evenly browned and adding more oil if necessary. Remove from heat. Preheat oven to 275°. Put shanks in heavy Dutch oven or roasting pan coated with nonstick spray. Combine tomatoes and all remaining ingredients and pour over shanks. Cover pan tightly. Braise 3 hours or more, until meat is very tender, almost falling off bone. Remove shanks to serving platter. Spoon vegetable gravy over top. To serve, sprinkle with chopped fresh parsley and serve with garlic mashed potatoes. Yields 8 to 10 servings.

Strawberries Romanoff

This is a wonderful light and cool dessert to follow a summer dinner. Very pretty served with a sprig of fresh mint on top.

1 cup sour cream
¼ cup light brown sugar
1 tablespoon granulated sugar
1 tablespoon Grand Marnier
2 pints fresh strawberries, washed,
    and hulled
Sweetened whipped cream

Process sour cream and sugars and Grand Marnier in blender or food processor until smooth. Chill. Just before serving, place strawberries in chilled wine or champagne glasses (cut in half if too large). Spoon sauce over strawberries and top with sweetened whipped cream. Yields 6 servings.

Grandma Judy's Lemon Chess Pie

2 cups sugar
4 large eggs
1 tablespoon all-purpose flour
1 tablespoon cornmeal
¼ cup milk
¼ cup (½ stick) melted butter, cooled
¼ cup fresh lemon juice
2 tablespoons grated lemon rind
1 unbaked, 9-inch, pastry piecrust

Preheat oven to 375°. Combine sugar with eggs and beat on high speed for 1 minute.

Combine flour and cornmeal and add to egg mixture. With beater running, gradually add milk, butter, lemon juice, and rind. Pour into piecrust. Bake in center of oven 45 minutes or until set and lightly browned. Yields 8 servings.

WRIGHT INN & CARRIAGE HOUSE

235 Pearson Drive
Asheville, NC 28801
(828) 251-0789 (phone)
(828) 251-0929 (fax)
(800) 552-5724 (toll free)
info@wrightinn.com
www.wrightinn.com

This elegant Victorian is ideal for a relaxing, romantic getaway. Award-winning gardens and an expansive gazebo front porch are awaiting your arrival. The inn is close to Biltmore Estate, downtown Asheville, and the Blue Ridge Parkway. Antiques, art, and crafts are just minutes from our front porch.

Nanna's Sweet Potato Casserole

This is a wonderful dish for a fall brunch.

6 sweet potatoes
½ cup (1 stick) butter
½ cup milk
1 tablespoon maple syrup
1½ cups brown sugar
¾ cup coconut
½ teaspoon ground cinnamon
¼ teaspoon ground nutmeg
10 mini-marshmallows

Peel, boil, and mash sweet potatoes. Preheat oven to 375°. Combine butter, milk, maple syrup, brown sugar, coconut, cinnamon, and nutmeg and blend well with sweet potatoes. Place mixture in well-greased 9 x 11-inch baking dish and bake 30 minutes. Sprinkle mini-marshmallows over dish and continue baking 10 to 12 minutes or until golden in color. Yields 8 to 10 servings.

BILTMORE VILLAGE INN

119 Dodge Street
Asheville, NC 28803
(828) 274-8707 (phone)
(828) 274-8779 (fax)
(866) 274-8779 (toll free)
info@biltmorevillageinn.com
www.biltmorevillageinn.com

The former home of George Vanderbilt's lawyer, this 1892 Queen-Anne Victorian is a designated local landmark and on the National Register. Fully restored, elegant in design, handsome in its museum-quality collections, it is furnished with every comfort. The unusually large bedrooms and baths have whirlpool tubs, fireplaces, even fireplaces in some bathrooms. It's located on a hilltop in the charming historic mountain city of Asheville, known for the Blue Ridge Parkway, the Biltmore Estate, music, theater, and countless outdoor activities.

Raspberry-Orange Croissants

6 large croissants
1 cup soft cream cheese
1 cup fresh or frozen raspberries

8 eggs
½ cup sugar
1 cup half-and-half
1 teaspoon ground nutmeg
1 teaspoon almond extract
½ cup orange marmalade
¼ cup orange juice

Lightly oil a 9 x 12-inch casserole dish. Split croissants and spread each half with cream cheese. Put raspberries on cream cheese and replace tops. Place croissants in casserole dish. Beat eggs and add sugar, half-and-half, nutmeg, and almond extract. Stir thoroughly and pour over croissants. Mix orange marmalade and orange juice in small bowl. Spoon over croissants to make glaze. Refrigerate 8 to 10 hours or overnight. When ready to bake, preheat oven to 350°. Bake about 40 minutes until custard is puffy and slightly browned. Cut apart to serve. Yields 6 servings.

White Chocolate Chip Coconut Cookies

1 cup (2 sticks) butter, softened
1 cup granulated sugar
1 cup brown sugar
2 teaspoons vanilla extract
2 tablespoons milk
2 eggs, lightly beaten
2½ cups all-purpose flour
1 teaspoon salt
1 teaspoon baking soda
1 teaspoon baking powder
1 cup packaged coconut
12 ounces white chocolate chips
1½ cups chopped pecans

Preheat oven to 350°. Lightly oil baking sheet. Cream butter with both sugars in mixer. (It's too hard to do by hand.) Add vanilla, milk, and eggs, beating until light and fluffy. Add flour, salt, baking soda, and baking powder to creamed mixture and beat to combine. By hand, stir in coconut, chocolate chips, and nuts. Drop dough by teaspoonfuls 1½ inches ap[art on] cookie sheets. Bake 12 mi[nutes.] sheets 1 minute and then remove t[o cool]ing racks. Yields 5 dozen cookies.

Biltmore Village Fruit Topping

1 (15-ounce) container ricotta cheese
1 (8-ounce) container lemon yogurt
¼ cup orange juice
1 teaspoon vanilla extract
½ cup sugar
1 teaspoon almond flavoring
1 teaspoon ground nutmeg
1 teaspoon grated orange rind

Spin all ingredients in blender until smooth. Store in covered container. Use 1 to 2 tablespoons over fresh fruit. Yields about 3 cups.

Caribbean Pears

4 pears
½ cup (1 stick) butter
1 cup brown sugar
½ cup orange juice
½ teaspoon coconut flavoring
3 cinnamon sticks
1 kiwifruit

Peel, halve, and core pears. Place face-down in baking dish. Preheat oven to 350°. In saucepan over low heat, melt butter and add brown sugar. Add orange juice and coconut flavoring. Break cinnamon sticks into stem lengths. Bring to low boil and pour over pears. Bake 30 minutes. Peel and cut kiwifruit in half lengthwise, then into thin slices. Place pears on plates, pour a little sauce over them, put cinnamon sticks as "stems," and arrange kiwifruit slices as "leaves." Yields 8 servings.

FOUR ROOSTER INN

403 Pireway Road
Tabor City, NC 28463
(910) 653-3878 (phone/fax)
(800) 653-5008 (toll free)
info@4roosterinn.com
www.4roosterinn.com

Four Rooster Inn is such a fine place, guests crow over the outstanding hospitality, beautiful antiques, and excellent food. Close to Myrtle Beach, South Carolina, it offers golf, shopping, and dining. Tabor City is called the "Yam Capital of the World." This most nutritious vegetable is celebrated the fourth weekend of each October with parades, festive dinners, and beauty pageants.

Apricot Conserve

2 cups dried apricots
1 cup dried cranberries
1 (20-ounce) can crushed pineapple, drained
1½ cups raisins
4 cups sugar
1 cup roasted, chopped walnuts

In large saucepan, barely cover apricots with water and cook over medium heat 15 to 20 minutes. In small saucepan, barely cover cranberries and cook over medium heat 15 to 20 minutes until tender. Drain fruits on paper towels. Mash apricots with fork until smooth. Return apricots and cranberries to large saucepan. Add pineapple, raisins, and sugar. Bring mixture just to boiling and turn off heat. Add walnuts. Spoon hot mixture into hot jars, leaving ¼-inch headspace. Wipe jar rims. Process in water bath 15 minutes. Yields 8 (½-pint) jars.

Tabor City Yam Bread

6 tablespoons butter
1 cup sugar
2 eggs
1 cup cooked and mashed sweet potatoes
¼ teaspoon cloves
½ teaspoon salt
¼ teaspoon baking soda
½ teaspoon ground nutmeg
2 cups all-purpose flour
2 teaspoons baking powder
¼ teaspoon ground cinnamon
⅛ to ½ cup milk
½ cup chopped nuts
Caramel icing (optional)

Preheat oven to 350°. Butter an 8 x 8-inch loaf pan. Blend together to creamy consistency butter and sugar. Beat eggs in thoroughly and add sweet potatoes. In separate bowl, blend together cloves, salt, soda, nutmeg, flour, baking powder, and cinnamon. Add dry ingredients to egg/potato mixture alternately with milk. Add nuts. Pour into loaf pan and bake 50 to 55 minutes. Top with homemade caramel icing, if desired. Freezes well. Microwave to reheat. Yields 1 loaf.

Note: May also be baked in lined muffin tins at 400° for 15 to 20 minutes.

Tabor City Brandy Sweet Potato Pie

2 cups mashed, baked sweet potatoes
½ cup half-and-half
1 cup sugar
½ cup (1 stick) butter
2 eggs, separated
¼ cup brandy
¼ teaspoon salt
¼ teaspoon ground nutmeg
1 (9-inch) unbaked, deep-dish pie shell

Blend mashed potatoes together with half-and-half until smooth. Preheat oven to 350°. In large bowl, cream sugar, butter, and egg yolks. Add brandy, salt, and nutmeg. Stir in potatoes. Beat egg whites until stiff and fold into potato mix. Pour into deep-dish pie shell. Bake 45 minutes or until knife inserted in center comes out clean. A dollop of real whipped cream seasoned with extra brandy adds a crowning touch. Yields 6 to 8 servings.

North Dakota

COUNTRY GARDEN BED & BREAKFAST

805 1st Avenue West
Williston, ND 58801
(701) 774-9643

Nestled in the heart of Williston, North Dakota, and located just blocks off the Lewis & Clark Trail, Country Garden Bed & Breakfast is close to numerous downtown shops you will want to explore. A variety of antique delights, eating establishments, and sources of entertainment are within walking distance. You will find many areas of interest located within a short driving distance from Country Garden, including Lewis & Clark State Park and Theodore Roosevelt National Park. Overlooking the Missouri River, Red Mike's Resort, a world-class golf course, is available for the golfing enthusiast. "Plain" Amish cuisine is the fare of the day and can be enjoyed in simple indoor surroundings or in the serenity you will find in the garden.

Peach Cobbler

1 stick butter
6 peaches, halved
1 plus 1 cup sugar
1 cup flour
1 teaspoon baking powder
1 teaspoon salt
1 cup milk

Preheat oven to 350°. Melt butter in 2-quart casserole in oven. In medium saucepan combine peaches and 1 cup sugar. Boil over medium heat until completely hot. In mixing bowl, beat together remaining 1 cup sugar, flour, baking powder, salt, and milk. Add flour mixture to melted butter—*don't* stir. Pour hot fruit into center—*don't* stir. Bake 1 hour. Yields 6 servings.

Chicken Baked in Cream

½ cup all-purpose flour
¾ teaspoon salt
½ teaspoon black pepper
½ teaspoon paprika
1½ teaspoons poultry seasoning
2 tablespoons butter
2 tablespoons vegetable oil
6 (7-ounce) boneless, skinless
   chicken breasts
2 cups heavy cream

Preheat oven to 300°. In large paper bag, combine flour, salt, pepper, paprika, and poultry seasoning. In large sauté pan, melt butter with oil over medium-high heat. Shake chicken, two or three at a time, in flour mixture. Place floured chicken in pan and sauté on both sides until golden brown, 8 to 10 minutes. Transfer the browned chicken to a 9 x 13-inch baking dish and pour cream over chicken. Sprinkle additional paprika to taste over chicken, cover tightly, and bake 2 hours or until the chicken is tender. Garnish with parsley or sage and serve immediately.

Amish Waffles & Fruit Sauce

Batter:
1 cup all-purpose flour
1 cup cake flour (sifted)
1½ cups milk
2½ teaspoons baking powder
2 eggs, well beaten
5 tablespoons melted butter
1 teaspoon vanilla extract

Fruit sauce:
1⅔ cup water
⅔ cup sugar
2 tablespoons white corn syrup
2 tablespoons cornstarch
1 (3-ounce) package raspberry gelatin
8 ounces frozen blueberries
8 ounces frozen raspberries

For batter, mix in order flours, milk, baking powder, eggs, butter, and vanilla, just until smooth. Bake in hot waffle iron.

For fruit sauce, combine water, sugar, corn syrup, and cornstarch in saucepan and cook over medium heat until thickened. Remove from heat and add gelatin, stirring until dissolved. Let cool and add berries. Serve warm over waffles with scoop of soft ice cream or dollop of whipped cream. Yields 3 to 4 waffles.

MISSOURI RIVER LODGE

140 42nd Avenue NW
Stanton, ND 58571
(701) 748-2023 (phone)
(877) 480-3498 (toll free)
moriverlodge@westriv.com
www.moriverlodge.com

Missouri River Lodge is located on a two-thousand-acre working ranch near Stanton. It's nested in a deep valley along the Missouri River and is surrounded by badland formations. There are over ten miles of hiking or biking trails, a boat dock and sandy private beach on the Missouri River, historical sites on the original Lewis and Clark Trail, and birding in five habitat zones. Bikes and electric golf carts can be rented on site.

Toasted Orzo with Peas, Onion, & Bacon

1½ cups orzo (rice-shaped pasta)
1¼ cups chopped onion
5 bacon slices, chopped
3¼ cups (or more) canned chicken broth
1½ cups frozen peas, thawed

Heat large nonstick skillet over medium heat. Add orzo and stir until beginning to color, about 10 minutes. Transfer orzo to small bowl. Add onion and bacon to same skillet. Sauté until bacon browns and onion is tender, about 15 minutes. Add broth and orzo and bring to boil. Reduce heat to medium low, cover, and simmer until broth is absorbed and orzo is tender, about 18 minutes. Mix in peas. Add more broth if mixture is dry. Cover and cook until peas are just warmed through, about 2 minutes. Season to taste with salt and pepper and serve. Yields 6 servings.

Potatoes and Shiitake Mushroom Gratin

6 tablespoons butter
24 ounces button mushrooms, coarsely chopped
24 ounces fresh shiitake mushrooms, stemmed, caps coarsely chopped
2 cups canned chicken broth
3 tablespoons minced garlic
2 teaspoons dried thyme
1 teaspoon crushed dried rosemary
3 pounds russet potatoes, peeled, cut into thick slices
2 cups freshly grated Parmesan cheese
2 cups half-and-half
2 cups whipping cream
1¼ teaspoon salt
1 teaspoon black pepper

Melt butter in large pot over high heat. Add mushrooms, garlic, thyme, and rosemary and sauté 1 minute. Add chicken broth and simmer until liquid evaporates, stirring often, about 18 minutes. Season with salt and pepper. Cool. Position oven racks in middle and bottom third of oven; preheat to 375°. Grease 13 x 9 x 2-inch glass baking dish. Arrange one-third of potatoes in dish, overlapping slightly. Top with half mushroom mixture. Sprinkle one-third of cheese on top. Add another layer: one-third of potatoes, remaining mushroom mixture, and one-third of cheese. Arrange remaining potatoes on top of cheese. Whisk half-and-half, cream, salt, and pepper in large bowl to blend; pour over potatoes. Cover loosely with foil. Place baking sheet on bottom rack in oven. Place baking dish on middle rack in oven and bake 1 hour 30 minutes, or until potatoes are tender and liquid thickens. Uncover. Using metal spatula, press on potatoes to submerge. Sprinkle remaining cheese over potatoes and bake until cheese melts and gratin is golden at edges, about 15 minutes longer. Let stand 10 minutes. Yields 12 servings.

Baked Scallops with Herbed Breadcrumb Topping

Orzo pilaf and stewed tomatoes simmered with sliced fennel bulb are nice side dishes. Classic chocolate mousse is the perfect finish.

2 tablespoons (¼ stick) butter
12 ounces bay scallops
Salt and pepper
1 cup fresh breadcrumbs made from crustless French bread
1 large garlic clove, minced
2 tablespoon chopped fresh parsley
1 tablespoon chopped fresh tarragon
Lemon wedges

Preheat oven to 450°. Melt butter in heavy-bottomed medium skillet. Grease 10-inch glass dish. Place scallops in single layer in prepared dish. Season with salt and pepper to taste. Add breadcrumbs and garlic to skillet. Stir until crumbs are crisp, about 5 minutes. Mix in parsley and tarragon. Top scallops with crumb mixture. Bake until topping is golden and scallops are opaque in center, about 10 minutes. Serve with lemon wedges. Yields 2 servings.

Ohio

MAPLEVALE FARM BED & BREAKFAST

3891 Oxford Millville Road (US 27 South)
Oxford, OH 45056-9045
(513) 523-8909 (phone/fax)
(877) 506-2753 (toll free)
Maplevalefarm@yahoo.com
www.maplevale.com

This wonderful circa-1856 farmhouse was built by John Martindell. He and Sarah, his wife, raised their seven children in the home. The Maplevale Farm originally encompassed 185 acres south of Oxford. The home is furnished with antiques and the linens have been selected with your comfort in mind. All guest rooms have satellite TV with VCR, data ports with high-speed Internet, and alarm clock radios with sound machine. The inn is minutes from Miami University, golf courses, Jungle Jim's International Market, Indiana's Antique Alley, Hueston Woods State Park, Cincinnati Bengals and Reds, and it's an hour from three major airports.

♣   ♣   ♣

Raspberry-Peach Trifle

16 ounces frozen peaches, thawed
12 ounces frozen raspberries, thawed
2 tablespoons sugar
1 (3½-ounce) package instant vanilla
    pudding mix
1¾ cups skim milk
12 ounces light whipped topping, thawed
1 (13½-ounce) fat-free pound cake,
    cut into 1-inch cubes
4 ounces (½ cup) orange juice

In large bowl combine peaches, raspberries, and sugar. Toss to coat. In mixing bowl combine pudding and milk with wire whisk and mix until well blended. Place pudding mix in refrigerator to set to soft for 5 to 10 minutes. Fold in half of whipped topping. Place half of pound cake cubes in bottom of trifle bowl and drizzle with half of orange juice. Arrange half of fruit mixture over cake and then half of pudding mixture. Repeat layers of cake, orange juice, fruit, pudding. Cover and chill at least 2 hours and top with remaining whipped topping before serving. Yields 8 to 10 servings.

Strawberry Soup

1 cup fresh strawberries, hulled
1 cup orange juice
¼ cup honey
¼ cup sour cream
½ cup sweet white wine
    (optional)

Process all ingredients together in blender until smooth. Cover and chill. Stir well before serving. Yields 3 cups.

Maplevale Farm Bed & Breakfast

Strawberry Bread

3 cups all-purpose flour
1 teaspoon baking soda
1 teaspoon salt
1 tablespoon ground cinnamon
2 cups sugar
2 cups finely chopped strawberries
2 tablespoons vegetable oil
4 eggs, beaten

Preheat oven to 325°. In medium bowl combine flour, baking soda, salt, cinnamon, and sugar. Combine strawberries, oil, and eggs. Fold dry mixture into strawberry mixture. Pour batter into mini muffin tins or loaf pans. Bake 25 minutes for mini muffins, 45 to 60 minutes for mini loaves. Yields 12 servings.

Whispering Pines Bed & Breakfast

P.O. Box 340
Dellroy, OH 44620
(330) 735-2824 (phone)
(330) 735-7006 (fax)
(866) 4LAKEVU (toll free)
romance@atwoodlake.com
www.atwoodlake.com

Whispering Pines is the ultimate romantic getaway, nestled on seven acres of gently rolling hills overlooking beautiful Atwood Lake with spectacular lake views in peaceful surroundings, spa tubs, fireplaces, and balconies. Lake activities including boating, swimming, fishing, beach area, and a wonderful park on the west end of the lake that has several walking/hiking trails. There is a golf course across the lake and many others in the area. The Amish area is a short drive, along with Warther's Museum and a large antique mall. Football Hall of Fame and Harry London Chocolate Factory are also a short drive.

Double Chocolate Chip Muffins

1¾ cups all-purpose flour
½ cup sugar
¼ cup cocoa powder
1 tablespoon baking powder
½ teaspoon salt
½ cup semisweet chocolate chips
2 eggs
½ cup (1 stick) melted butter, cooled
1 cup milk at room temperature
1 teaspoon vanilla extract

Preheat oven to 400°. In large bowl combine flour, sugar, cocoa, baking powder, salt, and chocolate chips. In another bowl whisk together eggs, butter, milk, and vanilla. Gently fold wet ingredients into dry ingredients until moistened. Do *not* overmix. Spoon into greased muffin tins. Bake 15 to 18 minutes. Yields 12 delicious muffins.

Sticky-Bun Cake

½ cup pecans
1 (48-ounce) package frozen
   dinner rolls
2 (3½-ounce) packages instant
   butterscotch pudding mix
   (Do *not* prepare according
   to directions.)
½ cup packed brown sugar
¼ cup (½ stick) butter
⅛ teaspoon ground cinnamon

Grease 10-inch Bundt pan. Sprinkle pecans on bottom of pan. Arrange frozen dough balls on top of pecans and on top of each other. Sprinkle pudding mix over dough balls. In small saucepan, cook and stir brown sugar, butter, and cinnamon until butter is melted. Pour mixture over dough balls. Spray a little oil on tinfoil and cover dough. Leave in oven 8 to 10 hours or overnight. When ready to bake, remove pan and preheat oven to 350°. Uncover dough and bake 30 minutes or until golden in color. Immediately invert cake onto serving plate. Cool slightly before serving. By putting this together the night before, dough will have defrosted and risen by morning. Yields 10 servings.

Double Chocolate Sour Cream Cookies

2¾ cups all-purpose flour
½ teaspoon baking soda
½ teaspoon baking powder
½ teaspoon salt
½ cup (1 stick) butter at
   room temperature
1½ cups sugar
1 square unsweetened chocolate,
   melted and cooled to
   room temperature
2 eggs at room temperature
1 cup sour cream at room temperature
1 teaspoon vanilla extract
2 cups chocolate chips

Sift together flour, baking soda, baking powder, and salt. In mixer, combine butter and sugar and mix well. Stir cooled chocolate into butter mixture. Add eggs and blend. Add sour cream and vanilla and blend. Mix in dry ingredients. Stir in chocolate chips. Chill dough 8 to 10 hours or overnight. When ready to bake, preheat oven to 400°. Drop dough by heaping teaspoonfuls on ungreased cookie sheet and bake 8 to 10 minutes. Remove from cookie sheet, cool on racks, and watch them disappear. Yields 4 to 6 dozen cookies.

CAMPBELL COTTAGE BED & BREAKFAST

932 West Lakeshore Drive
Kelleys Island, OH 43438
(877) 746-2740 (toll free)
JCKIOH@cs.com

Campbell Cottage Bed & Breakfast, on the western shore of Lake Erie's Kelleys Island, serves delicious breakfasts on the front porch and warm hospitality throughout the house. The spacious front porch welcomes you to an afternoon of relaxation and an evening filled with fantastic sunset views. Complimentary bicycles, homemade cookies and lemonade, queensize beds, and private baths provide a restful retreat.

Cottage Chocolate Cookies

1 cup (2 sticks) butter or margarine
½ cup firmly packed brown sugar
½ cup granulated sugar
2 eggs
2 tablespoons cold coffee
1 teaspoon vanilla extract
2 cups all-purpose flour
1 (3½-ounce) package instant chocolate pudding (Do *not* prepare according to directions.)
1 teaspoon salt
1 teaspoon baking soda
1 teaspoon ground cinnamon
1 cup chopped walnuts
1 (12-ounce) package white baking chips

Preheat oven to 375°. In mixing bowl with electric mixer on medium speed (or mix by hand), cream butter, sugars, eggs, coffee, and vanilla until light and fluffy. Add flour, pudding, salt, baking soda, and cinnamon and stir until well blended. Stir in nuts and white chips. Drop by rounded teaspoons 2 inches apart on cookie sheet. Bake 8 to 10 minutes or until edges are lightly browned. Cool on pan several minutes, then on wire rack. Yields 3 to 4 dozen cookies.

Pumpkin Pancakes

1½ cups all-purpose flour
1 teaspoon baking powder
¼ teaspoon baking soda
1½ teaspoons pumpkin pie spice
¼ teaspoon salt
1 egg
1½ cups milk
½ cup pumpkin
3 tablespoons oil

In medium bowl combine flour, baking powder, baking soda, pumpkin pie spice, and salt. In large bowl beat egg, milk, pumpkin, and oil. Add flour mixture to milk mixture and stir until blended but still lumpy. Pour about ½ cup batter per pancake onto hot griddle coated with small amount of oil. Cook, flipping cakes when bubbles are dry and edges are set. Serve with Apple Cider Syrup (see recipe below). Garnish with thin slices of red apple and sift confectioners' sugar over stack of pancakes when serving. Yields 8 (5-inch) pancakes.

Apple Cider Syrup

1 cup sugar
3 tablespoons biscuit mix
1 teaspoon ground cinnamon
¼ teaspoon ground nutmeg
2 cups cider
1 tablespoon lemon juice
¼ cup (½ stick) butter or margarine

Mix together dry ingredients in saucepan. Stir in cider and lemon juice. Cook over medium heat, stirring constantly until thick and bubbly. Remove from heat and stir in butter. Stir and boil for 1 minute. Serve in pitcher so each guest can pour desired amount on pancakes, waffles, or French toast. Refrigerate leftover syrup. Yields 3 cups syrup.

THE SIGNAL HOUSE

234 North Front Street
Ripley, OH 45167
(937) 392-1640 (phone/fax)
signalhouse@webtv.net
www.Thesignalhouse.com

This stately home on the Ohio River, known as the Signal House, welcomes you to the historic and scenic village of Ripley, Ohio. The Signal House leaves a mark in history through its involvement in the Underground Railroad. A lantern from a skylight in the attic signaled Rev. John Rankin that the waterfront was safe to transport slaves to freedom. Built in the 1830s, this Greek Italianate-style home features ornate plaster moldings that surround the twelve-foot ceilings, enhancing the charm of the twin parlors. Relish splendid views of the Ohio River from spacious rooms, or be our guest on one of the three relaxing porches. View the rolling hills and spectacular sunsets while anticipating a glimpse of a passing paddle wheeler comin' 'round the bend. Enjoy various museums, restaurants, and shops, including antiques and crafts. Imagine the grand drama of the past while strolling through Ripley's fifty-five-acre historical district. The surrounding areas offer unique towns, festivals, dramas, caves, a winery, herb farms, covered bridges, sternwheeler regatta, and lots of friendly people.

Super-Easy, Super-Yummy Apple Pie

Piecrust:
1½ cups all-purpose flour
2 teaspoons sugar
1 teaspoon salt
2 tablespoons milk
2 tablespoons oil

Filling:
¼ cup all-purpose flour
⅔ cup sugar
1 teaspoon ground cinnamon
½ cup sour cream
4 apples, peeled and sliced

Topping:
1 cup crushed cornflakes
⅓ cup all-purpose flour
⅓ cup firmly packed brown sugar
½ teaspoon ground cinnamon
¼ cup (½ stick) butter, softened

Preheat oven to 375°. For piecrust combine flour, sugar, and salt in medium bowl. Stir in milk and oil. Mix well. Pat in ungreased, 9-inch pie plate and flute edges. Combine filling ingredients in large bowl. Place in crust. Combine topping ingredients in small bowl. Sprinkle topping over pie. Bake 35 to 45 minutes until apples are tender and topping is golden brown. Enjoy. Yields 8 servings.

Nutty Popcorn

5 cups popping corn to equal
    10 cups popped
1 stick butter
1 teaspoon chili powder
1 teaspoon salt
½ teaspoon onion salt
1 (7- to 10-ounce) container mixed nuts
½ cup Parmesan cheese

Pop corn kernels. Preheat oven to 250°. Melt butter in saucepan. Add chili powder, salt, onion salt, and mix well. Pour popped corn in large, shallow baking dish. Pour butter mix over popcorn. Add nuts and Parmesan cheese and stir well. Bake 45 minutes. Stir often. Cool. Store in tight container. Yields about 10 servings.

Company Hash-Brown Potatoes

2 pounds frozen hash-brown potatoes
2 cups grated American cheese
½ cup diced onions
1 (10¾-ounce) can cream of celery soup
16 ounces sour cream and chives
½ cup (1 stick) melted butter
½ teaspoon celery salt
1 teaspoon salt
Pepper

Preheat oven to 350°. Mix ingredients together. Bake uncovered in 13 x 9-inch pan 1 hour. Yields 10 to 12 servings.

CAPTAIN MONTAGUE'S

229 Center Street
Huron, OH 44839
(419) 433-4756 (phone)
(800) 276-4756 (toll free)
judytann@aol.com
www.captainmontagues.com

This stately Southern Colonial manor, built by the owner of the local lumberyard in the 1870s and later purchased by Captain Montague, has welcomed guests internationally. Completely renovated, refurbished, and filled with antiques, exquisite reproductions, oriental and hook rugs, and accessories, the inn offers the finest in the romantic Victorian tradition. This Lake Erie paradise region is the largest tourist area in the state of Ohio. Locally, enjoy Cedar Point, voted the best amusement park in the world, boasting the most roller

The Signal House

coasters, Lake Erie Islands, historical sites and museums, nature preserves, and a host of other fun activities all year through. Huron is home to Ohio's oldest, continuous summer stock theater, the Huron Playhouse; and the city's "gem", the municipal boat basin and amphitheater, hosts free, live entertainment every weekend throughout the summer.

Cranberry Scones

2 cups unbleached flour
1 tablespoon baking powder
½ teaspoon salt
¼ cup sugar plus additional for sprinkling
1 cup dried cranberries
1¼ to 1½ cups heavy whipping cream
Melted butter

Preheat oven to 350°. Combine flour, baking powder, salt, ¼ cup sugar, and cranberries. Stir in cream with fork until dough holds together. Knead several times. Either pat into 10-inch circle and cut into eight wedges or make biscuit-style (8 or 9). Bake on ungreased cookie sheet or baking stone. Brush scones with melted butter and sprinkle with sugar. Bake 15 to 20 minutes until lightly browned. Yields 8 servings.

Raspberry Supreme Bundt Cake

1 (18-ounce) box yellow cake mix
½ cup sugar
2 (3½-ounce) boxes white chocolate instant pudding mix
1 cup vegetable oil
4 eggs
¼ cup vodka
¼ plus ¼ cup Chambord (raspberry liqueur)
¼ cup water
½ cup confectioners' sugar

Preheat oven to 350°. Mix cake mix, sugar, pudding mix, oil, eggs, vodka, ¼ cup

Chambord, and water in mixer at medium speed for 4 minutes. Spray Bundt pan with nonstick coating. Pour mixture into prepared pan. Bake 50 to 60 minutes. Cool at least 15 minutes. Turn onto plate and allow to cool for at least 15 more minutes. Combine remaining ¼ cup Chambord with confectioners' sugar. Pour over cake. Cover with plastic wrap and refrigerate. Serve as is or with a dollop of whipped topping. Yields 12 large pieces or 24 smaller ones.

Molly's Tea

1½ cups instant tea (pure)
1 (9-ounce) jar orange-flavored instant breakfast drink
1 (3-ounce) package lemonade mix
¾ cup sugar
1 teaspoon ground cinnamon
1 teaspoon ground cloves
¾ teaspoon ginger

Combine all ingredients until well blended. Store mix in airtight container. To make 1 cup of Molly's Tea use 1 cup hot water and stir in 2 teaspoons tea mix. Yields 3½ cups, enough for 24 servings.

Optional: Add a jigger of apricot brandy at the end.

Chutney-Cheddar Tea Sandwiches

4 ounces cream cheese, softened
1 cup (4 ounces) shredded Cheddar cheese
2 tablespoons chutney
1 teaspoon Dijon mustard
1 green onion, thinly sliced
12 slices whole wheat or pumpernickel bread, crusts removed
Butter, softened
Chopped parsley (optional)

In small mixer bowl, combine cream cheese, Cheddar cheese, chutney, mustard, and green onion. Beat at medium speed

until blended. Spread six bread slices with cheese mixture. Top with remaining bread slices to make six sandwiches. Cut each sandwich into three fingers. Spread one end of each finger sandwich with butter and press into chopped parsley. Cover with damp paper towels and plastic wrap until ready to serve. Yields 18 finger sandwiches.

Potato Surprise

4 to 5 medium baking or russet potatoes, scrubbed but not peeled
2 tablespoons butter
½ cup diced red onions
2 tablespoons all-purpose or unbleached flour
½ teaspoon salt
½ teaspoon black pepper
1 cup half-and-half
½ cup mayonnaise or salad dressing
1 tablespoon Dijon-style mustard
1 or 2 dashes Tabasco sauce
4 slices bacon, cooked and crumbled
1 teaspoon dried thyme leaves (or fresh), crumbled

Bake potatoes in microwave or conventional oven until fork tender. Cool and place in refrigerator at least 2 hours or overnight. Preheat over to 350°. Dice or cube potatoes. Melt butter in saucepan. Add onions. Sauté until soft, but not brown. Sprinkle with flour. Add salt and pepper. Slowly add half-and-half, cooking and stirring until sauce thickens. Remove from heat and cool slightly. Add mustard, Tabasco, and mayonnaise. Stir until well blended; sauce will be thick and creamy. Turn potatoes into buttered casserole. Cover with sauce. Sprinkle with crumbled bacon and thyme. Bake at least 30 minutes. Yields 4 to 6 servings.

BAILEY HOUSE BED & BREAKFAST

112 North Water Street
Georgetown, OH 45121
(937) 378-3087
Baileyho@bright.net
www.baileyhousebandb.com

The Bailey House was built in 1832 for the prominent Georgetown physician, Dr. George Bailey and his family of eight children. The Baileys were closely associated with the family of Ulysses S. Grant The Bailey House was purchased by current owner Nancy Purdy's great-grandfather and has been in the family ever since. It became a bed and breakfast in 1994. The Bailey House offers three guest rooms; each is spacious, inviting, and is furnished with antiques. Relax in the parlor or browse in the library. Delightful to any Civil War enthusiast, the library boasts many hours of reading on Gen. Ulysses S. Grant.

Apple French Toast

1 stick butter
1 cup packed brown sugar
2 tablespoons light corn syrup
4 large apples, peeled and sliced
3 eggs
1 cup milk
2 tablespoons vanilla extract
8 (¾-inch thick) slices French bread

In small saucepan, melt butter and add brown sugar and corn syrup. Cook over medium heat until bubbly. Pour mixture into greased 13 x 9-inch pan. Layer sliced apples on top. In bowl, beat eggs. Add milk and vanilla and mix well. Dip bread slices into egg mixture and layer on top of apples.

Cover and refrigerate 8 to 10 hours or overnight. When ready to bake, preheat oven to 350° and bake uncovered 35 minutes. To serve, invert each slice of bread onto serving plates and spoon apples on top. Yields 4 servings.

Bailey House Egg Casserole

9 eggs, beaten
1 pound bulk sausage, browned and drained
1½ cups shredded cheese
4 slices bread, cubed
Salt and pepper

Combine all ingredients in bowl. Pour into lightly greased 13 x 9-inch pan. Cover and refrigerate 8 to 10 hours or overnight. When ready to bake, preheat oven to 350° and bake uncovered 1 hour. Yields 8 servings.

CEDAR HILL BED & BREAKFAST

4003 SR 73 West
Wilmington, OH 45177
(937) 383-2525 (phone)
(877) 722-2525 (toll free)

Nestled in ten acres of woods, Cedar Hill offers quiet bird-watching or a walk in the woods. The Carriage House has three guest rooms, each with private bath, queen-size bed, TV, sitting area, and library. Guests may enjoy the Gathering Room with an open hearth fireplace, TV, VCR, CD player, and wet bar. Area attractions include Waynesville and Lebanon antique shops; Little Miami bike trail; golfing; King's Island; prime outlet shops; canoeing on the Little Miami River; British Isle Festival; Ohio Renaissance Festival; Ohio Sauerkraut Festival; The Theater at Wilmington College; Blue Jacket outdoor drama; Clinton County Corn Festival; Banana Split Festival; Historic Murphy Theater; and Valley Vineyard Wine Festival.

Leftover Bread/ Muffin Pudding

Stuck with leftover muffins or banana bread? Here's a great way to use them.

6 muffins or leftover bread
1 cup blueberries or blackberries (or other fruits as desired)
1 cup milk
2 eggs
½ cup sugar
1 teaspoon vanilla extract
1 cup boiling water
Cinnamon sugar

Preheat oven to 350°. Crumble muffins into 8 x 8-inch pan sprayed with coating. Sprinkle with fruit. Combine milk, eggs, sugar, vanilla, and water. Stir and pour over muffins. Sprinkle with cinnamon sugar. Bake 30 to 35 minutes. Can also use individual dishes (ramekins). Yields 4 to 6 servings.

Simple Sweet Scones

2½ cups all-purpose flour
1 tablespoon baking powder
½ teaspoon salt
½ cup (1 stick) cold unsalted butter
¼ cup sugar (use ⅓ cup for sweeter scones)
⅔ cup milk

Preheat oven to 425°. Put flour, baking powder, and salt into large bowl and stir to mix well. Cut in butter with pastry blender or rub in with your fingers until mixture looks like fine granules. Add sugar and toss to mix. Add milk and stir with a fork until soft dough forms. Form dough into ball, put onto lightly floured board, and give it ten to twelve kneads.

To make triangular scones, cut dough in half. Knead each half lightly into ball and turn smooth-side up. Pat or roll into 6-inch circles. Cut each circle into six to eight wedges. Place wedges slightly apart on ungreased cookie sheet. Bake 12 minutes or until medium brown on top. Put linen or cotton dish towel on wire rack; cover loosely with cloth and cool completely before serving. Yields 12 to 16 servings.

The Rum Cake

1 (18-ounce) box yellow cake mix
1 (3½-ounce) package vanilla instant
    pudding mix
4 eggs
½ cup cold water
½ cup vegetable oil
½ plus ½ cup rum
2 cups chopped walnuts
1 stick butter or margarine
1 cup sugar
¼ cup water

Preheat oven to 325°. Grease and flour Bundt cake pan. Mix together cake mix, vanilla pudding mix, eggs, cold water, oil and ⅓ cup rum. Spread walnuts on bottom of pan and pour batter on top. Bake about 1 hour. In small saucepan melt butter and stir in sugar, water, and remaining ½ cup rum. Mix until sugar is dissolved. Boil 5 minutes. While cake is still warm, prick all over with fork and pour glaze over all. Serve this in fall of the year for evening dessert. Guests have been known to ask for it at the breakfast table as well. Yields 12 servings.

WALDEN

WALDEN COUNTRY INN & STABLES

1119 Aurora Hudson Road
Aurora, OH 44202
(330) 562-5508 (phone)
(330) 562-8001 (fax)
(888) 808-5003 (toll free)
frontdesk@waldenco.com
www.waldenco.com

Make yourself at home in one of twenty-five spacious suites, each with private sanctuary, where remarkable architecture lives in harmony with the pastoral setting. Relax by the fireplace in a timeless rocking chair, or dream amidst Italian linens beneath cedar-paneled ceilings. Step into the Vermont slate shower lavished with European bath accessories, and then into a plush, cozy robe. Enjoy your morning coffee on a private patio while gazing at the beautiful woodlands and pastures that surround you. Trails, stables, golf, tennis, swimming, and theater are on the premises.

Curried Butternut Squash Bisque

1 large butternut squash
2 tablespoons diced onions
2 tablespoons diced celery
2 tablespoons plus 1 tablespoon butter
½ tablespoon (1½ teaspoons)
    curry powder
3 cups chicken stock
Salt and pepper
¼ cup heavy cream
⅓ cup sour cream
¼ tablespoon ground ginger
1 Gala apple, peeled, cored, and diced

1 tablespoon sugar
Pinch of cinnamon

Half, seed, and roast squash skin-side up at 350° until tender. Sauté onions and celery in 2 tablespoons butter in medium saucepan, being careful not to brown. Add curry and continue until aroma is apparent. Add squash and continue cooking for 2 minutes. Add stock, salt, and pepper and simmer for 20 minutes. Transfer to blender and purée. Return to saucepan, bring back to simmer, and add cream. Adjust seasonings if needed. Combine sour cream and ginger. Lightly brown remaining 1 tablespoon butter in medium sauté pan. Add apples, sugar, and cinnamon and cook just until tender. Pour squash into bowls, swirl in ginger cream, and top with apples. Yields 4 servings.

Gorgonzola Crusted Pork with Dried Fruits

10 ounces Gorgonzola cheese
½ cup chopped walnuts
⅓ cup breadcrumbs
½ teaspoon chopped fresh rosemary
2 tablespoons dried cherries
2 tablespoons dried apricots
2 tablespoons coarsely chopped
    dried figs
2 ounces brandy
2 cups prepared demi-glace
    (substitute Knorr Swiss)
2½ pounds pork tenderloin, trimmed,
    cut into 3-ounce medallions, and
    flattened to ½-inch thickness
Salt and pepper
Olive oil for coating

Combine cheese, walnuts, breadcrumbs, and rosemary and roll into log. Chill and cut into ¼-inch medallions. Soak fruits in brandy for 1 hour and drain, reserving brandy. Carefully warm brandy in 1 quart saucepan, remove from heat, and ignite to burn off. Add fruit and demi-glace. Season meat and grill to desired doneness. Top with cheese medallions and brown under broiler. Serve in pool of fruit sauce. Yields 6 servings.

The Inn at Cedar Falls

21190 State Route 374
Logan, OH 43138
(800) 65-FALLS (toll free)
www.innatcedarfalls.com

Mammoth rock formations, caves, and waterfalls share their breathtaking beauty in the Hocking Hills area that surrounds The Inn at Cedar Falls. Overnight accommodations include antique furnished rooms, cozy cottages, and 1840s log cabins. A unique dining experience awaits you in the double-wide log house, originally constructed in the 1840s with 18-inch-wide logs. The original plank floors remain.

Poppy Seed Muffins

3 cups all-purpose flour
2¼ cups sugar
1½ teaspoons baking powder
1½ tablespoons salt
1½ cups vegetable oil
1½ cups milk
3 eggs
½ teaspoon almond extract
1½ tablespoons poppy seeds

Preheat oven to 350°. Combine flour, sugar, baking powder, and salt. Mix oil, milk, eggs, almond extract, and poppy seeds. Mix together. Bake 20 to 25 minutes in greased muffin tins. Yields 12 muffins.

Almond Torte

1 cup all-purpose flour
1½ tablespoons sugar
¾ stick (6 tablespoons) butter
2 egg yolks
1 cup heavy cream
1 cup sugar
¼ teaspoon salt
1 cup sliced almonds
¼ teaspoon almond extract

Preheat oven to 325°. Combine flour, sugar, and butter in food processor until like coarse meal. Add yolks and mix until combined. Press into 9-inch tart pan with removable bottom. Bake 10 minutes. Meanwhile, prepare filling. Combine cream, sugar, and salt. Bring to boil over medium to medium-high heat, stirring frequently. Simmer over medium to medium-low heat 5 minutes, stirring occasionally. Add almonds and almond extract. Raise oven temperature to 375°. Pour filling into crust and bake 25 to 30 minutes or until lightly browned on top. Serve with raspberry sauce. Yields 6 to 8 servings.

Chocolate Decadence

16 (1-ounce) squares semisweet chocolate
⅔ cup butter
5 large eggs
¼ cup plus 2 tablespoons sugar
2 tablespoons all-purpose flour
2 cups fresh raspberries plus some
    for garnish
2 cups water
2 tablespoons cornstarch
2 tablespoons water
Whipped cream
Fresh raspberries

Line bottom of 9-inch springform pan with parchment paper. Combine chocolate and butter in top of double boiler. Bring water to a boil and reduce heat to low. Cook until chocolate has melted. Preheat oven to 400°. Place eggs in large mixing bowl. Gradually add chocolate mixture to eggs and beat at medium speed with electric mixer 10 minutes. Fold in 2 tablespoons sugar and flour. Pour into prepared pan. Bake 15 minutes. (Dessert will not be set in the center.) Remove from oven, cover, and chill thoroughly. Combine raspberries and water and remaining ¼ cup sugar in large saucepan. Bring to boil over medium-high heat, reduce heat, and simmer 30 minutes, stirring occasionally. Pour raspberry mixture through strainer into bowl, discarding seeds. Return raspberry mixture to pan. Combine cornstarch and water and add to raspberry mixture. Cook over medium heat, stirring constantly, until mixture comes to a boil. Boil 1 minute, stirring constantly. Cool completely and pour over chilled chocolate dessert. Garnish with whipped cream and fresh raspberries. Yields 8 to 10 servings.

Apple Raisin Clafouti

4 cups apples
¼ cup dark raisins
¼ cup golden raisins
¼ cup blanched almonds
2 tablespoons all-purpose flour
¾ cup heavy cream
⅓ cup plus 2 tablespoons sugar
2 eggs
1 tablespoon tawny port
¼ teaspoon salt
2 tablespoons cold butter
Whipped cream for topping

Peel, core, and cut apples into thick slices. Mix apples with raisins. Arrange in buttered, two-quart dish. Preheat oven to 350°. In food processor, grind almonds and flour until fine. Add cream, ⅓ cup sugar, eggs, port, and salt, and beat until well blended. Pour custard evenly over fruit. Dot with butter and sprinkle with remaining 2 tablespoons sugar. Bake 30 to 40 minutes or until top is golden. Let cool 20 minutes. Serve warm with dollop of whipped cream. Yields 6 servings.

VALLEY VIEW INN

32327 S.R. 643
New Bedford, OH 43824
(330) 897-3232 (phone)
(800) 331-8439 (toll free)
www.avalleyviewinn.com

This Christian-owned-and-operated Inn has ten spacious rooms with private baths. Located in quiet Amish Country, we cater to couples or groups of twenty. Activities in surrounding area include the world's largest Amish community, shopping, sightseeing, Amish cottage industries, steam engine train ride, historic sites, Longaberger Basket capital, Amish cooking and restaurants, live theater, cheese factories, biking paths, fishing, farmers' markets, fudge factory, quilt shops, furniture stores/shops, and more.

Fruit Slush

2 cups sugar
3 cups boiling water
1 (6-ounce) can frozen orange juice
　　concentrate
5 to 6 bananas, thinly sliced
1 (20-ounce) can crushed or chunk
　　pineapple with juice
1 (29-ounce) can peaches, cut into
　　small pieces
18 ounces lemon-lime soda

Dissolve sugar in boiling water in large bowl. Add orange juice. Slice bananas into mixture and add pineapple and peaches with juice. Add soda to help keep bananas from turning brown. After mixing all ingredients together, pour into container that can be placed in freezer (plastic is best). A shallow container is better than a deep one. Freeze until needed. Remove from freezer approximately 1 hour before serving. Chop up mixture and place in small dessert cups. This is a refreshing "dessert" that our guests love regardless of the season. Yields about 5 quarts.

Ham and Cheese Sandwich Puffs

2 cups cooked ham, cubed in
　　small pieces
2 cups grated Swiss cheese
½ cup mayonnaise
1 teaspoon prepared mustard
12 slices toasted white bread
6 eggs
2¼ cups milk

Combine ham and cheese and blend in mayonnaise and mustard. Spray glass dish with nonstick spray. Place six slices bread in pan. Spread mixture on slices and top with remaining six slices. Cut in half diagonally. In medium-size mixing bowl, beat eggs and add milk. Pour mixture slowly over sandwiches. Cover and chill 4 hours or overnight. When ready to serve, preheat oven to 325° and bake sandwich puffs 45 minutes to 1 hour or until custard sets. Serve on dishes and garnish with parsley. Yields 6 to 8 servings.

Honey Fruit Dressing

⅔ cup sugar
1 teaspoon dry mustard
1 teaspoon paprika
1 teaspoon celery seeds
¼ teaspoon salt
⅛ cup honey
⅓ cup vinegar
1 tablespoon lemon juice
1 teaspoon grated onion (optional)
1 cup vegetable oil

In a medium mixing bowl combine sugar, mustard, paprika, celery seeds, and salt. Add the honey, vinegar, lemon juice, and onion, if using. Pour the oil into the hot mixture very slowly, beating constantly. Keep refrigerated until ready to use. Delicious over breakfast fruit—melon, grapefruit, etc. Yields about 2¼ cups.

Valley View Inn

THE INN AT HONEY RUN

6920 County Road 203
Millersburg, OH 44654-9018
(330) 674-0011 (phone)
(330) 674-2623 (fax)
(800) 468-6639 (toll free)
www.innathoneyrun.com

Experience nature with a walk through sixty acres of woods and pastures. Enjoy the birds at our multiple feeders. Our full-service dining room features American regional cuisine. Located in Holmes County, known for its cheese houses, handcrafted quilts, and fine wood furniture, the inn features twenty-five guest rooms, many of them smoke free. The earth-sheltered honeycombs with twelve rooms offer a combination of luxury and privacy. Local activities include hiking trails on sixty acres; scenic bi-ways; challenging golf courses; history museums; summer theater; cheese houses; quilt shops; handmade furniture; antique shops; and Amish farms and stores.

Hot Buttered Tomato Soup

4 cups tomato juice
½ teaspoon basil leaves
½ teaspoon salt
1 teaspoon sugar
1 tablespoon brown sugar
Dash of garlic powder
2 tablespoons butter or margarine

Combine all ingredients except butter in saucepan. Bring to a boil, stirring occasionally. Reduce heat and simmer, uncovered for 5 minutes. Add butter and stir until melted. Yields 6 servings.

Broccoli Slaw

½ medium green pepper
½ small onion
½ medium tomato
1½ cups peeled and grated broccoli stems
¼ teaspoon salt
⅛ teaspoon pepper
6 tablespoons French dressing

Finely chop green pepper, onion, and tomato. Combine with grated broccoli. Stir in salt, pepper, and French dressing. Cover tightly with plastic wrap and chill several hours to blend flavors. Stir before serving. Yields 4 servings.

Chocolate Silk Pie

¾ cup (1½ sticks) butter
1 cup sugar
2 ounces unsweetened chocolate, melted and cooled
1 teaspoon vanilla extract
3 eggs
1 (9-inch) baked, cooled pastry shell
1 cup heavy cream
2 tablespoons confectioners' sugar
½ teaspoon vanilla extract
Grated chocolate

Cream butter and sugar until light and fluffy. Add melted chocolate and vanilla and beat until sugar is dissolved. Add eggs, one at a time, beating on high 2 minutes after each is incorporated. Spoon into pastry shell. Beat cream and confectioners' sugar until stiff peaks form and fold in vanilla. Cover top of pie with whipped cream. Garnish with grated chocolate. Yields 8 servings.

Buttermilk Pecan Chicken Breasts

½ cup buttermilk
1 egg, beaten
½ cup all-purpose flour
½ cup grated pecans
1⅓ tablespoons sesame seeds
Dash of paprika
½ teaspoon salt
Dash black pepper
6 (6-ounce) chicken breasts
¼ cup pecan pieces
¼ cup (½ stick) melted margarine

Preheat oven to 375°. Mix buttermilk and egg in small bowl. Combine flour, grated pecans, sesame seeds, paprika, salt, and pepper in medium bowl. Dip chicken in buttermilk mixture and cover with flour mixture. Coat 13 x 9 x 2-inch pan with vegetable spray. Place chicken in pan. Scatter pecan pieces over top of chicken

The Inn at Honey Run

breasts. Pour margarine over chicken to cover flour mix. Bake covered 20 minutes and then uncovered 10 minutes until chicken is golden brown. Yields 6 servings.

THE CINCINNATIAN HOTEL

601 Vine Street
Cincinnati, OH 45202
(513) 381-3000 (phone)
(513) 651-0256 (fax)

The grand walnut and marble staircase of this hotel's eight-story, sky-lit atrium is what you walk into. A European-style, luxury hotel, The Cincinnatian has 146 rooms and suites, with granite showers and oversized tubs. Relax with afternoon tea and enjoy music in the Cricket Lounge or dine in the four-star Palace restaurant.

Seared Jumbo Scallops

2 wonton skins
2 ounces clarified butter
1 teaspoon sesame seeds
1 tablespoon Yuzu lemon juice
2 tablespoons soy sauce
1 tablespoon sesame oil or olive oil
Salt and freshly ground pepper
1 cup mixed green salad or mesclun
¼ green mango, julienned
1 teaspoon chopped shallots
6 pieces U10 fresh scallops, cleaned

Preheat oven to 350°. Brush wonton skins on both sides with clarified butter. Spread some sesame seeds on one side of wonton skins. Bake until golden brown, about 4 to 5 minutes. Remove from oven and let cool. Make vinaigrette by mixing Yuzu juice with soy sauce and sesame oil or olive oil. Add salt and pepper to taste. Toss greens with mango, chopped shallots, and Yuzu dressing. Season scallops with salt and pepper. Sauté scallops in skillet with clarified butter until golden brown on both sides. Put salad on middle of plate, and put 3 scallops around the salad. Add the wonton skin on top of the salad. Drizzle some dressing around the plate. Serve lukewarm. Yields 2 servings.

Rack of Venison with Parsnips Purée

1 pound fresh parsnips, peeled, cut to dice
3 ounces bitter orange marmalade
1 teaspoon green peppercorns
Salt and freshly ground black pepper
1 (8-rib) venison rack
3 tablespoons olive oil
3 ounces Spicy Pear Chutney
    (prepared ahead of time)

Preheat oven to 425°. Fill large pot with water, add parsnips, and cook until tender. Purée parsnips with food processor. Add into parsnips orange marmalade and green peppercorns. Adjust seasoning with salt and pepper to taste. Keep parsnip purée warm. Season venison rack with salt and pepper. Heat ovenproof pan over high heat. When it is very warm, add oil and swirl pan. Add venison and sear meat on both sides until golden brown. Transfer pan to oven and roast venison for 10 to 13 minutes until rare or to taste (for rare, 115° to 125° on meat thermometer). Remove venison from oven and keep on warm area to rest for 5 to 10 minutes. Cut venison into eight pieces by following ribs. Serve 2 ribs per person with warm Parsnip Purée and Spicy Pear Chutney (see recipe below). Yields 4 servings.

Spicy Pear Chutney

2 tablespoons vegetable oil
½ tablespoon brown mustard seeds
½ tablespoon yellow mustard seeds
1 onion, diced
⅓ red bell pepper, cored and diced
⅓ yellow bell pepper, cored and diced
1 Serrano chile, chopped
1 teaspoon ground allspice
1 teaspoon ground ginger
    (or ½ teaspoon chopped
    fresh ginger)
¼ teaspoon cardamom powder
⅛ teaspoon ground cinnamon powder
¼ cup raisins
4 pears (Asian or Anjou),
    peeled and diced
1 Granny Smith apple, skin on, diced
1 cup brown sugar
¾ cup apple cider vinegar
Salt and pepper

Heat oil in large saucepan over high heat. Add mustard seeds, cover, and cook until popping stops. Reduce heat and add onion, bell peppers, and Serrano chile. Cook until onion and bell peppers are translucent. Stir in allspice, ginger, cardamom, and cinnamon and cook 2 more minutes. Add raisins, pears, apple, brown sugar, apple cider, and salt and pepper to taste. Cook, uncovered, over slow heat, until mixture is soft and aromatic, about 45 minutes. Chill before serving. Can be made ahead and kept four days in tight container. Yields about 4 cups.

MAPLE PLACE BED & BREAKFAST

418 West Maple
Enid, OK 73701
(580) 234-5858
thekislings@pldi.net
www.mapleplace.com

Specializing in traditional Oklahoma hospitality is the slogan made famous by Maple Place Bed & Breakfast. Our beautiful 1902 home is located in the heart of Enid, within walking distance to many cultural and entertainment venues. All of our mouth-watering meals are guaranteed to leave you feeling full. Breakfast is served to your room for a relaxing and romantic private dining experience. Corporate, government, and long-term rates are available.

4-Chippers

2 cups all-purpose flour
½ cup brown sugar
2 teaspoons baking powder
⅔ cup milk
½ cup (1 stick) melted butter
2 eggs
1 teaspoon vanilla extract

½ cup white chocolate chips
½ cup butterscotch chips
½ cup semisweet chocolate chips
½ cup peanut butter chips

Preheat oven to 350°. Combine flour, brown sugar, and baking powder in bowl and mix well. Whisk milk, butter, eggs, and vanilla in bowl until blended. Add milk mixture to flour mixture and stir just until moistened. Fold in chips. Fill greased muffin cups three-quarters full. Bake 18 to 20 minutes for standard muffin cups or 20 to 25 for jumbo muffin cups. Remove to wire rack to cool. Yields 1 dozen standard muffins.

Governor's Broccoli Cheese Soup

2 tablespoons finely chopped
    white onion
2 tablespoons butter
3 tablespoons all-purpose flour
Salt and pepper
2 cups milk
1 cup cubed Velveeta cheese
1 (10-ounce) package frozen
    chopped broccoli
1½ cups water
3 chicken bouillon cubes

In stockpot sauté onion in the butter until tender. Stir in flour and salt and pepper to taste. Cook until blended, stirring constantly. Blend in milk. Cook until thickened, stirring constantly. Add cheese and stir until it melts. Remove from heat. Combine broccoli, water, and bouillon in microwave safe dish. Microwave 7 minutes or until tender. Add unstrained broccoli mixture to the stockpot and mix well. Cook just until heated through, stirring frequently. Yields 4 servings.

THE GRANDISON INN AT MANEY PARK

1200 N. Shartel Drive
Oklahoma City, OK 73103
(405) 232-8778 (phone)
(405) 232-5039 (fax)
(800) 240-INNS (toll free)
grandison@juno.com
www.bbonline.com/ok/grandison

In 1996 longtime innkeepers Claudia and Bob Wright moved their bed and breakfast into a different building in a lovely part of town. Located at Maney Park, the Grandison now occupies a 1904 Victorian mansion with carved mahogany woodwork, a curved staircase, stained and leaded glass windows, and a spacious round front porch extending from a two-story corner bay. The Grandison has a main parlor and music parlor, a large dining room and full basement with meeting and conference rooms. It's the perfect place for weddings and receptions, retreats and conferences. Also available are a guest kitchenette and a gift shop with Grandison Keepsakes, antique collectibles, and artistically different gifts.

Sausage Cheese Biscuits

Our friend who is a contract baker gave up this recipe when she was too busy to cook for us one day. They are so easy to make and delicious, too.

2¼ cups baking mix
⅔ cup milk
1 cup shredded Cheddar cheese
1 cup cooked crumbled sausage

Preheat oven to 375°. In large bowl stir together baking mix and milk. Add cheese and sausage. Mixture should be sticky. (You may need to add additional milk.) Drop dough onto ungreased baking sheet. Bake 10 to 15 minutes. Serve warm or reheat in microwave for 10 seconds per biscuit. Yields 15 to 20 biscuits.

Salsa Eggs

This is one of the most asked for breakfasts at the Grandison Inn. It can feed two to twenty, depending on how many ramekins you have. It can also be made the night before—leaving the egg out until ready to bake.

½ cup (8 ounces) chipped ham
4 tablespoons salsa
4 eggs
½ cup shredded Cheddar cheese

Preheat oven to 400°. Spray 4 ramekins with nonstick spray. Place 2 tablespoons ham in bottom of each of 4 ramekins. Add 1 tablespoon salsa over ham. Break 1 egg over ham and salsa and bake ramekins about 10 minutes or until egg white is almost set. Cover each ramekin with ⅛ cup cheese. Put back in oven for 5 minutes or until the cheese is melted. Serve with croissants or muffins and fresh fruit. Yields 4 servings.

Pumpkin Nut Bread

When our kids were small we carved pumpkins one Halloween. We had so much pumpkin left over that we searched for a recipe that had pumpkin in it, and this was our favorite.

3⅓ cups all-purpose flour
1 teaspoon ground cinnamon
3 cups sugar
1 teaspoon ground nutmeg
2 teaspoons baking soda
1 teaspoon salt
2 cups pumpkin
⅔ cup water
4 eggs
1 cup chopped nuts
    (walnuts or hazelnuts)
1 cup olive oil
1 teaspoon vanilla extract

Preheat oven to 350°. Mix the flour, cinnamon, sugar, nutmeg, baking soda, and salt in bowl. Make a well in the mixture and add pumpkin, water, eggs, nuts, oil, and vanilla. Stir carefully, just enough to moisten dry ingredients. Pour batter into 8½ x 4½ x 2½-inch loaf pan. Bake about 1 hour. Yields 1 loaf.

Cake Mix Cookies

This recipe is from Dorthea Wright, a fraternity house mother for over ten years. She was always cooking for a crowd.

1 cup confectioners' sugar
1 (18.25-ounce) box Devil's Food Cake
2 tablespoons water
2 eggs
½ cup oil
1 teaspoon almond extract
½ cup chopped nuts (pecans or walnuts)

Preheat oven to 350°. Pour confectioners' sugar in bowl. Put cake mix, water, eggs, oil, extract, and nuts in bowl. Mix until dough forms. Break off cookie-size pieces and drop into bowl of sugar. Roll in sugar until it is in shape of a ball. Place balls on cookie sheet and bake 8 to 10 minutes. Yields 4 dozen cookies.

Note: Yellow Cake Mix goes well with vanilla or lemon extract.

MEADOWLAKE RANCH BED & BREAKFAST

3450 S 137th W Avenue
Sand Springs, OK 74063
(918) 494-6000 (phone)
(800) 256-5323 (toll free)
meadowlakeranch@cox.net
www.meadowlakeranch.com

Meadowlake Ranch is a year-round bed and breakfast with dude ranch activities from March thru October. It sits on nearly three hundred acres of wooded hills, lush valleys, high prairies, and spring-fed lakes. Our guests enjoy bluff-top log cabins, lakeside Indian tepees, horseback riding on scenic trails, fishing, hiking, canoeing, throwing tomahawks, and shooting black powder rifles. We are located just fifteen minutes west of Tulsa in former Indian territory on the site of one of the largest oil discoveries in Oklahoma. (Sadly, most of the oil was removed before we became the new owners.) This is an area of pristine natural beauty, rich in wildlife and cowboy and Indian heritage and tradition.

Meadowlake Mulch

Salad dressing:
Extra virgin olive oil
Red wine vinegar
Salt and pepper
1 teaspoon Spike or Greek seasoning

Salad:
2 heads iceberg lettuce
1 head red leaf lettuce
6 to 12 mushrooms, chopped
2 (14½-ounce) cans quartered
   artichoke hearts
½ purple onion, sliced
1 clove garlic, finely chopped
Romano and Parmesan cheese
6 strips well-cooked bacon, crumbled
1 (4-ounce) jar pimiento

Mix salad dressing with equal parts olive oil and red wine vinegar. Season with salt, pepper, and Spike to taste.

Tear and wash both iceberg and red leaf lettuce leaves in half. Place in very large bowl and drain. Add chopped mushrooms, artichoke hearts, onion, and garlic. Cover completely with grated Romano and Parmesan cheese. Pour dressing over salad and mix by hand. Knead and tear lettuce into smaller pieces. Sprinkle more cheese on top with crumbled bacon bits and pimiento. Yields 6 to 10 servings.

Tom's Country Breakfast

1 (10-count) can sourdough biscuits

Sausage gravy:
1 pound maple flavored pork sausage
Whole wheat flour
Garlic powder
Chili powder
2% milk

Eggs:
½ cup milk
10 large eggs
1 tablespoon chopped red bell pepper
1 tablespoon chopped yellow bell pepper
3 to 4 chopped fresh scallions
3 large portabella mushrooms, chopped
1 tablespoon Worcestershire sauce
Salt and pepper

Bake biscuits according to directions on package and keep warm.

Cook sausage over medium heat, flatten to ¼-inch thick to cook thoroughly. Drain cooked sausages on paper towels. Pour sausage grease into another skillet and heat to medium. Add enough whole wheat flour to saturate grease. Add garlic powder and pepper to taste, then slowly stir in enough 2% milk until gravy has proper consis-

tency, reduce heat to low and continue stirring occasionally until serving time.

Mix ½ cup milk with 10 eggs, red and yellow bell peppers, scallions, and mushrooms. Add Worcestershire sauce and salt and pepper to taste. Reheat first skillet to medium and add egg mix. Continually scrape eggs from bottom of skillet to mix with leftover sausage spices. Serve eggs with biscuits and gravy and sausage on side. Yields 4 servings.

Note: Don't expect light and fluffy eggs. This is heavy, hearty 'work-till-dark-and-dance-all-nite' country fare.

Myersy's Blackberry Cobbler

6 cups blackberries
1 cup sugar
2 (9-inch) piecrusts

Combine the blackberries with the sugar and pour into 1 piecrust. Cut other piecrust into strips and place on top of pie to cover. Place in cold oven, turn oven to 425°, and bake about 45 minutes. Serve with your favorite ice cream. Yields 12 servings.

DUFUR VALLEY BED & BREAKFAST

82439 Dufur Valley Road
P.O. Box 8
Dufur, OR 97021
(541) 467-2602 (phone)
(800) 846-7313 (toll free)
suzi@dufurvalley.com
www.dufurvalley.com

Just fifteen miles south of the Dalles in Dufur, Oregon, this historic Oregon farmhouse, built in 1912, has been restored to its original charm as well as expanded and is now open for your enjoyment as a premiere bed and breakfast. Dufur Valley Bed & Breakfast is the perfect vacation destination for the outdoor enthusiast, being uniquely surrounded by Mt. Hood, the Columbia River Gorge, and the Deschutes River. We are located close to both water and snow skiing, snowboarding, whitewater rafting, fishing, hunting, hiking, windsurfing, and scenic byways. Whether you are looking for an adventure or a quiet retreat, consider Dufur Valley Bed & Breakfast the next time you want to get away.

Yogurt Fruit Sauce

8 ounces lemon or lime yogurt
Dash of ground cinnamon
¼ to ½ cup heavy cream

In small bowl mix yogurt and cinnamon well. Add heavy cream and whip to desired consistency. Should be creamy and smooth. Yields 1½ cups.

Note: Serve with bowl of fresh-cut, assorted fruit. Can be stored in refrigerator for 1 week.

Herbed Steak and Pepper Omelet

¼ cup corn or olive oil
1 pound round or sirloin steak, cut into short, thin strips
2 cups thinly sliced peppers (green, red, or yellow or combination)
¼ cup chopped fresh chives
¼ cup chopped fresh basil
3 eggs
Dash of salt
Dash of pepper
Dash of nutmeg
¼ cup Mexican cheese mix (optional)

In fry pan, heat oil on medium high and sauté steak and peppers about 3 minutes. Add chives and basil and sauté for another 3 minutes. Set aside, cover, and keep warm. Coat cold, 8-inch skillet with cooking spray. Using fork, combine eggs, salt, pepper, and nutmeg until well mixed. Pour egg mixture into prepared pan and cook over medium heat. As eggs set, run spatula around edges and lift to allow uncooked egg portion to flow underneath. When eggs are set but still shiny, remove from heat and spoon steak mixture (about ½ cup) either into center for French omelet or to one side for regular omelet and then fold. Add Mexican cheese, if using, and spread evenly over filling before folding. Transfer to warm plate. Yields 1 serving.

Note: When making multiples, can be kept warm in foil on low oven.

Festive French Toast

8 eggs
1½ cups heavy cream
½ cup milk
1 tablespoon vanilla extract
½ teaspoon ground cinnamon
12 slices thick French bread
1½ cups crushed Rice Chex cereal
Fresh fruit, cut into bite-size pieces
Maple syrup
Confectioners' sugar
Nondairy whipped cream

Preheat griddle or fry pan to 375°. Whisk eggs, cream, milk, and vanilla together for 3 minutes (should be consistency of light batter). Add cinnamon and mix. Dip bread into mixture—do *not* soak—and then dip one side of bread into cereal. Place on griddle cereal-side down first. Turn when golden brown. Cook other side. Place two slices on warmed plate. Top with fresh fruit assortment. Drizzle syrup over all and dust with confectioners' sugar. Top with dollop of whipped cream and piece of fresh fruit. Yields 6 servings.

Variation: Go tropical and use fruits such as pineapple, kiwi, mango, or papaya. Add small amount of pineapple juice to maple syrup before drizzling. Top with toasted shredded coconut.

Apple Crêpes

Crêpes:
3 large eggs
1 cup milk
⅓ cup water
3 tablespoons melted butter
1 cup unbleached flour
¼ teaspoon salt

Filling:
3 tablespoons butter
3 large, tart cooking apples, peeled,
    cored, and sliced ½-inch thick
2 tablespoons firmly packed
    light brown sugar
½ teaspoon apple pie spice

Caramel sauce:
1½ cups heavy cream
⅔ cup firmly packed dark brown sugar
½ cup corn syrup
2 tablespoons butter
2 teaspoons vanilla extract

Confectioners' sugar
Whipped cream

Place crêpe ingredients into deep bowl. Using large whisk, beat batter vigorously by hand until mixture is smooth, about 30 seconds. Scrape bowl, if needed, and beat 15 seconds longer. Batter should be like smooth heavy cream. If needed, adjust batter consistency by adding more milk or more flour. Cover and refrigerate 1 to 3 hours, allowing mixture to absorb liquid and swell. Can be prepared 8 to 10 hours ahead of time. Bring batter to room temperature and stir before using. Strain batter if lumpy.

For filling, melt butter in skillet over medium-high heat. Add apples and sprinkle with sugar. Cook over medium heat until sugar melts and begins to turn amber color, 5 to 8 minutes. Apples will soften but still hold their shape. Sprinkle apples with apple pie spice and remove from stove. Keep warm.

For sauce, put cream in deep saucepan and warm over medium heat. Mix in sugar, corn syrup, and butter with whisk. Stir until sugar is dissolved, about 4 minutes. Remove from heat and stir in vanilla. Keep warm in hot water bath until ready to serve.

Heat prepared crêpe pan over medium-high heat until hot, but not smoking. Stir batter a few times. Remove pan from heat and ladle in ¼ cup batter, tilting and rotating pan quickly in all directions to coat entire surface evenly. Return pan to heat. In about 1½ minutes carefully turn crêpe and cook 30 seconds. Invert pan and release crêpe onto towel. Repeat until all batter is used. Cover crêpes with towel to keep warm until ready to use. To serve place crêpe on work surface and spoon filling on one quarter. Fold crêpe into quarters. Place two crêpes on warm plate and ladle on caramel sauce, but don't drown them. Dust with confectioners' sugar and top with dollop of whipped cream. Serve immediately. Yields 8 servings.

Mocha Nut Muffins

½ cup (1 stick) butter or margarine
¾ cup firmly packed brown sugar
3 tablespoons finely ground coffee
2 teaspoons vanilla extract
2 large eggs
¼ cup dark rum or water
1¾ cups all-purpose flour
1½ teaspoons baking powder
1 (12-ounce) bag semisweet chocolate chips
1 cup coarsely chopped walnuts

Preheat oven to 350°. With electric mixer, beat together butter, brown sugar, coffee, and vanilla until fluffy. Add eggs one at a time, then rum or water; beating well after each addition. Mix flour with baking powder. Add to batter, beating slowly to blend, then faster until batter is well mixed. Stir in chocolate chips and walnuts. Fill twelve greased muffin cups to rim with batter—mixture doesn't overflow when baked. Bake until golden brown around edges, about 20 minutes. Best served hot or warm. Yields 1 dozen muffins.

Excelsior Inn

754 East 13th Avenue
Eugene, OR 97401
(541) 342-6963 (phone)
(541) 342-1417 (fax)
(800) 321-6963 (toll free)
info@excelsiorinn.com
www.excelsiorinn.com

Welcome to Excelsior. The inn features fourteen rooms in an elegant European style. The restaurant is known for its fine cuisine and award-winning desserts. The Excelsior is conveniently located one block from the University of Oregon, across from Sacred Heart Medical Center. The Eugene area is host to a full calendar of fairs and festivals, including the Bach Festival, Art in the Vineyard, the Eugene Ballet Company, and Eugene Celebration. Many of Oregon's most scenic areas, such as the beautiful Oregon coast and majestic Cascade Mountains, are just a short drive away.

Risotto Alla Milanese

Generous pinch of saffron
10 cups veal and chicken stocks
1 cup (2 sticks) butter
2 onions, coarsely chopped
4 ounces bone marrow
2 pounds arborio rice
6 ounces (1¼ cups) Parmesan cheese, grated

Put generous pinch of saffron in cup with about ¼ cup hot stock. In soup pot, heat a little butter and sauté onions and bone marrow about 15 minutes. Remove onion, add rice, and stir a few minutes. Slowly add broth as needed. When rice is almost done, add broth mixture with saffron, remaining butter, and cheese. Serve on large platter with main course, such as Osso Bucco. Yields 8 to 12 servings.

Vitello Farcito con Funghi Salvia

16 (2-ounce) slices veal
Flour for dusting
¾ cup olive oil
16 sage leaves
16 thin slices prosciutto di Parma
16 thin slices Fontina cheese
4 plus 4 tablespoons butter
1 tablespoon chopped shallots
3 cups sliced mushrooms
1 cup Marsala
1 cup veal demi-glace
2 tablespoons truffle oil

Gently pound veal until slices are ¼-inch thick and dust with flour. In large sauté pan over medium-high heat add olive oil and when hot, quickly sear veal on both sides. Remove from heat and keep warm. Put sage leaf between prosciutto slice and slice of Fontina. Place this, Fontina-side up, on veal slice. In sauté pan over medium heat melt 4 tablespoons butter and add shallots, then mushrooms, and cook for 1 minute. Add Marsala and reduce by half. Slowly add demi-glace. When sauce is at proper consistency, add remaining 4 tablespoons butter, truffle oil, salt, and pepper. Top veal slices with sauce and serve at once. Yields 8 servings.

The Campbell House

THE CAMPBELL HOUSE

252 Pearl Street
Eugene, OR 97401
(541) 343-1119 (phone)
(541) 343-2258 (fax)
(800) 264-2519 (toll free)
campbellhouse@campbellhouse.com
www.campbellhouse.com

The Campbell House is located downtown, but tucked away from the traffic and buzz of downtown Eugene. It is an elegant, yet comfortable, turn-of-the-century Queen Anne-style house in the east Skinner Butte historic district. The inn is tastefully decorated, cozy, and inviting. It is near several of Eugene's best restaurants, shops, riverside paths, and the University of Oregon.

The Campbell House Scones

3 cups all-purpose flour
⅓ cup sugar
2½ teaspoons baking powder
½ teaspoon baking soda
¾ teaspoon salt
¾ cup (1½ sticks) firm butter, cut into small pieces
¾ cup chopped dried fruit or nuts (optional)
1 cup buttermilk
Cinnamon sugar

Preheat oven to 400°. In large bowl, stir together flour, sugar, baking powder, soda, and salt until thoroughly blended. Using pastry blender or knife, cut butter into flour mixture until it resembles coarse cornmeal. Stir in fruit or nuts, if desired. Make a well in center of butter-flour mixture. Add buttermilk all at once. Stir mixture with fork until dough pulls away from

sides of bowl. With hands, gather dough into ball and turn out onto lightly floured board. Divide dough into four parts and lightly pat each part into a circle. Cut each circle into four parts and place wedges on greased cookie sheet. Sprinkle scones with cinnamon sugar, if desired. Bake 12 minutes. Serve warm with jam and butter. Yields 16 scones.

Mediterranean Frittata

1 (12-ounce) can artichokes, drained and chopped
1 (6-ounce) can black olives, sliced
8 to 10 eggs
1 cup crumbled feta cheese
½ cup grated Parmesan cheese
½ cup cottage cheese
1 tablespoon minced garlic
2 teaspoons onion powder
2 teaspoons salt
1 tablespoon chopped parsley
1 small tomato, sliced

Preheat oven to 400°. Place artichokes and olives in greased round pie pan. In separate bowl whisk eggs and add cheeses, garlic, and spices. Pour egg mixture over artichokes and olives. Bake 35 minutes or until firm in center. Garnish with tomato slices and Parmesan cheese. Yields 4 servings.

Chile-Cheese Egg Puff

12 large eggs
½ cup all-purpose flour
1 teaspoon baking powder
1 pint (2 cups) cottage cheese
1 pound grated Monterey Jack cheese
8 ounces chopped green chiles
Chives
Salsa

Preheat oven to 350°. Beat eggs until lemon colored. Add flour, baking powder, cottage cheese, and Jack cheese. Blend until smooth. Stir in chiles. Pour into buttered 9 x 13-inch pan or individual oven boats. Bake for 35 minutes or until firm and set in middle. Garnish with chives and serve with salsa on the side. Yields 8 to 12 servings.

The Campbell House Honey Oats

1 cup vegetable oil
⅓ cup honey
1 teaspoon vanilla extract
½ teaspoon ground cinnamon
8 cups rolled oats
1 cup slivered almonds
1 cup chopped pecans
½ cup dried cranberries
½ cup raisins

Preheat oven to 300°. In small saucepan heat oil, honey, vanilla, and cinnamon together over low heat. In a large bowl mix rolled oats and nuts. Pour heated mixture over oats and nuts and spread on cookie sheet. Bake 60 minutes. After granola has cooled, fold in cranberries and raisins. Store in airtight container. Yields about 11 cups.

HOSTESS HOUSE

5758 N.E. Emerson St.
Portland, OR 97218-2406
(503) 282-7892 (phone)
(800) 760-7799 (toll free)
hostess@hostesshouse.com
www.hostesshouse.com

Providing outstanding hospitality since 1988, the Hostess House is centrally located for easy access to major arteries.

Guests are coddled and well fed, and they enjoy repeat visits to this outstanding home. You'll enjoy the City of Roses as you view an incredible rose garden, the Japanese Garden, Chinese Garden, and Interpretive Center. Visit historic sights and museums, tour wineries, golf, hike the nature trails, or take a cruise up the Columbia or Willamette Rivers.

German Apple Pancake

2 eggs, beaten
6 tablespoons milk
6 tablespoons all-purpose flour
¼ teaspoon salt
1½ tablespoons butter
1 cup thinly sliced cooking apples
¼ cup sugar
¼ teaspoon ground cinnamon

Preheat oven to 400°. Blend eggs, milk, flour, and salt with mixer or lightly in blender. Heat 9-inch round cake pan in oven until very hot. Put in butter and swirl in hot pan. Pour in batter. Quickly place apples around edge in sunburst fashion or just sprinkle sliced apples over top and push under batter. Combine sugar and cinnamon and sprinkle on top. Bake 20 to 25 minutes until golden. Serve immediately with hot Apple Cider Syrup (see recipe below). Yields 2 to 3 servings.

Apple Cider Syrup

1 cup sugar
2 tablespoons cornstarch
1 cinnamon stick
2 cups fresh, natural apple cider
2 tablespoons fresh lemon juice
¼ cup (½ stick) butter

Mix all ingredients except butter and cook, stirring until mixture boils and thickens. Boil 1 minute longer. Remove from heat and stir in butter. Serve immediately. Store

remaining syrup in refrigerator. Take cinnamon stick out after syrup cools. (Syrup freezes well, too.) Also goes well on French toast made with cinnamon bread. Yields about 2½ cups.

Crustless Quiche

½ cup bacon, fried and crumbled
2 tablespoons onion flakes
1 cup shredded Swiss cheese
2 cups skim milk
½ cup baking mix
4 eggs
¼ teaspoon salt
Dash of white pepper

Preheat oven to 350°. Combine meat, onion, and cheese. Coat 9-inch-square pan with nonstick spray and add meat mixture. Mix milk, baking mix, eggs, salt, and pepper on high in blender and pour over mixture in pan. Bake 50 minutes until knife comes out clean. Let sit 3 minutes before serving. Yields 4 servings.

Cinnamon-Apple Cake

1½ plus ¼ cups sugar
¾ cup (6 ounces) fat-free cream cheese
½ cup (1 stick) butter
1 teaspoon vanilla extract
2 eggs
1½ cups all-purpose flour
1½ teaspoons baking powder
¼ teaspoon salt
2 teaspoons ground cinnamon
3 cups chopped, peeled apples
    (about 2 large)

Preheat oven to 325°. Coat 8-inch springform pan with nonstick spray. Beat 1½ cups sugar, cream cheese, butter, and vanilla at medium speed until well blended, about 4 minutes. Add eggs, 1 at a time, beating after each addition. Combine flour, baking powder, and salt. Add flour mixture to creamed mixture and beat at low speed until blended. Combine remaining ¼ cup sugar with cinnamon. Combine 2 tablespoons cinnamon mixture with apples and stir apples into batter. Pour batter into prepared pan and sprinkle with remaining cinnamon sugar. Bake 1 hour and 15 minutes or until cake pulls away from sides of pan. Cool cake on wire rack and, because cake is so tender, cut with serrated knife. Yields 12 servings.

Cream Cheese Crêpes with Strawberry Topping

Crêpes:
⅔ cup all-purpose flour
½ teaspoon salt
3 eggs, beaten
1 cup skim milk
12 ounces light cream cheese, softened
¼ to ½ cup sour cream at
    room temperature
¼ cup sugar
1 teaspoon vanilla extract

Strawberry topping:
1 plus 1 pint freshly hulled strawberries
½ cup plus 2 tablespoons cold water
½ cup sugar
2 tablespoons cornstarch
Juice of 1 lemon

Combine flour, salt, and eggs and beat until smooth. Slowly add milk, mixing until blended. Pour ¼ cup batter into lightly greased, 8-inch crêpe pan, tilting pan to cover bottom. Cook at medium heat until lightly browned on both sides. Preheat oven to 325°. Combine cream cheese, sour cream, sugar, and vanilla and blend to spreading consistency. Spread about ¼ cup mixture on one side of each crêpe. Roll up like jelly roll. Place in 13 x 9-inch baking dish. Bake 15 to 20 minutes or until thoroughly heated.

To make topping, dice 1 pint berries and combine with ½ cup water and sugar.

Put on stove to boil. Mix cornstarch with remaining 2 tablespoons water and add to boiling mixture, stirring constantly until mixture is clear and thick. Add lemon juice. Put remaining pint of berries on crêpes and pour berry glaze over berries and crêpes. May top with whipped cream. Yields 8 servings.

Note: When strawberries are not in season, substitute sliced bananas for 1 pint fresh berries used on the crêpes.

Hostess House

Orange Sour Cream Yeast Roll

Yeast roll:
2¼ teaspoons (1 package) active dry yeast
¼ cup warm water
1¾ cups plus 1 cup all-purpose flour
¼ cup sugar
1 teaspoon salt
⅔ cup sour cream at room temperature
6 tablespoons melted butter
2 eggs
1 tablespoon orange zest

Filling:
2 tablespoons melted butter
¾ cup sugar
¾ cup toasted coconut
2 tablespoons grated orange peel

Glaze:
¼ cup sugar
⅓ cup sour cream
4 tablespoons butter
3 tablespoons orange juice
¼ cup toasted coconut

In small bowl dissolve yeast in warm water (110° to 115°). In large mixing bowl combine yeast mix, 1¾ cups flour, sugar, salt,

sour cream, butter, eggs, and orange peel. Beat 3 minutes on medium speed. Stir in enough remaining flour, about 1 cup, by hand, to form soft dough. Cover and let rise in warm place until doubled, 1 to 2 hours. Oil 9 x 13-inch pan.

For filling, combine butter, sugar, toasted coconut, and orange peel in small bowl. (To toast coconut, place it on baking sheet and bake in preheated 325° oven for 15 minutes, or until lightly browned. Watch carefully and stir frequently.) Knead dough 12 to 15 times. Divide and roll half the dough into 12-inch circle. Sprinkle with half of filling mixture. Cut into 12 wedges and roll each wedge, starting with wide end, to form crescent-shaped rolls. Repeat with remaining dough. Place rolls in pan making three rows of eight rolls each. Cover and let rise until doubled, 1 to 2 hours. Preheat oven to 350° and bake 25 to 30 minutes. Leave rolls in pan.

In small saucepan, combine glaze ingredients. Bring to a boil and stir for 3 minutes. Pour warm glaze over warm rolls. Sprinkle with coconut. Yields 24 rolls.

PINE MEADOW INN BED & BREAKFAST

1000 Crow Road
Merlin, OR 97532
(541) 471-6277 (phone)
(800) 554-0806 (toll free)
pmi@pinemeadowinn.com
www.pinemeadowinn.com

A distinctive retreat in a tranquil garden setting near the Rogue River, Pine Meadow Inn features organic and English gardens, Koi pond, and healthy gourmet breakfasts. Visitors are happy to discover nearby vineyards and wineries, day trips to Crater Lake,

Oregon Caves National Monument, Wildlife Images, the Oregon coast, California Redwoods, and rafting and fishing on the wild and scenic Rogue River.

Spiced Pear Fans

3 ripe pears (Red Anjou preferred)
½ cup apple juice (may also use apricot or peach)
½ cup sherry
1 teaspoon ground cinnamon
¼ teaspoon cloves
1 tablespoon brown sugar
¼ cup berry preserves
6 sprigs thyme or other herb, about 2 inches long

Cut each pear in half. With sharp knife cut core section away. Turn pear over on cutting board so it is face down. Cut pear into thin vertical slices, leaving pear intact so as to "fan out" on plate. (If you discard outer pieces on either side, it will be easier to lay fanned pear flat.) Coat baking dish with cooking spray and place each pear face down in dish, keeping pears intact. Preheat oven to 350°. Mix together juice, sherry, cinnamon, cloves, and brown sugar. Pour over pears in baking dish, reserving 1 tablespoon juice. Bake pears 20 to 30 minutes, depending on firmness of pears. While pears are baking, mix reserved juice with preserves and divide among six small individual serving plates. When pears are done, carefully place halves cut-side down on plates. Be careful to keep cut pears "intact"—they are easier to handle after they have cooled. Yields 6 servings.

Fresh Peach Sauce

This is a favorite way to use fresh peaches in the summertime. We serve this sauce with our fresh grapes, but you can also use this with strawberries or blueberries.

1 teaspoon dried orange zest
1 cup orange juice
2 tablespoons cornstarch
½ teaspoon ground cinnamon
2 tablespoons brown sugar
2 tablespoons granulated sugar
1 teaspoon vanilla extract
5 large ripe peaches, peeled and sliced or diced

In medium saucepan, stir together all ingredients except for peaches. Gently stir in peaches. Cook and stir until thickened and bubbly. Cook over low heat for 5 minutes more, stirring frequently. Yields 4 cups.

Granny Smith Oatmeal Waffle

If you're in a hurry, you can make pancakes from this batter without the one-hour wait. For pancakes, just reduce oil to 2 tablespoons.

1½ cups all-purpose flour
1 cup thick old-fashioned rolled oats
2 teaspoons baking powder
1½ teaspoons ground cinnamon
1 teaspoon baking soda
½ teaspoon salt
½ teaspoon ground nutmeg
½ teaspoon vanilla extract
1½ cups nonfat buttermilk
2 tablespoons brown sugar or honey
1 egg plus egg substitute equal to 2 eggs
4 tablespoons vegetable oil
2 medium Granny Smith apples, grated

Mix flour, oats, baking powder, cinnamon, baking soda, salt, and nutmeg. Add vanilla, buttermilk, brown sugar or honey, egg, egg substitute, and oil. Mix all together by hand, using as few strokes as possible and

gently fold in grated apple. Batter should be thick. Let sit for 1 hour before using. Bake in preheated waffle iron until done. Yields 4 to 6 waffles or 10 to 12 pancakes.

Chocolate Chip Orange Delights

Our guests love this "sweet dreams" treat by their bedside.

1 cup (2 sticks) butter, softened
1 cup firmly packed brown sugar
½ cup granulated sugar
2 eggs
1 teaspoon vanilla extract
1 teaspoon orange flavoring
1½ cups all-purpose flour
1 teaspoon baking soda
1 teaspoon ground cinnamon
½ teaspoon ground nutmeg
1 tablespoon dried grated orange zest
3 cups thick old-fashioned rolled oats
1 cup chocolate chips (can substitute raisins)

Preheat oven to 350°. In large bowl combine butter and sugars and beat together until creamy. Beat in eggs, vanilla, and orange flavoring. Stir in flour, baking soda, cinnamon, nutmeg, and grated orange peel. Mix well. Stir in oats and chocolate chips. Drop by rounded spoonfuls onto ungreased cookie sheet and bake 10 minutes. Let cool on cookie sheet 5 minutes or so, and place on paper towels to cool.

Note: We rotate pans after 5 minutes when baking cookies. Yields about 4 dozen cookies.

Dilled Fresh Veggie Frittata

Guests particularly enjoy this dish during the growing season, when they can stroll through our vegetable and fruit garden and see where the onions, asparagus, zucchini, and dill are grown.

1 tablespoon olive oil
½ cup asparagus tips
1 medium zucchini, sliced and quartered
8 eggs
Egg substitute equal to 4 eggs
2 cups nonfat cottage cheese
2 cups grated low-fat mozzarella cheese
½ cup chopped green onions
2 teaspoons dill plus extra for garnish

Preheat oven to 350°. Heat oil in skillet over medium heat and lightly sauté asparagus tips and zucchini. Be careful not to overcook. Combine eggs and egg substitute and beat until light and fluffy. Mix in cottage cheese and mozzarella cheese. Add green onions, sautéed vegetables, and dill, mixing until well blended. Pour into a 9 x 13-inch baking dish coated with nonstick spray. Sprinkle top with more dill. Bake 45 minutes or until a knife inserted into the center comes out clean. When using individual ramekins, reduce baking time to 30 minutes. You can prepare this the night before baking. Yields 8 servings.

Strawberries Romanoff Light

Our guests love this nonfat version of an old favorite, especially when they see us picking the strawberries from our organic gardens.

2 pints fully ripe strawberries
¼ cup sugar
½ cup fresh orange juice
Zest of ½ orange
¼ teaspoon ground cinnamon
⅛ teaspoon rum flavoring
½ cup nonfat sour cream

Wash and hull berries, cutting larger berries in half. Cover with paper towel and refrigerate. To make sauce, combine sugar, orange juice, and zest in small saucepan. Over high heat bring to a boil, reduce heat, and simmer for 10 minutes. Blend in cinnamon, rum flavoring, and sour cream. Cover and chill at least 30 minutes. Place berries in individual serving dishes and top with sauce. Yields 6 to 8 servings.

OVAL DOOR BED & BREAKFAST INN

988 Lawrence Street at Tenth
Eugene, OR 97401-2827
(541) 683-3160 (phone)
(541) 485-0260 (fax)
(800) 882-3160 (toll free)
ovaldoor@ovaldoor.com
www.ovaldoor.com

An inviting and elegant oasis in the heart of downtown Eugene, the Oval Door Inn features impeccable hospitality and an outstanding gourmet breakfast. The inn is in easy walking distance of many fine restaurants, the Hult Center for Performing Arts, downtown shops, business center, and only twelve blocks from the University of Oregon. The inn is in driving distance of Willamette Valley Wineries, the McKenzie River, the Oregon coast, and Willamette Pass. Golf, hiking, kayaking, biking, fishing, shopping, and skiing are all close-by activities.

Sweet Potato-Chive Biscuits

½ cup cooked and mashed sweet potatoes
  (about 2 medium)
⅓ cup milk
¾ cup brown sugar
1½ cups all-purpose flour
1½ teaspoons baking powder
6 tablespoons chilled butter
½ teaspoon salt
¼ teaspoon pepper
8 chive stems, minced
Melted butter

Preheat oven to 435°. In mixing bowl combine potatoes and milk. In another bowl combine sugar, flour, and baking powder. Using pastry blender cut butter into dry ingredients. Add salt, pepper, and chives. Add flour mix to potato mix and blend just until combined. On floured surface, roll dough out to ¾-inch thickness. Using round, 2-inch cookie cutter, cut out biscuits. Place on cookie sheet and brush with butter. Bake for 12 to 15 minutes or until golden. Yields 20 biscuits.

Carrot Cake Pancakes

¾ cup all-purpose flour
2 tablespoons ground cinnamon
1 teaspoon baking soda
½ teaspoon salt
¼ cup walnuts, chopped to pea size
  (optional)
¼ cup raisins
1 cup buttermilk
3 tablespoons melted butter,
  slightly cooled
1 egg
1 carrot, grated and squeezed through
  sieve, or cheesecloth, until dry
2 egg whites
1 tablespoon sugar

Cream cheese icing:
3 ounces cream cheese at room
  temperature
1 tablespoon soft butter
¼ cup sifted confectioners' sugar

Preheat griddle to 350°. Combine flour, cinnamon, baking soda, salt, nuts, and raisins in large bowl. In separate bowl combine buttermilk, butter, and egg with carrot. With mixer or hand beaters, whip egg whites with sugar until soft peaks

form. Combine dry ingredients with buttermilk mixture just until blended. Stir in one-fourth of egg whites until incorporated. Fold in remaining whites gently. Pouring ¼ cup batter onto griddle, cook pancakes until golden on both sides. Layer cakes on warm plate.

For icing, in small mixing bowl, combine cream cheese and butter until well blended. Slowly incorporate confectioners' sugar until completely mixed. Use pastry bag to decorate pancakes with icing. Serve with maple syrup. Yields 4 servings, 12 (3-inch) cakes.

Apple Gingerbread Bread Pudding

½ loaf gingerbread, cut in small cubes
1 Macintosh apple, peeled and diced
½ cup currants
2 cups milk
½ cup cream
½ vanilla bean, cut lengthwise
    and scraped
3 eggs
2 egg yolks
½ cup sugar
½ teaspoon ground cinnamon
Dash of salt
Confectioners' sugar

Place gingerbread in generously buttered 8 x 8 x 2-inch pan. Top with apple and currants. Scald milk, cream, and vanilla bean, including scrapings. In bowl combine eggs, egg yolks, sugar, cinnamon, and salt. Hand whip until mixed. Temper egg mixture with milk mixture. (That is, pour a little at a time hot milk mixture into egg mixture while hand whipping. Do this so not to scramble eggs.) Strain through sieve into prepared pan. Press gingerbread down to ensure complete coverage with liquid. Let sit for 30 minutes or overnight. When ready to bake, preheat oven to 350°. Cover pan loosely with foil. Bake in water bath about 1 hour and 30 minutes or until done. Remove foil during last 20 minutes of baking to brown top. Cut into squares, sprinkle with confectioners' sugar, and serve hot. Yields 6 to 9 servings.

Variation: You can use individual buttered ramekins for a better presentation.

Italian Benedict

4 eggs
2 English muffins
4 slices Canadian bacon
¼ cup ricotta cheese
2 teaspoons pesto
2 tablespoons Parmesan cheese
1 cup Tomato Cream Sauce
    (see recipe below)
1 tablespoon basil chiffonade
    (sliced in long strands)

Poach eggs to soft, almost 4 minutes. Do *not* overcook eggs. Toast English muffins. Heat Canadian bacon in microwave. In small bowl combine ricotta cheese and pesto. Spread 1 tablespoon on each toasted muffin. Top with Canadian bacon. Place muffins on baking sheet. Place each poached egg on top of a toasted English muffin. Sprinkle with Parmesan cheese. Place under broiler about 30 seconds, just until cheese is melted. Remove and set English muffin on each plate. Ladle ¼ cup Tomato Cream Sauce over egg and sprinkle with basil. Serve immediately. Yields 4 servings.

Tomato Cream Sauce

1 teaspoon olive oil
1 clove garlic, minced
1 cup canned diced tomatoes
    or chopped fresh tomatoes
1 teaspoon Italian seasoning
1 teaspoon chopped fresh basil
1 teaspoon sugar
2 tablespoons cream
Salt and pepper

In small saucepan, heat olive oil on medium heat. Quickly sauté garlic, until soft, not allowing it to turn brown. Add tomatoes, Italian seasoning, and basil and let simmer 15 to 20 minutes. Add sugar and reduce heat to low. Stir in cream. Add salt and pepper to taste. Yields 4 servings.

Maple Poached Pears

2 quarts water
1 cup pure maple syrup
    plus ½ cup for serving
1 cinnamon stick
1 vanilla bean pod, split open
1 tablespoon lemon juice
6 firm pears, your favorite
2 tablespoons mascarpone cheese
    (Italian soft cheese)
2 tablespoons sugar
½ teaspoon ground cinnamon
¼ cup whipping cream
½ cup poaching liquid (from above)
Cinnamon sugar for garnish

In large pot at least 5 inches deep bring water, 1 cup maple syrup, cinnamon stick, vanilla bean, and lemon juice to a boil. Peel pears and cut in half lengthwise. Remove core and stem. When poaching liquid comes to a boil, reduce heat and simmer pears until tender. Remove from liquid with slotted spoon. In small bowl, combine mascarpone, sugar, and cinnamon. Whip cream and fold into mixture. Keep refrigerated. In separate saucepan, heat remaining ½ cup maple syrup and add ½ cup of poaching liquid. Let cook until sauce is reduced by half. In center of small plate or shallow bowl, place 1 tablespoon cream to keep pear from sliding around. Place half pear, face up, on top of cream and ladle about 2 tablespoons sauce around bottom of bowl or plate. Place another dollop of cream into hole in pear. Sprinkle with cinnamon sugar. Serve immediately. Yields 6 servings.

SEA QUEST BED & BREAKFAST

95354 Highway 101
Yachats, OR 97498
(541) 547-3782 (phone)
(541) 548-3719 (fax)
(800) 341-4878 (toll free)
seaquest@newportnet.com
www.seaq.com

Sea Quest is located just yards from the breaking surf. Sea Quest's rooms are designed for privacy, each room having its own outside entrance and balcony. Generous private bathrooms complete with hot, bubbling Jacuzzi tubs top off your private suite. Furnished and decorated with your comfort in mind, Sea Quest has found the perfect mix of coastal fare and elegance.

Marjorie's Mom's Chocolate Banana Bundt

8 tablespoons (1 stick) butter
1 cup sugar
1 teaspoon vanilla extract
3 eggs
2 cups all-purpose flour
1 teaspoon baking powder
1 teaspoon baking soda
½ teaspoon salt
3 tablespoons sour cream
3 mashed bananas
1 cup chopped pecans
1 cup chocolate chips
2 cups confectioners' sugar
3 tablespoons coffee
1 cup melted chocolate chips

Preheat oven to 350°. In bowl and using electric mixer, cream together butter, sugar, and vanilla until fluffy. Add eggs, one at a time, mixing well. In another bowl mix flour, baking powder, baking soda, and salt. Add sour cream and bananas, then flour mixture, ending with pecans and chocolate chips. Pour batter into oiled and floured 10-inch Bundt pan. Bake 50 minutes. Mix together confectioners' sugar, coffee, and melted chocolate chips. Drizzle over cake. Yields 12 servings.

Breaded Breakfast Bacon

12 thick bacon slices
1 large egg
1 tablespoon water
1 teaspoon Dijon mustard
1 teaspoon Worcestershire sauce
1 cup fine breadcrumbs, plain or Italian

Preheat oven to 400°. Place bacon slices in single layer on baking sheet with rim. Bake 10 minutes and drain off fat. In long, shallow bowl, whisk egg with water. Add mustard and Worcestershire sauce and mix well. Place crumbs on wax paper. Remove bacon from baking sheet and coat each piece on both sides with egg mixture, then crumbs. Return to baking sheet and bake until crisp, about 15 minutes longer. Drain on paper towels. Yields 6 servings.

Hide the Eggs

4 tablespoons butter
4 tablespoons all-purpose flour
3 cups warm milk
1 (8-ounce) package cream cheese
1 heaping tablespoon mustard
1 clove garlic, minced
Salt
Dash of Tabasco
½ teaspoon paprika
8 to 10 eggs
Breadcrumbs for topping
Parmesan cheese for topping

Melt butter in saucepan and whisk in flour. Add milk and when sauce is bubbling, add cream cheese, mustard, and garlic. Season with salt, Tabasco, and paprika. Cook until sauce thickens and pour into casserole dish. Preheat oven to 350°. Break eggs one at a time into sauce as if you were poaching them. Sprinkle with breadcrumbs and Parmesan cheese. Bake for 15 to 25 minutes. Serve fresh from oven with hot biscuits. Yields 8 to 10 servings.

Grated Potatoes and Bacon

1 pound bacon, plain or peppered,
   thickly sliced is better
8 eggs
1 cup mayonnaise
2 cups grated cheese, Jack, Cheddar, Swiss
1 onion, chopped
1 pound potatoes, peeled and grated
Spike (seasoning)
Salt and pepper
Parsley for garnish

Cook bacon until crisp and crumble. Preheat oven to 375°. Beat eggs and mayonnaise and add cheese, onion, potatoes, and bacon. Bake 45 minutes. Sprinkle with Spike and salt and pepper to taste. Garnish with parsley. Yields 8 servings.

THE WATER STREET INN

421 N. Water Street
Silverton, OR 97381
(503) 873-3344 (phone)
(866) 873-3344 (toll free)
info@thewaterstreetinn.com
www.thewaterstreetinn.com

In historic downtown Silverton, a town people love, the previously named Wolfard

Hotel of 1890, now known as the Water Street Inn, offers modern luxuries in the elegance of a grand old home. In the winter, relax by the fire or watch a movie in your room. In summer, enjoy the backyard garden or front-porch swing. The inn has five guest rooms, all with private baths. Of interest in the area are the town of Silverton, the Oregon Garden botanical gardens, and home of Frank Lloyd Wright's Gordon House. In the summer activities include a concert series, Silver Falls State Park, Willamette Valley tulip and iris fields, day trips to Columbia Gorge, Mt. Hood, the Oregon coast, and winery tours.

Water Street Inn Maple Granola

¼ cup canola oil
⅓ cup honey
4 tablespoons maple syrup
1 teaspoon vanilla extract

1 teaspoon almond extract
4 cups old-fashioned oats
⅔ cup rice bran, oat bran, or wheat germ
1 teaspoon cinnamon
¾ cup slivered almonds (optional)
⅛ cup sesame seeds (optional)
⅛ cup sunflower seeds (optional)

Preheat oven to 300°. In small saucepan over medium heat, stir oil, honey, syrup, and extracts until honey melts, about 3 minutes. In large bowl, toss all remaining ingredients. Pour honey mixture over oat mixture and stir to coat. Spread combined ingredients onto baking pan in an even, sparse layer. Bake 50 minutes, stirring every 10 minutes, until golden brown and toasted. Place pan on wire rack to cool. When completely cool, transfer mixture to an airtight container. You can add raisins or dried fruit to taste in one-cup amounts if desired. Stays fresh up to two weeks if stored airtight. Recipe can be multiplied; use corresponding number of pans so mixture cooks evenly. Terrific sprinkled over vanilla, or any flavor, yogurt. Yields about 6 cups.

The Water Street Inn

WOLFE MANOR INN

586 B. Street
Ashland, OR 97520
(541) 488-3676 (phone)
(541) 488-4567 (fax)
sybil@wolfemanor.com
www.wolfemanor.com

Wolfe Manor Inn is a lovingly restored, 1910 Craftsman-style inn conveniently located in the quiet neighborhood of the Historic Railroad District, surrounded by beautiful English gardens with fountains, waterfall, and Koi pond. The town of Ashland offers many festivals and music programs year-round. There are also many outdoor activities available such as cross-country and downhill skiing, white-water rafting, jet boating, kayaking, and fishing. The Oregon Caves are a day trip away.

Bagels and Lox Benedict

6 plain bagels
12 slices thinly sliced smoked salmon
12 very thin slices red onion
12 poached eggs

Lemon-Caper Sauce:
2 cups vegetable broth
3 tablespoons cornstarch
1½ cups reduced-fat sour cream
3 tablespoons lemon juice
4 tablespoons drained capers
Salt and pepper
Fresh dill sprigs

Cut bagels in half horizontally and toast. Put 2 bagel halves on each plate and top each half with onion and salmon slice. Place egg on each half.

For Lemon-Caper Sauce, in 3-quart pan whisk broth and cornstarch until smooth. Stir over medium-high heat until boiling, 2 to 3 minutes. Whisk in sour cream, lemon juice, and capers. Stir frequently just until steaming, 2 to 3 minutes. Season to taste with salt and pepper. Spoon sauce equally over portions. Garnish with dill. Yields 6 servings.

Oatmeal Buttermilk Pancakes

Citrus syrup:
1¼ cups light corn syrup
3 tablespoons fresh lemon juice
2 tablespoons grated orange peel
1 tablespoon grated lemon peel
4 teaspoons sugar

Pancakes:
1¼ cups old-fashioned oatmeal
2 cups buttermilk
2 eggs or ½ cup egg substitute
1 cup all-purpose flour
3 tablespoons sugar
1 teaspoon baking soda
1 teaspoon baking powder
½ teaspoon salt
¼ cup vegetable oil
¾ cup coarsely chopped pecans

For syrup, mix all ingredients in small bowl, stirring until sugar dissolves. Let stand at least 1 hour. Can be made ahead and refrigerated for up to two weeks.

For pancakes, in medium bowl stir together oatmeal and buttermilk until coated well. Stir in eggs until blended. Stir in flour, sugar, baking soda, baking powder, salt, oil, and pecans. Preheat lightly greased griddle or large skillet, preferably nonstick. When hot, drop batter by ¼-cup measure. Immediately reduce heat to medium-low. Cook until bubbles appear around edges and bottom is golden. Turn and cook until cooked through.

For variety, add sliced bananas, fresh blueberries, or peeled and cored, thinly sliced apples to pancakes after pouring batter on griddle. Serve with Citrus Syrup and whipped cream with sprinkle of fresh grated nutmeg. Yields 16 pancakes.

Peach Pancakes with Peachy Berry Sauce

1 cup all-purpose flour
2 tablespoons cornmeal
1 tablespoon sugar
1 teaspoon baking powder
½ teaspoon baking soda
½ teaspoon ground cinnamon
⅛ teaspoon salt
2 to 4 large peaches for 1½ cups purée
½ cup milk
1 egg, beaten
2 tablespoons vegetable oil

Peachy berry sauce:
½ cup maple syrup
1 cup fresh raspberries, blackberries
   or blueberries, or combination
1 cup thinly sliced, peeled peaches
   or nectarines or combination
Whipped cream

In bowl stir together flour, cornmeal, sugar, baking powder, baking soda, cinnamon, and salt. Make well in center of dry mixture. Pit, peel, and quarter peaches and place in food processor bowl or blender container. Cover, process, or blend until smooth to make purée. In another bowl combine milk, peach purée, egg, and oil. Add peach mixture all at once to dry mixture. Stir just until moistened; batter should be lumpy. Pour ¼ cup batter onto hot, lightly greased griddle or heavy skillet. Cook over medium heat about 2 minutes on each side or until pancakes are golden brown, turning to second side when pancakes have bubbly surfaces and edges are slightly dry.

For Peachy Berry Sauce, in saucepan over medium heat bring maple syrup just to simmer. Remove from heat. Stir in fruit. Serve over Peach Pancakes. Yields 10 pancakes.

Grilled Portobello Mushrooms with Scrambled Eggs

4 portobello mushrooms
½ cup olive oil
2 tablespoons basalmic vinegar
Garlic pepper
8 large eggs
¼ cup milk
2 tablespoons chopped fresh parsley
1 tablespoon hot red pepper flakes
1 teaspoon seasoned salt
½ cup finely diced red bell pepper
¼ cup ricotta cheese

With damp paper towel wipe mushrooms on top side to clean. Using pastry brush, brush top and bottom of mushrooms with olive oil and vinegar. Sprinkle bottom side with garlic pepper and place top side up on baking sheet. Starting with top side, broil for 4 to 6 minutes on each side, depending on thickness of mushrooms. While mushrooms are broiling, whisk together eggs, milk, chopped parsley, hot pepper flakes, and seasoned salt. Over medium heat, sauté bell pepper in skillet in small amount of butter and add egg mixture. Add ricotta cheese. As egg mixture thickens, gently lift edges to allow uncooked egg to run under cooked eggs. Cook until eggs are set, but are still moist and shiny. Place one mushroom on each of four plates, bottom-side up, and top mushrooms with eggs. Good served with sliced tomatoes sprinkled with spices. Yields 4 servings.

Pennsylvania

MAYTOWN MANOR BED & BREAKFAST

25 West High Street
P.O. Box 275
Maytown, PA 17550
(717) 426-2116 (phone)
(866) 426-2116 (toll free)
innkeepers@maytownmanorbandb.com
www.maytownmanorbandb.com

Maytown Manor Bed & Breakfast provides an inviting and relaxing retreat near Lancaster, Pennsylvania. Built in 1880, this Federal-style brick house—the former Heistand Estate—offers three thoughtfully appointed guest rooms with private baths, a parlor featuring a fireplace and piano, a relaxing porch swing, hearty breakfasts, and complimentary snacks. Maytown Manor provides easy access to main attractions like Amish Country, Hershey Park, Nissley Winery, Gettysburg, and Harrisburg. There are unique restaurants, antique stores, farmers' markets, and outlet malls. Leave the hectic world behind; come home to a peaceful sanctuary and capture that "renewed" feeling.

❧ ❧ ❧

Colonial Innkeeper's Pie

Crust:
1 cup sugar
¾ cup warm water
½ cup cocoa
½ square semisweet baking chocolate
1 tablespoon margarine

Filling:
2 cups sugar
¼ cup (1 stick) margarine
¼ cup vegetable shortening
2 eggs
1 cup milk
1 teaspoon vanilla extract
2 cups all-purpose flour
1 teaspoon baking powder
Dash of salt

2 unbaked 8-inch pie shells

For crust, combine sugar, warm water, cocoa, chocolate, and margarine in double boiler until melted. Let cool. Divide cooled chocolate between pie shells.

For filling, combine sugar, margarine, and shortening. Beat in eggs, milk, vanilla, flour, baking powder, and salt until smooth. Preheat oven to 350°. Divide batter and spoon half over chocolate layer of each pie, working from outside in. Bake 30 to 40 minutes. Yields 2 pies, 12 to 16 servings.

Maytown Manor Bed & Breakfast

332

Broccoli and Bacon Quiche

2 cups cooked broccoli
1 (9-inch) unbaked piecrust
½ cup light mayonnaise
2 tablespoons all-purpose flour
2 eggs
½ cup milk or cream
2 cups three-cheese mix
    (Romano, Parmesan, and Asiago)
⅓ cup chopped spring onions
4 slices bacon, cooked and crumbled

Preheat oven to 350°. Lay broccoli in piecrust. Combine all remaining ingredients except bacon and pour into crust over broccoli. Top with bacon. Bake 45 minutes to 1 hour. Yields 6 servings.

Note: You can vary ingredients as desired. Other combinations include adding fresh or canned crab, chunks of ham, or excluding all meat for vegetarians.

Caramel French Toast

1 cup packed light brown sugar
½ cup (1 stick) butter
2 tablespoons light corn syrup
5 eggs
1½ cups milk
1 tablespoon vanilla extract
1 loaf French bread, cut into ¾-inch
    slices, estimate 2 per person
Cinnamon sugar

In medium saucepan over medium-low heat, mix and melt brown sugar, butter, and corn syrup. Coat 9 x 13-inch baking dish with nonstick spray. Pour butter mixture into baking dish. Whisk together eggs, milk, and vanilla. Arrange bread slices in baking dish. Pour egg mixture over bread slices, not missing any areas, and using all of mixture over bread slices. Cover baking dish and refrigerate 8 to 10 hours or overnight. When ready to bake, preheat oven to 350°. Uncover baking dish and bake 45 minutes to 1 hour. Serve directly from baking dish, inverting slices onto plates. Sprinkle with cinnamon sugar. Yields about 8 servings.

Sour Cream Softies

3 cups sifted all-purpose flour
1 teaspoon salt
½ teaspoon baking powder
½ teaspoon baking soda
½ cup (1 stick) butter
1¼ cups sugar
2 eggs
1 teaspoon vanilla extract
1 cup sour cream
Cinnamon sugar

Preheat oven to 400°. Measure flour, salt, baking powder, and soda into sifter. Cream butter with sugar and blend well. Beat in eggs and vanilla. Sift in flour mixture, adding alternately with sour cream, and blend well to make thick batter. Drop by rounded tablespoonfuls, four inches apart on greased cookie sheets, spread into 2-inch rounds and sprinkle with cinnamon sugar. Bake 12 minutes or until lightly golden around edges. Remove from sheets and cool completely on wire racks. Yields 12 softies.

Peachy Fruit Salad

1 (20-ounce) can peach pie filling
1 (20-ounce) can pineapple chunks
1 (15-ounce) can mandarin oranges
1 cup red or green grapes
2 bananas, sliced
1 cup marshmallows

Combine all ingredients. (If making ahead, omit bananas and marshmallows until ready to serve.) Makes 8 servings.

GOLDEN PHEASANT COUNTRY INN

763 River Road (Route 32)
Erwinna, PA 18920
(610) 294-9595 (phone)
(610) 294-9882 (fax)
(800) 830-4474 (toll free)
barbara@goldenpheasant.com
www.goldenpheasant.com

Golden Pheasant is an 1857 Bucks County fieldstone inn nestled between the Delaware River and Canal. It was originally built as a mule barge stop and is listed on the National Register of Historic Places. Creative French cuisine by Chef Michel Faure is served in the tavern with fireplace and greenhouse overlooking canal. Romantic lodging features four-poster canopy beds, fireplaces, and river views. The inn is near scenic roads and covered bridges, and it is sixty miles from Philadelphia or New York City and only twelve miles north of New Hope.

Golden Marnier Cheesecake

1¾ cups graham cracker crumbs
¼ plus ¾ cup sugar
2 teaspoons ground cinnamon
1 stick unsalted butter at room
    temperature
24 ounces cream cheese
1 cup sour cream
⅛ teaspoon salt
1½ teaspoons vanilla extract
4 large eggs
⅓ cup Grand Marnier liqueur

Generously butter springform pan. In medium mixing bowl stir together crumbs,

¼ cup sugar, and cinnamon. Melt butter. Add to mixture and stir. Press mixture around sides of pan, leaving ½ inch uncovered. Press mixture onto bottom. Place in refrigerator until ready to use. Adjust rack one-third from top of oven and preheat oven to 275°. In large bowl of electric mixer, beat cream cheese until soft and smooth. Add sour cream and beat well. Add remaining ¾ cup sugar and beat until smooth. Add salt, vanilla, and eggs, beating well after each addition. Remove from mixer and stir in liqueur. Pour filling into crumb crust. Level and smooth top with spatula. Bake 60 minutes. Remove and cool. Remove from pan to serve. Yields 12 servings.

Roasted Pheasant with Normandy Sauce

½ cup olive oil
8 pheasant halves with ribs and skin
    (4 hens, 3 pounds each)
20 shallots, peeled, trimmed, and sliced
Salt
Freshly ground black pepper
3 pounds (8 to 10) Granny Smith apples,
    peeled and quartered
½ plus 1 cup Calvados
2 cups chicken stock
2 tablespoons cornstarch
1 cup heavy cream
Pinch of cayenne

Rub oil over pheasants. Quickly brown them on all sides in skillet over medium-high heat. Place hens, breast-sides down, in large roasting pan. Add shallots to pan. Sprinkle with salt and pepper. Add apples and ½ cup Calvados. Cook about 45 minutes or until juices run clear. Remove hens, shallots, and apples from pan to serving dish. Pour off fat and return pan to stove. Add chicken stock and bring to a boil. Scrape bottom vigorously with wooden spoon. Reduce liquid by half. Pour deglazing liquid through fine sieve into large saucepan. Add cornstarch to saucepan. Add

remaining cup Calvados. Bring to a boil. Add heavy cream, pepper, and cayenne. Reduce to low heat. Stir. Serve sauce with roasted pheasant. Yields 8 servings.

French Onion Soup with Three Cheeses

6 tablespoons unsalted butter
1 pound (2 to 3 medium) yellow onions,
    thinly sliced
1 tablespoon all-purpose flour
6 cups chicken stock
Salt
Freshly ground black pepper
16 slices baguette, toasted
¾ cup grated Swiss cheese
¾ cup grated provolone cheese
¾ cup grated Emmentaler (cheese)

Melt butter in heavy, 4-quart saucepan. Add onions and sauté over low heat until soft. Sprinkle in flour and stir. Pour in stock. Season with salt and pepper. Cover and cook over low heat for 45 minutes, stirring occasionally. Divide soup into eight flame-proof bowls. Place two slices toasted bread on each bowl. Mix cheeses together and sprinkle on soup. Place bowls under broiler until cheese is melted and browned. Serve immediately. Yields 8 servings.

Grilled Salmon with Ginger Glaze

8 (6-ounce) salmon fillets,
    each ¾ to 1-inch thick
⅓ cup soy sauce
⅓ cup cream sherry
3 teaspoons sugar
1½ tablespoons grated ginger root
3 cloves garlic, minced
Vegetable oil
8 lemon wedges

Do not remove skin from fillets. Combine soy sauce, sherry, and sugar in small sauce-

pan. Heat over low heat until sugar is dissolved. Add ginger and garlic. Place salmon in non-reactive dish. Pour marinade over salmon. Cover with plastic wrap and marinate in refrigerator at least 3 hours. Remove salmon from marinade and transfer to plate. Brush oil on both sides. Thread each fillet lengthwise on two long skewers. Grill fish fillets flesh-side down first over medium-hot heat. Cook 5 minutes. Baste with marinade. Turn and grill skin-side down. Baste again. Do *not* overcook. Heat leftover marinade and serve with fish. Garnish with lemon wedges. Yields 8 servings.

Stuffed Pork Chops Provençal

2 plus 2 tablespoons olive oil
1 cup finely chopped onion
1 cup chopped mushrooms
¼ teaspoon each thyme, oregano,
    tarragon, and marjoram
2 teaspoons chopped garlic
½ cup Italian chopped parsley plus
    parsley for garnish
¼ teaspoon lemon juice
Salt and ground pepper
Fresh nutmeg
1 egg
2 cups dry bread cubes
4 double-rib pork chops, trimmed
½ cup dry white wine

Warm 2 tablespoons olive oil in frying pan. Add onions and cook gently until softened. Add mushrooms and sauté. Add herbs, garlic, parsley, lemon juice, salt, pepper, and nutmeg to taste. Pour into bowl and cool. Add egg and bread cubes. Mix. Make a pouch in each chop with small sharp knife. Season with salt and freshly ground pepper. Stuff chops with crumb mixture. Sauté chops in heavy ovenproof pan in remaining 2 tablespoons olive oil until brown. Turn once. Add wine. Preheat oven to 300°. Cover chops and bake until tender, about 25 minutes. Serve with chopped Italian parsley garnish. Yields 4 servings.

Chicken Chasseur

2 chickens (2½ to 3 pounds each)
Salt and pepper
Thyme
½ cup vegetable oil
¼ cup finely diced shallots or onions
1 tablespoon minced garlic
¾ pound mushrooms, thinly sliced
¾ cup white wine
½ cup brandy
1 pint tomatoes, peeled, seeded,
    and cubed
1 (14-ounce) can chicken broth
½ cup chopped parsley

Clean and disjoint chickens. Season with salt, pepper, and thyme to taste. Heat oil in large sauté pan. Add chicken pieces and brown carefully on all sides. To prepare sauce remove chicken and all but two ounces of sauté oil and add shallots, garlic, mushrooms, and wine. Remove pan from heat and add brandy to flame mixture. Return pan to heat and simmer until tender. Add tomatoes and chicken broth and mix well. Add chicken pieces and cook until tender, about 20 minutes. Sprinkle chopped parsley over individual servings. Yields 8 servings.

Wild Mushroom Soup

4 tablespoons butter
¼ cup minced shallots
½ pound shiitake mushrooms
½ pound oyster mushrooms
1 tablespoon minced thyme
3 cloves garlic, minced
8 cups chicken stock
1 pound russet potatoes,
    cut in 2-inch pieces
¼ cup Madeira wine
Salt and pepper
½ cup heavy cream (optional)
½ cup chopped Italian parsley

Melt butter in large heavy stockpot over medium-high heat. Add shallots and sauté 1 minute. Add mushrooms and sauté 5 minutes. Add thyme and garlic and sauté 8 minutes. Stir in chicken stock and potatoes. Bring to a boil. Reduce heat, cover, and simmer 25 minutes. Working in batches, purée soup in blender. Return soup to pot and add Madeira. Season with salt and pepper. Stir in cream if desired. Sprinkle with parsley and serve. Soup may be prepared two days ahead and refrigerated. Heat before serving. Yields 8 servings.

Mushroom Caps Stuffed with Crabmeat

16 large mushrooms
4 tablespoons olive oil
3 plus 1 tablespoon unsalted butter
    plus some for basting
9 tablespoons minced onions
3 cloves garlic, minced
½ cup crabmeat
3 tablespoons freshly chopped
    Italian parsley
3 tablespoons freshly chopped thyme
⅓ cup dried breadcrumbs
Salt
Freshly ground black pepper
⅓ cup freshly grated Parmesan cheese
⅓ cup dry white wine

Wash mushrooms and remove and chop stems. Heat oil in large sauté pan over high heat. Add 3 tablespoons butter. Add onions and sauté until clear. Add garlic and mushroom stems. Sauté until wilted. Add crabmeat and cook 5 minutes, stirring all ingredients. Add parsley, thyme, and breadcrumbs. Season with salt and pepper to taste and stir. Preheat oven to 350°. Pile mixture into mushroom caps. Sprinkle with cheese. Place mushroom caps in shallow dish. Add white wine. Bake 15 minutes, basting with butter if desired while cooking. Remove from oven and pour off wine. Serve hot. Yields 8 servings.

1870 Wedgwood Inns

111 W. Bridge Street
New Hope, PA 18938
(215) 862 2570 (phone)
(215) 862-3937 (fax)
stay@new-hope-inn.com
www.1870wedgwoodinn.com

An 1870 blue, Victorian Painted Lady, Wedgwood House is two blocks from village center on the National Registry of Historic Places. It is a warm, friendly, and hospitable inn. Each one of the inn's accommodations has a distinct personality. Rooms are graced with fresh-cut flowers all year round and are hand painted/stenciled by a New Hope artist. Guest rooms feature antiques, original art, scented English soaps, plush towels, extra pillows, plus brass ceiling fans, and some have double Jacuzzis, canopy four-poster beds, and fireplaces. There are private pool and tennis club privileges for guests, too. The Wedgwood, Umpleby House, and the Aaron Burr House are all owned and operated by the Glassman family, which also holds workshops for aspiring innkeepers, an inspiration for guests and potential innkeepers.

Wedding Cookies

½ cup confectioners' sugar plus sugar
    for rolling cookies
1 cup (2 sticks) butter or margarine,
    softened
2 cups all-purpose flour
⅛ teaspoon salt
½ teaspoon vanilla extract

Preheat oven to 400°. Add sugar to butter and mix until smooth. Add flour, salt, and vanilla and cream together. Mixture should be stiff. Roll dough into balls and bake 10 to 12 minutes. Roll cookies in confectioners' sugar before cooling. Yields 2 dozen cookies.

Chicken Salad with Honey-Mustard Dressing

2 cups cubed, cooked chicken
2 cups diced apples
½ cup chopped walnuts
½ cup chopped celery
½ cup mayonnaise
¼ cup honey
3 tablespoons Dijon mustard
Dash of dried rosemary

In large bowl combine chicken, apples, walnuts, and celery. Combine mayonnaise, honey, Dijon mustard, and rosemary in small bowl. Gently stir into chicken mixture. Cover and chill. To serve, spoon onto lettuce-lined plates. Yields 3 to 4 servings.

Jeanie's Sour Cream Coffee Cake

1⅔ cups sour cream
3 eggs
1½ cups sugar
1½ sticks soft margarine
3 cups all-purpose flour
1½ teaspoons baking soda
1½ teaspoons baking powder
½ teaspoon salt
⅓ cup sugar
1½ teaspoons ground cinnamon
1 cup walnuts

Preheat oven to 350°. Mix sour cream, eggs, sugar, and margarine. Blend until light and fluffy. In separate bowl, blend flour, baking soda, baking powder, and salt. Add wet ingredients to dry ingredi-

ents and mix well. Mix sugar, cinnamon, and walnuts in small bowl. In greased tube or Bundt pan, place half of batter and half of topping. Place remaining batter on top and sprinkle with remaining topping. Bake 45 to 50 minutes. Yields 12 servings.

Aaron Burr House
NEW HOPE, PENNSYLVANIA

THE AARON BURR HOUSE

80 West Bridge Street
New Hope, PA 18938
(215) 862-2343
stay@aaronburrhouse.com
www.aaronburrhouse.com

Aaron Burr House Bed & Breakfast is an 1873 Painted Lady, one block from New Hope Center in historic Bucks County. Each of the inn's accommodations has a distinct personality—hand-painted/stenciled by a New Hope artist—and features antiques, private bath, and air conditioning. Most have brass ceiling fans, and some have canopy four poster beds and/or fireplaces. Serving business and leisure travelers since 1990, the inn is on the bus line from New York City, is located midway between New York City and Philadelphia, and is three hours from Baltimore/ Washington, D.C. metro area.

Fresh Fruit Shortcakes

1 tablespoon plus ½ cup sugar
½ plus ½ teaspoon ground cinnamon
1 cup unbleached all-purpose flour
1 cup whole wheat flour
1 tablespoon baking powder
⅓ cup canola oil
⅔ cup skim milk
4 cups chopped and lightly sugared fresh fruit
1 cup low-fat vanilla yogurt

Preheat oven to 375°. Mix 1 tablespoon sugar with ½ teaspoon cinnamon in small bowl. Set aside to use as topping. Combine remaining ½ cup sugar, remaining ½ teaspoon cinnamon, flour, and baking powder. In another bowl, combine oil and milk. Stir oil mixture into flour mixture to form into ball. Drop by tablespoonfuls onto ungreased baking sheet and flatten. Sprinkle with cinnamon/sugar topping. Bake 10 to 12 minutes. To serve, place hot shortcakes on plate. Spoon fresh fruit onto shortcake and top with dollop of vanilla yogurt. Yields 4 dozen shortcakes.

Apple or Pear Fruit Tart

5 large ripe pears or apples
1 tablespoon lemon juice
10 tablespoons all-purpose flour
¾ teaspoon baking powder
6 tablespoons sugar
¼ cup vegetable oil
2 tablespoons milk
2 egg yolks
½ teaspoon vanilla extract
Pinch of salt
¼ cup (½ stick) butter
Sugar to sprinkle
¼ cup slivered almonds (optional)

Peel, core, and slice fruit. Sprinkle with lemon juice, turning gently to mix with fruit. In large mixing bowl, combine flour, baking powder, sugar, oil, milk, eggs, vanilla, and salt in that order. Pour batter into small tart molds or into muffin tins. Preheat oven to 400°. Arrange fruit slices on top. Dot with butter and sprinkle with sugar. Sprinkle almonds on top if desired. Bake 20 to 30 minutes, checking occasionally with toothpick. Yields 8 servings.

Espresso Chip Muffins

2 cups all-purpose flour
½ cup sugar
2½ teaspoons baking powder
2 teaspoons instant espresso powder
    (or 4 teaspoons instant coffee
    powder)
½ teaspoon salt (optional)
½ teaspoon ground cinnamon
1 cup milk, scalded and cooled
½ cup (1 stick) melted butter, cooled
1 egg, lightly beaten
1 teaspoon vanilla extract
¾ cup miniature semisweet
    chocolate chips

Preheat oven to 375°. In large bowl stir together flour, sugar, baking powder, espresso or coffee powder, salt, and cinnamon. In separate bowl mix milk (it must be cool or it will melt chocolate chips) butter, egg, and vanilla. Make a well in center of flour mixture. Pour in milk mixture and stir just until all ingredients are combined. Fold in chocolate chips. Divide batter among twelve muffin cups. Bake 15 to 20 minutes or until a toothpick inserted in center comes out clean. Yields 12 muffins.

Fresh Mango Bread

2 cups all-purpose flour
¼ teaspoon salt
¾ teaspoon baking soda
¾ teaspoon baking powder
1¼ cups sugar

2 eggs
2½ tablespoons butter
¼ cup milk
⅔ cup mashed mango (or peaches)
½ cup chopped nuts
1 tablespoon honey
1 tablespoon orange juice

Preheat oven to 350°. In medium-size bowl mix together dry ingredients. Add eggs, butter, and milk and blend lightly, just to wet. Do *not* overmix; that makes dough tough. Fold in mangos and nuts. Pour into standard, well-greased loaf pan. Bake 50 to 60 minutes. Brush with mix of honey and orange juice. Let stand on baking rack 15 minutes before serving. Yields 1 loaf.

Hanukkah Sweet Apple Latkes

2 eggs, well beaten
1½ cups orange juice, yogurt, or milk
2 cups all-purpose flour
1 teaspoon baking powder
Dash of salt
¼ cup sugar (if using juice)
    or ½ cup sugar (if using dairy)
3 medium-size apples, peeled and grated
Vegetable oil for frying
Confectioners' sugar for sprinkling

Mix eggs with orange juice, yogurt, or milk. In separate bowl combine flour, baking powder, salt, and sugar. Add dry ingredients and apples to egg mixture. Heat thin layer of oil in skillet over medium-high heat and drop 1 heaping tablespoon batter per latke into hot oil. Cook on each side until slightly golden and drain on paper towels. Sprinkle with confectioners' sugar and serve. Yields about 36 latkes.

1833 Umpleby House

111 West Bridge Street
New Hope, PA 18938
(215) 862-3936 (phone)
(215) 862-3937 (fax)
info@1833umplebyhouse.com
1833umplebyhouse.com

New Hope's Umpleby House is a luxury and upscale bed and breakfast inn. The circa 1833 Classic Revival, plaster-stone manor house is situated on two private parklike acres. The inn is conveniently located in the Historic District, the picturesque riverside village square of New Hope, Bucks County, Pennsylvania. The warm, friendly, and hospitable inn attracts business and leisure travelers, as well as groups seeking off-site meeting retreats. It is located midway between New York City and Philadelphia.

Apple Brown Betty

6 to 7 large apples
Water
2 tablespoons lemon juice
¾ cup packed brown sugar
1⅛ cups all-purpose flour
¾ teaspoon ground cinnamon
¼ teaspoon ground nutmeg
12 tablespoons butter, cut in small pieces
Whipped cream or ice cream for serving

Preheat oven to 350°. Peel and slice apples and put in large bowl of water with lemon juice to prevent browning. Combine brown sugar, flour, cinnamon, and nutmeg. Cut in butter with knife until mixture is crumbly. Lay apples in greased 9 x 13-inch baking pan. Sprinkle sugar mixture over apples. Bake 50 to 60 minutes. Serve warm with freshly whipped cream or vanilla ice cream. Yields 12 servings.

White Chocolate Strawberry Mousse

20 ounces white chocolate
1 quart fresh strawberries
½ cup strawberry preserves
2 cups heavy cream, whipped
8 egg whites, stiffly beaten

Melt chocolate in top of double boiler. Purée strawberries. Strain and reserve liquid. Place berries in 1-quart saucepan, add preserves, and cook over low heat until thickened. Remove from heat. Cool slightly. Fold into melted chocolate. Fold in whipped cream, reserving a small amount for garnish. Fold in egg whites. Garnish with fresh strawberries and whipped cream flavored with strawberry juice. Yields 8 to 10 servings.

Lemon Almond Biscotti

2½ cups all-purpose flour
1 teaspoon baking powder
½ teaspoon baking soda
1 teaspoon salt
4 large eggs
¾ cup sugar
1 tablespoon lemon zest
1½ teaspoons fresh lemon juice
1 cup toasted almonds
    or macadamia nuts

Line baking tray with parchment paper. Preheat oven to 325°. Sift together flour, baking powder, baking soda, and salt. In separate bowl, beat eggs and sugar until light in color. Beat in zest and lemon juice. Slowly add dry ingredients to egg mixture. Add nuts. Turn dough onto lightly floured surface and knead until smooth, about 2 minutes. Do *not* overwork dough. Divide dough in half, shaping into two logs. Bake about 30 minutes or until golden brown, remove from oven, and allow to cool completely. Reduce oven to 300°. Cut logs into

½-inch slices. Return to baking sheet and cook until toasted, 20 to 30 minutes. Yields 4 dozen biscotti.

Dinie's Grandmother's Apple Cake

5 to 6 apples, pared, cored, and sliced
1 tablespoon ground cinnamon
3 cups all-purpose flour
1 tablespoon baking powder
1 teaspoon salt
2 cups sugar
1 cup vegetable oil
4 eggs, lightly beaten
½ cup orange juice
2½ teaspoons vanilla extract
½ plus ¼ cup walnuts
2 plus 1 tablespoon honey

Preheat oven to 350°. Grease and flour 10-inch tube pan. Dust apples with cinnamon. In large bowl, mix flour, baking powder, salt, and sugar. Make a well in center of dry ingredients and add oil, eggs, orange juice, and vanilla. Combine for smooth batter. Spoon half of batter into prepared pan. Arrange half of sliced apples on top. Sprinkle with ½ cup walnuts and 2 tablespoons of honey. Cover with remaining batter. Top with remaining apples and ¼ cup walnuts. Drizzle remaining 1 tablespoon honey on top. Bake 1½ hours or until cake is golden and tester comes out clean. Yields 12 servings.

COCALICO CREEK BED & BREAKFAST

224 South Fourth Street
Denver, PA 17517
(717) 336-0271 (phone)
(888) 208-7334 (toll free)
cocalicocrk@dejazzd.com
www.cocalicocrk.com

The Cocalico Creek Bed & Breakfast is a 1920s inn overlooking pastures and spacious grounds with hillside gardens, blended with sounds of ducks splashing in ponds and creeks or an occasional Amish buggy passing by. The area attractions include historical sites, quilt/fabric shops, Amish crafts, farmer's markets, and antiques.

Cocalico Quick Corn Chowder

4 slices bacon, cut in small pieces
1 small onion, sliced
2 medium red potatoes, cubed
2 (14¾-ounce) cans creamed corn
1 (12-ounce) can evaporated milk
Salt and pepper
½ teaspoon dill

In 4-quart saucepan sauté bacon until almost cooked, add onion, and cook until onion becomes transparent. Add potatoes and enough water to cover. Cook until potatoes are tender. Do *not* overcook. Add corn, milk, salt and pepper to taste, and dill. Cook on low until heated through; stir occasionally to prevent sticking. Yields 4 servings.

Slow-Cooker Christmas Wassail

8 cups (2 quarts) apple juice
2 cups (1 pint) cranberry juice
¾ cup sugar
1 teaspoon bitters
2 sticks cinnamon
1 teaspoon allspice
Small orange, studded with cloves
1 cup light rum (optional)

Combine all ingredients in a 3-quart slow cooker. Cook on high 1 hour and then turn heat to low and steep 4 to 8 hours. Yields 12 servings.

Secret-Center Nut Bread

Filling:
6 ounces cream cheese
1 egg
2 tablespoons all-purpose flour
1 tablespoon rum or brandy extract
¾ cup sugar

Bread:
⅔ cup honey
⅔ cup milk
2½ cups all-purpose flour
⅓ cup sugar
1 teaspoon baking soda
1 teaspoon salt
½ cup shortening
1 teaspoon ground cinnamon
1 egg
1 cup chopped nuts

For filling combine cream cheese, egg, flour, rum or brandy extract, and sugar in large bowl. Preheat oven to 325°.

For bread combine honey and milk in separate bowl. Add flour, sugar, baking soda, salt, shortening, cinnamon, and egg. Blend at low speed until smooth. Stir in nuts. Spread half of batter in greased and floured, 9 x 5-inch loaf pan and pour fill-ing over batter. Carefully spoon remaining batter over filling. Bake 1 hour 25 minutes. Yields 8 to12 servings.

Dutch Apple Sour Cream Coffee Cake

¼ pound (1 stick) margarine
1 cup sugar
2 cups sifted all-purpose flour
2 eggs
1 cup sour cream
1 teaspoon baking powder
1 teaspoon baking soda
1 teaspoon vanilla extract
½ teaspoon salt

Filling:
¼ cup light brown sugar
2 teaspoons ground cinnamon
½ cup broken nuts
1 (20-ounce) can apple pie filling
½ cup raisins

Preheat oven to 350°. Cream margarine and sugar. Add flour, eggs, sour cream, baking powder, soda, vanilla, and salt. Place half of batter into greased and floured angel food cake pan.

For filling, mix brown sugar, cinnamon, and nuts together. Sprinkle half of mixture over batter. Add apple pie filling and raisins. Spoon remaining batter over fill-ing. Top with remaining sugar/cinnamon mixture and pat into batter with back of spoon. Bake 45 minutes. Yields 12 servings.

Brownie Pudding Cake

1 cup all-purpose flour
2 teaspoons baking powder
¾ cup sugar
¼ cup plus 2 tablespoons cocoa
½ teaspoon salt
½ cup milk
1 teaspoon vanilla extract

2 tablespoons liquid shortening
¾ cup walnuts (optional)
¾ cup brown sugar
1¾ cups hot water

Preheat oven to 350°. Blend together flour, baking powder, sugar, 2 tablespoons cocoa, and salt. Add milk, vanilla, and shortening. Mix until smooth. Add walnuts if desired. Pour into greased 8 x 8 x 2-inch pan. Mix brown sugar and remaining ¼ cup cocoa and sprinkle over batter. Pour hot water over entire batter. Do *not* stir. Bake 40 to 45 minutes. Yields 12 servings.

PACE ONE RESTAURANT & COUNTRY INN

P.O. Box 108
341 Thornton Road
Thornton, PA 19373
(610) 459-3702 (phone)
(610) 558-0825 (fax)
augustpace@msn.com
www.paceone.net

Pace One Restaurant & Country Inn is a historically renovated stone barn. It has won many awards for adaptive reuse of a historic building. Located in the heart of Brandywine Valley, Pace One is open seven days a week. Longwood Gardens, Brandywine River Museum, and Winterthur are just a few of the area attractions. Come and enjoy a wide selection of wines by the glass, a wood burning stove, and fresh seafood bar. Enjoy the bar before dinner or make an evening of it. Food is made from scratch—fresh and never boring. The menu and service blends well with the country setting.

Pace One's Romaine Salad

18 cups cleaned and chopped fresh
    romaine lettuce
¾ cup sun-dried cranberries
¾ cup crumbled blue cheese
1½ cups orange juice
½ cup raspberry vinegar
2 cups olive oil
¼ teaspoon salt
¼ teaspoon cracked black pepper

Toss lettuce, cranberries, and cheese. Combine remaining ingredients and mix into salad. Serve on chilled plate. Yields 6 servings.

Grilled Lamb Chops with Roasted Potatoes

2 cups balsamic vinegar
1 cup honey
1 large Idaho potato, cleaned and
    cut in ¼-inch slices
1 plus 1 tablespoon olive oil
Salt and pepper
2 Spanish onions, thinly sliced
4 lamb chops
1 ounce crumbled blue cheese
Baby arugula or chives

Preheat oven to 450°. Heat vinegar until reduced by half. Stir in honey and let cool.

Toss potato slices in 1 tablespoon oil and add salt and pepper to taste. Lay slices on sheet pan and bake for 12 minutes. Let cool. Sauté onions in remaining 1 tablespoon oil until caramelized and let cool. Grill lamb chops until medium rare, about 5 minutes. Place crumbled cheese on single potato slice, top with caramelized onions, and top with another potato slice. Repeat with remaining potato slices and put back in oven until cheese begins to melt, about 8 minutes. Surround potatoes with lamb chops and drizzle with balsamic glaze. Garnish with baby arugula or chives. Yields 4 servings.

Oatmeal-Crusted Salmon Stuffed with Apples

4 cups heavy cream
1 cup horseradish
½ teaspoon salt
½ teaspoon white pepper
2 tablespoons Dijon mustard
Juice of 2 oranges
Juice of 2 lemons
6 Granny Smith apples, cored, peeled,
    and diced
10 (7-ounce) salmon fillets
2 cups all-purpose flour
4 eggs, beaten
2 cups dry oatmeal

Simmer heavy cream for 5 minutes. Add horseradish, salt, and pepper. Simmer until cream begins to thicken. Mix mustard, orange juice, and lemon juice. Soak diced apples in mixture for several minutes. Cut a pocket in side of salmon and stuff with apples. Dip stuffed salmon in flour, then eggs, then oatmeal. Place breaded salmon on sheet pan and refrigerate until ready to fry. Preheat oven to 425°. Coat frying pan with butter and lightly brown salmon over medium heat. Transfer to baking sheet and bake 20 to 25 minutes. Place horseradish sauce on plate and top with cooked salmon. Yields 10 servings.

Pace One's New England Pudding

7 cups chunk pineapple
7 cups cubed apples
¼ cup lemon juice
1½ cups chopped walnuts
1 cup brown sugar
4 eggs
2 cups granulated sugar
2 cups all-purpose flour
¾ cup (1½ sticks) melted butter

Preheat oven to 350°. Drain pineapple completely. Cube apples and soak in lemon juice. Mix apples and pineapples and pour into large, ungreased baking pan. Top with walnuts and brown sugar. Whip eggs, add granulated sugar, and blend. Add flour and melted butter and mix completely. Spread topping over center of pan, being careful not to touch ends or sides. Bake until golden brown. Serve warm with vanilla ice cream. Yields 24 servings.

THE BECHTEL VICTORIAN MANSION INN

400 West King Street
East Berlin, PA 17316
(717) 259-7760 (phone)
(800) 331-1108 (toll free)
bechtelvictbb@aol.com

The Bechtel Victorian Mansion Inn is an 1897 Victorian in the National Historic District of East Berlin. Its nine bedrooms are decorated in country-Victorian style with period antiques, dolls, teddy bears, and toys. All guest rooms have private baths and air conditioning. Activities in the area include more than five hundred antique dealers, historic Gettysburg and York, bicycle trails, museums, fine dining, theater, and golf.

Belgian Waffles with Blueberry Sauce

Waffles:
2 cups all-purpose flour
1 tablespoon baking powder
1½ tablespoons sugar
¼ teaspoon ground cinnamon
⅛ teaspoon ground nutmeg
⅛ teaspoon ground ginger
4 large eggs
1 cup milk
½ cup melted butter
1 tablespoon vanilla extract

Blueberry sauce:
1 tablespoon cornstarch
1 (16-ounce) can blueberries in light syrup
Whipped cream

In medium bowl, sift together flour, baking powder, sugar, and spices. In large bowl beat eggs until thick and frothy. Add milk, butter, and vanilla and beat well. Stir in dry ingredients.

For sauce, in medium saucepan over medium heat, stir cornstarch into blueberries. Cook until syrup thickens, stirring constantly. Keep warm. Pour ¾ cup waffle batter onto preheated Belgian waffle grill. Cook until done. Top with blueberry sauce and whipped cream. Yields 4 large waffles.

Sausage Puff

½ pound bulk sausage,
    cooked and fat drained
½ cup shredded Swiss cheese
    (about 4 ounces)
½ cup Cheddar cheese (about 1 ounce)
1 large portobello mushroom, cut into
    small pieces
⅛ teaspoon black pepper

¼ teaspoon parsley
1 sheet frozen puff pastry, thawed
1 tablespoon melted butter

Preheat oven to 425°. Grease baking sheet. To make filling mix together sausage, cheeses, mushroom, pepper, and parsley. Unfold pastry onto lightly floured, 20-inch-long sheet of wax paper. Roll into 9 x 15-inch rectangle, using floured rolling pin. Spread filling down center of pastry sheet. Fold pastry over filling, folding short sides in first, and then fold over large sides envelope style. Pinch seams closed. Place seam-side down onto prepared baking sheet. Remove wax paper. Brush with melted butter. Bake 10 minutes. Reduce oven temperature to 375° and bake until golden brown, about 30 minutes or more. Transfer baking sheet to wire rack to cool slightly. Cut into slices. Yields 4 to 6 servings.

E. J. BOWMAN HOUSE BED & BREAKFAST

2672 Lititz Pike (Route 501)
Lancaster, PA 17601
(717) 519-0808 (phone)
(717) 519-0774 (fax)
(877) 519-1776 (toll free)
alice.ey@ejbowmanhouse.com
www.ejbowmanhouse.com

E. J. Bowman House Bed & Breakfast is centrally located in the heart of Amish Country in Lancaster County, Pennsylvania. The commodious 1860s, Italianate Victorian, family bed and breakfast and landscaped grounds have regained their elegance and historical significance in the village of Neffsville. Known locally as the "big yellow house," the E. J. Bowman

House showcases exquisite murals depicting the Lancaster of the late nineteenth century. Enjoy gracious service at gourmet breakfasts, afternoon teas, or other special family events. Lancaster County and Amish Country are quite well known for shopping, crafts, antiques, artistic or historical events, dining, and touring.

Fresh Apricot Almond Clafouti

This is a sweet, but tart, custard that is a wonderful departure from the traditional morning pastry offerings. Teamed with waffles or pancakes and fresh fruit, breakfast becomes a real feast guaranteed to satisfy all morning guests. We use apricots in this version, but you can substitute fresh seasonal fruit like cherries, pears, and cranberries, or any other soft fruit.

1 cup whole milk
¼ cup heavy cream
¼ cup packed brown sugar
⅓ cup granulated sugar
3 eggs
1 teaspoon vanilla extract
1 teaspoon almond extract
Dash of salt
⅔ cup all-purpose flour
10 to 14 apricots (depending upon size),
    halved and pitted
⅓ cup sliced almonds

Preheat oven to 350°. Coat a clafouti baking dish or 9-inch pie pan with cooking spray. Combine all ingredients except apricots and almonds in large bowl. Whisk until well combined. Pour about one-fourth of mixture into prepared pan and bake 5 minutes. Remove from oven. Arrange apricots on cooked custard. Pour remaining custard batter over apricots. Top with sliced almonds. Return to oven and bake 30 to 35 minutes until puffed. Remove from oven and let stand 5 to 10 minutes until set. Slice into wedges and plate. Sprinkle with confectioners' sugar, garnish with mint sprig, and serve warm with sweet freshly whipped cream if desired. Yields 4 servings.

Vanilla Orange Ginger Sauce

Fresh fruit is always a welcome treat at breakfast. Enhance the taste by serving this sweet sauce over the fruit.

> 2 cups fresh orange juice
>   (Do not use juice from concentrate.)
> 1 cup sugar
> 1 vanilla bean, split
> 5 slices crystallized ginger
> 2 tablespoons Grand Marnier (optional)

Combine orange juice, sugar, vanilla bean, and ginger in heavy-bottom, medium saucepan. Bring to a boil. Reduce heat and reduce to 1¼ cups. Strain. Add Grand Marnier if using. Chill until ready to use. Arrange fruit on chilled plates. Pour small amount of cold sauce over fruit. Garnish with mint sprigs and serve. Yields 3 cups.

Puff Pancake Turnover

In the late spring and summer we like to serve it with fresh berries or cherries that have been macerated with a little sugar and Chambord or other liqueur. In the fall serve with pears or apples and dried cranberries that have been cooked and softened in butter, brown sugar, cinnamon, and cider.

> 4 eggs, separated
> ½ cup milk
> 2 tablespoons all-purpose flour
> 2 tablespoons sugar
> 1 teaspoon vanilla extract
> Dash of salt
> 2 tablespoons melted butter
> Confectioners' sugar
> Fresh or cooked fruit in season for filling

Preheat oven to 450°. Whisk egg whites until stiff, but not dry. In small bowl mix milk, flour, sugar, vanilla, salt, and egg yolks. Fold small amount of beaten egg whites into pancake batter to lighten, and then gently fold batter into remaining egg whites. Put butter in nonstick, oven-safe pan or use pie plate that has been heated in oven for several minutes with butter. Be sure to coat sides of pan (or pie plate) with butter. Pour batter into pan and place in oven. Bake 10 minutes until golden brown and puffed. Slide pancake onto cutting board. Spoon fresh or cooked fruit on half of pancake. Sprinkle with confectioners' sugar. Gently fold pancake in half over fruit. Cut in halves or thirds. Place wedges onto warmed plates. Top with additional fruit. Dust with additional confectioners' sugar and serve. Yields 4 servings.

Egg Roulade

This is a wonderfully light egg entrée that combines fragrant herbs from the garden, the zest of a spicy mustard, and the earthy taste of turkey ham. We like to serve this with fresh tomato slices.

> 4 ounces goat cheese
> ¾ cup milk
> 2 tablespoons all-purpose flour
> 1 tablespoon pesto
> 12 eggs
> ½ cup diced red onion
> 1 teaspoon olive oil
> 2 tablespoons Dijon or other good
>   ground mustard
> 1 plus 1 plus ¼ cup shredded cheese
> 2 cups chopped smoked turkey ham
> Hollandaise sauce (optional)

Line bottom and sides of greased 15 x 10 x 1-inch baking pan with parchment paper. Coat paper with butter-flavored spray. Preheat oven to 375°. Beat goat cheese until smooth. Add milk, flour, and pesto and mix until combined. Whisk eggs until blended. Add to milk mixture. Pour into prepared pan. Bake 20 minutes until eggs are puffed and set. Do *not* overbake. While eggs are baking, sauté onion in oil until clear, about 5 minutes. Remove eggs from oven and spread with mustard. Sprinkle filling on eggs in following order: 1 cup cheese, turkey ham, onions, and finish with 1 cup cheese. Roll short side, peeling away parchment paper as you roll. Sprinkle top with remaining ¼ cup cheese and return to oven. Bake another 5 minutes until cheese is melted. Remove from oven and cool 2 to 3 minutes before slicing. Plate each slice and top with Hollandaise sauce. Yields 8 to 10 servings.

THE COLUMBIAN INN

360 Chestnut Street
Columbia, PA 17512
(717) 584-5869 (phone)
(800) 422-5869 (toll free)
inn@columbianinn.com
www.columbianinn.com

The Columbian is an 1897 Colonial Revival mansion with wraparound porches and unique staircase featuring a beautiful stained glass window in the river town of Columbia on the Susquehanna River. The National Watch and Clock Museum, the 1738 Wright's Ferry Mansion, and the restored 1850 First National Bank Museum are located in Columbia. We are within easy driving distance of Gettysburg, Hershey, and the Lancaster County Amish. There are many opportunities to hike or bike in the area. Round Top ski area is nearby. The Susquehanna River is great for fishing and canoeing. York County, which is just across the river, is noted for its manufacturing tours, including the Harley-Davidson final assembly plant with its Antique Motorcycle Museum, York Bar Bell, York Wallpaper, Pfaltzgraff, and a number of pretzel and potato chip factories.

Cucumber Quick Bread

3 eggs
2 cups sugar
2 cups grated, peeled and seeded
    cucumbers
1 cup vegetable oil
1½ teaspoons vanilla extract
3 cups all-purpose flour
1 cup chopped nuts
1½ teaspoons ground cinnamon
1 teaspoon baking soda
1 teaspoon salt
¼ teaspoon baking powder

Preheat oven to 350°. In mixing bowl beat eggs. Beat in sugar, cucumbers, oil, and vanilla until well blended. Combine flour, nuts, cinnamon, baking soda, salt, and baking powder and add to cucumber mixture. Beat just until combined. Pour into two greased 9 x 5-inch loaf pans. Bake 60 to 65 minutes. Cool 10 minutes, removing from pans to wire racks. Yields 2 loaves.

Granola

4 cups one-minute oatmeal
1 cup wheat bran
1 cup coconut
1 cup chopped pecans
2 tablespoons brown sugar
2 teaspoons ground cinnamon
⅓ cup honey
½ cup vegetable oil
1 teaspoon vanilla extract
¼ cup raisins
¼ cup craisins

Preheat oven to 250°. In large, shallow (2-quart) glass dish mix oatmeal, wheat bran, coconut, pecans, brown sugar, and cinnamon. In small saucepan combine and heat over low heat honey, oil, and vanilla. Pour over dry mixture and stir well. Toast mix 45 minutes, stirring every 15 minutes. Remove from oven and stir well. When cool, add raisins and craisins.

Store in airtight container. Yields about 2 quarts.

Herb and Cheese Egg Casseroles

7 eggs
1 cup milk
2 teaspoons sugar
4 cups shredded cheeses
    (Cheddar, Monterey Jack, Swiss)
4 ounces cream cheese, cubed
16 ounces small-curd cottage cheese
2 tablespoons margarine
½ cup all-purpose flour
1 teaspoon baking powder
1 teaspoon basil
1 teaspoon thyme
1 teaspoon marjoram

Preheat oven to 325°. Beat eggs, milk, and sugar together. Add shredded cheeses, cream cheese, cottage cheese, and margarine. Mix well and add flour, baking powder, and herbs. Pour into greased 9 x 13-inch pan (8 x 8-inch pan for half recipe). Bake 45 minutes or until knife comes out clean. Yields 12 servings.

Note: You can refrigerate the unbaked casserole 8 to 10 hours or overnight to blend flavors. From refrigerator bake 60 minutes.

Lemon Coconut Loaf

1 cup (2 sticks) butter, softened
2 cups sugar
3 plus 2 tablespoons lemon juice
4 eggs
3 cups all-purpose flour
2 teaspoons baking powder
½ teaspoon salt
1 cup milk
½ cup shredded coconut
2 teaspoons grated lemon peel
¼ cup confectioners' sugar

Preheat oven to 350°. In mixing bowl, cream butter, sugar, and 3 tablespoons lemon juice.

Add eggs, one at a time, beating well after each addition. Combine flour, baking powder, and salt. Add to creamed mixture alternately with milk. Stir in coconut and lemon peel. Pour into two, greased, 8 x 4-inch loaf pans. Bake 60 to 70 minutes. Cool 10 minutes. Remove from pan to wire rack. Combine confectioners' sugar and remaining 2 tablespoons lemon juice and brush over loaf. Yields 2 loaves.

Baked Peach Pancake

Pancake:
¼ cup (½ stick) butter
1 cup baking mix
¾ cup milk
4 eggs
1 (20-ounce) can sliced peaches, drained
¼ cup sugar
¼ teaspoon ground cinnamon

Honey-Raisin Syrup:
½ cup honey
¼ cup raisins
¼ cup (½ stick) butter
¼ teaspoon ground cinnamon

Preheat oven to 400°. Place 2 tablespoons butter in each of two 9-inch pie plates. Heat in oven until melted. Beat baking mix, milk, and eggs in small bowl, using wire whisk until smooth. Arrange half of peach slices in each pie plate. Divide batter evenly between plates. Sprinkle sugar and cinnamon over batter. Bake 20 to 25 minutes or until puffed and golden brown.

For Honey-Raisin Syrup, heat all ingredients in saucepan over medium heat, stirring occasionally, until hot. Pour over pancakes. We serve sausages on the side. Yields 8 servings.

ROSE MANOR BED & BREAKFAST

124 S. Linden Street
Manheim, PA 17545
(717) 664-4932 (phone)
(717) 664-1611 (fax)
(800) 666-4932 (toll free)
inn@rosemanor.net
www.rosemanor.net

Built in 1905, Rose Manor sits in a quiet neighborhood and is surrounded by herb gardens and roses. After a restful night's slumber, awaken to the music of chirping birds and the aroma of a hearty breakfast. Spend your day exploring the Pennsylvania Dutch countryside, visiting Amish farms, antiquing, outlet shopping, going to farmer's markets, bicycling, quilt shopping, or attending the Renaissance Faire. In addition, Rose Manor is a convenient starting point for day trips to Gettysburg and Longwood Gardens. Rose Manor's herbal theme is reflected in decorative touches throughout the house, as well as in our gourmet cooking.

Cheesy Seafood Sandwiches

2 cups shredded Cheddar cheese
1 (6½-ounce) can tuna in water,
    drained and flaked
1 (4½-ounce) can small shrimp,
    rinsed and drained
½ cup finely chopped celery
1 tablespoon dried minced onion
½ teaspoon dried dill weed
¾ cup prepared salad dressing
⅓ cup tartar sauce
Whole wheat bread, crusts removed

Mix cheese, tuna, and shrimp together. Add celery, onion, dill weed, mayonnaise, and tartar sauce. Spread on whole wheat bread. Yields 8 servings.

Guamanian Sandwiches

½ cup chopped, pitted black olives
¼ cup chopped scallions with green tops
2 cups grated sharp Cheddar cheese
½ cup mayonnaise
½ teaspoon curry powder
½ teaspoon chili powder
Party pumpernickel bread slices

Mix olives, scallions, cheese, mayonnaise, curry, and chili powder together well. Dollop on top of bread. Place under broiler and heat until bubbly. Garnish with black olive slices, if desired. Yields 15 to 20 servings.

Pennsylvania Dutch Breakfast Casserole

½ large loaf Italian bread, torn up
3 tablespoons softened butter
8 ounces sharp Cheddar cheese, grated
¼ pound sweet Lebanon bologna,
    cut in small pieces
1½ cups milk
⅛ cup white wine
2 teaspoons Dijon mustard
10 eggs
½ tablespoon dehydrated minced onion
¼ teaspoon freshly ground black pepper
Several drops of hot sauce
½ cup sour cream
2 cups grated Romano cheese

Coat 9 x 13-inch baking pan with non-stick spray. Lay bread over bottom surface, spreading with softened butter. Sprinkle with cheese and bologna. Beat together milk, wine, mustard, eggs, onion, pepper, and hot sauce. Pour over bread mixture in pan. Cover and refrigerate 8 to 10 hours or overnight. Remove from refrigerator 2 hours before baking. When ready to bake, preheat oven to 325° and bake covered 1 hour. Uncover, spread with sour cream, and sprinkle with Romano. Bake uncovered 10 minutes more or until lightly browned. Yields 8 to 10 servings.

Fruit Salad with Raspberry Fruit Dressing

Raspberry fruit dressing:
1 cup sour cream or plain yogurt
3 tablespoons raspberry vinegar
3 tablespoons honey
1 tablespoon seedless raspberry jam

Salad:
1 cup sliced kiwifruit
1 cup mandarin orange sections
1 cup sliced banana
1 cup green grapes
1 cup pineapple chunks

Shake all dressing ingredients in container and chill for 3 hours. Mix together fruits and top with dressing. Yields about 4 servings.

Blueberry Bread with Raspberry Glaze

2 cups all-purpose flour
1 cup sugar
½ teaspoon salt
1½ teaspoons baking powder
½ teaspoon baking soda
1 egg
¾ cup water
¼ cup vegetable oil
1 cup fresh or frozen blueberries
¼ cup raspberry preserves

Preheat oven to 350°. In large bowl combine flour, sugar, salt, baking powder, and baking soda. In small bowl, beat together egg, water, and oil. Stir into dry ingredients just until moistened. Fold in berries. Pour into greased and floured 9 x 5-inch loaf pan. Spoon preserves over batter and cut through batter with knife to swirl. Bake 65 to 70 minutes until toothpick inserted near center comes out clean. Cool 10 minutes and remove from pan to wire rack. Yields 1 loaf.

Note: You can substitute cranberries for blueberries and apricot preserves for raspberry preserves.

The Artist's Inn & Gallery

117 East Main Street
Terre Hill, PA 17581
(717) 445-0219 (phone)
(888) 999-4479 (toll free)
stay@artistinn.com
www.artistinn.com

Spend the night in an art gallery. Our antique-filled home in Terre Hill features the colored pencil pictures of the innkeeper. You'll feel like you've escaped to a simple, gentler time as horse-drawn buggies pass by the house and chimes play from the nearby church. All rooms feature gas fireplaces, Amish quilts, private baths, and antiques. Two rooms feature whirlpool tubs. Local attractions include Hershey, Pennsylvania, Amish Country, Mt. Hope Winery, Ephrata Cloister, Fulton Opera House, Antiques Capital of the USA, and outlet shopping.

❧   ❧   ❧

Raspberry, Apple, and Brie Purses

1 (single-sheet) package frozen puff pastry
4 ounces Brie cheese, chopped
2 apples, peeled, cored, and diced
2 tablespoons packed brown sugar
1 cup raspberries, drained
½ cup pecans
1 egg, lightly beaten

Preheat oven to 400°. Thaw puff pastry according to directions. Mix cheese, apples, brown sugar, raspberries, and pecans together in medium bowl to make filling. Spread pastry sheet on counter. Cut into 9 squares. Coat two muffin pans with cooking spray. Place pastry squares into muffin pan and top with heaping tablespoon filling. Pull all four corners of puff pastry together up over filling and twist so that they "stick" together. Repeat until muffin pan is full and fill second pan as needed. Brush egg wash over top of "purses" and bake about 20 minutes or until golden. Yields 4 servings.

Whoopies

2 cups brown sugar
1 cup vegetable oil
2 eggs
3 cups plus 5 tablespoons all-purpose flour
1 plus 1 cup milk
½ cup cocoa
¼ teaspoon salt
1½ plus 1 teaspoon vanilla extract
1 teaspoon baking soda
1 cup granulated (or confectioners') sugar
1 cup shortening
Confectioners' sugar for sprinkling

Preheat oven to 350°. Combine brown sugar, oil, eggs, 3 cups flour, 1 cup milk, cocoa, salt, 1½ teaspoons vanilla, and baking soda. Let mixture stand for 45 minutes. Drop by teaspoonfuls onto lightly greased cookie sheet. Bake two to three inches apart 5 to 10 minutes. Cool. Cook together remaining 5 tablespoons flour and 1 cup milk until thick. Cool thoroughly and add 1 cup sugar, shortening, and remaining 1 teaspoon vanilla. Beat mixture about 15 minutes or until it is no longer sugary, meaning that you can't taste granules. Place cream filling between two cookies and sprinkle with confectioners' sugar. Yields 3 to 4 dozen whoopies.

The Artist's Inn Corn Pudding

1 (14-ounce) can cream-style corn or 5 ears fresh corn with ¼ cup heavy cream
¼ cup sugar
2 eggs
1 cup milk
1 tablespoon all-purpose flour
Salt and pepper
Butter

Preheat oven to 350°. Mix all ingredients except butter in large bowl. Pour in greased casserole or baking dish and dot with butter. Bake uncovered until firm and slightly brown. Yields 4 to 6 servings.

Carrot Soufflé

1½ pounds carrots, sliced
½ cup (1 stick) butter
3 large eggs
¼ cup all-purpose flour
1½ teaspoons baking powder
1½ cups sugar
¼ teaspoon ground cinnamon

Cook carrots in boiling water 20 to 25 minutes or until tender. Drain. Preheat oven to 350°. Pour carrots and remaining ingredients into blender and purée until smooth. Pour into greased soufflé dish. Bake for a little over an hour or until set. Yields 10 to 12 servings.

Blue Heaven

2 cups blueberries
2 cups low-fat buttermilk
1 cup sugar
Whipped cream for topping

Pour ingredients into blender and purée. Pour into champagne glasses, stemware, or sundae cups. Freeze for several hours. Before serving, let thaw 30 minutes on counter. Serve with dollop of whipped cream and yellow nasturtium flower. Yields 4 servings.

WATCH BOX HOLLOW BED & BREAKFAST

RR 3, Box 1757
Port Royal, PA 17082
(717) 535-4596
watchboxbb@tricountyi.net
www.watchboxhollow.com

The Watch Box Hollow Bed & Breakfast is nestled in the oaks and pines of the Tuscarora Mountains, just a short walk to the Juniata River. Relax in a comfortable, eclectic antiques atmosphere and leave the rest of the world behind. A full breakfast is served each morning and local wines and beverages are served each evening. We can arrange a horse-drawn carriage or sleigh ride, a scenic airplane tour over Pennsylvania's mountains and farms, a trail ride on horseback, or a canoe adventure on the Juniata River. Bring your mountain bike or hike the trails on the Tuscarora Mountain. The surrounding area also offers four vineyards and wineries and four antique malls. Porch sitting and bird-watching during the day or a good book and chirping frogs at night are sometimes all you need.

Double Dip Cheesecake Toast

1 loaf homemade white bread
1 (8-ounce) tub cheesecake-flavored
    cream cheese, softened
3 eggs
4 cups milk
2 tablespoons vanilla extract
¼ cup premixed cinnamon and sugar
¼ cup (½ stick) butter
1 (12-ounce) bottle butter-flavored syrup
1 quart raspberries, blueberries,
    and/or strawberries

Cut ½-inch slices of bread and separate into pairs. Spread cream cheese lightly on both slices and press pairs together. Whip eggs in deep dish and stir in milk and vanilla. Dip "sandwiches" into batter on both sides and grill. Sprinkle one side with cinnamon and sugar mixture. A hearty bread is best; it can stand up to the cream cheese and double dip. Heat pan or griddle to 425° and generously cover with butter. This creates marbled look to one side of toast; place onto plates with this side up. Finish this breakfast creation with berries or your guest's favorite fruit on top. Yields 6 to 8 servings.

Breakfast Ham Steaks with Jim's Homemade Hickory Cherry Sauce

1 (10-ounce) jar maraschino cherries
    without stems
2 tablespoons hickory-smoked
    BBQ sauce
¼-inch slices ham steak from deli

Drain syrup off jar of cherries into glass measuring cup. Purée cherries in food processor or blender for 30 seconds. Stir cherries back into syrup. Stir in BBQ sauce.

Heat large frying pan to high (400°). Place ham steaks in pan and fry for several minutes. Drain any water and fat from pan. Lightly cover each slice with cherry sauce. Turn steaks over and simmer in sauce for a few more minutes. Serve with eggs and toast to your guests' liking. A sprig of parsley adds color. Yields about 1 cup sauce.

Golden Mushroom Soufflé

Prepare today; cook tomorrow.

4 plus 2 plus 2 tablespoons butter
5 plus 5 ounces plain
    or Parmesan croutons
1½ cups chopped celery
1½ cups chopped green
    and red bell peppers
¾ cup chopped Vidalia onion
¾ cup mayonnaise
¼ teaspoon pepper
1 pound fresh mushrooms, sliced
5 eggs
2½ cups milk
1 (10¾-ounce) can golden
    mushroom soup
½ cup shredded Parmesan cheese

Melt 4 tablespoons butter in bottom of 2½-quart casserole dish. Add half of croutons to bottom of dish. Melt 2 tablespoons butter in large, deep frying pan. Sauté celery, peppers, and onions. Remove from heat and stir in mayonnaise and pepper. In separate pan melt remaining 2 tablespoons of butter. Sauté mushrooms 3 to 4 minutes. Combine with vegetable mixture. Pour combined mixture over croutons in casserole dish. Beat together eggs and milk and stir in soup. Pour over casserole mixture and top with remaining croutons and Parmesan cheese. Refrigerate 8 to 10 hours or overnight. (You have to get up early to serve this casserole for breakfast, but the reviews are worth it.) When ready to bake, preheat oven to 425°. Bake casserole 20 minutes and then reduce heat to 375° and bake additional 50 minutes or until top is set and golden brown. Remove casserole from oven and allow to set 5 minutes before serving. Sprinkle each serving with Parmesan cheese. Yields 6 to 8 servings.

Apple-Cinnamon Oatmeal Pie with Caramel Apples

1 cup light corn syrup
1 stick butter
½ cup brown sugar
2 large eggs
2 teaspoons vanilla extract
4 envelopes apple-cinnamon oatmeal or baked-apple oatmeal
4 envelopes maple-and-brown-sugar oatmeal
1 (9-inch) unbaked pie shell
3 apples
2 cups caramel, custard-style yogurt

Place corn syrup in microwaveable mixing bowl. Add butter and microwave 30 seconds. Beat in eggs and vanilla. Stir in all eight envelopes of oatmeal. Pour into pie shell. Preheat oven to 375°. Peel and cut apples into small wedges. Press wedges from one apple into pattern on top of pie. Bake 45 minutes or until top is golden brown. Serve on colorful plate with dollop of custard and remaining apple slices to the side, or use vanilla custard and cubed cantaloupe. Yields 8 to 10 servings.

Easy Dozen Breakfast Muffins

12 flaky biscuits
12 eggs
1 cup milk
1 cup chopped onion
2 tablespoons butter
2 pounds ground sausage
2 cups chopped green/red peppers
2½ teaspoons no-salt herb mixture
3 cups shredded Cheddar cheese

Press biscuits into bottoms of two, six-cup extra large muffin tins and work dough up sides. Preheat oven to 425°. Beat eggs in large mixing bowl. Stir in milk. In deep pan, fry chopped onion in butter until soft. Add sausage, cook thoroughly, and drain fat. Add peppers and herb mix. Cook until peppers just begin to get tender. Add sausage mixture to egg mixture. Stir in cheese. Divide mixture among muffin cups. Bake 30 to 35 minutes or until lightly browned on top. Yields 12 muffins, 6 to 10 servings.

PINEAPPLE HILL BED & BREAKFAST

1324 River Road
New Hope, PA 18938
(215) 862-1790 (phone)
(888) 866-8404 (toll free)
ktriolo@pineapplehill.com
www.pineapplehill.com

Escape to romantic rooms, luxurious suites and scrumptious full breakfasts at our New Hope inn. We offer private balconies, fireplaces, canopy beds, and a secluded backyard pool. Excellent walking, biking, fishing, bird watching, and all that the Delaware River provides are a short walk away. For history buffs, there's Pennsbury Manor (one-time home of William Penn), Washington Crossing Park (the spot where George Washington invaded Trenton to turn the tide of the Revolutionary War), and the Pearl S. Buck house, to name just a few. New Hope and the surrounding areas are also home to excellent restaurants, art galleries, antique shops, and local and regional theater.

Delectable French Toast

2 eggs
½ cup milk
1 tablespoon sugar
1 teaspoon vanilla extract
Dash of ground cinnamon
2 large croissants, split horizontally

In bowl mix all ingredients except croissants. Soak croissant slices in mixture. Heat frying pan to low-medium heat and coat lightly with cooking spray. Lightly brown soaked croissants in frying pan, flipping after first side is done. Cook slowly so that mixture cooks throughout without needing to flatten croissants. Serve with confectioners' sugar and bacon slices or sausage. Also excellent with heated canned pie filling on top. Yields 2 servings.

Easy Breakfast Pie

½ cup chopped onion
½ cup chopped zucchini
2 ounces cooked mushrooms or ham
1¼ ounces shredded Cheddar cheese
1 cup milk
2 tablespoons sour cream
2 eggs or 3 egg whites
¾ cup buttermilk baking mix
Pinch of pepper

Preheat oven to 350°. Coat 9-inch pie plate with cooking spray. Spray small skillet also. Add onion, zucchini, and mushrooms or ham and cook about 2 minutes until onions are translucent. Spread onion mixture over bottom of pie plate. Sprinkle cheese on top. In bowl, combine milk, sour cream, eggs, baking mix, and pepper and blend with fork. Pour into pie plate. Bake until golden brown and puffy, 35 to 45 minutes. Cut into four slices, sprinkle with parsley, and serve with fruit garnish. Yields 4 servings.

Eggs in a Bed

White bread
Butter
Salt
Pepper
¾ cup grated Cheddar cheese
6 eggs
1½ cups milk

Coat 9 x 9-inch glass baking dish with cooking spray. Line bottom of dish with bread, cutting as necessary to fit snugly. Butter bread and then salt and pepper it. Sprinkle cheese on top. In bowl mix eggs and add milk. Pour over bread. Cover with tinfoil and refrigerate 8 to 10 hours or overnight. When ready to bake, put dish in cold oven and turn to 350°. Bake 1 hour. Serve with slice of tomato for garnish and favorite breakfast meat. Yields 4 servings.

Strawberry Dip

1 pint strawberries
2 tablespoons sour cream
2 tablespoons brown sugar
Mint sprig

Imagine a large plate as having three sections. Arrange strawberries, taking up one section. Place sour cream in dollop in second section, and place sugar in last section. Place mint sprig in sour cream for added color. Serve with two small plates for strawberry crowns. Dip each strawberry in sour cream, then roll in brown sugar, and eat. Yields 2 servings.

Baked Bananas

½ cup (1 stick) melted butter
3 tablespoons fresh lemon juice
6 firm, ripe, peeled bananas
⅓ cup brown sugar
1 teaspoon ground ginger
1 cup grated coconut
½ cup heavy cream

Preheat oven to 375°. Stir butter and lemon juice together and spread over bottom of baking dish. Put bananas in dish and coat with butter mixture. Mix brown sugar and ginger together in small bowl and pour over bananas, saving half. Bake bananas 10 minutes. Roll bananas over and pour on remaining sugar mixture. Bake another 5 minutes. Pour coconut over and bake 5 more minutes. Serve in fruit dishes. Pour heavy cream over each serving. Yields 6 servings.

The Beechmont Inn

315 Broadway
Hanover, PA 17331
(717) 632-3013 (phone)
(800) 553-7009 (toll free)
innkeeper@thebeechmont.com
www.thebeechmont.com

Whether your visit is for business or relaxation, our goal is to pamper you with great comfort and maybe a whirlpool tub or fireplace. A sumptuous breakfast is served each morning as you plan your day to explore Gettysburg National Military Park, search for antique treasures, or while away the hours hiking or fishing. You can also play numerous golf courses, excite the senses at farmers' markets, find hidden back roads in Amish country, and watch things being made during York County factory tours.

Cinnamon Spice Pancakes with Lemon Sauce

Pancakes:
2 large eggs, separated
2 cups all-purpose flour
½ cup oatmeal
2 teaspoons baking powder
1 teaspoon baking soda
Pinch of salt
2 teaspoons ginger
1 teaspoon ground cinnamon
½ teaspoon ground nutmeg
¼ teaspoon ground cloves
1½ cups buttermilk
2 tablespoons melted butter
1 tablespoon sugar
2 teaspoons dark molasses

Lemon Sauce:
1 cup sugar
2 to 3 tablespoons cornstarch
2 cups water
4 tablespoons butter
2 to 3 tablespoons grated lemon zest
¼ cup lemon juice

For lighter pancakes, separate eggs and beat egg whites in deep bowl on high speed until they hold moist peaks. Combine flour, oatmeal, baking powder, baking soda, salt, and spices in small bowl. Beat egg yolks in large bowl with buttermilk, butter, sugar, and molasses. Add flour mixture. Blend well. Add egg whites, folding them gently into batter until combined. Cook on buttered griddle over medium heat by pouring out batter to form pancakes 4 to 5 inches in diameter. Cook until edges are full of bubbles and then flip and cook another 1 to 2 minutes until golden brown.

For Lemon Sauce, in small pan, mix sugar with cornstarch. Add water and bring to a boil over high heat. Remove from heat and add butter, lemon zest, and lemon juice. Stir until butter melts. Serve with pancakes. Yields 4 servings.

Strawberry Corn Muffins

1 cup cornmeal
1 cup all-purpose flour
⅓ cup sugar
2½ teaspoons baking powder
¼ teaspoon salt
2 cups strawberries, cut in small pieces
1 cup vanilla yogurt
¼ cup canola oil
1 egg, slightly beaten

Preheat oven to 350°. Grease muffin pan or line with paper cups. In large bowl combine and whisk together cornmeal, flour, sugar, baking powder, and salt. Add strawberries and toss gently to coat with flour mixture. In small bowl, whisk together yogurt, oil, and egg. Add yogurt mixture to flour mixture and mix just until dry ingredients are combined. Do *not* overmix. Fill muffin cups about two-thirds full and bake 20 to 25 minutes. Yields 12 muffins.

Strawberry Salsa

6 tablespoons olive oil
2 tablespoons white balsamic vinegar
1 teaspoon sea salt or ½ teaspoon
   table salt
1 teaspoon sugar
2 cups chopped fresh strawberries
6 green onions, chopped
4 cups halved cherry tomatoes
¼ to ½ cup chopped fresh cilantro

Combine oil, vinegar, salt, and sugar and whisk together in medium bowl. Add strawberries, onions, tomatoes, and cilantro to oil mixture. Toss to coat. Chill at least 1 hour. Serve with your favorite egg

dish to add a delightful distinction. Can also be served with tortilla chips for an evening treat. Yields 6 to 7 cups.

Pennsylvania Dutch Soft Sugar Cookies

3½ cups all-purpose flour
1 teaspoon baking soda
1 teaspoon baking powder
1 teaspoon salt
2 cups sugar
1 cup (2 sticks) butter
2 eggs
1 tablespoon vanilla extract
1 cup buttermilk

Preheat oven to 375°. Sift together flour, baking soda, baking powder, and salt. Cream together sugar and butter. Add eggs one at a time and beat. Add vanilla and beat. Stir flour mixture into sugar mixture, alternating with buttermilk. Stir until smooth. Drop by tablespoonfuls (or use small ice cream scoop) onto greased cookie sheet (or for best results, use cookie sheet lined with parchment paper). Sprinkle tops with sugar. Bake 7 to 10 minutes. Remove cookies from sheet and cool on rack. Store in airtight container with wax paper between layers. Yields about 4 dozen.

Almond Ginger Cookies

2 cups all-purpose flour
2 teaspoons baking soda
1 teaspoon salt
1 teaspoon ground cinnamon
1 teaspoon ginger
½ teaspoon ground allspice
½ teaspoon ground nutmeg
½ teaspoon cloves
¾ cup vegetable oil
1 cup sugar
1 egg
4 tablespoons molasses

1 teaspoon vanilla extract
½ cup sliced almonds

Preheat oven to 350°. Sift together flour, baking soda, salt, and spices. Beat together oil and sugar until well blended. Add egg, molasses, and vanilla. Blend. Stir in dry ingredients and add almonds. Dough will be fairly stiff. Drop by tablespoonfuls onto greased cookie sheet. Bake for 10 minutes. Remove from baking sheet and cool. Store in an airtight container with slice of bread to preserve chewy texture. Yields about 2 dozen cookies.

THE BRICKHOUSE INN

452 Baltimore Street
Gettysburg, PA 17325
(717) 338-9337 (phone)
(717) 338-9265 (fax)
(800) 864-3464 (toll free)
stay@brickhouseinn.com
www.brickhouseinn.com

The Brickhouse Inn opened in July 1996 with three rooms and has since grown to ten rooms in two houses. The main building, built in 1898, houses eight guest rooms, two parlors, and two dining rooms. The second building is a circa 1830 home with an 1868 addition housing two guest rooms, each with private entrances and gas fireplaces. The original doors on the house and outside wall show bullet marks from the Civil War. The Brickhouse Inn is in the heart of Gettysburg within the downtown historic district. Conveniently located within walking distance of parts of the battlefield, restaurants, shops, and Civil War art galleries, The Brickhouse has much to offer its guests.

Breakfast Lasagna

2 cups white sauce
9 lasagna noodles, cooked and drained
8 ounces ham, diced
1 (8-ounce) package salami, diced
1 plus 1 plus 1 cup shredded cheese
    (Cheddar, Monterey Jack, Mozzarella)
1 dozen hard-cooked eggs, chopped
1 plus 1 tablespoon chives
Hollandaise sauce (optional)

Preheat oven to 350°. Grease 9 x 13-inch pan. Place ¼ cup white sauce in pan and spread to coat bottom. Place 3 noodles in bottom of pan. Sprinkle noodles with half of ham, half of salami, and 1 cup cheese. Sprinkle half of eggs over top and 1 tablespoon chives. Drizzle half of remaining white sauce (about ¾ cup) over top. Add second layer of 3 noodles, and remaining meats, eggs, chives, 1 cup cheese, and ½ cup of remaining sauce. Top with 3 remaining noodles. Spread remaining ¼ cup white sauce over noodles and top with remaining 1 cup cheese. Bake 40 to 45 minutes or until golden and bubbly. Remove from oven and let sit 10 minutes before serving. Serve topped with Hollandaise sauce, if desired. Yields 12 servings.

Cranberry-Apple French Toast

1 cup brown sugar
½ cup melted butter
1 teaspoon ground cinnamon
3 apples, peeled, cored, and thinly sliced
¾ cup chopped cranberries
6 eggs
1 cup milk
¾ cup half-and-half
2 teaspoons vanilla extract
1 loaf cinnamon bread, cut into
    1-inch slices
Maple syrup

Combine brown sugar, butter, and cinnamon in large bowl. Add apples and cranberries. Toss to coat well. Spread apple mixture in greased 9 x 13-inch pan. Whisk together eggs, milk, half-and-half, and vanilla. Dip bread slices in egg mixture. Arrange slices on top of apples in pan. Drizzle any remaining liquid over bread. Cover with plastic wrap and refrigerate 8 to 10 hours or overnight.

When ready to bake, preheat oven to 375°. Remove plastic wrap and cover pan with foil. Bake 45 minutes or until knife inserted in center comes out clean. Uncover and let sit 5 minutes. Invert pan onto cookie sheet so toast is served with apple layer on top. Serve immediately with maple syrup. Yields 10 servings.

Perfect Blueberry Muffins

2 cups plus 1 tablespoon all-purpose flour
1 cup plus 1 tablespoon sugar
2 teaspoons baking powder
½ teaspoon salt
2 cups fresh blueberries, rinsed,
    drained, and patted dry
Grated zest of 1 lemon
1 teaspoon ground coriander
½ cup milk
½ cup (1 stick) melted butter, cooled
1 egg, lightly beaten
1 teaspoon vanilla extract
½ teaspoon ground cinnamon
¼ teaspoon ground nutmeg

Preheat oven to 400°. Grease twelve-cup muffin tin. In large bowl, stir together 2 cups flour, 1 cup sugar, baking powder, and salt. Gently fold in blueberries, lemon zest, and coriander. In another bowl, whisk together milk, butter, egg, and vanilla until well blended. Add to dry ingredients, stirring just to combine. Spoon batter into prepared muffin tin. Combine remaining 1 tablespoon sugar, cinnamon, remaining 1 tablespoon flour, and nutmeg. Sprinkle over each muffin top. Bake 20 to 25 minutes or until toothpick inserted in center comes out clean. Cool in muffin tins. Yields 12 muffins.

Cinnamon Chip Coffee Cake

Topping:
2 tablespoons sugar
1 cup chopped pecans

Glaze:
½ cup semisweet chocolate chips
¼ cup (½ stick) butter

Cake:
1 cup (2 sticks) butter, softened
2 cups sugar
2 eggs
2 cups all-purpose flour
½ teaspoon salt
1½ teaspoons baking powder
1 cup sour cream
1 teaspoon vanilla extract

1¾ cups cinnamon chips

For topping, mix together in small bowl sugar and pecans. Sprinkle 3 tablespoons topping mixture into prepared muffin cups. Spoon half of batter into cups and smooth.

For glaze, melt chocolate chips and butter together in small saucepan over low heat. Set aside.

Preheat oven to 350°. Grease and flour tube pan. For cake batter, cream butter, and sugar until fluffy. Add eggs to the batter, beating until smooth. Gradually add flour, salt, and baking powder to the batter, blending well. Fold in sour cream and vanilla. Pour batter into tube pan. Drizzle half of chocolate glaze over batter. Sprinkle with half of the cinnamon chips and 4 to 5 tablespoons of topping. Spoon the remaining batter into pan. Smooth and sprinkle with remaining topping. Bake for 1 hour 15 minutes or until toothpick in center comes out clean. When done, remove the cake from the oven and immediately sprinkle with remaining cinnamon chips. Let it cool completely in pan. When it is cool, remove from pan. Reheat remaining glaze and drizzle over cake. Yields 16 to 20 servings.

FLOWERS & THYME BED & BREAKFAST

238 Strasburg Pike
Lancaster, PA 17602-1326
(717) 393-1460 (phone)
(717) 399-1986 (fax)
padutchbnb@aol.com
members.aol.com/padutchbnb

The Flowers & Thyme Bed & Breakfast is located in a country setting, overlooking a picturesque working farm. Surrounding the property of one and one-third acre are landscaped cottage gardens, herb bed, and a vegetable garden. You'll find tastefully created interiors here, as well as genuine hospitality and clean comfortable rooms with queen beds. All rooms have private in-suite baths. Bountiful country breakfasts are served in the spacious gathering room. Dinner with an Amish family can be arranged.

Best Omelet

2 tablespoons green bell pepper
½ tablespoon red bell pepper
2 tablespoons onion
¼ cup (½ stick) butter
8 large eggs, beaten
2 tablespoons Parmesan cheese
2 tablespoons milk
Pinch of salt and pepper
½ teaspoon garlic salt
2 tablespoons fresh parsley for topping

Sauté peppers and onion in butter over medium heat. Lower heat to medium low and add remaining ingredients except parsley. Cook until almost done and flip over briefly. Add favorite fillings such as cheeses or tomatoes and flip omelet halfway to cover. Sprinkle with parsley. Yields 6 servings.

Caramel Pear Pudding

1 cup all-purpose flour
⅓ cup sugar
½ cup milk
1½ teaspoons baking powder
½ teaspoon ground cinnamon
¼ teaspoon salt
¼ teaspoon ground cloves
4 medium pears, peeled and
    cut into cubes
½ cup pecans
⅓ cup brown sugar
¼ cup (½ stick) butter
¾ cup boiling water

Preheat oven to 375°. Combine flour, sugar, milk, baking powder, cinnamon, salt, and cloves. Stir in pears and pecans. Spoon into ungreased 2-quart baking dish. Combine brown sugar, butter, and water and pour over batter. Bake uncovered 45 to 50 minutes. Serve warm with whipped cream if desired. Yields 4 servings.

Coffeecake Cookies

1 (¼-ounce) package yeast
½ cup lukewarm water
1 teaspoon salt
¼ cup sugar
4 cups all-purpose flour
¾ cup shortening
1 cup milk
2 eggs, beaten
½ cup sugar
1 teaspoon ground cinnamon
4 tablespoons melted and
    browned butter
1½ cups confectioners' sugar
1 teaspoon vanilla extract

Dissolve yeast in water. Combine dry ingredients and cut in shortening. Scald milk and cool. Combine with eggs and yeast water. Add to flour and mix lightly until flour is moist. Do *not* knead. Refrigerate 8 to 10 hours or overnight. When ready to bake, preheat oven to 350°. Divide dough in half. Roll out each half into 9 x 10-inch size. Mix sugar with cinnamon and sprinkle on dough. Roll up and slice. Bake 8 to 10 minutes on second shelf of oven. Mix butter, confectioners' sugar, and vanilla until light and fluffy. Add enough hot water to make spreadable, if needed. Ice cookies. Yields 4 dozen.

Glazed Sour Cream Coffee Cake

Cake:
½ cup sugar
¼ cup (½ stick) butter
1 egg, beaten
½ teaspoon vanilla extract
1 cup all-purpose flour
½ teaspoon baking powder
¼ teaspoon salt
¾ cup sour cream
3 tablespoons brown sugar
3 tablespoons chopped nuts
½ teaspoon ground cinnamon
1 tablespoon browned butter

Glaze:
⅓ cup confectioners' sugar
½ teaspoon vanilla extract
1 to 2 teaspoons milk

Preheat oven to 350°. Cream together sugar and butter. Add egg and vanilla. Mix flour, baking powder, and salt and add alternately with sour cream to sugar mixture. In separate bowl combine brown sugar, nuts, and cinnamon. Spoon half of batter in greased and floured 8-inch round pan. Add nut filling on top and spoon browned butter over top. Bake 30 to 35 minutes. Cool 10 minutes.

For glaze, mix together well confectioners' sugar, vanilla, and milk and brush glaze on cake. Yields 6 to 8 servings.

Chicken Salad Supreme

1 cup mayonnaise
¼ cup lemon juice
1 teaspoon salt
¼ teaspoon ginger
4 cups cubed cooked chicken
1 cup halved seedless green grapes
½ cup sliced almonds

Combine mayonnaise, lemon juice, salt, and ginger. Add remaining ingredients and toss to combine. Serve on lettuce leaves. Yields 6 servings.

LOCUST BROOK LODGE

179 Eagle Mill Road
Butler, PA 16001
(724) 283-8453
ronni@isrv.com
locustbrooklodge.com/locustbrooklodge

Locust Brook Lodge is located in western Pennsylvania about thirty-five miles north of Pittsburgh. Nearby attractions include Moraine and McConnell's Mill State Parks, an Amish community, a large outlet mall, farmer's markets, craft, gift and antique shops, and many lovely historic homes.

Poached Eggs with Ham on Cornbread Rounds

Cornbread:
1¼ cups all-purpose flour
¾ cup cornmeal
¼ cup sugar
2 teaspoons baking powder
½ teaspoon salt plus for seasoning
1 cup buttermilk
¼ cup vegetable oil
1 egg, beaten

Cheese sauce:
1 tablespoon butter
1 tablespoon all-purpose flour
1 cup milk
1 teaspoon hot sauce
1 cup shredded Cheddar cheese
Salt and pepper

8 whole eggs
½ pound ham, thinly sliced

Preheat oven to 400°. Grease 9-inch square pan or four 3-inch-round pans. (Individual baking dishes work well.) Combine flour, cornmeal, sugar, baking powder, and salt. Stir in buttermilk, oil, and egg just until evenly moist. Bake in prepared pans 20 to 25 minutes or until lightly browned and wooden pick inserted in center comes out clean. Remove from oven, cool in pan a few minutes, and turn out on wire rack to cool completely. If baked in one pan, use 3-inch round cutter to cut four circles. Split rounds in half horizontally.

For cheese sauce, in small saucepan, heat butter and flour over medium heat. Slowly add milk, stirring constantly, and continue cooking until mixture begins to thicken. Add hot sauce and cheese, stirring until cheese is melted and blended. Season to taste with salt and pepper.

Poach eggs in poacher or in simmering water in shallow pan. To serve, place two cornbread rounds on each of four plates. Divide ham slices evenly among rounds. Place 1 egg on each round and top with cheese sauce. Yields 4 servings.

Chocolate Chip Sand Tarts

1 cup (2 sticks) butter
⅛ teaspoon salt
1 teaspoon almond extract
1¼ cups sugar
1 egg
2 cups all-purpose flour
2 cups chocolate chips
1 cup chopped walnuts

Preheat oven to 350°. Cream together butter, salt, almond extract, and sugar until light and fluffy. Beat in egg. Stir in flour. Add chocolate chips and nuts. Drop by teaspoonfuls on ungreased cookie sheet and bake 15 minutes or until lightly browned. Yields 4 dozen tarts.

Chocolate Brunch Waffles

1 quart fresh strawberries
Sugar to season plus ½ cup
2¼ cups all-purpose flour
1 tablespoon baking powder
¾ teaspoon salt
1 cup chocolate chips
¾ cup (1½ sticks) butter
1½ cups milk
3 eggs, lightly beaten
1 tablespoon vanilla extract

Wash, remove stems, and slice strawberries. Sweeten to taste with sugar (use bottled strawberry syrup in place of sugar if available) and set aside to marinate. Combine ½ cup sugar, flour, baking powder, and salt in large mixing bowl. Microwave chips and butter on high 1 minute; stir. Microwave additional 10 to 20 seconds until melted and smooth. Cool mixture and stir; batter will be thick. Stir in butter, milk, eggs, and vanilla. Cook in Belgian waffle maker. To serve, divide each waffle into four sections and place sections, point down, in dessert dishes, leaning edge of waffle on side of dish. You can add a scoop of ice cream or just top with berries, making sure to drizzle a little syrup on each serving. Yields 6 to 8 servings.

Buttermilk Coffee Cake

1 cup packed brown sugar
1 cup chopped nuts
⅓ plus ½ cup soft butter
3 cups plus 2 tablespoons
    all-purpose flour
4 teaspoons ground cinnamon
1½ cups granulated sugar
2 eggs
4 teaspoons baking powder
½ teaspoon salt
2 cups buttermilk
1 cup raisins

Preheat oven to 350°. In small bowl, combine brown sugar, nuts, ⅓ cup butter, 2 tablespoons flour, and cinnamon until mixture resembles coarse crumbs. In large mixing bowl cream remaining ½ cup butter and granulated sugar. Add eggs, one at a time, beating well after each addition. Combine remaining 3 cups flour, baking powder, and salt and add to mixing bowl alternately with buttermilk. Stir in raisins. Spread half of batter in greased 13 x 9-inch pan. Sprinkle with half of nut mixture. Carefully spread with remaining batter and sprinkle with remaining nut mixture. Bake 35 to 40 minutes or until wooden pick inserted near center comes out clean. Yields 8 to 12 servings.

THE INN AT NEW BERLIN

321 Market Street
New Berlin, PA 17855-0390
(570) 966-0321 (phone)
(570) 966-9557 (fax)
(800) 797-2350 (toll free)
visit@innatnewberlin.com
www.innatnewberlin.com

The Inn at New Berlin is an uptown experience in a rural setting, a clutch of quiet pleasures. We offer a select registry and an award-winning restaurant. The inn captures the spirit of the past with all the sophistication of today. Attractions include Penns Creek Pottery; Shade Mountain Winery; R. B. Winter State Park with hiking and biking; Roller Mills Antique Center; Knoebels Amusement park; Penns Cave; Reptileland; and Slifer House Museum.

The Valley Omelet

1 tablespoon butter
¼ cup loose sausage, crumbled
¼ cup cooked and diced potato
¼ cup crumbled bread, any variety
    (at the inn we use Challah,
    Jewish egg bread)
1 teaspoon parsley
Dash of salt
Dash of pepper
Dash of paprika
2 eggs
2 tablespoons milk
¼ cup Monterey Jack cheese, shredded

Melt butter in sauté pan over medium heat. Add sausage, potato, bread, parsley, salt, pepper, and paprika. Sauté until sausage is fully cooked. Keep warm. Whisk eggs and milk together and pour into lightly but-

tered 6-inch sauté pan. When egg mixture is cooked (omelet size), sprinkle top with shredded cheese and sausage mixture. To serve, slip out of pan onto plate. We garnish plate with a fanned strawberry and a dab of whipped cream studded with kiwi slices, or gently rim plate with parsley flakes. Yields 1 hearty serving.

Gabriel's Stuffed Acorn Squash

A popular vegetarian alternative at the inn and chosen by many non-vegetarians as well.

½ acorn squash, seeds removed
¾ cup freshly chopped mixed vegetables
    (broccoli, cauliflower, zucchini,
    summer squash, snow peas,
    scallions)
4 carrot slices
4 mushroom slices
Olive oil or butter
⅛ teaspoon basil
⅛ teaspoon oregano
⅛ teaspoon thyme
Pinch of salt
Pinch of pepper
¼ cup white wine
½ to 1 teaspoon lime juice
1 to 2 teaspoons brown sugar
½ cup grated Gouda cheese

Steam acorn squash in advance. Can be kept cool and in refrigerator until ready to use. Sauté mixed vegetables, carrots, and mushrooms in oil or butter until al dente. Add herbs, salt, and pepper. Add wine and lime juice to vegetables. Simmer for 3 to 4 minutes. Coat inside of acorn-squash-half with brown sugar. Heat in microwave 1 to 2 minutes just to take chill of refrigerator off. Preheat oven to 350°. Fill squash with vegetable mixture and top with Gouda cheese. Bake 15 minutes, or until heated through. Serve with rice, pasta, or potatoes. Garnish with fruit. Yields 1 serving.

Gabriel's Pear Streusel Topper

½ cup (1 stick) butter
1 tablespoon lemon juice
4 pears (peeled, cored, and sliced)
⅓ cup brown sugar
¼ teaspoon ground cinnamon
⅛ teaspoon ground nutmeg
⅛ teaspoon ginger
¼ cup chopped pecans

Melt butter in large sauté pan. Sprinkle lemon juice over pears and stir into melted butter. Add brown sugar, spices, and nuts. Cook slowly over low heat, stirring occasionally, until pears are somewhat softened, about 5 minutes. Serve over Belgian waffles or draped down center of 2 to 3 pieces of French toast. Plate with crisp lean bacon and festive fanned strawberry. Makes about 2 cups topping. Use ⅓ cup per serving. Yields 6 servings.

Key Lime Caesar Salad

½ cup Coco-Lopez
2 tablespoons melted butter
2 tablespoons flaked and
    sweetened coconut
2 cups 1-inch bread cubes
    (works best with dense bread)

1½ cups olive oil
½ cup red wine vinegar
2 teaspoons Dijon mustard
1 teaspoon white pepper
4 tablespoons Key lime juice
2 cups grated Asiago cheese
Romaine lettuce

Preheat oven to 350°. Mix Coco-Lopez, butter, and coconut. Toss with bread cubes and bake on greased cookie sheet 12 to 14 minutes or until light brown. Combine oil, vinegar, mustard, pepper, lime juice and cheese in 2-quart food processor. Process for 5 minutes until smooth. Toss lettuce pieces with dressing before plating. Top with croutons, and if springtime, an edible flower such as nasturtium, pansy, or marigold. Yields 6 to 8 servings.

Spring Festival Salad

1½ cups mixed seasonal greens (romaine, endive, arugula, radicchio)
2 tablespoons dried cranberries
2 tablespoons raisins
2 tablespoons toasted sliced almonds
2 tablespoons Gorgonzola cheese, crumbled
3 large grapefruit sections

Fluff mixed greens on salad plate. Sprinkle cranberries, raisins, almonds, and cheese on top of greens. Arrange grapefruit sections in a spiral on top of greens. A fanned strawberry can also be added to center of grapefruit wedges for extra pizzazz. Serve with salad dressing of choice. We always use a Honey-Walnut-Raspberry Vinaigrette, but a fat-free or low-cal alternative could also be used. Yields 1 generous serving.

Elderberry and Ginger Duckling

3 tablespoons sugar
⅓ cup cider vinegar
1 cup elderberry preserves
3 tablespoons brandy
1 tablespoon butter
1 teaspoon fresh ginger
    or ½ teaspoon ground ginger
4 duckling halves (12 ounces each)

Preheat oven to 350°. Combine all ingredients except ducklings in heavy saucepan over medium heat and bring to slow boil. Simmer on low heat 5 to 10 minutes, stirring constantly to avoid scorching. Remove from heat but keep warm. Bake ducklings in oven 25 to 30 minutes or until crispy. Drizzle sauce over ducklings and serve. Yields 4 servings.

Rhode Island

VANDERBILT HALL

41 Mary Street
Newport, RI 02840
(401) 846-6200 (phone)
(401) 846-0701 (fax)
(888) VAN-HALL (toll free)
info@vanderbilthall.com
www.vanderbilthall.com

Vanderbilt Hall is an AAA Four-Diamond, fifty-two-room luxury mansion that captures the elegance of the past in an atmosphere of comfort, style, and personalized service. Enjoy award-winning dining fireside in our restaurant, The Alva, or stop in to experience Newport's best martini bar. Vanderbilt Hall is located in the Historic Hill district of Newport and is just steps from intriguing shops, restaurants, art galleries, museums, historic mansions, and the scenic harbor.

Hot Chocolates

½ cup all-purpose flour
½ teaspoon baking powder
½ teaspoon ground cinnamon
Pinch of salt
¾ teaspoon cayenne
4 eggs
1½ cups sugar
1 teaspoon vanilla extract
1 pound bittersweet chocolate, melted
⅛ cup (¼ stick) melted butter

Preheat oven to 350°. Line baking tin with Silpat (a nonstick silicone mat used widely in restaurants, now available for home use) or grease lightly. Into large bowl, sift flour, baking powder, cinnamon, salt, and cayenne. In electric mixer whip eggs, sugar, and vanilla for 10 minutes on high. Add chocolate and butter and mix to combine. Remove bowl from electric mixer and carefully fold in dry ingredients just until combined. Scoop dough with small scoop and place onto prepared baking sheet. Place on center rack of oven and bake 15 to 20 minutes or until centers of cookies appear barely dry. Yields 50 tea cookies.

Raspberry-Almond Bars

2 cups all-purpose flour
1 cup sugar
¾ cup almond flour (pulverized almonds)
1 egg
1 teaspoon almond extract
1 cup (2 sticks) cubed and softened unsalted butter
1 cup seedless raspberry jam
½ cup sliced almonds

Preheat oven to 350°. Lightly grease 9 x 9-inch baking tin with butter. In electric mixer, combine flour, sugar, and almond flour on low speed. In separate bowl, whisk together egg and almond extract. To flour mixture, add butter piece by piece until all is used and flour mixture resembles coarse meal. Add egg mixture and just combine. Reserve 1 cup dough. The remaining dough should be pressed into prepared pan evenly. Spread jam over dough carefully; do not touch sides of pan with jam. Sprinkle small pieces of reserved dough over jam and finish with ½ cup sliced almonds. Bake about 25 minutes or until golden brown. Allow to cool, remove from tin, and slice in bite-size pieces for tea or larger pieces for dessert bars. Yields 12 dessert bars, 6 dozen bite-size pieces.

Cedar Roasted North Atlantic Salmon

4 (8-ounce) North Atlantic salmon fillets, with skin
1 teaspoon salt
1 teaspoon pepper
½ tablespoon parsley
½ tablespoon chives
½ tablespoon thyme
½ tablespoon dill
Olive oil

Preheat oven to 375°. Preheat large, nonstick skillet over medium-high. Gently season portions of salmon with salt, pepper, and herbs. When pan is hot coat with olive oil. Sear the salmon skin-side down, about 2 minutes. Flip fillets and continue to sear another 2 minutes. Prepare baking sheet by placing cedar plank in the middle of tray.

Put salmon portions, skin-side up, onto cedar shingle. Place salmon in oven and bake 7 to 10 minutes, or until salmon is fully cooked and just flaking. Remove from oven and place onto bed of risotto. Top each salmon with Golden Raisin-Basil Butter and serve with Frizzle-Fried Leeks (see recipes below). The butter will melt and essentially make a wonderful sauce for salmon. Yields 4 servings.

Golden Raisin-Basil Butter

½ stick unsalted butter, softened
3 tablespoons chopped fresh basil
2 tablespoons roughly chopped
    golden raisins
¼ teaspoon salt
1 tablespoon freshly ground
    black pepper

In small bowl combine all ingredients. On parchment or wax paper, place butter and roll into a tube, twisting ends to force butter to middle. Butter should be frozen or refrigerated until use. To use, simply unroll chilled butter and slice into disks. Place disks onto your favorite seafood or vegetable. Yields ¾ cup.

Frizzle-Fried Leeks

1 bunch leeks, tops removed,
    trimmed, and washed
1 cup milk
Vegetable oil as needed
1 cup all-purpose flour, seasoned with
    salt, pepper, and garlic

Split whites of leeks and carefully inspect for grit; if dirty, rewash. Finely julienne the leeks and soak in milk at least 1 hour. In home fryer or in thick-bottomed pot, carefully bring frying oil to 375°. Remove leeks from milk and shake off excess mois-

ture. Place leeks into seasoned flour and toss lightly until well coated. Shake off excess flour. Put leeks in frying oil and cook in small batches until golden brown. Remove from oil and place on absorbent paper towels. Reserve as garnish for salmon. Yields 4 servings.

Vanderbilt French Toast

5 eggs, well-beaten
¼ cup whole milk
1 tablespoon sugar
1 tablespoon Meyer's Dark Rum
½ teaspoon vanilla extract
¼ teaspoon salt
¼ teaspoon ground cinnamon
1 tablespoon freshly grated nutmeg
4 plus 4 slices thick Texas Toast,
    or egg-based bread (Slices should
    be ½- to ¾-inch thick.)
¼ cup seedless raspberry jam
¼ cup mascarpone cheese
Sweet cream butter
Confectioners' sugar
100% pure maple syrup

In shallow but wide bowl, combine eggs, milk, sugar, rum, vanilla, salt, cinnamon, and nutmeg. Whisk until well combined and emulsified. With offset spatula, spread four slices Texas Toast with raspberry jam. Spread remaining four with mascarpone cheese. Make four sandwiches by putting together jam slices with cheese slices. Preheat an electric griddle to 350°. When hot, grease griddle with butter. Dredge each sandwich, one at a time, in egg batter until well coated. Place coated toast onto griddle and cook 2 to 3 minutes per side or until golden brown and fully cooked. Remove from griddle, cut diagonally, and arrange four halves per plate to serve. Garnish with sprinkle of confectioners' sugar and serve with syrup. Yields 2 servings.

Johnny Cake & Blueberry Scones

1½ cups all-purpose flour
¾ cup Johnny Cake cornmeal (white)
2 teaspoons baking powder
¼ teaspoon salt
⅓ cup unsalted butter, chilled
    and finely diced
1 cup fresh or frozen Maine blueberries
1 large egg
½ cup milk
½ cup firmly packed light brown sugar
½ teaspoon pure vanilla
Whipped sweet-cream butter

Position oven rack to center and preheat to 375°. Lightly grease and flour baking sheet or use a Silpat (a nonstick silicone mat used widely in restaurants and now available for home use). In large bowl, blend flour, cornmeal, baking powder, and salt. Using a pastry blender cut butter into flour mixture until it resembles coarse meal. Add blueberries to meal. In small bowl, beat egg, milk, brown sugar, and vanilla until smooth. Add mixture to meal and gently stir just until combined. Turn dough onto lightly floured surface and shape into 8-inch circle. Pat down dough so that it is even across entire surface. Using floured, serrated knife, score circle into eight equal wedges, being sure not to cut all the way through dough. Bake 15 to 18 minutes, or just until golden brown. Remove from oven and serve hot with whipped sweet-cream butter. Yields 8 servings.

POINT PLEASANT INN & RESORT

333 Poppasquash Road
Bristol, RI 02809
(401) 253-0627 (phone)
(401) 253-0371 (fax)
(800) 503-0627 (toll free)
reservations@pointpleasantinn.com
www.pointpleasantinn.com

Point Pleasant Inn & Resort

Point Pleasant Inn & Resort is located in historic Bristol, Rhode Island, on a twenty-five-acre waterfront estate. Known as the Rockwell Mansion, the English manor has been restored to its original glory. It's all-inclusive and very exclusive, all the while managing to make you feel at home.

Eggs Rockwell

2 English muffins
2 tablespoons olive oil
4 eggs
4 slices tomato
4 slices bacon, cooked
12 medium shrimp, peeled, deveined, and cooked
¾ cup fresh lump crabmeat
8 spears asparagus, slightly steamed
Hollandaise sauce
Paprika

Split English muffins in half. Cut small hole in center of halves. Heat oil in skillet over medium heat. Place English muffin halves and circles in oil. Crack 1 egg in center of each muffin half. Cook eggs to medium, flipping once. Place each muffin, with egg, on heated plate. Top each half with slice of tomato and bacon (cut into 2 pieces). Add 3 shrimp and 3 tablespoons crabmeat per muffin half. Put 2 asparagus spears and muffin circle on top and pour on some Hollandaise sauce and paprika to taste. Yields 4 servings (½ muffin each).

THE SCHELL HAUS

117 Hiawatha Trail
Scenic Highway 11
Pickens, SC 29671
(864) 878-0078 (phone)
(877) 283-0661 (toll free)
schellhs@bellsouth.net
www.schellhaus.com

We welcome you to the Schell Haus, a Victorian-style home tucked away in the foothills of the Blue Ridge mountains. A full view of Table Rock, South Carolina's natural wonder, and wooded acreage surrounding the house provide the backdrop to your visit. Your stay will be relaxed and comfortable complemented by a full breakfast of unique recipes, including the accent of local seasonal fruits and berries. The Schell Haus's northwest South Carolina location is easily accessible from Furman and Clemson Universities, Asheville, Greenville, and Interstates 85 and 26. Excellent restaurants, shops, antiques, and entertainment are nearby.

Apricot Casserole

3 cups drained apricot halves
8 ounces light brown sugar
2 tubes Ritz crackers, crumbled
½ pound (2 sticks) butter, melted

Preheat oven to 300°. Layer half of apricots, sugar, crackers, and butter in casserole dish. Repeat layers. Cook in oven 1 hour. Serve as side dish or as fruit. Yields 6 servings.

Pumpkin Pancakes

½ cup all-purpose flour
½ cup cornmeal
2 teaspoons baking powder
1 teaspoon ground cinnamon
¼ teaspoon baking soda
¼ teaspoon salt
1 cup buttermilk
½ cup canned solid-pack pumpkin
3 tablespoons light or dark brown sugar
1 large egg
1 tablespoon vegetable oil
3 pears or apples
Butter
Confectioners' sugar
Maple syrup

Stir together flour, cornmeal, baking powder, cinnamon, baking soda, and salt. Mix well buttermilk, pumpkin, brown sugar, egg, and oil with wire whisk until blended and sugar dissolves. Add flour mixture and stir just until moistened. Drop batter by ¼ cupful onto hot griddle. Meanwhile, peel and slice pears or apples. Sauté in butter. To serve, top pancakes with fruit and sprinkle with confectioners' sugar. Serve maple syrup on side. Yields 4 servings.

Spicy Pumpkin Bread

3½ cups all-purpose flour
2 teaspoons baking soda
1 teaspoon baking powder
1 teaspoon salt
1 teaspoon ground cinnamon
1 teaspoon ground nutmeg
1 teaspoon ground allspice
½ teaspoon ground cloves
2½ cups granulated sugar
1 cup light brown sugar
1 cup corn oil
3 eggs
1 (15-ounce) can cooked pumpkin
1 cup buttermilk
1 cup diced pecans

Preheat oven to 350°. Coat three large loaf pans or seven mini-loaf pans with non-stick spray. Combine flour, baking soda, baking powder, salt, cinnamon, nutmeg, allspice, and cloves. In large bowl beat sugars and oil with electric beater until smooth. Add eggs and beat well. Add pumpkin, continuing to beat until smooth. Add dry ingredients, alternating with buttermilk and beating until batter is smooth. Fold in pecans. Pour into prepared loaf pans and bake 45 minutes or until knife inserted comes out clean. Let rest 10 minutes in pans and then turn out onto wire rack to cool. Serve warm or at room temperature, with sweet butter if desired. Yields 30 servings.

Pumpkintown Grits

6 cups water
2 cups quick-cooking grits
½ teaspoon salt
1 (15-ounce) can pumpkin
¼ cup (½ stick) butter
8 tablespoons brown sugar
1 teaspoon ground cinnamon
2 (7-ounce) jars marshmallow crème

Bring water to a boil in medium saucepan over high heat. Slowly add grits and salt, stirring with wire whisk. Reduce heat to low, cover, and cook 5 to 7 minutes or until thickened, stirring occasionally. Remove from heat, add pumpkin, and blend until smooth. Stir in butter, brown sugar, and cinnamon. Mix well. Preheat oven to 350°. Coat a 9 x 13-inch casserole with nonstick spray. Place pumpkin and grits mixture in casserole and spread top with marshmallow crème. Heat in oven until hot and top is golden. Yields 12 servings.

THE SHAW HOUSE BED & BREAKFAST

613 Cypress Court
Georgetown, SC 29440
(843) 546-9663

The Shaw House is a spacious two-story, colonial home in a serene, natural setting perfect for bird-watching. Large rooms with private baths, antiques and Southern hospitality greet all guests. The bed and breakfast is walking distance to downtown and near golf courses, beaches, gardens, antique shops, boat rides, and wonderful restaurants.

Hot Tomato Grits

2 slices bacon
2 (14-ounce) cans chicken broth
½ teaspoon salt
1 cup quick-cooking grits
2 tomatoes, peeled
2 tablespoons canned chopped green chiles
1 cup (4 ounces) shredded Cheddar cheese

Cook bacon in heavy skillet and drain. Add broth and salt. Bring to a boil. Stir in grits, tomatoes, and chiles. Return to boil. Reduce heat and simmer 15 to 20 minutes. Stir in cheese. Cover. Let stand 5 minutes. Enjoy a Southern breakfast. Yields 4 servings.

German Apple Pancakes

Pancake:
3 large eggs
¾ cup milk
¾ cup all-purpose flour
½ teaspoon salt
1½ tablespoons butter

Filling:
5 or 6 tart apples
½ stick butter
¼ cup brown sugar
½ teaspoon ground cinnamon
Confectioners' sugar

Preheat oven to 450°. Beat eggs, milk, flour, and salt until smooth. Melt butter in medium-size skillet. Pour in batter. Bake 15 minutes, reduce heat to 350°, and bake 10 minutes more.

For filling, heat apples, butter, brown sugar, and cinnamon until boiling. Pour in center of pancake. Sprinkle with confectioners' sugar. Serve with sausage or bacon. Yields 4 servings.

Sweet Potato Muffins

1½ cups sugar
½ cup vegetable oil
2 eggs
⅓ cup water
1¾ cups all-purpose flour
1½ teaspoons ground cinnamon
1 teaspoon ground nutmeg
1 teaspoon baking soda
½ teaspoon salt
1 cup cooked, mashed sweet potatoes
½ cup chopped pecans
½ cup raisins

Preheat oven to 350°. In large bowl mix sugar, oil, eggs, water, flour, cinnamon, nutmeg, soda, salt, potatoes, pecans, and raisins. Stir until well mixed. Pour into muffin pan and bake 25 minutes. Yields 4 to 6 servings.

Feather Eggs

French bread or cornbread
Cheddar cheese
¼ cup milk
1 egg
Salt and pepper
1 teaspoon mustard
Paprika
1 sprig of parsley

Preheat oven to 375°. Crumble French bread or cornbread in bottom of a ramekin. Sprinkle with cheese. Beat together milk, egg, salt and pepper to taste, and mustard. Bake 15 to 20 minutes. Sprinkle paprika on top. Garnish with sprig of parsley. Yields 1 serving.

Breakfast Casserole

2½ cups croutons
2 cups shredded Cheddar cheese
2 pounds sausage
4 eggs
2½ cups milk
1 (10¾-ounce) can cream of
    mushroom soup

Preheat oven to 350°. Place croutons in greased pan. Top with cheese and sausage. Beat eggs and mix with milk and soup. Pour mix over sausage. May be refrigerated overnight. Bake 1½ hours. Delicious with baked apples on side. Yields 4 servings.

BED &
BREAKFAST OF
SUMMERVILLE

304 South Hampton St.
Summerville, SC 29483
(843) 871-5275 (phone/fax)
ewrhodes@bellsouth.net

The Bed & Breakfast of Summerville is set in a quiet historic district where you will find privacy, comfort, and convenience. The country-style furnished guest house is on the grounds of a gracious circa 1865 home known as the Blake Washington House and is within walking distance of downtown Summerville, yet far enough away to be quiet and peaceful. Bed and Breakfast of Summerville offers bikes for touring the tree-lined streets. The swimming pool is available for registered guests from mid-May to mid-September.

Cranberry Cornbread

1½ cups cornmeal
1½ cups all-purpose flour
½ plus ¼ cup sugar
½ teaspoon baking soda
2 teaspoons baking powder
½ teaspoon salt
2 whole eggs, lightly beaten
1½ cups buttermilk
9 tablespoons melted butter
1 pint cranberries

Preheat oven to 375°. Blend together cornmeal, flour, ½ cup sugar, baking soda, baking powder, and salt. Make a well and add eggs, buttermilk, and butter. Stir until mixed. Toss cranberries with remaining ¼ cup sugar. Fold into batter. Pour into greased 9 x 13-inch pan. Bake 25 minutes or until golden brown. Yields 6 to 8 servings.

Note: Try with dried cherries or cranberries. Also good with sliced turkey sandwiches or hash. Great with butter or even honey.

THE
LAMPSTAND
BED &
BREAKFAST

9614 Charlotte Highway
Fort Mill, SC 29715
(803) 547-3100 (phone)
(866) 383-2059 (toll free)
lampstand@comporium.net
www.bbonline.com/sc/lampstand/index.html

The Lampstand Bed & Breakfast, a log house on six wooded acres, is a peacefully secluded sanctuary. Located south of Charlotte, there's plenty to see and do, unless you'd rather just rock on the porch. Here you can stay as busy or be as lazy as you like. Activities include antiquing galore, horseback riding, ballooning, Carolina Panther games, performing arts, and every kind of restaurant you can imagine.

Stuffed Breakfast Popovers

2 eggs
2 tablespoons vegetable oil
1 cup milk
1 cup all-purpose flour
1 teaspoon sugar
½ teaspoon salt

Preheat oven to 400°. Spray or grease 12-cup muffin or popover tin(s). Combine eggs and oil in medium bowl. Beat slightly. Gradually beat in remaining ingredients. Pour batter into cups until three-fourths full. Place on baking sheet in center of oven. Bake 45 to 50 minutes. Muffins will be brown and crunchy on outside, but hollow inside. Serve basket of hot popovers with assortment of side dishes. Each person stuffs his own, according to taste. Suggested fillings include scrambled eggs, bacon, ham, sausage crumbles, grated cheeses, fresh chopped herbs, even salsa. Yields 6 to 8 servings.

Fig Flowers

12 large fresh figs, washed and stemmed
4 large egg yolks
1 cup sugar
½ cup lemon juice
¼ pound (1 stick) unsalted butter,
    melted and cooled
Zest of 1 lemon
12 single mint leaves, washed

Slice figs four to five times lengthwise, from stem-end down, leaving bottom peel intact. Separate wedges to form flower shape. Whisk yolks until smooth in glass bowl. Blend in sugar, then lemon juice and butter. Whisk until well mixed. Microwave on medium-high, stirring every minute, until mixture coats back of wooden spoon, 4 to 5 minutes total. Pour into small container and place plastic wrap right on curd to prevent film. (Keeps well in refrigerator for up to 2 weeks.) Pipe or dollop lemon curd in center of each fig. Sprinkle lightly with lemon zest. Add mint leaf for accent. Yields 6 to 8 servings.

Bluenana Muffins

1 cup blueberries
1 cup pecans
¼ cup all-purpose flour
½ stick unsalted butter, softened
1 cup brown sugar
1 teaspoon ground nutmeg
1 egg
1 cup milk
½ cup honey
2 cups baking mix
1 cup mashed ripe banana

Preheat oven to 375°. Spray or grease 12-cup muffin tin(s). Coat blueberries and pecans in flour. Cream butter, sugar, and nutmeg in large mixer bowl. Beat in egg. Stir in milk and honey until blended. Add baking mix in three parts, blending well each time. Stir in bananas, just until blended. Fold in blueberries and pecans. Spoon into muffin tins until full. Bake 20 to 25 minutes. Yields 8 to 10 servings.

Benne Seed Wafers

This is an adaptation of an old Charleston recipe. There, sesame seeds are traditionally called benne seed. These wafers are light, crispy, and perfect for tea.

¼ pound (1 stick) butter
1 egg
1½ cups molasses
1 teaspoon vanilla extract
1 cup all-purpose flour
¼ teaspoon salt

¼ teaspoon baking soda
1 cup roasted unsalted sesame seeds

Preheat oven to 350°. Cover cookie sheets with foil, dull-side up. Cream together butter, egg, molasses, and vanilla. Stir in flour, salt, and baking soda. Stir in seeds just until blended. Drop by ½ teaspoonful (no more) onto foil 2 inches apart. Bake 8 minutes. Let cool. Peel off foil. Store in airtight container. Yields 10 dozen wafers.

Calendula Corn Patties with Cinnamon Apples

Calendula petals not only add warm golden color, but also are purported to have significant healing properties.

2 eggs, beaten
¼ cup vegetable oil
½ cup honey
2 cups all-purpose flour
1 cup yellow cornmeal
1 teaspoon baking powder
½ teaspoon salt
1½ cups buttermilk
1 (15½-ounce) can whole kernel corn, drained
1 cup grated Cheddar cheese
¼ cup dried calendula petals
4 cups dried apple slices
2 cups water
½ cup sugar
½ stick butter
1 tablespoon ground cinnamon

In bowl combine eggs, oil, and honey. In separate bowl combine flour, cornmeal, baking powder, and salt. Add flour mixture to egg mixture, alternating with buttermilk. Blend well. Stir in corn and cheese. Add calendula petals. Shape with hands into 3 x ½-inch-thick patties. Spray or grease griddle with vegetable oil. Fry 4 to 5 minutes on each side until light brown. Keep warm. Place apples and water in microwave dish with lid. Cover and cook

on high until water is absorbed and apples are soft, 5 to 10 minutes. Stir in sugar, butter, and cinnamon. Add more sugar, if needed. Serve warm over Calendula Corn Patties. Yields 6 servings.

Note: May substitute heated canned apples. Add extra sugar and cinnamon to taste.

THE 1790 HOUSE BED & BREAKFAST

[This inn is no longer in business.]

The 1790 House is a 212-year-old, West Indies-style, plantation owner's town home. Activities in the area include intra-coastal waterway cruises and excursions and high tea in the 1790 House Tea Room and Spice Emporium.

Baked French Toast

French toast:
1 loaf French or Italian bread
6 eggs or egg substitute equivalent
¾ cup whipping cream
¾ cup milk
2 tablespoons sugar
1 teaspoon vanilla extract
¼ teaspoon ground cinnamon
¼ teaspoon ground nutmeg
Salt

Honey butter:
¼ cup honey
½ stick butter, softened
1½ tablespoons whipping cream

Slice bread into ¾-inch slices. Arrange slices in baking pan, making sure slices fit tightly in pan. In large bowl combine eggs, ¾ cup whipping cream, milk, sugar, vanilla, cinnamon, nutmeg, and salt. Beat with wire whisk. Carefully pour over bread slices covering evenly and between slices. Cover with plastic wrap and refrigerate 8 to 10 hours or overnight. When ready to bake, preheat oven to 350°. Bake bread mixture 40 minutes until puffed and lightly golden.

For honey butter, whip honey and butter together until creamy. Add whipping cream and continue to whip until smooth. Place small dollop of honey butter on each piece of French toast and serve with warmed maple syrup. Yields 4 servings.

Apple Pie Pancakes

Batter:
2 cups all-purpose flour
3 teaspoons baking powder
½ teaspoon salt
1 tablespoon apple pie spice
¼ cup sugar
2 tablespoons apple butter
1 cup buttermilk
2 eggs
2 tablespoons oil
2 cups sliced Granny Smith apples

Lemon-honey butter:
½ stick butter, softened
¼ cup honey
Juice of ½ lemon

For batter combine flour, baking powder, salt, apple pie spice, and sugar in bowl. In separate bowl combine apple butter, buttermilk, eggs, and oil and blend with wire whisk. Carefully fold in dry ingredients. Pour batter by ¼ cup per pancake onto greased hot griddle. Place three or four slices of apple on top of each pancake. When bubbles appear, flip pancake.

For lemon-honey butter, mix butter, honey, and lemon juice together until creamy. Carefully brush lemon-honey butter on each pancake with pastry brush. Serve with warmed maple syrup and garnish with two or three slices of apple. Yields 6 to 8 servings.

COLVIN FARM BED & BREAKFAST

999 Halsellville Road
Chester, SC 29706
(803) 581-9916 (phone)
(803) 581-0368 (fax)
smower@chestertel.com
www.colvinfarmbandb.com

The Colvin Farm Bed & Breakfast is in the Olde English district of South Carolina. This bed and breakfast is a great country getaway. Area attractions include historic downtown Chester, Landsford Canal State Park, historic Brattonsville, TNT Motorsport Park, a number of Revolutionary War battle sites, Lake Monticello, and Chester State Park.

Carrot Cake Muffins with Cinnamon Glaze

2¼ cups all-purpose flour
1 tablespoon baking powder
2 plus 1 teaspoons ground cinnamon
¼ teaspoon ground nutmeg
¼ teaspoon ground allspice
¼ teaspoon salt
1 cup brown sugar
⅔ cup granulated sugar
1 cup flaked coconut
2 eggs
½ cup vegetable oil
½ cup plus 2 tablespoons buttermilk
3 carrots, grated
1 (8-ounce) can crushed pineapple
   with juice
1 tablespoon vanilla extract
1 cup sifted confectioners' sugar

Preheat oven to 375°. Lightly grease two muffin pans or use paper liners. In large bowl mix together flour, baking powder, 2 teaspoons cinnamon, nutmeg, allspice, and salt. Mix in sugars and coconut. In separate bowl, combine eggs, oil, ½ cup buttermilk, carrots, pineapple, and vanilla. Make a well in middle of flour mixture and add egg mixture. Mix until batter is moistened. (Do *not* overmix.) Fill muffin cups three-fourths full. Bake 20 to 25 minutes, or until top springs back when lightly tapped. Allow to cool. In small bowl, combine confectioners' sugar, remaining 1 teaspoon cinnamon, and remaining 2 tablespoons buttermilk. Mix until smooth and refrigerate until thickened. Drizzle over cooled muffins. Yields 24 muffins.

Chunky Applesauce

Homemade applesauce in just 10 minutes is wonderful. Serve it warm with hot fluffy biscuits and it's like hot apple pie for breakfast.

2 McIntosh apples
2 Granny Smith or other tart apples
1 cup water
Juice of ½ lemon
½ cup sugar
½ teaspoon ground cinnamon

Halve and core McIntosh apples and peel if you like. Cut each apple into six wedges. Halve and core tart apples and cut them into 1-inch chunks. Combine apples, water, and lemon juice in deep microwave-safe, 2½-quart casserole. Toss sugar and cinnamon together in small bowl and stir into apple mixture. Cook, uncovered, at full power 5 minutes. Stir, pressing apples into liquid, and return to microwave. Cook another 5 minutes. Using potato masher, coarsely mash apples, stirring them into liquid. If they do not mash easily, return to microwave for another 5 minutes. Allow applesauce to cool to room temperature. Cover and refrigerate. Applesauce thickens as it cools. Yields 4 servings.

French Toast Soufflé

10 cups 1-inch-cubed pieces
    sturdy white bread
1 (8-ounce) block Neufchatel
    cream cheese, softened
8 large eggs
1½ cups reduced-fat (2%) milk
⅔ cup half-and-half
½ plus ¾ cup maple syrup
½ teaspoon vanilla extract
3 tablespoons confectioners' sugar

Place bread cubes in 13 x 9-inch baking dish coated with cooking spray. Beat cream cheese at medium speed of mixer until smooth. Add eggs, one at a time, mixing well after each addition. Add milk, half-and-half, ½ cup maple syrup, and vanilla and mix until smooth. Pour cream cheese mixture over bread. Cover and refrigerate 8 to 10 hours or overnight. When ready to bake, remove bread mixture from refrigerator and let stand on counter 30 minutes. Preheat oven to 375°. Bake 50 minutes or until set. Sprinkle soufflé with confectioners' sugar and serve with remaining ¾ cup maple syrup. Yields 12 servings.

LIBERTY HALL INN

621 South Mechanic Street
Pendleton, SC 29670
(864) 646-7500 (phone)
(800) 643-7944 (toll free)
libertyhallinn@aol.com
www.bbonline.com/sc/liberty/

For the epitome of elegance in lodging and fine dining, you must experience Liberty Hall Inn, where the specialty of the house every day is Southern hospitality.

Points of interest include local craftsmen; historic tours of Woodburn and Ashtabula Plantations; choice golf course and lakes; the bustling campuses of Clemson University and Southern Wesleyan University, always alive with sporting and cultural events; town of Pendleton, founded 1790 and on the National Register of Historic Places.

Parmesan Potato Pancakes

These are good served with the Carolina Crab Cakes.

8 cups instant mashed potatoes
1 cup finely chopped onion
3 eggs
½ cup sour cream
½ cup heavy cream
Salt and pepper
Grated Parmesan cheese

Put potatoes and onions in mixing bowl. Add eggs, one at a time, until well combined. Add sour cream, heavy cream, and salt and pepper to taste. Gradually add Parmesan cheese until very stiff mixture is formed, generally 2 cups. Refrigerate. Place in cast-iron skillet coated with nonstick spray and light amount of olive oil. Cook on high heat until golden brown. Turn once. Serve with Carolina Crab Cakes. Yields 4 pancakes, 2 servings.

Carolina Crab Cakes

Pepper sauce:
1 (7½-ounce) can roasted red bell
    peppers, drained and washed
1 cup horseradish
3 tablespoons lobster base
¼ cup lemon juice
¼ cup minced garlic
1½ cups sour cream

Crab cakes:
1 (6-ounce) can claw crabmeat
1 egg
1 bunch scallions (about 4 to 6),
    finely sliced
2 tablespoons Worcestershire sauce
4 tablespoons Tabasco
¼ cup lemon juice
½ cup mayonnaise
¼ cup whole-grain mustard
2 tablespoons Old Bay Seasoning
1 cup (more or less) breadcrumbs

For pepper sauce, combine all ingredients in blender and mix thoroughly. Refrigerate.

For crab cakes, chop crabmeat into small pieces. Combine in mixing bowl with egg, scallions, Worcestershire, Tabasco, lemon juice, mayonnaise, mustard, and Old Bay. Mix well and add breadcrumbs slowly until mixture firm but still wet. Do *not* let mixture become dry. Should be able to form patty that holds and does not crumble. Refrigerate for at least 1 hour before using. Shape ingredients into patties (usually 2 to 3 inches in diameter). Place in cast-iron skillet coated with nonstick spray or olive oil. Cook on high heat until golden brown. Turn once. In large-mouth shallow bowl, place fresh greens in center. Stack crab cakes in center of greens. Crown with a lemon slice pierced with a frilly pick and positioned vertically. Garnish edges of bowl with swirls of pepper sauce and chopped parsley. Yields 2 servings.

♣   ♣   ♣

Pasta Cafe Leisure

2 slices raw bacon, chopped
2 tablespoons chopped garlic
4 tablespoons butter
½ cup crumbled blue cheese
1 cup heavy cream
1½ cups cooked penne pasta
1 (8-ounce) salmon fillet
3 scallions
Parsley
Paprika

Sauté bacon and garlic in butter in a large skillet. Once garlic is light brown, add blue cheese crumbles, heavy cream, and penne pasta. Stir and let simmer about 1 minute and remove from pan. Slice salmon fillet on diagonal and grill until desired doneness. Along with salmon, grill scallions for serving. Place pasta and sauce in large shallow bowl and top with scallions and bronzed salmon slices. Garnish edges of bowl with chopped parsley and light sprinkling of paprika for color. Yields 1 serving.

Pork Tenderloin Medallions with Rum Raisin Sauce

<u>Pork:</u>
1 (4 to 5 pound) pork loin
Garlic salt
Black pepper

<u>Sauce:</u>
2 cups spiced rum
2 cups golden raisins
6 cups water
1 pound brown sugar
¾ cup demi-glace powder
4 pears
Riesling wine

Preheat oven to 350°. Cut loin in half. Coat 4-inch-deep pan with nonstick spray. Place both halves of loin in pan. Season with garlic salt and black pepper. Cover with aluminum foil and roast 45 minutes.

For sauce, place rum, raisins, water, sugar, and demi-glace powder in saucepan and bring to slow boil over medium heat. When ready to serve, place a four-ounce ladle of sauce per serving in sauté pan over medium heat.

Drain and soak pears in wine. If using fresh pears, peel and poach in wine until tender. Cut two 1-inch thick medallions of pork and place on top of garlic mashed potatoes in center of plate. Place pear half slice-side down on stacked pork and top with generous ladle of warmed rum raisin sauce. Yields 8 servings.

ROSE STONE INN BED & BREAKFAST

504 E Fourth St.
Dell Rapids, SD 57022
(605) 428-3698
rosestoneinn@siouxvalley.net
www.bbonline.com/sd/rosestone

The Rose Stone Inn Bed & Breakfast was an old hotel built in 1908 for traveling salesmen arriving on the railroad. It is constructed of "rose-colored" quartzite quarried on the edge of town. It is part of the historic Main Street and included with many other downtown quartzite buildings on the National Register of Historic Places. The inn is decorated with antiques, collectibles, and warm cozy quilts, quilts, and more quilts. The breakfast is generous and referred to by guests as "delicious as it was beautiful to behold," "heavenly," and "incredible to the taste buds." Dell Rapids is a small country town along the Sioux River that turns into rapids and passes through the Dells located on the south edge of town. The city is located fifteen minutes from the intersection of Interstate 90 and 29 just outside of Sioux Falls.

Dutch Baby

4 eggs
1 cup milk (2% or whole)
1 teaspoon lemon extract
1 cup all-purpose flour
¼ cup (½ stick) butter

Preheat oven 425° Mix eggs in blender at high speed for 1 minute. Slowly add milk and lemon extract. Slowly add flour (one tablespoon at a time). Let rest for 1 to 2 minutes. Add butter in 7-inch pie plate and heat plate in oven until butter melts. Pour egg mixture into pie plate and bake 20 to 25 minutes. Baby should puff and turn golden brown. Yields 4 servings.

Hot Rum Buns

1 cup raisins
¾ cup rum
2 packages yeast (quick-rise yeast is best)
2 cups lukewarm water
1 (18.25-ounce) box yellow cake mix
1 plus 5¼ cups all-purpose flour
3 eggs
⅓ cup vegetable oil
1 teaspoon salt
3 tablespoons butter
¼ cup brown sugar
3 tablespoons cinnamon

Soak raisins in rum. Let stand. Dissolve yeast in water. Add cake mix, 1 cup flour, eggs, oil, and salt. Beat until bubbles form. Drain raisins and add ½ cup to flour mixture. Slowly add remaining 5¼ cups flour. Stir with a spoon. Let rise until doubled. Dough will be sticky. Roll out like cinnamon rolls. Spread dough with butter, sprinkle with brown sugar, cinnamon, and drained re-maining ¼ cup raisins. Roll up and cut into 16 rolls. Let rise until double in size. Pre-heat oven to 350°. Bake 20 to 30 minutes. Yields 16 servings.

Root Beer Float Cookies

Cookies:
1 cup sugar
1 cup (2 sticks) butter or margarine
3 eggs
1 cup brown sugar
½ cup buttermilk
2 teaspoons root beer extract
1 teaspoon vanilla extract
4 cups all-purpose flour
1 teaspoon baking soda
¼ teaspoon salt

Frosting:
2 cups powdered sugar
1 tablespoon half-and-half
2 teaspoons butter or margarine
2 teaspoons root beer extract

Preheat oven to 350°. Cream together sugar, butter, eggs, brown sugar, buttermilk, root beer extract, and vanilla. Add flour, baking soda, and salt. Beat until soft dough forms. Bake 10 to 12 minutes.

For frosting, combine powdered sugar, half-and-half, butter, and root beer extract. Frost cookies when cool. Yields 1 dozen cookies.

IRON MOUNTAIN INN

P.O. Box 30
Butler, TN 37640
(423) 768-2446
ironmtn@preferred.com
www.ironmountaininn.com

The Iron Mountain Inn is privacy and "Pampering Perfected" service. With 140 acres of secluded forested mountaintop, this is *the* place to go and leave the world behind. Northeast Tennessee is home to beautiful Laurel Creek Falls on the Appalachian Trail. Perhaps you prefer biking. The Dennis Cove area abounds with quiet scenic roads with surprises around each corner. Fish, swim, kayak, or just picnic on pristine Watauga Lake in your pontoon boat.

Iron Mountain Inn Surprise

For breakfast, it is a slushy or smoothie; for luncheon it is a cold soup; for dinner it is a sherbet refresher. It all depends on how hard you freeze it.

2 cups red or white wine*
2 cups sliced strawberries (fresh is best)
½ cup sugar
2 cups ice cubes

Put wine into blender. Add strawberries, sugar, and ice cubes. Process until smooth. Transfer to plastic freezer bag and freeze. Take out what you need for whichever variation of the recipe you are using. If using it as soup or a slush, give it a quick turn in blender to remix just before serving. Garnish with whole strawberry dipped in chocolate or sprig of fresh mint. Just try not to eat it all as you are making it. Yields 6 servings.

   *Note: There is a slightly different taste depending on which kind of wine you use. You may also substitute ginger ale or club soda.

French Scrambled Eggs

2 eggs
3 tablespoons milk
2 tablespoons white wine or champagne
2 (¼-inch) cream cheese squares
Chopped parsley
Chopped chives
Chopped basil

Whisk eggs, milk, and wine together. Roll cream cheese squares in mixture of herbs until coated. Heat nonstick fry pan over medium heat. Pour egg mixture into pan. Stir and scrape until no longer runny but not cooked. Add cream cheese and stir until dissolved and mixed with eggs. Cook to doneness you prefer. Serve with Italian Potato Cubes, bacon, or sausage. Yields 1 serving.

Italian Potato Cubes

3 tablespoons olive oil
2 teaspoons Italian seasoning
Salt and pepper
1 large Idaho baking potato, skin on, cleaned and cut into ¼-inch cubes

Mix together olive oil, Italian seasoning, and salt and pepper to taste. Roll potato cubes in oil mixture until coated. Cook in microwave 5 to 6 minutes or until tender; or cook on baking pan in 350° oven until tender, about 10 minutes. Yields 4 servings.

LITTLE GREENBRIER LODGE

3685 Lyon Springs Road
Sevierville, TN 37862
(865) 429-2500 (phone)
(800) 277-8100 (toll free)
littlegreenbrierlodge@worldnet.att.net
www.littlegreenbrierlodge.com

Little Greenbrier Lodge, circa 1939, is one of the oldest rustic lodges now operating as a bed and breakfast. It is perched on a mountainside only 150 yards from the entrance of the Great Smoky Mountain National Park and a main hiking trail. It's close to Cades Cove, Gatlinburg, and Pigeon Forge and has antique furniture, gorgeous views, and a full country breakfast.

Cooling Tropical Lemonade

12 ounces frozen lemonade concentrate
18 ounces frozen orange juice concentrate
24 ounces canned pineapple juice
1 gallon water
1 tablespoon vanilla extract
1 tablespoon almond extract
Sugar
15 mint sprigs

In large pitcher mix lemonade and orange juice concentrates, pineapple juice, water, vanilla, almond, and sugar to taste. Serve with mint sprig in each glass. Yields 15 servings.

Little Greenbrier Breakfast Bake

1 cup seasoned croutons
1½ cups grated Cheddar cheese
1 cup chopped ham (optional)
½ cup chopped portobello mushroom
⅓ cup chopped green bell pepper
⅓ cup chopped red bell pepper
⅓ cup chopped onion
1 cup chopped artichoke hearts
1½ cups grated Swiss cheese
10 eggs
2 cups half-and-half
Salt and pepper

Grease 9 x 13-inch pan and sprinkle with croutons, Cheddar cheese, ham, if using, mushrooms, veggies, and Swiss cheese in

that order. In large bowl beat eggs, half-and-half, and salt and pepper to taste until frothy. Pour egg mixture over layers. Cover pan and refrigerate 8 to 10 hours or overnight. When ready to bake, preheat oven to 350°. Remove cover and bake 1 hour. Let sit a few minutes before cutting. Yields 12 servings.

Little Greenbrier Sugar Cookies

½ pound (2 sticks) butter
1 cup vegetable oil
1 cup granulated sugar
2 cups confectioners' sugar
1 teaspoon vanilla extract
2 eggs
1 teaspoon baking soda
4⅓ cups all-purpose flour
1 teaspoon salt
1 teaspoon cream of tartar
Sugar to coat cookies

Preheat oven to 375°. In large bowl cream butter, oil, and both sugars. Add vanilla and eggs, then baking soda, flour, salt, and cream of tartar. Roll small pieces of dough into balls and roll in sugar. Place balls on cookie sheet and press down with bottom of glass that has been dipped in sugar. Bake 12 minutes or until edges are browned. Yields 3 dozen cookies.

CHRISTOPHER PLACE

1500 Pinnacles Way
Newport, TN 37821
(423) 623-6555 (phone)
(423) 613-4771 (fax)
(800) 595-9441 (toll free)
stay@christopherplace.com
www.christopherplace.com

Secluded in the scenic Smoky Mountains, Christopher Place was named one of the ten most romantic inns in America. Gatlinburg is nearby. You can hike waterfall trails, go horseback riding, raft on the river, visit Biltmore estate, shop the outlet malls, or just relax.

Coeur a la Crème with Raspberry Sauce

Crème:
8 ounces mascarpone cheese
¼ plus 1 cup heavy cream
1 teaspoon vanilla extract
1 tablespoon fresh lemon juice
1 tablespoon raspberry liqueur
½ cup sifted confectioners' sugar

Sauce:
1 pint fresh raspberries
1 tablespoon sugar
1 teaspoon fresh lemon juice

Cut piece of cheesecloth into four 6-inch squares. Dampen and wring out lightly. Press one square into each of four perforated heart-shaped ceramic molds. Whip cheese, ¼ cup cream, vanilla, lemon juice, and liqueur until well blended and refrigerate. Whip remaining 1 cup cream and confectioners' sugar until cream forms stiff peaks. Fold whipped cream into cheese mixture and spoon into molds.

Fold edges of cheesecloth over tops and refrigerate 3 hours.

For sauce purée raspberries, sugar, and lemon juice. Taste for sweetness. Strain and refrigerate. Unfold cheesecloth and invert molds onto serving plate. Lift off mold gently. Smooth with back of spoon and remove cheesecloth slowly. Spoon sauce onto plate around hearts and garnish with more fresh raspberries. Yields 4 servings.

Glazed Medallion Carrots

2 bunches carrots, peeled
3 tablespoons butter
2 tablespoons honey
1 tablespoon Dijon mustard
2 tablespoons white wine

Slice carrots in ¼-inch rounds. Steam in small amount of water, drain, and reserve liquid. Return liquid to pan and heat with remaining ingredients. Stir until well mixed. Add carrots and cook to reduce liquid to a glaze. Yields 4 servings.

Beef Medallions in Cognac Sauce

1 plus 1 tablespoon unsalted butter
¼ cup chopped shallots
1 teaspoon brown sugar
1 cup low-sodium chicken broth
½ cup canned beef broth
½ cup cognac
¼ cup whipping cream
2 (4- to 5-ounce) beef tenderloins
Salt and pepper

Melt 1 tablespoon butter in heavy, medium saucepan over medium heat. Add shallots and sauté until tender, about 4 minutes. Add brown sugar and stir 1 minute. Add chicken broth, beef broth, and cognac. Simmer until reduced to ½ cup, or about

20 minutes. Add cream. Sprinkle steaks with salt and pepper to taste and melt 1 tablespoon butter in skillet over medium-high heat. Add steaks and cook to desired temperature. Transfer to plate. Add sauce to skillet and bring to a boil, scraping up any brown bits. Add salt and pepper if desired. Slice steaks and fan on plates. Spoon sauce over. Garnish with chives. Yields 2 servings.

Cucumber, Radish, and Red Onion Salad

1 cucumber, peeled, halved, and seeded, cut into ¼-inch slices
2 radishes, cut into rounds
¼ cup sliced red onion
1 teaspoon olive oil
1 teaspoon lemon juice

Combine vegetables in bowl. In separate bowl whisk olive oil and lemon juice together. Add to vegetables and chill at least 1 hour. Yields 2 servings.

Note: This recipe is equally tasty with your favorite salad dressing or vinaigrette instead of olive oil and lemon juice.

Carrot-Onion Broth

1½ pounds carrots, diced small
½ cup minced onions
2 tablespoons butter
1 quart (4 cups) chicken stock
1 cup hot milk
Salt
White pepper
½ cup warm heavy cream

Sweat carrots, onions, and butter on low heat, covered, until tender. Do *not* brown. Add stock to pot and simmer until vegetables are tender. Purée soup in blender and pass through strainer and cheesecloth. Add hot milk and heat soup again. Do *not* let boil. Season with salt and white pepper to taste. At serving time, add heavy cream. Yields 6 to 8 servings.

HACHLAND HILL INN BED & BREAKFAST

1601 Madison Street
Clarksville, TN 37043
(931) 647-4084 (phone)
(931) 552-3454 (fax)

This famous inn is located on a wooded hill in downtown Clarksville. It has six guest rooms in the main inn. Three cottages, all cedar log, were built in the late 1700s: Honeymoon Cottage; Pioneer House; 1790 House. It is a special place for the honeymoon or a business getaway.

"Coq Au Vin"

4 boneless chicken breasts
½ teaspoon dry mustard
½ teaspoon onion powder
½ teaspoon dried basil
½ teaspoon dried sage
½ teaspoon dried oregano
½ stick butter
1 plus 1 cup water
1 cup good sherry wine
2 tablespoons cornstarch
¼ cup red wine
1 (4-ounce) can sliced mushrooms
1 cup rice
1 cup orange juice

Preheat oven to 350°. Place chicken breasts skin-side down in baking pan. Sprinkle with mustard, onion powder, basil, sage, and oregano. Dot with butter. Add 1 cup water and 1 cup good sherry wine. Cover and bake for 2 hours. Remove cover and allow chicken to brown. Drain juice from chicken and thicken with mixture of cornstarch and several tablespoons water. Add ¼ cup red wine and sliced mushrooms.

Cook rice in orange juice and remaining cup water until liquid is absorbed, about 14 minutes for converted rice. Season with salt, pepper, and plenty of butter. Yields 4 servings.

Tutti Fruiti

1 (20-ounce) can Alberta peaches, chopped
1 (20-ounce) can pineapple cubes
1 (20-ounce) can crushed pineapple
½ cup sliced maraschino cherries
3 cups sugar
1 cup bourbon or rum

Drain fruit juice into saucepan. Add sugar and boil 5 minutes. Add fruit and chill. Stir in Bourbon or rum and store in refrigerator. Yields 8 to 10 servings.

Hot Fudge Sauce

¼ pound (1 stick) butter
2¼ cups confectioners' sugar
⅔ cup evaporated milk
6 squares bitter chocolate

Mix all ingredients. Cook over hot water in double boiler for 30 minutes. Do *not* stir. Beat until smooth and serve. Serve with homemade ice cream and cookies. Yields about 3½ cups.

Egg Soufflé

3 cups rich cream sauce
½ teaspoon curry powder
½ teaspoon Worcestershire sauce
Salt and pepper
8 hard-cooked eggs, diced
¾ pound bacon, crisply cooked
    and crumbled

Preheat oven to 350°. To cream sauce add curry powder, Worcestershire sauce, and salt and pepper to taste. Make alternate layers of eggs, sauce, and bacon in 3-quart

baking dish. Finish with bacon and brown in oven 20 to 30 minutes. Yields 4 servings.

Duckling a l'Orange

1 young duck, 2 to 3 pounds
Salt and pepper
1 cup orange juice
4 oranges, sliced thin with rind
3 tablespoons cognac
3 tablespoons curaçao
    (Cointreau or Triple Sec)

Preheat oven to 350°. Split duck down middle. Place duck in roasting pan. Sprinkle with salt and pepper. Cover with orange juice and orange slices. Bake 2½ to 3 hours. Remove juices. Add salt and pepper to taste. Stir in cognac and curaçao. Thicken gravy and pour over duck. Remove pan from heat and sprinkle with cognac to flame. Yields 2 servings.

BLUE MOON FARM BED & BOARD

4441 North Chapel Road
Franklin, TN 37076
(615) 497-4518 (phone)
(800) 493-4518 (toll free)
relax@bluemoonfarmbb.com
www.bluemoonfarmbb.com

The guest house at Blue Moon Farm is an exclusive country hideaway for one special guest at a time. It is one hundred years old and a few short miles from Nashville in historic Franklin, Tennessee. Surrounded by wraparound balcony and pastoral rolling hillsides, guests can sit in a porch swing beside the perennial and water gar-

den. Sleep soundly in the down-draped, king-size featherbed and awake to a tray-delivered, gourmet, candlelight breakfast. Don't even bother to dress for breakfast. Our spa robes are comfy and cozy, especially designed for us by one of the finest robe tailors. This unique setting allows as much, or as little, host involvement as you solicit. Romance packages and gourmet dinner for two upon request. Once in a Blue Moon you find an escape as unique as you are.

Pork Tenderloin Sweet Potato Hash

¼ cup (½ stick) unsalted butter
4 (2-inch) pork tenderloin boneless chops
1 large sweet onion
2 tablespoons minced garlic
1 large sweet potato, cut in small dice
2 tablespoons minced pimientos
2 tablespoons minced fresh rosemary
Salt and pepper

Melt butter in large skillet. Brown and cook pork. Remove from pan to cool and retain drippings. Chop onion and sauté until translucent, about 5 minutes. Add garlic and sweet potato. In food processor coarsely shred pork. Return pork to pan. Add pimientos, rosemary, salt, and pepper. Mix well, patting mixture lightly into a large cake. Allow to cook 25 minutes on medium low without stirring. This will make a nicely browned surface when you flip. Then do the same on reverse side. Cut in quarters, serve with eggs on top and garnish with sprigs of fresh rosemary. Yields 4 servings.

Note: The orange color of the sweet potato contrasts well with eggs over easy and a rosemary garnish.

Almond-Chicken-Salad-Stuffed Tomato

2 skinless, boneless chicken breasts
1 cup honey mixed with 1 cup spicy
    brown mustard or Dijon mustard
Seasoned breadcrumbs
1 stick unsalted butter
1 red onion
1 stick celery
1 cup unsalted whole almonds,
    reserving 3 for garnish
2 tablespoons mayonnaise
Pinch of salt and pepper
1 teaspoon Italian seasoning
Squeeze of fresh lemon juice
Mixed lettuce greens
Medium ripe tomato
1 cup balsamic vinegar
1 cup extra virgin olive oil
Pinch of salt and pepper
Fresh orange or tangerine

Dip chicken breasts in honey-mustard mixture. Coat with breadcrumbs. Heat butter in skillet over medium-low heat. Sauté chicken. Cool and chill. Finely chop chicken, onion, celery, and almonds. Mix in mayonnaise, salt and pepper, Italian seasoning, and lemon juice. Put lettuce greens on plate and top with tomato sectioned into wedges but not cut through the bottom. You are creating a "bowl" to hold chicken salad. Place chicken salad in tomato. Garnish with 3 whole almonds. Combine vinegar, oil, and salt and pepper. Drizzle all with vinaigrette. Peel and section orange or tangerine, place 3 to 5 wedges alongside of stuffed tomato. Add a few stoned-wheat crackers or warm French bread. Yields 2 servings.

Peach Morning Tiramisù

Freshly picked peaches
1 teaspoon maple syrup
¼ teaspoon ground cinnamon
½ teaspoon sugar
½ teaspoon Triple Sec liqueur
2 tablespoons orange juice
¼ cup vanilla pudding or custard
Apricot sponge cake or ladyfingers
Bing cherries

Peel and slice peaches, allowing juices to drip into bowl. Add syrup, cinnamon, sugar, Triple Sec, and orange juice. Allow mixture to sit 30 minutes to glaze. In bottom of parfait glass, place pudding or custard. Place sponge cake or ladyfinger vertically, with bottom edge resting on custard and top edge protruding over top edge of glass. Use slotted spoon to place peaches over custard and bottom half of cake. Pour glaze over cake to absorb. Garnish with fresh Bing cherries for flavor and color contrast. Yields 2 servings.

Chocolate Tea Bread

¼ pound (1 stick) butter, softened
1 cup sugar
2 eggs
1½ cups all-purpose flour
2 tablespoons cocoa
1 teaspoon baking soda
1 teaspoon salt
½ teaspoon ground cinnamon
1 teaspoon vanilla extract
½ cup sour cream
½ cup chopped walnuts
⅓ cup miniature semisweet chocolate chips

Preheat oven to 350°. Cream butter and gradually add sugar, beating until light and fluffy. Add eggs, one at a time, beating well after each addition. Combine flour, cocoa, soda, salt, and cinnamon. Sift together. Stir flour mixture into egg mixture, blending well. Add vanilla. Stir in

sour cream, walnuts, and chocolate morsels. Spoon batter into two greased and floured 7½ x 3 x 2-inch loaf pans. Bake 55 minutes or until wooden toothpick inserted in center comes out clean. Cool in pans 10 minutes, remove from pans, and cool completely on wire rack. Yields 2 loaves.

PROSPECT HILL BED & BREAKFAST INN

801 W. Main Street, Hwy. 67
Mountain City, TN 37683
(423) 727-0139 (phone)
(800) 339-5084 (toll free)
judyH@prospect-hill.com
www.prospect-hill.com

Hospitality and history set Prospect Hill apart. Huge rooms offer king- and queen-size beds, choice of whirlpool tub for two or a large shower, "traditional" furnishings that are never stuffy. Enjoy robes, generous snack baskets, in-room TV, individual climate controls, and scented candles. Explore the Blue Ridge's many hidden treasures less than one hour away or enjoy the three-state view from our porches. Activities include hiking, biking, skiing, fly-fishing, boating, antiquing, and relaxing.

Southern Pound Cake

Cake:
2 cups sugar
1 cup solid vegetable shortening
6 large eggs
1 teaspoon vanilla extract
1 teaspoon almond extract
2 cups all-purpose flour
½ teaspoon salt

Frosting:
1 pound confectioners' sugar
¼ pound (1 stick) butter, softened
¼ cup milk
1 teaspoon vanilla extract

Preheat oven to 325°. Cream sugar and shortening by melting briefly in microwave. Add eggs and combine well with vanilla and almond. Sift together flour and salt. Fold into wet mixture. Do *not* overbeat because it will cause unsightly, large tunnels through cake. Grease, but do not flour, 10-inch Bundt pan. Bake 1 hour or until a knife comes out clean. Cool and remove from pan.

For frosting, mix together sugar, butter, milk, and vanilla until smooth. Allow cake to cool completely before frosting. Yields 12 servings.

Strawberry Crêpes

Crêpes:
6 eggs
4 teaspoons sugar
1 teaspoon salt
2 cups all-purpose flour
2 cups milk

Filling:
3 (10-ounce) boxes frozen strawberries
¼ to ⅓ cup sour cream

Sauce:
Juice from strawberries for filling
3 tablespoons cornstarch

For crêpes, heat saucepan over medium-low heat. Mix together eggs, sugar, and salt. Add alternately flour and milk. Beat thoroughly. Pour ¼ cup batter into pan and spread evenly. Turn when lightly browned. Brown second side. Remove to flat surface.

For filling, defrost strawberries overnight. Warm thoroughly in microwave. Drain berries, reserving juice for sauce. Stir in sour cream to taste.

For sauce, place strawberry juice in glass container. Add cornstarch and whisk together. Microwave off and on until sauce thickens. Use whisk to stir as sauce thickens.

To serve place about ⅛ cup filling in 5- to 6-inch line along one edge of crêpe. Roll up crêpe and place on serving plate. Pour or paint a stripe of strawberry sauce along length of crêpe, dust with confectioners' sugar, serve warm. Crêpes can be assembled and held in slightly warm oven (about 175°) until serving time. Serve with side of sausage and fruit garnish, including a strawberry and sauce. Yields 3 servings.

Chocolate Almond Muffins

6 tablespoons sugar
½ stick unsalted butter
2 eggs
1 teaspoon vanilla extract
1 teaspoon almond extract
1½ cups all-purpose flour
½ cup powdered cocoa
¼ teaspoon salt
3 teaspoons baking powder
¾ cup milk
½ to ¼ cup semisweet chocolate chips
Confectioners' sugar

Preheat oven to 425°. In medium-size ceramic mixing bowl place sugar and butter. Heat in microwave about 30 seconds, or until butter is melted. Add eggs and mix together thoroughly. Add extracts. Measure flour, cocoa, salt, and baking powder into sifter. Sift into egg mixture, add milk, and stir until mixed. Do *not* overmix. Stir in chocolate chips. Grease muffin pans with nonstick flavorless spray. Spoon just under ¼ cup mix into each cup, more if using large size tins. Bake 10 to 15 minutes. When done, a pick comes out clean and top is puffed and nearly pointed. Do *not* overcook. Allow to cool slightly before removing from pan. May also be cooked in molds. Dust with confectioners' sugar and serve with butter on side. Yields 7 to 9 servings.

Note: Add food coloring for seasonal effects. For a special touch, we color a small amount of cake mix red and some blue and make layers in the Bundt pan. Garnish with a sprig of mint or a small American flag.

Cinnamon Muffins

¼ pound (1 stick) butter, softened
1 cup sugar
2 eggs
1½ cups sifted all-purpose flour
2 teaspoons baking powder
Pinch of salt
1 tablespoon ground cinnamon
½ teaspoon allspice
½ cup milk

Preheat oven to 350°. Soften butter and sugar together in microwave. Beat in eggs. Sift together flour, baking powder, salt, cinnamon, and allspice and stir in egg mix, alternating with milk. Pour into greased muffin pans and bake 15 to 20 minutes or until a toothpick inserted in center comes out dry. Allow time for muffins to cool before removing from pan, or they will fall apart. Yields 15 to 16 muffins.

BUCKHORN INN

2140 Tudor Mountain Road
Gatlinburg, TN 37738
(865) 436-4668 (phone)
(865) 436-5009 (fax)
buckhorninn@msn.com
www.buckhorninn.com

Offering fine accommodations since 1938, Buckhorn Inn offers rooms, suites, cottages, and guest houses with breathtaking mountain views. It is the only inn in the county offering dinner every evening.

Tuscan Chicken and Artichoke Soup

4 celery ribs, diced
1 red onion, diced
4 garlic cloves, minced
2 tablespoons olive oil
8 cups (64 ounces) chicken broth
16 ounces quartered artichoke hearts
1 pound mushrooms, sliced
2 pounds cooked chicken breasts, chopped
2 bay leaves
1 tablespoon thyme
1 tablespoon oregano
1 tablespoon chopped parsley
¼ cup all-purpose flour
¼ cup white wine
¼ cup lemon juice

Sauté celery, onion, and garlic in olive oil until tender. Add chicken broth, artichoke hearts, mushrooms, chicken, bay leaves, thyme, oregano, and parsley and bring to a boil. Turn heat to low and simmer 30 minutes. Mix flour and wine and add to soup, stirring well. Add lemon juice. Yields 8 to 10 servings.

Crispy Salmon

1½ cups balsamic vinegar
¼ cup chicken broth
¼ pound (1 stick) butter, cut into pieces
¼ cup olive oil
4 salmon fillets with skin on
All-purpose flour
Salt and pepper

In small saucepan, bring vinegar to a boil. Reduce to ½ cup. Add chicken broth and butter and cook until butter is melted. Keep warm but do *not* boil. Heat oil in pan or iron skillet with ovenproof handle. Dredge fillets skin-side down in flour and

put in hot oil. Salt and pepper tops of fillet. Sauté until skin starts to brown, 3 to 4 minutes. Put in oven skin-side down and cook until done, 10 to 15 minutes. Serve skin-side up brushed with balsamic vinegar glaze on rice or couscous. Yields 4 servings.

Blueberry-Lemon Cheesecake

Crust:
1 stick unsalted butter, softened
¼ cup sugar
½ cup all-purpose flour
½ cup yellow cornmeal
Pinch of salt

Cheesecake:
4 (8-ounce) packages cream cheese, softened
1 cup softened mascarpone cheese
1½ cups sugar
2 large eggs
2 teaspoons finely chopped lemon zest
3 tablespoons freshly squeezed lemon juice

Topping:
3 cups fresh blueberries
½ cup sugar
1 tablespoon water
2 teaspoons freshly squeezed lemon juice

For crust, preheat oven to 350°. In mixer, combine butter and sugar and mix until smooth. Mix in flour, cornmeal, and salt until crumbly. Press into bottom of springform pan and bake about 20 minutes.

For cheesecake, decrease oven temperature to 325°. In mixer combine cream cheese, mascarpone, and sugar. Mix in eggs, lemon zest, and lemon juice. Spread batter over crust and place springform pan in rectangular baking pan. Fill pan one-third full of hot water. Bake in water bath until all but very center is set, about 1 hour. Remove cheesecake from water bath. With knife, loosen edges of cheesecake to prevent cracking. Refrigerate until cold.

For topping, combine blueberries, sugar, water, and lemon juice in saucepan. Over medium-low heat cook mixture 5 to 10 minutes until thick. Cool and spread over cheesecake. Yields 8 to 10 servings.

Cappuccino Brownies

Brownie:
8 ounces bittersweet chocolate (not unsweetened)
1 cup walnuts
1½ sticks unsalted butter
2 tablespoons instant espresso powder
1 tablespoon boiling water
1½ cups sugar
2 teaspoons vanilla extract
4 large eggs
1 cup all-purpose flour
½ teaspoon salt

Frosting:
8 ounces cream cheese, softened
6 tablespoons unsalted butter, softened
1½ cups confectioners' sugar
1 teaspoon vanilla extract
1 teaspoon ground cinnamon

Glaze:
6 ounces bittersweet chocolate
1½ tablespoons instant espresso powder
1 tablespoon boiling water
2 tablespoons unsalted butter
½ cup heavy cream

Preheat oven to 350°. Butter and flour 13 x 9-inch baking pan. Chop chocolate and walnuts and cut butter into pieces. In cup dissolve espresso powder in boiling water. In metal bowl set over saucepan of barely simmering water, melt chocolate and butter with espresso mixture, stirring until smooth. Remove bowl from heat and cool mixture to lukewarm. Stir in sugar and vanilla. Stir in eggs one at a time, stirring well after each addition, and stir in flour and salt just until combined. Stir in walnuts. Pour batter into baking pan and smooth top. Bake brownie layer in middle of oven 22 to 25 minutes, or until tester comes out with crumbs adhering. Cool brownie layer completely in pan on rack.

For frosting beat cream cheese and butter in bowl with an electric mixer until light and fluffy. Sift confectioners' sugar over mixture and add vanilla and cinnamon, beating until combined well. Spread frosting evenly over brownie layer. Chill brownie 1 hour or until frosting is firm.

For glaze chop chocolate. Dissolve espresso powder in boiling water. In metal bowl set over saucepan of barely simmering water, melt chocolate and butter with cream and espresso mixture, stirring until glaze is smooth. Remove bowl from heat and cool glaze to room temperature. Spread glaze carefully over frosting layer. Chill brownies, covered, at least 3 hours. Cut chilled brownies with sharp knife and serve chilled or at room temperature. Brownies keep, covered and chilled, three days. Yields 12 to 14 brownies.

NEWBURY HOUSE BED & BREAKFAST

5517 Rugby Highway (Hwy 52)
Rugby, TN 37733
(423) 628-2441 (phone)
(423) 628-2266 (fax)
(888) 214-3400 (toll free)
rugbytn@highland.net
www.historicrugby.org

Restored Newbury House Bed & Breakfast, built in 1880, was the first boarding house in Rugby colony. It offers six Victorian-furnished, air-conditioned bedrooms, four with private baths and two sharing a large bath in the hall. A parlor with ceiling fans, fireplace, and front verandah are relaxing places for quiet discussions. Cottages are also available. Come to the beautiful Cumberland Plateau of East Tennessee to a truly special historic village for your next getaway.

Shepherd's Pie

2 cups chopped onions
2 cups chopped celery
8 cups thinly sliced carrots
Margarine
10 cups cooked, chopped roast beef
　　or pot roast (about ½-inch pieces
　　or smaller)
4 cups brown gravy
2 beef bouillon cubes
　　or equivalent base
6 teaspoons parsley flakes
1 teaspoon sage
3 to 4 large bay leaves
2 teaspoons garlic powder
1 to 2 teaspoons salt
Mashed potatoes
2 tablespoons grated Cheddar cheese

Over medium-high heat sauté onions, celery, and carrots in margarine in large skillet just until tender. Combine with roast beef, gravy, bouillon, parsley, sage, bay leaves, garlic powder, and salt and simmer slowly about 20 minutes. Be sure to remove bay leaves before serving. Mixture should be thicker than stew but neither too dry nor too runny. Add more gravy if necessary. Put ¾ cup hot beef mixture into small, round casserole dishes. Cover to edges with mashed potatoes, smoothing with knife. Mark with tines of fork. Sprinkle middle with cheese. Place under broiler until lightly brown. Garnish with fresh parsley. After storage in refrigerator, more gravy may be needed. Yields about 20 servings.

Note: Do not use more sage as it overpowers other flavors.

Cream Scones

5 cups all-purpose flour
7½ teaspoons baking powder
5 tablespoons sugar
1¼ teaspoons salt
1 stick plus 2 tablespoons butter
5 eggs, beaten
¾ cup heavy cream or evaporated milk

Preheat oven to 400°. Combine flour, baking powder, sugar, and salt in large bowl. Cut in butter until mixtures resembles crumbs. Stir in beaten eggs and cream to make fairly stiff dough. Turn out on lightly floured surface and knead just until dough sticks together. Roll dough to 1-inch thick and cut into 2½-inch rounds with floured cutter. Arrange on ungreased baking sheet ¾-inch apart. (They should not touch.) Bake 12 to 15 minutes, just until tops are lightly browned. (Do *not* overbake because they will get hard.) Yields 25 (2½-inch round) scones.

Cottage Pie

10 pounds ground beef
8 large onions, diced
2 pounds carrots, diced
2 tablespoons ground sage
3 (6-ounce) cans tomato paste
5 ounces beef base
5 quarts (20 cups) water
4 tablespoons Kitchen Bouquet
Salt and pepper
4 cups all-purpose flour
4 cups warm water
Mashed potatoes
Grated cheese

Using large thick-bottomed pan, brown meat and onions (no fat is required). When meat looks crumbly, add carrots, sage, tomato paste, and beef base and stir. Then add water to cover mixture. Add Kitchen Bouquet to make liquid medium brown (not black brown). Allow to simmer until meat is tender, stirring occasionally to prevent burning. Add salt and pepper to taste. Bring to full boil. Skim off any excess fat. Mix flour with warm water to thick pouring paste and add this to boiling meat mixture. Allow flour to cook out, about 5 minutes, stirring all the time. Pour into baking pans up to half depth, at least about two inches deep. Cool completely until mixture is firm to touch. Preheat oven to 350°. Spread with mashed potatoes at least 1½ inches deep. Mark surface with fork. Bake about 1 hour. Sprinkle with cheese 5 minutes before removing from oven. Yields 20 servings.

Buttermilk Coconut Pie

½ stick butter or margarine
1 cup sugar
2 tablespoons all-purpose flour
Dash of salt
4 eggs, beaten lightly
2 teaspoons vanilla extract
1 cup buttermilk
1 cup grated coconut
1 (9-inch) unbaked pie shell

Preheat oven to 350°. Melt butter or margarine. Remove from heat and stir in sugar, flour, and salt. Add eggs, vanilla, and buttermilk and stir until well blended. Stir in coconut. Pour into unbaked pie shell. Bake 45 minutes, or until set and lightly browned. Serve topped with dollop of whipped cream and with sprinkle of coconut if available. Yields 8 servings.

Notes: Pie will puff up as it bakes, then sink as it cools. Can be served at room temperature or chilled. Should be kept in refrigerator if held from day to day.

RICHMONT INN

220 Winterberry Lane
Townsend, TN 37882
(865) 448-6751
richmontinn@aol.com
www.richmontinn.com

Rest your body and soul at the Richmont Inn in the Great Smoky Mountain National Park. Enjoy hiking, biking, fishing, picnicking, horseback riding, rafting, golfing, antiquing and craft shopping, wildflower walks, historic tours, and the theater.

Richmont Inn's Crème Brûlée Kahlúa

2 cups heavy cream
4 egg yolks
2½ tablespoons sugar
1 teaspoon pure vanilla extract
3 tablespoons Kahlúa
¼ cup sifted light brown sugar

Preheat oven to 325°. Heat cream in double boiler. In mixer beat egg yolks, gradually adding sugar. Remove cream from heat and pour into egg mixture slowly, stirring constantly. Add vanilla and Kahlúa. Pour into 3½-inch ramekins and place them into pan of warm water. Bake uncovered 50 minutes. When custard is set, remove from oven, sprinkle with brown sugar, and place under broiler about 2 minutes until sugar is caramelized. Chill

for minimum of 4 hours and serve. Yields 6 servings.

Richmont Inn Bacon

1 plus ½ cup bread flour
8 thick slices bacon, halved
1 cup light brown sugar
½ teaspoon black pepper
1 teaspoon thyme

Line sheet pan with aluminum foil, folding edges of foil over lip of pan to outside. Sprinkle aluminum foil with ½ cup bread flour. Preheat oven to 350°. Place bacon halves on sheet pan. In bowl, mix remaining 1 cup bread flour with sugar, pepper, and thyme and sprinkle mix on bacon. Turn bacon over and sprinkle other side. Bake about 30 minutes or until done to preferred crispness. Remove from oven and place on paper towel-lined pan to remove any excess fat. Serve immediately or keep warm in oven until ready to serve. Yields 4 servings.

French Toast a l'Orange with Rum-Soaked Bananas

2 bananas, sliced
2 tablespoons butter
¼ cup rum
3 large eggs
½ cup heavy whipping cream
1½ tablespoons sugar
¼ cup Triple Sec or Grand Marnier
1 teaspoon ground cinnamon
1 tablespoon dried orange peel
2 tablespoons unsalted butter
4 one-day-old croissants, halved
Confectioners' sugar
Thin slices of orange for garnish

Sauté sliced bananas in butter and rum and set aside. Beat eggs and gradually whip cream into eggs. Add sugar, Triple Sec, cinnamon, orange peel, and unsalted butter and whip lightly. Dip each half croissant into batter. Place on buttered griddle and cook over medium heat on both sides until golden brown. Place 4 tablespoons banana mix in center of croissant. Place remaining half croissant on top. Sprinkle with confectioners' sugar and garnish with thin orange slices. Yields 4 servings.

GENERAL MORGAN INN

111 N. Main Street
Greeneville, TN 37743
(423) 787-1000 (phone)
(423) 787-1001 (fax)
(800) 223-2679 (toll free)
genmorgan@xtn.net
www.generalmorganinn.com

The General Morgan Inn & Conference Center is located in downtown historic Greeneville, Tennessee, and offers elegant accommodations, fine dining, and unparalleled service and amenities.

Apple, Carrot, and Raisin Salad

½ cup raisins
½ cup orange juice
2½ cups shredded carrots
3 medium Golden Delicious apples, shredded
1 tablespoon shredded horseradish or 1½ teaspoons prepared
⅓ cup vegetable oil
Salt
Pepper

Combine raisins and orange juice to plump raisins. Drain raisins and reserve juice. Combine raisins, carrots, apples, and horseradish. Beat together reserved orange juice, oil, and salt and pepper to taste. Add dressing to carrot mixture and toss until all ingredients are thoroughly coated. Yields 10 servings.

Roast Duckling with Bigarade Sauce

Duck:
1 duckling
Salt
Pepper
2 to 3 parsley stems
1 thyme sprig
Small piece bay leaf

Sauce:
1½ tablespoons sugar
1 tablespoon water
1½ tablespoons dry white wine
1½ tablespoons cider vinegar
¼ cup orange juice concentrate
¼ cup red currant jelly
4 cups demi-glace
2 cups brown stock

Zest of 1 orange, julienned and blanched
Orange segments

Place duckling breast-side up on rack. Season with salt and pepper to taste. Place parsley, thyme, and bay leaf piece in duck cavity. Roast duckling until juices run barely pink. Remove duckling from pan and set aside. Degrease pan and reserve drippings. Cool, split in half, and partially bone duckling.

For sauce, combine sugar and water and caramelize mixture carefully. Add wine, vinegar, orange juice concentrate, and currant jelly. Mix well. Reduce by half. Add demi-glace and brown stock and bring to a boil. Add pan drippings. Reduce heat and simmer until mixture is reduced to 1 quart. Strain through cheesecloth and reserve.

For each serving brush duckling with small amount of sauce and reheat in very hot oven until duck is crisp. Reheat about ¼ cup of sauce per serving and add blanched orange zest and orange segments. Pool sauce on a plate and place duckling on sauce. Yields 4 to 6 servings.

Santa Fe-Style Black Bean Cakes

12 ounces dried black beans, soaked overnight
1 smoked ham hock
6 to 8 peppercorns
1 sprig fresh rosemary
1 sprig fresh thyme
3 to 4 parsley stems
5 whole cloves garlic
1 onion, minced
Chicken stock as needed
2 eggs
5 tablespoons cake flour
Salt and pepper
10 ounces crabmeat, picked
10 ounces corn kernels
Clarified butter or olive oil as needed
3 tablespoons chopped cilantro
1 (16-ounce) jar salsa

To large soup pot add beans and ham hock. In cheesecloth tie together peppercorns, rosemary, thyme, parsley, and garlic to make a bouquet garni. Add to pot with onion, and enough chicken stock to cover by about 3 inches. Simmer 1½ hours, or until beans are tender. Drain off liquid and discard bouquet garni. Purée beans to chunky paste. Stir in eggs and flour. Adjust seasoning with salt and pepper to taste. Form mixture into cakes. Sauté crabmeat and corn in clarified butter until hot. Adjust seasoning and add cilantro. Keep warm. Sauté bean cakes in butter or oil until heated through. Serve cakes on pool of salsa and top with crabmeat and corn mixture. Yields 10 servings.

Louisiana Chicken and Shrimp Gumbo

¼ pound andouille sausage, chopped
½ pound lean chicken meat, chopped
1 green pepper, chopped
2 ribs celery, chopped
1 jalapeño pepper, chopped
4 scallions, split and cut on bias
1 tablespoon chopped garlic
1 cup sliced okra
1 cup coarsely chopped tomato
13 cups chicken stock
1 cup cooked Carolina rice
1¼ cups all-purpose flour,
    baked to dark brown
1 tablespoon filé powder
1 teaspoon oregano
2 bay leaves
½ teaspoon dried thyme leaves
¼ teaspoon black pepper
1 teaspoon onion powder
4 ounces shrimp, chopped

Sauté andouille sausage and add chicken. Add green pepper, celery, jalapeño, scallions, garlic, okra, and tomatoes and sauté lightly. Add stock and rice. Add flour and filé, stirring to work out any lumps. Add seasonings; simmer 30 minutes. Add shrimp and simmer 2 minutes. Adjust seasoning to taste with salt and pepper. Yields 1 gallon.

Chocolate Sabayon Torte

9 egg yolks
½ cup sugar
¾ cup sherry
8 (1-ounce) squares sweet chocolate,
    melted
3 cups heavy cream, whipped
1 teaspoon vanilla extract
2 (¼-ounce) packages gelatin
¼ cup brandy
6 slices chocolate sponge cake
Simple syrup as needed (2 parts water,
    1 part sugar boiled until clear)
Chocolate whipped cream*
Cake crumbs
32 chocolate fans (or sliced chocolate)

Combine egg yolks, sugar, and sherry in small, glass bowl. Cook over simmering water until thickened and mixture falls in ribbons from spoon. Add melted chocolate and blend. Fold in whipped cream and add vanilla. Soften gelatin in brandy and place over simmering water to dissolve all crystals. Add to chocolate mixture. Moisten sponge cake slices with simple syrup. Place one layer in bottom of springform pan and add a layer of sabayon filling. Add second layer of sponge cake, followed by layer of filling, and top this with third layer of cake. Repeat procedure for second torte. Refrigerate tortes until filling is firm.

Ice tortes with chocolate whipped cream and mark each torte into 16 slices. Trim bottom edge of tortes with cake crumbs. Pipe dollop of chocolate whipped cream onto each slice. Lean fan of chocolate on each dollop. Yields 2 (10-inch) tortes.

Note: To make chocolate whipped cream, melt chocolate in double boiler and add to container of whipped cream until desired chocolaty-ness.

River Run Bed & Breakfast

120 Francisco Lemos St.
Kerrville, TX 78028
(830) 896-8353 (phone)
(830) 896-5402 (fax)
(800) 460-7170 (toll free)
riverrun@ktc.com
www.riverrunbb.com

River Run is a romantic getaway located in the heart of Texas hill country with six spacious guest rooms, all with queen-size beds and whirlpool tubs. The bed and breakfast serves a country breakfast each morning. Places of interest in the surrounding area include the National Center for American Western Art, Riverside Nature Center, Lost Maples State Natural Park, Kerrville Folk Festival, and Texas State Arts and Crafts Fair.

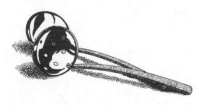

Mexican Bread Pudding

Known as the rose of fruits, the ancient Chinese considered the apricot to be a symbol of a sensual nature. Reputed to be the prime fruit in the Garden of Eden, it's possible that it was an apricot that Eve offered to Adam.

½ cup chopped dried apricots
½ cup melted margarine
1 French bread loaf, cut into
    2-inch cubes
½ cup sugar
4 large eggs
2 cups milk
2 teaspoons vanilla extract
½ teaspoon salt
1 teaspoon ground cinnamon

Cajeta sauce:
1 cup packed brown sugar
¼ cup apricot nectar
½ cup chopped pecans
½ cup coconut flakes
3 tablespoons apricot brandy

Preheat oven to 375°. Place apricots in glass bowl. Cover with water and microwave for 2 minutes. Melt margarine. Pour half into 2 x 8 x 12-inch glass baking pan. Spread bread cubes over bottom of pan. Place in oven for 15 minutes. In large bowl cream sugar into remaining margarine, beat in eggs, and then milk, vanilla, and salt. Remove bread cubes from oven. Drain apricots and sprinkle, along with cinnamon, over bread cubes. Evenly pour egg mixture over bread mixture. Place glass pan inside larger metal baking pan with ½ inch water on bottom. Loosely cover with sheet of foil. Bake 20 more minutes. Remove foil covering and bake additional 15 to 20 minutes or until toothpick inserted into center comes out dry. Remove from oven to cool 20 minutes.

For Cajeta sauce, mix brown sugar with apricot nectar in large glass bowl and microwave on high 3 minutes. Stir in chopped pecans and coconut flakes. Microwave additional 3 minutes. Remove and stir in apricot brandy. Spoon over top of bread pudding. Yields 10 to 12 servings.

The Dutchman's Date Loaf

1½ cups milk
1 cup uncooked old-fashioned oats
1 cup chopped dates
2 cups baking mix
⅔ cup granulated sugar
⅓ cup brown sugar
½ cup chopped walnuts
1 large egg
⅓ cup applesauce
⅓ cup canola oil

Preheat oven to 325°. Microwave milk until almost simmering. Place oatmeal and dates in large mixing bowl and stir in hot milk. Mix and set aside to cool to room temperature. In another bowl stir baking mix, sugars, and walnuts together.

After oat mixture has cooled, beat in egg, applesauce, and canola oil. Then stir mixture into dry ingredients, mixing well. Pour batter into buttered and floured Bundt pan. Bake 45 to 50 minutes or until top is crusty and golden. Cool on rack 10 minutes before removing from pan. Cool loaf on rack additional 20 minutes. Slice and enjoy. Yields 1 loaf.

Poached Apples with Raspberries

    6 medium baking apples
    1 cup water
    ½ plus ½ cup sugar
    1 tablespoon lime juice
    1 cup frozen raspberries

Cut, peel, and core apples using spiral apple cutter. Place apples in baking dish with water, ½ cup sugar, and lime juice. Poach apples in microwave until tender but not mushy. Drain poaching water. Place frozen raspberries in small glass container, add remaining ½ cup sugar and enough water to cover berries. Microwave for 2 minutes, stir, and pour over apples. Return to microwave for 2 minutes. Place on warmer and serve hot. Yields 10 servings.

THE BLUEBONNET INN BED & BREAKFAST

214 South Live Oak
Bellville, TX 77418
(979) 865-0027 (phone)
(979) 865-8229 (fax)
www.bluebonnet-inn.com

Specializing in hospitality, gourmet cooking, and retreats, the 1906 historic Bluebonnet Inn is furnished with impressive antiques and is located off the official Bluebonnet Trail of Texas. Austin County is the colonial capital of Texas with nearby activities, which include many historic markers and homes, antiquing, two state parks, shopping, golfing, biking, train spotting, as well as Round Top and Festival Hill.

❧ ❧ ❧

The Bluebonnet Inn Bed & Breakfast

Serious Vinaigrette Dressing

    ½ teaspoon dry mustard
    2 tablespoons salt
    1 teaspoon black pepper
    ¼ teaspoon seasoning salt
    1 tablespoon sugar
    ¼ cup water
    1½ tablespoons minced red onion
    2 tablespoons dried parsley
    2 tablespoons finely chopped bell pepper
    2 tablespoons finely chopped dill pickle
    2½ cups salad oil
    1½ cups white vinegar

Combine all ingredients in mixing bowl using whisk. Cover and refrigerate until ready to serve. Shake or beat before serving. Yields 1 quart, about 20 servings.

Molded French Cream Dessert

    2 (8-ounce) containers sour cream
        (do *not* use low fat)
    2 cups heavy whipping cream
    1½ cups plus 1 tablespoon sugar
    2 envelopes unflavored gelatin
    ½ cup cold water
    2 (8-ounce) packages cream cheese,
        softened
    2 teaspoons vanilla extract
    Fresh berries or mint leaves

Whisk together sour cream and whipping cream in medium saucepan. Gradually add 1½ cups sugar, whisking with each addition. Cook over low heat, whisking often, until warm. Sprinkle gelatin over cold water in small saucepan and let stand 1 minute. Cook over medium heat, stirring until gelatin dissolves. Add to sour cream mixture. Beat cream cheese at medium speed with electric mixer until light and fluffy. Gradually add sour cream mixture and vanilla, beating until smooth. Pour into lightly greased 8-cup mold, individual molds, or

Old Mulberry Inn Bed & Breakfast

2-quart bowl. Chill until firm or, if desired, up to 2 days. Unmold onto a serving platter. Put remaining 1 tablespoon sugar in with fresh berries in small bowl and cover to create syrup with berries. Let stand until ready to serve. Spoon on berry mixture for garnish, or mint leaves make a great alternate. Yields 12 to 14 servings.

Fudge Pie

5 tablespoons butter
3 squares unsweetened baking chocolate
4 eggs
2 cups sugar
¼ teaspoon salt
1 teaspoon vanilla extract
⅔ cup broken pecans
1 unbaked, 9-inch pie shell

Melt butter and chocolate in top of double boiler over low heat. Preheat oven to 350°. In mixing bowl beat eggs until light. Beat sugar, salt, and vanilla in with eggs. Add chocolate mixture, slightly cooled, and pecans. Mix thoroughly and pour into pie shell. Bake 40 minutes or until top is crusty and filling is set, though somewhat soft inside. Filling and crust will settle as pie cools. Serve with whipped cream and slice of strawberry. Yields 1 (9-inch) pie.

OLD MULBERRY INN BED & BREAKFAST

209 Jefferson St.
Jefferson, TX 75657
(903) 665-1945 (phone)
(800) 263-5319 (toll free)
mulberry@jeffersontx.com
www.oldmulberryinn.com

Built as a bed and breakfast, this grand plantation-style inn offers nineteenth-century charm and twenty-first-century comforts. Located in Jefferson's historic district, Old Mulberry Inn is within walking distance of downtown antique shops, restaurants, museums, and tour homes. Visitors may also take a romantic carriage ride around town, narrated tours, play a round of golf, or venture out on Cypress Bayou. Nearby are Caddo Lake (the largest natural lake in the state) and Lake O' the Pines. The casinos in Shreveport-Bossier City, Louisiana, are an hour away.

Alta's Stollen (German Coffee Cake)

This is a sweet yeast bread. No kneading is required. Mix it together at night, cover, and leave it to rise overnight; or mix it in the morning, cover it, and roll it out in the evening.

4 cups all-purpose flour
¼ pound (1 stick) butter, softened
¾ teaspoon salt
1 (¼-ounce) package dry yeast dissolved in 1½ cups warm milk
½ cup soft shortening
¼ to ½ cup sugar
2 whole eggs plus 1 yolk
Melted butter
Cinnamon
Sugar
Chopped nuts and dates
Dried fruit or candied fruit.

Combine flour, soft butter, salt, yeast, shortening, sugar, and eggs in large bowl until well mixed. Cover dough with plastic wrap and let rise at least six to eight hours. It will double in size or more. When ready to cook, preheat oven to 375°. Divide dough into 2 to 3 parts. Roll out one part at a time as thinly as possible on floured surface. Brush on melted butter and sprinkle with cinnamon and sugar. Sprinkle with chopped nuts and dates or fruits. Roll up dough into loaves and carefully transfer loaves to cookie sheet using large spatulas. Cover and let rise 30 minutes. Repeat with remaining dough. Bake about 30 minutes. Frost with butter cream frosting or drizzle with icing. Yields 2 or 3 loaves.

Fresh Plum Kuchen

½ plus ½ cup sugar
¼ pound (1 stick) butter, softened
2 eggs
¾ teaspoon almond extract
½ teaspoon vanilla extract
1 cup all-purpose flour
1 teaspoon baking powder
½ teaspoon salt
20 small plums, cut in half or 4 to
    5 large plums sliced into wedges
1 teaspoon ground cinnamon
¼ teaspoon ground nutmeg

Preheat oven to 350°. Cream ½ cup sugar and butter until light and fluffy. Beat in eggs, one at a time. Add almond and vanilla extracts. Whisk together flour, baking powder, and salt. Add to creamed mixture and blend well. Spread batter into greased and floured, 9-inch square cake pan. Arrange small plums cut-side down on batter. If using slices, place them slightly overlapping one another around edge of batter and fill in center, reversing direction. Combine remaining ½ cup sugar, cinnamon, and nutmeg and sprinkle on top. Bake 30 minutes. Cut into wedges and serve warm with whipped cream, if desired. Yields 8 to 10 servings.

Eggplant, Tomato, and Feta Muffins

1 medium eggplant
1 clove garlic
¼ cup olive oil
6 English muffins
8 ounces feta cheese, crumbled
2 tablespoons dried basil
12 slices tomato
Balsamic vinegar
Black pepper

Slice eggplant into 12 rounds about ⅜-inch thick. Salt both sides and arrange on paper towels on cookie sheets. Let sit 1 hour and then rinse and pat dry. Press garlic into measuring cup and add olive oil. Stir and then brush both sides of eggplant. Broil eggplant about 3 minutes each side about 5 inches from broiler. Spread muffin halves evenly with crumbled feta mixed with basil. (You may add a little softened butter to help bind mixture.) Broil a few minutes, being careful not to burn muffin edges. Set oven to bake at 350°. Top muffins with eggplant and tomato slices. Brush tomato with oil mixture. Bake about 5 minutes. Turn oven to broil and broil for about 5 minutes. Remove from oven and drizzle with balsamic vinegar. Top with freshly ground black pepper and serve immediately. Yields 6 servings.

Prize-Winning Fruit Salad

1 tablespoon butter
1 cup sugar
Juice of 2 lemons
1¼ cups water
3 tablespoons cornstarch
3 egg yolks
Cream
1 orange, peeled and quartered
2 apples, cored and quartered
2 bananas, sliced
1 cup seedless grapes, white or red
2 peaches, pitted and sliced
1 pint fresh strawberries
1 (15½-ounce) can pineapple
    chunks, drained
1 (15-ounce) can fruit cocktail,
    drained (optional)

Combine butter, sugar, lemon juice, water, cornstarch, and egg yolks. Heat in double boiler until thick. Cool. Dilute with cream to desired consistency. Cook dressing carefully if using a saucepan as dressing will scorch easily. Mix orange, apples, bananas, grapes, peaches, strawberries, pineapple, and fruit cocktail, if using, in bowl. Pour sauce over fruit, stir gently, and serve. Great as a starter course or after-breakfast "dessert" when served in footed sherbet dishes. Yields 12 servings or more.

A VICTORIAN LADY INN

421 Howard St.
San Antonio, TX 78212
(210) 224-2524 (phone)
(800) 879-7116 (toll free)
oli@swbell.net
www.viclady.com

A Victorian Lady Inn is a grand 1898 mansion in the heart of San Antonio. Enjoy casual elegance in a Victorian atmosphere with spacious rooms, fabulous breakfasts, and a sparkling pool. The surrounding area has many sights from the River Walk to the Alamo; to the Mission Trail. Many more downtown attractions are just a brief trolley ride away.

Irish Bread

3 cups all-purpose flour
2 tablespoons baking powder
½ teaspoon salt
½ cup sugar
¼ cup shortening
¼ cup (½ stick) butter or margarine
1 cup raisins
1 cup fresh fruit
1¼ cups milk
2 large eggs
1 tablespoon white vinegar

Preheat oven to 350°. Combine flour, baking powder, salt, and sugar in bowl. Cut shortening and butter into flour mixture with pastry blender or fork until mixture is crumbly. Stir in raisins and fresh fruit. In separate bowl whisk together milk, eggs, and vinegar. Add to fruit mix and stir until moistened. Pour batter into two greased, 8-inch, cast-iron skillets. Bake 35 to 40 minutes. Yields 16 slices.

Muffin Bread Pudding

4 cups cubed day-old French bread
3 eggs
1½ cups granulated sugar
2 tablespoons brown sugar
½ teaspoon ground nutmeg
½ stick butter, melted
2¾ cups whipping cream
Parsley sprigs

Coat 9 x 13-inch baking dish with nonstick spray. Preheat oven to 350°. Layer cubed bread into pan. In large bowl, lightly whip eggs. Add sugars and nutmeg and mix well. Add melted butter and stir until blended. Whisk in whipping cream. Pour over muffin mix. Bake 55 minutes. After 30 minutes, cover with tinfoil to avoid excessive browning. Garnish pan with parsley sprigs. Yields 12 to 16 servings.

Mini Sausage Frittatas

1 pound sausage with sage
1 small onion, chopped
1 cup grated Cheddar cheese
2 cups frozen hash browns, thawed
3 tablespoons all-purpose flour
8 eggs
1 cup ranch dressing
½ cup milk
Salsa

In medium skillet cook sausage and onion over medium heat until sausage is browned, crumbling it while it cooks. Drain well. Preheat oven to 350°. In large bowl, combine sausage, cheese, and hash browns and stir. Add flour and stir again. In another bowl, blend eggs, ranch dressing, and milk. Add to sausage mixture and blend well. Coat two 12-cup muffin tins with nonstick spray. Fill two-thirds full with sausage and egg mixture. Bake 10 to 15 minutes or until egg is set. Remove from muffin tins and serve hot. Place two to three mini frittatas on plate. Serve with ramekin of warm salsa. Yields 24 mini frittatas.

MOSES HUGHES RANCH

7075 W. FM 580
Lampasas, TX 76550-3662
(512) 556-5923
info@moseshughesranch.com
www.moseshughesranch.com

Historic Moses Hughes Ranch was built in 1856. It is situated on forty-five private acres with a spring-fed creek and abundant wildlife. Things to do and see in the area include shopping and dining in historic Lampasas, Colorado Bend State Park, Gorman Falls, Vanishing Texas River Cruise, eagle watching (in season), golfing, fishing, museums, historic sites, fabulous lakes, wineries, festivals, and special events.

Wrapped Baked Pears

½ cup sugar
4 teaspoons ground cinnamon
½ cup nuts

Moses Hughes Ranch

6 pears
2 tablespoons unsalted butter, cut into small pieces
1 pound puff pastry, chilled
1 egg, beaten

Mix sugar, cinnamon, and nuts in small bowl. Core pears carefully. Fill each pear with sugar mixture. Place 1 pat butter on top. Wrap each pear with puff pastry. Place pears on parchment-lined baking sheet and chill. When ready to bake, preheat oven to 400°. Lightly brush each wrapped pear with egg glaze and bake 20 to 25 minutes, or until pastry is puffed and golden brown. Yields 6 servings.

Al's Apple Thyme Puff Daddy

3 eggs
¾ cup all-purpose flour
¾ cup milk
2 tart green apples (such as Granny Smith), thinly sliced and sprinkled with lemon juice
¼ cup packed light brown sugar
2 tablespoons chopped fresh thyme
Maple syrup

Preheat oven to 425°. Coat 3-quart, ovenproof pan with nonstick spray. For batter combine eggs, flour, and milk in bowl just until blended (batter will be lumpy). Toss apple slices with brown sugar and thyme. Pour batter into pan. Arrange apples in center of batter and bake 20 to 25 minutes until puffed and golden brown. Cut into wedges and serve with maple syrup if desired. Yields 4 servings.

Cranberries in Wine Sauce

1 pound fresh cranberries
2 cups sugar
2 cups port wine
½ teaspoon ground cinnamon
½ teaspoon ground nutmeg
½ teaspoon ground cloves

Rinse cranberries in colander. In 3-quart saucepan combine cranberries, sugar, and wine. Bring to boil over high heat, stirring to dissolve sugar. Lower heat and continue to cook until berries begin to pop their skins, about 5 minutes. Stir in spices and remove from heat. Cool and refrigerate until ready to serve. Yields 6 to 8 servings.

Orange Tarragon French Toast

4 eggs
⅔ cup orange juice
½ cup milk
¼ cup sugar
½ teaspoon vanilla extract
¼ teaspoon ground nutmeg
¼ teaspoon ground cinnamon
½ teaspoon dried tarragon
4 cold French croissants
½ stick butter, melted
Confectioners' sugar
Maple syrup

Whisk together eggs, orange juice, milk, sugar, vanilla, nutmeg, cinnamon, and dried tarragon. Coat two 11 x 7-inch glass baking pans with nonstick spray. Cut croissants in half length-wise and place them tightly into baking pans. Pour egg mixture over croissants. Cover and refrigerate 8 to 10 hours or overnight. When ready to cook, preheat oven to 400°. Pour butter evenly over croissants. Bake 30 minutes. To serve, sprinkle each croissant with confectioners' sugar. Serve with syrup and garnish with fresh tarragon sprigs or a rosebud. Yields 4 servings.

A YELLOW ROSE BED & BREAKFAST

229 Madison
San Antonio, TX 78204
(210) 229-9903 (phone)
(210) 229-1691 (fax)
(800) 950-9903 (toll free)
yellowrose@ddc.net
www.ayellowrose.com

This 130-year-old Victorian bed and breakfast is located in the quiet neighborhood of the historic King William district in downtown San Antonio. Since it is only two blocks to the River Walk, restaurants, shopping, and the trolley, there is plenty to do. Or just relax in the spacious rooms with their high ceilings and luxurious amenities. All rooms have private entrances and porches, en suite baths, queen beds with nonallergenic feather toppers, radio/clock, iron and board, premium cable TV, hair dryer, and other first class comforts. Relax and delight in quiet sophistication, inn charm, and hotel privacy.

❧   ❧   ❧

Buttermilk Scones for Two

1 cup all-purpose flour
1½ tablespoons sugar
1 teaspoon baking powder
⅛ teaspoon baking soda
½ stick cold butter, cut into small pieces
3 tablespoons currants
¼ teaspoon grated orange rind
¼ to ⅓ cup buttermilk
⅛ teaspoon ground cinnamon
½ teaspoon sugar

Preheat oven to 375°. In large bowl, combine flour, sugar, baking powder, and baking soda. Add butter and rub with fingers to form fine crumbs. Stir in currants and orange rind. Make a well in center and pour in buttermilk. Stir with fork until dough holds together. Pat dough into ball and knead lightly on lightly floured board for 5 to 6 turns. Shape dough into smooth ball and place in greased 8- or 9-inch cake or pie pan. Combine cinnamon and sugar and sprinkle on top. Bake 10 minutes. With sharp knife, quickly cut a cross ½ inch deep across top of scone. Bake about 20 minutes more or until golden brown. Serve warm with butter and jam. Yields 2 servings.

Roasted Pancakes

Batter:
1 tablespoon unsalted butter
2 eggs
1 cup milk
1 cup unbleached all-purpose flour
¼ teaspoon salt

Topping:
½ stick butter
2 to 3 cups fresh fruit
Juice of 1 lemon
½ cup brown sugar
½ teaspoon ground cinnamon
¼ teaspoon ground nutmeg
½ cup slivered almonds
¼ cup confectioners' sugar

Preheat oven to 450°. Place butter in 10-inch pan and warm 5 minutes or until it melts. Coat pan completely with butter. In mixing bowl beat eggs and milk. Add flour and salt, beating with wire whisk until batter is smooth. Pour batter into quiche pan and bake 15 minutes. Reduce heat to 350° and bake 7 minutes.

For topping melt butter in medium saucepan over low heat and add fruit, lemon juice, brown sugar, cinnamon, and nutmeg. Stir over medium heat until fruit is soft and well coated. Serve over pancakes and top with almonds and confectioners' sugar. Garnish with raw fresh fruit—berries look especially good—or sectioned oranges. Yields 4 servings.

Blintz Soufflé

Batter:
1½ cups sour cream
½ cup orange juice
6 eggs
½ stick butter
1 cup all-purpose flour
⅛ cup sugar
2 teaspoons baking powder
½ teaspoon ground cinnamon

Filling:
16 ounces small-curd cottage cheese
2 egg yolks
1 tablespoon sugar
1 teaspoon vanilla extract
8 ounces cream cheese, softened

Topping:
½ cup sour cream
¼ cup fresh fruit or jam

For batter mix sour cream, orange juice, eggs, butter, flour, sugar, baking soda, and cinnamon in blender and blend thoroughly.

For filling, mix cottage cheese, egg yolks, sugar, vanilla, and cream cheese with mixer.

Stir together sour cream and fresh fruit for topping. In 9 x 13-inch casserole pan pour in half of batter. Pour filling over batter by tablespoonfuls and gently spread.

Put remaining batter over filling. This will look silly initially, but it will work. The layered mix may be left in refrigerator 8 to 10 hours or overnight. When ready to cook, preheat oven to 350°. Bake uncovered 50 to 60 minutes. Drizzle with topping. Sprinkle serving plate with confectioners' sugar and garnish soufflé with fresh berries. Yields 8 to 10 servings.

THE COOK'S COTTAGE & SUITES

703 West Austin
Fredericksburg, TX 78624
(210) 493-5101 (phone)
(210) 493-1885 (fax)
(210) 273-6471 (mobile)
stay@bed-inn-breakfast-tx.com
www.bed-inn-breakfast-tx.com

The Cook's Cottage & Suites is a nationally recognized bed and breakfast. It has been selected as "One of the Top 25 Most Romantic Places in America" by *Travel and Leisure* magazine. Enjoy chilled Texas wine and appetizers upon arrival. Marvel at the luxurious master bedroom, queen-size, four poster bed with antique lace and white silk. Relax in the garden spa room. Take a stroll through the flower, herb, and butterfly gardens. Nearby are such local sites as country wineries, antique shops, the Admiral Nimitz Museum, the Pioneer Museum, the George Bush Museum of the Pacific War, and the LBJ Ranch.

Tortilla Turtles

10 flour tortillas
Vegetable oil for frying
½ cup sugar
1½ teaspoons ground cinnamon
6 ounces miniature chocolate chips
4 ounces white chocolate chips
¼ pound (about ½ cup) unwrapped
   caramels

Cut tortillas into triangle-shaped wedges. Heat oil in frying pan and when hot, cook wedges in batches until crisp and lightly browned, turning to cook evenly. Drain on paper towels. Combine sugar and cinnamon and sprinkle over hot chips. In three microwave-safe containers, gently melt chocolate chips, white chocolate chips, and caramels separately in microwave on high. Start at 15-second increments. Stir until smooth. Using separate forks, dip tines into melted chocolates and caramels and drizzle over chips with sweeping motions. Allow to dry and harden before serving. Yields 80 tortilla chips.

Enchilada Suizas

3 cups shredded, cooked chicken
1 (4-ounce) can chopped green chiles
Salt
1 (10-ounce) can green chile
   enchilada sauce
1 (5-ounce) can evaporated milk
1 dozen corn tortillas
2 cups shredded pepper Jack cheese

Preheat oven to 425°. Mix together chicken, green chiles, and salt. Combine enchilada sauce and evaporated milk in small skillet over low heat. Dip tortillas in warm enchilada sauce mixture one at a time and fill with ¼ cup chicken mixture. Roll and place seam-side down in 13 x 9-inch baking dish. Pour over remaining sauce. Sprinkle with cheese and bake 15 minutes or until bubbly and hot. Yields 4 to 6 servings.

Gringo Migas

2 tablespoons butter or margarine
Dash of red pepper sauce
4 eggs, lightly beaten
2 tablespoons finely minced onion
2 tablespoons finely minced
    green bell pepper
1 fresh jalapeño, minced
¼ cup shredded Cheddar cheese
Crushed, crumbled tortilla chips
Thinly sliced ripe avocado
Hot tortillas, salsa, and refried
    beans for serving

Melt butter or margarine in nonstick skillet over medium heat. Stir red pepper sauce into eggs and pour into skillet. As soon as eggs begin to set, add onion, green pepper, and jalapeño pepper. When eggs are almost cooked, add cheese and turn heat to low. Stir in tortilla chips. Serve hot, garnished with thin avocado slices. Pass salsa and refried beans and, of course, hot tortillas. Yields 2 to 3 servings.

Texas Sunburst

4 flour tortillas, with notches cut out
    or edges scalloped
Vegetable oil for frying
Cinnamon sugar
¼ cup minced kiwifruit
¼ cup minced pineapple
¼ cup minced strawberries
¼ cup minced mangos
¼ cup minced papayas
Fresh mint leaves

From 2 flour tortillas cut out cactus shapes. Fry remaining 2 tortillas and cactus shapes in hot oil. Remove and immediately sprinkle with cinnamon sugar. Drain and keep airtight. Combine minced fruit and mound evenly in the center of each sunburst. Insert "cactus" in center of fruit and garnish with mint leaves. Serve immediately. Yields 2 servings.

HOLLY HILL HOMESTEAD & RETREAT

9076 TX Hwy 11 E
Hughes Springs, TX 75656
(903) 639-1318
Jolene@hollyhillhomestead.com
www.hollyhillhomestead.com

Rural and secluded, this quaint, old homestead features a large farmhouse, renowned herb gardens, and wildflowers, sun-bathed porches, walking trails, and extraordinary country dining. In beautiful northeast Texas there are numerous festivals: Christmas in October Festival at Holly Hill, Holly Hill Spring Festival, and Wildflower Trail Festivals. Some attractions or activities include the Daingerfield State Park, northeast Texas lakes area, Lake O' The Pines, golfing, antiquing, historical district, bird-watching, and biking.

Shepard's Pear Tart

Pastry for two-crust pie
4 ounces cream cheese
4 ounces ricotta cheese
3 Bosc pears
1 teaspoon finely chopped fresh rosemary
1 teaspoon finely chopped fresh sweet basil
½ teaspoon freshly ground black pepper
¾ cup plus 2 teaspoons sugar

Preheat oven to 350°. Roll piecrust into one large circle about 12 inches in diameter. Fold in quarters and transfer to baking stone or pizza pan. Unfold and center on pan. Mix together cheeses and spread on crust in 9-inch circle. Top with peeled and sliced pears. Sprinkle with rosemary, basil, and pepper. Top with ¾ cup sugar. Fold extra pastry up and over filling, pleating as you fold. This should leave an opening in center. Sprinkle crust with remaining 2 teaspoons sugar. Bake until brown and bubbling, about 45 minutes. Serve warm. Garnish with dollop of whipped cream and sprig of basil. Yields 6 to 8 servings.

Buttered Lemon Rice

2 cups water
¾ teaspoon salt
1 plus 3 tablespoons butter (½ stick)
1 cup raw rice
Grated zest and juice of 1 large lemon
2 tablespoons chopped red bell pepper
1 tablespoon minced lemon basil
    (optional)

In deep heavy-bottomed pan bring to boil water, salt and 1 tablespoon butter. Add rice slowly so boiling doesn't stop. Reduce heat to simmer, cover, and simmer 20 minutes without removing lid. Then check; rice should be tender. Add remaining 3 tablespoons butter, zest, lemon juice, bell pepper, and lemon basil. Serve immediately. Yields 4 servings.

Chicken Amandine

1 cup raw almonds
½ cup fresh parsley leaves
1½ cups fresh breadcrumbs
1 large egg
1 tablespoon water
6 (4- to 5-ounce) boneless, skinless
    chicken breasts
1½ plus 2½ tablespoons butter (½ stick)
¼ cup olive oil
½ cup freshly grated Parmesan cheese
¼ cup sliced almonds
1 teaspoon minced garlic
½ cup white wine
2 teaspoons lemon juice
1 cup sour cream

Chop almonds in food processor. Add parsley and process until almonds are finely chopped. Stir in breadcrumbs and put mixture in shallow bowl. Whisk together egg and water. Dip chicken in egg, then in breadcrumb mixture. Pat to adhere. Chill several hours to set. Melt 1½ tablespoons butter with oil in large skillet. Sauté chicken over medium heat until brown and crisp, about 4 minutes on each side. Sprinkle with cheese and set on warm platter. In same pan, melt remaining 2½ tablespoons butter and scrape bottom of pan. Add sliced almonds and garlic and sauté over medium heat until almonds begin to brown. Add wine and lemon juice. Heat until mixture begins to boil. Take from heat and stir in sour cream. Pour over chicken. Garnish with sprig of fresh parsley. Yields 6 servings.

Grandma's Lemon Griddle Cookies

Dough:
3½ cups all-purpose flour
1 cup sugar
1½ teaspoons baking powder
1 teaspoon salt
½ teaspoon baking soda
1 teaspoon ground ginger
1 teaspoon grated lemon rind
1 cup vegetable shortening
1 egg
7 tablespoons milk
1 tablespoon lemon juice

Lemon glaze:
Juice of 1 large lemon
Confectioners' sugar

Place flour, sugar, baking power, salt, baking soda, ginger, and lemon rind in mixing bowl in order given. Mix well with wire whisk. Cut shortening into flour mixture with pastry blender or two knives until mealy consistency forms. Whisk together egg, milk, and lemon juice. Make a well in dry ingredients and add liquid all at once. Mix with fork until moistened. Gather dough together and divide in half. Roll dough between two pieces of wax paper to thickness of just less than ¼ inch. Cut dough into large 3-inch squares. Heat griddle to 300° and transfer cookies with floured spatula. Brown on each side, about 5 minutes.

For glaze, combine lemon juice and enough confectioners' sugar to make thin icing. Brush lemon glaze on cookies while warm. Yields 2 dozen cookies.

THE CARLETON HOUSE

803 N. Main Street
Bonham, TX 75418
(903) 583-2779 (phone)
(800) 382-8033 (toll free)
information@carletonhouse.com
www.carletonhouse.com

Built in 1888, The Carleton House is located in the heart of historic downtown Bonham, Texas, just one hour northeast of Dallas. This newly renovated three-story Victorian, listed on the National Register of Historic Homes, features a large entrance hall, a parlor, dining room with ceiling mural, music room, breakfast area, and a large staircase leading to the bedrooms. The home, sitting on a landscaped half acre with remnants of its original gardens is also available for weddings and parties or just an evening stroll. The Carleton House is operated by individuals who appreciate art, music, antiques, good service, and great food. All of this is reflected in your experience.

Apricot-Cinnamon Scones

1½ cups all-purpose flour
1½ teaspoons baking powder
⅛ teaspoon baking soda
⅛ teaspoon salt
1 tablespoon sugar
3 tablespoons shortening
1 egg, beaten
¾ cup buttermilk
⅛ cup chopped dried apricots
⅛ cup cinnamon chips
2 tablespoons melted butter

Blend flour, baking powder, baking soda, salt, and sugar into large mixing bowl. Cut in shortening with pastry cutter. In separate bowl, whisk egg until light in color. Add buttermilk and mix well. Stir egg mix into dry ingredients just until moistened and let mixture sit for 5 minutes. Dough will be sticky. Stir in apricots and cinnamon chips. Preheat oven to 400°. On well-floured surface, spoon ⅛ cup batter and dust with additional flour. Carefully shape into elongated wedge, shake off excess flour, and place in greased, 8-inch pan coated with nonstick spray, point toward center. Continue in this manner until all dough is used and a circle is created. Bake 15 to 20 minutes until golden brown. Brush with butter. Can be served with favorite jam. Yields 10 scones.

ANT STREET INN

107 West Commerce
Brenham, TX 77833
(800) 805-2600 (toll free)
stay@antstreetinn.com
www.antstreetinn.com

In historic Brenham, home to Bluebonnets and Blue Bell Ice Cream, the Ant Street Inn combines the finest in hospitality, warmth, and elegance with the conveniences and personal service of a first class hotel. The inn is located midway between Houston and Austin and is the perfect place for an overnight or weekend getaway. Relax in rocking chairs on the back balcony overlooking the courtyard. Enjoy some of the many shops, restaurants, and night spots in the historic Ant Street area or dine in the Inn at the Capital Grill with your favorite beer or wine.

Blintz Soufflé with Blueberry Topping

Soufflé:
1 cup all-purpose flour
⅓ cup sugar
2 teaspoons baking powder
½ teaspoon ground cinnamon
1½ cups light sour cream
½ cup orange juice
1 (8-ounce) package fat-free
    cream cheese, softened
16 ounces light small-curd cottage cheese
7 eggs
½ stick butter, softened
1 teaspoon vanilla extract

Blueberry topping:
1 cup sugar
Dash of salt
¼ teaspoon ground nutmeg
5 tablespoons cornstarch
1 cup boiling water
1 cup blueberries
1 tablespoon lemon juice

Mix flour, sugar, baking powder, and cinnamon in large bowl. Add sour cream, orange juice, cheeses, eggs, butter, and vanilla and beat until thoroughly mixed. Coat 9 x 13-inch baking dish with cooking spray. Pour batter into dish. Cover and refrigerate overnight or at least 2 hours. When ready to cook, preheat oven to 350°. Bake 50 to 65 minutes.

For blueberry topping, mix sugar, salt, nutmeg, and cornstarch in saucepan. Add boiling water and stir. Heat to boiling, stirring constantly. Add blueberries and stir until thickened. Remove from heat and add lemon juice. Serve on top of soufflé. Yields 12 to 14 servings.

Chicken and Chiles

1 (10-ounce) can enchilada sauce
½ plus ⅓ cup sour cream
1 (4-ounce) can chopped green chiles,
    drained
1 (11-ounce) can Mexicorn, drained
1 (4-ounce) jar chopped pimientos,
    drained
1 (10-ounce) can chunk chicken packed
    in water, drained
⅓ cup yellow self-rising cornbread mix
2 teaspoons sugar
1 egg
1 tablespoon oil

Preheat oven to 400°. In 1½-quart casserole dish combine enchilada sauce and ½ cup sour cream. Stir in green chiles, corn, pimientos, and chicken. Microwave on high 5 minutes to heat ingredients. In mixing bowl combine cornbread mix and sugar. Form well in center. In another bowl mix egg, oil, and remaining ⅓ cup sour cream. Stir together and add to dry ingredients, mixing thoroughly. Drop dough by tablespoonfuls on top of chicken mixture. Bake 20 minutes. Yields 4 to 6 servings.

Apple Ricotta Brunch Biscuits

½ cup sugar
1 cup ricotta cheese
1 egg
½ teaspoon ground cinnamon
¼ cup sliced almonds
1 (17.3-ounce) can refrigerated
    buttermilk biscuits
1 small apple, peeled and
    cut into 8 wedges

Heat oven to 375°. Coat eight jumbo muffin cups or custard cups with nonstick spray. In small bowl combine sugar, cheese, and egg. Mix together. In another small bowl combine cinnamon and almonds and mix well. Separate dough into 8 biscuits. Press each biscuit evenly in bottom and up sides of prepared cups. Place 1 apple wedge in each cup. Spoon 2 rounded tablespoonfuls cheese mixture over each apple wedge and sprinkle with cinnamon mixture. Bake 20 to 25 minutes or until biscuits are deep golden brown and apples are tender. Remove biscuits from muffin cups. Cool 15 minutes. Serve warm. Store in refrigerator. Yields 8 servings.

Southwestern Egg Bake

10 (6-inch) corn tortillas plus several
    for garnishing
1 (11-ounce) can Mexicorn
16 eggs
1 cup milk
1 cup shredded Cheddar cheese
1 pound processed soft cheese
1 (10-ounce) can diced tomatoes
    and green chiles
1 cup salsa
1 cup sour cream
1 cup guacamole

Grease 13 x 9-inch casserole dish. Cut tortillas into quarters and line bottom and sides of dish. Drain corn and sprinkle on tortillas. Mix eggs and milk together and pour into dish. Sprinkle with Cheddar cheese. Cover and refrigerate 8 to 10 hours or overnight if desired. When ready to cook, preheat oven to 375°. Cover casserole with foil and bake 25 to 30 minutes in conventional radiant oven (less time in convection oven). Cut triangular pieces of tortillas and slip them around edges of casserole to decorate dish. Melt processed cheese, diced tomatoes, and green chiles together in microwave to use as sauce over casserole. Serve with salsa, guacamole, and sour cream on the side. Yields 12 servings.

ROSEVINE INN BED & BREAKFAST

415 South Vine
Tyler, TX 75702
(903) 592-2221 (phone)
(903) 592-5522 (fax)
info@rosevine.com
www.rosevine.com

Rosevine Inn Bed & Breakfast

Experience the old-fashioned concept of bed and breakfast at the Rosevine Inn, an excellent alternative to the ordinary hotel routine. We are in Tyler, Texas, "The Rose Capital of the World," and Tyler's first bed and breakfast. The Rosevine Inn is situated on one of the city's quaint brick streets near the Azalea district. The home is furnished with antiques and country collectibles. Numerous antique and craft shops are only a short distance away.

Orange Muffins

¾ cup vegetable oil
1 cup sugar
2 eggs
1½ cups all-purpose flour
1 teaspoon salt
1 teaspoon baking soda
1 teaspoon vanilla extract
¼ cup plus 1 tablespoon fresh orange juice
½ cup confectioners' sugar

Preheat oven to 350°. Combine oil, sugar, and eggs. Mix well. Add flour, salt, baking soda, vanilla, and ¼ cup orange juice. Blend. Pour into muffin pan coated with nonstick spray. Bake 10 to 15 minutes. Mix together the confectioners' sugar and remaining 1 tablespoon orange juice for glaze. Spread glaze on top of muffins. Yields 12 muffins.

Grape Jelly Meatballs

2 pounds ground beef
¼ cup minced onion
1 (12-ounce) jar chili sauce
8 ounces grape jelly

Preheat oven to 350°. Mix beef and onion and roll into balls. Bake until done, 30 to 45 minutes. Combine meatballs, sauce, and jelly in slow cooker and cook on low for 2 hours to marinate. Yields 8 servings.

Cucumber Dip

2 or 3 cucumbers
1 (8-ounce) package cream cheese, softened
⅓ (8-ounce) carton sour cream
Minced or grated onion, about 1 tablespoon
Juice of ½ lemon
Garlic powder
Tabasco sauce
Salt

Peel and grate cucumbers and drain off as much liquid as possible. With mixer on medium speed, combine cucumbers, cream cheese, and sour cream until well blended. Add onion, lemon juice, garlic powder, Tabasco, and salt to taste. Green food coloring may be added for appearance. Tastes great with Fritos. Yields about 2 cups.

Pink Salad

12 ounces cream-style cottage cheese
1 (3-ounce) package strawberry gelatin
1 (8-ounce) can crushed pineapple
¾ cup pecans
1 (10-ounce) carton non-dairy whipped topping

Empty cottage cheese into bowl. Pour in dry gelatin and stir until well blended. Add pineapple and pecans and fold in whipped topping. Yields 4 to 6 servings.

DOWELL HOUSE

1104 South Tennessee St.
McKinney, TX 75069
(972) 562-2456 (phone)
(800) 373-0551 (toll free)
info@DowellHouse.com
www.dowellhouse.com

Pamper yourself with a stay in one of McKinney's finest old historic homes. Located in a spacious, Federal/Classical-style home built in 1870, where parts of the original *Benji* movie were filmed, Dowell House has a rich history and an elegant ambience to share with you. Step back into an era when life was genteel and slow. Linger over a full, fresh breakfast in the formal dining room, and then relax in the sunny garden room with the second cup of coffee or enjoy the swing on the deck. Explore McKinney's many antique shops and galleries or drive along quaint streets lined with turn-of-the-century homes.

Besotted Pears

According to Websters, besotted *is a verb meaning to muddle with drunkenness, and these pears just may be muddled.*

4 firm pears (Bosc, if available)
2 cups red wine
2 cups water
1 cup sugar
2 tablespoons red hot candies
6 to 8 whole cloves
6 tablespoons cornstarch

Place pears in large glass or ceramic pot. Pour wine over pears. Add water so liquid will fully cover pears. Remove pears and add sugar, red hot candies, and whole cloves. Place pot over medium heat and stir vigorously to dissolve candies and sugar. When dissolved, lower heat and simmer while you prepare pears. Peel and core pears. Leave stem intact for presentation. Add prepared pears to wine sauce. Simmer until pears are slightly tender when pierced. Do *not* overcook or they will be mushy. When tender, remove from heat and let cool. Cover and refrigerate 8 to 10 hours or overnight. Just before serving, pour 1 cup wine sauce into saucepan over medium heat. Mix cornstarch with 1 cup water and add to saucepan, simmering until mixture is thickness of honey. Divide sauce among serving dishes and place pear in sauce. Garnish with mint sprig next to stem. Yields 4 servings.

Note: If you do not like the flavor of wine, use fruit juice.

BECKMANN INN & CARRIAGE HOUSE BED & BREAKFAST

222 E. Guenther Street
San Antonio, TX 78204
(210) 229-1449 (phone)
(210) 229-1061 (fax)
(800) 945-1449 (toll free)
beckinn@swbell.net
www.beckmanninn.com

Beckmann Inn is a Victorian bed and breakfast located downtown across from the landscaped River Walk in the beautiful King William historic district. A perfect location for business or leisure lodging. The inn is near the River Walk, the historic district, the Alamo, missions, the Mexican Market, the Botanical Garden, the zoo, the Institute of Texas Cultures, riverboat cruises, golf, Sea World, Fiesta Texas, Tower of Americas, and La Villita.

Butterscotch Caramel Coffee Cake

1 package frozen dinner rolls, about 24
½ cup sugar
1½ teaspoons ground cinnamon
½ cup chopped pecans
½ cup packed brown sugar
1 (4-ounce) package butterscotch
    pudding (not instant)
1 stick butter or margarine, sliced

Spray angel food cake pan. Place ingredients in pan in order given. Leave covered

on counter 8 to 10 hours or overnight. When ready to cook, preheat oven to 350°. Bake 30 minutes, covering with foil after 15 minutes. Yields 12 servings.

Southern Cornbread and Egg Casserole

1 cup yellow cornmeal
1 cup all-purpose flour
¼ teaspoon baking soda
1¼ cups buttermilk
1 large egg
2 tablespoons sugar
¼ cup vegetable oil
Salt and pepper
1½ cups Cheddar or Swiss cheese
¾ cup diced ham
8 large eggs
2 cups milk
Dash of Worcestershire sauce

Preheat oven to 375°. Mix cornmeal, flour, soda, buttermilk, egg, sugar, and oil. Pour mixture into 8- to 9-inch pan coated with nonstick spray. Bake 25 minutes or until done. When cool, crumble cornbread into large chunks and put into 14 x 11-inch sprayed pan. Salt and pepper to taste. Sprinkle cheese and ham on top. Whisk eggs, milk, and Worcestershire together and pour over cheese and ham. Reduce oven heat to 350° and bake 30 minutes or until done. Yields 8 servings.

WOODROW HOUSE BED & BREAKFAST

2629 19th Street
Lubbock, TX 79410
(806) 793-3330 (phone)
(800) 687-5236 (toll free)
innkeeper@woodrowhouse.com
www.woodrowhouse.com

Built specifically to be a bed and breakfast, Woodrow House is the culmination of four years of dreaming, planning, researching, and designing by the owners and hosts, David and Dawn Fleming. Woodrow House is named after David's paternal grandfather, George Woodrow Fleming (1914–1972). Woodrow "Woody" Fleming was a Texas Rancher, agribusinessman, cotton ginner, grain merchant, and entrepreneur. Located across the street from Texas Tech University, Woodrow House is within walking distance of virtually all university events and activities.

Hash Browns and Ham Casserole

12 ounces frozen hash browns
½ stick butter, melted
1 cup (¼ pound) shredded
    hot pepper cheese
1 cup shredded Swiss cheese
1 cup diced ham
4 eggs
½ cup light cream or milk
¼ teaspoon seasoned salt

Preheat oven to 425°. Thaw hash browns and mix with melted butter. Press in bottom and up sides of 9-inch pie pan to make crust. Bake 25 minutes. Remove from oven and let cool to room temperature. Mix remaining ingredients and pour over crust. Cover and refrigerate 2 hours or overnight if desired. When ready to cook, preheat oven to 350°. Uncover and bake 30 to 40 minutes. Yields 6 to 8 servings.

VIEH'S BED & BREAKFAST

18413 Landrum Park Road
Highway 675
San Benito, TX 78586
(956) 425-4651
Viehbb@aol.com
www.vieh.com

Vieh's Bed & Breakfast is at the tip of Texas. Enjoy a friendly atmosphere at this ranch-style home. Enjoy hearty breakfasts. The home is decorated with collectables and antiques. The area activities include bird-watching, butterfly watching, U.S. and Mexican shopping, golfing, tennis, a beach, and fine dining.

Lana's Cornmeal Pancakes

1 cup whole wheat flour
1 cup yellow cornmeal
1 tablespoon baking powder
1 teaspoon baking soda
1 teaspoon salt
2 tablespoons sugar or honey
1 egg, separated
¼ cup canola oil
1½ to 2 cups buttermilk

Sift flour, cornmeal, baking powder, baking soda, salt, and sugar together. Combine egg yolk, oil, and buttermilk and add to dry ingredients. Mix well. Beat egg white to peak stage and fold gently into batter. Spoon mixture onto hot, oiled griddle. (Animal figures are fun to make.) Cook both sides until golden brown. Yields 5 servings.

Lana's Grits, Spinach, and Sausage Quiche

1 cup grated cheese (Swiss, Cheddar, Monterey Jack)
½ pound hot sausage, cooked and crumbled
1 (10-inch) uncooked, buttered piecrust
2 cups milk or light cream
Pinch of sugar
Pinch of ground nutmeg
Dash of cayenne pepper
½ teaspoon salt
½ teaspoon pepper
1 cup leftover cooked grits
½ cup chopped frozen or fresh spinach, cooked and drained

Preheat oven to 400°. Sprinkle cheese and sausage over piecrust. In blender mix milk, sugar, nutmeg, cayenne, salt, pepper, grits, and spinach. Quickly blend these and gently pour into crust. Bake 12 minutes and then reduce temperature to 350° and cook for 40 to 50 minutes more. Yields 6 to 8 servings.

Vieh's Brownies

½ cup all-purpose flour
1 cup sugar
4 tablespoons cocoa
½ teaspoon salt
¼ cup canola oil
2 eggs
1 teaspoon vanilla extract
½ cup pecans
Hot Fudge Sauce (see page 390)

Preheat oven to 350°. Sift together flour, sugar, cocoa, and salt. Mix together oil, eggs, and vanilla. Combine dry ingredients with liquid ingredients and add pecans. Spray 9 x 9-inch glass baking dish and pour in mixture. Bake 25 minutes or until toothpick comes out clean when tested in center. To slice into squares, dip knife into glass of ice water, wipe, and slice. Serve with Hot Fudge Sauce (see recipe below). Yields 10 to 12 servings.

Hot Fudge Sauce

8 tablespoons cocoa
2 cups sugar
⅔ cup milk
2 tablespoons butter
1 teaspoon vanilla extract

In heavy quart saucepan, mix cocoa, sugar, milk, and butter well. Bring to boil and boil 6 minutes without stirring. Remove from heat. Add vanilla and mix well. Yields about 1½ cups.

GRUENE MANSION INN

1275 Gruene Road
New Braunfels, TX 78130
(830) 629-2641 (phone)
(830) 629-7375 (fax)
frontdesk@gruenemansioninn.com
www.gruenemansioninn.com

The Gruene Mansion Inn, a premier bed and breakfast, is located in the historic German community of New Braunfels, which hosts many German festivals annually, including Wurstfest in November and Wassilfest in December. Surrounded by authentic Texas history—Texas' oldest dance hall, Gruene Hall, and the Guadalupe River—the inn features thirty elegant Victorian rooms, each with private bath and entry. In addition to the Guadalupe River, Schlitterbahn Water Park has three locations in New Braunfels. Natural Bridge Caverns and Wildlife Ranch are only a few miles away.

Morning Glory Muffins

1 cup low-fat buttermilk
¾ cup bud-style bran cereal (100% bran)
½ cup golden raisins
½ cup grated carrots
1 egg
⅓ cup honey
¼ cup canola oil
1 teaspoon vanilla extract
1¼ cups whole wheat flour
1 teaspoon baking soda
1 teaspoon ground cinnamon
1 tablespoon honey-crunch wheat germ (optional)

Preheat oven to 425°. Coat 12-cup muffin pan with cooking spray. In medium bowl combine buttermilk, cereal, raisins, carrots, egg, honey, oil, and vanilla. Let stand 10 minutes. In large bowl, combine flour, baking soda, and cinnamon. Make a well in center and add buttermilk mixture. Stir enough to moisten flour. Divide batter evenly among muffin cups. Sprinkle tops with wheat germ, if using. Bake 15 to 20 minutes or until toothpick inserted in center comes out clean. Yields 12 servings.

Cranberry-Orange Muffins

1½ cups all-purpose flour
⅔ cup plus 2 tablespoons sugar
2 teaspoons baking powder
1 teaspoon ground cinnamon
1 teaspoon salt
½ teaspoon baking soda
¾ cup coarsely chopped fresh
    or frozen cranberries (do not thaw)
⅔ cup low-fat buttermilk
½ stick butter, melted
1 large egg, lightly beaten
4 teaspoons finely grated fresh
    orange zest
1 teaspoon vanilla extract
⅓ cup confectioners' sugar (optional)
2 teaspoons orange juice (optional)

Preheat oven to 400°. Line 12 medium muffin cups with paper liners. In medium bowl combine flour, ⅔ cup sugar, baking powder, cinnamon, salt, and baking soda and mix well. In small bowl toss cranberries with remaining 2 tablespoons sugar and stir into dry ingredients. Add buttermilk, butter, egg, orange zest, and vanilla. Mix just until dry ingredients are moistened. Spoon batter into prepared muffin cups, filling almost full. Bake 20 minutes or until golden brown. Let cool 5 minutes before transferring to cooling rack. If desired, mix sugar and orange juice to form a glaze and drizzle over muffins. Serve warm. Yields 12 muffins.

WASHINGTON SCHOOL INN

P.O. Box 536
543 Park Ave.
Park City, UT 84060
(435) 649-3800 (phone)
(435) 649-3802 (fax)
(800) 824-1672 (toll free)
washinn@xmission.com
www.washingtonschoolinn.com

Nestled among the majestic mountains of Park City the Washington School Inn Bed & Breakfast delights guests with unexpected luxuries and a wide range of services. Conveniently located two blocks from the Town Ski Lift, it is the perfect place to stay on your ski vacation. When the snow melts and summer arrives, Park City and the surrounding area abound with hordes of activities such as the famed Summer Concert Series, the Annual Art Show, the Senior PGA Tour, and the Annual Rodeo. Whether it's summer or winter, the bed and breakfast's convenient location near Salt Lake City makes it a perfect mountain getaway for your Utah vacation.

Southwest Corn Pie

- 3 large eggs
  1 cup cream-style corn
  1 (10-ounce) package frozen corn
  ½ cup finely chopped green onions
  ½ cup yellow cornmeal
  1 cup sour cream
  4 ounces Monterey Jack cheese,
      cut into ½-inch cubes
  4 ounces Cheddar cheese,
      cut into ½-inch cubes
  ½ cup canned green chiles
  ½ teaspoon salt
  ¼ teaspoon Worcestershire sauce
  ½ cup diced red pepper (optional, for color)

Preheat oven to 375°. Grease 10-inch pie plate. In large bowl beat eggs. Add remaining ingredients and stir thoroughly. Pour into pie plate and bake uncovered 1¼ hours. Serve with your favorite salsa and sour cream on the side. Yields 6 servings.

Ginger Snaps

  ¾ cup shortening
  ½ cup granulated sugar
  ½ cup brown sugar
  ¼ cup molasses
  1 egg
  2 cups all-purpose flour
  1 teaspoon baking soda
  1 teaspoon ground cinnamon
  ½ teaspoon cloves
  ½ teaspoon ginger
  ½ teaspoon salt

Cream shortening and sugars. Add molasses and egg. Add dry ingredients. Chill dough for 1 hour. Preheat oven to 375°. Make dough into small balls and roll in sugar. Bake 9 minutes. Yields approximately 2 to 3 dozen cookies.

Pompushkas

  1 cup cottage cheese
  ¼ cup sour cream
  2 tablespoons sugar
  1 teaspoon ground cinnamon
  ¼ teaspoon salt
  1 cup all-purpose flour
  2 eggs
  Milk

Combine all ingredients, using enough milk for chosen consistency. May add blueberries or bananas if desired. Cook batter on hot griddle as you would pancakes. Serve warm with maple syrup. Yields 12 to 14 pancakes.

SkyRidge Inn

P.O. Box 750220
Torrey, UT 84775
(435) 425-3222 (phone/fax)
skyridge@color-country.net
www.skyridgeinn.com

SkyRidge is situated in the heart of Utah's magnificent red-rock canyon country on seventy-five acres complete with unparalleled views of Capitol Reef National Park,

Boulder Mountain and Torrey's valley. The three-story inn features a collection of antiques, contemporary art, and ethnic and folk sculpture. SkyRidge Gallery exhibits paintings, photographs, jewelry, Navajo folk art and much more throughout the inn. During the summer and fall the Park Service invites you to enter the ancient orchards planted by pioneers in Fruita and pick your own fruit. SkyRidge is also an ideal getaway for those seeking a few days of serenity within an environment of sheer beauty. Whether you enjoy adventuresome days filled with exploring or glorious hours of relaxation, we have it all!

Pecan Griddle Cakes

1 cup all-purpose flour
1 cup whole wheat flour
2 tablespoons brown sugar
1¾ teaspoons baking powder
½ teaspoon salt
2½ cups low-fat milk
1 large egg plus 1 large egg white
2 tablespoons melted unsalted butter
1 teaspoon orange zest
1 teaspoon vanilla extract
⅔ cup chopped pecans
Confectioners' sugar for dusting
Maple syrup

Preheat oven to 200°. Blend flours, brown sugar, baking powder, and salt in medium bowl. Whisk milk, egg and egg white, butter, orange zest, and vanilla in large bowl to blend. Whisk in dry ingredients. Batter should be fairly thin, thinner than regular pancakes. Add more milk if necessary. Add pecans. Spray griddle or skillet with non-stick spray. Using ¼-cup measure, pour batter onto griddle. Cook until bubbles appear and griddle cakes are golden. Turn and cook top side of griddle cakes. Transfer to baking sheet and keep warm in oven while cooking others. Place griddle cakes, three to plate, and sprinkle with confectioners' sugar. Serve with warmed maple syrup. This pairs excellently with maple-flavored breakfast sausage or bacon. Yields 8 servings.

Apple-Stuffed Croissants

4 Granny Smith apples, peeled, cored, and chopped into medium dice
¼ cup granulated sugar
¼ cup brown sugar
1 tablespoon molasses
1 plus ½ teaspoon ground cinnamon
8 ounces cream cheese
¼ cup coarsely chopped pecans
1 teaspoon grated orange rind
1 plus 1 teaspoon vanilla extract
2 eggs
1 cup milk
¼ teaspoon ground nutmeg
6 croissants
Confectioners' sugar
1 cup sweetened, chopped fruit (optional)

Preheat oven to 350°. In 7 x 11-inch or 2½-quart baking dish toss apples with sugars, molasses, and 1 teaspoon cinnamon. Bake 45 minutes until apples are golden. Mix cream cheese, pecans, orange rind, and 1 teaspoon vanilla together and add to apple mixture. Continue with recipe or refrigerate 8 to 10 hours or overnight. In shallow bowl beat together eggs, milk, remaining 1 teaspoon vanilla, remaining ½ teaspoon cinnamon, and nutmeg. Heat griddle. Heat apple mixture in microwave until hot. Split croissants and spread 2 to 3 tablespoons apple mixture on bottom section. Place top of croissant on mixture sandwich style. Dip croissants in egg mixture and toast on griddle until golden brown on both sides. Place croissants on individual plates or serving platter and sprinkle liberally with confectioners' sugar. Top with fruit and serve. Yields 6 servings.

Note: This pairs wonderfully with sausage or ham.

Sue Kallin's Blue Ribbon Cinnamon Rolls

2½ plus 3¼ cups all-purpose flour
1½ tablespoons yeast
1 tablespoon salt
¾ plus 2 cups sugar
1¼ cups scalded milk
1 cup shortening
1¼ cups water
3 eggs
10 tablespoons cinnamon
Melted butter

SkyRidge Inn

1 pound confectioners' sugar
¼ cup milk
¼ tablespoon vanilla extract
Dash of salt

Liberally grease two 9 x 9-inch baking pans. Mix 2½ cups flour, yeast, salt, and ¾ cup sugar in large mixing bowl. Scald milk. Add shortening and water to milk to cool to 110°. Pour milk mixture into flour mixture and mix. Stir in eggs, one at a time. Mix remaining 3¼ cups flour, one at a time, into mixture until dough begins to pull away from bowl. Dough will be very soft. Grease large bowl liberally with shortening. Put dough into bowl and turn dough to coat with shortening. Cover and let dough rise until double. When doubled, punch dough down and turn onto heavily greased counter. Coat hands with shortening. Divide dough into two equal parts. Working with half at a time, pat dough to 12 x 12-inch square. Mix remaining 2 cups sugar with cinnamon and sprinkle dough heavily with mixture. Roll dough toward you in jellyroll fashion and cut into nine equal rolls. Place rolls in one baking pan. Follow same procedure with other section of dough. Let rise until at least double. Preheat oven to 375°. Bake rolls 20 to 30 minutes or until golden brown. Drizzle with melted butter while hot. Mix confectioners' sugar, milk, vanilla, and salt together and drizzle icing, in swirls, over cinnamon rolls. Yields 18 servings.

Legacy Inn

337 North 100 East
Manti, UT 84642
(435) 835-8352 (phone/fax)
stay@legacyinn.com
www.legacyinn.com

The Legacy Inn is a charming Victorian bed and breakfast in the heart of central Utah's Mormon country. Our little touches make the difference—scrumptious chocolate truffles for every guest, hearty country breakfast, and our warm hospitality to make you feel right at home. Enjoy the view of the majestic Manti Temple while you relax on the front porch with a glass of our refreshing mint lemonade and a big soft ginger cookie.

Mint Lemonade

Mint Syrup:
10 cups water
Fresh mint (enough to fill
    6-quart saucepan)
5 cups sugar

Lemonade:
1 (12-ounce) can all-natural
    frozen lemonade
4⅓ (12-ounce) cans water
1½ cups mint syrup

To make mint syrup, bring 10 cups water, sugar, and mint to a simmer to dissolve sugar. Turn off heat and let steep 1 hour or more. Strain mint from syrup and discard. Mint syrup may be stored in jar in refrigerator.

To make lemonade, mix together frozen lemonade, remaining 4⅓ cans water, and mint syrup. Stir and serve over ice. Garnish with fresh mint sprigs. Yields about 2½ quarts.

Big Soft Ginger Cookies

1½ sticks butter, softened
¼ cup dark molasses
½ teaspoon ground cloves
¾ teaspoon ground cinnamon
1 cup sugar
1 teaspoon baking soda
2 teaspoons ground ginger
1 egg
2¼ cups all-purpose flour
¼ cup chopped, candied ginger

Preheat oven to 350°. Mix butter, molasses, cloves, cinnamon, sugar, soda, and ginger. Beat until fluffy and add egg, flour, and candied ginger. Mix until well blended. Shape into golf-ball-size rounds and roll in sugar. Place on baking sheet and bake about 8 minutes or until barely browned. Let cool 2 minutes before removing to cooling rack. Yields about 4 dozen cookies.

Cali Cochitta Bed & Breakfast Inn

110 South 200 East
Moab, UT 84532
(435) 259-4961 (phone)
(435) 259-4964 (fax)
(888) 429-8112 (toll free)
calicochitta@lasal.net
www.moabdreaminn.com

One of the first homes built in Moab, Cali Cochitta, "House of Dreams," is a late 1800s Victorian home, restored and renovated to its original classic style. It is located in the heart of spectacular red rock country and offers a wonderland of breathtaking panoramas. At least one morning during your stay, we urge you to wake early. Sit on the front porch with a cup of freshly ground coffee, tea, or freshly squeezed juice and enjoy a southern Utah sunrise. It's a sensory experience you'll not soon forget. Enjoy hiking, mountain biking, river rafting, rock climbing, golfing, fishing, four wheeling, and cross-country skiing in nearby Lasal mountains.

Apple Streusel Coffee Cake

1 cup whole pecans
⅓ cup packed light brown sugar
1 cup plus 2 tablespoons granulated sugar
1½ teaspoons ground cinnamon
2 cups plus ½ cup unbleached
    all-purpose flour
1½ plus ½ sticks butter, softened
1½ teaspoons plus ½ teaspoon pure vanilla
4 egg yolks
½ plus ¼ cup sour cream
½ teaspoon baking powder
½ teaspoon baking soda
¼ teaspoon salt
1 Granny Smith apple, peeled, cored,
    and sliced ¼-inch thick
2 teaspoons lemon juice

In food processor combine nuts, brown sugar, 2 tablespoons granulated sugar, and cinnamon. Process until nuts are coarsely chopped. Remove ¾ cup and reserve for filling. Add ½ cup flour, ½ stick butter, and ½ teaspoon vanilla to remaining nut mixture. Combine until crumbly. Set aside for topping. Preheat oven to 350°. Grease 9-inch springform pan and line bottom with wax or parchment paper. Grease and flour paper. In small bowl combine egg yolks, ¼ cup sour cream, and remaining 1½ teaspoons vanilla. In large bowl combine remaining 2 cups flour, remaining 1 cup sugar, baking powder, baking soda, and salt. Stir until blended. Add remaining 1½ sticks butter and remaining ½ cup sour cream. Using electric mixer, beat 2 minutes at medium-high speed. Add egg yolk mixture slowly, beating 20 seconds after each addition. Pour two-thirds of batter into prepared pan. Smooth surface with spatula and sprinkle with remaining ¾ cup nut filling mixture. Place apple slices over filling. Drop remaining batter over apples and spread evenly with spatula. Sprinkle with reserved topping mixture. Sprinkle lemon juice on top. Bake 55 to 65 minutes or until center springs back when pressed lightly. If cake appears too brown after 45 minutes, cover loosely with foil. Remove from oven and cool in pan on rack. Gently remove sides of pan. If desired, remove cake from pan bottom. Use large spatula and gently slide under cake and paper, loosening entire bottom of cake. Carefully slide onto serving plate. Yields 12 to 16 servings.

THE OLD MINERS' LODGE

615 Woodside Avenue
P.O. Box 2639
Park City, UT 84060-2639
(435) 645-8068 (phone)
(435) 645-7420 (fax)
stay@oldminerslodge.com
www.oldminerslodge.com

The Old Miners' Lodge is located in the national historic district of the colorful resort town of Park City, Utah. This charming bed and breakfast inn was established in 1889 as a boarding house for local silver miners seeking fortune in Park City's ore-rich mountains. Today, the spirited warmth and hospitality of Park City's illustrious past is still alive in this building, which has been lovingly restored to its original splendor. Guests can walk ten yards down the street to access the Town Run Ski Bridge, allowing them to ski to Park City Mountain Resort's Town Ski Lift and back to our door at the end of the day. Historic Main street, with its many restaurants, shops, and galleries, is just one short block away. And the town of Park City offers exceptional year-round recreation, including skiing, snowboarding, snowmobiling, biking, hot-°air ballooning, golf, tennis, hiking, horseback riding, concerts, and festivals.

Multi-Grain Pancakes

3 whole eggs
4 cups 1% low-fat milk
¾ cup melted margarine
1 cup brown sugar
3 cups instant oatmeal
2¼ cups all-purpose flour
1 cup wheat germ, toasted
1 tablespoon baking soda
½ tablespoon baking powder
1 tablespoon ginger
1 tablespoon ground cinnamon
½ tablespoon cloves

Combine eggs (or equivalent egg substitute) with milk, margarine, and brown sugar. Combine remaining ingredients and mix well. Mix together wet and dry ingredients. Let batter rest 15 minutes to allow oatmeal to absorb moisture. Use ⅓ cup batter per pancake and cook in greased skillet until bubbles form and edges turn slightly brown. Turn pancake and cook until brown on bottom. Yields 10 servings.

Corn Waffles

5 cups all-purpose flour
⅓ cup baking powder
2½ teaspoons salt
3¾ cups yellow cornmeal
½ cup sugar
10 eggs, separated
6¼ cups buttermilk or sour milk
2½ cups applesauce
10 tablespoons (1¼ sticks) melted butter
2½ cups frozen corn kernels, thawed

In large bowl, combine flour, baking powder, salt, and cornmeal. Beat sugar and egg whites to soft peak stage and set aside. Beat yolks until thick and lemon colored and beat in milk, applesauce, and melted butter. Add to dry ingredients and mix just until blended. Stir in one-third of egg white mix and gently fold in remaining two-thirds. Gently fold in corn. Cook in greased waffle iron. Yields 20 servings.

Note: To make sour milk, add 1 teaspoon lemon juice to each cup of milk. Let stand 10 minutes to sour.

Honey Pecan Butter

1 cup pecan pieces
½ cup (1 stick) unsalted butter
   at room temperature
½ cup light clover honey

Preheat oven to 350°. Toast pecan pieces in single layer on cookie sheet 3 minutes. Let cool completely. Combine pecans, butter, and honey in food processor. Pulse on and off several times to blend. Pecans should remain chunky. Yields 10 servings.

Raspberry Syrup

2 cups frozen raspberries, thawed
½ cup hot water
1½ cups sugar
½ cup light corn syrup
1 tablespoon lemon juice

Blend raspberries and hot water in blender or food processor. Strain into medium saucepan, rubbing strainer until all juice is extracted and just seeds are left. Discard seeds. Add sugar and corn syrup to raspberry juice. Stir to combine well. Add lemon juice. Bring syrup to a boil and boil for 1 minute. Remove from heat and skim off foam. Yields about 3 cups.

SOUTH SHIRE INN

124 Elm Street
Bennington, VT 05201
(802) 447-3839 (phone)
(802) 442-3537 (fax)
relax@southshire.com
www.southshire.com

Located in the heart of historic Bennington in southwestern Vermont, our romantic Victorian inn combines elegance with comfort. Spacious guest rooms in the main inn include private baths, phones, air conditioning, and original fireplaces, while the Carriage House rooms offer the added luxury of whirlpool baths and TV/VCR. The inn is within easy walking distance of Bennington's downtown shops and restaurants. Bennington is a historic town that was settled in 1761. Local attractions include the Bennington Battle Monument, the Bennington Museum, and Grandma Moses Schoolhouse.

Barbara's Cranberry Pie

2 cups raw cranberries
½ cup walnuts
¼ plus ¾ cup sugar
2 eggs
1½ sticks butter, melted
1 cup all-purpose flour
1 teaspoon almond flavoring

Grease 9½-inch pie pan. Preheat oven to 325°. Chop cranberries and nuts together and place in bottom of pan. Sprinkle with ¼ cup sugar. Beat eggs. Add remaining ¾ cup sugar, butter, flour, and almond flavoring. Pour over cranberries. Bake 40 to 45 minutes or until toothpick comes out clean. Yields 6 to 8 servings.

Oatmeal Raisin Cookies

1½ cups all-purpose flour
1 teaspoon salt
1 teaspoon baking soda
1 teaspoon ground cinnamon
¼ teaspoon ground cloves
⅛ teaspoon ground nutmeg
1 cup shortening
1 cup brown sugar
1 cup granulated sugar
2 eggs
3 cups oatmeal
1 cup raisins

Preheat oven to 350°. Mix flour, salt, soda, and spices together. Cream shortening. Add sugars and cream together thoroughly. Mix in eggs. Blend in dry ingredients. Stir in oatmeal and raisins. Form into walnut-size balls. Place on lightly greased cookie sheet and flatten. Bake 12 to 15 minutes. Yields 5 dozen cookies.

BRASS LANTERN INN

717 Maple Street
Stowe, VT 05672
(802) 253-2229 (phone)
(800) 729-2980 (toll free)
info@brasslanterninn.com
www.brasslanterninn.com

Nestled at the foot of majestic Mt. Mansfield in Vermont's scenic Green Mountains is the alluring village of Stowe. A church steeple rises above this classic New England town, the mystique and natural beauty of which compel one to come and explore. At the edge of this genuine two-hundred-year-old village is the Brass Lantern Inn, a traditional bed and breakfast inn. An 1800s farmhouse and carriage barn, the inn is restored to reflect its rich history while providing modern comfort in its authentic atmosphere. The inn offers nine guest rooms, each with its own identity and decor. Furnished with antiques and handmade quilts, all guest rooms have planked floors and private baths. Most offer spectacular views, and some have fireplaces and/or whirlpool tubs.

Andy's Crêpes

Crêpes:
2 eggs
1½ cups milk
½ teaspoon salt
1 cup all-purpose flour
2 tablespoons melted butter

Filling:
4½ Granny Smith apples, pared, cored, and sliced
3 tablespoons melted butter
⅔ cup brown sugar
Zest of 1 orange
¼ cup raisins
¼ cup maple syrup
Cornstarch

Mix crêpe ingredients and let rest 30 minutes. Cook in black pan or Teflon, using ¼ cup batter per crêpe. Make crêpes with all batter and set aside covered to keep warm.

Mix filling ingredients, except cornstarch, in saucepan on moderate heat and cook 5 minutes. Reserve three-fourths of juice. Whisk cornstarch 1 teaspoon at a time to saucepan until thick. Fill crêpes with apple filling, roll up, and spoon reserved juice over crêpes. Garnish with orange zest and any remaining apple slices or any seasonal fruits. Yields 10 crêpes.

THATCHER BROOK INN

P.O. Box 490
Waterbury, VT 05676
(802) 244-5911 (phone)
(802) 244-1294 (fax)
(800) 292-5911 (toll free)
info@thatherbrook.com
www.thatcherbrook.com

Thatcher Brook Inn is a faithfully restored, 1899 Victorian mansion on the Vermont Register of Historic Buildings. Our twenty-four guest rooms are all exquisitely decorated, some with fireplaces or whirlpools. Enjoy the restaurant for a fine dining experience or Bailey's Fireside Tavern for the lighter appetite. Proclaimed "One of the top ten romantic inns in the country," Thatcher Brook is centrally located near Stowe, Mad River Valley, Burlington, and Montpelier. Visit Lake Champlain, climb Mount Mansfield, canoe or kayak any of the streams or lakes. The inn is a short walk to Ben and Jerry's Ice Cream factory.

Sweet-Potato-Crusted Salmon

1 large sweet potato
1 large egg, beaten
1 teaspoon thyme
1 teaspoon rosemary
½ cup plus 1 tablespoon all-purpose flour
2 (6-ounce) salmon fillets
½ cup cream
1 tablespoon Dijon mustard
1 sprig fresh rosemary
3 tablespoons butter

Preheat oven to 350°. Shred sweet potato and mix with egg, thyme, rosemary, and 1 teaspoon flour. Mixture should be slightly moist; if not add more egg. Heat sauté pan over medium heat. Put salmon, top-side down, in ½ cup flour. Then tap to remove excess flour. (Flour will help sweet potato mixture stick to salmon.) Press sweet potato mixture on floured side. Sear, crust-side down, in hot sauté pan. Finish in oven for 5 minutes. Pour cream into sauté pan and add mustard, rosemary, and butter. Reduce by half, about 2 minutes. Remove and discard rosemary. Strain sauce if needed. Serve salmon over mound of rice pilaf. Spoon sauce over salmon, drizzling down side. Yields 2 servings.

Apple Cheddar Pork Roulade

1 (2-pound) pork tenderloin
2 tablespoons butter
2 Granny Smith apples
Dash of ground cinnamon
8 ounces Cheddar cheese, shredded
Salt and pepper
½ cup maple syrup
½ cup balsamic vinegar

Butterfly tenderloin and pound flat. Preheat oven to 375°. Heat butter in sauté pan. Add apples and cinnamon. Cook about 3 to 4 minutes and add cheese. Spread mixture on pork and roll and tie with butcher's twine. Season with salt and pepper. Roast 25 minutes. Mix maple syrup and vinegar in small saucepan and heat, reducing by half, about 15 minutes. Keep sauce warm. Carve two slices per person and arrange on mashed potatoes. Drizzle sauce over top of pork and garnish with apple slices. Yields 4 servings.

Mushrooms a la Thatcher

4 ounces crabmeat
4 ounces cream cheese
1 to 2 teaspoons dill
1 to 2 teaspoons parsley
1 to 2 teaspoons thyme
2 teaspoons lemon juice
Salt and pepper
10 to 15 button mushrooms (depending on size)
Vermont Cheddar cheese, shredded
⅓ cup white wine

Preheat oven to 400°. Put crabmeat, cream cheese, dill, parsley, thyme, lemon juice, and salt and pepper to taste in mixing bowl and mix well. Remove stems from mushrooms. Stuff mushrooms with crab mix and sprinkle top with cheese. Bake until cheese melts and mushrooms are soft, 7 to 10 minutes. Arrange on plate with wedge of lemon and sprinkle with chopped parsley. Yields 2 servings.

Note: Use a pool of white wine in bottom of pan to bake mushrooms.

Artichoke Meuniere

5 whole garlic cloves plus extra
    for sautéing
1 quart water
2 fresh lemons, quartered
15 peppercorns
¾ cup white wine
2 large fresh artichokes
16 ounces cream cheese
1 (13½-ounce) can artichoke hearts,
    drained and chopped
2 teaspoons lemon juice
Salt and pepper
4 ounces fresh Parmesan, shredded
Mesclun or red lettuce
Parsley sprigs

Preheat oven to 400° and roast garlic until lightly browned and soft, about 20 minutes. Chop finely and set aside. In large saucepan, put water, lemon quarters, peppercorns, and wine to make poaching liquid. Bring to a boil and add fresh artichokes. Let simmer about 20 minutes. Remove and let cool. Cut artichokes into quarter sections and clean around heart. Reserve quarter sections. Using mixer, blend cream cheese, canned artichoke hearts, roasted garlic, and lemon juice. Mix well. Season with salt and pepper to taste. Reheat oven to 400°. On baking sheet sprayed with nonstick spray, make four 4-inch circles with Parmesan cheese. Bake 5 minutes and let cool for 1 to 2 minutes. While cheese is still soft, place small juice glass on cheese circle and mold cheese to glass, forming a cup. Let cool. Warm cream cheese dip in microwave and spoon into Parmesan cups. Sauté fresh artichoke quarters in oil with extra garlic, lemon juice, and salt and pepper. Arrange Parmesan cups on four plates, each with small amount of mesclun or chopped red leaf lettuce as a bed for quartered sections of sautéed artichokes. Serve with fresh lemon and parsley sprigs. Yields 2 to 4 servings.

FITCH HILL INN

258 Fitch Hill Road
Hyde Park, VT 05655-9363
(802) 888-3834 (phone)
(802) 888-7789 (fax)
(800) 639-2903 (toll free)
innkeeper@fitchhillinn.com
www.fitchhillinn.com

Fitch Hill Inn is located away from the highway with over three acres of lawn, flower gardens, and woods, plus spectacular views of the Green Mountains. The Fitch Hill Inn's grounds have a park-like feel that, along with well-appointed comfortable rooms, award-winning breakfasts, and warm hospitality, will leave you refreshed, rejuvenated, and ready to face the everyday world again. Although in a peaceful setting the inn is close to such sights as the village of Stowe, Ben and Jerry's Ice Cream factory, Stowe Mountain, Smuggler's Notch and Jay Peak ski areas. There are also numerous antique shops and dozens of great restaurants in the area.

"Shipwreck"

2 tablespoons butter or margarine
4 medium potatoes, peeled and sliced
½ cup chopped onion
¾ cup diced ham
6 eggs, lightly beaten
1 cup grated Vermont Cheddar cheese

In large skillet, melt butter or margarine over medium heat. Add potatoes and cook until almost tender, flipping occasionally. Add onion and continue cooking until onion and potatoes are tender. Reduce heat slightly and add ham and eggs. Cook, stirring frequently, until eggs are set. Sprinkle cheese on top of mixture and cover, cooking just until cheese is melted. Remove from heat and serve. Yields 4 servings.

Cranberry Eggnog Muffins

Batter:
1 cup coarsely chopped cranberries
2 tablespoons plus 1 cup sugar
2¼ cups all-purpose flour
1 tablespoon baking powder
½ teaspoon salt
2 eggs
¾ cup eggnog
⅓ cup margarine, melted
1 teaspoon almond extract

Streusel topping:
½ cup sugar
½ cup all-purpose flour
½ cup chopped pecans
¼ cup (½ stick) margarine

Preheat oven to 400°. For batter, in small bowl combine cranberries with 2 tablespoons sugar. In large bowl stir together flour, remaining 1 cup sugar, baking powder, and salt. In separate bowl, beat eggs, eggnog, margarine, and almond extract. Add mixture, all at once, to dry ingredients. Stir just until moistened. Fold in cranberries. Fill well-greased or sprayed muffin tins two-thirds full.

Combine streusel topping ingredients, cutting in margarine until crumbly. Sprinkle on top of muffins. Bake 20 to 25 minutes or until muffins test done. Cool in tins for 5 minutes and remove to wire rack. Yields 12 muffins.

Peach Pecan Muffins

2 cups all-purpose flour
1 cup chopped pecans
1 cup sugar
2 teaspoons baking powder
1 egg, lightly beaten
1 cup (8-ounce container) peach yogurt
¼ pound (1 stick) butter or margarine, melted
1 teaspoon vanilla extract
1 cup peeled and chopped peaches
Turbinado sugar (optional)

Preheat oven to 400°. In large bowl, combine flour, pecans, sugar, and baking powder. In separate bowl, combine egg, yogurt, butter, and vanilla and mix well. Stir wet ingredients into dry ingredients just until moistened. Fold in peaches. Fill greased or lined muffin cups two-thirds full. Sprinkle tops lightly with turbinado sugar if desired. Bake 15 to 20 minutes or until muffins test done. Cool in pan 5 to 10 minutes before removing to wire rack. Yields 8 jumbo muffins or 16 regular muffins.

RED CLOVER INN

7 Woodward Road
Mendon, VT 05701
(802) 775-2290 (phone)
(800) 752-0571 (toll free)
innkeepers@redcloverinn.com
www.redcloverinn.com

Down a winding country road amidst thirteen acres, this 1840s restored farmhouse estate offers guests warmth, pampering, and exceptional gourmet fare. From enticing rooms with antiques, some with whirlpools and cozy fires, to sumptuous breakfasts, candlelight dining with soft music and an award-winning wine list, the atmosphere is relaxed and welcoming.

Espresso Bar-B-Que Sauce

1 small onion, finely diced
4 cloves garlic, chopped
2 tablespoons vegetable oil
½ cup espresso
½ cup Worcestershire sauce
¾ cup ketchup
¼ cup cider vinegar
2 tablespoons brown sugar
2 tablespoons chili powder
1 tablespoon dry mustard

In medium saucepan sauté onions and garlic in oil until translucent. Add remaining ingredients and simmer 30 minutes. Yields about 2 cups.

Note: This sauce is excellent on duck, beef, chicken, or shrimp.

Savory Herbed Cheesecake

Crust:
1 cup Parmesan cheese
1 cup breadcrumbs
5 tablespoons melted butter

Filling:
1½ pounds cream cheese
¾ pound goat cheese
¼ pound blue cheese
4 eggs
½ cup buttermilk
1½ teaspoons salt
½ teaspoon pepper
1 tablespoon chopped garlic
1 tablespoon chopped shallots
2 tablespoons chopped fresh parsley
1 tablespoon chopped fresh basil
1 tablespoon chopped fresh oregano
1 tablespoon chopped fresh thyme

Preheat oven to 350°. Combine crust ingredients and press mixture into bottom of 10-inch springform pan.

For filling, cream three cheeses together.

Add eggs, one at a time, scraping bowl after each egg. Add buttermilk, salt, pepper, garlic, shallots, parsley, basil, oregano, and thyme and mix well. Pour batter into crust. Bake in a bain-marie (water bath) 45 to 50 minutes. Turn off oven and allow cheesecake to stay in oven for 1 hour. Serve cold. Yields 6 to 8 servings.

Bourbon-Marinated Salmon

Marinade:
½ cup bourbon
½ cup soy sauce
2 teaspoons chopped garlic
¼ cup packed brown sugar
Salt and pepper

6 (6-ounce) salmon fillets, boned
1 tablespoon oil

Whisk together marinade ingredients. Marinate salmon fillets 3 to 24 hours. Heat sauté pan and sear salmon. Finish in 375° oven if needed. Cooking times vary depending on degree of preferred doneness. Yields 6 servings.

DORSET INN

8 Church Street
Dorset, VT 05251
(802) 867-5500 (phone)
(802) 867-5542 (fax)
(877) DORSET-9 (toll free)
info@dorsetinn.com
www.dorsetinn.com

Welcoming guests since 1796, the Dorset Inn is Vermont's oldest, continuously operated inn. Befitting the eighteenth century atmosphere of the Dorset Inn, an outstanding honest American fare is offered, featuring the talents of its excellent Chef/Owner Sissy Hicks. Located six miles north of Manchester, Vermont, facing the village green, the inn is ideally located for leisurely exploration of Dorset's many rural amenities. Craft and antique shops, a handsome stone church, a general store, and the oldest professional summer stock theater company in the state can also be found in this small, pleasant community.

Potato-Crusted Halibut

5 Idaho potatoes
½ cup lemon juice
½ cup heavy cream
Salt and pepper
Dill, minced (for red snapper only)
6 (6-ounce) halibut or red snapper fillets
3 teaspoons spicy seasoning
Flour
2 tablespoons oil

Peel potatoes and put in cold water. Be sure to keep potatoes covered with water or lemon juice as you peel or grate them or they turn a nasty brown color. Put lemon juice in medium mixing bowl and coarsely grate potatoes into juice. Keep tossing potatoes in juice as you add them. When all potatoes are grated, add heavy cream, salt, pepper (and some dill if using red snapper instead of halibut). You should have a thick, not too milky, mixture. Sprinkle fillets with some spicy seasoning and dredge lightly in flour. Hold fillet in one hand and pat potato mixture on evenly until whole fillet is covered. Place on parchment paper on plate. (Dredging fillets in flour helps to hold potato onto fish). When ready to cook, heat oil in sauté pan. Place 2 fillets at a time into oil. Fry until nicely browned and crisp. Flip over and brown other side. Place in roasting pan. Continue this procedure until all pieces are crispy on both sides, but not completely cooked. Preheat oven to 450° and roast 10 minutes or until fish are cooked through. Yields 6 servings.

Crème Brûlée

4 cups heavy cream
1 vanilla bean
    or 1 teaspoon vanilla extract
Pinch of salt
9 egg yolks
¾ cup plus 2 tablespoons sugar
9 tablespoons natural sugar
    or brown sugar

Preheat oven to 300°. Combine cream, vanilla, and salt in saucepan over medium heat and cook 5 minutes or until mixture begin to "shimmer." Mix egg yolks and sugar in bowl. Add cream mixture and stir until dissolved. Strain into another bowl and skim air bubbles off top. Pour into ten individual serving ramekins or large soufflé dish and, again, skim off bubbles. Place ramekins in pan of hot water and cover pan tightly with foil. Bake 55 to 60 minutes. Chill at least 6 hours. When ready to serve, sprinkle each ramekin with 1 tablespoon natural or brown sugar and broil 35 to 40 seconds. Yields 10 servings.

Bread Pudding

1 French baguette
¼ cup bourbon
4 cups plus 1 cup milk
2 cups half-and-half
1 cup sugar
6 whole eggs
4 egg yolks
1 teaspoon vanilla extract
1 teaspoon ground cinnamon
½ teaspoon ground nutmeg
1 cup raisins
Whiskey Sauce (see next recipe)

Slice baguette diagonally into 12 slices. Place in large mixing bowl and soak with bourbon and 1 cup milk. While bread is soaking, heat 4 cups milk with half-and-half. Heat to scalding stage. Mix sugar, eggs, yolks, vanilla, cinnamon, and nutmeg. When milk is scalded, whisk in egg mixture. Spread raisins in 9 x 13-inch bak-

ing pan. Lay bread on top. Pour milk mixture over bread and press down with your hands to make sure bread is totally soaked. Preheat oven to 350°. Place bread pudding pan in water bath (shallow pan of warm water to surround food with gentle heat while cooking in oven). Bake uncovered about 1 hour or until firm and browned on top. Serve with Whiskey Sauce and topped with whipped cream. Yields 10 to 12 servings.

Whiskey Sauce

½ pound (2 sticks) butter
2 cups sugar
2 eggs
1 cup bourbon

Melt butter in double boiler. While butter is melting, mix sugar with eggs in small bowl. Whisk mixture into butter. Stir until sugar is dissolved and eggs have thickened, about 5 minutes. Pull from heat and cool to room temperature. Whisk in bourbon. Yields 2 cups.

Note: Be careful. This sauce will knock your socks off, but it is *so* good with the bread pudding.

Roasted Corn Soup

4 cups corn kernels
1 tablespoon sugar
2 plus 2 tablespoons vegetable oil
1 onion, sliced
4 cloves garlic, crushed
½ teaspoon Tabasco
½ tablespoon Worcestershire sauce
1 teaspoon turmeric
Salt and pepper
4 cups (2 pints) heavy cream
3 cups chicken stock
3 tablespoons roux*

Preheat oven to 400°. Toss corn with sugar and 2 tablespoons oil in small bowl. Spread corn on cookie sheet and put into oven for about 20 minutes. Shake and toss often to make sure kernels are roasting evenly and turning golden brown. Remove from oven and let stand. (You can also roast corn on the cob on grill, toss with sugar, and cut off cob.) Heat remaining 2 tablespoons oil in medium pot. Add onion and garlic and sauté about 5 minutes until onions are soft. Add roasted corn, Tabasco, Worcestershire, turmeric, and salt and pepper to taste. Toss briefly. Add heavy cream and chicken stock and bring to a boil. Reduce heat, simmer about 20 minutes, and whisk in roux. Simmer another 10 minutes. Purée in food processor until smooth. Yields 12 cups.

*Note: To make the roux heat 1½ tablespoons butter in skillet. Slowly add 1½ tablespoons flour. Stir to make a paste and cook until light brown.

Award-Winning Venison Chili

2 pounds venison
⅓ cup diced bacon
2 tablespoons vegetable oil
2 onions, diced
1 tablespoon minced garlic
¼ cup chili powder
1 tablespoon ground cumin
2 teaspoons dried oregano
1 teaspoon salt
2 teaspoons ground black pepper
2 chipotle peppers, rehydrated and diced
2 (28-ounce) cans crushed tomatoes
1 (15-ounce) can black beans

Smoke venison on an outdoor grill over dampened wood chips about 20 minutes (for flavor, not to cook meat). Dice smoked venison into very small pieces. Place diced bacon in large sauté pan over medium heat. Render fat from bacon. Leave bacon and fat in pan and add venison. Stir meat until thoroughly browned. Remove from heat. Heat oil in large pot over medium heat. Add onions and garlic. Sauté until soft, about 5 minutes. Add chili powder, cumin, oregano, salt, pepper, and chipotle peppers. Stir. Add tomatoes. Bring to boil and then turn down to simmer. Simmer

about 10 minutes and add venison and black beans. Serve with toppings of chopped scallions or onions and sour cream. Yields 4 to 6 servings.

ENGLISH ROSE INN

195 Mountain Road
Route 242
Montgomery Center, VT 05471
(802) 326-3232 (phone)
(802) 326-2001 (fax)
(888) 303-3232 (toll free)
stay@theenglishroseinn.com
www.englishroseinnvermont.com

The English Rose Inn is an 1850s farmhouse beautifully decorated in romantic Victorian charm featuring fourteen guest rooms and suites. Lace curtains, hardwood floors, crocheted and heirloom quilts adorn the antique-filled rooms. Vermont winter sports include downhill or cross-country skiing and snowshoeing at Hazen's Notch. Summer offers all the beauty of the Vermont outdoors: golfing, mountain biking, cycling the rail trail, and hiking the Long Trail.

Devonshire Mushrooms

1 tablespoon butter or margarine
8 ounces white button mushrooms
1 garlic clove, crushed
2 tablespoons finely chopped onion
¼ cup white wine
4 tablespoons sour cream
2 tablespoons chopped fresh parsley

In sauté pan heat butter over medium heat and sauté mushrooms, garlic, and onion

5 minutes. Add white wine and cook 5 more minutes. Remove pan from heat and stir in sour cream. Top with parsley and serve immediately. Yields 2 servings.

Fergie's Lime-Crusted Haddock

1 lime
1½ cups fresh breadcrumbs
2 plus 2 tablespoons melted butter
4 (6-ounce) haddock fillets, skinned
Salt and pepper

Preheat oven to 400°. Grate zest from lime into small bowl. Cut lime in half and squeeze juice into another bowl. Combine breadcrumbs, lime zest, 2 tablespoons butter, and half of lime juice. Place fillets in shallow baking dish. Season with salt and pepper to taste. Combine remaining lime juice and remaining 2 tablespoons butter and drizzle over and around fillets. Coat each fillet evenly with breadcrumb mixture. Bake 10 to 12 minutes or until breadcrumbs are golden. Yields 4 servings.

Lady Chatterley's Chicken

4 (6-ounce) boneless, skinless
  chicken breasts
Salt and pepper
½ teaspoon dried thyme
  or 1 tablespoon fresh
¼ cup slivered almonds
1½ cups plain breadcrumbs
½ cup all-purpose flour
2 eggs, beaten
2 tablespoons butter
2 tablespoons olive oil

Lightly pound chicken breasts to make uniform in size and season each breast with salt and pepper to taste. Mix thyme and almonds with breadcrumbs. Coat chicken breasts with flour, shaking off excess. Dip chicken in beaten eggs and coat with breadcrumb mixture. On medium heat melt butter and olive oil in sauté pan and add chicken breasts. Cook breasts on each side until golden brown or until cooked through, about 8 minutes on each side. Serve with your favorite potatoes or mixed green salad. Yields 4 servings.

English Shepherd's Pie

5 large potatoes
2 tablespoons butter
¼ cup milk or whipping cream
Salt and pepper
1 pound lean ground beef
1 large tomato, chopped
6 sliced mushrooms
2 tablespoons chopped parsley
2 tablespoons tomato paste
1 dash Worcestershire sauce
1 cup commercial brown gravy
1 (12-ounce) package frozen peas

Cook potatoes in boiling salted water, drain, cool, and peel. Mash in large bowl with butter and milk and season to taste with salt and pepper. Sauté beef until browned, stirring to keep meat crumbly. Season to taste with salt and pepper. Add tomato, mushrooms, parsley, tomato paste, Worcestershire sauce, and gravy. Stir to mix. Add peas and cook about 5 minutes. Preheat oven to 400°. Turn mixture into casserole, spread potatoes evenly over meat, and bake 40 minutes until top is crispy. Yields 4 to 6 servings.

STONE HILL INN

89 Houston Farm Road
Stowe, VT 05672
(802) 253-6282 (phone)
(802) 253-7415 (fax)
stay@stonehillinn.com
www.stonehillinn.com

Stone Hill Inn is a perfect romantic getaway. All rooms feature a fireside, two-person Jacuzzi, king-size bed, and many thoughtful touches. Come unwind, and just enjoy being together. The area of Stowe has unlimited possibilities for activities all seasons. In the winter there is downhill skiing, cross-country skiing, romantic sleigh rides, snowshoeing, tobogganing, and snowmobiling. In the summer there is hiking, golf, canoeing, horseback riding, scenic gondola rides to the top of Mt. Mansfield, glider rides, fly-fishing, and biking. You can also visit museums, galleries, wineries, Vermont cheese and syrup producers, the Ben and Jerry's Ice Cream factory, the Cold Hollow Cider Mill, and the Vermont Teddy Bear factory.

Marinated Shrimp

2 pounds shrimp, peeled but not cooked
1½ cups olive oil
½ cup freshly chopped parsley
4½ teaspoons dried basil
3 teaspoons dried oregano
12 cloves garlic, minced
4½ teaspoons salt
2 tablespoons pepper
4 tablespoons lemon juice
Lemon wedges

Thaw shrimp, if necessary. Combine oil, parsley, basil, oregano, garlic, salt, pepper, and lemon juice. Reserve one-third of marinade to baste during cooking. Pour remaining marinade over shrimp, stirring well. Chill at least 1 hour. Remove shrimp from marinade and discard used marinade. Put shrimp on skewers and grill or broil, basting with reserved marinade, 3 minutes on each side. Serve with lemon wedge for garnish. Yields 4 servings.

Strawberry-Blueberry Crêpes

Crêpes:
1 cup cold water
1 cup cold milk
4 eggs
½ teaspoon salt
2 cups all-purpose flour
4 tablespoons melted butter

Filling:
2 (8-ounce) packages cream cheese, softened
1 pint sour cream
¾ cup confectioners' sugar

Sauce:
2 cups fresh strawberries
½ cup sugar

Toppings:
3 to 4 cups lightly sweetened strawberries and blueberries
Whipped cream
Fresh mint

To make crêpes, mix all ingredients in blender until smooth. Refrigerate 2 to 3 hours. Heat lightly oiled skillet or crêpe pan. Spoon 3 to 4 tablespoons batter into pan and lift and tilt to form 6-inch crêpe. Brown lightly on one side. Cool and stack between layers of wax paper or parchment paper. These can be made ahead and refrigerated. They even freeze well.

To make filling, beat cream cheese, sour cream, and confectioners' sugar with electric mixer.

To make sauce, crush strawberries and mix thoroughly with sugar.

Preheat oven to 350°. Spoon room temperature crêpes with 3 to 4 tablespoons of filling. Roll and place seam-side down in baking pan. Heat 5 to 7 minutes. Remove from oven, place on serving plate, and top with sauce, whole fruit, and whipped cream. Garnish with fresh mint leaves. Yields 12 to 14 servings.

Tomato and Vidalia Onion Quiche

1 (9-inch) piecrust
1 cup shredded mozzarella cheese
1 cup shredded Cheddar cheese
2 medium tomatoes, seeded and chopped
1 medium (or ½ large) Vidalia onion, thinly sliced
1 teaspoon dried basil or 1 tablespoon freshly chopped basil
¼ teaspoon garlic salt
Cracked pepper
3 eggs
1 cup milk
3 tablespoons grated Parmesan cheese

Preheat oven to 400°. Spread piecrust into 9-inch pie pan, pressing up against sides and into bottom. Trim crust, if necessary. Prick with fork all over. Bake pie shell about 7 to 9 minutes, until brown spots just start to appear. Remove pie shell from oven and reduce oven temperature to 350°. Sprinkle cheeses across bottom of pie shell. Layer tomatoes and onions over cheeses. Sprinkle basil, garlic salt, and pepper on top. Beat eggs and milk together and pour over other ingredients. Sprinkle with Parmesan. Bake 45 to 50 minutes or until set. Yields 6 servings.

Chicken Curry Spread

2 cups grated Monterey Jack cheese
2 (3-ounce) packages cream cheese, softened
¼ plus ¾ cup chopped green onions
⅔ cup finely chopped chutney
3 teaspoons curry powder
1 teaspoon ginger
½ teaspoon salt
3 medium chicken breasts, cooked and shredded
1 cup sour cream
½ teaspoon garlic powder
¼ teaspoon paprika
¼ teaspoon pepper
¼ to ½ cup chopped raisins
½ cup slivered or sliced almonds, toasted

Beat cheeses and ¼ cup green onions with chutney, curry powder, ginger, and salt. Thinly spread onto large platter and chill. Combine chicken with sour cream, garlic powder, paprika, and pepper. Spread over cheese mixture and refrigerate 4 to 24 hours. Just before serving, sprinkle remaining ¾ cup green onions around edge of cheese mixture and sprinkle raisins and toasted almonds over center. Serve with milk and crackers. Yields about 8 cups.

Banana Chocolate Chip Nut Bread

1½ cups sugar
¼ pound (1 stick) butter
2 large eggs, lightly beaten
2¼ cups all-purpose flour
½ teaspoon baking powder
¾ teaspoon baking soda
½ teaspoon salt
1¼ cups mashed banana
1 teaspoon vanilla extract
¼ cup buttermilk
1 cup chopped walnuts
1 cup semisweet chocolate morsels

Preheat oven to 350°. Coat an 8½ x 4½-inch loaf pan with nonstick spray. Beat sugar and butter at medium speed with electric mixer until well blended. Add eggs, beating well. Combine flour and baking powder, soda, and salt in separate bowl. Add to butter mixture, beating well. Combine banana, vanilla, buttermilk, nuts, and chocolate morsels. Add to flour mixture, beating well. Pour batter into loaf pan.

Bake 1 hour and 15 minutes or until tester comes out clean. Yields 1 loaf.

I. B. MUNSON HOUSE BED & BREAKFAST

37 South Main Street, Route 7
Wallingford, VT 05773
(802) 446-2860 (phone)
(888) 519-3771 (toll free)
stay@ibmunsoninn.com
www.ibmunsoninn.com

The I. B. Munson House is a beautiful Victorian mansion, circa 1856, nestled in the quaint village of Wallingford. It features high ceilings, arched windows, clawfoot tubs, period antiques, and six working fireplaces. The house has fourteen rooms, including seven guest rooms, all with private baths. A full gourmet breakfast is included.

Strawberry and Banana French Toast

5 eggs
¾ cup milk
¼ teaspoon baking powder
1 tablespoon pure vanilla
1 loaf French bread, cut into thick slices
1 (20-ounce) bag frozen whole strawberries
4 ripe bananas
1 cup sugar
1 tablespoon apple pie spice
2 tablespoons cinnamon sugar

Combine eggs, milk, baking powder, and vanilla. Pour over bread and refrigerate

8 to 10 hours or overnight. Preheat oven to 450°. Combine strawberries, bananas, sugar, and apple pie spice. Put into greased baking dish and top with prepared bread. Sprinkle with cinnamon sugar. Bake 20 to 25 minutes. Yields 8 servings.

Lisa's Chocolate Chip-Off-the-Block Muffins

4½ cups all-purpose flour
1 cup firmly packed brown sugar
½ cup granulated sugar
4 teaspoons baking powder
1 teaspoon baking soda
1 teaspoon salt
2 cups buttermilk
¾ cup vegetable oil
1½ teaspoons vanilla extract
3 eggs
1 cup chocolate chips

In large bowl, combine flour, sugars, baking powder, baking soda, and salt and mix well. Add buttermilk, oil, vanilla, and eggs. Stir just until dry ingredients are moistened. Fold in chocolate chips. Batter can be baked immediately or stored in tightly covered container in refrigerator up to 5 days. When ready to bake, preheat oven to 375°. Grease bottoms only of desired number of muffin cups or line with paper baking cups. Stir batter, fill cups two-thirds full. Bake 20 to 25 minutes or until toothpick inserted in center comes out clean. Immediately remove from pan. Serve warm. Yields 24 servings.

Charlie's Grilled Eggplant

1 large eggplant
4 tablespoons salt
¼ cup olive oil
8 ounces fontina or mozzarella cheese, grated
2 large tomatoes, chopped
Chopped basil for garnish

Slice eggplant into ¼-inch slices, sprinkle with salt, and place in colander for 30 minutes to 1 hour. Rinse and pat dry. Preheat oven to 350°. Brush eggplant slices with olive oil and grill on both sides. Top eggplant with grated cheese and chopped tomatoes. Place on baking sheet prepared with nonstick spray. Bake until cheese melts. Serve garnished with chopped basil if desired. Yields 4 servings, two eggplant slices per person.

Auntie Audrey's Goat Cheese Egg Cups

1 (8-count) package crescent rolls
4 ounces goat cheese
12 eggs
1 tablespoon parsley flakes

Roll out crescent roll dough and cut into eight squares. Place squares in muffin tins with edges overlapping top to form cup. Bake per directions on package until golden brown. Divide goat cheese among cups immediately. Scramble eggs, overfill each cup, top with parsley, and serve. Yields 8 servings.

STOWEFLAKE

P.O. Box 369
1746 Mountain Road
Stowe, VT 05672-0369
(802) 760-1053 (phone)
(800) 253-2232 (toll free)
info@stoweflake.com
www.stoweflake.com

In the heart of Stowe enjoy luxurious accommodations, a fifty-thousand-square-foot, world-class spa, endless onsite activities, including indoor and outdoor pools, golf facilities, tennis, cross-country skiing, snowshoeing, horse-drawn sleigh/carriage rides, and even a hot-air balloon. Savor the delectable selections of Executive Chef Jeffrey Weiss in one of two award-winning restaurants, Winfield's Bistro and Charlie B's Pub and Restaurant.

I. B. Munson House Bed & Breakfast

Vermont Cheddar "Ornaments"

A festive hors d'oeuvre or perfect accompaniment to your favorite holiday salad.

8 ounces low-fat Cabot Cheddar, grated
2 eggs plus 1 egg
½ cup plus 4 tablespoons
    all-purpose flour
1 teaspoon freshly chopped sage
½ teaspoon kosher salt
⅛ teaspoon ground white pepper
1 ounce dried cranberries
1½ cups ground pepita or pumpkin seed

Preheat oven to 400°. Place cheese, 2 eggs, ½ cup flour, sage, salt, and pepper in food processor. Mix about 10 seconds or until ingredients form together. Place in mixing bowl and fold in dried cranberries. Form into about 18 balls, ½ ounce each. Whip remaining egg and 1 teaspoon water in bowl. In separate bowls put remaining flour, and pepita or pumpkin seed. First dredge "ornaments" in flour, then in egg wash, and finally in pumpkin seeds. Bake on Teflon cookie sheet 10 minutes. Yields 18 ornaments.

Pumpkin Vermont Chèvre

6 soup-bowl-size pumpkins
1 tablespoon butter
2 tablespoons all-purpose flour
⅛ teaspoon cayenne
Salt and cracked black pepper
6 eggs, separated
12 ounces Jonah crabmeat
2 sage leaves, cut in thin strips
6 ounces Vermont chèvre

Preheat oven to 350°. Cut tops off pumpkins, remove seeds, and place pumpkins in large deep pan with about 4 cups water. Cover and bake 40 minutes. Remove pumpkins from oven and scoop flesh out,

reserving shell. Purée flesh in food processor until smooth. Place in heavy-bottom pot with butter, flour, cayenne, and salt and pepper to taste. Cook over low heat until dry. Remove from heat, add egg yolks, and transfer to stainless steel bowl. Fold in crab, sage, and goat cheese. Whip egg whites to stiff peaks and add to mixture. Pipe mixture back into pumpkin, raise oven temperature to 375° and bake about 13 minutes. Yields 6 servings.

Mt. Mansfield Foraged Morel Mushroom Cappuccino

2 cloves garlic, minced
3 whole shallots, minced
1 tablespoon unsalted butter
3 ounces dried morels*,
    rehydrated to 7-ounce size
⅛ cup sherry
2 quarts mushroom stock
    (rehydrated liquid)
2 plus ½ cups heavy whipping cream
4 sprigs freshly picked thyme, minced
3 teaspoons beurre manié (equal parts
    softened butter and flour)
Salt and freshly ground pepper

Sweat garlic and shallots in unsalted butter in saucepan over medium heat until translucent. Add sliced morels and stir for 1 minute. Deglaze with sherry. Reduce until dry. Add stock (rehydrated liquid) and bring to simmer. Reduce to one-third. Slowly whisk in 2 cups heavy cream. Bring to boil. Add half of minced thyme and simmer for 15 minutes. Whisk in balls of beurre manié to thicken. Simmer 15 more minutes. Season with salt and freshly ground pepper to taste. Whip remaining thyme with remaining ½ cup cream until soft peaks form. Spoon on top of soup. Garnish with morel dust. Yields 6 (6-ounce) bowls.

*Note: Save 2 dried morels and grind in coffee grinder for morel dust to garnish.

THE RICHMOND VICTORIAN INN

191 East Main Street
Richmond, VT 05477
(802) 434-4410 (phone)
(802) 434-4411 (fax)
(888) 242-3362 (toll free)
innkeeper@richmondvictorianinn.com
www.richmondvictorianinn.com

Nestled in the foothills of the Green Mountains, The Richmond Victorian Inn is a lovely restored 1850s Victorian. The six guest rooms of the inn are decorated in a country Victorian style and include many antiques. Twelve miles east of Burlington and Lake Champlain, many recreational opportunities, including the Long Trail, boating, fishing, and downhill and cross-country skiing are within a few minutes' drive. Or you can sit on the front porch and watch the world go by or curl up in a rocker with a good book.

Blueberry Cream Cheese Casserole

12 slices sourdough or white bread
1 plus 1 (8-ounce) package cream cheese
¾ plus ¾ cup blueberries, fresh or frozen
12 eggs
2 cups milk
⅓ cup Vermont maple syrup
1 teaspoon ground cinnamon

Cut bread in half on diagonal. Place half in buttered 13 x 9-inch pan or casserole dish. Cut 1 package cream cheese into 1-inch cubes and place over bread. Top with ¾ cup blueberries. Repeat process with remaining bread, cream cheese, and blueberries. In separate bowl beat eggs and add milk, maple syrup, and cinnamon. Mix well and pour over bread layers. Cover with foil and refrigerate 8 to 10 hours or overnight.

When ready to cook, remove casserole from refrigerator. Preheat oven to 350° and bake casserole, covered, 30 minutes. Uncover and bake 25 to 30 minutes more, or until knife inserted near center comes out clean. Serve warm with blueberry or Vermont maple syrup and bacon or sausage. Yields 8 servings.

Gingerbread Pancakes with Orange Sauce

Batter:
2 cups baking mix
1 egg
1⅓ cups milk, low-fat or whole
¼ cup molasses
1½ teaspoons ground ginger
1 teaspoon ground cinnamon
½ teaspoon ground cloves

Orange sauce:
1 cup sugar
¼ pound (1 stick) butter or margarine
¼ cup water
1 egg, well beaten
Grated peel of 1 large orange
Juice of orange, up to 3 tablespoons
1 package cream cheese, cut in cubes
    (or use a 1-inch scoop), for garnish

Beat baking mix, egg, milk, molasses, and spices with whisk or hand beater until smooth. For each pancake pour scant ¼ cup batter onto hot griddle. (Grease griddle using shortening or similar, if necessary). Cook until pancakes are bubbly and dry around edges. Carefully turn (pancakes are delicate) and cook other sides until golden brown.

For orange sauce, heat all ingredients to boiling over medium heat, stirring constantly. Place two pancakes on each plate and garnish with cube of cream cheese. Spoon orange sauce over pancakes and serve warm with bacon or sausage and fried apples. Yields 7 to 9 servings.

Orange Praline French Toast

French toast:
1 loaf day-old, French, Italian, or
    sourdough bread, sliced ½-inch thick
¼ plus ¼ cup orange liqueur
    (Triple Sec or similar)
Grated zest of 1 large orange
    (remove peel and slice for garnish)
1 teaspoon ground cinnamon
¼ teaspoon ground nutmeg
8 eggs
⅔ cup orange juice
2 cups milk
½ cup sugar
1 teaspoon vanilla extract

Praline topping:
½ cup chopped pecans
½ cup firmly packed brown sugar
¼ cup all-purpose flour
1 teaspoon ground cinnamon
2 teaspoons grated orange zest
3 tablespoons melted butter
Confectioners' sugar
Mint sprigs for garnish

Butter 13 x 9-inch baking pan or casserole dish. Place half of bread slices in bottom of pan and brush with half of Triple Sec. Sprinkle with half of orange zest, cinnamon, and nutmeg. Cover with remaining slices of bread and repeat. Whisk together eggs, orange juice, milk, sugar, and vanilla. Pour mixture over bread. Cover and refrigerate 8 to 10 hours or overnight. When ready to bake, preheat oven to 350°. Remove casserole from refrigerator and uncover. To make topping, combine pecans, brown sugar, flour, cinnamon, and orange zest in small bowl until well blended. Add butter and mix well. Sprinkle over casserole. Bake, uncovered, 30 to 35 minutes, or until knife inserted near center comes out clean. To serve, sprinkle with sifted confectioners' sugar and garnish with slices of peeled orange and mint sprig, if desired. Yields 10 to 12 servings.

the Inn at Manchester

THE INN AT MANCHESTER

Historic Route 7 A
Manchester Village, VT 05254
(802) 362-1793 (phone)
(802) 362-3218 (fax)
(800) 273-1793 (toll free)
stay@innatmanchester.com
www.innatmanchester.com

The Inn at Manchester is a Victorian inn featuring casual elegance and warm hospitality in a country atmosphere with in-town conveniences. Come for "peace, pancakes and pampering." Activities in the surrounding area include golf, horseback riding, fly-fishing, canoeing, biking, hiking, and shopping. There is the Southern Vermont Arts Center, Robert Todd Lincoln's Hildene, the American Museum of Fly-fishing, and the Bennington Museum.

Cottage Cakes

1 cup cottage cheese
4 eggs, beaten
4 tablespoons melted butter or margarine
½ cup all-purpose flour

Whisk cottage cheese, eggs, and butter together. Fold in flour. Bake on pancake griddle, using medium-high heat. Serve with Vermont maple syrup and apricot sauce. Yields 2 to 4 servings.

Carrot Cake

Cake:
1½ cups vegetable oil
2 cups sugar
4 eggs
3 cups grated carrots
2 cups all-purpose flour
2 teaspoons baking powder
2 teaspoons baking soda
1 teaspoon ground cinnamon
1 teaspoon salt
1 cup chopped pecans

Icing:
¼ pound (1 stick) butter or margarine
8 ounces cream cheese
1 teaspoon vanilla extract
2 cups confectioners' sugar

Preheat oven to 350°. For cake, combine oil and sugar and beat on medium speed. Add eggs one at a time. Mix until well blended. Add carrots. Combine flour, baking powder, soda, cinnamon, salt, and nuts. Pour into three 8-inch tins or two 9-inch tins, greased and floured. Bake 30 to 35 minutes. Cool cake.

For icing, cream together butter and cream cheese. Add vanilla. Add sugar and beat well. Frost cake. Yields 12 to 15 servings.

Sour Cream Waffles

3 eggs, separated
¾ cup sour cream
¾ cup buttermilk
1 stick butter, melted
1½ cups all-purpose flour
½ teaspoon baking soda
2 teaspoons baking powder
1 tablespoon sugar

Beat egg yolks and add sour cream, buttermilk, and melted butter. Sift together flour, baking soda, baking powder, and sugar. Add to eggs and mix well. Beat egg whites until stiff. Fold into batter. Cook in heated waffle iron. Great with Vermont maple syrup, or our favorite, warm raspberry sauce and vanilla ice cream. Yields 4 servings.

Apricot Cheese Bread

2 cups water
½ cup cut up dried apricots
½ cup light raisins
¼ plus 1½ cups sugar
8 ounces cream cheese, softened
½ pound (2 sticks) butter
1½ teaspoons vanilla extract
4 eggs
2 cups all-purpose flour
1½ teaspoons baking powder
½ cup chopped pecans

Preheat oven to 325°. Grease and flour Bundt pan. In saucepan combine water, apricots, raisins, and ¼ cup sugar. Bring to a boil and let simmer 15 to 20 minutes. Drain well. In mixing bowl combine remaining 1½ cups sugar, cream cheese, butter, and vanilla. Beat until creamed. Add eggs, beating in one at a time. Combine flour, baking powder, and nuts and add gradually to creamed mixture. Gently fold into apricot mixture. Turn into pan and bake 65 to 70 minutes. Cool completely on wire rack. Yields 12 to 16 servings.

WINDHAM HILL INN

311 Lawrence Drive
West Townshend, VT 05359
(802) 874-4080 (phone)
(802) 874-4702 (fax)
(800) 944-4080 (toll free)
windham@sover.net
www.windhamhill.com

Windham Hill Inn sits on 160 acres at the end of a Green Mountain hillside country road, surrounded by rock-wall-bordered fields and forests and breathtaking views. Friendly innkeepers and staff welcome you to this country estate with its sparkling rooms, memorable gourmet meals, relaxing ambiance, and closeness to nature. Relax in four elegantly furnished common rooms with wood-burning fireplaces, a Steinway grand piano, and an eight-hundred-disc CD library. Guest rooms feature antiques, locally-crafted furnishings, hardwood floors, and oriental rugs.

Maine Crab "Cosmopolitan"

Chutney:
⅓ cup cider vinegar
1 tablespoon minced ginger
1 clove garlic, chopped
2 cups sliced dried apricots
¼ cup dried cranberries
¼ cup golden raisins
¼ cup sugar
Pinch of cayenne
Pinch of salt
Water as needed

¾ cup (4 ounces) fresh Maine crabmeat
½ cup cranberry juice
1 tablespoon premium vodka
4 ounces crème fraîche or sour cream
Chervil sprigs for garnish

For chutney, combine vinegar, ginger, and garlic in blender and process 1 minute. In heavy-bottomed, medium saucepan pour vinegar mixture and add apricots, cranberries, raisins, sugar, cayenne, and salt. Add just enough water to cover. Bring to a boil and then reduce to simmer. Cook, stirring occasionally, until mixture is very thick, 30 to 45 minutes. Taste for seasonings and add more salt or cayenne to taste. Pour onto cookie sheet and cool to room temperature. Store covered in refrigerator up to a month.

To serve, place 2 tablespoons chilled chutney in bottom of each of four chilled martini glasses. Top with 3 tablespoons crabmeat and 2 tablespoons cranberry juice. Stir vodka into crème fraiche and spoon sparingly on top of crabmeat. Garnish with chervil sprigs and serve. Yields 4 servings.

Pan-Seared Diver Scallops

Vinaigrette:
7 tablespoons butter
1 teaspoon smooth Dijon mustard
½ teaspoon salt
⅛ teaspoon freshly ground black pepper
Dash of Cholula hot sauce
½ cup grapeseed or canola oil

Scallops:
2 tablespoons grapeseed or canola oil
12 (U-10) diver scallops
    (under 10 scallops to the pound)
16 ounces baby spinach
Salt
Freshly ground black pepper
9 slices bacon, diced and cooked crisply

For vinaigrette, place small saucepan over medium-low heat and add butter. Cook until butter turns brown and develops nutty aroma, 5 to 8 minutes. Combine butter with mustard, salt and pepper, hot sauce, and oil in blender and emulsify. Transfer to small bowl and reserve.

To prepare scallops, place medium sauté pan over high heat and add oil. Season six scallops with salt and pepper. When pan begins to smoke, add scallops to pan. Cook 1 to 2 minutes or until bottoms are nicely browned. Then turn scallops over and sear other side. Cook 1 minute more, until scallops feel firm to touch. Remove from heat and keep warm. Repeat process with remaining scallops. In same pan, wilt spinach over high heat and season with salt and pepper. Divide spinach among six warm dinner plates, placing mound in center of each. Place two scallops on top of each

mound and spoon vinaigrette over top and around plate. Sprinkle with bacon and serve. Yields 6 servings.

Molasses-Glazed Salmon

Crust:
4 cups toasted pumpkin seeds
1 cup toasted sesame seeds
4 tablespoons minced garlic
1 teaspoon salt
1½ teaspoons freshly ground black pepper
½ cup canola oil

Molasses glaze:
1 cup molasses
½ cup rice wine vinegar

Salmon:
2 tablespoons grapeseed or canola oil
6 (6-ounce) salmon fillets, skin removed
Salt
Freshly ground black pepper
1½ pounds Swiss chard, cleaned and
    roughly chopped

For crust, combine ingredients in food processor until mixture is thick and spreadable (you may need to add extra oil) and reserve.

For glaze, combine molasses and vinegar in small saucepan and reduce by one-third. Set aside and keep warm.

For salmon, preheat oven to 450°. Place large sauté pan over high heat and add about 1 tablespoon oil. Season fillets with salt and pepper to taste. When pan begins to smoke, add three fillets and cook 3 to 4 minutes until salmon are crispy brown on bottom. Turn over and sear 2 to 3 minutes more. Transfer to ovenproof platter or baking sheet. Repeat process with remaining salmon. Place about ½ cup crust on top of each fillet. Transfer salmon to oven and bake 6 to 8 minutes or until fillets are firm to touch. In same sauté pan, wilt chard over high heat and season with salt and

pepper. Divide chard among six warm dinner plates, placing a mound in center of each. Place one fillet on top of each mound of chard, drizzle with molasses glaze, and serve. Yields 6 servings.

Buttery Jam Tart Cookies

10 tablespoons (1¼ sticks) butter
½ cup sugar
1 egg
1 teaspoon almond extract
1 teaspoon vanilla extract
2 tablespoons milk
2½ cups all-purpose flour
¼ teaspoon baking soda
¼ teaspoon salt
16 ounces favorite jam

Preheat oven to 350°. In mixing bowl cream together butter and sugar until light and fluffy. Add egg, almond, vanilla, and milk. Mix until thoroughly combined. In small bowl, mix flour, baking soda, and salt. Add dry ingredients to wet ingredients and mix completely. Cut dough into 36 pieces with fluted, round, 2-inch-diameter cookie cutter. Place one cookie round onto parchment-lined cookie sheet and place small amount of jam on top. Cut out center of second cookie with small cookie cutter of any desired shape, reserving center. Place second cookie atop jam. Crimp edges of two cookies slightly to prevent jam from seeping between layers while cookies bake. Place reserved cut-out center on top of cookie for decorative touch, if desired. Repeat process with remaining dough rounds, placing each jam-filled cookie about 2 inches apart on baking sheet. Bake 10 to 12 minutes or until light golden brown. Yields 18 cookies.

Virginia

BLUEMONT BED & BREAKFAST

18562 US Hwy. Business 340
Luray, VA 22835
(540) 743-1268 (phone)
(888) IN-LURAY (toll free)
innkeeper@bluemontbb.com
www.bluemontbb.com

Bluemont Bed & Breakfast is a hilltop retreat located in the Shenandoah Valley countryside. Guests are pampered with a full country breakfast, snacks, beverages, and evening dessert. All of our guests love our "million dollar" views of the Blue Ridge and Massanutten Mountains, located two miles south of Luray.

Brownie Caramel Nut Tart

1 (9-inch) unbaked piecrust
½ cup chopped nuts (walnuts or pecans)
20 caramels, unwrapped
1 (14-ounce) can condensed milk
1 egg, beaten
2 tablespoons melted butter
6 ounces semisweet melted chocolate chips

Place pastry shell in tart pan with removable bottom. Sprinkle nuts into piecrust. Preheat oven to 325°. In saucepan over low heat melt caramels with ⅔ cup condensed milk. Spread mixture over nuts. In separate bowl, combine egg and melted butter and remaining milk. Mix well. Stir in melted chips. Pour mixture over caramel layer. Bake 30 minutes or until center is set. Cool. Serve warm or chilled. Refrigerate leftovers. Yields 8 servings.

Cinnamon Crunch Coffeecake

1 cup all-purpose flour
½ teaspoon baking powder
⅛ teaspoon baking soda
½ teaspoon ground cinnamon
¼ teaspoon salt
⅓ cup butter
¼ plus ¼ cup packed brown sugar
½ cup granulated sugar
1 egg
½ cup buttermilk or ½ cup milk plus
    1 teaspoon lemon juice
½ cup chopped apples
¼ cup chopped walnuts or pecans
½ teaspoon ground cinnamon
¼ teaspoon ground nutmeg

Mix flour, baking powder, baking soda, cinnamon, and salt. In separate bowl, cream butter, ¼ cup brown sugar, and granulated sugar until blended. Add egg and beat until light and fluffy. Add dry ingredients and stir in milk. Mix thoroughly. Fold in apples. Pour into greased, 8-inch square pan. Mix remaining ¼ cup brown sugar, nuts, cinnamon, and nutmeg and sprinkle over batter. Cover and refrigerate 8 to 10 hours or overnight. When ready to bake, set pan out while preheating oven to 350°. Bake 25 to 30 minutes or until toothpick inserted comes out clean. Cut into squares and serve warm with whipped cream. Yields 6 to 8 servings.

Brownie Chocolate Chip Cheesecake

1 package brownie mix (snack size)
3 (8-ounce) packages cream cheese, softened
1 (14-ounce) can sweetened condensed milk
3 eggs at room temperature
2 teaspoons vanilla extract
¾ plus ¼ cup mini chocolate chips
    (reserve some to sprinkle
    on cheesecake)
1 teaspoon all-purpose flour

Prepare brownie mix according to package directions, but bake in 9- or 10-inch springform pan for cheesecake base. Cool thoroughly. Once cooled, line walls of springform pan with wax paper or parchment paper so cheesecake does not stick when removing from pan. Preheat oven to 300°. In large mixing bowl beat cream cheese until fluffy. Add condensed milk and beat until smooth. Add eggs one at a time and blend after each. Add vanilla.

Mix well. In small bowl toss ¾ cup chips with flour to coat and stir into cheese mixture. Pour over brownie base. Sprinkle remaining ¼ cup chips evenly over top. Bake about 45 minutes. Cake should not form cracks on top. Watch carefully so as not to overcook. Center should appear slightly soft. It will firm as it cools. Cool to room temperature on cooling rack. Cover and chill overnight. Remove side of pan. Cut into serving pieces. Refrigerate leftovers. Yields 12 servings.

CAPE CHARLES HOUSE BED & BREAKFAST

645 Tazewell Ave.
Cape Charles, VA 23310
(757) 331-4920 (phone)
(757) 331-4960 (fax)
stay@capecharleshouse.com
www.capecharleshouse.com

Cape Charles House is the recent recipient of the Virginia Governor's Award for hospitality. It is a romantic getaway with comfortable elegance and antiques in a small town on Chesapeake Bay. Here you will find history, galleries, antiques, birdwatching, beaches, bikes, sunsets, and golf packages. The bed and breakfast offers gourmet breakfast, complimentary wine and cheese, tea and sweets. The rooms are large and sunny with private baths, some with Jacuzzis.

Stuffed Peach Croissants

1½ cups half-and-half
4 eggs
¼ cup Triple Sec
½ teaspoon almond flavoring
1 teaspoon ground nutmeg
4 baked croissants
4 to 6 ounces cream cheese, softened
⅓ cup chopped pecan or walnut meats
2 to 3 peaches, peeled and sliced
Cinnamon

Make custard mixture by combining half-and-half, eggs, Triple Sec, almond flavoring, and nutmeg in medium bowl and beat well. Coat 9 x 13-inch baking dish with nonstick spray. Slice croissants in half lengthwise and place in baking dish. Open each croissant, spread cream cheese on bottom half, and sprinkle with ground nuts. Place sliced peaches over nuts and sprinkle with cinnamon. Dip tops of croissants into custard mixture and place on filled bottoms. Pour custard mixture over croissants. At this point you can cover and refrigerate 8 to 10 hours or overnight or bake at 375° for 15 minutes until custard is set. If croissants are browning too quickly, loosely cover baking dish with foil. When baked, carefully cut around each croissant, lightly dust with confectioners' sugar, and lift onto warmed serving plate. Serve with warm maple syrup. Yields 4 servings.

Savory Asparagus Croissants

1½ cups half-and-half
4 eggs
⅛ teaspoon cayenne
2 teaspoons spicy mustard
1 teaspoon ground nutmeg
½ teaspoon salt
White sesame seeds
Black sesame seeds or poppy seeds
4 baked croissants

1½ cups shredded Swiss cheese
16 asparagus spears, cooked
Garlic salt
Ground pepper
Dill weed

For custard mixture combine half-and-half, eggs, cayenne, mustard, nutmeg, and salt in medium bowl and beat well. Coat 9 x 13-inch baking dish with nonstick spray. Slice croissants in half lengthwise. Place croissants in baking dish. Open each one and sprinkle bottom half with part of cheese. Place 4 asparagus spears on top of each one and sprinkle with garlic salt, ground pepper, and small amount of dill weed. Sprinkle remaining cheese over asparagus. Dip tops of croissants into custard mixture and place them on top of filled croissant bottoms. Pour custard mixture over all. Top each croissant with a few white and black sesame seeds. At this point you can cover and refrigerate 8 to 10 hours or overnight or bake at 375° for 15 minutes or until custard is set. If croissants brown too quickly, loosely cover baking dish with foil. When baked, carefully cut around each croissant and lift onto warmed serving plate. Yields 4 servings.

Calico Quesadillas

4 large eggs
¼ cup water
¼ cup chopped red pepper
4 spring onions, sliced
½ cup corn (can be frozen)
½ cup fresh cilantro, chopped
1 teaspoon garlic salt
½ teaspoon freshly cracked pepper
½ teaspoon cumin
4 small flour tortillas
1 cup shredded Mexican cheese blend
Salsa
Sour cream

Lightly coat medium frying pan with nonstick spray. Preheat oven to 450°. In bowl combine eggs and water and beat well. Heat frying pan over medium-high heat and add egg mixture. Begin to scramble eggs and then add red pepper, green onions, corn, cilantro, garlic salt, pepper, and cumin. Continue to scramble until eggs are set. Lightly spray cookie sheet. Place tortillas on sheet and divide cooked egg among tortillas, placing mixture just on half of tortilla with some cheese. Fold other half over eggs and cheese, creasing at folded edge to secure. Bake 3 to 5 minutes or until nicely browned. Top tortilla crescent with tablespoon of salsa, dollop of sour cream, and sprinkle of chopped fresh cilantro. Serve with Rosemary Roasted Potatoes and baked tomato half. Yields 4 servings.

THE INN AT MONTICELLO

Route 20 South
1188 Scottsville Road
Charlottesville, VA 22902
(434) 979-3593
stay@innatmonticello.com
www.innatmonticello.com

The Inn at Monticello is a beautiful historic property very close to Thomas Jefferson's Monticello. The inn is also close to Ashlawn-Highlands, home of President James Monroe, the University of Virginia, the city of Charlottesville, and Skyline Drive and the Blue Ridge Parkway. Our guests come from all over the world and enjoy the elegance of our home, but they especially rave about our breakfasts.

Peaches and Crème Brûlée French Toast

1 plus ½ stick butter
1 plus ½ cup packed brown sugar
¼ cup corn syrup
10 (1-inch thick) slices bread
6 eggs
1½ cups half-and-half
1 teaspoon vanilla extract
1 teaspoon Triple Sec
¼ teaspoon salt
½ cup rum or peach brandy
Fresh or frozen peaches

In heavy saucepan, melt 1 stick butter with brown sugar and corn syrup, stirring until smooth. Pour into 15 x 10-inch baking pan coated with nonstick spray (glass dish works best). Place bread over mixture. Mix eggs, half-and-half, vanilla, Triple Sec, and salt together with whisk. Pour over bread.

Cover and refrigerate 8 to 10 hours or overnight. When ready to bake, allow mixture to sit at room temperature 30 minutes. Preheat oven to 350° and bake 30 to 35 minutes. While baking, melt remaining ½ stick butter in microwave and add rum or peach brandy and remaining ½ cup brown sugar. Heat 30 seconds. Add fresh or frozen peaches. Place one piece of French toast, cut on the diagonal, on each plate, brown sugar-side up. Spoon peaches over top. This dish is very rich. Yields 10 servings.

Florentine Eggs

8 eggs, slightly beaten
¼ cup plus 2 tablespoons melted butter
8 ounces Swiss cheese, grated
8 ounces feta cheese, crumbled
1 cup cottage cheese
1 (12-ounce) package frozen chopped spinach, thawed and squeezed dry
1 teaspoon ground nutmeg
3 tablespoons all-purpose flour
1 cup half-and-half
1 cup milk
8 ounces grated Monterey Jack cheese
½ teaspoon salt
¼ teaspoon white pepper
Dash of Tabasco

Preheat oven to 350°. Beat eggs and ¼ cup butter. Combine eggs and butter with Swiss, feta, and cottage cheese in large bowl. Stir in spinach and nutmeg. Mix well. Divide into eight greased ramekins and bake 30 minutes. While baking, make cheese sauce. In saucepan heat remaining 2 tablespoons butter, stir in flour, and cook 1 to 2 minutes until creamy, stirring constantly. Add half-and-half and milk and cook until sauce begins to thicken and boil, stirring constantly. Stir in Monterey Jack cheese, salt, pepper, and Tabasco. Continue cooking until cheese has melted. Remove eggs from ramekins onto plates and spoon two to three large spoonfuls of cheese sauce over eggs. Serve quickly before they cool. Yields 8 servings.

The Inn at Monticello

Eggs a la Jefferson

10 slices bacon
½ pound fresh mushrooms
Salt and pepper
16 eggs
1½ cups shredded Cheddar cheese
¾ cup sour cream
4 green onions, chopped

Coat 10 x 15-inch glass pan with nonstick spray. Fry and crumble bacon. Slice mushrooms. Salt and pepper eggs to taste and soft scramble them; do *not* overcook. Place eggs as first layer in pan, then bacon, mushrooms, and cheese. Put dollops of sour cream over mixture and sprinkle with green onions. Cover and place in refrigerator if not using immediately. When ready to cook, let eggs come to room temperature, about 40 minutes. Preheat oven to 350°. Bake 20 to 25 minutes until warmed through and cheese is bubbly. Serve with thin slices of fresh tomato. Yields 10 servings.

Banana Coconut Coffee Cake

1 (18-ounce) package moist deluxe cake mix, yellow or white
1 (3.8-ounce) box vanilla instant pudding
4 eggs
1 cup sour cream
½ cup vegetable oil
¼ cup water
¼ cup sugar
1 cup coconut
½ cup chopped nuts
2 to 3 mashed bananas

Preheat oven to 350°. Coat large tube pan with nonstick spray. Combine cake mix, pudding mix, eggs, sour cream, oil, water, and sugar. Beat until smooth with electric mixer. Add coconut, nuts, and bananas by hand. Pour batter into pan and bake 45 to 50 minutes. Test with cake tester. Yields 12 servings.

SYCAMORE HILL HOUSE & GARDENS

110 Menefee Mountain Lane
Washington, VA 22747
(540) 675-3046
sycamore@shentel.net
www.sycamorehillhouseandgardens.com

Sycamore Hill House & Gardens is situated on fifty-two acres atop Menefee Mountain near Washington, Virginia. Enjoy the pastoral beauty of the countryside and the Blue Ridge Mountains. The house has light hardwood floors and oriental rugs throughout and is furnished in a classic contemporary style. Kerri Wagner's famous plants, from lush African violets to the most exotic orchid or seven-foot weeping fig tree, fill every corner of this sunny house. The bed and breakfast was created in 1987 as a garden-wildlife-inspired retreat for those seeking privacy and relaxation. Marvelous original art graces each room. Nearby is Skyline Drive, Luray Caverns, Old Rag Mountain, antiques, art and crafts shops, golf, tennis, ballooning, canoeing, and horseback riding.

Roasted Jalapeño Salsa

4 cups chopped, peeled, and seeded roasted jalapeño peppers
4 cups diced fresh tomatoes
2 cups chopped yellow onion
2 teaspoons salt
4 large cloves garlic, finely minced
2 cups white vinegar

Combine all ingredients in large saucepan on stove, bring to a boil, cover, and let simmer gently 10 minutes. The mixture should be like thick soup. Ladle salsa into sterilized pint jars, cover with sterilized lids, and process in boiling water bath 25 minutes. Remove jars from canning bath and let cool. Lids of canning jars should seal into a vacuum while cooling. Label with canning date and store in cool, dark cupboard. Yields 6 pints.

Cinnamon-Apple Puff

1 large Granny Smith apple, cored, peeled, and thinly sliced
1 plus 2 tablespoons butter
3 large eggs
½ cup all-purpose flour
½ cup whole milk
1 teaspoon sugar
Dash of salt
2 tablespoons cinnamon sugar
Juice of 1 lemon

Liberally grease 9- to 10-inch fluted quiche dish. Preheat oven to 475°. Sauté apple in 1 tablespoon butter until slightly tender. Spread apple slices evenly in quiche dish. In small bowl beat eggs and add flour, milk, sugar, and salt. Mix until well blended and pour over apple slices. Place quiche dish in oven for 10 minutes. Remove from oven, dot with remaining 2 tablespoons butter, and sprinkle with cinnamon sugar. Return to oven for 5 minutes. Bring to table puffed and golden and sprinkle lemon juice over puff. Cut in four wedges and serve. Yields 4 servings.

Note: When you pour on lemon juice, puff will sizzle and hiss, but also deflate. It's fun to present it and always get "oooohs," and "aaaahs."

Shrimp and Cheese Pie

8 slices firm white bread,
    crusts removed
4 tablespoons melted butter
1 cup grated Swiss cheese
2 green onions, chopped
2 tablespoons chopped fresh parsley
½ pound small, pre-cooked shrimp
    (thawed, frozen shrimp work fine)
3 large eggs
½ teaspoon salt
1 teaspoon Dijon-style mustard
1½ cups whole milk
½ cup sour cream

Diagonally cut each bread slice in half. Dip in melted butter and arrange half of slices in unbuttered 8 to 9-inch deep dish pie plate or baking dish. Sprinkle with half of cheese, onions, parsley, and shrimp. Add remaining bread to cover and sprinkle with remaining cheese, onions, parsley, and shrimp. In small bowl, beat together eggs, salt, mustard, milk, and sour cream. Pour mixture over layered bread. Cover tightly with foil and refrigerate 8 to 10 hours or overnight. When ready to bake, remove from refrigerator and preheat oven to 350°. Bake 45 to 50 minutes until pie is puffed and golden. Let stand a few minutes and slice into six wedges. Serve warm. Yields 6 servings.

WHITE FENCE BED & BREAKFAST

275 Chapel Road
Stanley, VA 22851
(540) 778-4680 (phone)
(540) 778-4773 (fax)
(800) 211-9885 (toll free)
innkeeper@whitefencebb.com
www.whitefencebb.com

The White Fence Bed & Breakfast is an 1890 Victorian on three acres. There are two spacious private cottage suites and one bed-and-breakfast suite with a queen bed, TV-VCR, fireplace, and two-person whirlpool. A continental breakfast is delivered to your door every morning. Activities available in the area include canoeing on the Shenandoah River; year-round horseback riding; famous Luray Caverns; Shenandoah National Park and Skyline Drive; and wineries.

Peach Soup

5 large ripe peaches, peeled and quartered
¼ cup sugar
1 cup plain yogurt plus some for garnish
¼ cup orange juice
¼ cup lemon juice
¼ cup cream sherry

Purée peaches with sugar in food processor or blender. Blend in yogurt. Add orange and lemon juices. Add sherry and mix until smooth. Refrigerate 8 to 10 hours or overnight and pour into dishes to serve. With a little vanilla yogurt on end of a fork, drizzle a design on top and garnish with mint leaf. Yields 8 to 10 servings.

Rum Raisin Muffins

¾ cup sugar
6 tablespoons butter, softened
1 cup sour cream
1 egg
1 cup raisins, soaked overnight
    in ⅓ cup rum
2 cups all-purpose flour
½ teaspoon baking soda
1 teaspoon baking powder
¼ teaspoon salt
¼ teaspoon ground nutmeg

Preheat oven to 375°. Cream sugar with butter and add sour cream and egg. Gently stir in raisins, including rum. Add flour, baking soda, baking powder, salt, and nutmeg. Grease muffin tin(s) well. Bake 17 to 19 minutes. Yields 11 to 12 muffins.

Ginger Pancakes with Maple Pecan Syrup

¾ cup water
1 cup buttermilk
2 eggs
¼ cup brown sugar
2 tablespoons melted butter
2 cups all-purpose flour
1¾ teaspoons baking powder
1¾ teaspoons baking soda
½ teaspoon salt
¼ plus ¼ teaspoon ground cinnamon
¼ teaspoon ground cloves
1 teaspoon ground ginger
1½ cups maple syrup
½ cup chopped pecans

Beat water, buttermilk, and eggs together. Add brown sugar, butter, flour, baking powder, baking soda, salt, ¼ teaspoon cinnamon, cloves, and ginger. Spoon dough on griddle and cook until edges are dry. Turn and cook other side. Keep pancakes warm in 275° oven. Mix remaining ¼ teaspoon cinnamon, syrup, and pecans in small pan and heat on low until warm. Serve with pancakes. Yields 6 servings.

GREENOCK HOUSE INN

249 Caroline Street
Orange, VA 22960
(540) 672-3625 (phone)
(540) 672-5029 (fax)
(800) 841-1253 (toll free)
info@greenockhouse.com
www.greenockhouse.com

Our passion is food! We love to share that passion. At our beautiful Victorian farmhouse on over five gorgeous acres, you can sit on the wraparound porch to enjoy your evening hors d'oeuvres and wine. In the morning, indulge in a gourmet breakfast including one of our pastry chef's sinful desserts.

Italian Potato Omelets

1 red pepper, julienned
½ large onion, julienned
1 tablespoon olive oil
2 cloves garlic, minced
1 teaspoon crushed
    fresh black peppercorns
2 teaspoons Italian seasoning
4 medium potatoes, microwaved
    3 to 4 minutes and cut into
    small cubes
3 tablespoons capote capers
2 eggs
1 tablespoon water
2 teaspoons olive oil
Provolone cheese

Sauté red pepper and onion in oil with garlic, black pepper, and Italian seasoning. Add potatoes and capers. Blend and heat thoroughly. Beat eggs and water together well. Heat oil in skillet. Pour egg mixture into pan. Let egg set up. Push egg in from sides of pan, tipping pan to let liquid part run under and cook. You may scrape liquid towards outside if needed. Fill with two, half-circle slices Provolone cheese and scoop of potato filling. Fold omelets onto round plates. Yields 6 to 8 omelets.

Blueberry Gems

Blueberry curd:
1 (16-ounce) package
    frozen blueberries
8 eggs
½ pound (2 sticks) butter
3½ cups sugar
1 teaspoon lemon juice

Gems:
Prepared frozen puff pastry sheets
1 quart fresh blueberries
½ cup sugar

For the curd, defrost blueberries. Purée in food processor. Drain in strainer, saving juice. When drained, you should have 10 fluid ounces liquid. If short, add similar juice like cranberry-raspberry to make up difference. Beat eggs together. Blend berry juice, butter, sugar, and lemon juice in double boiler. Heat slowly. Whisk eggs into curd mixture when butter is mostly melted. At this point, mixture should be warm, but not hot. If it is too hot, eggs will curdle. Stir constantly until thick enough to coat back of spoon. Remove from heat and chill overnight. Add puréed solids when curd is cool to preserve fresh blueberry flavor. Store in refrigerator until ready to prepare gems. This makes just under 2 quarts curd. You can use curd for gems, scones, breads, and other desserts. Blueberry curd freezes very well. Freeze any you don't use for other items.

Set frozen puff pastry sheet out to soften slightly. Grease 8 mini muffin pans. Preheat oven to 400°. To make gems, cut pastry sheet into 2-inch squares and press a square into each muffin pocket so points extend out handkerchief-style. Fill each cup about two-thirds full of blueberries. Sprinkle each cup with ½ teaspoon sugar. Bake 10 to 12 minutes or until puff pastry is golden. Remove from oven. Immediately spoon about 2 teaspoons blueberry curd into each cup so it melts over blueberries and fills puff. Top each cup with single blueberry to garnish. Serve immediately or reheat in warm oven to crisp puff pastry. Yields 4 servings (2 gems per serving).

Swedish Limpa Bread

⅓ cup water
1 tablespoon honey
⅔ cup orange juice
⅔ cup beer (with body)
1½ tablespoons butter
1½ tablespoons sugar
1 teaspoon salt
1 teaspoon fennel seed
2 teaspoons orange zest
⅓ cup rye flour
⅔ cup bread flour
3 cups all-purpose flour
2 tablespoons active dry yeast

Blend water, honey, juice, beer, and butter in microwave-safe container. Heat just until butter is melted. Measure sugar, salt, fennel, zest, flours, and yeast into mixing bowl. Using bread-kneading attachment, blend dry ingredients. Add warm liquid ingredients all at once. Let knead 5 to 10 minutes. Dough will form smooth ball. Set bowl covered in warm place to rise until double in size. Punch down. Split dough in two. Form into rounds and let rest on counter for 10 minutes. Form into loaves and press into greased loaf pans. Let rise just until mounding over top of pans. When risen, preheat oven to 350° and bake 18 to 20 minutes, or until loaf sounds hollow if thumped from bottom. Yields 1 loaf.

Vegetable Mélange Stuffed Mushrooms

6 leaves bok choy
½ red pepper
½ Spanish onion
1 teaspoon fresh rosemary
¼ teaspoon ground rosemary
3 tablespoons white balsamic vinegar
6 to 8 large mushroom caps, cleaned

Preheat oven to 375°. Blend all ingredients except mushrooms in food processor until chopped enough to fit in mushroom caps but not puréed. Cook over low heat in skillet to meld flavors and cook onion. Fill mushroom caps slightly mounded. Bake 6 to 8 minutes. You can speed up process by microwaving caps before filling and then broiling them for 1 minute to brown. The filling holds well refrigerated. Yields 6 to 8 servings.

WILLIAM MILLER HOUSE

1129 Floyd Ave.
Richmond, VA 23220
(804) 254-2928 (phone/fax)
innkeeper@ourfanhomes.com
www.ourfanhomes.com

This Greek-Revival-style home was built by William Miller, proprietor of the Rogers and Miller Marbleworks, in 1869. The house remained in the Miller family until the thirties. Keeping the charm of the original marble mantles, period window glass, and other architectural details, the owners have added the "necessities" of today, including central air conditioning and newly tiled baths. A full gourmet breakfast is served each morning on a collection of platters from travels in Europe.

Poached Eggs on Asparagus

1 pound (about 20) asparagus spears, trimmed
½ stick plus 1 tablespoon butter
¼ cup all-purpose flour
1 cup half-and-half
3 ounces Boursin cheese
8 eggs
½ teaspoon salt
1 teaspoon vinegar
Pepper
Ground paprika for garnish

Cook asparagus in medium skillet in boiling water just until tender, about 3 minutes. Drain and return asparagus to skillet. In medium saucepan melt ¼ cup butter over medium heat. Blend in flour and mix until smooth. Gradually blend in half-and-half, mixing until smooth. Crumble cheese and mix into sauce and keep warm until service. To poach eggs, bring pot of salted water and vinegar to a boil. Slide whole eggs into water one at a time. When water returns to a boil, reduce heat to low and simmer until eggs are set. Watch carefully and remove eggs when yolks are still soft, about 2 to 2½ minutes. Remove eggs from water and drain on paper-lined plate. Season with salt and pepper to taste. Add remaining 1 tablespoon butter to asparagus in skillet and stir over medium heat. Divide asparagus among four plates. Spoon 2 eggs over asparagus on each plate and spoon cheese sauce over each plate. Garnish with sprinkle of paprika and serve. Yields 4 servings.

MIDDLE GROVE INN BED & BREAKFAST

37175 Jeb Stuart Road
Purcellville, VA 20132
(540) 338-0918 (phone)
(540) 338-3947 (fax)
stay@middlegroveinn.com
www.middlegroveinn.com

Middle Grove Inn sits on three-plus acres of gently rolling open meadow. You can enjoy walking around the property or sitting in the Rose Tea Garden watching the hummingbirds, butterflies, and birds that inhabit the area. The inn is located on a dirt and gravel road one mile from the one-hundred-year-old General Store, where you can get a tube of toothpaste, enjoy a cup of coffee, and read the morning newspaper, or mail a letter in the post office. The inn has four guest rooms and various common rooms, a swimming pool, Jacuzzi, billiard table, exercise room, and various porches and gazebos.

Cornmeal Scrapple

2 cups ground pork or 1½ cups ground chicken and ½ cup cut up lean pork
2 cups lean ground beef
3 cups beef broth
1½ teaspoons salt
Dash of cayenne
1 cup cornmeal

Combine pork, beef, and broth in medium or large saucepan. Bring to a boil, stirring to crumble. Add salt and cayenne. Gradually sprinkle in cornmeal, stirring constantly. Cook 30 minutes over low heat, stirring frequently. Coat a 10-inch tube pan with nonstick spray and spoon in meat mixture. Chill until firm. Cut into ½-inch slices and fry in hot oil until brown, turning once. Serve with mashed potatoes, cooked sauerkraut, and warm rice pudding. Yields 10 to 12 servings.

Banana Bread

⅓ cup applesauce
¼ cup honey
2 tablespoons molasses
1 egg, well beaten or ¼ cup egg substitute
2 cups bran flakes or raisin bran cereal
1 cup all-purpose flour
½ cup whole wheat flour
2 teaspoons baking powder
½ teaspoon salt
½ teaspoon baking soda
½ cup chopped nuts (walnuts or pecans)
1½ cups mashed banana
1 tablespoon water
1 teaspoon vanilla extract

Preheat oven to 350°. Cream applesauce, honey, and molasses together. Add egg and bran flakes. Sift together flours, baking powder, salt, and baking soda. Add nuts. Combine bananas and water. Add to creamed mixture alternately with dry ingredients. Stir in vanilla. Pour in 9 x 5 x 3-inch pan coated with vegetable spray. Bake 1 hour and 5 minutes or until toothpick comes out clean in center. Yields 1-pound loaf.

Cheese and Green Chile Pie

8 ounces sharp Cheddar cheese, shredded
8 ounces part skim Mozzarella cheese, shredded
3 eggs, slightly beaten
    or ¾ cup egg substitute
1 (5-ounce) can fat-free evaporated milk
1 (4-ounce) can chopped green chiles

Preheat oven to 350°. Combine cheeses, eggs, and milk. Line 9 x 13-inch glass dish with chiles and cover with egg mixture. Bake about 40 minutes or until lightly brown and firm. Cool slightly and cut into bite-size pieces. May be frozen and reheated. Yields 12 to 15 servings.

THE HIDDEN BED & BREAKFAST

7632 Michelle Court
Manassas, VA 20109-2959
(703) 330-0951 (phone)
(703) 257-7104 (fax)
(800) 830-5685 (toll free)
davealdrich@designstravel.com
www.designstravel.com

The Hidden Bed & Breakfast is a one-thousand-square-foot apartment bed and breakfast with full kitchen, living room with working fireplace, bedroom and private bath, and a screened-in porch and private entrance. Located in the town of the first and third battles of the Civil War, the Hidden Bed & Breakfast is close to many historical locations. The bed and breakfast is eleven miles from the metro (subway) into Washington, D. C., and seventy-two miles from the entrance to the Shenandoah National Park. Activities in the immediate area include a small ski area in the winter, a water park (SplashDown) in the summer, Civil War reenactments, and horseback riding.

Fettuccine with Fresh Peas and Ham

2 tablespoons butter or margarine
1 small onion (or scallion), finely chopped
12 ounces ham
1 cup heavy cream
Freshly ground salt and pepper
2½ cups shelled green peas
    or 2½ cups frozen peas
1 pound fettuccine

In frying pan melt butter over low heat. Add onion and sauté, stirring frequently, until translucent, about 3 minutes. Add ham and cream. Simmer, stirring frequently, for another 5 minutes. Season to taste with salt and pepper and keep warm. In large pot boil water with salt. Add peas and pasta and cook until pasta is al dente. Drain peas and pasta and arrange on warm platter. Pour cream mixture over top and toss well. Serve at once. Yields 6 servings.

Lemon or Lime Sorbet

You need an ice cream machine to make this recipe.

1 ripe cantaloupe or honeydew melon
Grand Marnier or Crème de Menthe
2 cups sugar
2 cups water
1½ cups fresh lemon or lime juice
    (about 6 to 8 whole fruits)
1 tablespoon grated lemon or lime zest

Before making sorbet, use small melon baller to scoop out honeydew or cantaloupe (or mix) and marinate balls in liqueur 2 to 3 hours. Combine sugar and water in medium saucepan and bring to boil over medium-high heat. Reduce heat to low and simmer until sugar dissolves, 3 to 4 minutes. Cool completely—stick pan in freezer 15 to 20 minutes. When totally cooled, add lemon or lime juice and zest. Pour mixture and melon balls into freezer bowl machine and turn on for 30 minutes. You have to be careful how many melon balls you put in because inside of freezer drum is only so large, so you may want to do freezing in two parts, breaking up liquid mixture and melon balls into equal parts. Then transfer mixture into freezer container and allow to sit about 2 hours or overnight. Yields 6 to 8 servings.

Caesar Salad

1 large or 2 medium heads
    romaine lettuce
2 large cloves garlic
¾ teaspoon freshly ground Kosher salt
1¼ teaspoons freshly ground
    black pepper
10 fat anchovies, drained, patted dry
    (if they have pimiento rolled
    in them, even better)
2 large egg yolks
3 tablespoons fresh lemon juice
2 tablespoons balsamic vinegar
1 tablespoon Dijon mustard
1 teaspoon Worcestershire sauce
½ cup olive oil
Parmesan cheese
Fried Parsley Croutons (see next recipe)

To crisp lettuce, separate leaves, rinse under cold water, and pat dry. Break into 2-inch pieces. Roll in clean paper towels, place in plastic bag, and seal. Refrigerate until cold and crisp, at least 1 hour. (Do not skip this step. It makes all the difference to have the romaine leaves snap with coldness.) In container of electric blender, combine garlic, salt, pepper, and anchovies. At high speed, blend until garlic and anchovies are finely chopped. Add egg yolks, lemon juice, vinegar, mustard, and Worcestershire sauce. Blend until mixture is smooth. Turn blender on high and with machine running, remove center of lid and slowly pour in olive oil in thin, steady stream. Blend until all oil is added and dressing is smooth and creamy. Set aside or refrigerate until ready to add to salad, up to 4 hours. Place crisped lettuce pieces in very large salad bowl. Pour dressing over salad and sprinkle with grated cheese and croutons. Toss until lettuce and Fried Parsley Croutons (see next recipe) are coated with dressing and cheese. Serve immediately. Yields 6 first-course servings.

Fried Parsley Croutons

¼ to ½ cup olive oil plus that again
2 plus 2 large cloves garlic, chopped in
    fairly large pieces
6 cups (¾-inch cubes) *fresh* Italian bread
    (do not remove crust)
2 tablespoons finely chopped
    flat parsley

To flavor olive oil, heat oil and garlic in large skillet until oil is hot and garlic is fragrant. I prefer to leave all garlic in oil and start with half of cubed bread. By turning continually, croutons have an even brown color. I like to have several cubes with "slightly darker burn spots" on them giving a very deep garlic flavor to salad. Remove first half of croutons and add ¼ to ½ cup olive oil again to frying pan with remaining 2 cloves garlic. Add remaining half of bread cubes to oil in skillet. Toss to coat and sauté until golden brown over medium-high heat. Sprinkle parsley over croutons and toss gently to coat. Cool croutons completely. Use immediately or store in airtight container up to one day ahead of serving. Yields 6 cups.

HARMONY HILL BED & BREAKFAST

929 Wilson Hill Road
Arrington, VA 22922
(434) 263-7750 (phone)
(877) 263-7750 (toll free)
innkeeper@harmony-hill.com
www.harmony-hill.com

Harmony Hill offers a unique setting—rustic, romantic, and relaxed. This log home in the foothills of the Blue Ridge has five spacious, air-conditioned rooms, private baths, and king-size or queen-size beds featuring handmade quilts. Some rooms have fireplaces, whirlpool tubs, and window seats. A hearty, country breakfast is served. While here, guests enjoy visiting any of numerous antique shops and wineries. You can hike to the top of Crabtree Falls, ride the Blue Ridge Parkway, golf or ski at Wintergreen. Other sites nearby are Natural Bride, Monticello, Ash Lawn, University of Virginia, and Appomattox.

Tea Room Scones

2 cups unbleached all-purpose flour
2 teaspoons baking powder
½ teaspoon salt
¼ teaspoon baking soda
1 teaspoon dried lemon peel
6 tablespoons cold butter
½ cup currants
½ cup buttermilk
1 large egg
1 tablespoon milk
1 tablespoon sugar

Preheat oven to 425°. Lightly grease large baking sheet. In large bowl combine flour, baking powder, salt, baking soda, and lemon peel. With pastry blender or two knives, cut in butter until mixture resembles coarse crumbs. Mix in currants with fork. In a cup beat together buttermilk and egg and add to flour mixture. Mix lightly with fork until mixture clings together and forms ball of soft dough. Turn dough onto lightly floured surface and knead gently, turning 5 to 6 times. With floured rolling pin, roll dough to ½-inch thickness. With floured 2-inch biscuit cutter, cut dough into rounds. Place scones one inch apart on baking sheet. Pat dough scraps together, roll out again, and cut out more scones. Lightly brush tops of scones with milk and sprinkle with sugar. Bake scones for 10 to 12 minutes or until golden brown. Yields 10 to 12 scones.

Biscotti Regina (Italian Sesame Cookies)

1 stick unsalted butter, softened
1 cup sugar
2 teaspoons vanilla extract
4 plus 2 eggs
3½ cups unbleached white flour
6 teaspoons baking powder
½ teaspoon salt
4 tablespoons wheat germ
4 tablespoons stone-ground
    yellow cornmeal
2½ cups unhulled sesame seeds

Preheat oven to 425°. Cream butter, sugar, and vanilla until very light and fluffy. Beat in 4 eggs very well. Mix flour, baking powder, salt, wheat germ, and cornmeal and stir into butter mixture gradually. With hands, shape mixture into rolls about 2 inches long and ¾ inch in diameter. Beat remaining 2 eggs, dip cookies in egg, and roll in sesame seeds. Place on ungreased baking sheet and bake 12 minutes or until brown. Cool on rack. Yields 5 dozen cookies.

Rob's Hash Brown Potatoes

6 large potatoes, peeled and diced
¼ plus ¼ teaspoon salt, divided
1 tablespoon shortening
½ small onion, diced
2 tablespoons diced sweet pepper,
    green, red, or yellow
¼ teaspoon black pepper
½ teaspoon hot pepper sauce
    (or 1 chopped fresh jalapeño
    pepper with seeds)
¾ teaspoon Italian seasoning
1 teaspoon grated Parmesan cheese

Cook potatoes in boiling water with ¼ teaspoon salt until just tender. Drain. Heat 12-inch iron skillet and when hot, add shortening and onion. When onion starts to become tender, add sweet pepper. When onion is transparent, add potatoes and cover. Cook, stirring occasionally. When potatoes start to brown, add remaining ¼ teaspoon salt, black pepper, and hot pepper sauce and stir. Continue cooking until potatoes get crusty. Add Italian seasoning. Place in serving dish and sprinkle with Parmesan cheese. Yields 6 to 8 servings.

Cantaloupe Bread

1 cup sugar
½ large cantaloupe, puréed and drained
    to make 1 cup cantaloupe
⅓ cup vegetable oil
1 teaspoon vanilla extract
2 eggs
1½ cups all-purpose flour
2 teaspoons baking powder
½ teaspoon ground cinnamon
½ teaspoon salt
¼ teaspoon ground cloves
½ cup coarsely chopped walnuts
    or pecans

Preheat oven to 350°. Grease bottom only of loaf pan. Mix sugar, 1 cup cantaloupe purée, oil, vanilla, and eggs in large bowl. Blend flour, baking powder, cinnamon, salt, and cloves with whisk. Add to sugar mixture. Stir in nuts. Pour batter in loaf pan and bake 45 to 55 minutes or until toothpick inserted in center comes out clean. Cool 10 minutes. Loosen sides of loaf from pan and remove loaf. Cool completely on wire rack before slicing. Store tightly wrapped in refrigerator up to one week or can be frozen up to three months. Yields 1 loaf.

THE INN AT FAIRFIELD FARM

5305 Marriott Lane
Hume, VA 2263
(540) 364-2627 (phone)
(540) 364-3564 (fax)
(877) 324-7344 (toll free)
stay@MarriottRanch.com
www.MarriottRanch.com

The Inn at Fairfield Farm, located near the center of the Marriott Ranch's forty-two hundred acres, is a historic bed and breakfast with ten guest rooms offering private baths, fireplaces, afternoon teas, and three-course breakfasts. Once J. Willard Marriott's personal retreat, now Marriott Ranch is open to the public. Come and enjoy our "West" atmosphere back east. The ranch also offers horseback riding and catering.

Cranberry Date Scones

3 cups all-purpose flour
½ cup plus 2 teaspoons sugar
½ teaspoon salt
½ teaspoon baking soda
Zest of 1 orange
1½ sticks butter, softened
½ cup dried cranberries
1 cup chopped walnuts
½ cup chopped dates
1 cup buttermilk
Milk or cream for brushing
2 teaspoons allspice
2 teaspoons ground cinnamon
2 teaspoons mace

Preheat oven to 375°. Sift together flour, ½ cup sugar, salt, and baking soda. Add orange zest. Cream butter and fold dry ingredients into butter. Gently stir in cranberries, walnuts, and dates. Stir in buttermilk. Roll dough onto floured board, knead slightly, and roll out to 1½ inches thick. Cut into triangles. Brush with milk or cream. Sprinkle with remaining 2 teaspoons sugar, allspice, cinnamon, and mace. Bake 20 minutes on buttered and floured or parchment-covered baking sheets. Yields 4 to 6 servings.

L'AUBERGE PROVENÇALE

P.O. Box 190
White Post, VA 22663
(540) 837-1375 (phone)
(540) 837-2004 (fax)
(800) 638-1702 (toll free)
cborel@shentel.net
www.laubergeprovençale.com

Transport yourself to sunny Provence at L'Auberge Provençale in the heart of Virginia Hunt Country. The inn is nationally acclaimed for its French cuisine and romantic accommodations, Provençale fabrics, antiques, fireplaces, flower and herb gardens. Area activities include hiking, biking, golf, antiquing, horseback riding, canoeing, and kayaking. It is a short drive to the Shenandoah National Park and Skyline Drive.

Hubbard Squash Soup

1 leek, chopped, white part only
1 medium onion, diced
2 cloves garlic
½ stick butter
2 pounds Hubbard squash
1 large potato, peeled and chopped
⅛ teaspoon fresh nutmeg
4 cups (1 quart) chicken stock
1 cup heavy cream
Salt and pepper

In 6-quart saucepan sauté leeks, onion, and garlic in butter over medium heat 5 min-

utes. Add squash, potato, nutmeg, and chicken stock and simmer 20 to 30 minutes until vegetables are tender. In blender, purée soup. Strain and return to pot. Reheat with cream and salt and pepper to taste. Yields 6 servings.

Sweetbreads with Port Wine and Capers

2 pounds sweetbreads
2 quarts water
1 teaspoon salt plus some for seasoning
½ teaspoon pepper plus some for seasoning
6 bay leaves
⅓ cup red wine vinegar
1 stick plus 2 plus 2 tablespoons
    unsalted sweet butter
Juice of ½ lemon
2 medium shallots, chopped
1 cup port
1 cup concentrated veal stock
2 teaspoons baby capers

Rinse sweetbreads in bowl with slow running water for 4 hours. Clean and devein. In large saucepan, boil water with salt and pepper, bay leaves, and vinegar. Purge sweetbreads into water, reduce heat, and simmer 20 minutes. Drain and let sweetbreads cool. Using heavy skillet as weight, place skillet on top of sweetbreads for ½ hour until they are slightly flattened. Dust sweetbreads with flour and salt and pepper. Sauté sweetbreads in skillet in 1 stick butter until slightly golden. Squeeze lemon juice over them. Remove from heat. Remove sweetbreads from pan and place on warm plate. With clean towel, wipe residue from skillet and add 2 tablespoons butter and cook shallots until soft. Add port and veal stock and reduce by half over medium heat. Add capers and season with salt and pepper. Remove pan from heat and add remaining 2 tablespoons butter. Arrange sweetbreads on plate. Pour sauce with capers around sweetbreads. Serve. This dish may be prepared in advance up to time of sautéing sweetbreads. Yields 4 servings.

Orange Blossom Waffles with Mangos and Nutmeg Cream

Mangos:
1 cup sugar
¾ cup water
2 tablespoons Peach Schnapps liqueur
1 tablespoon chopped mint or basil
2 mangos, peeled and sliced

Nutmeg cream:
2 cups heavy whipping cream
2 tablespoons sugar
1 tablespoon grated nutmeg

Waffles:
1 cup all-purpose flour
1 teaspoon baking powder
2 tablespoons sugar
1 pinch salt
1 cup milk
1 egg
2 tablespoons peanut oil
1 tablespoon orange blossom water

For mangos, bring sugar, water, Peach Schnapps, and herbs to boil. Remove from heat and let cool to room temperature. Pour over sliced mangos and refrigerate.

For nutmeg cream, whip heavy cream, sugar, and grated nutmeg until soft peaks form. Refrigerate until ready to use.

For waffles, preheat waffle iron and mix flour, baking powder, sugar, and salt together. In separate bowl, mix milk, egg, oil, and orange blossom water. Whisk wet ingredients into dry ingredients until well blended. Pour enough batter to cover waffle iron bottom and cook until golden brown. Cut waffle into three wedges and fan out on half of plate. Fan out 5 to 6 mango slices on other half of plate. Pour a little maple syrup on waffles and dollop a little nutmeg cream in center of plate. Garnish with sprig of mint or basil. Yields 3 large waffles.

Smoked Rabbit with Chanterelle Mushrooms

1½ cups olive oil
½ cup white wine vinegar
2 sprigs fresh tarragon, chopped
2 sprigs fresh thyme, chopped
6 cloves garlic, chopped
1 large onion, chopped
1 teaspoon salt
1 teaspoon pepper
2 (2½-pound) rabbits
3 tablespoons butter
1½ cups chanterelle
    or morel mushrooms
1½ cups heavy cream
Salt and pepper
2 pounds fresh pasta,
    cooked and drained

In large baking dish, combine oil, vinegar, tarragon, thyme, garlic, onion, salt, and pepper. Add rabbits, cover and marinate overnight in refrigerator, turning two times. Remove rabbits from marinade and place in hot smoker. Smoke 45 minutes, turning every 15 minutes. Allow rabbits to cool after smoking. Bone rabbits and cut meat into bite-size pieces. In large frying pan, melt butter and sauté mushrooms 8 to 10 minutes. Add cream and reserved rabbit and bring to a boil. Reduce heat and cook, stirring constantly, until cream thickens and coats spoon. Sprinkle with salt and pepper. Add reserved pasta and heat through. Place some rabbit pieces in center of each serving plate and surround with pasta. Pour remaining mushroom sauce over top and serve immediately. Yields 8 servings.

❧ ❧ ❧

HERITAGE HOUSE BED & BREAKFAST

P.O. Box 427
291 Main Street
Washington, VA 22747
(540) 675-3207 (phone)
(540) 675-1340 (fax)
(888) 819-8280 (toll free)
hhbb@shentel.net
www.heritagehousebb.com

Heritage House, a historic 1837 manor house, is superbly located in the heart of Washington, Virginia, and just one short block from the world-renowned Inn at Little Washington. In its fabled past, the house served as Confederate headquarters to Civil War Gen. Jubal Early and remained a private residence until 1985, when it opened its doors as a bed and breakfast.

Situated at the foothills of the beautiful Blue Ridge Mountains, the village of Washington is just a short drive to Shenandoah National Park and Skyline Drive. Visit nearby award-winning wineries, hike, horseback ride, or canoe the Shenandoah. Whatever the season you will marvel at the beautiful and unspoiled vistas in Rappahannock County.

Cranberry Lace Cookies

⅔ cup all-purpose flour
½ teaspoon salt
½ teaspoon baking soda
½ cup old-fashioned rolled oats
1½ sticks unsalted butter, softened
⅔ cup granulated sugar
⅔ cup light brown sugar
1 large egg, lightly beaten
1 teaspoon vanilla extract
2 cups pecan pieces
⅔ cup dehydrated cranberries

Preheat oven to 350°. In small bowl whisk together flour, salt, and baking soda. Stir in rolled oats. In medium bowl cream butter and sugars. Add egg and beat. Beat in vanilla. Fold in flour mixture. Mix in

Heritage House Bed & Breakfast

pecans and cranberries. Form mixture into 1-inch balls and place on parchment paper on cookie sheet about 2½ inches apart. Bake 10 to 12 minutes until golden brown and lacy. Yields 50 to 75 cookies.

Grandma Roth's Strawberry Shortbread

2 cups all-purpose flour
1 cup self-rising flour
1 cup vegetable shortening
¾ teaspoon salt
1 cup sugar
⅔ cup cold water (chill with ice)
1½ pounds strawberries, chopped,
    and sweetened to taste if desired
1 pint whipping cream

Preheat oven to 350°. Mix flours, shortening, salt, sugar, and water. Mix together to make dough. Roll out to ¼-inch thickness and cut into 1 x 4-inch strips. Bake on ungreased pan 5 minutes or until golden brown. Layer shortbread with strawberries and top with hand-whipped cream. Yields 8 servings.

Spiced Apple-Pear Sauce (Waffle topping)

1 cup apple cider
¼ cup lemon juice
½ cup granulated sugar
⅓ cup light brown sugar
1 teaspoon ground cinnamon
¼ teaspoon nutmeg
2½ pounds apples, peeled, cored,
    and coarsely chopped
2 pounds under-ripe pears, peeled,
    cored, and coarsely chopped

Mix cider, lemon juice, sugars, cinnamon, and nutmeg. Add apples and pears to mix-

ture. Bring to a boil in nonreactive saucepan. Reduce heat and simmer 15 minutes or until tender. Cool and refrigerate until use. To serve, warm allotted portion in microwave oven and spoon over waffles. Yields 10 to 12 servings.

Eggs Florentine

1 (4-ounce can) mushroom pieces,
    drained and finely chopped
½ cup finely chopped onion
¼ cup finely chopped green onions
1 (26-ounce) can condensed cream of
    mushroom soup
2 cups sour cream
2 tablespoons Dijon mustard
½ teaspoon Tabasco
1 teaspoon dried basil
1 teaspoon dried oregano
2 cups mozzarella cheese
2 pounds chopped spinach, drained well
12 eggs
Parmesan cheese
Paprika
6 English muffins, halved

Preheat oven to 365°. Mix together mushroom pieces, onion, green onions, soup, sour cream, Dijon mustard, Tabasco, basil, and oregano. Add mozzarella cheese and spinach. Fill 12 ramekins three-quarters full of mixture. Break 1 egg over each ramekin and heavily sprinkle with Parmesan cheese and paprika. Bake 25 to 30 minutes. Remove from ramekins (eggs facing up). Serve over warmed English muffin halves. Yields 12 servings.

THE MARTHA WASHINGTON INN

150 West Main Street
Abingdon, VA 24210
(276) 628-3161 (phone)
(276) 628-8885 (fax)
(888) 888-5252 (toll free)
info@themartha.com
www.marthawashingtoninn.com

The Martha Washington Inn is located in Abingdon's historic district, across the street from the Barter Theatre. True Southern hospitality and a loving preservation of the original architecture set the stage for discriminating travelers seeking a relaxing stay in the southwestern highlands of Virginia. Fine and casual dining and distinctive shops provide guests with a most memorable stay. Enjoy the warm Southern nights in a rocking chair on our oversized front porch or experience the charm and historic character of the State Theatre of Virginia by catching a performance at the Barter Theatre. With all of the restored historic homes and buildings, it is clear why the area is referred to as "little Williamsburg."

Bourbon-Glazed Ham

1 large ham
1 cup chopped carrots
1 cup chopped onion
1 cup chopped celery
4 cups water
1 cup bourbon
1 cup honey
1 teaspoon cloves

Preheat oven to 375°. Place ham, vegetables, and water in roasting pan and cook until ham reaches internal temperature of 165°. Mix together bourbon, honey, and cloves for glaze. Remove ham from pan. Score with knife in criss-cross pattern. Brush with glaze. Return ham to 300° oven 20 to 30 minutes. Yields 8 to 10 servings.

Hominy Soufflé

½ cup diced country ham
4 cups white hominy
½ cup diced red pepper
Salt and pepper
2 cups heavy cream
2 whole eggs
½ teaspoon ground nutmeg

Preheat oven to 350°. Cook country ham in frying pan until crisp. Put in mixing bowl with hominy and red pepper and salt and pepper to taste. Whisk together heavy cream, eggs, and nutmeg. Fold hominy mixture into cream. Coat 9-inch casserole dish and add mixture. Place casserole dish in water bath and bake 45 minutes or until soufflé mixture is firm. Yields 6 to 8 servings.

Chocolate Cranberry Nougat Bars

1 pound almonds
4 egg whites
1¼ cups sugar
1 cup corn syrup
2½ cups honey
¼ cup water
1 cup dried cranberries
10 ounces chocolate

Blend almonds in food processor until small but not powdery. Whip egg whites to stiff peaks. Combine sugar, corn syrup, honey, and water in heavy-bottom saucepan. Stir to dissolve sugar and bring to a boil over medium-high heat. Drizzle syrup into egg whites, stirring constantly. Fold in almonds and cranberries and stir until ball

forms. Spread mixture out onto pan lined with parchment paper. Nougat should be about ½ inch thick. Melt chocolate in double boiler. Slice cooled nougat into bars and dip into chocolate. Yields 3 to 4 dozen servings.

She Crab Bisque

5 tablespoons butter
½ cup diced onion
½ cup diced red pepper
⅓ cup all-purpose flour
½ gallon shrimp stock
10 ounces fresh crabmeat
4 cups (2 pints) heavy cream
½ cup sherry
Salt and pepper

Melt butter in soup pot. Sauté onions and peppers until tender. Stir in flour to make a roux. Cook roux 5 minutes on medium heat, stirring constantly. Whisk shrimp stock into roux a little at a time to avoid lumps. Add crabmeat and simmer 20 minutes. Add heavy cream, sherry, salt, and pepper. Yields about 3 quarts, 8 to 10 servings.

THE MOUNTAIN ROSE INN

1787 Charity Hwy.
Woolwine, VA 24185
(276) 930-1057 (phone)
(276) 930-2165 (fax)
info@mountainrose-inn.com
www.mountainrose-inn.com

Historical country elegance in the beautiful Blue Ridge Mountains, the Mountain Rose Inn is a 190-year-old farmhouse with five rooms, all with private baths, working

fireplaces, satellite TV, air conditioning, and porches. It is near Blue Ridge Parkway and Chateau Morrisette winery. The inn offers elegant three-course breakfasts, 100 private acres, swimming pool, hiking, and trout stream. Voted "Best Bed & Breakfast" in 2001 and 2002 by City Magazine.

Peach Smoothies

4 medium peaches
2 bananas
1 teaspoon almond extract
½ cup plain yogurt
2 tablespoons honey
6 ice cubes

Place all ingredients in blender and purée until smooth. Pour into fancy stem glasses and garnish with slice of peach and fresh mint. Yields 6 servings.

Banana Buttermilk Pecan Pancakes

3 cups all-purpose flour
1½ teaspoons baking soda
1½ teaspoons salt
3 tablespoons sugar
1 teaspoon allspice
1 teaspoon ground nutmeg
¾ cup coarsely chopped pecans
3 eggs
3 cups buttermilk
3 tablespoons vegetable oil
2 bananas

Sift flour, baking soda, salt, sugar, allspice, and nutmeg together into large bowl. Stir in pecans. Mix eggs, buttermilk, and oil together. Mash bananas and add to buttermilk mixture. Combine dry ingredients with buttermilk mixture. Pour ¼ cup batter for each pancake onto hot greased griddle. Cook until bubbles form and then turn and finish cooking. Serve with Hot

Whiskeyed Maple Syrup (see next recipe).
Yields 10 servings.

Hot Whiskeyed Maple Syrup

2 cups maple syrup
2 sticks butter
1 teaspoon ground cinnamon
½ teaspoon allspice
½ teaspoon mace
2 tablespoons whiskey

In saucepan, bring all ingredients except whiskey to a boil, whisking often. Reduce heat and bring down to simmer. Once simmering, add whiskey and then serve. Yields 3 cups.

Mushroom Oven Omelet

1 cup Mexican salsa
1 cup canned, sliced mushrooms
¼ cup Parmesan cheese
2 cups shredded Mexican-blend cheese
6 eggs
1 cup sour cream

Preheat oven to 350°. Coat 9-inch pie dish with nonstick spray. Spread salsa on bottom of dish. Sprinkle mushrooms over salsa, then cheeses over mushrooms. Blend eggs and sour cream in blender until smooth. Pour egg mixture over cheeses. Bake uncovered for 30 to 40 minutes until set. Serve garnished with additional sour cream. Yields 6 to 8 servings.

The Highland Inn of San Juan Island

P.O. Box 135
Friday Harbor, WA 98250
(888) 400-9850 (toll free)
helen@highlandinn.com
www.highlandinn.com

The Highland Inn Bed and Breakfast is located on the desirable, exclusive west side of San Juan Island, where three resident pods of Orca whales feed and play from May through October. Be lulled to sleep with the sounds of the whales blowing and splashing. There are historic sites, hiking trails, a lavender farm, an alpaca farm, our own vineyard, art galleries, and many fine restaurants.

Chèvre Squash Gratin Casserole

3 tablespoons unsalted butter
1 large onion, halved and thinly sliced
2 pounds yellow crookneck and zucchini
    squash, sliced ¼ inch thick
Salt
Freshly ground pepper
8 ounces chèvre at room temperature
½ cup heavy whipping cream
½ cup freshly grated Parmesan cheese
½ cup dry breadcrumbs

Preheat oven to 350°. Grease 9 x 13-inch baking dish. Melt butter in skillet, add onion, and sauté until translucent. Arrange half of squash slices in prepared dish. Season with salt and pepper to taste. Spread half of onion over squash slices. Repeat layers. Season with salt and pepper. Crumble chèvre into blender. Add cream. Pour over squash and onion layers. Combine Parmesan and breadcrumbs. Sprinkle over top. Bake 40 minutes. Yields 8 to 10 servings.

Artichoke Frittata

16 ounces frozen artichoke hearts
1 onion, chopped
Butter
1¼ cups half-and-half
6 eggs
1 tablespoon Worcestershire Sauce
2 teaspoons dry mustard
1 teaspoon seasoning salt
2 English muffins, broken up
½ pound grated Monterey Jack cheese
¼ cup Italian breadcrumbs
¼ cup Parmesan cheese

Defrost artichoke hearts and chop in blender. Butter 8- or 9-inch square pan. Preheat oven to 350°. Spread with artichokes. Sauté onion in a little butter and spread over artichokes. Blend half-and-half with eggs, Worcestershire, dry mustard, and seasoning salt. Pour half mix over artichokes and blend English muffins into other half of egg mixture until smooth. Pour muffin mix over artichokes and add Monterey Jack cheese. Sprinkle breadcrumbs and Parmesan cheese over that. You may also sprinkle with paprika and chopped parsley as desired. Bake 45 minutes to 1 hour or until center is set. Cool slightly and cut into squares. This may also be baked in individual ramekins. Yields 6 servings.

Mrs. King's Cookies

1 pound (4 sticks) butter
2 cups brown sugar
2 cups granulated sugar
4 eggs
2 teaspoons vanilla extract
Grated zest and juice of 1 orange
4 cups all-purpose flour
2 teaspoons baking powder
2 teaspoons salt
2 teaspoons baking soda
2 cups white chocolate chips
2 cups semisweet chocolate chips
3 cups raisins
3 cups chopped nuts
2 cups old-fashioned rolled oats
3 cups orange almond granola,
    or any good granola

Preheat oven to 350°. Blend butter and sugars until creamy. Add eggs, vanilla, grated zest, and orange juice and beat until well mixed. Mix flour, baking powder, salt, and baking soda and stir into egg mixture just until blended. Add chips, raisins, nuts, oats, and granola. When well mixed, shape into Ping-Pong or golf-ball size and bake on ungreased cookie sheet 8 to 10 minutes or just until cookies turn brown around edges. Best when warm from oven. Dough keeps refrigerated or frozen. Bake cookies fresh as needed. Yields 6 to 8 dozen cookies.

Cottage Cheese Delight

1 cup milk
1 cup all-purpose flour
1 pint low-fat cottage cheese
6 eggs
1 stick butter or margarine, melted
16 ounces Monterey Jack cheese, grated
Breadcrumbs or crushed leftover
    croissant crumbs
Sour cream or vanilla yogurt
Fresh berries or fruit conserve

Preheat oven to 350°. Blend milk, flour, cottage cheese, eggs, and butter. Grease 8 or 9-inch square pan. Sprinkle Monterey Jack cheese over pan. Pour egg mixture over cheese. Dust with breadcrumbs (they add a buttery, crunchy topping). Bake 45 minutes. Cut into squares and top with sour cream or vanilla yogurt, and fresh berries or fruit conserve. Recipe may be doubled for 24 guests. Use 9 x 13-inch pan and bake 1 hour and 15 minutes, or until set and cracks appear in center. The recipe may be baked a day ahead and reheated on serving plate in oven or microwave. Leftovers make great blintzes as filling for crêpes. Top with sour cream and fruit. Yields 12 servings.

TRUMPETER INN BED & BREAKFAST

318 Trumpeter Way
Friday Harbor, WA 98250
(360) 378-3884 (phone)
(800) 826-7926 (toll free)
swan@rockisland.com
www.trumpeterinn.com

The Trumpeter Inn is situated on five acres within the serene and bucolic rolling pastures of the San Juan Valley, located only one and a half miles from the picturesque town of Friday Harbor on San Juan Island. The inn features six beautifully appointed bedrooms, all with private baths, floor-length robes and slippers, spa amenities, and fireplaces, CD players, and private decks in the inn's two king suites. Gourmet sweets are served in the afternoon and delectable breakfasts greet guests each morning. Outdoor Jacuzzi tub, hammock, and lovely rose gardens are in the surroundings.

Magic Strawberry Pancake Basket

Strawberry cream filling:
3 pints strawberries, stems removed,
    and halved
½ cup confectioners' sugar
2 cups sour cream
¼ cup brown sugar

Pancake basket:
2 eggs
½ cup milk
¼ teaspoon salt
½ cup all-purpose flour
1 tablespoon butter or margarine

One to two hours before serving combine strawberries and confectioners' sugar. Mix sour cream and brown sugar. Refrigerate until ready to use.

To make pancake basket, place rack in center of oven and preheat oven to 450°. In a small bowl, mix eggs, milk, salt, and flour. Put butter in pie or quiche dish (or individual ramekins). Place in oven for 2 minutes or until butter melts. Swirl to coat bottom and immediately pour in egg batter. Bake 15 minutes, reduce oven temperature to 350°, and bake 8 to 10 minutes more, or until puffed and golden brown. Remove from oven, lift out basket, and place on serving plate. Spoon strawberries in center and top with sour cream mixture. If made in pie dish, cut in wedges to serve. Yields 6 servings.

Fresh Fruit-Walnut Torte

Crust:
1⅓ cups all-purpose flour
3 tablespoons sugar
1 stick chilled butter, cut into
    small pieces
1 cup ground walnuts
1 egg yolk
⅓ cup seedless raspberry jam

Filling:
1½ cups light brown sugar
1 large egg
1¼ cups coarsely chopped walnuts
½ cup shredded coconut
5 tablespoons all-purpose flour
½ teaspoon baking powder
Fresh fruit of choice
½ cup currant jelly

For crust, combine flour and sugar in food processor. Cut in butter until mix resembles coarse crumbs. Blend in walnuts. With processor running, add egg yolk and mix just until dough comes together. Remove dough from processor and press into bottom and 1 inch up sides of 9-inch springform pan. Spread flat surface of dough with jam.

For filling, beat brown sugar and egg in bowl with electric mixer until very thick, about 10 minutes. Preheat oven to 350°. Mix in walnuts, coconut, flour, and baking powder. Batter will be very thick. Spread batter evenly over jam in prepared crust and bake 30 minutes. Reduce oven temperature to 300° and continue baking until filling is set and top has browned, about 25 minutes longer. Arrange fresh fruit on top. Heat current jelly and pour over fruit to glaze. Yields 6 to 8 servings.

Smoked Salmon Quiche

2 (8-inch) baked pie shells,
    lightly browned
8 ounces smoked salmon
    (vacuum packed garlic-
    or pepper-flavored is great)
1 cup sautéed vegetables
    (e.g. zucchini, tomatoes, and onions)
4 eggs
8 ounces cream cheese
1 cup half-and-half
1 cup whole milk
½ teaspoon salt
¼ teaspoon ground black pepper
Sour cream
Caviar

Preheat oven to 375°. Top baked pie shells with crumbled salmon and then sautéed vegetables. Blend in blender or mixer remaining ingredients, through pepper, and pour into pie shells. Bake 35 minutes or until set and lightly browned on top. Cut each pie in quarters. Top with sour cream and caviar. Yields 8 servings.

The Guest House Bed & Breakfast

1121 S. W. 160th
Seattle, WA 98166
(206) 439-7576 (phone)
(866) 439-7576 (toll free)
info@guesthousebnb.com
www.guesthousebnb.com

The Guest House Bed & Breakfast, your Pacific Northwest getaway, is minutes from downtown Seattle, Seattle's Cruise Ship Terminal, Safeco Field, and Sea-Tac Airport. Wake to a superb hot breakfast while enjoying piles of pillows, down comforters, tailored robes, handmade soaps, and fresh-cut flowers. Take a dip in the hot tub or stroll the brick pathway to the vegetable and flower gardens. Activities available include the Pike Place Market, Pioneer Square, Seattle Art Museum, Paul Allen's Experience Music Project, Tillicum Village on Blake Island, Spirit of Washington Dinner Train, Washington State History Museum, Dale Chihuly's Museum of Glass, and Mount Rainier.

Moist Banana Bread

2 fresh eggs
2 very ripe bananas, mashed
½ cup canola oil
¼ cup plus 1 tablespoon buttermilk
1 teaspoon vanilla extract
1¾ cups all-purpose flour
1½ cups sugar
1 teaspoon baking soda
½ teaspoon salt
1 cup chopped pecans

Preheat oven to 350°. Place eggs, mashed bananas, canola oil, buttermilk, and vanilla

in medium mixing bowl and beat with electric mixer until creamy and well blended. Combine flour, sugar, soda, and salt and add to egg mixture. Beat at low speed just until all dry ingredients are incorporated. Stir in chopped pecans. Pour batter into lightly greased 8½ x 4¼-inch loaf pan or two 7 x 3½-inch loaf pans. Bake 45 minutes or until toothpick placed in center of loaf comes out clean. Remove from oven to cooling rack for 20 minutes. Run knife around edges of pan to loosen and remove from loaf pans to cool on rack. Yields 1 large loaf or 2 medium loaves.

Note: This banana loaf welcomes our guests each morning with freshly brewed coffee and hot tea. It also freezes well.

Orange French Toast

4 fresh eggs
⅓ cup orange juice
½ teaspoon cardamom
1 teaspoon orange zest
¼ cup (½ stick) butter or margarine
8 slices day-old French bread
Confectioners' sugar

Preheat oven to 450°. Place eggs in small casserole dish and beat well with wire whisk. Pour orange juice in glass bowl, add cardamom, and whisk well to incorporate. Pour orange juice mixture into eggs along with orange zest and whisk until well blended. Place 4 tablespoons butter in lightly greased, large cookie sheet with sides (jelly roll pan). Place pan in oven until butter is melted. Remove pan from oven and dip each side bread slices in egg mixture and place on baking sheet in single layer. Return to oven and bake 6 minutes. With spatula, turn bread slices once and return to oven for additional 6 minutes. Serve immediately dusted with confectioners' sugar and garnish with violas fresh from the garden. Yields 4 servings.

DeVoe Mansion Bed & Breakfast

208 133rd Street East
Tacoma, WA 98445
(253) 539-3991 (phone)
(888) 539-3991 (toll free)
innkeeper@devoemansion.com
www.devoemansion.com

DeVoe Mansion Bed & Breakfast

Nestled on one and a half acres of beautiful grounds, this National Historic Register inn is yours to call home while exploring the beautiful Pacific Northwest and the Tacoma-Seattle area. It is a perfect destination for business or pleasure. The inn offers four antique-filled guest rooms, private baths with soaking tubs, and all the amenities fine lodging affords. Early morning gourmet coffee and a leisurely multicourse breakfast featuring seasonal specialties make your stay remarkable. Activities in the area include museums, antiquing, fine dining, gardens, zoo and aquarium, NW Trek Wildlife Park, shopping, kayaking, concerts, and theater.

Italian Parmesan Egg

1 slice Canadian bacon
1 egg
1 tablespoon whipping cream
1 tablespoon Parmesan cheese
Basil

Preheat oven to 350°. Coat individual ramekin cup with nonstick spray. Place bacon in bottom of cup. Place egg on top of bacon followed by whipping cream and then Parmesan cheese. Garnish top with basil. Bake 12 to 15 minutes or until edges just start to turn light brown. Using rubber spatula, loosen all edges and remove from cup. Garnish with fresh basil leaves. Serve with grilled, garlic-roasted, new potatoes. Yields 1 serving.

Cranberry Pear Dumplings

3 cups sliced, peeled, and cored pears
2 tablespoons flour
1 (16-ounce) can whole-cranberry sauce
¼ cup sugar
1 teaspoon ground nutmeg
1 (6-count) package biscuits
1 tablespoon melted butter
Half-and-half or light cream (optional)
Fresh mint (optional)

Place pears in 1½-quart microwave-safe bowl and sprinkle with flour to lightly coat pears. Put cranberry sauce on top of pears. Combine sugar and nutmeg and sprinkle over pears and cranberries, reserving enough of mixture to sprinkle tops of dumplings. Cover and cook on high for 8 to 10 minutes, or until mixture is bubbly and pears are slightly tender, stirring once. Preheat oven to 400°. Snip edges of biscuits to within ½-inch of center to form flower petals. Place biscuits on top of warm pear mixture and brush with melted butter. Sprinkle with remaining sugar and nutmeg mixture. Bake uncovered 10 to 12 minutes or until dumplings are golden. Serve warm. Garnish with cream, fresh mint, and an edible flower. This makes an excellent fruit-and-bread starter for breakfast, or serves as a good dessert course. Yields 4 to 6 servings.

Note: You can roll out your biscuits and use any shape cookie cutter for different dumplings. Making your own biscuits or scones for this recipe is worth the effort.

Raspberry-Filled Orange Cookies

¾ cup sugar
¼ cup softened margarine
3 ounces softened cream cheese
1 teaspoon orange flavoring
2 teaspoons grated orange zest
1 egg
2¼ cups all-purpose flour
¾ teaspoon baking powder
½ cup seedless raspberry preserves
½ cup white vanilla chips
2 teaspoons oil

Preheat oven to 350°. In large bowl combine sugar, margarine, and cream cheese.

Mix well. Add orange flavoring, orange zest, and egg. Blend well. Add flour and baking powder and mix well. Shape dough into 1-inch balls. Place 2 inches apart on ungreased cookie sheet. With thumb or wooden spoon handle dipped in flour make indentation in center of each cookie. Spoon ¼ teaspoon preserves into hole. Bake cookies 11 to 13 minutes. Cool 2 minutes on rack and then remove to wire rack to cool completely. In glass bowl microwave vanilla chips and oil, stirring chips to make them smooth. (Don't overcook or they will burn.) Drizzle melted chips over cookies and allow to cool. Serve with your favorite cup of tea and a good book. Yields 3 dozen cookies.

SALISBURY HOUSE

750 16th Avenue East
Seattle, WA 98112
(206) 328-8682 (phone)
(206) 720-1019 (fax)
sleep@salisburyhouse.com
www.salisburyhouse.com

Salisbury House offers gracious in-city accommodations to the discerning vacationer or business traveler. It is situated on a tree-lined residential street just minutes from downtown and the convention center. Shops, restaurants, and the park are all within walking distance. Leave the car and take advantage of Seattle's excellent transit system. Built in 1904, Salisbury House has been a bed and breakfast since 1985. Guest rooms have comfy queen-size beds, crisp white sheets, down comforters, private baths, and high-speed wireless Internet service.

❧   ❧   ❧

Autumn Berry Bread

½ cup granulated sugar
1 cup brown sugar
1 stick butter at
    room temperature
2 eggs
1 cup buttermilk
3 cups all-purpose flour
1 teaspoon baking soda
1 teaspoon baking powder
1 teaspoon salt
1 cup cranberries, fresh or frozen
1 cup blueberries

Preheat oven to 375°. Grease two small loaf pans. Cream sugars and butter in large bowl. Beat in eggs and add buttermilk. In medium bowl mix flour, soda, baking powder, and salt. Add to sugar and butter mixture. Add cranberries and mix well. Add blueberries and mix in just enough to incorporate them. The idea is to have blueberries remain mostly whole but cranberries break apart slightly and give bread a pink hue. Spread in loaf pans and bake about 45 minutes or until knife comes out clean. This bread freezes nicely and is good served warm or at room temperature. Yields 2 loaves.

Mexican Quiche

6 eggs
¼ cup all-purpose flour
1 teaspoon baking powder
1½ cups grated Jack cheese
1½ cups cottage cheese
3 tablespoons melted butter
1 (8-ounce) can diced green chiles

Preheat oven to 350°. Beat eggs. Add flour and baking powder and mix with wire whip. Fold in Jack and cottage cheeses with rubber spatula. Add butter and chiles and mix well. Pour into greased, 9-inch quiche pan or glass pie plate. Bake about 30 minutes until set and browned slightly on top. Cool 5 to 10 minutes and serve with dollop of fresh salsa and sliced tropical fruit. Yields 6 servings.

Salisbury House

Winter Quiche with Leeks and Brie

Crust:
½ cup all-purpose flour
3 tablespoons cold unsalted butter
1 tablespoon cold vegetable shortening
¼ cup ice water

Filling:
2 cups thinly sliced leeks,
    only white and light green parts
2 tablespoons olive oil
1 small clove garlic, minced
3 eggs
½ cup milk or half-and-half
¼ teaspoon dried thyme
    (¾ teaspoon fresh)
¼ teaspoon dried sage
    (¾ teaspoon fresh)
Salt and pepper
½ cup Brie, cut into chunks

Preheat oven to 425°. For crust, mix flour with butter and shortening in medium bowl using pastry blender or fork. Slowly add water until mixture begins to bond. Form ball with hands, handling as little as possible and adding only enough water to keep mixture together. Roll out and place in 9-inch pie tin or quiche pan. Bake 5 to 10 minutes until crust browns slightly.

While crust is baking, make filling. Rinse leeks well in sieve, removing any mud. Shake dry and sauté in olive oil with minced garlic until soft and tender. Remove from heat. In small bowl mix eggs, milk, and herbs and season with salt and pepper to taste. Into partially cooked crust spread leeks and garlic and sprinkle evenly with chunks of Brie. Pour egg mixture over top and bake 15 minutes. Reduce heat to 350° and bake another 10 minutes until quiche is set and top is slightly brown. Let cool slightly before serving. Yields 4 servings.

PUGET VIEW GUESTHOUSE

7924 61st Avenue NE
Olympia, WA 98516
(360) 413-9474
pugetview@hotmail.com
www.bbonline.com/wa/pugetview

Puget View Guesthouse is a secluded cottage on the shore of Puget Sound. Since 1984, guests have come to appreciate its peaceful beauty and comfortable hospitality. Tall firs, Olympic Mountains, and island views complete a perfect setting for relaxation. The cottage interior is complete with queen-size bed, private bath, sitting room with sofa sleeper, dining area, refrigerator, and microwave. A "continental plus" breakfast is served at your door.

All-Season Quick Bread

2 sticks margarine
2 cups sugar
4 eggs
1 teaspoon vanilla extract
1½ teaspoons baking soda
1 teaspoon salt
1½ cups all-purpose flour
1 cup whole wheat flour
1½ cups applesauce
Cinnamon
Nutmeg
Chopped walnuts (optional)
Raisins (optional)
Confectioners' sugar

Preheat oven to 375°. Cream margarine and sugar. Add eggs and vanilla. Add baking soda, salt, and flours. Season applesauce with cinnamon and nutmeg to taste and add to flour mixture. Stir in walnuts and/or raisins, if desired. Grease and flour three 7 x 3-inch loaf pans. Bake about 30 minutes or until toothpick comes out clean. Dust with confectioners' sugar just before serving. Yields 3 loaves.

Poppy Seed Bread

3 cups all-purpose flour
1½ teaspoons salt
1½ teaspoons baking powder
2½ cups sugar
1½ cups milk
1⅛ cups (1 cup plus 2 tablespoons)
    vegetable oil
1½ tablespoons poppy seed
3 eggs
1½ teaspoons vanilla extract
1½ teaspoons almond extract

Preheat oven to 350°. Put all ingredients in mixer bowl and mix 2 minutes at medium speed of mixer. Pour into two greased and floured bread pans and bake about 1 hour. Let cool 10 to 15 minutes on wire rack and remove from pans. While bread is best served warm with butter, it also freezes well for future use. Yields 2 loaves.

KANGAROO HOUSE

1459 North Beach Road
P.O. Box 334
Eastsound, WA 98245-0334
(360) 376-2175 (phone)
(888) 371-2175 (toll free)
Innkeeper@KangarooHouse.com
www.KangarooHouse.com

The Kangaroo House is a centrally located, Craftsman home on Orcas Island. Casual comfort with a stone fireplace, garden hot tub, and delicious full breakfasts await guests. Families are welcome. Activities include hiking, cycling, whale watching, sea kayaking, bird-watching, relaxing, relaxing, and more relaxing. Kangaroo House was rated number one in the nation for friendliest staff.

Challah French Toast

Crushed cornflakes
6 eggs, slightly beaten
2 cups half-and-half
¼ cup rum
1 tablespoon orange zest
1 cup sugar
½ teaspoon ground cinnamon
½ teaspoon ground nutmeg
1 loaf challah bread, sliced
Melted margarine for cooking

Place cornflakes in plastic bag and crush moderately with rolling pin. Do *not* crush to powder. Whisk together eggs, half-and-half, rum, orange zest, sugar, and spices. Dip challah slices in egg mixture, then in crushed cornflakes to coat. Let sit 10 to 15 minutes to absorb. Sauté in melted margarine until crispy and golden brown. Dust with confectioners' sugar or serve with maple syrup. Yields 8 servings.

Ginger Poached Pears

6 cups water
2 cups sugar
¼ cup peeled and sliced ginger root
5 drops yellow food coloring
3 tablespoons lemon juice
4 pears

Combine water, sugar, sliced ginger, food coloring, and lemon juice in large, nonreactive pot and cook over medium heat until sugar dissolves. Reduce heat to simmer. Peel and halve pears. Use melon baller to remove core and paring knife to remove "flower part" at bottom. Add pear halves to poaching liquid and simmer until pears are tender, being careful to pierce only cut surface to preserve appearance. Place a weight on pears to keep them submerged and prevent oxidation of surfaces. When fork tender, remove from heat and let stand in liquid 8 to 10 hours or overnight for good color saturation. When ready to use, reduce about 1 cup of liquid to a syrup. To serve, remove pear halves from liquid, slice, and fan to pleasing arrangement and spoon small quantity of ginger syrup over pear. Yields 8 servings.

Kangaroo House

TURTLEBACK FARM INN

1981 Crow Valley Road
Eastsound, WA 98245
(360) 376-4914 (phone)
(800) 376-4914 (toll free)
turtleback@interisland.net
www.turtlebackinn.com

An Orcas Island landmark, Turtleback Farm Inn offers intimate lodging, personal attention, quality service, and generous amenities. Set on eighty acres of tranquil countryside with grazing sheep, crowing roosters, shimmering ponds, and well-tended gardens, the restored Farmhouse and newer Orchard House provide a haven for those anxious to experience the wide range of island activities: whale watching, sea kayaking, sailing, deep-sea and fresh-water fishing, hiking, bird-watching, and summer swimming in the park. Enjoy excellent dining at many local restaurants and shopping at the various artisan shops and studios that dot the island.

Warm Chocolate-Espresso Pudding Cakes

1½ sticks butter
6 ounces bittersweet chocolate, chopped
4½ tablespoons unbleached white flour
2 teaspoons freezer-dried espresso powder or 2 tablespoons hot espresso
2 tablespoons unsweetened cocoa
5 large eggs, separated
⅓ cup sugar
1½ tablespoons Kahlúa
½ teaspoon vanilla extract

Preheat oven to 350°. In small pan combine butter and chocolate. Heat over low heat until melted and smoothly mixed. Mix in flour, espresso powder, and cocoa. In large bowl, beat egg whites until they begin to peak. Beat in sugar, 1 tablespoon at a time. Continue beating until whites are shiny and hold stiff, but not dry, peaks. Beat together yolks until well blended and add Kahlúa and vanilla to cocoa-flour mixture. Gently fold in beaten whites. Pour about ½ cup batter into each of eight buttered ramekins or custard cups. For ease of handling, set ramekins on cookie sheet and bake until edges begin to firm but center is still soft when pressed, about 11 to 12 minutes. Let cool a few minutes and invert on dessert plates. Serve with coffee ice cream. Yields 8 servings.

Savory Torte

Egg crepes:
1 cup milk
1 cup unbleached white flour
4 eggs
2 tablespoons melted butter
Pinch of salt

Filling:
1 bunch spinach, cleaned, stemmed, and chopped or 10 ounces frozen chopped spinach
½ pound mushrooms, chopped
2 tablespoons butter
8 ounces cream cheese
Pinch of salt
Ground black pepper
¼ teaspoon ground nutmeg

Mix crepe ingredients well in blender and let batter sit. Batter should resemble heavy cream. Heat 10-inch skillet over medium-high heat. Add butter to pan before you make your first crêpe. After initial crêpe is cooked, you should not need to add more butter. While tilting the pan, add just enough batter to thinly cover bottom of pan. Cook until bubbles pop, about 1 minute. Turn over and brown other side. This recipe should make six large crêpes.

For filling, sauté spinach and mushrooms in butter until tender and most moisture has evaporated. Add cream cheese and seasonings and mix well. Season to taste. Keep warm.

Preheat oven to 350°. Place large rectangle of foil on counter. Cook one crêpe and place in middle of foil. Spread one-fifth of filling over crêpe and top with second crêpe. Repeat until you have five crêpes covered with spinach mixture. Top with final crêpe and seal in foil. Place in oven a few minutes to be sure torte is evenly warm. Cut into eight wedges and serve with dollop of sour cream and snipped chives or a few snipped green onion tops. Yields 8 servings.

Note: For a more substantial meal, chopped and sautéed ham can be added to filling.

Blintz Soufflé

Soufflé:
1 stick butter, softened
6 eggs plus 2 egg yolks
1 cup sour cream
½ cup orange juice
1 cup all-purpose flour
2 teaspoons baking powder
2 plus 1 tablespoons sugar
8 ounces cream cheese, cut up
1 pound cottage cheese
1 teaspoon vanilla extract

Fruit sauce:
2 tablespoons butter
1 cup fresh berries or summer fruit such as peaches, nectarines, or apricots
3 tablespoons sugar
½ cup orange juice

Preheat oven to 350°. Butter 13 x 9-inch baking pan. Blend butter, 6 eggs, sour cream, orange juice, flour, baking powder, and 2 tablespoons sugar. Pour half of mixture into bottom of prepared pan. Set remaining half aside. Combine remaining 1 tablespoon sugar, cream cheese, cottage cheese, 2 egg yolks, and vanilla in food processor, processing until smooth. Drop by spoonfuls over batter in bottom of pan. With knife, spread top layer as smoothly as possible over bottom layer. Pour remaining half of batter mixture over top. (Unbaked soufflé may be covered and refrigerated 8 to 10 hours or overnight until ready to bake. If convenient, bring soufflé to room temperature.) Bake uncovered 50 to 60 minutes or until still soft but golden.

While baking, make fruit sauce by melting butter in saucepan. Add remaining ingredients. Cook over low heat until fruit is soft. If fresh fruit is not available, frozen berries or fruit can be substituted. Serve immediately over soufflé and sprinkle nuts on top. Yields 12 servings.

CHINABERRY HILL

302 Tacoma Avenue North
North Tacoma, WA 90403
(253) 272-1282
chinaberry@wa.net
www.chinaberryhill.com

Surrounded by one-hundred-year-old trees, cascading greenery, and captivating views of the Sound, this 1889 grand Victorian offers bright, spacious suites and guest cottage in a remarkable hillside garden setting. Within a few blocks of museums, galleries, antique shops, waterfront restaurants, and several parks, Chinaberry Hill is just five minutes from the Tacoma Dome and University campuses.

Cinnamon Pears

¼ cup pine nuts
2 bananas, sliced
2 ripe Bartlett or Bosc pears
½ cup frozen apple juice concentrate
1 teaspoon ground cinnamon
¾ pound red seedless grapes
12 ounces vanilla bean yogurt

Preheat skillet to medium high. Pour in pine nuts and stir constantly with spatula until brown. Pour into small bowl and set aside. Using four dessert dishes, put 10 to 12 banana slices into four dessert dishes. Quarter pears and remove core, slicing half a pear into each dish. Spread 2 tablespoons frozen apple juice on top of each bowl of pears and sprinkle with cinnamon. Add grapes and top with yogurt and pine nuts. Yields 4 servings.

Corn and Cheddar Quiche

1 (9-inch) piecrust
1 egg, separated, plus 4 whole eggs
1 cup whipping cream
½ large sweet onion, diced
1 medium red pepper, diced
2 tablespoons butter
1 teaspoon salt
½ teaspoon ground pepper
1 tablespoon all-purpose flour
½ cup plus ¼ cup shredded
    sharp Cheddar cheese
4 to 6 green onions, diced
1½ cups frozen white shoe peg corn

Preheat oven to 400°. Roll out piecrust for 9½-inch glass pie dish. Flour bottom lightly to prevent sticking and arrange in dish, fluting edges. Using pastry brush (I actually use a paper towel), cover inside of crust with egg white and set aside to dry. (The yolk from this egg can be added to whole eggs). Beat eggs in mixing bowl, add cream, and mix thoroughly. Sauté onion and red pepper in butter over medium-high heat, using large skillet or stockpot. When onion is clear, add salt, pepper, flour, and ½ cup cheese, stirring until cheese is melted. Add egg and cream mixture, mixing thoroughly. Stir in green onions and corn until uniformly distributed and pour mixture into piecrust. Top with remaining ¼ cup cheese. Place in oven on cookie sheet and bake 45 minutes, or until center is set and top is golden brown. Yields 4 to 6 servings.

Orange Butter Croissant French Toast

2 day-old butter croissants
1 medium orange
3 large eggs
1 teaspoon sugar
1 teaspoon orange oil
½ teaspoon almond extract
½ cup orange juice
½ cup whipping cream
Confectioners' sugar

Preheat electric griddle to 350° or large, nonstick skillet to medium high. Slice croissants in half horizontally, using bread knife. Using a micro-plane or zester, remove approximately 1 tablespoon zest from orange and put into mixing bowl large enough for dipping croissants. Add eggs, sugar, orange oil, and almond extract and whisk until eggs are thoroughly beaten. Add orange juice and whipping cream and mix thoroughly. Dip croissants into batter, turning twice (do not saturate) and place cut-side up on griddle, cooking for 3½ to 4½ minutes. Turn and cook face down for another 3 to 4 minutes until golden brown. Place croissants overlapping on plates and dust with confectioners' sugar. Garnish with slices of orange, cut open on one side and twisted over top of croissants. Serve with butter and maple syrup. Yields 2 servings.

INN AT SHIP BAY

326 Olga Road
Eastsound, WA 98245
(360) 376-5886 (phone)
(360) 376-4675 (fax)
(877) 276-7296 (toll free)
shipbay@rockisland.com
www.innatshipbay.com

We are a quiet and pastoral country inn at the top of a bluff overlooking Ship Bay, in Eastsound, on Orcas Island. Inn at Ship Bay is centered around the historic Adams Orchard House, built in 1869 by Michael Adams, one of the early pioneers of Orcas Island's storied past. We offer clean, comfortable waterfront accommodations and excellent and unpretentious dining in an atmosphere of warmth and hospitality, located only minutes from Eastsound and Moran State Park. Our grounds also are graced by the presence of many deer, bald eagles, and other wildlife. We are proud to be stewards of this historic property and are firmly committed to maintaining this very special environment.

Honey Oat Granola

4½ cups regular rolled oats
1 cup each toasted wheat germ
    and sunflower seeds
½ cup toasted walnuts
½ cup almonds
½ cup coconut
⅔ cup firmly packed dark brown sugar
¼ cup salad oil
2½ cups nonfat dry milk
½ teaspoon salt
½ cup honey
½ plus ½ cup vegetable oil
2 teaspoons vanilla extract

Preheat oven to 300°. In large bowl combine oats, wheat germ, sunflower seeds, walnuts, almonds, and coconut. In saucepan combine brown sugar, oil, milk, salt, and honey. Stir over medium-high heat until mixture is runny (don't boil too long). Pour over oats mixture and mix thoroughly with hands. Spread mixture on two cookie sheets, each covered with ½ cup oil. Bake 45 minutes. Stir every 15 minutes while cooking. When out of oven, sprinkle with vanilla. Allow to cool on pan. Break up granola and store in airtight container. Yields about 8 cups.

Zucchini Nut Muffins

1 egg
¼ cup oil
⅛ cup milk
1½ cups flour
½ cup granulated sugar plus some
    for sprinkling
½ cup brown sugar
1 teaspoon ground cinnamon
½ teaspoon baking soda
½ teaspoon salt
½ teaspoon baking powder
1 cup grated zucchini
1 cup chopped nuts

Preheat oven to 350°. Mix egg, oil, and milk together and add remaining ingredients. Mix until combined. Scoop into 8-cup muffin tin sprayed with nonstick vegetables coating or greased. Sprinkle with granulated sugar. Bake 25 minutes. Yields 8 large muffins.

ABENDBLUME PENSION

12570 Ranger Road
P.O. Box 981
Leavenworth, WA 98826
(509) 548-4059 (phone)
(509) 548-9032 (fax)
(800) 669-7634 (toll free)
abendblm@rightathome.com
www.abendblume.com

Abendblume Pension invites you to surround yourself with romance and luxury. Inspired by fine European country inns, Abendblume is one of the area's finest award-winning bed and breakfasts. Many guest rooms have fireplaces, marble showers, spas, and balconies. Here, the gracious hospitality is warm, personal, and discreet, with taste and style and quietly refined pleasures. Nestled in the Cascade Mountains, Abendblume Pension is in the Bavarian town of Leavenworth, Washington, and this elegant Austrian chalet boasts spectacular lodging.

Danish Pancakes

2 eggs, separated
2 cups low-fat buttermilk
2 cups all-purpose flour
2 tablespoons sugar
2 tablespoons baking powder
½ teaspoon baking soda
½ teaspoon salt
½ teaspoon ground cardamom
½ teaspoon vanilla extract
4 tablespoons melted unsalted butter
Vegetable oil
Confectioners' sugar

Beat egg whites in medium-size bowl until stiff but not dry. Reserve. Combine yolks, buttermilk, flour, sugar, baking powder, baking soda, salt, cardamom, vanilla, and melted butter in bowl and mix until smooth. Fold in egg whites. Pour about ¾ teaspoon oil into each round of an aebleskiver pan and heat over medium-high heat on top of stove. Add heaping tablespoon batter, or enough to fill each round about three-quarters full. When bubbly around edges, turn each round upside down with chopsticks or fork. Continue cooking, turning frequently, until rounds are golden on all sides and done in middle, about 5 minutes. Remove each cake as it is done and drain on paper towels. Keep warm in 200° oven until all rounds are cooked. Sprinkle with confectioners' sugar. Yields 6 servings.

Sherry Cinnamon Swirl Cake

Cake:
1 (18 ounce) box yellow cake mix
    (pudding free)
1 (7.5-ounce) box instant vanilla pudding
¾ cup sherry wine
¾ cup vegetable oil
1 teaspoon ground nutmeg
4 eggs

Topping:
½ cup chopped walnuts
½ cup sugar
2 tablespoons ground cinnamon

Glaze:
¼ pound (1 stick) butter
¼ cup water
1 cup sugar
¼ cup sherry wine
Confectioners' sugar

Preheat oven to 325°. Mix cake ingredients and set batter aside. Mix topping ingredients. Sprinkle ¼ cup topping into well-greased and floured heavy Bundt pan. Pour in half of batter and top with remaining topping. Marbleize with knife and bake 45 to 50 minutes. Check during last 10 minutes for doneness. Test with toothpick.

For glaze, melt butter in saucepan. Stir in water and sugar. Boil 5 minutes, stirring constantly. Remove from heat. Stir in sherry. Pour glaze over cake while still in pan. Allow cake to absorb glaze, about 30 minutes. Then invert onto cake plate and dust with confectioners' sugar if desired. Yields 12 servings.

Apple Syrup

1 cup sugar
2 tablespoons cornstarch
¼ teaspoon ground nutmeg
¼ teaspoon ground cinnamon
1 pint apple juice
Splash of lemon
½ stick butter

Combine all ingredients and heat over medium heat until desired thickness. Serve warm. Yields 14 servings.

Brone Koken

½ pound (2 sticks) butter
1 cup sugar
1 teaspoon vanilla extract
2 tablespoons Lyle's golden syrup
2 cups all-purpose flour
1 teaspoon baking soda

Preheat oven to 350°. Cream butter and sugar, add vanilla and syrup, and then add flour and soda. Roll into logs long enough to fit on cookie sheet and about 1 inch thick. Bake until light brown, 5 to 10 minutes. As soon as you take logs out of oven, cut slices 1 to 2 inches wide on diagonal. Yields 10 servings.

Ravenscroft Inn

533 Quincy Street
Port Townsend, WA 98368
(360) 385-2784 (phone)
(800) 782-2691 (toll free)
info@ravenscroftinn.com
www.ravenscroftinn.com

Ravenscroft Inn is a Charleston single-house design among the Victorian homes of the northwest historic seaport town. From the verandas are glorious water and mountain views. Activities in the surrounding area include whale watching, sailing, and kayaking; scuba diving, and ferry rides. There are also many shops, a historic walking tour, museums, and historic Fort Worden.

Smoked Salmon Timbales

Timbales:
4 plus 1 tablespoons diced green chiles
6 tablespoons cottage cheese
½ pound smoked salmon
2 cups grated Swiss cheese
6 eggs

1½ cups milk
3 teaspoons paprika
Dash of onion salt
3 tablespoons Parmesan cheese

Sauce:
3 tablespoons butter
3 tablespoons all-purpose flour
1½ cups milk
¾ to 1 cup grated smoked Cheddar cheese
Paprika

Preheat oven to 350°. Spray six 8-ounce ramekins with nonstick pan coating. Place 1 teaspoon chiles in bottom of each ramekin. Next, spoon in 1 tablespoon cottage cheese. Chop or shred smoked salmon and put equal amounts in each ramekin. Place grated Swiss cheese on top. In separate bowl, mix together eggs, milk, paprika, onion salt, and Parmesan cheese. Ladle mixture into each ramekin and give mixture a little time to soak down through layers. Add more mixture to each ramekin, if necessary, to fill each to top. Bake 30 minutes or until custard has risen and top is brown. Remove from oven and let rest. Timbales will fall a little.

While timbales are baking, make sauce. Melt butter, add flour, and stir rapidly. Add milk to make a roux (white sauce). Add cheese and stir until melted. To serve, invert timbales out of ramekin onto plate. Pour cheese sauce over top of each timbale. Sprinkle top with paprika and garnish as desired. Yields 6 servings.

Note: The recipe has many different twists and turns. The timbales can be made with seafood (shrimp, crab, etc.), leftover turkey after Thanksgiving, ham, bacon bits, spicy breakfast sausage, for a few suggestions. The cheese sauce can be changed to Swiss cheese with ham timbales, a Gouda cheese sauce with seafood or turkey. Let your imagination create your own version.

West Virginia

HIGHLAWN INN

171 Market Street
Berkeley Springs, WV 25411
(304) 258-5700 (phone)
(888) 290-4163 (toll free)
info@highlawninn.com
www.highlawninn.com

Highlawn Inn is a complex of bed and breakfasts in four restored buildings. These include the original Highlawn Inn, the Carriage House, Aunt Pearl's, and the Bathkeeper's Quarters. Victorian charm and warm hospitality greet you with superb accommodations. Choose from a wealth of activities such as an easy stroll down the hill; bathe in historic warm mineral springs; yield to the relaxing fingers of a massage therapist; hike nearby mountains; or treasure hunt from nearly one hundred antique and collectible dealers in two malls and a sprinkling of stores.

Confetti-Herb Squash

2 cups cooked, drained, and mashed
    yellow squash,
2 eggs, well beaten
½ cup undiluted evaporated milk
½ stick margarine, melted

Highlawn Inn

1 tablespoon sugar
1 tablespoon all-purpose flour
¾ cup grated Swiss cheese
Salt and pepper
2 tablespoons freshly
    chopped tarragon
1 tablespoon freshly chopped basil
½ cup chopped onions
¼ cup each red and green
    chopped peppers
Breadcrumbs

Preheat oven to 350°. Combine ingredients, except breadcrumbs, in large bowl in order given and mix well. Pour into buttered, 2-quart, glass casserole. Top with breadcrumbs. Bake about 1 hour or until center is set. Yields 6 servings.

Note: This dish can easily be doubled. It can also be prepared ahead and baked later.

Baked French Toast

1 cup dark brown sugar
½ cup (1 stick) butter
2 tablespoons dark molasses
1 teaspoon allspice
2 tablespoons ground cinnamon
1 teaspoon ginger
2 tablespoons pure vanilla
¼ cup brandy
1 loaf French bread, cut into ¾-inch slices
5 eggs
1½ cups canned milk

Coat 9 x 13-inch baking dish with nonstick spray. In saucepan over low-medium heat mix and melt brown sugar, butter, molasses, allspice, cinnamon, ginger, and vanilla. Add brandy. Line prepared dish with bread slices. Blend eggs and milk and add to sugar mixture. Pour mixture over bread slices. Cover dish and refrigerate 8 to 10 hours or overnight. When ready to bake, preheat oven to 350°. Uncover dish and bake about 30 minutes or until set. Yields 8 servings.

Note: For different texture, use leftover croissants. Sliced peaches or other fruits may be added for variation.

Sandy's Crazy Herbs Omelet

3 tablespoons vegetable oil
8 eggs, well beaten
1 cup shredded mozzarella cheese
2 plum tomatoes, sliced
1 tablespoon chopped fresh oregano
    (about 3 sprigs)
1 tablespoon chopped fresh tarragon
    (about 4 sprigs)
2 tablespoons coarsely cut opal basil
    (about 6 leaves)
½ cup tomato sauce
⅓ cup cooked zucchini
2 tablespoons chopped, sautéed onion

Heat vegetable oil in stainless steel frying pan over low-medium heat. Pour in half of eggs. Add cheese and distribute tomato slices on top. Combine herbs and sprinkle half on top. Gently pour in remaining eggs. Mix tomato sauce with zucchini and onion and add by spoonfuls on top of eggs. Sprinkle remaining herbs on top. Watch pan constantly, shaking and lifting edges to let mixture run under edges until omelet is set. (It may be necessary to cut hole in center with fork to set.) Slide omelet onto heated plate. Cut into wedges and serve. Garnish with lots of fresh basil leaves. Yields 4 servings.

♣   ♣   ♣

GILLUM HOUSE BED & BREAKFAST

35 Walnut Street
Shinnston, WV 26431
(304) 592-0177 (phone)
(304) 569-1882 (fax)
(888) 592-0177 (toll free)
relax@gillumhouse.com
www.gillumhouse.com

The Gillum House is known for low-fat, low-cholesterol food that tastes wonderful. Our slogan is "Where you are treated like a guest but feel like family." Welcome back to Granny's house. Our local attractions include historic sites, rail trails (one is fifty feet from the inn), glass factory tours, covered bridges, and outdoor adventure and sports. Golf, fishing, hunting, birding, white-water rafting, kayaking, hiking, biking, antiques, and drive-in movies are all available near the Gillum House.

French Bread a la Gillum

2½ cups warm water
1½ (¼-ounce) packets active dry yeast
2 tablespoons sugar
2 tablespoons unsweetened applesauce
6 to 7 cups all-purpose flour
Cornmeal

Pour warm water into large bowl. Add yeast and sugar. Wait 5 minutes. If yeast starts clumping to surface, it is proofed, meaning it is working. Add applesauce, stir, and gradually add flour, mixing well after each addition until stiff dough is formed. Turn out onto lightly floured surface. Knead well, about 10 minutes. During kneading you may lift dough and bang it hard on surface (this is a great bread to make when upset—it relieves tensions). Place ball of dough back in bowl, cover, and let rise until double in bulk. Once again, turn out on lightly floured surface, divide in half and knead well to work out all air bubbles. Coat French bread pan with nonstick spray and coat with cornmeal. Shape into 2 long loaves, gash tops diagonally ¼-inch deep every 2 inches, and place in pan. Cover

Gillum House Bed & Breakfast

and let rise until double in bulk. Preheat oven to 350° and bake 40 to 45 minutes. Brush tops lightly with butter and serve hot from oven. Yields 2 loaves.

Wheat-Free Low-Fat Banana Muffins

¾ cup soy flour
¾ cup brown rice flour
1 cup sugar
1 teaspoon baking soda
⅓ cup unsweetened applesauce
1 teaspoon vanilla extract
4 egg whites
3 large bananas, mashed
1 cup chocolate chips (optional)

Preheat oven to 375°. Sift dry ingredients together in large bowl. Add remaining ingredients and mix. Coat mini muffin pans with nonstick spray. Fill muffin pans and bake 16 minutes. Remove from pans to wire rack to cool as soon as possible. Yields 3 dozen mini muffins.

Gillum Pumpkin Chocolate Chip Muffins

1⅓ cups all-purpose flour
⅔ cup sugar
1 teaspoon ground cinnamon
½ teaspoon ground nutmeg
½ teaspoon allspice
½ teaspoon ginger
½ teaspoon cloves
1 teaspoon baking soda
¼ teaspoon baking powder
4 egg whites
1 cup pumpkin purée
½ cup unsweetened applesauce
1 cup chocolate chips

Preheat oven to 375°. Sift dry ingredients into medium-size bowl. Add remaining

ingredients and mix gently. Coat mini muffin pans with nonstick spray. Scoop batter (1-inch scoop can be used for speed and ease) into pans. Bake 16 minutes. Yields 3 dozen mini muffins.

Kathleen's Bottomless Tossed Salad

1 head iceberg lettuce, torn
1 bunch romaine lettuce, torn
¾ cup sliced baby carrots
½ green bell pepper, chopped
¼ cup chopped fresh basil leaves
2 stalks celery, thinly sliced
1 head radicchio, chopped (optional)
2 large tomatoes, seeded and chopped
1 large cucumber, seeded and sliced
1 (14-ounce) can black olives, drained
    and rinsed
Seasoned croutons (optional)
3 medium radishes, thinly sliced
1 hard-cooked egg, quartered

Combine all ingredients, except egg, in large bowl. Toss and serve topped with egg quarters arranged in "star" pattern around a black olive. Put croutons in separate bowl to keep crisp. Yields 8 servings.

Sugar-Free Oatmeal-Apple Muffins

1 cup whole wheat flour
3 teaspoons baking powder
½ teaspoon ground nutmeg
2 teaspoons ground cinnamon
⅜ teaspoon stevioside powder
1½ cups rolled oats
4 egg whites
¾ cup skim milk
¼ cup unsweetened applesauce
1 medium apple, cored and shredded
¾ cup chopped raisins

Preheat oven to 375°. In medium bowl sift whole wheat flour, baking powder, nutmeg,

cinnamon, and stevioside (or Splenda) and thoroughly mix. Empty sifter remains into bowl, add oatmeal, and mix. Add remaining ingredients and mix gently. Spray mini muffin pans with nonstick spray. Scoop batter (use 1-inch scoop) into muffin pans and bake 15 minutes. Yields 3 dozen mini muffins.

WASHINGTON HOUSE INN

216 South George Street
Charles Town, WV 25414
(304) 725-7923 (phone)
(800) 297-6957 (toll free)
emailus@washingtonhouseinnwv.com
www.washingtonhouseinnwv.com

In charming colonial Charles Town, nestled in the Blue Ridge Mountains where the Shenandoah and Potomac Rivers meet, the Washington House Inn is a wonderful example of late Victorian architecture. Built in 1899 the inn is graced with antique furnishings, carved oak mantles, telephones, data ports, cable televisions, and spacious guest rooms. Take a leisurely stroll to the charming colonial Main Street. Hike the mountain trails of the Blue Ridge or bike along the restored C&O towpath. The Shenandoah and Potomac Rivers offer exciting white-water rafting, kayaking, and serene bird-watching, or simply float down the peaceful river for a quiet summer day.

Orange Sour Cream Nut Sauce

1 cup sour cream
⅓ cup orange juice
⅓ cup confectioners' sugar
⅓ cup chopped nuts

Blend all ingredients together and serve with melon. Yields 2 cups.

Baked Eggs and Cheese

6 tablespoons melted butter
½ cup all-purpose flour
1 teaspoon baking powder
7 eggs
1 cup milk
16 ounces small-curd cottage cheese
16 ounces grated Swiss cheese
4 ounces cream cheese
1 tablespoon fresh chives

Preheat oven to 350°. Mix melted butter with flour and baking powder. Blend in eggs. Add remaining ingredients. Pour into greased 13 x 9-inch dish and bake 30 minutes until casserole is slightly browned. Yields 6 servings.

Eggs Sausage Soufflé

Crusty bread
1 pound sausage, browned
5 eggs
1½ cups milk
½ teaspoon dry mustard
1 (10¾-ounce) can cream of
    mushroom soup
½ cup milk
1 cup grated Cheddar cheese

Tear bread into pieces and cover bottom of greased 9 x 13-inch dish. Put crumbled sausage on top of bread. Blend eggs, milk,

and dry mustard together and pour over sausage and bread. Mix soup, milk, and cheese together and pour over top. Refrigerate 8 to 10 hours or overnight. When ready to bake, preheat oven to 325° and bake until brown, about 45 minutes, or at 350° about 30 minutes. Yields 6 servings.

Cinnamon Raisin Bread French Toast

8 ounces cream cheese
¼ cup strawberry jam
12 slices cinnamon-raisin bread
6 eggs
1½ cups milk

Blend cream cheese and jam. Spread on bread slice and top with another. Repeat to make 6 "sandwiches." Beat eggs and add milk. Soak bread in egg mixture. Brown on griddle using medium-high heat. Yields 6 servings.

Famous Pumpkin Dip

1 (15-ounce) can pumpkin
8 ounces cream cheese
2 cups confectioners' sugar
½ teaspoon ground ginger
½ teaspoon ground nutmeg
½ teaspoon vanilla extract
1 teaspoon ground cinnamon

Blend all ingredients together. Use ginger snaps for dipping. Yield about 4 cups.

THE BAVARIAN INN & LODGE

Route 3, Box 30
Shepherdstown, WV 25443
(304) 876-2551 (phone)
(304) 876-9355 (fax)
info@bavarianinnwv.com
www.bavarianinnwv.com

Nestled on the inn's eleven-acre estate is the Greystone Mansion, where guests are invited to dine in warm elegance. Award-winning international cuisine is served amid the mansion's dark hardwoods, stone fireplaces, and fine furnishings. Casual dining and entertainment is a staple of the Rathskeller, a richly paneled hideaway in the European pub tradition—fine German and continental cuisine overlooking the Potomac River. The inn has seventy-two luxuriously appointed guest rooms with fireplaces and whirlpool baths. Five minutes from Antietam Battlefield and Harpers Ferry historical sites, the inn offers access to Cress Creek Golf Club, biking along the C&O Canal, tennis, fitness room and putting green on property, and outlet shopping minutes away.

Jaegerschnitzel (Veal Cutlet Hunter Style)

½ pound fresh button mushrooms, sliced
Butter
4 strips bacon, chopped
4 shallots, chopped
2 tablespoons dry white wine
1 tablespoon plus ½ cup all-purpose flour
Salt and pepper
4 (8-ounce) veal steaks

Sauté mushrooms in butter. In separate pan sauté bacon until golden brown and add shallots and wine. Thicken lightly with 1 tablespoon flour. Combine mushrooms with bacon mixture and simmer lightly 5 minutes. Lightly salt and pepper veal steaks to taste and lightly turn in flour. Cook steaks in separate pan in butter until done. Serve veal steaks on preheated plates and top with mushroom sauce. Yields 4 servings.

Duck Strudel with an Armagnac Chestnut Jus

4 (8-ounce) duck breasts
½ medium onion, finely diced
2 celery ribs, finely diced
1 clove garlic, minced
¼ cup raisins
1 Granny Smith apple, peeled and diced
8 dried prunes, soaked in brandy overnight
Sage, thyme, rosemary, nutmeg, and ground cloves
2 slices rye bread, diced
9 x 11-inch sheet puff pastry
2 large eggs, lightly beaten
⅓ cup Armagnac or brandy
⅓ cup Crème de Marrons (chestnut cream)
1 cup beef broth
½ ounce cornstarch
2 tablespoons water

Preheat oven to 375°. Roast duck breasts skin-side down 35 minutes. Remove from oven and let cool. Save juice and fat from pan to sauté remaining ingredients. Remove and save skin from duck. Slice duck breast into quarter-size pieces and set aside. Sauté onion, celery, and garlic in juice from duck until tender. Add raisins, apple, prunes, spices to taste, and duck meat. Cook 2 minutes longer and let cool. Fold rye bread into mixture to thicken. Roll puff pastry out to about ⅛-inch thickness. Add duck mixture and roll, tucking ends in so no mixture is exposed. Brush strudels with

beaten eggs. Reduce oven temperature to 350° and bake 30 minutes or until golden brown. Combine Armagnac, Crème de Marrons, and beef broth. Bring to a boil. Mix cornstarch and water together. Add slowly to liquids until desired consistency is achieved. Spoon over duck. Yields 4 servings.

Bavarian Inn Sauerbraten

1½ cups red wine vinegar
3 cups water
1 medium white onion, sliced
2 tablespoons whole peppercorns
½ cup pickling spices
Salt
1 sliced carrot
1 (4-pound) piece beef bottom round, rump, or chuck
2½ tablespoons shortening
¼ cup white sugar
¼ cup all-purpose flour
2 gingersnaps
½ cup red wine

Mix vinegar, water, onion, peppercorns, pickling spices, salt, and carrot in glass, enamel, or earthenware bowl. Place meat in bowl, cover, and refrigerate. Allow meat to marinate for three days, turning several times. Drain meat and wipe dry, saving remaining brine for gravy. Grease heavy roasting pan with shortening. Preheat oven to 325°. Brown meat on all sides in roasting pan and bake in oven 25 minutes per pound. When meat is almost done, sprinkle sugar over meat and bake another 5 to 10 minutes until sugar is fully dissolved. Thicken remaining marinade with flour and gingersnaps. Mix well and pour over meat. Roast meat for additional ½ hour until gravy is creamy and thick. Remove meat, stir wine into gravy, and strain. Yields 8 servings.

❧ ❧ ❧

Bavarian Inn Sauerkraut

1 gallon store-bought sauerkraut
3 tablespoons butter
12 ounces ground smoked pork
½ onion, julienned
2 juniper berries
1 bay leaf
3 cups chicken stock
1 cup dry white wine
1 tablespoon caraway seeds
½ cup cornstarch

Place sauerkraut in strainer and wash three times with cold water. Sauté butter, ground pork, onion, and juniper berries until pork is browned. In large pan combine sauerkraut and pork mixture with remaining ingredients except cornstarch. Allow to simmer for 1 hour, stirring every 10 minutes. Remove bay leaf. Combine cornstarch and ½ cup chilled water, adding slowly to finished sauerkraut until desired consistency is met. Yields 1 gallon.

THE JAMES WYLIE HOUSE BED & BREAKFAST

208 East Main Street
White Sulphur Springs, WV 24986
(304) 536-9444 (phone)
(800) 870-1613 (toll free)
www.jameswylie.com

The James Wylie House enjoys a history of hospitality dating back almost two hundred years. The bed and breakfast offers six guest units and travelers find easy comfort and a memorable breakfast. Convenient to the house are activities for the whole family, including fishing, golf, rafting, biking, canoeing, and hiking. Nearby are the historic Oakhurst Links and the renowned Greenbrier resort.

Banana Nut Bread

4 very ripe medium bananas
1 cup coarsely chopped walnuts
    or pecans
2½ cups self-rising flour
½ cup brown sugar
½ cup granulated sugar
3 tablespoons vegetable oil
1 egg
⅓ cup milk

Preheat oven to 350°. Grease bottom only of 9 x 5 x 3-inch bread pan. In small bowl mash bananas and add nuts. In large bowl mix flour and sugars until well blended. Add oil, egg, and milk. After mixing thoroughly, add banana mixture. Pour into pan. Bake 60 minutes. Cool in pan for 10 minutes and remove to finish cooling. Serve whipped cream cheese for spreading. Yields 1 loaf.

Sweet Corn and Bacon Quiche

8 slices bacon, cut into pieces
1 Pillsbury ready-to-use piecrust
2 cups corn
1 cup grated Cheddar cheese
5 eggs
1½ cups half-and-half
½ teaspoon salt
Pinch of cayenne

Preheat oven to 450°. Cook bacon until browned and drain on paper towels. Place piecrust in 10-inch quiche dish. Spread corn, cheese, and bacon evenly over crust. Beat eggs, half-and-half, salt, and cayenne. Pour egg mixture over corn, cheese, and bacon. Bake 10 minutes and reduce heat to 350°. Continue baking 20 to 25 more minutes until set in center. Let stand a few minutes and cut into wedges. Yields 6 to 8 servings.

French Toast with Cinnamon Cream Syrup

Toast:
3 eggs
¼ cup all-purpose flour
2 teaspoons sugar
⅛ teaspoon salt
1 cup milk
¼ teaspoon orange zest
8 slices egg bread

Cinnamon Cream Syrup:
1 cup sugar
½ cup light corn syrup
¼ cup water
½ teaspoon ground cinnamon
½ cup evaporated milk

For toast, beat eggs, flour, sugar, and salt until smooth. Add milk and orange zest. Soak bread in mixture until saturated. Heat butter in skillet or on griddle until melted. Cook bread until golden brown.

For syrup, combine sugar, corn syrup, and water in small saucepan. Bring to a boil over medium heat, stirring constantly. Cook and stir 2 minutes. Remove from heat and cool 5 minutes. Stir in milk. Serve warm over French toast. Yields 4 servings.

THOMAS SHEPHERD INN

Corner of Duke and German Streets
P.O. Box 3634
Shepherdstown, WV 25443
(304) 876-3715 (phone)
(888) 889-8952 (toll free)
info@thomasshepherdinn.com
www.thomasshepherdinn.com

Nestled in the beautiful lower Shenandoah Valley along the Potomac, the Thomas Shepherd Inn is a place where life slows down long enough for you to enjoy it. Wonderful restaurants and unique shops are within a few blocks in our historically preserved small town, as is Shepherd College. The inn is only minutes away from Civil War landmarks such as Antietam Battlefield and Harpers Ferry and outdoor activities like hiking on the Appalachian Trail, biking on the C&O Canal Path or water fun on the Potomac River. Come for any of the many fairs and festivals in the area, like the Contemporary American Theater Festival, the Dulcimer Festival, or the Mountain Heritage Arts and Crafts Festival.

Strawberry Gazpacho

2 quarts (2 pounds) strawberries,
    rinsed and halved
1 ripe mango, pitted, peeled, and diced
2 kiwifruits, peeled and diced
¼ cup sugar
1 cup white grape juice
3 tablespoons lime or lemon juice
Vanilla lowfat yogurt for garnish

Purée strawberries with sugar in food processor until smooth. Pour into bowl and stir in grape and lemon or lime juice. Add diced mango and kiwifruits and refrigerate 2 hours. Serve gazpacho in soup bowl with spoonful of yogurt on top. Yields 6 servings.

Hot Fruit Compote

8 cups chopped fruit*
1 tablespoon lemon juice
½ cup sugar (optional)
1 teaspoon ground cinnamon
1 teaspoon ground ginger
⅓ cup packed brown sugar
2 cups old-fashioned oats
1½ sticks butter, softened

Preheat oven to 350°. Combine fruit and lemon juice in lightly greased 3-quart baking dish and toss well. If using tart fruit like cranberries or rhubarb pour sugar evenly over fruit. Combine cinnamon, ginger, brown sugar, oats, and butter and sprinkle evenly over fruit. Bake 45 minutes. Yields 12 servings.

*Note: Use following combinations: 6 cups apples + 1 can whole berry cranberry sauce or 6 cups peaches + 2 cups blueberries or 6 cups apples + 2 cups rhubarb.

Mexican Soufflé

8 eggs
1 cup milk
1 pound Colby-Jack cheese, shredded
1 (12-ounce) package small-curd cottage cheese
¼ cup melted butter
½ cup all-purpose flour
1 teaspoon baking powder
1 (4-ounce) can chopped mild chiles
1 tablespoon breadcrumbs
1 tablespoon Parmesan cheese

Preheat oven to 350°. In large bowl beat together eggs and milk with electric mixer. Add cheeses and melted butter and stir. Mix in flour and baking powder. Fold in chiles and pour mixture into 3-quart baking dish coated with nonstick spray. Sprinkle breadcrumbs and Parmesan on top. Place dish in pan of hot water and bake 40 to 50 minutes

or until inserted knife comes out clean. Cut into rectangles and serve with fruit salsa. Yields 8 to 10 servings.

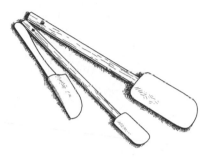

Baked Blueberry-Pecan French Toast

French toast:
1 large French bread baguette, cut in 1-inch slices
6 large eggs
1 cup milk
½ teaspoon ground nutmeg
1 teaspoon vanilla extract
¾ plus ¼ cup packed brown sugar
1 cup chopped pecans
4 tablespoons plus 1 teaspoon unsalted butter
2 cups blueberries

Syrup:
1 cup blueberries
½ cup pure maple syrup
1 teaspoon fresh lemon juice

Layer baguette slices in bottom of 9 x 13-inch greased baking dish. Whisk together eggs, milk, nutmeg, vanilla, and ¾ cup brown sugar in large bowl and pour over bread. Cover and chill mixture for 8 hours or overnight. Preheat oven to 350°. Spread pecans on baking sheet and toast in oven until fragrant, about 4 minutes. Toss pecans with 1 teaspoon butter and sprinkle over bread mixture. Increase oven to 400°. Sprinkle blueberries over bread mixture. Cut remaining 4 tablespoons butter in

pieces and heat with remaining ¼ cup brown sugar in saucepan over medium heat until butter is melted. Drizzle butter mixture over bread and bake 20 to 30 minutes or until liquid is bubbling.

For syrup, cook blueberries and maple syrup in small saucepan over medium heat until blueberries have burst, about 5 minutes. Pour syrup through a sieve into a pitcher, pressing on solids to extract all juice. Stir in lemon juice and reheat before serving. Serve French toast with syrup. Yields 6 to 8 servings.

BERKELEY SPRINGS SPA & INN

New Hope Road
Berkeley Springs, WV 25411
(304) 258-4536
www.bsspa.com

We cater to couples on that romantic getaway. Guests enjoy beautifully appointed guest rooms, five-course, candlelit dinners, and a full-service spa. Inn amenities include in-ground pool and outdoor Jacuzzi year-round; Satellite TV and VCR in every room with twelve hundred videos in the collection at the inn; bikes and bike racks for off-site trips; a full service spa (manicure, pedicure, facials, tanning, massage, full-service beauty salon, steam, sauna, and Jacuzzi); guest library with parlor games. Area activities include golf, horseback riding, biking, antiquing, shopping, historical sites, the C&O Canal, and rails-to-trails conversion project.

Chicken & Corn Tortilla Soup

2 large onions, large dice
2 tablespoons fresh garlic
Butter or olive oil
½ gallon fresh chicken stock
2 cans Italian-style tomatoes
2 cups fresh corn
2 large boneless chicken breasts
1 tablespoon oregano
3 tablespoons ground cumin
1 tablespoon chili powder

Sauté onions and garlic in salted butter (or olive oil). Add chicken stock, tomatoes, corn, and chicken. Simmer until chicken is thoroughly cooked. Remove chicken to let cool. Add oregano, cumin, and chili powder to soup. Shred chicken and add back to soup. Serve with crushed tortilla chips, Monterey Jack cheese, and diced scallions. Yields 2 servings.

Fresh Salmon Wrapped in Phyllo Dough

1 (single-sheet package) phyllo dough
Melted butter
4 (4-ounce) salmon fillets
1 to 2 tablespoons chopped fresh dill
    plus 4 sprigs
1 (6-ounce) bottle clam juice
1 cup Chardonnay wine
2¼ cups heavy whipping cream
Chives or parsley

Preheat oven to 350°. Brush phyllo dough with melted butter or use nonstick spray as alternative. Divide sheet in quarters. Place a salmon fillet in center of each quarter and top with dill sprig. Wrap salmon in phyllo dough as you would a burrito. Coat with nonstick spray as browning agent. Bake salmon about 25 minutes or until cooked through and phyllo dough is browned. In small skillet combine clam juice and Chardonnay and reduce by half. Add whipping cream and dill and simmer until thickened. Cut each phyllo wrap on diagonal in center of salmon. Place one piece on bed or rice (your favorite variety) and stand other half at an angle on top of first piece. Spoon dill sauce over salmon and rice. Garnish with chives or parsley. Complete with favorite vegetable. Yields 4 servings.

Fresh Peach Ice Cream

4 cups half-and-half
1½ cups sugar
½ cup nonfat dry milk
6 cups peeled, pitted, and sliced
    fresh peaches
6 tablespoons lemon juice
5 teaspoons vanilla extract
Dash of salt

Combine half-and-half, sugar, and dry milk in blender or food processor and process until smooth. Pour into large bowl. Without cleaning blender or processor, purée peaches until smooth. Add to sugar mixture and mix well. Add lemon juice, vanilla, and salt. Pour into ice cream maker and freeze according to manufacturer's instructions. Yields 6 to 8 servings.

THE CEDAR HOUSE

92 Trenol Heights
Milton, WV 25541
(888) 743-5516 (toll free)
vickersc@Marshall.edu
www.bbonline.com/wv/cedarhouse

Relax in this contemporary hilltop home on six acres with view of surrounding hills and bird-watching on the outside deck. Hand-dipped chocolates are a specialty. Nearby attractions include Blenko Glass Co. and Gibson Glass, makers of hand-blown glass; Milton covered bridge; Marshall University; Old Central City antique shops; Huntington Art museum, outstanding glass and gun collections; Civil War collection at Marshall University library; public golf courses; Beech Fork State Park, hiking trails and fishing; West Virginia State Capitol complex.

Summer Chicken Salad

5 chicken breasts, cooked and cubed
1 cup diced celery
1 cup quartered red seedless grapes
1 cup pecan pieces
1 cup drained crushed pineapple
1½ cups mayonnaise
1 teaspoon seasoned salt
¼ teaspoon ginger

Mix all ingredients thoroughly, adjusting seasonings to taste. Chill and serve on leaf lettuce or bed of mixed salad greens. Garnish with slices of melon, strawberries, kiwi, or other fruit. Yields 6 servings.

Mother's Cranberry Salad

1 cup sugar
1 cup finely chopped cranberries
1 cup finely chopped apples
1 (3-ounce) package cherry
    or lemon gelatin
1 cup boiling water
¾ cup pineapple juice
½ cup quartered seedless red grapes
½ cup pecan pieces

Add sugar to cranberries and apples. Let it stand. In another bowl dissolve gelatin in water and add pineapple juice. Stir in cranberry mixture, pineapple juice, grapes, and nuts. Pour into individual molds or 7 x 11-inch casserole dish and refrigerate until set. Serve over leaf lettuce and garnish with teaspoon of mayonnaise and pecan halves or pieces. Yields 8 servings.

Martha's Chicken-Broccoli Casserole

Casserole:
2 (10-ounce) packages chopped broccoli
3 ounces shredded Cheddar cheese
1 whole chicken or 6 breast halves
1 (10¾-ounce) can cream of chicken or celery soup, undiluted
⅓ cup chicken broth
1 cup mayonnaise
1 tablespoon lemon juice
Dash of curry powder

Topping:
2 cups herb-seasoned dressing mix
⅔ cup chicken broth
½ cup margarine

Cook broccoli in salted water, drain, and arrange in 9 x 13-inch baking dish. Sprinkle grated cheese over broccoli. Cook chicken in seasoned water, reserving broth. Preheat oven to 350°. Cut chicken into bite-size pieces and arrange over broccoli-cheese mixture. Mix soup, ½ cup broth, mayonnaise, lemon juice, and curry powder. Pour over chicken and broccoli.

Mix topping ingredients together and spread over casserole. Bake 30 minutes. Yields 6 servings.

Spoon Bread

1 quart milk
1 cup grits
1 stick margarine
1 teaspoon salt
3 eggs

Preheat oven to 350°. Heat milk in saucepan over low heat. Stir in grits and cook until thickened. Remove from heat and add margarine and salt. Cool mixture. Beat in eggs, one at a time. Pour into buttered casserole and bake 40 to 45 minutes. Yields 6 to 8 servings.

Carol's Bread Sticks

½ cup (1 stick) butter
2 cups self-rising flour
2 teaspoons sugar
¾ cup milk
Sesame seeds

Preheat oven to 400°. Melt butter in 7 x 11-inch baking pan. Mix flour, sugar, and milk together just until flour is moistened. Let rise 1 minute. Knead gently on floured cloth and roll out to fit baking pan. Cut lengthwise in center of dough, then crosswise in 1-inch strips, making sticks 3½ inches x 1 inch. Lift four or five strips at a time and roll in melted butter. Sprinkle sesame seeds on top. Bake 15 to 18 minutes or until golden brown. Yields 6 servings.

Breakfast Casserole

6 eggs
6 tablespoons all-purpose flour
½ cup (1 stick) margarine
1 (10-ounce) package chopped broccoli or spinach
8 ounces American or Cheddar cheese, grated
3 (8-ounce) containers small-curd cottage cheese

Preheat oven to 350°. Combine all ingredients. Bake in buttered casserole dish for 60 minutes. Let stand 15 minutes before serving. Yields 4 servings.

HILLBROOK INN

Route 2, Box 152
Charles Town, WV 25414
(304) 725-4223 (phone)
(304) 725-4455 (fax)
(800) 304-4223 (toll free)
reservations@hillbrookinn.com
www.hillbrookinn.com

A European-style, country house hotel cascading down a limestone ridge on fifteen levels with two thousand panes of glass flooding the interior with light, the

Hillbrook Inn

Hillbrook Inn is adorned with old wood, polished brass, and oriental carpets. Add the flicker of candles, the warmth of a fire, Flemish oils, African masks, dramatic contemporary sculpture, and a library lined with books and the ambience is complete. For dinner, there are seven spectacular courses with wine and fragrant herbs from the kitchen dooryard and trout from a nearby farm. Sophisticated yet unpretentious, elegant and eclectic is the Hillbrook Inn.

Chocolate Pâté

Pâté:
4 cups (1 quart) heavy cream
4 (16-ounce) packages semisweet
    chocolate, chopped
2 ounces unsweetened chocolate,
    chopped
2 pounds pecan halves

Bourbon cream:
4 cups (1 pint) heavy cream
½ cup bourbon
½ teaspoon vanilla extract
⅔ cup sugar

For pâté, bring cream to a boil and turn off heat. Add chopped chocolates and stir until completely smooth and silky. Fold in pecans and pour into plastic-lined pâté pan or you may use loaf pans. Refrigerate at least 24 hours.

For bourbon cream, stir ingredients together until sugar dissolves. Slice pâté and serve with bourbon cream drizzled over plate, under or over pâté. Yields 40 servings.

Mustard-Crusted Rack of Lamb

2 (8-rib) racks of lamb, French trimmed
3 tablespoons coarse-grained mustard
1 tablespoon freshly chopped garlic
1 tablespoon freshly chopped shallots
3 tablespoons extra virgin olive oil
1 teaspoon cracked black pepper
Pinch of salt
Pinch of ground cloves
3 tablespoons fresh breadcrumbs

Preheat oven to 400°. Sear racks on all sides in hot skillet and place on baking sheet bone-side down. Stir together remaining ingredients except for breadcrumbs. Spread generous layer of mixture over top of racks. Cover with breadcrumbs. Bake 10 minutes for medium rare. Let stand 10 minutes before slicing. Yields 4 servings.

THE GENEVA INN

N2009 State Road 120
Lake Geneva, WI 53147
(262) 248-5685 (fax)
(800) 441-5881 (toll free)
luxury@genevainn.com
www.genevainn.com

Located directly on the shores of Geneva Lake, discover intimate accommodations decorated to reflect the peaceful comfort of a traditional English country inn. Lakeside private balconies and oversized vintage or whirlpool baths; thick fluffy bathrobes; bedtime chocolates; continental buffet breakfast; private marina; and exercise facilities are only a few of the amenities that await you at the Geneva Inn. There is also spectacular cuisine at the Grandview Restaurant overlooking Geneva Lake. Lake Geneva offers a variety of boutiques, shops, and galleries. Nearby are championship golf courses, public beaches, horseback riding, biking, cross-country or downhill skiing, parasailing, fishing, ice-skating, snowmobiling, and a variety of area attractions.

Jumbo Lump Crab Cakes

Crab cakes:
16 ounces (1 pound) jumbo
    lump crabmeat
¼ cup heavy cream
2 tablespoons all-purpose flour
Pinch of salt
Pinch of ground white pepper

Sweet corn-basil relish:
1 ear fresh corn, shucked
1 tomato, diced
½ red onion, diced
1 tablespoon olive oil
1 tablespoon honey
3 to 4 basil leaves, julienned
Juice of 1 lime
Salt and pepper

For crab cakes, combine ingredients in medium mixing bowl and gently stir with spatula, being careful not to overmix crab. Using small ice cream scoop, form into eight cakes. Place medium, nonstick sauté pan over medium heat and cook cakes until golden brown, about 2 minutes each side.

For relish, place corn in medium sauté pan and sauté 1 to 2 minutes with ¼ cup water. Once cooked, drain water, cut kernels from cob, and chill. When cool, combine corn with remaining ingredients and pour over crab cakes. Garnish with fresh chives and lemon. Yields 4 servings.

❧   ❧   ❧

Seared Dayboat Scallops over Green Olive Risotto

Salad:
½ cup julienned sun-dried tomatoes
1 bulb fennel, shaved
1 tangerine, segmented
1 shallot, julienned
1 teaspoon tarragon leaves
1 tablespoon rice wine vinegar
1 tablespoon extra virgin olive oil
1 teaspoon honey
Salt and pepper

Risotto:
½ cup diced shallots
2 plus 2 tablespoons butter
1 cup Arborio rice
⅓ cup dry white wine
1 plus 1 cup vegetable stock
3 cups water
¼ cup grated Parmesan cheese
¼ cup diced green olives
1 tablespoon diced golden raisins
1 stick cinnamon
2 bay leaves
Salt and pepper
1 tablespoon heavy cream

Scallops:
2 tablespoons olive oil
6 fresh scallops in shell
2 tablespoons butter

Combine salad ingredients in small mixing bowl and whisk until incorporated. Season to taste and set aside.

For risotto, in large skillet sweat shallots until soft in 2 tablespoons butter over medium heat. Add rice and stir 2 to 3 minutes. Add wine, stirring until absorbed. Increase heat to medium high and stir in 1 cup hot vegetable stock. Cook, uncovered, stirring frequently, until broth is absorbed. Continue stirring and add remaining 1 cup broth and water, allowing each cup to be absorbed before adding another, until rice is tender and mixture has creamy consistency. It will take 25 to 30 minutes. Stir in cheese, olives, raisins, cinnamon stick, bay leaves, salt and pepper to taste, cream, and remaining 2 tablespoons butter. Stir until mixture is creamy, about 2 minutes.

For scallops, in large sauté pan heat olive oil over medium-high heat. Sear scallops until golden brown on each side, 2 to 3 minutes for each side. Serve on top of risotto. Put salad on top of scallops. Yields 6 servings.

Hot Crab and Artichoke Dip

1 (8-ounce) package cream cheese, softened
½ cup sour cream
2 tablespoons mayonnaise
1 tablespoon lemon juice
1¼ teaspoons Worcestershire sauce
½ teaspoon dry mustard
Pinch of garlic salt
1 tablespoon milk
¼ cup grated Cheddar cheese
1 (6-ounce) can crabmeat
1 (16-ounce) can artichoke hearts, drained and chopped
Paprika

Preheat oven to 325°. In large bowl mix cream cheese, sour cream, mayonnaise, lemon juice, Worcestershire sauce, mustard, and garlic salt until smooth. Add enough milk to make mixture creamy. Stir in half of cheese. Fold crabmeat and artichoke hearts into cream cheese mixture. Pour into greased 1-quart casserole. Top with remaining cheese. Bake until mixture

is bubbly and browned on top, about 30 minutes. Sprinkle top with paprika and serve with toasted French bread. Yields about 3 cups.

Hungarian Gulyás Soup

5 cups beef stock or broth
4 cups water
3 medium onions, peeled and chopped
4 to 5 ribs celery, diced
2 (16-ounce) cans diced tomatoes
1 tablespoon caraway seeds
Salt and white pepper
1 pound beef tips, browned
4 potatoes, peeled and diced
¼ cup finely chopped fresh parsley
Sour cream

Bring stock and water to boil. Add onions, celery, tomatoes, caraway seeds, and salt and pepper to taste. To stock, add beef tips and potatoes and simmer 45 minutes or until meat is fork tender. Ladle into bowls and top with parsley and sour cream. Yields 6 to 8 servings.

TRILLIUM

E 10596 East Salem Ridge Road
La Forge, WI 54639
(608) 625-4492
www.bbonline.com/wi/trillium/index.html

Trillium is an eighty-five-acre family farm that offers a private fully-furnished guest cottage with full bath, complete kitchen, porch, stone fireplace, generous breakfast, woods and fields, variety of livestock and privacy. Within a few miles of the farm are state historic sites, antique stores, restaurants, three rivers, lakes,

numerous trout streams, horseback riding stables, canoe rentals, hiking trails, bird-watching, cheese factories, the largest Amish community in Wisconsin, ethnic and seasonal festivals, and more.

Whole Wheat Bagels

This recipe requires about 2½ to 3 hours of preparation and baking time.

1½ cups warm water
3 tablespoons honey
2 tablespoons active dry yeast
2 large eggs, beaten
2 tablespoons oil
1 teaspoon salt
4 cups whole wheat flour
1 to 2 cups all-purpose flour to prevent dough from sticking

In large mixing bowl combine warm water, honey, and yeast. Allow yeast to completely dissolve (12 to 15 minutes) until mixture is frothy. Stir in eggs; add oil; stir in salt. One cup at a time, stir in whole wheat flour to form very soft dough. Add enough all-purpose flour to form firm dough. Turn dough out onto floured surface, using extra flour as needed. Work dough by kneading 15 minutes. Place dough in oiled bowl, cover, put in warm spot, and let rise for an hour or so until doubled in volume. Punch dough down. Turn out onto floured surface and divide dough into eighteen equal portions. Using large saucepan bring to a boil 2 quarts water plus 2 tablespoons sugar. Roll each dough section out into rope shape about 8 inches in length. Shape into bagels. One at a time, drop bagels into boiling water, 3 or 4 at a time, until they float, about 2 minutes. Remove bagels to a clean, dry dishtowel. Preheat oven to 400°. Place individual bagels on ungreased cookie sheets and bake 15 to 20 minutes. Yields 18 bagels.

Note: Once completely cooled, store any unused portions in airtight container.

Cherry Cobbler

This recipe requires about 1 hour 20 minutes of preparation and baking time.

¼ plus 1 cup sugar
3 tablespoons melted butter
1 cup all-purpose flour
¼ teaspoon salt
1 teaspoon baking powder
½ cup milk
3½ cups pitted fresh cherries
1 tablespoon cornstarch
1 cup boiling water

In medium-size mixing bowl, combine ¾ cup sugar, butter, flour, salt, and baking powder. Stir in milk. Grease 9-inch baking dish (glass pie pan works well) with butter. Preheat oven to 350°. Place prepared cherries in baking dish evenly over baking surface. Spoon batter over cherries. In small bowl, combine remaining 1 cup sugar with cornstarch. Stir in boiling water. Pour mixture over batter on top of cherries because as cobbler bakes, surface will smooth out over bubbling cherries. Yields 8 servings.

Note: This recipe is excellent when served topped with whipped cream. After completely cool, store any unused portion in airtight container in refrigerator.

Poppy Seed Puffs

This recipe requires about 2½ hours preparation and baking time.

2 tablespoons honey
1 tablespoon melted butter
1 cup plain yogurt
¼ cup warm water
1 tablespoon active dry yeast
1 egg
1 teaspoon salt
2 teaspoons poppy seeds
2¼ cups whole wheat flour

In small saucepan melt together honey, butter, and yogurt. In small bowl, combine warm water and yeast and allow to sit 10 to 15 minutes until thoroughly dissolved. Place warm butter mixture in medium-size mixing bowl. Add dissolved yeast mixture. Stir together. Mix in egg.

Add salt, then poppy seeds. One cup at a time, stir in whole wheat flour to form soft dough. Turn dough out onto floured surface and knead dough 12 to 15 minutes, using small amount of additional flour to prevent sticking. Place dough in oiled bowl, cover, set in warm place, and allow to rise at least 1 hour. Punch down dough and divide into 12 equal portions. Form each portion into ball of dough and place in oiled muffin tin. Cover and let rise 30 minutes. Preheat oven to 400°. Place muffin tin in oven and bake 15 to 20 minutes until nicely browned. Yields 12 puffs.

Note: Store unused portions of baked puffs in an airtight container. Puffs are most tasty when eaten the day baked.

EAGLE HARBOR INN

9914 Water Street
Ephraim, WI 54211
(920) 854-2121 (phone)
(800) 324-5427 (toll free)
nedd@eagleharbor.com
www.eagleharbor.com

Eagle Harbor Inn is a graciously appointed nine-room inn, all with private baths, some with whirlpools and fireplaces. The inn offers a main street location in Ephraim's historic district. It is an easy walk to Ephraim's white-sand beach, wonderful shops, and intriguing galleries.

Trillium

...d Danish

...cup plus 1½ cups plus 2 tablespoons
    butter
1 plus 1 cup all-purpose flour
2 tablespoons plus 1 cup water
1 teaspoon almond extract
3 eggs
1½ cups confectioners' sugar
1½ teaspoons vanilla extract
2 tablespoons warm water

Blend ½ cup butter, 1 cup flour, and 2 table-spoons water together. Spread into two strips 3 x 12 inches. Bring 1½ cups butter and 1 cup water to a boil. Remove from heat. Add almond extract and remaining 1 cup flour. Cook over low heat until mixture forms ball. Beat in eggs. Spread on top of dough strips. Bake at 350° for 60 minutes. Mix together confectioners' sugar, remaining 2 tablespoons butter, vanilla, and warm water. Frost Danish when cool. Yields 16 slices.

Cinnamon Pecan Coffee Cake

2¼ cups unbleached flour
½ teaspoon salt
1 plus 1 teaspoon ground cinnamon
¼ teaspoon ginger
1 cup brown sugar
¾ cup granulated sugar
¾ cup corn oil
1 cup chopped pecans
1 teaspoon baking soda
1 teaspoon baking powder
1 egg, beaten
1 cup buttermilk

Preheat oven to 350°. Grease a 13 x 9 x 2-inch pan. Mix flour, salt, 1 teaspoon cinnamon, ginger, sugars, and oil together, reserving ¾ cup mixture for topping. Add nuts and remaining 1 teaspoon cinnamon to reserved ¾ cup topping mixture. Add baking soda, baking powder, egg, and buttermilk to flour mixture. Pour batter into

greased pan and sprinkle on topping. Bake 35 to 45 minutes. Yields 12 servings.

Nedd's Apple Cake

3 cups all-purpose flour
1 tablespoon baking powder
½ teaspoon salt
4 large Granny Smith apples,
    peeled and sliced
¼ cup plus 1¾ cups sugar
1 teaspoon ground cinnamon
1 cup corn oil
4 large eggs
½ cup fresh orange juice
2 teaspoons vanilla extract

Preheat oven to 350°. Combine flour, baking powder, and salt. Combine apples, ¼ cup sugar, and cinnamon. In large bowl beat oil, eggs, remaining 1¾ cups sugar, orange juice, and vanilla. Add flour mixture to egg mixture and stir until blended. Layer cake batter with apple mixture in greased 9 x 13-inch pan and bake 50 to 60 minutes. Yields 16 servings.

Cherry Streusel

<u>Muffin batter:</u>
1½ cups unbleached all-purpose flour
¼ cup granulated sugar
¼ cup packed brown sugar
2 teaspoons baking powder
¼ teaspoon salt
1 teaspoon ground cinnamon
1 egg, slightly beaten
¼ cup (½ stick) melted unsalted butter
½ cup milk
1 cup cherries
1 teaspoon grated lemon zest

<u>Streusel topping:</u>
½ cup chopped pecans
½ cup packed dark brown sugar
¼ cup unbleached flour
1 teaspoon ground cinnamon
1 teaspoon grated lemon zest
2 tablespoons melted unsalted butter

Preheat oven to 350°. Line 12 muffin cups with paper liners. For muffin batter, sift flour, sugars, baking powder, salt, and cinnamon together into medium-size mixing bowl and make well in center. Place egg, melted butter, and milk in well. Stir with wooden spoon just until ingredients are combined. Quickly stir in cherries and lemon zest. Fill each muffin cup three-fourths full with batter.

For streusel topping, combine pecans, brown sugar, flour, cinnamon, and lemon zest in small bowl. Pour in melted butter and stir to combine. Sprinkle mixture evenly over top of each muffin. Bake until nicely browned and firm, 20 to 25 minutes. Yields 1 dozen muffins.

WHITE LACE INN

16 North 5th Avenue
Sturgeon Bay, WI 54235
(920) 743-1105 (phone)
(920) 743-8180 (fax)
(877) 948-5223 (toll free)
romance@whitelaceinn.com
www.WhiteLaceInn.com

Romance and relaxation in Door County begin as you follow the winding garden paths that link the four historic homes and their eighteen inviting rooms. Door County is truly a playground for all seasons. Outdoor recreation includes eleven golf courses, miles of biking and hiking trails, beaches, horseback riding, and kayaking. In the winter, there are more than 100 miles of trails for cross country skiing and snowmobiling. In addition, there are wonderful shops, galleries, museums, and fine restaurants, many right in Sturgeon Bay and within walking distance of the White Lace Inn.

Scandinavian Fruit Soup

3 cups apple cider
1 lemon, cut in half lengthwise
    and thinly sliced
1 orange, cut in half lengthwise
    and thinly sliced
½ cup golden raisins or to taste
2 sticks cinnamon
½ teaspoon ground cinnamon
⅛ teaspoon allspice
Pinch of ground cloves
5 pounds peaches, sliced
5 pounds pears, sliced
1 (16-ounce) can cherries

In large kettle combine cider, lemon, orange, raisins, cinnamon sticks, ground cinnamon, allspice, and cloves. Cover and simmer until rinds are soft, about 20 minutes. Add fruits. Simmer another 15 minutes. Yields 20 servings.

Note: This recipe makes a large amount. You can cut recipe in half. Serve soup warm or cold. Great served warm or cold over rice pudding. Keeps at least a week in refrigerator.

Cherie's Creamy Rice Pudding

2½ cups medium-grain rice
2 tablespoons butter (optional)
1½ cups sugar
2½ plus 1½ cups half-and-half
2 teaspoons vanilla extract
4 eggs
1 cup golden raisins

Cook rice in 5½ cups water in covered heavy kettle over low heat until water is just absorbed, 15 to 20 minutes. Turn heat off and let sit with lid on about 10 minutes. Add butter, sugar, and 2½ cups half-and-half. Turn heat on and barely simmer on low about 30 to 40 minutes, stirring every 10 minutes. In separate large bowl,

mix together vanilla, eggs, and remaining 1½ cups of half-and-half. To egg mixture, add hot rice mixture 1 tablespoon at a time, stirring constantly until at least half rice mixture is in egg mixture. Then pour mixture back into original pan and cook 10 minutes covered and 10 minutes uncovered, stirring every 5 minutes. Add raisins and cook another 5 minutes. Cool 15 minutes, stirring occasionally. Refrigerate in glass or plastic container. A sprinkle of nutmeg or cinnamon may be added as garnish when served. Yields 6 to 8 servings.

Note: You can serve warm (not hot) after you make it, reheating slightly in microwave or serve chilled. Always use medium-grain rice and heavy kettle. If rice starts to stick to bottom of pan while cooking, remove from burner and let stand for 5 minutes. You can substitute chopped dried apricots, dried cherries, or experiment.

Cherry Almond Cream Cheese French Toast

1 loaf white bread, cubed
4 cups frozen Door County cherries,
    rinsed and drained
16 ounces softened cream cheese
½ plus ½ cup sugar
1 plus 1 teaspoon almond extract
½ cup sour cream
½ loaf French bread, cut in
    10 (1-inch) slices
7 eggs
1½ cups milk
1½ cups half-and-half
¼ cup confectioners' sugar
1 cup sliced almonds

Place bread cubes in greased 9 x 13-inch pan. Spread cherries over cubes. Microwave cream cheese to soften. Add ½ cup sugar, 1 teaspoon almond extract, and sour cream to cream cheese. Spread over cherries. Place bread slices over cherries. Beat eggs well, add remaining ½ cup sugar,

remaining 1 teaspoon alm
milk, and half-and-half and
Pour egg mixture over bread
and refrigerate 8 to 10 hours or overnight. When ready to cook, preheat oven to 350°. Bake covered with tinfoil 40 to 50 minutes. Uncover for last 10 minutes to brown slightly. Let sit about 10 minutes. Sprinkle top with confectioners' sugar and almonds before slicing. Yields 10 servings.

Veggie Hash Brown Egg Bake

½ cup (1 stick) butter
1 (32 ounce) package frozen hash
    browns, thawed
1 tablespoon onion salt
2 bunches green onions, chopped
2 cups plus 1 cup grated Cheddar cheese
¾ loaf white bread, crust removed
    and cubed
¼ cup chopped green pepper
¼ cup chopped red pepper
¼ cup chopped yellow pepper
1 (8-ounce) package fresh mushrooms,
    thinly sliced
2 cups grated Monterey Jack cheese
1 large tomato, thinly sliced
7 eggs, beaten
1½ cups milk
1½ cups half-and-half
1 teaspoon dry mustard
Salt and pepper
Paprika or cayenne (optional)
Dash of parsley flakes (optional)

Mix butter with hash browns. Spread hash browns into greased 9 x 13-inch pan. Sprinkle with onion salt. Bake 20 minutes. Let cool. Sprinkle green onions, then 2 cups Cheddar cheese over hash browns. Place bread cubes over cheese. Microwave peppers together for 2 minutes. Sprinkle pepper mixture and mushrooms over bread. Sprinkle Monterey Jack over veggies. Place tomato slices over cheese, then remaining 1 cup Cheddar over tomato. Beat eggs and add milk, half-and-half, dry mustard, salt and pepper to taste and beat together. Pour over pan evenly. Sprinkle top with paprika or cayenne pepper and parsley flakes, if using. Cover and refrigerate 8 to 10 hours or overnight. When ready to cook, preheat oven to 350° and bake 45 minutes covered with aluminum foil, then uncovered for 15 minutes to let brown slightly. Let sit about 10 minutes before slicing. Yields 10 servings.

HISTORIC BENNETT HOUSE BED & BREAKFAST

825 Oak Street
Wisconsin Dells, WI 53965
(608) 254-2500
www.historicbennetthouse.com

Historic Bennett House was built in 1863 and is listed on the National Register of Historic places. It was owned by Henry Hamilton Bennett, who was a pioneer photographer of the Wisconsin Dells area. His work is in the Smithsonian, and his photographs are world renowned. The Bennett Museum is located a half-block from the home in downtown Dells. Breakfast is served rather formally on fine china, crystal glasses, and silver utensils. Our guests enjoy this inviting and relaxing breakfast, and they use this time to exchange stories and experiences as well as to enjoy the food.

Rhubarb Bread Extraordinaire

1½ cups packed light brown sugar
⅔ cup vegetable oil
1 egg at room temperature
1 cup buttermilk
1 teaspoon salt
1 teaspoon baking soda
1 teaspoon vanilla extract
2½ cups all-purpose flour
2 cups diced rhubarb
½ cup chopped walnuts
½ cup granulated sugar
2 tablespoons butter, softened

Preheat oven to 350°. Coat two 8 x 4-inch bread pans with nonstick spray. Combine brown sugar with oil and beat until smooth. Stir in eggs, buttermilk, salt, soda, vanilla, and flour. Blend just until moistened. Fold in rhubarb and nuts. Pour into prepared pans. Combine granulated sugar and butter until crumbly. Sprinkle over batter. Bake 50 to 55 minutes, or until toothpick inserted in center comes out clean. Turn onto racks to cool. Yields 2 loaves.

Gail's Bennett House Original

3 plus 4 tablespoons butter
3 tablespoons all-purpose flour
2 cups milk
1½ cups Cheddar cheese
1½ cups processed cheese
5 hard-cooked eggs
1 (10½-ounce) can asparagus cuts, drained
1 cup Italian breadcrumbs
Salt and pepper
¼ pound honey ham, chopped

Preheat oven to 350°. Melt 3 tablespoons butter in medium pan over low heat. Add flour and milk and stir until thickens. Add both cheeses and stir until melted. Remove from heat. Slice 3 eggs and crumble 2. Drain asparagus. Melt remaining 4 tablespoons butter in saucepan. Add breadcrumbs (more if necessary) and stir until browned. Pour one-third of cheese sauce on bottom of quiche pan Add one-third of asparagus. Add one-third of eggs and salt and pepper to taste. Add one-third of ham. Pour over more cheese sauce. Repeat layers until all ingredients have been used except breadcrumbs. Sprinkle breadcrumbs over all and bake until heated through. Yields 4 servings.

Eggs Bennett

12 large eggs
2 tablespoons water
Salt and pepper
½ cup sour cream
½ pound honey ham, chopped
⅓ cup grated sharp Cheddar cheese

Preheat oven to 350°. Coat quiche dish and medium fry pan with nonstick spray. Beat eggs well in bowl and add water. Add salt and pepper to taste. Scramble eggs in fry pan, using a high-heat spatula to turn eggs. Remove from heat and place in quiche dish. Spread sour cream over eggs and work in so flavor is throughout. Sprinkle chopped ham over eggs. Sprinkle grated Cheddar cheese over all. Bake 8 to 10 minutes. Yields 4 servings.

Frozen Banana Pineapple Cups

3 cups water
1½ cups sugar
1 (6-ounce) can frozen orange juice, thawed
1 (20-ounce) can crushed pineapple, undrained
2⅔ cups mashed bananas

Combine all ingredients, mix well, and pour into 9 x 13-inch pan. Freeze 24 hours. Take out 20 to 30 minutes before serving. Scrape out amount desired. Refreeze remaining mix. Yields 12 servings.

THE WASHINGTON HOUSE INN

W 62, N 573 Washington Avenue
Cedarburg, WI 53012
(262) 375-3550 (phone)
(800) 554-4717 (toll free)
whinn@execpc.com
www.washingtonhouseinn.com

The Washington House was Cedarburg's first inn, built in 1846. In 1886 the original structure was replaced by the present Victorian cream, city brick building. The Washington House existed as a hotel until the 1920s, when it was converted into offices and apartments. In 1983 its ownership changed hands and the building was renovated to restore the Washington House to its original use as an inn. It is listed on the National Register of Historic Places. The Romance of country Victorian comes alive as you enter Cedarburg's historic bed and breakfast inn. A lovely collection of antique Victorian furniture, marble trimmed fireplace and fresh-cut flowers offer you a warm reception. A comfortable, elegant room awaits you.

Sunrise Farm Biscuits

4 cups biscuit mix
1½ cups buttermilk
1 cup chopped ham
1½ cups shredded Swiss cheese
¾ cup finely chopped scallions

Preheat oven to 450°. Mix biscuit mix with buttermilk. Add chopped ham, Swiss cheese, and scallions. Let it sit 10 minutes. Spray cookie sheet. Drop biscuits by heaping tablespoonfuls onto sheet. Bake 8 to 10 minutes. Remove from oven and imme-diately remove from pan. Serve with butter, preserves, or apple butter. Yields 18 to 20 biscuits.

Kate's Pineapple Walnut Soda Bread

4 cups all-purpose flour
¾ cup sugar
1 tablespoon baking powder
1 teaspoon baking soda
¼ teaspoon cream of tartar
½ teaspoon salt
¾ cup (1½ sticks) margarine
    or butter, softened
1 cup crushed pineapple, well drained
⅔ cup chopped walnuts
1½ cups buttermilk
2 eggs

Preheat oven to 325°. Mix flour, sugar, baking powder, baking soda, cream of tartar, and salt together. Cut in margarine, using pastry blender. Add pineapple and walnuts. Toss to mix. Whisk together buttermilk and eggs and add to dry ingredients. Pour into greased 9-inch round pan. Bake 1 hour and 10 minutes. Yields 1 round loaf.

Blueberry Tea Cake

¾ plus ¾ cup sugar
½ cup plus 2 cups all-purpose flour
1 teaspoon ground cinnamon
½ plus ½ cup butter, softened
2 teaspoons baking powder
½ teaspoon salt
1 egg, beaten
½ cup milk
1½ cups blueberries

Mix ¾ cup sugar, ½ cup flour, and cinnamon. Cut in ½ cup butter to form crumbs and set aside for topping. Preheat oven to 350°. Mix remaining 2 cups flour, baking powder, and salt. Cream together remaining ½ cup butter and remaining ¾ cup sugar and add egg. Add dry ingredients to creamed mixture alternately with milk. Fold in blueberries. Pour cake mixture into greased and floured 9 x 13-inch pan. Top with crumb topping. Bake 40 minutes. Yields 1 cake.

JUSTIN TRAILS RESORT

7452 Kathryn Avenue
Sparta, WI 54656
(608) 269-4522 (phone)
(800) 488-4521 (toll free)
info@justintrails.com
www.justintrails.com

Justin Trails Resort is your center for recreation, relaxation, and romantic atmosphere set in a private valley surrounded by hardwood forests. There is lodging in cabins and suites with whirlpools and fireplaces. Recreate with disc golf, Nordic skiing, snowshoeing, dog sledding, snow tubing, star-studded sky, hiking trails, bird-watching, ponds, and gardens.

Migas

1 medium potato, sliced
½ cup chopped red bell pepper
½ cup chopped green bell pepper
½ cup chopped onion
½ cup chopped mushrooms
4 eggs, scrambled
½ teaspoon salt
½ teaspoon white pepper
½ teaspoon ground cumin
½ teaspoon thyme
½ cup corn chips
Salsa
Italian parsley

Sauté potato, peppers, and onion until tender. Add mushrooms, scrambled eggs, salt and pepper, cumin, thyme, and corn

...r heat to cook eggs until they ...hine. Serve with salsa on the ...h with Italian parsley or other herbs. Yields 6 servings.

and sugar and sprinkle top. Bake 15 to 20 minutes. Yields 24 medium cupcakes.

Chocolate Cream Cheese Raspberry Muffins

<u>Muffins:</u>
1 cup sugar
⅔ cup canola oil
2 eggs
1 teaspoon almond extract
3 cups all-purpose flour
1 teaspoon salt
2 teaspoons baking soda
2 teaspoons baking powder
½ cup cocoa
½ cup milk
1 cup vanilla yogurt

<u>Filling:</u>
1 cup fresh or frozen raspberries
8 ounces reduced-fat cream cheese
⅓ cup sugar
1 cup milk chocolate chips
1 egg
¼ teaspoon salt
1 tablespoon lemon juice

<u>Topping:</u>
1 teaspoon ground cinnamon
½ cup sugar

Preheat oven to 375°. For muffins, cream sugar and oil, add eggs and almond extract, and beat. Mix flour, salt, baking soda, baking powder, and cocoa and add alternately to egg mixture with milk and yogurt. Fill paper-lined cupcake tins one-third full with batter.

For filling, sprinkle fresh or frozen raspberries on top of batter. Do not thaw raspberries. Beat cream cheese, sugar, chips, egg, salt, and lemon juice together until smooth. Drop full teaspoon of cheese mixture in each cupcake tin. Cover with small scoop of cupcake batter. Mix cinnamon

Pumpkin Pie Chocolate Chip Muffins

2 cups brown sugar
1 cup canola oil
4 eggs
1 cup pumpkin
2 cups chocolate chips
1½ cups plain yogurt
½ cup crystallized ginger
2 teaspoons orange zest
3½ cups all-purpose flour
2 teaspoons baking soda
1 teaspoon salt
1 teaspoon ground nutmeg
1 tablespoon ground cinnamon
1 tablespoon ground ginger
¼ teaspoon cloves

Preheat oven to 375°. Cream sugar and oil. Add eggs. Beat. Stir in pumpkin, chocolate chips, yogurt, crystallized ginger, and orange zest. Mix dry ingredients together. Add one-third to liquids and gently stir. Add one-third more and gently stir, but do *not* blend. Add remaining dry ingredients and stir just until moist. Use ice cream scoop to pour batter into paper-lined, medium-size muffin tins. Bake 15 minutes. (340° in convection oven for 17 minutes.) Yields 2½ dozen muffins.

The Inn at Pine Terrace

351 Lisbon Road
Oconomowoc, WI 53066
(262) 567-7463 (phone)
(262) 567-7532 (fax)
innkeeper@innatpineterrace.com
www.innatpineterrace.com

This twelve-guest-room restored Victorian mansion welcomes travelers to an uncommon European-styled elegance that is enhanced by many contemporary amenities. Activities enjoyed by the inn's guests include hiking, bird-watching, cycling, roller blading, golf, tennis, swimming (in the inn's outdoor pool or at local beaches), horseback riding, elegant and casual dining at local and area restaurants, museums, antiquing, numerous festivals, and concerts.

Peach Appetizer

½ cup cider vinegar
½ cup loosely packed light brown sugar
½ cup granulated sugar
½ cup seeded and diced sweet red pepper
½ cup peeled and diced white onion
⅓ cup white raisins
1 tablespoon finely chopped garlic
1 tablespoon grated ginger
½ teaspoon salt
1½ pounds firm fresh peaches
    (or nectarines), blanched to
    remove pit and skin, diced

Place vinegar and sugars in saucepan over medium heat and bring to a boil. Add red pepper, onion, raisins, garlic, ginger, and salt. Simmer 15 minutes. Add peaches (or nectarines) and simmer additional 15 minutes. For thicker syrup, mixture can be simmered a bit longer to reduce liquid. Remove from heat and allow to cool at room temperature. Mixture can then be refrigerated for up to two weeks. Serve at room temperature over chunk of cream cheese with crackers. Yields 2½ cups.

Cheddar Spread

1 pound sharp Cheddar cheese, grated
¾ cup mayonnaise
1 small onion, finely chopped
1 clove garlic, pressed
⅛ teaspoon Tabasco
2 tablespoons minced chives
2 tablespoons green onion tops
1 cup chopped pecans
1 cup strawberry or raspberry preserves

Combine all ingredients except preserves in bowl and mix thoroughly. Put in ramekin, two-cup mold, or ceramic dish. Chill for several hours. Mixture will come together when chilled. Take out of mold and serve with preserves on the side. Cocktail rye bread, water wafers, or butter crackers work well with this hors d'oeuvre. Yields 4 cups.

Fried Walnuts

6 to 8 cups water
4 cups walnuts
¼ cup brandy or bourbon
½ cup sugar
Vegetable oil or canola oil
2 tablespoons salt mixed with
    ½ teaspoon paprika and
    ½ teaspoon black pepper

Bring water and liquor to a boil in large kettle. Add nuts and boil 1 to 2 minutes. Remove nuts and rinse thoroughly under very hot water. Drain and while still hot place nuts in separate bowl and toss with sugar until sugar melts. Heat oil (1½ inches) in frying pan to about 360°. Add 2 cups nuts at a time and fry 3 to 5 minutes or until golden brown. (Be careful when adding nuts to oil because it will splatter.) Drain. Spread nuts in single layer on cookie sheet and sprinkle with paprika mixture. Cover tightly and store at room temperature for up to a week or freeze indefinitely. Yields 4 cups.

The Inn at Pine Terrace

THE HILLCREST INN & CARRIAGE HOUSE

540 Storle Avenue
Burlington, WI 53105
(262) 763-4706 (phone)
(262) 763-7871 (fax)
(800) 313-9030 (toll free)
hillcrest@thehillcrestinn.com
www.thehillcrestinn.com

The Hillcrest Inn & Carriage House is a romantic, luxurious, and private wooded four-acre estate with magnificent view. English flower gardens and walking paths abound. The stately 1908 Edwardian home with elegant carriage house offers period antiques, lovely decor, queen-size beds, fireplaces, and whirlpools. Activities while visiting the inn include biking, nature walks, golf, antiques, boating, skiing, shopping, swimming, and horseback riding. Lake Geneva, Old World Wisconsin, and the Bristol Renaissance Faire are nearby.

Victorian Cobbler

1 (12-ounce) bag frozen raspberries
1 (12-ounce) bag frozen strawberries,
    blueberries, or cranberries
½ cup chopped pecans
½ plus ½ cup sugar
½ cup chocolate chips
½ cup (1 stick) melted butter
2 eggs
1 cup all-purpose flour

Preheat oven to 350°. Place berries, nuts, ½ cup sugar, and chocolate chips in 9 x 13-inch pottery or porcelain baking dish. In

The Hillcrest Inn & Carriage House

Preheat oven to 350°. Combine eggs, flour, and baking powder in large bowl. Stir in cheeses. In skillet melt butter and lightly sauté onion and drained artichokes in seasoned salt. Stir artichoke mixture into cheese mixture and blend well. Pour into greased 9 x 13-inch baking dish. Bake uncovered 1 hour until mixture is set and golden brown. Let stand a few minutes. Cut into 8 portions and serve on plates. Garnish with dollop of sour cream and fresh or dried basil leaves. Yields 10 to 12 servings.

Chocolate Cream Cheese Whispers in Raspberry Sauce

Raspberry sauce:
1 cup raspberry juice from fresh
   or frozen berries
1 tablespoon cornstarch

Whispers:
½ cup chocolate chips
1½ tablespoons butter
1 (3-ounce) package cream cheese,
   softened
3 tablespoons confectioners' sugar
1 (15-count) package mini phyllo shells.
Chocolate leaf dessert decorations
   (optional)

To prepare raspberry sauce, bring raspberry juice to boil in small saucepan. Add cornstarch, whisk to incorporate, and cook until thickened. Sauce may be made in advance and refrigerated.

For whispers, combine chocolate chips and butter in small microwave-safe bowl. Microwave on high, stirring at 20-second intervals, until melted and smooth. In another small bowl combine cream cheese and confectioners' sugar and beat until smooth. Assemble by placing 2 tablespoons raspberry sauce on each dessert plate. Place 1 or 2 phyllo shells on sauce. In each shell place 1 teaspoon cream cheese mixture and 1 teaspoon chocolate mixture. Serve immediately or store in refrigerator

medium bowl combine remaining ½ cup sugar, butter, eggs, and flour. Spread batter over berry mixture. Bake 40 minutes or until top is golden brown and berry mixture is bubbly. Spoon into custard cups and serve warm. Yields 8 servings.

Chocolate Pecan Strudel

1 (16-ounce) package frozen
   phyllo dough
1 egg, beaten
1 tablespoon water
12 ounces chocolate chips
4 tablespoons half-and-half
½ cup chopped pecans, chopped
Confectioners' sugar (optional)

Thaw dough at room temperature 30 minutes. Preheat oven to 350°. Mix egg and water in small bowl. Microwave chocolate chips and half-and-half in medium bowl 1½ minutes or until chocolate is almost melted. Stir until chocolate is completely

cookie sheet. Spread chocolate mixture evenly on pastry to within ½ inch of edges. Starting at long edge, roll pastry, placing seam down on cookie sheet and tucking ends to seal. Brush with egg mixture. Bake 35 minutes. Cool. May be prepared in advance and wrapped in foil until serving time. Slice into ¾-inch pieces. Place on dessert plate and dust with confectioners' sugar if desired. Yields 8 servings.

Cheesy Artichoke Egg Bake

10 eggs
½ cup all-purpose flour
1 teaspoon baking powder
1 (16-ounce) carton cottage cheese
2 cups shredded colby Jack cheese
¼ cup (½ stick) butter
½ cup chopped onion
1 (13-ounce) can artichoke hearts
1 teaspoon seasoned salt
Sour cream
Fresh or dried basil leaves

up to 1 hour. If desired, decorate with shaved chocolate or chocolate dessert decorations. Yields 8 servings.

ANTON-WALSH HOUSE

202 Copper Street
Hurley, WI 54534-1339
(715) 561-2065
info@Anton-Walsh.com
www.Anton-Walsh.com

An intimate and historic bed and breakfast inn located in downtown Hurley, Wisconsin, the Anton-Walsh House features three uniquely styled rooms, each with a private bathroom. A hearty breakfast spotlighting the bounties of the wilderness and the dairy state is included with each night of your stay. Located in Wisconsin's north woods, the inn is a half-hour to one hundred waterfalls and Alpine skiing. Built in 1896, this inn is historic yet offers in-room, high-speed Internet connections.

Wild Rice Pudding with Cranberries

3 cups cooked wild rice*
   (Broken grain works especially well.)
¾ cup maple syrup
1 tablespoon vanilla extract
1 teaspoon ground cinnamon
3 eggs
1 cup sweetened dried cranberries
½ teaspoon ground nutmeg
   or ½ whole nutmeg, grated
3 cups heavy cream
Cinnamon sugar mix

Preheat oven to 350° with rack in center. Mix rice, maple syrup, vanilla, cinnamon, eggs, cranberries, and nutmeg thoroughly. Then stir in heavy cream. Pour entire mixture into large, flat casserole or individual ceramic bowls. Sprinkle top with cinnamon sugar mix. Bake 1 hour. Allow to cool 10 minutes before serving. Yields 6 hearty servings.

  *Note: It is very important that the rice is fully cooked and tender before mixing into this dish.

Eggs da Vinci

¼ cup heavy cream
½ whole nutmeg, grated
4 ounces finely chopped prosciutto ham
Freshly ground black pepper
12 ounces well-washed fresh spinach
4 egg yolks
Juice of ½ lemon (3 tablespoons)
½ teaspoon cayenne
½ pound (2 sticks) cold unsalted butter, cut into 10 pieces
4 English muffins, split, buttered, and toasted under broiler
8 poached eggs
Shredded Asiago cheese

In omelet pan, reduce heavy cream by about half. Add nutmeg, prosciutto, and black pepper. Add spinach, turning often to coat it with seasoned, reduced cream. Cook only lightly until spinach has wilted, but is not soggy or overdone. Whisk together egg yolks, lemon juice, and cayenne in top of double boiler (or better yet, in a stainless steel bowl that can be set over pot of simmering water). Add 2 pieces butter and set over simmering water. Whisking constantly, add more butter as other pieces melt into sauce. When sauce has thickened, remove from heat. On each plate, arrange two toasted English muffin halves. Top with creamed spinach and prosciutto. Place poached egg on spinach and top with sauce. Sprinkle with shredded Asiago cheese. Yields 4 servings.

WINDY HILLS

393 Happy Jack Road
Cheyenne, WY 82007
(307) 632-6423 (phone)
(307) 632-8906 (fax)
windycooki@aol.com
www.windyhillswyo.com

Guests of Windy Hills experience warm western Wyoming hospitality at its finest in our sixty-acre retreat. Located in the Laramie Mountains, it is nestled in the hills overlooking Granite Lake and the Medicine Bow National Forest. Guests can enjoy very private and varied upscale accommodations. A spectacular spa in a natural western setting will invigorate the senses after hiking, fishing, or canoeing on the lake.

American Danish English Crust

Unsalted butter
6 English muffins, halved
12 thin slices Havarti cheese
Honey
Fresh tomatoes, peaches, strawberries,
    or Granny Smith apples

Preheat oven broiler. Butter each English muffin half. Place buttered muffins on cookie sheet. Broil until golden brown. Place slice of cheese on each muffin half. Drizzle with honey. Broil until cheese is melted. Garnish with fresh tomatoes, peaches, strawberries, or Granny Smith apples. Yields 12 servings.

Gazpacho Dip

½ cup Italian dressing
1 (16-ounce) jar salsa
1 teaspoon garlic powder
½ teaspoon pepper
½ teaspoon salt
1 teaspoon coriander
1 teaspoon freshly chopped parsley
5 green onions, thinly sliced
1 (4-ounce) can chopped black olives
1 (4-ounce) can green chiles, do *not* drain
3 tomatoes, chopped
4 avocadoes, chopped
Tostado chips
1 cup sour cream (optional)

Combine Italian dressing, salsa, garlic powder, pepper, salt, coriander, parsley, onions, black olives, and chiles in bowl. Mix well. Chill at least 2 hours before serving. Stores well for 2 weeks. Fold in tomatoes and avocadoes. Serve on tostados. Garnish with dollop of sour cream. Yields 30 servings.

Windy Hills Egg Blossom

12 thin slices ham
Unsalted butter
3 slices French bread, divided into quarters
12 eggs
Salt and pepper
Fresh tarragon leaves or chives

Preheat oven to 400°. Coat 12-cup muffin pan with nonstick spray. Fit ham slice into each muffin cup. Ends will hang over sides. Butter bread and place quarter piece on top of ham. Crack egg on top of bread in each cup. Bake 15 to 20 minutes. Season eggs with salt and pepper and garnish with tarragon or chives. Remove muffins with two spoons. Yields 12 muffins.

Green Tea Tonic

This simple tonic cleanses, tones, and soothes when you are oh, so tired.

2 teaspoons powdered green tea
½ cup boiling water

Steep green tea in boiling water for 10 minutes and allow to cool. Apply tonic to face with cotton balls or gauze. Can be used daily. Yields ½ cup.

OLD STONE HOUSE BED & BREAKFAST

135 Wolf Creek Road
Ranchester, WY 82839
(307) 655-9239
oldstone@fiberpipe.net
www.wyomingbnb-ranchrec.com/osh.html

Old Stone House is a beautifully restored 1899 cattle baron's home, built of stone at the base of the Big Horn Mountains. A carved stone lion guards the grand parlor's rustic splendor from its place over the mantel. Rooms have private baths, king-size or queen-size beds, and breakfast is always a special occasion. Area attractions include the Big Horn Mountains with over one million acres for hiking, mountain biking, climbing, boating, fishing, camping, photography, and hunting. Opportunities for horseback riding, hang gliding, golfing, and even polo matches are in the area. Historical places to see include several museums, historic homes, forts, and historic downtown areas. The Battle of the Little Big Horn National Monument is one hour to the north.

Old Stone House Bed & Breakfast

Baked Scotch Eggs

Eggs:
18 ounces pork/turkey sausage
½ cup freshly chopped parsley
Pinch of ground sage
Pinch of ground thyme
Freshly ground pepper
12 eggs, hard-cooked and peeled
¾ cup all-purpose flour
Salt and pepper
2 beaten eggs
1 cup dry breadcrumbs

Dipping sauce:
2 cups mayonnaise
¼ cup white wine
1 tablespoon dry mustard
Salt
½ teaspoon Worcestershire sauce
⅛ teaspoon cayenne
1 tablespoon fresh lemon juice

Mix sausage with parsley, sage, thyme, and pepper and divide into twelve patties. Wrap each egg in sausage, covering egg completely. At this point you can refrigerate until ready to cook. Preheat oven to 450°. Combine flour with salt and pepper to taste. Roll sausage-covered eggs in flour mixture. Roll in beaten eggs, then in breadcrumbs. Place eggs on cooking sheet and bake 30 minutes.

For dipping sauce, mix ingredients together. This too can be made ahead and refrigerated. To serve, cut eggs into four lengthwise wedges and serve around small condiment dish on each guest's plate along with a toasted English muffin. Extra eggs are put whole in serving bowl on the table for seconds. Yields 12 servings.

Lemon Zucchini Bread

3 cups all-purpose flour
1 tablespoon baking powder
1 cup vegetable oil
2 cups sugar
2 tablespoons grated lemon zest
¼ cup lemon juice
3 eggs
1 pound grated zucchini
1 cup chopped pecans

Preheat oven to 350°. Mix flour and baking powder together in small bowl. In separate bowl mix oil, sugar, lemon zest, and lemon juice. Add eggs one at a time, beating after each addition. Add flour mixture to egg mixture and mix well. Add zucchini and pecans. Grease two 4 x 8-inch loaf pans and divide batter between them. Bake about 50 minutes or until toothpick comes out clean. Cool. Yields 24 servings. This bread freezes well.

Spicy Chicken Breast

4 boneless, skinless chicken breasts
1 teaspoon chopped fresh garlic
3 plus 4 tablespoons melted butter
3 tablespoons extra virgin olive oil
Salt and pepper
1 (16-ounce) jar garlic Alfredo sauce
⅓ cup extra dry vermouth
1 tablespoon extra hot pepper sauce
1 pound farfalle pasta, cooked and
   drained
½ cup chopped fresh parsley

Sauté chicken breasts and garlic in 3 tablespoons butter and olive oil over medium heat until done, about 10 minutes on each side. Season to taste with salt and pepper. Hold warm until serving. Mix Alfredo sauce, vermouth, remaining 4 tablespoons butter, and hot pepper sauce together. Heat through, being careful not to overcook sauce. Place serving of hot pasta on pasta plates, cover with sauce, and add chicken breasts. Sprinkle with parsley. Yields 4 servings.

Very Lemon Cookies

Cookies:
½ cup vegetable shortening
2 tablespoons butter
1 cup sugar
½ teaspoon vanilla extract
½ teaspoon lemon extract
1½ tablespoons fresh lemon zest
¼ teaspoon lemon juice
1½ cups all-purpose flour
1½ teaspoons baking powder
½ teaspoon baking soda

Frosting:
½ pound confectioners' sugar
¼ cup (½ stick) butter
¼ cup lemon juice

Preheat oven to 350°. With electric mixer cream together shortening, butter and sugar. Add vanilla, lemon extract, zest, and juice, beating mixture until smooth. Sift together flour, baking powder, and baking soda. Add to creamed mixture to form dough. Chill dough about 2 hours. Make 50 balls of cookie dough. (We freeze any dough balls that we may want to save for future use.) Placing on ungreased baking sheet and slightly flatten with spatula. Bake 8 to 10 minutes or until edges are just turning brown. Cookies will be thin and crisp. Cool cookies on rack.

For frosting, mix ingredients together with electric mixer. (We also freeze unused frosting for future use.) Frost cookies and chill about 30 minutes to firm frosting before serving. Yields 50 cookies.

A. DRUMMOND'S RANCH BED & BREAKFAST

399 Happy Jack Road
Cheyenne-Laramie, WY 82007
(307) 634-6042
adrummond@juno.com
www.adrummond.com

A. Drummond's Ranch Bed & Breakfast is situated between Laramie and Cheyenne in Wyoming ranch country. Tucked into a south-facing hillside, this lovely facility captures the serenity of its views of Rocky Mountain National Park to the south and Medicine Bow National Forest to the west. A beautiful gourmet breakfast is served at a time of the guests' choosing. Everything is made from scratch. As an added delight, the fragrance of homemade bread pervades the home almost every morning. Silver, china, crystal, and linens grace every meal creating an elegant but friendly ambiance. Guests are welcome to bring their own horses and ride in the fifty-five thousand acres of National Forest just down the road, take a hike at their leisure, rent a mountain bike, cross-country ski, or simply slow down and relax.

Yeast Waffles

1 (¼-ounce) package yeast
1¼ cups warm water
1½ cups all-purpose flour
¼ cup milk (skim or whole)
3 tablespoons butter
1½ tablespoons honey
1 teaspoon salt
2 large eggs

The night before or 8 to 10 hours before serving, dissolve yeast in warm water in 2-quart ceramic bowl. Mix in flour and cover with plastic wrap and set aside. When ready to cook, put milk, butter, honey, and salt in microwave and zap on high for about 30 seconds. Stir until butter is melted. Beat eggs well and whisk into flour mixture until well blended. About 15 minutes before baking, add liquid mixture and blend well. Cook waffles in preheated waffle iron about 5 to 6 minutes. This makes three waffles; it can be doubled. Serve with butter and maple syrup. Yields 2 to 3 servings.

Stuffed French Toast

1½ cups milk (skim or whole)
6 eggs
1 teaspoon vanilla extract
Butter at room temperature
8 slices frozen Texas toast
    or thick slices of bread
Low-fat cream cheese at
    room temperature
Diced apricots, peaches, strawberries,
    or any fruit or preserves
Brown sugar
Orange slice
Cherry Almond Sauce

Mix milk, eggs, and vanilla together in glass or ceramic bowl until well blended and smooth. Grease 8 x 8-inch glass pan. Lightly spread butter on one side of each piece of bread, and lightly spread other side with cream cheese. Place four bread slices, butter-side down, in pan and put fruit or preserves on each slice from edge to edge. Sprinkle lightly with about ¼ teaspoon brown sugar per slice of bread. Place remaining slices of bread on top with cream-cheese-side down and butter on top. Pour milk mixture over all and cover with plastic wrap. Refrigerate 8 to 10 hours or overnight. When ready to cook, preheat oven to 375° and bake about 35 minutes. Toast will puff up and turn golden brown on top. Serve with slice of orange, twisted and placed on top. Serve with real maple syrup or with Cherry Almond Sauce (see next recipe). Yields 6 servings.

Cherry Almond Sauce

1 (20-ounce) can cherry pie filling
¼ cup (½ stick) butter
⅓ cup packed brown sugar
¼ cup light corn syrup
½ teaspoon almond extract

Put all ingredients in small saucepan, mix well, and heat over low heat until well blended. Serve hot in small pitcher to pour over stuffed French toast or yeast waffles. Yields 2 cups.

Sheepwagon Carrot Cake

1⅓ cups water
1 cup raisins
1¼ cups sugar
2 cups grated carrots
1 teaspoon butter
1 teaspoon ground cinnamon
1 teaspoon cloves
1 teaspoon ground nutmeg
2⅓ cups all-purpose flour
½ teaspoon salt
2 teaspoons baking powder
1 cup chopped nuts (optional)

In medium saucepan mix together water, raisins, sugar, carrots, butter, and spices. Simmer over low heat for 5 minutes. Remove from heat, cover, and let rest 12 hours or overnight. When ready to cook, preheat oven to 300°. Sift together flour, salt, and baking powder. Mix dry ingredients with liquid ingredients well and pour equal portions into two loaf pans. Bake about 50 minutes. Cool and wrap in foil. Yields 2 loaves.

Blueberry Muffins

4 eggs at room temperature
2 cups sugar
1 cup light olive oil
1 teaspoon vanilla extract
1 cup whole wheat flour
3 cups all-purpose flour
1 teaspoon baking soda
2 teaspoons baking powder
1 teaspoon salt
2 cups light sour cream
3 cups fresh or frozen blueberries

Preheat oven to 400°. Put thirty muffin cups in tins. Beat eggs in metal or ceramic bowl on medium to high speed until well blended and gradually add sugar while still beating. Continue beating at slightly lower speed and slowly pour in oil, then vanilla. In separate bowl, combine flours, baking soda, baking powder, and salt. Alternately add dry ingredients and sour cream to egg mixture until well blended. Gently fold in blueberries and spoon into muffin cups about three-quarters full. Bake 20 minutes in conventional oven. Yields 30 muffins.

Note: You can make this with only all-purpose flour. This recipe can easily be halved or doubled, and you can freeze any leftovers.

THE HUFF HOUSE INN

240 E. Deloney
P.O. Box 1189
Jackson Hole, WY 83001
(307) 733-4164 (phone)
(307) 739-9091 (fax)
huffhousebnb@blissnet.com
www.jacksonwyomingbnb.com

At the Huff House Inn, a block and a half off the town square, you can truly experience downtown Jackson's unique shops, restaurants, museums, galleries, and activities. Then at day's end, withdraw to the inn's quietly elegant ambience. Mature cottonwoods and majestic pines protect you from Jackson's vibrant activity. The Huff House Inn features three spacious guest rooms in the main house and four recently built guest cottages, all with private baths. While retaining a sense of Jackson Hole as it was in the early part of this century, the Huff House's comfortable furnishings make your stay a warm and relaxing home away from home.

Orange Thyme Pancakes

2 cups all-purpose flour
1 teaspoon salt
2 teaspoons baking soda
¼ cup sugar
½ teaspoon ground thyme
2 eggs
1¾ cups orange juice
¼ cup (½ stick) melted butter

Mix dry ingredients in bowl. Beat eggs in separate bowl. Add orange juice and melted butter. Mix liquids into dry ingredients. If batter seems stiff, add a little more orange juice. Drop batter on griddle. Turn when bubbles start to form on top. Serve with Orange Butter Syrup (see next recipe). Yields 8 servings.

Orange Butter Syrup

½ cup (1 stick) melted butter
3 tablespoons cornstarch
⅔ cup sugar
1 tablespoon orange zest
2 cups orange juice
2 cups pure maple syrup

In small pan add butter, cornstarch, sugar, zest, and orange juice. Stir over medium heat until thickened to make orange butter. Mix equal parts of orange butter and maple syrup together. Heat in microwave until hot. Serve. Yields about 4½ cups.

Oven Omelets

¼ cup (½ stick) melted butter
18 eggs
1 cup milk
1 cup sour cream
1½ teaspoons salt
Chopped onion
¾ cup grated sharp Cheddar cheese
Sliced tomatoes

Preheat oven to 325°. Divide butter between two quiche pans. Mix together with a whisk eggs, milk, sour cream, and salt. Divide mixture between quiche pans. Top each with a little chopped onion and cheese and place sliced tomatoes to cover pans. Bake 40 minutes or until knife comes out clean. Cut each into six pieces. Yields 12 servings.

ADVENTURERS' COUNTRY BED & BREAKFAST

3803 I-80 S. Service Road
Cheyenne, WY 82009
(307) 632-4087 (phone/fax)
wht2@aol.com
www.bbonline.com/wy/adventurers/

Adventurers' Country Bed & Breakfast is located on Raven Cry Ranch and accepts children and board for your animals. There are four guest rooms and a suite—all with private bathrooms—a picturesque roaming front porch, and a beautiful courtyard. Activities in the area include Cheyenne Frontier Days, rodeos, old-fashioned melodramas, state capital, horse-drawn coach rides, and Cheyenne trolley rides.

♣   ♣   ♣

Grilled Stuffed Peach French Toast

4 tablespoons peach preserves
1 (8-ounce) package cream cheese, softened
1 (1-pound) loaf French bread, sliced 1-inch thick
6 eggs, beaten
1 cup milk or half-and-half
1 teaspoon sugar
1 teaspoon vanilla extract
Fresh peaches, sliced
Confectioners' sugar

Combine peach preserves and cream cheese in blender. Make pocket in each piece of French bread. Stuff each slice with 2 tablespoons of mixture. Put bread in single layer in large pan or dish. With wire whisk combine eggs, milk, sugar, and vanilla until well blended. Pour mixture over bread slices. Turn over once, carefully, so as not to tear bread, but just to coat evenly. Cover with plastic wrap and refrigerate 8 to 10 hours or overnight. When ready to cook, remove from refrigerator and take off plastic wrap about 30 minutes before grilling. Oil grill and brown each piece of filled bread well on both sides. Do *not* punch down bread. Serve each slice of toast with fresh peaches dusted with confectioners' sugar. Also good to serve a warmed maple syrup to drizzle over peaches. Yields 10 servings.

Sausage and Wild Rice

1 (6-ounce) package Uncle Ben's Long Grain and Wild Rice
1 pound bulk breakfast sausage
1 medium onion, chopped
½ green pepper, chopped
½ cup sliced mushrooms
¼ cup (½ stick) butter
¼ cup all-purpose flour
1½ cups chicken stock
Black pepper
¼ cup heavy cream

Cook rice according to package directions. Cook sausage, breaking into small pieces as it cooks and drain off all fat. Add onion, green pepper, mushrooms, and butter to sausage. Sauté just until onion is tender. Sprinkle with flour and mix well. Add chicken stock and black pepper. Stir and cook until thickened. Mix in heavy cream and remove from heat. At this point you may refrigerate cooked rice and sausage mixture separately. If you do this, bring ingredients to room temperature before baking. When ready to complete casserole, preheat oven to 350°. Combine rice and sausage and pour into buttered 2-quart dish. Bake 30 to 45 minutes until hot and bubbly. Yields 4 to 6 servings.

♣   ♣   ♣

Adventurers' Country Bed & Breakfast

Brunch Egg Bake

12 ounces shredded Cheddar cheese
12 ounces shredded mozzarella cheese
½ onion, chopped
½ green bell pepper, chopped
¼ cup (½ stick) butter or margarine
8 ounces ham, cooked and julienned
1 tomato, chopped
½ cup all-purpose flour
1¾ cups milk
2 tablespoons snipped fresh parsley
8 eggs, beaten
Seasoned salt

Preheat oven to 350°. In large bowl lightly toss cheeses together. Sprinkle half of cheese mixture in ungreased 13 x 9-inch baking dish. Cook onion and green pepper in margarine until tender. Arrange ham over vegetables. Sprinkle remaining cheese over meat. Place chopped tomato on top. In large bowl with wire whisk blend flour, milk, parsley, and eggs and pour over layers in baking dish. Add seasoned salt to taste. Bake 35 to 45 minutes until mixture is set and top is browned. Let stand 10 minutes. Cut into squares. Yields 12 servings.

Swiss Cheese and Vegetable Quiche

Pastry for 1 (9-inch) crust
1 cup shredded Swiss cheese
1 small tomato, diced
1 small green pepper, diced
1 small onion, diced
1 small yellow squash, diced
4 eggs, beaten
1 teaspoon Dijon mustard
Salt
1 cup half-and-half

Preheat oven to 350°. Lightly coat quiche pan with nonstick spray and line with pastry crust. Layer Swiss cheese, tomato, pepper, onion, and squash in crust. In small bowl blend eggs, mustard, salt to taste, and half-and-half. Pour evenly over vegetables in crust. Bake 45 minutes or until knife inserted 1 inch from center comes out clean. Yields 6 servings.

Cream Cheese Pound Cake

1½ cups (3 sticks) butter (no substitutes)
    at room temperature
1 (8-ounce) package cream cheese
    at room temperature
2½ cups sugar
6 eggs at room temperature
3 cups all-purpose flour
1 teaspoon vanilla extract
Brandy Sauce (see recipe below)

Preheat oven to 300°. In large bowl cream butter and cream cheese and gradually add sugar, beating until light and fluffy, 5 to 7 minutes. Add eggs, one at a time, beating well after each addition. Gradually add flour and beat just until blended. Stir in vanilla. Pour into greased and floured 10-inch tube pan. Bake 1½ hours or until cake is done. Do *not* overcook. Cool in pan 15 minutes before removing to wire rack. Cool completely. Serve with Brandy Sauce (see recipe below). Yields 12 servings.

Brandy Sauce

1 egg, beaten
1 cup sugar
¼ cup (½ stick) butter
4 tablespoons brandy
¾ cup whipping cream

In saucepan combine egg, sugar, and butter. Cook and stir until thick and boiling. Remove from heat and carefully stir in brandy. Slowly stir in whipping cream and cool slightly. Yields 1⅓ cups.

THE HOWDY PARDNER BED & BREAKFAST

1920 Tranquility Road
Cheyenne, WY 82009
(307) 634-6493 (phone)
(307) 634-2822 (fax)
janp9999@aol.com
www.howdypardner.net

The Howdy Pardner is authentic western hospitality. This ranch-style inn stands on a hill surrounded by ten acres of rolling grasslands dotted with pine and fir trees just five miles from the middle of downtown. Be prepared for a big "Howdy" from the innkeeper when you arrive. The landscaped yard reveals a horseshoe-shaped fish pond, a genuine 1820s sheepherder wagon, two timeworn hand plows, and a vintage black carriage with red wheels. Throughout the inn, little signs reveal clever quotes and quips with an Old West flavor. The guest rooms have private baths. Plan for a great time on the Wyoming range.

Sour Cream Coffee Cake

¾ cup (1½ sticks) butter
1½ cups granulated sugar

3 eggs or egg substitute equivalent
2 cups sour cream
3 cups all-purpose flour*
2 teaspoons vanilla extract
1½ teaspoons baking soda
1½ teaspoons baking powder
½ teaspoon salt
¾ cup packed brown sugar
2 teaspoons ground cinnamon
1 cup chopped nuts
Raisins, if desired
1½ cups confectioners' sugar
2 tablespoons water
½ teaspoon vanilla extract

Preheat oven to 350°. Cream together butter, granulated sugar, eggs, and sour cream. Add flour, vanilla, baking soda, baking powder, and salt. Mix brown sugar, cinnamon, nuts, and raisins if using. Place in layers with batter in lightly greased Bundt pan or angel food cake pan. Bake 1 hour. Let stand 10 minutes. Combine confectioners' sugar, water, and vanilla to make glaze. Drizzle over cake. Yields 12 servings.

*Note: You can use half wheat and half white but increase baking powder and soda to 2 teaspoons. Freeze well to serve later.

Baked Cheese Grits

3 cups water
1 teaspoon salt
¾ cup uncooked grits, regular
    or quick type (*not* instant)
¾ stick (6 tablespoons) butter
    or margarine
½ pound Velveeta cheese, cut in chunks
1 large dash Tabasco
2 eggs well-beaten or use egg beaters

Preheat oven to 325°. Bring water to boil in medium saucepan over high heat and add salt and grits. Cook until thick, about 5 minutes. Add butter, cheese, Tabasco, and eggs. Pour mixture into 8 x 12-inch, lightly greased dish and bake 40 to 45 minutes. Sprinkle with paprika before serving. Yields 8 to 10 servings.

HUNTER PEAK RANCH

P.O. Box 1731, Painter Rt.
Cody, WY 82414
(307) 587-3711
hpr@wtp.net
www.nezperce.com/ranchhp.html

Hunter Peak Ranch is a neat place to stay while recreating in the mountains of northwest Wyoming. Activities on and near the ranch include horseback riding, fishing, hiking, lawn games, Ping-Pong, reading, touring Yellowstone Park, cross-country skiing, snowmobiling, river and snow tubing, photography, and constructive loafing.

Rice & Vegetable Casserole

2 plus 2 cups chopped tomatoes, fresh,
    frozen, or canned
2 plus 2 cups chopped vegetables*
1 cup rice (either all white
    or half white and half brown)
1 cup hot water (use less with frozen
    or canned tomatoes)
1 tablespoon vinegar
2 tablespoons chicken or beef bouillon
Dash of hot sauce
2 cups shredded cheese, any flavor
    or combination

Preheat oven to 350° (325° for glass pan). Layer 2 cups tomatoes in 9 x 9-inch pan coated with nonstick spray. Next, layer 2 cups vegetables. Spread rice over vegetables. Layer remaining 2 cups vegetables, then remaining 2 cups tomatoes. Combine water, vinegar, bouillon, and hot sauce and pour over mixture. Cover with foil. Bake 1½ hours. Remove foil and cover with cheese. Return to oven until cheese melts, about 20 minutes. Yields 8 servings.

*Note: Use any combination of onion, broccoli, cauliflower, carrot, mushroom, cabbage, squash, or others.

Cabbage Salad

¾ cup sugar
2 tablespoons salt
⅔ cup vegetable oil
1 cup white vinegar
1 head cabbage, chopped
1 green pepper, sliced
1 onion, sliced

Combine sugar, salt, oil, and vinegar in saucepan and boil. Pour hot mixture over chopped vegetables. Do not stir until completely cold. Then stir and serve. Store in jar in refrigerator. This will keep fresh for months. Yields 6 to 8 servings.

THE LOCKHART INN

109 West Yellowstone Avenue
Cody, WY 82414
(307) 587-6074 (phone)
(800) 377-7255 (toll free)
info@codyvacationproperties.com
www.CodyVacationProperties.com

The Lockhart Inn is truly your "home away from home" for people who enjoy personal service as well as western hospitality. Enjoy fresh mountain air, blue skies,

The Lockhart Inn

Creamed Cheese Scrambled Eggs

8 eggs (farm-fresh are best)
Splash of half-and-half
Several shakes garlic salt
    and dried parsley
1 (8-ounce) package cream cheese,
    softened

Mix all ingredients and cook in medium, 2-inch-deep skillet over medium heat. Yields 6 to 8 servings.

and beautiful mountain views as you relax on the spacious veranda outside the inn. It is located in the town of Cody, Wyoming, which was founded by its namesake William "Buffalo Bill" Cody. The Lockhart Inn is just minutes from the Buffalo Bill Historical Center, Old Trail Town, and the Cody Nite Rodeo, and walking distance to all major attractions and restaurants.

Oatmeal Cinnamon Pancakes

¼ teaspoon ground cinnamon
½ cup oatmeal
2 cups pancake mix
Water
1 teaspoon vanilla extract

Add cinnamon and oatmeal to basic pancake mix and add water to desired consistency. Add vanilla, more if desired. Mix well, let stand, and adjust amount of water. Cook as directed on package. You are now ready for a great treat. Yields 6 servings.

Artichoke Gorgonzola Omelet

8 eggs
1 (13-ounce) can artichoke hearts
1 cup grated Gorgonzola cheese
2 small tomatoes, chopped
½ cup pitted and chopped olives
1 onion, chopped
8 ounces mushrooms, sliced

Coat frying pan with nonstick spray. Beat eggs gently in bowl. Drain artichokes and rinse. Slightly chop them, but do not make mushy. Mix eggs and artichokes with remaining ingredients and cook over medium heat, tossing eggs and veggies and cheese. Yields 4 servings.

Index of Cities & Inns

Berkeley Springs Spa & Inn, 441
Bernerhof Inn, The, 246–47
Big Bay, Michigan
        Big Bay Lighthouse Bed & Breakfast, 194
Big Bear Bed & Breakfast, 11
Big Mill Bed & Breakfast, 272
Biltmore Village Inn, 303
Birchwood Inn, 183
Blair House Carousel Inn, 38
Blake House Inn, 269
Blooming Garden Inn, 276
Blue Bell Inn, The, 135
Bluebird House, 129
Bluebonnet Inn Bed & Breakfast, The, 378
Bluemont Bed & Breakfast, 409
Blue Moon Farm Bed & Board, 369
Blue Spruce Inn, 73
Bonham, Texas
        Carleton House, The, 385
Bonne Terre, Missouri
        Victorian Veranda Bed & Breakfast, 219
Bonnie Castle Bed & Breakfast, 111
Bonnie's Parsonage 1908 Bed &
        Breakfast, 194–95
Boothbay, Maine
Kenniston Hill Inn, 163
Boulder, Colorado
        Inn on Mapleton Hill, The, 78–79
Bozeman, Montana
        Silver Forest Inn, 228–29
Bradford, New Hampshire
        Candlelite Inn, 244
        Rosewood Country Inn, 245–46
Brampton Bed & Breakfast Inn, 171
Branson, Missouri
        Branson Hotel Bed & Breakfast Inn,
        The, 221
Brass Lantern Inn, 169, 396
Breckenridge, Colorado
        Hunt Placer Inn, 81
Brenham, Texas
        Ant Street Inn, 385–86
Brewster, Cape Cod, Massachusetts
        Captain Freeman Inn, The, 179
Brickhouse Inn, The, 349
Brickyard Barn Inn, The, 141
Bridge Creek Inn, 35
Brierwreath Manor Bed & Breakfast, 122
Brigadoon Bed & Breakfast, 193
Bristol, Rhode Island
        Point Pleasant Inn & Resort, 357
Brooklyn, Michigan
        Dewey Lake Manor Bed & Breakfast, 199
Bross Hotel Bed & Breakfast, 78

Brunswick, Maine
        Brunswick Bed & Breakfast, 168
Bryson City, North Carolina
        Fryemont Inn, The, 301
Buckhorn Inn, 371–72
Bunker Hill Bed & Breakfast, 184
Burlington, Iowa
        Schramm House Bed & Breakfast,
        The, 131–32
Burlington, Wisconsin
        Hillcrest Inn & Carriage House, The, 453
Butler, Pennsylvania
        Locust Brook Lodge, 352
Butler, Tennessee
        Iron Mountain Inn, 366

C

Cali Cochitta Bed & Breakfast Inn, 393
Calistoga, California
        Foothill House, 57
Camai Bed & Breakfast, 13
Campbell Cottage Bed & Breakfast, 309
Campbell House, The, 323
Candlelite Inn, 244
Candor, New York
        Edge of Thyme, The, 261–62
Cape Carteret, North Carolina
        Harborlight Guest House, 284
Cape Charles, Virginia
        Cape Charles House Bed & Breakfast, 410
Cape May, New Jersey
        Chalfonte Bed & Breakfast, The, 250
        Mainstay Inn, The, 252
        Queen Victoria Bed & Breakfast, The, 253
Cape Neddick, Maine
        Cape Neddick House, 160
Capitola, California
        Inn at Depot Hill, The, 64
Captain Cook, Hawaii
        Mara's Dive Bed & Breakfast, 116
Captain Ezra Nye House, 188
Captain Fairfield Inn, The, 160
Captain Freeman Inn, The, 179
Captain Jefferds Inn, The, 157
Captain Montague's, 310–11
Captain Wohlt Inn Bed & Breakfast, 215
Captain's Choice Bed & Breakfast, 185
Carleton House, The, 385
Carolina Inn, The, 284
Carriage House Bed & Breakfast, 140
Carson City, Nevada
        Deer Run Ranch Bed & Breakfast, 233
Casa Tierra Bed & Breakfast, 18

Cedarburg, Wisconsin
        Washington House Inn, The, 451
Cedar Crest Victorian Inn, 289–90
Cedar Grove Mansion Inn, 213
Cedar Hill Bed & Breakfast, 312
Cedar House, The, 442
Center Conway, New Hampshire
        Lavender Flower Inn, The, 243
Chalet Inn, The, 300
Chalfonte Bed & Breakfast, The, 250
Chama, New Mexico
        Gandy Dancer Bed & Breakfast Inn, 255
Chapel Hill, North Carolina
        Carolina Inn, The, 284
        Inn at Bingham School, The, 278–79
Charlestown, Massachusetts
        Bunker Hill Bed & Breakfast, 184
Charles Town, West Virginia
        Hillbrook Inn, 443
Charlottesville, Virginia
        Inn at Monticello, The, 411
Cheshire, Massachusetts
        Harbour House Inn Bed & Breakfast, 181
Chester, South Carolina
        Colvin Farm Bed & Breakfast, 362
Chestertown, Maryland
        Brampton Bed & Breakfast Inn, 171
        Inn at Mitchell House, The, 173
Chestertown, New York
        Friends Lake Inn, 259
Chestnut Charm Bed & Breakfast, 130
Cheyenne, Wyoming
        Adventurers' Country Bed & Breakfast, 460
        Howdy Pardner Bed & Breakfast, The, 461
        Windy Hills, 456
Cheyenne-Laramie, Wyoming
        A. Drummond's Ranch Bed & Breakfast, 458
Chicago Pike Inn, 199
Chichester-McKee House, 71
Chimney Hill Farm Estate, 251
Chimney Rock, North Carolina
        Wicklow Inn, The, 288
Chinaberry Hill, 431
Chretien Point Plantation, 151
Christopher Place, 367
Cincinnati, Ohio
        Cincinnatian Hotel, The, 316
Cincinnati's Weller Haus Bed & Breakfast,
        Inc., 146
Cinnamon Bear Inn, 67
Clarksville, Tennessee
        Hachland Hill Inn Bed & Breakfast, 368
Cloverdale, California
        Shelford House Bed & Breakfast Inn, The, 39

Index of Recipes